Corporate Finance

THIRD EDITION

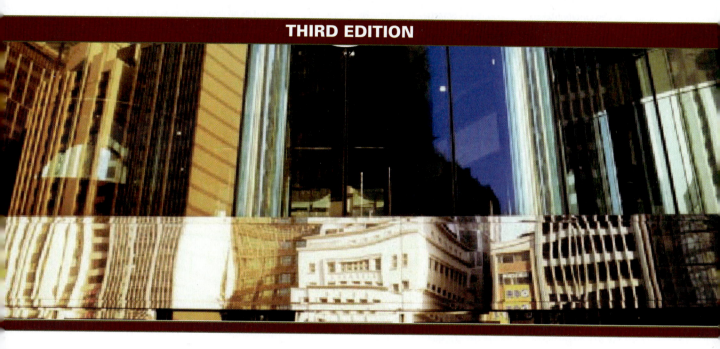

JOHN R. GRAHAM

Duke University

SCOTT B. SMART

Indiana University

WILLIAM L. MEGGINSON

University of Oklahoma

SOUTH-WESTERN
CENGAGE Learning™

Australia • Brazil • Japan • Korea • Mexico • Singapore • Spain • United Kingdom • United States

SOUTH-WESTERN
CENGAGE Learning

Corporate Finance, 3rd Edition
John R. Graham, Scott B. Smart, and
William L. Megginson

VP of Editorial, Business: Jack W. Calhoun

Publisher: Joe Sabatino

Executive Editor: Michael R. Reynolds

Sr. Developmental Editor: Susanna C. Smart

Sr. Marketing Comm. Manager: Jim Overly

Marketing Coordinator: Suellen Ruttkay

Marketing Manager: Nate Anderson

Content Project Manager: Scott Dillon

Manager of Technology, Editorial:
Matt McKinney

Manager of Media, Editorial: John Barans

Media Editor: Scott Fidler

Sr. Frontlist Buyer, Manufacturing:
Kevin Kluck

Production Service/Compositor: Integra

Copyeditor: Matt Darnell

Proofreader: Christine Gever

Sr. Editorial Assistant: Adele Scholtz

Sr. Art Director: Michelle Kunkler

Internal Design: Juli Cook/Plan-It-
Publishing, Inc.

Cover Design: Jennifer Lambert/Jen2Design

Cover Image: © Wilhelm Scholz / Stone

For product information and technology assistance, contact us at
Cengage Learning Customer & Sales Support, 1-800-354-9706

For permission to use material from this text or product,
submit all requests online at **cengage.com/permissions**
Further permissions questions can be emailed to
permissionrequest@cengage.com

Library of Congress Control Number: 2009931539

PKG ISBN-13: 978-0-324-78291-2

PKG ISBN-10: 0-324-78291-8

ISBN-13: 978-0-324-78296-7

ISBN-10: 0-324-78296-9

South-Western Cengage Learning
5191 Natorp Boulevard
Mason, OH 45040
USA

Cengage Learning products are represented in Canada by Nelson Education, Ltd.

For your course and learning solutions, visit **academic.cengage.com**

Purchase any of our products at your local college store or at our preferred online store **www.ichapters.com**

Printed in the United States of America
1 2 3 4 5 6 7 13 12 11 10 09

To my wife Suzanne, my parents, my sister Beth, and my children - Matt, Laura, and Rebecca.
Thanks for all the love, support, and patience.

—John Graham

To Susan, Bobby, and Mary Anne, who bring joy to my life every day.

—Scott Smart

To my father, who showed the way.

—Bill Megginson

GET UP CLOSE

Individual Talents.
Combined Strengths.

with Today's Leading Corporate Finance Authors.

One of the most prolific and widely cited scholars of this generation

JOHN R. GRAHAM

John Graham is the D. Richard Mead Professor of Finance at Duke University where he also serves as the Director of the Duke/*CFO* Global Business Outlook survey. He is coeditor of the *Journal of Finance* and has published more than three dozen scholarly articles in journals such as the *Journal of Financial Economics*, the *Review of Financial Studies*, the *Journal of Finance*, the *Journal of Accounting and Economics*, and many others. John is one of the most prolific and widely cited scholars of his generation, and he is a three-time winner of the Jensen Prize for the best corporate finance paper published in the *Journal of Financial Economics*. John is a Research Associate with the National Bureau of Economic Research, and he has received recognition for outstanding teaching and faculty contributions at Duke and the University of Utah.

Award-winning master teacher and pioneer in innovative teaching technology

SCOTT B. SMART

Scott Smart has been a member of the Finance Department at Indiana University since 1990. He has published articles in scholarly journals such as the *Journal of Finance*, the *Journal of Financial Economics*, the *Journal of Accounting and Economics*, and the *Review of Economics and Statistics*. His research has been cited by the *Wall Street Journal*, *Business Week*, and other major newspapers and periodicals. Professor Smart holds a Ph.D. from Stanford University and has been recognized as a master teacher, winning more than a dozen teaching awards at the graduate level. Some of his consulting clients include Intel and Unext.

International finance researcher and well-recognized finance consultant

WILLIAM L. MEGGINSON

Bill Megginson is Professor and Rainbolt Chair in Finance at the University of Oklahoma's Michael F. Price College of Business. From 2002 to 2007, he was a voting member of the Italian Ministry of Economics and Finance's Global Advisory Committee on Privatization. During spring 2008, he was the Fulbright Tocqueville Distinguished Chair in American Studies and Visiting Professor at the Université-Paris Dauphine. He has published refereed articles in several top academic journals, including the *Journal of Economic Literature*, the *Journal of Finance*, the *Journal of Financial Economics*, the *Journal of Financial and Quantitative Analysis*, and *Foreign Policy*. Dr. Megginson holds a Ph.D. in Finance from Florida State University. He has visited 70 countries and has served as a privatization consultant for the New York Stock Exchange, the OECD, the IMF, the World Federation of Exchanges, and the World Bank.

About the Authors

*This accomplished author team, led by award-winning author and nationally acclaimed finance scholar **John Graham**, helps build a bridge between academic rigor and corporate finance practices. Together, the authors offer more than 50 years of combined research, writing, and teaching experience at all levels.*

Corporate Finance:
Linking Theory to What Companies Do, 3e
GET CLOSER.

> "This edition provides a deeper understanding of the connection between financial theory and what companies actually do."
>
> *– Author John Graham*

PREFACE

New Lead Author John Graham Brings Students Closer to Finance As It Is Practiced in Business Today.

Readers of *Corporate Finance*, **3e** will immediately notice the most significant change to our book—the **addition of John Graham** as lead author. John is one of the most prolific and widely cited scholars of his generation. Through a partnership between Duke University and *CFO Magazine*, John also serves as director of the *CFO* Global Business Outlook survey, and is therefore keenly aware of how CFOs around the world put finance theory into practice. Thus, in joining this book, John brings to the table not only an unparalleled reputation as a teacher and scholar, but also an active connection to the business world. With John on the team, we are in a unique position to deliver a text that reflects a solid grounding in theory, emphasizes new developments in scholarship, and yet maintains a focused, real-world emphasis. That emphasis is a key component of this revision and is highlighted in a new subtitle: *Linking Theory to What Companies Do*. Virtually every chapter in this edition reveals John's contributions as a scholar, writer, and teacher. New features in each chapter help students see how the theory they are learning is put into action by financial executives.

Anchoring Student Learning in the Latest Corporate Theory and Practice.

Professors who teach corporate finance at the M.B.A. level consistently tell us they want a book that has modern content, global integration, and an appropriate level of theoretical rigor. However, professors also say that M.B.A. students respond best when they see a clear connection between the theory taught in the classroom and what they will do on the job. Every chapter of *Corporate Finance: Linking Theory to What Companies Do,* 3e provides direct evidence from *CFO Magazine* executive surveys and other sources that connects textbook theory to corporate finance practice. We show students how CFOs spend their time, what analysis CFOs rely on to back up their most important decisions, and how financial practices vary across countries. We also highlight areas where emerging research offers new approaches for solving financial problems.

OBJECTIVE AND PRIMARY GOALS OF THIS EDITION

Get Closer to the Practice of Finance Today.

The overriding objective that guided our work was to create a **focused, topically cutting-edge text grounded in modern theory**. We wanted the book to have a truly global perspective and to reach students through the use of innovative and engaging technologies. We want to motivate and enhance student learning, facilitate ease and effectiveness of instruction, and provide valuable content.

Above all, our desire was that students would take away from the book a deeper understanding of the connection between financial theory and what companies actually do. To achieve these objectives, we focused our energies on **five primary goals**.

Get Closer to the Topics That Matter Most.

Goal 1: Focus on Important Topics.

This goal drove the development and revision of the overall text structure as well as the topics covered within each chapter. With this goal in mind, we designed a book that covers **classic corporate finance concepts**, such as risk and return, capital budgeting, and capital structure, **as well as emerging theories** that we feel are likely to have an impact in the business world as current students progress in their careers. More importantly, every chapter includes new material illustrating how financial management works in real companies. Each chapter begins with an opening vignette entitled, "*What Companies Do*." These chapter openers help students see, right from the start, that managers and investors really make decisions using the tools presented in the book.

As students delve into each chapter, they will encounter evidence from the *CFO* **Global Business Outlook** survey and other sources that demonstrate how companies use financial theory—or in some cases, we even discuss why the textbook theory does not line up with practice particularly well. Students will also have opportunities to **hear from business leaders directly through dozens of new video clips** that not only provide direct reinforcement that the textbook material is relevant for business decision making, but also touch on recent developments, such as the lingering effects of the financial crisis.

Professors Find Thorough Coverage.
Students Find Keys to Job Interview Success.

To professors, the important topics are those that cover the traditional lexicon of corporate finance. But to students, what often matters most is the skill they need to locate and succeed in their first job. With a challenging labor market, students' concerns about job placement are higher than ever. In this edition we offer students a new feature in each chapter that will help them land the job they desire. Through conversations with dozens of

> "From classic corporate finance concepts to emerging theories, readers see how financial management works in real organizations."
>
> *– Author Scott Smart*

corporate recruiters as well as current and former students, we've developed an **inventory of actual job interview questions that our students have encountered** in their own interviews. These questions appear in the margins of the text at exactly the spot where the textbook provides answers. Students often ask us about the technical topics they should review before they meet with recruiters, and now they can see for themselves which topics surface again and again in actual job interviews.

"This edition delivers a more global view of corporate finance than you'll find in any other corporate finance text."

– Author Bill Megginson

Get Closer to Theory in Practice Today.

Goal 2: Make Theory Discussions Intuitive and Practical.
We feel it's important to expose M.B.A. students to cutting-edge thinking in corporate finance. The art of doing this in an intuitively appealing and practical manner rests on the ability to synthesize, interpret, and communicate complex ideas in a way that readers can easily digest, and to link theoretical material to real business practices. Throughout the text, we illustrate concepts with step-by-step examples, many of which utilize real data. We've expanded the **number of end-of-chapter problems that come with live solutions**, so students can see (on video or through flash animation) demonstrations of important solution techniques and linkage to the theory presented in the book.

Get Closer to An Integrated Global Approach.

Goal 3: Provide a Truly Global Perspective.
We incorporate a seamless global perspective throughout the text rather than confine global issues to a single chapter that few instructors have time to cover. Every chapter has a unique feature entitled, *"What Companies Do Globally,"* **designed to compare corporate finance practices around the world.** For example, right from the start, in Chapter 1, we show that the extent to which CFOs agree with the goal of shareholder value maximization varies dramatically across countries. Perhaps not surprisingly, then, in Chapter 8, we show that the reliance that firms place on decision-making tools linked to value maximization, such as NPV and IRR, varies dramatically across countries as well.

In addition, many of the *"What Companies Do"* chapter openers involve companies from foreign markets. Chapter 4's opener, for example, discusses the consequences for a Canadian firm of a credit downgrade by one of the rating agencies. The result of our efforts to integrate international material throughout the book is that we offer **students a more global view of corporate finance than any other corporate finance text.**

Get Closer to a Fulfilling Student Learning Experience.

Goal 4: Engage and Motivate Student Learning.
To maintain high reader interest, we use a relaxed, conversational writing style. We know it is crucial for students to develop sharp quantitative skills to succeed in our field. Nevertheless, when we present mathematical topics, such as the variance of a portfolio

of assets or pricing an option using Black and Scholes, we do more than simply present the equations along with "plug and chug" examples. We convey the intuition beneath the surface, urging readers to contemplate not just how an equation works, but also why it works.

More Approachable Presentation. More Flexibility in Practice.
Writing clearly, incorporating real examples, and asking students interesting questions are some of the ways that we try to **make the quantitative material more approachable**. Beyond writing, we have added features that encourage students to come to class prepared to learn. Each chapter has **online homework problems** that randomly vary the numeric value of the inputs so that students cannot collaborate on solutions. For example, two students would solve an assigned problem that is identical in every way except that the equity beta is 1.2 (1.7) for the first (second) student, the cost of debt is 8% (9%), etc. These inputs randomly vary for each student, as does the correct answer. The end result is that students solve nearly identical problems individually. Because these problems are completed online and graded automatically, the instructor can assign nightly homework that compels students to keep up to date on the course with little time required on the instructor's part.

Get Closer to the Ideal Learning Environment with *SmartFinance* Online Tools.

Goal 5: Use Technology to Clarify and Motivate.
We developed *SmartFinance*, **an integrated technology package**, to engage, motivate, and at times entertain students, while helping them master financial concepts on their own time and at their own pace. A variety of dynamic **videos** allow students to hear firsthand about exciting recent developments in financial research and to learn from business professionals why the material contained in the text is relevant. The **flash animated concept reviews and problem solutions** let students review some of the more difficult concepts at any time and as many times as they like. **Nearly 100 short video interviews** with leading scholars and practitioners give students access to "virtual guest speakers" and help build the bridge between theory and practice that we feel is so important. In-residence and online M.B.A. students as well as executive M.B.A. students who have used the *SmartFinance* tools have offered almost unanimous praise for these features. In fact, the most common complaint we hear from students is, "Why can't we have more of this?"

In this edition, we have also added **new videos of the author team solving end-of-chapter problems**. Our experience is that some students struggle to understand how to solve finance problems until a professor walks them through the solution step-by-step. We do that for you, with the goal of helping students understand and retain important solution techniques.

"Engage, motivate, and reach students in ways they learn best with the variety of SmartFinance online tools that let them learn and review at their own pace, on their own time."

– Author Scott Smart

SMARTFinance

Smart Practices Video

Tom Cole, Co-Head, Global Banking, Deutsche Bank Securities

"By the end of 2008, the noninvestment grade credit spread was 1400 basis points."

See the entire interview at
SMARTFinance

ORGANIZATION OF THE TEXT

Streamlined Coverage. Full Understanding.

We divided the text into 9 parts that include 25 chapters plus 2 additional Web chapters. The nine part titles are:

Part 1: Introduction
Part 2: Valuation, Risk, and Return
Part 3: Capital Budgeting
Part 4: Capital Structure and Payout Policy
Part 5: Long-Term Financing
Part 6: Options, Derivatives, and International Financial Management
Part 7: Short-Term Financing Decisions
Part 8: Special Topics
Part 9: Web Chapters

Quality Content and Flexible Approach Shaped by Feedback from Students and Instructors.

This structure evolved from a number of iterations and refinements based on user feedback. Classroom tests using this structure confirm its effectiveness. Of course, those professors who prefer an alternative structure will find the text is flexible in that alternative sequences generally work well.

Part 1 includes three introductory chapters that provide background and review. Discussions focus on the scope of corporate finance and coverage of financial statement and cash flow analysis, with a chapter on the time value of money. Because of differences in course prerequisites, some professors may assign these chapters and cover them in class, while others may include them as review that students can use to confirm their understanding of the course prerequisites. The chapters work well in both of these situations. Through careful integration of **CFO survey results**, these early chapters help to motivate students to pursue the topics covered in the rest of the book. **Part 2 includes three chapters—one on bond and stock valuation and two on risk and return.** These chapters give students a solid understanding of risk, return, and value that serves as the conceptual base upon which subsequent discussions are built.

Part 3 includes three chapters devoted to capital budgeting processes and techniques, cash flow and capital budgeting, and cost of capital and project risk. **Part 4 on capital structure and payout policy** includes six chapters. They cover market efficiency, an overview of long-term financing, capital structure theory and taxes, balancing the benefits and costs of debt, the link between capital structure and capital

"We are committed to continuously improving this text to emphasize the relevance of theory to today's student and to bring both student and instructor closer to finance as it's practiced today."

– *Author Scott Smart*

budgeting, and payout policy. These chapters contain accessible presentations of recent research related to the covered topics. **Part 5 includes two chapters on long-term financing**. They focus on investment banking and the public sale of equity securities and long-term debt and leasing.

Part 6 includes three chapters—two on options (options basics and Black and Scholes and beyond) and one on international financial management. **Part 7 contains three short-term financing chapters**—one on strategic and operational financial planning and two on short-term financial management. **Part 8 includes two special topics chapters**—one on mergers, acquisitions, and corporate governance and the other on bankruptcy and financial distress. Finally, **Part 9 includes two Web chapters**—one covering venture capital and private equity, and one on risk management and financial engineering. For ultimate flexibility, these optional chapters are available at the text website **www.cengage.com/finance/graham** and are not printed in the book.

MAJOR IMPROVEMENTS IN THE THIRD EDITION

Get Closer to Theory Students Find Relevant.
Get Closer to What Companies Are Practicing Today.

We are committed to continuous improvement of *Corporate Finance*, **3e**. In this edition we placed a renewed emphasis on **linking theory to what companies do** and on **helping students see the relevance of what they are learning.**

In the previous edition, each chapter began with an "Opening Focus," and each contained a feature highlighting global financial practices called "Comparative Corporate Finance." All of these have been replaced with more recent examples and data, and they have been retitled, "*What Companies Do*," "*What Companies Do Globally*," and "*What CFOs Do*," to reflect our new emphasis on financial practice.

WHAT COMPANIES DO

WHAT COMPANIES DO GLOBALLY

WHAT CFOs DO

"*What Companies Do*" highlights intriguing examples from real companies, timely topics and even finance stories from today's media to show how finance theory applies to today's business challenges. *See pages 66, 248, 372, and 505 for examples.*

"*What Companies Do Globally*" describes corporate finance practices around the world and the effects of the recent global financial crises. *See pages 139, 261, and 522 for examples.*

"*What CFOs Do*" are new features in many of this edition's chapters that illustrate how senior executives rely on financial theory to make key decisions. *See pages 26, 233, and 487 for examples.*

Dozens of new *Job Interview Questions* appear in the margins throughout the text. These questions, shared with us by both the recruiters who asked the questions and students confronted by them, help students see that firms expect them to apply the finance theory they have learned. Not only will these questions help students interview well, they also serve the purpose of motivating students to master the related material. *See pages 123, 416, and 556 for examples.*

New Smart Practices Videos Demonstrate Cutting-Edge Thinking and Practices by Business Leaders Today.

Smart Ethics Video

Andy Bryant, Executive Vice President of Finance and Enterprise Services, Chief Administrative Officer, Intel Corp.

"I never thought that ethics would be a value-add to a company, but today I believe it counts as part of your market cap."

See the entire interview at **SMARTFinance**

We have also added **dozens of new video clips from interviews with scholars and business leaders**. These clips educate students about new developments in the field and demonstrate how practicing managers use the concepts they learned in their corporate finance classes. References in the text connect videos to relevant content within the book.

More End-of-Chapter Video Solutions

The **inventory of solutions to end-of-chapter problems has expanded dramatically, with new solutions delivered on video** so students can not only see how to reach a solution, but they can also hear commentary on why a particular problem is important, how and when they might encounter such a problem in practice, and the connection between the problem and the theory behind it.

CHAPTER CONTENT IMPROVEMENTS

Streamlined Approach Offers More Than Ever Before.

In this edition, we worked hard to streamline the content, and even while adding new features, we succeeded in reducing the length of most chapters. In addition to providing a more streamlined text, we made significant improvements to many chapters.

Many chapters contain new material reflecting the causes and consequences of the recent financial crisis. For example, the opening story in Chapter 1 discusses a major decision faced by a CFO whose constituents (e.g., investors and board members) had conflicting views on how to manage the firm's cash resources during a credit crunch.

Chapters 12–14 cover the traditional approach to capital structure, including the Modigliani and Miller propositions, and theories such as the trade-off between taxes and bankruptcy costs, signaling, agency costs, and the pecking order. However, we introduce **a new approach to optimal capital structure decision making**, one that reflects emerging research and shows students how to trade off the marginal costs and benefits of debt to arrive at an optimal capital structure. In a nutshell, companies should issue debt until the marginal cost of doing so equals the marginal benefit of the next increment of debt. We use accessible language and colorful graphics to illustrate these concepts, leaving the students with a deep understanding of how capital structure decisions should be made. *See pages 451 and 472.*

Chapter 15 has been rewritten to emphasize current trends in dividend and share repurchase policy, linking in an accessible way to recent research. *See page 484.*

Chapter 16 discusses the dramatic upheaval in the investment banking industry from 2007 to 2009 and explains how the industry has changed as a result of the financial crisis. *See page 506.*

Chapter 25 offers the most complete discussion of corporate bankruptcy that can be found in any introductory corporate finance text. At a time when bankruptcies have reached historic highs, this material is very topical and will equip students to think through the various legal issues and incentives that occur when a company becomes distressed. *See page 841.*

THE END RESULT
Get Closer to What Students Need, What Professors Want.

The Book That's Best for Students. The Package Perfect for Professors.
In the final analysis, a textbook must cover the topics that professors believe are important and it must do so using a level of rigor appropriate for its readers—in this case, graduate students. Beyond that, professors want a book that students can and will use as a resource to succeed in the classroom and in the workplace. We believe that *Corporate Finance: Linking Theory to What Companies Do*, **3e** delivers the best our profession has to offer in terms of modern theory and practice. The book effectively engages students in learning, both in a linear fashion on the written page and interactively using the computer. We hope you'll try it. We are confident that if you do, whether you are a professor, student, or practicing professional, you will be glad you did.

Get a Closer Look at *Corporate Finance*, 3e Now.

"The book's streamlined approach still emphasizes the balance of modern theory, practical applications, and integrated technology essential for today's M.B.A. course."

– Author John Graham

ONLINE TEXT SUPPLEMENTS

Get Closer with Integrated Online Support and Technology Strengths.

"The best instructional technology combines the latest learning tools that appeal to today's variety of learners with content that truly supports course priorities."

– Author Scott Smart

FOR INSTRUCTORS

Get Closer to Providing All the Learning Support Students Need with Time-Saving Supplements.

Instructor's Manual with Test Bank provides comprehensive, time-saving support in one convenient place.

Prepared by Jana Cook, Oklahoma Christian University, the Instructor's Manual is designed to support novice instructors and finance veterans alike. This comprehensive resource includes chapter overviews, lecture guides organized by section, enrichment exercises, and answers to concept review questions. (0-538-46660-X)

Solutions Manual.

Revised by William T. Chittenden, Texas State University, and Jeffrey Whitworth, University of Houston, Clear Lake, the Solutions Manual includes all solutions for end-of-chapter problems. (0-324-78330-2)

Test Bank.

The Test Bank, revised by Daniel Pace, University of West Florida, has been thoroughly updated and expanded, and is available in Word files, as well as in *ExamView* computerized testing. (0-324-78329-9)

New Algorithmic ExamView Computerized Testing Software saves time and provides unlimited testing options.

This easy-to-use test creation software allows instructors to test students' comprehension of corporate finance with all of the proven questions from the printed test bank. Algorithmic flexibility allows key numeric inputs by students providing almost unlimited options in test questions that can vary by student if the professor so desires. Compatible with Microsoft Windows, *ExamView* lets instructors add or edit questions, instructions, and answers, and select questions randomly, by number, or by previewing them on the screen. Instructors can also create and administer quizzes online, whether over the Internet, a local area network (LAN), or a wide area network (WAN). (0-324-78292-6)

Up-to-Date PowerPoint® Presentation Slides bring lectures to life.

Engaging PowerPoint slides are available to visually clarify concepts and bring dynamic energy to classroom lectures. Each year, some of the key graphs and tables in these slides will be updated so professors can bring the latest real-world information with them to class. A brief student version is also available for students to use as an aid to note-taking. For your convenience, you can download slides from the text companion website at **www.cengage.com/finance/graham**. (0-324-78328-0)

Leading Aplia™ for Finance Homework Solution and Course Management System Provides Time-Saving Support.
Now instructors can equip students with the tools to improve their understanding of corporate finance with the best-selling homework solution in educational publishing today. Trusted by more than 650 institutions and 500,000 students, **Aplia for Finance** helps you prepare students for success with an easy-to-use course management system, auto-graded homework problem sets, a variety of tutorials, and much more.

For more information on how **Aplia for Finance** can benefit instructors and students alike, visit **www.aplia.com/finance** today!

Online *SmartFinance* Tools Offer Additional Learning Resources for Students.
Instructors can discover all of the dynamic *SmartFinance* tutorials, animations, videos, and interactive practice tools that reinforce learning at appropriate points within the text. For a full description of these *SmartFinance* resources, see the "For Students" section of the Preface below, or visit **www.cengage.com/finance/smartfinance**. (0-324-78297-7)

Get Closer to Professional Colleagues Who Share a Commitment to Exceptional Instruction.

Graham/Smart/Megginson *Corporate Finance*, 3e Community Website – www.cengage.com/community/graham

Visit the *Corporate Finance*, **3e Community Website** for your opportunity to learn more about innovative corporate finance features and new technology. Share instructional insights and ideas with peers. Learn from the successes of others and stay current with the latest financial developments. Each quarter, author John Graham will post PowerPoint slides that summarize the results from the latest Global Business Outlook survey.

FOR STUDENTS
Get Closer to Today's Students with Outstanding Technology Tools.
Online Suite of *SmartFinance* Tools.
Time-saving online *SmartFinance* tools further reinforce learning at appropriate points within the text with integrated tutorials, interactive practice, and videos from leading academics as well as finance researchers who highlight key theories and concepts. (0-324-78297-7)

Smart Concepts Provide Step-by-Step Animated Tutorials.

Smart Concepts. These animated concept review tutorials, organized by chapter, explain key topics step-by-step, offering students opportunities to review more difficult

chapter material at their own pace and at convenient times. Students can also decide how much or what parts of the review they want to cover. An icon in the text directs students to **www.cengage.com/finance/smartfinance** to explore these review tutorials.

Smart Solutions Help Students Sharpen Critical Thinking Skills.

Smart Solutions. Now students can refine their problem-solving skills with these animated and video-based clear solution steps. Firsthand coaching guides students in how to identify the right technique to apply to particular problems. New, comprehensive whiteboard solutions show the text authors completing problems. An icon in the text directs students to **www.cengage.com/finance/smartfinance** when Smart Solutions correspond with content in the text.

Smart Ideas Video

Malcolm Baker, Harvard University

"If you start to believe that markets aren't efficient, then that has consequences for corporate finance."

See the entire interview at
SMARTFinance

Smart Ideas Videos. Students learn from the leading academic researchers behind theories or concepts discussed in class with Smart Ideas Videos. Each brief video clip runs only two to three minutes, but is packed with powerful information. Video clips feature leaders in the field of finance, such as Robert Schiller (Yale), Elroy Dimson (London School of Business), Andrew Karolyi (Cornell University), Kenneth French (Dartmouth College), Raghu Rajan (University of Chicago), Mitchell Petersen (Northwestern University), and many, many more. An icon in the text directs students to **www.cengage.com/finance/smartfinance** at appropriate points within the book to view these short video clips.

Smart Practices Videos introduce business leaders using cutting-edge practices to maximize financial performance.

Smart Practices Videos. Business and industry leaders discuss how they capitalize on their companies' financial performance using cutting-edge practices. These videos can help show students why corporate finance is a vital topic regardless of their functional areas. Presidents and CFOs of major corporations, such as Andy Bryant, of Intel Corp., as well as corporate recruiters, are featured interviewees. An icon in the text directs students to **www.cengage.com/finance/smartfinance** at appropriate points within the text.

Smart Practices Video

Michael Mack, Jr., Chief Financial Officer, John Deere

"We evaluate the beta of the assets we invest in by looking at peer companies."

See the entire interview at
SMARTFinance

Smart Ethics Videos show the impact of ethics on the bottom line.

Smart Ethics Videos. These videos show how both academics and business executives view ethics and the impact that ethical or unethical behavior can have on the company's bottom line. An icon in the text directs students to **www.cengage.com/finance/smartfinance** to view these clips.

Smart Quizzing provides interactive practice for exams.

Smart Quizzing. The SmartFinance website provides true/false and multiple-choice quiz questions for each chapter to test student knowledge. Answers confirm students are correct or explain errors.

Research Like the Pros Do with Thomson ONE–*Business School Edition (BSE)*

Use the same tool professional brokers and analysts rely upon every day to access leading financial data sources with Thomson ONE–BSE!

This web-based portal provides integrated access to Thomson Financial content for financial analysis. This dynamic educational version reflects the financial resources used daily by actual Wall Street analysts and is the ideal tool for completing online research, projects, and special end-of-chapter activities in the text. An access card for Thomson ONE–BSE is provided with each new textbook. *If your text is used and does not contain an access card, you can purchase access at **www.cengage.com/thomsonone***.

Aplia™ for Finance Homework Solution Brings Students Closer to the Grade They Want.

Now students can improve their performance and understanding of corporate finance with the best-selling homework solution in educational publishing today, trusted by more than 650 institutions and 500,000 students. **Aplia for Finance** prepares students for success with auto-graded homework problem sets, a variety of tutorials, an easy-to-use course management system, and much more. (0-324-65314-3)

For more information on how this tool could benefit you, visit **www.aplia.com/finance** today!

Cengage Learning's *Global Economic Watch* Presents the Latest Financial Developments as They Happen.

From credit collapse and surging unemployment to bailouts and bankruptcies, keep up with the latest pivotal events making history right now, hour by hour, with **Cengage Learning's Global Economic Watch for Finance**. You'll see how today's financial turmoil transforms academic theory into intense real-life challenges that affect every business sector. *The Watch* includes a content-rich blog; real-time database with hundreds of relevant and vetted articles, videos, and podcasts; thorough timeline and overview of events leading to the global economic crises; and numerous other learning and teaching resources. For more information, visit **www.cengage.com/thewatch**.

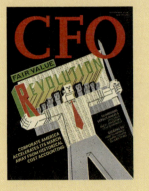

Get Closer, Stay Closer to What Today's CFOs Are Thinking Right Now!

Current Global Business Outlook CFO Survey Results Updates Online Reflect the Most Recent Developments.

Stay abreast of the most recent thinking and developments of today's CFOs with regular online updates. Instructors can access a PowerPoint Slide deck personally developed by John Graham for his own corporate finance course. This deck contains the most recent results of the Duke University/*CFO Magazine* Global Business Outlook quarterly survey. A link connects instructors to an online discussion that walks through the slides. Materials highlight today's most important trends and current concerns related to the world of corporate finance. It's one more way today's corporate finance course gets closer to the current economic environment.

ACKNOWLEDGMENTS

Most people realize that creating a textbook is a collaborative venture. As authors, we truly appreciate all the people who helped plan, edit, produce, and launch our book. Although only three people are listed as authors on the title page, we wish to acknowledge the debt we owe to those who have worked so closely with us.

Over the years, numerous other publishing company professionals have helped mold this book. First on this list is our editor, Susan Smart, who did a fantastic job helping the three of us communicate and stay on track. Nate Anderson, our marketing manager, contributed creative marketing suggestions to achieve a successful launch. We also want to thank Mike Reynolds, Bill Hendee, Jim Overly, Scott Dillon, and everyone else at Cengage Learning who helped make our final product something in which we could all take pride. Several people made written contributions to the book and its supplements. We are particularly grateful to Dubos Masson and Joe Guzinski for their written contributions to specific chapters, and Bill Chittenden and Jeff Whitworth for their close attention in verifying the Solutions Manual and suggesting numerous changes. We thank Daniel Pace for revising the test bank, Jeff Whitworth, again, for his contributions to the revision of the PowerPoint slides, and Jana Cook for her updating of the Instructor's Manual. We thank Larry Gitman for his masterful editing, creative thinking, and oversight. We also thank *CFO Magazine* for their part in many of the surveys that appear throughout the book.

Technology is an extremely important part of this book, and we wish to express our deep appreciation to Cengage Learning for their financial and professional support.

Though it would be nice to pretend that our skills as authors are so advanced that we did not have to make repeated passes at writing the chapters you see today, in fact, this book has benefited immeasurably from the feedback we have received from reviewers and survey and focus group participants. We would like to thank the following people for their insightful comments and constructive criticism of the text:

John Affleck-Graves
University of Notre Dame
Keldon Bauer
Illinois State University
Efraim Benmelech
Harvard University
Brian Bolton
University of New Hampshire
Daniel J. Borgia
Florida Gulf Coast University
Carol Marie Boyer
Long Island University
Ivan Brick
Rutgers University
Arturo Bris
IMD
Amy Burnett
St. Edwards University
Chao Chen
California State University–Northridge
Indudeep Chhachhi
Western Kentucky University
James Cotter
Wake Forest University
Arnold Cowan
Iowa State University
Pete Crabb
Northwest Nazarene University
Charles Cuny
Texas A&M University
Massi De Santis
Dartmouth University
Karen Denning
West Virginia University
Elroy Dimson
London Business School
James S. Doran
University of Texas
Daniel Ebels
University of Michigan
Melissa Frye
University of Central Florida
Lawrence R.Glosten
Columbia University

Richard Gritta
University of Portland
John Hall
University of Arkansas–Little Rock
Joel Harper
Florida Atlantic University
Del Hawley
University of Mississippi
Edith Hotchkiss
Boston College
J. Christopher Hughen
Bowling Green State University
Steve Jordan
University of Virginia
Kathleen Kahle
University of Arizona
John N. Kallianiotis
University of Scranton
Andrew Karolyi
Cornell University
Shady Kholdy
California Polytechnic University–Pomona
Nikolay Kosturov
University of Oklahoma
Praveen Kumar
University of Houston
Michael Kwag
Boston University
Chun-I Lee
Loyola Marymount University
James S. Linck
University of Georgia
David Lins
University of Illinois–Champaign
John Longo
Rutgers University
Evgeny Lyandres
Boston University
Edmund H. Mantell
Pace University
Ike Mathur
Southern Illinois University–Carbondale
Felix Meschke
Arizona State University

Vassil Mihov
Texas Christian University
David B. Milton
Bentley College
Roger Morin
Georgia State University
Charles Mossman
University of Manitoba
Jim Musumeci
Southern Illinois University–Carbondale
Ralph A. Pope
Cal State/Sacramento University
Raghu Rajan
University of Chicago
Narendar V. Rao
Northeastern Illinois University
Ramesh Rao
Oklahoma State University
Lee Redding
University of Michigan
Bill Reese
Tulane University
Patricia Ryan
Colorado State University
Mukunthan Santhanakrishnan
Idaho State University
James Schallheim
University of Utah
James Seward
University of Wisconsin–Madison

Dennis Sheehan
Penn State University
Betty Simkins
Oklahoma State University
Mark Simonson
Arizona State University
Andrew Spieler
Hofstra University
Timothy G. Sullivan
Bentley College
Ronald Sverdlove
Long Island University
Alex Tang
Morgan State University
Olaf Thorp
Babson College
Sorin Tuluca
Fairleigh Dickinson University
Harry Turtle
Washington State University
Joseph Vu
DePaul University
Kam-Ming Wan
University of Texas, Dallas
Susan White
University of Maryland
Rohan Williamson
Georgetown University
Mela Wyeth
Charleston Southern University
David A. Zalewski
Providence College

We would like to thank the following instructors for sharing their experience with support pieces and assisting us in the development of the ancillary materials that continue to be carried over to this edition.

Shyam Bhandari
Bradley University
John Crocket
George Mason University
J. David Diltz
University of Texas–Arlington

Kenneth Kim
University of Wisconsin–Milwaukee
Hany Shawky
University at Albany
Tie Su
University of Miami

A key feature of our book is that we integrate video clips of academics and finance professionals throughout the text. The following academics provided critical contributions to this text by sharing their insights and views on modern financial thought. Our interviews with them appear in Smart Ideas Videos and Smart Ethics Videos.

Ed Altman
New York University
Malcolm Baker
Harvard University
Utpal Bhattacharya
Indiana University
Michael Brennan
UCLA
James Brickley
University of Rochester
Robert Bruner
University of Virginia
Jennifer Conrad
University of North Carolina
Francesca Cornelli
London Business School
David Denis
Purdue University
Diane Denis
Purdue University
Elroy Dimson
London School of Business
Darrell Duffle
Stanford University
Mara Faccio
Purdue University
Kenneth French
Dartmouth College
Jon Garfinkel
University of Iowa
Steven Kaplan
University of Chicago
Andrew Karolyi
Cornell University
Scott Lee
Texas A&M University
Chris Lundblad
University of North Carolina
Ike Mathur
Southern Illinois University–Carbondale

David Mauer
University of Texas at Dallas
Mitchell Petersen
Northwestern University
Annette Poulsen
University of Georgia
Manju Puri
Duke University
Raghu Rajan
University of Chicago
Jay Ritter
University of Florida
Myron Scholes
Stanford University and Chairman of Platinum Grove Asset Management
Lemma Senbet
University of Maryland
William Sharpe
Stanford University and co-founder of Financial Engines
Robert Shiller
Yale University
Laura Starks
University of Texas
Avanidhar Subrahmanyam
UCLA
Anjan Thakor
Washington University
Sheridan Titman
University of Texas
Greg Udell
Indiana University
Theo Vermaelen
INSEAD
Rohan Williamson
Georgetown University
Kent Womack
Dartmouth College

We are also grateful to the following individuals who shared their insights based on their experience practicing corporate finance. Our interviews with them appear in Smart Practices Videos and Smart Ethics Videos.

Beth Acton
Chief Financial Officer, Comerica
Greg Barsch
President, Ravello Enterprises
David Baum
Co-Head of M&A for the Americas,
Goldman Sachs
Robert Blanding
Corporate Controller, Intel Corp.
Andy Bryant
Executive Vice President of Finance and
Enterprise Systems, Intel Corp.
Dan Carter
Executive Vice President, Chief Financial
Officer, Charlotte Russe
David Childress
Asset Liability Manager,
Ford Motor Company
Tom Cole
Co-Head, Global Banking,
Deutsche Bank Securities
Ron Dollens
Chief Executive Officer (retired),
Guidant Corp.
John Eck
President of Broadcast and Network
Operations, NBC
Lorenzo Flores
VP of Finance and Corporate Controller,
Xilinx Corp.
Scott Frame
Federal Reserve Bank of Atlanta
Jay Goodgold
Managing Director, Equities Division,
Goldman Sachs
David Haeberle
Chief Executive Officer,
Command Equity Group

Jeff Kauffman
Portfolio Manager, Blue Collar Fund,
George Weiss Associates
Herbert Kelleher
Founder, Southwest Airlines
Vince LoForti
Chief Financial Officer, Overland Storage Inc.
Cynthia Lucchese
Chief Financial Officer, Hillenbrand Industries
Walter Lukken
Chairman (former), CFTC
Ben Lytle
Chairman Emeritus, Anthem Inc.
Michael Mack, Jr.
Chief Financial Officer, John Deere
Jon Olson
Chief Financial Officer, Xilinx Corp.
Frank Popoff
Chairman of the Board (retired),
Dow Chemical
Neil Powell
Corporate Controller, Intel Corp.
Todd Richter
Managing Director, Bank of America Securities
Paul Savastano
Director of Information Technology,
Sprint Corp.
Jackie Sturm
Director of Finance for Technology and
Manufacturing, Intel Corp.
Gregg Summerville
President, Tecumseh Capital
Greg Swearingen
VP, Investor Relations, Teradata Corp.
Jeff Thermond
CEO, Woven Systems
Keith Woodward
Vice President of Finance, General Mills

Last, but certainly not least, the authors wish to thank their families and friends who provided invaluable support and assistance.

JRG, SBS, WLM   July 2009

Brief Contents

Contents

PART 2   Valuation, Risk, and Return

PART 3 Capital Budgeting

PART 4   Capital Structure and Payout Policy

PART 7   Short-Term Financing Decisions

PART 8   Special Topics

PART **1**

Introduction

Welcome to the study of *corporate finance*. In this book, you will learn the theoretical concepts that guide everyday decisions made by financial managers. The emphasis here is not just on describing the concepts but also on linking theory to what firms actually do. Part 1 of the text includes three chapters that set the stage for what follows. These chapters describe the scope of corporate finance and review two key tools that are used widely in finance: financial statement and cash flow analysis; and the time value of money.

Chapter 1 begins with a description of corporate finance and the five basic corporate finance functions (financing, financial management, capital budgeting, risk management, and corporate governance) as well as its core principles—such as investors demanding a higher return to bear risk. It then presents a brief review of the legal forms of business organizations, placing greatest emphasis on the competitive advantages and characteristics of corporations. Finally, the chapter focuses on the goals of the corporate financial manager and on the related issues of agency costs and ethics.

A recent survey reports that chief financial officers (CFOs) spend more of their time working on accounting-related tasks than on any other activity, so an understanding of basic accounting principles is clearly important to practicing financial managers. Chapter 2 provides a broad overview of the most important source of accounting information: a firm's financial statements. Our focus is on how managers use this information, not on how accountants construct the statements. Chapter 2 also explains the differences between profits and cash flows and why financial experts argue that "cash is king." Finally, we demonstrate how to construct a variety of financial ratios that analysts use to highlight how a firm performs over time and how it fares relative to competitors.

Chapter 3 introduces the time value of money, one of the most fundamental concepts in finance. The intuition behind this concept is simple: a dollar today is worth more than a dollar in the future. That's because a dollar invested today will grow to more than a dollar in the future. Managers need tools that allow them to make appropriate comparisons between costs and benefits that, in most business situations, are spread out over time. The techniques described in Chapter 3 enjoy widespread use in major corporations, but they are also helpful in making routine decisions such as choosing a home mortgage, saving for retirement, and evaluating different credit card offers.

The Scope of Corporate Finance

What Companies Do
Managing in a Financial Crisis

In October 2008, Jon Olson, CFO of Xilinx Corp., pondered an interesting offer presented to him by a hedge fund that held a large stake in Xilinx bonds. Xilinx had sold the bonds for $1,000 each in March 2007; the bonds paid an interest rate of just over 3% and were convertible into roughly 32 shares of Xilinx common stock. The company issued the bonds not because it needed the proceeds to operate, but because it wanted to distribute cash to its stockholders through a share repurchase program while simultaneously enjoying a tax deduction on the interest Xilinx paid on the debt. Since the bond was issued, world financial markets were roiled by an almost unprecedented financial crisis. U.S. stock indexes fell by 30% or more, financial institutions such as Merrill Lynch, Lehman Brothers, and Bear Stearns had liquidated or been acquired, and some credit markets in which corporations previously could readily borrow money had nearly stopped functioning.

Xilinx's bondholders needed cash, which prompted them to contact Olson. They proposed to sell roughly $1 billion in bonds back to Xilinx for $750 million, a 25% loss from the purchase price the previous year. Xilinx could entertain this offer because it had a long history of generating positive cash flow and had built up a large cash reserve over time. Xilinx produced programmable logic devices (PLDs), but it was a "fabless" company, meaning that it did none of its own manufacturing. As a consequence, most of the firm's costs were variable rather than fixed; thus, when sales moved up and down with the business cycle, costs moved proportionately and the company remained profitable most of the time.

Olson sought input from members of his board of directors, as well as from the firm's largest stockholders. Some board members thought the opportunity to retire a $1,000 loan for only $750 was too good to pass up. Others worried that the deepening financial crisis would ultimately cause a large drop in the company's revenues, and they advised Olson to hoard every penny the company made until the economy improved. Shareholders who had watched Xilinx stock drop by one-third since early 2007 advised Olson not to buy back the bonds but instead to accelerate the share repurchase program. Olson wondered which option was best as he watched the U.S. stock market continue its downward slide.

Source: Author's interview with Jon Olson, October 2008.

1.1 WHAT IS CORPORATE FINANCE?

Corporate finance is the practice of managing the money that flows in and out of businesses. The example that opens this chapter illustrates several of the important decisions that senior financial managers face on the job. Like Jon Olson, most CFOs must weigh the pros and cons of different options for raising money, investing it, and distributing profits back to investors. In managing their firm's finances, senior managers consider the interests of many different stakeholders including customers, suppliers, lenders, stockholders, and others. In this text, our goal is to describe *what* financial managers do and also *why* they do it. In other words, we believe that it is important for students to understand not only how finance is practiced in the business world but also the theory that shapes those everyday practices.

What Financial Managers Do

The scope of corporate finance is extremely broad, as is the variety of jobs available to people with financial training. In fact, the range of activities in which financial managers engage is so diverse that it is sometimes a challenge to give a succinct answer to the question, "What do financial managers do?" The practice of corporate finance involves five basic, related functions:

1. Raising capital to support a company's operations and investment programs—the **financing function**.
2. Managing a firm's day-to-day cash flows, including payments to suppliers and receipts from customers, determining optimal holdings of short-term assets such as cash and inventory, and developing short- and intermediate-term financial plans to ensure that the firm will have adequate financial resources to operate—the **financial management function**.
3. Selecting the best projects in which to invest the firm's resources, based on each project's perceived risk and expected return—the **capital budgeting function**.
4. Managing the firm's exposure to risk in order to maintain the optimum risk–return trade-off and therefore maximize shareholder value—the **risk management function**.
5. Developing a corporate governance structure capable of ensuring that managers act ethically and in stockholders' interests—the **corporate governance function**.

On a daily basis, financial managers spend their time engaged in one or more of these five activities. Figure 1.1 shows the results from a recent survey of CFOs who were asked to assess the value to their firms of different activities performed by the finance staff. This is by no means an exhaustive list, but it illustrates the scope of corporate finance as well as the relative importance of different roles in which financial professionals are engaged. What kinds of problems confront managers in each of the five functions?

Financing   Businesses raise money in one of two ways: either *externally* from investors or creditors, or *internally* by retaining operating cash flows. Most companies raise the bulk of the funding they require each year internally. When companies raise external financing they can do so either by selling an ownership interest or by borrowing money from creditors. In business terms, an ownership interest (e.g., a security such as common stock) is called **equity**, and money borrowed from creditors is termed **debt**. In their early years, corporations usually raise equity capital privately, often from professional investors such as **venture capitalists**, who specialize in high-risk/high-return investments in fast-growing firms. After a corporation "goes public" by selling its stock through an **initial public offering (IPO)**, it has the option to raise cash by selling more stock later.

Smart
Practices
Video

Tom Cole, Co-Head, Global
Banking, Deutsche Bank
Securities

*"To be good at finance you
have to understand how
businesses work."*

See the entire interview at
SMARTFinance

FIGURE 1.1

Which Finance Functions Add the Most Value?

Source: Servaes and Tufano, "CFO Views on the Importance and Execution of the Finance Function" (Deutsche Bank, 2006).

When a corporation sells securities to investors, it raises capital in a **primary market transaction**. In such a transaction, money flows from investors to firms and then firms invest the money to exploit investment opportunities. Investors who hold firms' securities can trade them with other investors. Such **secondary market transactions** (trades between investors) generate no cash for the firm, but the existence of an active secondary market does make firms' securities more attractive to investors, increasing their price.

Corporations can obtain debt financing either by selling bonds directly to investors or by borrowing money from a commercial bank or other financial intermediary. The largest and most creditworthy firms raise large amounts of short-term funding by issuing **commercial paper** directly to investors in the **money market**, the market for debt instruments maturing in one year or less. Longer-term debt instruments include **notes** (debt with original maturities of less than seven years) and various types of corporate **bonds** (debt with original maturities of more than seven years). Most corporations also borrow at least some money from commercial banks. The importance of bank financing, relative to capital market financing, has been declining for large U.S. corporations for several decades. However, bank financing remains important for smaller businesses. Commercial banks also continue to be an important source of financing in most countries.

Notice in Figure 1.1 that three of the four items rated by CFOs as "most valuable" to their companies involve the financing function. At the top of the list is "capital structure," meaning the mix of debt and equity securities issued by the company. Next is "debt issuance and management," with "bank relationships" listed fourth. It may be surprising that "equity issuance" appears near the bottom of the list, but in fact most firms rarely issue new shares to investors. Doing so is costly, and typically the market reacts negatively to a new equity offering.

Financial Management   The finance function is charged with managing the firm's operating cash flows as efficiently as possible. Part of this requires the finance staff to ensure that the firm has adequate working capital (i.e., current assets net of current liabilities) to operate smoothly day to day. Managing working capital involves obtaining seasonal financing, building inventories sufficient to meet customer needs, paying suppliers, collecting from customers, and investing surplus cash.

In Figure 1.1, CFOs cite "working capital management" as the third most valuable thing that they do for their companies. "Financial analysis and planning," which includes planning for and monitoring working capital needs, is cited as being quite important, and "cash management" appears about halfway down the list.

Capital Budgeting For two reasons, capital budgeting—selecting the best projects in which to invest the firm's resources—is a critical function. First, the scale of capital investment projects is usually quite large. Second, companies can prosper in a competitive economy only by seeking out the most promising new products, processes, and services to deliver to customers. Companies such as Intel, General Electric, Deutsche Telekom, and Toyota regularly make huge capital investments, the outcomes of which drive the value of their firms and the wealth of their owners. For these and other companies, the annual capital investment budget can run to several billion dollars.

Figure 1.1 reports that CFOs cite "making investment decisions" as the sixth most valuable activity in which they are engaged. Of course, one of the biggest investments that a firm can undertake is buying another firm, and CFOs also say that "merger, acquisition, and disposal decisions" have a large effect on firm value.

Risk Management Eighth on the CFO's list of most valuable finance activities is risk management. Historically, risk management has involved identifying a firm's risk exposure and using insurance products or self-insurance to manage that exposure. The risk management function now includes identifying, measuring, and managing all types of risk exposure. Common examples include losses that can result from adverse interest-rate movements, changes in commodity prices, and fluctuations in currency values. The techniques for managing these risks are among the most sophisticated of all corporate finance practices. The risk management task begins with quantifying the sources and size of a firm's risk exposure and deciding whether to simply accept these risks or to actively manage them.

Some risks are easily insurable, such as the risk of loss due to fire, employee theft, or product liability. Firms can reduce some other risks by *diversifying*. For example, rather than use a sole supplier for a key production input, a firm might choose to contract with several suppliers even if doing so means purchasing the input above the lowest attainable price.

However, modern risk management focuses on market-driven risks. Today risk managers use complex financial instruments to **hedge**, or offset, market risks such as interest-rate and currency fluctuations. The four most common instruments in the risk manager's arsenal are *forwards*, *futures*, *options,* and *swaps*. Companies also make commonsense choices to reduce risks, such as aligning the maturity structure of their assets and liabilities or locating a plant near important offshore suppliers or customers to attenuate currency risk.

Corporate Governance The existence of a well-functioning corporate governance system is extremely important to the modern corporation. Good management does not occur in a vacuum. Instead, it results from a corporate governance system that hires and promotes qualified, honest people and that structures employees' financial incentives to motivate them to maximize firm value.

An optimal corporate governance system is extremely difficult to develop in practice, not least because the incentives of stockholders, managers, and other stakeholders often conflict. A firm's stockholders want managers to work hard and to protect the shareholders' interests, but it is rarely profitable for any *individual* stockholder to expend time and resources monitoring managers to see if they are acting appropriately. An individual

Smart
Concepts

See the concept explained step-by-step at

SMARTFinance

Smart Practices Video

Jeff Thermond, CEO, Woven Systems

"Given that the financial markets are as messed up as they are, why should someone even contemplate a career in finance?"

See the entire interview at

SMARTFinance

JOB INTERVIEW QUESTION

What are the pros and cons of the Sarbanes-Oxley Act as it relates to corporate governance?

stockholder would personally bear all the costs of monitoring management, but the benefit of such monitoring would accrue to all shareholders. Likewise, managers may feel the need to increase the wealth of owners, but they also want to protect their own jobs. Managers rationally do not want to work harder than necessary if others will reap most of the benefits. Finally, managers and shareholders may effectively run a company to benefit themselves at the expense of creditors or other stakeholders who do not have a direct say in corporate governance.

As you might expect, several mechanisms have been designed to mitigate these problems. A strong board of directors is an essential element in any well-functioning governance system, because it is the board's duty to hire, fire, pay, and promote senior managers. The board develops *fixed* (salary) and *incentive* (bonus and stock-based) compensation packages to align managers' and shareholders' incentives. Auditors play a governance role by certifying the validity of firms' financial statements. The **Securities and Exchange Commission (SEC)**, a federal agency established in 1934, is charged with oversight of the fair reporting of financial information to investors in public companies (those whose shares are listed for trading in a public securities market). In the United States, accounting scandals and concerns about auditors' conflicts of interest prompted the SEC to require the CFOs of large firms to personally certify their firms' earnings numbers. Note in Figure 1.1 the importance that CFOs assign to tasks such as "external financial reporting," "regulatory compliance," and "internal audit," all of which are related to how the firm is governed.

Despite the efforts of the SEC, corporate scandals near the turn of the century revealed numerous shortcomings in U.S. corporate governance practices. In response, Congress passed the **Sarbanes–Oxley Act of 2002**. This act imposed a host of new requirements on firms, including restrictions on board membership, executive compensation, relationships with auditors, and many others. The legislation also required firms to provide extensive documentation of the internal controls they put in place to protect investors from fraud. The costs of complying with the Sarbanes–Oxley Act prompted many small firms to choose private over public ownership or to raise capital in markets outside the United States.

Just as companies struggle to develop an effective corporate governance system, so do countries. Governments establish legal frameworks that either encourage or discourage the development of competitive businesses and efficient financial markets. For example, a legal system should permit efficiency-enhancing mergers and acquisitions but should block business combinations that significantly restrict competition. It should provide protection for creditors and minority shareholders by limiting the opportunities for managers or majority shareholders to expropriate wealth.

The Principles behind Managerial Decisions

The theory of corporate finance provides managers with a set of principles that they can use to make wise financial decisions. These principles apply to a wide range of practical business problems, as you'll see while progressing through the book. Five core principles form the theoretical bedrock of corporate finance.

The Time Value of Money   Suppose you win $100 in a contest and you can choose to receive your prize immediately or in a year. Which would you choose? Most people would rather have the money immediately rather than wait for it. That is not merely a matter of impatience. If you have $100 in hand today, you can invest it and earn interest, accumulating more than $100 in one year. Thus we have the first core principle of finance:

> *The opportunity to earn a return on invested funds means that a dollar today is worth more than a dollar in the future.*

This principle is important because most business decisions involve a trade-off between spending money today and receiving money in the future. That is precisely the trade-off that companies face when they build new manufacturing facilities, broadcast commercials on television, or hire new employees. Financial managers use time-value-of-money (TMV) tools to determine how much cash a firm must generate in the future in order to justify today's expenditures on new investments.

Compensation for Risk   Now consider another proposition. You have just won $100 dollars and are given the opportunity to double your money. The flip of a coin will determine the outcome. If the coin comes up heads then you win $200, but if it comes up tails then you win nothing. Would you take the risk and go for $200, or would you count yourself lucky to walk away with $100?

In this situation, most people choose the certain $100 prize over the 50-50 chance at $200. Given that you have an equal likelihood of winning $200 or winning nothing, elementary statistics tells us that the expected value of the gamble is $100. But why take that risk when you can get $100 for sure? To entice people to play this game, we might increase the prize for flipping a "heads" to something above $200, or we might change the game so that the probability of winning the $200 prize is greater than 50%. In either case, inducing people to accept the gamble means changing the game so that the expected payoff *exceeds* $100, the value of the sure thing. This leads to the second core finance principle:

> *Investors expect compensation for bearing risk.*

There are many business applications of this principle. For example, suppose a consumer products firm is weighing two investment proposals, both of which require an investment of $10 million. The first proposal is to distribute a product in Canada that has had prior success in the United States. The second proposal calls for investing in basic research and development (R&D) to develop new products in a market niche where the company currently has no presence.

Intuitively, the second investment seems riskier than the first. If that intuition is correct, then investors will demand a higher return on the R&D project. Accordingly, in evaluating the two projects, financial managers must recognize that the R&D project must generate higher future cash flows than the alternative project in order to justify an investment of $10 million.

Don't Put All Your Eggs in One Basket   In 1990, Harry Markowitz shared the Nobel Prize in economics for his work showing how investors could improve the performance of their investments through diversification. His insights contributed to a boom in mutual funds, an industry that pools investors' funds so they can achieve greater diversification. Most people understand that they can reduce the risk of their investments by diversifying, but Markowitz's insight went deeper than that. He showed how diversification could actually improve the performance of a portfolio relative to its risk. Thus, Markowitz was an early pioneer in developing the third core finance principle:

> *Investors can achieve a more favorable trade-off between risk and return by diversifying their portfolios.*

Markets Are Smart   On January 28, 1986, the world was shocked when the spacecraft *Challenger* exploded shortly after launching. Months later, a presidential commission reported its finding that cold temperatures at launch time compromised the integrity of

O-rings in the rocket boosters, which led to the explosion. Physicist Richard Feynman famously demonstrated the problem by dunking a piece of O-ring rubber into ice water to show that it was slow to return to its original shape when cold.

Several companies—including Rockwell International, Lockheed, Martin Marietta, and Morton Thiokol—had contracts to produce components of the space shuttle. Stock prices of all four firms fell when the shuttle exploded. But while the prices of Rockwell, Lockheed, and Martin Marietta dropped about 2.5%, Morton Thiokol's stock fell almost 12%, with much of that drop taking place within 20 minutes of the accident. What was Morton Thiokol's role in the space shuttle program? It made the solid rocket boosters. In other words, prices in the market quickly reflected—accurately, as it turned out—investors' perceptions of which company made the component that was critical in causing *Challenger*'s demise.[1] This illustrates the fourth core principle of finance:

Capital markets are, for the most part, efficient.

By "efficient" here we simply mean that prices of stocks, bonds, and other financial assets reflect all the information to which investors have access. If markets are "informationally efficient," then only *new* information (by definition, information that no one knows or can reliably predict) moves stock prices. Therefore, in an efficient market it is difficult for any individual, even a professional money manager, to do a better-than-average job of predicting which stocks will perform particularly well and which ones will disappoint investors.

No Arbitrage   The term *arbitrage* refers to a trading strategy in which an investor simultaneously buys and sells the same asset in different markets at different prices to earn an instant, risk-free profit. For example, suppose a currency trader learns that in New York she can exchange $2 for £1 but that in London £1 will buy only $1.90. If the trader is clever, she will recognize the profit opportunity here. She could convert £1 million into $2 million in New York and then transfer those funds to the London market, converting them there into £1,052,632. Without taking any risk at all she earns a £52,632 profit, and she will keep repeating that trade until the exchange rate between dollars and pounds is the same in New York and London. Because opportunities like this one are almost always too good to last, we have the fifth core finance principle:

Arbitrage opportunities are extremely scarce.

The notion that arbitrage opportunities should be very hard to find—and should not last very long if they are uncovered—has many applications in modern finance. These applications range from understanding the impact of **capital structure** and dividend decisions on firm value to pricing exotic financial securities such as options. In fact, the no-arbitrage principle may well be the most powerful of all the core principles and also the least understood.

Each year tens of thousands of MBA students select finance as their major. We believe that the popularity of finance stems from the exciting and rewarding career opportunities available to students who master the five basic functions outlined here. Although this book stresses the roles that financial managers play in large corporations, successful careers in finance are by no means limited to the Fortune 500 firms or to the corporate sector. In the next section we discuss the pros and cons of different organizational forms adopted by business owners and managers in the United States and abroad.

---

[1]For a full description of the stock market's reaction to the *Challenger* disaster, see Maloney and Mulherin (2003).

Concept Review Questions

1. What are the five basic corporate finance functions?
2. What are the core principles of finance? Describe some ways in which managers might use the core principles of finance when performing the basic corporate finance functions.

1.2 Legal Forms of Business Organization

Companies exist so that people can organize to pursue profit-making ventures in a formal, legally secure manner. This section examines how companies organize themselves legally and discusses the costs and benefits of each major form.

The three key legal forms of business organization in the United States have historically been the sole proprietorship, the partnership, and the corporation. These have recently been joined by a fourth type, the limited liability company (LLC). The sole proprietorship is the most common form of organization. The corporation is by far the dominant form in terms of aggregate sales and profits. In addition to these key forms, there are two very important "hybrid" organizational forms, the limited partnership and the S corporation. We will examine all these forms, beginning with the sole proprietorship.

Sole Proprietorships

A **sole proprietorship** is a business with a single owner. In fact, there is no legal distinction between the business and the owner. The business is the owner's personal property, it exists only as long as the owner lives and chooses to operate it, and all business assets belong to the owner. Furthermore, the owner bears liability for all the company's debts and pays income taxes on its earnings. Sole proprietorships are the most common type of business in the United States, accounting for about three-fourths of all business tax returns filed each year. However, proprietorships receive less than 6% of all business income and employ less than 10% of the workforce.

Simplicity and ease of operation constitute the principal benefits of the proprietorship. However, this organizational form suffers from weaknesses that in most cases limit the firm's long-run growth potential. These include the following:

1. *Limited life*. By definition, a proprietorship ceases to exist when the founder retires or dies. Although the founder/entrepreneur can pass the assets of the business on to a third party, most of what makes the business valuable is tied to the proprietor personally. Furthermore, changes in ownership of successful companies can trigger large tax liabilities.
2. *Limited access to capital*. A proprietorship can obtain operating capital from only two sources: reinvested profits and personal borrowing by the entrepreneur. In practice, both of these sources are easily exhausted.
3. *Unlimited personal liability*. A sole proprietor is personally liable for all the debts of the business, including judgments awarded a plaintiff in a successful lawsuit. The United States is the most litigious society in history (each year some 20 *million* lawsuits are filed in state courts alone), and a single jury verdict can destroy even the most successful business.

Partnerships

A (general) **partnership** is essentially a proprietorship with two or more owners who have joined their skills and personal wealth. As in a sole proprietorship, there is no legal distinction between the business and its owners, each of whom can execute contracts binding on the other(s) and each of whom is personally liable for all the partnership's debts. This sharing of legal responsibility is known as **joint and several liability**.

Though nothing requires the owners to formalize the terms of their partnership in a written *partnership agreement*, most partnerships create such a document. In the absence of a partnership agreement, the business dissolves whenever one of the partners retires or dies. Furthermore, unless there is a partnership agreement specifying otherwise, each partner shares equally in business income and each has equal management authority. As with a proprietorship, partnership income is taxed only once: at the personal level.

In addition to the tax benefits and ease of formation that partnerships share with proprietorships, the partnership allows a large number of people to pool their capital and expertise to form a much larger enterprise. Partnerships enjoy more flexibility than proprietorships in that the business need not automatically terminate following the retirement or death of one partner. Industries in which partnerships are usually the dominant form of organization include accounting, consulting, engineering, law, and medicine.

The drawbacks of the partnership form resemble those of the sole proprietorship:

1. *Limited life.* The life of the firm can be limited, particularly if only a few partners are involved. Problems may also result from the instability inherent in long-term, multi-person business associations.
2. *Limited access to capital.* For operating capital the firm is still limited to retained profits and personal borrowings.
3. *Unlimited personal liability.* This disadvantage is accentuated because the partners are subject to joint and several liability.

As firms grow larger, the competitive disadvantages of the proprietorship and partnership organizational forms tend to become extremely burdensome. Almost all successful companies eventually adopt the corporate organizational form.

In many ways, a **limited partnership (LP)** combines the best features of the (general) partnership and the corporate organizational forms. In any limited partnership, there must be one or more **general partners**, each of whom has unlimited personal liability. Because only the general partners operate the business and are legally exposed, they usually receive a greater-than-proportional (in terms of their capital contribution) share of partnership income. Most of the participants in the partnership are **limited partners**. They have the limited liability of corporate shareholders, but their share of the profits from the business is taxed as partnership income. The limited partners, however, must be totally passive. They contribute capital to the partnership but cannot have their names associated with the business; neither can they take an active role in the operation of the business, even as employees. In return for this passivity, the limited partners face no personal liability for business debts. This means that, although limited partners can lose their equity investment in the business, tax authorities (or other plaintiffs) cannot sue the limited partners personally for payment of their claims. It should be emphasized that limited partners share in partnership income, which is taxed as ordinary personal income for the partners.

Limited partnerships are ideal vehicles for funding long-term investments that generate large noncash operating losses in the early years of the business, because these losses *flow through* directly to the limited partners. This means the limited partners can (under specified conditions) use the tax losses to offset taxable income from other sources. Disadvantages of LPs include a shallow secondary market for securities and difficulties with monitoring and disciplining the general partner(s). In some cases, registering an LP with the SEC allows secondary-market trading of partnership interests; this can reduce or even eliminate the illiquidity problem.

Corporations

Under U.S. law, a **corporation** is a separate legal entity with many of the economic rights and responsibilities enjoyed by individuals. A corporation can sue and be sued, it can own property and execute contracts in its own name, and it can be tried and convicted for crimes committed by its employees.

The corporate organizational form has several key competitive advantages over other forms, including the following:

1. *Unlimited life.* Once created, a corporation has perpetual life unless it is explicitly terminated.
2. *Limited liability.* The firm's shareholders cannot be held personally liable for the firm's debts.
3. *Separable contracting.* Corporations can contract individually with managers, suppliers, customers, and ordinary employees, and each individual contract can be renegotiated, modified, or terminated without affecting other stakeholders.
4. *Improved access to capital.* The company itself, rather than its owners, can borrow money from creditors, and it can also issue various classes of preferred and common stock to equity investors. Furthermore, the ownership claims themselves (shares of common stock) can be freely traded among investors, without obtaining the permission of other investors, if the corporation is a **public company**—that is, one whose shares are listed for trading in a public securities market.

As a legal entity, a corporation is owned by the **shareholders** who hold its shares of stock. Shares of stock carry voting rights, and shareholders vote at an annual meeting to elect the firm's directors. The directors include key corporate personnel as well as outsiders who are typically successful private businesspeople or executives of other major corporations. The **board of directors** is responsible for hiring and firing managers and for setting overall corporate policies. The rules dictating voting procedures and other parameters of corporate governance appear in the firm's **corporate charter**, the legal document created at the corporation's inception to govern the firm's operations. The charter can be changed only by a vote of the shareholders.

Also, in contrast to the practice in almost all other countries, incorporation in the United States is executed at the state rather than at the national level and is governed primarily by state law, not federal law. Nonetheless, all 50 states have broadly similar rules for incorporation and corporate governance. At the federal level, of course, it is the SEC's job to regulate the financial reporting of public corporations.

Corporations may issue two forms of stock—*common* and *preferred*—each with slightly different rights and privileges. Shareholders of common and preferred stock, as owners of the firm's equity securities, are often called **equity claimants**. Shareholders of preferred stock typically have higher-priority access to the corporation's earnings and bear less risk than shareholders of common stock. In exchange, they generally do not have the right to vote. Therefore, we refer to common stockholders as the firm's ultimate owners. Common stockholders vote periodically to elect the members of the board of directors and, occasionally, to amend the firm's corporate charter.

It is important to note the division between owners and managers in a large corporation. The **president** or **chief executive officer (CEO)** is responsible for managing day-to-day operations and carrying out the policies established by the board. The board expects regular reports from the CEO regarding the firm's current status and future direction. However, the CEO and the board serve at the will of the shareholders. The separation between owners and managers leads to **agency costs**, the costs that arise from conflicts of interest between shareholders and managers. These costs—and the agency problems that cause them—are discussed in greater depth in Section 1.3.

Although corporations dominate economic life around the world, this form has some competitive disadvantages. Many governments tax corporate income at both company and personal levels. This treatment, commonly called the **double-taxation problem**, has traditionally been the single greatest disadvantage of the corporate form in the United States. But the Jobs and Growth Tax Relief Reconciliation Act of 2003 substantially reduced this problem by lowering personal tax rates on dividends and capital gains.

Table 1.1 illustrates the double-taxation problem by comparing the tax burden faced by investors in a corporation with the taxes owed by the owners of a partnership. Both businesses earn $100,000 of pre-tax income. We assume that the corporation in our example is taxed at the top corporate income-tax rate of 35% ($T_c = 0.35$) and that the partnership's investors face the top personal income-tax rate, which is also 35% ($T_p = 0.35$). The tax law now allows the corporation's shareholders to treat received dividends as capital gains, and we will assume that shareholders face the top personal capital gains tax rate of 15% ($T_{cg} = 0.15$). As the law currently stands, the partners receive after-tax disposable income of $65,000 [$100,000 × (1 − 0.35)] and shareholders receive net disposable income of $55,250 [$100,000 × (1 − 0.35) × (1 − 0.15)]. As this example shows, a partnership (or proprietorship) enjoys a small tax advantage over a corporation.[2]

Table 1.1	**Taxation of Business Income for Corporations and Partnerships _after_ Passage of the Jobs and Growth Tax Relief Reconciliation Act of 2003**	
	CORPORATION	**PARTNERSHIP**
Operating income	$100,000	$100,000
Less: Corporate profits tax ($T_c = 0.35$)	35,000	0
Net income	65,000	$100,000
Cash dividends or partnership distributions	65,000	$100,000
Less: Personal tax on dividends ($T_{cg} = 0.15$)	9,750	
Less: Personal tax on partnership income ($T_p = 0.35$)		35,000
After-tax disposable income	$ 55,250	$ 65,000

In contrast to a regular corporation, an **S corporation** (previously called a _Subchapter S corporation_) allows shareholders to be taxed as partners while still retaining their limited liability status as corporate shareholders. This type of company is an ordinary corporation (or _C corporation_), in which the shareholders have elected to be treated as S-corporation shareholders. To be eligible for S status, a firm must meet several requirements: it must have 100 or fewer shareholders, the shareholders must be individuals or certain types of trusts (not corporations), the S corporation cannot issue more than one class of equity security, and it cannot be a _holding company_ (cannot hold a controlling fraction of the stock in another company).

[2]Although the exact tax rates may change under President Obama's administration, the double-taxation problem is likely to remain.

If a corporation meets these requirements, then S-corporation status allows the company's operating income to escape separate taxation at the corporate level.[3] Instead, each shareholder claims as personal income a proportionate fraction of total company profits and pays tax on this profit at his own personal tax rate. As with a limited partnership, S-corporation status yields the limited liability benefit of the corporate form along with the favorable taxation of the partnership form. In addition, an S corporation can easily become a regular C corporation should it outgrow the 100-shareholder ceiling or need to issue multiple classes of equity securities. Given the inherent flexibility of this type of organization, it is common for successful companies to begin life as S corporations and to retain S status until they decide to go public, at which time they are required to become regular corporations.

Limited Liability Companies

The **limited liability company (LLC)** combines the partnership's pass-through taxation with the S corporation's limited liability. All 50 U.S. states allow LLCs, which are easy to set up. The IRS allows an LLC's owners to elect taxation as either a partnership or a corporation, and many states allow one-person LLCs and a choice between a finite or infinite company life. Even though LLCs can be taxed as partnerships, their owners face no personal liability for the other partners' malpractice, making this type of company especially attractive for professional service firms. Given the limited liability feature and the flexibility of LLCs, we expect that they will continue to gain significant "organizational market share" in the years to come.

Concept Review Questions	3. What are the costs and benefits of each of the three major organizational forms? Why do you think that the various "hybrid" forms of business organization have proven so successful?
	4. Comment on the following statement: "Sooner or later, all successful private companies that are organized as proprietorships or partnerships must become corporations."

1.3 GOALS OF THE CORPORATE FINANCIAL MANAGER

In widely held corporations, the owners typically do not manage the firm. This raises an interesting question: Whose interests should managers serve? Shareholders? Creditors? Customers? Employees? The traditional answer given in finance textbooks is that managers should operate the firm in a way that maximizes shareholder wealth. As a practical matter, that recommendation is difficult to implement, partly because managers may be tempted to pursue their own interests rather than shareholders' interests.

What Should a Financial Manager Try to Maximize?

Should a financial manager try to maximize corporate profits, shareholder wealth, or something else? In the sections that follow, we hope to convince you that managers should seek to maximize shareholder wealth.

Smart Practices Video

Herbert Kelleher, Founder, Southwest Airlines

"Shareholder value maximization is devoid of meaning unless you tell me how you're going to do it."

See the entire interview at

SMART**Finance**

---

[3] According to the 2009 *Statistical Abstract of the United States*, about 65% (3.684 million of 5.671 million) of all corporations filing 2005 tax returns were S corporations, which indicates both the popularity of this organizational form and the relatively small *average* size of U.S. businesses.

Maximize Profit?   Some people believe that the manager's objective is to maximize profits, and it is common to see compensation plans designed so that managers receive larger bonuses for increasing reported earnings. To achieve profit maximization, the financial manager takes those actions that make a positive contribution to the firm's profits. Thus, for each alternative, the financial manager should select the one with the highest expected profit. From a practical standpoint, this objective translates into maximizing earnings per share (EPS).

Although it seems a plausible objective, profit maximization suffers from several flaws. First, EPS figures are inherently backward-looking, reflecting what has happened rather than what will happen. Second, some short-run decisions (e.g., forgoing maintenance) to boost EPS can actually destroy value in the long run. Third, even if managers strive to maximize profits over time, they should not ignore the timing of those profits. A large profit that arrives many years in the future may be less valuable than a smaller profit earned today. (Remember the first core principle of finance: the time value of money.) Fourth, a manager cannot maximize profits without knowing how to measure them, and conventional barometers of profit come from accrual-based accounting principles rather than from a focus on cash flow.

JOB INTERVIEW QUESTION

What problems might be encountered if a firm ties its bonuses to earnings per share?

Finally, focusing solely on earnings ignores risk. When comparing two investment opportunities, managers should not always choose the one they expect to generate the highest profits. They must consider the risks of the investments as well. The third core principle in corporate finance is that a trade-off exists between risk and return. Higher cash flow generally leads to higher share prices, whereas higher risk results in lower share prices. Therefore, an investment project with high profits and high risk could be less valuable than one with lower profits and lower risk.

Maximize Shareholder Wealth?   Modern finance asserts that the proper goal of the firm is to maximize the wealth of shareholders, where wealth is measured by the firm's stock price. This stock price reflects the timing, magnitude, and risk of the *cash flows* that investors expect a firm to generate over time. When considering alternative strategies, financial managers should undertake only those actions that they expect will increase the firm's share price.

Why does finance preach the wisdom of maximizing share value as the primary corporate objective? Why not focus instead on satisfying the desires of corporate **stakeholders** such as customers, employees, suppliers, and creditors? A firm's shareholders are sometimes called its **residual claimants**, meaning that they can exert claims only on the firm's cash flows that remain after all other claimants are satisfied in full. It may help to visualize a queue with all the firm's stakeholders standing in line to receive their share of the firm's cash flows. Shareholders stand at the end of this line. If the firm cannot pay its employees, suppliers, creditors, and the tax authorities, then shareholders receive nothing. Shareholders earn a return on their investment only after all other stakeholders' claims have been met. In other words, maximizing shareholder returns usually implies that the firm must also satisfy customers, employees, suppliers, creditors, and other stakeholders first.[4]

Furthermore, by accepting their position as residual claimants, shareholders agree to bear more risk than other stakeholders do. If firms did not operate with the goal of maximizing shareholder wealth in mind, then shareholders would have little incentive to accept the risks necessary for a business to thrive. To understand this point, consider how a firm would operate if it were run solely in the interests of its creditors. Given that creditors receive only a fixed return, would such a firm be inclined to make risky investments, no matter how profitable? Only shareholders have the proper incentives to make risky, value-increasing investments.

---

[4]This statement is, we admit, overly simplistic, because conflicts of interest can exist between a firm's shareholders and its other constituents. Even so, from a legal perspective, shareholders profit only when the firm meets its contractual obligations to other stakeholders.

WHAT COMPANIES DO GLOBALLY

Views on Corporate Goals and Stakeholder Groups

Although the perspective of maximizing shareholder value enjoys widespread acceptance in the United States, its appeal internationally is more limited. Figure 1.2 reports survey evidence on this question from the United Kingdom, the Netherlands, Germany, and France. In each country, researchers asked CFOs to rate the importance of alternative corporate goals and different stakeholder groups. Of all the CFOs surveyed, those in Britain put the highest value on maximizing shareholder wealth—but even for them, other goals were more important. In France, maximizing shareholder wealth was rated as least important among all the choices.

Parallel responses appear in a question about the "importance" of various stakeholder groups. British managers placed far more emphasis on satisfying shareholders than did French and German managers. The French said that shareholders were less important than "the general public," suggesting that they view firms as agents of social welfare as much as vehicles for the creation of private wealth. But in all four countries, managers rated the interests of customers, employees, and management above those of shareholders. Note once again, however, that this view is not entirely inconsistent with maximizing shareholder value because satisfying the other stakeholder groups may be a prerequisite for generating shareholder wealth.

FIGURE 1.2

What Global Companies Do

Source: Brounen et al. (2004, FM).

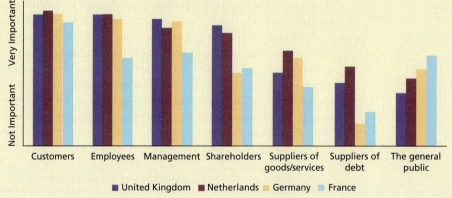

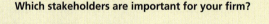

How Can Agency Costs Be Controlled in Corporate Finance?

We have argued that financial managers should pursue the goal of maximizing share-holder wealth. Thus, managers act as *agents* of the owners who have hired them and given them decision-making authority. In practice, managers also care about their personal wealth, job security, lifestyle, prestige, and perquisites. Such concerns cause managers to pursue objectives other than maximizing shareholder wealth. Shareholders recognize the potential for managers' self-interested behavior, and they use a variety of tools to limit this behavior. The term *agency costs* refers to costs that arise as a result of these conflicts between owners and managers.

Types of Agency Costs   The conflict of interest between owners and managers gives rise to **agency problems**. Shareholders can attempt to overcome agency problems by various means: (1) relying on market forces to exert managerial discipline; (2) incurring the monitoring and bonding costs necessary to supervise managers; and/or (3) structuring executive compensation packages that align the interests of managers and stockholders.

Several market forces constrain the behavior of a firm's managers. In recent years, large investors have become more active in management. This is particularly true for *institutional investors* such as mutual funds, life insurance companies, and pension funds, which often hold large blocks of stock. Activist institutional investors use their influence to put pressure on underperforming management teams, occasionally applying enough pressure to replace the CEO.

An even more powerful form of market discipline is the **hostile takeover**, which involves the acquisition of one firm (the *target*) by another (the *acquirer*) through an open-market bid for a majority of the target's shares. By definition, a takeover attempt is hostile if the target firm's senior managers resist (or simply do not support) the acquisi-tion. Bidders in hostile deals may believe that they can improve the value of the target company, and thereby make a profit on their investment, by replacing incumbent manage-ment. Managers naturally find this threatening and erect a variety of barriers to thwart potential acquirers. Nevertheless, the constant threat of a takeover provides additional motivation for managers to act in the interests of the firm's owners.

In addition to these market forces, other devices exist that encourage managers to behave in shareholders' interests or that limit the consequences when managers misbe-have. *Monitoring expenditures* pay for audits and control procedures that alert sharehold-ers when managers pursue their own interests too aggressively.[5] *Bonding expenditures* protect against the potential consequences of dishonest acts by managers. Directors can make bonding expenditures, or managers can themselves make these expenditures to reassure the firm's directors of their benevolent intentions. This can be done, for example, by accepting a portion of their total pay in the form of delayed compensation.

Use of Compensation Contracts to Control Agency Costs   Another way to align managerial and stockholder interests is through **executive compensation plans**. The objective is to design such plans to give managers the incentive to act in the best interests of the owners. Incentive compensation plans tie managerial wealth to the firm's share price by paying managers with shares of stock or **stock options**. (Stock options give the manager the right to purchase stock at a fixed price, usually the market price of the stock

---

[5]But, you may ask, "Who monitors the monitors?" In the wake of Enron's bankruptcy, Enron's auditor—Arthur Andersen—experienced the consequences of failing to alert shareholders to the company's problems. Audit clients abandoned the firm in droves and many of the firm's partners quit, so Arthur Andersen closed its accounting/auditing services and then returned as a consulting firm, Accenture. Thus, the market disciplined the auditors for their failure to impose discipline on Enron.

at the time the manager receives the options.) The key idea is that managers will have an incentive to take actions that maximize the stock price, because this will increase their wealth along with that of the other shareholders.

Although experts agree that an effective way to motivate management is to tie compensation to performance, many have scrutinized compensation plans in recent years. Individual and institutional investors, as well as the SEC, have publicly questioned the appropriateness of the multimillion-dollar compensation packages received by some corporate executives. Average levels of CEO compensation in other developed countries tend to be much lower than in the United States.

Large pay packages may be justified by exceptional increases in shareholder wealth, yet academic studies generally find only a modest positive relationship between CEO compensation and share price. These generous pay packages are also extremely controversial in cases where managers of poorly performing companies still receive large payouts. For example, while the U.S. stock market (especially Nasdaq) suffered one of its worst yearly declines in decades during 2000, the average total compensation of 365 CEOs of the companies in *Business Week*'s survey rose by 18%, to $13.1 million. More recently, there has been an uproar as executives of the financial sector received large paydays while their employees and shareholders suffered. Further controversy arose with the discovery that some executives were backdating their option grants, setting the terms of the options in a way that maximized value to managers without disclosing that fact to the public.

Why Ethics are Important in Corporate Finance

In recent years, the media and others have questioned the legitimacy of actions taken by certain businesses. Examples range from the $1.2 million that former Merrill Lynch CEO John Thain spent redecorating his office, shortly after Bank of America acquired Merrill in 2008, to the billions stolen by Bernard Madoff through his massive Ponzi scheme. The global financial crisis, beginning in 2007 and continuing as this book went to press, focused attention on a wide range of ethical issues. Did mortgage lenders lower their credit standards in order to make a quick profit on loan originations while passing on the risk of subprime mortgages to other investors? Did a lack of due diligence by rating agencies cause them to fail to warn investors of the risks of exotic mortgage-backed securities and credit default swaps? Should financial institutions like American International Group (AIG) pay bonuses to managers even after receiving billions in federal bailout dollars?

The last time ethical concerns received as much attention in the media was after the Enron collapse in late 2001. In response to a series of corporate scandals Congress passed the Sarbanes–Oxley Act of 2002, a law that requires firms to provide extensive documentation of the internal controls they put in place to protect investors from fraud. Among other things, Sarbanes–Oxley requires the CFO to personally vouch for the accuracy of numbers in the financial statements. In all likelihood, one response to the current global financial crisis will be the enactment of new laws placing limits on the risks that financial institutions can take. Already, firms that receive money under the Troubled Asset Relief Program (TARP) face limits on the compensation they can pay to top personnel.

More and more firms are now directly addressing the issue of ethics by establishing corporate ethics policies and guidelines and by requiring employee compliance with them. Frequently, employees are required to sign a formal pledge to uphold the firm's ethics policies. Such policies typically apply to employee actions in dealing with all corporate stakeholders, including the public at large. *Ethical behavior is therefore viewed as both necessary and perfectly consistent with achieving the firm's goal of maximizing shareholder wealth.*

Smart Ethics Video

Andy Bryant, Executive Vice President of Finance and Enterprise Services, Chief Administrative Officer, Intel Corp.

"I never thought that ethics would be a value-add to a company, but today I believe it counts as part of your market cap."

See the entire interview at
SMARTFinance

SUMMARY

- Corporate finance activities can be grouped into five basic functions: the financing function, the financial management function, the capital budgeting function, the risk management function, and the corporate governance function.

- The practice of corporate finance rests on a foundation of five core principles dealing with the time value of money, the trade-off between risk and return, diversification, efficient markets, and no arbitrage.

- The three key legal forms of business organization in the United States are sole proprietorships, partnerships, and corporations. Sole proprietorships are most common, but corporations dominate economically. A new, fourth form, the limited liability company, has recently become popular because of its flexibility and the favorable tax treatment it offers.

- The goal of the firm's managers should be to maximize shareholder wealth, not to maximize profits. Maximizing profits focuses on the past rather than the future, ignores the timing of profits, relies on accounting values rather than future cash flows, and ignores risk. Maximizing shareholder wealth is socially optimal because shareholders are residual claimants who profit only after all other claims are paid in full.

- Agency costs that result from the separation of ownership and management must be addressed satisfactorily for companies to prosper. These costs can be overcome (or at least reduced) by relying on the workings of the market for corporate control, incurring monitoring and bonding costs, and using executive compensation contracts designed to align the interests of shareholders and managers.

KEY TERMS

agency costs	equity claimants	president
agency problems	executive compensation plans	primary market transaction
board of directors	financial management function	public company
bonds	financing function	residual claimants
capital budgeting function	general partners	risk management function
capital structure	hedge	S corporation
chief executive officer (CEO)	hostile takeover	Sarbanes–Oxley Act of 2002
commercial paper	initial public offering (IPO)	secondary market transactions
corporate charter	joint and several liability	Securities and Exchange
corporate finance	limited liability company (LLC)	Commission (SEC)
corporate governance function	limited partners	shareholders
corporation	limited partnership (LP)	sole proprietorship
debt	money market	stakeholder
double-taxation problem	notes	stock options
equity	partnership	venture capitalists

QUESTIONS

1-1. Why must a financial manager have an integrated understanding of the five basic finance functions? Why is the corporate governance function considered a finance function? Has the risk management function become more important in recent years?

1-2. Which of the five core principles of finance relate to the five basic finance functions? Based on the descriptions provided in the chapter, in what ways do these core principles relate to the basic finance functions?

1-3. What are the advantages and disadvantages of the different legal forms of business organization? Could the limited liability advantage of a corporation also lead to an agency problem? Why? What legal form would an upstart entrepreneur likely prefer?

1-4. Can there be a difference between maximizing profits and maximizing shareholder wealth? If so, what could cause this difference? Which of the two should be the goal of the firm and its management?

1-5. Define a corporate *stakeholder*. Which groups are considered to be stakeholders? Would shareholders also be considered stakeholders? Compare, in terms of economic systems, the principle of maximizing shareholder wealth with the principle of satisfying stakeholder claims.

1-6. What is meant by an *agency cost* or *agency problem*? Do these interfere with maximizing shareholder wealth? Why or why not? What mechanisms minimize these costs/problems? Are executive compensation contracts effective in mitigating them?

1-7. Are ethics critical to the financial manager's goal of maximizing shareholder wealth? How are the two related? Is establishing corporate ethics policies and requiring employee compliance enough to ensure ethical behavior by employees?

PROBLEMS

Smart Solutions

See the problem and solution explained step-by-step at **SMARTFinance**

Legal Forms of Business Organization

1-1. **a.** Calculate the tax disadvantage to organizing a U.S. business as a corporation, as compared to a partnership, under the following conditions. Assume that all earnings will be paid out as cash dividends. Operating income will be $500,000. The tax rate on corporate profits is 35%, the average personal tax rate for the partners is 35%, and the capital gains tax rate on dividend income is 15%.

b. Now recalculate the tax disadvantage using the same income but with the maximum tax rates that existed before 2003. (These rates were 35% on corporate profits and 38.6% on personal investment income.)

Goals of the Corporate Financial Manager

1-2. Consider the following simple corporate example with one stockholder and one manager. There are two mutually exclusive projects in which the manager may invest (see the top of the next page) and two possible manager compensation plans that the stockholder may choose to employ. The manager may be paid a flat $300,000 or receive 10% of corporate profits. The stockholder receives all profits net of manager compensation.

a. Which project maximizes shareholder wealth? Which compensation contract does the manager prefer if this project is chosen?

b. Which project will the manager choose under a flat compensation arrangement?

Project #1		Project #2	
Probability	**Gross Profit**	**Probability**	**Gross Profit**
33.33%	$0	50%	$600,000
33.33%	$3,000,000	50%	$900,000
33.33%	$9,000,000		

  c. Which compensation contract aligns the interests of the stockholders and the manager so that the manager will act in the best interest of the stockholders?

  d. What do the answers tell you about structuring management pay contracts?

THOMSON ONE | Business School Edition

Access financial information from the Thomson ONE–Business School Edition website for the following problem(s). Go to http://tobsefin.swlearning.com/. If you have already registered your access serial number and have a username and password, click **Enter**. Otherwise, click **Register** and follow the instructions to create a username and password. Register your access serial number and then click **Enter** on the aforementioned website. When you click Enter, you will be prompted for your username and password (please remember that the password is case sensitive). Enter them in the respective boxes and then click **OK** (or hit **Enter**). From the ensuing page, click **Click Here to Access Thomson ONE–Business School Edition Now!** This opens up a new window that gives you access to the Thomson ONE–Business School Edition database. You can retrieve a company's financial information by entering its ticker symbol [provided for each company in the problem(s)] in the box below "Companies." For further instructions on using the Thomson ONE–Business School Edition database, please refer to "A Guide for Using Thomson ONE–Business School Edition."

1-3. Examine the insider activities of Johnson & Johnson (ticker symbol, JNJ). Under the Filings tab, click on the Daily 144 List in the Insider Analytics box. Does there appear to be a preponderance of proposed buying or selling of JNJ shares? Does this suggest that an agency problem exists?

2

Financial Statement and Cash Flow Analysis

What Companies Do
Financial Signs of a Slowing Economy

How can a financial manager know that a slowing economy is directly affecting her company? One of the best indicators of financial stress is an increase in the time that customers take to pay their bills. A clear signal that the U.S. economy was under stress was provided by the release of a 2007 survey of U.S. companies. The study—conducted by REL, a consulting firm, and *CFO Magazine*—documented a sharp increase in the average "days' sales outstanding", the average number of days' sales that are outstanding as uncollected accounts receivable. The survey found that average days' sales outstanding increased from 39.7 days in 2006 to 41.0 days in 2007. Although this may not seem like a dramatic increase, the report pointed out that days' sales outstanding rarely increased by more than half a day from one year to the next. Thus the 1.3-day increase was a strong sign that American companies were having trouble collecting on the credit they had extended.

Source: "Dealing with the Downturn: Accounts not Receivable," The Economist (September 6, 2008), page 74. Copyright © 2008 by The Economist. All rights reserved. Reprinted by permission.

Smart Practices Video

Jon Olson, Chief Financial Officer, Xilinx Corp.

"It is really important that you know some of the basics of accounting."

See the entire interview at

SMARTFinance

Accounting is called the language of business. However, finance professionals and accountants use accounting information in different ways. Accountants construct financial statements using an **accrual-based approach**. This means that accountants record revenues at the point of sale and costs when they are incurred, not necessarily when a firm receives or pays out cash.

In contrast, finance professionals use a **cash flow approach** that focuses on current and prospective inflows and outflows of cash. The financial manager must convert relevant accounting and tax information into cash inflows and cash outflows so that companies and investors can use this information for analysis and decision making.

This chapter describes how finance professionals use accounting information to analyze the firm's cash flows and financial performance. We begin with a brief review of the four major financial statements. Next, we use these statements to demonstrate key concepts involved in cash flow analysis. Finally, we discuss some popular financial ratios used to analyze a firm's financial performance.

2.1 FINANCIAL STATEMENTS

Although our discussion in this chapter is based on U.S. accounting statements and conventions, the principles covered are quite general. Many national governments require public companies to generate financial statements based on widely accepted accounting rules. In the United States, these rules are the Generally Accepted Accounting Principles (GAAP), developed by the Financial Accounting Standards Board (FASB). The FASB is a nongovernmental, professional standards body that examines controversial accounting topics and issues standards that, in terms of their impact on accounting practices, almost have the force of law.

The Securities and Exchange Commission (SEC) regulates publicly traded U.S. companies as well as the nation's stock and bond markets. Every industrialized country has an agency similar to the SEC, and most developed countries mandate that companies generate financial statements following international accounting standards (IAS). These are broadly similar to GAAP, although GAAP rules tend to place greater emphasis on public information disclosure than do IAS rules. Also, in response to the accounting scandals of 2001 and 2002, the Sarbanes–Oxley Act of 2002 established the Public Company Accounting Oversight Board (PCAOB), which effectively gives the SEC authority to oversee the accounting profession's activities.

The SEC has long required that U.S. companies and all non-U.S. companies wishing to sell securities on American financial markets report results based on GAAP. In late August 2008, however, the Commission voted to publish for public comment a proposal that could lead to the use of International Financial Reporting Standards (IFRS) by U.S. issuers beginning in 2014. If ultimately adopted, this proposed policy change will dramatically impact American financial reporting.

Reporting financial information, both externally to investors and internally to managers, is clearly something that is very important to senior financial executives. The following What CFOs Do feature shows that they spend more time on this activity than on anything else.

The SEC requires four key financial statements: (1) the balance sheet, (2) the income statement, (3) the statement of retained earnings, and (4) the statement of cash flows. In this section, we review the information these statements present using the financial statements from the 2010 stockholders' report of the Global Petroleum Corporation (GPC). Though fictional, GPC's accounts are based on actual statements of the five largest international petroleum companies, so the values constructed for GPC reflect those of a globally active oil company.

WHAT CFOs DO

CFO Survey Evidence

Surveys of corporate financial managers show that practitioners spend a large fraction of their working time on financial reporting and analysis. The chart below shows that "management reporting/accounting" and "financial planning and analysis" are the two most time-consuming tasks that financial managers routinely perform, each accounting for almost 21 hours per month. The related tasks of "external financial reporting/accounting," "internal audit," and "accounting policies" together account for an additional 30 hours per month, clearly demonstrating that managers continually use the analytical tools described in this chapter.

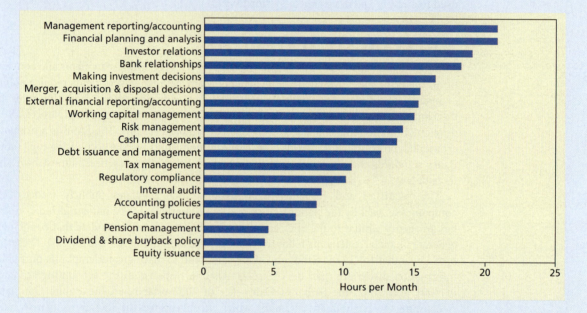

Source: Henri Servaes and Peter Tufano, "A Global Survey of Corporate Capital Structure & Treasury Risk Management Practices & Policies," Deutsche Bank (2006).

Balance Sheet

A firm's balance sheet presents a "snapshot" view of the company's financial position at a specific moment in time. By definition, a firm's assets must equal the combined value of its liabilities and stockholders' equity. Thus, creditors and equity investors finance all of a firm's assets.

Balance sheets consist of three sections that list firms' assets and liabilities as well as the claims of the stockholders. Assets and liabilities appear in descending order of *liquidity*, the length of time it takes to convert accounts into cash during the normal course of business. The most liquid asset (cash) appears first, and the least liquid (fixed assets) comes last. Similarly, accounts payable represents the obligations the firm must pay with cash within the next year. The last entry on the balance sheet, stockholders' equity, quite literally never matures.

Table 2.1 presents Global Petroleum Corporation's balance sheet as of December 31, 2010. As is standard practice in annual reports, the table also shows the prior year's (2009) accounts for comparison. The following accounts appear among GPC's assets:

Table 2.1   Balance Sheet for Global Petroleum Corporation

GLOBAL PETROLEUM CORPORATION BALANCE SHEETS AT DECEMBER 31, 2009 AND 2010 ($ IN MILLIONS)

ASSETS	2010	2009	LIABILITIES AND STOCKHOLDERS' EQUITY	2010	2009
Current assets			Current liabilities		
Cash and cash equivalents	$ 440	$ 213	Accounts payable	$ 1,697	$1,304
Marketable securities	35	28	Notes payable	477	587
Accounts receivable	1,619	1,203	Accrued expenses	440	379
Inventories	615	530	Total current liabilities	$2,614	$2,270
Other (mostly prepaid expenses)	170	176	Long-term liabilities		
Total current assets	$2,879	$2,150	Deferred taxes	$ 907	$ 793
Fixed assets			Long-term debt	1,760	1,474
Gross property, plant, and equipment	$9,920	$9,024	Total long-term liabilities	$2,667	$2,267
Less: Accumulated depreciation	3,968	3,335	Total liabilities	$5,281	$4,537
Net property, plant, and equipment	$5,952	$5,689	Stockholders' equity		
			Preferred stock	$ 30	$ 30
Intangible assets and others	758	471	Common stock ($1 par value)	373	342
			Paid-in-capital in excess of par	248	229
Net fixed assets	$6,710	$6,160	Retained earnings	4,271	3,670
			Less: Treasury stock	614	498
			Total stockholders' equity	$4,308	$3,773
Total assets	**$9,589**	**$8,310**	**Total liabilities and stockholders' equity**	**$9,589**	**$8,310**

- Cash and cash equivalents *are assets such as checking account balances at commercial banks that can be used directly as means of payment.*
- Marketable securities *represent liquid short-term investments, which financial analysts view as a form of "near cash."*
- Accounts receivable *represent the amount customers owe the firm from sales made on credit.*
- Inventories *include raw materials, work in process (partially finished goods), and finished goods held by the firm.*
- Gross property, plant, and equipment *is the original cost of all real property, structures, and long-lived equipment owned by the firm.*
- Net property, plant, and equipment *represents the difference between their gross value and* accumulated depreciation—*the cumulative expense recorded for the depreciation of fixed assets since their purchase. Governments allow companies to depreciate (to charge against taxable earnings) a fraction of a fixed asset's cost each year. This charge reflects a decline in the asset's economic value over time. The one fixed asset that is not depreciated is land, because it seldom declines in value.*
- *Finally,* intangible assets *include items such as patents, trademarks, copyrights, or (in the case of petroleum companies) mineral rights entitling the company to extract oil and gas on specific properties. Although intangible assets are usually no more than legal rights, they are often extremely valuable—as demonstrated by our discussion of the market value of global brands in this chapter's What Companies Do Globally feature.*

WHAT COMPANIES DO GLOBALLY

Assessing the Market Value of Global Brands

RANK 2008	RANK 2007	BRAND	2008 BRAND VALUE ($ MILLION)	2007 BRAND VALUE ($ MILLION)	PERCENT CHANGE	COUNTRY OF OWNERSHIP
1	1	Coca-Cola	66,667	65,324	2%	U.S.
2	3	IBM	59,031	57,091	3%	U.S.
3	2	Microsoft	59,007	57,709	1%	U.S.
4	4	GE	53,086	51,569	3%	U.S.
5	5	Nokia	35,942	33,696	7%	Finland
6	6	Toyota	34,050	32,070	6%	Japan
7	7	Intel	31,261	30,954	1%	U.S.
8	8	McDonald's	31,049	29,398	6%	U.S.
9	9	Disney	29,251	29,210	0%	U.S.
10	20	Google	25,590	17,837	43%	U.S.
11	10	Mercedes-Benz	25,577	23,568	9%	Germany
12	12	Hewlett-Packard	23,509	22,197	6%	U.S.
13	13	BMW	23,298	21,612	8%	Germany
14	16	Gillette	22,069	20,415	8%	U.S.
15	15	American Express	21,940	20,827	5%	U.S.
16	17	Louis Vuitton	21,602	20,321	6%	France
17	18	Cisco	21,306	19,099	12%	U.S.
18	14	Marlboro	21,300	21,283	0%	U.S.
19	11	Citi	20,174	23,443	−14%	U.S.
20	19	Honda	19,079	17,998	6%	Japan

How much is a global brand name worth? Interbrand Corporation, a New York–based consulting firm, has been trying to answer this question for several years, and *Business Week* has been publishing the rankings annually since 2001. The table above details what this firm considers the 20 most valuable brands of 2008 and also lists the value of those brands in 2007. The total brand values are large and are dominated by brands of U.S.-based companies. Additionally, the rankings are remarkably stable from year to year; the 2008 ranking listed the same 20 brands as in 2007, though the ranking of some (particularly Google and Citi) changed significantly.

Although American companies are not required to disclose estimated brand values in their financial statements, large publicly traded British and Australian firms must do so. Brand values do, however, have a major impact on U.S. accounting rules in one important area: accounting for the "goodwill" created when a firm is acquired by another company for more than the acquired firm's book value. This premium over book value represents the higher market (versus book) value of intangible assets such as patents, copyrights, and trademarks as well as brand names and business relationships that are not accounted for at all. The Financial Accounting Standards Board requires acquirers to periodically assess the fair value of assets they purchase through acquisitions. If the fair value of those assets declines significantly over time then firms must recognize "goodwill impairment," meaning that the value of their intangible assets has also declined. Charges arising from goodwill impairment can have a dramatic effect on reported earnings.

Source: Reproduced from the September 29, 2008 issue of *BusinessWeek* by special permission, copyright © by The McGraw-Hill Companies, Inc.

Now turn your attention to the liabilities and owners' equity parts of the balance sheet. Current liabilities include the following accounts:

- Accounts payable, *amounts owed for credit purchases by the firm.*
- Notes payable, *outstanding short-term loans, typically from commercial banks.*
- Accrued expenses, *costs incurred by the firm that have not yet been paid. Examples of accruals include taxes owed to the government and wages due employees.*

Accounts payable and accruals are often called *spontaneous liabilities* because they tend to change directly with changes in sales.

Next is the long-term liabilities section. There are two main categories of long-term liabilities: deferred taxes and long-term debt.

- *In the United States and many other countries, laws permit firms to construct two sets of financial statements, one for reporting to the public and one for tax purposes. For example, when a firm purchases a long-lived asset, it can choose to depreciate the asset rapidly for the purpose of obtaining large, immediate tax write-offs. When the firm constructs financial statements for release to the public, however, it may choose a different depreciation method—perhaps one that results in higher reported earnings in the early years of the asset's life. The* deferred taxes *entry is a long-term liability that reflects the difference between the taxes that firms actually pay and the tax liabilities they report on their public financial statements.*
- Long-term debt *represents debt that matures more than one year in the future.*

The stockholders' equity section provides information about the claims against the firm held by investors who own preferred and common shares. It shows the following accounts:

- *The* preferred stock *entry shows the proceeds from the sale of preferred stock ($30 million for GPC). This form of ownership has preference over common stock when the firm distributes income and assets.*
- *Next, two entries show the amount paid in by the original purchasers of* common stock: *The* common stock *entry equals the number of outstanding common shares multiplied by the* par value *per share.* Paid-in-capital in excess of par *equals the number of shares outstanding multiplied by the original selling price of the shares, net of the par value. The combined value of common stock and paid-in-capital equals the proceeds the firm received when it originally sold shares to investors.*
- Retained earnings *are the cumulative total of the earnings that the firm has reinvested since its inception. Be sure you know that retained earnings are not a reservoir of unspent cash. When the retained earnings "vault" is empty, it is because the firm has already reinvested the earnings in new assets.*
- *Finally, the* treasury stock *entry records the value of common shares that the firm currently holds in reserve. Usually, treasury stock appears on the balance sheet because the firm has reacquired previously issued stock through a share repurchase program.*

GPC's balance sheet (Table 2.1) shows that the firm's total assets increased by $1,279 million from 2009 to 2010. Other significant changes in GPC's balance sheet include sizable increases in cash, accounts receivable, and intangible assets coupled with a massive ($896 million) increase in gross property, plant, and equipment. Balancing these increases in asset accounts is an increase of $393 million in accounts payable plus $601 million in new retained earnings. In other words, GPC financed increases in asset accounts mainly by borrowing more from suppliers (accounts payable) and by reinvesting profits (retained earnings). We will discover additional insights into these changes when we look more closely at the statement of cash flows.

Income Statement

Table 2.2 presents Global Petroleum Corporation's income statement (also called the profit-and-loss statement, or P&L) for the year ended December 31, 2010. As with the balance sheet, GPC's income statement includes data from 2009 for comparison.[1]

In the vocabulary of accounting, income (also called *profit, earnings,* or *margin*) equals revenue minus expenses. A firm's income statement, however, has several measures of "income" appearing at different points:

- Gross profit *is the first income measure. It is the amount by which* sales revenue *exceeds the* cost of goods sold *(the direct cost of producing or purchasing the goods sold).*
- *Next, a firm deducts from gross profits various operating expenses, including selling expense, general and administrative expense, and depreciation expense.[2] The resulting* operating profit *($1,531 million for GPC) represents the profits earned from the sale of products, although this amount does not include financial and tax costs.*
- Other income, *earned on transactions directly related to producing and/or selling the firm's products, is added to operating income to yield* earnings before interest and taxes (EBIT). *When a firm has no "other income," its operating profit and EBIT are equal.*
- *Next, the firm subtracts* interest expense—*representing the cost of debt financing— from EBIT to find its* pretax income. *For example, GPC subtracts $123 million of interest expense from EBIT to find pretax income of $1,548 million.*
- *The final step is to subtract taxes from pretax income to arrive at* net income, *or net profits after taxes ($949 million for GPC). Net income is the proverbial "bottom line" and the single most important accounting number for both corporate managers and external financial analysts.*

Note in Table 2.2 that, although GPC incurred a total tax liability of $599 million during 2010, only the $367 million *current* portion must be paid immediately.[3] The remaining $232 million in deferred taxes must be paid eventually, but these are noncash expenses for year 2010.

Based on its income statement, GPC had an average tax rate during 2010 of about 39% ($599 million in taxes divided by $1,548 million of pretax income). For financial decision-making purposes, the financial manager would focus on the firm's *marginal tax rate*: the rate applicable to the next dollar of earnings. Throughout this text, the assumed tax rates are always marginal tax rates.

---

[1]When reporting to shareholders, firms typically also include a so-called common-size income statement wherein all entries are expressed as a percentage of sales.

[2]Companies frequently include depreciation expense in manufacturing costs—the cost of goods sold—when calculating gross profits. In this text we show depreciation as an expense in order to isolate its effect on cash flows.

[3]Corporations are subject to federal corporate tax rates that are progressive and range between 15% and 39%. Personal tax rates are also progressive, and the federal rate ranges from 10% to 35%.

Table 2.2   Income Statement for Global Petroleum Corporation

GLOBAL PETROLEUM CORPORATION INCOME STATEMENTS FOR
THE YEARS ENDED DECEMBER 31, 2009 AND 2010 ($ IN MILLIONS)

	2010	2009
Sales revenue	$12,843	$9,110
Less: Cost of goods sold[a]	8,519	5,633
Gross profit	$ 4,324	$3,477
Less: Operating and other expenses	1,544	1,521
Less: Selling, general, and administrative expenses	616	584
Less: Depreciation	633	608
Operating profit	$ 1,531	$ 764
Plus: Other income	140	82
Earnings before interest and taxes (EBIT)	$ 1,671	$ 846
Less: Interest expense	123	112
Pretax income	$ 1,548	$ 734
Less: Taxes		
Current	367	158
Deferred	232	105
Total taxes	599	263
Net income (net profit after tax)	$ 949	$ 471
Less: Preferred stock dividends	3	3
Earnings available for common stockholders	$ 946	$ 468
Less: Dividends	345	326
To retained earnings	$ 601	$ 142
Per-share data[b]		
Earnings per share (*EPS*)	$ 5.29	$ 2.52
Dividends per share (*DPS*)	$ 1.93	$ 1.76
Price per share	$ 76.25	$71.50

[a]Annual purchases have historically represented about 80 percent of cost of goods sold. Using this relationship, its credit purchases in 2010 were $6,815 and, in 2009, they were $4,506.
[b]Based on 178,719,400 and 185,433,100 shares outstanding as of December 31, 2010 and 2009, respectively.

The next entries in the income statement indicate distributions of net income:

- *If a firm has preferred stock, it deducts preferred stock dividends from net income. For example, GPC paid $3 million in dividends on its $30 million of preferred stock outstanding during both 2009 and 2010.*
- *Net income net of preferred stock dividends is* earnings available for common stockholders. *Dividing earnings available for common stockholders by the number of shares of common stock outstanding results in* earnings per share (EPS). *Earnings per share represents the amount earned during the period on each outstanding share of common stock. GPC's earnings per share for 2010 is $5.29, which represents a significant increase from the 2009 EPS of $2.52. Actual EPS for the past 12 months, such as those shown on GPC's income statement, are sometimes called* trailing EPS. *Estimates of earnings for the next 12 months are often called* leading EPS.

WHAT CFOs DO

CFO Survey Evidence

In a recent study, Graham, Harvey, and Rajgopal (2005) asked CFOs to identify the most important financial measures that they reported to outside investors. The pie chart to the right shows that the overwhelming response was earnings. The study also reported that CFOs believed that reporting higher earnings than the same quarter in the prior year was the most important earnings "benchmark" for firms to achieve, even more important than beating Wall Street analysts' earnings forecasts. The importance of earnings stands in contrast to our recommendation that managers focus on cash flows.

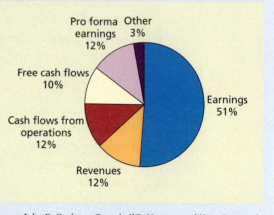

Source: John R. Graham, Campbell R. Harvey, and Shiva Rajgopal, "The Economic Implications of Corporate Financial Reporting," *Journal of Accounting and Economics* 40 (2005), pp. 3–73.

■ *The final entry in the income statement is the cash* dividend per share (DPS) *paid to common stockholders. GPC's dividend per share during 2010 is $1.93, up slightly from the 2009 DPS of $1.76.*

Statement of Retained Earnings

This third key financial statement reconciles the net income earned during a given year, and any cash dividends paid, with the change in retained earnings between the start and end of that year. Table 2.3 presents the statement of retained earnings for Global Petroleum Corporation for the year ended December 31, 2010; it shows that the company began

Table 2.3	Statement of Retained Earnings for Global Petroleum Corporation

GLOBAL PETROLEUM CORPORATION STATEMENT OF RETAINED EARNINGS FOR THE YEAR ENDED DECEMBER 31, 2010 ($ MILLION)

Retained earnings balance (January 1, 2010)		$ 3,670
Plus: Net income (for 2010)		949
Less: Cash dividends (paid during 2010)		
Preferred stock	$ 3	
Common stock	345	
Total dividends paid		348
Retained earnings balance (December 31, 2010)		**$4,271**

the year with $3,670 million in retained earnings and had net income after taxes of $949 million. From its net income GPC paid a total of $348 million in preferred and common stock dividends. At year-end, retained earnings were $4,271 million. Thus, in 2010 the net increase for GPC was $601 million ($949 million net income minus $348 million in dividends).

Note two points about GPC's retained earnings between 2009 and 2010. First, 2010 was a very good year for GPC in terms of increased sales and profits. GPC's net income more than doubled, rising from $471 million in 2009 to $949 million in 2010. Thus it is not surprising that the amount of earnings retained during 2010 ($601 million) was much larger than in 2009 ($142 million).[4]

Second, observe that GPC's increased dividend payment was far smaller proportionally than was the increase in net income. Another way to phrase this is to say that GPC's **dividend payout ratio**—the fraction of current earnings available for common stockholders paid out as dividends—declined. Specifically, its dividend payout ratio declined from 69.7% ($326 million ÷ $468 million) in 2009 to 36.5% ($345 million ÷ $946 million) in 2010.

Statement of Cash Flows

The statement of cash flows provides a summary of a firm's cash flows over the year. This statement isolates the firm's operating, investment, and financing cash flows and reconciles them with changes in its cash and marketable securities during the year. Table 2.5 presents GPC's statement of cash flows for the year ended December 31, 2010. This table appears in Section 2.2, where we present some important cash flow concepts and measures and then show how to use those data to prepare the statement of cash flows.

Notes to Financial Statements

Besides the four key financial statements themselves, the "notes" to financial statements can be extremely useful to financial managers and analysts. A public company's financial statements include explanatory notes keyed to the relevant accounts in the statements. These notes provide detailed information on the accounting policies, calculations, and transactions that underlie entries in the financial statements. For example, the notes to General Motors' 2007 financial statements cover 49 of the 134 pages in its annual report.

Notes typically provide additional information about a firm's revenue recognition practices, income taxes, fixed assets, leases, and employee compensation plans. Professional security analysts find this information particularly useful, and they routinely scour the notes when evaluating the firm's performance and value.

Concept Review Questions	1. Are balance sheets and income statements prepared with the same purpose in mind? How are these two statements different, and how are they related? 2. Which statement is of greatest interest to creditors? Which would be of greatest interest to stockholders? 3. Why are the notes to financial statements important to professional security analysts?

---

[4] Also note that the relative increase of the two broadest measures of income (EBIT and net income) was far greater than that of sales revenue. Whereas sales increased by 41% (from $9,110 million to $12,843 million), EBIT and net income increased by 98% and 101%, respectively. This suggests that the firm's extensive use of fixed-cost assets (refineries, pipelines, tankers, etc.) imparts a high degree of *operating leverage*, meaning that a given percentage increase (decrease) in sales yields a much larger percentage increase (decrease) in operating profits (the same as with EBIT). Chapter 9 discusses the concept of operating leverage more fully.

2.2 Cash Flow Analysis

Although financial managers are interested in the information in the firm's accrual-based financial statements, their primary focus is on cash flows. Without adequate cash to pay obligations on time, to fund operations and growth, and to compensate owners, the firm will fail. The financial manager and other interested parties can gain insight into the firm's cash flows over a given time period by using some popular measures of cash flow and by analyzing the firm's statement of cash flows.

The Firm's Cash Flows

In the process of evaluating a firm's cash flows, analysts view cash and marketable securities as perfect substitutes. Both represent a reservoir of liquidity that increases with *cash inflows* and decreases with *cash outflows*.

A firm's total cash flows can be conveniently divided into (1) operating flows, (2) investment flows, and (3) financing flows. The **operating flows** are cash inflows and outflows directly related to the production and sale of products or services. **Investment flows** are cash flows associated with the purchase or sale of fixed assets and business equity. Clearly, purchases result in cash outflows, whereas sales generate cash inflows. The **financing flows** result from debt and equity financing transactions. Taking on new debt (short-term or long-term) results in a cash inflow; repaying existing debt requires a cash outflow. Similarly, the sale of stock generates a cash inflow, whereas the repurchase of stock or payment of cash dividends results in a cash outflow. In combination, the operating, investment, and financing cash flows during a given period affect the firm's cash and marketable securities balances.

Monitoring cash flow is important for the firm's financial managers and for outside analysts trying to estimate the firm's worth. Managers and analysts track a variety of cash flow measures. Among these, one of the most important is free cash flow.

Smart Practices Video

Greg Swearingen, VP, Investor Relations, Teradata Corp.

"Free cash flow is getting at the discretionary cash flows available to invest."

See the entire interview at
SMARTFinance

Free Cash Flow   The measure of **free cash flow (FCF)** is the amount of cash flow available to investors—the providers of debt and equity capital. It represents the net amount of cash flow remaining after the firm has met all operating needs and has made all required payments on both long-term (fixed) and short-term (current) investments. Free cash flow for a given period can be calculated in two steps.

First, we find the firm's **net operating profits after taxes (NOPAT)**, the firm's earning before interest and after taxes:[5]

$$NOPAT = EBIT \times (1 - T)$$ **(Eq. 2.1)**

where

EBIT = earnings before interest and taxes
  T = corporate tax rate

Adding depreciation back into NOPAT yields operating cash flow (OCF), which is the amount of cash flow generated by the firm's operations.

$$OCF = NOPAT + Depreciation$$ **(Eq. 2.2)**

Note that because depreciation is a noncash charge, we add it back when determining OCF. **Noncash charges**—such as depreciation, amortization, and depletion allowances—are

---

[5]A related indicator of a firm's financial performance is *earnings before interest, taxes, depreciation, and amortization* (EBITDA). Analysts use EBITDA to compare profitability of companies because it measures revenue minus all expenses other than interest, taxes, depreciation, and amortization. It thereby eliminates the effects of financing and accounting decisions. Although EBITDA is a good measure of profitability, it does not measure cash flows.

expenses that appear on the income statement but do not involve an actual outlay of cash. Almost all firms list depreciation on their income statements, so we focus on depreciation in our presentation. But when amortization or depletion occur in a firm's financial statements, you would treat them in a similar manner.

Substituting Equation 2.1 for NOPAT into Equation 2.2, we obtain a single equation for operating cash flow:

$$\text{OCF} = [\text{EBIT} \times (1 - T)] + \text{Depreciation} \qquad \textbf{(Eq. 2.3)}$$

Substituting the values from GPC's 2010 income statement (from Table 2.2) and assuming a 35.85% tax rate ($T = 35.85\%$), as implied by GPC's 2010 income statement, we get GPC's operating cash flow:

$$\text{OCF} = \$1,671 \times (1.00 - 0.3585) + \$633 = \$1,072 + \$633 = \$1,705$$

Hence, GPC's OCF was $1,705 million.

Next we convert operating cash flow to free cash flow (FCF). To do so, we deduct the firm's net investments (denoted by Delta, the "change" symbol Δ) in fixed and current assets from operating cash flow, as shown in the following equation:

$$\text{FCF} = \text{OCF} - \Delta\text{FA} - (\Delta\text{CA} - \Delta\text{AP} - \Delta\text{accruals}) \qquad \textbf{(Eq. 2.4)}[6]$$

where

$$\Delta\text{FA} = \text{change in gross fixed assets}$$
$$\Delta\text{CA} = \text{change in current assets}$$
$$\Delta\text{AP} = \text{change in accounts payable}$$
$$\Delta\text{accruals} = \text{change in accrued expenses}$$

Spontaneous current liability changes occur automatically with changes in sales. They must therefore be deducted from current assets in order to find the net change in short-term investment. From the preceding calculation, we know that GPC's OCF in 2010 was $1,705 million. Using GPC's 2009 and 2010 balance sheets (Table 2.1), we can calculate the changes in gross fixed assets, current assets, accounts payable, and accruals between 2009 and 2010:

$$\Delta\text{FA} = \$9,920 - \$9,024 = \$896$$
$$\Delta\text{CA} = \$2,879 - \$2,150 = \$729$$
$$\Delta\text{AP} = \$1,697 - \$1,304 = \$393$$
$$\Delta\text{accruals} = \$440 - \$379 = \$61$$

Substituting these values into Equation 2.4 yields the following expression:

$$\begin{aligned} \text{FCF} &= \$1,705 - \$896 - (\$729 - \$393 - \$61) \\ &= \$1,705 - \$896 - \$275 \\ &= \$534 \end{aligned}$$

The second line of this FCF calculation shows that, after subtracting $896 million in fixed asset investment and $275 million in current asset investment net of accounts payable and accruals, GPC had free cash flow in 2010 of $534 million available to pay its investors.

---

[6]This equation is often presented as:

$$\text{FCF} = \text{OCF} - \text{Capital Expenditures} + \text{Depreciation} - \Delta\text{WC}$$

where:

$$\text{Capital Expenditures} - \text{Depreciation} = \Delta\text{FA}$$
$$\Delta\text{CA} - \Delta\text{AP} - \Delta\text{Accruals} = \Delta\text{WC}, \text{ where WC is net working capital}$$

We will use free cash flow in Chapter 4 to estimate the value of a firm. At this point, suffice it to say that FCF is an important measure of cash flow used by corporate finance professionals.

Inflows and Outflows of Cash   Table 2.4 classifies the basic inflows and outflows of the cash of corporations (assuming other things are held constant). For example, a $1,000 increase in accounts payable would be an *inflow of cash*. A $2,500 increase in inventory would be an *outflow of cash*.

Table 2.4 The Inflows and Outflows of Corporate Cash	
INFLOWS	**OUTFLOWS**
Decrease in any asset	Increase in any asset
Increase in any liability	Decrease in any liability
Net income (profit after taxes)	Net loss
Depreciation and other noncash charges	Dividends paid
Sale of common or preferred stock	Repurchase or retirement of stock

A few additional points about the classifications in Table 2.4 are worth noting:

1. A *decrease* in an asset (such as inventory) is an *inflow of cash* because cash that has been tied up in the asset is released and can be used for some other purpose, such as repaying a loan. In contrast, an *increase* in inventory (or any other asset) is an *outflow of cash* because additional inventory ties up more of the firm's cash. Similar logic explains why an increase in any liability is an inflow of cash and why a decrease in any liability is an outflow of cash.

2. Our earlier discussion noted why depreciation and other noncash charges are considered cash inflows. Logic suggests that if net income is a cash inflow then a *net loss* (negative net profit after taxes) is a cash outflow. The firm must balance its losses with an inflow of cash from, say, selling off some of its fixed assets (reducing an asset) or increasing external borrowing (increasing a liability). Can a firm have a *net loss* (negative NOPAT) and still have positive operating cash flow? Yes, as Equation 2.2 indicates, this can occur when depreciation and other noncash charges during the period are greater than the net loss. The statement of cash flows treats net income (or net losses) and depreciation and other noncash charges as separate entries.

EXAMPLE

On June 30, 2008, and on March 31, 2008, Procter & Gamble Co.® (P&G) (ticker symbol, PG) reported the following balances, in millions of dollars, in certain current asset and liability accounts.

Account	June 30, 2008	March 31, 2008
Cash	$ 3,313	$ 3,737
Investment securities	228	341
Accounts receivable	6,761	6,934
Inventory	8,416	8,427
Accounts payable	6,775	5,535
Short-term debt	13,084	13,287

In terms of current assets, cash, short-term investments, accounts receivable, and inventory declined during the second quarter of 2008, providing inflows of cash for P&G. It may seem strange to think of a *decrease* in cash balances as a *source* of cash, but it simply means that P&G used some of its cash flow to support other activities. On the liabilities side, accounts payable increased, representing another source of cash inflow, and short-term debt declined, representing an outflow of cash for P&G.

Developing the Statement of Cash Flows

Accountants construct the statement of cash flows by using the income statement for a given year along with the beginning- and end-of-year balance sheets. The procedure involves classifying balance sheet changes as inflows or outflows of cash; obtaining income statement data; classifying the relevant values into operating, investment, and financing cash flows; and presenting them in the proper format.[7]

Global Petroleum Corporation's statement of cash flows for the year ended December 31, 2010, appears in Table 2.5. Note that the statement assigns positive values to all cash inflows and negative values to all cash outflows. Notice also that, in the investment activities section, the statement of cash flows records the increase in *gross* fixed assets—rather than *net* fixed assets—as a cash outflow. Depreciation accounts for the difference between changes in gross and net fixed assets, but depreciation expense appears in the operating activities section of the statement. The focus on changes in gross fixed assets avoids double-counting depreciation in the statement. For a similar reason, the statement does not show a specific entry for the change in retained earnings as an inflow (or outflow) of cash. Instead, the factors that determine the change in retained earnings (i.e., profits or losses and dividends) appear as separate entries in the statement.

By adding up the totals in each category—operating, investment, and financing activities—we obtain the net increase (decrease) in cash and marketable securities for the year. As a check, this value should reconcile with the actual yearly change in cash and marketable securities obtained from the beginning- and end-of-year balance sheets.

By applying this procedure to GPC's 2010 income statement and 2009 and 2010 balance sheets, we obtain the firm's 2010 statement of cash flows (see Table 2.5). It shows that GPC experienced a $234 million increase in cash and marketable securities in 2010. Looking at GPC's 2009 and 2010 balance sheets in Table 2.1, we see that the firm's cash increased by $227 million and that its marketable securities increased by $7 million. The $234 million net increase in cash and marketable securities from the statement of cash flows reconciles with the total change of $234 million in these accounts during 2010. Therefore, GPC's statement of cash flows reconciles with the balance sheet changes.

Interpreting the Statement

The statement of cash flows allows the financial manager and other interested parties to analyze the firm's cash flow over time. Unusual changes in either the major categories of cash flow or in specific items offer clues to problems a firm may be experiencing. For example, an unusually large increase in accounts receivable or inventories, resulting in major cash outflows, may signal credit or inventory problems. All of the financial

---

[7]For a description and demonstration of the detailed procedures for developing the statement of cash flows, see any recently published financial accounting text—for example, Chapter 14 of *Corporate Financial Accounting* (Warren, Reeve, and Duchac 2009).

Table 2.5 Statement of Cash Flows for Global Petroleum Corporation

GLOBAL PETROLEUM CORPORATION STATEMENT OF CASH FLOWS FOR THE YEAR ENDED DECEMBER 31, 2010 ($ MILLION)

Cash flow from operating activities		
Net income (net profit after tax)	$949	
Depreciation	633	
Increase in accounts receivable	(416)	
Increase in inventories	(85)	
Decrease in other current assets	6	
Increase in accounts payable	393	
Increase in accrued expenses	61	
Cash provided by operating activities		$1,541
Cash flow from investment activities		
Increase in gross fixed assets	($896)	
Increase in intangible and other assets	(287)	
Cash provided (consumed) by investment activities		($ 1,183)
Cash flow from financing activities		
Decrease in notes payable	($110)	
Increase in deferred taxes	114	
Increase in long-term debt	286	
Changes in stockholders' equity	(66)	
Dividends paid	(348)	
Cash provided (consumed) by financing activities		($ 124)
Net increase in cash and marketable securities		**$ 234**

statements we've discussed in this chapter are important, and each of them provides some useful information that cannot be found in the others. However, because financial analysts place so much emphasis on cash flow and because the statement of cash flows provides the clearest and most complete view of the cash coming in and going out of a business, this statement is probably the most important single statement.

Financial managers and analysts can also prepare a statement of cash flows developed from projected, or pro forma, financial statements. They use this approach to determine if the firm will need additional external financing or will generate excess cash that could be reinvested or distributed to shareholders.

Analysis of Global Petroleum Corporation's statement of cash flows for 2010 indicates no major problems for the company. GPC used the $1,541 million of cash from operating activities primarily to purchase an additional $896 million in property, plant, and equipment and to increase intangibles and other fixed assets by $287 million. Financing activities were basically a wash: increases in deferred taxes and long-term debt contributed a combined cash inflow of $400 million. Roughly offsetting these inflows of cash were outflows from a

JOB INTERVIEW QUESTION

"As an investor, if you could look at only one financial statement, which one would you choose?"

reduction of notes payable ($110 million), payment of common and preferred stock dividends ($348 million), and a net reduction in common stock outstanding of $66 million. In addition to cash provided by net income ($949 million) and depreciation ($633 million), GPC realized major cash inflows by increasing accounts payable ($393 million) and long-term debt ($286 million). The $1,183 million increase in fixed, intangible, and other assets was unusually large, by recent standards, but consistent with the significant growth in revenue that occurred during 2010.

One financially encouraging step taken by GPC in 2010 was to increase its net working capital by $385 million. **Net working capital** is defined as current assets minus current liabilities. It is a measure of the firm's overall liquidity; higher values reflect greater solvency, and vice versa. GPC's net working capital at the end of 2009 was −$120 million. As of December 31, 2010, its net working capital had risen to a positive level of $265 million. GPC engineered this $385 million increase by increasing its investment in current assets by $729 million while increasing its current liabilities by only $344 million. *Cash and marketable securities*, *accounts receivable*, and *inventories* increased by $234 million, $416 million, and $85 million, respectively, while the *other* current assets decreased by $6 million. Large increases occurred in two of the three categories of current liabilities—accounts payable ($393 million) and accrued expenses ($61 million)—although they were partially offset by a $110 million decline in notes payable. In general, it appears that GPC is growing and is managing its cash flows reasonably well.

Concept Review Questions	4. How do depreciation and other noncash charges act as sources of cash inflow to the firm? Why does a depreciation allowance exist in the tax laws? For a profitable firm, is it better to depreciate an asset quickly or slowly for tax purposes? Explain.
	5. What is operating cash flow (OCF)? How does it relate to net operating profits after taxes (NOPAT)? What is free cash flow (FCF), and how is it related to OCF?
	6. Why is the financial manager likely to have great interest in the firm's statement of cash flows? What type of information can interested parties obtain from this statement?

2.3 Assessing Financial Performance Using Ratio Analysis

Assessing a firm's financial statements is of interest to shareholders, creditors, and the firm's own management. A firm often wants to compare its financial condition to that of similar firms, but doing so can be very tricky. For example, suppose you are introduced to a man named Jeff who tells you that he runs a company that earned a profit of $10 million last year. Would you be impressed by that? What if you knew that Jeff's last name was Immelt? Most people would agree that a profit of $10 million would be a great disappointment for General Electric, the firm run by Jeff Immelt, because GE's annual profit is typically in the billions.

The point here is that the amounts of sales, profits, and other items that appear on a firm's financial statements are difficult to interpret unless we have some way to put the numbers in perspective. To analyze financial statements, we need relative measures that, in effect, normalize size differences. Effective analysis of financial statements is thus based on the use of *ratios* or *relative values*. **Ratio analysis** involves calculating and interpreting financial ratios to assess a firm's performance and status.

Using Financial Ratios

Different constituents of a firm will focus on different types of financial ratios. Creditors are primarily interested in ratios that measure the firm's short-term liquidity and its ability to make interest and principal payments. A secondary concern of creditors is profitability; they want assurance that the business is healthy and will continue to be successful. Present and prospective shareholders focus on ratios that measure the firm's current and future levels of risk and return, because these two dimensions directly affect share price. The firm's managers use ratios to generate an overall picture of the company's financial health and to monitor its performance from period to period. They carefully examine unexpected changes in order to isolate developing problems.

An additional complication of ratio analysis is that a normal ratio in one industry may be highly unusual in another. For example, the net profit margin ratio measures the net income generated by each dollar of sales. (We will show later how to compute this ratio.) Net profit margins vary dramatically across industries. An outstanding net profit margin in the retail grocery industry would look paltry in the software business.

Therefore, when making subjective judgments about the health of a given company, analysts usually compare the firm's ratios to two benchmarks. First, analysts compare the financial ratios in the current year with previous years' ratios. In doing so, they hope to identify trends that will aid in evaluating the firm's prospects. Second, analysts compare the ratios of one company with those of other "benchmark" firms in the same industry (or to an industry average obtained from a trade association or third-party provider).

JOB INTERVIEW QUESTION

How would you identify firms that may be financially weak in the short term?

We will use the 2010 and 2009 balance sheets and income statements for Global Petroleum Corporation, presented in Tables 2.1 and 2.2, to demonstrate ratio calculations. (To simplify the presentation, we have deleted the *millions* after GPC's values.) The ratios presented in this chapter can be applied to nearly any company. Of course, many companies in different industries use ratios that focus on aspects peculiar to their industry.[8] We will cover the most common financial ratios, which are grouped into five categories: liquidity, activity, debt, profitability, and market ratios.

Liquidity Ratios

Liquidity ratios measure a firm's ability to satisfy its short-term obligations *as they come due.* Because a common precursor to financial distress or bankruptcy is low or declining liquidity, liquidity ratios are good leading indicators of cash flow problems. The two basic measures of liquidity are the *current ratio* and the *quick (acid-test) ratio.*

The **current ratio**, one of the most commonly cited financial ratios, measures the firm's ability to meet its short-term obligations. It is defined as current assets divided by current liabilities. So GPC's current ratio on December 31, 2010, is computed as follows:

$$\text{Current ratio} = \frac{\text{Current assets}}{\text{Current liabilities}} = \frac{\$2,879}{\$2,614} = 1.10$$

How high should the current ratio be? The answer depends on the type of business and on the costs and benefits of having too much versus not enough liquidity. For example, a current ratio of 1.0 would be acceptable for a utility but might be unacceptable for a manufacturer. The more predictable a firm's cash flows, the lower the acceptable current

---

[8]For example, airlines pay close attention to the ratio of revenues to passenger miles flown. Retailers diligently track the growth in same-store sales from one year to the next.

ratio. Because the business of oil exploration and development has notoriously unpredict-able annual cash flows, GPC's current ratio of 1.10 indicates that the firm takes a fairly aggressive approach to managing its liquidity.

The **quick (acid-test) ratio** is similar to the current ratio except that it *excludes* inventory, which is usually the least-liquid current asset.[9] The generally low liquidity of inventory results from two factors. First, many types of inventory cannot be easily sold because they are partially completed items, special-purpose items, and the like. Second, inventory is typically sold on credit, so it becomes an account receivable before being converted into cash. The quick ratio is calculated as follows:

$$\text{Quick ratio} = \frac{\text{Current assets} - \text{Inventory}}{\text{Current liabilities}} = \frac{\$2,879 - \$615}{\$2,614} = 0.866$$

The quick ratio for GPC in 2010 is 0.866.

The quick ratio provides a better measure of overall liquidity *only* when a firm's inventory cannot be easily converted into cash. If inventory is liquid, then the current ratio is a preferred measure. Because GPC's inventory is mostly petroleum and refined products that can be readily converted into cash, the firm's managers will probably focus on the current ratio.

Activity Ratios

Activity ratios measure the speed with which the firm converts various accounts into sales or cash. Analysts use activity ratios as guides to assess how efficiently the firm manages its assets and its accounts payable.

Inventory turnover provides a measure of how quickly a firm sells its goods. Here is the calculation for GPC's 2010 *inventory turnover ratio*:

Smart Practices Video

Greg Barsch, President, Ravello Enterprises

"We needed six to 12 inventory turns per year."

See the entire interview at

SMARTFinance

$$\text{Inventory turnover} = \frac{\text{Cost of goods sold}}{\text{Inventory}} = \frac{\$8,519}{\$615} = 13.85$$

In the numerator we used cost of goods sold, rather than sales, because firms value inventory at cost on their balance sheet. Note also that, in the denominator, we used the *ending* inventory balance of $615. If inventories are growing over time or exhibit seasonal patterns then analysts sometimes use the *average* level of inventory throughout the year, rather than the ending balance, to calculate this ratio.

The resulting turnover of 13.85 indicates that the firm basically sells out its inventory 13.85 times each year, or slightly more than once each month. This value is most meaningful when compared with that of other firms in the same industry or with the firm's past inventory turnover. An inventory turnover of 20.0 is not unusual for a grocery store, whereas a common inventory turnover for an aircraft manufacturer is 4.0. GPC's inventory turnover is in line with those for other oil and gas companies, and it is slightly above the firm's own historic norms.

We can easily convert inventory turnover into an **average age of inventory** by dividing the turnover figure into 365 (the number of days in a year). For GPC, the average age of inventory is 26.4 days (365 ÷ 13.85), meaning that GPC's inventory balance turns over about every 26 days.

---

[9]An alternate and more precise definition of the quick (acid-test) ratio is (cash + marketable securities + accounts receivable) ÷ current liabilities. This definition eliminates inventory as well as prepaid and other current assets from the numerator. For convenience, though, we use the more common approximation shown in the text.

EXAMPLE

Inventory ratios, like most other financial ratios, vary a great deal from one industry to another. For example, on December 27, 2008, Intel Corp. reported inventory of $3.74 billion and cost of goods sold of $16.74 billion for the year ended December 27, 2008. This implies an inventory turnover ratio for Intel of about 4.48 and an average age of inventory of about 81 days. With the rapid pace of technological change in the semiconductor industry, Intel cannot afford to hold inventory too long.

In contrast, for the year ended December 31, 2008, the Boeing Company reported cost of goods sold of $50.13 billion and inventory of $15.61 billion. Boeing's inventory turnover ratio is thus 3.21, and its average age of inventory is about 114 days.

Clearly, the differences in these inventory ratios reflect differences in the economic circumstances of the industries. Whereas the value of semiconductors declines as they age, which also occurs in the aerospace business, but at a much slower pace.

The **average collection period**, or *average age of accounts receivable,* is useful in evaluating credit and collection policies.[10] To compute this measure, we divide the firm's average daily sales into the accounts receivable balance. As shown in the following equations, it takes GPC on average 46 days to receive payment from a credit sale:

$$\text{Average daily sales} = \frac{\text{Annual sales}}{365} = \frac{\$12,843}{365} = \$35.19$$

$$\text{Average collection period} = \frac{\text{Accounts receivable}}{\text{Average daily sales}} = \frac{\$1,619}{\$35.19} = 46.0 \text{ days}$$

The average collection period is meaningful only in relation to the firm's credit terms. If GPC extends 30-day credit terms to customers, then an average collection period of 46 days may indicate a poorly managed credit or collection department (or both). On the other hand, a longer collection period could be the result of an intentional relaxation of credit-term enforcement in response to competitive pressures. If the firm had offered customers 45-day credit terms then the 46-day average collection period would be quite acceptable. Clearly, one would need additional information to evaluate the effectiveness of the firm's credit and collection policies.

Firms use the **average payment period** to evaluate their payment performance. This metric measures the average length of time it takes a firm to pay its suppliers. The average payment period equals the firm's average daily purchases divided into the accounts payable balance.

Before calculating average daily purchases an analyst may need to estimate the firm's annual purchases, because they are not reported on a firm's published financial statements. Instead, annual purchases are included in its cost of goods sold. GPC's annual purchases in 2010 were estimated at 80% of the cost of goods sold, as shown in footnote *a* to its income statement in Table 2.2.

Using the annual purchase estimate of $6,815, GPC's average payment period in 2010 indicates that the firm usually takes 90.9 days to pay its bills:

---

[10]The average collection period is sometimes called the *days' sales outstanding* (DSO). As with the inventory turnover ratio, the average collection period can be calculated using either end-of-year accounts receivable or the average receivables balance for the year. We discuss the evaluation and establishment of credit and collection policies in Chapter 22.

$$\text{Average daily purchases} = \frac{\text{Annual purchases}}{365} = \frac{\$6,815}{365} = \$18.67$$

$$\text{Average payment period} = \frac{\text{Accounts payable}}{\text{Average daily purchases}} = \frac{\$1,697}{\$18.67} = 90.9 \text{ days}$$

Like the average collection period, the average payment period is meaningful only in light of the actual credit terms the firm's suppliers offer. If GPC's suppliers extend, on average, 60-day credit terms, then the firm's average payment period of 90.9 days suggests that the firm is slow in paying its bills. Paying suppliers 30 days later than the agreed-upon terms could damage the firm's ability to obtain additional credit and could raise the cost of any credit that it does obtain.

However, if suppliers grant GPC average credit terms of 90 days then its 90.9-day average payment period is very good. Clearly, an analyst would need further information to draw definitive conclusions about the firm's overall payment policies from the average payment period measure.

The **fixed asset turnover** measures the efficiency with which a firm uses its *fixed assets.* The ratio tells analysts how many dollars of sales the firm generates per dollar of investment in fixed assets. The ratio equals sales divided by net fixed assets:

$$\text{Fixed asset turnover} = \frac{\text{Sales}}{\text{Net fixed assets}} = \frac{\$12,843}{\$6,710} = 1.91$$

GPC's fixed asset turnover in 2010 is 1.91. Stated another way, GPC generates almost $2 in sales for every dollar of fixed assets. As with other ratios, the "normal" level of fixed asset turnover varies widely from one industry to another.

The **total asset turnover** ratio indicates the efficiency with which a firm uses *all its assets* to generate sales. Like the fixed asset turnover ratio, total asset turnover indicates how many dollars of sales a firm generates per dollar of asset investment. All other factors being equal, analysts favor a high turnover ratio: it indicates that a firm generates more sales (and, ideally, more cash flow for investors) from a given investment in assets.

GPC's total asset turnover in 2010 equals 1.34, calculated as follows:

$$\text{Total asset turnover} = \frac{\text{Sales}}{\text{Total assets}} = \frac{\$12,843}{\$9,589} = 1.34$$

When using the fixed asset and total asset turnover ratios, an analyst must be aware that they are calculated using the historical costs of fixed assets. Because some firms have significantly newer or older assets than do others, comparing fixed asset turnovers of those firms could be misleading. Firms with newer assets tend to have lower turnovers than those with older assets, which have lower book (accounting) values. A naive comparison of fixed asset turnover ratios for different firms may lead an analyst to conclude that one firm operates more efficiently than another when, in fact, the firm that appears to be more efficient simply has older (i.e., more fully depreciated) assets on its books.

Debt Ratios

Firms finance their assets from two broad sources, equity and debt. Equity comes from stockholders, whereas debt comes in many forms from many different lenders. Firms borrow from suppliers, banks, and investors who buy publicly traded bonds. *Debt ratios* measure the extent to which a firm uses money from creditors rather than from stockholders to finance its operations. Because creditors' claims must be satisfied before firms can distribute earnings to stockholders, current and prospective investors pay close attention to the debt on the balance sheet. The more indebted the firm, the higher the probability that it will be unable to satisfy the claims of all its creditors.

Fixed-cost sources of financing, such as debt and preferred stock, create financial leverage that magnifies both the risk and the expected return on the firm's securities.[11] In general, the more debt a firm uses in relation to its total assets, the greater its financial leverage. That is, the more a firm borrows, the riskier its outstanding stock and bonds and the higher the return that investors require on those securities. In Chapters 12 and 13, we discuss in detail the effect of debt on the firm's risk, return, and value. This explains our focus on the use of debt ratios when assessing a firm's indebtedness and its ability to meet the fixed payments associated with debt—a way of quantifying financial leverage.

Broadly speaking, there are two types of debt ratios. One type focuses on *balance sheet* measures of outstanding debt relative to other sources of financing. The other type, known as **coverage ratios**, focuses more on *income statement* measures of the firm's ability to generate sufficient cash flow to make scheduled interest and principal payments. Investors and credit-rating agencies use both types of ratios to assess a firm's creditworthiness.

The **debt ratio** measures the proportion of total assets financed by the firm's creditors. The higher this ratio, the greater is the firm's reliance on borrowed money to finance its activities. The ratio equals total liabilities divided by total assets. GPC's debt ratio in 2010 was 0.551, or 55.1%:

$$\text{Debt ratio} = \frac{\text{Total liabilities}}{\text{Total assets}} = \frac{\$5,281}{\$9,589} = 0.551 = 55.1\%$$

This figure indicates that the company has financed more than half of its assets with debt.

A close cousin of the debt ratio is the **assets-to-equity (A/E) ratio**, sometimes called the **equity multiplier**:

$$\text{Assets-to-equity ratio} = \frac{\text{Total assets}}{\text{Common stock equity}} = \frac{\$9,589}{\$4,278} = 2.24$$

This is calculated as total assets divided by common stock equity. Note that the denominator of this ratio uses only common stock equity of $4,278 ($4,308 of total equity minus $30 of preferred stock equity). The resulting value indicates that GPC's assets in 2010 were 2.24 times greater than its equity. This value seems reasonable given that the debt ratio indicates slightly more than half (55.1%) of GPC's assets in 2010 were financed with debt. The high equity multiplier indicates high debt and low equity, whereas a low equity multiplier indicates low debt and high equity.

An alternative measure that focuses solely on the firm's long-term debt is the **debt-to-equity ratio**. It is calculated as long-term debt divided by stockholders' equity. The 2010 value of this ratio for GPC is as follows:

$$\text{Debt-to-equity ratio} = \frac{\text{Long-term debt}}{\text{Stockholders' equity}} = \frac{\$1,760}{\$4,308} = 0.409 = 40.9\%$$

GPC's long-term debts were therefore only 40.9% as large as its stockholders' equity.

---

[11]By *fixed cost* we mean that the cost of this financing source does not vary over time in response to changes in the firm's revenue and cash flow. For example, if a firm borrows money at a variable rate, then the interest cost of that loan is *not* fixed through time although the firm's *obligation* to make interest payments is "fixed" regardless of the level of the firm's revenue and cash flow.

A word of caution: Both the debt ratio and the debt-to-equity ratio use book values of debt, equity, and assets. Analysts should be aware that the *market values* of these variables may differ substantially from book values.

The **times interest earned ratio** measures the firm's ability to make contractual interest payments. It equals earnings before interest and taxes divided by interest expense. A higher ratio indicates a greater capacity to meet scheduled payments. The times interest earned ratio for GPC in 2010 was equal to 13.59, indicating that the firm could experience a substantial decline in earnings and still meet its interest obligations:

$$\text{Times interest earned} = \frac{\text{Earnings before interest and taxes}}{\text{Interest expense}} = \frac{\$1,671}{\$123} = 13.59$$

Profitability Ratios

Several measures of profitability relate a firm's earnings to its sales, assets, or equity. *Profitability ratios* are among the most closely watched and widely quoted financial ratios. Many firms link employee bonuses to profitability ratios, and stock prices react sharply to unexpected changes in these measures.

The **gross profit margin** measures the percentage of each sales dollar remaining after the firm has paid for its goods. The higher the gross profit margin, the better. GPC's gross profit margin in 2010 was 33.7%:

$$\text{Gross profit margin} = \frac{\text{Gross profit}}{\text{Sales}} = \frac{\$4,324}{\$12,843} = 0.337 = 33.7\%$$

The **operating profit margin** measures the percentage of each sales dollar remaining after deducting all costs and expenses *other than* interest and taxes. As with the gross profit margin, the higher the operating profit margin, the better. This ratio tells analysts what a firm's bottom line looks like before deductions for payments to creditors and tax authorities. GPC's operating profit margin in 2010 was 11.9%:

$$\text{Operating profit margin} = \frac{\text{Operating profit}}{\text{Sales}} = \frac{\$1,531}{\$12,843} = 0.119 = 11.9\%$$

The **net profit margin** measures the percentage of each sales dollar remaining after deducting all costs and expenses *including* interest, taxes, and preferred stock dividends. GPC's net profit margin of 7.4% in 2010 is calculated as follows:[12]

$$\text{Net profit margin} = \frac{\text{Earnings available for common stockholders}}{\text{Sales}}$$

$$= \frac{\$946}{\$12,843} = 0.074 = 7.4\%$$

For the quarter ending on June 30, 2008, Microsoft reported a net profit margin of 27.1%, nearly 8 times larger than the 3.4% net profit margin reported by Wal-Mart one month later. This example shows how net profit margins vary widely across industries.

Probably the most closely watched financial ratio of them all is *earnings per share* (EPS), which the investing public considers to be an indicator of corporate success. The earnings per share measure represents the number of dollars earned on behalf of each

---

[12]Some analysts calculate (1) the net profit margin by excluding the financing costs associated with debt and (2) preferred stock dividends by using in the numerator NOPAT rather than earnings available for common stockholders. Applying this formula results in a measure of after-tax operating profits. Here we use the more comprehensive measure of overall profits on sales.

outstanding share of common stock. Many firms tie management bonuses to specific EPS targets. Earnings per share are calculated as follows:

$$\text{Earnings per share} = \frac{\text{Earnings available for common stockholders}}{\text{Number of shares of common stock outstanding}}$$

$$= \frac{\$946}{178.7} = \$5.29$$

Smart Ethics Videos

Frank Popoff, Chairman of the Board (retired), Dow Chemical

"Overstating or understating the performance of the enterprise is anathema . . . it's just not done."

See the entire interview at

SMARTFinance

The value of GPC's earnings per share in 2010 was \$5.29.[13] This figure represents the dollar amount *earned* on behalf of each share of common stock outstanding. Note that EPS is not the same as dividends. The amount of earnings actually *distributed* to each shareholder is the *dividend per share*; as noted in GPC's income statement (Table 2.2), this value rose to \$1.93 in 2010 from \$1.76 in 2009.

The **return on total assets (ROA)**, often called the *return on investment* (ROI), measures management's overall effectiveness in using the firm's assets to generate returns to common stockholders.[14] The return on total assets for GPC in 2010 was equal to 9.9%:[15]

$$\text{Return on total assets} = \frac{\text{Earnings available for common stockholders}}{\text{Total assets}}$$

$$= \frac{\$946}{\$9,589} = 0.099 = 9.9\%$$

A closely related measure of profitability is the **return on common equity (ROE)**, which captures the return earned on the common stockholders' (owners') investment in the firm. For a firm that uses only common stock to finance its operations, the ROE and ROA figures will be identical. With debt or preferred stock on the balance sheet, these ratios will usually differ. When the firm earns a profit, even after making interest payments to creditors and paying dividends to preferred stockholders, the firm's ROE will exceed its ROA. Conversely, if the firm's earnings fall short of the amount it must pay to lenders and preferred stockholders, then the ROE will be less than ROA. For GPC, the return on common equity for 2010 was 22.1%, substantially above GPC's return on total assets:

$$\text{Return on common equity} = \frac{\text{Earnings available for common stockholders}}{\text{Common stock equity}}$$

$$= \frac{\$946}{\$4,278} = 0.221 = 22.1\%$$

DuPont System of Analysis   Financial analysts sometimes conduct a deeper analysis of the ROA and ROE ratios using the **DuPont system**. This approach uses both income statement and balance sheet information to break the ROA and ROE ratios into component

---

[13]We state all per-share values strictly in dollars and cents, as do company reports. Per-share values are not stated in millions, unlike the dollar values used to calculate these and other ratios.

[14]Naturally, all other things being equal, firms prefer a high ROA. However, as we will see later, analysts must be cautious when interpreting financial ratios. We recall an old Dilbert comic strip in which Wally suggests boosting his firm's ROA by firing the security staff. The reduction in expenses would boost the numerator while the reduction in security would lower the denominator.

[15]Some analysts prefer using NOPAT in the numerator, rather than using earnings available for common stockholders, in order to more clearly focus the ratio on the productivity of assets without regard to their cost of financing. Here we use the more general formula for ROA.

pieces. It highlights the influence of both the net profit margin and the total asset turnover on a firm's profitability. In the DuPont system, the return on total assets equals the product of the net profit margin and total asset turnover:

$$\text{ROA} = \text{Net profit margin} \times \text{Total asset turnover}$$

By definition, the net profit margin equals earnings available for common stockholders divided by sales, and total asset turnover equals sales divided by total assets. When we multiply these two ratios together the sales figure cancels, resulting in the familiar ROA measure:

$$\text{ROA} = \frac{\text{Earnings available for common stockholders}}{\text{Sales}} \times \frac{\text{Sales}}{\text{Total assets}}$$

$$= \frac{\$946}{\$12{,}843} \times \frac{\$12{,}843}{\$9{,}589} = 0.074 \times 1.34 = 0.099 = 9.9\%;$$

$$\text{ROA} = \frac{\text{Earnings available for common stockholders}}{\text{Total assets}} = \frac{\$946}{\$9{,}589} = 0.099 = 9.9\%$$

Naturally, the ROA value for GPC in 2010 obtained using the DuPont system is the same value we calculated before. Yet now, seeing its two component parts, we can think of the ROA as a product of how much profit the firm earns on each dollar of sales and the efficiency with which the firm uses its assets to generate sales. Holding the net profit margin constant, an increase in total asset turnover increases the firm's ROA. Similarly, holding total asset turnover constant, an increase in the net profit margin increases ROA.

We can push the DuPont system one step further by multiplying the ROA by the *assets-to-equity* (A/E) *ratio,* or the *equity multiplier.* The product of these two ratios equals the return on common equity:

$$\text{ROE} = \text{ROA} \times \text{A/E}$$

For a firm that uses no debt and has no preferred stock, the ratio of assets to equity equals 1 and so the ROA equals the ROE. For all other firms, the ratio of assets to equity exceeds 1.

Smart Concepts

See the concept explained step-by-step at

SMARTFinance

We can apply this version of the DuPont system to GPC and thereby recalculate its return on common equity in 2010:

$$\text{ROE} = \frac{\text{Earnings available for common stockholders}}{\text{Total assets}} \times \frac{\text{Total assets}}{\text{Common stock equity}}$$

$$= \frac{\$946}{\$9{,}589} \times \frac{\$9{,}589}{\$4{,}278} = 0.099 \times 2.24 = 0.221 = 22.1\%;$$

$$\text{ROE} = \frac{\text{Earnings available for common stockholders}}{\text{Common stock equity}} = \frac{\$946}{\$4{,}278}$$

$$= 0.221 = 22.1\%$$

Observe that GPC's ratio of assets to equity was 2.24. This means that GPC's return on common equity was more than twice as large as its return on total assets. Note also that if GPC's return on total assets were a *negative* number then the firm's return on common equity would be even more negative than its ROA.

The advantage of the DuPont system is that it allows the firm to break its return on common equity into three components tied to the financial statements: (1) a profit-on-sales component (net profit margin) that ties directly to the income statement; (2) an efficiency-of-asset-use component (total asset turnover) that ties directly to the balance sheet; and (3) a "financial leverage use" component (an assets-to-equity ratio) that also ties directly to the balance sheet. Analysts can then study the effect of each of these factors on the overall return to common stockholders, as demonstrated in the following Example.[16]

EXAMPLE

The 2010 ratio values for the ROE, ROA, assets-to-equity ratio, total asset turnover, and net profit margin calculated earlier for GPC are shown below, along with the 2010 industry averages for globally active oil companies.

Ratio	GPC	Industry Average
Return on common equity (ROE)	22.1%	19.7%
Return on total assets (ROA)	9.9%	12.1%
Assets-to-equity (A/E) ratio	2.24	1.63
Total asset turnover	1.34	1.42
Net profit margin	7.4%	8.5%

We begin the analysis of GPC's 2010 performance with its return on common equity of 22.1%, which is noticeably above the industry average of 19.7%. To learn why GPC's ROE outperformed the industry, we look at two components of ROE: ROA and the assets-to-equity (A/E) ratio. We see that GPC's ROA of 9.9% was well below the industry average of 12.1%. But thanks to its greater use of leverage—an A/E ratio of 2.24 for GPC versus 1.63 for the industry—GPC was able to generate a higher ROE than the average firm.

Looking further at the two components of ROA (the net profit margin and the total asset turnover), we see that GPC's total asset turnover of 1.34 is very close to the industry average of 1.42. However, its net profit margin of 7.4% is below the industry average of 8.5%, which caused GPC's ROA to be below the industry average, too. Clearly, GPC was less able than its competitors to manage costs and generate a profit on sales.

In summary, GPC compensated for its below-average ROA by using significantly more leverage than its competitors. Clearly, GPC took greater risk in order to compensate for low profits on sales. The firm should focus on its income statement to improve its profitability and also should consider reducing its leverage to moderate its risk. It appears that GPC has problems in both its income statement (net profit margin) and its balance sheet (assets-to-equity ratio).

---

[16]Keep in mind that the ratios in the DuPont system are interdependent and that the equation is just a mathematical identity. It is easy to draw questionable conclusions about lines of causality using the DuPont system. For example, consider this farcical version of the formula:

$$\text{ROE} = \frac{\text{Earnings available for common stockholders}}{\text{Sales}} \times \frac{\text{Sales}}{\text{Assets}} \times \frac{\text{Assets}}{\text{CEO age}} \times \frac{\text{CEO age}}{\text{Common stock equity}}$$

In this equation, we might interpret the third term on the right as the efficiency with which a CEO of a given age manages the firm's assets. If a younger CEO manages the same quantity of assets then this ratio would increase and, holding all other factors constant, we could say that the firm's ROE would increase. This is clearly silly, but mathematically this expression ultimately gives you the firm's ROE.

Market Ratios

Market ratios relate the firm's market value, as measured by its current share price, to certain accounting values. These ratios provide insight into how investors think the firm is performing, and they also reflect the common stockholders' assessment of the firm's past and expected future performance. Here we consider two popular market ratios, one that focuses on earnings and another that considers book value.

JOB INTERVIEW QUESTION

What financial ratios might you review in order to gain insight into how investors think a firm is performing?

The **price/earnings (P/E) ratio** measures the amount investors are willing to pay for each dollar of the firm's earnings. Investors often use the P/E ratio, the most widely quoted market ratio, as a barometer of a firm's long-term growth prospects and of investor confidence in the firm's future performance. A high P/E ratio indicates investors' belief that a firm will achieve rapid earnings growth in the future; hence, companies with high P/E ratios are referred to as *growth stocks.* Simply stated, investors who believe that future earnings are going to be higher than current earnings are willing to pay a lot for today's earnings, and vice versa.

Using the per-share price of $76.25 for Global Petroleum Corporation on December 31, 2010, and its 2010 EPS of $5.29, the P/E ratio at year-end 2010 is

$$\text{Price/earnings (P/E) ratio} = \frac{\text{Market price per share of common stock}}{\text{Earnings per share}} = \frac{\$76.25}{\$5.29}$$

$$= 14.41$$

This figure indicates that investors were paying $14.41 for each dollar of GPC's earnings. GPC's price/earnings ratio one year before (on December 31, 2009) had been almost twice as high at 28.37 ($71.50 per share stock price ÷ $2.52 earnings per share).

The **market/book (M/B) ratio** provides another assessment of how investors view the firm's performance. It relates the market value of the firm's shares to their book value. The stocks of firms that investors expect to perform well in the future—improving profits, growing market share, launching successful products, and so forth—typically sell at higher M/B ratios than firms with less attractive prospects. Firms that investors expect to earn high returns relative to their risk typically sell at higher M/B multiples than those expected to earn low returns relative to risk.

To calculate the M/B ratio for GPC in 2010, we first need to find its *book value per share of common stock:*

$$\text{Book value per share} = \frac{\text{Common stock equity}}{\text{Number of shares of common stock outstanding}}$$

$$= \frac{\$4,278}{178.7} = \$23.94$$

We then compute the M/B ratio by dividing the book value into the current price of the firm's stock:

$$\text{Market/book (M/B) ratio} = \frac{\text{Market value per share of common stock}}{\text{Book value per share of common stock}}$$

$$= \frac{\$76.25}{\$23.94} = \$3.19$$

Investors are currently paying $3.19 for each $1.00 of book value of GPC's stock. Clearly, investors expect GPC to continue to grow in the future: they are willing to pay more than book value for the firm's shares.

7. Which of the categories and individual ratios described in this chapter would be of greatest interest to each of the following parties?
   a. Existing and prospective creditors (lenders)
   b. Existing and prospective shareholders
   c. The firm's management

8. How could analysts use the availability of cash inflow and cash outflow data to improve on the accuracy of the liquidity and debt coverage ratios presented previously? What specific ratio measures—using cash flow rather than financial statement data—would you calculate to assess the firm's liquidity and debt coverage?

9. Assume that a firm's total assets and sales remain constant. Would an increase in each of the ratios below be associated with a cash inflow or a cash outflow?
   a. Current ratio   d. Average payment period
   b. Inventory turnover   e. Debt ratio
   c. Average collection period   f. Net profit margin

10. Use the DuPont system to explain why a slower-than-average inventory turnover could cause a firm with an above-average net profit margin to have a below-average return on common equity.

11. How can you reconcile investor expectations for a firm with an above-average M/B ratio and a below-average P/E ratio? Could the age of the firm have any effect on this ratio comparison?

SUMMARY

- The four key financial statements are (1) the balance sheet, (2) the income statement, (3) the statement of retained earnings, and (4) the statement of cash flows. Companies typically include with these statements detailed notes describing the technical aspects of the financial statements.

- A firm's total cash flows can be conveniently divided into (1) operating flows, (2) investment flows, and (3) financing flows. Operating cash flow (OCF) measures the amount of cash flow generated by the firm's operations; it is calculated by adding any noncash charges (the main one being depreciation) to the firm's net operating profits after taxes (NOPAT). The value of NOPAT is calculated as earnings before interest and taxes (EBIT) multiplied by 1 minus the tax rate.

- More important than OCF to financial analysts is free cash flow (FCF), the amount of cash flow available to investors. Free cash flow equals operating cash flow less the firm's net investments in fixed and current assets.

- The statement of cash flows summarizes the firm's cash flows over a specified period of time, typically one year. It presents operating, investment, and financing cash flows. When interpreting the statement, an analyst typically looks for unusual changes in either the major categories of cash flow or in specific items to find clues to problems that the firm may be experiencing.

- Financial ratios are a convenient tool for analyzing the firm's financial statements to assess its performance over a given period. Analysts use various financial ratios to assess a firm's liquidity, activity, debt, profitability, and market value. The DuPont system uses both income statement and balance sheet data to assess a firm's profitability, particularly the returns earned on both the total asset investment and the owners' common stock equity in the firm.

KEY TERMS

accrual-based approach	average age of inventory	cash flow approach
activity ratios	average collection period	common stock
assets-to-equity (A/E) ratio	average payment period	coverage ratios

current ratio	inventory turnover	par value
debt ratio	investment flows	preferred stock
debt-to-equity ratio	liquidity ratios	price/earnings (P/E) ratio
deferred taxes	long-term debt	quick (acid-test) ratio
dividend payout ratio	market/book (M/B) ratio	ratio analysis
dividend per share (DPS)	net operating profits after taxes	retained earnings
DuPont system	(NOPAT)	return on common
earnings per share (EPS)	net profit margin	equity (ROE)
equity multiplier	net working capital	return on total
financing flows	noncash charges	assets (ROA)
fixed asset turnover	operating flows	times interest earned ratio
free cash flow (FCF)	operating profit margin	total asset turnover
gross profit margin	paid-in-capital in excess of par	treasury stock

QUESTIONS

2-1. What information (explicit and implicit) can be derived from financial statement analysis? Does the standardization required by GAAP add greater validity to comparisons of financial data between companies and industries?

2-2. What role does the Sarbanes–Oxley Act of 2002 play in financial reporting? Are there possible shortcomings to relying solely on financial statement analysis to value companies?

2-3. Distinguish between the types of financial information contained in the various financial statements. Which statements provide information on a company's performance over a reporting period? Which present data on a company's current position? What sorts of valuable information may be found in the notes to financial statements? Describe a situation in which the information in the notes would be essential to making an informed decision about the value of a corporation.

2-4. If you were a commercial credit analyst charged with the responsibility of making an accept–reject decision on a company's loan request, with which financial statement would you be most concerned? Which financial statement is most likely to provide pertinent information about a company's ability to repay its debt?

2-5. Suppose someone were to define operating cash flow as "net income plus depreciation plus interest expense multiplied by 1 minus the tax rate." Is this definition equal to the definition of operating cash flow in this text (assuming the firm pays interest on debt)? If not, then reduce the difference between the two definitions to a simple calculation. (*Hint:* Consider the tax advantages of debt.) Moreover, are the two definitions the same if the firm is composed entirely of equity (i.e., if there is no debt, which means there is no interest expense)?

2-6. Suppose a supplier allows payment for inventory 30 days from delivery and the firm is able to sell all of the inventory within 15 days of delivery. How does this affect free cash flow?

2-7. Firm Q has a low times interest earned ratio relative to its industry. However, corporate officers indicate that the ratio is low because Firm Q depreciates assets faster than the industry norm. Is this a credible reason? How would viewing the firm's gross profit margin help illuminate this situation?

2-8. You have determined that, for Firm X, $\{\Delta CA - \Delta AP - \Delta accruals\}$ is negative. Does this affect the firm's operating cash flow and free cash flow positively, negatively, or not at all?

2-9. Suppose a firm has volatile sales and consequently does not finance with much debt. How does this affect the times interest earned ratio, the debt-to-equity ratio, and the equity multiplier?

2-10. How is the DuPont system useful in analyzing a firm's ROA and ROE? What information can analysts infer by breaking ROE into contributing ratios? What is the mathematical relationship between each of the individual components (net profit margin, total asset turnover, and assets-to-equity ratio) and ROE? Can ROE be raised without affecting ROA? How?

PROBLEMS

Financial Statements

2-1. Use the financial statements below to answer the questions about S&M Manufacturing's financial position at the end of the calendar year 2010.

S&M Manufacturing, Inc.
Balance Sheet as of December 31, 2010 ($ thousand)

Assets		Liabilities and Equity	
Current assets		Current liabilities	
Cash	$ 140,000	Accounts payable	$ 480,000
Marketable securities	260,000	Notes payable	500,000
Accounts receivable	650,000	Accruals	80,000
Inventories	800,000	Total current	$1,060,000
Total current assets	$1,850,000	liabilities	
Fixed assets		Long-term debt	
Gross fixed assets	$3,780,000	Bonds outstanding	$1,300,000
Less: Accumulated	1,220,000	Bank debt (long-term)	260,000
depreciation		Total long-term debt	$1,560,000
Net fixed assets	$2,560,000	Stockholders' equity	
Total assets	$4,410,000	Preferred stock	$ 180,000
		Common stock (at par)	200,000
		Paid-in capital	810,000
		in excess of par	
		Retained earnings	600,000
		Total stockholders' equity	$1,790,000
		Total liabilities and equity	$4,410,000

S&M Manufacturing, Inc.,
Income Statement for Year Ended December 31, 2010 ($ thousand)

Sales revenue		$6,900,000
Less: Cost of goods sold		4,200,000
Gross profits		$2,700,000
Less: Operating expenses		
Sales expense	$ 750,000	
General and administrative expense	1,150,000	
Leasing expense	210,000	
Depreciation expense	235,000	
Total operating expenses		2,345,000
Earnings before interest and taxes		$ 355,000
Less: Interest expense		85,000
Net profit before taxes		$ 270,000
Less: Taxes		81,000
Net profits after taxes		$ 189,000
Less: Preferred stock dividends		10,800
Earnings available for common stockholders		$ 178,200
Less: Dividends		75,000
To retained earnings		$ 103,200

Per share data

Earnings per share (EPS)	$1.43
Dividends per share (DPS)	$0.60
Price per share	$15.85

a. How much cash and near cash does S&M have at year-end 2010?

b. What was the original cost of all of the firm's real property that is currently owned?

c. How much in total liabilities did the firm have at year-end 2010?

d. How much did S&M owe for credit purchases at year-end 2010?

e. How much did the firm sell during 2010?

f. How much equity did the common stockholders have in the firm at year-end 2010?

g. What is the cumulative total of earnings reinvested in the firm from its inception through the end of 2010?

h. How much operating profit did the firm earn during 2010?

i. What is the total amount of dividends paid out by the firm during the year 2010?

j. How many shares of common stock did S&M have outstanding at year-end 2010?

2-2. Obtain financial statements for Microsoft for the last five years either from its website (http://www.microsoft.com) or from the SEC's online EDGAR site (http://www.sec.gov/edgar/searchedgar/webusers.htm). First, look at the statements without reading the notes. Then read the notes carefully, concentrating on those regarding executive stock options. Do you have a different perspective after analyzing the notes?

Cash Flow Analysis

Smart Solutions

See the problem and solution explained step-by-step at **SMARTFinance**

2-3. Given the balance sheets and selected data from the income statement of GSM Industries that follow, answer parts (a)–(d).

a. Use Equation 2.1 to calculate the firm's net operating profits after taxes (NOPAT) for the year ended December 31, 2010.

b. Use Equation 2.2 to calculate the firm's operating cash flow (OCF) for the year ended December 31, 2010.

c. Use Equation 2.4 to calculate the firm's free cash flow (FCF) for the year ended December 31, 2010.

d. Interpret, compare, and contrast your cash flow estimates in parts (b) and (c).

GSM Industries Balance Sheets ($ million)

	December 31	
	2010	**2009**
Assets		
Cash	$ 3,500	$ 3,000
Marketable securities	3,800	3,200
Accounts receivable	4,000	3,800
Inventories	4,900	4,800
Total current assets	$16,200	$14,800
Gross fixed assets	$31,500	$30,100
Less: Accumulated depreciation	14,700	13,100
Net fixed assets	$16,800	$17,000
Total assets	$33,000	$31,800

Liabilities and Stockholders' Equity

Accounts payable	$ 3,600	$ 3,500
Notes payable	4,800	4,200
Accruals	1,200	1,300
Total current liabilities	$ 9,600	$ 9,000
Long-term debt	$ 6,000	$ 6,000
Common stock	$11,000	$11,000
Retained earnings	6,400	5,800
Total stockholders' equity	$17,400	$16,800
Total liabilities and stockholders' equity	$33,000	$31,800

Income Statement Data

Depreciation expense	$1,600
Earnings before interest and taxes (EBIT)	4,500
Taxes	1,300
Net profits after taxes	2,400

2-4. Classify each of the following items as an inflow (I) or an outflow (O) of cash or as neither (N).

Item	Change ($)	Item	Change ($)
Cash	+600	Accounts receivable	−900
Accounts payable	−1,200	Net profits	+700
Notes payable	+800	Depreciation	+200
Long-term debt	−2,500	Repurchase of stock	+500
Inventory	+400	Cash dividends	+300
Fixed assets	+600	Sale of stock	+1,300

Assessing Financial Performance Using Ratio Analysis

2-5. A *common-size income statement* for Aluminum Industries' 2009 operations follows. Using the firm's 2010 income statement presented in Problem 2-12, develop the 2010 common-size income statement (see footnote 1) and compare it with the 2009 statement. Which areas require further analysis and investigation?

Aluminum Industries, Inc. Common-Size Income Statement
for the Year Ended December 31, 2009

Sales revenue ($35,000,000)		100.0%
Less: Cost of goods sold		65.9
Gross profit		34.1%
Less: Operating expenses		
Selling expense	12.7%	
General and administrative expenses	6.3	
Lease expense	0.6	
Depreciation expense	3.6	
Total operating expense		23.2
Operating profit		10.9%
Less: Interest expense		1.5
Net profit before taxes		9.4%
Less: Taxes (rate = 40%)		3.8
Net profits after taxes		5.6%

2-6. Assume current liabilities are $10,000, the current ratio is 2.0, and the quick ratio is 1.0. How much does the firm have in inventory and how much does the firm have in current assets?

2-7. Suppose a firm's inventory turnover is 4.5 annually and its average collection period is 90 days. Assuming a 365-day year, how many days (on average) elapse between receiving inventory and collecting payment from selling the inventory?

2-8. A firm's return on total assets is 6% and its return on common equity is 9%. What is the firm's debt ratio?

2-9. Firm A is composed entirely of equity and has an ROA that is twice as large as Firm B's. However, both firms have the same ROE. What does this imply about Firm B's debt ratio and debt-to-equity ratio? (Supply values for both ratios.)

2-10. A firm has earnings available for common stockholders of $15 million with an asset base of $1.25 billion and equity of $75 million. Assuming that equity does not change, how would the firm's return on total assets and return on common equity be affected if the asset base were reduced to $1 billion? Demonstrate by calculating ROA and ROE before and after the asset base reduction.

2-11. The partially complete 2010 balance sheet and income statement for Challenge Industries are given below, followed by selected ratio values for the firm based on its completed 2010 financial statements. Use the ratios along with the partial statements to complete the financial statements. (*Hint:* Use the ratios in the order listed to calculate the missing statement values that need to be installed in the partial statements.)

Challenge Industries, Inc.
Balance Sheet as of December 31, 2010 ($ thousand)

Assets		Liabilities and Equity	
Current assets		Current liabilities	
Cash	$ 52,000	Accounts payable	$150,000
Marketable securities	60,000	Notes payable	?
Accounts receivable	200,000	Accruals	80,000
Inventories	?	Total current liabilities	?
Total current assets	?	Long-term debt	$425,000
Fixed assets (gross)	?	Total liabilities	?
Less: Accumulated	240,000	Stockholders' equity	
depreciation		Preferred stock	?
Net fixed assets	?	Common stock (at par)	150,000
Total assets	?	Paid-in capital in excess	
		of par	?
		Retained earnings	390,000
		Total stockholders' equity	?
		Total liabilities and	?
		stockholders' equity	

Challenge Industries, Inc.
Income Statement for the Year Ended December 31, 2010 ($ thousand)

Sales revenue		$4,800,000
Loss: Cost of goods sold		?
Gross profits		?
Less: Operating expenses		
Sales expense	$690,000	
General and administrative expense	750,000	
Depreciation expense	120,000	
Total operating expenses		1,560,000
Earnings before interest and taxes		?
Less: Interest expense		35,000
Earnings before taxes		?
Less: Taxes		?
Net income (Net profits after taxes)		?
Less: Preferred dividends		15,000
Earnings available for common stockholders		?
Less: Dividends		60,000
To retained earnings		?

Challenge Industries, Inc.
Ratios for the Year Ended December 31, 2010

Ratio	Value
Total asset turnover	2.00
Gross profit margin	40%
Inventory turnover	10
Current ratio	1.60
Net profit margin	3.75%
Return on common equity	12.5%

2-12. Manufacturers Bank is evaluating Aluminum Industries, Inc., which has requested a $3 million loan, to assess the firm's risk. On the basis of the debt ratios for Aluminum, along with the industry averages and Aluminum's recent financial statements (which follow), evaluate and recommend appropriate action on the loan request.

Aluminum Industries, Inc.
Income Statement for the Year Ended December 31, 2010

Sales revenue		$30,000,000
Less: Cost of goods sold		21,000,000
Gross profit		$ 9,000,000
Less: Operating expenses		
Selling expense	$3,000,000	
General and administrative expenses	1,800,000	
Lease expense	200,000	
Depreciation expense	1,000,000	
Total operating expense		$6,000,000

Operating profit	$3,000,000
Less: Interest expense	1,000,000
Net profit before taxes	$2,000,000
Less: Taxes (rate = 40%)	800,000
Net profits after taxes	$1,200,000

Aluminum Industries, Inc. Balance Sheet as of December 31, 2010

Assets		Liabilities and Stockholders' Equity	
Current assets		Current liabilities	
Cash	$ 1,000,000	Accounts payable	$ 8,000,000
Marketable securities	3,000,000	Notes payable	8,000,000
Accounts receivable	12,000,000	Accruals	500,000
Inventories	7, 500,000	Total current liabilities	$16,500,000
Total current assets	$23,500,000	Long-term debt (including financial	$20,000,000
Gross fixed assets (at cost)		leases)	
Land and buildings	$11,000,000	Stockholders' equity	
Machinery and equipment	20,500,000	Preferred stock (25,000 shares, $4 dividend)	$ 2,500,000
Furniture and fixtures	8,000,000	Common stock (1 million shares, $5 par)	5,000,000
Gross fixed assets	$39,500,000	Paid-in capital in excess of par value	4,000,000
Less: Accumulated depreciation	13,000,000	Retained earnings	2,000,000
Net fixed assets	$26,500,000	Total stockholders' equity	$13,500,000
Total assets	$50,000,000	Total liabilities & stockholders' equity	$50,000,000

Industry Averages

Debt ratio	0.51
Debt-to-equity ratio	1.07
Times interest earned ratio	7.30

2-13. A firm's price/earnings ratio is 20.0 with earnings available for common stockholders of $45 million. Assuming there are 27 million shares outstanding, what is the firm's stock price?

2-14. Tracey White, owner of the Buzz Coffee Shop chain, has decided to expand her operations. Her 2010 financial statements follow. Tracey can buy two additional coffeehouses for $3 million, and she has the choice of completely financing these new coffeehouses with either a 10% (annual interest) loan or by issuing new common stock. She also expects these new shops to generate an additional $1 million in sales. Assuming a 40% tax rate and no other changes, which financing option results in the better ROE? Should Tracey buy the two coffeehouses? Why or why not?

Buzz Coffee Shops, Inc. 2010 Financial Statements

Balance Sheet		Income Statement	
Current assets	$ 250,000	Sales	$500,000
Fixed assets	750,000	−Costs and expenses	200,000
Total assets	$1,000,000	@40%	
Current liabilities	$ 300,000	Earnings before interest	$300,000
Long-term debt	0	and taxes (EBIT)	
Total liabilities	$ 300,000	−Interest expense	0
Common equity	$ 700,000	Net profit before taxes	$300,000
Total liabilities and	$1,000,000	−Taxes @40%	120,000
stockholders' equity		Net income	$180,000

Use the following information for Problems 2-15 and 2-16.

Income Statements for the Year Ended December 31, 2010

	Heavy Metal Manufacturing (HMM)	Metallic Stamping Inc. (MS)	High-Tech Software Co. (HTS)
Sales	$75,000,000	$50,000,000	$100,000,000
−Operating expenses	65,000,000	40,000,000	60,000,000
Operating profit	$10,000,000	$10,000,000	$ 40,000,000
−Interest expenses	3,000,000	3,000,000	0
Earnings before taxes	$ 7,000,000	$ 7,000,000	$ 40,000,000
−Taxes (rate = 40%)	2,800,000	2,800,000	16,000,000
Net income	$ 4,200,000	$ 4,200,000	$ 24,000,000

Balance Sheets as of December 31, 2010

	Heavy Metal Manufacturing (HMM)	Metallic Stamping Inc. (MS)	High-Tech Software Co. (HTS)
Current assets	$ 10,000,000	$ 5,000,000	$ 20,000,000
Net fixed assets	90,000,000	75,000,000	80,000,000
Total assets	$100,000,000	$80,000,000	$100,000,000
Current liabilities	$ 20,000,000	$0,000,000	$ 10,000,000
Long-term debt	40,000,000	40,000,000	0
Total liabilities	$ 60,000,000	$50,000,000	$ 10,000,000
Common stock	$ 15,000,000	$10,000,000	$ 25,000,000
Retained earnings	25,000,000	20,000,000	65,000,000
Total common equity	$ 40,000,000	$30,000,000	$ 90,000,000
Total liabilities and common equity	$100,000,000	$80,000,000	$100,000,000

2-15. Use the DuPont system to compare the two heavy metal companies shown above (HMM and MS) during 2010.

    a. Which of the two companies has a higher return on common equity? What is the cause of the difference between the two?

    b. Calculate the return on common equity of the software company HTS. Why is this value so different from those of the heavy metal companies calculated in part (a)?

    c. Compare the leverage levels between the industries. Which industry receives a greater contribution from return on total assets? Which industry receives a greater contribution from the assets-to-equity (A/E) ratio?

    d. Can you make a meaningful DuPont comparison across industries? Why or why not?

2-16. Referring back to Problem 2-15, perform the same analysis with real data. Download last year's financial data from Ford Motor Company (http://www.ford.com), General Motors (http://www.gm.com), and Microsoft (http://www.microsoft.com). Which ratios demonstrate the greatest difference between Ford and General Motors? Which of the two is more profitable? Which ratios drive the greater profitability?

2-17. Use the following 2010 financial data for Greta's Gadgets, Inc., to determine the effect of using additional debt financing to purchase additional assets. Assume that an additional $1 million of assets is purchased with 100% debt financing at a 10% annual interest rate.

Greta's Gadgets, Inc.

Income Statement for the Year Ended December 31, 2010		**Balance Sheet as of December 31, 2010**	
		Assets	
Sales	$4,000,000	Current assets	$ 0
−Costs and expenses @90%	3,600,000	Fixed assets	2,000,000
Earnings before interest & taxes	$ 400,000	Total assets	$2,000,000
		Liabilities and Stockholders' Equity	
−Interest (.10 × $1,000,000)	100,000		
Earnings before taxes	$ 300,000	Current liabilities	$ 0
−Taxes @40%	120,000	Long-term debt @10%	1,000,000
Net income	$ 180,000	Total liabilities	$1,000,000
		Common stock equity	$1,000,000
		Total liabilities and stockholders' equity	$2,000,000

    a. Calculate the current (2010) net profit margin, total asset turnover, assets-to-equity ratio, return on total assets, and return on common equity for Greta's.

    b. Now, assuming no other changes, determine the impact of purchasing the $1 million in assets using 100% debt financing at a 10% annual interest rate. Further, assume that the newly purchased assets generate an additional $2 million in sales and that the costs and expenses remain at 90% of sales. For this problem, assume a tax rate of 40%. What is the effect on the ratios calculated in part (a)? Is the purchase of these assets justified on the basis of the return on common equity?

c. Assume that the newly purchased assets in part (b) generate only an extra $500,000 in sales. Is the purchase justified in this case?

d. Which component ratio(s) of the DuPont system is (are) not affected by the change in sales? What does this imply about the financial risk?

2-18. The financial statements of Access Corporation for the year ended December 31, 2010, follow.

Access Corporation Income Statement for the Year Ended December 31, 2010

Sales revenue		$160,000
Less: Cost of goods sold[a]		106,000
Gross profit		$ 54,000
Less: Operating expenses		
Selling expense	$16,000	
General and administrative expense	10,000	
Lease expense	1,000	
Depreciation expense	10,000	
Total operating expense		37,000
Operating profit		$ 17,000
Less: Interest expense		6,100
Net profit before taxes		$ 10,900
Less: Taxes @40%		4,360
Net profits after taxes		$ 6,540

[a]Access Corporation's annual purchases are estimated to equal 75% of the cost of goods sold.

Access Corporation Balance Sheet as of December 31, 2010

Assets		Liabilities and Stockholders' Equity	
Cash	$ 500	Accounts payable	$ 22,000
Marketable securities	1,000	Notes payable	47,000
Accounts receivable	25,000	Total current liabilities	$ 69,000
Inventories	45,500	Long-term debt	$ 22,950
Total current assets	$ 72,000	Total liabilities	$ 91,950
Land	$ 26,000	Common stock[a]	$ 31,500
Buildings and equipment	90,000	Retained earnings	$ 26,550
Less: Accumulated		Total liabilities and	$150,000
depreciation	38,000	stockholders' equity	
Net fixed assets	$ 78,000		
Total assets	$150,000		

[a] The firm's 3,000 outstanding shares of common stock closed 2010 at a price of $25 per share.

a. Use the preceding financial statements to complete the following table. Assume that the industry averages given in the table are applicable for both 2009 and 2010.

b. Analyze Access Corporation's financial condition as it relates to (1) liquidity, (2) activity, (3) debt, (4) profitability, and (5) market value. Summarize the company's overall financial condition.

Access Corporation's Financial Ratios

Ratio	Industry Average	Actual 2009	Actual 2010
Current ratio	1.80	1.84	_____
Quick (acid-test) ratio	.70	.78	_____
Inventory turnover	2.50	2.59	_____
Average collection period[a]	37 days	36 days	_____
Average payment period[a]	72 days	78 days	_____
Debt-to-equity ratio	50%	51%	_____
Times interest earned ratio	3.8	4.0	_____
Gross profit margin	38%	40%	_____
Net profit margin	3.5%	3.6%	_____
Return on total assets (ROA)	4.0%	4.0%	_____
Return on common equity (ROE)	9.5%	8.0%	_____
Market/book (M/B) ratio	1.1	1.2	_____

[a] Based on a 365-day year and on end-of-year figures.

Smart Solutions

See the problem and solution explained step-by-step at **SMARTFinance**

2-19. Given the following financial statements, historical ratios, and industry averages, calculate the MBA Company's financial ratios for 2010. Analyze its overall financial situation both in comparison with industry averages and over the period 2008–2010. Break your analysis into an evaluation of the firm's liquidity, activity, debt, profitability, and market value.

MBA Company Income Statement for the Year Ended December 31, 2010

Sales revenue		$10,000,000
Less: Cost of goods sold[a]		7,500,000
Gross profit		$ 2,500,000
Less: Operating expenses		
Selling expense	$300,000	
General and administrative expense	650,000	
Lease expense	50,000	
Depreciation expense	200,000	
Total operating expense		1,200,000
Operating profit (EBIT)		$ 1,300,000
Less: Interest expense		200,000
Net profits before taxes		$ 1,100,000
Less: Taxes (rate = 40%)		440,000
Net profits after taxes		$ 660,000
Less: Preferred stock dividends		50,000
Earnings available for common stockholders		$ 610,000
Earnings per share (EPS)		$ 3.05

[a] Annual credit purchases of $6.2 million were made during the year.

MBA Company Balance Sheet as of December 31, 2010

Assets			Liabilities and Stockholders' Equity		
Current assets			Current liabilities		
Cash	$	200,000	Accounts payable	$	900,000
Marketable securities		50,000	Notes payable		200,000
Accounts receivable		800,000	Accruals		100,000
Inventories		950,000	Total current liabilities		$ 1,200,000
Total current assets		$ 2,000,000	Long-term debt (including		$ 3,000,000
Gross fixed assets		$12,000,000	financial leases)		
(at cost)			Stockholders' equity		
Less: Accumulated		3,000,000	Preferred stock (25,000 shares,		$ 1,000,000
depreciation			$2 dividend)		
Net fixed assets		$ 9,000,000	Common stock		600,000
Other assets		$ 1,000,000	(200,000 shares, $3 par)[a]		
Total assets		$12,000,000	Paid-in capital in excess of par		5,200,000
			Retained earnings		1,000,000
			Total stockholders' equity		$ 7,800,000
			Total liabilities and stockholders'		$12,000,000
			equity		

[a]On December 31, 2010, the firm's common stock closed at a price of $27.50 per share.

Historical and Industry Average Ratios for MBA Company

Ratio	Actual 2008	Actual 2009	Industry Average 2010
Current ratio	1.40	1.55	1.85
Quick (acid-test) ratio	1.00	0.92	1.05
Inventory turnover	9.52	9.21	8.60
Average collection period[a]	45.0 days	36.4 days	35.0 days
Average payment period[a]	58.5 days	60.8 days	45.8 days
Fixed asset turnover	1.08	1.05	1.07
Total asset turnover	0.74	0.80	0.74
Debt ratio	0.20	0.20	0.30
Debt-to-equity ratio	0.25	0.27	0.39
Times interest earned ratio	8.2	7.3	8.0
Gross profit margin	0.30	0.27	0.25
Operating profit margin	0.12	0.12	0.10
Net profit margin	0.067	0.067	0.058
Return on total assets (ROA)	0.049	0.054	0.043
Return on common equity (ROE)	0.066	0.073	0.072
Earnings per share (EPS)	$1.75	$2.20	$1.50
Price/earnings (P/E) ratio	12.0	10.5	11.2
Market/book (M/B) ratio	1.20	1.05	1.10

[a]Based on a 365-day year and on end-of-year figures.

Smart Solutions

See the problem and solution explained step-by-step at **SMARTFinance**

2-20. Choose a company that you would like to analyze and then obtain its financial statements. Now, select another firm from the same industry and obtain its financial data. Perform a complete ratio analysis on each firm. How well does your selected company compare with its industry peer? Which components of your firm's ROE are superior, and which are inferior?

THOMSON ONE | Business School Edition

Access financial information from the Thomson ONE–Business School Edition website for the following problem(s). Go to http://tobsefin.swlearning.com/. If you have already registered your access serial number and have a username and password, click **Enter**. Otherwise, click **Register** and follow the instructions to create a username and password. Register your access serial number and then click **Enter** on the aforementioned website. When you click Enter, you will be prompted for your username and password (please remember that the password is case sensitive). Enter them in the respective boxes and then click **OK** (or hit **Enter**). From the ensuing page, click **Click Here to Access Thomson ONE–Business School Edition Now**! This opens up a new window that gives you access to the Thomson ONE–Business School Edition database. You can retrieve a company's financial information by entering its ticker symbol [provided for each company in the problem(s)] in the box below "Companies." For further instructions on using the Thomson ONE–Business School Edition database, please refer to "A Guide for Using Thomson ONE–Business School Edition."

2-21. Compare the profitability of Wal-Mart Stores Inc. (ticker symbol, WMT) and Target Corp. (ticker symbol, TGT) for the latest year. Using the return on total assets (ROA) and return on common equity (ROE) measures, determine which firm is more profitable. Use the DuPont system to determine what drives the difference in the profitability of the two firms.

2-22. Analyze the cash flows of Southwest Airlines (ticker symbol, LUV) over the last five years. Calculate the operating cash flow (using Equation 2.2) and the free cash flow (using Equation 2.4) for each of the last five years. Do the operating cash flows you calculated match the Net Cash Flow from Operating Activities on the 5-Year Annual Cash Flow Statement? If they are different, why are they different?

MINI-CASE: FINANCIAL STATEMENT AND CASH FLOW ANALYSIS

Jaedan Industries has the following account balances as of December 31, 2010. The firm's dividend payout ratio is 25% and the tax rate is 34%. The firm's stock price on December 31, 2009, was $42.89 and on December 31, 2010, it was $56.82. Construct an income statement, balance sheet, statement of retained earnings, and statement of cash flows for 2010. Also determine the firm's free cash flow and calculate the liquidity, activity, debt, profitability, and market ratios for Jaedan Industries. Perform a DuPont analysis and compare the firm to the industry ratios (see last table in this sequence). Highlight any financial strengths and weaknesses that Jaedan Industries may have.

Jaedan Industries Account Balances
for the Year Ending December 31, 2010

Sales	$42,000,000
Cost of goods sold (COGS)	63%
Portion of COGS that represents purchases	75%
Selling, general, and administrative expenses	$1,621,000
Depreciation	$800,000
Interest rate on short- and long-term debt	10%
Cash balance	$3,689,000
Accounts receivable	$5,423,000
Marketable securities	$1,836,000
Inventory	$4,118,000
Fixed assets	$14,811,000
Accumulated depreciation (does not include depreciation for 2010)	$5,160,000
Accounts payable	$3,136,000
Notes payable	$706,000
Accruals	$500,000
Long-term bonds outstanding	$3,046,000
Preferred stock (at par)	$100,000
Retained earnings (does not include retained earnings for 2010)	$1,628,819
Common stock (at par)	$4,000,000
Paid-in capital in excess of par	$4,500,000
Tax rate	34%
Dividend payout ratio (common stock)	25%
Dividends on preferred stock	8% of par
Number of shares of common stock outstanding	1 million
Terms of trade on accounts receivable	35 days
Terms of trade on accounts payable	45 days

To aid in your calculations, the financial statements from 2009 are given below.

Jaedan Industries Income Statement
for the Year Ending December 31, 2009

Sales	$38,578,155
Less: Cost of goods sold	27,004,709
Gross profit	$11,573,447
Less: Operating expenses:	
Selling, general, and administrative expenses	$ 1,000,000
Depreciation	700,000
Earnings before interest and taxes	$ 9,873,447
Less: Interest expense	375,000
Earnings before taxes	$ 9,498,447
Less: Taxes	3,229,472
Net income	$ 6,268,975
Less: Dividends paid	1,575,244
To retained earnings	$ 4,693,731

**Jaedan Industries Balance Sheet
as of December 31, 2009**

Assets		Liabilities and Equity	
Cash	$ 871,319	Accounts payable	$ 2,946,000
Marketable securities	3,587,000	Notes payable	684,000
Accounts receivable	2,867,500	Accruals	350,000
Inventories	3,210,000	Total current liabilities	$ 3,980,000
Total current assets	$10,535,819	Long-term debt	$ 3,046,000
Fixed assets	$11,879,000	Preferred stock	$ 100,000
Less: Accumulated	5,160,000	Common stock (at par)	$ 4,000,000
depreciation		Paid-in capital in excess of par	$ 4,500,000
Net fixed assets	$ 6,719,000	Retained earnings	$ 1,628,819
Total assets	$17,254,819	Total liabilities and equity	$17,254,819

The industry ratios for 2009 and 2010 are as follows.

Industry Ratios

	2009	2010
Liquidity ratios		
Current ratio	2.89	3.26
Quick ratio	1.42	2.19
Activity ratios		
Inventory turnover	6.71	6.59
Average collection period	35.12	36.17
Average payment period	50.73	49.63
Fixed asset turnover	4.32	4.76
Total asset turnover	2.14	2.33
Debt ratios		
Debt ratio	41.93%	39.36%
Assets-to-equity ratio	165.82%	163.13%
Debt-to-equity ratio	31.26%	30.23%
Times interest earned	15.72	16.81
Profitability ratios		
Gross profit margin	22.19%	23.74%
Operating profit margin	19.32%	20.89%
Net profit margin	15.11%	17.97%
Earnings per share	$4.36	$4.58
Return on total assets	32.34%	41.87%
Return on common equity	53.63%	68.30%
Market ratios		
Price/earnings ratio	5.41	5.97
Market/book ratio	4.19	4.32

3

The Time Value of Money

What Companies Do

Take the Money and … Park?

Facing a projected 2009 budget deficit of several hundred million dollars, Chicago Mayor Richard Daley struck a deal to lease the city's 36,000 parking meters to an investor group that included Morgan Stanley. Morgan and its partners would pay Chicago $1.2 billion up front; in return, they would have the right to collect revenue from parking meters for the next 75 years. The deal also allowed for increases in meter rates. The least expensive parking fees would rise from $1 per hour to $2 by 2013, while fees for the choice, downtown spots would rise from $3 to $6.50.

Asked to vote on approval for the deal with just 72 hours notice, Chicago City Aldermen voted in favor of the deal by a 40-5 margin. Alderman Richard Mell, whose son-in-law Governor Rod Blagojevich was under investigation for allegedly trying to sell Barack Obama's Senate seat to the highest bidder, explained his vote by arguing that the deal was a "once-in-a-lifetime shot to grab this pool of money." Local restaurant owner Alderman Thomas Tunney said: "This value in today's market is an unbelievable deal."

But was it an unbelievable deal for the city of Chicago or for Morgan Stanley (who coincidentally employs Richard Daley's son) and its partners? In order to answer that question, you must know how to compare an up-front payment with a stream of cash payments that occur over many years. This chapter will show you how to make that comparison.

Sources: Aldermen approve Chicago parking meter lease, http://newsblogs.chicagotribune.com/ clout_st/2008/12/aldermen-deba-1.html (December 4, 2008); Chicago "leasing" parking meters, http://taxpayer.wordpress.com/2008/12/03/chicago-leasing-parking-meters/ (December 3, 2008); Mayor scoffs at criticism on parking meter increases, http://newsblogs.chicagotribune.com/clout_ st/2008/12/mayor-scoffs-at.html (December 5, 2008); Chicago sells rights to city parking meters for $1.2 billion, http://ohmygov.com/blogs/general_news/archive/2008/12/24/chicago-sells-right-to-city-parking-meters-for-1-2-billion.aspx (December 24, 2008); Mayor Richard Daley warns of big budget deficit on Chicago budget, http://archives.chicagotribune.com/2008/jul/30/local/ chi-daley-chicago-budget-30-jul30 (July 30, 2008).

SMARTFinance Use the learning tools at www.cengage.com/finance/smartfinance

Finance is primarily concerned with the *voluntary transfer of wealth* between individuals and across time. The transfer of wealth *between individuals* occurs in financial markets through **financial intermediaries**. It can involve creditors lending money to borrowers in exchange for future repayment with interest, or investors purchasing an ownership claim in an entrepreneur's venture in exchange for a share in future profits.

Likewise, transferring wealth *across time* can take two forms. The first involves determining what the value of an investment made today will be worth at a specific future date. The second determines the value today of a cash flow to be received at a specific date in the future. We refer to the first as determining the **future value** of an investment and the second as determining the **present value** of a future cash flow.

These wealth transfers are voluntary "trades" of cash today for promises of greater payments in the future. These trades make all parties better off. Savers spend less than they earn today, and they lend or invest their savings so that they can consume more tomorrow. Borrowers may be better off as well. For example, an entrepreneur with a new invention borrows from investors to build a business that may enrich both the investors and the entrepreneur. In sum, financial markets improve the welfare of savers, entrepreneurs, and ordinary citizens by allowing borrowing, lending, and investing to occur most efficiently.

The remainder of this chapter addresses this issue of the **time value of money**. Section 3.1 describes how to compute the *future value* of a lump sum invested today at a given interest rate. In Section 3.2, we show how to compute the *present value* today of a cash flow to be received in the future, assuming investors can earn the same returns as on investments of comparable risk. Specifically, we present the technique for calculating the present value of a *lump sum*. Sections 3.3 and 3.4 describe the procedures for calculating the future value and present value, respectively, of a *stream of cash flows*. Section 3.5 demonstrates several special applications of time value of money techniques.

3.1 Future Value of a Lump Sum Received Today

The Concept of Future Value

Saving today allows investors to earn interest on their savings and enjoy higher future consumption. A person who invests $100 today at 5% interest expects to receive $105 in one year, representing $5 interest plus the return of the $100 originally invested. In this example, we say that $105 is the *future value* of $100 invested at 5% for one year.

We can calculate the future value of an investment over a specified period of time by applying either *simple interest* or *compound interest*. **Simple interest** is interest paid only on the initial principal of an investment. **Principal** is the amount of money on which the interest is paid. To demonstrate, if the investment in our previous example pays 5% simple interest, then the future value in any year equals $100 plus the product of the annual interest payment and the number of years. In this case, its future value would be $110 at the end of year 2 [$100 + (2 × $5)], $115 at the end of year 3 [$100 + (3 × $5)], $120 at the end of year 4 [$100 + (4 × $5)], and so on.

Compound interest is interest earned on both the principal amount and the interest earned in previous periods. To demonstrate compound interest, assume that you can deposit $100 into a risk-free account paying 5% interest annually. At the end of year 1, your account will have a balance of $105. This represents the initial principal of $100 plus 5% ($5) in interest. This future value is calculated as follows:

$$\text{Future value at end of year 1} = \$100 \times (1 + 0.05) = \$105$$

WHAT COMPANIES DO GLOBALLY

Taking It to the Bank

This chapter is all about comparing cash flows over time. Businesses and individuals use the tools explained in this chapter when they are investing or borrowing money. For these kinds of transactions to take place on a large scale, there must be some kind of institution that facilitates the flow of money between borrowers and lenders. Probably the first such institution that comes to mind is a bank, but access to banking services varies widely around the world. The following graph shows the number of bank branches per 100,000 people in 22 countries. Spain leads the world with 95 branches per 100,000 people; at the other end of the spectrum are countries such as Nigeria and Bolivia. In general, citizens in more developed economies have easier access to banks, and firms in those countries are less likely to face financing constraints when they want to invest in new plants, equipment, and other types of assets.

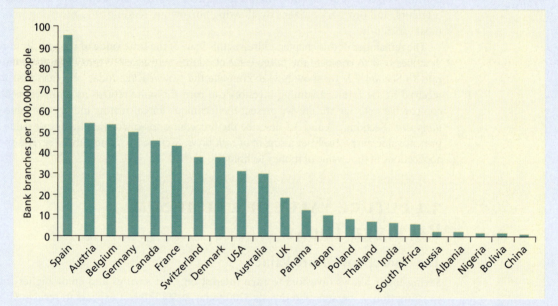

Source: Thorsten Beck, Asli Demirgüç-Kunt, and Maria Soledad Martinez Peria, "Reaching Out: Access to and Use of Banking Services across Countries," *Journal of Financial Economics* 85 (July 2007), pp. 234–266.

A surprise emerging from the graph is that China ranks last with just 1.33 banks per 100,000 people. Does this mean that Chinese citizens have very limited access to banking services? Not necessarily. The per capita figure for China is skewed downward because of the nation's extraordinarily high population. And by another measure—the number of bank ATMs per square kilometer—China ranks above the countries of Australia and Canada. Despite the imperfections in any particular measure of access to banking services, the ratio of branches to population hints at an important link between the presence of vibrant financial institutions and the development of a nation's economy.

If you leave this money in the account to earn compound interest for another year, then you will be paid interest at the rate of 5% on the *new principal* of $105. In other words, the bank will pay 5% interest both on the original principal of $100 and on the first year's interest of $5. At the end of this second year, there will be $110.25 in your account. This amount represents the principal at the beginning of year 2 ($105) plus 5% of the $105 ($5.25) in interest.[1] The future value at the end of the second year is computed as follows:

$$\text{Future value at end of year 2} = \$105 \times (1 + 0.05) = \$110.25$$

Substituting the first equation into the second one yields the following:

$$\begin{aligned} \text{Future value at end of year 2} &= \$100 \times (1 + 0.05) \times (1 + 0.05) \\ &= \$100 \times (1 + 0.05)^2 \\ &= \$110.25 \end{aligned}$$

Therefore, $100 deposited at 5% *compound* annual interest will be worth $110.25 at the end of two years.

It is important to recognize the difference in future values that results from compound versus simple interest. Although the difference between the account balances for simple versus compound interest in this example ($110 versus $110.25) seems rather trivial, the difference grows exponentially over time. With simple interest this account would have a balance of $250 after 30 years [$100 + (30 × $5)]; with compound interest, the account balance after 30 years would be $432.19.

The Equation for Future Value

Because financial analysts routinely use compound interest, we generally use compound rather than simple interest throughout this book. Equation 3.1 gives the general algebraic formula for calculating the future value, at the end of *n* years, of a lump sum invested today at an interest rate of *r* percent per period:

$$FV = PV \times (1 + r)^n \tag{Eq. 3.1}$$

where

FV = future value of an investment,
PV = present value of an investment (the lump sum),
 r = interest rate per period (typically 1 year),
 n = number of periods (typically years) that the lump sum is invested.

The following Example illustrates how you might use the concept of future value to evaluate an investment in a bank certificate of deposit (CD).

EXAMPLE

You have an opportunity to invest $100 cash in a CD that pays 6% annual interest. You would like to know how much your CD will be worth at the end of five years.

Substituting PV = $100, *r* = 0.06, and *n* = 5 into Equation 3.1 gives the future value at the end of year 5:

$$FV = \$100 \times (1 + 0.06)^5 = \$100 \times (1.3382) = \$133.82$$

Your CD will have an account balance of $133.82 at the end of the fifth year. This result is presented graphically, as a **time line**, in Figure 3.1.

---

[1] Said differently, compound interest includes the beneficial effect of "earning interest on your interest." In this example, during the second year you earn $5 interest on your initial $100 principal, plus you earn another $0.25 interest on the interest you earned (and saved) the first period. All total, in the second period you earn $5.25 in interest ($5 + $0.25).

FIGURE 3.1

Time Line for the Future Value of $100 Invested for Five Years at a 6% Interest Rate

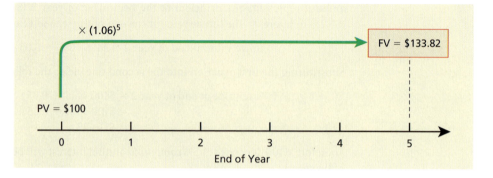

$\times (1.06)^5$

FV = $133.82

PV = $100

| | | | | | |
|0|1|2|3|4|5|

End of Year

In addition to algebra, there are two popular methods for simplifying future value calculations. One method is to use a *financial calculator*. To compute FV in the preceding example, you would simply input the number of years (5), the interest rate (6), and the amount of the initial deposit ($100); the calculator then returns the future value of $133.82. The second method is to use a *financial spreadsheet* such as Excel. Figure 3.2 shows a simplified spreadsheet illustrating the key inputs, the cell formula for the output, and the future value of $133.82.

FIGURE 3.2

An Excel Spreadsheet Used to Solve a Time Value of Interest Problem—in This Case, Future Value

Microsoft Excel - Book1

File   Edit   View   Insert   Format   Tools   Data   Window   Help

Binomial ▾ Equity ▾ FX ▾ Futures ▾ Bonds ▾ Exotic ▾ | Compute | ? Explain Help

B9

	A	B	C	D	E	F
1	Present value	$100				
2	Number of period	5				
3	Interest rate	6%				
4	**Future Value**	**$133.82**				
5		*Formula B4. FV(B3, B2,0,B1)*				
6						

A Graphic View of Future Value

Remember that we measure future value at the *end* of a given period. Figure 3.3 shows the relationship between various interest rates, the number of periods interest is earned, and the future value of $1. The figure shows two key points about future value: (1) the higher the interest rate, the higher the future value; and (2) the longer the period of time, the higher the future value. Note that for an interest rate of 0% the future value always equals the present value ($1), but for any interest rate greater than zero the future value is greater than the present value of $1.

Concept Review Questions

1. If compounding occurs once per year, will a deposit made in an account paying compound interest yield a higher future value after one period than an equal-size deposit in an account paying simple interest? What about future values for investments held longer than one period?

2. How would the future value of a deposit be affected by (a) a *decrease* in the interest rate or (b) an *increase* in the holding period? Why?

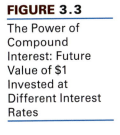

FIGURE 3.3

The Power of Compound Interest: Future Value of $1 Invested at Different Interest Rates

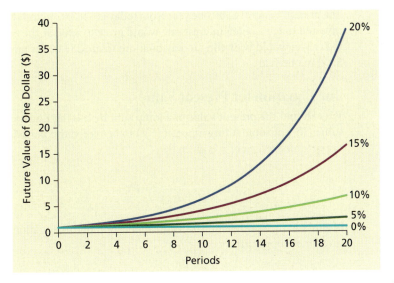

3.2 PRESENT VALUE OF A LUMP SUM

So far we have examined how to project the amount of cash that will build over time as an initial investment earns interest. Now we reverse that focus, asking what an investor would pay today in exchange for receiving a lump-sum payment at some point in the future. In other words, we want to know the *present value* of the future payment.

The Concept of Present Value

In finance, we use the term **discounting** to describe the process of calculating present values. The technique of discounting helps us to answer this question: If I can earn r percent on my money, then what is the most I'd be willing to pay *now* for the opportunity to receive FV dollars n periods from today? This process is actually the inverse of compounding interest:

■ compounding *tells us the future value of present dollars invested at a given interest rate;*
■ discounting *helps us determine the present value of a future amount, assuming an opportunity to earn a given return (r) on the money.*[2]

To see how this works, suppose an investment will pay you $300 one year from now. How much would you be willing to spend today to acquire this investment if you can earn 6% on an alternative investment of equal risk? To answer this question, you must determine how many dollars you would have to invest at 6% today in order to have $300 one year from now. Let PV equal this unknown amount, and use the same notation as in our discussion of future value:

$$PV \times (1 + 0.06) = \$300$$

Solving this equation for PV gives us

$$PV = \frac{\$300}{(1 + 0.06)} = \$283.02$$

---

[2]This interest rate, r, is variously referred to as the *discount rate,* the *required return,* the *cost of capital,* the *hurdle rate,* or the *opportunity cost of capital.*

The present value of $300 one year from today is $283.02 in today's dollars. That is, $283.02 invested today at a 6% interest rate would grow to $300 at the end of one year. Therefore, today you would be willing to pay no more than $283.02 for an investment that pays you $300 in one year.

The Equation for Present Value

We can find the present value of a lump sum by solving Equation 3.1 for PV. The present value (PV) of some future amount (FV) to be received n periods from now, assuming an opportunity return of r, is given by

$$PV = \frac{FV}{(1+r)^n} = FV \times \frac{1}{(1+r)^n} \qquad \text{(Eq. 3.2)}$$

The following Example illustrates an application of this equation to the case of a corporate investment opportunity.

Calculator

Input	Function
1700	PV
8	N
8	I
	CPT
	FV
Solution	918.46

EXAMPLE

Pam Verity, the financial manager of the Wildcatter Oil Drilling Company, can purchase from Sam Long, the owner of Petroleum Land Management Company, the right to a $1,700 royalty payment eight years from now. Pam believes her company's opportunity cost should be 8% on investments of this level of risk (i.e., this is the amount of return she believes she can earn on other investments of similar risk). How much should Pam be willing to pay for the right to the royalty payment? Substituting FV = $1,700, $n = 8$, and $r = 0.08$ into Equation 3.2 yields

$$PV = \frac{\$1,700}{(1+0.08)^8} = \frac{\$1,700}{1.85093} = \$918.46$$

Pam finds that the present value of this $1,700 royalty payment is $918.46. If Sam offers this investment opportunity today at a price of $918.46 or less, then Pam should accept the offer; if the price is higher then she should reject it. Figure 3.4 shows this process in a time line.

FIGURE 3.4

Time Line for the Present Value of $1,700 to Be Received in Eight Years at an 8% Discount Rate

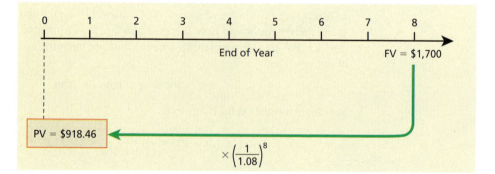

As with future values, there are two popular methods for simplifying present value calculations: financial calculators and spreadsheets.

A Graphic View of Present Value

For investors who expect to receive cash in the future, Figure 3.5 sends two important messages. First, the present value of a future cash payment declines the longer investors must wait to receive it. Second, the present value declines as the discount rate rises. Of course, for a discount rate of 0% the present value always equals the future value ($1). However, for any discount rate greater than zero, the present value falls below the future value.

FIGURE 3.5

The Effects of Discounting: Present Value of $1 Discounted at Different Interest Rates

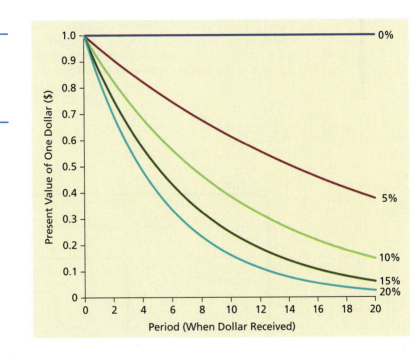

Concept Review Questions

3. How are the present value and the future value of a lump sum related definitionally? Mathematically?

4. How would the present value be affected by (a) an *increase* in the discount rate or (b) a *decrease* in the time period until the cash flow is received? Why?

3.3 FUTURE VALUE OF CASH FLOW STREAMS

Financial managers frequently must evaluate *streams* of cash flows that occur in future periods. Though this is mechanically more complicated than computing the future or present value of a single cash flow, the same basic techniques apply.

Two types of cash flow streams are possible: the mixed stream and the annuity. A **mixed stream** is a series of unequal payments reflecting no particular pattern. An **annuity** is a stream of equal periodic cash flows over a stated period of time. Either of these cash flow patterns can represent *inflows* of returns earned on investments or *outflows* of funds invested to earn future returns. Because certain shortcuts are possible when evaluating an annuity, we discuss mixed streams and annuities separately.

Finding the Future Value of a Mixed Stream

The future value of any *stream* of cash flows measured at the end of a specified year is the sum of the future values of the individual cash flows at that year's end. This future value is sometimes called the *terminal value*. The following Example demonstrates such a calculation.

EXAMPLE

Assume we want to determine the balance in an investment account earning 9% annual interest, given the following five end-of-year deposits: $400 in year 1, $800 in year 2, $500 in year 3, $400 in year 4, and $300 in year 5. These cash flows appear on the time line in Figure 3.6, which also depicts the future value calculation for this mixed stream of cash flows.

Note that the first cash flow, which occurs at the end of year 1, earns interest for four years (end of year 1 to end of year 5). Similarly, the second cash flow, which occurs at the end of year 2, earns interest for three years (end of year 2 to end of year 5), and so on. The future value of the mixed stream is $2,930.70.[3] The five deposits, which total $2,400 before interest, have grown by nearly $531 at the end of five years as a result of the interest earned.

FIGURE 3.6

Time Line for the Future Value at the End of Five Years of a *Mixed Cash Flow Stream* Invested at a 9% Interest Rate

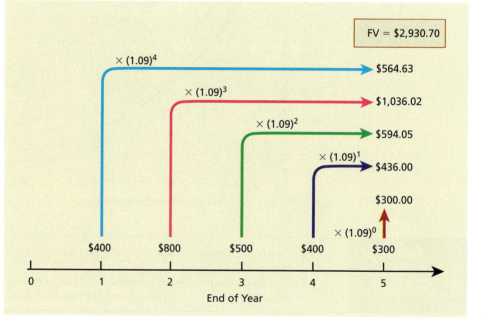

Letting CF_t represent the cash flow at the end of year t, the future value of an n-year mixed stream of cash flows (FV) can be expressed as follows:

$$FV = CF_1 \times (1 + r)^{n-1} + CF_2 \times (1 + r)^{n-2} + \cdots + CF_n \times (1 + r)^{n-n} \qquad \text{(Eq. 3.3)}$$

Substituting the annual cash flows and the 9% interest rate into Equation 3.3, we would calculate the value for each year (shown to the right of the time line). These values would total $2,930.70.

We can simplify the notation for Equation 3.3, as shown in Equation 3.3a, by using the summation symbol, Σ. Doing so gives us a shorthand way of saying that the *future value of*

---

[3]There is a $0.01 rounding difference between the future value given on the time line compared to the future value of $2,930.71 computed using a calculator or spreadsheet.

this n-year mixed stream is equal to the sum of the future values of individual cash flows from periods 1, 2, 3, ..., *n*:

$$FV = \sum_{t=1}^{n} CF_t \times (1 + r)^{n-t}$$

(Eq. 3.3a)

Though summations economize on the notation needed to express most of the equations presented in this chapter, for clarity we present equations in their "noncondensed" format wherever possible and use the summation notation sparingly.

Types of Annuities

Before looking at future value computations for annuities, we distinguish between the two basic types of annuities: the ordinary annuity and the annuity due. An **ordinary annuity** is an annuity for which the payments occur *at the end of each period.* An **annuity due** is one for which the payments occur *at the beginning of each period.*

To demonstrate these differences, assume you want to choose the better of two annuities as a personal investment opportunity. Both are five-year, $1,000 annuities, but annuity A is an ordinary annuity and annuity B is an annuity due. Although the amount of each annuity totals $5,000, the timing of the cash flows differs; each cash flow arrives one year sooner with the annuity due than with the ordinary annuity. As you might expect (given the core principle of the time value of money), for any positive interest rate, *the future value of an annuity due is always greater than the future value of an otherwise identical ordinary annuity.*[4] Why? Because you receive the first cash flow today in the annuity due, giving you a longer time to earn interest.

Finding the Future Value of an Ordinary Annuity

We can calculate the future value of an ordinary annuity using the same method demonstrated earlier for a mixed stream.

Calculator

Input	Function
1000	PMT
5	N
7	I
	CPT
	FV
Solution	5750.74

EXAMPLE

Assume you wish to save money on a regular basis to finance an exotic vacation in five years. You are confident that, with sacrifice and discipline, you can force yourself to deposit $1,000 annually at the *end of each* of the next five years into a savings account paying 7% annual interest. The time line in Figure 3.7 depicts this situation graphically.

We can use Equation 3.3 to compute the future value (FV) of this annuity. We simply use the assumed interest rate (*r*) of 7% and plug in the known values of each of the five yearly (*n* = 5) cash flows (CF_1 to CF_5), as follows:

$$FV = CF_1 \times (1 + r)^{n-1} + CF_2 \times (1 + r)^{n-2} + \cdots + CF_n \times (1 + r)^{n-n}$$
$$FV = CF_1 \times (1 + r)^{5-1} + CF_2 \times (1 + r)^{5-2} + \cdots + CF_5 \times (1 + r)^{5-5}$$
$$= \$1,000(1.07)^4 + \$1,000(1.07)^3 + \$1,000(1.07)^2 + \$1,000(1.07)^1 + \$1,000(1.07)^0$$
$$= \$1,310.80 + \$1,225.04 + \$1,144.90 + \$1,070 + \$1,000 = \$5,750.74$$

The year-1 cash flow of $1,000 earns 7% interest for four years, the year-2 cash flow earns 7% interest for three years, and so on. The future value of this ordinary annuity is $5,750.74.

---

[4]Ordinary annuities arise frequently in corporate finance. Therefore, throughout this book, unless otherwise specified the term "annuity" refers to an ordinary annuity.

Time Line for the Future Value at the End of Five Years of an *Ordinary Annuity* of $1,000 per Year Invested at a 7% Interest Rate

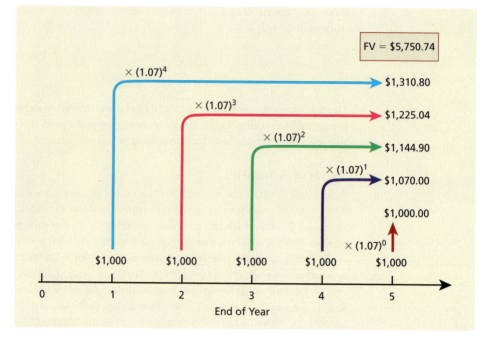

Making this calculation for a longer annuity would become cumbersome. Fortunately, a shortcut formula exists that simplifies the future value calculation of an ordinary annuity. Using the acronym PMT to represent the annuity's annual payment, Equation 3.4 gives the future value of an annuity that lasts for *n* years, assuming an interest rate of *r* percent:

$$FV = PMT \times \frac{(1 + r)^n - 1}{r}$$ **(Eq. 3.4)**

EXAMPLE

We can demonstrate that Equation 3.4 yields the same answer we obtained using the previous model by plugging in the values PMT = $1,000, *n* = 5, and *r* = 0.07:

$$FV = \$1,000 \times \frac{(1.07)^5 - 1}{0.07} = \$1,000 \times \frac{1.40255 - 1}{0.07}$$
$$= \$1,000 \times 5.7507 = \$5,750.74$$

Once again, we find the future value of this ordinary annuity to be $5,750.74.

Instead of using algebra, we could simplify future value calculations for annuities by using financial calculators or spreadsheets.

Finding the Future Value of an Annuity Due

The calculations used to find the future value of an annuity due involve only a slight change to those already used for an ordinary annuity. For the annuity due, the question is: How much money will you have at the end of five years (to finance your exotic vacation) if you deposit $1,000 annually at the *beginning of each year* into a savings account paying 7% annual interest?

FIGURE 3.8

Time Line for the Future Value at the End of Five Years of an *Annuity Due* of $1,000 per Year Invested at a 7% Interest Rate

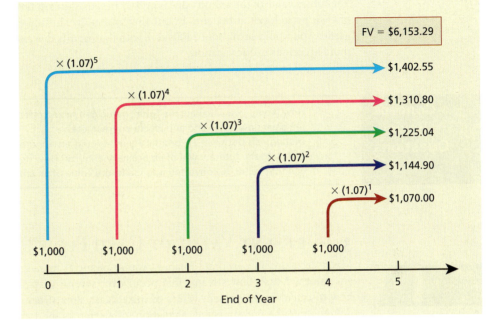

Figure 3.8 depicts this scenario graphically on a time line. Note that the ends of years 0 through 4 are respectively equivalent to the beginnings of years 1 through 5. As expected, the $6,153.29 future value of the annuity due is greater than the $5,750.74 future value of the comparable ordinary annuity. Because the cash flows of the annuity due occur at the beginning of the year, the cash flow of $1,000 at the beginning of year 1 earns 7% interest for five years, the cash flow of $1,000 at the beginning of year 2 earns 7% interest for four years, and so on. Comparing this to the ordinary annuity, you can see that each $1,000 cash flow of the annuity due earns interest for one more year than the comparable ordinary annuity cash flow. As a result, the future value of the annuity due is greater than the future value of the comparable ordinary annuity.

We can convert the equation for the future value of an ordinary annuity, Equation 3.4, into an expression for the *future value of an annuity due*, denoted FV(annuity due). To do so, we must take into account that each cash flow of an annuity due earns an additional year of interest. Therefore, we simply multiply the Equation 3.4 formula by $1 + r$:

$$\text{FV(annuity due)} = \text{PMT} \times \frac{(1+r)^n - 1}{r} \times (1 + r) \qquad \textbf{(Eq. 3.5)}$$

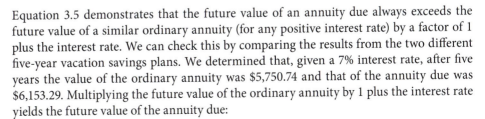

Equation 3.5 demonstrates that the future value of an annuity due always exceeds the future value of a similar ordinary annuity (for any positive interest rate) by a factor of 1 plus the interest rate. We can check this by comparing the results from the two different five-year vacation savings plans. We determined that, given a 7% interest rate, after five years the value of the ordinary annuity was $5,750.74 and that of the annuity due was $6,153.29. Multiplying the future value of the ordinary annuity by 1 plus the interest rate yields the future value of the annuity due:

$$\text{FV(annuity due)} = \$5,750.74 \times 1.07 = \$6,153.29$$

The future value of the annuity due is greater because its cash flow occurs at the beginning of each period, not at the end. In our illustration, by shifting each saving date one year earlier, you would earn about $400 more with the annuity due and could enjoy a somewhat more luxurious exotic vacation.

Concept Review Questions

5. How would you calculate the future value of a mixed stream of cash flows, given the cash flow dates and applicable interest rate?
6. Distinguish between an ordinary annuity and an annuity due. How would you calculate the future value of an ordinary annuity? How (for the same cash flows) can that value be converted into the future value of an annuity due?

3.4 PRESENT VALUE OF CASH FLOW STREAMS

Many decisions in corporate finance require financial managers to calculate the present values of cash flow streams that occur over several years. In this section, we show how to calculate the present values of mixed cash flow streams and annuities. We also demonstrate the present value calculation for an important cash flow stream known as a *perpetuity*.

Finding the Present Value of a Mixed Stream

The present value of any cash flow stream is the sum of the present values of the individual cash flows. To calculate the present values of all kinds of cash flow streams, we can apply the same techniques we used to calculate present values of lump sums.

Smart Practices Video

Cynthia Lucchese,
Chief Financial Officer,
Hillenbrand Industries

"At Hillenbrand, even the most basic financial tools are important."

See the entire interview at
SMARTFinance

Calculator

Input	Function
2nd	CLR TVM
	CF
2nd	CLR WORK
	↓
4000	ENTER ↓↓
8000	ENTER ↓↓
5000	ENTER ↓↓
4000	ENTER ↓↓
3000	ENTER ↓↓
	NPV
9	ENTER ↓↓
	CPT
Solution	19047.58

EXAMPLE

Shortly after graduation you receive an inheritance that you use to purchase a small bed-and-breakfast inn as an investment (and a weekend escape). Your plan is to sell the inn after five years. The inn is an old mansion, so you know that appliances, furniture, and other equipment will wear out and need to be replaced or repaired on a regular basis. You estimate these expenses over the five years of your ownership as follows: $4,000 during year 1, $8,000 during year 2, $5,000 during year 3, $4,000 during year 4, and $3,000 during year 5. For simplicity, assume that the expense payments will be made at the end of each year.

Because you have some of your inheritance left over after purchasing the inn (the deceased was indeed generous), you want to set aside a lump sum today from which you can make annual withdrawals to meet the estimated expenses when they come due, as shown on the time line in Figure 3.9. Suppose you can invest the lump sum in a bank account that pays 9% interest. To determine the amount of money you need to put in the account, you must calculate the present value of the stream of future expenses, using 9% as the discount rate.

Alternatively, we can use a financial calculator (or an Excel spreadsheet) to determine the present value of each annual cash flow. In the end, we add together the present value of each year's cash flows and find that the present value of the mixed stream is $19,047.58. This is the lump-sum amount you will need to set aside today to fund the estimated expenses over the five years.

FIGURE 3.9

Time Line for the Present Value of a 5-Year *Mixed Stream* Discounted at a 9% Interest Rate

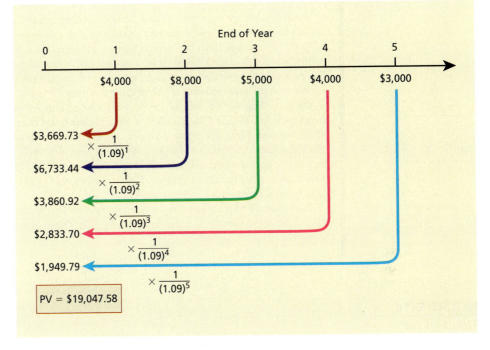

As you no doubt suspect, there is a general formula for computing the present value of a stream of future cash flows. Continuing to let CF_t represent the cash flow at the end of year t, we can express the present value of an n-year mixed stream of cash flows as

$$PV = \left[CF_1 \times \frac{1}{(1+r)^1}\right] + \left[CF_2 \times \frac{1}{(1+r)^2}\right] + \cdots + \left[CF_n \times \frac{1}{(1+r)^n}\right]$$

$$= \sum_{t=1}^{n} CF_t \times \frac{1}{(1+r)^t}$$

(Eq. 3.6)

If we substitute into Equation 3.6 the cash flows shown on the time line in Figure 3.9 and the 9% discount rate, we obtain the present value figure of $19,047.58.

Finding the Present Value of an Ordinary Annuity

We can find the present value of an ordinary annuity in a way similar to that for a mixed stream: discount each payment and then add up each payment's present value to find the annuity's present value.

EXAMPLE

A principal equipment supplier has approached Braden Company, a producer of plastic toys, with an offer for a service contract. Extruding Machines Corporation (EMC) offers to take over all of Braden's equipment repair and servicing for five years in exchange for a one-time payment today. Braden's managers know their company spends $7,000 on maintenance at the end of every year, so EMC's service contract would reduce Braden's cash outflows by $7,000 each year for five years.

(continued)

Because these are equal annual cash benefits, Braden can determine what it should be willing to pay for the service contract by valuing it as a five-year ordinary annuity with a $7,000 annual cash flow. If Braden requires a minimum return of 8% on all its investments, how much should it be willing to pay for EMC's service contract? The time line in Figure 3.10 shows calculation of the present value of this annuity.

We find the present value of this ordinary annuity by using the same method used in the preceding section to find the present value of a mixed stream. That is, we discount each end-of-year $7,000 cash flow back to time 0 and then sum the present values of all five cash flows. As Figure 3.10 shows, the present value of this ordinary annuity (EMC's service contract) is $27,948.97. If Braden were to initially deposit $27,948.97 into an account paying 8% annual interest, then it could withdraw $7,000 at the ends of years 1 through 5. After the final withdrawal (at the end of year 5), the account balance would exactly equal zero.

Therefore, if EMC offers the service contract to Braden for a lump-sum price of $27,948.97 or less then Braden should accept the offer. Otherwise, Braden should continue to perform its own maintenance.

FIGURE 3.10

Time Line for the Present Value of a 5-Year *Ordinary Annuity* Discounted at an 8% Interest Rate

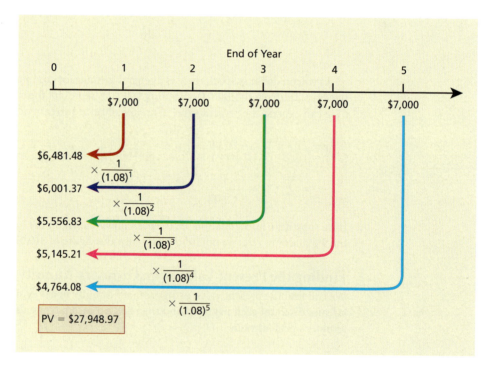

As with the future value of an annuity, a shortcut formula simplifies the present value calculation for an annuity. Here letting PMT denote the annual cash flow, we can use the following formula to calculate the present value of an *n*-year ordinary annuity:

$$PV = \frac{PMT}{r} \times \left[1 - \frac{1}{(1+r)^n}\right]$$

(Eq. 3.7)

EXAMPLE

We can use Equation 3.7 to calculate the present value of the service contract EMC has offered to Braden Company. Substituting in $n = 5$ years, $r = 0.08$, and PMT = $7,000, we once again find the present value of this ordinary annuity to be $27,948.97:

$$PV = \frac{\$7,000}{0.08} \times \left[1 - \frac{1}{(1.08)^5}\right] = \frac{\$7,000}{0.08} \times [1 - 0.6806] = \$27,948.97$$

By now, you know that we can simplify these computations by using a financial calculator or a spreadsheet.

Finding the Present Value of an Annuity Due

We can find the present value of an annuity due in much the same way we found the present value of an ordinary annuity. Remember that each cash flow for an annuity due occurs one period earlier than for an ordinary annuity. Thus, an annuity due would have a larger present value than an ordinary annuity with the same cash flows, discount rate, and life.

To find the present value of the annuity due, we use the same method used to find the present value of an ordinary annuity, with one difference: each of the cash flows of the annuity due occurs one year earlier—at the beginning rather than the end of the year. The expression for the present value of an *annuity due*, shown in Equation 3.8, is similar to that for the present value of an *ordinary annuity* given in Equation 3.7:

$$PV(\text{annuity due}) = \frac{PMT}{r} \times \left[1 - \frac{1}{(1 + r)^n}\right] \times (1 + r) \qquad \textbf{(Eq. 3.8)}$$

Comparing Equations 3.7 and 3.8, you can see that the present value of an annuity due is merely the present value of a similar ordinary annuity multiplied by $1 + r$.

EXAMPLE

To demonstrate, assume the Braden Company wishes to find the present value of the five-year service contract at an 8% discount rate, and assume also that each of the maintenance expenditures occurs *at the beginning of the year.* This means that the first payment for maintenance expenses would occur today.

The present value of this annuity due is simply $(1 + r)$ times the value of the ordinary annuity: PV(annuity due) = $27,948.97 $\times$ 1.08 = $30,184.89. If Braden pays its maintenance costs at the start of each year, then the most that it should be willing to pay EMC for the service contract increases by more than $2,000, to $30,184.89.

Finding the Present Value of a Perpetuity

A **perpetuity** is an annuity with an infinite life; it promises to pay the same amount at the end of every year *forever.* One of the first, and certainly the most famous, perpetuities in modern history was the massive "consol" bond issue sold by the British government after the Napoleonic Wars ended in 1815. This bond issue got its name from the fact that it consolidated all the existing British war debts into a single issue that paid a constant annual amount of interest in perpetuity. The issue itself never matured, meaning that the principal was never to be repaid.

Currently, not many corporations or governments issue perpetual bonds.[5] Perhaps the simplest modern example of a perpetuity is preferred stock issued by corporations. Preferred shares promise investors a constant annual (or quarterly) dividend payment forever. Though "forever" is a difficult time period to measure, we simply express the lifetime (n) of this security as infinity (∞) and then modify our basic valuation formulation for an annuity accordingly. We wish to determine the present value of an annuity (PV) that pays a constant annual dividend amount (PMT) for a perpetual number of years ($n = \infty$) discounted at a rate r. Here, the summation notation helps us express the desired formula:

$$PV = PMT \times \sum_{t=1}^{\infty} \frac{1}{(1+r)^t} \qquad \textbf{(Eq. 3.9)}$$

Fortunately, Equation 3.9 also comes in a simplified version, which states that the present value of a perpetuity equals the annual, end-of-year payment divided by the discount rate (in decimal form). Equation 3.10 gives this straightforward expression for the present value of a perpetuity:

$$PV = PMT \times \frac{1}{r} = \frac{PMT}{r} \qquad \textbf{(Eq. 3.10)}$$

JOB INTERVIEW QUESTION

How can you quickly estimate the present value of a long-lived cash flow stream that is growing at a constant rate over time?

EXAMPLE

In September 2008, following a series of tumultuous events that included the bankruptcy of Lehman Brothers and the bailout of insurance giant AIG, Warren Buffett expressed his faith in the U.S. markets by purchasing perpetual preferred stocks from Goldman Sachs. These shares had no maturity and promised to pay $500 million annually in dividends. Assuming that Buffett wanted a 10% annual return on his investment, the purchase price would be:

$$PV = \frac{\$500 \text{ million}}{0.10} = \$5 \text{ billion}$$

A $5 billion purchase price makes sense because each year Buffett would receive $500 million in dividends, exactly the 10% return that he sought.

Finding the Present Value of a Growing Perpetuity

By definition, perpetuities pay a constant periodic amount forever. However, few aspects of modern life are constant, and most of the cash flows we care about have a tendency to grow over time. This is true for income such as wages and salaries, dividend payments from corporations, and Social Security payments from governments.[6] Inflation is only one factor that drives increasing cash flows. Because of this tendency for cash flows to grow over time, we must determine how to adjust the present value of a perpetuity formula to account for expected growth in future cash flows.

---

[5]Some long-term bonds are nearly perpetuities. In July 1993, the Walt Disney Company sold $300 million of bonds that matured in the year 2093, 100 years after they were issued. The market dubbed these "Sleeping Beauty bonds" because their maturity matched the amount of time that Sleeping Beauty slept before being kissed by Prince Charming in the classic story.

[6]Unfortunately, this is also true for expense items such as rent and utilities, car prices, and tuition payments.

Suppose we want to calculate the present value of a stream of cash flows growing forever ($n = \infty$) at rate g. Given an opportunity cost of r, the present value of the **growing perpetuity** is given by the following equation, which is sometimes called the **Gordon growth model:**[7]

$$PV = \frac{CF_1}{r - g} \quad (r > g) \qquad \text{(Eq. 3.11)}$$

Note that the numerator in Equation 3.11 is CF_1, the first year's cash flow that occurs exactly one year from today. This cash flow is expected to grow at a constant annual rate (g) from now until the end of time. We can determine the cash flow for any specific future year (t) by applying the growth rate (g) as follows:

$$CF_t = CF_1 \times (1 + g)^{t-1}$$

EXAMPLE

Assume that Gil Bates is a philanthropist wishing to endow a medical foundation with sufficient money to fund ongoing research. Gil is particularly impressed with the research proposal submitted by the Smith Cancer Institute (SCI). The Institute requests an endowment sufficient to cover its expenses for medical equipment, which for the next year will total $10 million, and then grow by 3% per year in perpetuity afterwards.

Assume that the Institute can earn an 11% return on Gil's contribution. How much must Gil contribute in order to finance the Institute's medical equipment expenditures in perpetuity? Equation 3.11 tells us that the present value of these expenses equals $125 million, computed as follows:

$$PV = \frac{\$10{,}000{,}000}{0.11 - 0.03} = \frac{\$10{,}000{,}000}{0.08} = \$125{,}000{,}000$$

Gil would have to make an investment of $90,909,091 ($10,000,000 ÷ 0.11, using Equation 3.10) to fund a nongrowing perpetuity of $10 million per year. The remaining $34.1 million supports the 3% annual growth in the payout to SCI.

Smart Concepts
See the concept explained step-by-step at
SMARTFINANCE

Concept Review Questions

7. How would you calculate the present value of a mixed stream of cash flows, given the cash flows and an applicable required return?
8. Given the present value of an ordinary annuity and the applicable required return, how can this value be easily converted into the present value of an otherwise identical annuity due? What is the fundamental difference between the cash flow streams of these two annuities?
9. What is a perpetuity, and how can you conveniently calculate its present value? How do you find the present value of a growing perpetuity?

3.5 SPECIAL APPLICATIONS OF TIME VALUE

Financial managers frequently apply time value of money techniques to solve other types of problems. In such cases the analyst already knows the future or present values, and he solves the equations presented earlier for the unknown variable. Examples of unknown

---

[7]For this formula to work, the discount rate must be greater than the growth rate. If cash flows were to grow at a rate equal to or greater than the discount rate, then the present value of the stream would be infinite.

variables in these instances are the cash flow (CF or PMT), interest or discount rate (r), or number of time periods (n).

Here we consider six of the more common time value applications and refinements: (1) compounding more frequently than annually; (2) stated versus effective annual interest rates; (3) calculating deposits needed to accumulate a future sum; (4) loan amortization; (5) implied interest or growth rates; and (6) number of compounding periods.

Compounding More Frequently Than Annually

In many applications, interest compounds more frequently than once a year. Financial institutions compound interest semiannually, quarterly, monthly, weekly, daily, or even continuously. This section explores how the present and future value techniques change if interest compounds more than once a year.

Semiannual Compounding   The **semiannual compounding** of interest involves two compounding periods within the year. Instead of the stated interest rate being paid once per year, one-half of the rate is paid twice a year.

To demonstrate, consider an opportunity to deposit $100 in a savings account paying 8% interest with semiannual compounding. After the first six months, your account grows by 4%, to $104. Six months later, the account again grows by 4%, to $108.16. Notice that after one year, the total increase in the account value is $8.16, or 8.16% ($8.16 ÷ $100). This return slightly exceeds the stated rate of 8% because semiannual compounding allows you to earn *interest on interest* during the year. Table 3.1 shows the growth of the account value every six months for the first two years. At the end of two years, the account value reaches $116.99.

Table 3.1	**The Future Value from Investing $100 at 8% Interest Compounded *Semiannually* over Two Years**		
PERIOD (MONTHS)	**BEGINNING PRINCIPAL (1)**	**FUTURE VALUE FACTOR (2)**	**FUTURE VALUE AT END OF PERIOD [(1) × (2)] (3)**
6	$100.00	1.04	$104.00
12	104.00	1.04	108.16
18	108.16	1.04	112.49
24	112.49	1.04	116.99

Quarterly Compounding   As the name implies, **quarterly compounding** describes a situation in which interest compounds four times per year. An investment with quarterly compounding pays one-fourth of the stated interest rate every three months.

For example, assume that after further investigation you find an institution that will pay 8% interest compounded quarterly. After three months, your $100 deposit grows by 2%, to $102. Three months later the balance again increases 2%, to $104.04. By the end of the year, the balance reaches $108.24. Table 3.2 tracks the growth in the account every three months for two years. At the end of two years, the account is worth $117.16. Notice that with quarterly compounding your account grows to a greater amount ($117.16) than it does with semiannual compounding ($116.99).

Table 3.2 The Future Value from Investing $100 at 8% Interest Compounded Quarterly over Two Years

PERIOD (MONTHS)	BEGINNING PRINCIPAL (1)	FUTURE VALUE FACTOR (2)	FUTURE VALUE AT END OF PERIOD [(1) × (2)] (3)
3	$100.00	1.02	$102.00
6	102.00	1.02	104.04
9	104.04	1.02	106.12
12	106.12	1.02	108.24
15	108.24	1.02	110.40
18	110.40	1.02	112.61
21	112.61	1.02	114.86
24	114.86	1.02	117.16

As you should expect by now, *the more frequently interest compounds, the greater the amount of money that accumulates.*

A General Equation   We can generalize the preceding examples in a simple equation. Suppose that you invest a lump sum, denoted by PV, at *r* percent per year for *n* years. If *m* equals the number of times per year that interest compounds, then the future value grows as shown in the following equation:

$$FV = PV \times \left(1 + \frac{r}{m}\right)^{m \times n} \qquad \text{(Eq. 3.12)}$$

Notice that if *m* = 1 then this equation reduces to Equation 3.1. The next several examples verify that Equation 3.12 yields the same ending account values after two years as shown in Tables 3.1 and 3.2.

EXAMPLE

We have calculated the amount that you would have at the end of two years if you deposited $100 at 8% interest compounded semiannually and quarterly. For semiannual compounding, *m* = 2 in Equation 3.12; for quarterly compounding, *m* = 4. Substituting the appropriate values for semiannual and quarterly compounding into Equation 3.12 yields the following results.

For semiannual compounding:

$$FV = \$100 \times \left(1 + \frac{0.08}{2}\right)^{2 \times 2} = \$100 \times (1 + 0.04)^4 = \$116.99$$

For quarterly compounding:

$$FV = \$100 \times \left(1 + \frac{0.08}{4}\right)^{4 \times 2} = \$100 \times (1 + 0.02)^8 = \$117.16$$

Continuous Compounding   As we switch from annual to semiannual to quarterly compounding, the interval during which interest compounds gets shorter and the number of compounding periods per year gets larger. In principle, there is almost no limit to this process—interest could be compounded daily, hourly, or second by second. **Continuous compounding**, the most extreme case, occurs when interest compounds literally at every moment. In this case, m would approach infinity in Equation 3.12, which converges to the following expression:

$$\text{FV(continuous compounding)} = \text{PV} \times e^{r \times n} \qquad \textbf{(Eq. 3.13)}$$

The number e is an irrational number that is useful in mathematical applications involving quantities that grow continuously over time; its value is approximately 2.7183.[8] As before, increasing the frequency of compounding—in this case, by compounding every single instant—increases the future value of an investment.

EXAMPLE

To find the value at the end of two years of your $100 deposit in an account paying 8% annual interest compounded continuously, we substitute PV = $100, $r = 0.08$, and $n = 2$ into Equation 3.13:

$$\text{FV(continuous compounding)} = \$100 \times e^{0.08 \times 2} = \$100 \times 2.7183^{0.16}$$
$$= \$100 \times 1.1735 = \$117.35$$

The future value with continuous compounding is equal to $117.35. As expected, continuous compounding leads to an amount that is greater than the future value of interest compounded semiannually ($116.99) or quarterly ($117.16).[9]

Stated versus Effective Annual Interest Rates

Consumers and businesses must make objective comparisons of loan costs or investment returns over different compounding periods. To put interest rates on a common basis for comparison, we distinguish between *stated* and *effective annual interest rates*. The **stated annual rate** is the contractual annual rate charged by a lender or promised by a borrower. The **effective annual rate (EAR)**, or the *true annual return*, is the annual rate of interest *actually* paid or earned. Why the difference? The effective annual rate reflects the impact of compounding frequency; the stated annual rate does not. We can best illustrate the differences between stated and effective rates with numerical examples.

Using the notation introduced previously, we can calculate the *effective annual rate* by substituting values for the stated annual rate (r) and the compounding frequency (m) into Equation 3.14:

$$\text{EAR} = \left(1 + \frac{r}{m}\right)^m - 1 \qquad \textbf{(Eq. 3.14)}$$

We demonstrate the application of this equation in the following Example.

---

[8]In one of the more esoteric uses of the Internet, the first 5 million digits of the number e appear at the URL http://antwrp.gsfc.nasa.gov/htmltest/gifcity/e.5mil. Only the first million will be covered on the exam.

[9]The Excel function for continuous compounding is "=exp(argument)". For example, suppose you want to calculate the future value of $100 compounded continuously for five years at 8%. To find this value in Excel, first calculate the value of $e^{(0.08 \times 5)}$ using "=exp(.08*5)" and then multiply the result by $100.

EXAMPLE

You want to take out a loan to purchase equipment for a small business that you are starting. A community bank offers you a loan with an 8% stated annual rate. You are so excited at actually getting the loan that you forget to ask the bank officer about the compounding period. Before you call the bank to ask, you do some calculations on your own. You wish to find the effective annual rate associated with an 8% stated annual rate ($r = 0.08$) when interest is compounded annually ($m = 1$); semiannually ($m = 2$); and quarterly ($m = 4$). Substituting these values into Equation 3.14 produces the following results.

For annual compounding:

$$\text{EAR} = \left(1 + \frac{0.08}{1}\right)^1 - 1 = (1 + 0.08)^1 - 1$$
$$= 1.08 - 1 = 0.08 = 8.0\%$$

For semiannual compounding:

$$\text{EAR} = \left(1 + \frac{0.08}{2}\right)^2 - 1 = (1 + 0.04)^2 - 1$$
$$= 1.0816 - 1 = 0.0816 = 8.16\%$$

For quarterly compounding:

$$\text{EAR} = \left(1 + \frac{0.08}{4}\right)^4 - 1 = (1 + 0.02)^4 - 1$$
$$= 1.0824 - 1 = 0.0824 = 8.24\%$$

The results mean that 8% compounded semiannually is equivalent to 8.16% compounded annually. Analogously, 8% compounded quarterly is equivalent to 8.24% compounded annually. These values demonstrate two important points: (1) the stated and effective rates are equivalent for annual compounding; and (2) the effective annual rate increases with increasing compounding frequency. You are now better prepared with information about the interest rate before you call the bank.

Not surprisingly, the maximum effective annual rate for a given stated annual rate occurs when interest compounds continuously. The effective annual rate for this extreme case can be found by using the following equation:

$$\text{EAR(continuous compounding)} = e^r - 1 \qquad \textbf{(Eq. 3.14a)}$$

For the 8% stated annual rate ($r = 0.08$), substituting into Equation 3.14a results in an effective annual rate of 8.33%, as follows:

$$\text{EAR} = e^{0.08} - 1 = 1.0833 - 1 = .0833 = 8.33\%$$

At the consumer level in the United States, "truth-in-lending laws" require disclosure on credit cards and loans of the **annual percentage rate (APR)**. The APR is the *stated annual rate* charged on the credit account or loan. It is calculated as the periodic rate (the interest rate per period) multiplied by the number of periods in one year. For example, a bank credit card that charges 1.5% per month would have an APR of 18% (1.5% per month × 12 months per year). In this example, is the 18% APR the actual cost of the credit card? Not necessarily—which is why you must read the fine print on credit card agreements. To find the actual cost of this credit card account, you need to calculate the **annual percentage yield (APY)**. The APY is the same as the *effective annual rate*, which (as discussed earlier) reflects the impact of compounding frequency. For this credit card example, 1.5% per month interest has an APY of $(1.015)^{12} - 1 = 0.1956$, or 19.56%. This means that paying interest at 1.5% monthly is the same as paying 19.56%, if interest were charged annually. If the stated rate is 1.75% per month, as is the case with many U.S. credit card accounts, then the APY is a whopping 23.14%. If you are carrying a positive credit card balance at this interest rate, you will want to pay it off as soon as possible!

Calculating Deposits Needed to Accumulate a Future Sum

Suppose that a firm or a person wishes to determine the annual deposit needed to accumulate a certain amount of money at some point in the future. For example, assume that you want to buy a house five years from now and estimate that an initial down payment of $20,000 will be required. You wish to make equal end-of-year deposits into an account paying annual interest of 6%, so you must determine what size annuity will result in a lump sum of $20,000 at the end of year 5. We can derive the solution by using the equation for the future value of an ordinary annuity.

Previously we applied Equation 3.4 to find the future value (FV) of an n-year ordinary annuity. Solving that equation for PMT (which in this case is the required annual deposit) yields

$$PMT = \frac{FV}{\left[\frac{(1+r)^n - 1}{r}\right]}$$

(Eq. 3.15)

Once this is done, we need only substitute the known values of FV, r, and n into the right-hand side of the equation to find the annual deposit required.

Calculator

Input	Function
20000	FV
5	N
6	I
	CPT
	PMT
Solution	3547.93

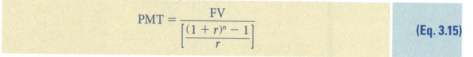

EXAMPLE

As a demonstration of this formula, you would need to make equal annual end-of-year deposits of $3,547.93 each year for five years in order to accumulate $20,000 (the FV) at the end of five years ($n = 5$), given an interest rate of 6% ($r = 0.06$):

$$PMT = \frac{\$20,000}{\left[\frac{(1.06)^5 - 1}{0.06}\right]} = \$3,547.93$$

Loan Amortization

Loan amortization refers to a borrower making equal periodic payments over time to fully repay a loan. For instance, with a conventional 30-year home mortgage, the borrower makes the same payment each month for 30 years until the mortgage is completely repaid. To *amortize* a loan (i.e., to calculate the periodic payment that pays off the loan), you must know the total amount of the loan (the amount borrowed), the term of the loan, the frequency of payments, and the interest rate.

In terms of the time value of money, the loan amortization process involves finding a level stream of payments (over the term of the loan) with a present value (calculated at the loan interest rate) equal to the amount borrowed. Lenders use a **loan amortization schedule** to determine these payments and the allocation of each payment to interest and principal.

For example, suppose you borrow $25,000 at 8% annual interest for five years to purchase a new car. To demonstrate the basic approach, we first amortize this loan assuming that you make payments at the end of years 1 through 5. We then modify the annual formula to compute the more typical monthly auto loan payments. To find the size of the annual payments, the lender determines the amount of a five-year annuity discounted at 8%

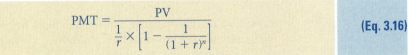

that has a present value of $25,000. This process is actually the inverse of finding the present value of an annuity.

Earlier, we found the present value (PV) of an n-year ordinary annuity using Equation 3.7. Solving that equation for PMT, the annual loan payment, yields

$$PMT = \frac{PV}{\frac{1}{r} \times \left[1 - \frac{1}{(1+r)^n}\right]}$$

(Eq. 3.16)

Calculator

Input	Function
25000	PV
5	N
8	I
	CPT
	PMT
Solution	6261.41

EXAMPLE

To find the annual payment required on the five-year, $25,000 loan with an 8% annual rate, we have only to substitute the known values of PV = $25,000, $r = 0.08$, and $n = 5$ into the right-hand side of the equation:

$$PMT = \frac{\$25,000}{\frac{1}{0.08} \times \left[1 - \frac{1}{(1.08)^5}\right]} = \$6,261.41$$

Thus, you will need five annual payments of $6,261.41 to fully pay off this $25,000 loan.

Again, we can also calculate the annual cash flow (PMT) using either a financial calculator or spreadsheet.

Each loan payment consists partly of interest and partly of the loan principal. Columns 3 and 4 of the loan amortization schedule in Table 3.3 show the allocation of each loan payment of $6,261.41 to interest and principal. Observe that the portion of each payment representing interest (column 3) declines over the repayment period while the portion going to principal (column 4) increases. This pattern is typical of amortized loans. With level payments, the interest component declines and a larger portion of each subsequent payment is left to repay principal.

Table 3.3   Loan Amortization Schedule for $25,000 Principal, 8% Interest Rate, Five-Year Repayment Period

END OF YEAR	LOAN PAYMENT (1)	BEGINNING-OF-YEAR PRINCIPAL (2)	PAYMENTS		END-OF-YEAR PRINCIPAL [(2) − (4)] (5)
			INTEREST [0.08 × (2)] (3)	PRINCIPAL [(1) − (3)] (4)	
1	$6,261.41	$25,000.00	$2,000.00	$4,261.41	$20,738.59
2	6,261.41	20,738.59	1,659.09	4,602.32	16,136.27
3	6,261.41	16,136.27	1,290.90	4,970.51	11,165.76
4	6,261.41	11,165.76	893.26	5,368.15	5,797.61
5	6,261.41	5,797.61	463.81	5,797.60	0.01[a]

[a]This value should be zero, but there is an insignificant difference (due to rounding) of one cent.

Computing amortized loan payments is the present value formulation that people use most frequently in their personal lives to calculate auto loan and home mortgage payments. Because lenders typically require monthly (rather than annual) payments on consumer loans, we now demonstrate amortization calculations using monthly payments. First, Equation 3.16a is simply a modified version of Equation 3.16:

$$PMT = \frac{r}{(1+r)^n - 1} \times (1+r)^n \times PV \qquad \text{(Eq. 3.16a)}$$

Second, we can generalize this formula to more frequent compounding periods by dividing the interest rate by m and then multiplying the number of compounding periods by m. This changes the equation as follows:

$$PMT = \frac{\frac{r}{m}}{\left(1+\frac{r}{m}\right)^{m \times n} - 1} \times \left(1 + \frac{r}{m}\right)^{m \times n} \times PV \qquad \text{(Eq. 3.16b)}$$

EXAMPLE

We can use Equation 3.16b to calculate what your *monthly* car payment will be if you borrow $25,000 for five years at 8% annual interest. Once again, PV will be the $25,000 amount borrowed but now the periodic interest rate ($r \div m$) will be 0.00667, or 0.667% per month (0.08 per year $\div$ 12 months per year). There will be $m \times n = 60$ compounding periods (12 months/year $\times$ 5 years = 60 months). Substituting these values into Equation 3.16b yields a monthly auto loan payment of $506.96:

$$PMT = \frac{\frac{0.08}{12}}{\left(1+\frac{0.08}{12}\right)^{12 \times 5} - 1} \times \left(1 + \frac{0.08}{12}\right)^{12 \times 5} \times \$25,000$$

$$= \frac{0.00667}{(1.00667)^{60} - 1} \times (1.00667)^{60} \times \$25,000$$

$$= \$506.96$$

To test your command of the monthly payment formula, compute the monthly mortgage payment for a home purchased using a 30-year, $100,000 loan with a fixed 7.5% annual interest rate. Note that there will be 360 compounding periods (30 years $\times$ 12 months/year).[10]

Implied Interest or Growth Rates

Analysts often calculate the compound annual interest or *growth rate* (annual rate of change in value) of a series of cash flows. Once the cash flow streams are known, the calculations required for finding interest rates and growth rates are the same. We examine each of three possible cash flow patterns: lump sums, annuities, and mixed streams.

Lump Sums In the simplest situation, you want to find the interest or growth rate of a single cash flow over time. Assume that you invested $1,000 in a stock mutual fund in December 2005 and that now, in December 2010, this investment is worth $2,150. What was your compound annual rate of return over the five-year period?

As it happens, this is easy to determine because we are unconcerned about the investment's value during any of the intervening years. We simply want to know what compound annual rate of return (r) converted a $1,000 investment (PV) into a future amount (FV)

---

[10]To find the solution, just enter the formula "=pmt(.00625,360,100000)" in Excel. The first argument in this function is the monthly interest rate, 7.5% divided by 12.

worth $2,150 in five years ($n$). Note that the number of years of growth (or interest) is the difference between the latest and earliest numeric year. In this case, $n = 2010 - 2005 = 5$ years. Note that there are only five years of growth: the earliest year (2005) serves as the base year (i.e., time 0), which is followed by five years of change (2005 to 2006, 2006 to 2007, 2007 to 2008, 2008 to 2009, and 2009 to 2010).

Finding r involves manipulating Equation 3.1 so that we have the value to be determined—in this case, $(1 + r)^n$—on the left-hand side of the equation and, on the right-hand side, the two known values (FV and PV):

$$(1 + r)^n = \frac{FV}{PV} \qquad \text{(Eq. 3.17)}$$

By substituting the known values, we obtain the following:

$$(1 + r)^5 = \frac{\$2,150}{\$1,000} = 2.150$$

This says that 1 plus the rate of return $(1 + r)$, compounded for five years ($n = 5$), equals 2.150. Our final step is to calculate the fifth root of 2.150. We can do this simply by raising 2.150 to the one-fifth power using the y^x key on a financial calculator, and then subtracting 1:

$$r = (2.150)^{0.20} - 1 = 1.1654 - 1 = 0.1654 = 16.54\% \text{ per year}$$

Annuities Sometimes people need to find the interest rate associated with an annuity, such as the equal annual end-of-year payments on a loan. To demonstrate, assume that your friend John Jacobs can borrow $2,000 to be repaid in equal annual end-of-year amounts of $514.18 for the next five years. He wants to find the interest rate on the loan and asks for your assistance.

You realize that John is really asking an annuity valuation question, so you use a variant of the present value of an annuity formula shown in Equation 3.7:

$$PV = PMT \times \left\{ \frac{1}{r} \times \left[1 - \frac{1}{(1 + r)^n} \right] \right\}$$

You wish to determine the interest rate (r) that will equate the present value of a five-year ($n = 5$) annuity (PV = $2,000) to a stream of five equal annual payments (PMT = $514.18 per year). Because you know PV and PMT, you can rearrange Equation 3.7, putting the unknown value on the left-hand side and the known values on the right:

$$\left\{ \frac{1}{r} \times \left[1 - \frac{1}{(1 + r)^5} \right] \right\} = \frac{PV}{PMT} = \frac{\$2,000}{\$514.18} = 3.8897$$

The term on the left-hand side is extremely difficult to solve directly for r, so the best option is to use a financial calculator or Excel to find the solution, which is 9.00%.[11]

Mixed Streams As demonstrated in the previous discussion, finding the unknown interest or growth rate for a lump sum or an annuity is relatively simple. However, finding the unknown interest or growth rate for *a mixed stream* is difficult when you are using only formulas. It can be accomplished by an iterative trial-and-error approach that eventually yields the interest rate that would cause the present value of the stream's inflows to just equal the present value of its outflows. This calculation is often referred to as finding the *yield to maturity* or *internal rate of return* (IRR).

---

[11]If you type "=rate(5,−514.18,2000,0,0,0)" then Excel will report that the interest rate on this loan is 9%.

A much simpler way to make this calculation is to use a financial calculator or spreadsheet that has the IRR function built into it. With such an approach, an analyst can input all the cash flows—both outflows (as negative numbers) and inflows—and then use the IRR function to calculate the unknown interest rate. This approach is discussed and demonstrated in later chapters on bonds and capital budgeting.

Number of Compounding Periods

Occasionally, for either a lump sum or an annuity, the financial analyst wants to calculate the unknown number of time periods necessary to achieve a given cash flow goal. We consider this calculation here for both lump sums and annuities.

Lump Sums If we know the present (PV) and future (FV) amounts along with the interest rate (*r*), then we can calculate the number of periods (*n*) necessary for a present amount to grow to equal the future amount.

Suppose, for example, that you plan to deposit $1,000 in an investment that is expected to earn an 8% annual rate of interest, and you want to know how long it will take to triple your money (to accumulate $3,000). Stated differently, at an 8% annual interest rate, how many years (*n*) will it take for $1,000 (PV) to grow to $3,000 (FV)? We can express this problem simply by rearranging the basic future value formula (Equation 3.1) to express the unknown value, *n*, on the left-hand side and then plugging in the known values for FV, PV, and *r*:

$$FV = PV \times (1 + r)^n$$

$$(1 + 0.08)^n = \frac{FV}{PV} = \frac{\$3,000}{\$1,000} = 3.000$$

$$(1.08)^n = 3.000$$

Now what? How do we find the exponent value (*n*) that will turn 1.08 into 3.000? We do so by first taking natural logarithms of both sides of this formula and then expressing the unknown number of years (*n*) as a ratio of two log values, as follows:

$$\ln(1.08)^n = \ln(3.000)$$

$$n = \frac{\ln(3.000)}{\ln(1.08)} = \frac{1.0986}{0.0770} = 14.275$$

The result is 14.275 years. This means that, given an 8% annual rate of interest, it will take about 14.3 years for your $1,000 deposit to triple in value to $3,000. We could also use a financial calculator or spreadsheet to directly solve for the unknown number of periods for a lump sum.[12]

Annuities Occasionally we want to determine the unknown life of an annuity that is intended to achieve a specified objective, such as to repay a loan of a given amount with a stated interest rate and equal annual end-of-year payments.

To demonstrate, assume that you can borrow $20,000 at a 12% annual interest rate with annual end-of-year payments of $3,000. You want to know how long it will take to fully repay the loan's interest and principal. In other words, how many years (*n*) will it take to repay a $20,000 (PV), 12% (*r*), loan if the payments of $3,000 (PMT) are made at the end of each year?

---

[12]To solve this problem in Excel, type "=nper(0.08,0,–1000,3000,0)".

You have probably deduced already that this is similar to the problem we addressed earlier of determining the unknown interest rate in an annuity. The difference is that now we know that $r = 0.12$ and we want to determine the number of years (n). To solve for n, substitute the values you know and rearrange Equation 3.7 until you have an expression that looks like this:

$$1-\left(\frac{0.12(\$20,000)}{\$3,000}\right)=(1+0.12)^n$$

$$0.2=1.12^n$$

Next, you can use logarithms to solve for n much as we did in the previous problem:

$$\ln(0.2)=-n\times[\ln(1.12)]$$

$$\ln(0.2)/\ln(1.12)=\frac{-1.6094}{0.1133}=-n$$

$$n=14.2 \text{ years}$$

Calculator

Input	Function
20000	PV
12	I
-3000	PMT
	CPT
	N

Solution: 14.20

This means that you will have to repay $3,000 at the end of each year for 14 years and about $600 (0.20 × $3,000) at the end of 14.2 years in order to fully repay the $20,000 loan at 12%.

Concept Review Questions

10. What effect does increasing compounding frequency have on (a) the future value of a given deposit and (b) its effective annual rate (EAR)?
11. Under what condition would the stated annual rate equal the effective annual rate for a given deposit? How do these rates relate to the annual percentage rate (APR) and annual percentage yield (APY)?
12. How would you determine the size of the annual end-of-year deposits needed to accumulate a given future sum at the end of a specified future period? What impact does the magnitude of the interest rate have on the size of the deposits needed?
13. What relationship exists between the calculation of the present value of an annuity and amortization of a loan? How can you find the amount of interest paid each year under an amortized loan?
14. How can you find the interest or growth rate for (a) a lump-sum amount, (b) an annuity, and (c) a mixed stream?
15. How can you find the number of time periods needed to repay (a) a single-payment loan and (b) an installment loan requiring equal annual end-of-year payments?

SUMMARY

- In order to compare decision alternatives, financial managers use future value and present value techniques to equate cash flows occurring at different times. Managers rely primarily on present value techniques and commonly use financial calculators or spreadsheet programs to streamline their computations.
- The future value in a lump-sum calculation applies compound interest to the present value (the initial investment) over the period of concern. The higher the interest rate and the longer the period of time, the higher the cash flow's future value.
- The present value of a lump sum is the amount of money today that is equivalent to the given future amount, considering the rate of return that can be earned. The present value calculation discounts the future value at the given interest rate. The higher the interest rate and the further in the future the cash flow occurs, the lower its present value.
- The future value of any cash flow stream—mixed stream, ordinary annuity, or annuity due—is the sum of the future values of the individual cash flows. Future values of annuities are easy to calculate because they have the same cash flow each period; future values of mixed streams are more difficult to establish. The future value of an ordinary annuity (end-of-period cash flows) can be converted into the future value of an

annuity due (beginning-of-period cash flows) by multiplying the ordinary value by 1 plus the interest rate.

- The present value of a cash flow stream is the sum of the present values of the individual cash flows. Present values of annuities, which have the same cash flow each period, can be calculated easily using the annuity formula. The present value of an ordinary annuity can be converted to the present value of an annuity due by multiplying the ordinary value by 1 plus the interest rate. The present value of an ordinary perpetuity—an infinite-lived annuity—is found by dividing the amount of the annuity by the interest rate.

- Some special applications of time value include compounding interest more frequently than annually, stated and effective annual rates of interest, deposits needed to accumulate a future sum, loan amortization, implied interest or growth rates, and number of compounding periods. The more frequently interest is compounded at a stated annual rate, the larger the future amount that will be accumulated and the higher the effective annual rate.

- The annual deposit needed to accumulate a given future sum is found by manipulating the future value of an annuity equation. Loan amortization involves rearranging the present value of an annuity equation to determine the equal periodic payments necessary to fully repay loan principal and interest over a given time at a given interest rate. An amortization schedule allocates each payment to principal and interest.

- Implied interest or compound annual growth rates can be found using the basic future value equations for lump sums and annuities; mixed streams, however, require an iterative trial-and-error approach. Given present and future cash flows and the applicable interest rate, the unknown number of periods can be found using the basic equations for future values of lump sums and annuities. Using a financial calculator or spreadsheet greatly simplifies these calculations.

KEY TERMS

annual percentage rate (APR)	future value	principal
annual percentage yield (APY)	Gordon growth model	quarterly compounding
annuity	growing perpetuity	semiannual compounding
annuity due	loan amortization	simple interest
compound interest	loan amortization schedule	stated annual rate
continuous compounding	mixed stream	time line
discounting	ordinary annuity	time value of money
effective annual rate (EAR)	perpetuity	
financial intermediaries	present value	

QUESTIONS

3-1. The price of a security is the sum of all of the discounted future cash flows associated with the security. Assuming that future cash flows do not change and that the price of the security increases, is the discount rate for the security increasing, decreasing, or stable?

3-2. A particular business deal allows you the choice of receiving $1,000 today or receiving $2,000 10 years from today. How would your choice change based on your ability to invest money at a low versus a high rate of interest?

3-3. If a firm's required return were 0%, would the time value of money matter? As these returns rise above 0%, what impact would the increasing return have on future value? On present value?

3-4. If a series of cash flows are valued using the future value of an annuity, will the valuation of the cash flows increase or decrease as the interest rate increases? What is your answer if the cash flows are valued using the present value of an annuity?

3-5. What happens to the present value of a cash flow stream when the discount rate increases? Place this in the context of an investment. If the required return on an investment goes up but the expected cash flows do not change, would you be willing to pay the same price for the investment or would you pay more or less for this investment than before interest rates changed?

3-6. Examine the formula for the present value of an annuity. What happens to the present value as the number of periods increases? What distinguishes an annuity from a perpetuity? Why is there no future value of a perpetuity?

3-7. Does the EAR increase or decrease as the number of compounding periods per year increases?

3-8. With regard to repaying a loan, an increase in which of the following variables—interest rate, number of periods, loan amount—will increase the periodic loan payment?

3-9. If you assume market interest rates are expected to increase over the term of the loan, would you prefer a loan with a fixed interest rate for the life of the loan or rather a loan with a variable rate that changes in response to market interest rates? (Assume that both loans start with the same interest rate.) Would your answer change if market interest rates are expected to decrease over the term of the loan?

3-10. Suppose you need to know the interest rate that sets a series of periodic future cash flows equal to a given present amount X. Is there a direct solution for finding the interest rate?

3-11. A person plans to retire today and expects to begin living off $50,000 received annually beginning one year from now and continuing until death. The person currently has $700,000 in savings that earns 10% interest annually. How long will the savings be able to accommodate this retirement plan?

Problems

Future Value of a Lump Sum Received Today

3-1. You have $1,500 to invest today at 7% interest compounded annually.
   a. How much will you have accumulated in the account at the end of the following number of years?
      1. Three years
      2. Six years
      3. Nine years
   b. Use your findings in part (a) to calculate the amount of interest earned in
      1. The first three years (years 1 through 3)
      2. The second three years (years 4 through 6)
      3. The third three years (years 7 through 9)
   c. Compare and contrast your findings in part (b). Explain why the amount of interest earned increases in each succeeding three-year period.

Present Value of a Lump Sum

Smart Solutions

See the problem and solution explained step-by-step at **SMARTFinance**

3-2. An Indiana state savings bond can be converted to $100 at maturity six years from purchase. If the state bonds are to be competitive with U.S. savings bonds, which pay 8% annual interest, at what price must the state sell its bonds?

3-3. You just won a lottery that promises to pay you $1 million exactly 10 years from today. Because the state in which you live guarantees the $1 million payment, opportunities exist to sell the claim today for an immediate lump-sum cash payment.
   a. What is the least you will sell your claim for if you could earn the following rates of return?
      1. 6%
      2. 9%
      3. 12%
   b. Rework part (a) under the assumption that the $1 million payment will be received in 15 rather than 10 years.
   c. Based on your findings in parts (a) and (b), discuss the effect of the rate of return and the time until receipt of payment on the present value of a future sum.

Future Value of Cash Flow Streams

3-4. Dixon Shuttleworth is considering three investment options. The first investment offers a 5% return for the first five years, a 10% return for the next five years, and a 20% return thereafter. The second investment offers 10% for the first 10 years and 15% thereafter. The third investment offers a constant 12% rate of return. Determine which of these investments is the best for Dixon if he plans to invest a lump sum today and keep his money invested for the following number of years.

    a. 15 years

    b. 20 years

    c. 30 years

3-5. Lauren Blanding's employer offers workers a two-month paid sabbatical every seven years. Lauren, who just started working for the firm, plans to spend her sabbatical touring Europe at an estimated cost of $25,000. To finance her trip, Lauren plans to make six annual deposits of $2,500 each, starting at the end of her first year and continuing through the end of her sixth year, into an investment account earning 8% interest.

    a. Will Lauren's account balance at the end of seven years be enough to pay for her trip?

    b. Suppose Lauren increases her annual contribution to $3,150. How large will her account balance be at the end of seven years?

3-6. Robert Williams is considering an offer to sell his medical practice, allowing him to retire five years early. He has been offered $500,000 for his practice and can invest this amount in an account earning 10% per year, compounded annually. The practice is expected to generate the following cash flows. Should Robert accept this offer and retire now? (*Hint:* Assume that the practice has a sale value of $0 at the end of five years.)

End of Year	Cash Flow
1	$150,000
2	150,000
3	125,000
4	125,000
5	100,000

    a. Based soleley on your calculations, should Robert accept this offer and retire now?

    b. If Robert retires early then he will no longer have to work. What impact (if any) does this fact have on your answer to part (a)? Explain.

3-7. Gina Coulson has just contracted to sell a small parcel of land that she inherited a few years ago. The buyer is willing to pay either $24,000 now (year 0) or the series of payments shown in the following table. Gina plans to invest any received payments in an account that earns 7% annual interest. Gina wants to buy a house five years from now, so she wants to select the option that has the highest future value at that time.

Mixed Stream	
Year	Payment
1	$ 2,000
2	4,000
3	6,000
4	8,000
5	10,000

    a. What is the future value of the lump sum five years from now?

    b. What is the future value of the mixed stream five years from now?

c. Based on your findings in parts (a) and (b), which alternative should Gina take?

d. If Gina could earn 10% rather than 7% on the funds, would your recommendation in part (c) change? Explain.

3-8. For the following questions, assume an annual annuity of $1,000 and a required return of 12%.

Smart Solutions

See the problem and solution explained step-by-step at **SMARTFinance**

a. What is the future value of an *ordinary annuity* for 10 years?

b. If you earned an additional year's worth of interest on this annuity, what would be the future value?

c. What is the future value of a 10-year *annuity due*?

d. What is the relationship between your answers in parts (b) and (c)? Explain.

3-9. Starratt Alexander would like to invest specified amounts in each of four investment opportunities described below. For each opportunity, determine the amount of money Starratt will have at the end of the given investment horizon.

Investment A: Invest a lump sum of $2,750 today in an account that pays 6% annual interest and leave the funds on deposit for exactly 15 years.

Investment B: Invest the following amounts at the *beginning* of each of the next five years in a venture that will earn 9% annually and measure the accumulated value at the end of exactly five years.

Beginning of Year	Amount
1	$ 900
2	1,000
3	1,200
4	1,500
5	1,800

Investment C: Invest $1,200 at the *end of each year* for the next 10 years in an account that pays 10% annual interest, and determine the account balance at the end of year 10.

Investment D: Make the same investment as in investment C, but place the $1,200 in the account at the *beginning of each year.*

3-10. Kim Edwards and Chris Phillips are both newly minted 30-year-old MBAs. Kim plans to invest $1,000 per month into her 401(k) beginning next month; Chris intends to invest $2,000 per month, but he does not plan to begin investing until 10 years after Kim begins investing. Both Kim and Chris will retire at age 67, and the 401(k) plan averages a 12% annual return, compounded monthly. Who will have more 401(k) money at retirement?

Present Value of Cash Flow Streams

3-11. Given the mixed streams of cash flows shown in the following table, answer parts (a) and (b).

	Cash Flow Stream	
Year	A	B
1	$ 50,000	$ 10,000
2	40,000	20,000
3	30,000	30,000
4	20,000	40,000
5	10,000	50,000
Totals	$150,000	$150,000

a. Find the present value of each stream, using a 15% discount rate.

b. Compare the present values, and explain why they vary even though both streams pay $150,000 over five years.

3-12. In each of the next five years, you must make a large payment as indicated in the table below. You want to set aside money today, earning 8% interest, which will be sufficient to pay these bills.

Year	Payment
1	$ 5,000
2	4,000
3	6,000
4	10,000
5	3,000

a. How much money do you need today?

b. What effect would an increase in the rate of return have on your answer to part (a)? Explain.

3-13. Ron Nail has just received two offers for his seaside home. The first offer is for $1 million today. The second offer is for an owner-financed sale with a payment schedule as follows:

Year	Payment
0 (today)	$200,000
1	200,000
2	200,000
3	200,000
4	200,000
5	300,000

Assuming no differential tax treatment between the two options and that Ron earns a rate of 8% on his investments, which offer should he take?

3-14. An investment pays $80 per year for 10 years, with the first payment due one year from now. What would you pay to acquire this investment if you can earn 7% on your money?

3-15. Assume that you just won the state lottery. Your prize can be taken either in the form of $40,000 at the end of each of the next 25 years (i.e., $1 million over 25 years) or as a lump sum of $500,000 paid immediately.

a. If you expect to be able to earn 5% annually on your investments over the next 25 years, which alternative should you take? Why?

b. Would your decision in part (a) be altered if you could earn 7% rather than 5% on your investments? Why?

c. At approximately what interest rate would you be indifferent between the two plans?

3-16. For the following questions, assume that the annuity pays $250 per year and that the discount rate is 10%.

a. What is the present value of a 5-year annuity?

b. What is the present value of a 10-year annuity?

c. What is the present value of a 100-year annuity?

d. What is the present value of a $250 perpetuity?

e. Do you detect a relationship between the number of periods of an annuity and its resemblance to a perpetuity?

Smart
Solutions

See the problem and solution explained step-by-step at **SMARTFinance**

3-17. Use the following table of cash flows to answer parts (a)–(c). Assume an 8% discount rate.

End of Year	Cash Flow
1	$10,000
2	10,000
3	10,000
4	12,000
5	12,000
6	12,000
7	12,000
8	15,000
9	15,000
10	15,000

  a. Calculate the present value of the cash flow stream by summing the present value of each individual cash flow.
  b. Now, calculate the present value by summing the present value of the three separate annuities (one current and two deferred).
  c. Which computational method would you prefer for a long series of cash flows with embedded annuities?

3-18. Joan Wallace, corporate finance specialist for Big Blazer Bumpers, has been given the task of funding an account to cover anticipated future warranty costs. Warranty costs are expected to be $5 million per year for three years, with the first costs expected to occur four years from today. How much will Joan have to place into an account today earning 10% per year to cover these expenses?

3-19. Landon Lowman, star quarterback of the university football team, is thinking about forgoing his last two years of eligibility and making himself available for the professional football draft. Scouts estimate that Landon could receive a signing bonus of $1 million today along with a five-year contract for $3 million per year (payable at the end of the year). They further estimate that he could negotiate a contract for $5 million per year for the remaining seven years of his career.

  The scouts believe, however, that Landon will be a much higher draft pick if he improves by playing out his eligibility. If he stays at the university, he is expected to receive a $2 million signing bonus in two years along with a 5-year contract for $5 million per year. After that, the scouts expect Landon to obtain a five-year contract for $6 million per year to take him into retirement.

  Assume that Landon can earn a 10% return over this time. Should Landon stay or go?

3-20 Kate Snead has been offered four investment opportunities, all equally priced at $45,000. Because the opportunities differ in risk, Kate's required returns (i.e., applicable discount rates) are not the same for each opportunity. The cash flows and required returns for each opportunity are summarized below.

Opportunity	Cash Flows		Required Return
A	$7,500 at the end of 5 years		12%
B	**End of Year**	**Amount**	15%
	1	$10,000	
	2	12,000	
	3	18,000	
	4	10,000	
	5	13,000	
	6	9,000	

(continued)

Opportunity	Cash Flows	Required Return
C	$5,000 at the *end* of each year for the next 30 years.	10%
D	$7,000 at the *beginning* of each year for the next 20 years.	18%

    a. Find the present value of each of the four investment opportunities.
    b. Which, if any, opportunities are acceptable?
    c. Which opportunity should Kate take?

3-21. Assume you wish to establish a college scholarship of $2,000 paid at the end of each year for a deserving student at the high school you attended. You would like to make a lump-sum gift to the high school to fund the scholarship into perpetuity. The school's treasurer assures you that they will earn 7.5% annually forever.

    a. How much must you give the high school today to fund the proposed scholarship program?
    b. If you wanted to allow the amount of the scholarship to increase annually after the first award (end of year 1) by 3% per year, how much must you give the school today to fund the scholarship program?
    c. Discuss the differences in your response to parts (a) and (b).

3-22. Matt Sedgwick, ticket manager for the Birmingham Buffalo professional football team, has come up with an idea for generating income. Matt wants to sell lifetime (perpetual) season ticket packages. Each package will guarantee its purchaser 10 season tickets, which cost $200 per ticket per year, for life. What is the minimum selling price that Matt will have to charge for the ticket packages if the required return is 10%?

Special Applications of Time Value

3-23. Assume that you deposit $10,000 today into an account paying 6% annual interest and leave it on deposit for exactly eight years.

    a. How much will be in the account at the end of eight years if interest is compounded as follows?
        1. Annually
        2. Semiannually
        3. Monthly
        4. Continuously
    b. Calculate the effective annual rate (EAR) for (1) through (4) of part (a).
    c. Based on your findings in parts (a) and (b), what is the general relationship between the frequency of compounding and EAR?

3-24. You plan to make a single deposit of $2,000 in an investment account today at a stated interest rate of 8%, which is expected to apply to all future years.

    a. How much will you have in the account at the end of 10 years if interest is compounded as follows?
        1. Annually
        2. Semiannually
        3. Daily (assume a 360-day year)
        4. Continuously
    b. What is the effective annual rate for each compounding period in part (a)?
    c. How much greater will your investment account balance be at the end of 10 years if interest is compounded continuously rather than annually?
    d. How does the compounding frequency affect the future value and effective annual rate for a given deposit? Explain in terms of your findings in parts (a)–(c).

3-25. Jason Spector is comparing interest rates on several different one-year investments.

Stated Rate	Compounding
6.10%	Annual
5.90%	Semiannual
5.85%	Monthly

   a. Which investment offers Jason the highest effective annual rate (EAR)?

   b. Now assume that Jason wishes to invest his money for only six months and that the stated annual compounded rate of 6.10% is not available. Which of the remaining investments should Jason choose?

3-26. Calculate the EAR for the following stated interest rates and determine which proposed rate offers the most attractive return.

   a. 12% compounded monthly

   b. 12.5% compounded quarterly

   c. 13% compounded semiannually

   d. 13.25% compounded annually

3-27. Answer parts (a)–(c) for each of the following cases.

Case	Amount of Initial Deposit ($)	Stated Annual Rate, r (%)	Compounding Frequency, m (times/year)	Deposit Period (years)
A	2,500	6	2	5
B	50,000	12	6	3
C	1,000	5	1	10
D	20,000	16	4	6

   a. Calculate the future value at the end of the specified deposit period.

   b. Determine the effective annual rate.

   c. Compare the stated annual rate (r) to the effective annual rate (EAR). What relationship exists between compounding frequency and the stated and effective annual rates?

3-28. Tara Cutler is newly married and is already preparing for a surprise trip to Europe with her husband on their tenth wedding anniversary. Tara plans to invest $5,000 per year until that anniversary (end of year 10) and plans to make her first $5,000 investment on their first anniversary. If she earns an 8% rate on her investments, how much will she have saved for their trip if the interest is compounded in each of the following ways?

   a. Annually

   b. Quarterly

   c. Monthly

3-29. Melissa Gould wants to invest today in order to assure there are adequate funds for her son's college education. She estimates that her son will need $20,000 at the end of 18 years; $25,000 at the end of 19 years; $30,000 at the end of 20 years; and $40,000 at the end of 21 years. How much will Melissa have to invest in a fund today if the fund earns the following interest rate?

   a. 6% per year with annual compounding

   b. 6% per year with quarterly compounding

   c. 6% per year with monthly compounding

3-30. John Tye has just been hired as the new corporate finance analyst at I-Ell Enterprises and has received his first assignment. John is to take the $25 million in cash received from a recent divestiture and use part of these proceeds to retire an outstanding $10 million bond issue and the remainder to repurchase common stock. However, the bond issue cannot be retired for another two years. If John can place the funds necessary to retire this $10 million debt into an account earning 6% compounded monthly, then how much of the $25 million remains to repurchase stock?

3-31. Find the present value of a 3-year, $20,000 ordinary annuity deposited into an account that pays 12% interest compounded monthly. Calculate the present value of the annuity in the following ways:

   a. As three single cash flows discounted at the stated rate of interest
   b. As three single cash flows discounted at the effective annual rate
   c. As a 3-year annuity discounted at the effective annual rate

3-32. You intend to retire 20 years from today with $800,000 in savings. Assuming you earn 8% annual interest on your investments and intend to make annual payments into your retirement account starting next year, what is the minimum payment you can make to realize your retirement goal?

3-33. To supplement your planned retirement in exactly 42 years, you estimate that you need to accumulate $220,000 by the time you retire. You plan to make equal annual end-of-year deposits into an account paying 8% annual interest.

   a. How large must the annual deposits be at the end of each of the next 42 years in order to create the $220,000 fund by the end of 42 years?
   b. If you can afford to deposit only $600 per year into the account, how much will you have accumulated by the end of the forty-second year?

3-34. Determine the annual deposit required to fund a future liability of $12,000 per year. You will fund this future liability over the next five years, with the first deposit to occur one year from today. The future $12,000 liability will last for four years, with the first payment to occur at the end of seven years from today. If you can earn 8% on this account, how much will you have to deposit at the end of each year over the next five years to fund the future liability?

3-35. Mary Sullivan, capital outlay manager for Waxy Widgets, has been instructed to establish a contingency fund to cover the expenses over the next two years (24 months) associated with repairing defective widgets from a new production process. The Waxy Widgets controller wants to make equal monthly cash deposits into this fund. If Mary faces the following monthly repair costs and has $1 million to start the fund today, what will be her monthly payments into the fund necessary to cover all repair costs? Mary will make her first payment one month from today, and the fund will earn 6%, compounded monthly.

Months	Repair Costs per Month
1–4	$500,000
5–12	$250,000
13–24	$100,000

3-36. Craig and LaDonna Allen are trying to establish a college fund for their son Spencer, who turned 3 today. They plan for Spencer to withdraw $10,000 on his eighteenth birthday and $11,000, $12,000, and $15,000 on his subsequent birthdays. They want to fund these withdrawals with a 10-year annuity, with the first payment to occur one year from today, and expect to earn an average annual return of 8%.

   a. How much will the Allens have to contribute each year to achieve their goal?
   b. Create a schedule showing the cash inflows (including interest) and outflows of this fund. How much will be in the fund on Spencer's sixteenth birthday?

3-37. Joan Messineo borrowed $15,000 at a 14% annual interest rate to be repaid over three years. The loan is amortized into three equal annual end-of-year payments.

    a. Calculate the annual end-of-year loan payment.

    b. Prepare a loan amortization schedule showing the interest and principal breakdown of each of the three loan payments.

    c. Explain why the interest portion of each payment declines with the passage of time.

3-38. You are planning to purchase a building for $40,000 and you have $10,000 to apply as a down payment. You may borrow the remainder under the following terms: a 10-year loan with semiannual repayments and a stated interest rate of 6%. You intend to make $6,000 payments, applying the excess over your required payment to the reduction of the principal balance.

    a. Given these terms, how long (in years) will it take you to fully repay your loan?

    b. What will be your total interest cost?

    c. What would your total interest cost be if you made no prepayments and instead repaid your loan by strictly adhering to its terms?

3-39. Use a spreadsheet to create amortization schedules for the following five scenarios. What happens to the total interest paid under each scenario?

    a. Scenario 1:

        Loan amount—$1 million

        Annual interest rate—5%

        Term—360 months

        Prepayment—$0

    b. Scenario 2: Same as Scenario 1 except annual interest rate is 7%

    c. Scenario 3: Same as Scenario 1 except term is 180 months

    d. Scenario 4: Same as Scenario 1 except prepayment is $250 per month

    e. Scenario 5: Same as Scenario 1 except loan amount is $125,000

3-40. Suppose you make monthly mortgage payments of $2,545 and have 10 years left on the mortgage (next payment due next month). Assuming a 6.6% stated annual interest rate for the mortgage, how much would you need today to pay off the mortgage? Also, how much interest would you owe on the next mortgage payment?

3-41. Find the rates of return required to do the following:

    a. Double an investment in 4 years

    b. Double an investment in 10 years

    c. Triple an investment in 4 years

    d. Triple an investment in 10 years

3-42. You are given the series of cash flows shown in the following table.

	Cash Flows		
Year	A	B	C
1	$500	$1,500	$2,500
2	560	1,550	2,600
3	640	1,610	2,650
4	720	1,680	2,650
5	800	1,760	2,800
6		1,850	2,850
7		1,950	2,900
8			2,060
9			2,170
10			2,280

a. Calculate the compound annual growth rate for each cash flow stream from year 1 through the final year shown.

b. If year-1 values represent initial deposits in a savings account paying annual interest, then what is the annual rate of interest earned on each account?

c. Compare and discuss the growth rate and interest rate found in parts (a) and (b), respectively.

3-43. Which one of the following investments produces the best annual percentage return?

a. Purchase a security for $100.00 and then sell the security for $119.10 three years later.

b. Purchase a security for $50.00 and sell the security for $55.00 after one year.

c. Purchase a security for $200.00 and sell the security for $237.62 after two years.

d. Purchase a security for $150.00 and sell the security for $300.00 after ten years.

3-44. Imagine that you are a professional personal financial planner. One of your clients asks you the following questions. Use the time value of money techniques to develop appropriate responses to each question.

a. "I borrowed $75,000 and am required to repay it in six equal (annual) end-of-year installments of $16,000. What rate of interest am I paying?"

b. "I need to save $37,000 over the next 15 years to fund my three-year-old daughter's college education. If I make equal annual end-of-year deposits into an account that earns 7% annual interest, how large must these deposits be?"

3-45. Log on to MSN Money (http://www.investor.msn.com) and select five stocks to analyze. Use their rates of return over the last five years to determine today's value of $1,000 invested in each stock five years ago. What is the compound annual rate of return for each of the five stocks over the 5-year period?

3-46. The viatical industry offers a rather grim example of present value concepts. A firm in this business, called a viator, purchases the rights to the benefits from a life insurance contract from a terminally ill client. The viator may then sell claims on the insurance payout to other investors. The industry began in the early 1990s as a way to help AIDS patients capture some of the proceeds from their life insurance policies for living expenses.

Suppose a patient has a life expectancy of 18 months and a life insurance policy with a death benefit of $100,000. A viator pays $80,000 for the right to the benefit and then sells that claim to another investor for $80,500.

a. From the point of view of the patient, this contract is like taking out a loan. What is the compound annual interest rate paid on the loan if the patient lives exactly 18 months? What if the patient lives 36 months?

b. From the point of view of the investor, this transaction is like lending money. What is the compound annual interest rate earned on the loan if the patient lives 18 months? What if the patient lives just 12 months?

3-47. Determine the length of time required to double the value of an investment, given the following rates of return.

a. 4%

b. 10%

c. 30%

d. 100%

3-48. You are the pension fund manager for Tanju's Toffees, and the CFO has just asked you to calculate the minimum annual return required on the pension fund in order to make all required payments over the next five years *and* not diminish the current fund balance of $500 million.

a. Determine the rate of return if outflows are expected to exceed inflows by $50 million per year.

b. Determine the rate of return with the following fund cash flows.

End of Year	Inflows	Outflows
1	$55,000,000	$100,000,000
2	60,000,000	110,000,000
3	60,000,000	120,000,000
4	60,000,000	135,000,000
5	64,000,000	145,000,000

c. Consider the cash flows in part (b). What will happen to your asset base if you earn 10%? If you earn 20%?

3-49. Jill Chew wishes to select the best of four retirement annuities. In each case, in exchange for paying a single premium today she will receive equal annual end-of-year cash benefits for a specified number of years. She considers the annuities to be equally risky and is not concerned about their differing lives. Her decision will be based solely on the rate of return that she will earn on each annuity. The key terms of each of the four annuities are shown in the following table.

Annuity	Premium Paid Today	Annual Benefit	Life (years)
A	$30,000	$3,100	20
B	25,000	3,900	10
C	40,000	4,200	15
D	35,000	4,000	12

a. Calculate to the nearest whole percent the rate of return on each of the four annuities Jill is considering.

b. Given Jill's stated decision criterion, which annuity would you recommend?

3-50. Determine which of the following three investments offers you the highest rate of return on your $1,000 investment over the next five years.

Investment 1: $2,000 lump sum to be received in five years.

Investment 2: $300 at the end of each of the next five years.

Investment 3: $250 at the beginning of each of the next five years.

a. Which investment offers the highest return?

b. Which offers the highest return if the payouts are doubled (i.e., to $4,000, $600, and $500)?

c. What causes the big change in the returns on the annuities?

3-51. Consider the following three investments of equal risk. Which offers the greatest rate of return?

Year	A	B	C
		Investment	
0	−$10,000	−$20,000	−$25,000
1	0	$ 9,500	$20,000
2	0	$ 9,500	$30,000
3	$24,600	$ 9,500	−$12,600

3-52. You plan to start saving for your son's college education. He will begin college when he turns 18 years old and will need $4,000 at that time and in each of the following three years. You will make a deposit at the end of this year in an account that pays

6% compounded annually as well as an identical deposit at the end of each year, with the last deposit occurring when he turns 18. If an annual deposit of $1,484 will allow you to reach your goal, how old is your son now?

THOMSON ONE | Business School Edition

Access financial information from the Thomson ONE–Business School Edition website for the following problem(s). Go to http://tobsefin.swlearning.com/. If you have already registered your access serial number and have a username and password, click **Enter**. Otherwise, click **Register** and follow the instructions to create a username and password. Register your access serial number and then click **Enter** on the aforementioned website. When you click Enter, you will be prompted for your username and password (please remember that the password is case sensitive). Enter them in the respective boxes and then click **OK** (or hit **Enter**). From the ensuing page, click **Click Here to Access Thomson ONE–Business School Edition Now!** This opens up a new window that gives you access to the Thomson ONE–Business School Edition database. You can retrieve a company's financial information by entering its ticker symbol [provided for each company in the problem(s)] in the box below "Companies." For further instructions on using the Thomson ONE–Business School Edition database, please refer to "A Guide for Using Thomson ONE–Business School Edition."

3-53. What is the current price per share (previous close) of Amazon (ticker symbol, AMZN)? What is the three-year total return for Amazon? If Amazon were to continue at this same growth rate, what will be the value of a share of Amazon in three years? If you owned 1,000 shares of Amazon, how much would they have been worth three years ago (assuming the same growth rate)?

3-54. What are the annual growth rates in total assets for Caterpillar (ticker symbol, CAT) and Boeing (ticker symbol, BA) over the last four years? What are the annual growth rates in total interest income for both firms? If total assets and total interest income were to continue to grow at the rates you calculated for the next five years, what would total assets and interest income be for both firms?

MINI-CASE: THE TIME VALUE OF MONEY

It is December 31, 2010, and 35-year-old Camille Henley is reviewing her retirement savings and planning for her retirement at age 60. She currently has $55,000 saved (which includes the deposit she just made today) and invests $2,000 per year (at the end of the year) in a retirement account that earns about 10% annually. She has decided that she is comfortable living on $40,000 per year (in today's dollars) and believes she can continue to live on that amount as long as it is adjusted annually for inflation. Inflation is expected to average 2.86% per year for the foreseeable future. After researching information on average life expectancy for females of her background, her plan will assume she lives to age 88. She will withdraw the amount needed for each year during retirement at the beginning of the year. So, on December 31 at age 60, she will make her last deposit of $2,000 and the following day (January 1) she will withdraw her first installment for retirement.

1. If Camille continues on her current plan, will she be able to accomplish it?

2. How would the situation change if Camille were to start placing her $2,000 annual savings into her retirement account on January 1st of each year rather than December 31 of each year? Assume that the investment still pays interest at the end of the year.

3. If Camille resumes making her deposits at the end of the year, how much would she have to save each year to accomplish her objective?

4. Assume that Camille continues with her current plan. What interest rate would she have to earn on her investment to make it work?

5. If Camille wishes to leave a $50,000 perpetuity to her alma mater, starting one year from the year she turns 88, then how much extra money would she need to have on December 31 of the year she turns 88? Assume that the investment will earn 10%.

6. Rework the previous question for the case where Camille wants the university investment to grow by 5% per year.

PART 2

Valuation, Risk, and Return

Above all, finance is about valuation. The tools of finance allow you to value objects ranging from financial assets, such as stocks and bonds, to physical assets, such as new manufacturing facilities. The three chapters in this section introduce the concepts and techniques that are critical to the valuation process.

Chapter 3 introduced the notion that "time is money." In Chapter 4, we apply time value of money (TVM) concepts to estimate the prices of bonds, preferred stock, and common stock. To value these securities, you must first understand their basic characteristics—such as when each instrument pays cash to investors and what rights investors have if the cash flows they are promised do not materialize. Once you know what cash flows to expect from a particular security, estimating the price becomes a relatively straightforward application of the TVM mathematics.

Of course, investors know that the cash flows they expect from an investment can be quite different from the cash flows they actually receive. This is the notion of risk, the subject of Chapters 5 and 6. In Chapter 5, we begin by showing some historical evidence, from the United States and many other countries, that suggests a trade-off exists between risk and return. Assets that require investors to accept more risk must offer investors the expectation of higher returns. We devote much of this chapter to carefully defining the terms *risk* and *return*. A somewhat counterintuitive lesson emerging from this chapter is that how we define risk depends on whether we are trying to measure the risk of a single asset, such as a share of IBM stock, or a whole portfolio of assets, such as the Standard & Poor's (S&P) 500.

Chapter 6 delves deeper into risk and return, and it introduces perhaps the most famous financial model of all time—the capital asset pricing model, or CAPM. The CAPM suggests that the expected return on any asset depends on three variables: the risk-free interest rate, the expected return on the overall market portfolio, and the systematic risk of the asset, as measured by beta. Beta captures the correlation between an individual asset's returns and returns on other assets. Alternative models exist for measuring the expected returns on risky assets, but none have gained as much acceptance, especially in the corporate finance realm, as the CAPM.

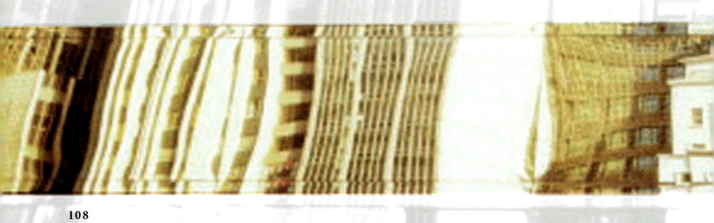

What Companies Do
Junk on TV

As the global economy cooled in 2008, CanWest Media Inc., a subsidiary of Canada's largest media company, struggled to remain profitable while ad revenues were dropping at its Canadian and Australian TV stations and newspapers. Watching closely were the three major credit rating agencies—Standard & Poor's, Fitch, and Moody's—as well as a relative newcomer, DBRS. The business of these firms was to assess the probability that CanWest (or any other firm with publicly traded debt) would default on its obligations and then to assign a rating to CanWest bonds that reflected the assessed level of risk. In late November, DBRS dropped its CanWest rating to B, which placed CanWest's bonds in the "highly speculative" junk bond class. Citing declining ad revenues, a DBRS spokesperson said that this "could put CanWest Media into a negative free cash flow situation by the end of fiscal 2009."

Sources: "CanWest Media Downgraded," thestar.com (November 29, 2008); "DBRS Downgrades Ratings of CanWest Media," The Globe and Mail *(November 29, 2008).*

4

Valuation

Our objective in this chapter is to describe the basic models used to value debt and equity securities. Though we do not wish to understate the complexities of security valuation, a relatively straightforward framework exists that investors can use to value many types of financial assets, including bonds and stocks. This framework states that *the value of any asset equals the present value of all future benefits accruing to the asset's owner.*

Why do corporate managers need to understand how to price bonds and stocks? First, firms occasionally approach the bond and stock markets to raise capital for new investments. Understanding how investors in these markets value the firm's securities helps managers determine how to finance new projects. Second, firms periodically make investments by acquiring privately held companies, just as they unload past investments by selling divisions. In either case, knowing how the market values a firm guides a manager's expectations regarding the appropriate price for an acquisition or divestiture. Third, a company's stock price provides an external, independent performance assessment of top management, one that a diligent board of directors watches closely. Surely managers who will be judged based on their firm's stock price need to understand the determinants of that price. Fourth, finance theory suggests that the objective of corporate management should be to maximize the firm's stock price—but how can managers take actions to maximize that stock price if they don't know what causes stock prices to be high or low?

4.1 Valuation Fundamentals

The owner of an asset is entitled to the benefits generated by the asset. These benefits may be tangible, like the interest payments on a bond, or intangible, like the pleasure experienced from viewing a beautiful painting. In either case, *the value of any asset equals the present value of all its future benefits.* Finance theory focuses primarily on tangible benefits, typically the cash flows paid by an asset over time. The value of a bond equals the present value of interest and principal payments to be paid by the borrower (issuer) to the lender (bondholder). The value of common stock equals the present value of dividends and other cash payments that investors expect firms to distribute to them. The value of an apartment complex equals the present value of future rent payments less the cost of operating and maintaining the property. In each case, the asset's worth is determined by the value today of the future benefits the asset is expected to convey to its owner.

This implies that pricing an asset requires knowledge of both its future benefits and the appropriate discount rate that converts future benefits into a present value. For some assets, such as U.S. government bonds, investors know with near certainty what will be the future benefit stream. For investments such as common stock, which give investors an ownership stake in a company, the benefit stream is less predictable. Investors must consider how much cash the firm will generate, how much cash the firm will reinvest to finance growth, and how much it will distribute to shareholders. Generally, *the greater the uncertainty about an asset's future benefits, the higher the discount rate investors will apply when discounting those benefits to the present.*

Consequently, the valuation process links an asset's risk and return to determine its price. Holding future benefits constant, an inverse relationship exists between risk and value. If two investments promise identical cash payments in the future, then investors will pay a higher price for the one with the more credible promise. In equilibrium, riskier assets must offer higher returns in order to attract investors.

The Fundamental Valuation Model

Chapters 5 and 6 present an in-depth analysis of the relationship between risk and return. For now, assume that we know the market's required rate of return on a specific investment. How can we use that market rate of return to determine the prices of different types of securities? Equation 4.1 expresses the fundamental valuation model as follows:

$$P_0 = \frac{CF_1}{(1+r)^1} + \frac{CF_2}{(1+r)^2} + \cdots + \frac{CF_n}{(1+r)^n}$$

(Eq. 4.1)

In this equation, P_0 represents the asset's price today (at time 0), CF_1 represents the asset's expected cash flow at time 1, CF_2 represents the expected cash flow in time 2, ..., and r is the required return—in other words, the discount rate that captures the asset's risk. The letter n stands for the asset's life, the period over which it distributes cash flows to investors, which is usually measured in years. As you will see, n may be a finite number, as in the case of a bond that matures in 30 years, or it may be infinite, as in the case of a common stock with an indefinite life span. In either case, this equation provides us with a method to value almost any type of asset.

JOB INTERVIEW QUESTION

In general, what determines the value of any asset, and how would you go about estimating today's value of an asset?

EXAMPLE

As part of its effort to stay in business during the 2008–2009 recession, General Motors announced that it would attempt to find an investor willing to engage in a sale–leaseback transaction involving GM's headquarters facility, the Renaissance Center in Detroit. In this transaction, GM would transfer ownership of the building complex to another party and would commit to lease the property over several years. How much could GM hope to raise from this transaction? Suppose that GM promised to lease the facility for $10 million per year for 10 years. Assuming a discount rate of 10%, the present value of that payment stream would be almost $61.5 million:

$$P_0 = \frac{\$10\ \text{million}}{(1+0.10)^1} + \frac{\$10\ \text{million}}{(1+0.10)^2} + \cdots + \frac{\$10\ \text{million}}{(1+0.10)^{10}}$$

$$= \$61,445,671$$

Would a buyer pay $61 million for the Renaissance Center? Perhaps, but the equation neglects several important details. First, GM might default on its promise to make lease payments, and this risk suggests that a buyer might use a discount rate higher than 10% when calculating the present value of GM's payments. Second, the owner would most likely be able to rent the property for more than 10 years, either to GM or to other parties.

With this simple framework in hand, we now turn to the problem of pricing bonds. Though bond pricing techniques can be complex, we focus on "plain vanilla" bonds: those that promise a fixed payment stream over a finite time period. Among the largest issuers of such *fixed-income* securities are national governments and large, multinational corporations.

Concept Review Questions

1. Why is it important for corporate managers to understand how to price bonds and stocks?
2. Holding constant an asset's future benefit stream, what happens to its price if the asset's risk increases?
3. Holding constant an asset's risk, what happens to its price if the asset's future benefit stream increases?
4. Discuss how one might use Equation 4.1 to determine the price per acre of farmland.

4.2 BOND VALUATION

The Basics of Bond Valuation

Bonds are debt instruments used by business and government to borrow large sums of money, often from a diverse group of lenders. Though bonds come in many varieties, most bonds share certain basic characteristics. First, a bond promises to pay investors a fixed amount of interest, called the bond's **coupon**. Borrowers usually make coupon payments semiannually. Second, bonds have a limited life, or **maturity**. When the bond matures, the borrower repays investors a lump sum known as the bond's *face value, principal value,* or **par value**. Third, a bond's **coupon rate** equals the bond's annual coupon payment divided by its par value. Fourth, a bond's **coupon yield** equals the coupon payment divided by the bond's current market price (which does not always equal its par value). To illustrate, suppose that a company issues a bond with a $1,000 par value and promises to pay investors $35 every six months. The bond's *coupon* is $70 per year, and its *coupon rate* is 7% ($70 ÷ $1,000). If the current market value of this bond is $980, then its *coupon yield* is 7.14% ($70 ÷ $980).

A contract known as the **bond indenture** specifies the cash flow that the bond issuer pays to bondholders. Let's assume that a bond pays annual interest at a stated coupon rate i, that M represents the bond's par value, that the bond matures in n years, and that r is the required return on the bond. Each year, bondholders expect to receive a coupon payment, C, that is equal to the product of the coupon rate and par value (i.e., $C = i \times M$); at maturity, the bondholders expect the borrower to repay the par value. The bond's price equals the present value of its future cash flows. Equation 4.2 shows that the bond's price is merely the sum of the present value of the coupon payments (an annuity) plus the present value of its par value.

$$\text{Price} = \left[\frac{C}{(1+r)^1} + \frac{C}{(1+r)^2} + \cdots + \frac{C}{(1+r)^n}\right] + \left[\frac{M}{(1+r)^n}\right]$$

Present value of coupon payments   Present value of par value

(Eq. 4.2)

EXAMPLE

On January 1, 2010, Worldwide United had outstanding a $1,000 par value bond with a 9.125% coupon rate, which we will assume pays interest at the end of each calendar year. The bond matures at the end of 2020, in exactly 11 years. In 2010, investors required bonds of similar risk to pay a return of 8%. The annual coupon C on this bond is 0.09125 × $1,000 = $91.25. The bond's cash flows appear below the time line in Figure 4.1. Substituting these values into Equation 4.2, we obtain the following result:

$$\text{Price} = \left[\frac{91.25}{(1+0.08)^1} + \frac{91.25}{(1+0.08)^2} + \cdots + \frac{91.25}{(1+0.08)^{11}}\right] + \left[\frac{1,000}{(1+0.08)^{11}}\right]$$
$$= \$651.43 + \$428.88 = \$1,080.31$$

The required return on Worldwide United bonds compensates investors for the risk that the company will fail to make all scheduled payments to investors. For some borrowers, the risk of default is so slight that investors in the market essentially treat their bonds as being risk free.

FIGURE 4.1

Time Line for
Bond Valuation:
Worldwide United
$9\frac{1}{8}$% Coupon,
$1,000 Par Bond,
Maturing in
December 2020;
Required
Return 8%

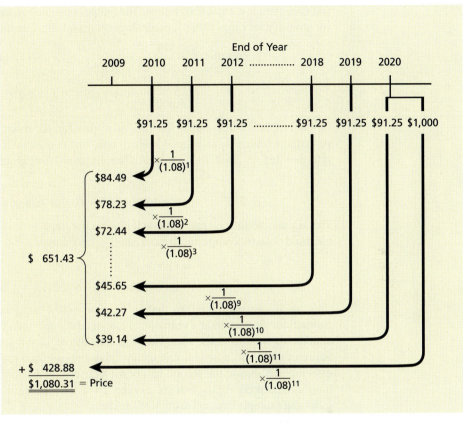

Risk-Free Bonds

A **risk-free bond** is a bond that has no chance of default by its issuer. In practice, investors view only those bonds issued by the most creditworthy national governments as risk-free instruments. The world's largest issuer of risk-free bonds is the U.S. Treasury. Treasury securities come in a wide range of maturities, ranging from just a few weeks to 30 years. Some countries offer even longer maturity on their government bonds. In 2005, Japan issued 40-year bonds for the first time, and the United Kingdom and France have issued 50-year bonds. Most of these securities make semiannual coupon payments, but some short-term Treasury securities, called *discount* or *zero-coupon* bonds, do not make coupon payments at all. Instead they sell at a discount relative to par value, as the next section illustrates.

Zero-Coupon Treasuries   Pure discount instruments, such as U.S. Treasury bills, promise investors a single fixed payment on a specified future date. They make no intermediate interest payments and so are sometimes called **zero-coupon bonds**. How can bonds that pay no interest be attractive investments? That's where the word *discount* comes into play. Investors purchase Treasury bills at a discount from their par value. If held to maturity, Treasury bills offer a dollar return equal to the difference between the par value and the purchase price. For example, an investor might purchase a Treasury bill maturing in six months for $9,800. When the bill matures, the U.S. Treasury pays $10,000, the par value of the bill, and the investor earns a $200 return. The bill pays no coupon interest. Using Equation 4.2, we can solve for r to obtain the percentage return on this investment as follows:

$$\$9,800 = \frac{\$10,000}{1 + r}$$

$$r = \left(\frac{\$10,000}{\$9,800}\right) - 1 = 1.0204 - 1 = 0.0204 = 2.04\%$$

Of course, 2.04% represents the rate of return for six months, so we could state the percentage return on an annual basis in either of two ways. If we multiply the 6-month rate, denoted r_{6mo}, by 2, then we obtain the simple-interest annual rate of 4.08%:

$$r_{simple} = r_{6mo} \times 2$$
$$= 0.0204 \times 2 = 0.0408 = 4.08\%$$

This is a simple-interest rate because it ignores the impact of compounding. Alternatively, we could obtain a compound annual rate, r_{ann}, as follows:

$$r_{ann} = \left(1 + r_{6mo}\right)^2 - 1$$
$$= (1 + 0.0204)^2 - 1 = 0.0412 = 4.12\%$$

This rate represents the return that an investor would earn at the end of one year if she invested for six months at a semiannual rate of 2.04% and then reinvested the proceeds for another six months at the same rate. The annual rate slightly exceeds the simple-interest figure of 4.08% because this calculation takes into account the investor's opportunity to earn interest, during the second half of the year on the original principal and also on the interest earned during the first six months. To see how this works in practice, consider the following example from a Treasury bill auction.

The Treasury conducts periodic auctions of bills with maturities ranging from 4 to 26 weeks. The following quote, obtained from the Treasury website (http://www.treasury .gov), illustrates bill pricing in a typical auction:

Term	Issue Date	Maturity Date	Discount Rate (%)	Investment Rate (%)	Price per $100	CUSIP
182-DAY	5-23-2009	11-19-2009	0.295	0.300	99.850861	912795S51

The first entry indicates that this particular bill matures in 182 days, or about six months. The second item gives the date of the auction in which the bill was sold, and following that appears the bill's maturity date. The fourth and fifth entries in the quote are measures of the bond's yield, which we will discuss shortly. The sixth item is the bond's price, and the final item in the quote is the bill's CUSIP,[1] essentially a tracking number that allows traders to communicate with each other about a specific security. Look at the next-to-last number in the quote, 99.850861; it represents the market price of the bill (as determined by the auction) per $100 of par value. If an investor submitted a successful bid to purchase bills having a par value of $10,000, then the purchase price for this order would be $9,985.09. If the investor purchases bills and holds them to maturity, then the dollar return on that investment will be just $14.91, which is the difference between the $10,000 par value and the purchase price. The percentage return is calculated as follows:

$$\frac{(\$10,000 - \$9,985.09)}{\$9,985.09} = 0.001493 = 0.1493\%$$

---

[1] CUSIP stands for the Committee on Uniform Securities Identification Procedures. A CUSIP number identifies most securities, including stocks of all registered U.S. and Canadian companies as well as U.S. government and municipal bonds.

However, this is the return over just six months. We could annualize the return by using simple interest as follows:

$$0.001493 \times \left(\frac{365}{182}\right) = 0.00300 = 0.300\%$$

Notice that this number, 0.300%, appears in the bond quotation shown previously. Bond traders call it the **bond equivalent yield**, and it is a simple-interest measure of an investor's annual return from holding a Treasury bill.[2] We can substitute the equation above into the equation on the bottom of page 116 and then rearrange terms to arrive at a Treasury bill pricing formula that looks more like the present value pricing relationship given in Equation 4.1:

$$\frac{(\$10,000 - \$9,985.09)}{\$9,985.09} = 0.001493 = \frac{0.00300}{\left(\frac{365}{182}\right)};$$

$$\text{Price} = \frac{\$10,000}{\left[1 + 0.00300\left(\frac{182}{365}\right)\right]} = \$9,985.09$$

In other words, the price of the bond equals the $10,000 payment that it will make in six months, discounted using a 182-day interest rate. In this equation, the interest rate (0.300%) is multiplied by the fraction of the year that will have elapsed at the bond's maturity date. This equation can be stated in a more general form as follows:

$$\text{Price} = \frac{\text{Par}}{\left[1 + r\left(\frac{1}{2}\right)\right]} = \frac{\text{Par}}{\left(1 + \frac{r}{2}\right)}$$

where we have made the simplifying assumption that the bill matures in exactly one-half year (or that 1/2 approximates $182 \div 365$). In this equation, r represents the market's required return on the bill, and we divide it by 2 because the bill matures in six months.[3] When conversing about current market conditions, Treasury bill traders will often refer to a bill's return rather than its price. It should be clear that if you know the bill's return then you can calculate its price, and vice versa. (Also note that, as the price of a bill or bond increases, its return falls.) You can use the previous equation to price most pure discount bonds. Just discount the par value at an appropriate interest rate to obtain the price.

The six-month Treasury bill that sold for $9,985.09 in May 2009 offered investors a very low return: less than one-half of 1% per year. That return was low by historical standards, but yields on some Treasury bills were actually below zero a few months earlier. This means that investors paid the U.S. Treasury a little *more* than $10,000 in exchange for the promise that the Treasury would repay them exactly $10,000 a few months later. Why would anyone accept a negative return on their investment? In September 2008 Lehman

---

[2]In this market it is traditional to calculate one other measure of the bill's return, the **bank discount yield**:

$$\frac{\$10,000 - \$9,985.09}{\$10,000}\left(\frac{360}{182}\right) = 0.00295 = 0.295\%$$

Note that this number appears just before the bond equivalent yield in the price quote. This is a poor measure of an investor's return for several reasons, but traders nonetheless use it to communicate with each other about current prices in the market. The important lesson here is not to memorize the differences between bond equivalent and bank discount yields but rather to understand that the price of a Treasury bill is just the present value of the cash payment made at maturity.

[3]Here's a pop quiz. Does the value r in this equation represent the simple-interest or rather the compound-interest annual return? *Answer:* Since the equation calculates the 6-month rate by simply dividing the annual rate by 2, it follows that r is a simple-interest rate.

Brothers, the 158-year-old investment bank, filed for bankruptcy; this set off fears that other investment banks and even some large commercial banks, might soon follow suit. Investors pulled their money out of other short-term investments and used those funds to buy Treasury bills. At least some investors were so concerned that there was no other safe place to invest that they were willing to pay the U.S. government for keeping their money safe as the financial crisis escalated.

Coupon-Paying Treasuries Valuing coupon-paying instruments, such as Treasury notes and bonds, requires only a slight modification to the pricing equation for discount bonds. Treasury notes and bonds, like Treasury bills, are risk free in that they are backed by the full faith and credit of the U.S. government. Unlike Treasury bills, however, notes and bonds make interest payments every six months, and they also have longer maturities than bills. It is easy to modify the general bond pricing equation (Equation 4.2) to fit the characteristics of coupon-paying notes or bonds:

$$\text{Price} = \frac{\frac{C}{2}}{\left(1 + \frac{r}{2}\right)^1} + \frac{\frac{C}{2}}{\left(1 + \frac{r}{2}\right)^2} + \frac{\frac{C}{2}}{\left(1 + \frac{r}{2}\right)^3} + \cdots + \frac{\frac{C}{2} + \$1{,}000}{\left(1 + \frac{r}{2}\right)^{2n}} \qquad \textbf{(Eq. 4.3)}$$

In this equation, C refers to the annual coupon payment, so $C/2$ represents the semiannual payment. Observe that, in the last period, the bond makes its final coupon payment and repays the par value or principal (in this case, $1,000). As before, r represents the discount rate or, equivalently, the market's required rate of return on this bond.[4] The bond matures in n years, so there are $2n$ semiannual payments. The bond's price is the sum of the present value of interest payments and the present value of the par value.

EXAMPLE

Suppose that six months ago the Treasury issued a new 5-year, $1,000 par value note that paid a coupon rate of 4%.

Assume that the bond just made its first interest payment, so the next one will be due in six months. Since the bond was first issued, market conditions have changed and investors now require a return of 5% per year. What is the price of the bond?

Given its coupon rate, the bond pays $40 in interest per year, or $20 every six months. Thus, we have

$$\text{Price} = \frac{\$20}{\left(1 + \frac{0.05}{2}\right)^1} + \frac{\$20}{\left(1 + \frac{0.05}{2}\right)^2} + \frac{\$20}{\left(1 + \frac{0.05}{2}\right)^3} + \cdots + \frac{\$20}{\left(1 + \frac{0.05}{2}\right)^8} + \frac{\$1{,}020}{\left(1 + \frac{0.05}{2}\right)^9} = \$960.15$$

The bond has nine interest payments remaining (plus the principal repayment) and is worth $960.15.[5]

---

[4]Notice once again that this equation calculates the present value of payments arriving every six months by taking the annual interest rate (r) and dividing by 2 to obtain a semiannual rate. Hence the value r in this equation represents a simple-interest rate, which is conventional for quoting rates in the bond market. Remember that, whenever we calculate an annual interest rate by multiplying a semiannual rate by 2 (or calculate a semiannual rate by dividing an annual rate by 2), we are dealing with simple rather than compound interest.

[5]You can easily use Excel to calculate this number. First, enter the bond's nine payments in cells A1 through A9 on a spreadsheet. Next, in any empty cell, type the formula "= NPV(.025,A1:A9)"; Excel will then produce the price of the bond. (Here ".025" represents the 2.5% semiannual interest rate.)

In this example, the bond's price is below its par value. We say that a bond sells at a **discount** when its price is less than par value.[6] The bond sells at a discount because its coupon rate, 4%, offers a return lower than that currently required by the market, 5%. If investors demand a 5% return, then the only way they can get it from a bond that pays 4% interest is to purchase the bond at a discount. At a price of $960.15, the bond offers a coupon yield of 4.17% ($40 ÷ $960.15), still not up to the 5% required return. For investors who purchase this bond and hold it to maturity, the total return will reflect both the interest payments and a capital gain of $39.85 ($1,000 − $960.15) when the Treasury repays the $1,000 principal at maturity. Combined, the interest payments and capital gain generate a return of 5%. The same logic can work in reverse. Suppose that the market's required return on this bond was 3% rather than 5%. When the market requires only a 3% return, a bond that pays 4% interest is quite attractive. Investors would purchase this bond, driving its price above par value. In that case, the bond would sell for a **premium**. Substituting 3% for 5% in the preceding equation, you can verify that the market price of the bond would be $1,041.80.

Risky Bonds

How do you know what return the market "requires" for a particular bond? Your intuition probably tells you that the riskier the bond, the higher the rate of return the market will require. Yet putting that language into quantitative terms is a challenge. Because Treasury bonds provide a riskless stream of cash flows, you can deduce the market's required rate of return if you know the market price of a T-bond. Suppose that a Treasury bond with $1,000 par value matures in exactly 2.5 years and pays a 6% coupon. You observe that the market price of this bond is $988.63. Because this bond sells at a discount, you know that the market requires a return on the bond greater than the coupon rate. But how much greater? To answer this question, just use the bond pricing equation (Equation 4.3) to solve for the discount rate that equates the present value of the bond's cash flows to its current price:

$$\frac{\$30}{\left(1+\frac{r}{2}\right)^1} + \frac{\$30}{\left(1+\frac{r}{2}\right)^2} + \frac{\$30}{\left(1+\frac{r}{2}\right)^3} + \frac{\$30}{\left(1+\frac{r}{2}\right)^4} + \frac{\$1,030}{\left(1+\frac{r}{2}\right)^5} = \$988.63$$

By using a financial calculator or spreadsheet program (or by trial and error), you can solve this equation to find $r/2 = 0.0325$, so $r = 0.065$ or 6.5%. In this equation, the value of r is called the bond's **yield to maturity (YTM)**.[7] The yield to maturity of any bond is the discount rate that equates the present value of the bond's cash flows to its market price. For Treasury bonds, the yield to maturity measures the market's required return.

Valuing an ordinary corporate bond involves the same steps: write down the cash flows, determine an appropriate discount rate, and calculate the present value. The discount rate on a corporate bond should be higher than on a Treasury bond with the same maturity because corporate bonds carry **default risk**, the risk that the corporation may not make all scheduled payments. Bond traders often speak of the "yield spread" between Treasury bonds and corporate bonds. The **yield spread** is the difference in yield to maturity between two bonds or two classes of bonds with similar maturities but different degrees of risk.

---

[6]Because this bond trades below par value, it sells at a discount. However, it is not a pure discount bond like a Treasury bill.

[7]A bond's yield to maturity is also called its **internal rate of return (IRR)**. It can be calculated using a financial calculator or spreadsheet. In Excel, you can calculate a bond's YTM by using the "=IRR" function (see Problem 4-11 for an illustration).

EXAMPLE

Assume that a 1-percentage-point spread exists between 10-year Treasury bonds and 10-year, high-quality corporate bonds. If the yield to maturity on 10-year Treasury bonds is 7%, then the yield to maturity on a 10-year corporate bond would be 8%.

Suppose you want to determine the price of a 10-year corporate bond with a 9% coupon. Substitute $C = \$90$, $r = 0.08$ (8%), and $n = 10$ into Equation 4.3, which gives the answer

$$\text{Price} = \frac{\$45}{\left(1 + \frac{0.08}{2}\right)^1} + \frac{\$45}{\left(1 + \frac{0.08}{2}\right)^2} + \frac{\$45}{\left(1 + \frac{0.08}{2}\right)^3} + \cdots + \frac{\$45}{\left(1 + \frac{0.08}{2}\right)^{19}} + \frac{\$1,045}{\left(1 + \frac{0.08}{2}\right)^{20}}$$

$$= \$1,067.95$$

The bond's price should therefore be $1,067.95.

Bonds may seem like safe investments. Investors who purchase Treasury bonds or high-quality corporate bonds can be fairly confident that promised cash payments will be made as scheduled. But all bonds are not created equal, and bond yields vary widely based on the market's assessment of the borrower's financial condition. Furthermore, the U.S. tax code contains special tax breaks for certain types of bond issuers, and those tax benefits also affect bond yields.

Bond Issuers   A simple way to classify bonds is based upon the identity of the issuer. Large companies that need money to fund new investments and to fulfill other needs issue **corporate bonds**. Corporations issue bonds with maturities ranging from 1 to 100 years. When a company issues a debt instrument with a maturity of 1 to 10 years, the instrument is usually called a *note* rather than a bond, but notes and bonds are essentially identical instruments. Most corporate bonds have a par value of $1,000 and pay interest semiannually. **Municipal bonds** are issued by local and state government entities. In the United States, federal law gives local and state governments a significant tax break by exempting interest received on municipal bonds from the bondholder's federal income tax. Obviously, this makes municipal bonds especially attractive to investors who face high marginal income tax rates. The tax exemption on municipal bond interest allows state and local governments to raise money at lower interest rates than they would otherwise be able to do.

The world's largest bond issuer is the U.S. Treasury. **Treasury bills** are debt instruments that mature in less than a year. The maturities of **Treasury notes** range from 1 to 10 years, and maturities of **Treasury bonds** extend up to 30 years. The federal government issues bonds to raise money to cover budget deficits, and investors generally regard Treasury bills, notes, and bonds as very safe investments.

Some federal government agencies and government-sponsored enterprises (GSEs) issue their own bonds, called **agency bonds**, to finance operations. The government charges these organizations with the task of providing credit for certain sectors of the economy such as farming, real estate, and education. The Federal Home Loan Bank (FHLB), the Federal National Mortgage Association (FNMA or "Fannie Mae"), the Government National Mortgage Association (GNMA or "Ginnie Mae"), and the Federal Home Loan Mortgage Corporation (FHLMC or "Freddie Mac") are the major mortgage-related agencies that issue bonds. Agency debt is not necessarily backed by the full faith and credit of the Treasury, so investors recognize that agency debt carries a small amount of additional risk relative to Treasury securities. However, during the 2008 U.S. financial crisis, both Fannie Mae and Freddie Mac experienced severe financial difficulties due to the decline in residential real estate prices and associated mortgage defaults. To prevent these GSEs from defaulting on their debt, the federal government essentially took over both entities, receiving stock in exchange for capital infusions of up to $100 billion in each. Therefore, although there was no explicit legal commitment for the government to guarantee the debts of the GSEs, regulators chose to do so.

Bond Ratings   For information on the likelihood that a particular bond issue may default, investors turn to bond rating agencies such as Moody's, Standard & Poor's, and Fitch. These organizations provide an independent assessment of the risk of most publicly traded bond issues, and they assign a letter **bond rating** to each issue in order to indicate its degree of risk. Table 4.1 lists the major bond-rating categories provided by each of the agencies and the interpretation associated with each rating class. Bonds rated Baa3 or higher by Moody's, and BBB– or higher by S&P and Fitch, are classified as investment-grade. Lower-rated bonds are called noninvestment-grade, high-yield, or **junk bonds**. The term "junk bonds" has a pejorative connotation but simply means that these bonds are riskier than investment-grade bonds. For example, for bonds in the investment-grade category, the probability of default is extremely low, perhaps as low as 1%. In contrast, a recent study put the probability of a B-rated bond defaulting in its first year at almost 8%.[8]

Table 4.1	Bond Ratings		
RATING DESCRIPTION	**MOODY'S**	**S&P AND FITCH**	
Highest quality	Aaa	AAA	Investment-grade bonds
High quality	Aa1, Aa2, Aa3	AA+, AA, AA–	
Upper medium	A1, A2, A3	A+, A, A–	
Medium	Baa1, Baa2, Baa3	BBB+, BBB, BBB–	
Noninvestment-grade	Ba1	BB+	Junk (speculative) bonds
Speculative	Ba2, Ba3	BB, BB–	
Highly speculative	B1, B2, B3	B+, B, B–	
Very risky, default	Caa1 or lower	CCC+ or lower	

JOB INTERVIEW QUESTION

When is a bond considered to be a junk bond?

Figure 4.2 shows a plot of the yield spread between 10-year high-yield bonds and 10-year Treasury bonds from 1978 through the third quarter of 2008. Note that the yield spread was more than 10 percentage points in 1990 (a recession year) and again during the financial crisis of 2008. Spreads were also unusually high during 2000–2002, a period that included a recession and the 9/11 terrorist attacks. In contrast, the low points in the figure occur in 1978, 1984, 1993, 1996, 2004, and 2006—all periods of relative prosperity. The tendency

---

[8]See Phoa and Fabozzi (2002). Altman and Karlin (2008) reported that in the 3rd quarter of 2008, one-year-ahead forecasts of default rates based on current yield spreads between junk bonds and Treasuries were predicting a default rate of more than 11%.

of spreads to widen during recessions and to narrow during economic expansions simply reflects the higher likelihood of default when business conditions deteriorate. For example, in 1990 and 1991 roughly one in ten high-yield bond issuers defaulted, and in 2002 that figure reached one in eight borrowers.[9]

FIGURE 4.2

Yield Spread between 10-Year Treasury and High-Yield Bonds

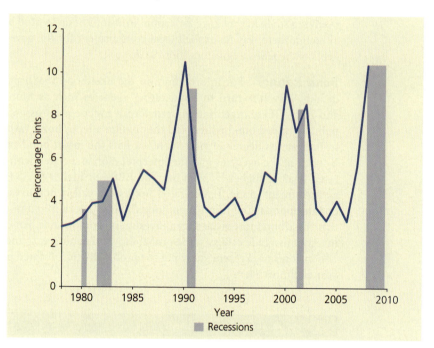

In our discussion of risk-free bonds, we stated that the yield to maturity on Treasury bonds was a good estimate of the market's required return on these instruments. Is the same true for junk bonds? In 2008, the YTM on a typical junk bond was 10 percentage points above the yield on Treasuries. Did investors really expect a return that was 10 percentage points higher than they could get on Treasury bonds? The answer is no, because investors do not expect high-yield bonds to make all promised payments all of the time. In other words, an investor who holds a portfolio of high-yield bonds expects that some of these bonds will default, so the actual return that the investor earns will be less than the promised return (i.e., less than the yield to maturity, which assumes that the borrower makes all payments on time).

The vast majority of corporate bonds do not default, so investors typically receive the cash flows that they are promised when the bonds are purchased. However, this does not mean that bonds are risk-free, even if they do not default. The next section explores how market forces affect bond prices.

JOB INTERVIEW QUESTION

If a B-rated bond's yield to maturity is 8%, then is 8% also the market's required return on that bond?

Bond Prices

Bond Price Quotations   The prices of bonds are quoted in the financial press. In each edition of the *Wall Street Journal*, quotations for the prior trading day's 40 most active fixed-coupon corporate bonds are reported. Their format is demonstrated below for a few bonds traded on Monday, December 8, 2008.

---

[9]The source for Figure 4.2 and the default rate data is Altman and Karlin (2008).

COMPANY (TICKER)	COUPON	MATURITY	LAST PRICE	LAST YIELD	EST SPREAD	UST
Citigroup (C.HFL)	5.500	Apr 2013	91.942	7.720	562	5
General Mills (GIS.GD)	6.000	Feb 2012	96.709	7.172	387	6
Altria GP (MO.HC)	9.700	Nov 2018	103.327	9.179	540	10

Smart Practices Video

Tom Cole, Co-Head, Global Banking, Deutsche Bank Securities

"By the end of 2008, the noninvestment grade credit spread was 1400 basis points."

See the entire interview at

SMARTFinance

JOB INTERVIEW QUESTION

If yield spreads on junk bonds are currently high, what might that tell you about expected default rates on junk bonds?

The first column of the bond quotations lists the bond issuer's name and ticker symbol. The second column shows the annual coupon rate, and the third column reports the maturity date. Corporate bond prices are quoted as a percent of par value, with par typically set at $1,000. For example, the first row of the table indicates that the Citigroup bond, paying a coupon rate of 5.5% and maturing in April 2013, recently sold for $919.42 (or 91.942% of par value). Given the price, coupon, and maturity date, the fifth column calculates the bond's yield to maturity, which equals 7.72%.

The estimated spread (EST SPREAD) in the sixth column equals the difference in yield to maturities between the given bond and a Treasury bond at roughly the same maturity. By convention, these spreads are quoted in terms of **basis points** (100 basis points equals 1 percentage point). Corporate bonds offer higher yields than Treasury bonds because they are riskier, so the yield spread is always a positive number. The seventh column specifies what we mean by a "similar" bond. The column heading "UST" stands for U.S. Treasury, and the numbers in the column refer to the maturity of the Treasury security to which each corporate bond is compared when calculating the estimated spread. Looking at those two columns, we see that the Citigroup bond offers a yield that is 562 basis points (or 5.62 percentage points) above the yield on a Treasury bond maturing in five years. The 5-year Treasury bond is a relevant comparison because the Citigroup bond's maturity is roughly five years away.

As you might expect, bond spreads bear a direct relationship to default risk. The greater the risk that the borrower may default on its debts, the higher the spread that borrower-issued bonds must offer investors in order to compensate them for the risk they take. For investors, estimating the default risk of a particular bond issue is a crucial element in determining what the required return on the bond should be. Bond ratings are helpful in making such estimates.

Bond Price Behavior   The market value of a bond changes constantly. One factor that can cause a bond's price to move is simply the passage of time. Whether a bond sells at a discount or a premium, its price will converge to par value (plus the final interest payment) as time elapses and the maturity date draws near. This is easy to understand if you imagine a bond that will mature in one day. The final cash flow of the bond is its par value plus the last coupon payment. If this final payment is to arrive tomorrow, then you can determine the bond's price simply by discounting this payment for one day, revealing that the price and the final payment are virtually identical. In addition to the passage of time, economic forces can cause movements in a bond's price. When the required return on a bond changes, the bond's price changes in the opposite direction. You can see this inverse relationship between price and required return in the bond pricing equation. The higher the bond's required return, the lower its price (and vice versa). How much a bond's price responds to changes in required returns depends on several factors, but among the most important is the bond's maturity.

Figure 4.3 shows how the prices of two bonds change as their required returns change. To focus on the effects of changes in required returns on bond prices, assume that both bonds are free of default risk. Both pay a 6% coupon, but one matures in 2 years whereas the other matures in 10 years. The figure indicates that, when the required return equals the coupon rate (6%), both bonds trade at their $1,000 par value. However, as the required return increases, the bonds' prices fall. The rate of decline in the 10-year bond's price far exceeds that of the 2-year bond. Likewise, as the required return decreases, the prices of both bonds increase; but the 10-year bond's price increases much faster than that of the 2-year bond. The general point is that *the prices of long-term bonds display greater sensitivity to changes in interest rates than do the prices of short-term bonds.*[10]

FIGURE 4.3

The Relationship between Prices and Yields for Bonds with the Same 6% Coupon Rate but Differing Times to Maturity

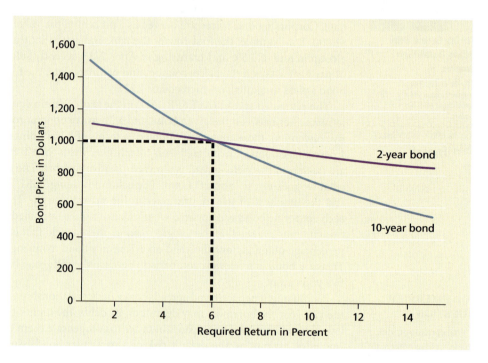

Figure 4.3 illustrates that the most important risk for bond investors to consider is usually **interest-rate risk**, the risk that changes in market interest rates will cause fluctuations in a bond's price. Changes in the required returns on bonds can occur as a result of economy-wide forces, such as increases in inflation and/or firm-specific factors, such as a decline in the creditworthiness of the borrower. The experience of France Telecom illustrates what can happen to corporate bonds when business conditions deteriorate. In an attempt to refinance its massive short-term debt obligations, France Telecom conducted what was once the largest-ever corporate bond offering by selling the equivalent of $16.4 billion worth of bonds to investors around the world. France Telecom simultaneously issued bonds in three different currencies: U.S. dollars, euros, and British pounds. Days after successfully floating its bonds, France Telecom announced that it would not be able to retire as much short-term debt as it had originally anticipated, thereby signaling to the market that its cash flows were weaker than expected. Prices and yields of

[10]There can be exceptions to this rule in certain unusual circumstances. For example, the prices of short-term bonds that sell at a deep discount can be more sensitive to interest-rate movements than the prices of bonds with longer maturities that sell at a premium. A better measure of a bond's sensitivity to interest rate movements is its *duration*, a metric that considers both the timing and the magnitude of the cash payments that the bond makes during its life.

France Telecom bonds responded accordingly. For example, the required return on France Telecom's 5-year dollar bonds, issued with a 7.2% coupon, rose to about 8.5%. The following equation shows that this increase in the required return was associated with a decline in price of $52.07, or 5.2%, from the original $1,000 par value:

$$\frac{\$36}{\left(1+\frac{0.085}{2}\right)^1} + \frac{\$36}{\left(1+\frac{0.085}{2}\right)^2} + \frac{\$36}{\left(1+\frac{0.085}{2}\right)^3} + \cdots + \frac{\$36}{\left(1+\frac{0.085}{2}\right)^9} + \frac{\$1,036}{\left(1+\frac{0.085}{2}\right)^{10}} = \$947.93$$

The same effect can occur in reverse. Consider what might have happened if France Telecom's business had improved suddenly after the bond issue. Suppose that the bond market became convinced that France Telecom's brighter cash flow outlook lowered the risk of the 5-year bonds. If investors lowered their required return on these bonds to 6.5%, then the price of the 5-year bonds would have risen to $1,029.48.

EXAMPLE

On May 15, 2007, the U.S. Treasury issued a 30-year bond paying a coupon rate of 4.75% on a par value of $1,000. The auction price of this bond was $986.05, resulting in a yield to maturity of 4.84%. Soon thereafter, the U.S. economy was in recession and, by the time the bond had made its fourth semiannual payment, its yield had fallen to 3.70%. What was the bond's price now?

After making four coupon payments, this bond had 56 payments remaining: two payments per year for the next 28 years. Use Equation 4.2 to calculate the price of the bond:

$$\frac{\$23.75}{\left(1+\frac{0.037}{2}\right)^1} + \frac{\$23.75}{\left(1+\frac{0.037}{2}\right)^2} + \frac{\$23.75}{\left(1+\frac{0.037}{2}\right)^3} + \cdots + \frac{\$23.75}{\left(1+\frac{0.037}{2}\right)^{55}} + \frac{\$1,023.75}{\left(1+\frac{0.037}{2}\right)^{56}} = \$1,182.12$$

Compared to its price when issued, the value of the bond had risen by almost 20% in response to a decline in the required rate of return from 4.84% to 3.70%.

You might argue that this entire discussion is irrelevant if an investor plans to hold a bond to maturity rather than sell it. If the bond is held to maturity then there is a good chance that the investor will receive all interest and principal payments as promised, so any price increase (or decrease) that occurs between the purchase date and the maturity date is just "on paper." Though the tax code may ignore investment gains and losses until investors realize them, financial economists argue that gains and losses matter whether or not investors realize them by selling assets. For example, when the France Telecom bond's value falls from $1,000 to $947.93, an investor holding the bond experiences an opportunity loss: the bond's lower price means that the investor no longer has the opportunity to invest $1,000 elsewhere.

Thus far, we have maintained a simplifying assumption in our valuation models. You can see that assumption embedded in Equation 4.1 and Equation 4.2, which both assume that a single discount rate (r) can be applied to determine the present value of cash payments made at any and all future dates. In other words, the models assume that investors require the same rate of return on an investment that pays cash one year from now and on one that pays cash ten years from now. In reality, required rates of return depend on the exact timing of cash payments, as the next section illustrates.

5. What is the difference between the terms *coupon, coupon rate,* and *yield to maturity* for a bond?
6. Who are the major issuers of bonds? What role do bond ratings play in evaluating bonds? What are junk bonds?
7. Why are bond prices and interest rates inversely related?

4.3 Advanced Bond Valuation: The Term Structure of Interest Rates

A quick glance at actual prices and yields of bonds having different maturities reveals an important fact: yields vary with maturity. That is, if you examine the yield to maturity on a number of bonds that are similar (e.g., all Treasury bonds) except that they mature at different times, you will find that yields are not the same for short-term and long-term bonds. The *Wall Street Journal* and many other financial publications regularly display a graph that plots the relationship between YTM and maturity for a group of similar bonds. Finance professionals refer to this graph as the **yield curve**, and they call the relationship between yield to maturity and time to maturity the **term structure of interest rates**.

Evaluating the Yield Curve

Figure 4.4 shows how the yield curve for U.S. government bonds looked at four different dates. Usually, long-term bonds offer higher yields than short-term bonds, and the yield curve slopes upward. This was the case in January 1983 and in July 1993. However, the level of the yield curve was much higher in 1983 than in 1993. Differences in expected inflation rates in those two years largely explain why the yield curve was so much higher in 1983. In the 24 months just prior to January 1983, the annual rate of U.S. inflation had averaged about 6%. Assume that investors expected inflation to remain roughly at that level in the near term. Investors who purchased short-term Treasury bills in January 1983 earned a return of about 7.5%, slightly higher than the expected inflation rate. In contrast, in the 24 months prior to July 1993, the annual inflation rate averaged just under 3%. In July 1993, T-bills offered a return of just over 3%, again just slightly above the inflation rate at that time. The general lesson here is that the yields offered by bonds must be sufficient to offer investors a positive **real return**. The real return on an investment approximately equals the difference between its stated or **nominal return** and the inflation rate.

The other two lines in Figure 4.4 illustrate that the shape of the yield curve can change over time. In July 2006, the yield curve was nearly flat, with yields on short-term and long-term bonds hovering around 5%. But by February 2007, the yield curve had inverted, with short-term yields lying slightly above long-term yields. Inverted yield curves typically occur prior to and during recessions.[11] In fact, Duke University economist Campbell Harvey (1993) argues that economic forecasts based on the slope of the yield curve perform as well as or better than many forecasts produced using complex statistical models. Research in this area shows that the yield curve works well as a predictor of economic

---

[11]One possible explanation for this phenomenon is that investors, when faced with the prospect of a recession, anticipate that the weakening economy will lead to lower inflation (or perhaps deflation) in the long term. Expectations of lower long-term inflation may cause long-term interest rates to fall below short-term rates. Go to http://www.smartmoney.com/bonds/ and click the link for the "Living Yield Curve" to see how the yield curve has behaved in the United States since 1977.

FIGURE 4.4

Yield Curves for
U.S. Government
Bonds

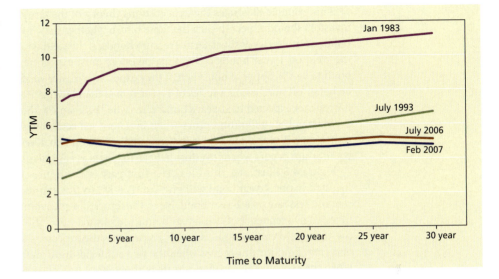

activity not only in the United States but also in Canada, Germany, and other large industrialized economies.[12]

Term Structure Theories

Economists have studied the yield curve intensely for several decades, trying to understand how it behaves and what it portends for the future. From this research we have learned that economic growth forecasts incorporating (the slope of) the yield curve perform better than forecasts that ignore the yield curve. Can the yield curve also tell us something about the direction in which interest rates are headed? The answer is a highly qualified yes. To understand the logic underlying the hypothesis that the slope of the yield curve predicts interest-rate movements, we first consider expectations theory.

Expectations Theory   Russell wants to invest $1,000 for two years. He does not want to take much risk, so he plans to invest the money in U.S. Treasury securities. Consulting the Treasury website, Russell learns that 1-year Treasury bonds currently offer a 3% YTM and that 2-year bonds offer a 3.5% YTM. At first, he thinks that his decision about which investment to purchase is easy. He wants to invest for two years and the 2-year bond pays a higher yield, so why not just buy that one? Thinking a bit more, Russell realizes that he could invest his money in a 1-year bond and reinvest the proceeds in another 1-year bond when the first bond matures. Whether that strategy will ultimately earn a higher return than simply buying the 2-year bond depends on what the yield on a 1-year bond will be one year from now. If, for example, the 1-year bond rate rises to 5%, then Russell will earn 3% in the first year and 5% in the second year for a grand total of 8% (8.15% after compounding). Over the same period, the 2-year bond offers just 3.5% per year or 7% total (7.12% after compounding). Obviously, in this scenario, Russell earns more by investing in two 1-year bonds than in one 2-year bond. But what if the yield on a 1-year bond is just 3% next year? In that case, Russell would earn 6% over two years (or 6.09% after compounding) and so would be better off buying the 2-year bond. If next year's yield on the 1-year bond is about 4%, then both investment strategies will earn approximately the same return over the two years.

---

[12]See Bonser-Neal and Morley (1997).

This example illustrates the **expectations theory** of the term structure: in equilibrium, investors should expect to earn the same return whether they invest in long-term Treasury bonds or in a series of short-term Treasury bonds. If the yield on 2-year bonds is 3.5% when the yield on 1-year bonds is 3%, then investors must expect next year's yield on a 1-year bond to be 4%. Suppose not. Then, if they expected a higher yield than 4%, investors would be better off purchasing a series of 1-year bonds than buying the 2-year bond. Conversely, if investors expected next year's bond rate to be less than 4% then they would flock to the 2-year bond. Equilibrium occurs when investors' expectations are such that the expected return on a 2-year bond equals the expected return on two 1-year bonds. In our example, equilibrium occurs when investors believe that next year's interest rate will be 4%.

Figure 4.5 illustrates this idea. The first part of the figure shows that the value of $1 invested in one 2-year bond will grow to $(1 + r)^2$. In this expression, r represents the current interest rate on a 2-year bond. Next, the figure shows that investors expect each dollar invested in a sequence of two 1-year bonds to grow to $(1 + r_1)[1 + E(r_2)]$. Here, r_1 represents the current 1-year bond rate and $E(r_2)$ represents the expected 1-year bond rate in the second year. Equilibrium occurs when the two strategies have identical expected returns, or when the expected 1-year interest rate is about 4%.[13]

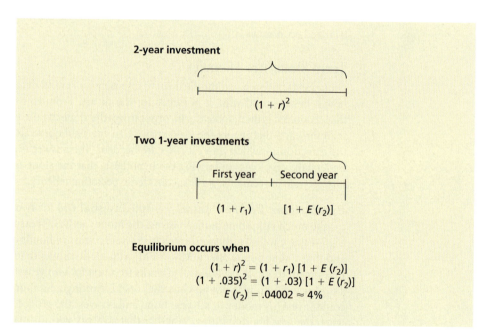

Expectations theory says that if the yield curve is upward sloping—that is, if long-term bond yields exceed short-term bond yields—then investors must expect short-term yields to rise. According to the theory, it is only when investors expect short-term rates to rise that they are willing to forgo the higher current yield on a long-term bond and instead purchase a short-term bond. Conversely, when the yield curve inverts and short-term yields exceed long-term yields, investors must expect short-term rates to fall. Only then would they willingly accept the lower yield on long-term bonds.

---

[13]When we solve for the expected interest rate in year 2 that equates the returns on two 1-year investments to the returns on one 2-year investment, we are solving for the **forward interest rate**. Under expectations theory, forward interest rates provide unbiased forecasts of future spot interest rates. That is, forward interest rates predict where interest rates are headed.

Liquidity Preference Theory Unfortunately, the slope of the yield curve does not always provide a reliable signal of future interest-rate movements, perhaps because expectations theory ignores several factors that may be important to investors and may influence the shape of the yield curve. The first factor is that investors may have a preference for investing in short-term securities. As we have seen, for a given change in the required return, the prices of long-term bonds fluctuate more than the prices of short-term bonds; this added risk might deter some investors from investing in long-term bonds. To attract investors, perhaps long-term bonds must offer a return that exceeds the expected return on a series of short-term bonds. Therefore, when the yield curve slopes upward, we cannot be sure whether this is a result of investors expecting interest rates to rise or simply a reflection of long-term rates being higher to compensate for risk. The **liquidity preference theory** of the term structure recognizes this issue and states that the slope of the yield curve is influenced not only by expected interest-rate changes, but also by the liquidity premium that investors require on long-term bonds.

Preferred Habitat Theory Interpreting the slope of the yield curve as a signal of future interest-rate movements is more challenging if certain investors always purchase bonds with a particular maturity. For instance, pension funds that promise retirement income to investors, as well as life insurance companies that provide death benefits to policyholders, have very long term liabilities. These companies may have a strong desire to invest in long-term bonds (the longest available in the market) in order to match the maturity of their liabilities, even if long-term bonds offer lower expected returns than a series of short-term bonds. Indeed, demand for very long term bonds by pension funds and life insurance companies is one of the driving forces behind the recent decisions of some governments to issue bonds with maturities as long as 50 years. Economists use the **preferred habitat theory** (or the *market segmentation theory*) to describe the effect of this behavior on the yield curve. Short-term bond rates may exceed long-term rates because the demand for long-term bonds is high relative to their supply. This demand drives up long-term bond prices and so drives down their yields. If investors purchasing long-term bonds have a strong preference to invest in those securities despite their low yields, then the downward-sloping yield curve does not necessarily imply that investors expect interest rates to fall.[14]

Our understanding of the yield curve continues to evolve. It appears that the slope of the yield curve provides information that is helpful in forecasting interest rates but that this information is not sufficient to generate forecasts with great accuracy. For now, the most important points are that (1) bond prices derive from the present values of their cash flows and (2) prices of long-term bonds generally fluctuate more than those of short-term bonds in response to interest-rate changes. We now turn our attention from pricing bonds to pricing stocks.

Concept Review Questions	8. What is the yield curve? What type of information does it provide? 9. Briefly compare and contrast the three theories that have been offered to explain yield-curve behavior. Which theory is generally accepted?

---

[14]Do you have a favorite place to go and enjoy a beer with your peers? Is the price of beer there the lowest price in town? If not, then you are behaving according to the preferred habitat theory. You prefer to go to a particular establishment to socialize, even though you could buy the same beer at another location for less money. In the same way, some investors might prefer to invest in long-term bonds even though a series of short-term bonds offered a higher expected return.

4.4 STOCK VALUATION

In this section, we examine valuation models for two types of stock: preferred and common. Even though the characteristics of bonds and stocks seem quite different, the principles involved in valuing debt and equity are much the same. However, applying those principles to equity securities can be challenging. Therefore, we begin with preferred stock, a security that resembles debt as much as it does equity.

Preferred Stock Valuation

Smart
Practices
Video

Todd Richter, Managing
Director, Bank of America

*"The concepts of value, the
things that drive value, don't
change."*

See the entire interview at
SMART**Finance**

Neither a pure debt nor a pure equity instrument, preferred stock exhibits characteristics of both. Like bonds, preferred stock usually pays investors a fixed cash flow stream over time. The fixed cash flow, the *preferred dividend*, is typically expressed as a percentage of par value, similar to a bond's coupon rate. However, if firms do not generate enough cash flow to meet preferred dividend payments then preferred shareholders, unlike bondholders, cannot force the firm into bankruptcy after failure to make a promised payment. In that sense, preferred stockholders are in a legal position similar to that of common shareholders, although preferred shares generally do not carry the right to vote. Most preferred stock is *cumulative*; this means that, if a firm skips a preferred dividend payment, then it cannot pay dividends to common shareholders until it makes up for all unpaid dividends to preferred shareholders. Finally, like equity, preferred stock typically has no fixed maturity date. For that reason, we treat preferred stock as a security with an infinite life in our valuation formulas.

In Chapter 3, you learned a shortcut for valuing a *perpetuity*—an annuity with an infinite life. To find today's value of a preferred stock, PS_0, we use Equation 3.10 for the present value of a perpetuity, dividing the preferred dividend, D_P, by the required rate of return on the preferred stock, r_P:

$$PS_0 = \frac{D_P}{r_P}$$

EXAMPLE

In 1947, Alcoa, Inc., issued preferred stock paying an annual dividend of $3.75. Moody's and Standard & Poor's both rated Alcoa's preferred shares at the low end of the investment grade category. Suppose that, in December 2009, investors required a return on Alcoa preferred stock of 6⅛%. What would be the market price of the shares assuming that the next dividend is paid in one year?

$$\text{Price} = \frac{\$3.75}{0.06125} = \$61.22$$

Now suppose the rating agencies upgrade Alcoa's credit rating and, as a result, investors lower their required return to 5.5%. What happens to the preferred stock price?

$$\text{Price} = \frac{\$3.75}{0.055} = \$68.18$$

As a source of capital for American industry, preferred stock has been in decline for at least six decades and now represents well under 5% of the net external financing for U.S. companies each year. This is at least partly due to tax factors. The U.S. tax code treats preferred dividends more like dividends on common stock than interest on bonds. Firms cannot deduct preferred dividends as business expenses as they can interest payments on debt. Individuals who receive preferred stock dividends from domestic corporations are subject to the same 15% maximum tax rate that is levied on common stock dividends received.[15] Because preferred shares offer a fixed dividend, the prospect of earning large capital gains (which are generally taxed at the same preferential rates as common and preferred dividends) on them is small relative to the potential for gains on common stock. Consequently, preferred stocks face a tax disadvantage relative to bonds at the corporate level and, at the investor level, a capital gain disadvantage relative to common stocks.

Common and preferred stocks do enjoy one type of comparative tax advantage over debt. In order to avoid taxing cash payments between corporate parents and subsidiaries, Congress has allowed corporations that receive cash dividends on stock they own to exclude a large fraction of those receipts from corporate tax. For this reason, corporations have become the principal holders of preferred stock in the United States. Additionally, businesses sometimes issue new preferred stock as part of merger and acquisition transactions, especially when the company being purchased has preferred stock outstanding. In these cases, the acquiring firm often issues its own preferred shares to replace those previously issued by the target company. Acquirers commonly issue *convertible preferred stock*—shares that the holder can convert into a prespecified number of shares of common stock—in exchange for the common stock of the target firm.

EXAMPLE

In September 2008 the "Sage of Omaha," Warren Buffett, invested $5 billion in Goldman Sachs. In exchange, Buffett's company, Berkshire Hathaway, received preferred shares paying a 10% dividend. Buffett also received the right to buy shares of Goldman common stock (which was trading at about $120 at the time) for $115 per share. News of the transaction boosted Goldman shares and the shares of other financial institutions, and the media wondered whether Buffett's investment signaled the end of that summer's dramatic financial crisis. The jump in Goldman's shares left Buffet with a 24-hour profit (on paper) of nearly $750 million.

Preferred stock also plays a key role in one other small but extremely influential area of American finance—venture capital financing. Venture capital firms raise and invest billions of dollars each year in private firms, usually those with high growth potential. Venture capitalists frequently structure their investments in these high-risk, high-return companies in the form of convertible preferred stock.

The Basic Common Stock Valuation Equation

As expressed in Equation 4.1, the value of a share of common stock equals the present value of all future benefits that investors expect it to provide. Unlike bonds, which have contractual cash flows, common stocks have cash flows that are noncontractual and unspecified. What are the benefits expected from a share of common stock? When you buy a share of stock, you may expect to receive a periodic dividend payment from the firm, and you probably hope to sell the stock for more than its purchase price. But when you sell the stock, you are simply passing the rights to future benefits to the new buyer.

[15]In late 2008, dividends and capital gains were taxed at the same rate. However, there was talk in Washington of raising dividend tax rates above the rates on long-term capital gains.

The buyer purchases the stock from you in the belief that the future benefits—dividends and capital gains—justify the purchase price. This logic extends to the next investor who buys the stock from the person who bought it from you, and so on ad infinitum. Simply put, the value of common stock equals the present value of all future dividends that investors expect the stock to distribute, even if those dividends are not expected to be paid until many years in the future.[16]

The easiest way to understand this argument is as follows. Suppose that an investor buys a stock today for price P_0, receives a dividend equal to D_1 at the end of one year, and immediately sells the stock for price P_1. The return on this investment is easy to calculate:

$$r = \frac{D_1 + P_1 - P_0}{P_0}$$

The numerator of this expression equals the dollar profit or loss from receiving the dividend and net gain in stock price. Dividing that by the purchase price converts the return into percentage form. Rearrange this equation to solve for the current stock price:

$$P_0 = \frac{D_1 + P_1}{1 + r} \qquad \text{(Eq. 4.4)}$$

This equation indicates that the value of a stock today equals the present value of cash that the investor receives in one year. But what determines P_1, the selling price at the end of the year? Use Equation 4.4 again, changing the time subscripts to reflect that the price next year will equal the present value of the dividend and selling price received two years from now:

$$P_1 = \frac{D_2 + P_2}{1 + r}$$

Now, take this expression for P_1 and substitute it back into Equation 4.4:

$$P_0 = \frac{D_1 + \dfrac{D_2 + P_2}{1 + r}}{1 + r} = \frac{D_1}{(1 + r)^1} + \frac{D_2 + P_2}{(1 + r)^2}$$

This expression states that the price of a stock today equals the present value of the dividends it will pay over the next two years, plus the present value of the selling price in two years. Again we could ask, what determines the selling price in two years, P_2? By repeating the last two steps over and over, we can determine the price of a stock today:

$$P_0 = \frac{D_1}{(1 + r)^1} + \frac{D_2}{(1 + r)^2} + \frac{D_3}{(1 + r)^3} + \frac{D_4}{(1 + r)^4} + \frac{D_5}{(1 + r)^5} + \cdots \qquad \text{(Eq. 4.5)}$$

Comparing Equation 4.5 to the general valuation equation, Equation 4.1, we see that the equations are identical except that the cash flows (CF) in Equation 4.1 are replaced with the common stock dividends (D) in Equation 4.5.

The price today equals the present value of the entire dividend stream that the stock will pay. To calculate this price, an analyst must have two inputs: the future dividends

---

[16]Firms can distribute cash directly to shareholders in forms other than dividends. For instance, many firms regularly buy back their own shares. Also, when an acquiring firm buys a target, it may distribute cash to the target's shareholders. In this discussion, we assume for simplicity that cash payments always come in the form of dividends, but the logic of the argument holds if we allow for other forms of cash payments as well.

and the appropriate discount rate. Neither input is easy to estimate. The discount rate, or the rate of return required by the market on this stock, depends on the stock's risk. We defer until Chapters 5 and 6 a full discussion of how to measure a stock's risk and how to translate that risk into a required rate of return. Here we focus on the problem of estimating dividends. In most cases, analysts can formulate reasonably accurate estimates of dividends one year in the future. The real trick is to determine how quickly dividends will grow over time. Our discussion of stock valuation centers on three possible scenarios for dividend growth: zero growth, constant growth, and variable growth. After discussing these dividend models, we present the free cash flow approach to valuing an enterprise.

Zero Growth

The simplest approach to dividend valuation, the **zero growth model**, assumes a constant dividend stream. If dividends do not grow, then we can write

$$D_1 = D_2 = \cdots = D$$

Plugging the constant value D for each dividend payment into Equation 4.5, you can see that the valuation formula simply reduces to the equation for the present value of a perpetuity:

$$P_0 = \frac{D}{r}$$

In this special case, the formula for valuing common stock is identical to that for valuing preferred stock.

EXAMPLE

Ryder System, Inc. (ticker symbol, R), a provider of transportation and supply chain management solutions, paid a dividend of $0.15 per quarter, or $0.60 per year, without interruption from March 1989 to November 2004. Perhaps after 15 years of receiving the same dividend, investors believed that Ryder would continue to pay this steady dividend indefinitely. What price would they be willing to pay for Ryder stock?

The answer depends on investors' required rate of return. If investors demand a 10% return on Ryder stock then the stock should be worth $0.60 ÷ 0.10, or $6 (making the simplifying assumption that the dividend is paid once per year).[17] In fact, in the spring of 2005, Ryder stock traded in the vicinity of $40 to $45 per share. This implies one of two things: either investors required a rate of return on Ryder stock that was much less than 10%, which is implausible, or investors expected dividends to grow even though they hadn't for a long time. That expectation was partially realized when the firm increased its dividend, for the first time in 16 years, to $0.16 per quarter in February 2005; as of May 2009, Ryder had raised the quarterly dividend to $0.23, a 53% increase since the end of the 15-year streak of constant dividends.

---

[17]If you do not make this assumption, you can apply the same formula to quarterly dividends as long as you make an appropriate adjustment in the interest rate. For example, if investors expect a 10% effective annual rate of return on Ryder stock, then they expect a quarterly return of $(1.10)^{0.25} - 1$, or 2.41%. Using this figure, you can recalculate the stock price by dividing $0.15, the quarterly dividend, by 0.0241 to obtain $6.22. Why is Ryder stock more valuable in this calculation? Ryder's dividends arrive more often than once a year, so the present value of the dividend stream is greater.

Constant Growth

Of all the relatively simple stock valuation models that we consider in this chapter, the **constant growth model** is probably the most used in practice. This model assumes that dividends will grow at a constant rate, g. If dividends grow at a constant rate forever, then we can calculate the value of that cash flow stream by using the formula (given in Equation 3.11) for a growing perpetuity. Denoting next year's dividend as D_1, we can determine the value today of a stock that pays a dividend growing at a constant rate:[18]

$$P_0 = \frac{D_1}{r - g}$$

(Eq. 4.6)

The constant growth model in Equation 4.6 is commonly called the **Gordon growth model** after Myron Gordon, who popularized this formula during the 1960s and 1970s.

EXAMPLE

Few public companies have achieved a longer streak of uninterrupted increases in dividends than Integrys Energy Group, Inc. (ticker symbol, TEG), a holding company that provides administrative support primarily to its regulated utility subsidiaries. Integrys increased its dividend every year for 20 years, from 1988 to 2009. Over this period, the compound annual dividend growth rate was 2.75%. Suppose that investors expected an annual dividend of $2.79 in 2010. Although this dividend is paid quarterly, we assume that the entire dividend is received in May 2010 and is expected to continue to grow at 2.75% annually. What should be the price of TEG stock in May 2009?

Suppose that investors require a 10% rate of return on the stock of Integrys. Substituting into the constant growth model, Equation 4.6, we obtain the following value for TEG stock in May 2009:

$$P_0 = \frac{\$2.79}{0.100 - 0.0275} = \$38.48$$

In May 2009, Integrys shares traded in the $25–$30 range, so our estimate of the stock's value is a little too high. Remember that, in 2009, the U.S. was in the midst of a deep recession. During such a time, investors probably lower their expectations of dividend growth and raise their required return on stocks because investors perceive the risk of equity investments to be particularly high when the economy is weak. In the example above, if we reduce our forecast of dividend growth to 2% and increase the expected return to 12%, we would obtain a new estimate of $27.90, very close to the stock's actual market value in May 2009.

Smart Concepts

See the concept explained step-by-step at

SMARTFinance

We do not want to oversell the accuracy of the constant growth model. We based our calculations on a reasonable set of assumptions, using the long-run growth rate in dividends for g and the long-run rate of return on Integrys stock for r. By making small adjustments to the dividend, the required rate of return, or the growth rate, we could easily obtain an estimate for Integrys stock that matches the current market price in May 2009. Yet we could also obtain a very different price with an equally reasonable set of assumptions. For instance, decreasing the required rate of return to 9% and increasing the dividend growth rate to 3% increases the price to $46.50! Obviously, analysts want to estimate the inputs for Equation 4.6 as precisely as possible, but the amount of uncertainty inherent in estimating required rates of return and growth rates makes obtaining precise valuations very difficult.

---

[18]To apply this equation, one must assume that $r > g$. Of course, dividends at some firms may grow very rapidly for a short time, so that $g > r$ temporarily. We treat the case of firms that grow rapidly for a finite period later in the discussion. In the long run, it is reasonable to assume that r must eventually exceed g.

Nevertheless, the constant growth model provides a useful way to think about stock valuation problems, highlighting the important inputs and in some cases providing price estimates that seem fairly reasonable. But the model should not be applied blindly to all types of firms, especially not to those enjoying rapid (albeit temporary) growth.

Variable Growth

The zero growth and constant growth common stock valuation models just presented do not allow for any shift in expected growth rates. However, many firms go through periods of relatively fast growth followed by a period of more stable growth. Valuing the stock of such a firm requires a **variable growth model**, one in which the dividend growth rate can vary. Using our earlier notation and letting D_0 equal the last or most recent per share dividend paid, g_1 the initial (fast) growth rate of dividends, g_2 the subsequent (stable) growth rate of dividends, and N the number of years in the initial growth period, we can write the general equation for the variable growth model as follows:

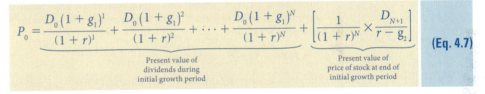

$$P_0 = \underbrace{\frac{D_0(1+g_1)^1}{(1+r)^1} + \frac{D_0(1+g_1)^2}{(1+r)^2} + \cdots + \frac{D_0(1+g_1)^N}{(1+r)^N}}_{\substack{\text{Present value of} \\ \text{dividends during} \\ \text{initial growth period}}} + \underbrace{\left[\frac{1}{(1+r)^N} \times \frac{D_{N+1}}{r-g_2} \right]}_{\substack{\text{Present value of} \\ \text{price of stock at end of} \\ \text{initial growth period}}}$$ (Eq. 4.7)

As indicated by the labels, the first part of the equation calculates the present value of the dividends expected during the initial growth period and the second part represents the present value of the stock price calculated at the end of the initial growth period, which is found using the constant growth model. The following Example demonstrates the application of this formula.

EXAMPLE

A food company has developed a new fat-free ice cream and, as the popularity of the product increases, the firm (unlike its customers) will grow quite rapidly—perhaps as much as 20% per year. Over time, as the market share of this new food increases, the firm's growth rate will reach a steady state. At that point, the firm may grow at the same rate as the overall economy, perhaps 5% per year. Assume that the market's required rate of return on this stock is 14%.

To value the food company's stock, you need to break the future stream of cash flows into two parts: the first consists of the period of rapid growth, and the second is the constant growth phase. Suppose that the firm's most recent (year-0) dividend was $2 per share. You anticipate that the firm will increase the dividend by 20% per year for the next three years, after which time it will grow at 5% per year indefinitely. The expected dividend stream looks like this:

Fast Growth Phase ($g_1 = 20\%$)		Stable Growth Phase ($g_2 = 5\%$)	
Year	Dividend	Year	Dividend
0	$2.00	4	$3.63
1	2.40	5	3.81
2	2.88	6	4.00
3	3.46	7	4.20

(continued)

The value of the dividends during the fast growth phase is calculated as follows:

$$\text{PV of dividends in fast growth phase} = \frac{\$2.40}{(1.14)^1} + \frac{\$2.88}{(1.14)^2} + \frac{\$3.46}{(1.14)^3}$$

$$= \$2.11 + \$2.22 + \$2.33 = \$6.66$$

The stable growth phase begins with the dividend paid four years from now. The final term of Equation 4.7 is actually Equation 4.6, which indicates that the value of a constant growth stock at time t equals the dividend one year later (at time $t + 1$) divided by the difference between the required rate of return and the growth rate. Applying that formula here means valuing the stock at the end of year 3, just before the constant growth phase begins:

$$P_3 = \frac{D_4}{r - g_2} = \frac{\$3.63}{0.14 - 0.05} = \$40.33$$

Don't forget that $40.33 is the price of the stock three years from now. Today's present value equals $40.33 ÷ (1.14)^3 = \$27.22$. This represents the value today of all dividends that will occur in year 4 and beyond. Putting the pieces together yields the following expression for the stock's total value:

$$P_0 = \$6.66 + \$27.22 = \$33.88$$

This calculation is depicted on the time line in Figure 4.6. It can be shown more compactly in this single algebraic expression:

$$P_0 = \frac{\$2.40}{(1.14)^1} + \frac{\$2.88}{(1.14)^2} + \frac{\$3.46 + \$40.33}{(1.14)^3} = \$33.88$$

The numerator of the last term contains both the final dividend payment of the fast growth phase, $3.46, and the present value *as of the end of year 3* of all future dividends, $40.33. The value of the firm's stock using the variable growth model is $33.88. This value can be calculated efficiently using a financial calculator or spreadsheet.

FIGURE 4.6

Time Line for Variable Growth Valuation

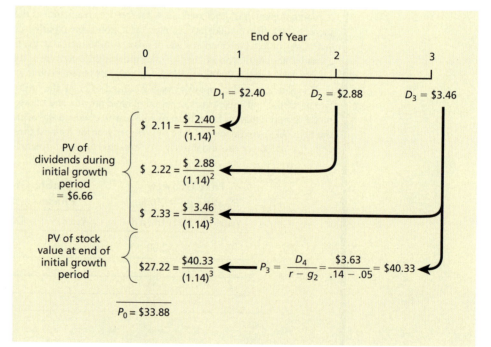

How to Estimate Growth

By now it should be apparent that a central component in many stock pricing models is the growth rate. Unfortunately, analysts face a tremendous challenge in estimating a firm's growth rate, whether that rate applies to dividends, earnings, sales, or almost any other measure of financial performance. A firm's rate of growth depends on several factors, but among the most important are the size of the investments it makes in new and existing projects and the rate of return that those investments earn.

A simple but rather naive method for estimating how fast a firm will grow relies on information from financial statements. This approach acknowledges the importance of new investments in driving future growth. First, calculate the magnitude of new investments that the firm can make by determining its *retention rate* (RR), the fraction of the firm's earnings that it retains. Second, calculate the firm's return on common equity, ROE, to estimate the rate of return that new investments will generate. The product of those two values is the firm's expected growth rate, *g*:

$$g = \text{RR} \times \text{ROE}$$

(Eq. 4.8)

EXAMPLE

Simon Manufacturing traditionally retains 75% of its earnings to finance new investments and pays out 25% as dividends. Last year, Simon's net income was $44.6 million and the book value of its equity was $297.33 million, resulting in a return on common equity (ROE) of 15%. Substituting into Equation 4.8 and multiplying the retention rate by the return on common equity, we estimate Simon's expected growth rate as follows:

$g = 0.75 \times 0.15 = 0.1125$

This approach estimates Simon's growth to be 11.25%.

An alternative approach to estimating expected growth rates makes use of historical data. Analysts track a firm's sales, earnings, and dividends over several years in an attempt to identify growth trends. But how well do growth rates from the past predict growth rates in the future? Unfortunately, the correlation between past and future growth rates for most firms is surprisingly low. Chan, Karceski, and Lakonishok (2003) report that future growth is almost completely unrelated to past growth—there is very little persistence in growth rates over time. They argue that analysts tend to be too optimistic about the expected future growth of firms that have had high growth rates in the past.

That expected growth rates are largely unpredictable should not come as a great surprise. One of the most fundamental ideas in economics is that competition limits the ability of a firm to generate abnormally high profits for a sustained period of time. If one company identifies a profitable business opportunity then people notice, and entrepreneurs (or other companies) attempt to enter the same line of business. As more and more firms enter, profit (or its rate of growth) falls. If the industry becomes sufficiently competitive then, at some point, profits will fall to such a low level that some firms will exit. As firms exit, profits for the remaining firms rise again. The constant pressure created by these competitive forces means that it is rare to observe a firm with a consistent, long-term growth trend. Perhaps one reason companies like Microsoft and Intel are so well known is that their histories of exceptional long-run growth are so uncommon.

Although it may be extremely difficult to predict how rapidly firms will grow, there is no doubt that stock prices reflect the value of firms' expected growth opportunities. Consider the consumer products firm Procter & Gamble (P&G). In late 2008, most analysts predicted that P&G would generate earnings of about $4.28 per share in fiscal year 2009. Suppose investors believed that P&G would stop reinvesting earnings to finance new investments and that P&G would simply distribute all its earnings to investors. If P&G could distribute $4.28 per share in perpetuity and if the required return on P&G stock were 10%, then the price of P&G stock would be $42.80 ($4.28 ÷ 0.10). In fact, the price of P&G stock in December 2008 fluctuated around $62.50. That price clearly implied that investors expected P&G to make new investments that would increase earnings and dividends over time.

We generalize this idea as follows. The price of any stock can be divided into two parts. The first part is the amount that investors would be willing to pay if a firm generated a constant annual earnings stream (E) in perpetuity and distributed it to investors. The second part represents the additional present value associated with expected future growth opportunities, or PVGO. Mathematically, we have

$$P_0 = \frac{E_1}{r} + \text{PVGO}$$

This equation indicates that the current stock price equals the present value of a perpetual earnings stream *plus* the present value of growth opportunities. For Procter & Gamble, the present value of growth opportunities in late 2008 was about $19.70: the difference between the actual $62.50 stock price and $42.80, the present value of a constant earnings stream of $4.28 per share.

What If There Are No Dividends?

After seeing the different versions of the dividend growth models, students usually ask: "What about firms that don't pay dividends?" Though many large, well-established firms in the United States pay regular dividends, most companies do not pay dividends at all. Of the thousands of companies listed on the NYSE, AMEX, and Nasdaq, as many as 80% pay no cash dividends in a given year. Fama and French (2001) report that the percentage of U.S. firms paying cash dividends fell from 66.5% in 1978 to 20.8% in 1999, though the trend reversed somewhat by 2003. Nonetheless, the long-term trend is for fewer firms to pay dividends, a trend that reflects a shift in the characteristics of U.S. public corporations. Specifically, the fraction of relatively young firms rose with the boom of the initial public offering (IPO) market in the 1990s, especially in the technology sector. Younger firms with excellent growth prospects are traditionally less likely to pay dividends than are more mature firms. However, even controlling for the changing characteristics of listed firms, the overall propensity for a given type of firm to pay dividends has fallen over time.

Can we apply the stock valuation models covered thus far to firms that pay no dividends? Yes and no. On the affirmative side, firms that do not currently pay dividends may begin paying them in the future. In that case, we simply modify the equations presented earlier to reflect that the firm pays its first dividend not within one year but rather several years in the future. However, from an entirely practical standpoint, predicting when firms will begin paying dividends and what the dollar value of those far-off dividends will be is virtually impossible. Consider the problem of forecasting dividends for a company like Google. Since its IPO in August 2004, Google has paid no cash dividends even though its revenues have increased from about $3.2 billion to $21.8 billion in 2008. The company was consistently profitable and had accumulated $15.8 billion in cash reserves. Is Google ready

WHAT COMPANIES DO GLOBALLY

Factors that Influence U.S. Investors in Foreign Markets

This chapter is primarily about valuing stocks and bonds. But when investors decide whether to buy stock in companies located in other countries, many factors influence that decision beyond a simple valuation analysis. Leuz, Lins, and Warnock have studied the factors that influence the extent to which U.S. investors hold shares in foreign markets. One factor the authors studied is the degree of family control over firms in different countries. To be more specific, the authors determine the percentage of firms in each country in which family members held a larger stake than any

other investor. Evidently, firms controlled by families are less attractive to U.S. investors: the trend line in the following graph shows that, as the percentage of firms controlled by family shareholders rises, investment by U.S. investors falls. More generally, this study finds that U.S. investors invest less in countries where legal protections for outside investors are poor and where the quality of accounting information is low.

Source: Christian Leuz, Karl V. Lins, and Francis E. Warnock, "Do Foreigners Invest Less in Poorly Governed Firms?" *Review of Financial Studies*, published online on October 8, 2008.

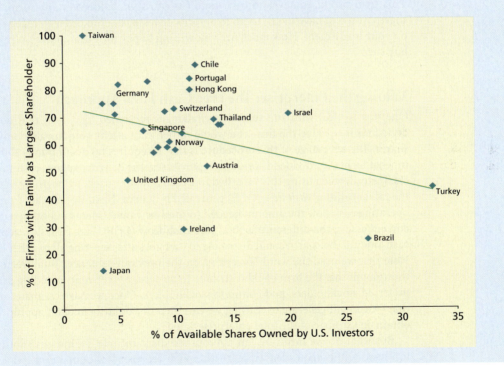

to start paying dividends, will it continue to reinvest income to finance growth, or will it be acquired by another firm? In all likelihood, investors will have to wait several years to receive Google's first dividend, and there is no way to determine with any degree of precision when that will happen.

Perhaps firms that don't pay dividends will repurchase stock instead. In that event, we modify the valuation equations to focus on cash payments made to shareholders—whether the payments come in the form of dividends or share buybacks. However, some firms neither pay dividends nor engage in share repurchases, in which case we are still left with the valuation problem for no-dividend firms.

Analysts confronted with the problem of valuing firms that do not pay dividends have several alternative models at their disposal. Each of these models has strengths and weaknesses, and each should be applied with caution. Before discussing the details of those models, we want to comment on another question we hear frequently: What happens if a company never plans to pay a dividend, repurchase shares, or otherwise distribute cash to investors? Students point to a firm like Oracle that has been in business for many years and certainly has sufficient cash flow to pay dividends. Don't thousands of investors buy and sell Oracle shares every day with no expectation of ever receiving dividends? Our answer to this question is that, for a stock to have value, there must be some expectation that the firm will distribute cash to investors in some form at some point in the future. That cash could come in the form of dividends or share repurchases. If the firm is acquired by another company for cash, then the cash payment will come when the acquiring firm purchases the shares of the target. Investors must believe that they will receive cash at some point in the future. If you have a hard time believing this, we invite you to buy shares in the Graham, Smart, & Megginson Corporation, a firm expected to generate an attractive revenue stream from selling its products and services. This firm promises never to distribute cash to shareholders in any form. If you buy shares, you will have to sell them to another investor later in order to realize any return on your investment. How much are you willing to pay for these shares? Why would you buy them?

Valuing the Enterprise: The Free Cash Flow Approach

One way to deal with the valuation challenges presented by a firm that does not pay dividends is to value the firm as a whole rather than attempting to value only the firm's shares. The advantage of this procedure is that it requires no assumptions about when or in what form (i.e., dividends or share repurchases) the firm distributes cash to stockholders. Instead, when using this so-called free cash flow approach, we begin by asking what is the total *operating cash flow* (OCF) generated by a firm. Next, we subtract from the firm's operating cash flow the amount needed to fund new investments in both fixed assets and current assets; the difference is total **free cash flow (FCF)**. Free cash flow represents the cash amount that a firm could distribute to investors after meeting all its other obligations. Note that we used the word "investors" in the previous sentence. Total free cash flow is the amount that the firm could distribute to *all types of investors*, including bondholders, preferred stockholders, and common stockholders. Once we have estimates of the FCFs that a firm will generate over time, we can then discount them at an appropriate rate to obtain an estimate of the total enterprise value.

But what do we mean by "an appropriate discount rate"? This is a subtle issue, but to illustrate the main idea we recall that FCF represents the total cash available for *all* investors. For investors in a given firm, debt is not as risky as preferred stock, and preferred stock is not as risky as common stock. This means that bondholders, preferred shareholders, and common stockholders each have a different required return in mind when they buy the firm's securities. Somehow we have to capture these varying required rates of return to come up with a single discount rate that can be applied to the free cash flows available to all three types of investors. This type of discount rate is known as the **weighted average cost of capital (WACC)**. The WACC is the after-tax weighted average required return on all types of securities issued by the firm, where the weights equal the percentage of each type of financing in the firm's overall capital structure. For example, suppose that a firm finances its operation with 50% debt and 50% common stock equity. Suppose further that this firm pays an after-tax return of 8% on its outstanding debt and that investors require a 16% return on the firm's shares of common stock. Then the WACC for this firm would be calculated as

$$\text{WACC} = (0.50 \times 8\%) + (0.50 \times 16\%) = 12\%$$

If we obtain forecasts of the FCFs and if we discount those cash flows at a 12% rate, then the resulting present value is an estimate of the total value of the firm.

When analysts value free cash flows, they use the same types of models we have used to value dividend streams. We could assume that a firm's free cash flows will experience zero, constant, or variable growth, and in each instance the procedures and equations would be the same as those introduced earlier for dividends—except now we would substitute FCF for dividends.

Recall that our goal in using the free cash flow approach was to develop a method for valuing a firm's shares of common stock without making assumptions about its dividends. The free cash flow approach begins by estimating the total value of the firm. To find out what the firm's shares of common stock are worth (V_S), we subtract from the total enterprise value (V_F) the value of the firm's debt (V_D) and the value of the firm's preferred stock (V_P). Equation 4.9 expresses this mathematically:

$$V_S = V_F - V_D - V_P \qquad \textbf{(Eq. 4.9)}$$

We already know how to value bonds and preferred shares, so this step is relatively straightforward. Once we subtract the value of debt and preferred stock from the total enterprise value, the remainder equals the total value of the firm's shares of common stock. Simply divide this total by the number of shares outstanding to calculate the value per share, P_0.

EXAMPLE

Had a good cup of coffee lately? Probably the best-known purveyor of coffee is Starbucks Corp. (ticker symbol, SBUX). Its stock traded in the $50–$60 range during the first calendar quarter of 2005. At the end of its 2004 fiscal year (September 30, 2004), Starbucks had debt with a market value of about $200 million, had issued no preferred stock, and had 398.79 million shares of common stock outstanding. Its fiscal year–2004 free cash flow, calculated using the techniques presented in Chapter 2, was about $233 million. Its revenues and operating profits grew at compound annual rates of about 27% and 38%, respectively, between fiscal years 2002 and 2004. Indeed, many consumers were buying Starbucks coffee during that period. At the same time the coffee market was growing, competition was beginning to heat up. Analysts predicted that Starbucks would experience about 25% annual growth in FCF from the end of 2004 through 2008, followed by 10% annual growth thereafter as a result of competition and maturation of the market.[19] We assume that Starbucks' WACC equals 12%.

The following table illustrates the calculations that an analyst might have made to estimate the value of Starbucks as of 2005. The analysis begins with forecasts for Starbucks' free cash

(continued)

---

[19]The analysts' forecast of 10% growth is unrealistic because it exceeds the expected GDP growth at that time. Given the infinite time horizon, a firm that grows faster than GDP would ultimately become the market.

flow, starting with the actual free cash flow in 2004 and projecting to 2009, the beginning of the stable growth phase.

End of Fiscal Year	Growth Status	Growth Rate (%)	FCF Calculation	FCF
2004	Historic	—	Given	$233,000,000
2005	Fast	25	$233,000,000 \times (1.25)^1$	$291,250,000
2006	Fast	25	$233,000,000 \times (1.25)^2$	$364,062,500
2007	Fast	25	$233,000,000 \times (1.25)^3$	$455,078,125
2008	Fast	25	$233,000,000 \times (1.25)^4$	$568,847,656
2009	Stable	10	$568,847,656 \times (1.10)^1$	$625,732,422

Letting $D_t = \text{FCF}_t$ in Equation 4.7 and substituting $N = 4$, $r = 0.12$, and $g_2 = 0.10$, we can estimate Starbucks' enterprise value at the beginning of 2005, V_{F2005}:

$$V_{F2005} = \frac{\$291,250,000}{(1.12)^1} + \frac{\$364,062,500}{(1.12)^2} + \frac{\$455,078,125}{(1.12)^3} + \frac{\$568,847,656}{(1.12)^4}$$

$$+ \left[\frac{1}{(1.12)^4} \times \frac{\$625,732,422}{0.12 - 0.10} \right]$$

$$= \$264,044,643 + \$290,228,396 + \$323,915,621 + \$361,512,969 + \$19,883,210,000$$

$$= \$21,122,911,629$$

Substituting Starbucks' enterprise value (V_F) of $21,122,911,629, its debt value (V_D) of $200 million, and its preferred stock value (V_P) of $0 into Equation 4.9, we obtain its total common stock share value:

$$V_S = \$21,122,911,629 - \$200,000,000 - \$0$$

$$= \$20,922,911,629$$

Dividing the total share value by the 398,790,000 shares outstanding at the beginning of 2005 yields the per-share value of Starbucks' stock, P_{2005}:

$$P_{2005} = \frac{\$20,922,911,629}{398,790,000} = \$52.47$$

Our estimate of $20,922,911,629, or $52.47 per share, for Starbucks' total common stock value at the beginning of calendar year 2005 was within its actual trading range of $50–$60 per share during the first calendar quarter of 2005.

Smart Practices Video

Todd Richter, Managing Director, Bank of America

"For each and every company that I analyze I try to build a sector model."

See the entire interview at
SMARTFinance

The free cash flow approach offers an alternative to the dividend discount model that is especially useful when valuing shares that pay no dividends. As we'll see in the next section, security analysts have several alternative approaches at their disposal for estimating the value of shares, some of which do not rely on the discounted cash flow methods that we have studied so far.

Concept Review Questions

10. What preferred stock features resemble the characteristics of bonds more than common stock?
11. In the 1990s, many finance professionals interpreted the booming stock market as a sign that investors were requiring lower future returns on common stocks than they had in the past. Explain.
12. Using a dividend forecast of $2.79, a required return of 10%, and a growth rate of 2.75%, we obtained a price for Integrys of $38.48. Holding all these assumptions fixed, what will the price of the stock be one year later? What price increase from the original value of $38.48 does your new estimate represent (in percentage terms)? Explain.
13. How can analysts use the free cash flow approach to resolve the valuation challenge presented by firms that do not pay dividends? Compare and contrast this model with the dividend valuation models.

JOB INTERVIEW QUESTION

"How would you value a potential acquisition target?"

4.5 OTHER APPROACHES TO COMMON STOCK VALUATION

So far we have used discounted cash flow (DCF) techniques to value stocks. In some cases, analysts need to value firms that do not currently pay dividends or generate free cash flow. In these cases, or when they simply want an alternate estimate of value to compare to the DCF estimate, analysts use other methods that rely on a firm's financial statements or on data regarding the market prices of similar companies.

Book Value

Book value refers to the value of a firm's equity shown on its balance sheet. "Book equity" reflects the historical cost of the firm's assets, adjusted for depreciation, net of the firm's liabilities. Because of its backward-looking emphasis on historical cost figures, book value is less than market value for most companies most of the time. Book value does not incorporate information about a firm's potential to generate future cash flows, whereas market values are inherently forward-looking. An exception to this general rule occurs when firms experience financial distress. In some cases, such as when a firm's earnings prospects are very poor, the book value of equity may actually exceed its market value. For example, in early January of 2009, Citigroup's book value of equity was $18.10 while its shares were trading at $7.15. This situation was fairly common for financial institutions during that time because of the ongoing financial industry meltdown in the U.S. economy.

Liquidation Value

To calculate **liquidation value**, analysts estimate the amount of cash that would be left over if a firm sold all of its assets and paid off its liabilities. Liquidation value may be more or less than book value, depending on the marketability of the firm's assets and the depreciation charges that have been assessed against fixed assets. For example, an important asset on many corporate balance sheets is real estate. The value of raw land appears on the balance sheet at historical cost, but in many cases its market value is much higher. In that case, liquidation may exceed book value. In contrast, suppose the largest assets on a firm's balance sheet are highly customized machine tools that were purchased two years ago. If the firm depreciates these tools on a straight-line basis over five years, then the value shown on the books would equal 60% of the purchase price. However, there may be little or no secondary market for tools that have been customized for the firm's manufacturing processes. If the firm goes bankrupt and the machine tools must be liquidated, they may sell for much less than book value.

Price/Earnings Multiples

How do you decide what a house is worth? Most home buyers use information about recent sales of similar homes (e.g., homes in a certain location or of a given size) to decide how much they are willing to offer for a particular property. Likewise, managers, analysts, and investment bankers sometimes estimate the value of a particular firm by looking at the market prices of similar firms (e.g., firms in the same industry). Usually comparisons among similar firms focus not on the firms' stock prices per se but rather on the stock price relative to earnings.

The *price/earnings* (P/E) *ratio* reflects what investors are willing to pay for each dollar of earnings. The ratio simply equals the current stock price divided by annual earnings per share (EPS). The EPS used in the denominator of the P/E ratio may reflect either the earnings that analysts expect a firm to generate over the next year or earnings from the previous year.[20] An analyst using this method to value a stock might proceed as follows. First, forecast what the firm's EPS will be in the next year. Second, calculate a "normal" P/E ratio for firms in that industry. As the following discussion about P/E ratios highlights, it is important to consider what the *normal* growth rate is when determining the normal P/E ratio. Third, multiply the forecasted EPS by the industry P/E ratio to arrive at an estimate of what the stock price should be.

The financial press frequently ties a firm's P/E ratio to its growth prospects, using logic similar to the following. Suppose one firm has a P/E ratio of 50 while another has a P/E ratio of 20. Why would investors pay $50 per dollar of earnings for the first company and only $20 per dollar of earnings for the second? One possibility is that investors expect the first firm's earnings to grow more rapidly than those of the second firm. But you should be cautious in assuming that higher P/E ratios necessarily imply faster growth.

To see why, review Equation 4.6. It indicates that the price of a stock depends on three variables: the dividend next period, the required rate of return, and the dividend growth rate. We can modify this formula by assuming that a firm pays out a constant percentage of its earnings as dividends. If we denote this payout percentage as d and next year's earnings per share as E_1, then we can rewrite Equation 4.6 as follows:

$$P_0 = \frac{dE_1}{r - g}$$

In the numerator we have replaced the next year's dividend with the payout ratio multiplied by next year's earnings. Now, divide both sides of this equation by E_1 to obtain

$$\frac{P_0}{E_1} = \frac{d}{r - g}$$

On the left-hand side is the P/E ratio. Observe that if g increases then so does the P/E ratio. This provides some justification for the common notion that stocks with high P/E ratios have high growth potential. However, either an increase in the dividend payout or a decrease in the required return will also increase the P/E ratio. Therefore, when comparing P/E ratios of different firms, one cannot conclude that the firm with the higher P/E ratio necessarily has better growth prospects. In addition, interpreting a P/E ratio is virtually impossible when the firm's earnings are negative or close to zero. For example,

[20]Analysts refer to "leading" or "trailing" P/E ratios depending on whether the earnings number in the denominator is a forecast or a historical number.

WHAT COMPANIES DO

How Investment Bankers Value Companies

When one firm attempts to acquire another, both the bidder and the target firm may hire an investment banker to provide fairness opinions, written reports that provide the banker's expert opinion regarding the fairness of the price offered by the bidder. Matt Cain and David Denis have investigated which methods bankers use in their fairness opinions to value target firms. As the chart shows, bankers almost always perform a discounted cash flow valuation as part of their analysis, but they sometimes use other methods. In a slight majority of acquisitions, bankers value the target company by using comparisons to public-firm multiples such as P/E ratios. Bankers also use transaction multiples (price paid relative to target earnings in recent acquisitions) and transaction premia (what bidders have paid for targets, above and beyond their market values, in recent deals) when advising their clients.

Source: Matt Cain and David Dennis, "The Information Content of Fairness Opinions in Negotiated Mergers," Working paper (August 2008).

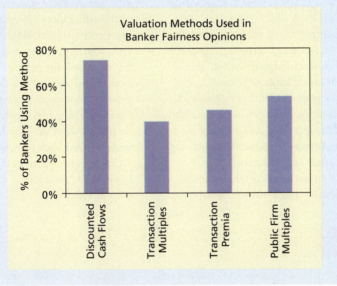

When one firm attempts to acquire another, both the

imagine that some firm in some year barely earns a profit, reporting an EPS of $0.01. Even if the firm's stock price is only $1 per share, it's P/E ratio will be 100. In such a case, the astronomical P/E ratio is an artifact of low current earnings rather than an indicator of growth potential. A potential solution to this problem is to use something other than earnings in the denominator of the ratio. For example, when earnings are near or below zero, analysts might create multiples by dividing stock prices by cash flow per share or book value per share, rather than by earnings per share.[21]

---

[21]Investment bankers use many different multiples to estimate the value of a firm. One variant of the P/E ratio uses EBITDA (earnings before interest, taxes, depreciation, and amortization), rather than earnings, in the denominator. Bankers sometimes argue that EBITDA provides a clearer measure of a firm's earning power than does net income. Ever the skeptic, Warren Buffett wondered in one of his annual reports whether advocates of the EBITDA measure ignored depreciation because they thought the tooth fairy paid for capital expenditures.

| Concept Review Questions | 14. Why is using either book value or liquidation value inconsistent with the concept of a "going concern"? |
| | 15. Why is it dangerous to conclude that a firm with a high P/E ratio will probably grow faster than a firm with a lower P/E ratio? |

Summary

- Conceptually, valuing bonds and stocks means discounting the stream of cash flows that will accrue to a security holder over that security's life. The sum of the discounted cash flows is the security's value.
- The appropriate discount rate to use to value a bond or stock is based primarily on the risk of that security's cash flows. Payments on Treasury securities are discounted at a risk-free rate; all other debt and equity securities are discounted at higher rates to reflect their higher risk.
- Bond issuers include corporations, municipalities, the U.S. government, and federal government agencies. Bond ratings help investors judge default risk; low-rated, high-risk bonds are called junk bonds.
- Ordinary bonds make periodic fixed cash payments, called coupons, to investors. Bond prices move in the opposite direction of interest rates, and prices of long-term bonds are generally more sensitive to interest-rate movements than are prices of short-term bonds.
- The term structure of interest rates is the relationship between time to maturity and yield to maturity for bonds having similar risk. A graphic representation of the term structure is called the yield curve.

- Preferred stock has no maturity and pays a constant periodic dividend. Therefore, preferred shares can be valued using the formula for the present value of a perpetuity.
- Common stock is often difficult to value; this is due to the inherent difficulty of determining which risk-adjusted discount rate is most "appropriate" and also to the difficulty of estimating dividends (or other cash payments to shareholders) far into the future.
- Discounting dividends to determine the stock price does not work well for certain firms, particularly those that have no history of paying dividends. When valuing such firms, analysts may value free cash flows to determine the enterprise value, which can be reduced to total common stock share value by deducting the value of all debt and preferred stock from the total enterprise value.
- Other approaches to valuing common stock include book value, liquidation value, and market multiples such as P/E ratios.

Key Terms

agency bonds	forward interest rate	risk-free bond
bank discount yield	free cash flow (FCF)	term structure of interest rates
basis points	Gordon growth model	Treasury bills
bond equivalent yield	interest-rate risk	Treasury bonds
bond indenture	internal rate of return (IRR)	Treasury notes
bond rating	junk bonds	variable growth model
book value	liquidation value	weighted average cost of capital
constant growth model	liquidity preference theory	(WACC)
corporate bonds	maturity	yield curve
coupon	municipal bonds	yield spread
coupon rate	nominal return	yield to maturity (YTM)
coupon yield	par value	zero growth model
default risk	preferred habitat theory	zero-coupon bond
discount	premium	
expectations theory	real return	

QUESTIONS

4-1. A firm issues a bond at par value. Shortly thereafter, interest rates fall. If you calculated the coupon rate, coupon yield, and yield to maturity for this bond after the decline in interest rates, which of the three values would be highest and which would be lowest? Explain.

4-2. Twenty-five years ago, the U.S. government issued 30-year bonds with a coupon rate of about 8%. Five years ago, the U.S. government sold 10-year bonds with a coupon rate of about 5%. Suppose that the current coupon rate on newly issued 5-year Treasury bonds is 2.5%. For an investor seeking a low-risk investment maturing in five years, do the bonds issued 25 years ago with a much higher coupon rate provide a more attractive return than the new 5-year bonds? What about the 10-year bonds issued five years ago?

4-3. What's a simple way to assess and compare the default risk of publicly traded bonds? Describe how a bond's interest rate risk is related to its maturity.

4-4. Under expectations theory, what does the slope of the yield curve reveal about the future path of interest rates? If the yield curve is typically upward sloping, what would this imply about the long-term path of interest rates if expectations theory were true?

4-5. In times of economic distress or uncertainty, many investors start buying high-quality bonds. What effect does this have on the prices of high-quality bonds and their associated yield to maturity?

4-6. Visit a website that posts an up-to-date yield curve. What is the current yield on long-term Treasury bonds? Next, using the web or the financial section of a newspaper, find the current prices of several outstanding preferred stocks. Make sure that the preferred shares you choose pay a fixed dividend and are not convertible into common stock. For each preferred stock, divide the annual dividend that the stock pays by the current market price. What should you expect to find?

4-7. Go to http://www.stockcharts.com/charts/YieldCurve.html and then click on the animated yield-curve graph. Answer the following questions:
a. Is the yield curve typically upward sloping, downward sloping, or flat?
b. Notice the behavior of the yield curve and the S&P 500 between July 28, 1998, and October, 19, 1998. In August 1998, Russia defaulted on billions of dollars of foreign debt. Then came the news in late September that, at the behest of the Federal Reserve, 15 financial institutions would infuse $3.5 billion of new capital into the Long-Term Capital Management hedge fund, which had lost nearly $2 billion in the previous month. Comment on these events as they related to movements in the yield curve and the S&P 500 that you see in the animation.

4-8. At http://www.nber.org/cycles.html, you can find the official beginning and ending dates for U.S. business cycles according to the National Bureau of Economic Research (NBER). For example, the NBER indicates that the U.S. economy was in recession from January 1980 to July 1980, from July 1981 to November 1982, and from July 1990 to March 1991. Next, go to http://www.smartmoney.com/onebond/index.cfm?story=yieldcurve and click on the animation of the Living Yield Curve. Pause the animation at November 1978. Then, click one frame at a time until May 1980. Pause again at November 1981, and then click one frame at a time until August 1982. Let the animation play again until you reach March 1989. What association do you notice between the shape of the yield curve and the NBER's dates for recessions?

4-9. Go to http://www.smartmoney.com/onebond/index.cfm?story=yieldcurve and click on the animation of the Living Yield Curve. Make a note of the overall level of the yield curve from about mid-1979 to mid-1982, and compare that to the level of the curve for most of the 1990s. What accounts for the differences in yield-curve levels in these two periods?

4-10. The value of common stocks cannot be tied to the present value of future dividends because many firms don't pay dividends. Comment on the validity, or lack thereof, of this statement.

4-11. A common fallacy in stock market investing is assuming that a good company makes a good investment. Suppose we define a "good company" as one that has experienced rapid growth in the recent past. Explain the reasons why shares of "good companies" may or may not turn out to be "good investments."

4-12. Why is the book value of equity typically less than its market value? Can you describe a scenario in which the liquidation value of equity would exceed its market value?

PROBLEMS

Valuation Fundamentals

4-1. A best-selling author decides to cash in on her latest novel by selling to an investor the rights to the book's royalties for the next four years. Starting in one month, the royalty stream will be $400,000, and that stream will decline at the rate of 5% per month for the next 11 months. Royalties in the second year will be $150,000 per month, followed by flat monthly royalties of $100,000 and $50,000 per month in the third and fourth years, respectively. If the investor requires a 0.5% return *per month* on this investment, what should he pay for the royalty stream?

Bond Valuation

4-2. A 5-year bond pays interest annually. The par value is $1,000, and the coupon rate equals 7%. If the market's required return on the bond is 8%, then what is the bond's market price?

4-3. A bond that matures in two years makes semiannual interest payments. The par value is $1,000, the coupon rate equals 4%, and the bond's market price is $1,019.27. What is the bond's yield to maturity?

4-4. A bond makes two $45 interest payments each year. Given that the bond's par value is $1,000 and its price is $1,050, calculate the bond's coupon rate and coupon yield.

4-5. A bond with a $1,000 par value makes semiannual interest payments. Its coupon rate is 8% and its coupon yield is 6%. What is the bond's price?

4-6. Calculate the price of a 5-year, $1,000 par value bond that makes semiannual payments, has a coupon rate of 8%, and offers a yield to maturity of 7%.

Smart Solutions
See the problem and solution explained step-by-step at SMARTFinance

4-7. Recalculate the price of the bond in Problem 4-6 assuming a YTM of 9%. What is the relationship between the prices you have calculated in these two problems and the bond's par value? Explain.

4-8. A bond pays a $100 annual coupon and it matures in four years. If investors require a 10% return on this investment, what is the bond's price?

4-9. A bond pays a $100 annual coupon in two $50 semiannual installments. The bond matures in four years. If investors require an annual return of 10% on this bond also, should its price be higher than, lower than, or identical to the price of the bond in Problem 4-8? Use Equation 4.3 and let $r = 0.10$. What price do you obtain? Can you explain the apparent paradox?

Smart Solutions
See the problem and solution explained step-by-step at SMARTFinance

4-10. Two bonds offer a 5% coupon rate, paid annually, and sell at par ($1,000). One bond matures in two years and the other matures in ten years.
  a. What are the YTMs on each bond?
  b. If the YTM changes to 4%, then what happens to the price of each bond?
  c. What happens if the YTM changes to 6%?

4-11. A bond makes annual interest payments of $75. The bond matures in four years, has a par value of $1,000, and sells for $975.30. Calculate the YTM of this bond using a financial calculator or Excel as follows:

- Enter the price of the bond in cell A1, but enter the price as a *negative* number.
- Enter the four remaining payments that the bond makes in cells A2–A5.
- Enter the formula "=IRR(A1:A5, .05)" into any empty cell.
- The value ".05" in the formula simply represents a guess (i.e., 5%) of what the YTM will turn out to be; Excel searches iteratively for the correct value, but you have to give Excel a starting value or guess to begin (it doesn't much matter how good your guess is).
- The formula should calculate a YTM of 8.25%. (*Hint:* If you see only 8% when you enter the formula, use the "Format" command to force Excel to display the additional digits that occur after the decimal point.)

4-12. A $1,000 par value bond offers a 6% coupon that it pays in two semiannual installments. The bond matures in five years, and its price is $1,019.50. What is its YTM?

4-13. A $1,000 par value bond offers a 2% coupon that it pays semiannually. The bond matures in eight years, and its price is $919.25. What is its YTM?

4-14. Two bonds make semiannual interest payments of $40. One bond matures in two years and the other matures in ten years. Both bonds currently sell at par ($1,000), meaning that they offer a YTM of 8%. Calculate the price of each bond if the YTM drops to 6%, and then calculate the price of each bond if the YTM rises to 10%. Comment on the patterns that you observe.

4-15. Suppose that a 5-year Treasury bond with a $1,000 par value offers a coupon rate of 6%, paid semiannually. If the YTM on the bond is 6.5%, what is the bond's price?

4-16. What is the price of a 15-year, $1,000 par value bond with a 7% coupon that pays interest semiannually if we assume that its yield to maturity is 8%? What would be the price of the bond if its YTM were 9%? Compute the percentage change in price: (new price − initial price) ÷ initial price. Repeat the exercise for a 10-year, $1,000 bond with a 7% coupon paying interest semiannually using the same two yields. What do you notice about the percentage change in price for the 10-year bond versus that for the 15-year bond?

Advanced Bond Valuation: The Term Structure of Interest Rates

Smart Solutions

See the problem and solution explained step-by-step at **SMARTFinance**

4-17. A one-year Treasury security offers a 4% yield to maturity (YTM). A two-year Treasury security offers a 4.25% YTM. According to the expectations hypothesis, what is the expected interest rate on a one-year security next year?

4-18. A one-year Treasury bill offers a 6% YTM. The market's consensus forecast is that 1-year T-bills will offer 6.25% next year. What is the current yield on a 2-year T-bill if the expectations hypothesis holds?

4-19. We can use the yield curve to price a 3-year, $1,000 bond with 5% annual coupons as follows:

$$\frac{\$50}{(1 + 0.060)^1} + \frac{\$50}{(1 + 0.061)^2} + \frac{\$50}{(1 + 0.063)^3} + \frac{\$1,000}{(1 + 0.063)^3} = \$965.74$$

What is the yield to maturity for the bond (i.e., what single discount rate will produce the same bond price)? Given the manner in which the bond is priced, what is the expected 1-year interest rate for next year?

Stock Valuation

4-20. City Power & Light has preferred stock outstanding that pays an annual dividend of $8 per share. If investors demand a 10% return on this stock, what is the price?

4-21. Suppose that a company's preferred shares sell for $33 and that they pay an annual dividend of $4. What rate of return do investors require on these shares?

4-22. Investors demand a 12% return on a particular preferred share that sells for $65. What is the annual dividend on this stock?

4-23. Omega Healthcare Investors pays a dividend on its Series B preferred stock of $0.539 per quarter. If the price of Series B preferred stock is $25 per share, then (a) what quarterly rate of return does the market require on this stock and (b) what is the effective annual required return?

4-24. Zenith Propulsion, Inc., is expected to pay a dividend next year of $2.45 per share. Investors think that Zenith will continue to increase its dividend by 5% each year for the foreseeable future.

  a. If the required rate of return on Zenith stock is 13%, then what is Zenith's stock price?

  b. Investors expect Zenith to pay out 50% of its earnings as dividends. What is Zenith's price/earnings ratio? (Here P/E is defined as current price divided by next year's earnings.)

  c. Maintaining all the other assumptions, recalculate Zenith's stock price and P/E ratio if investors expect dividends to grow at 8% per year rather than at 5%.

4-25. A company recently announced an increase of their quarterly dividend from $0.05 to $0.06 per share. This continued a long string of double-digit percentage increases in dividends. Suppose you want to use the dividend growth model to value this firm's stock. You believe that dividends will keep growing at 10% per year indefinitely, and you think the market's required return on this stock is 11%. Let's assume that the firm pays dividends annually and that the next dividend is expected to be $0.23 per share. The dividend will arrive in exactly one year. What would you pay for the stock right now? Suppose you buy the stock today, hold it just long enough to receive the next dividend, and then sell it. What rate of return will you earn on that investment?

4-26. One year from today, investors anticipate that the stock of Groningen Distilleries, Inc., will pay a dividend of $3.25 per share. After that, investors believe that the dividend will grow at 20% per year for three years before settling down to a long-run growth rate of 4%. The required rate of return on Groningen stock is 15%. What is the current stock price?

Smart Solutions
See the problem and solution explained step-by-step at **SMARTFinance**

4-27. On September 22, 2010, Wireless Logic Corp. (WLC) paid its annual dividend of $1.25 per share. Because WLC's financial prospects are particularly bright, investors believe that the company will increase its dividend by 20% per year for the next four years. After that, WLC is expected to increase the dividend at a more modest annual rate of 4%. Investors require a 16% return on WLC stock, and WLC always makes its dividend payment on September 22 of each year.

  a. What is the price of WLC stock on September 23, 2010?

  b. What is the price of WLC stock on September 23, 2011?

  c. Calculate the percentage change in price of WLC stock from September 23, 2010, to September 23, 2011.

  d. For an investor who purchased WLC stock on September 23, 2010, received a dividend on September 22, 2011, and sold the stock on September 23, 2011, what was the total rate of return on the investment? How much of this return came from the dividend, and how much came from the capital gain?

e. What is the price of WLC stock on September 23, 2014?

f. What is the price of WLC stock on September 23, 2015?

g. For an investor who purchased WLC stock on September 23, 2014, received a dividend on September 22, 2015, and sold the stock on September 23, 2015, what was the total rate of return on the investment? How much of this return came from the dividend, and how much came from the capital gain? Comment on the differences between your answers to this question and your answers to part (d).

4-28. Suppose that today's date is March 30, 2010, and that the stock of E-Pay, Inc., pays a dividend every year on March 29. The most recent dividend was $1.50 per share. You expect the company's dividends to increase at a rate of 25% per year through March 29, 2013. After that, dividends will probably increase at 5% per year. Investors require a 14% return on E-Pay stock. Calculate the price of the stock on the following dates: March 30, 2010; September 30, 2011; and March 30, 2014.

Smart Solutions

See the problem and solution explained step-by-step at **SMARTFinance**

4-29. In the spring of 2005, analysts predicted that The Finish Line (ticker symbol, FINL), a specialty retailer offering athletic footwear and apparel, would generate earnings per share of $1.70 over the next 12 months. Finish Line stock was trading at about $19. Assuming that investors required a 10% return on this stock, calculate the present value of growth opportunities (PVGO) per share.

4-30. Roban Corporation is considering going public but is unsure of a fair offering price for the company. Before hiring an investment banker to assist in making the public offering, managers at Roban have decided to make their own estimate of the firm's common stock value. The firm's CFO has gathered data for performing the valuation using the free cash flow valuation model.

The firm's weighted average cost of capital is 12%, and it has $1,400,000 of debt at market value and $500,000 of preferred stock at its assumed market value. The estimated free cash flows over the next five years, 2011 through 2015, are given below. Beyond 2015, the firm expects its annual free cash flow to grow by 4% indefinitely.

Year (t)	Free cash flow (FCF_t)
2011	$250,000
2012	290,000
2013	320,000
2014	360,000
2015	400,000

a. Estimate the value of Roban Corporation's entire company by using the free cash flow approach.

b. Use your answer to part (a), along with the previous data, to find Roban Corporation's common stock value.

c. If the firm plans to issue 220,000 shares of common stock, then what is its estimated value per share?

4-31. Assume that you have an opportunity to buy the stock of Pedal Systems, Inc., an IPO being offered for $13 per share. Although you are very much interested in owning the company, you are concerned about whether it is fairly priced. In order to determine the value of the shares, you have decided to apply the free cash flow approach to the firm's financial data that you've assembled from a variety of sources. The following table summarizes the key values you have compiled.

Free Cash Flow

Year (t)	FCF$_t$	Other Data
2011	$ 750,000	Growth rate of FCF beyond 2014 = 3%
2012	850,000	Weighted average cost of capital = 9%
2013	1,000,000	Market value of all debt = $2,500,000
2014	1,150,000	Market value of preferred stock = $1,200,000
		Number of shares of common stock outstanding = 1,000,000

a. Use the free cash flow approach to estimate Pedal Systems' common stock value per share.

b. Judging on the basis of your answer to part (a) and the stock's offering price, should you buy the stock?

c. Upon further analysis, you find that the growth rate in FCF beyond 2014 will be 4% rather than 3%. What effect would this finding have on your responses in parts (a) and (b)?

Other Approaches to Common Stock Valuation

4-32. A firm follows a policy of paying out 50% of its earnings as dividends. Next year's earnings are expected to be $10 per share. The long-run growth rate of dividends for this firm is 5%, and investors require a 15% rate of return on the stock. What is the firm's P/E ratio?

4-33. Dauterive Barber Shops (DBS) specializes in providing quick and inexpensive haircuts for middle-aged men. The company retains about half of its earnings each year and pays the rest out as a dividend. Recently, the company paid a $3.25 dividend. Investors expect the company's dividends to grow modestly in the future, about 4% per year, and they require a 9% return on DBS shares. Based on next year's earnings forecast, what is DBS's price/earnings ratio? How would this P/E ratio change if investors believed that DBS's long-term growth rate was 6% rather than 4%? Retaining the original assumption of 4% growth, how would the P/E ratio change if investors became convinced that DBS was not very risky and were willing to accept a 7% return on their shares going forward?

THOMSON ONE | Business School Edition

4-34. Look up the bond ratings in the 10-K reports of Best Buy (ticker symbol, BBY) and Radio Shack (ticker symbol, RSH). (*Hint:* You can access the 10-K reports under the Filings tab: click on the 10-K link in the Filings box.) Which company has the better ratings? Which company's bonds are considered "investment grade"? Is this what you would expect given the companies' respective leverage and profitability ratios?

4-35. Using Equation 4.8, what is the growth rate for Coca Cola (ticker symbol, KO)? (*Hint:* The relevant data can be found on the Worldscope Income Statement Ratios Report.) Assuming that Coke will maintain this growth rate forever and has just paid a dividend, what rate of return do investors require on Coke? Use the latest available closing price as the current stock price. How does this required rate of return compare with the compound annual stock return over the last five years? Did Coke's return over this period adequately compensate shareholders?

4-36. Are the "A" shares of Berkshire Hathaway (ticker symbol, BRK) currently under- or overpriced? Using Berkshire Hathaway's five-year average Price/Earnings Ratio–Close (this can be found on the Worldscope Overview, Statistical Analysis Report), determine the price per share using the median EPS estimate for the next fiscal year end (which can be found on the Thomson Estimates Tearsheet, under Estimates). Is this estimate higher or lower than the latest closing price for Berkshire Hathaway?

MINI-CASE: BOND AND STOCK VALUATION

Five years ago, Laissez-Faire Recliners issued $10,000,000 of corporate bonds with a 30-year maturity. The bonds have a coupon rate of 10.125%, pay interest semiannually, and have a par value of $1,000 per bond. The bonds are currently trading at a price of $879.625 per bond. A 25-year Treasury bond with a 6.825% coupon rate (paid semiannually) and $1,000 par is currently selling for $975.42.

1. Determine the yield spread between the corporate bond and the Treasury bond. If you are considering an investment in Laissez-Faire's bonds (that will be held to maturity) and require an 11% rate of return, would you purchase the bonds? Why or why not?

2. Alternatively, you are considering a purchase of Laissez-Faire's preferred stock. Assume that the preferred stock has a current market price of $42, a par value of $50, and a dividend amounting to 10% of par. Would you be willing to buy the firm's preferred stock? Why or why not? Your required rate of return for investments of this type is 12.5%.

3. Now assume that Laissez-Faire has EPS of $1.89, has 750,000 common shares outstanding, and has recently paid a dividend of $0.65 per share. Additionally, the firm generated a net income of $1,417,500 and has common stockholders' equity of $6,000,000 (book value). You believe the firm is in a constant state of growth, and your required rate of return for investments of this risk level is 18%. The firm's common stock is currently trading for $45 per share. Based upon this information, would you be willing to purchase shares of common stock in the firm? Why or why not? Use both the present value of cash flows model and the free cash flow approach to determine your answer. The firm's current FCF is $109,237. Use the firm's weighted average cost of capital of 15.83% as the appropriate discount rate.

4. Would your decision to purchase shares of Laissez-Faire's common stock change if—rather than expecting the firm to experience a constant rate of growth—you expect the following variable growth pattern?
   - Fast growth of 25% for years 1 through 6
   - Moderate growth of 20% for years 7 through 10
   - Stable growth of 15% for years 11 and beyond

5

The Trade-off between Risk and Return

What Companies Do

You Want a Piece of Me?

How do hedge funds, mutual funds, and other companies in the business of managing money try to attract investors? One way is by providing investment opportunities that are unique. Such opportunities can be very attractive to investors seeking to lower the risk of their overall investment portfolios through diversification. The key to forming a well-diversified portfolio is investing in assets that are not highly correlated with each other, so that the ups and downs in one part of a portfolio are offset by assets in other parts of the portfolio.

It was precisely this principle that motivated the national bank of Dubai (Emirates, NBD) to establish the Hero Global Football Fund. In Europe, soccer teams rarely trade players as is the custom in U.S. professional sports. Instead, when a player moves from one team to another, the transfer typically involves a cash payment from the new club to the old one. The Hero Fund purchases the contract rights to emerging soccer stars from the small clubs where players typically start their careers. The fund makes this investment with the hope that, as players develop, larger clubs will later pay to acquire those rights. For example, consider the history of the 2008 European Footballer of the Year, Cristiano Ronaldo. When Ronaldo was just 16, his rights were purchased for €450,000, and, just two years later, Manchester United paid €12.2 million to add him to their roster.

If the payoffs to soccer players' contracts do not rise and fall in sync with other investments such as stocks and bonds, then fund investors could benefit from the diversification that comes from adding these investments to their portfolios. However, an important lesson from the financial crisis which began in 2007 is that, during periods of severe economic distress, many types of investments move in the same direction at the same time. The benefits of diversification can be elusive at precisely the time when they are most needed.

Sources: Ceri Jones, "Transferring Football's Profits," Interactive Investor *(May 12, 2006);*
"Investors Target Profit from Football's Talented Youth," TheSportBlog, www.guardian.co.uk;
Skip Sauer, *"Pure Play in Soccer: Hedge Fund Invests in Portuguese Stars,"* Wall Street Journal
(July 5, 2006); "Dubai Bank Sees Profit in Tomorrow's Soccer Stars," International Herald Tribune
(November 6, 2008).

Perhaps the most important question in finance is, "What is it worth?" For an investor contemplating a stock purchase or a corporate manager weighing a proposal to build a new plant, placing a value on risky assets is fundamental to the decision-making process. The most common procedure for valuing a risky asset involves three basic steps: (1) determining the asset's expected cash flows, (2) choosing a discount rate that reflects the asset's risk, and (3) calculating the present value. Finance professionals apply these three steps, known as **discounted cash flow (DCF) analysis**, to value a wide range of real and financial assets. Chapter 3 introduced you to the rather mechanical third step of this process, converting a sequence of future cash flows into a single number reflecting an asset's present value. In this chapter and the next, we emphasize the second step in DCF analysis—determining the appropriate discount rate.

Matching a discount rate to a specific asset requires answers to two critical questions. First, how risky is the asset, investment, or project? Second, how much return should the project offer, given its risk? This chapter offers an answer to the first question, showing how different ways of defining and measuring risk apply to individual assets as compared with portfolios (collections of different assets). The central insight here is that some risks, especially those affecting many different securities at the same time, are more important than others. Investors need a means to quantify the risks that matter—those risks that cannot be diversified away by holding a balanced portfolio.

Building on this foundation, Chapter 6 provides a solution to the second problem: determining the required return for an asset with a particular risk level. The capital asset pricing model (CAPM) proposes a specific way to measure risk and to determine what compensation investors should expect in exchange.

The CAPM's most basic insight, and indeed that of all asset pricing models, is that a trade-off exists between risk and return. This trade-off is clearly evident when you examine the historical record of different types of investments. In countries around the world, historical capital market data offer compelling evidence that investors cannot earn higher returns unless they are willing to bear greater risks.

5.1 Risk and Return Fundamentals

A Historical Overview of Risk and Return

During the past 30 years, the percentage of U.S. households that own common stock more than doubled to roughly 50%. Although stock ownership varies by country, it increased rapidly in most industrialized countries over the past three decades. What accounts for the increasing global popularity of stocks?

Figure 5.1 provides one answer to this question. The figure compares the long-run performance of alternative investments in several countries for the period 1900–2008. Each graph in the figure shows how the value of one local currency unit (e.g., one dollar, one pound, one Swiss franc) would have grown over time if it had been invested in January 1900 in one of three asset classes: common stocks, long-term government bonds, or short-term government bills. In addition, the graphs plot the inflation rate in each country over the last 109 years.

A quick glance at Figure 5.1 reveals an inescapable conclusion: In the United States, the United Kingdom, France, the Netherlands, Switzerland, and Spain, common stocks outperformed the other asset classes. For example, $1 invested in U.S. stocks at the start of 1900 would have been worth $14,276 by the end of 2008, whereas $1 invested in government bonds or bills would have reached just $242 or $71, respectively. In the

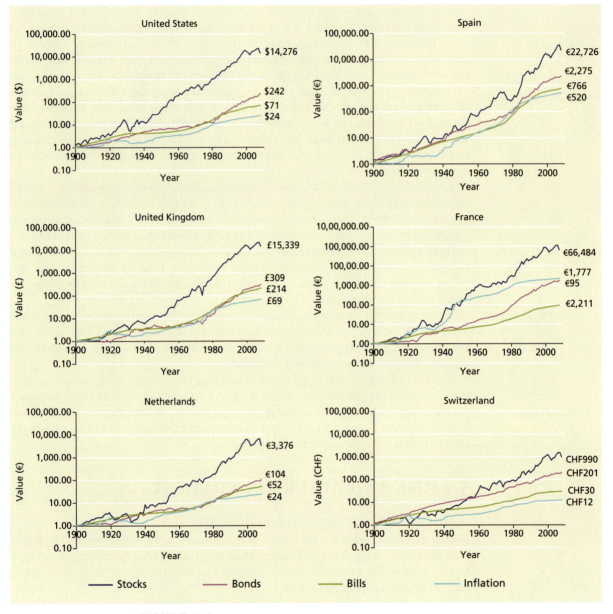

FIGURE 5.1

Value of Alternative Investments in Different Countries, 1900–2008

Each graph shows how the value of one local currency unit would have grown from 1900 to 2008 if it had been invested in stocks, bonds, or bills. In most countries around the world, stocks earn higher returns in the long run compared to bonds and bills.

Source: Dimson, Elroy; Triumph of the Optimists: 101 Years of Global Investment Returns, Elroy Dimson, Paul Marsh, and Mike Staunton. Published by Princeton University Press. Additional updates provided by Dimson et al. Reprinted with permission of Princeton University Press.

United Kingdom, a £1 investment in common stocks in 1900 grew to £15,339 in 2008, compared to £309 for bonds and £214 for bills. In Switzerland, investors earned almost 5 times as much by investing their francs in stocks rather than bonds (2008 accumulated value of SF990 versus SF201). Though the performance of equities relative to bonds and bills varied by country, common stocks earned higher long-term returns than govern-ment bonds and bills in each country shown in Figure 5.1, and in many other countries as well.

Figure 5.1 reveals a second important lesson about the relationship between investment returns and inflation. Looking at the U.S. graph, we see that prices rose by a factor of 24 since 1900. This means the purchasing power of $1 in 1900 was equivalent to the purchas-ing power of $24 in 2008. Why do we include inflation in a graph focusing on investment returns? When people invest, they forgo the opportunity to spend their money today in exchange for the opportunity to consume more tomorrow. Economists refer to the increase in purchasing power that an investment provides as its **real return**. An asset that merely keeps pace with inflation offers a real return of zero and fails to deliver increased future consumption.

For example, suppose that a boy born on January 1, 1900, received one share of stock in Millennium Company from a generous relative and held it for a lifetime. Imagine that the price of this stock was $1 at the time. Over the next 109 years, the Millennium Company never paid a dividend. Its stock price reached $24 by January 1, 2009. What could our elderly investor purchase if he sold his stock on his 109th birthday? Given the 24-fold rise in prices, one share of Millennium stock would buy no more or less than it did in 1900.[1]

With the concept of real return in mind, look again at Figure 5.1. Notice that, in every country except France, the lines for bond and bill returns generally lie above the line for inflation, but not by much. In the United States, individuals who invested only in bills over the past 109 years would have increased their purchasing power by a factor of about 3 ($71 ÷ $24 = 2.96), compared to a tenfold purchasing power increase for bond investors ($242 ÷ $24 = 10.1).[2] Both U.S. bills and bonds provided a positive real return during the century. But the real returns on these instruments pale in comparison to the real return generated by common stocks. Investors who held U.S. stocks over the century would have increased their purchasing power almost 600 times ($14,276 ÷ $24 = 595). Even in France, the only country in Figure 5.1 where bond and bill returns trail the inflation rate, equities earn positive real returns. In light of this evidence, the rising tide of stock ownership is hardly surprising.

Table 5.1 looks at the data on U.S. and U.K. long-term returns from another perspec-tive. The first column shows the average annual real return on each asset class; the second column gives the standard deviation of annual returns.[3] Recall from statistics that the standard deviation measures the dispersion of a random variable around its average. Thus, we can interpret it as a measure of the uncertainty of the return associated with each asset class. The third and fourth columns list the highest and lowest single-year real returns for each investment.

---

[1]Comparisons of this type are a bit tricky. Suppose it cost $72 to visit a dentist in January 2009. That price is roughly equivalent to $3 in 1900. But if you invented a time-travel device, would you be eager to have your dental work done in 1900, even if it only cost $3? The quality of goods and services improves over time, just as their prices increase, but it is difficult to adjust price indexes to capture quality enhancements.

[2]Actually, once you consider the taxes that bond and bill investors would pay, the increase in purchasing power they provide is even less.

[3]Table 5.1 also shows statistics for inflation. You can closely approximate the real return on an investment by subtract-ing the inflation rate from the nominal (actual) return, which of course means that you can add the real return to the inflation rate to obtain the nominal return. For example, Table 5.1 shows that U.S. stocks earned an average annual real return of 8.1% while inflation averaged 3.1% annually. The nominal average annual return on equities must there-fore be roughly equal to the sum of these figures, 11.2%. A more precise definition of the real return is:

$$\text{Real rate} = \left(\frac{1 + \text{Nominal rate}}{1 + \text{Inflation rate}} \right) - 1$$

Table 5.1 Real Returns on U.S. and U.K. Investments, 1900–2008

This table provides evidence of a positive relationship between risk and return. Stocks offer higher real returns on average compared to bonds and bills, but stock returns are much more volatile than are returns on bonds and bills.

ASSET	MEAN RETURN (%)	STANDARD DEVIATION (%)	HIGHEST YEAR (%)	LOWEST YEAR (%)
United States				
Stocks	8.1	20.4	56.5	−38.0
Bonds	2.6	10.0	35.1	−19.4
Bills	1.1	4.7	19.8	−15.1
Inflation	3.1	4.9	20.5	−10.7
United Kingdom				
Stocks	7.0	20.0	96.7	−57.1
Bonds	2.2	13.8	59.0	−30.1
Bills	1.2	6.3	42.4	−15.4
Inflation	4.2	6.6	24.9	−26.0

Source: Dimson, Elroy; Triumph of the Optimists: 101 Years of Global Investment Returns, Elroy Dimson, Paul Marsh, and Mike Staunton. Published by Princeton University Press. Additional updates provided by Dimson et al. Reprinted with permission of Princeton University Press.

Smart Ideas Video

Elroy Dimson, London Business School

"The worldwide average equity premium has been somewhere in the 4 to 5 percent range."

See the entire interview at

SMARTFinance

The table indicates that higher returns on equity investments come at a cost—namely, higher volatility. In the United States, the average annual real return on equity was 8.1%; average real returns on bonds and bills were just 2.6% and 1.1%, respectively. However, the annual standard deviation of U.S. common stock returns was 20.4%. Furthermore, the spread between the best (+56.5%) and worst (−38.0%) years was an astounding 94.5%! By comparison, the standard deviations of bond and bill returns were much lower, just 10.0% and 4.7%. The story was much the same in the United Kingdom, with average real equity returns of 7.0% compared to 2.2% for bonds and 1.2% for bills. The standard deviation of U.K. equity returns was 20.0%, but this figure was 13.8% for bonds and just 6.3% for bills. The fundamental lesson here is that equities, although they earn higher average returns than bonds or bills, also fluctuate much more. Conversely, markets offer very little reward (about 1% annually in real terms and close to zero when taxes are considered) to investors who opt for the relative safety of government bills.

Financial economists refer to the difference in equity returns and returns on safe investments as the **equity risk premium**. For example, simply by taking the difference in U.S. stock and bond returns from Table 5.1, we obtain a rough estimate of the U.S. equity risk premium of 5.5% (or a 7.0% premium on stocks versus bills). In the United Kingdom, equities earned a premium of 4.8% over bonds and of 5.8% over bills. As we will see in subsequent chapters, the equity risk premium plays an important role in many financial models. Investment banks, consulting firms, and large corporations need estimates of the risk premium in order to set acceptable rates of return on investment opportunities and to value whole companies. The data in Table 5.1 tell us what the equity risk premium has been historically, but that may or may not prove to be a useful forward-looking estimate of the future risk premium. Even so, analysts use historical equity risk premium figures as a starting point for many different types of analysis.

EXAMPLE

Suppose an investment banker wants to estimate the value of a firm that a client may acquire. The banker projects the firm's cash flows going forward and decides to discount them at a rate comparable to the expected return on the overall U.S. stock market.

How can the analyst make a long-term projection of U.S. equity returns? By consulting Table 5.1, the analyst sees that the premium on equities versus bills averaged about 7.0% over the last 109 years. Suppose that, at the time of this analysis, the yield on short-term Treasury bills is 1.0%. Adding the 7.0% equity premium to this figure yields an 8.0% forecast for equity returns.[4] Using historical data is a common but very rough approach to estimating the future equity risk premium. We discuss alternative methods in Chapter 9.

CFO Survey Evidence on the Equity Risk Premium

One way to estimate the equity risk premium is to ask experts what return they expect equities to earn relative to safe assets such as Treasury bonds or bills. Welch (2000, 2001) and Graham and Harvey (2008) report survey evidence suggesting that financial experts expect a risk premium between 4% and 7%. Figure 5.2 shows quarterly survey results based on the Duke University CFO Survey. From 2000 to 2008 (3rd quarter), CFOs expected an

FIGURE 5.2

U.S. CFOs' Forward-Looking View of the Equity Risk Premium

Source: Duke University/ *CFO Magazine* Global Business Outlook (www .cfosurvey.org); accessed March 2009.

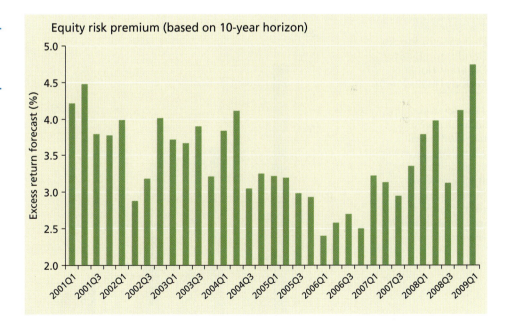

Equity risk premium (based on 10-year horizon)

[4]This is an approximation. The exact formula is much like the one that links real returns to nominal returns and inflation:

$$\text{Equity premium} = \left(\frac{1 + \text{Equity return}}{1 + \text{Bond return}} \right) - 1$$

In addition, it is preferable to calculate the equity premium each year and then take the average across the years rather than first calculating average equity and bond returns across the years and then calculating the risk premium based upon differences in those averages. For instance, if we calculate the equity risk premium in the United States year by year, we obtain 5.9% rather than the 5.5% figure obtained by subtracting average U.S. bond returns from average equity returns.

average risk equity risk premium of roughly 3.5% based on a 10-year horizon. However, the estimates vary over time, ranging from about 4.7% in late 2000 to 2.4% in early 2006. Overall, these estimates are lower than both the historical average risk premium and survey results gathered before the market drop of 2000–2001.

The term *equity risk premium* implies that stocks are riskier than bonds or bills. Certainly a comparison of the standard deviations of stock, bond, and bill returns in Table 5.1 and Table 5.2 (in the What Companies Do Globally feature to follow) supports this conclusion. But the volatility of stocks relative to bonds or bills depends on the time horizon over which we measure investment returns. The standard deviations in Tables 5.1 and 5.2 reflect year-to-year fluctuations in each asset's returns. However, it is possible to perform these calculations using longer horizons. For example, we might measure the returns on stocks, bonds, and bills over 2-year intervals and then calculate the standard deviation of 2-year returns for each instrument. Repeating these calculations over various time horizons, we find an interesting pattern: Return volatilities fall as the investment horizon lengthens. Stocks do not necessarily exhibit greater volatility than bills and bonds at long horizons.

Figure 5.3 illustrates this phenomenon using a 205-year sample of U.S. investment returns.[5] Assuming a 1-year investment horizon, the standard deviation of stocks is 2 times greater than the standard deviation of bonds. (The standard deviation is 3 times

FIGURE 5.3

The Standard Deviation of Stocks, Bonds, and Bills for Different Holding Periods (1802–2006)

Although stock returns are much more volatile than bond and bill returns using an annual investment horizon, at longer horizons the volatility of stock returns relative to other investment alternatives falls dramatically.

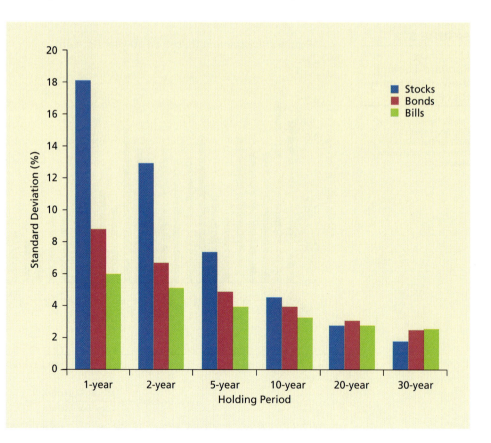

[5]We thank Jeremy Siegel for granting permission to use this figure, which appears in the fourth edition of his book entitled *Stocks for the Long Run* (New York: McGraw-Hill, 2007).

greater than that for government bills.) As the horizon increases, the standard deviation of all three investments declines, but it declines most rapidly for stocks. With a 20-year holding period, stocks, bonds, and bills have nearly identical standard deviations. At longer horizons, stocks actually have a lower standard deviation than either bonds or bills.

A bit of conventional wisdom among financial advisors is that investors should hold a greater fraction of their wealth in stocks if they do not need to tap their savings for many years. This idea also underlies a relatively new investment product whose popularity has grown dramatically in recent years—the *life-cycle mutual fund*. These funds automatically shift an investor's assets from stocks to bonds as the investor ages (i.e., as the investment horizon falls). This asset allocation strategy is based in part on the notion that stocks are less risky over long horizons than over shorter ones.

So are stocks riskier than bonds? In the short run, the answer is absolutely yes. In the long run, it is harder to say. Relative to the risk of investing in bonds or bills, the risk of buying stocks appears to decline rapidly as the investment horizon lengthens. However, we must temper that conclusion with an important observation: even with 204 years of data to examine, we have fewer than seven independent (non-overlapping) 30-year periods from which to draw conclusions. The data indicate that stocks and bonds have had a similar degree of risk for long holding periods. Of course, this conclusion is predicated on the belief that an investor is absolutely sure that she will not need access to the funds during a 30-year holding period. If there is a chance that funds must be withdrawn after, say, 5 or 10 years, then the greater riskiness of stocks over the shorter period becomes relevant. Furthermore, bonds have outperformed stocks over some relatively long periods. For instance, consider the most recent 20-year period in the United States. A $1,000 investment in stocks initiated on January 1, 1989, would have grown to $4,953 by December 31, 2008; but $1,000 invested in bonds over the same period would have grown to $6,762. Therefore, we are hesitant to conclude that the risk of investing in stocks and bonds is similar over long horizons.

Risk Aversion

To understand why riskier investments offer a premium, it is necessary to make some assumptions describing the preferences and behavior of investors. Most financial models begin with the assumption that investors are **risk-averse**. Risk aversion does not imply that investors always shun risk. Instead, risk aversion means that investors require compensation for taking risk.

Here's a simple illustration that makes the point. Suppose a friend offers you the following gamble. You roll a fair die. If the number 6 comes up, you win $6,000; otherwise, you win nothing. Your friend offers to let you play this game for a $1,000 fee. Would you play? Assuming that the die is fair, the probability that you will roll a 6 and win $6,000 is one-sixth, or 16.67%. Thus, we can calculate your expected payoff (or expected dollar return) from playing the game as follows:

$$\text{Expected payoff} = \text{Expected winnings} - \text{Fee}$$
$$= (16.67\% \times \$6,000) - \$1,000$$
$$= \$0$$

Statisticians refer to a gamble like this one as a **fair bet**, meaning that it offers an expected payoff of zero. Risk-averse investors will not accept a fair bet because it exposes them to risk without offering compensation in return. To persuade risk-averse investors to play this game, either the odds would have to be tilted in their favor (e.g., paying the $6,000 payoff

WHAT COMPANIES DO GLOBALLY

The Equity Risk Premium in the United States and Europe (1900–2008)

Table 5.2 shows average annual real returns on common stocks, government bonds, and government bills from 1900 to 2008 for nine different countries. Several robust patterns emerge from the table. First, in every country, the average return is lowest for bills and highest for common stocks, with bond returns falling in between. Second, the same pattern holds for standard deviations across countries. Bills exhibit the least year-to-year volatility while stocks show the most volatility. If we accept volatility as a measure of risk, this pattern makes sense because we expect riskier investments to pay higher returns over time. In other words, *investors seeking higher returns must generally accept more risk.*

Observe that, in real terms, bills are not actually risk-free investments. Remember, the real return on an investment approximately equals the nominal return minus the inflation rate. In France, the average real return on bills falls below zero. Assuming that no one expects a negative return when investing, the negative average returns on bills suggest that investors in France encountered higher-than-expected inflation over time. That risk helps explain the growing worldwide popularity of inflation-indexed bonds. The coupon and principal payments on inflation-linked bonds (also called *linkers*) rise and fall with the inflation rate, so unexpected changes in inflation cannot cause the real returns of these bonds to turn negative.

The final two columns in Table 5.2 show the equity risk premium (relative to bonds and bills) in each country. The premium relative to bills ranges from a high of 9.8% in Italy to a low of 5.0% in Switzerland. The 7.0% U.S. premium takes sixth place among these nations. Keep in mind that these figures represent the historical equity risk premium in each country, which may or may not be a good forecast of the future risk premium.

(continued)

Table 5.2   The Equity Risk Premium in the United States and Europe, 1900–2008

COUNTRY	STOCKS		BONDS		BILLS		EQUITY RISK PREMIUM	
	MEAN RETURN (%)	STANDARD DEVIATION (%)	MEAN RETURN (%)	STANDARD DEVIATION (%)	MEAN RETURN (%)	STANDARD DEVIATION (%)	STOCKS VS. BONDS	STOCKS VS. BILLS
France	5.7	23.3	0.7	13.1	−2.3	9.7	5.7	8.8
Germany	8.1	32.2	0.7	15.5	0.3	10.2	8.1	8.7
Italy	6.0	29.2	−0.4	14.2	−2.6	11.6	7.2	9.8
Netherlands	6.8	21.7	1.8	9.5	0.8	5.0	5.6	6.1
Spain	5.8	22.2	2.0	11.8	0.5	5.9	4.2	5.3
Sweden	9.6	22.9	3.2	12.5	2.2	6.9	7.1	7.5
Switzerland	6.0	19.9	2.9	7.8	0.9	5.0	3.0	5.0
United Kingdom	7.0	20.0	2.2	13.8	1.2	6.3	5.0	5.8
United States	8.1	20.4	2.6	10.0	1.1	4.7	5.9	7.0

Source: Dimson, Elroy; Triumph of the Optimists: 101 Years of Global Investment Returns, Elroy Dimson, Paul Marsh, and Mike Staunton. Published by Princeton University Press. Additional updates provided by Dimson et al. Reprinted with permission of Princeton University Press.

A careful reader may notice one troubling pattern in the table. Thus far, we have used the standard deviation of returns as a proxy for risk, a practice that seems to work well when comparing one asset class with another. In every country, the data show a positive link between the standard deviation of returns and the average return when we compare bills to bonds or bonds to stocks. Can we extend this logic to compare one country to another? Germany and the United States had nearly identical average returns on stocks, but the volatility of the German equity market was more than 50% greater than in the United States. Similarly, equity volatility in Sweden and France was nearly the same, but Sweden's average annual stock return was 9.6% compared to just 5.7% in France.

Perhaps the positive relationship between risk and returns that holds from one asset class to another does not hold across national boundaries. Another explanation, and one to which we will return later in this chapter, is that the standard deviation of returns may not be the best measure of risk.

for rolling a 6 *or* a 5), the payoff increased (e.g., paying $10,000 for rolling a 6), or the entry fee reduced so that the expected payoff becomes positive.[6]

We can extend this example to capital markets. The data in Table 5.1 illustrate that stocks outperform bonds on average, but the high standard deviation of stock returns implies that sometimes they perform quite poorly. The year 2008, for example, witnessed sharp declines in nearly all international stock indexes, but investors in U.S. Treasury bonds earned nearly 26%—the best year for Treasuries since 1995. Yet many investors persisted in holding stocks in their investment portfolios. These investors presumably anticipated that stocks would continue to earn higher average returns than bonds, providing compensation for the higher risks associated with equity securities. Because the numbers in Table 5.1 show a consistent positive relationship between an asset's volatility and its average return, we conclude that the data are consistent with the hypothesis that investors are generally risk averse.

Of course, it is possible that some investors care only about the returns on their investments, totally disregarding risk. **Risk-neutral** investors prefer investments with higher returns whether or not they entail greater risk. Theoretically, a risk-neutral investor is indifferent between accepting or declining our die-throwing gamble because it offers a zero expected return. But such an investor would accept the bet with only the slightest favorable modification, such as increasing the payoff from $6,000 to $6,001. Adding one dollar would generate a small but positive expected payoff, and someone unconcerned with the risk of the proposition would roll the die. Similarly, a risk-neutral investor would be willing to buy stocks, regardless of their risk, as long as they offer even a tiny premium over other investments.

Finally, we can define an almost pathological **risk-seeking** investor. A risk-seeking individual *prefers* to take risks and will invest in a risky asset even when its expected return falls below that of a safer alternative. Risk-seeking investors may purchase investments with negative expected returns. A risk-seeking investor might accept the die-throwing bet even if the payoff from rolling a six was just $4,000 (i.e., when there is a negative expected payoff). Risk-seeking investors would jump at the opportunity to buy stocks even if they offered lower returns than bonds. Clearly, the evidence on stock and bond returns does

---

[6]Risk aversion is closely related to the principle in economics known as diminishing marginal utility. *Diminishing marginal utility* means that the incremental increase in utility from having additional wealth becomes smaller as wealth increases. As Arnold Schwarzenegger put it: "Money doesn't make you happy. I now have $50 million, but I was just as happy when I had $48 million."

not support the notion that most people exhibit risk-seeking behavior when they invest their savings. Even so, examples of risk-seeking behavior easily come to mind. Lottery tickets and Las Vegas casinos give investors the opportunity to make high-risk "investments" with negative average returns.

The most plausible explanation for the relationship, observed in capital markets, between risk and return is that investors are risk averse. High-risk investments must offer the prospect of high returns in order to attract investors. For a risk-averse investor, the ideal portfolio is the one that offers the most favorable trade-off between risk and return. The rest of this chapter deals with the search for that portfolio, a search that begins with precise definitions of *risk* and *return*.

Concept Review Questions	1. Suppose the real return on a risk-free investment is barely above zero. Would a cautious investor do almost as well to hide her money inside a mattress rather than buy a Treasury bill? 2. Is purchasing insurance an example of risk-averse, risk-neutral, or risk-seeking behavior? Explain.

5.2 Basic Risk and Return Statistics

Return of a Single Asset

The total gain or loss on an investment over a given period of time is called the investment's return. The **return** on an asset includes the change in its value (either a gain or loss) as well as any cash distributions (such as dividends or interest payments). The mathematical expression for the return on an asset from time t to $t + 1$ is given by

$$R_{t+1} = \frac{P_{t+1} - P_t + CF_{t+1}}{P_t}$$

(Eq. 5.1)

Here P_{t+1} represents the asset's price at time $t + 1$, P_t is the price at time t, and CF_{t+1} is the cash flow paid by the asset at time $t + 1$. The numerator represents the dollar return on this investment from time t to time $t + 1$. Dividing that return by the initial price of the asset, P_t, converts this dollar return into a fractional return, and multiplying this result by 100 yields a percentage return. This equation measures returns after the fact, or *ex post*.

But uncertainty about asset returns forms the very fabric of portfolio theory. Thus, we need a measure of an asset's *ex ante*—that is, its expected—return. Estimating expected returns is extremely difficult, and we defer a more detailed discussion of that process to the next chapter. However, as a starting point, suppose that the past tells us something useful about the future. By observing returns on an investment or a group of similar investments over time (as in Table 5.1), we may surmise that the average return earned in the past provides a reasonable estimate of the average return going forward.

A technical issue arises when using average historical returns to estimate expected returns. To illustrate the problem, look at the returns earned by a stock from 2007 to 2010:

2007	+23.9%
2008	−18.2%
2009	+20.2%
2010	+12.2%

What was the average annual return on this stock over these years? The simplest way to answer this question is to calculate the **arithmetic average return** by adding up the annual returns and dividing the sum by the number of observations (in this case, 4). From 2007 to 2010, the arithmetic average return was 9.525%.

An alternative approach is to calculate the, **geometric average return**. The geometric average represents the *compound* annual return earned by an investor who bought and held the stock for four years. We can calculate the geometric average of a series of annual returns over *t* years using Equation 5.2:

$$\text{Geometric average return} = \left[(1 + R_1)(1 + R_2)(1 + R_3)\cdots(1 + R_t)^{1/t} - 1\right] \qquad \textbf{(Eq. 5.2)}$$

Applying this formula to our example yields a geometric average return of 0.081, or 8.1%.

Observe that the arithmetic average exceeds the geometric average by about 1.4% in this example. If returns vary over time, then the geometric average will always fall below the arithmetic mean, and the difference between the two figures increases with greater volatility in returns.

For example, let's compare the arithmetic and geometric average real returns, as well as the standard deviation of returns, for common stock investments in Australia and Japan.[7]

Country	Geometric Average (%)	Arithmetic Average (%)	Standard Deviation (%)
Australia	7.3	8.9	18.1
Japan	3.8	8.6	30.1

During the twentieth century, the arithmetic average real return on equities in Australia was 8.9%, which is 1.6 percentage points higher than the geometric average return of 7.3%. Over the same period, Japanese equities earned an arithmetic average annual return of 8.6% while the geometric average was just 3.8%, a difference of 4.8 percentage points. The gap between the arithmetic average and the geometric average is 3 times as large in Japan as it is in Australia. The reason is that Japanese stocks were much more volatile than Australian stocks during the past century: the standard deviation of real returns in Japan was 30.1%, compared to just 18.1% in Australia.

In Tables 5.1 and 5.2 we examined the equity risk premium by comparing the average returns on stocks and bills over 109 years. The returns in those tables are arithmetic averages. We know that stock returns display more volatility than do bill returns, so the difference between the arithmetic and geometric average returns for stocks should be much higher than the same difference for bills (just as the difference is higher for Japan than for Australia). Therefore, we will obtain a higher estimate of the equity risk premium if we take the difference in arithmetic averages between stocks and bills than if we use geometric average returns.

But which number, the arithmetic or the geometric mean, serves as a better estimate of expected returns? Keep in mind that arithmetic and geometric means measure different things. The arithmetic mean is an estimate of the return that one might expect, on average, in a single period. The geometric mean represents the average annual compound return one might expect after a series of repeated "draws" from a distribution of returns.

---

[7]*Source:* Dimson, Elroy; Triumph of the Optimists: 101 Years of Global Investment Returns, Elroy Dimson, Paul Marsh, and Mike Staunton. Published by Princeton University Press. Additional updates provided by Dimson et al. Reprinted with permission of Princeton University Press.

When the purpose of calculating the average return from historical data is to estimate the expected return one period ahead, most economists advocate using the arithmetic mean, and we will follow that convention.

Risk of a Single Asset

Definitions of risk involve a degree of subjectivity. To most people, the word "risk" connotes the possibility of a bad outcome: perhaps earning a negative return on an investment or, even worse, losing the entire sum of money invested. However, most financial models do not define risk strictly in terms of unfavorable outcomes. There are several reasons for this, but the simplest explanation arises from the properties of historical returns. An examination of the year-to-year returns earned by different types of investments yields an interesting symmetry: Those assets that earn the highest returns in good times often earn the lowest returns in bad times. For example, the Nasdaq Composite Index, a U.S. stock index heavily weighted with high-tech companies (which tend to have higher-than-average risk), rose 82% in 1999; yet over the 31 months beginning in January 2000, the index declined by 68%. In contrast, the Standard & Poor's 500 Index (S&P 500), a collection of 500 large firms from a wide variety of industries, rose nearly 20% in 1999; over the next 31 months, it fell by 36%.

A **probability distribution** tells us what outcomes are possible and associates a probability with each outcome. Suppose we have been told that the returns offered by some investment follow a particular probability distribution. Unfortunately, the probability distribution for almost any real-world investment cannot be known with certainty. But by plotting a histogram showing the relative frequencies of different outcomes in the past, we can gain insight into the underlying, unknown distribution.

Figure 5.4 is a histogram of annual common stock returns in the United States from 1900 to 2008. You can see that stock returns tend to cluster near the middle of the histogram, with extremely good and bad years occurring infrequently. If you draw a smooth curve that just touches the top of each bar in the picture, you will generate a curve that is somewhat bell shaped. This looks somewhat like the familiar **normal distribution** curve.

FIGURE 5.4

Histogram of Real Stock Returns in the United States (1900–2008)

Source: Dimson, Elroy; Triumph of the Optimists: 101 Years of Global Investment Returns, Elroy Dimson, Paul Marsh, and Mike Staunton. Published by Princeton University Press. Additional updates provided by Dimson et al. Reprinted with permission of Princeton University Press.

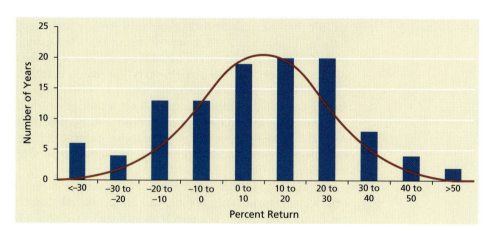

The normal distribution has several properties that make it useful in financial modeling. First, the distribution is symmetric around its mean. This symmetry implies that the probability of an outcome in the far right tail (e.g., very high returns) matches the probability of an outcome in the far left tail (e.g., very low returns). The normal distribution's symmetry makes it easy to determine the probabilities of events that fall within certain ranges. For example, about 68% of the time a normally distributed random variable falls within one standard deviation of the mean, and about 95% of the time it falls within two standard deviations of the mean. Second, just two characteristics—the mean and variance—fully describe the normal distribution. Therefore, if returns follow a normal distribution, then investors need only estimate the mean and variance of the underlying distribution in order to understand the statistical properties of stock returns.

But does the normal distribution reasonably approximate returns on the assets available to investors in the real world? A glance at Figure 5.4 suggests that the approximation is a good one, though not perfect. One problem is that the histogram appears to be more "lumpy" than a normal curve. Even after 109 years of stock market history, there still may not be enough data to generate a perfectly smooth histogram.

Beyond that, histograms of stock returns often exhibit an elongated right tail, indicating that very high returns occur more frequently than very low returns. This "right skewness" appears most dramatically when returns are measured over horizons of a year or more. In part, the skewness results from the limited liability protection afforded stockholders of corporations. The minimum possible return on a share of common stock is −100%, because a stock's price cannot fall below zero. On the other hand, there is no upper limit on a stock's return, resulting in the long right tail in histograms of past returns.[8]

If we were to compare the histogram in Figure 5.4 to the same type of diagram for bond returns, we would find that the likelihood of very low returns on stocks is greater than on bonds, but so is the likelihood of very high returns. If investments that offer a good chance of making a very high return also carry a substantial risk of very low returns, then perhaps a reasonable way to define risk is to focus on the *dispersion* of returns. The most common measure of dispersion used as a proxy for financial risk is the *variance*, or its square root, the *standard deviation*. A distribution's variance equals the expected value of squared deviations from the mean. Suppose we treat the return on an investment as a random variable denoted R, with a mean (expected value) of $E(R)$. Equation 5.3 gives the variance of returns for this investment, usually denoted by the Greek letter sigma squared, or σ^2:

$$\text{Variance} = \sigma^2 = E\{[R - E(R)]^2\} \qquad \textbf{(Eq. 5.3)}$$

Here E stands for "expected value of" and $E(R)$ denotes the mean return.

If we knew all possible returns that an investment might earn, along with the probability attached to each outcome, then we could calculate the variance using these probabilities. Consider the following hypothetical example. Suppose that a firm is involved in product liability litigation, and a decision in the case is expected today. If the firm's defense succeeds then its stock will rise 15%. You assess the probability of a successful defense to be 0.55 (slightly better than even odds). If the firm loses the case, its stock will drop 10%. We can calculate today's expected return and variance for this stock as follows:[9]

$$\text{Expected return} = 0.55(15\%) + 0.45(-10\%) = 3.75\%;$$
$$\text{Variance} = 0.55(15\% - 3.75\%)^2 + 0.45(-10\% - 3.75\%)^2 = 154.7\%^2$$

---

[8]A distribution that allows for right skewness and more closely matches long-term historical return data is the *lognormal* distribution. When economists say that returns are distributed lognormally, this simply means that if you take the logarithm of stock returns then the resulting values are distributed normally. Like the normal distribution, the lognormal distribution is fully described by its mean and variance.

[9]In the variance calculation, we are using percentage figures for returns rather than decimals—that is, 15 percent rather than 0.15. If we used decimals, the expected return and variance would be 0.0375 and 0.01547.

Notice the peculiar units of measure in the variance calculation—percent squared! Rather than worry about how to interpret these admittedly odd units, simply take the square root to convert variance to standard deviation:

$$\text{Standard deviation} = \sigma = \sqrt{154.7\%^2} = 12.4\%$$

There may be special cases when it makes sense to calculate the variance of returns for an investment using this probability-based approach. In most cases, however, it is simply not feasible to list either the full set of returns that an investment might earn or their associated probabilities. Instead, financial analysts often gather historical data and estimate the variance and standard deviation from these observations. In that case, we can use Equation 5.4 to calculate the variance:

JOB INTERVIEW QUESTION

Given annual return data for your company's stock for the immediate past 10 years, how would you measure its return and risk?

$$\text{Variance} = \sigma^2 = \frac{\sum_{t=1}^{N}(R_{it} - \overline{R_i})^2}{N - 1} \qquad \textbf{(Eq. 5.4)}$$

Here R_{it} represents the return on a particular investment i during period t, and $\overline{R_i}$ represents the asset's sample mean return over the sample's N periods (replacing the unobservable expected return, $E(R)$).[10] As usual, the formula for standard deviation is simply the square root of the variance.

EXAMPLE

To demonstrate, let's estimate the standard deviation for the Standard and Poor's 500 Stock Index and for the pharmaceutical firm Merck, using 10 years of data (1995–2004). The following table shows that the S&P 500 earned an arithmetic average return of 13.8% compared to Merck's 13.4% average.

| | ANNUAL RETURN (%) | |
Year	S&P 500	Merck
2004	10.7	−29.0
2003	28.2	−11.2
2002	−21.6	−1.2
2001	−12.1	−36.0
2000	−9.8	41.8
1999	20.4	−7.5
1998	28.7	41.3
1997	33.5	35.6
1996	21.8	24.0
1995	38.0	76.5
Average	**13.8**	**13.4**

---

[10]If you have the historical returns loaded into an Excel spreadsheet, you can use the formula "=var()" to calculate variance and "=stdev()" to calculate standard deviation.

Using Equation 5.4, we find the S&P 500's variance is

$$\sigma^2_{S\&P500} = \frac{(10.7\% - 13.8\%)^2 + (28.2\% - 13.8\%)^2 + \ldots + (38.0\% - 13.8\%)^2}{10 - 1}$$

$$= 444.6\%^2$$

Taking the square root of this figure gives a standard deviation of 21.1%.
For Merck, we find that the variance is

$$\sigma^2_{Merck} = \frac{(-29.0\% - 13.4\%)^2 + (-11.2\% - 13.4\%)^2 + \ldots + (76.5\% - 13.4\%)^2}{10 - 1}$$

$$= 1{,}296.1\%^2$$

Taking the square root once more, we obtain an estimate of 36% for Merck's standard deviation.

The preceding Example illustrates more than how to calculate the variance or standard deviation from historical data. The S&P 500 and the Merck stock earned similar average returns over this period. But notice that Merck's standard deviation was about 70% higher than the S&P 500's (36.0% ÷ 21.1% = 1.7). This raises two interesting questions. First, why are the returns on an individual stock so much more volatile than the returns on a portfolio of stocks (as represented by the stock index)? Second, if Merck stock exhibits more volatility than does the S&P 500, then is Merck a riskier investment? And if Merck is riskier, shouldn't its shareholders earn higher returns as a reward for bearing that risk? Section 5.3 addresses the first of these questions, and Section 5.4 answers the second.

Concept Review Questions

3. "Variance measures the dispersion of an investment's returns, both above and below the average; however, a measure of risk should focus only on the bad outcomes." Comment.

4. An investor purchases a share of stock for $20 on January 2, 2010, and sells it for $30 a year later. Is the 2010 rate of return on this investment 50%? What do you need to know to be sure?

5.3 RISK AND RETURN FOR PORTFOLIOS

Portfolio Returns

So far, we have calculated risk and return only for single assets. The most valuable insights regarding the trade-off between risk and return come when we examine what happens when investors combine individual assets to form *portfolios*.

Consider a simple portfolio consisting of just two assets. Denote the fraction (or weight) invested in each asset by w_1 and w_2.[11] The expected return on this portfolio, $E(R_p)$, is a

Smart Ideas Video

Darrell Duffie, Stanford University

"In order to short a stock, you have to find someone willing to lend the shares."

See the entire interview at **SMARTFinance**

[11]At a broader level, you can think of w_1 and w_2 as representing the fraction of an investor's total wealth invested in two classes of assets. Note that the sum of w_1 and w_2 must be 1.0, but the individual weights can be either positive or negative. A negative value of w_1 means that the investor short-sells the first asset. *Short selling* means borrowing the asset from someone else, selling it, and investing the proceeds in the second asset.

simple weighted average of the expected returns of the two assets, $E(R_1)$ and $E(R_2)$, in the portfolio:

$$E(R_p) = w_1 E(R_1) + w_2 E(R_2) \qquad \text{(Eq. 5.5)}$$

Smart Concepts

See the concept explained step-by-step at

SMARTFinance

Suppose the expected returns on assets 1 and 2 are 10% and 20%, respectively. If an investor creates a portfolio invested 30% in asset 1 and 70% in asset 2, then the portfolio's expected return equals:

$$E(R_p) = 0.30(10\%) + 0.70(20\%) = 17\%$$

The equation for the portfolio's expected return is linear. This means the expected return on this portfolio increases at a constant rate as the proportion invested in asset 1 falls and the proportion invested in asset 2 rises. The general expression for the expected return of a portfolio with N assets is a natural extension of the two-asset case:

$$E(R_p) = w_1 E(R_1) + w_2 E(R_2) + w_3 E(R_3) + \cdots + w_N E(R_N) \qquad \text{(Eq. 5.6)}$$

When estimating expected returns using historical averages, replace the terms $E(R_i)$ in the equation with $\overline{R}_i$.

EXAMPLE

Suppose that you want to invest one-third of your money in corporate bonds, one-third in large-firm stocks, and one-third in small-company stocks. You think that the expected returns on the asset classes are (respectively) 6.1%, 13.0%, and 17.7%. What is the expected return on your portfolio?

$$E(R_p) = \left(\frac{1}{3}\right)6.1\% + \left(\frac{1}{3}\right)13.0\% + \left(\frac{1}{3}\right)17.7\% = 12.3\%$$

Portfolio Variance: An Example

Determining the variance or standard deviation of a portfolio is a bit more complicated. First, look at Table 5.3. The table shows three years of monthly returns on four stocks. The first column of data lists returns for MeadWestvaco Corp. (Mead), a major producer and distributor of paper and wood products, including office and school supplies. The second column reports monthly returns on the stock of Boise Cascade, distributor of paper and building products and owner of more than 2 million acres of timberland in the United States.[12] The next two columns contain returns for Nike, the well-known designer and marketer of athletic footwear and apparel, and Arrow International, producer of disposable catheters and related products for critical and cardiac care. Underneath the series of monthly returns are each stock's average monthly return and standard deviation.

---

[12]Boise Cascade sold its forest products assets to a private equity group and then changed its name to OfficeMax.

Table 5.3 Monthly Returns and Descriptive Statistics for Individual Stocks and Portfolios

MONTH	MEAD CORP.	BOISE CASCADE	NIKE INC.	ARROW INTERNATIONAL	HALF MEAD, HALF BOISE	HALF NIKE, HALF ARROW
1	−2.35%	−3.02%	12.17%	−10.76%	−2.68%	0.71%
2	6.89%	3.33%	17.45%	−12.08%	5.11%	2.68%
3	1.03%	4.31%	8.18%	−12.21%	2.67%	−2.02%
4	37.11%	24.81%	7.80%	4.35%	30.96%	6.07%
5	−11.01%	−1.55%	−2.01%	13.02%	−6.28%	5.51%
6	11.71%	8.58%	4.20%	1.97%	10.14%	3.08%
7	−1.80%	−9.62%	−17.95%	4.83%	−5.71%	−6.56%
8	−8.60%	−6.13%	−10.10%	7.12%	−7.37%	−1.49%
9	−7.87%	0.58%	21.91%	−11.85%	−3.64%	5.03%
10	4.73%	−2.06%	−1.54%	6.11%	1.33%	2.29%
11	−0.40%	−2.98%	−17.86%	10.57%	−1.69%	−3.64%
12	21.72%	17.40%	8.01%	−3.13%	19.56%	2.44%
13	−14.24%	−12.65%	−8.20%	9.70%	−13.45%	0.75%
14	−19.17%	−15.72%	−37.50%	24.35%	−17.45%	−6.57%
15	16.70%	17.06%	39.76%	−20.57%	16.88%	9.60%
16	−0.36%	−6.29%	9.62%	8.76%	−3.33%	9.19%
17	−11.00%	−10.56%	−1.29%	−3.12%	−10.78%	−2.21%
18	−18.05%	−10.64%	−6.86%	1.52%	−14.35%	−2.67%
19	0.50%	6.76%	9.89%	1.87%	3.63%	5.88%
20	6.33%	8.14%	−9.57%	4.57%	7.24%	−2.50%
21	−12.82%	−10.59%	1.57%	2.11%	−11.70%	1.84%
22	23.80%	8.00%	−0.31%	10.82%	15.90%	5.26%
23	−8.05%	0.65%	6.73%	−7.60%	−3.70%	−0.44%
24	18.68%	16.97%	31.22%	1.30%	17.82%	16.26%
25	−3.27%	−2.07%	−1.42%	−7.18%	−2.67%	−4.30%
26	−9.19%	−2.58%	−29.03%	4.74%	−5.89%	−12.14%
27	−8.40%	−1.65%	4.15%	3.25%	−5.02%	3.70%
28	12.40%	11.40%	3.11%	0.93%	11.90%	2.02%
29	3.44%	0.77%	−1.70%	−1.33%	2.11%	−1.51%
30	−6.41%	0.20%	2.46%	2.32%	−3.11%	2.39%
31	9.51%	2.93%	13.24%	−3.80%	6.22%	4.72%
32	12.42%	1.38%	5.15%	−0.18%	6.90%	2.49%
33	−16.73%	−19.21%	−6.14%	1.33%	−17.97%	−2.40%
34	−3.03%	−3.19%	5.45%	2.01%	−3.11%	3.73%
35	15.83%	12.18%	7.35%	−0.38%	14.01%	3.49%
36	−0.10%	6.62%	6.36%	5.55%	3.26%	5.95%
Average monthly return	1.11%	0.88%	2.06%	1.08%	0.99%	1.57%
Standard deviation	13.00%	9.88%	14.53%	8.42%	11.12%	5.21%

Notice that Nike stock earned the highest average monthly return (2.06%) during this period but also had the highest standard deviation (14.53% per month). Boise Cascade stock produced the lowest returns (just 0.88% per month), but it was also much less volatile than Nike stock, with a standard deviation of 9.88%. Mead Corp. shares offered the second-highest monthly return at 1.11%, with volatility second only to Nike's. Arrow International's average monthly return was 1.08%; it was the least volatile stock, with a standard deviation of 8.42%. Though there is not a one-to-one correspondence between stocks' average returns and standard deviations, this example offers some support for the notion that a trade-off exists between volatility and returns. However, you will soon see that a stock's standard deviation sometimes yields a misleading estimate of its risk.

The last two columns of Table 5.3 illustrate the monthly returns that an investor would have earned by forming portfolios of these stocks. One portfolio consists of half Mead stock and half Boise Cascade stock; likewise, the other portfolio contains equal amounts of Nike and Arrow International stock. Because you know that the average monthly returns on Mead and Boise were 1.11% and 0.88%, respectively, you might guess that the monthly return on the Mead–Boise portfolio would fall in between these two figures. Exactly right! The *return on a portfolio* is simply the weighted average of the returns of the stocks in the portfolio. Because this portfolio consists of equal amounts (50%) of each stock, its return is 0.99%—exactly halfway between Mead's return and Boise's. Similarly, the average monthly return on the Nike–Arrow portfolio is 1.57%, which is exactly the midpoint between the returns of Nike and Arrow.

Look closely at the standard deviation of these portfolios, starting with the combination of Mead and Boise Cascade. Mead's standard deviation is 13.00% and Boise's is 9.88%. Your intuition might suggest that an equally weighted portfolio of these stocks would have a standard deviation halfway between Mead's and Boise's, or 11.44%. In fact, the portfolio's standard deviation is a little less, 11.12%. But note that the portfolio's volatility still falls between that of Mead and Boise, as you anticipated.

Now turn to the Nike–Arrow portfolio. Recalling that the respective standard deviations for Nike and Arrow are 14.53% and 8.42%, you conjecture that the standard deviation of a 50-50 portfolio should be about halfway between these two figures, 11.48%. Or perhaps, learning from the Mead–Boise example, you guess that the portfolio's standard deviation will be a bit less than the midpoint. In fact, the standard deviation is just 5.21%! *The portfolio exhibits less volatility than do either of the stocks it contains.* More importantly, it achieves a substantial reduction in risk while still offering a return that exceeds the return on Arrow International. In other words, by choosing a portfolio containing both Nike and Arrow, instead of holding only Arrow stock, an investor simultaneously obtains higher returns and lower risk, the best of both worlds. How can this happen?

The Importance of Covariance

The risk reduction achieved in these portfolios occurs because fluctuations in one asset partially offset fluctuations in the other. This effect is especially dramatic in the Nike–Arrow portfolio because the best months for Nike stock were often the worst months for Arrow, and vice versa. Examine months 26 and 31 for prominent examples of this phenomenon. In contrast, the best (worst) periods for Boise were typically periods in which Mead stock also performed well (poorly); months 33 and 35 illustrate this tendency. In general, the risk of a portfolio will depend crucially on whether the returns on the portfolio's components move *together*, as in the Mead–Boise case, or *in opposite directions*, as did Nike and Arrow during these three years.

In the concept of **covariance**, statistics provides a way to measure the co-movements of two random variables. Continuing with our use of R_1 and R_2 to represent returns on two different assets, we find that the covariance of returns between them, denoted by σ_{12}, is given by

$$\text{Cov}(R_1, R_2) = \sigma_{12} = E\{[R_1 - E(R_1)][R_2 - E(R_2)]\} \qquad \textbf{(Eq. 5.7)}$$

To calculate the covariance directly from this equation, an analyst would have to know the probability distribution describing returns for assets 1 and 2. In virtually all practical applications, this probability distribution is unknown, so analysts estimate the covariance using historical data. Given a sample of N periods during which returns on the assets are observed, the formula for covariance becomes:[13]

$$\text{Cov}(R_1, R_2) = \sigma_{12} = \frac{\left[\sum_{t=1}^{N}(R_{1t} - \overline{R}_1)(R_{2t} - \overline{R}_2)\right]}{N-1} \qquad \textbf{(Eq. 5.8)}$$

Examine the numerator of this formula. Imagine that stocks 1 and 2 tend to *move together*, as did Mead and Boise Cascade in the previous example. If both stocks experience above-average returns then both terms in parentheses will be positive, yielding a positive product when multiplied together. Similarly, if both stocks realize below-average returns then both terms in parentheses will be negative, again resulting in a positive product when multiplied. Thus, two assets that tend to move together will have a *positive* covariance. (For example, the covariance between Mead and Boise is 0.0114.)

Conversely, suppose the two stocks move in *opposite directions*, as did Nike and Arrow International. When Nike earns above-average returns, Arrow's will be below average. The product in the numerator will be negative. Likewise, if Arrow's returns are atypically high then Nike's will be unusually low, again resulting in a negative product. Consequently, two assets that tend to move in opposite directions will have a *negative* covariance. (The covariance between Nike and Arrow is -0.0087.) When two assets move independently—that is, when one asset's return is completely unrelated to the return on the other asset—then the covariance will be zero.

Covariance figures can be difficult to interpret because they depend on the units of measurement. A covariance calculation for stock returns will yield very different numerical results depending on whether the stock returns are measured in percentages, decimals, or dollars. Does the 0.0114 covariance between Mead and Boise indicate a strong or weak tendency for these two stocks to move together? A standardized measure, one that does not depend on units of measure, would help answer this question.

---

[13]Perhaps you are wondering why we divide by $N - 1$ (here and in the variance formula) when there are N observations in the sample. The reason is that estimating variance or covariance first requires estimating a mean, and you use one degree of freedom in doing so. If you had the full population of returns for an investment—rather than just a sample—then you could divide by N. Excel gives you the option, when calculating variance or standard deviation, to use formulas that are appropriate for either a sample or a population. In virtually all practical applications, the sample formula is appropriate. An unfortunate quirk of Excel is that its only formula for calculating covariance, "=covar()", divides by N and is therefore, strictly speaking, inaccurate for a sample. However, in a reasonably large sample, dividing by N versus $N - 1$ makes little difference.

Fortunately, the correlation coefficient is such a measure. Denoted by the Greek letter rho (ρ), the correlation coefficient between two random variables is shown in Equation 5.9:

$$\text{Correlation coefficient} = \rho_{12} = \frac{\sigma_{12}}{\sigma_1 \sigma_2} \qquad \text{(Eq. 5.9)}$$

The **correlation coefficient** standardizes the covariance measure. It divides covariance by the product of the standard deviation of each asset. Looking back at the formula for covariance, you can see that, like variance, it is measured in units of "percent squared." Notice that the denominator of the correlation coefficient equation multiplies two figures together that are each measured in percentage units. Therefore, both the numerator and denominator are in percent-squared units that cancel each other out. The correlation coefficient is a unit-free measure of the co-movement of two assets. It ranges between a minimum value of -1.0 and a maximum value of $+1.0$. If the correlation coefficient between two assets reaches 1.0 then they are said to exhibit *perfect positive correlation*. Of course, *perfect negative correlation* occurs when the correlation coefficient between two assets is -1.0.

We now can apply this formula to calculate and then compare the correlation between Mead and Boise Cascade to that of Nike and Arrow International:

$$\text{Correlation of Mead and Boise} = \frac{0.00114}{(0.13)(0.0988)} = 0.89$$

$$\text{Correlation of Nike and Arrow} = \frac{-0.0087}{(0.1453)(0.00842)} = -0.71$$

These figures indicate a fairly strong tendency for Mead and Boise returns to move together. This is not surprising, given that they operate in many of the same industry segments. The figures also indicate a somewhat weaker tendency for Nike and Arrow to move in opposite directions. This negative correlation between Nike and Arrow is unusual. Why would good times for Nike translate into bad times for Arrow, and vice versa? Perhaps if people are getting lots of exercise and are spending a lot of money on Nike products, then they are less likely to have heart attacks or other ailments that would make them customers of Arrow International!

Although such reasoning might appeal to someone with a dark sense of humor, we are skeptical. Common macroeconomic factors—such as changes in interest rates, inflation, and economic growth—should affect Nike and Arrow in similar ways, and those common factors tend to generate a positive correlation between most pairs of stocks. The negative correlation between Nike and Arrow is more likely explained by the statistical sampling techniques that were used. When we are using a sample to estimate the value of some underlying parameter (like the correlation coefficient), it is always possible that by chance we have drawn an unusual sample. As a matter of practice, it is wise to draw samples from different periods to determine if the statistical estimates obtained from one period are applicable in other periods. Though there may be exceptions, a strong negative correlation between two stocks is a relatively rare occurrence.

Variance of a Two-Asset Portfolio

In Table 5.3, you saw the monthly returns on two equally weighted portfolios as calculated by taking a 50-50 weighted average of the individual stock returns in each month. The portfolio containing Nike and Arrow International stock exhibited low volatility; the explanation for that phenomenon, we now know, lies in the notion of covariance or correlation. In fact, the variance of any two-asset portfolio depends on three factors: the weight w_i invested in each asset, the variance σ_i^2 of each asset, and the covariance σ_{ij} between the two assets. Equation 5.10 provides the general formula for a two-asset portfolio's variance:

$$\text{Portfolio variance} = \sigma_p^2 = w_1^2 \sigma_1^2 + w_2^2 \sigma_2^2 + 2w_1 w_2 \sigma_{12} \qquad \textbf{(Eq. 5.10)}$$

Looking back at Equation 5.9, we see that the covariance can be expressed as follows:

$$\sigma_{12} = \rho_{12} \sigma_1 \sigma_2 \qquad \textbf{(Eq. 5.11)}$$

Plugging this new expression for covariance into Equation 5.10 yields

$$\text{Portfolio variance} = \sigma_p^2 = w_1^2 \sigma_1^2 + w_2^2 \sigma_2^2 + 2w_1 w_2 \rho_{12} \sigma_1 \sigma_2 \qquad \textbf{(Eq. 5.12)}$$

Observe the importance of the correlation between assets 1 and 2 in this expression. If ρ_{12} is positive then the third term in the equation is positive, leading to a higher overall portfolio variance. Conversely, if ρ_{12} is negative then the third term serves to reduce the variance of the portfolio.

EXAMPLE

What is the standard deviation for a portfolio containing 40% Nike and 60% Arrow International stock? Using the figures from Table 5.3 and the correlation coefficient between Nike and Arrow of -0.71, you can calculate the portfolio standard deviation in two steps. First, calculate the variance:

$$\sigma^2 = (0.4)^2 (0.1453)^2 + (0.6)^2 (0.0842)^2 + 2(0.4)(0.6)(-0.71)(0.1453)(0.0842)$$
$$= 0.00176$$

Then, take the square root to obtain the standard deviation, 0.0420 (or 4.20%). Notice that this portfolio has an even lower standard deviation than the 50-50 portfolio in the table.

The equation for portfolio variance allows quick recomputations if the portfolio weights change. Figure 5.5 plots the monthly return and standard deviation for many different combinations of (A) Mead–Boise and (B) Nike–Arrow. Note that the

FIGURE 5.5(A)

Average Return and Standard Deviation for Portfolios of Mead and Boise Cascade

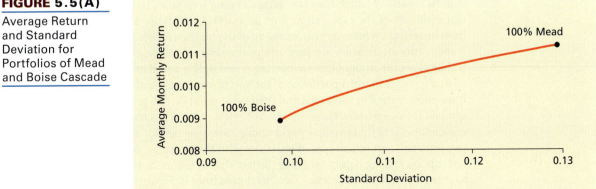

FIGURE 5.5(B)

Average Return and Standard Deviation for Portfolios of Nike and Arrow International

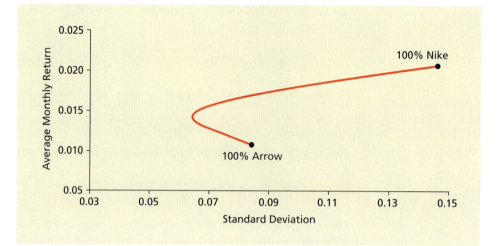

Mead–Boise portfolios trace out an upward-sloping arc. The figure shows that, if you add Mead stock to a portfolio containing only Boise shares, then the portfolio's average return and standard deviation increase. Intuitively, we might conclude that Mead is a riskier stock than Boise because the former has a higher standard deviation and because adding Mead shares to Boise stock increases the overall volatility of the portfolio.

JOB INTERVIEW QUESTION

You own a low-volatility stock. If you buy some shares of a high-volatility stock, will your portfolio volatility go up? Upon what does the answer depend?

But that intuition is not always correct. Look at the backward-bending arc representing alternative portfolios of Nike and Arrow. Adding some Nike shares to a portfolio invested 100% in Arrow stock results in an increase in the portfolio's average return (because Nike's average return is higher than Arrow's), but the portfolio's standard deviation falls—at least up to a point. Holding a portfolio of Nike and Arrow, rather than only Arrow stock, gives investors the best of both worlds: higher returns and less volatility. Indeed, this is the key implication of diversifying and is the basis for the adage, "Don't keep all your eggs in one basket." But this example raises questions about using standard deviation as a measure of risk. If adding a few Nike shares to the portfolio makes the portfolio less volatile, can we really say that Nike is riskier than Arrow just because its standard deviation is higher?

The key lesson from Figure 5.5 is that the volatility of a two-asset portfolio depends on the correlation between the two assets. Figure 5.6 illustrates this point in a general setting with two assets, A and B. Note the change in the y-axis label. In this diagram, we presume that estimates of the expected returns on assets A and B are available (perhaps derived from historical average returns), enabling us to plot the expected returns of the portfolios. If these two investments are perfectly positively correlated ($\rho = +1.0$), then portfolios will lie along the straight line connecting A and B. If A and B are perfectly negatively correlated ($\rho = -1.0$), then portfolios of the two investments lie along the kinked line going from point A back to the y-axis and then up to point B. The graph indicates that, in this special case, one particular combination of assets A and B has zero risk. Though it is virtually impossible to find two real-world stocks displaying perfect negative correlation, investors can construct other types of securities with this property. As you will see later in the text, option pricing theory relies on the fact that investors can combine two risky assets to create a portfolio that is risk-free. The dotted lines in Figure 5.6 illustrate intermediate cases in which the value of ρ falls between $+1.0$ and -1.0. It is clear that, as the correlation becomes less positive (the dashed lines move away from the solid line AB), the portfolio risk (standard deviation) is reduced for each level of expected return.

FIGURE 5.6

Portfolio Performance with Different Values of ρ

As the correlation between the returns of assets A and B falls, the volatility of portfolios of A and B declines.

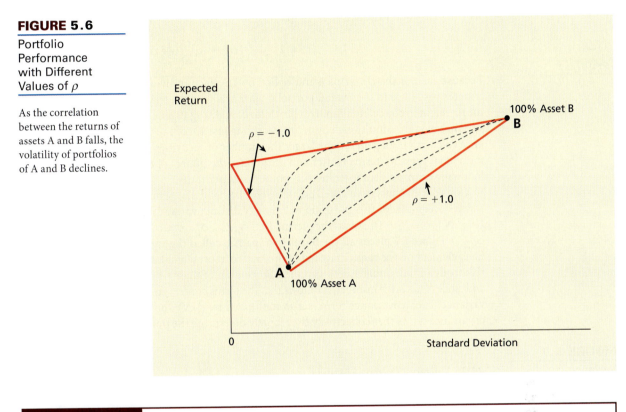

---

5. "If two assets are negatively correlated then, when one has a positive return, the other will have a negative return. A portfolio of these assets will not make any money." Are these statements correct?
6. If you pick two stocks at random, would you guess that their returns are positively correlated, independent, or negatively correlated? Why?
7. Imagine that two stocks have the same average return (10%) and the same standard deviation (30%). Would the average return on a 50-50 portfolio of these two stocks be equal to, greater than, or less than 10%? Would the portfolio standard deviation be equal to, greater than, or less than 30%?

5.4 SYSTEMATIC AND UNSYSTEMATIC RISK

What Drives Portfolio Risk?

A simple modification extends the variance equation to a portfolio with more than two assets. Remember, the equation for portfolio variance consists of three elements: portfolio weights, variances of individual assets, and covariances (or correlations) of pairs of assets. We can express the variation equation for a portfolio with three stocks as

$$\sigma_p^2 = w_1^2\sigma_1^2 + w_2^2\sigma_2^2 + w_3^2\sigma_3^2 + 2w_1w_2\sigma_{12} + 2w_1w_3\sigma_{13} + 2w_2w_3\sigma_{23} \qquad \textbf{(Eq. 5.13)}$$

You can see the importance of the covariance between assets in a portfolio by applying this equation to an equally weighted portfolio of three stocks. With one-third of the portfolio invested in each security, we calculate the portfolio variance as follows:

$$\text{Portfolio variance} = \sigma_p^2 = \frac{1}{9}\sigma_1^2 + \frac{1}{9}\sigma_2^2 + \frac{1}{9}\sigma_3^2 + 2\left(\frac{1}{3}\right)\left(\frac{1}{3}\right)\sigma_{12} + 2\left(\frac{1}{3}\right)\left(\frac{1}{3}\right)\sigma_{13} + 2\left(\frac{1}{3}\right)\left(\frac{1}{3}\right)\sigma_{23}$$

Because each of the σ^2 terms is multiplied by 1/9, each individual stock's variance contributes very little to the overall portfolio variance. Instead, the covariance terms receive more weight in the calculation. In a portfolio containing 10 assets, each individual stock's variance would be multiplied by 1/100, receiving just 1% of the weight in the overall variance calculation. In general, the larger the number of securities in a portfolio, the less the individual variance terms matter and the greater the impact of the covariance terms. The following example demonstrates this point mathematically.

Consider an equally weighted portfolio consisting of a large number N of securities. The variance formula for this portfolio will have N distinct variance terms ($\sigma_1, \sigma_2, \ldots, \sigma_N$) and $N^2 - N$ [or $N(N-1)$] covariance terms ($\sigma_{12}, \sigma_{13}, \ldots, \sigma_{1N}, \sigma_{21}, \sigma_{23}, \ldots, \sigma_{2N}, \ldots, \sigma_{N1}, \sigma_{N2}, \ldots, \sigma_{N,N-1}$). Figure 5.7 places all the terms in a matrix, called the *variance-covariance matrix*. Each element on the main diagonal of this matrix represents the contribution to portfolio risk from an individual asset's variance. Since each of these terms is multiplied by $(1/N)^2$ and since N is a large number, it follows that the terms contribute very little to the portfolio variance. Each covariance term is also multiplied by $(1/N)^2$, but there are so many more covariance terms that collectively they largely determine the portfolio's variance.

FIGURE 5.7

Variance-Covariance Matrix and Portfolio Variance Equation for an Equally Weighted Portfolio of *N* Stocks

Variance-Covariance Matrix

Stock	1	2	3	⋯	*N*
1	$\left(\frac{1}{N}\right)^2\sigma_1^2$	$\left(\frac{1}{N}\right)^2\sigma_{12}$	$\left(\frac{1}{N}\right)^2\sigma_{13}$	⋯	$\left(\frac{1}{N}\right)^2\sigma_{1N}$
2	$\left(\frac{1}{N}\right)^2\sigma_{21}$	$\left(\frac{1}{N}\right)^2\sigma_2^2$	$\left(\frac{1}{N}\right)^2\sigma_{23}$	⋯	$\left(\frac{1}{N}\right)^2\sigma_{2N}$
3	$\left(\frac{1}{N}\right)^2\sigma_{31}$	$\left(\frac{1}{N}\right)^2\sigma_{32}$	$\left(\frac{1}{N}\right)^2\sigma_3^2$	⋯	$\left(\frac{1}{N}\right)^2\sigma_{3N}$
⋮	⋮	⋮	⋮	⋮	⋮
N	$\left(\frac{1}{N}\right)^2\sigma_{N1}$	$\left(\frac{1}{N}\right)^2\sigma_{N2}$	$\left(\frac{1}{N}\right)^2\sigma_{N3}$	⋯	$\left(\frac{1}{N}\right)^2\sigma_N^2$

Portfolio Variance Equation

$$\sigma_p^2 = N\left(\frac{1}{N}\right)^2\overline{\sigma^2} + N(N-1)\left(\frac{1}{N}\right)^2\overline{\sigma_{ij}}$$

$$\sigma_p^2 = \frac{\overline{\sigma^2}}{N} + \left(\frac{N-1}{N}\right)\overline{\sigma_{ij}}$$

A final illustration will clarify our main point. The matrix in Figure 5.7 contains N variance terms and $N(N-1)$ covariance terms. Each variance and covariance term is multiplied by $(1/N)^2$. Suppose that the average stock in this portfolio has a variance equal to $\overline{\sigma^2}$ and that, across any pair of stocks (say, stock i and stock j), the average covariance is $\overline{\sigma_{ij}}$. Then the portfolio variance equation can be written as shown at the bottom of Figure 5.7.

As the number N of stocks in the portfolio becomes very large, the variance term $N(1/N)^2 \, \overline{\sigma^2}$ approaches zero. This means the average variance of individual stocks has no impact on portfolio variance. As N increases, the second term in the equation converges to $\overline{\sigma_{ij}}$, indicating that what really determines the risk of a large portfolio is the average covariance between all pairs of securities. A large portfolio consisting of securities that are, on average, only weakly correlated with each other will have a lower variance than a portfolio that consists of highly correlated securities.

Figure 5.8 plots the relationship between the number of securities in a portfolio and the portfolio's variance given by this equation. For investors, the figure contains both good and bad news. The good news is that as the number of securities in the portfolio increases, the portfolio's variance declines. Given the proliferation of low-cost mutual funds available today, investors can construct portfolios containing hundreds of securities, thereby reducing the variance of their investment portfolio to some degree. The bad news is that the marginal risk reduction benefit of adding more securities to the portfolio decreases as the number of securities in the portfolio increases. Not even a very well diversified portfolio can eliminate all risk.

FIGURE 5.8

Effect of
Diversification on
Portfolio Variance

Adding more securities
to a portfolio lowers
the portfolio's volatility,
but the incremental
benefit of adding more
securities declines
as the number of
securities rises.

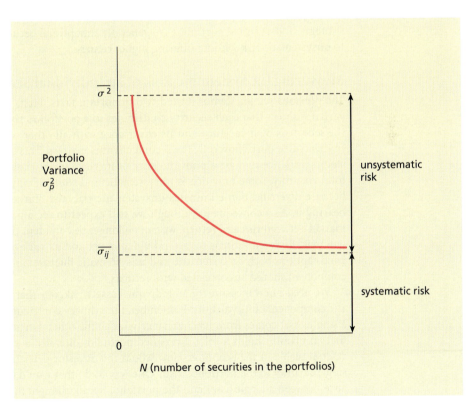

Because some risks systematically affect almost all securities, there is a limit to the risk reduction achievable by adding more securities to a portfolio. The average covariance term $\overline{\sigma_{ij}}$ represents this limit. No matter how diversified a portfolio becomes, its variance cannot fall below the average covariance of securities in the portfolio. Financial economists give this type of risk special names: undiversifiable risk, **systematic risk**, or market

risk. Similarly, the risk that diversification eliminates is called diversifiable risk, **unsystematic risk**, idiosyncratic risk, or unique risk.

In real-world terms, what exactly is systematic risk? This is a difficult question to answer, and we explore it in more depth in the next chapter. For now, we just say that systematic risks are those that are common across all types of securities. Fluctuations in gross domestic product, inflation, oil prices, or interest rates can be thought of as systematic risks, and so might certain political factors. For example, the legal system governing investors and markets in a given country can influence systematic risk because that system determines the level of protection given to minority shareholders, creditors, and ordinary investors. When investors perceive that the legal system protects their interests, their willingness to trade and invest in securities increases and so the returns they require for bearing risk decline.

If investors can cheaply eliminate some risks through diversification, then we should not expect a security to earn higher returns for risks that can be eliminated through diversification. Investors can expect compensation only for bearing systematic risk (i.e., risk that cannot be diversified away). Refer back to the Example following Equation 5.4, which showed that the average return on Merck stock was about the same over 10 years as the average return on the S&P 500 *even though* Merck stock was much more volatile than the index. An undiversified investor who held only Merck stock had to bear twice as much volatility as an investor who owned the S&P 500, even though both investors earned the same reward. This is not to say that Merck was or is a bad investment. The point is that holding Merck (or any other individual company's stock) *in isolation* is a poor investment strategy. Undiversified portfolios are generally suboptimal because they expose investors to unsystematic risk without offering higher returns.

Measuring the Systematic Risk of an Individual Security

The previous section demonstrated two important facts. First, the formula for portfolio variance shows that each security contributes to a portfolio's risk through two channels, the security's own variance and its covariance with all other securities in the portfolio. In diversified portfolios, only the second channel matters. This implies that an individual stock's variance may be a poor measure of its risk. The variance of a stock captures its total volatility, some of which is unsystematic and some of which is systematic. Second, because diversification eliminates unsystematic risk, the market provides no reward for bearing it. As a consequence, though we still expect to see a positive relationship in the market between risk and return, we can no longer be confident that a positive relationship will exist between returns on an individual asset and its variance. Again, a stock's variance captures both its systematic and unsystematic fluctuations, but only the systematic component should be correlated with returns.

We need a new measure for an individual asset's risk, one that captures only the systematic component of its volatility. Remember, the primary contribution to portfolio risk from a single asset comes from its covariance with all the other assets in the portfolio. Imagine that an investor holds a fully diversified portfolio—literally, a portfolio containing every asset available in the economy. How would this investor determine the contribution of a single security to the portfolio's risk? One way to do that would be to measure the covariance between a single asset and the portfolio. Recall, though, the difficulty that nonstandard units cause for interpreting covariance calculations. A standardized measure would be preferable, and finance theory gives us just such a measure in the concept of *beta*:

$$\beta_i = \frac{\sigma_{im}}{\sigma_m^2}$$

(Eq. 5.14)

The **beta** of asset i (β_i) equals the covariance of the asset's returns with the returns on the overall portfolio, divided by the portfolio's variance. As you will see in the next chapter, the portfolio we refer to here is known as "the market portfolio," a value-weighted portfolio of all available assets.[14] A security's beta gives us a standardized measure of its covariance with all other assets, or a measure of its systematic risk. If the market rewards only systematic risk and if beta captures the systematic risk of an individual asset, then we should observe a positive relationship between values of beta and returns in the market.

Observe that the formula for an asset's beta closely resembles that of the correlation coefficient:

$$\beta_i = \frac{\sigma_{im}}{(\sigma_m)(\sigma_m)} ;$$

$$\rho_i = \frac{\sigma_{im}}{(\sigma_i)(\sigma_m)}$$

The equations are identical except in one respect: The denominator of the correlation coefficient multiplies the standard deviations of the asset and the market, whereas the denominator of the beta formula squares the standard deviation of the market. This small adjustment to the denominator makes the interpretation of beta a little different from that of the correlation coefficient. First, unlike ρ, beta has no maximum or minimum value. Second, beta indicates how much the individual asset's return moves, on average, when the market moves by 1%. For example, if a stock has a beta of 1.5, then, when the market return increases by 1%, the stock return will (on average) increase by 1.5%.

EXAMPLE

Now that we understand the beta measure of a stock's risk, how does it compare to the measure we started with, standard deviation? Comparing the monthly returns on each of the four stocks listed in Table 5.3 to returns on the overall stock market, suppose you calculate the following statistics:

Stock	Covariance with Market
Mead	0.0031
Boise	0.0026
Nike	0.0011
Arrow	−0.0003

If the variance of market returns were 0.0028, then the betas of the four stocks would be as follows:

Mead   1.11   Boise   0.93   Nike   0.39   Arrow   −0.11

These betas contain several surprises. First, based on comparison of the standard deviations of each stock in Table 5.3, we concluded that Nike was the riskiest security. Comparing the betas, however, suggests that Nike is less risky than either Mead or Boise Cascade. Recall

(continued)

---

[14]The modifier "value-weighted" means that the fraction invested in a particular security is equal to that security's total market value as a percentage of the market value of all securities. For example, if the total market value of all securities in the market is $10 trillion and if the total market value of a certain company's stock equals $100 billion, then the fraction of that stock in a value-weighted portfolio would be 0.01, or 1%.

the dramatic risk reduction achieved in the Nike–Arrow portfolio. Apparently, much of the volatility of Nike and Arrow was unsystematic (i.e., the volatility was uncorrelated with the broader market). Thus, neither Nike nor Arrow contribute much risk to a portfolio.

The second surprise is that Arrow's beta is negative (though just barely). This is surprising because, over the long term, economic booms tend to lift returns on all types of stocks and recessions tend to lower them. As a result, most stocks have positive betas. To find a security that usually blossoms when the market swoons, and vice versa, is something of an anomaly. Some natural resource companies, such as gold mining companies, have negative betas. There are only a few such companies, whose stocks are often characterized as "defensive" because their returns tend to hold up in an economic downturn. Arrow's −0.11 beta probably results from our drawing an unusual sample from the historical record and so is likely not a generalizable long-term finding.

The third surprise is the relationship between the betas and the returns of these four companies. If the market rewards investors only for bearing systematic risk and if beta measures systematic risk, then we should expect to see a positive relationship between beta and returns. Here, Nike delivered the highest return but had a relatively low beta. Nike's standard deviation was the highest of the group, so we might be tempted to conclude that market returns are more strongly correlated with total risk (standard deviation) than with systematic risk (beta). For a variety of reasons, such a conclusion would be premature at this point.

Smart Concepts

See the concept explained step-by-step at

SMARTFinance

Limitations of Beta

In the real world, beta is by far the most popular way to measure the risk of a common stock. And, in general, beta risk and expected returns are correlated as one would expect. However, the beta measure is not perfect. For one thing, the relation between beta and returns is weak at times. In our example, Nike stock had the highest returns yet Nike also had the next-to-smallest beta. This implies that there may be other dimensions to the risk–return trade-off that are not captured by beta. Researchers have found that other risk characteristics may be related to the size of the company or to the ratio of its market value to its book value of assets. Chapter 6 explores the relationship between beta and expected returns in greater depth. For now, the important point is that a stock's variance (or standard deviation) measures its total risk but that total risk contains both systematic and unsystematic components. Only the systematic part is priced in the market because only this part contributes to risk in a well-diversified portfolio. The beta metric is one way to measure the systematic risk of an asset, but researchers have found that stock returns seem also related to other risk characteristics.

Concept Review Questions

8. Would you expect a portfolio consisting only of U.S. stocks to have a higher or lower variance than a portfolio consisting of stocks from the United States, Japan, the United Kingdom, France, and Germany?

9. Suppose you track the stock of a company and notice that its value swings wildly from month to month. You do some research on the Internet and find several sites reporting relatively low betas for this firm. Is this possible, or are the websites miscalculating?

10. Why should investors not use a stock's standard deviation as a way to measure the stock's risk?

SUMMARY

- In the United States and in most other countries, stocks have historically earned higher average returns than bonds but stock returns have also been more volatile. However, the difference between the volatility of stock and bond returns depends on the investment horizon. The longer the horizon, the smaller the difference between the volatility of stock and bond returns.

- Individuals save and invest money in order to increase their purchasing power over time, so the most relevant measure of an investment's return is its real return.

- Most investors are risk-averse, which means that they expect compensation for bearing risk.

- The return of an asset measures the amount by which it increases an investor's wealth over time. When calculating average returns from historical data, an analyst must decide whether to compute the arithmetic

or geometric average. We follow the common practice of using the arithmetic average to define a stock's expected return.

- Risk can be defined in many ways, including the chance of a loss and the dispersion of returns around the average. Sophisticated financial models recognize that a better measure of risk captures an investment's contribution to the overall variability of a portfolio. This is the only type of risk that the market should reward; we call it systematic risk.

- The systematic risk of any asset depends on its covariance with other assets. One measure of systematic risk is beta, which equals the ratio of the covariance of an asset's returns with the overall market's return, divided by the variance of the market's returns.

KEY TERMS

arithmetic average return
beta
correlation coefficient
covariance
discounted cash flow (DCF) analysis
equity risk premium

fair bet
geometric average return
normal distribution
probability distribution
real return
return

risk-averse
risk-neutral
risk-seeking
systematic risk
unsystematic risk

QUESTIONS

5-1. When using discounted cash flow analysis to value an asset, explain why it is important to measure the risk of the asset and to associate an expected return with that risk measure.

5-2. When we examine historical investment return data from many different countries, what trade-off becomes apparent?

5-3. Why are investors more concerned with the real returns than the nominal returns on their investments?

5-4. You observe that the price of some financial asset falls, but you do not believe that the expected future cash flows from the investment have changed. After the price decline, what has happened to the asset's expected return?

5-5. What is meant by the term *risk premium*? Why must riskier assets offer a risk premium?

5-6. How does the long-run historical U.S. equity risk premium compare to the risk premium that financial experts say they expect when they respond to surveys? How does the historical equity risk premium in the United States compare to the equity risk premium in other countries?

5-7. What is the basis for the claim that, relative to other investments, stocks are not as risky in the long run as they are in the short run?

5-8. How does risk affect the decision-making process of risk-averse and risk-neutral individuals?

5-9. How do historical data on investment returns align with the assumption that most investors are risk-averse?

5-10. An investor purchases a bond at par value, and the bond pays a coupon rate of 8%. Assume that the firm pays interest just once per year. The investor holds the bond for one year and sells it just after it makes its first coupon payment. Will the investor's total return on this investment equal 8%? Why or why not?

5-11. Given a series of historical returns on some investment, what is the relationship between the arithmetic and geometric average returns obtained from this series? Why is this important when comparing average returns on alternative investments?

5-12. If two securities are considered "uncorrelated," does this mean that their correlation coefficient is −1.0?

5-13. Can variance and standard deviation ever be negative? Can the two measures ever be zero?

5-14. Can the covariance ever be negative? Can the covariance ever have a different sign than the associated correlation coefficient?

5-15. Security A sells for $25.00 and has a guaranteed 1-year return of 4% (i.e., a future price of $26.00). Security B has the potential to be $50.00 with a probability of 1% or $25.76 with a probability of 99% (i.e., an expected price of $26.00). If we assume that investors are risk-averse, should Security B sell for more than $25.00, less than $25.00, or exactly $25.00? Answer this question again under the assumption that investors are risk-neutral.

5-16. How does the variance of a portfolio compare to the weighted average of the variances of the securities in the portfolio? Explain.

5-17. Suppose that the returns on two stocks are perfectly negatively correlated (i.e., the correlation coefficient is −1.0). Does this imply that, whenever the price of one security goes up, the price of the other security goes down?

5-18. Under what circumstances can you construct a risk-free portfolio with only risky securities? What would be the required return on such a portfolio?

5-19. What is the basis for saying that the variance of an individual asset is not a good measure of that asset's risk?

5-20. Explain why covariance matters more than variance in determining the risk of a large portfolio.

5-21. Suppose that a portfolio consists of 10 stocks. In the equation defining the variance of this portfolio:

   a. How many terms will be linked to the variance of the individual stocks in the portfolio?

   b. How many terms will be linked to the covariance between pairs of assets in the portfolio?

5-22. Describe two measures of the risk of an investment. How do these measures differ?

5-23. What constitutes total risk, and how is it measured? Of the two components of total risk, which one can investors eliminate? What is the remaining risk, and how is it measured?

5-24. Explain why the curve in Figure 5.8 does not reach all the way down to the x-axis.

5-25. Why do we say that the market rewards only systematic risk with higher expected returns?

5-26. What is the logic behind the claim that a stock's beta provides a better measure of its systematic risk than does its standard deviation?

PROBLEMS

Risk and Return Fundamentals

5-1. According to Figure 5.1, what would be the real value in 2008 of a £1 investment placed in British stocks in 1900?

5-2. Suppose you know that the current yield to maturity on Swedish government bonds is 3%. Use this data and figures from Table 5.2 to formulate a long-term forecast of the return on Swedish stocks. Is this figure in nominal or real terms?

5-3. Would a risk-averse person accept a gamble that offered a 50% chance of making $1,000 and a 50% chance of losing $1,000? Why or why not? Would a risk-seeking person accept the gamble?

5-4. A particular gamble offers a 50% chance of winning $1,000 and a 50% chance of losing $900. Can you say for sure whether a risk-averse person would accept this gamble? Why or why not? What would a risk-neutral person do?

See the problem and solution explained step-by-step at **SMARTFinance**

5-5. Return to the die-throwing example of a fair bet described in Section 5.1 under "Risk Aversion." If we view the $1,000 entry fee as the price of playing the game, then what is the expected percentage return on this investment? Calculate the expected percentage return on the game if the entry fee is $900. Repeat the calculation if the entry fee equals $800. What general relationship does this reveal between the price of an asset and its expected return (holding expected future cash flows constant)?

5-6. A risk-averse investor owns a stock portfolio worth $1 million. The investor believes that over the next year this portfolio's value will either rise by 20% or fall by 10%, with each outcome being equally likely. An investment bank offers the investor the following proposition: One year from today, the bank will pay the investor $100,000 if her portfolio value has decreased; otherwise, she receives nothing. In return, the investor must pay the investment bank $50,000 today. Does the investor accept the deal?

Basic Risk and Return Statistics

5-7. On January 3, 2009, you purchased 100 shares of stock for $45 per share. On January 3, 2010, you received a dividend of $2 per share, after which you immediately sold your shares for $48 each. What was your dollar return on this investment? What was your percentage return? Is your return for 2009–2010 different if you keep the shares instead of selling them?

5-8. Figure 5.1 shows that £1 invested in U.K. government bonds at the beginning of 1900 would be worth £309 at the end of 2008, but U.K. *prices* over the same period rose by a factor of 68.

    a. What is the real value at the end of 2008 of a £1 investment in U.K. bonds made at the start of 1900?

    b. Table 5.1 reports that the average annual real return on U.K. bonds for the period 1900–2008 was 2.2% (more precisely, 2.25%). Starting with £1 in January 1900, to what amount should a bond investment grow by December 31, 2008? Why is this answer so different from the answer to part (a)?

5-9. In 2008, the U.S stock market fell by about 37%. Suppose that the long-run arithmetic average return on this market is 12% per year. At that rate, how many years would it take the index to recover its losses? How would your answer change if you decided to use the geometric average return rather than the arithmetic average? Assume that the geometric average nominal return is 10%.

5-10. Calculate the expected return and standard deviation for an investment with the following probability distribution:

Return (%)	Probability (%)
−10	20
5	20
10	20
15	30
25	10

5-11. You are weighing the risk and return characteristics of a particular investment. You believe that the return of this investment can be characterized by the probability distribution that follows:

Return (%)	Probability (%)
−16	12.5
−8	12.5
0	12.5
4	12.5
8	12.5
12	12.5
16	12.5
32	12.5

a. Calculate the expected return and standard deviation for this investment.

b. Suppose that the returns listed in the first column are *not* points on a probability distribution. (In other words, ignore the probabilities in the second column.) Instead, imagine that they are the actual returns earned by this investment over the last eight years. Calculate the arithmetic average return and the standard deviation using this 8-year sample. Comment on any differences between your answers to this question and those in part (a).

c. Next, suppose we list 100 different possible outcomes for an investment's returns, each of which might occur with probability 1%. We then ask you to calculate the expected return and standard deviation using that probability distribution. Conceptually, how would your answers change if we ask you to calculate the expected return and standard deviation using 100 years' worth of historical returns?

Risk and Return for Portfolios

5-12. Using the probability distribution below, determine the mean, variance, and standard deviation of all four securities.

Probability	Security A	Security B	Security C	Security D
15%	8%	−1.88%	1.94%	3%
35%	5%	−4.28%	3.14%	3%
20%	−4%	−11.48%	6.74%	3%
30%	−6%	−13.08%	7.54%	3%

a. Compute the correlation coefficient between: Security A and Security B; Security A and Security C; Security A and Security D.

b. Which security is the risk-free security? Explain your answer using the statistical measures that have already been computed.

c. Because Security B has all negative returns, can one simply assume it is perfectly negatively correlated with Security A?

d. Should the correlation between the risk-free security and any risky security be zero?

5-13. Compute the correlation coefficient between the two securities below:

Probability	Security A	Security B
20%	7%	9%
40%	5%	6%
30%	7%	4%
10%	15%	6%

A friend argues, "Two securities are uncorrelated, so one of the securities must be the risk-free security." How valid is this statement based on the calculation of the correlation coefficient in this instance?

5-14. Compute the mean, variance, and standard deviation for the following three securities:

Probability	Security A	Security B	Security C
15%	8%	6%	6.8%
35%	5%	3%	3.8%
20%	−4%	2%	−0.4%
30%	−6%	10%	3.6%

a. Compute the covariance and correlation coefficient between Security A and Security B.

b. Find the portfolio mean, variance, and standard deviation for a portfolio with 40% invested in Security A and 60% invested in Security B.

c. Calculate the mean, variance, and standard deviation of returns for Security C. Compare your answer to part (b). (*Hint:* Notice that, in each row of the table, the return on Security C equals 40% of the return on Security A plus 60% of the return on Security B.)

5-15. Calculate the covariance and correlation coefficient for two assets with the following returns over the past year.

Month	Asset #1	Asset #2
Jan.	0.05	0.02
Feb.	0.10	0.06
Mar.	−0.02	−0.11
Apr.	0.01	0.09
May	0.07	0.08
June	−0.12	−0.06
July	0.03	0.04
Aug.	0.08	0.11
Sep.	−0.05	−0.01
Oct.	−0.07	−0.04
Nov.	0.04	0.05
Dec.	0.00	0.01

5-16. Go to http://www.yahoo.com and then click on the link labeled "Finance." The next screen asks you to enter a ticker symbol; type in "PMCS" (the ticker symbol for PMC–Sierra, a company that designs and develops high-speed broadband communications equipment) and hit "Get Quotes." You will then see current information about this stock as well as a number of additional links to explore. (*Note to students:* If PMCS does not bring up a stock quote for PMC Sierra, then the company may well have been acquired or gone out of business since this writing; continue with this problem using another company of your choice.)

Start by clicking "Historical Prices." At the top of the next page, you are given several choices about the time period over which you want to collect data. In the "Start" boxes, enter "June, 30, 2006." In the "End" boxes, type in "June, 30, 2009." Also click "Monthly" to indicate that you want monthly data rather than daily or weekly data. Next, click on the link "Get Prices" to see a table containing 37 months of data for this company. The table gives you the price at the beginning (open) and end (close) of each month as well as the high and low prices during the month. It also tells you how many shares were traded during the month. The final column contains the "Adjusted Close," a month-end price that reflects dividend payments, stock dividends, and/or stock splits.

You can calculate the monthly return just by calculating the percentage difference in adjusted closing prices. For example, the adjusted close in December 2006 was $6.71 and in January 2007 it was $6.30. Therefore, the percentage return during January 2007 was −6.11% [(6.30 − 6.71) ÷ 6.71]. Click the link labeled "Download To Spreadsheet" below the table and save the file when prompted. This should save the data in a comma-delimited file (with the .csv file extension) that you can open in Excel. Alternatively, you can download the file "Problem 5-16.xls" from the text's website.

a. Using the series of adjusted closing prices, calculate the return for PMC–Sierra stock in each month from January 2007 through December 2009.

b. Using the "=average()" function in Excel, calculate the average monthly return.

c. What is the geometric average monthly return?

d. Using the functions "=var()" and "=stdev()" in Excel, calculate the variance and standard deviation of monthly returns.

e. Repeat parts (a)–(d) to obtain monthly data from December 2006 to December 2009 for Broadcom, Inc., another producer of broadband semiconductor products (ticker symbol, BRCM). Calculate the monthly returns for Broadcom; then calculate the average, variance, and standard deviation of Broadcom's returns.

f. Calculate the covariance and correlation coefficient between the returns on PMC–Sierra and Broadcom. How would you characterize the correlation between these two stocks? Is that surprising or expected?

g. Imagine that you constructed a portfolio equally invested in PMC–Sierra and Broadcom stock. Calculate the return that this portfolio would have earned each month during 2007–2009 using this equation:

$$\text{Portfolio monthly return} = 0.50(\text{PMC monthly return}) + 0.50(\text{Broadcom monthly return})$$

Now use Excel to calculate the average value of the monthly return series you just constructed. What is the average monthly portfolio return?

h. Calculate the portfolio's return using Equation 5.5 with $w_1 = w_2 = 0.50$. You will use your answers to parts (b) and (e), the average returns on each stock, in place of the expected returns shown in Equation 5.5. Verify that your answer here is the same as in part (g).

i. Use the "=stdev()" function in Excel to calculate the standard deviation of the monthly returns on the 50-50 portfolio. Next, calculate the portfolio's standard deviation using Equation 5.10 (or Equation 5.12). Do the two answers match?

j. Compare the standard deviations of PMC and Broadcom returns, obtained in parts (d) and (e), to the standard deviation of the 50-50 portfolio's returns. How does the portfolio standard deviation compare to the standard deviations of the individual shares? How is that comparison tied to the correlation coefficient from part (f)?

5-17. Repeat the steps outlined previously to download historical prices from June 2006 to June 2009 for C. R. Bard, maker of surgical and diagnostic medical devices (ticker symbol, BCR), and York Water Company, water supplier to York and Adams counties in Pennsylvania (ticker symbol, YORW). You can obtain the data from Yahoo! or simply download the file "Problem 5-17.xls" from the text's website.

a. Calculate the average monthly return, variance, and standard deviation for each of the two stocks.

b. Calculate the covariance and correlation coefficient between C. R. Bard and York. Are these two stocks strongly or weakly correlated over this period?

c. Calculate the return that a portfolio invested equally in each company would have earned in each month during July 2007–June 2009. Next, calculate the monthly average return on the portfolio and the standard deviation of the portfolio's returns.

d. How does the average portfolio return compare to the average returns on the individual stocks?

e. How does the portfolio standard deviation compare to the standard deviations of the individual stocks? How is this related to the correlation between the two stocks?

5-18. You observe the following returns on two different stocks over the past several years:

Year	Stock 1 (%)	Stock 2 (%)
2002	5	3
2003	25	14
2004	−8	1
2005	13	9
2006	12	13
2007	1	−1
2008	−17	2
2009	−5	11
2010	46	20

a. Calculate the arithmetic average return for each stock over these nine years.

b. Calculate the geometric average return for each stock over the same period.

c. Compare your answers to parts (a) and (b), and explain the general points that these calculations illustrate.

d. For each stock, calculate the value of $1,000 invested at the beginning of 2002, assuming that you hold the stock until the end of 2010.

e. Calculate the standard deviation of returns for each stock, and then calculate the covariance and correlation coefficient between stock 1 and stock 2. (*Hint:* Be sure to use $N - 1$ in the denominator because you are using a sample of data.)

f. Using the historical arithmetic average return for each stock as an estimate of its expected return, calculate the expected return and standard deviation for a portfolio consisting of 35% stock 1 and 65% stock 2.

Smart
Solutions

See the problem and solution explained step-by-step at SMARTFinance

5-19. You are given the following data on two stocks:

	Stock 1	Stock 2
Expected return	10%	14%
Standard deviation	20%	40%
Correlation coefficient		0.50	

a. Calculate the expected return and standard deviation of the following portfolios, where w_1 and w_2 represent the fractions invested in stock 1 and stock 2, respectively. Plot these figures on a graph similar to Figure 5.6.

w_1	w_2	$E(R)$	σ
75%	25%		
50%	50%		
25%	75%		

b. Suppose an investor currently has $1,000 invested in stock 2 but would like to invest more. She borrows $250 worth of stock 1 from a broker, agreeing to return the shares in one year. Immediately after receiving these borrowed shares, the investor sells them in the market and then uses the $250 proceeds to increase her investment in stock 2. This investment approach is called *short selling*. What are the new portfolio weights (w_1 and w_2), and what is the expected return and standard deviation of this portfolio? Add these to your graph from part (a). Give an intuitive explanation of what the graph shows.

5-20. Asset 1 has an expected return of 10% and a standard deviation of 20%. Asset 2 has an expected return of 20% and a standard deviation of 50%. The correlation coefficient between the two assets is 0.0. Calculate the expected return and standard deviation for each of the following portfolios, and plot them on a graph:

Portfolio	% Invested in Asset 1	% Invested in Asset 2
A	100	0
B	75	25
C	50	50
D	25	75
E	0	100

Now, repeat these calculations after changing just one assumption: suppose the standard deviation of asset 1 equals zero. In other words, asset 1 pays a risk-free (because it never varies) return of 10%. How does the graph of the expected return and standard deviation for various portfolios change in this case?

5-21. Earlier this year you invested in a grocery store chain and added the stock to your portfolio. The purchase price was $40 per share. The end of the year is just a few days away, and your grocery stock currently sells for $22. If you sell the stock and realize the $18-per-share loss, then you can deduct that loss from income for tax purposes. But you feel that the stock is an important part of your overall portfolio and believe it may bounce back. You'd like to go ahead and realize the loss, in order to capture the tax deduction, and then immediately repurchase the stock and restore it to your portfolio. Unfortunately, the tax authorities impose something called the "wash sale rule," which disallows the tax deduction when you repurchase the stock within 30 days of selling it. How can you use the concept of correlation to capture the tax loss without missing out on the potential benefits from owning the stock that might occur immediately after your sale?

5-22. Security X has a mean return of 8% and an associated standard deviation of 36%. Security Y has a mean return of 12% and an associated standard deviation of 46%.

a. If we assume that the correlation coefficient is -1.0, then what is the portfolio variance when 56.10% of the portfolio is invested in Security X and the rest is invested in Security Y?

b. If the correlation coefficient is 1.0, then what is the portfolio variance when 460% of the portfolio is invested in Security X and the rest is invested in Security Y? (*Note:* The weight for Security Y is negative, which indicates short selling.)

c. Assume that short selling is permitted. Does perfect correlation then allow one to eliminate all portfolio risk?

d. Based on your calculations, can all portfolio risk be eliminated if short selling is *not* permitted? If so, then what must the correlation coefficient equal?

Systematic and Unsystematic Risk

5-23. You hold a portfolio consisting of N different stocks, and the average variance of a stock in your portfolio is 0.16. (Remember, variance is measured in units of "percent squared"—the average standard deviation would be 0.4 or 40%.) The average covariance between a pair of stocks in your portfolio is 0.12.

  a. Calculate the variance and standard deviation of your portfolio if $N = 5$.

  b. Repeat these calculations assuming that $N = 10$ and $N = 100$. What lesson do these calculations illustrate?

5-24. Suppose that you form an equally weighted portfolio of 100 different stocks.

  a. In the equation defining the variance of this portfolio, how many terms represent the variance of individual stocks?

  b. What weight is associated with each variance term when calculating the portfolio's variance?

  c. How many terms in the portfolio variance equation represent the covariance or correlation between a pair of stocks?

5-25. Calculate the standard deviation of the following three-asset portfolio.

Statistic	Asset		
	1	2	3
Standard deviation	30%	25%	10%
Correlation with 1	1.00	0.75	0.25
Correlation with 2	0.75	1.00	0.40
Correlation with 3	0.25	0.40	1.00
Portfolio weight	50%	30%	20%

5-26. You observe that the standard deviation of a particular stock is 40% per year; the standard deviation on a broad market index is 25% per year. If the correlation coefficient between the stock and the market index is 0.8, then what is the stock's beta?

5-27. You observe that the standard deviation of a particular stock is 60% per year; the standard deviation on a broad market index is 25% per year. If the correlation coefficient between the stock and the market index is 0.8, then what is the stock's beta? Holding fixed the market's standard deviation as well as the correlation between the market and the stock, how does an increase in a stock's standard deviation affect its beta? Repeat the problem assuming that the stock's standard deviation is just 15%.

THOMSON ONE | Business School Edition

5-28. Calculate the arithmetic average and standard deviation of monthly returns for Apple Computer Inc. (ticker symbol, AAPL), Dell Computer Corp. (ticker symbol, DELL), and General Mills (ticker symbol, GIS) over the last 12 months. (*Note:* You can obtain price data in ThomsonONE under Prices → Overviews → Datastream Market Data → Actual Value Price History Report.)

  Assume you have an equally weighted portfolio (equal *amount of money invested* in each security) of AAPL, DELL, and GIS. Calculate the arithmetic average and standard deviation of the monthly returns for the equally weighted portfolio. Repeat the calculations while assuming that you have a value-weighted portfolio (equal *number of shares* in each security) of these three companies.

How do the average returns and standard deviations of the three individual securities compare to the average returns and standard deviations of the portfolios? Is there a benefit to combining the securities into a portfolio? Does your answer change if you are comparing the average return and standard deviation for the equally weighted portfolio versus the value-weighted portfolio?

5-29. Calculate the monthly geometric average over the last 12 months for Apple, Dell, and General Mills. How do the geometric averages compare to the arithmetic averages computed in Problem 5-28? Which is the better "average" return—arithmetic or geometric?

5-30. Using Equation 5.14, calculate the betas for Apple, Dell, and General Mills using monthly returns for the last 12 months. Use the S&P 500 as the market index (DSMnemonic S&PCOMP). How would you expect these betas to change if you were to use the Nasdaq (DSMnemonic NASCOMP) or the Dow Jones Industrial Average (DSMnemonic DJINDUS) as the market index?

MINI-CASE: THE TRADE-OFF BETWEEN RISK AND RETURN

The end-of-year stock prices for KFD Corporation for the past six years, and annual dividends per share, are as follows:

Year	Stock Price	Dividends
2009	$85.23	$0.22
2008	$79.14	$0.18
2007	$37.86	$0.14
2006	$45.99	$0.10
2005	$23.33	$0.10
2004	$14.67	—

You have the following expectations for KFD's stock price during 2010:

Outlook	Probability	Stock Price
Good	45%	$93.42
Average	35%	$89.15
Bad	20%	$81.87

You think KFD will pay a dividend of $0.22 during 2010, regardless of the economic outlook.

1. Calculate the annual returns on KFD Corporation's stock for the years 2005–2009. Determine the geometric and arithmetic means for the returns as well as the variance and standard deviation of the arithmetic mean.

2. Forecast the overall expected return and standard deviation for KFD's stock during 2010.

You are now considering the possibility of adding KFD stock to your portfolio, which currently consists of equal weights of Mellon Corporation and Insignia Enterprises.

The expected returns and standard deviation of expected returns for Mellon and Insignia are:

	Mellon Corporation	**Insignia Enterprises**
Expected return	23.14%	18.93%
Standard deviation	26.56%	20.77%

The correlation coefficients among the three corporations are:

	Mellon Corporation	**Insignia Enterprises**	**KFD Corporation**
Mellon Corporation	1.0000		
Insignia Enterprises	0.5385	1.0000	
KFD Corporation	0.4233	0.3982	1.0000

3. Calculate the expected return, variance, and standard deviation of a portfolio consisting of 30% Mellon Corporation, 60% Insignia Enterprises, and 10% KFD Corporation.

4. The correlation coefficient between KFD Corporation and the market is 0.2532, while the variance of the market is 0.04. Determine the beta for KFD Corporation.

6

Risk, Return, and the Capital Asset Pricing Model

What Companies Do
Will the CAPM Cause a Train Wreck?

In most industries, the only restrictions that companies face when setting prices for their goods and services are the restraints placed upon them by competition. But this is not the case for railroads, which have been regulated by the federal government for more than a century. Currently, a little-known regulatory body, the Surface Transportation Board (STB), is charged by Congress with resolving railroad rate disputes and approving proposed railroad mergers. In its analysis of the rates that railroads charge customers, the STB determines what should be an acceptable rate of return for railroad companies and, in light of that, assesses whether railroad company revenues are adequate or inadequate to achieve that rate of return.

In response to pressure from railroad customers, the STB announced in 2007 that it would consider changing the method it used to calculate the cost of capital (or required rate of return) for railroad companies. The new method under consideration would estimate required returns using the Capital Asset Pricing Model (CAPM). In shifting to the CAPM, the STB would be adopting a technique already widespread in U.S. industry. Calculating the cost of capital is something that U.S. corporations do as a matter of routine, and the vast majority of those companies rely on the CAPM for their analysis. Railroads protested the move, fearing that the new model would generate lower estimates of their capital costs that would, in turn, put downward pressure on railroad shipping prices.

Sources: www.stb.dot.gov; Platts Coal Outlook (November 5, 2007).

Chapter 5 introduced the basic elements of portfolio theory, starting with a simple observation: Investments that historically have offered the highest average returns have also displayed the greatest volatility. The positive relationship between returns and volatility in the historical data makes sense in a world populated by risk-averse investors. If riskier investments did not offer the prospect of higher returns, then they could not survive in the market. Yet total volatility (i.e., the variance or standard deviation of returns) has serious flaws as a measure of risk. Investors can easily reduce volatility through diversification. Accordingly, investors can expect rewards only for bearing *systematic* risk, the risk that cannot be diversified away. Asset pricing models attempt to quantify systematic risk and to determine the rate of return investors expect as compensation for bearing this risk. Remember, the price of a financial asset equals the present value of its future cash flows. If we know the return that the market requires on a given asset, then we know the rate at which the market discounts the asset's cash flows, information that is necessary in order to determine the asset's price.

For decades, beta stood alone as the most popular metric for an investment's systematic risk. *Beta* measures the sensitivity of an investment's returns to fluctuations in overall market returns. By definition, the beta of the overall market is 1.0. Investments with below-average systematic risk have betas below 1.0, and those with above-average systematic risk have betas greater than 1.0. Put another way, high-beta investments increase the systematic risk exposure of a portfolio whereas low-beta investments decrease that exposure. If investors concern themselves only with systematic risk and if beta measures that risk accurately, then we anticipate a positive relationship between beta and returns. This is the crux of the *capital asset pricing model* (CAPM).

This chapter traces the development of the CAPM, explaining its intellectual foundations as well as its practical impact. We explain how recent criticisms led to modifications to the original CAPM as well as to entirely new approaches to asset pricing. We conclude with a discussion of the current state of the "CAPM controversy" and descriptions of the leading alternatives to the CAPM.

6.1 Efficient Risky Portfolios

The Efficient Frontier with Two Assets

Are some portfolios better than others? For risk-averse investors, the answer is clearly yes. Recall the portfolios we examined containing different combinations of Nike and Arrow International shares in Figure 5.5(B). An investor holding a portfolio consisting entirely of Arrow shares could unambiguously improve the portfolio's performance by selling some Arrow shares and using the proceeds to buy Nike stock. By doing so, the investor increases the portfolio's return while simultaneously decreasing its standard deviation, at least up to a point. In this example, diversification achieves two goals at once—increasing portfolio returns and decreasing portfolio volatility.

Figure 6.1 illustrates this phenomenon for two generic stocks, A and B. Stock A has an expected return of 6% and a standard deviation of 20%, while Stock B has an expected return of 17% and a standard deviation of 50%. The curve connecting A and B, called the **feasible set**, plots the expected return and standard deviation for all possible portfolios of these two stocks. By glancing at the figure, we know that the correlation between the returns for A and B falls below 1.0—otherwise, portfolios of A and B would lie on a straight, upward-sloping line connecting the two points. Analogously, because the arc connecting A and B does not bend all the way back to the *y*-axis, the correlation between A and B exceeds −1.0. Figure 6.1 therefore illustrates an intermediate case, where stocks are imperfectly correlated. You might observe this pattern when plotting the data of any two stocks picked at random.

FIGURE 6.1

Expected Return
and Standard
Deviation for
Portfolios of Two
Assets A and B

Note that portfolios
C and D are efficient
portfolios.

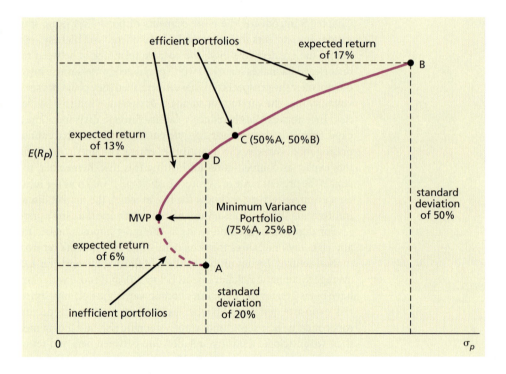

Because the arc initially bends backward toward the *y*-axis, an investor can construct a portfolio of A and B that has less volatility than either A or B alone. By trial and error (or by using calculus), you can find the combination of A and B shares that results in the portfolio marked MVP, the **minimum variance portfolio**. No other combination of assets A and B yields a portfolio with a lower standard deviation. For the sake of illustration, suppose that investing 75% in A and 25% in B results in the MVP. How can an investor use this information?

Examine the two segments of the arc separated by the point MVP. An investor allocating money between A and B should avoid buying shares in company A exclusively because another portfolio that offers a higher return for the same level of volatility exists on the arc. That portfolio is represented by point D in the figure. Notice that portfolios A and D both have a standard deviation of 20%, but the expected return on portfolio D is 13% compared to portfolio A's expected return of just 6%.

The same statement could be made for any portfolio lying on the dashed portion of the arc, from A to MVP. At any point on this segment, another portfolio exists with the same standard deviation and a higher expected return. Therefore, all portfolios lying on the dashed segment from A to MVP (i.e., all portfolios with less than 25% invested in B) are **inefficient portfolios**. We say that a portfolio is inefficient if it offers a lower expected return than another portfolio with the same standard deviation. Faced with the investment opportunities portrayed in Figure 6.1, an investor knows that 25% is the minimum rational investment in stock B. Any smaller investment in B results in an inefficient portfolio.

By the same token, all portfolios lying on the solid red segment connecting MVP and B qualify as **efficient portfolios**. A portfolio is efficient if it offers the highest expected return among the group of portfolios with equal or less volatility. In other words, if you mark any point on the arc from MVP to B, you will notice that no other portfolio promises a higher expected return without adding more volatility. The terms **efficient set** and **efficient frontier** refer to all the points on the solid red arc from MVP to B. Investors want to hold portfolios that lie on the efficient frontier because those portfolios maximize expected returns for any given level of volatility.

If the minimum rational investment in asset B is 25%, can we say that a portfolio containing 50% B would be even better? Not necessarily. The answer depends on the investor's tolerance for risk. A 50-50 portfolio is plotted as point C in Figure 6.1. This portfolio provides a higher expected return than the MVP but at the cost of higher volatility. Some very risk-averse investors might decide that C's additional return is inadequate compensation for the extra risk, whereas other investors might think the extra compensation is sufficient. Portfolio theory says that no risk-averse investor should choose an inefficient portfolio (lying between A and MVP), but choosing among efficient portfolios involves subjective assessments that vary from one investor to another, depending on each investor's tolerance for risk.

The Efficient Frontier with Many Assets

Figure 6.2 generalizes these concepts to a market with more than two investments. The arc and the area beneath it represent the new feasible set. Each point underneath the arc corresponds to a specific security. The feasible set simply consists of all possible portfolios formed by combining these assets.

FIGURE 6.2

The Efficient Frontier with Many Assets

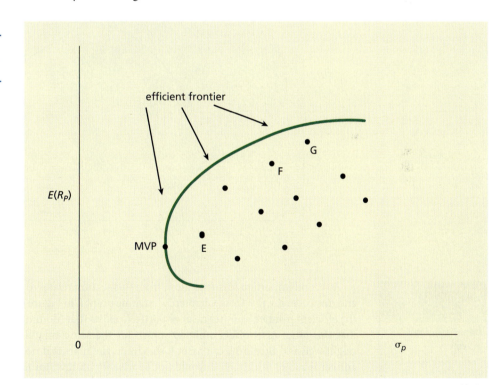

As before, the upward-sloping portion of the arc forming the northwest boundary of the feasible set is the efficient frontier. Each point on the efficient frontier is formed by combining individual securities into a portfolio that has the highest possible return for a given level of volatility. Inefficient portfolios in this figure include points such as E, F, and G. For each of these assets, a portfolio on the frontier exists offering a higher expected return for the same risk.

We must make two important remarks here. First, in describing the feasible set and efficient frontier (EF) in Figures 6.1 and 6.2, we have often used the terms "stock" or "share" to describe the individual investments available to investors. However, the important lessons of portfolio theory apply to the full universe of investment classes, not just to common stocks. For example, the feasible set consists not only of portfolios that might be formed by purchasing shares in companies listed on the New York Stock Exchange but also portfolios that include assets such as corporate and government bonds, real estate, and even exotic investments such as precious metals or art. Furthermore, there is no reason to restrict the feasible set to domestic investments. It also includes stocks and bonds that trade in foreign countries. Chapter 5 demonstrated that diversification reduces portfolio risk, and that lesson applies here. *The broader the range of investments included in the feasible set, the greater the risk reduction achievable through diversification.* Figure 6.3 illustrates the point by showing hypothetical efficient frontiers for different feasible sets encompassing an expanding array of investment choices.

FIGURE 6.3

The Effect of Expanding the Set of Investment Alternatives on the Efficient Frontier (EF)

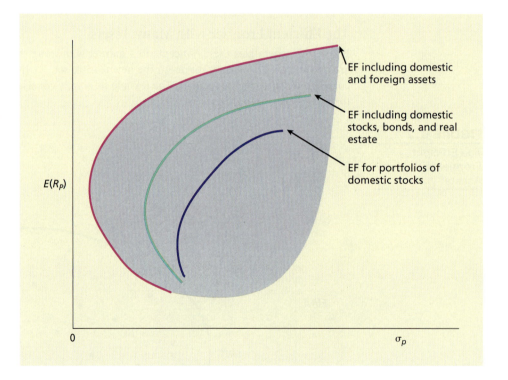

A second important lesson to glean from this section relates to the concepts of systematic and unsystematic risk from Chapter 5. Examine point E in Figure 6.2. Because E lies beneath the efficient frontier, another asset or portfolio exists that "dominates" E, by which we mean that this other asset offers a higher return for the same volatility. If that is the case, you might well ask, then how can asset E survive in the market if no one wants to own it? The answer is subtle. Although it would not be wise for an investor to hold asset E in isolation, it does not follow logically that investors will avoid E entirely. In fact, investors may need to hold some fraction of their wealth in E to construct a portfolio that lies on the efficient frontier. For example, suppose that asset E exhibits very low correlation with the other assets in the feasible set. Adding such an asset to a portfolio reduces the portfolio's level of systematic risk. In that case, investors will be willing to hold asset E as part of their portfolios even if it offers a relatively low return.[1]

---

[1]In other words, the risk of a portfolio that contains asset E is less than it would be if asset E were removed. Insurance provides a concrete example of this phenomenon. Because fire and casualty insurance companies price their policies to

EXAMPLE

A few simple calculations illustrate the main points to take away from this section. Chapter 5 examined the risk and return characteristics of two different portfolios: one containing shares of Mead Corp. and Boise Cascade, the other containing shares of Nike and Arrow International. Table 6.1 calculates the expected monthly return and standard deviation for 16 different portfolios consisting of various combinations of these four stocks.[2] Figure 6.4 plots the expected return and standard deviation for each portfolio. Notice how closely the shape of the set in this figure resembles those shown in Figures 6.2 and 6.3. You could trace the boundary of this set by drawing lines connecting portfolios 2 through 8 in the figure, and the upward-sloping portion of that boundary (including portfolios 3, 4, and 8) would roughly trace out the efficient frontier.

Table 6.1   Expected Return (per month) and Standard Deviation for Various Portfolios

	PERCENTAGE INVESTED IN EACH STOCK				PORTFOLIO CHARACTERISTICS	
PORTFOLIO NUMBER	MEAD CORP.	BOISE CASCADE	NIKE INC.	ARROW INTERNATIONAL	EXPECTED RETURN (PER MONTH)	STANDARD DEVIATION
1	0	0	0	100	1.08	8.42
2	0	50	0	50	0.98	5.34
3	0	25	25	50	1.28	4.37
4	0	0	50	50	1.57	5.12
5	25	0	50	25	1.58	8.14
6	10	10	70	10	1.75	10.99
7	5	5	85	5	1.91	12.70
8	0	0	100	0	2.06	14.53
9	50	0	0	50	1.09	6.95
10	25	25	25	25	1.28	7.31
11	20	20	40	20	1.44	8.17
12	0	50	50	0	1.47	10.93
13	50	0	50	0	1.59	11.88
14	0	100	0	0	0.88	9.88
15	50	50	0	0	0.99	11.12
16	100	0	0	0	1.11	13.00

Note: Portfolios 3 through 8 are efficient portfolios.

---

make a profit, the average purchaser of fire insurance loses money. As a consequence, purchasers of fire insurance can expect negative returns on their policies, on average. Is it irrational to buy fire insurance? Absolutely not. A fire insurance policy pays off big at precisely the time that the value of an investor's home declines sharply (i.e., when the home is reduced to ashes). For most people, a home represents a significant fraction of total wealth. Because the correlation between the return on a home and the return on a fire insurance policy is negative, combining them in a portfolio makes sense. Fire insurance reduces overall portfolio risk, even though most individuals can expect to lose money on the fire insurance component of their portfolios.

[2]The data for these calculations come from Table 5.3.

Take a moment to examine a few inefficient portfolios lying beneath the efficient frontier in Figure 6.4. Portfolio 9, for example, is clearly inferior to portfolios 3 and 4, both of which offer higher returns and lower standard deviations than portfolio 9. For the same reason, portfolio 5 dominates portfolios 11–12 and 14–16.

FIGURE 6.4

Expected Return (per month) and Standard Deviation for Various Portfolios

The data points for each numbered portfolio in this figure appear in the final two columns of Table 6.1.

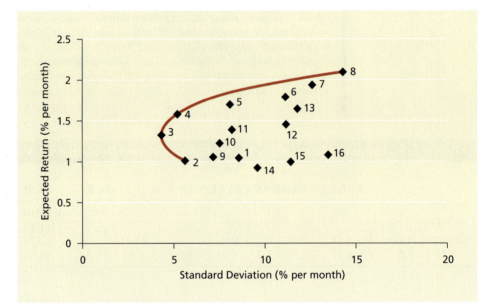

JOB INTERVIEW QUESTION

Under what circumstances might you advise a client to add a stock to his or her portfolio even though you expect the stock to earn a low return?

Portfolio 1, consisting entirely of Arrow International stock, falls well below the efficient frontier. Does this mean investors should stay away from Arrow stock? Not at all. Notice that portfolios 3 and 4, both of which lie on the efficient frontier, contain significant investments in Arrow. Arrow's returns are negatively correlated with returns on each of the other three stocks and so, when investors mix Arrow shares with other stocks, the resulting portfolios benefit from diversification. Notice that the portfolios containing no Arrow shares fall below the frontier, again with the exception of portfolio 8.[3] By itself, Arrow International looks like a bad investment, offering relatively low returns and relatively high risk. But Arrow shines in a portfolio!

> **Concept Review Questions**
>
> 1. Is the minimum variance portfolio always an efficient portfolio? Is an efficient portfolio always the minimum variance portfolio?
> 2. An efficient portfolio is one that maximizes expected return for any given level of risk. Is it equivalent to define an efficient portfolio as one that minimizes risk for any level of expected return?
> 3. How is the efficient frontier affected by expanding the types of assets included in the feasible set?
> 4. Examine portfolio 10 in Table 6.1 and Figure 6.4. This portfolio contains equal investments in all four stocks. Why do you think it falls below the efficient frontier?

---

[3]Investors wanting to create a portfolio with the highest possible expected return, no matter how risky, have just one choice—invest everything in the stock with the highest expected return, Nike. However, that conclusion will change in the next section when we allow investors to borrow and lend while forming portfolios.

6.2 Risk-Free Borrowing and Lending

Portfolios of Risky and Risk-Free Assets

By plotting the expected return and standard deviation for portfolios of two or more assets, we have seen that these portfolios define a set with a curved boundary. The lower the correlation between the assets in the portfolio, the more this boundary curves back toward the y-axis (i.e., the more that diversification reduces risk in a portfolio). Now we introduce a new possibility. What happens if investors can add a risk-free investment to their portfolios?

By definition, the expected return equals the actual return on a risk-free investment. That is, investors holding the risk-free asset get exactly the return they expected when they bought it. There is no uncertainty about what return the asset will generate. In reality, no investment is completely free of risk, but a U.S. Treasury bill comes close to that ideal. Keep in mind that, when they buy U.S. T-bills, investors are lending money to the government—albeit on a very short-term basis.

For now, assume that a truly risk-free investment exists. Denoting its return by R_f, we can write the following equations:

$$E(R_f) = R_f$$

$$\text{Var}(R_f) = \sigma_{Rf}^2 = 0;$$

$$\text{Std. dev.}(R_f) = \sigma_{Rf} = 0$$

Imagine that an investor currently holds a diversified mutual fund of risky securities with an expected return equal to $E(R_{MF})$ and a variance of σ_{MF}^2. We can treat this mutual fund as a single asset. Now form a portfolio by allocating weights w_{Rf} to the risk-free asset and w_{MF} to the mutual fund. In other words, w_{Rf} is the percentage invested in the risk-free asset, and w_{MF} is the percentage held in the mutual fund. You can derive the expected return and variance of this new, two-asset portfolio using the standard equations for any two-asset portfolio:

$$E(R_p) = w_{Rf}R_f + w_{MF}R_{MF}$$

$$\text{Var}(R_p) = \sigma_p^2 = (w_{Rf})^2\sigma_{Rf}^2 + (w_{MF})^2\sigma_{MF}^2 + 2(w_{Rf})(w_{MF})\text{Cov}(R_f, R_{MF})$$

Because the risk-free asset's return has no variance, $\sigma_{Rf}^2 = 0$. Likewise, if the risk-free return is constant then it does not covary with any other asset, so $\text{Cov}(R_f, R_{MF}) = 0$. Therefore, the equation for the variance of a portfolio consisting of a risky asset and a risk-free asset reduces to

$$\text{Var}(R_p) = \sigma_p^2 = w_{MF}^2\sigma_{MF}^2$$

Now taking the square root to obtain the standard deviation of this portfolio yields

$$\sigma_p = w_{MF}\sigma_{MF}$$

The standard deviation of this two-asset portfolio increases linearly as the fraction invested in the risky asset increases. Geometrically, that means that portfolios of risky and risk-free assets lie along the straight line shown in Figure 6.5. Point A in the figure represents a portfolio invested 50% in the risk-free asset and 50% in the risky asset.

But what about point B? How can investors form portfolios of risky and risk-free assets that lie above and to the right of the risky asset, MF? The answer is that investors can *borrow* money to invest in risky assets.

FIGURE 6.5

Portfolios of Risky and Risk-Free Assets

Portfolio A reflects 50% invested in the risk-free asset, and 50% invested in the risky asset MF, whereas portfolio B reflects the use of borrowing to invest more than 100% of the investor's funds in the risky asset MF.

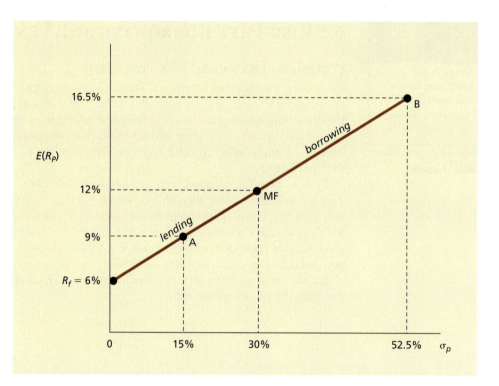

Consider an individual who has $1,000 to invest. Assume that the risk-free asset pays 6% and that the expected rate of return on the mutual fund she wants to buy is 12% with a standard deviation of 30%. She could put all of her money in the risky asset and reach point MF in the figure, she could put all of it in the risk-free asset and reach point R_f, or she could buy some of both and reach an intermediate point such as point A. But what if she can borrow money at 6% interest? By borrowing money and investing the proceeds in the risky asset, she can increase the fraction of her portfolio invested in MF to more than 100%. In other words, she invests all of her own money *plus* borrowed funds in the risky security. For instance, if she invests $750 of borrowed money then she effectively invests 175% of her initial wealth in MF. The expected return on her portfolio is shown in the following equation:

$$E(R_p) = -0.75(6\%) + 1.75(12\%) = 16.5\%$$

The first term on the right-hand side of this equation, $-0.75(6\%)$, reflects the fact that borrowing is just the opposite of lending. The investor borrows an amount equal to 75% of her initial wealth. The minus sign indicates that her return on these borrowed funds will be negative—she must pay 6% interest on the amount she borrows. However, she reinvests the $750 (plus her own $1,000) in the mutual fund that has a higher expected return. Because the mutual fund's expected return exceeds the interest rate on her loan, she expects to magnify her rate of return relative to what she could earn if she were to use only her own money. In this case, her expected return is 16.5%.

Of course, the downside to all this is the risk that the *actual return* on the mutual fund may turn out to be less than expected. Suppose that the mutual fund earns a 0% return. At the end of the year, the total value of her portfolio will be just what it was at the beginning, $1,750. Of this total, however, $795 belongs to the lender ($750 principal and $45 interest). Our investor, who began the year with $1,000, now has just $955, a loss of 4.5%. The general pattern illustrated by this numerical example is that the return on a portfolio financed with borrowed money fluctuates more than the return on the portfolio's under-lying assets, as demonstrated by the following calculations.

If the mutual fund's return is	Then her return after investing the borrowed money is
18%	27%
12%	16.5%
6%	6%
0%	−4.5%
−6%	−15%

To see how volatile this portfolio is, just use the equation for standard deviation:

$$\sigma_p = w_{MF}\sigma_{MF} = 1.75(30\%) = 52.5\%$$

The lesson here is straightforward. *The greater the amount of money invested in the risky asset, the higher will be the expected return and volatility of the portfolio. The greater the investment in the risk-free asset, the lower will be the portfolio's volatility and return.*

Finding the Optimal Portfolio

The opportunity to borrow and lend at the risk-free rate fundamentally changes an investor's portfolio selection problem. In a world with only risky assets, risk-averse investors search for portfolios that lie on the efficient frontier and then select, from that set of portfolios, the one that best matches their tolerance for risk. Though all investors can rule out many portfolios as inefficient (e.g., those underneath the frontier), there can be no agreement on which of the portfolios on the frontier is best. It is a matter of individual taste.

Figure 6.6 demonstrates how adding a risk-free asset alters the picture. The graph shows the familiar feasible set and efficient frontier. Point R_f on the vertical axis indicates the

FIGURE 6.6

A New Efficient Frontier

When individuals can invest in both risky and risk-free securities, a new efficient frontier emerges. The new efficient frontier is defined by a line that starts at point R_f and is tangent to the old frontier at point M, which represents the optimal risky portfolio.

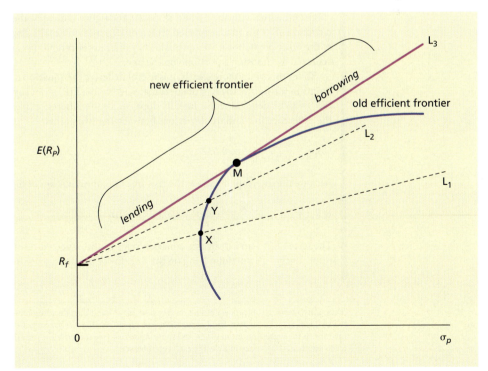

return available on the risk-free security. In this world, any investor can form a portfolio consisting of the risk-free asset and any other risky portfolio. For instance, the line marked L_1 represents all portfolios that an investor might create by combining the risk-free asset with risky portfolio X. Notice that some of these portfolios lie outside the old feasible set, meaning that the availability of a risk-free security opens up new investment opportunities.

The portfolios that lie along line L_1 are inferior to those on line L_2, which are formed by combining the risk-free asset with risky portfolio Y. For any portfolio on line L_1, a portfolio exists on line L_2 that has the same standard deviation and a higher expected return. But other portfolios exist that dominate those on line L_2. Only when investors reach line L_3, which combines the risk-free asset with risky portfolio M, have they maximized the expected return on their portfolio for a given standard deviation. In other words, *line L_3 defines a new efficient frontier.* Risky portfolios X and Y, which lie along the old efficient frontier in a world without a risk-free asset, are no longer efficient. To reach this new efficient frontier, investors first search for the point of tangency on the line connecting the risk-free asset to the old efficient frontier. That is, investors first determine the composition of portfolio M. Next, investors allocate their wealth between portfolio M and the risk-free asset according to their risk preferences. This amounts to deciding where on the line they want their portfolios to lie. Investors who are very risk averse will invest heavily in the risk-free asset, thereby locating their portfolios near point R_f. Investors who are less risk averse will allocate more of their money to the risky asset, perhaps even borrowing money to structure a portfolio lying to the right of point M.[4]

EXAMPLE

Suppose that Rachel can borrow or lend at the risk-free rate of 3%. She needs to decide which of seven risky portfolios she should hold in combination with a position in the risk-free asset. Figure 6.7 plots the standard deviation and expected return of each portfolio. To determine which portfolio is best, she draws a line from the risk-free rate to each dot in the figure and chooses the line with the highest slope. As the figure indicates, the portfolio with a standard deviation of 19% and an expected return of 15% maximizes the slope. Investing money in any of the other portfolios is suboptimal. They offer lower returns for any level of risk than can be achieved by choosing a portfolio on the line.

To see this point more clearly, it is useful to derive the equation of the line in Figure 6.7. Two points in the figure, the first at coordinates $[\sigma_p = 0\%, E(R) = 3\%]$ and the second at $[\sigma_p = 19\%, E(R) = 15\%]$, determine this line. Its slope equals the difference in expected returns divided by the difference in standard deviations between the two points:

$$\text{Slope} = \frac{15\% - 3\%}{19\% - 0\%} = 0.632$$

Because the intercept occurs at the risk-free rate, the equation of the line is

$$E(R_p) = 3\% + \left[\frac{15\% - 3\%}{19\%}\right]\sigma_p = 0.03 + 0.632\sigma_p$$

The terms $E(R_p)$ and σ_p in this equation refer to the expected return and standard deviation, respectively, of a portfolio lying on the line. Every portfolio on this line reflects some mixture

---

[4]Economists refer to this process of first finding portfolio M and then deciding how to allocate funds between M and the risk-free asset as the **two-fund separation principle**. When a risk-free asset exists, the optimal strategy for all investors is to invest some money in M and some in the risk-free security. The only thing that changes from one investor to another is how much to invest in each type of asset.

FIGURE 6.7

Finding the
Optimal Portfolio

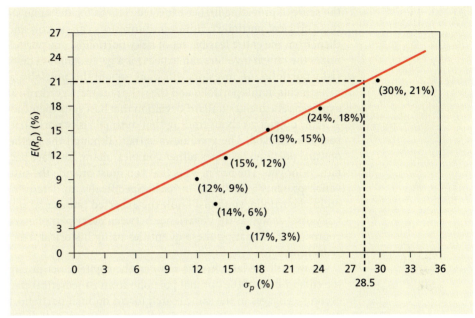

of the risk-free asset and the "optimal" risky portfolio. Investors can alter the mix of risky and risk-free assets according to their own tolerance for risk.

Suppose that Rachel, who has a very high tolerance for risk, reasons that she should hold the risky portfolio with the highest expected return (i.e., the (30%, 21%) portfolio in the top right portion of the figure). This portfolio offers a return of 21%, much higher than the "optimal" (19%, 15%) portfolio identified previously. Rachel might ask, "If I don't mind the fact that this portfolio has a standard deviation of 30%, why would I bother investing in something with a lower expected return?"

The answer is that another approach will allow Rachel to construct a portfolio with the same expected return, 21%, but with less risk. Start by calculating what mix of the risk-free asset and the "optimal" portfolio produces a 21% expected return. Let w represent the fraction invested in the risk-free asset, leaving $1 - w$ to be invested in the optimal portfolio:

$$E(R_p) = 21\% = w(3\%) + (1 - w)(15\%);$$
$$w = -0.5 = -50\%$$

Rachel should borrow an amount equal to 50% of her wealth, allowing her to invest 150% in the optimal portfolio. What will be the standard deviation of this new portfolio? It is equal to the standard deviation of the risky portfolio multiplied by the fraction invested in that portfolio:

$$\sigma_p = 1.5(19\%) = 28.5\%$$

Figure 6.7 highlights the advantage of this portfolio. By borrowing funds and investing them in the optimal risky portfolio, Rachel achieves her target expected return of 21% but with a standard deviation of 28.5% rather than 30%.

Before going on, let's summarize what we know so far. Because all risky assets are not perfectly correlated, investors should diversify. Diversification allows investors to eliminate unsystematic risk. Some diversified portfolios will perform better than others in the sense of providing higher expected returns for the same standard deviation. We call these efficient portfolios. However, if investors can borrow and lend at the risk-free rate then, from the entire feasible set of risky portfolios, one portfolio will emerge that maximizes the return investors can expect for a given standard deviation. This is the **optimal risky portfolio**. All investors will want to hold this portfolio, and they will change their investments in this portfolio and the risk-free asset in order to achieve the combination of expected return and standard deviation that best suits their individual preferences.

How do you go about finding that optimal risky portfolio? We have good news and bad news for you. The good news is that, although the mathematics of solving for the optimal portfolio becomes rather complex, many software packages can do the computations for you. The bad news is that you must provide the software with a set of inputs, which presents a challenge in itself. Specifically, to determine the composition of the optimal portfolio, you must know the expected return and standard deviation for every risky asset as well as the covariance between every pair of assets. Even taking the simple approach of estimating these quantities using historical data involves a lot of number crunching.

As we will see later in this chapter, the capital asset pricing model (CAPM) tells us the composition of the optimal portfolio from a theoretical standpoint. Recognizing that everyone engages in the same search for an optimal portfolio, the CAPM makes certain assumptions to derive its prediction that the optimal portfolio is just the market portfolio. The CAPM provides a novel and practical way to assess the expected return of any risky asset by using beta to measure its sensitivity to the market portfolio.

Concept Review Questions	5. If the covariance between two risky assets is zero, then portfolios of these two assets will lie along a backward-bending curve. The covariance between a risky and a risk-free asset is zero, yet portfolios of these two assets lie along a straight line. Explain.
	6. Explain how investors can use leverage (i.e., borrowed money) to increase both the expected return and the risk of their portfolios.
	7. How does an investor's portfolio selection problem change when risk-free borrowing and lending is possible?
	8. Explain the following statement: With risk-free borrowing and lending there is only one optimal risky portfolio, but there are still many efficient portfolios.

6.3 EQUILIBRIUM AND THE MARKET PORTFOLIO

The Market Portfolio

The preceding analysis suggests that all investors should search for the composition of the optimal portfolio. That search begins when investors form estimates of the expected returns, standard deviations, and covariances for all risky assets in the economy. Think for a moment about how investors might arrive at these estimates. First, they might look at the historical record to see how asset prices moved in the past. Second, they may examine other sources of public information, such as documents available from the Securities and Exchange Commission's EDGAR database (http://www.sec.gov/edgar.shtml). Third, they could listen to the opinions of analysts in the media or subscribe to one of the popular investment newsletter services. The point is, in their search for the optimal portfolio, different investors will sift through similar information sources to arrive at their estimates of expected returns, standard deviations, and covariances. Because they rely on similar information sources, investors may develop similar expectations for how investments will perform in the future. Although it is clearly true that differences of opinion exist from one investor to another, economists adopt the assumption of **homogeneous expectations** as a way to consider how the market will reach equilibrium.

If all investors agree on the risk-and-return characteristics of specific assets, then they will all agree on the shape of the efficient frontier. Given knowledge of the risk-free rate, every investor will find the same point of tangency with the efficient frontier—that is, the same optimal portfolio. Because this portfolio allows investors to maximize expected return for any level of standard deviation, all investors want to hold it.

In economics, equilibrium occurs in a market when the market price equates the quantity demanded and supplied of a good. If all investors demand to hold the same portfolio then, in equilibrium, this must be the portfolio that is supplied by the market. Economists refer to this portfolio, designated by point M in Figure 6.6, as the **market portfolio**. In theory, the market portfolio literally consists of every available asset, with each asset weighted by its market value relative to the total market value of all assets. In practice, forming the market portfolio is extremely difficult. Fortunately, we can approximate it with a value-weighted, diversified portfolio of many different assets, such as the Standard & Poor's 500 Stock Index.

The Capital Market Line

Under the assumption of homogeneous expectations, portfolio M in Figure 6.6 receives a special designation, the market portfolio. The line connecting point M to the risk-free rate, L_3, is referred to as the **capital market line (CML)**. The CML quantifies the relationship between expected return and standard deviation for portfolios consisting of the risk-free asset and the market portfolio:

$$E(R_p) = R_f + \left[\frac{E(R_m) - R_f}{\sigma_m}\right]\sigma_p \qquad \text{(Eq. 6.1)}$$

This equation indicates that the expected return on any portfolio, $E(R_p)$, equals the risk-free rate plus a premium that depends on the portfolio's risk, σ_p. The term in brackets measures the risk premium on the market portfolio relative to its standard deviation. Sometimes called the reward-to-risk ratio, or the **market price of risk**, the bracketed term is what investors try to maximize as they search for the optimal risky portfolio. Risk-averse investors want as much reward as they can obtain for a given level of risk.

The CML defines the efficient frontier when investors have common beliefs and can borrow and lend at the risk-free rate. Investors should only hold portfolios that are located on the CML. But what does this imply regarding the expected return and risk for individual assets, some of which do not lie on the CML? The capital asset pricing model, to which we now turn, answers this question.

Concept Review Questions

9. Do investors want to maximize or minimize the market price of risk? Why?
10. Refer to the equation for the CML. Is it possible to construct a portfolio such that σ_p exceeds σ_m? How?

6.4 THE CAPITAL ASSET PRICING MODEL (CAPM)

The Security Market Line

The basic CAPM was developed almost simultaneously during the mid-1960s by William Sharpe (1964), John Lintner, and Jan Mossin (1966); it was quickly embraced by academic researchers and, in time, by practitioners as well. The reason for the CAPM's widespread acceptance is not hard to understand—for the first time, researchers and practitioners had a model that generated specific predictions about the risk–return characteristics of individual assets, and this relation was driven by how each asset *covaries* with the market portfolio.

The formal development of the CAPM requires several assumptions about investors and markets. Rather than present a detailed list of these assumptions, we present the logic of the CAPM as it flows from the material we have covered so far.

1. Investors are risk averse and require higher returns on riskier investments.
2. Because investors can diversify, they care only about the systematic (or undiversifiable) risk of any investment.
3. The market offers no reward for bearing unsystematic risk because it can be diversified away.
4. Some portfolios are better than others. Portfolios that maximize expected return for any level of risk are efficient portfolios.
5. If investors can borrow and lend at the risk-free rate, then there exists a single risky portfolio that dominates all others. Only portfolios consisting of the risk-free asset and the optimal risky portfolio are efficient.
6. If investors have homogeneous expectations then they will agree on the composition of the optimal portfolio. In equilibrium, the optimal portfolio will be the market portfolio.
7. The central insight of the CAPM is that if all investors hold the market portfolio then—when evaluating the risk of any specific asset—they will be concerned with the covariance of that asset with the overall market. The implication is that any measure of an asset's systematic risk exposure must capture how it covaries with the rest of the market. An asset's beta provides a quantitative measure of this risk, and therefore the CAPM predicts a positive, linear relationship between expected return and beta. In the CAPM, beta risk (or market risk) is the only risk that is priced.

The **capital asset pricing model (CAPM)** indicates that the expected return on a specific asset, $E(R_i)$, equals the risk-free rate plus a premium that depends on the asset's beta, β_i, and the expected risk premium on the market portfolio, $E(R_m) - R_f$:

$$E(R_i) = R_f + \beta_i\left[E(R_m) - R_f\right] \tag{Eq. 6.2}$$

Recall that beta measures an asset's correlation with a broader portfolio—in this case, the market portfolio. The higher the beta of a security, the greater the security's exposure to systematic risk and the higher the expected return it must offer investors. Although there are three variables (R_f, β_i, and $E(R_m)$) on the right-hand side of the CAPM equation, only beta changes from one security to the next. For that reason, analysts classify the CAPM as a **single-factor model**, meaning that just one variable explains differences in returns across securities.

Figure 6.8 plots the CAPM equation on a diagram with the expected return on the y-axis and beta on the x-axis. The intercept of this line is R_f, and its slope is $E(R_m) - R_f$. According to the CAPM, the equilibrium expected returns of all securities must plot on

JOB INTERVIEW QUESTION

How would you estimate the expected return of a stock?

this line, which is called the **security market line (SML)**. An asset that offered an expected return above the line, like asset A, would be underpriced. Investors would snap up this stock, driving up its price and driving down its expected return until it falls to the SML. Conversely, if an asset's expected return fell below the line, as depicted by point B, then it would be overpriced. Investors would then divest their holdings of this asset, driving its price down and its expected return up until it reaches the SML.

FIGURE 6.8

The Security
Market Line

In equilibrium, all
assets should be on the
SML. Prices of assets
not on the SML would
be bid up or down until
they lie on the SML.

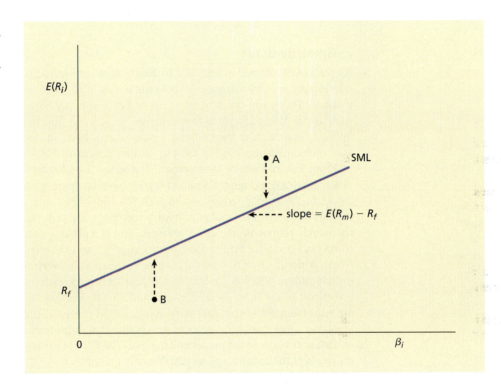

EXAMPLE

Suppose that the risk-free rate is 5% and that the expected return on the market portfolio is 11%. If a particular stock has a beta of 1.5 (50% higher than the market portfolio's beta), what is its expected return?

$$E(R) = 5\% + 1.5(11\% - 5\%) = 14\%$$

Because this stock has a relatively high beta, its expected return exceeds the expected return of the market portfolio. What if the stock had a beta of 1.0, equal to the beta of the market portfolio? Then

$$E(R) = 5\% + 1.0(11\% - 5\%) = 11\%$$

In this case, the stock displays average systematic risk and so its expected return equals the market portfolio's return. Finally, suppose that you could find a stock with a beta of 0.0:

$$E(R) = 5\% + 0.0(11\% - 5\%) = 5\%$$

(continued)

Here the expected return equals the risk-free rate. Does that mean that this stock is identical to a Treasury bill? Not exactly. An investor who buys a Treasury bill and holds it to maturity earns a certain nominal return. Not so with a zero-beta stock, whose realized return is not locked in like that of a T-bill. However, a stock that has a zero beta has zero exposure to systematic risk, so its returns fluctuate independently of market returns. Because the stock carries no systematic risk, its expected return in equilibrium is equivalent to a risk-free government security.

Estimating Betas

As the CAPM gained acceptance in business, a cottage industry developed with firms offering proprietary estimates of beta for virtually all listed common stocks in the U.S. markets. Today you can find estimates of betas in many libraries by looking in sources such as the *Value Line Investment Survey*, or you can find them online at sites such as Yahoo! Finance (http://www.finance.yahoo.com). Even so, you may want to construct your own estimates using the most up-to-date data available. Here's how to do it.

From Yahoo! Finance we downloaded a series of weekly returns on two stocks, as well as a market index. Figure 6.9 shows scatter plots comparing the weekly returns on these stocks to the weekly return on the S&P 500 Index. Plot A of the figure depicts weekly returns on Coach Inc., maker of luxury handbags and other fashion accessories, against the weekly return on the S&P 500 Index. Plot B replaces Coach returns with returns on ConAgra Foods, the largest food-service supplier and the second-largest food retailer in North America. Plot A shows a positive correlation between returns on Coach and the market index. Whether returns on the market are correlated with returns on ConAgra is difficult to say from visual inspection of Plot B. The lines drawn through each figure are regression lines estimated using Excel. Recall from statistics that regression analysis identifies a line through a series of data points that minimizes the sum of squared errors or distances between the points and the line. The *slope* of the regression line indicates how much effect the changes in one variable have on another.

In this instance, the slope of the regression lines indicates the extent to which movements in individual stocks are associated with movements in the overall market. In other words, the regression line's slope equals the stock's beta.[5] Notice that the regression line appears much steeper for Coach than for ConAgra—Coach stock has a higher beta. The general tendency is for Coach shares to perform very well (poorly) when the overall stock market is up (down). In contrast, returns on ConAgra stock display much less sensitivity to market movements, as indicated by its low beta of 0.11. These patterns make perfect sense. ConAgra produces food, and people have to eat in good times and bad. Coach, a company whose website uses the slogan, "Luxury within your reach," makes products such as a $500 leather handbag for carrying small dogs. People indulge in these products much more in good times than in bad.

Estimating a regression line yields additional information besides the beta of a stock. Typically, the regression output includes a variety of other statistics about the regression. One of the most useful of these statistics is the regression *R*-squared value. The *R*-squared measures "goodness of fit" and ranges from a minimum value of 0% (if there is no relationship between two variables) to 100% (if one variable is perfectly linked to another). In the

---

[5]Sometimes analysts use net returns or excess returns rather than actual returns to generate these plots. Thus, the *y*-axis would plot the actual return on a stock net of the risk-free rate while the *x*-axis would show the net return on the market index.

FIGURE 6.9

Scatterplots of Weekly Returns for Coach Inc., ConAgra, and Citigroup against the S&P 500 Index

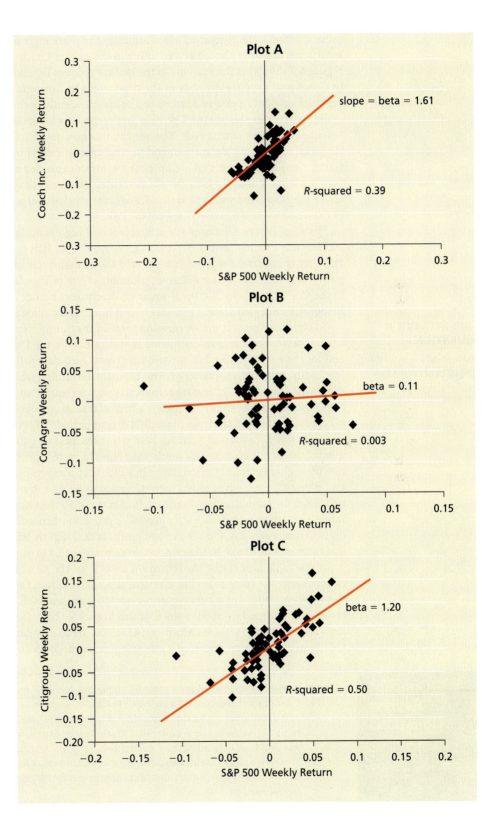

present context, the *R*-squared value indicates the percentage of variability in the stock's return that can be explained by variability in the market's return. The *R*-squared values in Figure 6.9 show that fluctuations in the market account for about 39% of the movements in Coach and for virtually none of the movements in ConAgra. At least over this sample period, ConAgra stock moved more or less independently of the overall market.

But what does this mean? The volatility of any stock contains two components: systematic and unsystematic risk. The systematic component reflects the extent to which the stock moves with the market, and the unsystematic component results from random fluctuations in the stock that are unrelated to (or unexplained by) the market.[6] Therefore, the regression *R*-squared indicates the percentage of an asset's volatility that is systematic. Given the *R*-squared values in Figure 6.9, we can say that a larger fraction of Coach's than of ConAgra's volatility reflects systematic risk.

Plot C of Figure 6.9 shows the scatterplot and regression line for Citigroup, a financial services holding company. At 1.20, Citigroup's beta falls between the betas of Coach and ConAgra, but the regression *R*-squared shows that systematic risk represents a larger proportion of total risk for Citigroup than for either of the other two firms. According to the CAPM, the beta (not the *R*-squared) determines a stock's expected return, but the *R*-squared value nonetheless provides useful information about statistical fit.

To conclude this section, we mention some of the thorny issues encountered when estimating betas. To obtain the estimates in Figure 6.9, we used weekly data for each stock and for the market index, but we could also have used data gathered at other frequencies (e.g., daily, monthly, or quarterly). The factors determining which type of data to use are somewhat subjective. For instance, from statistics we learn that larger samples often yield better estimates. But in the context of a financial market, collecting a larger sample may necessitate gathering data from more distant time periods. We collected 74 *weekly* observations spanning 1.5 years to form our beta estimates. Had we gathered the same number of *monthly* observations, our data would have covered more than 6 years. Over time, companies often change the mix of industries in which they compete by acquiring new businesses and divesting themselves of old ones. Consequently, data drawn from several years ago may not reflect the current risks of a particular stock. So then why not use 74 *daily* observations? The reason is that illiquidity presents a problem when using daily data. Many stocks do not trade every day. On the average business day, slightly less than 2% of NYSE-listed stocks and about 10% of Nasdaq stocks do not trade at all. On days when no trading occurs, it is impossible to measure the return on a stock for the same reason that a homeowner cannot know the value of his home unless he actually sells it. Deciding which type of data to use when estimating a beta requires evaluating the trade-off between having the most up-to-date information about a stock (which argues for high-frequency data) against having a large sample of returns (which argues for low-frequency data). Practitioners using the CAPM in business and researchers analyzing the model both confront these trade-offs.

JOB INTERVIEW QUESTION

How would you estimate the stock beta for a particular company?

Concept Review Questions	11. Why does an underpriced asset lie above the security market line?
	12. Running a regression with an individual asset's return as the dependent variable and the market's return as the independent variable yields two estimates of systematic risk: beta and *R*-squared. Explain how these metrics relate to systematic risk and how they differ from each other.
	13. You run regressions on two different stocks. One stock has a higher beta, and the other has a higher *R*-squared. According to the CAPM, which stock would have a higher expected return?

[6]Recall that unsystematic risk can be diversified away but systematic risk cannot be.

and French discovered that small firms earn consistently higher average returns than large firms and, similarly, that firms with high book-to-market ratios earn higher returns than firms with low book-to-market ratios. Controlling for these two effects, Fama and French found almost no relationship between beta and returns. In other words, the SML was not just "too flat"; it was completely flat.

Where does all of this leave us? From an academic point of view, the answer is uncertain. The empirical and theoretical shortcomings of the CAPM are by now well documented, and though the literature offers several alternative asset pricing models, none has emerged as the CAPM's clear heir apparent. As a matter of practice, however, the CAPM still reigns supreme in the corporate finance realm. Just as most U.S. firms look to the CAPM to estimate the required return on their shares, most brokerage and investment advisory firms still offer estimates of betas as part of their service package. Whether this will be the case in another 10 or 20 years is anyone's guess. To prepare you for that uncertain future, we now briefly review the leading alternative to the CAPM: the Fama-French (F-F) three-factor model.

Concept Review Questions	14. What does it mean to say that early tests of the CAPM indicated that the SML was "too flat"?
	15. Suppose that, on average, individuals become more risk averse during recessions and less risk averse during economic booms. How might this complicate tests of the CAPM?

6.6 THE FAMA-FRENCH MODEL

Smart Ideas Video

Kenneth French, Dartmouth College

"The three-factor model is an application of the arbitrage pricing theory."

See the entire interview at **SMARTFinance**

We have already mentioned the criticisms leveled at the CAPM by Eugene Fama and Ken French in their series of papers beginning in the early 1990s. It is one thing to criticize a theoretical model, but it is another thing entirely to suggest an improvement. Fortunately, Fama and French did both. Fama and French (1992, 1996, 2002a) sought to explain "the cross-section of expected returns," or why some stocks earn higher average returns than others. They make two key points in attacking the CAPM and presenting their alternative. The first point is that two factors, the size of a firm and the ratio of its equity's book value to its market value, are systematically related to returns. Looking back through the historical record, Fama and French find that small firms earn higher returns than large firms, even after holding beta constant, and that firms with high book-to-market ratios (*value stocks*) outperform firms with low book-to-market ratios (*glamour stocks*). The second point is that, controlling for firm size and market-to-book ratio, beta has little or no impact on returns. Why then did early tests of the CAPM indicate that high-beta stocks earned higher returns than low-beta stocks? Perhaps high-beta stocks tend to originate with small firms with high book-to-market ratios. Fama and French argue that if you look at a group of firms of similar size (and similar book-to-market ratio), then within that group the high-beta stocks earn about the same returns as low-beta stocks.

The mathematical expression of the **Fama-French (F-F) model** is

$$R_i - R_f = \alpha + \beta_{i1}\left(R_m - R_f\right) + \beta_{i2}\left(R_{small} - R_{big}\right) + \beta_{i3}\left(R_{high} - R_{low}\right) \qquad \text{(Eq. 6.3)}$$

The risk premium on stock *i* equals a constant term, α, plus a risk premium that depends on the stock's sensitivity to each factor and the risk premium for each factor. The term β_{i1}

is the sensitivity of stock i to the market factor, and $(R_m - R_f)$ is the familiar risk premium on the market. The β_{i2} term is the stock's sensitivity to the size factor, and $(R_{small} - R_{big})$ is the added expected return on small stocks compared to large stocks. Finally, β_{i3} represents the stock's sensitivity to the book-to-market ratio, with $(R_{high} - R_{low})$ representing the book-to-market risk premium. If the Fama-French model explains the cross-section of expected returns, then the average value of α should be close to zero.

What really distinguishes the Fama-French approach from the CAPM is its entirely empirical approach to modeling asset prices. Fama and French do not derive their pricing equation from a rigorous theoretical model, nor do they offer mathematical arguments for why these three factors (rather than some other set of factors) predict returns. Certainly, one can tell plausible stories to explain why small firms are riskier than large firms or why firms with high book-to-market ratios are riskier than those with low book-to-market ratios. For instance, a firm with dim prospects and teetering on the edge of financial disaster would probably have a very small market capitalization. That same firm might have a significant amount of equity "on the books" either from past external financing or accumulated profits. In that case, the firm would not only be small but also would have a high book-to-market ratio. Such a firm would indeed be very risky and would be priced by the market to reflect that investors demand a high expected return for holding this stock.[7]

But critics of Fama and French have their own stories. According to the three-factor model, a firm with a low book-to-market ratio is less risky and will offer lower returns than a firm with a high ratio. But what sorts of firms often have low book values and high market values (i.e., a low book-to-market ratio)? New firms, especially those in high-technology industries, often fit this description. In the late 1990s, stocks in the Internet sector had astronomical market values relative to their book values. Critics of Fama-French say that it is hard to conceive that investors viewed these as low-risk firms. Perhaps investors become too pessimistic about some firms, driving down their market values and pushing up their book-to-market ratios. Over time, investors learn that they underestimated these firms, and they drive prices back up. The reverse happens for low book-to-market firms, generating the positive correlation observed in the historical data.

The Fama-French model adopts the view that the market factor is not the only factor affecting asset returns. Some researchers have found that liquidity risk influences asset prices, with investors demanding higher returns on less liquid stocks (or stocks where the degree of liquidity is more uncertain). Other researchers argue that the "momentum" of a stock's returns affects future expected returns. In practice, these additional risks can easily be added in the expected return equation (Equation 6.3) as fourth and fifth factors, each with its own beta.

Other researchers have found that firms with better corporate governance systems outperform those with weaker governance, and still others have found that country-level factors, such as whether a nation enforces insider trading restrictions, influence stock returns. Recently, Bansal and Yaron (2004) argue that stocks' returns can be explained by risks associated with economic uncertainty and long-run growth prospects. At present, it seems clear that the search will continue for a more powerful model for explaining asset returns.

Smart Practices Video

Gregg Summerville,
President, Tecumseh Capital

"The risk you run is that sometimes the low valuations on value stocks are justified."

See the entire interview at
SMARTFinance

Smart Ideas Video

Chris Lundblad,
University of North Carolina

"If you look at the relationship between a value firm's cash flows and the business cycle you see that these firms are very risky."

See the entire interview at
SMARTFinance

Smart Ideas Video

Avanidhar Subrahmanyam,
UCLA

"We found that the higher the standard deviation of volume, the higher the expected return, which implies that liquidity risk is priced."

See the entire interview at
SMARTFinance

---

[7]Students sometimes find it counterintuitive that a firm with poor prospects would be priced to offer a high return. It may help to think of junk bonds. When firms with outstanding debt get into financial trouble, their bonds may slip from investment grade to the junk category. As this happens, the price on the bonds declines, but the yield on the bond (interest paid divided by price) rises. That is, investors demand very high expected returns for holding junk bonds (or stock in distressed companies).

6.7 THE CURRENT STATE OF ASSET PRICING THEORY

What is the state of asset pricing theory early in the twenty-first century? There are several competing models to describe asset returns, but no clear leader among those models has emerged. Even so, there are several valuable conclusions that we can draw based on the material in this chapter and Chapter 5. First, investors demand compensation for taking risk because they are risk averse. This fact in itself is important to keep in mind as you think about market valuations. To see why, imagine that a cultural shift takes place and investors generally become still more risk averse. Why might this occur? In 2008, the value of equity markets around the world dropped precipitously. Furthermore, the Ponzi scheme concocted by Bernard Madoff collapsed and investors lost billions. Other investors were burned by the collapse of financial stocks such as Lehman Brothers and Bear Stearns. Events such as these cause investors to reassess the risks they are taking and could move some investors to adopt a more risk-averse posture. What is the implication of an increase in the population's aversion to risk? As risk aversion rises, the compensation that a risky investment must offer to attract investors increases. As more and more investors pull out of stocks, market prices fall and expected returns rise.

Second, there is widespread agreement that systematic risk drives returns. At a minimum, this tells us that investors should hold diversified portfolios rather than invest a large fraction of their wealth in just a few securities. This is important advice to remember as you begin your career. Over time, you may accumulate stock options or other forms of equity in your employer. Holding a large fraction of your financial wealth in the firm for which you work is very risky, as Bear Stearns employees discovered in 2008 when the company went bankrupt. Large investments in your own firm's equity result in an undiversified financial portfolio that is highly correlated with your most valuable asset—your own human capital, which is tied to the prospects of your employer.

As an aside we point out here that, when it comes to diversification, what is good for individual investors is not necessarily good for firms. It is clearly advisable for investors to hold diversified portfolios, but it does not logically follow that companies should invest in many different industries to diversify their holdings. An individual can diversify across many different industries at very low cost, perhaps by following a strategy as simple as investing in mutual funds. For a firm, diversification is much more costly. One way that firms often diversify is by acquiring other businesses. But when one firm buys another, the acquirer must usually pay a significant premium over the target's market value in order to gain control. Furthermore, managers who are successful at operating a firm in one line of business may be less successful in other industries. There may also be a "managerial capacity" constraint that makes it difficult for firms to manage many different businesses at once. The bottom line is that investors can diversify at low cost on their own, so they have no reason to pay a premium for firms to diversify on their behalf. In fact, recent research in finance has documented just the opposite: investors tend to place *lower* values on diversified firms than on those that are more focused.

Smart Ideas Video

Diane Denis, Purdue University

"At this point it's fairly well documented that diversified firms don't seem to do as well as undiversified firms."

See the entire interview at **SMARTFinance**

Third, you can measure systematic risk in several different ways depending on the asset pricing model you choose. In the CAPM, beta captures the systematic risk of any investment. Each asset in the Fama-French three-factor model has several betas that capture its sensitivity to each of the factors. In the end, each model has its advantages and disadvantages.

Fourth, despite its flaws, the CAPM is still widely used in practice in both corporate finance and investment-oriented professions. Understanding how to estimate and interpret expected returns using the CAPM is part of the required tool kit for business school graduates. In time, perhaps, finance theory will provide a model that is indisputably superior to the CAPM that will make its way into practice.

Concept Review Question	17. Summarize the lessons of asset pricing theory that go beyond specific asset pricing models such as the CAPM and the Fama-French model.

Summary

- Finance teaches that markets reward investors for bearing risk, but only systematic risk. Unsystematic risk is not rewarded because it can be eliminated through diversification. Asset pricing models attempt to measure systematic risk and to quantify the trade-off between systematic risk and returns.
- Some portfolios are better than others. In general, risk-averse investors should hold only efficient portfolios—in other words, portfolios that maximize expected returns for any level of risk.
- If investors can borrow and lend at the risk-free rate, then a unique efficient risky portfolio exists. Investors must first attempt to learn the composition of this portfolio. Then they can divide their wealth between the efficient risky portfolio and the risk-free asset according to their own risk preferences.

- According to the CAPM, the optimal risky portfolio is the market portfolio, a value-weighted combination of all the assets in the economy.
- The CAPM predicts a linear positive relationship between expected returns and betas. The beta measures the systematic risk exposure of a particular asset. The graphical representation of the relationship between expected returns and beta is called the security market line.
- Early empirical tests offered some support for the CAPM, but the weight of the evidence now suggests that the CAPM offers an incomplete explanation of why some assets earn higher average returns than do others.
- A leading alternative to the CAPM is the Fama-French three-factor model. It has yet to completely supplant the CAPM—especially in the corporate finance realm, where the CAPM is widely used.

Key Terms

capital asset pricing model (CAPM)
capital market line (CML)
efficient frontier
efficient portfolio
efficient set
Fama-French (F-F) model

feasible set
homogeneous expectations
inefficient portfolio
market portfolio
market price of risk
minimum variance portfolio (MVP)

optimal risky portfolio
rational expectations
security market line (SML)
single-factor model
two-fund separation principle

QUESTIONS

6-1. Define the terms *feasible set* and *efficient set*.

6-2. Why is the efficient frontier generally a curved arc rather than a straight line?

6-3. Suppose that you adopt the rule of investing only in portfolios that have the minimum level of risk possible at a given expected return. If you follow this rule, will you always hold an efficient portfolio? (Assume that there is no risk-free asset; only risky assets are available.)

6-4. Suppose that there are only two risky assets. One offers a higher return than the other, but it also has a higher standard deviation. Will one of these assets always lie on the efficient frontier? Will one of them always be inefficient if held alone?

6-5. Suppose that the rate of inflation is negatively correlated with the rate of return in the stock market. A few years ago, the U.S. Treasury began issuing inflation-indexed bonds, bonds that pay a variable interest rate that rises and falls with the rate of inflation. Explain the effect of this new security on the feasible set available to investors.

6-6. For portfolios of risky and risk-free assets, the relationship between expected return and standard deviation is linear. Why?

6-7. Suppose that you have a friend who likes to invest in technology stocks. "Sure, they're risky," he says, "but the technology sector can go up 50% in a year. You'll never achieve that kind of return with a diversified portfolio." How should you respond?

6-8. In Japan, interest rates on short-term government bonds have been just over 0% for the last several years. If you could borrow and lend at a risk-free rate of 0%, would using borrowed money to finance part of your portfolio still increase the risk of your position?

6-9. Refer to Figure 6.1. Suppose that a risk-free rate were available in this diagram and that the level of this risk-free rate was such that the tangent line from R_f to the efficient frontier went through point C. From that level, if the risk-free interest rate rises (and nothing else changes) then what happens to the composition of the optimal portfolio?

6-10. How does the homogeneous expectations assumption lead to the CAPM's conclusion that the optimal risky portfolio is the market portfolio?

6-11. Consumers generally prefer low prices rather than high prices, yet we say that investors want to maximize the market price of risk (i.e., the slope of the CML). Explain this apparent paradox.

6-12. According to the CAPM, is it possible in equilibrium for an asset with a variance greater than zero (i.e., an asset other than the risk-free asset) to have an expected return that is below the risk-free rate?

6-13. Suppose that stock A has a higher variance than stock B. According to the CAPM, can stock A survive in the market if its expected return is lower than that for stock B?

6-14. Suppose that a mutual fund has a beta equal to 0.75. Is it necessarily the case that the standard deviation of returns on the fund is less than the standard deviation of market returns?

6-15. Suppose that investors generally become less risk averse. What effect would this have on stock prices and on expected returns?

6-16. If an asset lies above the SML, is it underpriced or overpriced? Why?

6-17. Is the expected return on a stock with a $\beta = 2.0$ twice the expected return on a stock with a $\beta = 1.0$?

6-18. Stock A has a beta of 1.5, and stock B has a beta of 1.0. Assume that the CAPM holds and then determine whether each of the following statements is true or false.

  a. Stock A has a higher expected return than stock B.

  b. The expected return on stock A is 50% higher than the expected return on the market portfolio.

  c. In a regression with the individual stock's return as the dependent variable and the market's return as the independent variable, the R-squared value is higher for stock A than it is for stock B.

6-19. You borrow shares of stock A, sell them, and invest the proceeds in stock B (i.e., you short-sell A and buy B). What must happen in order for this transaction to be profitable?

6-20. What is the CAPM beta for the risk-free security and the market portfolio? Is the risk-free security uncorrelated with the market portfolio?

6-21. In a regression using an asset's returns as the dependent variable, y, and returns on a market index as the independent variable, *x*, interpret both the regression slope coefficient and the regression *R*-squared value.

6-22. Beta estimates may be obtained from data gathered at different frequencies (daily, weekly, monthly, etc.). Explain the trade-offs that analysts confront when choosing the data's frequency.

6-23. What problems do researchers encounter when trying to test the validity of the CAPM?

6-24. What evidence supporting the CAPM have researchers found?

6-25. What data would you need when using the CAPM to estimate the required return on equity for a particular company? What data would you need when using the Fama-French model to perform the same analysis?

6-26. Describe the similarities and differences between the CAPM and the Fama-French model.

PROBLEMS

Some of the following problems require you to download monthly returns on several stocks from the Yahoo! website. Step-by-step instructions for gathering these data may be found in Chapter 5's Problem 5-16 on page 187.

Risk-Free Borrowing and Lending

6-1. Security X has an expected return of 8% with an associated standard deviation of 28%. Security Y has an expected return of 10% with an associated standard deviation of 36%. Assuming a covariance of −0.023732, find the portfolio's expected return and standard deviation for the following portfolios:

Weight of X	Weight of Y
20%	80%
40%	60%
60%	40%
80%	20%

Which portfolio appears to be the minimum variance portfolio (MVP)? Aside from the MVP, which portfolios are efficient?

6-2. Security Y is a risk-free security with an expected return of 5%. Security Z has an expected return of 10% with an associated standard deviation of 28%. Find the expected portfolio return and standard deviation for the following portfolios:

Weight of Y	Weight of Z
20%	80%
40%	60%
60%	40%
80%	20%

Does the slope of expected portfolio return versus portfolio risk (measured as standard deviation) change? Answer this question by comparing the slope between the first two portfolios and the last two portfolios. Is the risk–return trade-off simply a straight line in this instance?

6-3. Refer to Table 6.1 and Figure 6.4. Suppose that you can borrow and lend at the risk-free rate of 0.5% per month. Under these circumstances, which risky portfolio is optimal to hold in combination with the risk-free asset?

6-4. Repeat Problem 6-3 with a risk-free rate of 1.3% per month.

Smart Solutions

See the problem and solution explained step-by-step at **SMARTFinance**

6-5. The expected return on a particular stock is 15%, and its standard deviation is 38%. The risk-free return is 4%. Calculate the expected return and standard deviation on the following portfolios:

% Risky	% Risk-free	E(R)	Standard Deviation
75	25	___	___
50	50	___	___
25	75	___	___
150	−50	___	___

6-6. You have the following data on three different risky assets:

Statistic	Asset A	Asset B	Asset C
Expected return (%)	10	14	12
Standard deviation (%)	20	40	30
Correlation coefficient between:			

A & B = 0.5; A & C = 0.1; B & C = −0.35

a. Calculate the expected return and standard deviation for each of the following portfolios:

% in A	% in B	% in C	E(R)	Standard Deviation
100	0	0	___	___
0	100	0	___	___
0	0	100	___	___
50	50	0	___	___
50	0	50	___	___
0	50	50	___	___
10	40	50	___	___
30	30	40	___	___
40	20	40	___	___
50	40	10	___	___
0	75	25	___	___

b. Considered in isolation, which asset lies on the efficient frontier?
c. Which of the portfolios are efficient, and which are inefficient?

6-7. If the market has an expected return of 13% and a standard deviation of 28% and if the risk-free rate is 5%, explain how you can construct a portfolio with an expected return of 20%. What will be the standard deviation of this portfolio?

6-8. Refer to the numbers given in Problem 6-7. Explain how you can create a portfolio with a standard deviation of 16%. What will be the expected return on this portfolio?

Smart Solutions
See the problem and solution explained step-by-step at **SMARTFinance**

Equilibrium and the Market Portfolio

6-9. You must allocate your wealth between two securities. Security 1 offers an expected return of 10% and has a standard deviation of 30%. Security 2 offers an expected return of 15% and has a standard deviation of 50%. The correlation between the returns on these two securities is 0.25.

a. Calculate the expected return and standard deviation for each of the following portfolios, and plot them on a graph:

% Security 1	% Security 2	E(R)	Standard Deviation
100	0	_____	_____
80	20	_____	_____
60	40	_____	_____
40	60	_____	_____
20	80	_____	_____
0	100	_____	_____

b. Based on your calculations in part (a), which portfolios are efficient and which are inefficient?

c. Suppose that a risk-free investment is available that offers a 4% return. If you must divide your wealth between the risk-free asset and one of the risky portfolios in the preceding table, which risky portfolio would you choose?

d. Repeat your answer to part (c) assuming that the risk-free return is 8% rather than 4%. Can you provide an intuitive explanation for why the optimal risky portfolio changes?

e. Now suppose that you can short-sell either security, investing the proceeds in the other. Calculate the expected return and standard deviation of the following portfolios and then add them to your graph in part (a).

% Security 1	% Security 2	E(R)	Standard Deviation
140	−40	_____	_____
120	−20	_____	_____
−20	120	_____	_____
−40	140	_____	_____

6-10. In this problem, you will use several Excel 2007 features to map out a portfolio frontier. Assume there are two stocks available in the market with the following characteristics:

Stock	E(R)	Standard Deviation
1	12%	35%
2	18%	60%

Correlation coefficient = 0.15

Follow these instructions to create an Excel data table that will allow you to rapidly calculate the expected return and standard deviation for a large number of portfolios consisting of these two assets. Plotting the figures will enable you to see the portfolio frontier.

a. Starting in cell A2 and going down to cell A5, type in the following numbers:

−0.50;   −0.49;   −0.48;   −0.47

You can see that the pattern is to decrease the number in increments of 0.01 as you move down the column. Highlight all four numbers and grab the lower corner of the highlighted rectangle. As you drag the corner down, Excel will recognize the pattern and fill out the rest of the column (or you can use a formula to accomplish this task). Stop when cells A2 through A202 are full, with numbers that begin with −0.50 and increase until you reach the value 1.50 in cell A202. The numbers in this column represent the fraction of the portfolio invested in the first stock. Because this value ranges from −0.50 to 1.50, this problem will allow short-selling (i.e., borrowing to purchase). That is, the investor can take a short position of up to 50% of her wealth, investing the proceeds in the other stock.

b. In cell B1, type an Excel formula that will calculate the standard deviation of a portfolio consisting of these two stocks. This formula will use a cell reference to A1 instructing Excel to look in column A for the portfolio weight to place in stock 1. Note, however, that cell A1 is empty so far. Type the following formula in cell B1:

=((A1^2)*(0.35^2)+(1−A1)^2*(0.60^2)+2*A1*(1−A1)*0.35*0.60*0.15)^0.5

c. In cell C1, type an Excel formula that will calculate the expected return of a portfolio consisting of these two stocks. Again, this formula will reference cell A1 in telling Excel where to find the percentage invested in stock 1. Type the following formula in cell C1:

=A1*0.12+(1−A1)*0.18

d. Now, to create the data table, highlight the entire rectangle from cell A1 to cell C202. Once this is highlighted, select the "Data" menu and then under the "Data Tools" grouping choose "What-If Analysis." In the blank space that says "Column input cell," type "A1" and hit OK. Excel will automatically calculate the standard deviation (in column B) and the expected return (in column C) for every possible portfolio.

  1. What is the minimum variance portfolio?
  2. For an investor to create an efficient portfolio, what is the minimum rational investment in security 1?
  3. If an investor is willing to endure a portfolio standard deviation of 35%, how much can the investor increase the portfolio's expected return by diversifying rather than by holding security 1 alone?

e. Finally, use Excel's chart functions to create a "Scatter" plot as the type of graph you want to create. Tell Excel that the data series are in columns ranging from cells B2:C202. Add titles and headers if you like before producing the graph on a separate sheet.

6-11. The stock of Adams Teleped Corp. offers an expected return of 8% and has a standard deviation of 55%. Shares of Feldman Cosmetics, Inc., have an expected return of 13% and a standard deviation of 40%. The correlation coefficient between the two assets' returns is −0.2.

a. Plot each stock on a graph with standard deviation on the *x*-axis and expected return on the *y*-axis.

b. Calculate the expected return and standard deviation of the following portfolios, and add them to the graph from part (a):

% Adams	% Feldman	E(R)	Standard Deviation
100	0	———	———
80	20	———	———
60	40	———	———
50	50	———	———
40	60	———	———
20	80	———	———
0	100	———	———

c. Now suppose that the investor can short-sell Adams shares and invest the proceeds in Feldman stock. Calculate and plot (on the same graph) the expected return and standard deviation of the following portfolios:

% Adams	% Feldman	E(R)	Standard Deviation
−10	110	_____	_____
−30	130	_____	_____
−50	150	_____	_____

d. Can the situation depicted in this problem persist in a general equilibrium setting? That is, can one stock survive in the market when another stock with a lower standard deviation offers a higher expected return?

The Capital Asset Pricing Model (CAPM)

6-12. The risk-free asset pays 5%, the market portfolio's expected return is 13%, and its standard deviation is 35%. What is the slope of the capital market line?

6-13. The expected return on a particular asset is 10%, and its beta is 1.5. The risk-free return is 2%, and the expected return on the market portfolio is 14%. Does this asset lie on, above, or below the security market line? Explain.

6-14. A particular stock has a beta of 1.2 and an expected return of 10.2%. The expected risk premium on the market portfolio is 6%. What is the expected return on the market portfolio?

6-15. If a stock has a beta of 1.5 and the standard deviation of the market is 30%, what is the covariance between the stock and the market?

6-16. Assume that the expected risk premium on the market portfolio is 8% and that the risk-free rate is 5%. What is the beta of an asset with an expected return of 15%?

Smart Solutions

See the problem and solution explained step-by-step at **SMARTFinance**

6-17. Suppose a risk-free security pays a 6% return and the market portfolio has an expected return of 10%. What is the expected return on a portfolio that has $6,000 invested in the risk-free security and $4,000 invested in the market portfolio? What is the beta of the portfolio? Does the beta correspond to the portfolio weight invested in the market portfolio?

6-18. Suppose the risk-free security pays a 5% return and the market portfolio has an expected return of 12%. What is the expected return on a portfolio that has $2,000 borrowed at the risk-free rate and $12,000 invested in the market portfolio? What is the beta of the portfolio? If the beta exceeds 1, does it mean that the associated portfolio on the Capital Market Line (CML) has leverage (i.e., does the portfolio contain borrowed funds)?

6-19. Security A, Security B, and Security C have expected returns of 12%, 18%, and 9%, respectively. Assuming a risk-free rate of 3% and a market premium (equal to $[E(R_m) - R_f]$) of 6%, what are the betas for the three securities? If a portfolio comprises 20% of Security A, 45% of Security B, and 35% of Security C, then what is the portfolio's expected return and beta? Does the portfolio beta equal $0.20(\beta_A) + 0.45(\beta_B) + 0.35(\beta_C)$?

6-20. Compute the slope of the security market line (SML) using two securities: the risk-free security and the market portfolio. Next, use two random securities X and Y (assume X has a greater expected return than Y) to calculate the slope of the SML and demonstrate that it is the same as the previous calculation. (*Hint:* Substitute $R_f + \beta_x[E(R_m) - R_f]$ for the expected return of Security X and $R_f + \beta_y[E(R_m) - R_f]$ for the expected return of Security Y.) Describe how the slope of the SML is related to the expected return on the market portfolio.

6-21. A portfolio on the capital market line (CML) represents a combination of the risk-free security and the market portfolio. The portfolio's expected return is $w_{Rf}R_f + w_mE(R_m)$, where w_{Rf} and w_m (the portfolio weights of the risk-free security and the market portfolio, respectively) sum to 100%. Demonstrate how this equation for the portfolio's expected return is equivalent to $R_f + w_m[E(R_m) - R_f]$. (*Hint:* Substitute $1 - w_m$ for w_{Rf}.) What are the equations for the variance and standard deviation of a given portfolio on the CML relative to the market portfolio? (Let σ_m represent the standard deviation of the market portfolio.)

6-22. Let w_Q and w_S be the respective weights in the market portfolio for Portfolio Q and Portfolio S, which are both on the capital market line. Using $R_f + w_Q[E(R_m) - R_f]$ to denote the expected return on Portfolio Q and $R_f + w_S[E(R_m) - R_f]$ to denote the expected return on Portfolio S, calculate the slope of the CML (assume Security S has the greater expected return). In what manner is the slope of the CML related to the market portfolio?

Smart Solutions

See the problem and solution explained step-by-step at **SMARTFinance**

6-23. Luxury Products Inc. (LPI) stock has a beta of 1.2 and a standard deviation of 43%. Assuming a risk-free rate of 4% and an expected return on the market portfolio of 9%, what is the expected return of LPI? Suppose that the standard deviation of the market portfolio is 30%. It is possible to find a portfolio on the capital market line that has the same expected return as LPI. To construct that portfolio, how much must you invest in the risk-free asset and how much must you invest in the market portfolio? What is the standard deviation of the CML portfolio with an expected return identical to that of LPI? Compare the standard deviations of the CML portfolio and LPI. Why does LPI have a higher standard deviation?

The Fama-French Model

6-24. The expected risk premium on small stocks relative to large stocks is 6%, and the expected risk premium on low book-to-market stocks relative to high book-to-market stocks is 4%. Assume that the expected risk premium on the overall stock market relative to the risk-free rate is 5%. A particular stock has a market beta of 0.8, a size beta of 0.2, and a book-to-market beta of 0.4. If the risk-free rate is 4%, what is the expected return on this stock according to the Fama-French model?

THOMSON ONE Business School Edition

6-25. Calculate the monthly returns for Whirlpool Corporation (ticker symbol, WHR) and FedEx Corp. (ticker symbol, FDX) over the last 12 months. Using the S&P 500 as the market index (click on Indices, enter DSMnemonic as: S&PCOMP), calculate the betas of WHR and FDX by running a regression between the market returns and the individual security returns. (*Hint:* Using Excel will simplify this process.) How do your beta estimates compare to the reported betas on ThomsonONE? Based on your calculations and Equation 6.2, have WHR and FDX performed as expected? Use the rate on the current 10-year Treasury note as the risk-free rate.

6-26. Using the weights in the following table, calculate the arithmetic average and standard deviation of monthly returns for a portfolio of Whirlpool and FedEx over the last 12 months.

Whirlpool Weight	FedEx Weight
0%	100%
10%	90%
20%	80%
30%	70%
40%	60%
50%	50%
60%	40%
70%	30%
80%	20%
90%	10%
100%	0%

Graph the monthly returns and standard deviations. Which of these portfolios are efficient? Which weight combination results in the minimum variance portfolio?

6-27. Using the weights below, the current 10-year Treasury note rate, and the return for a portfolio consisting of 50% WHR and 50% FDX, calculate the arithmetic average and standard deviation of monthly returns over the last 12 months.

Treasury Note Weight	Whirlpool/FedEx Portfolio Weight
0%	100%
10%	90%
20%	80%
30%	70%
40%	60%
50%	50%
60%	40%
70%	30%
80%	20%
90%	10%
100%	0%

Graph the monthly returns and standard deviations. Which of these portfolios is efficient? Which weight combination results in the minimum variance portfolio?

MINI-CASE: RISK, RETURN, AND THE CAPITAL ASSET PRICING MODEL

Andrea Corbridge is considering forming a portfolio consisting of Kalama Corp. and Adelphia Technologies. The two corporations have a correlation of −0.1789, and their expected returns and standard deviations are as follows:

	Kalama Corp.	Adelphia Technologies
Expected return (%)	14.86	23.11
Standard deviation (%)	23.36	31.89

1. Calculate the frontier for all possible investment combinations of Kalama Corp. and Adelphia Technologies (from 0% to 100%, in 1% increments). Determine the optimal risky portfolio if the risk-free rate is 3%.

2. Andrea has $50,000 and wants to earn a 19% expected return on her investment. What is the optimal manner in which to structure her portfolio—both in dollar amounts and in weights relative to her $50,000—based on the preceding information?

3. Andrea is also seriously considering buying some stock in Medford Barnett Corporation (MBC). The stock prices of MBC and the S&P for the past 25 months are tabulated below. Andrea estimates that MBC will earn a 14% return during the next year, and she expects the market to earn a 12% return during the same time period. In addition, she expects the relationship exhibited between the S&P and MBC to remain as it has in the past. Assuming that Andrea would be pulling MBC into a fully diversified portfolio, is buying the MBC shares a good decision?

Month	S&P	MBC
1	1,198.41	58.04
2	1,228.81	65.36
3	1,220.33	48.48
4	1,234.18	53.32
5	1,191.33	57.59
6	1,191.50	49.23
7	1,156.85	55.57
8	1,180.59	50.99
9	1,203.60	64.10
10	1,181.27	50.45
11	1,211.92	50.65
12	1,173.82	51.23
13	1,130.20	46.68
14	1,114.58	51.09
15	1,104.24	50.75
16	1,101.72	59.80
17	1,140.84	52.78
18	1,120.68	49.22
19	1,107.30	53.47
20	1,126.21	49.26
21	1,144.94	48.55
22	1,131.13	61.32
23	1,111.92	48.06
24	1,058.20	58.88
25	1,050.71	46.19

PART 3

Capital Budgeting

Investment decisions have great impact on the long-term success or failure of a business. How companies decide to invest the money that shareholders and lenders entrust to them largely dictates whether they will thrive or wither over time. The process of analyzing and prioritizing investment opportunities is called *capital budgeting*. This section illustrates the analysis performed by financial managers when determining which investment opportunities their firms should pursue and which they should avoid.

Chapter 7 describes several techniques that firms use to justify their investment choices. Although simple techniques such as payback analysis enjoy widespread use in practice, the best method for analyzing most capital investment projects is the net present value (NPV) method. Chapter 7 explains the conceptual underpinnings of the NPV approach and highlights the strengths and weaknesses of other capital budgeting methods.

The first step in analyzing an investment opportunity is estimating the incremental cash inflows and outflows associated with the investment. Chapter 8 uses an extended case example to illustrate how to generate the cash flow numbers, which are an essential part of NPV analysis. In addition to listing the various types of cash flows commonly occurring in large investment projects, the chapter also explains how to deal with issues such as inflation or excess capacity when estimating project cash flows.

The second step in an NPV calculation is estimating a discount rate that is appropriate given the risk of the investment opportunity under consideration. Chapter 9 shows how the process of finding the right discount rate depends on the nature of the investment opportunity and on the firm's financial structure. In this chapter we introduce a key concept in finance, the *weighted average cost of capital* (WACC). Almost all large companies calculate their WACC as part of their capital budgeting decision process.

What Companies Do

How Falling Petroleum Prices Affect the Profitability of Oil-Shale Investments

How do oil companies make extremely large, long-term capital budgeting decisions when the global price for a barrel of petroleum can rise from $71 to $147, and then fall back below $65, within a 13-month period? This was the challenge facing financial managers at Petro-Canada and other major oil companies building multibillion-dollar oil-shale mining and processing facilities in Canada's Athabasca Basin in late 2008. All told, Canada's oil sands may hold 1.75 *trillion* barrels of oil, and international petroleum companies have been stepping up their investment sharply after oil prices began surging in early 2004.

When oil prices peaked in July 2008, Petro-Canada announced that the Fort Hills oil-shale project (in which the company holds a 60% interest) would cost $14.1 billion to complete, but the company expressed confidence that this investment would meet its required return. By late October, however, oil prices had dropped by more than 50% and the price tag for completing the Fort Hills project had risen to $23.8 billion, potentially damaging the project's viability for Petro-Canada and other major investors. In total, the French oil company, estimated that oil prices would need to stay at around $90 per barrel for the company to achieve a 12.5% internal rate of return on its investment. As 2008 drew to a close, all the major oil companies were reconsidering whether to continue making massive oil-shale investments in light of the volatility in petroleum prices.

Sources: Carrie Tait, "Winners and Losers in Oil Patch Shakeout," Financial Post (October 28, 2008), p. FP8; "Larger Companies to Dominate in Oil Sands, Total Chief Predicts," Financial Post (September 20, 2008), p. FP7; oil price data from U.S. Department of Energy, Energy Information Administration (http://www.eia.doe.gov).

7

Capital Budgeting Processes and Techniques

On a daily basis, firms make decisions that have financial consequences. Some decisions, such as extending credit to a customer or ordering inventory, have consequences that are short-lived. Moreover, managers can reverse such short-term actions with relative ease. In contrast, some decisions that managers face have a long-term impact on the firm and can be difficult to unwind once started. Major investments in plant and equipment fit this description, but so might spending on advertising designed to build brand awareness and loyalty among consumers. The terms **capital investment** and **capital spending** refer to investments in these kinds of long-lived assets, and the term **capital budgeting** refers to the process of identifying which of these investment projects a firm should undertake.

The capital budgeting process involves three basic steps:

1. Identifying potential investments
2. Analyzing the set of investment opportunities, isolating those that will create shareholder value, and prioritizing them if necessary
3. Implementing and monitoring the investment projects selected

The capital budgeting process begins with an idea and ends with implementation and monitoring. Ideas for investment projects can come from anywhere within the firm. Marketing may want the firm to spend money to reach new customers. Operations may want new equipment to realize production efficiencies. Engineering may want resources for research and development. Information Systems may want to upgrade the firm's computer network for more efficient information-sharing across the company. Each group will undoubtedly have a compelling story to justify spending money on its pet project. The analyst will consider the risk and return of each proposal; some projects will be approved and others rejected.

Without understating the importance of Steps 1 and 3, our focus in this chapter is the second step in the process: analyzing the merits of investment proposals. In practice, firms justify their capital investments using many different techniques, which range from simple to sophisticated. In this chapter, we describe some of these techniques and highlight their strengths and weaknesses. In the end, the preferred technique for evaluating most capital investments is called "net present value."

7.1 INTRODUCTION TO CAPITAL BUDGETING

A Capital Budgeting Problem

When managers evaluate different investment opportunities, they need analytical tools that weigh the merits of investment projects on several dimensions. For example, some projects take longer to pay off than do others, some involve larger up-front costs, and some require the firm to take more risk. To decide which investments to undertake, managers need an analytical tool that: (1) is easy to apply and easy to explain to nonfinancial personnel; (2) focuses on cash flow, not accounting-based measures such as profit; (3) accounts for the time value of money; (4) adjusts for differences in risk across projects; and (5) leads to higher firm value in any company (and higher stock prices in public firms).

In this chapter we discuss several different capital budgeting methods and evaluate whether they fulfill the conditions (1)–(5) just described. To provide a common framework for this discussion, we apply each of the decision-making techniques in this chapter to a single, simplified business problem currently facing Global Wireless Incorporated, a (fictitious) U.S.-based worldwide provider of wireless telephone services. Wireless carriers

WHAT CFOs DO

CFO Survey Evidence

Table 7.1 lists several of the capital budgeting methods covered in this chapter and indicates how widely they are used, according to a survey of U.S. CFOs. We argue in this chapter that the *net present value* (NPV) and *internal rate of return* (IRR) are theoretically preferable to methods such as *payback, discounted payback*, or *accounting rate of return*.[1] Apparently CFOs agree, because most of them say that the IRR and NPV methods are their preferred tools for evaluating investment opportunities. The payback approach is also widely used. It is interesting that the popularity of NPV and IRR is particularly high among large firms and firms with CFOs who have MBA training, whereas the payback approach sees wider use in smaller firms. The payback approach, as the name suggests, focuses on how quickly an investment produces sufficient cash flow to recover its up-front costs. Smaller firms probably have less access to capital than large firms, which may explain why smaller firms rely so heavily on the payback method.

Table 7.1 Popularity of Capital Budgeting Techniques	
TECHNIQUE	**PERCENT OF CFOs ROUTINELY USING TECHNIQUE**[a]
Internal rate of return	76%
Net present value	75%
Payback	57%
Discounted payback	29%
Accounting rate of return	20%
Profitability index	12%

[a]Note that these rounded percentages are drawn from the responses of a large number of CFOs and that many respondents use more than one technique.

Source: Reprinted from *Journal of Financial Economics*, 60, J.R. Graham and C.R. Harvey, "The Theory and Practice of Corporate Finance: Evidence from the Field," pp. 187–243, Copyright 2001, with permission from Elsevier.

are scrambling to attract and retain customers in today's highly competitive market. According to customer surveys, the number one reason for selecting a given carrier (or for switching to a new one) is the quality of service. Customers who lose calls as they commute to work or travel from one business location to another are apt to switch if another carrier offers fewer service interruptions.

Against this backdrop, Global Wireless is contemplating a major expansion of its wireless network in two different regions. Figure 7.1 depicts the projected cash inflows and outflows of each project over the next five years. By investing $250 million, Global Wireless could add up to 100 new cell sites to its existing base in Western Europe, giving

---

[1]We do not cover the accounting rate of return method in this book, even though it sees some use in practice. In a nutshell, this method evaluates investments based on their accounting earnings, usually relative to the book value of the assets required to undertake the investment.

FIGURE 7.1

Global Wireless
Investment
Proposals

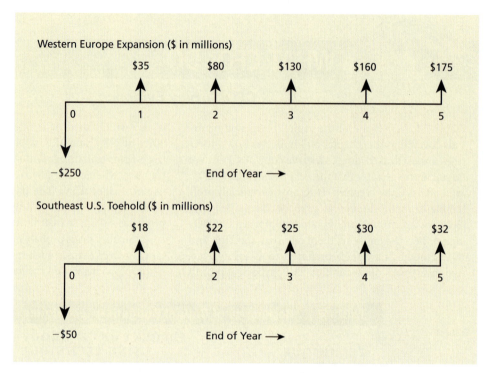

it the most comprehensive service area in that region. Company analysts project that this investment could generate year-end net after-tax cash inflows that could grow over the next five years, as outlined in the following table:

Initial Outlay	−$250 million
Year 1 inflow	$35 million
Year 2 inflow	$80 million
Year 3 inflow	$130 million
Year 4 inflow	$160 million
Year 5 inflow	$175 million

Alternatively, Global Wireless could make a much smaller investment to establish a toehold in a new market in the Southeast of the United States. For an initial investment of $50 million, Global Wireless believes it can create a southeast network with its hub centered in Atlanta, Georgia. The projected end-of-year cash flows associated with this project are as follows:

Initial outlay	−$50 million
Year 1 inflow	$18 million
Year 2 inflow	$22 million
Year 3 inflow	$25 million
Year 4 inflow	$30 million
Year 5 inflow	$32 million

Which investment should Global Wireless make? If the company can undertake both investments, should it do so? If it can make only one investment, which one is better for shareholders? We will see how different capital budgeting techniques lead to different investment choices, starting with the payback methods.

Concept Review Question	1. What characteristics does management desire in a capital budgeting technique?

7.2 PAYBACK METHODS

The Payback Decision Rule

The payback method is the simplest of all capital budgeting decision-making tools; it enjoys widespread use, particularly among small firms. The **payback period** is the amount of time it takes for a given project's cumulative net cash inflows to recoup the initial investment. *Firms using the payback approach define a maximum acceptable payback period and accept only those projects that have payback periods less than the maximum; all other projects are rejected.* If a firm decides that it wants to avoid any investment that does not "pay for itself" within three years, then the payback decision rule is to accept projects with a payback period of three years or less and to reject all other investments. If several projects satisfy this condition, then firms may prioritize investments based on which ones achieve payback more rapidly. The decision to use three years as the cutoff point is somewhat arbitrary, and there are no hard-and-fast guidelines that establish what the "optimal" payback period should be. Nevertheless, suppose that Global Wireless uses 3.00 years as its cutoff value for purposes of payback analysis. What investment decision would it make?

EXAMPLE

The investment to expand the wireless network in Western Europe requires an initial outlay of $250 million. According to the firm's cash flow projections, this project will bring in just $245 million in its first three years ($35 million in year 1 + $80 million in year 2 + $130 million in year 3) and $405 million after four years ($245 million in the first three years + $160 million in year 4). So the firm will fully recover its $250 million initial outlay sometime during year 4. Because the firm needs to recover only $5 million ($250 million initial outlay − $245 million recovered in the first three years) in year 4, we can estimate (assuming cash flow occurs at a constant rate throughout the year) the fraction of year 4 as 0.03 (by dividing the $5 million that needs to be recovered in year 4 by the $160 million expected to be recovered in that year). *The payback period for Western Europe is therefore 3.03 years, so Global Wireless would reject the investment because this payback period is longer than the firm's maximum 3.00-year payback period.*

The toehold investment in the Southeast U.S. project requires just $50 million. In its first two years, this investment generates $40 million in cash flow ($18 million in year 1 + $22 million in year 2). By the end of year 3, it produces a cumulative cash flow of $65 million ($40 million in the first two years + $25 million in year 3). Thus, the project earns back the initial $50 million at some point during year 3. It needs to recover $10 million ($50 million initial outlay − $40 million recovered in the first two years) in year 3. We can estimate the fraction of year 3 as 0.40 (by dividing the $10 million that needs to be recovered in year 3 by the $25 million expected to be recovered that year). *The payback for the Southeast U.S. project is therefore 2.40 years. Global Wireless would undertake the investment because this payback period is shorter than the firm's maximum 3.00-year payback period.*

JOB INTERVIEW QUESTION

A firm requires a 4-year payback period on investments in its home country. Should it shorten the required payback period when it invests overseas?

Pros and Cons of the Payback Method

Arguments for the Payback Method   Simplicity is the main virtue of the payback approach. Once a firm estimates a project's cash flows, it is a simple matter of addition to determine when the cumulative net cash inflows equal the initial outlay. The intuitive appeal of the payback method is strong. It sounds reasonable to expect a good investment to pay for itself in a fairly short period of time. Indeed, the time value of money suggests that, other things being equal, a project that brings in cash flow faster ought to be more valuable than one with more distant cash flows. Small firms, which typically operate with limited financing, tend to favor payback because it is simple and because receiving more cash flow sooner allows them more financial flexibility. Some managers say that establishing a short payback period is one way to account for a project's risk exposure. They argue that projects that take longer to pay off are intrinsically riskier than those that recoup the initial investment more quickly, partly because forecast errors tend to increase with the length of the payback time period. The payback period is a popular decision-making technique in highly uncertain situations, where it is frequently used as the primary technique. It is used frequently for international investments made in unstable economic/political environments and for risky domestic investments such as oil drilling and new business ventures.

Another justification given for using the payback method is that some firms face financing constraints. Advocates of the payback rule argue that it makes sense for cash-strapped firms to use payback because it indicates how quickly the firm can generate cash flow to repay debt or to pursue other investment opportunities. Career concerns may also lead managers to prefer the payback rule. Particularly in large companies, managers rotate quite often from one job to another. To obtain promotions and to enhance their reputations, managers seek investments that enable them to point to success stories at each stage of their careers. A manager who expects to stay in a particular position in the firm for only two or three years may prefer to undertake investments that recover costs quickly instead of those that have payoffs far in the future.

Arguments against the Payback Method   Despite these apparent virtues, the payback method suffers from several serious problems. First, the payback cutoff period is simply a judgment with little or no connection to maximizing shareholder value. How can we be sure that projects that pay back within three years will do more for shareholder wealth than those that pay back within two years or four years? Second, the way the payback method accounts for the time value of money is crude to an extreme. The payback method assigns a 0% discount rate to cash flows that occur before the cutoff point. That is, if the payback period is three years then cash flows that occur in years 1, 2, and 3 receive equal weight in the payback calculation. Beyond the cutoff point, the payback method implicitly assigns an infinite discount rate to all future cash flows, thereby ignoring them. In other words, cash flows in year 4 and beyond receive zero weight (or have zero present value) in today's decision to invest or not invest.[2] Third, using the payback period as a way to control for project risk is equally crude. Finance teaches that riskier investments should offer higher returns. If it is true that riskier projects have longer payback periods, then the payback rule simply rejects all such investments even if they offer higher returns in the long run. Managers who naively follow the payback rule tend to underinvest in long-term projects that could offer substantial rewards for shareholders. Fourth, there is an *agency problem* to the extent that career concerns lead managers to favor projects with quick payoffs. Agency problems should be resolved

---

[2]We know that the present value of a future cash flow becomes smaller and smaller as we apply higher and higher discount rates. Discounting at an infinite interest rate results in a future cash flow having zero present value.

through a firm's governance mechanisms, not by adopting a suboptimal decision rule. Firms could reduce incentives for managers to focus on short-term successes by rewarding them for their efforts in meeting the short-term goals of long-term projects (e.g., staying on budget, meeting revenue forecasts), as well as for long-term results.

Discounted Payback

The **discounted payback** rule is essentially the same as the payback rule except that, in calculating the payback period, managers first discount the cash flows. In other words, the discounted payback method calculates how long it takes for a project's discounted cash flows to recover the initial outlay. This represents a minor improvement over the simple payback method because it does a better job of accounting for the time value of cash flows that occur within the payback cutoff period. As with the ordinary payback rule, discounted payback totally ignores cash flows that occur beyond the cutoff point.

EXAMPLE

Suppose that Global Wireless uses the discounted payback method with a discount rate of 18% and a cutoff period of three years. The following schedules show the present value (PV) of each project's cash flows during the first three years. For example, $29.7 million is the present value of the $35 million that the Western Europe investment is expected to earn in its first year, $57.5 million is the present value of the $80 million that the project is expected to earn in its second year, and so on.

Present Value	Western Europe Project ($ million)	Southeast U.S. Project ($ million)
PV of year 1 inflow	29.7	15.3
PV of year 2 inflow	57.5	15.8
PV of year 3 inflow	79.1	15.2
Cumulative PV years 1–3	166.3	46.3

Recall that the initial outlay for the Western Europe expansion project is $250 million but is only $50 million for the Southeast U.S. toehold project. After three years, neither project's cumulative present value of cash flows exceeds its initial outlay. Clearly, then, neither investment satisfies the condition that the discounted cash flows recoup the initial investment within three years. Therefore, Global Wireless would reject both projects.

Pros and Cons of Discounted Payback

The discounted payback rule has most of the same advantages and disadvantages as ordinary payback analysis, and its primary appeal remains its relative simplicity. Discounted payback does correct the payback rule's problem of implicitly applying a 0% discount rate to all cash flows that occur before the cutoff point. However, like the ordinary payback rule, the discounted payback approach ignores cash flows beyond the cutoff point—applying, in essence, an infinite discount rate to these cash flows. So even though it's an improvement over the simplest version of the payback rule, discounted payback analysis is still likely to lead managers to underinvest in profitable projects with long-run payoffs.

By now you may have noticed some common themes in our discussion of the pros and cons of different approaches to capital budgeting. Neither payback method factors all the cash flows of a project into the decision-making process. Neither method properly accounts for the time value of money, and neither deals adequately with differences in risk from one investment to another. Despite these criticisms, both payback and discounted payback are widely used in practice because of their simplicity and broad intuitive appeal. Given the uncertain nature of forecasting project cash flows, some analysts find these simple techniques effective in making good investment decisions. We now turn our attention to a method that solves all these difficulties and therefore enjoys widespread support from both academics and business practitioners.

Concept Review Questions

2. What factors account for the popularity of the payback method? In what situations is it often used as the primary decision-making technique? Why?
3. What are the major flaws of the payback and discounted payback approaches?

7.3 NET PRESENT VALUE

Net Present Value Calculations

A project's **net present value (NPV)** equals the sum of its cash inflows and outflows, discounted at a rate that is consistent with the project's risk. Calculating an investment's NPV is relatively straightforward. First, write down the net cash flows that the investment will generate over its life. Second, discount these cash flows at an interest rate that reflects the risk inherent in the project. Third, add up the discounted cash flows to obtain the NPV, and invest in the project only when that value exceeds zero.[3]

$$NPV = CF_0 + \frac{CF_1}{(1+r)^1} + \frac{CF_2}{(1+r)^2} + \frac{CF_3}{(1+r)^3} + \cdots + \frac{CF_N}{(1+r)^N}$$ **(Eq. 7.1)**

In this expression, CF_t represents net cash flow in year t, r is the discount rate, and N denotes the life of the project. The cash flows in each year may be positive or negative, though we usually expect projects to generate cash outflows initially and cash inflows later on. For example, suppose that the initial cash flow, CF_0, is a negative number representing the outlay necessary to get the project started, and suppose that all subsequent cash flows are positive. In this case, the net present value can be defined as the *present value of future cash inflows minus the initial outlay.* The NPV decision rule says that firms should invest when the sum of the present values of future cash inflows exceeds the initial project outlay. That is, NPV > $0, which occurs when

$$-CF_0 < \frac{CF_1}{(1+r)^1} + \frac{CF_2}{(1+r)^2} + \frac{CF_3}{(1+r)^3} + \cdots + \frac{CF_N}{(1+r)^N}$$

Simply stated, the *NPV decision rule* is:

NPV > $0:   invest
NPV < $0:   do not invest

---

[3]What about investments with NPV = $0? A zero NPV represents a break-even point. When an investment's NPV is positive, a firm creates wealth for its shareholders; when the NPV is negative, the firm destroys wealth by undertaking the project. Yet when its NPV is zero, an investment will increase the book value of a firm's assets but neither create nor destroy wealth. In this case, shareholders are generally indifferent to whether the firm accepts or rejects the project.

Why Does the NPV Rule Generally Lead to Good Investment Decisions?

Remember that the firm's goal in choosing investment projects is to maximize shareholder wealth. Conceptually, the discount rate (r) in the NPV equation represents an opportunity cost, the highest rate of return investors can obtain in the marketplace on an investment with risk equal to that of the project under consideration. When the NPV of a cash flow stream equals zero, that stream of cash flows provides a rate of return exactly equal to the shareholders' required return. Therefore, when a firm finds a project with a positive NPV, it must offer an expected return that exceeds the shareholders' requirements.

A firm that consistently finds positive-NPV investments expects to surpass the shareholders' requirements and enjoy a rising stock price. Clearly, the acceptance of positive-NPV projects is consistent with the firm's value-creation goal. Conversely, if the firm makes an investment with a negative NPV, the investment will decrease value and shareholder wealth. A firm that regularly makes negative-NPV investments can expect to see its stock price lag as it generates lower-than-required returns for stockholders.

Drawing on what we already know about valuing bonds, we can develop an analogy to drive home the point about the relationship between stock prices and the NPV rule. Suppose that, at a given moment in time, investors require a 5% return on 5-year Treasury bonds. This means that if the U.S. Treasury issues 5-year, $1,000 par value bonds paying an annual coupon of $50, then the market price of these bonds will be $1,000 (same as the par value):[4]

$$\$1,000 = \frac{\$50}{(1.05)^1} + \frac{\$50}{(1.05)^2} + \frac{\$50}{(1.05)^3} + \frac{\$50}{(1.05)^4} + \frac{\$1,050}{(1.05)^5}$$

Now apply NPV logic. If an investor purchases one of these bonds for $1,000, then the NPV equals zero because the bond's cash flows precisely satisfy the investor's expectation of a 5% return:

$$NPV = \$0 = -\$1,000 + \frac{\$50}{(1.05)^1} + \frac{\$50}{(1.05)^2} + \frac{\$50}{(1.05)^3} + \frac{\$50}{(1.05)^4} + \frac{\$1,050}{(1.05)^5}$$

Next imagine that, in a fit of election-year largesse, the U.S. Congress decrees that the coupon payments on all government bonds will double, so this bond now pays $100 in interest per year. If the bond's price remains fixed at $1,000, this investment's NPV will suddenly switch from zero to positive. At a price of $1,000, the bond is underpriced if Congress raises the bond's coupon to $100:

$$NPV = \$216.47 = -\$1,000 + \frac{\$100}{(1.05)^1} + \frac{\$100}{(1.05)^2} + \frac{\$100}{(1.05)^3} + \frac{\$100}{(1.05)^4} + \frac{\$1,100}{(1.05)^2}$$

Of course, the bond's price will not remain at $1,000. Investors will quickly recognize that—with a price of $1,000 and a coupon of $100—the return offered by these bonds substantially exceeds the required rate of 5%. Investors will flock to buy the bonds, rapidly driving up bond values until prices reach the point at which buying bonds becomes a zero-NPV investment once again. In the new equilibrium, the bond's price will rise by $216.47, exactly the amount of the NPV that was created when Congress doubled the coupon payments:

$$NPV = \$0 = -\$1,216.47 + \frac{\$100}{(1.05)^1} + \frac{\$100}{(1.05)^2} + \frac{\$100}{(1.05)^3} + \frac{\$100}{(1.05)^4} + \frac{\$1,100}{(1.05)^5}$$

---

[4]Though Treasury bonds pay interest semiannually, we assume annual interest payments here to keep the example simple.

NPV and Stock Price The same forces that drove up the bond's price in the previous section will drive up a firm's stock price when it makes a positive-NPV investment, as shown in Figure 7.2. The figure depicts a firm that investors believe will pay an annual dividend of $4 per share in perpetuity. If investors require a 10% return on this firm's stock, the price will be $40.[5] What happens if the firm makes a new investment that is as risky as the stock just described? If the return on this investment is greater than 10% then it will have a positive NPV. Investors will recognize that the firm has made an investment that exceeds their expectations and so will raise their forecast of future dividends, perhaps to $4.10 per year. At that level the new stock price will be $41. The same thing happens in reverse if the firm makes an investment that earns a return below 10%. At this rate the project has a negative NPV. Shareholders recognize that this investment's cash flows fall below their expectations, so they lower their estimates of future dividends to $3.90 per year. As a consequence, the stock price falls to $39.

FIGURE 7.2

The NPV Rule and Shareholder Wealth

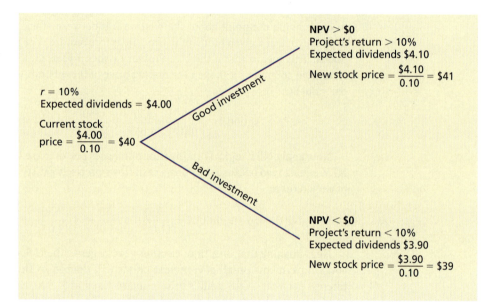

Now apply this process to Global Wireless. Suppose its shareholders demand an 18% return on their shares. According to the principles discussed in Chapter 4, the price of Global Wireless stock will reflect the value of all future cash distributions that investors expect from the company, discounted at a rate of 18%. But what if Global Wireless discovers it can make an investment that offers a return substantially above 18%? By definition, such an investment has a positive NPV; by undertaking it, Global Wireless will increase the price of its stock as investors realize that the company is able to distribute higher-than-anticipated cash flows as a result of the investment. How far will the stock price rise? Simply divide the project's NPV (which represents the amount of wealth the project is expected to create) by the number of outstanding shares. The result is the amount by which Global Wireless's stock price should increase.

---

[5]Remember that the price of a stock that pays a constant dividend in perpetuity equals the annual dividend divided by the required rate of return—in this case, $4 \div 0.10 = \$40$.

EXAMPLE

What are the NPVs of the investment opportunities now facing Global Wireless? Time lines depicting the NPV calculations for the Global Wireless projects under review appear in Figure 7.3. Discounting each project's cash flows at 18% yields the following results:[6]

$$NPV_{\text{Western Europe}} = -\$250 + \frac{\$35}{(1.18)^1} + \frac{\$80}{(1.18)^2} + \frac{\$130}{(1.18)^3} + \frac{\$160}{(1.18)^4} + \frac{\$175}{(1.18)^5} = \$75.3$$

$$NPV_{\text{Southeast U.S.}} = -\$50 + \frac{\$18}{(1.18)^1} + \frac{\$22}{(1.18)^2} + \frac{\$25}{(1.18)^3} + \frac{\$30}{(1.18)^4} + \frac{\$32}{(1.18)^5} = \$25.7$$

Both projects increase shareholder wealth, so both are worth undertaking. One could say that both projects earn more than the firm's 18% required return and are therefore acceptable. However, if the company can make only one investment, it should choose to expand its presence in Western Europe. That investment is expected to increase shareholder wealth by $75.3 million, whereas the Southeast U.S. investment is expected to increase wealth by only about one-third as much. If Global Wireless has 100 million shares of common stock outstanding, then accepting the Western Europe project should increase the stock price by about $0.75 ($75.3 million ÷ 100 million shares). Accepting the Southeast U.S. investment would increase the stock price by only about $0.26 ($25.7 million ÷ 100 million shares).

Smart
Practices
Video

Jon Olson, Chief Financial Officer, Xilinx Corp.

"On more complex decisions, we use NPV."

See the entire interview at
SMARTFinance

Pros and Cons of NPV

The net present value method solves all the problems we have identified with the payback and discounted payback. First, the NPV rule focuses on cash flow. Second, when properly applied, the NPV method makes appropriate adjustments for the time value of money. Third, the decision rule to invest when NPVs are positive and to refrain from investing when NPVs are negative reflects the firm's need to compete for funds and does not rely on an arbitrary judgment of management. Fourth, the NPV approach offers a relatively straightforward way to control for differences in risk among alternative investments: cash flows on riskier investments should be discounted at higher rates. Fifth, the NPV method incorporates all the cash flows that a project generates over its life, not just those that occur in the project's early years. Sixth, the NPV gives a direct estimate of the change in shareholder wealth resulting from a given investment.

Although we are enthusiastic supporters of the NPV approach, especially when compared with the other decision methods examined thus far, the NPV rule has its own weaknesses. Relative to alternative capital budgeting tools, the NPV rule seems less intuitive to some users. For some, that Global Wireless's Southeast U.S. project has an NPV of $25.7 million is less intuitive than saying that the investment pays back its initial cost in 2.4 years.

---

[6]Of course, you can compute this using a financial calculator or in Excel via the "=NPV" function. Imagine that you have all the Western Europe project's cash flows in column A of a spreadsheet, with the initial outlay in row 1, the first year's inflow in row 2, and so on. In any blank cell, type the formula "=NPV(0.18,A2:A6)+A1". Excel will return the value $75.3, which represents the NPV of the project. Observe that the NPV function contains as its first argument the discount rate, followed by the cash flows from year 1 to year 5 (contained in rows 2–6). By design, Excel's NPV function assumes that the first cash flow listed in the function (in this case, the cash flow in cell A2) occurs one year after the initial investment. We add the initial cash outflow, contained in cell A1, as a separate argument to get the total project NPV. Remember, the numerical value in cell A1 equals −$250, so by adding this negative number we are *subtracting* the initial cash outflow from the present value of the cash inflows in years 1–5. Excel's NPV function assumes that the project's cash flows are equally spaced through time and occur at the end of each period.

FIGURE 7.3

NPV of Two Global Wireless Projects at 18% ($ million)

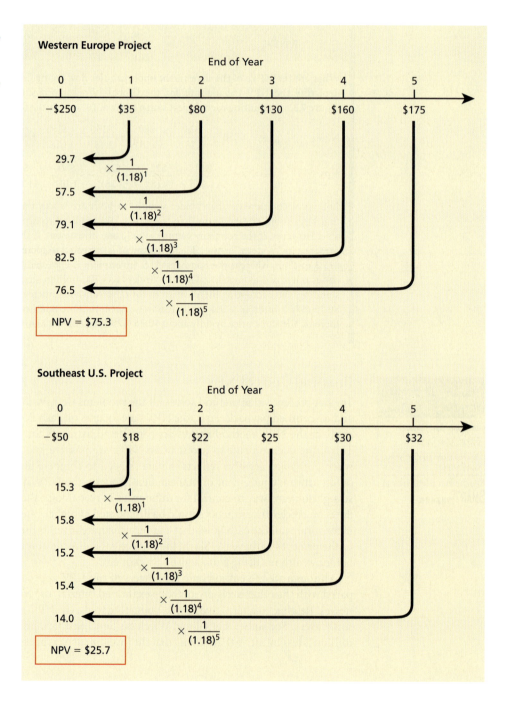

Western Europe Project

End of Year

0	1	2	3	4	5
−$250	$35	$80	$130	$160	$175

$29.7 \quad \times \dfrac{1}{(1.18)^1}$

$57.5 \quad \times \dfrac{1}{(1.18)^2}$

$79.1 \quad \times \dfrac{1}{(1.18)^3}$

$82.5 \quad \times \dfrac{1}{(1.18)^4}$

$76.5 \quad \times \dfrac{1}{(1.18)^5}$

NPV = $75.3

Southeast U.S. Project

End of Year

0	1	2	3	4	5
−$50	$18	$22	$25	$30	$32

$15.3 \quad \times \dfrac{1}{(1.18)^1}$

$15.8 \quad \times \dfrac{1}{(1.18)^2}$

$15.2 \quad \times \dfrac{1}{(1.18)^3}$

$15.4 \quad \times \dfrac{1}{(1.18)^4}$

$14.0 \quad \times \dfrac{1}{(1.18)^5}$

NPV = $25.7

Though the mathematics of an NPV calculation can hardly be called sophisticated, it is still easier to calculate a project's payback period than its NPV.

There is one other subtle drawback to the NPV rule, and it results from our inability to incorporate the value of managerial flexibility when calculating a project's NPV. What we have in mind by "managerial flexibility" are options that managers can exploit to increase the value of an investment. For example, if a firm makes an investment that turns out better than expected, managers have the option to expand that investment, making it even more valuable. Conversely, if a firm invests in a project that does not generate as much positive cash flow as anticipated, then managers have the option to scale back the investment and redeploy resources to more productive uses. The NPV method (like the other methods studied in this chapter) does a poor job of capturing the value of managerial flexibility. Incorporating the value of these options into the analysis requires a highly sophisticated approach that relies on the use of decision trees and the principles of option pricing. We offer a brief introduction to valuing investments with option-like characteristics in Chapter 9, but an in-depth discussion of the real options technique is deferred until Chapter 19.

Whereas most large corporations apply the NPV method—perhaps in conjunction with other capital budgeting tools—the NPV rule has a close cousin, known as the *internal rate of return*, that is even more widely used. The internal rate of return (discussed in Section 7.4) uses essentially the same mathematics as NPV does for evaluating a project's merits. The output of internal rate of return analysis is a single, intuitively appealing number that represents the return an investment earns over its life. *In most cases, the internal rate of return yields investment recommendations that are in agreement with the NPV rule, although important differences between the two approaches arise when ranking alternative projects.*

Economic Value Added

Net present value analysis is appealing for making capital budgeting decisions because it is both theoretically sound and easy to implement. In recent years, a variant of NPV analysis called **economic value added** (**EVA®**), or, more generically, shareholder value added (SVA), has become popular with many firms. A registered trademark of Stern Stewart & Company, EVA is based on the century-old idea of **economic profit**. In accounting, we say that a firm earns a profit if its revenues are greater than its costs. But when economists use the term *economic profit* they refer to how much profit a firm earns relative to a competitive rate of return. If a firm earns zero economic profit, then its accounting profits are positive and just sufficient to satisfy the returns required by the firm's investors. If a firm's economic profits are positive then its stock price will rise because it is out-earning its cost of capital and investor expectations. Similarly, a firm may be earning a positive *accounting* profit, but if that profit does not cover the firm's cost of capital then *economic* profits are negative.

EXAMPLE

On April 23, 2009, Microsoft reported an accounting profit of $2.98 billion. Just prior to that disclosure, Microsoft's market capitalization was roughly $170 billion, so reported earnings represented a return of just 1.75% relative to the value of shareholders' investment in the company—a rate of return similar to what investors in AAA-rated corporate bonds were earning at the time. Microsoft's economic profits for the quarter were therefore negative because they were lower than the company's cost of capital (one component of which was shareholders' required return for investing in Microsoft stock).

EVA establishes a benchmark for managers that measures their performance in each period based on whether they earn an economic profit. The EVA metric subtracts "normal profit" from an investment's cash flow to determine whether the investment is adding value for shareholders. As we have already explained, NPV also provides a measure of value added, so it should not be surprising that these methods are quite similar.

To illustrate how the EVA method works, consider an investment that requires $5 million of capital funding. For simplicity, assume that the invested capital never depreciates and generates annual cash flow of $600,000 in perpetuity. Finally, assume that the firm making this investment has a 12% cost of capital. The formula used to calculate EVA for a particular year is:

$$EVA = \text{Cash flow} - [(\text{Cost of capital}) \times (\text{Invested capital})]$$
$$= \$600,000 - 0.12(\$5,000,000) = \$0$$

An EVA of zero means that the project earns exactly its cost of capital. That is, the project covers all costs including the cost of funds—but does not earn any economic profit above and beyond that amount.

To determine whether the project should be undertaken, an analyst would calculate the EVA in every year and then discount the future EVAs back to the present at the cost of capital; if the resulting value is positive, then the investment is worthwhile. In this case, because EVA every year is zero (and the present value of all future EVAs is also zero), we conclude that this investment provides a break-even return for shareholders. What would the NPV method say? Using the perpetuity shortcut to value the investment's inflows, we find that the NPV is also zero,

$$NPV = -\$5,000,000 + \frac{\$600,000}{0.12} = \$0$$

so the two methods yield the same conclusion.

EVA uses the same basic cash flows as NPV and evaluates the economics of an investment "one year at a time," whereas NPV compares the incremental net cash inflows over the investment's life (discounted to the present at the firm's cost of capital) to the net cash outflows required by the investment. Technically, discounting the time series of annual EVAs at the firm's cost of capital should result in the project's NPV. Thus NPV and EVA are fully compatible and yield the same capital budgeting decisions. The appeal of EVA is its integration of NPV analytical techniques into day-to-day managerial decision making.

| Concept Review Questions | 4. What does it mean if a project has an NPV of $1 million? |
| | 5. What do NPV and EVA have in common, and how do they differ? |

7.4 INTERNAL RATE OF RETURN

Finding a Project's IRR

As methods used for evaluating investment projects, payback and discounted payback suffer from common problems—the complete or partial failure to make adjustments for the time value of money and for risk. Alternative methods, such as NPV, correct these shortcomings. Perhaps the most popular and most intuitive of these alternatives is known as the **internal rate of return (IRR)** method. An investment's internal rate of return is analogous to a bond's *yield to maturity* (YTM), a concept introduced in Chapter 4. Recall that the YTM of a bond is the discount rate that equates the present value of the bond's future cash flows to its market price. The YTM measures the compound annual return an investor earns by purchasing a bond and holding it until maturity (provided that all payments are made as promised and that interest payments can be reinvested at the same rate). Likewise, the IRR of an investment project is the compound annual rate of return on the project, given its up-front costs and subsequent cash flows.

A project's IRR is the discount rate that causes the net present value of all project cash flows to equal zero:

$$NPV = CF_0 + \frac{CF_1}{(1+r)^1} + \frac{CF_2}{(1+r)^2} + \cdots + \frac{CF_{N-1}}{(1+r)^{N-1}} + \frac{CF_N}{(1+r)^N} = \$0 \qquad \textbf{(Eq. 7.2)}$$

To find a project's IRR, we must begin by specifying the project's cash flows. Next we use a financial calculator, spreadsheet, or even trial and error to find the discount rate that equates the present value of cash flows to zero. Once we have the IRR calculated, we compare it with a prespecified hurdle rate established by the firm. The hurdle rate is the firm's minimum acceptable return for a given project, so *the IRR decision rule is to invest only if the project's IRR exceeds the hurdle rate; otherwise, reject the project.*

JOB INTERVIEW QUESTION

What is the relationship between the NPV and IRR of a given project?

But where does the hurdle rate come from? How do firms decide whether to require projects to exceed a 10% hurdle or a 20% hurdle? The answer provides insight into another advantage of IRR over capital budgeting methods that focus on a project's payback period. A company should set the hurdle rate at a level that reflects market returns on investments that are just as risky as the project under consideration. For example, if the project at hand involves expanding a chain of fast-food restaurants, then the hurdle rate should reflect the returns that other fast-food businesses offer investors. Thus the IRR method, like the NPV method, establishes a hurdle rate or a decision criterion that is *market based*—unlike the payback approaches, which establish arbitrary thresholds for investment approval. In fact, *for a given project, the hurdle rate used in IRR analysis should be the discount rate used in NPV analysis.*

Figure 7.4 is an **NPV profile**, which plots a project's NPV (on the *y*-axis) against various discount rates (on the *x*-axis). The NPV profile illustrates the relationship between a typical project's NPV and its IRR. By "typical" we mean a project with initial cash outflows and subsequent cash inflows. In this case, the NPV declines as the discount rate used to calculate the NPV increases. Not all projects have this feature, as we will soon see. The green line in Figure 7.4 plots the NPV of a project at various discount rates. When the discount rate is relatively low, the project has a positive NPV. When the discount rate is high,

FIGURE 7.4

NPV Profile

The NPV is positive when the IRR is greater than the hurdle (i.e., discount) rate, and the NPV is negative when the IRR is less than the hurdle rate.

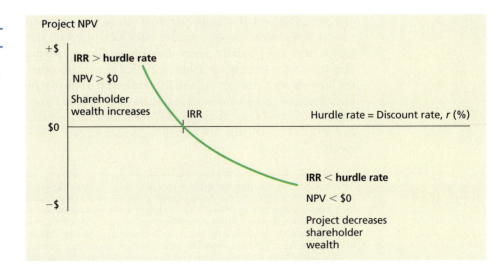

the project has a negative NPV. *At some discount rate, the NPV of the project will equal zero, and that rate is the project's IRR.*

EXAMPLE

Suppose that Global Wireless requires its analysts to calculate the IRR of all proposed investments. The company agrees to undertake only those investments that offer an IRR exceeding 18%, a rate that Global Wireless believes to be an industry standard. Figure 7.5 presents a time line depicting the IRR calculation procedure for the two Global Wireless projects. To obtain the IRR for each project under consideration, just solve these two equations:

$$\$0 = -\$250 + \frac{\$35}{\left(1 + r_{WE}\right)^1} + \frac{\$80}{\left(1 + r_{WE}\right)^2} + \frac{\$130}{\left(1 + r_{WE}\right)^3} + \frac{\$160}{\left(1 + r_{WE}\right)^4} + \frac{\$175}{\left(1 + r_{WE}\right)^5};$$

$$\$0 = -\$50 + \frac{\$18}{\left(1 + r_{SE}\right)^1} + \frac{\$22}{\left(1 + r_{SE}\right)^2} + \frac{\$25}{\left(1 + r_{SE}\right)^3} + \frac{\$30}{\left(1 + r_{SE}\right)^4} + \frac{\$32}{\left(1 + r_{SE}\right)^5}$$

Here r_{WE} is the IRR for the Western Europe project and r_{SE} is the IRR for the Southeast U.S. project. Solving these equations yields:[7]

$r_{WE} = 27.8\%;$

$r_{SE} = 36.7\%$

Because both investments exceed the hurdle rate of 18%, Global Wireless would like to undertake both projects. But what if it can invest in only one project or the other? Should the company invest in the Southeast U.S. project because it offers a higher IRR than the alternative?

ADVANTAGES OF THE IRR METHOD

A number of advantages make the IRR one of the most widely used methods for evaluating capital investments. First, the IRR makes an appropriate adjustment for the time value of money. The value of a dollar received in the first year is greater than the value of a dollar received in the second year. Even cash flows that arrive several years in the future receive some weight in the analysis (unlike payback, which totally ignores distant cash flows). Second, the hurdle rate itself can be based on market returns obtainable on similar investments. Because market rates vary based on the risks of different instruments, firms can similarly choose different hurdle rates for projects with different risks. This takes away some of the subjectivity that creeps into other methods. Third, because the "answer" that emerges from an IRR analysis is a rate of return, its meaning is easy for both financial and nonfinancial managers to grasp intuitively. (But we will see that the IRR's intuitiveness has its drawbacks, particularly when ranking investments with different IRRs.) Fourth, the IRR technique focuses on cash flow rather than on accounting measures of income.

---

[7]Of course, you can make this calculation using a financial calculator or Excel. Here's how to use Excel to solve for the IRR. Put the numbers for the Western Europe project in column A of a spreadsheet, and put the numbers for the Southeast U.S. project in column B. In row 1, type in the cash outflow for each project, entering the values as negative numbers. In rows 2–6 of the spreadsheet, enter the cash inflows in each year. Then, in any empty cell, type "=IRR(A1:A6, 0.10)" to calculate the IRR of the Western Europe project. The cells A1:A6 contain the relevant cash flows, and the value "0.10" is just a starting value that Excel uses to begin searching for the IRR. Likewise, enter the formula "=IRR(B1:B6, 0.10)" in any empty cell to calculate the IRR of the Southeast U.S. investment.

FIGURE 7.5

IRR of Two Global
Wireless Projects
($ million)

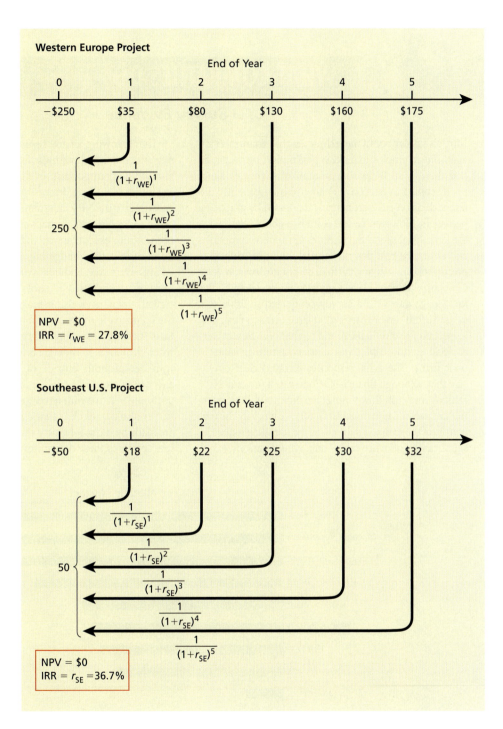

Western Europe Project

End of Year

0	1	2	3	4	5
−$250	$35	$80	$130	$160	$175

$$\frac{1}{(1+r_{WE})^1}$$

$$\frac{1}{(1+r_{WE})^2}$$

250

$$\frac{1}{(1+r_{WE})^3}$$

$$\frac{1}{(1+r_{WE})^4}$$

$$\frac{1}{(1+r_{WE})^5}$$

NPV = $0
IRR = r_{WE} = 27.8%

Southeast U.S. Project

End of Year

0	1	2	3	4	5
−$50	$18	$22	$25	$30	$32

$$\frac{1}{(1+r_{SE})^1}$$

$$\frac{1}{(1+r_{SE})^2}$$

50

$$\frac{1}{(1+r_{SE})^3}$$

$$\frac{1}{(1+r_{SE})^4}$$

$$\frac{1}{(1+r_{SE})^5}$$

NPV = $0
IRR = r_{SE} = 36.7%

Problems with the Internal Rate of Return

Although it represents a substantial improvement over payback analysis, the IRR technique has some quirks and problems that in certain situations should concern analysts. Some of these problems arise from the mathematics of the IRR calculation, but other difficulties come into play only when companies must discriminate between **mutually**

WHAT COMPANIES DO

CFO Survey Evidence

Much is known about the techniques that financial managers *should* employ to make capital budgeting decisions, and there is an increasing amount of survey evidence (as discussed in Section 7.1) about how frequently different decision rules are actually employed by practicing managers. However, far less is known about *who* makes the key capital spending decisions in modern companies and about the role that managerial rank and individual prestige play in swaying the final corporate decision. John Graham, Campbell Harvey, and Manju Puri help fill this knowledge gap with a survey conducted in 2006 that asked 10,700 senior managers at large firms to rank how important various financial and reputational factors were in deciding how capital was allocated across divisions in their firms. The 1,180 responses received clearly indicate that, although financial factors (e.g., a project's NPV ranking and cash flow timing) are important in decision making, several non financial factors—especially the reputation of the manager submitting the spending request—significantly influence capital budgeting decisions.

The following chart summarizes how frequently respondents listed various factors as being "important" or "very important" in their firms' capital budgeting decision making. In most firms, capital is allocated according to the NPV rule, managerial reputation, financial constraints, and, perhaps surprisingly, the "gut feel" of the senior executive who makes the final decision.

In most capital budgeting decisions, the CEO plays an important role, and this is especially true for the one-third of firms whose CEO holds an MBA. Delegation of capital budgeting decision-making to lower levels within the company is more common when the CEO's workload increases (in larger, more complex companies), when the CEO's knowledge is less important (for CEOs with backgrounds outside of finance and accounting and without an MBA), when incentive compensation is used, and in firms with fewer growth opportunities. This survey also makes clear that capital budgeting decisions are made by the most senior executives and that companies approach these decisions with great care.

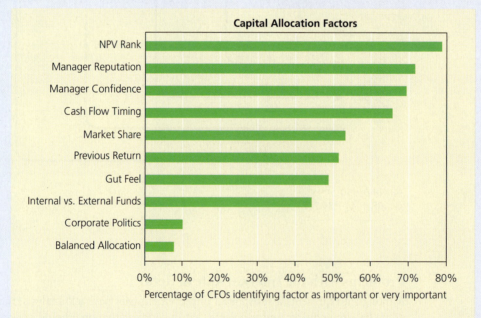

Source: John R. Graham, Campbell R. Harvey, and Manju Puri, "Capital Allocation and Delegation of Decision-Making Authority Within Firms," Working Paper, Duke University and NBER, 2008.

exclusive projects. If two projects offer IRRs in excess of the hurdle rate but the firm can invest in only one, which project should it pursue? It turns out that the intuitive answer—select the project with the highest IRR—sometimes leads to bad decisions.

We can identify two classes of problems that analysts encounter when evaluating investments using the IRR technique. The first class can be described as "mathematical problems," which are difficulties in interpreting the numbers obtained from solving an IRR equation. For example, consider a simple project with cash flows at three different points on the time line:

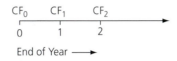

Here CF_0 is the immediate cash flow when the project begins, and CF_1 and CF_2 are cash flows that occur at the end of years 1 and 2, respectively. Note that conceptually the values of CF_0, CF_1, and CF_2 could be either positive or negative. Solving for this project's IRR means setting the net present value of all these cash flows equal to zero:

$$\text{NPV} = CF_0 + \frac{CF_1}{(1 + r)^1} + \frac{CF_2}{(1 + r)^2} = \$0$$

Note that this equation involves terms such as $[1/(1 + r)^1]$ and $[1/(1 + r)^2]$. In other words, this is a quadratic equation in terms of $[1/(1 + r)]$. Solving a quadratic equation can result in a variety of possible outcomes, including (1) a unique solution, (2) multiple solutions, and (3) no real solution. The following examples illustrate some of the problems that may arise when interpreting solutions to an IRR equation.[8]

Lending versus Borrowing   A firm establishes a hurdle rate of 20% for new investments. Consider two projects with cash flows occurring at just two dates: now and one year from now.

Project	Cash Flow Now	Cash Flow in One Year	IRR	NPV (20%)
1	−$100	+$150	50%	+$25
2	+$100	−$150	50%	−$25

The first project displays the familiar pattern of an initial cash outflow followed by a cash inflow. Most investment projects probably fit this profile. But the second project begins with a cash inflow followed by a cash outflow. What kinds of projects in the real world follow this pattern? Think of a firm that is cutting timber. The timber is cut and sold immediately at a profit, but when harvesting is complete, the company must replant the forest at considerable expense. Similarly, consider an optional warranty sold with a new car. The warranty seller receives payment up front but may have to pay claims later on.

---

[8]Another problem is commonly called the **reinvestment rate assumption**. This problem arises because IRR involves an implicit assumption that, in order to actually earn the calculated IRR on the project's full initial cash outlay, the firm must be able to reinvest its *intermediate cash inflows*—cash inflows received during the project's life—at a rate equal to the IRR. Most analysts much prefer NPV's more conservative assumption that intermediate cash inflows can be reinvested at the firm's cost of capital. Clearly, NPV's more conservative reinvestment rate assumption has appeal, because it doesn't presume that other projects earning the IRR are available for reinvestment of intermediate cash inflows. On this technical point, we likewise favor NPV.

Both projects described in the table have a 50% IRR, but are the two projects equally desirable? It should be intuitive to you that project 1 is superior because it generates net cash inflows over time whereas project 2 generates net cash outflows. Indeed, the NPVs bear this out: project 1 generates a positive $25 NPV and project 2 yields a negative $25 NPV.

The problem we are confronting here is known as the **lending-versus-borrowing problem**. We can think of project 1 as analogous to a loan. Cash flows out today in exchange for a larger amount of cash in one year. When we lend money, a higher interest rate (or a higher internal rate of return) is preferable, other things held constant. In contrast, project 2 is analogous to borrowing money. We receive cash up front but have to pay back a larger amount later. When borrowing money, a lower interest rate (or a lower IRR) is preferred, other factors held constant. Therefore, we can modify the internal rate of return decision rule as follows:

1. When projects have initial cash outflows and subsequent cash inflows, invest when the project IRR exceeds the hurdle rate.
2. When projects have initial cash inflows and subsequent cash outflows, invest when the project IRR falls below the hurdle rate.

Figure 7.6 illustrates this situation. The NPV of project 1 falls when the discount rate rises, as we would expect. This means that if the IRR exceeds the hurdle rate then the project's NPV is positive, but if the IRR falls below the hurdle rate then the NPV is negative. So in this case it makes sense to follow the usual rule of accepting projects when the IRR exceeds the hurdle rate. In contrast, the NPV of project 2 actually rises as the discount rate rises. This counterintuitive relationship holds because the firm is essentially borrowing money in project 2. The higher the rate at which the firm discounts the amount it will have to repay, the lower the present value of that payment and the higher the NPV of the project. In this case, it makes sense to accept projects only when the IRR falls short of the firm's hurdle rate.

FIGURE 7.6

Lending versus Borrowing

The green line is the NPV profile for project 1, which is a loan made by the firm; it shows that as the IRR exceeds the hurdle rate, the loan's NPV is positive. The orange line is the NPV profile for project 2, which involves the firm borrowing money; it shows that the higher the rate at which the loan payments are discounted, the higher the NPV.

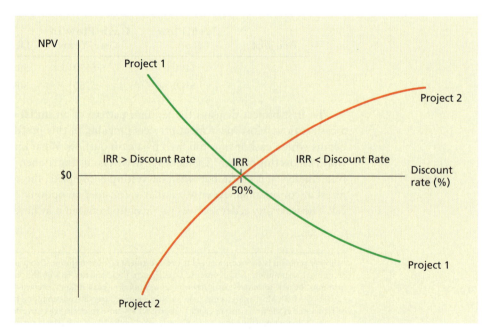

Multiple IRRs   A second difficulty with the IRR method can occur when a project's cash flows alternate between negative and positive values—that is, when the project generates an alternating series of net cash inflows and outflows. In that case, there may be more than one solution to the IRR equation. As an example, consider a project with the following stream of cash flows:

Year	CF ($ million)
0	+100.0
1	−460.0
2	+791.0
3	−602.6
4	+171.6

Admittedly, this project has a rather strange sequence of alternating net cash inflows and outflows, but it is not hard to think of real-world investments that generate cash flow streams that flip back and forth like this. Consider, for example, high-technology products. A new product costs money to develop. It generates plenty of cash for a year or two but then quickly becomes obsolete. Obsolescence necessitates more spending to develop an upgraded version of the product, which then generates cash again. The cycle continues indefinitely.

Figure 7.7 presents the NPV profile for a project with the cash flow just described at various discount rates. Observe that there are four points on the graph at which the project's NPV equals zero. In other words, there are four IRRs for this project, including $IRR_1 = 0\%$, $IRR_2 = 10\%$, $IRR_3 = 20\%$, and $IRR_4 = 30\%$. How does one apply the IRR decision rule in a situation such as this? Suppose that the hurdle rate for this project is 15%. Two of the four IRRs on this project exceed the hurdle rate and two fall below the hurdle

FIGURE 7.7

Multiple IRRs

This project's NPV profile fluctuates below and above the discount rate axis because the project's cash flows change signs a number of times.

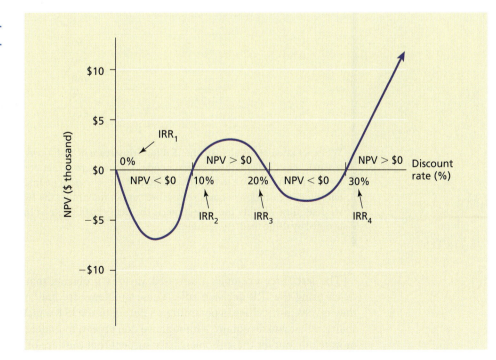

rate. Should the firm invest or not? The only way to know is to check the NPV. On the graph we see that, at a discount rate of 15%, the project's NPV is positive; hence the firm should invest.

The general rule of thumb is that the maximum number of IRRs that a project can have equals the number of sign changes in the cash flow stream. Therefore, in the typical project with cash outflows up front and cash inflows later on, there is just one sign change and there will be at most one IRR. In the previous example, there are four sign changes in the cash flow stream and four different IRRs. *If you must evaluate a project with more than one sign change in the cash flows, beware of the multiple IRR problem.* In this situation, analyze the NPV profile because using the IRR alone may lead to an incorrect investment.

No Real Solution   After entering the cash flows from a particular investment into a calculator or a spreadsheet, you may receive an error message indicating that there is no solution to the problem. For some cash flow patterns, it is possible that there is no real discount rate that equates the project's NPV to zero. In these cases, the only solution to the IRR equation involves imaginary numbers, hardly something that we can compare with a firm's hurdle rate.

EXAMPLE

When we first looked at the Global Wireless Western Europe expansion project, we examined cash flows over a 5-year project life. Let's modify the example a little. Suppose that the project life is six years rather than five and that, in the sixth year, the firm must incur a large negative cash flow (an outflow). The modified cash flow projections look like this:

Year	Western Europe Project ($ million)
0	−250
1	35
2	80
3	130
4	160
5	175
6	−355

When we attempt to calculate the IRR for this stream of cash flows, we find that Excel (or our financial calculator) returns an error code. The problem is that, for this stream of cash flows, there is no real solution to the IRR equation. That is, there is no interest rate at which the present value of cash flows equals zero. If we cannot determine the IRR of this project, how can we determine whether the project meets the firm's hurdle rate of 18%? These problems can be avoided by using the NPV technique.

The last three examples illustrated various problems that analysts may encounter when using the IRR decision rule. These problems are mathematical in the sense that they involve difficulties in obtaining a solution to the IRR equation or in interpreting the solution that you do obtain. Although we don't mean to underemphasize the importance of watching out for these problems, we suspect that they are of secondary importance in practice. In other words, most investment projects that you will evaluate using the IRR method will probably have a unique solution with little ambiguity about whether the project involves borrowing or lending (because most projects involve cash outflows up front followed by cash inflows). However, two additional problems may arise when analysts use the IRR method to prioritize projects or to choose between mutually exclusive projects. These problems are examined in the next section.

IRR, NPV, and Mutually Exclusive Projects

The Scale Problem   Suppose a friend promises to pay you $2 tomorrow if you lend him $1 today. If you make the loan and your friend fulfills his end of the bargain, then you will have made an investment with a 100% IRR.[9] Now consider a different case. Your friend asks you to lend him $100 today in exchange for $150 tomorrow. The IRR on that investment is 50%, exactly half the IRR of the first example. Both of these loans offer very high rates of return. Assuming that you trust the friend to repay you in either case, which investment would you choose if you could choose only one? The first investment increases your wealth by $1, and the second increases your wealth by $50. Even though the rate of return is lower on the second investment, most people would prefer to lend the larger amount because of its substantially greater monetary payoff.

The point of these examples is to illustrate the *scale problem* inherent in IRR analysis. When choosing between mutually exclusive investments, we cannot conclude that the one offering the highest IRR will necessarily create the most wealth. When several alternative investments offer IRRs that exceed a firm's hurdle rate, choosing the investment that maximizes shareholder wealth involves more than picking the project with the highest IRR. For example, take another look at the investment opportunities faced by Global Wireless, opportunities that vary dramatically in scale.

EXAMPLE

Here again are the NPV and IRR figures for the two investment alternatives.

Project	IRR	NPV (18%)
Western Europe	27.8%	$75.3 million
Southeast U.S.	36.7%	$25.7 million

If we had to choose just one project on the basis of IRR, then we would invest in the Southeast U.S. project. But we have also seen that the Western Europe project generates a much higher NPV, meaning that it creates more wealth for Global Wireless shareholders; hence, the NPV criterion tells us to expand in Western Europe rather than in the Southeast United States. Why the conflict? It's because the scale of the Western Europe expansion is roughly five times that of the Southeast U.S. project. Even though the Southeast U.S. investment provides a higher rate of return, the opportunity to make the much larger Western Europe investment (an investment that also offers a return well above the firm's hurdle rate) is more attractive.

JOB INTERVIEW QUESTION

"How would you evaluate an automation investment?"

Fortunately for analysts who prefer to use the IRR method, there is a resolution to the scale problem. The technique involves calculating the IRR for a hypothetical project with cash flows equal to the difference in cash flows between the large-scale (here, Western

---

[9]The IRR is 100% per day in this example, which is not a bad return if you annualize it.

Europe) and small-scale (Southeast U.S.) investments. Call this hypothetical project the **incremental project**. The logic of our approach runs as follows. We already know that both investments have IRRs that exceed the hurdle rate and that, because of limits in funding or managerial talent, we can invest in only one. But we can think of the Western Europe investment as consisting of two investments rolled into one. From this perspective, the Western Europe project equals the sum of the Southeast U.S. project and the incremental project. If we examine the incremental project's IRR and find that it also exceeds our hurdle rate, then by accepting the Western Europe project we are essentially making two investments, not just one. Thus, in accepting the Western Europe project, it is as if we are accepting one project with cash flows identical to those of the Southeast U.S. investment *and* another project with cash flows equal to those of the incremental project.[10]

Year	Incremental CF [Western Europe − Southeast U.S.] ($ million)
0	−200
1	17
2	58
3	105
4	130
5	143

The IRR of this cash flow stream equals 25.8%. Because this is higher than the 18% hurdle rate, we conclude that we would like to accept the incremental project *and* the Southeast U.S. project—but, of course, the only way to do both is to accept the Western Europe project!

The Timing Problem Managers of public corporations often receive criticism for neglecting long-term investment opportunities for the sake of meeting short-term financial performance goals. We prefer to remain noncommittal on whether corporate managers, as a rule, put too much emphasis on short-term performance. However, we do agree that a naive reliance on the IRR method can lead to investment decisions that unduly favor investments with short-term payoffs. The following Example illustrates the problem we have in mind.

EXAMPLE

A company wants to evaluate two investment proposals. The first involves a major effort in new product development. The initial cost is $1 billion, and the company expects the project to generate relatively meager cash flows in the first four years—followed by a big payoff in year 5. The second investment is a significant marketing campaign to attract new customers. It, too, has an initial outlay of $1 billion, but it generates significant cash flows almost immediately and lower levels of cash in the later years. A financial analyst prepares cash flow projections and calculates each project's IRR and NPV as shown in the following table (the firm uses 10% as its hurdle rate).

---

[10]The *incremental project cash flows* are found by subtracting the year-to-year cash flows of the small-scale project from those of the large-scale project. Here we subtract each year's cash flow of the Southeast U.S. project from the comparable year's cash flow of the Western Europe project. The cash flows of both projects are shown in Figure 7.1 on page 234.

Cash Flow	Product Development ($ million)	Marketing Campaign ($ million)
Initial outlay	−1,000	−1,000
Year 1	0	450
Year 2	50	350
Year 3	100	300
Year 4	200	200
Year 5	1,500	100
Technique		
IRR	14.1%	15.9%
NPV (@10%)	$184.44	$122.44

The analyst observes that the first project generates a higher NPV whereas the second offers a higher IRR. Bewildered, he wonders which project to recommend to senior management.

Even though both projects require the same initial investment and both last for five years, the marketing campaign generates more cash flow in the early years than the product development proposal. Therefore, in a relative sense the payoff from product development occurs later than the payoff from marketing. We know from our Chapter 4 discussion of interest-rate risk that when interest rates change, long-term bond prices move more than short-term bond prices. The same phenomenon is at work here. Figure 7.8 plots the NPV profiles for the two proposals on the same set of axes. Notice that the line plotting NPVs for the product development proposal is much steeper than the other. In simple terms, this

FIGURE 7.8

NPV Profiles that Demonstrate the Timing Problem

The timing problem can lead to NPVs and IRRs that yield different investment recommendations. At any discount rate below 12.5%, product development is preferred due to its higher NPV, although the marketing campaign has a higher IRR.

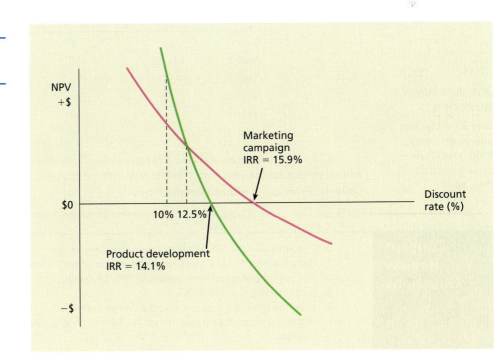

means the NPV of that investment is much more sensitive to the discount rate than is the NPV of the marketing campaign.

Each investment's IRR appears in Figure 7.8 where the NPV lines cross the *x*-axis. Figure 7.8 shows that both IRRs exceed the hurdle rate of 10% and that the marketing campaign has the higher IRR. The two lines intersect at a discount rate of 12.5%, where the NPVs of the two projects are equal. At discount rates below 12.5%, product development (which has a longer-term payoff) has the higher NPV. At discount rates above 12.5%, the investment in the marketing campaign offers a larger NPV. Given that 10% is the required rate of return on investments for this particular firm, it should choose to spend the $1 billion on product development. However, if the firm bases its investment decision solely on achieving the highest IRR, it will choose the marketing campaign instead.

In summary, we can say that if the timing of cash flows is very different from one project to another, then the project with the highest IRR may or may not have the highest NPV. As in the case of the scale problem, the timing problem can lead firms to reject investments they should accept. We want to emphasize that both the timing problem and the scale problem occur only when firms must choose between mutually exclusive projects. In the previous example, if the firm can invest in both projects then the analyst should recommend that it do so.

For firms that must prioritize projects and leave some acceptable ones on the table, there are two ways to avoid the timing trap. First, using NPV will lead to the correct decision when evaluating projects with very different cash flow patterns over time. Second, analysts can compare the long- and short-term projects' incremental cash flows, the same technique we used to deal with the IRR's scale problem. For example, calculating the incremental cash flows of the product development and the marketing campaign options by subtracting the marketing campaign cash flows from those associated with product development, we obtain the following:

Cash Flow	[Product Development − Marketing Campaign] ($ million)
Year 0	0
Year 1	−450
Year 2	−300
Year 3	−200
Year 4	0
Year 5	1,400

The IRR of this incremental cash flow stream is 12.5%. Because the IRR on the incremental project exceeds the firm's hurdle rate (10%), it makes sense for the analyst to recommend investing in product development.

Smart Concepts

See the concept explained step-by-step at

SMARTFinance

JOB INTERVIEW QUESTION

Does IRR always rank projects the same as NPV? Is the IRR ranking easier to understand? If not, why?

Concept Review Questions

6. Describe how the IRR and NPV approaches are related.
7. Suppose the IRR for a given project exceeds a firm's hurdle rate. Does this mean that the project must have a positive NPV? Explain.
8. What causes multiple IRRs?
9. Describe the scale problem and the timing problem. Explain the potential effects of these problems on using IRR versus NPV to choose among mutually exclusive projects.

7.5 PROFITABILITY INDEX

Calculating the Profitability Index

A final capital budgeting tool to discuss is the **profitability index (PI)**. Like the IRR, the profitability index is a close cousin of the NPV approach. For simple projects that have an initial cash outflow (CF_0) followed by a series of inflows ($CF_1, CF_2, \ldots, CF_N$), the PI is expressed mathematically as the present value of a project's cash inflows divided by the initial cash outflow:[11]

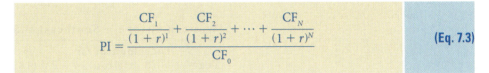

$$PI = \frac{\dfrac{CF_1}{(1+r)^1} + \dfrac{CF_2}{(1+r)^2} + \cdots + \dfrac{CF_N}{(1+r)^N}}{CF_0}$$

(Eq. 7.3)

The decision rule to follow when evaluating investment projects using the profitability index is to invest when the PI is greater than 1.0 (i.e., when the present value of cash inflows exceeds the initial cash outflow) and to refrain from investing when the PI is less than 1.0. Note that if the PI is above 1.0 then the NPV > $0. This means that *the NPV and PI decision rules will always yield the same investment recommendation when we are simply trying to accept or reject a single project.*

EXAMPLE

To calculate the PI for each of Global Wireless's investment projects, compute the present value of its cash inflows from years 1–5 and then divide by the initial cash outflow to obtain the following result:

Project	PV of CF (1–5) ($ million)	Initial Outlay ($ million)	PI
Western Europe	325.3	250	1.3
Southeast U.S.	75.7	50	1.5

Both projects have a PI that exceeds 1.0, so both are worthwhile. However, observe that if we rank projects based solely on PI then the Southeast U.S. project looks better.

Because the NPV, IRR, and PI methods are so closely related, they share many of the same advantages relative to payback analysis; there is no need to reiterate those advantages here. However, it is worth pointing out that the PI and the IRR share an important flaw. Both suffer from the *scale problem* described earlier. Recall that our NPV calculations suggested that the Western Europe project created more value for shareholders than the Southeast U.S. endeavor, whereas the IRR and PI comparisons suggest just the opposite project ranking. The latter two analyses identify the Southeast U.S. project as the superior investment because they ignore the differences in scale between the two projects. For the Southeast U.S. project, the PI indicates that project cash inflows exceed the initial cash outflow by 50% on a present value basis. The present value of cash inflows for the Western

---

[11]An alternate definition is PI = NPV/CF_0. Although this formula reduces the calculated PI by 1.00, it results in the same ordering of projects as when Equation 7.3 is used.

Europe investment exceeds the initial cash outflow by just 30%. But the Western Europe project is much larger and, as our NPV figures reveal, generates considerably more wealth for Global Wireless stockholders.

We have seen how the scale problem can be solved by looking at the IRR of an incremental project. In the same way, we can modify our PI analysis to solve its scale problem. First, calculate the incremental cash flows on the Western Europe investment relative to the Southeast U.S. investment. Next, take the present value of these incremental cash flows in years 1–5. Finally, divide this present value by the incremental initial cash outflow. If the profitability index on the incremental project exceeds 1.0, then invest in the larger project.

[Western Europe − Southeast U.S.]		
Year	Incremental CF ($ million)	PV (18%)
0	−200	−200.0
1	17	14.4
2	58	41.7
3	105	63.9
4	130	67.1
5	143	62.5

$$PI = \frac{\$14.4 + \$41.7 + \$63.9 + \$67.1 + \$62.5}{\$200.0} = \frac{\$249.6}{\$200.0} = 1.25$$

Because the PI of the incremental project equals 1.25, we should choose the large-scale project: the Western Europe expansion proposal.

The Profitability Index and Capital Rationing

At several points in this chapter, we have asked the following question: If a firm must choose between several investment opportunities, all of which are worth taking, how does it prioritize projects? We have seen that the IRR and PI methods sometimes rank projects differently than the NPV does, though it is often possible to reconcile differences in each method by examining incremental cash flows between projects.

There is a fundamental question that we have avoided until now. If the firm has many projects with positive NPVs (or investments with acceptable IRRs), why not accept all of them? One possibility is that the firm simply does not have enough money to finance all of its attractive investment opportunities. But surely in most years large, publicly traded firms could raise money by issuing new shares to investors and then use the proceeds to undertake any and all appealing investments.

Yet if you watch firms closely over a period of time, you will notice that most do not issue new shares very often. As Chapter 11 discusses more fully, it seems that firms prefer to finance investments with internally generated cash flow and will only infrequently raise money in the capital markets by issuing new equity. There are several possible reasons for this apparent reluctance to issue new equity. First, when firms announce their intention to raise new equity capital, they may send an unintended negative signal to the market. Perhaps investors will interpret the announcement as a sign that the firm's existing investments are not doing very well. Perhaps the decision to issue new shares will be seen as an indication that managers believe the firm's stock is overvalued. In either case, investors may react negatively to this announcement, causing the stock price to fall. Undoubtedly, managers will try to persuade investors that the funds being raised will be invested in profitable projects, but convincing investors that this is the firm's true motive will be an uphill struggle.

A second reason why managers may avoid issuing new equity is that it would dilute their ownership stake in the firm (unless they participate in the offering by purchasing some of the new shares). A smaller ownership stake means that managers control a shrinking block of votes, raising the potential of a corporate takeover or other threat to their control of the firm.

In conversations with senior executives, we often hear a third reason why firms do not fund every investment project that looks promising. Behind each idea for a new investment is a person, someone who may have an emotional attachment to the idea or a career-building motivation for proposing it. Upper-level managers are wise to be a little skeptical of the cash flow forecasts they see on projects with favorable NPVs or IRRs. It is a given that every cash flow forecast will prove to be wrong, but if the forecasting process is unbiased then half the time forecasts will be too pessimistic and half the time too optimistic. Which half is likely to surface on the radar screen of a CFO or CEO in a large corporation? Rationing capital is one mechanism by which senior managers impose discipline on the capital budgeting process. By doing so, they hope to weed out some investment proposals that have an optimistic bias built into their cash flow projections.

Whatever the motivation for their behavior, managers cannot always invest in every project that offers a positive NPV. In such an environment, **capital rationing** occurs. Given a set of attractive investment opportunities, managers must choose a combination of projects that maximizes shareholder wealth, subject to the constraint of limited funds. In this environment, ranking projects using the PI can be very useful. Once managers rank projects, they select the investment with the highest PI. If the total amount of capital available has not been fully exhausted, then managers invest in the project with the second-highest PI, and so on until no more capital remains to invest. By following this routine, managers will select a portfolio of projects that in aggregate generates a higher NPV than any other combination of projects.

As shown in the *What Companies Do* box on page 248, a study of CEOs and CFOs by Graham, Harvey, and Puri (2008) found that NPV rank is the most popular consideration in allocating capital to projects under capital rationing. After NPV, U.S. CFOs ranked manager reputation, manager confidence, cash flow timing, protecting market share, and previous return history of the project proposer as (respectively) the second through sixth most popular considerations in capital allocation decisions. We note with interest that non-U.S. CFOs tended to view the same set of considerations of greatest importance, but in a slightly different order. Here we focus solely on NPV rank, the most popular consideration. Clearly the other, more behavioral factors must be included when making the final decision.

Table 7.2 illustrates this technique. A particular firm has five projects to choose from, all of which have positive NPVs and IRRs that exceed the firm's hurdle rate of 12%. Notice that the first project has the highest IRR and the highest PI, but project 5 has a larger NPV. This is our familiar scale problem. Suppose that the firm can invest no more than $300 million this year. What portfolio of investments maximizes shareholder wealth?

You can see that there are several combinations of projects that satisfy the constraint of investing no more than $300 million. If we begin by accepting the project with the highest PI and continue to accept additional projects until we bump into the $300 million capital constraint, then we will invest in projects 1, 2, and 3. With these three projects, we have invested just $250 million, but this does not leave us with enough capital to entertain either

Table 7.2   **Capital Rationing and the Profitability Index**

YEAR	PROJECTS ($ MILLION)				
	1	2	3	4	5
0	−70	−80	−100	−150	−200
1	30	30	40	50	90
2	40	35	50	55	80
3	50	55	60	60	80
4	55	60	65	90	110
Technique					
NPV	$59.2	$52.0	$59.6	$38.4	$71.0
IRR	44%	36%	36%	23%	28%
PI	1.8	1.6	1.6	1.3	1.4

project 4 or 5. The total NPV obtainable from the first three projects is $170.8 million. No other combination of projects that satisfies the capital constraint yields a higher aggregate NPV. For example, investing in projects 3 and 5—thereby using up the full allotment of $300 million in capital—generates a total NPV of just $130.6 million. Likewise, investing in projects 1, 2, and 4 (another combination that utilizes all $300 million in capital) generates an aggregate NPV of $149.6 million.

We are simplifying a bit here. Strictly speaking, the method we've outlined can, in theory, lead to suboptimal investment decisions. For example, consider a firm that has a capital budget of $180 million and three investment opportunities. One requires an investment of $100 million and has an NPV of $15 million. The other two investments each require an initial investment of $90 million, and each provides an NPV of $10 million. If the firm ranks the projects based on NPV then it will invest in the first project and earn an NPV of $15 million. No additional investments are possible because the firm does not have enough capital to pursue them. However, if the firm decided to pass on the $100 million investment and pursue the two smaller investments, it would invest $180 million (thus exhausting the available capital) and earn an NPV of $20 million. In situations such as these, if the process of ranking projects based on NPV does not fully exhaust a firm's capital constraint, then the only way to determine the optimal combination of investments is to calculate the NPV of every combination that satisfies the capital constraint.[12]

Concept Review Questions

10. How are the NPV, IRR, and PI approaches related?
11. Why doesn't choosing the projects with the highest PIs (within the budget constraint) always lead to the best capital rationing decisions?

---

[12]Sorting projects according to the PI and selecting from that list until capital runs out may not maximize shareholder wealth when capital is rationed not only at the beginning of an investment's life, but also in all subsequent periods. This method can also lead to suboptimal decisions when projects are interdependent—that is, when one investment is contingent on another. In these situations, more-complex decision tools, such as integer programming, may be required.

WHAT COMPANIES DO GLOBALLY

CFO Survey Evidence

Surveys of corporate financial managers around the world reveal both major similarities and significant differences in the use of different capital budgeting techniques. The graph below documents how frequently managers in the United States, the United Kingdom, Germany, France, Brazil, and Australia use internal rate of return, net present value, payback period, real option analysis, and accounting rate of return. Internal rate of return and NPV are used by over 70% of managers of U.S companies and a majority or near-majority of Australian, Brazilian, and British managers, but the propensity to use either of these theoretically preferred methods of capital budgeting decision making is below 50% in all other countries. In fact, payback is the most frequently employed decision-making tool in all countries besides the United States.

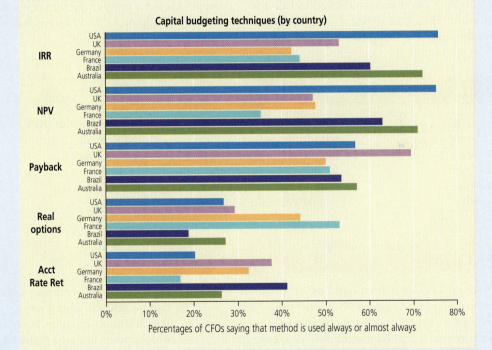

Sources: John R. Graham and Campbell R. Harvey, "The Theory and Practice of Corporate Finance: Evidence from the Field," *Journal of Financial Economics* 60 (2001), pp. 187–243; Dirk Brounen, Abe de Jong, and Kees Koedijk, "Corporate Finance in Europe: Confronting Theory with Practice," *Financial Management* 33 (Winter 2004), pp. 71–101; "Narratives in Managers' Corporate Finance Decisions," Les Coleman, Krishnan Maheswaran, and Sean Pinder, Working Paper, University of Melbourne, 2008.

SUMMARY

- The capital budgeting process involves identifying, isolating, prioritizing, implementing, and monitoring long-term investment proposals that are consistent with the firm's strategic goals.

- Other things being equal, managers would prefer an easily applied capital budgeting technique that considers cash flow, recognizes the time value of money, fully accounts for expected risk and return, and (when applied) leads to higher stock prices.

- Though simplicity is a virtue, the simplest approaches to capital budgeting do not always lead firms to make the best investment decisions.

- Capital budgeting techniques include the payback period and discounted payback period, which are less sophisticated techniques because they do not explicitly deal with the time value of money and are not tied to the firm's goal of maximizing shareholder wealth. Techniques that are more sophisticated include net present value (NPV), internal rate of return (IRR), and profitability index (PI). These methods always give the

same accept–reject decisions but do not necessarily rank projects the same.

- Using the IRR approach can lead to poor investment decisions when projects have cash flows that alternate between net inflows and outflows.

- Although the NPV and IRR techniques give the same accept–reject decisions, these techniques do not always agree when ranking mutually exclusive projects. The IRR technique may provide suboptimal project rankings when different investments have very different scales or when the timing of cash flows varies dramatically from one project to another. However, the scale and timing problems of IRR can be eliminated by finding the IRR of the *incremental project*.

- The most straightforward and, theoretically, the best decision technique is NPV.

- The profitability index (PI) is a close cousin of the NPV approach, but it suffers from the same scale problem as the IRR approach. The PI approach is most useful in capital rationing scenarios.

KEY TERMS

capital budgeting	economic value added (EVA®)	net present value (NPV)
capital investment	incremental project	NPV profile
capital rationing	internal rate of return (IRR)	payback period
capital spending	lending-versus-borrowing	profitability index (PI)
discounted payback	problem	reinvestment rate
economic profit	mutually exclusive projects	assumption

QUESTIONS

7-1. In statistics you learn about Type I and Type II errors. A Type I error occurs when a statistical test rejects a hypothesis when the hypothesis is actually true. A Type II error occurs when a test fails to reject a hypothesis that is actually false. We can apply this type of thinking to capital budgeting. A Type I error occurs when a firm rejects an investment project that would actually enhance shareholder wealth. A Type II error occurs when a firm accepts a value-decreasing investment, an investment it should have rejected.

    a. Describe the features of the payback rule that could lead to Type I errors.

    b. Describe the features of the payback rule that could lead to Type II errors.

    c. Which error do you think is more likely to occur when firms use payback analysis? Does your answer depend on the length of the maximum payback period? You can assume a "typical" project cash flow stream, meaning that most cash outflows occur in the early years of a project.

7-2. Holding the maximum payback period fixed, which method has a more severe bias against long-lived projects: payback or discounted payback?

7-3. In what way is the NPV consistent with the principle of maximizing shareholder wealth? For a firm that uses the NPV rule to make investment decisions, what consequences result if the firm misestimates shareholders' required returns and consistently applies a discount rate that is "too high"?

7-4. "Cash flow projections more than a few years out are not worth the paper they're written on. Therefore, using payback analysis, which ignores long-term cash flows, is more reasonable than making wild guesses, which the NPV approach requires." Respond to this comment.

7-5. "Smart analysts can massage the numbers in NPV analysis to make any project's NPV look positive. It is better to use a simpler approach, such as payback, that gives analysts fewer degrees of freedom to manipulate the numbers." Respond to this comment.

7-6. A particular firm's shareholders demand a 15% return on their investment, given the firm's risk. However, this firm has historically generated returns in excess of shareholder expectations, with an average return on its portfolio of investments of 25%.
 a. Looking back, what kind of stock price performance would you expect to see for this firm?
 b. A new investment opportunity arises, and the firm's financial analysts estimate that the project's return will be 18%. The CEO wants to reject the project because it would lower the firm's average return and hence the firm's stock price. How do you respond?

7-7. Does an investment need to show a positive EVA in each period in order to be considered worthwhile?

7-8. What are the potential problems with using the IRR as a capital budgeting technique?

7-9. Suppose a project has a discounted payback period equal to the life of the project (assuming a 10% discount rate). What is the NPV of the project, and what is the IRR?

7-10. Why is the NPV considered to be theoretically superior to all other capital budgeting techniques? Reconcile this reasoning with the prevalence in practice of using the IRR. How would you respond to your CFO if she instructed you to use the IRR technique to make capital budgeting decisions on projects with cash flow streams that alternate between inflows and outflows?

7-11. Outline the differences between NPV, IRR, and PI. What are the advantages and disadvantages of each technique? Do they agree with regard to simple accept–reject decisions?

7-12. Under what circumstances will the NPV, IRR, and PI techniques provide different capital budgeting decisions? Are these differing results found in the analysis of independent or mutually exclusive projects? Why are the differences found in one type of project analysis and not the other?

7-13. What is the only relevant decision for independent projects if an unlimited capital budget exists? How does your response change if the projects are mutually exclusive? How does your response change if the firm faces capital rationing?

7-14. Project A costs $1,000 and has annual cash flows of $400, $600, and $300. Project B costs $1,500 and has annual cash flows of $500, $500, $500, and $10,000. Based on having the shortest payback period, which project is better? Is this really the best decision? If not, what is the problem with payback period criteria?

PROBLEMS

Payback Methods

7-1. Suppose that a 30-year U.S. Treasury bond offers a 4% coupon rate, paid semiannually. The market price of the bond is $1,000, equal to its par value.
 a. What is the payback period for this bond?
 b. With such a long payback period, is the bond a bad investment?
 c. What is the discounted payback period for the bond, assuming that its 4% coupon rate is the required return? What general principle does this example illustrate regarding a project's life, its discounted payback period, and its NPV?

7-2. The cash flows associated with three different projects are as follows:

Cash Flows	Alpha ($ million)	Beta ($ million)	Gamma ($ million)
Initial outflow	−1.5	−0.4	−7.5
Year 1	0.3	0.1	2.0
Year 2	0.5	0.2	3.0
Year 3	0.5	0.2	2.0
Year 4	0.4	0.1	1.5
Year 5	0.3	−0.2	5.5

a. Calculate the payback period of each investment.

b. Which investments does the firm accept if the cutoff payback period is three years? Four years?

c. If the firm invests by choosing projects with the shortest payback period, which project would it invest in?

d. If the firm uses discounted payback with a 15% discount rate and a 4-year cutoff period, which projects will it accept?

e. One of these projects should almost certainly be rejected, but it may be accepted if the firm uses payback analysis. Which one?

f. One of these projects almost certainly should be accepted (unless the firm's opportunity cost of capital is very high), but it may be rejected if the firm uses payback analysis. Which one?

7-3. Nader International is considering investing in two assets—A and B. The initial outlay and annual cash flows for each asset are shown in the following table for the assets' assumed 5-year lives. The firm requires a 12% return on each of these equally risky assets. Nader's maximum payback period is 2.5 years, and its maximum discounted payback period is 3.25 years.

	Asset A ($200,000)	Asset B ($180,000)
Year (t)	Cash Flow (CF_t)	Cash Flow (CF_t)
1	$70,000	$80,000
2	80,000	90,000
3	90,000	30,000
4	90,000	40,000
5	100,000	40,000

a. Calculate the payback period for each asset, assess its acceptability, and indicate which asset is best in terms of this criterion.

b. Calculate the discounted payback for each asset, assess its acceptability, and indicate which asset is best in terms of this criterion.

c. Compare and contrast your findings in parts (a) and (b). Assuming that they are mutually exclusive, which asset would you recommend to Nader? Why?

Net Present Value

7-4. Calculate the net present value for the following 20-year projects. Comment on the acceptability of each. Assume that the firm has an opportunity cost of 14%.

a. Initial cash outlay is $15,000; cash inflows are $13,000 per year.

b. Initial cash outlay is $32,000; cash inflows are $4,000 per year.

c. Initial cash outlay is $50,000; cash inflows are $8,500 per year.

7-5. Michael's Bakery is evaluating a new electronic oven. The oven requires an initial cash outlay of $19,000 and will generate after-tax cash inflows of

$4,000 per year for eight years. For each of the costs of capital listed, (1) calculate the NPV, (2) indicate whether to accept or reject the oven, and (3) explain your decision.

a. The cost of capital is 10%.

b. The cost of capital is 12%.

c. The cost of capital is 14%.

7-6. Using a 14% cost of capital, calculate the NPV for each of the projects shown in the following table and indicate whether or not each is acceptable.

Initial Cash Outflow (CF$_0$):	Project A $20,000	Project B $600,000	Project C $150,000	Project D $760,000	Project E $100,000
Year (t)	Cash Inflows (CF$_t$)				
1	$3,000	$120,000	$18,000	$185,000	$ 0
2	3,000	145,000	17,000	185,000	0
3	3,000	170,000	16,000	185,000	0
4	3,000	190,000	15,000	185,000	25,000
5	3,000	220,000	15,000	185,000	36,000
6	3,000	240,000	14,000	185,000	0
7	3,000	—	13,000	185,000	60,000
8	3,000	—	12,000	185,000	72,000
9	3,000	—	11,000	—	84,000
10	3,000	—	10,000	—	—

7-7. Scotty Manufacturing is considering the replacement of one of its machine tools. Three alternative replacement tools—A, B, and C—are under consideration. The cash flows associated with each are shown in the following table. The firm's cost of capital is 15%.

Initial Cash Outflow (CF$_0$):	A $95,000	B $50,000	C $150,000
Year (t)	Cash Inflows (CF$_t$)		
1	$20,000	$10,000	$58,000
2	20,000	12,000	35,000
3	20,000	13,000	23,000
4	20,000	15,000	23,000
5	20,000	17,000	23,000
6	20,000	21,000	35,000
7	20,000	—	46,000
8	20,000	—	58,000

a. Calculate the NPV of each alternative.

b. Using NPV, evaluate the acceptability of each tool.

c. Rank the tools from best to worst in terms of NPV.

7-8. Erwin Enterprises has 10 million shares outstanding with a current market price of $10 per share. There is one investment available to Erwin, and its cash flows are listed below. Erwin has a cost of capital of 10%. Given this information, determine the impact on Erwin's stock price and firm value if capital markets fully reflect the value of undertaking the project.

Smart Solutions

See the problem and solution explained step-by-step at **SMARTFinance**

Initial Cash Outflow: $10,000,000

Year	Cash Inflow
1	$3,000,000
2	4,000,000
3	5,000,000
4	6,000,000
5	9,800,000

7-9. Project LMN has an initial cost of $10,000 and annual cash inflows of $2,825, $3,192, $3,607, and $4,076 in years 1–4. What is the NPV assuming a 12% discount rate? When the project was completed, none of the cash flows were reinvested. Sum up the cash flows and determine the annual return on the project based on the initial $10,000 investment. Why is the annual return on the project below the 12% discount rate?

7-10. A certain investment requires an initial cash outflow of $12 million and subsequently produces annual cash inflows of $1.4 million in perpetuity. A firm evaluating this investment has a cost of capital of 10%. What is the investment's NPV? What is the EVA each period? What is the present value of the stream of EVAs?

Internal Rate of Return

7-11. For each of the projects shown in the following table, calculate the internal rate of return.

Initial Cash Outflow (CF$_0$):	Project A $72,000	Project B $440,000	Project C $18,000	Project D $215,000
Year (t)		Cash Inflows (CF$_t$)		
1	$16,000	$135,000	$7,000	$108,000
2	20,000	135,000	7,000	90,000
3	24,000	135,000	7,000	72,000
4	28,000	135,000	7,000	54,000
5	32,000	—	7,000	—

7-12. William Industries is attempting to choose the better of two mutually exclusive projects for expanding the firm's production capacity. The relevant cash flows for the projects are shown in the following table. The firm's cost of capital is 15%.

Initial Cash Outflow (CF$_0$):	Project A $550,000	Project B $358,000
Year (t)		Cash Inflows (CF$_t$)
1	$110,000	$154,000
2	132,000	132,000
3	165,000	105,000
4	209,000	77,000
5	275,000	55,000

a. Calculate the IRR for each of the projects.
b. Assess the acceptability of each project based on the IRRs found in part (a).
c. Which project is preferred, based on the IRRs found in part (a)?

7-13. A project costs $4,000 and has annual cash flows of $1,090, $1,188, $1,295, and $1,411 in years 1–4. The firm has a discount rate of 9%. Find the following for the project.
a. Payback period
b. Discounted payback period

c. NPV

d. IRR

Smart Solutions

See the problem and solution explained step-by-step at **SMARTFinance**

7-14. Project Z has an initial cost of $6,000 and has annual cash inflows of $1,725, $1,984, $2,281, and $2,624 in years 1–4. Assuming a 15% discount rate, find the following for the project.

a. Discounted payback period

b. NPV

c. Profitability index

d. IRR

Smart Solutions

See the problem and solution explained step-by-step at **SMARTFinance**

7-15. Contract Manufacturing, Inc., is considering two alternative investment proposals. The first proposal calls for a major renovation of the company's manufacturing facility. The second involves replacing just a few obsolete pieces of equipment in the facility. The company will choose one project or the other this year, but it will not do both. The cash flows associated with each project appear below, and the firm discounts project cash flows at 15%.

Year	Renovate	Replace
0	−$9,000,000	−$1,000,000
1	3,500,000	600,000
2	3,000,000	500,000
3	3,000,000	400,000
4	2,800,000	300,000
5	2,500,000	200,000

a. Rank these investments based on their NPVs.

b. Rank these investments based on their IRRs.

c. Why do these rankings yield mixed signals?

d. Calculate the IRR of the incremental project. Reconcile your answer to this question with those from parts (a) and (b).

7-16. Consider a project with the following cash flows and a firm with a 15% cost of capital.

End of Year	Cash Flow
0	−$20,000
1	50,000
2	− 10,000

a. What are the two IRRs associated with this cash flow stream?

b. If the firm's cost of capital falls between the two IRR values calculated in part (a), should it accept or reject the project?

7-17. Jess Oil, an oil exploration company, is considering drilling a new well in an established field. Estimates indicate that a cash outflow of $480,000 will be incurred at time 0 for drilling and preparing the well for production. The well is expected to generate cash inflow of about $1,560,000 in the first year, and a $120,000 cash outflow will be required in the second year to shut down the well and clean up the site.

a. What are the two IRRs associated with the drilling decision?

b. Calculate the project's NPV at each of the following discount rates: 0%, 50%, 100%, 150%, 200%, and 250%. Use these points to draw the project's NPV profile.

c. Should the firm drill the proposed well if its cost of capital is 25%?

7-18. A certain project has the following stream of cash flows:

Year	Cash Flow
0	$ 17,500
1	− 80,500
2	138,425
3	− 105,455
4	30,030

a. Fill in the following table:

Cost of Capital (%)	Project NPV
0	_____
5	_____
10	_____
15	_____
20	_____
25	_____
30	_____
35	_____
50	_____

b. Use the values developed in part (a) to draw an NPV profile for this project.

c. What is this project's IRR?

d. Describe the conditions under which the firm should accept this project.

7-19. Both Old Line Industries and High Tech, Inc., use the IRR to make investment decisions. Both firms are considering investing in a more efficient $4.5 million mail-order processor. This machine could generate after-tax savings of $2 million per year over the next three years for both firms. However, owing to the risky nature of its business, High Tech has a much higher cost of capital (20%) than does Old Line (10%). Given this information, answer parts (a)–(c).

a. Should Old Line invest in this processor?

b. Should High Tech invest in this processor?

c. Based on your answers in parts (a) and (b), what can you infer about the acceptability of projects across firms with different costs of capital?

7-20. Butler Products has prepared the following estimates for an investment it is considering. The initial cash outflow is $20,000, and the project is expected to yield cash inflows of $4,400 per year for seven years. The firm has a 10% cost of capital.

a. Determine the NPV for the project.

b. Determine the IRR for the project.

c. Would you recommend that the firm accept or reject the project? Explain your answer.

Smart Solutions

See the problem and solution explained step-by-step at **SMARTFinance**

7-21. Reynolds Enterprises is attempting to evaluate the feasibility of investing $85,000, CF_0, in a machine with a 5-year life. The firm has estimated the cash inflows associated with the proposal as shown below. The firm has a 12% cost of capital.

End of Year (t)	Cash Inflows (CF_t)
1	$18,000
2	22,500
3	27,000
4	31,500
5	36,000

a. Calculate the payback period for the proposed investment.
b. Calculate the NPV for the proposed investment.
c. Calculate the IRR for the proposed investment.
d. Evaluate the acceptability of the proposed investment using NPV and IRR. What recommendation would you make relative to implementation of the project? Why?

7-22. Sharpe Manufacturing is attempting to select the best of three mutually exclusive projects. The initial cash outflow and after-tax cash inflows associated with each project are shown in the following table.

Cash Flows	Project X	Project Y	Project Z
Initial cash outflow (CF_0)	$80,000	$130,000	$145,000
Cash inflows (CF_t), years $t = 1-5$	$27,000	$41,000	$43,000

a. Calculate the payback period for each project.
b. Calculate the NPV of each project, assuming that the firm's cost of capital is 13%.
c. Calculate the IRR for each project.
d. Summarize the preferences dictated by each measure and indicate which project you would recommend. Explain why.

7-23. Wilkes, Inc., must invest in a pollution control program in order to meet federal regulations and stay in business. There are two programs available to Wilkes: an all-at-once program that will be immediately funded and implemented, and a gradual program that will be phased in over the next three years. The immediate program costs $5 million, whereas the phase-in program will cost $1 million today and $2 million per year for the following three years. If the cost of capital for Wilkes is 15%, which pollution control program should Wilkes select?

Profitability Index

7-24. JK Products is considering investing in either of two competing projects that will allow the firm to eliminate a production bottleneck and meet the growing demand for its products. The firm's engineering department narrowed the alternatives down to two—status quo (SQ) and high tech (HT). Working with the accounting and finance personnel, the firm's CFO developed the following estimates of the cash flows for SQ and HT over the relevant 6-year time horizon. The firm has an 11% required return and views these projects as equally risky.

	Project SQ	Project HT
Initial Outflow (CF_0):	$670,000	$940,000
Year (t)	Cash Inflows (CF_t)	
1	$250,000	$170,000
2	200,000	180,000
3	170,000	200,000
4	150,000	250,000
5	130,000	300,000
6	130,000	550,000

a. Calculate the net present value of each project, assess its acceptability, and indicate which project is best in terms of NPV.
b. Calculate the internal rate of return of each project, assess its acceptability, and indicate which project is best in terms of IRR.
c. Calculate the profitability index of each project, assess its acceptability, and indicate which project is best in terms of PI.

d. Draw the NPV *profile* for projects SQ and HT on the same set of axes; then use this diagram to explain why the NPV and the IRR show different preferences for these two mutually exclusive projects. Discuss this difference in terms of both the scale problem and the timing problem.

e. Which of the two mutually exclusive projects would you recommend that JK Products undertake? Why?

7-25. A consumer products firm finds that its brand of laundry detergent is losing market share, so it decides that it needs to "freshen" the product. One strategy is to maintain the current detergent formula but repackage the product. The other strategy involves a complete reformulation of the product in a way that will appeal to environmentally conscious consumers. The firm will pursue one strategy or the other but not both. Cash flows from each proposal appear below, and the firm discounts cash flows at 13%.

Year	Repackage	Reformulate
0	−$3,000,000	−$25,000,000
1	2,000,000	10,000,000
2	1,250,000	9,000,000
3	500,000	7,000,000
4	250,000	4,000,000
5	250,000	3,500,000

a. Rank these investments based on their NPVs.

b. Rank these investments based on their IRRs.

c. Rank these investments based on their PIs.

d. Draw NPV profiles for the two projects on the same set of axes and discuss these profiles.

e. Do these investment rankings yield mixed signals?

f. Calculate the IRR of the incremental project. Reconcile your answer to this question with your answer to parts (a) and (b).

7-26. Lundblad Construction Co. recently acquired 10 acres of land and is weighing two options for developing the land. The first proposal is to build 10 single-family homes on the site. This project would generate a quick cash payoff as the homes are sold over the next two years. Specifically, Lundblad estimates that it would spend $2.5 million on construction costs immediately and that it would receive $1.6 million as cash inflows in each of the next two years.

The second proposal is to build a strip shopping mall. This project calls for Lundblad to retain ownership of the property and to lease space for retail businesses that would serve the neighborhood. Construction costs for the strip mall are also about $2.5 million, and the company expects to receive $350,000 annually (for each of 50 years, starting one year from now) in net cash inflows from leasing the property. Lundblad's cost of capital is 10%.

a. Rank these projects based on their NPVs.

b. Rank these projects based on their IRRs.

c. Rank these projects based on their PIs. Do these rankings agree with those based on NPV or IRR?

d. Draw NPV profiles for these projects on the same set of axes. Use this graph to explain why, in this case, the NPV and IRR methods yield mixed signals.

e. Which project should Lundblad choose? Calculate the IRR of the incremental project to verify your answer.

f. Which project should Lundblad choose if its cost of capital is 13.5%? 16%? 20%?

7-27. Evaluate the following three projects in terms of the profitability index. Assume a cost of capital of 15%.

	Project		
	Liquidate	**Recondition**	**Replace**
Initial Cash Outflow:	**−$100,000**	**−$500,000**	**−$1,000,000**
Year 1 cash inflow	$50,000	$100,000	$500,000
Year 2 cash inflow	60,000	200,000	500,000
Year 3 cash inflow	75,000	250,000	500,000

   a. Rank these projects by their PIs.

   b. If the projects are independent, which would you accept according to the PI criterion?

   c. If these projects are mutually exclusive, which would you accept according to the PI criterion?

   d. Apply the NPV criterion to the projects, rank them according to their NPVs, and indicate which you would accept if they are independent and mutually exclusive.

   e. Compare and contrast your answer from part (c) with your answer to part (d) for the mutually exclusive case. Explain this result.

7-28. You have a $10 million capital budget and must make the decision about which investments your firm should accept for the coming year. Use the following information on three mutually exclusive projects to determine which investment your firm should accept. The firm's cost of capital is 12%.

	Project 1	**Project 2**	**Project 3**
Initial Cash Outflow:	**−$4,000,000**	**−$5,000,000**	**−$10,000,000**
Year 1 cash inflow	$1,000,000	$2,000,000	−$4,000,000
Year 2 cash inflow	2,000,000	3,000,000	−6,000,000
Year 3 cash inflow	3,000,000	3,000,000	−5,000,000

   a. Which project do you accept on the basis of NPV?

   b. Which project do you accept on the basis of PI?

   c. If these are the only investments available, which one do you select?

   d. Now assume that another independent project is available to you. This new project has a cost of $5 million and an NPV of $1.5 million. Given the availability of this new project, which of the mutually exclusive projects do you accept?

   e. Is the NPV or PI the better technique in the situation described in part(d)? Why?

7-29. Project ABC has an initial cost of $1,000 and generates cash inflow of $2,000 at the end of year 1. Project QRS has an initial cost of $10,000 and has annual cash inflows of $4,400, $4,840, and $5,324 in years 1–3. Assuming a 10% discount rate, calculate the net present value and profitability index for both projects. Which project is better in terms of NPV? Which project is better in terms of PI?

7-30. Project X has an initial cost of $3,300 and annual cash inflows of $1,232, $1,380, $1,545, and $1,731 in years 1–4. Project Y has an initial cost of $5,000 and annual cash inflows of $1,413, $1,596, $1,804, $2,038, and $2,303 in years 1–5. The discount rate is 12% for Project X and 13% for Project Y.

   a. What is the discounted payback period for each project?

   b. Which project is better given a maximum discounted payback of 42 months?

   c. Which project is better in terms of NPV?

   d. Which project is better in terms of PI?

THOMSON ONE | Business School Edition

7-31. Locate the 10-K report (filed January 29, 2005) for Wilsons The Leather Experts, Inc. (ticker symbol, WLSN). Search the 10-K report for the term "internal rate of return." What rate of return did Wilsons expect to earn on its stores?

7-32. Locate the 10-K report (filed September 30, 2005) for Chordiant Software Inc. (ticker symbol, CHRD). Search the 10-K report for the term "net present value." What does Chordiant evaluate using net present value? What discount rate(s) did Chordiant use in calculating net present value?

MINI-CASE: CAPITAL BUDGETING PROCESSES AND TECHNIQUES

Durango Cereal Company is considering adding two new kinds of cereal to its product line—one geared toward children and the other toward adults. The company is currently at full capacity and will have to invest a large sum in machinery and production space. However, given the nature of cereal production, the investment in machinery will be more costly for the children's cereal (Poofy Puffs) than for the adult cereal (Filling Fiber). The expected cash flows for the two cereals are:

Year	Poofy Puffs	Filling Fiber
0	−$24,890,000	−$13,500,000
1	12,950,000	7,230,000
2	10,923,000	8,100,000
3	8,231,000	8,629,000
4	7,242,000	5,238,900

Management requires a minimum return of 15% in order for the project to be acceptable. The discount rate for projects of this level of risk is 10%. Management requires projects with this type of risk to have a minimum payback of 1.75 years.

Assuming the projects are independent and ignoring the issue of scale, what should Durango Cereal Company do? Include calculations for the payback method, the discounted payback method, net present value, internal rate of return, and profitability index in your analysis. Revisit the problem considering the scaling issue. Which project should the company consider, if any?

What Companies Do

Wells Fargo Outbids Citigroup to Purchase Wachovia amid Market Turmoil

How do you determine what price to bid when acquiring a company during a period of extreme financial market stress? This was the question that faced Wells Fargo in October 2008 when it decided to make a $15.1 billion, all-stock offer to acquire Wachovia, the sixth-largest U.S. commercial bank. The bid was surprising for several reasons, but especially because it trumped a deal negotiated one week previously between Citigroup, Wachovia, and the U.S. Federal Deposit Insurance Corporation (FDIC). That deal called for Citigroup to acquire Wachovia's banking operations for $2.2 billion and for the FDIC to absorb all losses above $42 billion that Citigroup might suffer on Wachovia's troubled $312 billion mortgage portfolio. The Wells Fargo offer required no government guarantee and was supported by Wachovia's management.

Citigroup objected to the Wells Fargo offer and sought a court injunction to block the deal. After the injunction was denied, Citigroup dropped its opposition to the Wells Fargo offer but followed up with a lawsuit asking for $60 billion in damages. What made all these competing offers especially surprising was that Wachovia was on the verge of bankruptcy, pushed toward ruin by losses on its mortgage-related assets. In fact, later in October Wachovia would disclose a *quarterly* loss of $23.9 billion and reveal that panicked depositors had withdrawn $26 billion, or 24% of the bank's deposits, in the previous few weeks. Still, Wells Fargo's managers pointed out that they were seizing what would likely be a once-in-a-generation opportunity to acquire a major rival bank with a large branch network on the U.S. East Coast, where Wells was very weak, for less than 15% of Wachovia's book value.

Source: Financial Times, *various issues (October 2008).*

Cash Flows and Capital Budgeting

The Wells Fargo acquisition of Wachovia is a large-scale capital budgeting problem. In an acquisition, the buyer must decide if the future cash flows obtained by purchasing the target firm justify the initial investment. In that respect, an acquisition resembles many other projects in which companies routinely invest. This chapter describes procedures for determining just what a project's relevant cash flows will be—that is, the inputs for the capital budgeting decision tools from Chapter 7.

8.1 TYPES OF CASH FLOWS

Cash Flow, Accounting Profit, and Taxes

When accountants prepare financial statements for external reporting, they have a different purpose in mind than financial analysts have when they evaluate the merits of an investment. Accountants want to produce financial statements that fairly and accurately represent the state of a business at a particular moment in time and also over a period of time. Thus, accountants measure the inflows and outflows of a business's operations on an accrual basis rather than on a cash basis. Accountants typically will not record the full cost of an asset as an expense if they expect the asset to confer benefits to the firm over a long period of time. The best example of this approach is **depreciation**. If a firm spends $1 billion on an asset that it plans to use over 10 years, accountants may count only one-tenth of the purchase price, or $100 million, as a current-year depreciation expense.

Clearly, financial executives place significant emphasis on earnings in financial reporting. But because cash is the lifeblood of the firm, they should place primary emphasis on cash flows when analyzing projects and making investment decisions. Therefore the focus in capital budgeting is on cash flows rather than earnings. In part, this emphasis simply recognizes that, no matter what earnings a firm may show on an accrual basis, it cannot survive for long unless it generates enough cash to pay its bills. The importance placed on cash flow in capital budgeting also reflects the time value of money. If a firm sells a product for $1,000, the value of that sale is greater if the customer pays immediately rather than 30 or 90 days in the future.

Much of this chapter focuses on which cash flows you should include when calculating a project's NPV. It is also important to highlight which cash flows should *not* be included. Though perhaps counterintuitive at first, financing cash flows should not be included in the cash flows of a capital budgeting analysis. In most cases, the cash flow effects of financing choices are handled in the discount rate, not in cash flows. Consider interest deductions. Often the weighted average cost of capital (WACC) is used as the discount rate, and WACC is based on the *after-tax* cost of debt (i.e., the product of the cost of debt and one minus the corporate marginal tax rate, which reflects the benefit of interest tax deductions). Given that the benefit of interest deductions is already incorporated in the discount rate, it would be incorrect to also adjust project cash flows for interest deductions: doing so would amount to double-counting their effects. We highlight this issue because the double counting mistake is often made in practice.

When determining cash flows, it is important to consider the cost of paying corporate taxes to the government. Remember, we evaluate a project from the perspective of the stockholder. Taxes paid to the government reduce the cash flows available to be paid out to shareholders; therefore, when performing capital budgeting analysis, all cash flows should be measured on an after-tax basis. In the previous paragraph we emphasized that cash flow effects from financing, such as the tax savings from interest deductions, are captured in the discount rate. Therefore, the taxes that are subtracted from cash flows should be determined *as if* the company had no debt. This means that the after-tax cash flows used in capital budgeting are those for an all-equity project (i.e., one without debt financing), and any financing effects are captured in the discount rate. This sounds tricky at first but really boils down to two simple rules: (1) calculate after-tax cash flows as if the firm uses only equity financing, and (2) capture any financing effects in the discount rate (i.e., incorporate the after-tax cost of debt in the WACC discount rate).

The existence of different tax jurisdictions (local, state, national, international) means that determining taxes paid can be somewhat complicated in the real world. To keep you focused on the important issues, in this chapter we use simplified illustrations to emphasize the principles involved in measuring after-tax cash flows. Also, to minimize distraction, throughout the chapter we assume that the marginal corporate income tax rate equals 40%.

Depreciation

A second tax-related principle relevant for measuring cash flows concerns noncash expenses such as depreciation. Accountants are required to spread the cost of a machine over the life of that machine (e.g., by recording an annual depreciation expense of $100 million for 10 years for a machine that cost $1 billion and has a 10-year life). Financial analysts, who care about cash flows rather than accounting rules, instead recognize the full cost of the machine when the initial purchase is made (e.g., $1 billion in the first year). Although it might be tempting to think that depreciation can be totally ignored by the financial analyst, this is not the case. Depreciation deductions create real cash flows because they reduce the taxes that a firm owes to the government; and, as emphasized in the previous paragraph, taxes paid to the government must be factored into our cash flow estimates. As described more fully in what follows, there are two ways to calculate cash flow benefits of depreciation and other noncash charges. The first method is to add noncash expenses back to after-tax earnings. Alternatively, we can ignore noncash expenses when calculating after-tax earnings but then add to cash flow the tax savings created by noncash deductions.[1]

EXAMPLE

Let's take a look at two ways to treat noncash expenses when deriving cash flow numbers for a simple project. Suppose that today a firm spends $30,000 in cash to purchase a fixed asset that it plans to fully depreciate on a straight-line basis over three years.

Using this machine, the firm produces 10,000 units each year. The product sells for $3 and costs $1 to make. The following is an income statement for a typical year of this project:

Sales	$30,000
Less: Cost of goods	10,000
Gross profit	$20,000
Less: Depreciation	10,000
Pre-tax income	$10,000
Less: Taxes (40%)	4,000
Net income	$6,000

(continued)

---

[1]Deriving accurate cash flow numbers from real financial statements issued by real companies is considerably more complex than the following simple example might lead you to believe.

How much cash flow does this project generate in a typical year? There are two methods for arriving at the answer. In the first, start with net income and add back depreciation (because there is no cash outlay for depreciation):

Cash flow = Net income + Depreciation

$$= \$6,000 + \$10,000 = \$16,000$$

In the second method, you calculate after-tax net income by initially ignoring depreciation expense and then adding back the tax savings generated by the depreciation deduction:

Sales	$30,000	
Less: Cost of goods	10,000	
Pre-tax income	$20,000	
Less: Taxes (40%)	8,000	
After-tax income	$12,000	
Plus: Depreciation tax savings	4,000	(40% × $10,000)
Cash flow	$16,000	

The largest noncash item for most investment projects is depreciation. Analysts must know the magnitude and timing of depreciation deductions for a given project because these deductions affect the amount of taxes the firm will pay. Treating depreciation properly is complicated by laws that allow firms to use several different depreciation methods. For example, in the United States and the United Kingdom, firms can (and do) keep separate sets of books: one for tax purposes and one for financial reporting purposes, with different depreciation methods used for each set. As a result, most U.S. and U.K. firms use accelerated depreciation methods for tax purposes and straight-line depreciation for financial reporting. In contrast, the law in Japan, Sweden, and Germany requires that the income firms report to the tax authorities be substantially the same as the income they report to investors. Naturally, firms in these countries desire the tax benefits of accelerated depreciation, so they usually depreciate assets using such methods as double-declining balance or "sum of the years' digits."[2] Because we are interested in the cash flow consequences of investments and because depreciation affects cash flow only through taxes, when determining project cash flows we will consider only the depreciation method that a firm uses for tax purposes.

JOB INTERVIEW QUESTION

How does depreciation factor into NPV calculations? It is a noncash expense, so does it matter?

Table 8.1 illustrates the tax depreciation allowed in the United States on various classes of equipment. The Tax Reform Act of 1986 set forth a **modified accelerated cost recovery system (MACRS)**, which defined the allowable annual depreciation deductions for various classes of assets. Automobiles used for business purposes fall under the 3-year class, computer equipment is part of the 5-year class, and most manufacturing equipment is part of the 7-year class. A quick glance at the table reveals that U.S. tax laws allow firms to take larger depreciation deductions in the early years of an asset's life. The cash flow

---

[2]The International Forum on Accountancy Development (IFAD) maintains a website where you can find a brief overview of accounting standards in 62 different countries, all benchmarked against international accounting standards (IAS).

impact of this system is to accelerate the tax benefits associated with depreciation, thereby improving cash flows in the early years.[3]

Table 8.1	Tax Depreciation Schedules by Asset Class					
YEAR(S)	**3-YEAR**	**5-YEAR**	**7-YEAR**	**10-YEAR**	**15-YEAR**	**20-YEAR**
1	33.33	20.00	14.29	10.00	5.00	3.75
2	44.45	32.00	24.49	18.00	9.50	7.22
3	14.81	19.20	17.49	14.40	8.55	6.68
4	7.41	11.52	12.49	11.52	7.70	6.18
5		11.52	8.93	9.22	6.93	5.71
6		5.76	8.93	7.37	6.23	5.28
7			8.93	6.55	5.90	4.89
8			4.45	6.55	5.90	4.52
9				6.55	5.90	4.46
10				6.55	5.90	4.46
11				3.29	5.90	4.46
12					5.90	4.46
13					5.90	4.46
14					5.90	4.46
15					5.90	4.46
16					2.99	4.46
17–20						4.46
21						2.25

Note: U.S. tax depreciation allowed for various MACRS asset classes. Figures represent the percentage of asset value depreciable in each year.

Smart Practices Video

Cynthia Lucchese, Chief Financial Officer, Hillenbrand Industries

"It's important to estimate the savings from capital equipment investments."

See the entire interview at
SMARTFinance

Fixed Asset Expenditures

Many capital budgeting decisions involve the acquisition of a fixed asset. The cost of a fixed asset often appears as the initial cash outflow for a project (assuming that the firm pays the full purchase price in one cash payment). Additional factors that influence the cash consequences of fixed asset acquisitions include installation costs and the proceeds from sales of existing fixed assets.

In many cases, the cost of installing new equipment can be a significant part of a project's initial outlay. Firms combine the asset's purchase price and its installation cost to arrive at the asset's depreciable tax basis. Though depreciation itself is not a cash outflow, we have seen that depreciation deductions affect future cash flows by lowering taxes.

---

[3]That is, the tax benefits accrue faster than would be the case under straight-line depreciation. An observant reader of Table 8.1 will notice that it stipulates four years of depreciation deductions for assets in the 3-year asset class, six years of deductions for the 5-year class, and so on. There appears to be one "extra year" of depreciation for each asset class because the first year's deduction reflects an assumption that, on average, investments in fixed assets are in service for just one-half of the first year. The last half-year of depreciation deductions for an asset falling in the N-year class occurs in year $N + 1$. Special rules apply to real estate assets. In general, land is not depreciable. In contrast, the law does allow depreciation deductions for structures, with the depreciable life of the structure depending on whether it is a commercial or residential property.

Depreciation deductions also influence taxes when firms sell old fixed assets. Specifically, when a firm sells an old piece of equipment, there is a tax consequence if the selling price does not equal the old equipment's book value. A firm that sells an asset for more than its book value must pay taxes on the difference. If the asset is sold for less than its book value, then the firm can treat the difference as a tax-deductible expense.

EXAMPLE

Electrocom Manufacturing purchased $100,000 worth of new computers three years ago. Because of the speed at which technology changes, it must now replace the computers with newer, faster ones. Because computers qualify as 5-year equipment under MACRS depreciation rules, the company has depreciated 71.20% of the old machines' cost, leaving a book value of $28,800. Electrocom sells its old computers to another firm for $10,000, so the sale price is $18,800 less than the book value. This allows Electrocom to report a loss on the sale of $18,800. Assuming that Electrocom's business is otherwise profitable, the company can use this loss to shelter other sources of current income, resulting in a tax savings of $7,520 (40% of $18,800).

Working Capital Expenditures

Consider a retail firm evaluating the opportunity to open a new store. This endeavor would have costs associated with the necessary fixed assets—shelving, cash registers, and merchandise displays. There are also important costs related to purchasing inventory, stocking shelves, and the timing of how quickly the firm collects receivables or pays liabilities.

Just as a firm must account for cash expenditures on fixed assets, so must it consider the cash inflows and outflows associated with changes in net working capital. **Net working capital** equals the difference between current assets and current liabilities. Frequently, the term **working capital** is used to refer to what is more correctly known as "net working capital." An increase in net working capital represents a cash outflow. Note that net working capital increases if current assets rise (e.g., if the firm buys more inventory) or if current liabilities fall (e.g., if the firm pays down accounts payable). Therefore, any increase in a current asset account or any decrease in a current liability account results in a cash outflow.[4] Conversely, a decrease in net working capital represents a cash inflow. Net working capital decreases when current assets fall (as when the firm sells inventory) or when current liabilities increase (as when the firm borrows from suppliers). A decrease in any current asset or an increase in any current liability also results in a cash inflow.

---

[4]Of course, one important current asset account is cash. It may seem counterintuitive to argue that increases in the balance of the cash account should be treated as a cash outflow. However, consider again the example of a new retail store. If the company opens a new store, then a small amount of cash will have to be held in that store for transactions purposes. Holding fixed the amount of cash that the firm maintains in all of its other stores and in its corporate accounts, it follows that opening a new store requires a net increase in the firm's cash holdings. If the firm did not open the new store then it could invest the new store's cash in a different project. Thus, there is an opportunity cost (because the cash is not earning profit in a different project) that must be accounted for as a use of cash when opening a new store. Now, consider what happens if the company decides to close one of its stores. The cash kept in reserve at that location can be redeployed for another use, so reducing cash at that store represents a cash inflow to the firm as a whole. As we will see in Chapter 22, cash management tools have become so sophisticated today that few investments require significant changes in cash holdings. Changes in the other working capital items (e.g., inventory, receivables, and payables) typically have a much larger cash flow impact than changes in cash balances.

EXAMPLE

Have you ever noticed the cottage industries that spring up around certain big events? Think about the booths that open in shopping malls near the end of each year and sell nothing but calendars. Suppose you are evaluating the opportunity to operate one of these booths from November to January. You begin by ordering (on credit) $15,000 worth of calendars. Your suppliers require a $5,000 payment on the first day of each month starting in December. You anticipate that you will sell—entirely on a cash basis—30% of your inventory in November, 60% in December, and 10% in January. You also plan to keep $500 in the cash register until you close up shop on February 1. Your balance sheet at the beginning of each month looks like this:

	Oct. 1	Nov. 1	Dec. 1	Jan. 1	Feb. 1
Cash	$0	$ 500	$ 500	$ 500	$ 0
+Inventory	$0	$15,000	$10,500	$1,500	$ 0
−Accounts payable	$0	$15,000	$10,000	$5,000	$ 0
Net working capital	$0	$500	$1,000	−$3,000	$ 0
Monthly net working capital change	NA	+$500	+$500	−$4,000	+$3,000

Remember, net working capital is just current assets minus current liabilities. Also recall that an increase in net working capital leads to a decrease in cash flow (and vice versa), as shown below.

$500 cash outflow from October to November
$500 cash outflow from November to December
$4,000 cash inflow from December to January
$3,000 cash outflow from January to February

Observe that, at the start of November, purchases of inventory are entirely on credit and so the increase in inventory is exactly offset by an increase in accounts payable. The only working capital cash outflow occurs because you must raise $500 to put in the cash register. During November, sales reduce your inventory by $4,500 (inflow), but you have to pay suppliers $5,000 (outflow). You still have the same amount in the cash register as before, $500, so on net you have an outflow of $500, exactly equal to the increase in net working capital from the prior month. During the month of December, sales reduce your inventory by $9,000 (inflow), and you pay $5,000 to suppliers (outflow). That leaves you with cash inflow of $4,000, equal to the decrease in net working capital during the month. By February 1, sales reduce your inventory by the remaining $1,500 in calendars (inflow), you empty $500 from the cash register (inflow), and you pay the last $5,000 to suppliers (outflow). The net effect is a $3,000 cash outflow during January.[5]

Terminal Value

Some investments have a well-defined life span. The life span may be determined by the physical life of a piece of equipment, the length of time until a patent expires, or the period of time covered by a leasing or licensing agreement. Often, however, investments have an indefinite life.

---

[5]This example focuses on the working capital cash flows associated with the project. We have not considered any fixed asset investment up front. Nor are we considering the profits from selling calendars at a markup or the labor costs of operating the booth.

When managers invest in an asset with a long life span, they typically do not forecast cash flows more than 5 to 10 years into the future. One reason is that forecasts more than 5 to 10 years in the future have so much error that the fine detail of an item-by-item cash flow projection is not very meaningful. Instead, managers project detailed cash flow estimates for 5 to 10 years and then calculate a project's terminal value as of some future date. The **terminal value** is a number intended to reflect the value of a project at a given point in the future, and there are a number of ways to estimate this value.

Perhaps the most common approach to calculating terminal value is to take the final year of cash flow projections and make an assumption that all future cash flows from the project will grow at a constant rate. For example, in valuing a large acquisition, many firms project cash flows from the target company for five years into the future. After that, they assume that cash flows will grow at a long-run equilibrium rate, such as the growth rate in gross domestic product (GDP) for the economy.[6]

EXAMPLE

When Wells Fargo purchased Wachovia in October of 2008, global financial markets were in turmoil and both banks were suffering. Nonetheless, Wells Fargo clearly expected conditions to eventually improve and for Wachovia to generate positive cash flows. Suppose that analysts at Wells Fargo project that their acquisition of Wachovia will generate the following stream of cash flows:

Year 1	$0.50 billion
Year 2	1.00 billion
Year 3	1.25 billion
Year 4	1.50 billion

In year 5 and beyond, analysts believe that cash flows will continue to grow at 2.5% per year. What is the terminal value of this investment? Recall from Chapters 3 and 4 that we can determine the present value of a stream of cash flows growing at a perpetual rate, g, by using the formula

$$PV_t = \frac{CF_{t+1}}{r - g}$$

We know that the cash flow in year 5 is 2.5% more than in year 4, or $1.5375 billion. Put this figure in the numerator of the equation. We also know that $g = 2.5\%$. Suppose that Wells Fargo discounted the cash flows of this investment at 11%. Using the formula, we can determine that the present value, *as of year 4*, of cash flows in years 5 and beyond is equal to

$$PV_s = \frac{\$1.5375}{0.11 - 0.025} = \$18.09$$

This means that the terminal value, or the value of the project as of the end of year 4, is $18.09 billion. To determine the entire value of the project, simply discount this figure (along with all the other cash flows) at 11% to obtain a total value of $15.1 billion.[7]

---

[6]We emphasize that, if companies assume that an investment's cash flows will grow at some rate in perpetuity, then the rate of growth in GDP (for either the local or the world economy) serves as a maximum potential long-run growth rate. Why? If an investment generates cash flows that grow forever at a rate that exceeds the growth of GDP, then eventually that one investment would become the entire economy.

[7]Note that this is the *gross* present value, not the *net* present value, because we are not deducting any up-front cost for acquiring Wachovia.

Notice in the preceding Example that the terminal value was very large relative to all the other cash flows. Discounting the terminal value for four years at 11%, we find that $11.92 billion of the project's total $15.1 billion present value comes from the terminal value assumptions. Those proportions are not uncommon for long-lived investments, illustrating just how important estimates of terminal value can be in assessing an investment's merit. Analysts must think carefully about the assumptions they make when calculating terminal value. For example, the growth rate used to calculate a project's terminal value is often less than the long-run growth rate of the economy. A factory with fixed capacity might offer zero growth in cash flows, or growth that just keeps pace with inflation, once the firm reaches its capacity constraints.

Several other methods enjoy widespread application in terminal value calculations. One method calculates terminal value by multiplying the final year's cash flow estimate by a market multiple, such as a price-to-cash-flow ratio for publicly traded firms with characteristics similar to those of the investment. For example, the last specific cash flow estimate for the Wachovia acquisition was $1.5375 billion in year 5. Wells Fargo might observe that the average price-to-cash-flow ratio for companies in this industry is 10. Multiplying $1.5375 billion by 10 results in a terminal value estimate of $15.4 billion, quite close to the estimate obtained from the perpetual growth model. One hazard in using this approach is that market multiples fluctuate over time, which means that—even if Wachovia has generated $1.5375 billion in cash flow as anticipated when year 5 finally arrives—the market may place a much lower value on that cash flow than it did when the acquisition originally took place. Another tricky issue is determining just which "comparable firms" to include in the industry multiple.

Other approaches to this problem use an investment's book value or its expected liquidation value to estimate the terminal value figure. Using book value is most common when the investment involves physical plant and equipment with a limited useful life. In such a case, firms may plausibly assume that, after several years of depreciation deductions, the asset's book value will be zero. Depending on whether the asset has fairly standard characteristics that would enable other firms to use it, its liquidation value may be positive or it may be zero.[8] Some assets may even have negative terminal values if disposing of them incurs substantial costs. Projects that involve the use of substances hazardous to the environment fit this description. When an investment has a fixed life span, part of the terminal value or terminal cash flow may also include recovery of working capital investments. When a retail store closes, for example, the firm realizes a cash inflow from liquidating inventory and from being able to redeploy the cash that had been maintained in the store for transaction purposes.

Incremental Cash Flow

We have seen that many investment problems have similar types of cash flows that analysts must estimate: initial outlays on fixed assets, working capital outlays, operating cash flow, and terminal value. Yet for all these different sources of cash flow, there is one overriding and essential concept: only cash flows incremental to the project matter. To paraphrase the oath taken by witnesses in TV courtroom dramas, analysts must focus on "all incremental cash flow and nothing but incremental cash flow." But at times it can be complicated to determine which cash flows for a given project are incremental and which are not.

---

[8] Asplund (2000) estimates that firms can expect to recover no more than 20–50% of the original purchase cost of a new machine. This is true even for assets with reasonably active secondary markets.

Consider, for example, the incremental cash flows associated with a student's decision to get an MBA degree. Many of the incremental outflows are obvious: tuition and fees, the cost of textbooks, and possible relocation expenses. What about room and board? These don't count because, whether or not a student decides to pursue an MBA, she must still eat and have a place to sleep. Therefore, room and board expenditures are not incremental to the decision to go back to school.[9]

The cash inflows associated with investing in an MBA degree are more difficult to estimate. For most students an MBA degree offers the opportunity to earn higher pay after graduation than they earned before returning to school. Furthermore, most students expect their pay to increase at a faster rate than it would had they not obtained an MBA. The net cash flow equals the increase in salary a student would earn with an MBA minus the salary the student would have earned without an MBA—after taxes, naturally.

EXAMPLE

Norman Paul earns $70,000 per year as an engineer for an auto manufacturer, and he pays taxes at a flat rate of 35%. He expects salary increases each year of about 5%. Lately, Norm has been thinking about going back to school to earn an MBA. A few months ago he spent $1,000 to enroll in a Graduate Management Admission Test (GMAT) study course. He also spent $2,000 visiting various MBA programs in the United States. From his research on MBA programs, Norm has learned a great deal about the costs and benefits of the degree. At the beginning of each of the next two years, his out-of-pocket costs for tuition, fees, and textbooks will be $35,000. He expects to spend roughly the same amount on room and board in graduate school that he spends now. At the end of two years, he anticipates he will receive a job offer with a salary of $100,000 and that his pay will increase by 8% per year over his career (about the next 30 years). The schedule of incremental cash flows for the next few periods, *excluding* the salary Norm gives up if he goes back to school (more on that later), looks like this:

Year 0	−$35,000
Year 1	−$35,000
Year 2	+$15,503

We remark that Norm's cash outflows do not include money already spent on the GMAT review course and on visits to MBA programs. These are **sunk costs**, costs that have already been spent and are not recoverable if Norm decides to keep working rather than go back to school. The cash inflow figure for year 2 requires some explanation. Had Norm stayed at his current job for the next two years and not returned to school, his pay would have increased to $77,175. Therefore, the difference between that figure and his $100,000 post-MBA salary represents a net cash inflow of $22,825. If we assume that Norm pays about 35% of his earnings in taxes, then the after-tax inflow would be $14,836. In year 3, Norm expects to earn 8% more, or $108,000, compared to what he would have earned at his old job, $81,034. The after-tax cash inflow in year 3 equals $17,528. If you carry these steps out for 30 years, you will quickly see that the MBA has a substantial positive NPV at almost any reasonable discount rate.

---

[9]Of course, the amount of money you spend on housing and food may differ depending on whether you are a student or a working professional. The difference in spending would be an incremental cash flow, but it could be an incremental inflow (if these costs are lower in graduate school) or an outflow (if the MBA program is located in a city with a high cost of living).

Incremental cash flows show up in surprising forms. One type of incremental cash outflow that firms must measure when launching a new product is due to **cannibalization**. This means that, whenever a firm introduces a new product, some of the new product's sales may come at the expense of the firm's existing products. In the food products industry, sales of a low-fat version of a popular product may reduce sales of the original (presumably higher-fat) version.[10]

Opportunity Costs

We made a number of simplifying assumptions in the preceding Example. For instance, we assumed that Norm received his pay in a lump sum each year and that he faced a flat tax rate. Actually, the incremental salary that Norm earns arrives monthly, and his higher earnings may be taxed at a higher rate. All these effects are easy to account for, although the calculations become a bit more tedious.

However, the one major error in our analysis of Norm's investment problem is that we ignored a significant opportunity cost. Undertaking one investment often means giving up an alternative. In capital budgeting, the **opportunity costs** of one investment are the cash flows on the alternative investment that the firm (or in this case, the individual) decides *not* to make. If Norm did not attend school, he would earn $70,000 ($45,500 after taxes) the first year and $73,500 ($47,775 after taxes) the second year. This is Norm's *opportunity cost* of quitting work to obtain an MBA, and it is just as important in the overall calculation as his out-of-pocket expenses for tuition and books. And though the NPV of Norm's MBA remains positive, the value falls substantially once we incorporate the opportunity costs. Every MBA student knows that opportunity costs are real, not just hypothetical numbers. For example, the number of students applying to MBA programs worldwide rises during economic downturns and falls during booms; the most plausible explanation of this countercyclical phenomenon is that potential MBA students have higher opportunity costs when the economy is strong.

What kinds of opportunity costs do businesses encounter in capital budgeting problems? One interesting example arises when one company buys another by exchanging the target firm's shares for shares in the acquiring firm. In July 2000, for instance, JDS Uniphase exchanged $41 billion worth of its stock to acquire the shares of SDL. Later, as the market for high-technology stocks dropped precipitously, JDS was forced to "write down" the value of its investment in SDL. As a result, JDS reported the largest ever fiscal year loss, roughly $50 billion, during the summer of 2001. Some "experts" stated that the cash flow consequence of this transaction was nil—firms just traded pieces of paper, and no one paid or received cash. This view ignores JDS's opportunity cost. Though it may be true that JDS could not have raised $41 billion in cash had it attempted to sell the same number of shares it gave to SDL shareholders in the acquisition, JDS certainly could have raised a substantial amount of cash from a stock sale. The amount of cash that JDS gave up by issuing shares to pay for the acquisition, rather than selling them, is the opportunity cost of the acquisition.

Probably the most common type of opportunity cost encountered in capital budgeting problems involves the alternative use of an asset owned by a firm. Suppose that a company owns raw land purchased years ago in anticipation of an expansion opportunity and that it is now ready to expand by building new facilities on the land. Even though the firm may have paid for the land many years ago, using the land for expansion entails an incremental

Smart Concepts
See the concept explained step-by-step at **SMARTFinance**

---

[10]On a capital budgeting exam, one of our students mentioned that a firm needed to be wary that its new product should not "cannibalize the existing sales force." Needless to say, that's not the kind of cannibalization we have in mind—although it would certainly constitute an incremental cash outflow!

opportunity cost. The opportunity cost is the cash that could be raised if the firm sold the land or leased it for another purpose. That cost should be factored into the NPV calculation for the firm's expansion plans; otherwise, the company might embark on a negative-NVP project if it thinks of the land as being "free."

In the next section we work through an extended example of a capital budgeting project, illustrating how to apply the principles from this section to calculate the project's cash flows each year. Before getting into the details, we want to remind you of the big picture. Cash flows are important because they are necessary to calculate a project's NPV, and estimating the NPV is important because it provides an estimate of the increase or decrease in shareholder value that will occur if the firm invests.[11] This suggests that, on average, firms invest in positive-NPV projects. The chapter-opening What Companies Do feature offered evidence supporting this big picture by showing that what matters is not only the amount of investment that firms undertake but also how efficiently they invest.

Concept Review Questions

1. Why do changes in net working capital cause changes in cash flows?
2. For what kinds of investments would terminal value account for a substantial fraction of the total project NPV, and for what kinds of investments would terminal value be relatively unimportant?
3. A real estate development firm owns a fully leased 40-story office building. A tenant recently moved its offices from two stories of the building, leaving the space temporarily vacant. If the real estate firm considers moving its own offices into this 40-story office building, what cost should it assign for the space? Is the cost of the vacant space zero because the firm paid for the building long ago (a cost that is sunk), or is there an incremental opportunity cost?
4. Suppose that an analyst makes a mistake and calculates the NPV of an investment project by discounting the project's contribution to net income each year rather than by discounting its cash flows. Would you expect the NPV based on net income to be higher or lower than the NPV calculated using cash flows?

8.2 Cash Flows for OldMovies.com

OldMovies.com is a (fictitious) profitable Internet-based movie club selling classic movies on DVD to its membership. The company is considering a proposal to expand its movie selection to include international films. Management believes that many lovers of classic movies also enjoy international movies and so the company has a built-in clientele for the new movie offerings. If the company decides to undertake this project, it will begin selling international movie DVDs next month when its new fiscal year begins. The company accepts projects with positive NPVs, and it uses a 10% discount rate to calculate NPV.

Up-front costs associated with the investment include $50,000 in computer equipment (which falls under the MACRS 5-year asset class) and $4,500 in inventory ($2,500 of which is purchased on credit). For transactions purposes, the firm plans to increase its cash balance by $1,000 immediately. The firm does not expect to begin selling DVDs until the new fiscal year begins, though it is entitled to take the first half-year of MACRS depreciation in

---

[11]McConnell and Muscarella (1985) demonstrate the connection between capital investment decisions and shareholder value by showing that stock prices rise on average when firms publicly announce significant new capital investment programs.

WHAT COMPANIES DO GLOBALLY

Is a High Investment Rate Good for a Nation's Economic Health?

Most people would accept as given that a high investment rate (measured as capital investment spending as a percentage of GDP) is strongly correlated with rapid growth in industrial production and overall employment. However, as the following table makes clear, no such strong relationship exists for industrialized countries over the period 1990 to 2006. The industrialized country with the highest investment rate, Japan, actually saw industrial production fall by 6% between 1990 and 1998 before rising by only 12% over the subsequent eight years. Even more surprisingly, total employment in Japan declined by 21% between 1990 and 2006. Similarly, the large continental European economies of France, Germany, and Italy had above-average investment rates through most of the period from 1990 to 2006, but industrial production grew more slowly than the average for all industrial countries and, moreover, France and Italy experienced large net employment *declines* over these 16 years. Country-specific factors help explain the exceptional performance of two of the smaller countries in the table, Ireland and Norway. Ireland adopted an explicit open-market strategy during the 1980s and attracted large net inflows of foreign direct investment thereafter—with a spectacular payoff in industrial production plus a more muted (but still significant) increase in employment. Norway benefited from an investment boom due to exploration and development of massive North Sea petroleum deposits. However, by far the best-performing large economy was the United States. Despite having a below-average investment rate throughout this period, industrial production increased by 53% and employment by 23% between 1990 and 2006. The moral is clear: How *efficiently* capital is invested is far more important to a nation's economic health than how *much* is invested.

Source: International Monetary Fund, *International Financial Statistics Yearbook 2007* (Washington, DC).

COUNTRY	CAPITAL INVESTMENT SPENDING (AS % OF GDP)			INDUSTRIAL PRODUCTION INDEX (1995 = 100)			TOTAL EMPLOYMENT INDEX (1995 = 100)		
	1990	1998	2006	1990	1998	2006	1990	1998	2006
United States	18.0	20.2	20.0	86.5	118.6	139.4	93.4	107.3	116.1
Canada	20.7	20.5	22.0	88.8	110.6	128.1	112.6	109.6	106.1
Japan	32.8	26.3	24.1	105.3	99.0	111.3	101.7	105.0	80.0
France	23.4	18.8	21.1	100.4	108.1	118.3	113.6	98.1	89.6
Germany	24.6	21.6	17.8	103.2	107.1	128.4	100.0	99.4	108.4
Ireland	21.0	23.4	28.4	62.1	152.2	270.4	90.7	114.1	105.8
Italy	22.2	19.6	21.2	93.5	103.3	105.9	107.7	99.1	104.6
Spain	25.4	23.3	30.6	96.9	111.3	126.6	104.5	109.6	163.9
Norway	23.3	26.7	21.7	86.5	107.9	104.8	97.7	108.2	113.6
Sweden	21.3	17.1	17.9	87.8	111.5	139.2	124.7	100.0	85.5
Switzerland	28.3	23.4	22.1	97.0	108.4	132.9	119.4	94.5	90.6
United Kingdom	20.2	18.1	17.6	94.1	103.0	132.4	102.5	105.7	115.2
Industrial country average	**22.6**	**21.4**	**21.1**	**95.2**	**108.5**	**124.2**	**102.4**	**101.7**	**100.5**

the current fiscal year.[12] The average selling price of OldMovies.com's DVDs is currently $13.50, and company executives believe that DVD prices will increase over time at a 2% annual rate. OldMovies.com knows that some of its suppliers will provide it with DVDs on credit. In addition to relying on this trade credit, the firm expects to finance the proposed project using cash flow generated from its existing business.

Like most new business ventures, this one will not be profitable immediately. Managers expect unit sales volume to increase rapidly in the first few years before reaching a long-run stable growth rate. As sales volume increases, the firm expects gross profit margins to widen slightly. The firm does allow credit sales to customers with excellent payment histories. Expanding sales volume will require increases in current assets as well as additional spending on fixed assets. OldMovies.com pays taxes at a 40% rate.

Table 8.2 shows projections for the international film project. The first two rows list anticipated selling prices and unit volumes in each of the next six years. Underneath that appears a series of projected income statements. Top-line revenue simply equals the product of expected selling price and unit volume each year. The figures for cost of goods sold and selling, general, and administrative expenses (SG&A) reflect management's belief that costs as a percentage of sales will fall slightly as volume increases. Depreciation expense each year is determined by spending on fixed assets and the MACRS schedule for 5-year equipment.

Table 8.2 Projections for OldMovies.com's International Films DVD Proposal

YEAR:	0	1	2	3	4	5	6
Price per unit	$ 13.50	$ 13.77	$ 14.05	$ 14.33	$ 14.61	$ 14.91	$ 15.20
Units	0	4,000	10,000	16,000	22,000	24,000	25,000
Abbreviated Projected Income Statements							
Revenue	$ 0	$55,080	$140,454	$229,221	$321,482	$ 357,722	$380,080
−Cost of goods sold	0	41,861	105,341	169,623	234,682	259,349	273,657
Gross profit	$ 0	$ 13,219	$ 35,113	$ 59,598	$ 86,800	$ 98,373	$ 106,423
−SG&A expenses	0	8,262	19,664	29,799	35,363	35,772	38,008
−Depreciation	10,000	18,000	13,800	14,280	23,872	25,208	18,512
Pre-tax profit	−$10,000	−$13,043	$ 1,649	$ 15,519	$ 27,565	$ 37,393	$ 49,903
Abbreviated Projected Balance Sheets							
Cash	$ 1,000	$ 2,000	$ 2,500	$ 3,000	$ 3,200	$ 3,300	$ 3,500
Accounts receivable	0	4,590	11,705	19,102	26,790	29,810	31,673
Inventory	4,500	7,344	18,727	30,563	42,864	47,696	50,677
Current assets	$ 5,500	$13,934	$ 32,932	$ 52,665	$ 72,854	$ 80,806	$ 85,850
Gross P&E	$50,000	$60,000	$ 65,000	$ 90,000	$130,000	$145,000	$ 155,000
−Accum. deprec.	10,000	28,000	41,800	56,080	79,952	105,160	123,672
Net P&E	$40,000	$32,000	$ 23,200	$ 33,920	$ 50,048	$ 39,840	$ 31,328
Total assets	$45,500	$45,934	$ 56,132	$ 86,585	$122,902	$120,646	$ 117,178
Accounts payable	$ 2,500	$ 4,320	$ 11,016	$ 17,978	$ 25,214	$ 28,057	$ 29,810

[12]However, in most end-of-chapter problems we make the simplifying assumption that the first available depreciation deduction comes one year after the initial investment.

Beneath the income statement appears a series of balance sheets. Each shows the project's total asset requirements (including both current and fixed assets) as well as the trade credit financing available from suppliers in the form of accounts payable. As mentioned previously, any additional project funding will consist of internally generated funds from the OldMovies.com side of the business. To determine whether this project represents an investment opportunity worth taking, we determine its cash flows through time and discount them at 10% to calculate the project's NPV. As part of this calculation, we estimate the value of the endeavor beyond the sixth year. In other words, we estimate the project's terminal value.

Year-0 Cash Flow

The firm has cash outlays of $50,000 for computer equipment immediately. The MACRS rules allow a depreciation deduction of 20%, or $10,000, in the first year. Because the company has no other expenses or revenues, the project's incremental pre-tax profit this year is −$10,000. However, the $10,000 loss does not represent a cash outflow because it derives entirely from a noncash depreciation expense. Assuming that it can be deducted from the firm's profits, this expense will save OldMovies.com $4,000 in taxes (40% × $10,000). The firm purchases $4,500 in inventory and adds $1,000 to its cash account. Accounts payable totaling $2,500 are used to finance a portion of these outlays, resulting in an initial working capital investment of $3,000 ($4,500 inventory + $1,000 cash − $2,500 accounts payable). Therefore, the net cash flow for year 0 is as follows:

Increase in gross fixed assets	−$50,000
Tax savings	4,000
Initial working capital investment	− 3,000
Net cash flow	−$49,000

Year-1 Cash Flow

Notice in Table 8.2 that gross plant and equipment (P&E) increases by $10,000 in year 1. This means that OldMovies.com has purchased $10,000 in additional computer equipment or other fixed assets. Depreciation in the first full year of operation equals $18,000, the difference between accumulated depreciation in year 1 and year 0. That figure combines a depreciation charge of 32% of the initial $50,000 investment in fixed assets ($16,000) and a deduction of 20% of the current-year $10,000 investment in fixed assets ($2,000).

With sales volume increasing, the firm also makes additional investments in working capital. Cash balances increase by $1,000, receivables by $4,590, and inventories by $2,844. Partially offsetting the increase in current assets is an increase in accounts payable of $1,820. Therefore, net working capital increases by $6,614, a net cash outflow for the firm.

At a sales volume of 4,000 units in its first year of operation, the international film DVD business earns a pre-tax loss of $13,043. To convert this figure into cash flow, we must make two adjustments. First, if OldMovies.com can charge this loss against profits in its other operations, then the loss will generate tax savings of $5,217 (40% × $13,043). Second, we need to add depreciation expense back into the pre-tax loss because depreciation involves no cash outlay. Together these adjustments result in a net operating cash inflow of $10,174 (−$13,043 + $18,000 + $5,217).

Combining each source of cash flow, we can determine the net cash flow for the project's first full year as follows:

Increase in gross fixed assets	−$10,000
Change in working capital	− 6,614
Operating cash inflow	10,174
Net cash flow	−$ 6,440

Year-2 Cash Flow

We repeat the steps followed in year 1 to determine cash flow for year 2.

First, gross fixed assets increase by $5,000. Depreciation for year 2 is $13,800 (the difference between accumulated depreciation in year 2 and year 1). The depreciation in year 2 equals the sum of allowable depreciation on assets purchased up front (19.20% × $50,000), assets purchased in year 1 (32% × $10,000), and assets purchased in year 2 (20% × $5,000).

Sales continue to rise in year 2, requiring a large investment in working capital. Total current assets increase by $18,998, but accounts payable rises by $6,696. The net increase in working capital equals $12,302 and results in a cash outflow.

In year 2, the firm earns a small pre-tax profit of $1,649. After taxes of $660 are deducted, the net earnings amount to $989. Add to that figure the depreciation expense of $13,800 to arrive at operating cash inflow of $14,789. Here are the total net cash flows in year 2:

Increase in gross fixed assets	−$ 5,000
Change in working capital	− 12,302
Operating cash inflow	14,789
Net cash flow	−$ 2,513

Table 8.3 illustrates the annual net cash flows for the international films DVD project all the way through the sixth year. As you can see, project cash flows are not positive until the fifth year. From the stream of cash flows shown in Table 8.3, it is clear that the project will not generate a positive NPV. However, just because the year-by-year cash flow projections end in year 6 does not mean that the project ends at that time. To complete our analysis, we must estimate the project's terminal value.

Table 8.3 Annual Cash Flow Estimates for OldMovies.com

	YEAR 0	YEAR 1	YEAR 2	YEAR 3	YEAR 4	YEAR 5	YEAR 6
New fixed assets	−$50,000	−$10,000	−$ 5,000	−$25,000	−$40,000	−$15,000	−$10,000
Change in working capital	− 3,000*	− 6,614	− 12,302	− 12,771	− 12,953	− 5,109	− 3,291
Operating cash flow	4,000	10,174	14,789	23,591	40,411	47,644	48,454
Net cash flow	−$49,000	−$ 6,440	−$ 2,513	−$14,180	−$12,542	$ 27,535	$ 35,163

* Represents the initial working capital investment.

Terminal Value

We produce two different terminal value estimates for this project. In the first, we assume that by year 6 the project has reached a steady state, meaning that cash flows will continue to grow at 2% per year indefinitely. In the second, we assume that the firm sells its investment at the end of year 6 and receives a cash payment equal to the project's book value.

In year 6, the project generates a net cash inflow of $35,163. If we assume that cash flows beyond the sixth year grow at 2% per year and discount those cash flows at 10%, then we can determine the terminal value of the project *as of the end of year 6* as follows:

$$\text{Terminal value} = \frac{\$35,866}{0.10 - 0.02} = \$448,325$$

Observe that the numerator of this expression is 2% greater than the cash flow in year 6 ($35,866 = 1.02 × $35,163). Remember, when valuing a stream of cash flows that grows at a perpetual rate, the *value today* equals *next year's cash flow* divided by the difference between the discount rate and the growth rate. Thus, to determine the terminal value in year 6, we must use the cash flow for year 7 in the numerator.

As a second approach, assume that the terminal value of the project simply equals the book value at the end of year 6. At that time, the firm owns fixed assets worth $31,328. If the firm liquidates its current assets ($85,850) and pays off outstanding trade credit ($29,810), it will generate an additional $56,040 in cash. The terminal value then equals the sum of these two items, $87,368. Notice that this value is about one-fifth of the value we obtained using the perpetual growth model. The magnitude of that difference should not surprise us too much. In general, a profitable, growing business will have a market value that exceeds its book value.

International Films DVD Project NPV

Putting all this together, we arrive at two different estimates of the project's NPV, depending on which estimate of terminal value we use. Assuming that this business will continue to increase profits forever, we arrive at the following value:

$$\text{NPV} = -\$49,000 - \frac{\$6,440}{(1.1)^1} - \frac{\$2,513}{(1.1)^2} - \frac{\$14,180}{(1.1)^3} - \frac{\$12,542}{(1.1)^4} + \frac{\$27,535}{(1.1)^5}$$
$$+ \frac{\$35,163 + \$448,325}{(1.1)^6} = \$213,862$$

However, if we assume that the terminal value is only equal to book value after six years, then we arrive at the following:

$$\text{NPV} = -\$49,000 - \frac{\$6,440}{(1.1)^1} - \frac{(\$2,513)}{(1.1)^2} - \frac{\$14,180}{(1.1)^3} - \frac{\$12,542}{(1.1)^4} + \frac{\$27,535}{(1.1)^5}$$
$$+ \frac{\$35,163 + \$87,368}{(1.1)^6} = \$10,111$$

In this example, the project yields a positive NPV no matter which terminal value estimate we choose, so investing will increase shareholder wealth. But in many real-world situations, especially those involving long-lived investments, the "go" or "no-go" decision depends critically on terminal value assumptions. It is not at all uncommon for the perpetual growth approach to produce a positive NPV while the book value approach shows a negative NPV. In that case, managers must think more deeply about the long-run value of their enterprise.

To review the material covered so far, when developing cash flow figures for an NPV calculation, analysts should start with after-tax earnings (excluding interest expense) and add back any noncash deductions such as depreciation. Next, cash outflows for increased investments in fixed assets or working capital should be subtracted (or added if fixed assets or working capital decline). Although these steps are relatively easy to follow once

---

Smart Practices Video

David Nickel, former Controller for Legal and Risk Management, Intel Corp.

"Capital budgeting is the key theme for deciding which programs get funded."

See the entire interview at **SMARTFinance**

JOB INTERVIEW QUESTION

"How would you explain NPV calculations to a nonfinancial manager?"

you've practiced them, there is surprising evidence that most firms don't calculate project cash flows correctly. Meier and Tehran (2007) surveyed 127 companies and found that only 46% calculated project cash flows in the proper manner. The most common error is one we've already warned you about—deducting interest expenses from cash flows.

Concept Review Questions	
	5. Embedded in the analysis of the international films DVD proposal is an assumption about how OldMovies.com's customers will behave when they are able to choose from a new set of DVDs. What is that assumption?
	6. What other ways might OldMovies.com estimate the terminal value of this project?
	7. Suppose that Congress passes a new MACRS schedule that reclassifies computers as 3-year equipment rather than 5-year equipment. In general, what impact would such legislation have on this project's NPV?

8.3 CASH FLOWS, DISCOUNTING, AND INFLATION

At least since the mid-1940s, inflation has been a pervasive element of the macroeconomic environment in most countries. Inflation rates can vary dramatically across countries and across time within a given country. There are several ways to deal with inflation in capital budgeting analysis, but a simple way to characterize the proper treatment of inflation is as follows: If inflation is in the cash flows, it must also be in the discount rate. Stated differently, if inflation is in the numerator then be sure that it's also in the denominator. Likewise, if the numerator ignores inflation then so, too, must the denominator.

In Chapter 5, we commented on the difference between the nominal rate of return and the real rate of return on an investment. The *nominal return* reflects the actual dollar return, and the *real return* measures the increase in purchasing power (above and beyond inflation) gained by holding a certain investment. In general, if the inflation rate is high then so, too, will be the nominal rate of return offered by various investments, because investors will demand a return that not only keeps pace with inflation but also offers a positive real return.

EXAMPLE

Imagine that a movie ticket today costs $10. If you have $1,000, you have the resources to watch 100 movies. Now suppose that you put $1,000 into a mutual fund that earns a 23% nominal return over the next year. Suppose also that the inflation rate for that year turned out to be 6%. By the end of the year, each movie ticket costs $10.60. Your money has grown to $1,230, so you have enough to purchase 116 movie tickets. In other words, your purchasing power increased by 16% during the year, which represents your real return on the mutual fund.

Remember that we formalized the relationship between the nominal rate of return, the inflation rate, and the real rate via the following equation:[13]

$$(1 + \text{Nominal rate}) = (1 + \text{Inflation rate}) \times (1 + \text{Real rate})$$

---

[13]Students may be more familiar with approximating the nominal rate as the real rate plus the inflation rate. By Equation 8.1, the nominal rate actually equals the real rate plus the inflation rate *plus* the product of the real rate and the inflation rate. Hence the accuracy of the simpler approximation declines as either the real rate or the inflation rate increases. In our movie ticket example, for instance, the real rate plus the inflation rate equals 22% whereas the true nominal rate equals 23%.

We can rearrange the terms to solve for the real interest rate as follows:

$$\text{Real rate} = \frac{1 + \text{Nominal rate}}{1 + \text{Inflation rate}} - 1 \qquad \textbf{(Eq. 8.1)}$$

Plugging in the figures from our movie ticket example, we find that the real rate of return is just a little more than 16%:

$$\text{Real rate} = \frac{1 + 0.23}{1 + 0.06} - 1 = 0.1604 = 16.04\%$$

In most cases, when firms establish a discount rate for capital budgeting purposes, the discount rate reflects then-current market rates of return. As we have seen, embedded in market interest rates is an assumption about inflation or, more precisely, an estimate of expected inflation. Therefore, if we use a market interest rate in the denominator of an NPV calculation, then we must be careful that the cash flow estimates in the numerator are **nominal cash flows**, which reflect the same inflation rate that the interest rate does. We refer to this prescription as Inflation Rule 1. It is a natural rule because the cash flows and interest rates in everyday life are expressed in nominal terms.

> *Inflation Rule 1*—When we discount cash flows at a nominal interest rate, embedded in the discount rate is an estimate of expected inflation; therefore, we must employ the same inflation assumption when forecasting project cash flows.

EXAMPLE

Refer again to Table 8.2. Notice that two factors cause the project's revenues to rise over time. The first factor is that the average price of a DVD increases 2% each year. In this Example, 2% is the underlying inflation rate, meaning that all prices rise, on average, 2% per year. The second factor causing revenues to rise is the increase in sales volume. Multiplying price by quantity gives us revenue in *nominal terms*—that is, the actual dollar revenue figure that the firm expects to generate each year. Because the cash flow projections for the project include a 2% inflation rate, the discount rate used to calculate the NPV should be a nominal rate.

As long as the 10% discount rate used by OldMovies.com reflects current market returns, the company is treating inflation properly. It is discounting nominal cash flows with a nominal discount rate.

Occasionally, an investment's cash flow projections may be stated in *real* terms. **Real cash flows** reflect only current prices and do not incorporate upward adjustments for expected inflation. When project cash flows are stated in real terms, the proper discount rate to use in calculating the NPV is a real rate.

EXAMPLE

An alternative way to construct Table 8.2 would be to use the current-year price of DVDs, $13.50, all the way through the analysis. If we took that approach—and were careful also to use current-year labor costs, current-year prices for fixed assets, and so on—then we would be stating cash

(continued)

flows in real terms. For example, calculating revenues in all future years using today's DVD price of $13.50 yields real revenues that are about 2% lower in year 1 than shown in Table 8.2; in year 2, real revenues are about 4% less than in the table. In general, to convert nominal cash flows into real cash flows, we "discount" the nominal figures by the rate of inflation. By doing so, we restate cash flows to reflect today's prices, not future prices that have been driven upward by inflation. With cash flows stated in real terms, the real rate is the appropriate discount rate to use. From Equation 8.1, we can calculate the real rate for OldMovies.com as follows:

$$\text{Real rate} = \frac{1 + 0.10}{1 + 0.02} - 1 = 0.0784 = 7.84\%$$

Using a real rate to discount real cash flows should result in the same project NPV as using a nominal rate to discount nominal cash flows. To demonstrate this, we have restated all the project's cash flows in real terms in the following equations. For example, the net cash flow in year 1 of −$6,440 has been restated in real terms by deflating the nominal cash figure by the inflation rate:

$$\frac{-\$6,440}{1.02} = -\$6,314$$

Similarly, we restate the nominal cash flow in year 2 in real terms as

$$\frac{-\$2,513}{(1.02)^2} = -\$2,415$$

Converting cash flows in every year (except the cash flows that occur today) from nominal to real terms and then discounting at the real rate of 7.84% yields the following NPV:[14]

$$\text{NPV} = -\$49,000 - \frac{\$6,314}{(1.0784)^1} - \frac{\$2,415}{(1.0784)^2} - \frac{\$13,362}{(1.0784)^3} - \frac{\$11,587}{(1.0784)^4}$$

$$+ \frac{\$24,939}{(1.0784)^5} + \frac{\$31,224 + \$398,100}{(1.0784)^6} = \$213,862$$

When cash flows ignore the effects of inflation (i.e., when cash flows are in real terms), it is necessary to discount those cash flows with a discount rate that also excludes the impact of inflation: the real rate. This leads to Inflation Rule 2.

Inflation Rule 2—When project cash flows are stated in real rather than in nominal terms, the appropriate discount rate is the real rate.

Discounting real cash flows at a real interest rate should yield the same NPV as discounting nominal cash flows at a nominal rate. Errors occur when a firm discounts real cash flows using a nominal interest rate or discounts nominal cash flows using a real discount rate. Figure 8.1 is a matrix illustrating the four possible scenarios under which firms can choose to project cash flows in nominal or in real terms and to discount those cash flows using a nominal or real discount rate.

A 2007 study examined how companies handle inflation when making capital budgeting decisions. Companies are evenly split in terms of using real cash flows or nominal cash flows in their NPV analysis. Across all companies, about two-thirds of firms match the discount rate appropriately to the cash flows in terms of inflation adjustment. That is,

---

[14]Note that we are once again using the perpetual growth approach to estimate the project's terminal value. In addition, the equation shows a discount rate of 7.84%, but we are actually using 7.8431% to obtain exactly the same NPV figure as before.

FIGURE 8.1

Capital Budgeting and Inflation

	Nominal Cash Flows	Real Cash Flows
Nominal Discount Rate	✓	NPV understated
Real Discount Rate	NPV overstated	✓

two-thirds of the firms either discount real cash flows with a real discount rate or discount nominal cash flows with a nominal rate. However, a surprising one-third of companies say that they use a real discount rate to discount nominal cash flows or a nominal rate to discount real cash flows—when both approaches are incorrect, as we've just discussed.[15] This study highlights the importance of properly adjusting for inflation in capital budgeting analysis.

Concept Review Questions

8. Look back at the cash flow projections for OldMovies.com's international films DVD project. Are the depreciation deductions stated in nominal or in real terms?
9. Can you think of a project for which it might be easier to project real cash flows than to project nominal cash flows?

8.4 Special Problems in Capital Budgeting

Real business situations are more complex and occur in more varieties than any textbook can reasonably convey. In this section, we examine common business decisions with special characteristics that make them a little more difficult to analyze than the examples we have covered thus far. We will see that, although the analysis may require a little more thinking, the principles involved are the same ones discussed throughout this chapter and Chapter 7.

Equipment Replacement and Equivalent Annual Cost

Assume that a firm must purchase an electronic control device to monitor its assembly line. Two types of devices are available, and both meet the firm's minimum quality standards, but they differ in three dimensions. First, one device (A) costs less than the other (B). Second, the cheaper device (A) requires higher maintenance expenditures. Third, the less expensive device does not last as long as the more expensive one, so it will have to be replaced sooner. The sequence of expected *cash outflows* (we have omitted the negative signs for convenience, and for simplicity we are ignoring taxes and depreciation) for each device are listed in the following table.

---

[15]Meier and Tarhan (2007). Another key finding of the study is that companies add a "fudge factor" to their hurdle rate; that is, they will not pursue a project unless its expected return *exceeds* the company's cost of capital by about 5 percentage points. The amount by which a firm fudges the hurdle rate is related to financial flexibility considerations, managers' confidence in the estimates of beta, financial health of the firm, and the past performance of the particular industry.

Device	End of Year				
	0	1	2	3	4
A	$12,000	$1,500	$1,500	$1,500	$ 0
B	$14,000	$1,200	$1,200	$1,200	$1,200

Notice that the maintenance costs do not rise over time. Let us assume that this means the expected rate of inflation equals zero, in which case the nominal discount rate and the real discount rate are one and the same.[16] Suppose this firm uses a real discount rate of 7%. The present value of each stream of cash flows is then as follows:

Device	PV
A	$15,936
B	$18,065

Purchasing and operating device A seems to be much cheaper than B (remember that we are looking for a lower PV because these are cash outflows). But this calculation ignores the fact that using device A will necessitate a large replacement expenditure in year 4, one year earlier than device B. We need to capture the value of replacing device B less frequently than device A.

One way to do this is to look at both machines over a 12-year time horizon. Over the next 12 years, the firm will replace device A four times and device B three times. At the end of the twelfth year both machines must be replaced, and thus begins another 12-year cycle. Table 8.4 shows the streams of cash flows over the cycle. Notice that, in the years when one of the devices must be replaced, the firm must pay both the maintenance cost on the old device and the purchase price of the new device. The present value (using a 7% discount rate) of cash flows over the entire 12-year period is:

Device	PV
A	$48,233
B	$42,360

Taking into account the greater longevity of device B, it is the better choice.

An alternative approach to this problem is called the **equivalent annual cost (EAC) method**. The EAC method begins by calculating the present value of cash flows for each device over its lifetime. We have already seen that the PV for operating device A for three years is $15,936 and that the PV for operating device B for four years is $18,065. Next, the EAC method asks, what annual expenditure over the life of each machine would have the same present value? That is, the EAC solves each expression as follows:

$$\$15{,}936 = \frac{X}{(1.07)^1} + \frac{X}{(1.07)^2} + \frac{X}{(1.07)^3} \qquad X = \$6{,}072$$

$$\$18{,}065 = \frac{Y}{(1.07)^1} + \frac{Y}{(1.07)^2} + \frac{Y}{(1.07)^3} + \frac{Y}{(1.07)^4} \qquad Y = \$5{,}333$$

---

[16]Of course, if inflation were positive then we would restate the cash flows (building in an inflation assumption) before discounting the cash flows at the nominal interest rate.

	DEVICE	
Table 8.4 Twelve-Year Replacement Cycle for 3-Year and 4-Year Projects		
YEAR	**A**	**B**
0	$12,000	$14,000
1	1,500	1,200
2	1,500	1,200
3	13,500	1,200
4	1,500	15,200
5	1,500	1,200
6	13,500	1,200
7	1,500	1,200
8	1,500	15,200
9	13,500	1,200
10	1,500	1,200
11	1,500	1,200
12	1,500	1,200
PV (7%)	**$48,233**	**$42,360**

Note: At the end of 12 years, the firm will have to replace equipment regardless of whether it chooses device A or B; thus, a new 12-year cycle begins.

In the first equation, the variable X represents the annual cash flow from a 3-year annuity that has the same present value as the actual purchase and operating costs of device A. If the firm purchases A and keeps replacing it every three years for the indefinite future, then the firm will incur a sequence of cash flows over time with the same present value as a perpetuity of $6,072. In other words, $6,072 is the *equivalent annual cost* of device A. Likewise, in the second equation, Y represents the annual cash flow from a 4-year annuity with the same present value as the purchase and operating costs of device B. If the firm buys B and replaces it every four years, then the firm will incur a sequence of cash flows having the same present value as a perpetuity of $5,333. The firm should choose the device with the lower EAC, device B.

In solving the problem of choosing between equipment with unequal lives, we assumed that the firm will continue to replace worn-out equipment with similar machines for a long period of time. That may not be a bad assumption in some cases. Here's a different situation. What if new technology makes old equipment obsolete? For example, suppose the firm in our example believes that in three years a new electronic device will be available that is more reliable, less costly to operate, and longer lived. If this new device becomes available in three years, the firm will replace whatever device it is using at the time with the newer model. Furthermore, the superior attributes of the new model imply that the salvage value for either of the old devices will be zero. How should the firm proceed?

Knowing that it will replace the old device with an improved one in three years, the firm can simply discount cash flows for three years:

$$PV_A = \$12,000 + \frac{\$1,500}{(1.07)^1} + \frac{\$1,500}{(1.07)^2} + \frac{\$1,500}{(1.07)^3} = \$15,936$$

$$PV_B = \$14{,}000 + \frac{\$1{,}200}{(1.07)^1} + \frac{\$1{,}200}{(1.07)^2} + \frac{\$1{,}200}{(1.07)^3} = \$17{,}149$$

In this case, the best device to purchase is A rather than B. Remember that B's primary advantage was its longevity. In an environment in which technological developments make old machines obsolete, longevity is not much of an advantage.

Excess Capacity

Firms often operate at less than full capacity. In such situations, managers encourage alternative uses of the excess capacity because they view it as a free asset. Although it may be true that the marginal cost of using excess capacity is zero in the very short run, using excess capacity today may accelerate the need for more capacity in the future. When that is so, managers should charge the cost of accelerating new capacity development against the current proposal for using excess capacity.

Imagine a retail department store chain with a regional distribution center in western Canada. At the moment, the distribution center is not fully utilized. Managers know that in two years, as new stores are built in the region, the firm will need to invest $2 million Canadian (cash outflow) in order to expand the distribution center's warehouse. A proposal surfaces to lease all the excess space in the warehouse for the next two years at a price that would generate cash inflow of $125,000 per year. If the company accepts this proposal, then it will have no excess capacity. Thus, to hold inventory for new stores coming on line in the next few months, the firm must begin expansion immediately. The incremental investment in this expansion is the difference between investing $2 million now versus investing $2 million two years from now. The incremental cash inflow is, of course, the $125,000 lease cash flows that are received today and one year from today. Should the firm accept this offer? Assuming a 10% discount rate, the NPV of the project is shown as follows:[17]

$$NPV = \$125{,}000 - \$2{,}000{,}000 + \frac{\$125{,}000}{(1.1)^1} + \frac{\$2{,}000{,}000}{(1.1)^2} = -\$108{,}471$$

Observe that here we treat the $2 million investment in the second year as a cash inflow because, by building the warehouse today, the firm avoids having to spend the money two years later. Even so, the NPV of leasing excess capacity is negative. However, a clever analyst might propose a counteroffer derived from the follow equation:

$$NPV = X - \$2{,}000{,}000 + \frac{X}{(1.1)^1} + \frac{\$2{,}000{,}000}{(1.1)^2} = \$0$$

Here X represents the amount of the lease cash inflow (received today and again in one year) that would just make the firm indifferent to the proposal. Solving the equation, we see that if the lease cash inflows are $181,818 then the project NPV equals zero. Therefore, if the firm can lease its capacity for a price *above* $181,818 Canadian, then it should do so.

---

[17]Again, for simplicity we ignore depreciation here. A more complete analysis would take into account the changes in depreciation deductions that this decision would trigger.

Concept Review Questions	10. Under what circumstance is the use of the equivalent annual cost method to compare substitutable projects with different lives more efficient computationally than the use of the present value of multiple investments over a common period? (Assume that both projects terminate in the same year.)
	11. In almost every example so far, firms must decide to invest in a project immediately or not at all. But suppose that a firm could invest in a project today or it could wait one year before investing. How could you use NPV analysis to decide whether to invest now or later?
	12. Under what circumstances is the cost of excess capacity zero? Think about why the cost of excess capacity normally is not zero.

8.5 THE HUMAN FACE OF CAPITAL BUDGETING

This chapter illustrates which cash flows financial analysts should discount and which cash flows they should ignore when valuing real investment projects. Deciding which costs are incremental and which are not, incorporating the myriad of tax factors that influence cash flows, and measuring opportunity costs properly are all much more complex in practice than can be conveyed in a textbook. The nuances of capital budgeting are best learned through practice.

There is another factor that makes real-world capital budgeting more complex than textbook examples—the human element. Neither the ideas for capital investments nor the financial analysis used to evaluate them occurs in a vacuum. Almost any investment proposal important enough to warrant a thorough financial analysis has a champion behind it, someone who believes that the project is a good idea or at least that the project will advance the individual's own career. When companies allocate investment capital across projects or across divisions, they must recognize the potential for an optimistic bias to creep into the numbers. This bias can arise through intentional manipulation of the cash flows to make an investment look more attractive, or it may simply arise if the analyst calculating the NPV is also the cheerleader advocating the project in the first place.

One way that companies attempt to control for this bias is by putting responsibility for analyzing an investment proposal under an authority that is independent from the individual or group proposing the investment. For example, it is common in large firms for a particular group to have the responsibility of conducting the financial analysis required to value any potential acquisition targets. In this situation, financial analysts play a kind of gatekeeper role, protecting shareholders' interests by steering the firm away from negative-NPV investments. Naturally, these independent analysts face intense pressure from the advocates of each project to portray the investment proposal in its best possible light. Consequently, financial experts need to know more than just which cash flows count in the NPV calculation. They must also have a sense of what is reasonable when forecasting a project's profit margin and its growth potential. Analysts must also defend their assumptions, explaining why their (often more conservative) projections do not line up with those offered by the managers advocating a certain investment.

Generally the CFO is primarily responsible for the analysis of proposed projects. Typically the CFO submits an analysis coupled with a recommendation to the decision makers, which for major investments would likely include the CEO, an investment committee, and possibly the board of directors. A survey of CEOs and CFOs found that, of those respondents who claimed to provide major input into financial decisions, about 36% of the CEOs and only about 11% of the CFOs indicated they made the final investment decisions, in isolation, without the advice of others.[18] It is therefore apparent that CEOs are much

---

[18]Graham, Harvey, and Puri (2008).

WHAT CFOs DO

CFO Survey Evidence

Throughout this chapter we have stressed that managers should focus on cash flows rather than accounting earnings, both in intrafirm financial analysis (including capital budgeting assessments) and in the financial data they report to external stakeholders. Do practicing managers actually follow this advice? Unfortunately, survey evidence clearly suggests that financial managers place far greater emphasis on accounting earnings, especially earnings per share, than they do on any other financial metric. The following graph describes how 401 financial executives ranked the importance of company metrics provided to outsiders. Over half (51%) of the respondents listed earnings as the most important metric they report, with pro forma earnings and revenues the two next most important measures reported. Cash flows from operations and free cash flows, two of the metrics we stress in this chapter, were selected by only 12% and 10% of respondents, respectively.

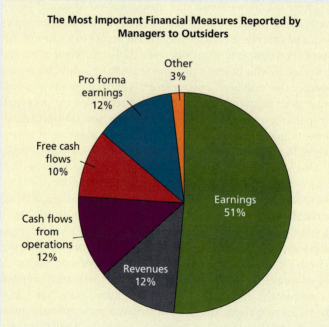

The Most Important Financial Measures Reported by Managers to Outsiders

Other 3%

Pro forma earnings 12%

Free cash flows 10%

Cash flows from operations 12%

Revenues 12%

Earnings 51%

The researchers conducting this survey also reported the disquieting fact that 78% of responding managers admitted a willingness to sacrifice firm value to smooth reported earnings. In response to the question, "How large a sacrifice in value would your firm make to avoid a bumpy earnings path?" 52% of managers reported a willingness to make a small sacrifice, 24% said they would make a moderate sacrifice, and 2% said they would make a large sacrifice to smooth reported profits. This clearly suggests that many managers will forgo positive-NPV investment opportunities so as not to disrupt reported earnings per share.

Source: Reprinted from *Journal of Accounting and Economics,* 40, John R. Graham, Campbell R. Harvey, and Shiva Rajgopal, Figure 2 and Table 9 of "The Economic Implications of Corporate Financial Reporting," pp. 3–73, Copyright 2005, with permission from Elsevier.

more involved in these decisions than are CFOs and that other parties (possibly investment committees and boards of directors) must play a major role in making capital budgeting decisions. Clearly the CFO's staff is primarily responsible for analysis and recommendations on proposed capital expenditures.

Many experienced managers say that they have never seen an investment with a negative NPV. In saying this, they do not mean that all investments are good investments but rather that all analysts know enough about NPV analysis to make any investment look attractive. Small adjustments to cash flow projections and discount rates can often tilt a project's NPV from negative to positive. In this environment, another skill comes into play in determining which project receives funding. We refer to this skill as economic intuition, as opposed to number crunching. Most good investments have a compelling intuition behind them—a reason, based on sound economic logic, that the investment's NPV *should* be positive. The best financial analysts can not only provide the numbers that underscore a good investment's value but can also explain why the investment makes sense, emphasizing the competitive opportunity that makes one investment's NPV positive and another's negative. We return to this commonsense element of capital budgeting in Chapter 9.

Smart Ideas Video

Raghu Rajan, University of Chicago

"Capital budgeting is not just about estimating cash flows and discount rates, but is also a lot about horse trading."

See the entire interview at

SMARTFinance

Concept Review Question	13. What role does the human factor play in the capital budgeting decision process? Could it cause a negative-NPV project to be accepted?

SUMMARY

- Certain types of cash flow are common to many different kinds of investments. These include cash expenditures on fixed assets and working capital, operating cash flow, and terminal value estimates.
- The costs of financing an investment, such as interest paid to lenders and dividends paid to shareholders, should not be counted as part of a project's cash outflows. The discount rate captures the financing costs, so deducting interest expense and dividends from a project's cash flows would be double-counting.
- To find working capital cash flow, calculate the change in net working capital from one period to the next. Increases in working capital represent cash outflows, whereas decreases in working capital represent cash inflows.
- To find operating cash flow, calculate after-tax net income and add back any noncash expenses.
- To find terminal value or terminal cash flow, employ one of several methods, such as the perpetual growth model or book value.

- Only the incremental costs associated with a project should be included in NPV analysis. The analyst should avoid including sunk costs.
- Opportunity costs should be included in cash flow projections.
- Discount nominal cash flows at a nominal rate and discount real cash flows at a real rate. Failure to match the type of cash flow with the correct discount rate will either overstate or understate the value of a project.
- One approach to evaluating alternative equipment purchases with unequal lives is to determine the equivalent annual cost of each type of equipment and choose the one that is least expensive.
- When confronted with proposals to use excess capacity, think carefully about the true cost of that capacity. It is rarely zero.
- When analyzing capital budgeting projects, it is important to consider human factors and make sure that the project, in addition to having a positive NPV, makes sense.

KEY TERMS

cannibalization
depreciation
equivalent annual cost (EAC) method
modified accelerated cost recovery
    system (MACRS)

net working capital
nominal cash flows
opportunity costs
real cash flows
sunk costs

terminal value
working capital

QUESTIONS

8-1. In capital budgeting analysis, why do we focus on cash flow rather than accounting profit?

8-2. Should the costs of evaluating a project be included as a portion of the project's cost?

8-3. Is the ability to use money allocated to a project for another purpose an example of a sunk cost?

8-4. Explain how depreciation creates a cash inflow even though there is no cash inflow or outflow associated with the depreciation deductions themselves.

8-5. In the technology industry, product prices and production costs typically decline over time. If you are putting together cash flow projections for a new high-tech product, explain how you would construct your forecasts to state them in nominal terms. What if you wanted to state them in real terms?

8-6. Is a negative change in net working capital a problem? (Assume that profitability and sales are maintained.)

8-7. To finance a certain project, a company must borrow money at 10% interest. How should it treat interest payments when it analyzes the project's cash flows?

8-8. Answer questions (a) through (d), which concern the role of depreciation in capital budgeting analysis.

    a. Does depreciation affect cash flow in a positive or negative manner?

    b. From a net present value perspective, why is accelerated depreciation preferable?

    c. Is it acceptable to utilize one depreciation method for tax purposes and another for financial reporting purposes?

    d. Which depreciation method is relevant for determining project cash flows?

8-9. In what sense does an increase in accounts payable represent a cash inflow?

8-10. List several ways to estimate a project's terminal value.

8-11. What are the tax consequences of selling an investment asset for more than its book value? Does this have an effect on project cash flows that must be accounted for in relevant cash flows? What is the effect if the asset is sold for less than its book value?

8-12. Why must incremental after-tax cash flows, rather than total cash flows, be evaluated in project analysis?

8-13. Differentiate between sunk costs and opportunity costs. Which of these costs should be included in incremental cash flows and which should be excluded?

8-14. Before entering graduate school, a student estimated the value of earning an MBA at $300,000. Based on that analysis, he decided to go back to school. After completing the first year, he ran the NPV calculations again. How would you expect the NPV to look after the student has completed one year of the program? Specifically, what portion of the analysis must be different than it was the year before?

8-15. Punxsutawney Taxidermy Inc. (PTI) operates a chain of taxidermy shops across the Midwest, with a handful of locations in the South. A rival firm, Heads Up Corp., has a few midwestern locations, but most of its shops are located in the South. PTI and Heads Up decide to consolidate their operations by trading ownership of a few locations. PTI will acquire four Heads Up locations in the Midwest and, in exchange, will relinquish control of its southern locations. No cash will change hands in the transaction. Does this mean that an analyst working for either company can evaluate the merits of this deal by assuming that the project has no initial cash outlay? Explain.

8-16. "If a company's practice is to calculate project NPVs using nominal cash flows and a nominal discount rate, then it must have a forecast for expected inflation; however, if the company discounts real cash flows at the real rate, then developing an inflation forecast is unnecessary." Is this statement true or false? Why?

8-17. Explain why the EAC method helps firms evaluate alternative investments with unequal lives.

8-18. Why isn't excess capacity free?

PROBLEMS

Types of Cash Flows

8-1. Currently, a firm has $30 million in cash, $20 million in accounts receivable, $45 million worth of inventory, and $10 million in taxes payable. The firm typically pays cash for its inventory, which makes it necessary to keep a large amount of cash on hand. The firm is considering financing its inventory by borrowing from suppliers in the future. Analysis provides a projection of the future working capital accounts: $10 million in cash, $20 million in accounts receivable, $60 million in inventory, $40 million in accounts payable for the inventory, and $10 million in taxes payable.

   a. Calculate the present and future projected net working capital for the firm.
   b. Based on the change in net working capital, does the financing of inventory appear to be a potentially beneficial practice for the firm?
   c. If the firm decided to go with a *just-in-time* inventory process that reduced the current inventory to $5 million and the current cash account to $15 million (other accounts remaining the same), would this reduce the change in net working capital even further than the inventory financing scheme?

8-2. A project's annual (operating) cash flows for the next five years are $1.2 million, $1.4 million, $1.7 million, $2 million, and $2.5 million. Assuming a discount rate of 15% and a terminal growth rate of 4%, answer the following questions.

   a. What is the terminal value for assessing the cash flows after the fifth year?
   b. What is the total value of the cash flows of the firm?
   c. What proportion of the total cash flow value depends on the terminal value?

8-3. The terminal value of a project's cash flow is $51.5 million: $3.605 million ÷ (10% − 3%). What is the equivalent price-to-cash-flow ratio that would produce this same terminal value? (*Hint:* You will need to reduce the $3.605 million projected cash flow by one growth period.)

8-4. The final projected cash flow for a firm is $4.2 million and, using a price-to-cash-flow ratio of 16.5, generates a terminal value of $69.3 million. Given a 14% discount rate, what terminal growth rate will produce the same terminal value? If a terminal growth rate of 4.2% is considered appropriate, then is the terminal value of $69.3 million an overestimation or an underestimation? Using 4.2% as the terminal growth rate, what is the terminal value? What price-to-cash-flow ratio does this value reflect?

8-5. A project costs $10 million dollars and is expected to have the following annual cash flows: $5.6 million, $6.272 million, and $7.025 million. What is the NPV of the project if we assume a 12% discount rate? After two years, the project has realized cash flows totaling $15 million (much beyond projections); however, to realize a third year of cash flow from the project, another $6 million investment must be made. Assume that the third-year projected cash flow is $6.6 million (down from the original $7.025 million) and that the discount rate is still 12%. Should the firm continue with the project? (Be sure to compute the NPV of the additional $6 million investment before making your decision.) Should the project's previous success influence the analysis?

8-6. Calculate the present value of depreciation tax savings on a depreciable asset with a purchase price of $5 million and zero salvage value, assuming a 10% discount rate, a 34% tax rate, and the following types of depreciation.

  a. The asset is depreciated over a 3-year life according to Table 8.1.

  b. The asset is depreciated over a 7-year life according to Table 8.1.

  c. The asset is depreciated over a 20-year life according to Table 8.1.

8-7. A certain piece of equipment costs $32 million plus an additional $2 million to install. This equipment qualifies under the 5-year MACRS category. For a firm that discounts cash flows at 12% and faces a tax rate of 34%, what is the present value of depreciation tax savings associated with this equipment? By how much would that number change if the firm could treat the $2 million installation cost as a deductible expense (rather than including it as part of the depreciable cost of the asset)?

8-8. The government is considering a proposal to allow depreciation deductions that are even more accelerated than those specified by MACRS.

  a. For which type of company would this change be more valuable: a company facing a 10% tax rate or one facing a 30% tax rate?

  b. If companies take larger depreciation deductions in the early years of an investment, what will the impact be on reported earnings? On cash flows? On project NPVs? How do you think the stock market might respond if the tax law changes to allow more-accelerated depreciation?

8-9. Taylor United is considering overhauling its equipment to meet increased demand for its product. The cost of equipment overhaul is $3.8 million plus $200,000 in installation costs. The firm will depreciate the equipment modifications under MACRS using a 5-year recovery period. Additional sales revenue from the overhaul should amount to $2.2 million per year, and additional operating expenses and other costs (excluding depreciation) will amount to 35% of the additional sales. The firm has an ordinary tax rate of 40%. Answer the following questions about Taylor United for each of the next six years.

  a. What additional earnings before depreciation and taxes will result from the overhaul?

  b. What additional earnings after taxes will result from the overhaul?

  c. What incremental operating cash flows will result from the overhaul?

8-10. Wilbur Corporation is considering replacing a machine. The replacement will cut operating expenses by $24,000 per year for each of the five years the new machine is expected to last. Although the old machine has a zero book value, it has a remaining useful life of five years. The depreciable value of the new machine is $72,000. Wilbur will depreciate the machine under MACRS using a 5-year recovery period and is subject to a 40% tax rate on ordinary income. Estimate the incremental operating cash flows attributable to the replacement. Be sure to consider the depreciation in year 6.

8-11. Advanced Electronics Corporation is considering purchasing a new packaging machine to replace a fully depreciated machine that will last five more years. The new machine is expected to have a 5-year life and depreciation charges of $4,000 in year 1, $6,400 in year 2, $3,800 in year 3, $2,400 in year 4 and also in year 5, and $1,000 in year 6. The firm's estimates of revenues and expenses (*excluding* depreciation) for the new and old packaging machines are shown in the following table. Advanced Electronics is subject to a 40% tax rate on ordinary income.

	New Packaging Machine		Old Packaging Machine	
Year	**Revenue**	**Expenses**	**Revenue**	**Expenses**
1	$50,000	$40,000	$45,000	$35,000
2	51,000	40,000	45,000	35,000
3	52,000	40,000	45,000	35,000
4	53,000	40,000	45,000	35,000
5	54,000	40,000	45,000	35,000

a. Calculate the operating cash flows associated with each packaging machine. Be sure to consider the depreciation in year 6.

b. Calculate the incremental operating cash flows resulting from the proposed packaging machine replacement.

c. Use a time line to depict the incremental cash flows found in part (b).

8-12. Premium Wines, a producer of medium-quality wines, has maintained stable sales and profits over the past eight years. Although the market for medium-quality wines has been growing by 4% per year, Premium Wines has been unsuccessful in sharing this growth. To increase its sales, the firm is considering an aggressive marketing campaign that centers on regularly running ads in major food and wine magazines and running TV commercials in large metropolitan areas. The campaign is expected to require an *annual* tax-deductible expenditure of $3 million over the next five years. Sales revenue, as noted in the following income statement for 2009, totaled $80 million. If the proposed marketing campaign is not initiated then sales are expected to remain at this level for each of the next five years, 2010–2014. With the marketing campaign, sales are expected to rise to the levels shown in the sales forecast table for each of the next five years; cost of goods sold is expected to remain at 75% of sales; general and administrative expense (exclusive of any marketing campaign outlays) is expected to remain at 15% of sales; and annual depreciation expense is expected to remain at $2 million. Assuming a 40% tax rate, find the relevant cash flows over the next five years associated with Premium Wines' proposed marketing campaign.

Premium Wines Income Statement for the Year Ended December 31, 2009

Sales revenue		$80,000,000
Less: Cost of goods sold (75%)		60,000,000
Gross profits		$20,000,000
Less: Operating expenses		
General and administrative expense (15%)	$12,000,000	
Depreciation expense	2,000,000	
Total operating expense		$14,000,000
Net profits before taxes		$ 6,000,000
Less: Taxes (rate = 40%)		2,400,000
Net profits after taxes		$ 3,600,000

Premium Wines Sales Forecast

Year	Sales Revenue
2010	$82,000,000
2011	84,000,000
2012	86,000,000
2013	90,000,000
2014	94,000,000

8-13. Barans Manufacturing is assessing the incremental cash flows associated with the proposed replacement of an existing stamping machine by a new, technologically advanced one. Given the following costs related to the proposed project, explain whether each would be treated as a *sunk cost* or an *opportunity cost* in developing the incremental cash flows associated with the proposed replacement decision.

  a. Barans would be able to use the same dies and other tools, which had a book value of $40,000, on the new stamping machine that it used on the old one.

  b. Barans would be able to link the new machine to its existing computer system in order to control its operations. Because the old stamping machine did not have a computer control system, the firm's excess computer capacity could be leased to another firm for an annual fee of $17,000.

  c. Barans would have to obtain additional floor space to accommodate the larger new stamping machine. The space that would be used is currently being leased to another company for $10,000 per year.

  d. Barans would use a small storage facility to store the increased output of the new stamping machine, a storage facility that was built by Barans three years ago at a cost of $120,000. Because of this structure's unique configuration and location, it is currently of no use to either Barans or any other firm.

  e. Barans would retain an existing overhead crane, which it had planned to sell for its $180,000 market value. Although the crane was not needed with the old stamping machine, it would be used to position raw materials on the new stamping machine.

8-14. Blueberry Electronics is exploring the possibility of producing a new handheld device that will serve both as a cell phone and as a basic PC with Internet access. Which of the following items are relevant for the project's analysis?

  a. The company has spent R&D funds while working on a prototype of the new product.

  b. The company's current-generation product has no cell-phone capability. The new product would therefore make the old one obsolete in the eyes of many consumers.

  However, Blueberry expects that other companies will soon bring to market products combining cell phone and PC features, and these will also reduce sales on Blueberry's existing products.

  c. The company has incurred costs of ramping up for production of the new device.

  d. Increases in receivables and inventory will occur as production increases.

Cash Flows

8-15. New York Pizza is considering replacing an existing oven with a new, more sophisticated oven. The old oven was purchased three years ago at a cost of $20,000, and this amount was being depreciated under MACRS using a 5-year recovery period. The oven has five years of usable life remaining. The new oven being considered costs $30,500, requires $1,500 in installation costs, and would be depreciated under MACRS using a 5-year recovery period. The old oven can currently be sold for $22,000 without incurring any removal or cleanup costs. The firm pays taxes at a rate of 40% on both ordinary income and capital gains. The revenues and expenses (*excluding* depreciation) associated with the new and the old ovens for the next five years are given in the following table.

	New Oven		Old Oven	
Year	Revenue	Expenses	Revenue	Expenses
1	$300,000	$288,000	$270,000	$264,000
2	300,000	288,000	270,000	264,000
3	300,000	288,000	272,000	264,000
4	300,000	288,000	271,000	264,000
5	300,000	288,000	270,000	264,000

  a. Calculate the initial cash outflow associated with replacement of the old oven by the new one.
  b. Determine the incremental cash flows associated with the proposed replacement. Be sure to consider the depreciation in year 6.
  c. On a time line, depict the relevant cash flows found in parts (a) and (b) associated with the proposed replacement decision.

8-16. Speedy Auto Wash is contemplating the purchase of a new high-speed washer to replace the existing washer. The existing washer was purchased two years ago at an installed cost of $120,000; it was being depreciated under MACRS using a 5-year recovery period. The existing washer is expected to have a usable life of five more years. The new washer costs $210,000 and requires $10,000 in installation costs; it has a 5-year usable life and would be depreciated under MACRS using a 5-year recovery period. The existing washer can currently be sold for $140,000 without incurring any removal or cleanup costs. To support the increased business resulting from purchase of the new washer, accounts receivable would increase by $80,000, inventories by $60,000, and accounts payable by $116,000. At the end of five years, the existing washer is expected to have a market value of zero; the new washer could be sold to net $58,000 after removal and cleanup costs and before taxes. The firm pays taxes at a rate of 40% on both ordinary income and capital gains. The estimated profits before depreciation and taxes over the five years, for both the new and the existing washer, are shown in the following table.

	Profits before Depreciation and Taxes	
Year	New Washer	Existing Washer
1	$86,000	$52,000
2	86,000	48,000
3	86,000	44,000
4	86,000	40,000
5	86,000	36,000

  a. Calculate the initial cash outflow associated with the replacement of the existing washer with the new one.
  b. Determine the incremental cash flows associated with the proposed washer replacement. Be sure to consider the depreciation in year 6.
  c. Determine the terminal cash flow expected at the end of year 5 from the proposed washer replacement.
  d. On a time line, depict the relevant cash flows associated with the proposed washer replacement decision.

8-17. TransPacific Shipping is considering replacing an existing ship with one of two newer, more efficient ones. The existing ship is three years old, cost $32 million, and is being depreciated under MACRS using a 5-year recovery period. Although the existing ship has only three years (years 4, 5, and 6) of depreciation remaining under MACRS, it has a remaining usable life of five years. Ship A, one of the two possible replacement ships, costs $40 million to purchase and $8 million to outfit for service. It has a 5-year usable life and will be depreciated under MACRS using a 5-year recovery period. Ship B costs $54 million to purchase and $6 million to outfit. It also has a 5-year usable life and will be depreciated under MACRS using a 5-year recovery period. Increased investments in net working capital will accompany the decision to acquire ship A or ship B. The purchase of ship A would result in a $4 million increase in net working capital; that of ship B would result in a $6 million increase in net working capital. The projected profits before depreciation and taxes with each alternative ship and the existing ship are given in the following table.

Profits before Depreciation and Taxes

Year	Ship A	Ship B	Existing Ship
1	$21,000,000	$22,000,000	$14,000,000
2	21,000,000	24,000,000	14,000,000
3	21,000,000	26,000,000	14,000,000
4	21,000,000	26,000,000	14,000,000
5	21,000,000	26,000,000	14,000,000

The existing ship can currently be sold for $18 million and will not incur any removal or cleanup costs; at the end of five years, it can be sold to net $1 million before taxes. Ships A and B can be sold to net (respectively) $12 million and $20 million before taxes at the end of the 5-year period. The firm is subject to a 40% tax rate on both ordinary income and capital gains.

a. Calculate the initial outlay associated with each alternative.

b. Calculate the operating cash flows associated with each alternative. Be sure to consider the depreciation in year 6.

c. Calculate the terminal cash flow at the end of year 5 associated with each alternative.

d. Depict on a time line the relevant cash flows associated with each alternative.

8-18. The management of Kimco is evaluating the possibility of replacing their large mainframe computer with a modern network system that requires much less office space. The network would cost $500,000 (including installation costs) and would generate $125,000 per year in operating cash flows (accounting for taxes and depreciation) over the next five years due to efficiency gains. The mainframe has a remaining book value of $50,000 and would be immediately donated to a charity for the tax benefit. Kimco's discount rate is 10% and its tax rate is 40%. On the basis of NPV, should management install the network system?

8-19. Pointless Luxuries Inc. (PLI) produces unusual gifts targeted at wealthy consumers. The company is analyzing the introduction of a new device designed to attach to the collar of a cat or dog. This device emits sonic waves that neutralize airplane engine noise, so that pets traveling with their owners will enjoy a more peaceful ride. PLI estimates that developing this product will require up-front capital expenditures of $10 million, costs that will be depreciated on a straight-line basis for five years. PLI believes that it can sell the product initially for $250. The selling price will increase to $260 in years 2 and 3 before falling to $245 and $240 in years 4 and 5, respectively. After five years the company will withdraw the product from the market and replace it with something else. Variable costs are $135 per unit. PLI forecasts a sales volume of 20,000 units the first year with subsequent increases of 25% (year 2), 20% (year 3), 20% (year 4), and 15% (year 5). Offering this product will force PLI to make additional investments in receivables and inventory. Projected end-of-year balances appear in the following table.

	Year 0	Year 1	Year 2	Year 3	Year 4	Year 5
Accounts receivable	$0	$200,000	$250,000	$300,000	$150,000	$0
Inventory	$0	$500,000	$650,000	$780,000	$600,000	$0

The firm faces a tax rate of 34%. Assume that cash flows arrive at the end of each year, except for the initial $10 million outlay.

  a. Calculate the project's contribution to net income each year.
  b. Calculate the project's cash flows each year.
  c. Calculate two NPVs, one using a 10% discount rate and one using 15%.
  d. A PLI financial analyst reasons as follows: "With the exception of the initial outlay, the cash flows from this project arrive in more or less a continuous stream rather than at the end of each year. Therefore, by discounting each year's cash flow for a full year, we are understating the true NPV. A better approximation is to move the discounting six months forward (e.g., discount year-1 cash flows for half a year, year-2 cash flows for 1.5 years, and so on), as if all the cash flows arrive in the middle of each year rather than at the end." Recalculate the NPV (at 10% and 15%) while maintaining this proposed assumption. How much difference does it make?

8-20. TechGiant Inc. (TGI) is evaluating a proposal to acquire Fusion Chips, a young company with an interesting new chip technology. This technology, when integrated into existing TGI silicon wafers, will enable TGI to offer chips with new capabilities to companies with automated manufacturing systems. TGI analysts have projected income statements for Fusion five years into the future. These projections appear in the income statements at the top of page 308, along with estimates of Fusion's asset requirements and accounts payable balances each year. These statements are designed assuming that Fusion remains an independent, stand-alone company. If TGI acquires Fusion, then analysts believe that the following changes will occur.

  1. TGI's superior manufacturing capabilities will enable Fusion to increase the gross margin on its existing products to 45%.
  2. TGI's massive sales force will enable Fusion to increase sales of its existing products by 10% above current projections (so that, for example, if Fusion is acquired then it will sell $110 million, rather than $100 million, in 2010). This increase will occur as a consequence of regularly scheduled conversations between TGI salespeople and existing customers and will not require added marketing expenditures. Operating expenses as a percentage of sales will be the same each year as currently forecasted (ranging from 10% to 12%). The fixed asset increases that are currently projected through 2014 will be sufficient to sustain the 10% increase in sales volume each year.
  3. TGI's more efficient receivables and inventory management systems will allow Fusion to increase its sales as previously described without making investments in receivables and inventory beyond those already reflected in the financial projection. TGI also enjoys a higher credit rating than Fusion and so, after the acquisition, Fusion will be able to obtain credit from suppliers on more favorable terms. Specifically, Fusion's accounts payable balance will be 30% higher each year than the level currently forecast.

FUSION CHIPS

Income Statements for Years Ended December 31 ($ thousand)

	2010	2011	2012	2013	2014
Sales	$100,000	$150,000	$200,000	$240,000	$270,000
−Cost of goods sold	60,000	90,000	120,000	144,000	162,000
Gross profit	$ 40,000	$ 60,000	$ 80,000	$ 96,000	$108,000
−Operating expenses	12,000	17,250	22,000	25,200	27,000
−Depreciation	12,000	18,000	24,000	28,800	32,400
Pre-tax income	$ 16,000	$ 24,750	$ 34,000	$ 42,000	$ 48,600
−Taxes	5,440	8,415	11,560	14,280	16,524
Net income	$ 10,560	$ 16,335	$ 22,440	$ 27,720	$ 32,076

Assets and Accounts Payable on December 31 ($ thousand)

	2009	2010	2011	2012	2013	2014
Cash	$ 400	$ 400	$ 525	$ 600	$ 600	$ 600
Accounts receivable	6,000	7,000	10,500	14,000	16,800	18,900
Inventory	10,000	12,500	18,750	25,000	30,000	33,750
Total current assets	$16,400	$ 19,900	$ 29,775	$ 39,600	$ 47,400	$ 53,250
Plant and equipment						
Gross	$80,000	$113,000	$166,500	$226,000	$283,200	$336,900
Net	50,000	71,000	106,500	142,000	170,400	191,700
Total assets	$66,400	$ 90,900	$136,275	$ 181,600	$217,800	$244,950
Accounts payable	$ 7,500	$ 13,500	$ 20,250	$ 27,000	$ 32,400	$ 36,450

Note: The 2009 figures represent the amounts currently on Fusion's balance sheet.

4. TGI's current cash reserves are more than sufficient for the combined company, so Fusion's existing cash balances will be reduced to $0.

5. Immediately after the acquisition, TGI will invest $50 million in fixed assets to manufacture a new chip that integrates Fusion's technology into one of TGI's best-selling products. These assets will be depreciated on a straight-line basis for eight years. After five years, the new chip will be obsolete, and no additional sales will occur. The equipment will be sold at the end of year 5 for $1 million. Before depreciation and taxes, this new product will generate $20 million in (incremental) profits the first year, $30 million the second year, and $15 million in each of the next three years. TGI will have to invest $3 million in net working capital up front, all of which it will recover at the end of the project's life.

6. Both companies face a tax rate of 34%.
   a. Calculate the cash flows generated by Fusion as a stand-alone entity in each year from 2010 to 2014.
   b. Assume that Fusion will reach a "steady state" by 2014, which means that its cash flows will then grow by 5% per year in perpetuity. If Fusion discounts cash flows at 15%, then what is the present value (as of the end of 2014) of all cash flows that Fusion will generate from 2015 forward?
   c. Calculate the present value as of 2009 of Fusion's cash flows from 2010 forward. What does this NPV represent?
   d. Suppose that TGI acquires Fusion. Recalculate Fusion's cash flows from 2010 to 2014, making all the changes previously described in items 1–4 and 6.

e. Assume that Fusion's cash flows will grow at a steady 5% per year after 2014. Calculate the present value of these cash flows as of 2014, assuming the discount rate is 15%.

f. If we ignore item 5 in the list of changes, what is the PV (as of 2009) of Fusion's cash flows from 2010 forward? Use a discount rate of 15%.

g. Finally, calculate the NPV of TGI's investment to integrate its technology with Fusion's. Considering this in combination with your answer to part (f), what is the maximum price that TGI can pay for Fusion? Assume a discount rate of 15%.

8-21. A project generates the following sequence of cash flows over six years:

Year	Cash Flow ($ million)
0	−59.00
1	4.00
2	5.00
3	6.00
4	7.33
5	8.00
6	8.25

a. Calculate the NPV over the six years. The discount rate is 11%.

b. This project does not end after the sixth year but instead will generate cash flows far into the future. Estimate the project's terminal value, assuming that cash flows after year 6 will continue at $8.25 million per year in perpetuity, and then recalculate the investment's NPV.

c. Calculate the terminal value assuming that cash flows after the sixth year grow at 2% annually in perpetuity, and then recalculate the NPV.

d. Using market multiples, calculate the terminal value by estimating the project's market value at the end of year 6. Specifically, calculate the terminal value while assuming that, at the end of year 6, the project's market value will be 10 times greater than its most recent annual cash flow. Recalculate the NPV.

Cash Flows, Discounting, and Inflation

8-22. Sherry Bishop of Thayer Industries is considering investing in a capital project that costs $1.2 million. The project is expected to generate after-tax operating cash flows equal to $500,000 in the first year and declining by $100,000 per year until the end of the project's life in five years. Assume that Thayer's nominal discount rate for this project is 12% and that the annual inflation rate is 3%.

a. Calculate the project's NPV, assuming that the problem's cash flows are given in nominal terms. Would you accept this project?

b. Calculate the real values of future cash flows.

c. Recalculate the project's NPV, using the real cash flows and the appropriate real discount rate. Does your accept–reject decision change from your answer in part (a)?

8-23. A certain investment will require an immediate cash outflow of $4 million. At the end of each of the next four years, the investment will generate cash inflows of $1.25 million.

a. Assuming that these cash flows are in nominal terms and that the nominal discount rate is 10.25%, calculate the project's NPV.

b. Now assume that the expected rate of inflation is 5% per year. Recalculate the project's cash flows in real terms, discount them at the real interest rate, and verify that you obtain the same NPV.

8-24. The engineers in the aircraft manufacturing division of a diversified conglomerate want the firm to fund a certain investment proposal. The investment will require an initial outlay of $75 million and will generate the following net cash inflows over five years:

Year	Cash Inflow ($ million)
1	10
2	20
3	20
4	30
5	40

This project will compete for funds with one proposed by the company's consumer products division. The alternative project requires an initial $55 million outlay and will generate the following net cash inflows over five years:

Year	Cash Inflow ($ million)
1	10
2	12
3	14
4	20
5	25

In the airline division, it is common practice to state all project cash flows in nominal terms, but such flows are stated in real terms in the consumer products division. The expected rate of inflation is 5%, and the required real rate of return on investments in both divisions is 8%. Which project should the firm accept if it can accept only one?

Special Problems in Capital Budgeting

8-25. Semper Mortgage wishes to select the best of three possible computers, each expected to meet the firm's growing need for computational and storage capacity. The three computers—A, B, and C—are equally risky. The firm plans to use a 12% cost of capital to evaluate each of them. The initial outlay and annual cash flows over the life of each computer are shown in the following table.

Initial Outlay (CF_0)	Computer A $50,000	Computer B $35,000	Computer C $60,000
Year (t)		Cash Inflows (CF_t)	
1	$7,000	$ 5,500	$18,000
2	7,000	12,000	18,000
3	7,000	16,000	18,000
4	7,000	23,000	18,000
5	7,000	—	18,000
6	7,000	—	—

a. Calculate the NPV for each computer over its life. Rank the computers in descending order based on their NPVs.

b. Use the equivalent annual cost approach to evaluate and rank the computers in descending order based on the EAC criterion.

c. Compare and contrast your findings in parts (a) and (b). Which computer would you recommend that the firm acquire? Why?

8-26. Seattle Manufacturing is considering the purchase of one of three mutually exclusive projects for improving its assembly line. The firm plans to use a 14% cost of capital to evaluate these equal-risk projects. The initial outlay and annual cash flows over the life of each project are shown in the following table.

Initial Outlay (CF$_0$)	Project X $156,000	Project Y $104,000	Project Z $132,000
Year (t)	Cash Inflows (CF$_t$)		
1	$34,000	$56,000	$30,000
2	50,000	56,000	30,000
3	66,000	—	30,000
4	82,000	—	30,000
5	—	—	30,000
6	—	—	30,000
7	—	—	30,000
8	—	—	30,000

a. Calculate the NPV for each project over its life. Rank the projects in descending order based on NPV.
b. Use the equivalent annual cost approach to evaluate and rank the projects in descending order based on the EAC.
c. Compare and contrast your findings in parts (a) and (b). Which project would you recommend that the firm purchase? Why?

8-27. As part of a hotel renovation program, a company must choose between two grades of carpet to install. One grade costs $22 per square yard and the other costs $28. The costs of cleaning and maintaining the carpets are identical, but the less expensive carpet must be replaced after six years whereas the more expensive one will last nine years before it must be replaced. Which grade should the company choose? The relevant discount rate is 13%.

8-28. Gail Dribble is a financial analyst at Hill Propane Distributors. Gail must provide a financial analysis of the decision to replace a truck used to deliver propane gas to residential customers. Given its age, the truck will require increasing maintenance expenditures if the company keeps it in service. Similarly, the market value of the truck declines as it ages. The current market value of the truck, as well as the market value and required maintenance expenditures for each of the next four years, appears below.

Year	Market Value ($)	Maintenance Cost ($)
Current	7,000	0
1	5,500	2,500
2	3,700	3,600
3	0	4,500
4	0	7,500

The company can purchase a new truck for $40,000. The truck will last 15 years and will require annual end-of-year maintenance expenditures of $1,500. At the end of 15 years, the new truck's salvage value will be $3,500.
a. Calculate the equivalent annual cost of the new truck using a discount rate of 9%.
b. Suppose the firm keeps the old truck one more year and sells it then rather than selling it now. What is the opportunity cost associated with this decision? What is the present value of the cost of this decision as of today? Restate this cost in terms of year-1 dollars.

c. Based on your answers to (a) and (b), is it optimal for the company to replace the old truck immediately?

d. Suppose the firm decides to keep the truck for another year. Next, Gail must analyze whether replacing the old truck after one year makes sense or whether the truck should stay in use for still another year. As of the end of year 1, what is the present value of the cost of using the truck and selling it at the end of year 2? Restate this answer in year-2 dollars. Should the firm replace the truck after two years?

e. Suppose that the firm keeps the old truck in service for two years. Should it replace it rather than keep it in service for the third year?

Smart Solutions

See the problem and solution explained step-by-step at **SMARTFinance**

8-29. A firm that manufactures and sells ball bearings currently has excess capacity. The firm expects that it will exhaust its excess capacity in three years, at which time it will spend $5 million to build new capacity. Suppose that this firm can accept additional manufacturing work as a subcontractor for another company. By doing so, the firm will receive net cash inflows of $250,000 immediately and in each of the next two years. However, the firm will also have to spend $5 million two years earlier than originally planned to bring new capacity online. Should the firm take on the subcontracting job? The discount rate is 12%. What is the minimum cash inflow that the firm would require (per year) to accept this job? For simplicity you may ignore depreciation.

THOMSON ONE | Business School Edition

8-30. Calculate Sara Lee Corporation's (ticker symbol, SLE) cash flow for the last four years, using the formula Cash flow = Net income + Depreciation. Do these figures match Sara Lee's net cash flow from operating activities? If not, list three specific reasons why they are different.

8-31. Using the most recent two years' data, does the change in accumulated depreciation equal the net change in property, plant, and equipment for General Electric (ticker symbol, GE)? If not, why might they be different? Using the average tax rate (income taxes divided by pre-tax income), what was the tax savings from depreciation for the most current year?

8-32. What has caused the change in net working capital over the last three years for Family Dollar Stores, Inc. (ticker symbol, FDO)?

MINI-CASE: CASH FLOWS AND CAPITAL BUDGETING

Kirk Tiberius is the financial manager for MicroDryer Enterprises, a company that manufactures microwave dryers. Using microwaves eliminates shrinkage of cotton and wool because clothing can be dried at a much lower surface temperature. The firm currently offers a full-size microwave dryer that is extremely energy efficient and dries clothes much faster than conventional dryers. However, it seems that the American consumer is either uninterested in energy efficiency or unwilling to purchase the rather high-priced full-size microwave dryer. Thus, MicroDryer Enterprises is considering development of a new product: a countertop microwave dryer that could be used in dorm rooms, apartments, hotels, or RVs. Kirk's job is to determine the financial feasibility of this venture based on sales and cost estimates provided by the marketing division and others. Kirk has been provided with the following estimates.

- *Expected annual sales in year 1 are 235,000 units. (Sales are expected to increase at a rate of 15% a year through year 4, at which point sales will decrease at a rate of 20% a year through year 10.)*
- *No sales cannibalization is expected to occur.*
- *Expected sales price is $250 per unit in today's dollars.*
- *Expected development costs of the product (at time 0) are $50,000,000, which will be depreciated over 10 years using the straight-line method.*
- *Annual fixed costs of production are $1,000,000 in today's dollars.*
- *Variable costs of production are estimated to be $100 per unit in today's dollars.*
- *Variable costs, fixed costs of production, and the sales price will increase at the rate of inflation each year, which is expected to be 2.89% annually.*
- *The tax rate for MicroDryer Enterprises' is 34%.*
- *The inventory balance is 35% of revenues, accounts payable are 50% of inventory, and accounts receivable are 10% of revenue.*
- *The expected life of project is not known, so the company has estimated that cash flows after the tenth year will increase at an annual rate of 3.5%.*
- *The firm's nominal discount rate is 11%.*

Based on this information, what recommendation should Kirk make concerning the countertop microwave dryer project? Use nominal values for your analysis.

9

Cost of Capital and Project Risk

What Companies Do

Alcoa's Cost of Capital

Quick—what do you think the cost of capital is for a typical publicly traded American corporation? Because such firms routinely finance massive investment programs by issuing debt and equity securities, virtually all public companies have a "weighted average cost of capital" that their managers consider to be the cost of funding investment projects. However, very few companies state their cost of capital publicly. Alcoa Inc. is different; not only does it specify that its cost of capital is 9%, it goes to great lengths to measure how efficiently that capital is employed by benchmarking its own return on capital against the return earned by the most profitable 100 members of the S&P 500.

When Alcoa first stated its cost of capital in 2004, the company was not achieving the return on investment of over 14% earned by the 100 best-performing S&P 500 firms. But it soon caught and then surpassed the competition. Alcoa achieved an 8.3% return in 2005, which increased to 16.2% in 2006 and 16.1% (excluding investment in growth projects) in 2007. As the world's leading producer of aluminum and aluminum products, Alcoa's capital investment spending tops $3.6 billion per year, so the company has good reason to measure its cost of capital carefully.

But how did Alcoa come up with a 9% cost of capital? As we will discuss in this chapter, a company should determine a *weighted average cost of capital* (WACC) by determining the after-tax cost of each major source of financing the company plans to tap for funds and then computing an average cost that is based on the fraction of total funding it wishes to draw from each source. We can calculate Alcoa's 9% WACC by applying this chapter's techniques to the company's reported end-of-2007 values for long-term debt outstanding ($6.36 billion), common stock outstanding ($28 billion market value), average after-tax cost of debt (3.83%), and the return demanded by Alcoa's shareholders (10.2%). This means that if Alcoa can earn 9.0% or more on its capital investments, the company will be able to fully repay its debtholders and have enough left over to more than pay the required return demanded by stockholders.

Sources: Alcoa Inc. news releases (January 24, 2004, and January 9, 2008); Alcoa Inc. 2007 Annual Report, downloaded from the company website (http://www.alcoa.com).

This chapter concludes our coverage of capital budgeting, as we focus on the risk dimension of project analysis. To calculate NPV, an analyst must evaluate the risk of a project and decide what discount rate adequately rewards investors for bearing that risk. Often, the best place to discover clues for solving this problem is the market for the firm's securities. The chapter begins with a discussion of how managers can look to the market to calculate a discount rate that properly reflects the risk of a firm's investment projects. Even when managers are confident that they have estimated project cash flows carefully and have chosen a proper discount rate, they should perform additional analysis to understand the causes and effects of a project's risk. Their tools include break-even analysis, sensitivity analysis, simulation, and decision trees—all covered in this chapter. We conclude with sections on real options and on strategy, that describe the sources of value in investment projects and illustrate how NPV analysis can sometimes understate the value of certain investments.

9.1 Choosing the Right Discount Rate

Cost of Equity

JOB INTERVIEW QUESTION

How would you estimate the cost of capital for our company?

What discount rate should managers use to calculate a project's NPV? This is a difficult question and is sometimes the source of heated discussions when firms evaluate capital investment proposals. Conceptually, when a company establishes a project's discount rate, that rate should reflect the opportunity costs of investors who can choose to invest either in the firm's project or in similar projects undertaken by other firms. This is a rather roundabout way of saying that a project's discount rate must be high enough to compensate investors for the project's risk. One implication of this statement is that, if a firm undertakes many different investment projects of various degrees of risk, then managers err if they apply a single, firmwide discount rate to value each investment. In principle, the appropriate discount rate to use in NPV calculations should vary from one investment to another if the risks vary across investments. Hence it is interesting that, in a survey of CFOs, Graham and Harvey (2001) found that a little more than half of the respondents always or almost always use a company-wide discount rate and that the other half always or almost always use a risk-matched discount rate for a particular project. Suffice it to say that CFOs appear to be fairly evenly split regarding the use of a company-wide versus a project-specific discount rate in NPV calculations.

To simplify things at the start, we consider a firm that finances its operations using only equity and invests in only one industry. Because the company has no debt, its investments must provide returns sufficient to satisfy just one type of investor: common stockholders. Because the firm invests in only one industry, we will assume that all its investments are *equally risky*. Therefore, when calculating the NPV of any project that this firm might make, its managers can use the required return on equity, often called the *cost of equity*, as the discount rate. If the firm uses the cost of equity as its discount rate then, by definition, any project with a positive NPV will generate returns that exceed shareholders' required returns.

To quantify shareholders' return expectations, managers look to the market. Recall from Chapter 6 that, according to the CAPM, the expected or required return on any security equals the risk-free rate *plus* the security's beta multiplied by the expected market risk premium:

$$E(R_i) = R_f + \beta_i[E(R_m) - R_f] \qquad \text{(Eq. 9.1)}$$

Managers can estimate the return that shareholders require if they know (1) their firm's stock beta, (2) the risk-free rate, and (3) the expected market risk premium.

Figure 9.1 summarizes the responses of 392 CFOs to a survey question of Graham and Harvey (2001) regarding the types of risk they feel are important when adjusting cash flows or discount rates. Note the primary importance given to market risk as measured by beta in the CAPM.

FIGURE 9.1

Risk Adjustments to Cash Flows and Discount Rates

More than 70% of CFOs always or almost always adjust cash flows or discount rates for market risk. Also popular among CFOs are adjustments for interest rate, foreign exchange, and business cycle risks.

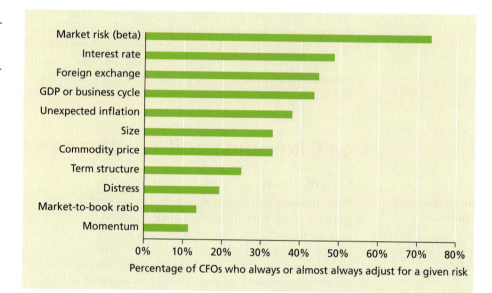

Percentage of CFOs who always or almost always adjust for a given risk

EXAMPLE

Carbonlite Inc. manufactures bicycle frames that are both extremely strong and very light. The firm finances its operations 100% with equity and is now evaluating a proposal to build a new manufacturing facility that will enable it to double its output within three years. Because Carbonlite sells a luxury good, its fortunes are sensitive to macroeconomic conditions; its stock has a beta of 1.5. Carbonlite's financial managers observe that the current interest rate on risk-free government bonds is 5%, and they expect that the return on the overall stock market will be about 11% per year in the future. Given this information, Carbonlite should calculate the NPV of the expansion proposal using a discount rate of 14%:

$$E(R) = 5\% + 1.5(11\% - 5\%) = 14\%$$

To reiterate, Carbonlite should use its cost of equity capital, 14%, to discount cash flows because we have assumed both that the company has no debt on its balance sheet and that undertaking any of Carbonlite's investment proposals will not alter the firm's risk. If either assumption is invalid, then the cost of equity is not the appropriate discount rate.

In the preceding Example, Carbonlite's stock beta is 1.5 because sales of premium bicycle frames are highly correlated with the state of the economy. Therefore, Carbonlite's investment in new capacity is riskier than an investment in new capacity by a firm producing a product whose sales are relatively insensitive to economic conditions. For example, managers of a food processing company might apply a lower discount rate to an expansion project than would Carbonlite's managers because the stock of a food processor has a lower beta. The general lesson is that the same type of capital investment project (such as capacity expansion, equipment replacement, or new product development) may require different discount rates in different industries. The level of systematic risk varies from one industry to another; so, too, should the discount rate used in capital budgeting analysis.

Several other factors affect betas, which in turn affect project discount rates. One of the most important factors is a firm's cost structure—specifically, its mix of fixed and variable costs. The greater the importance of fixed costs in a firm's overall cost structure, the more volatile will be its cash flows and the higher will be its stock beta (all other factors held constant). **Operating leverage** measures the tendency of operating cash flow volatility to increase with fixed operating costs. Mathematically, the definition of operating leverage can be expressed as

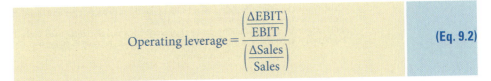

$$\text{Operating leverage} = \frac{\left(\dfrac{\Delta \text{EBIT}}{\text{EBIT}}\right)}{\left(\dfrac{\Delta \text{Sales}}{\text{Sales}}\right)} \qquad \textbf{(Eq. 9.2)}$$

where EBIT is earnings before interest and taxes (see Chapter 2) and the symbol Δ (Greek uppercase delta) denotes "change in." Operating leverage equals the percentage change in earnings before interest and taxes divided by the percentage change in sales. When a small percentage increase (decrease) in sales leads to a large percentage increase (decrease) in EBIT, then the firm has high (low) operating leverage. The connection between operating leverage and the relative importance of fixed and variable costs is easy to see in the following Example.

EXAMPLE

Carbonlite Inc. uses robotic technology to paint its finished bicycle frames whereas its main competitor, Fiberspeed Corp., offers customized, hand-painted finishes. Robots represent a significant fixed cost for Carbonlite, but robots help keep variable costs low. Fiberspeed incurs very low fixed costs, but it has high variable costs because of the time required to paint frames by hand. Both firms sell their bike frames at an average price of $1,000 apiece. Last year each firm made a profit of $1 million on sales of 10,000 bicycle frames, as shown in Table 9.1. Suppose that next year both firms experience a 10% increase in sales volume to 11,000 frames, holding constant all the other figures. Carbonlite's fixed costs do not change, and its EBIT will increase by $600 ($1,000 price minus $400 variable costs) per additional frame sold. Thus Carbonlite's EBIT will increase 60% from $1 million to $1.6 million while Fiberspeed's EBIT grows from $1 million to $1.3 million, an increase of just 30%. Because Carbonlite has higher fixed costs and lower variable costs, its profits increase more rapidly in response to a given increase in sales than do Fiberspeed's profits. In short, Carbonlite has more operating leverage. Figure 9.2 shows this graphically. The figure shows two lines, one tracing out the relationship between sales growth (from the base of 10,000 bicycles per year) and EBIT growth (from the $1 million EBIT base) for Carbonlite, the other illustrating the same linkage for Fiberspeed.[1] Because of its greater operating leverage, the line for Carbonlite is much steeper than the one for Fiberspeed. Even though Carbonlite and Fiberspeed compete in the same industry, they may well use different discount rates in their capital budgeting analysis because operating leverage increases the risk of Carbonlite's cash flows relative to Fiberspeed's.

[1]These comparisons are based on a reference point of 10,000 bikes per year sold for $1,000 per bike and an EBIT of $1 million. All changes described and shown in Figure 9.2 assume these points of reference in each case. Clearly, the sensitivity of these values to change will vary depending on the point of reference utilized.

Table 9.1 **Financial Data for Carbonlite Inc. and Fiberspeed Corp.**

ITEM	CARBONLITE	FIBERSPEED
Fixed cost per year	$5 million	$2 million
Variable cost per bike frame	$400	$700
Sale price per bike frame	$1,000	$1,000
Contribution margin[a] per bike frame	$600	$300
Last year's sales volume	10,000 frames	10,000 frames
EBIT [b]	$1 million	$1 million

[a]**Contribution margin** is the sale price per unit minus the variable cost per unit. For Carbonlite, $1,000 − $400 = $600 per bike; for Fiberspeed, $1,000 − $700 = $300 per bike.
[b]EBIT equals sales volume multiplied by the contribution margin *minus* fixed costs. For Carbonlite, (10,000 × $600) − $5,000,000 = $1,000,000; for Fiberspeed, (10,000 × $300) − $2,000,000 = $1,000,000.

FIGURE 9.2

Operating
Leverage for
Carbonlite and
Fiberspeed

The higher operating
leverage of Carbonlite
is reflected in its steeper
slope, demonstrating
that its EBIT is more
responsive to changes
in sales than is the EBIT
of Fiberspeed.

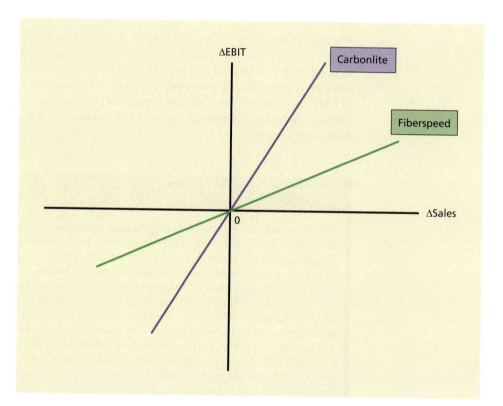

We have seen that Carbonlite's sales are extremely sensitive to the business cycle because the firm produces a luxury item. We have also observed that, because of its high operating leverage, Carbonlite's profits are quite sensitive to changes in sales. These factors contribute to Carbonlite's relatively high stock beta of 1.5 and its correspondingly high cost of equity of 14%. One other factor looms large in determining whether firms have high or low stock betas. Remember that Carbonlite's financial structure is 100% equity. In practice it is much more common to see both debt and equity on the right-hand side of a firm's balance sheet. When firms finance their operations with debt and equity, the presence of debt creates **financial leverage**, which leads to a higher stock beta. The effect of financial leverage on stock betas is much the same as the effect of operating leverage. When a firm borrows money, it creates a fixed cost that it must repay regardless of whether sales are high or low.[2] As was the case with operating leverage, an increase (decrease) in sales will lead to sharper increases (decreases) in earnings for a firm with financial leverage than for a firm that has only equity on its balance sheet.

Table 9.2 illustrates the effect of financial leverage on the volatility of a firm's cash flows and on its beta. The table compares two firms, A and B, which are identical in every respect except that Firm A finances its operations with 100% equity whereas Firm B uses 50% equity and 50% long-term debt with an interest rate of 8%. For simplicity, we assume that neither firm pays taxes. Firms A and B sell identical products at the same price, they both have $100 million in assets, and they face the same production costs. Suppose that, over the next year, both firms generate EBIT equal to 20% of total assets, or $20 million. Firm A pays no interest and so it can distribute all $20 million to its shareholders, a 20% return on their $100 million investment. Firm B pays 8% interest on $50 million for a total interest cost of $4 million. After paying interest, Firm B can distribute $16 million to shareholders, which represents a 32% return on their investment of $50 million. On the other hand, suppose both firms have EBIT equal to just 5% of assets, or $5 million. Firm A pays out all $5 million to its shareholders, a return of 5%. Firm B pays out $4 million in interest, leaving just $1 million for shareholders, a return of only 2%. Therefore, in periods when business is good, shareholders of Firm B earn higher returns than shareholders of Firm A, and the opposite happens when business is bad.

Table 9.2   The Effect of Financial Leverage on Shareholder Returns

ACCOUNT	FIRM A	FIRM B
Assets	$100 million	$100 million
Debt	$ 0	$ 50 million
Equity	$100 million	$ 50 million
When ROA = 20%		
EBIT	$20 million	$20 million
Less: Interest	0	$(0.08 \times \$50$ million$) = \$4$ million
Cash to equity	$20 million	$16 million
ROE	$20 million/$100 million = 20%	$16 million/$50 million = 32%
When ROA = 5%		
EBIT	$5 million	$5 million
Less: Interest	0	$(0.08 \times \$50$ million$) = \$4$ million
Cash to equity	$5 million	$1 million
ROE	$5 million/$100 million = 5%	$1 million/$50 million = 2%

The inclusion of debt as part of a firm's capital structure complicates our selection of the discount rate in two ways. First, debt creates financial leverage, which increases a firm's stock beta relative to the value it would obtain if the firm financed investments only with

---

[2]We use the term "fixed cost" here to mean a cost that does not vary with sales rather than simply a cost that is constant over time. Even when a firm agrees to a loan with a variable interest rate, which means that interest payments are not constant over time, the cost of repaying the debt does not generally vary as a function of sales.

equity. Second, when a firm issues debt, it must satisfy two groups of investors rather than one. Cash flows generated from capital investment projects must be sufficient to meet the return requirements of bondholders as well as stockholders. Therefore, a firm that issues debt cannot discount project cash flows using only its cost of equity capital: it must choose a discount rate that reflects the expectations of both investor groups. Fortunately, finance theory offers a way to find that discount rate.

Weighted Average Cost of Capital (WACC)

In Chapter 5, we learned that the expected return on a portfolio of two assets equals the weighted average of the expected returns of each asset in the portfolio. We can apply that idea to the problem of selecting an appropriate discount rate for a company that has both debt and equity in its capital structure. Imagine that Lox-in-a-Box Inc., a chain of kosher fast-food stores, has outstanding $100 million worth of common stock on which investors require a return of 15%. In addition, the firm has outstanding $50 million in bonds that offer a 9% return.[3] What rate of return must the firm earn on its investments to satisfy both groups of investors?

The answer lies in a concept known as the **weighted average cost of capital (WACC)**. Let D and E denote the market value of the firm's debt and equity securities, respectively, and let r_d and r_e represent the rate of return that investors require on bonds and shares. The WACC is the simple weighted average of the required rates of return on debt and equity, where the weights equal the percentage of each type of financing in the firm's overall capital structure:

$$\text{WACC} = \left(\frac{D}{D+E}\right)r_D + \left(\frac{E}{D+E}\right)r_E$$

As a practical matter, firms in many countries can deduct interest payments to bondholders when they calculate taxable income. If a firm's interest payments are tax deductible and if the corporate tax rate equals T_c, then interest deductibility reduces the cost of debt from r_D, which ignores interest tax deductibility, to $(1 - T_c)r_D$, where the $(1 - T_c)$ term captures the interest deductibility. This expression is known as the *after-tax cost of debt*. To accommodate interest deductibility, the WACC formula becomes

$$\text{WACC} = \left(\frac{D}{D+E}\right)(1 - T_c)r_D + \left(\frac{E}{D+E}\right)r_E \qquad \text{(Eq. 9.3)}$$

Plugging in the values from our example and assuming that the firm must pay one-third of its cash flows to tax authorities, we find that the WACC for Lox-in-a-Box is 12%:

$$\text{WACC} = \left(\frac{\$50}{\$50+100}\right) \times \left(1 - \frac{1}{3}\right) \times 9\% + \left(\frac{\$100}{\$50+\$100}\right) \times 15\% = 12\%$$

How can Lox-in-a-Box managers be sure that earning 12% return on its investments will satisfy the expectations of both bondholders and shareholders? Suppose the company is considering a new investment project that will cost $60. The firm's financial analysts expect this project to generate pre-tax cash flows of $10.80 per year in

---

[3]The return we have in mind here is the yield to maturity (YTM) on the firm's bonds. Unless the bonds sell at par, the coupon rate and the YTM will be different, but the YTM provides a better measure of the return that investors who purchase the firm's debt can expect. If there is a nontrivial probability of the firm defaulting on its debt, then the YTM actually overstates the expected return on the bonds. For now, we keep things simple by assuming that the likelihood of default is very low; then the YTM provides a close approximation to the expected return on debt.

perpetuity. If the corporate tax rate is one-third, then the after-tax annual cash flow equals $10.80 \times (1 - 0.33)$, or $7.20. A careful reader may wonder why, in calculating the after-tax cash flow, we ignored the interest expense that Lox-in-a-Box will pay because it uses debt to finance part of this project. Recall that in Chapter 3 we emphasized keeping the investment decision separate from the financing decision. One implication of this approach is that we exclude interest expense when estimating cash flows for an NPV analysis. That is, as discussed at the start of Chapter 8, we measure cash flows as if the firm uses only equity financing. Rather than adjust our cash flow numbers to capture this tax benefit, we will capture the value of interest tax shields by discounting cash flows at the WACC, which captures the interest tax savings by using the *after-tax* cost of debt. By multiplying the required return on debt by 1 minus the corporate tax rate, we account for the value of debt's tax benefits by lowering the discount rate rather than by raising our cash flow figures.

Let's calculate the NPV of this project using the WACC as the discount rate:[4]

$$\text{NPV} = -60 + \frac{7.2}{0.12} = 0$$

A project with a zero NPV qualifies as "barely acceptable," meaning that it just manages to satisfy the demands of the firm's investors. We can check to be sure that the project meets both shareholders' and bondholders' expectations.

Suppose Lox-in-a-Box sets up this project as a stand-alone firm that is financed two-thirds with equity ($40) and one-third with debt ($20). Because Lox-in-a-Box finances this new investment with $20 of debt paying 9% interest, they must pay debtholders $1.80 in interest each year, but the after-tax interest cost to the firm is $1.20 [i.e., $20 \times 0.09 \times (1 - 0.33)$]. If the project's after-tax cash flows, ignoring interest, equal $7.20, then subtracting the $1.20 after-tax interest charge leaves $6 for shareholders. Equity investors contributed $40 to the project, so the $6 cash flow they receive in perpetuity represents a 15% return, exactly equal to the required return on equity. Overall, then, Lox-in-a-Box managers can be sure that a 12% return on its investments will satisfy the required returns of both bondholders and shareholders.

The WACC is of critical importance to almost all firms. Companies that use the WACC to evaluate real investments know that a higher WACC implies investments must pass a higher hurdle before they can generate shareholder wealth. If an event beyond the firm's control increases the firm's WACC, then both its existing assets and its prospective investment opportunities become less valuable.

The WACC formula can be modified to accommodate more than two sources of financing. For instance, suppose a firm raises money by issuing equity E, long-term debt D, and preferred stock P. We assume that dividends to common and preferred shareholders are not tax-deductible but that interest payments are. Denoting the respective required return on each security by r_E, r_D, and r_P, we can determine the WACC as follows:

$$\text{WACC} = \left(\frac{E}{E + D + P}\right) r_E + \left(\frac{D}{E + D + P}\right) r_D (1 - T_c) + \left(\frac{P}{E + D + P}\right) r_P$$

---

[4] Recall that the present value of a perpetuity equals the annual cash flow divided by the discount rate, so the second term on the right-hand side of this equation is just the present value of the project's cash inflows; the first term is the project's cost.

EXAMPLE

The S. D. Williams Company has 1 million shares of common stock outstanding, which currently trade at a price of $50 per share. The company believes that its stockholders require a 15% return on their investment. The company also has $47.1 million (par value) in 5-year, fixed-rate notes with a coupon rate of 8% and a yield to maturity of 7%. Because the yield on these bonds is less than the coupon rate, they trade at a premium. The current market value of the 5-year notes is $49 million. Lastly, the company has 200,000 outstanding preferred shares, which pay an $8 annual dividend and currently trade for $80 per share. What is the company's WACC if the corporate tax rate is 35%?

Begin by calculating the market value of each security. S. D. Williams has $50 million in common stock, $49 million in long-term debt, and $16 million in preferred stock for a total capitalization of $115 million. Next, determine the required rate of return on each type of security. The rates on common stock, long-term debt, and preferred stock are 15%, 7%, and 10%, respectively. Plug all these values into the WACC equation to obtain 9.8%:

$$\text{WACC} = \left(\frac{\$50}{\$115}\right)0.15 + \left(\frac{\$49}{\$115}\right)0.07(1-0.35) + \left(\frac{\$16}{\$115}\right)0.10$$

$$= 0.098 = 9.8\%$$

Now we have seen two approaches for determining the correct discount rate to apply when addressing capital budgeting problems. A firm that uses all equity should discount project cash flows using the cost of equity, and a firm that uses both debt and equity should discount cash flows using the WACC. Both recommendations are subject to the important proviso that the company makes investments in only one line of business—or, stated differently, that the firm discounts cash flows using the WACC only when the project under consideration is very similar to the risk and financing choices of the firm's existing assets. Evaluating investments that deviate significantly from a firm's existing investments requires a different approach. To understand that approach, we need to revisit the CAPM and see how it is related to the WACC.

Connecting the WACC to the CAPM

The CAPM states that the required return on any asset is directly linked to the asset's beta. By now we are used to thinking about betas of shares of common stock, but there is nothing about the CAPM that restricts its predictions to common stock. When a firm issues bonds or preferred stock, the required returns on those securities should reflect their systematic risks (i.e., their betas) just as the required returns on the firm's common shares should. Because both preferred stock and bonds generally make fixed, predictable cash payments over time, measuring the rate of return that investors require on these securities is relatively easy, even without knowing their betas. For preferred stock, the dividend yield (dividend/price) provides a good measure of required returns; for debt, the yield to maturity does the same, at least for high-grade debt with relatively low default risk. However, this doesn't mean we can't estimate the beta of a bond or a share of preferred stock. Calculating the beta of a bond or preferred share is no different than calculating the beta of common stock—just estimate the covariance between returns on the security of interest and returns on the market, then divide by the variance of the market's returns.

WHAT COMPANIES DO GLOBALLY

Does Opening Up to the World Reduce the Cost of Capital?

What happens to the cost of capital when a nation decides to open up to foreign investors? Finance theory suggests that capital account liberalization—as the process of allowing in foreign capital is called—should reduce the cost of capital by increasing the pool of investors that might supply firms in that country with debt and equity capital. Empirical evidence strongly supports this idea.

A recent academic study found that three important things happen when emerging economies open their stock markets to foreign investors. First, the average cost of equity falls by 240 basis points. The graph demonstrates how dividend yields change in the years before $(-5 \text{ to } -1)$ and after $(+1 \text{ to } +5)$ capital account liberalization, which is year 0 in the figure. Second, the nation's overall capital stock increases by an average of 1.1 percentage points per year, meaning that companies invest more in productive assets. Third, the growth rate of output per worker rises by 2.3 percentage points per year. Since the cost of capital falls, investment increases sharply and the productivity of workers rises rapidly. When countries open their stock markets, the policy lesson is clear: Let foreign capital in!

Source: Peter Blair Henry, "Capital Account Liberalization, The Cost of Capital, and Economic Growth," *American Economic Review, Papers and Proceedings* 93 (May 2003), pp. 91–106.

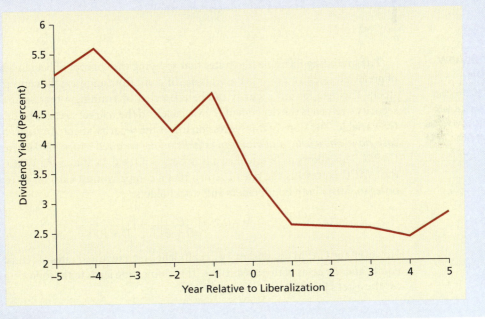

Smart Ideas Video

Chris Lundblad, University of North Carolina

"The benefit from liberalization is that you may be able to pursue projects that were formerly unavailable."

See the entire interview at
SMARTFinance

Remember, though, that returns on preferred shares and bonds are generally not as sensitive as returns on common stocks to the market's up-and-down movements. This implies that the beta of a firm's bonds is usually lower than the beta of its shares. A lower beta translates to a lower expected return, but that is exactly what we expect. Bonds, because they are less risky than stocks, offer lower expected returns.

EXAMPLE

Suppose an analyst gathers monthly returns on the bonds of a large corporation. Because interest rates and bond prices fluctuate from month to month, bond returns fluctuate as well. The analyst calculates the covariance between returns on the bonds and returns on a well-diversified portfolio of securities, then divides by the variance of returns on the portfolio to obtain an estimate of the bond's beta. The number obtained is 0.125. Assuming that the risk-free rate of interest is 4% and that the market portfolio's expected return is 12%, the analyst estimates the required return on the bonds using the CAPM equation:

$$r_D = 4\% + 0.125 \times (12\% - 4\%) = 5\%$$

Of course, there is another way to estimate the debt beta. Suppose the analyst observes that a firm's bonds offer a yield to maturity of 5%. Making the same assumptions as before about the risk-free rate (4%) and the expected return on the market (12%), the analyst could estimate the debt beta indirectly by solving this equation:

$$5\% = 4\% + \beta_D(12\% - 4\%);$$

$$\beta_D = 0.125$$

The **debt beta** is 0.125. Not surprisingly, the debt beta is close to zero because the bond's returns are not highly correlated with the market portfolio.

JOB INTERVIEW QUESTION

A firm has $100 million in publicly traded debt outstanding. How would you calculate the CAPM beta for this debt?

The preceding Example illustrates that applying the concept of beta to a bond, a share of preferred stock, or any other asset is no different from applying the concept to common stock. The beta for any security can be estimated by running a regression in which the security's return is the dependent (Y) variable and the market's return is the independent (X) variable. The slope of this regression line is the security's beta. *Any asset that generates cash flows has a beta, and that beta establishes the required return on the asset through the CAPM.* This allows us to establish a link between the CAPM and the WACC. Recall that the WACC represents the rate of return that a company must earn on its investments in order to satisfy both bondholders and stockholders:[5]

$$\text{WACC} = \left(\frac{D}{D+E}\right)r_D + \left(\frac{E}{D+E}\right)r_E$$

However, the CAPM establishes a direct link between required rates of return on debt and equity and the betas of these securities. This connection leads to the following relationship for the asset's beta, β_A:

$$\beta_A = \left(\frac{D}{D+E}\right)\beta_D + \left(\frac{E}{D+E}\right)\beta_E \qquad \text{(Eq. 9.4)}$$

Equation 9.4 states that the beta of a firm's assets equals the weighted average of the firm's debt and equity betas.[6] An **asset beta** is simply a measure of the systematic risk of a company's real assets, or the covariance of the cash flows generated by those assets and

---

[5]For simplicity, we will assume a zero corporate tax rate to begin this example.
[6]Again, we are just applying a basic concept from portfolio theory. If an investor holds a portfolio of two securities, then the beta of the portfolio is equal to the weighted average of the betas of the securities in the portfolio.

the market, divided by the variance of cash flows from the market portfolio. Suppose a company owns a factory that it uses to produce tires. The cash flows of this operation will vary in response to changes in the business cycle and other factors. The factory's asset beta measures the systematic risk of the cash flow stream generated by the factory.

The asset beta on the left-hand side of Equation 9.4 captures the risk of a physical asset. The terms on the right-hand side illustrate how the risk of the asset is allocated between debt and equity investors. For instance, suppose a firm has manufacturing assets with a beta of 1.0. If the firm is financed entirely with equity, then

$$\beta_A = 1.0 = \left(\frac{\$0}{\$0 + E}\right)\beta_D + \left(\frac{E}{\$0 + E}\right)\beta_E = \beta_E$$

When there are no bondholders, shareholders bear all the risk associated with the firm's assets, so the asset beta and the equity beta both equal 1.0. However, suppose that the same firm decides to raise 20% of the funding by issuing relatively safe bonds with a beta of 0.125. The assets of this firm have not changed, so the asset beta still equals 1.0. The firm's bonds are substantially less risky than the firm's assets, and equity holders must therefore bear all the residual risk. Using the previous equation and substituting 0.125 for the debt beta and 0.2 and 0.8 for the fractions of debt and equity financing, respectively, we find that

$$\beta_A = 1.0 = (0.2)(0.125) + (0.8)\beta_E$$

$$\beta_E = \frac{1.0 - (0.2)(0.125)}{0.8} = 1.219$$

Compared to the all-equity firm, the firm with 20% debt has a much higher equity beta. That is exactly what we would expect given our previous discussion of the effects of financial leverage on equity betas. There is a "law of conservation of risk" at work here. The fundamental risk of a firm depends on the risk of the assets in which it chooses to invest. This is what the asset beta captures. The firm can allocate that risk between different types of investors any way it sees fit. A firm may offer investors a security, such as a bond, that has relatively low risk, but this doesn't alter the fact that the firm's underlying assets are still risky. If bondholders are not bearing this risk, then the risk must fall to shareholders. The more promises a firm makes to provide investors with a "safe" return (i.e., the more debt it issues), the greater the risk surrounding the returns that the firm can provide to shareholders.

It is easy to see the effect of leverage on equity betas if we make the assumption that the debt beta equals zero. Given that assumption, rearranging terms in Equation 9.4 yields

$$\beta_E = \beta_A\left(1 + \frac{D}{E}\right) \qquad \text{(Eq. 9.5)}$$

JOB INTERVIEW QUESTION

What is the difference between an unlevered and levered equity beta?

In this equation we can see, once again, that if the firm has zero debt then the asset beta equals the equity beta. For firms that use debt, the term $[1 + (D/E)]$ will be greater than 1.0, which in turn means that $\beta_E > \beta_A$. Holding the asset beta—the risk of the firm's assets—constant, the more money the firm raises by issuing debt, the greater its financial leverage and the higher its equity beta.

It is worthwhile to stop and recall our original objective: to find the right discount rate for capital budgeting projects. When a new project is very similar to a firm's existing projects, managers should discount cash flows using the WACC. However, the WACC does not apply when a firm is considering a project outside its normal line of business or when a firm has many different lines of business under one corporate umbrella. In the latter

WHAT CFOs DO

CFO Survey Evidence

Finance theory suggests that managers should use the firm's weighted average cost of capital to evaluate only those investment projects that are similar to the firm's existing assets and should use a different discount rate—one adjusted for project-specific risks—to evaluate investments in other projects. Do practicing managers actually follow this advice? On balance, they generally do not, though a growing fraction of managers do adjust for project risk in a theoretically correct manner. The following table reports the responses of 401 financial executives to

the question, "How frequently would your company use the following discount rates when evaluating a new project in an overseas market?" Nearly three-fifths (58.79%) of the respondents said they would always or almost always use the same company-wide discount rate used to evaluate new international projects. On the other hand, a majority of responders (50.95%) also reported that they would adjust the discount rate to account for project and country risks, and over one-third said that they would adjust the discount rate to account for country risks.

How frequently would your company use the following discount rates when evaluating a new project in an overseas market?

RESPONSE	ALWAYS OR ALMOST ALWAYS (%)	MEAN RESPONSE (0 = NEVER, 4 = ALWAYS)
The discount rate for our entire company	58.79	2.50
A risk-matched discount rate for this particular project (considering both country and industry)	50.95	2.09
The discount rate for the overseas market (country discount rate)	34.52	1.65
A divisional discount rate (if the project line of business matches a domestic division)	15.61	0.95
A different discount rate for each component cash flow that has a different risk characteristic (e.g., depreciation vs. operating cash flows)	9.87	0.66

Source: Reprinted from Journal of Financial Economics, 60, John R. Graham and Campbell R. Harvey, Table 5 from "The Theory and Practice of Corporate Finance: Evidence from the Field," pp. 187–243. Copyright 2001 with permission from Elsevier.

case, the WACC represents the required rate of return on the firm's "average" investment, but some divisions of a company may be inherently riskier than others. Consider our earlier example of Lox-in-a-Box. If managers at Lox-in-a-Box believe that the firm should vertically integrate by investing in a salmon-fishing fleet, they should not discount cash flows from that investment at the firm's WACC. The risks of salmon fishing hardly resemble those of running a fast-food chain, and it is the latter that are reflected in the firm's WACC. Applying the WACC to all projects will tend to overstate the NPVs of projects that are more risky than average and to understate the NPVs of projects that are less risky than average. Managers can solve this problem by focusing their attention on the asset betas of specific projects, sometimes called project betas.

Asset Betas and Project Discount Rates

JOB INTERVIEW QUESTION

A conglomerate is considering the launch of a new product. How would you determine the discount rate for assessing this project?

General Electric Corp. (ticker symbol, GE) is a diversified conglomerate with significant investments in such diverse industries as lighting, aircraft engine manufacturing, broadcasting, and financial services. Suppose that GE's WACC is 13%. When GE evaluates a proposal to replace existing equipment in its aircraft engine division, it should not necessarily calculate the NPV using a 13% discount rate because engine manufacturing may be more or less risky than the average GE investment. The WACC tells GE that to keep investors happy it must earn on average 13% across all its investments, but GE should discount its most risky investments at rates above 13% and its least risky investments at lower rates. Similarly, if GE decides to invest in a brand-new line of business, it should not use its WACC as the hurdle rate for that investment. In short, for each investment it undertakes, GE must assess the underlying risk of that project's cash flows and determine a discount rate appropriate for the risk level of that project. To do this, GE should measure the asset betas of different investments.

Suppose that GE decides to diversify into oil and gas production. How can its managers determine an appropriate rate at which to discount cash flows from new investments in this industry? The answer is that GE's managers should look to the market. By looking at characteristics of existing oil and gas firms whose securities trade in the market, GE analysts can gain considerable insight into the risks and required returns in that industry.

As a starting point, GE managers should look for firms that compete in only one industry: oil and gas production. A firm that competes in a single line of business is called a **pure play**, so GE wants to find pure-play firms in the oil and gas business. Two such firms are Berry Petroleum Co. (ticker symbol, BRY) and Forest Oil Corp. (ticker symbol, FST). Table 9.3 lists several characteristics of these two firms that should be of interest to analysts at GE. Note that even though both companies produce oil and gas, the equity beta of Forest Oil (0.90) is almost 40% higher than the equity beta of Berry Petroleum (0.65). If both of these firms operate in the same industry, then why are their stock betas so different? One possibility is that the companies use different production technologies with different degrees of operating leverage. Another is that the companies make different financing decisions, with one firm using more debt than the other. Indeed, Table 9.3 shows that Forest obtains 39% of its financing from debt but that Berry borrows just 14%. Even if the underlying risks of the two firms are identical—that is, even if their asset betas are equal—Forest's greater use of financial leverage will result in a higher stock beta. In any case, GE is not interested in the risk of Berry Petroleum and Forest Oil shares because GE does not plan to purchase oil and gas stocks. Rather, GE plans to invest in assets required to produce oil and gas, so GE managers need to know the asset beta for this industry.

We make two assumptions to simplify this example. First, we assume that the debt of both companies has very little risk and so their debt betas equal zero. Second, we ignore

Table 9.3   Data for Berry Petroleum and Forest Oil[a]

	BERRY PETROLEUM	FOREST OIL
Stock beta	0.65	0.90
Debt (D) proportion	0.14	0.39
Equity (E) proportion	0.86	0.61
D/E ratio	0.16	0.64
Asset beta[b]	0.56	0.55

[a]Data taken from Value Line Investment Survey.
[b]Using Equation 9.4 for β_A and assuming $\beta_D = 0$.

taxes for now. Given the information in the table, we can use Equation 9.4 to calculate the asset betas, β_A, for each firm:

$$\beta_A = (0.14)(0) + (0.86)(0.65) = 0.56 \quad \text{for Berry Petroleum;}$$

$$\beta_A = (0.39)(0) + (0.61)(0.90) = 0.55 \quad \text{for Forest Oil}$$

The calculations show that, despite the rather large differences in equity betas between the two companies, Berry and Forest have nearly identical asset betas. This should not be too surprising given that they make similar investments with similar risks and rewards. The differences in the equity betas apparently are driven by differences in leverage between the two firms. When we remove the effects of leverage on an equity beta in this way, we are calculating a figure that analysts sometimes refer to as an **unlevered equity beta**. Therefore, *when a firm uses no leverage, its equity beta equals its asset beta*, so an unlevered beta simply tells us how risky the equity of a company might be if it used no leverage at all.[7]

An analyst at GE might calculate asset betas for many other pure plays in this industry, starting with each firm's equity beta and unlevering it if necessary. Next, the analyst might average across all those firms to arrive at a final asset beta estimate. This is a measure of the risk of the underlying assets in which GE plans to invest. The next step is to incorporate GE's own capital structure into the analysis by "relevering" the asset beta. In other words, once GE estimates the oil and gas asset beta, it must adjust this beta upward if GE's capital structure contains both debt and equity. With this "relevered beta" in hand, the analyst calculates the appropriate project discount rate using the CAPM.

EXAMPLE

To determine the appropriate discount rate for a proposed investment in oil and gas production, a financial manager at GE calculates asset betas for several pure-play firms in the industry and averages them to arrive at an industry asset beta of 0.55. Next, the analyst determines that the oil investment would ideally be financed with 20% debt and 80% equity (implying a debt/equity ratio of 0.25). Assuming a debt beta of zero, the analyst then uses Equation 9.5 to calculate the relevered project beta:

$$\beta_{GE} = \beta_A \left(1 + \frac{D}{E} \right) = 0.55(1 + 0.25) = 0.69$$

Suppose that the risk-free rate of interest equals 6% and that the expected risk premium on the market equals 7%. By plugging these figures (and also the relevered project beta) into the CAPM equation, the analyst obtains the rate of return that a GE stockholder would require on this oil and gas investment, 10.83%, as follows:

$$E(R) = 6\% + 0.69(7\%) = 10.83\%$$

There is one more step necessary to find the right discount rate for GE's investment in this industry. The analyst should calculate a project WACC (sometimes called a *divisional WACC* because it applies to the firm's oil and gas division) using Equation 9.3. As noted previously, the project is ideally financed with 20% debt and 80% equity. Suppose also that investors expect a return of 6.5% (just over the risk-free rate) on GE's bonds. Then the project WACC is

$$\text{WACC}_{project} = 6.5\%(20\%) + 10.83\%(80\%) = 9.96\%$$

---

[7]In mid-1996, Conrail was the target of takeover bids from two rivals, Norfolk Southern and CSX. See Thompson (2000) for an extended illustration of how the investment bank Lazard Frères & Co. used the concepts of levered and unlevered betas to calculate the WACC in its valuation of Conrail.

Smart
Ethics
Video

Robert Bruner, University
of Virginia

*"We discovered a remarkable
degree of convergence among
the best practitioners."*

See the entire interview at

SMARTFinance

We do not want to overstate the precision of this process. Calculating the discount rate requires several steps, each of which involves estimating an uncertain number. If the GE analyst arrives at a figure of 9.96% for the oil and gas discount rate, as shown in the preceding Example, then the report might show that the appropriate discount rate should be "between 9 and 11 percent." There is certainly room to argue around this figure, but notice that it is less than the company-wide WACC of 13% that we assumed for GE.

The following rules summarize the main lessons about finding the right discount rate for an investment project.

1. If an all-equity firm invests in an asset that is similar to its existing assets, then the cost of equity is the appropriate discount rate to use in NPV calculations.
2. If a firm with both debt and equity invests in an asset that is similar to its existing assets, then the WACC is the appropriate discount rate to use in NPV calculations.
3. In conglomerates, the WACC reflects the return that the firm must earn on average across all its assets in order to satisfy investors, but using the WACC to discount cash flows of any one investment can lead to mistakes. The reason for this is that a particular investment may be more or less risky than the firm's average investment and so, in turn, require a higher or lower discount rate than the WACC.
4. When a firm invests in an asset that is different from its existing assets, it should look for pure-play firms to find the right discount rate. Firms can calculate an industry asset beta by unlevering the betas of pure-play firms. Then it must relever the industry asset beta based on the acquiring firm's existing capital structure. Given the relevered industry asset beta, firms can determine an appropriate discount rate using the CAPM.

Nothing in the real world is as simple as matters that are portrayed in textbooks. One important item that we have omitted thus far in our discussion of asset betas is the effect of taxes on project discount rates. The opportunity to deduct interest payments reduces the after-tax cost of debt and changes the relationship between asset betas and equity betas in this way:

$$\beta_E = \beta_A \left[1 + (1 - T_c)\frac{D}{E} \right] \qquad \text{(Eq. 9.6)}$$

Fortunately, the four main rules listed previously do not change when we add taxes to the picture—only the calculations change. When a firm is making an "ordinary" investment, it can use Equation 9.3 to determine its after-tax WACC to serve as the discount rate in NPV calculations. Alternatively, when a firm invests in a new line of business, it can use Equation 9.6 to calculate asset betas for pure-play firms to arrive at an industry asset beta. As before, once analysts have an industry beta in hand, they simply relever it if necessary to reflect their own firm's capital structure; then they plug the beta into the CAPM to find the right discount rate for the investment.

A Note on the Equity Risk Premium

When managers use the CAPM to determine the cost of equity for an investment project, they must know three things: (1) the project or asset beta, (2) the risk-free rate, and (3) the expected risk premium on the market portfolio. In this chapter, we have already shown how to use the betas of the firm's securities to estimate its asset beta. Measuring the risk-free rate is a straightforward exercise in obtaining current market rates on government bills or bonds. Now we turn our attention to measuring the expected risk premium on the market portfolio.

In the CAPM, you recall, the market portfolio is a value-weighted combination of all assets in the economy. At present, we are unaware of any market index that attempts to incorporate every type of asset. When using the CAPM, most practitioners and academics use the returns on a broad-based stock index as a proxy for the true market portfolio. Accordingly, rather than try to estimate the expected risk premium on the market portfolio, analysts usually focus on the expected equity risk premium: the difference in expected returns between a well-diversified portfolio of common stocks and a risk-free asset such as a U.S. Treasury bill.

Since 1900, the average real return on stocks outpaced the average real return on U.S. Treasury bills by about 5.4% per year. But in the CAPM, what matters is not the actual equity risk premium from the past but rather the expected equity risk premium looking forward. Though many analysts trust the historical evidence and simply plug in a figure close to 6% for the term $E(R_m - R_f)$, a naive reliance on long-run historical averages is not the only approach for estimating the expected risk premium. Using an unbiased estimate is important because an error in the risk premium translates directly into an error in a project's discount rate and thus in its NPV.

One variable that analysts can use to obtain a forward-looking estimate of the risk premium is the market's aggregate earnings yield, which is the reciprocal of the price-to-earnings ratios. For example, to calculate the earnings yield for the S&P 500, add up the earnings of all 500 companies and divide by the aggregate market value of these firms. Corporate earnings fluctuate with the business cycle, so analysts usually try to smooth out, or *normalize*, these temporary effects before using the earnings yield to estimate the risk premium. In the United States, the long-run average value of the earnings yield is about 7%, a little less than the average real return on stocks. It should come as no surprise that the earnings yield is closely related to the real return on stocks. After all, stocks represent a claim on corporate earnings.

A second forward-looking method for estimating the equity risk premium uses the dividend growth model. Recall that this model calculates the present value of a perpetual dividend stream growing at a constant rate, g:

$$P_0 = \frac{D_1}{r - g}$$

Rearranging this equation shows that the required return on the stock equals the sum of the dividend yield and the dividend growth rate:

$$r = \frac{D_1}{P_0} + g$$

To use this model when estimating the equity risk premium, we must think of the equation in aggregate, macroeconomic terms. In other words, r represents the (real) required return on the stock market rather than the required return on a specific stock. The ratio D_1/P_0 represents the aggregate dividend yield, and g represents the (real) growth rate of aggregate dividends. From 1872 to 1950, the expected equity risk premium derived from this model almost exactly matched the actual risk premium measured using average historical returns (a little more than 4%). From 1950 to 2000, however, the average real return on equities was much higher than predicted by the dividend growth model.[8]

---

[8]The opposite has been true since 2000: real equity returns have been *lower* on average than the dividend growth model would predict.

Smart Ideas Video

Chris Lundblad, University of North Carolina

"How should we incorporate the risks of investments in emerging economies?"

See the entire interview at **SMARTFinance**

Perhaps the most direct forward-looking approach is simply to gather forecasts of the equity premium made by experts. Yale economist Ivo Welch did just that by surveying finance and economics professors in 1998 and again in 2001 (Welch 2000b, 2001). The result was that the average equity premium forecast declined considerably from 1998 to 2001, a period in which U.S. stocks earned low average returns. When Welch asked professors in 2001 for a forecast of the arithmetic average equity premium over the next 30 years, their average prediction was 5.5%, in contrast to 7.1% in the 1998 survey.[9] Graham and Harvey (2002) later performed a similar survey of chief financial officers and found an expected equity risk premium of about 4%.

All three forward-looking indicators—the earnings yield, the dividend growth model, and the consensus of academic experts and practitioners—point toward a future equity risk premium that is lower than the average historical premium.

Concept Review Questions

1. Why is using the cost of equity to discount project cash flows inappropriate when a firm uses both debt and equity in its capital structure?
2. Two firms in the same industry have very different equity betas. Offer two reasons why this can occur.
3. For a firm considering expansion of its existing line of business, why is the WACC, rather than the cost of equity, the preferred discount rate if the firm has both debt and equity in its capital structure?
4. The cost of debt, r_D, is generally less than the cost of equity, r_E, because debt is a less risky security. A naive application of the WACC formula might suggest that a firm could lower its cost of capital (thereby raising the NPV of its current and future investments) by using more debt and less equity in its capital structure. Give one reason why using more debt might not reduce a firm's WACC even if $r_D < r_E$.
5. Explain the difference between a levered beta and an unlevered equity beta.

9.2 A CLOSER LOOK AT RISK

JOB INTERVIEW QUESTION

What do you believe the equity risk premium is today? Why?

So far, the only consideration we have given to risk in our capital budgeting analysis is selecting the right discount rate. But it would be simplistic to say that, given a stream of cash flows, an analyst's work is done once he has discounted those cash flows using a risk-adjusted discount rate to determine the NPV. Managers generally want to know more about a project than just its NPV. They want to know the sources of uncertainty and the downside risk as well as the quantitative importance of each source. Managers need this information to decide whether a project requires additional analysis, such as market research or product testing. Managers also want to identify a project's key value drivers so they can closely monitor them after an investment is made.

Break-Even Analysis

When firms make investments, they do so with the objective of earning a profit. But another objective that sometimes enters the decision process is avoiding losses. Therefore, managers often want to know what is required for a project to break even. **Break-even analysis** can be expressed in many different ways. For instance, when a firm introduces

---

[9] Even more recently, Fernandez (2009) asked more than a thousand finance professors from around the world what market risk premium they used in their teaching and consulting. On average, U.S. professors reported a market risk premium of 6.5%.

a new product, it may want to know the level of sales at which incremental net income turns from negative to positive. When evaluating a new product launch over several years, managers might ask what growth rate in sales the firm must achieve in order to reach a project NPV of zero. When considering a decision to replace old production equipment, a firm might calculate the level of production volume needed to generate cost savings equal to the cost of the new equipment.

EXAMPLE

Take another look at Table 9.1, which shows price and cost information for Carbonlite Inc. and Fiberspeed Corp. How many bicycle frames must each firm sell to achieve a break-even point with EBIT equal to zero? We can obtain the answer by dividing fixed costs by the contribution margin, which is the per-unit sales price minus the per-unit variable cost:

Carbonlite break-even point = $5,000,000 ÷ ($1,000 − $400) = 8,333 frames;
Fiberspeed break-even point = $2,000,000 ÷ ($1,000 − $700) = 6,667 frames

Figures 9.3(A) and 9.3(B) illustrate the break-even point for each firm. Despite its $600 contribution margin, Carbonlite's high fixed costs result in a break-even point at higher sales volume than does Fiberspeed's break-even point. This is not surprising, since we already know that Carbonlite's production process results in higher operating leverage than Fiberspeed's.

Break-even analysis is popular among practitioners in part because it gives them clear targets. From break-even calculations, managers can derive specific targets for different functional areas in the firm (e.g., produce at least 10,000 units, gain at least a 5% market

FIGURE 9.3(A)

Break-Even Production Level for Carbonlite

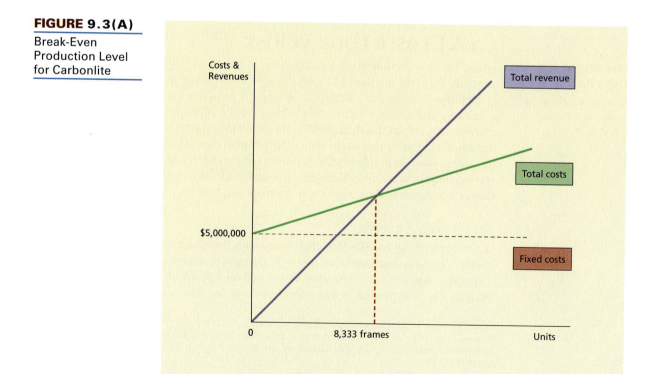

FIGURE 9.3(B)

Break-Even
Production Level
for Fiberspeed

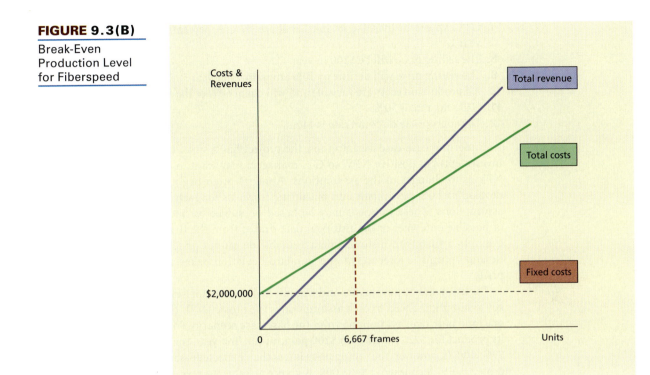

share, hold variable costs to no more than 65% of the selling price). As always, we encourage managers to use break-even analysis in the context of net present values rather than
earnings. A project that reaches the break-even point in terms of net income would still
destroy shareholder value if it does not recover the firm's cost of capital.

Sensitivity Analysis

Most capital budgeting problems require analysts to make many different assumptions
before arriving at a final NPV. For instance, forecasting project cash flows may require
assumptions about the selling price of output, costs of raw materials, market share, and
many other unknown quantities. Managers use **sensitivity analysis** to explore the importance of each individual assumption, holding all other assumptions fixed, on the project's
NPV. A common way of conducting sensitivity analysis is first to establish a "base case"
set of assumptions for a particular project and then to calculate its NPV based on those
assumptions. Next, managers allow one variable to change while holding all others fixed,
recalculating the NPV based on that one change. By repeating this process for all the
uncertain variables in an NPV calculation, managers can see how sensitive the NPV is to
changes in baseline assumptions.

   Imagine that Greene Transportation Incorporated (GTI) has developed a new skateboard equipped with a gyroscope for improved balance. GTI estimates that this project
has a positive NPV of $236,000 under the following base-case assumptions:

1. The project's life is five years.
2. The project requires an up-front investment of $7 million.
3. GTI will depreciate the initial investment on a straight-line basis for five years.
4. One year from now, the skateboard industry will sell 500,000 units.
5. Total industry unit volume will increase by 5% per year.
6. GTI expects to capture 5% of the market in the first year.

7. GTI expects to increase its market share by one percentage point each year after year 1.
8. The selling price will be $200 in year 1.
9. The selling price will decline by 10% annually after year 1.
10. All production costs are variable and will equal 60% of the selling price.
11. GTI's tax rate is 30%.
12. The appropriate discount rate is 14%.

Under the base-case assumptions, the project has a small (relative to the $7 million investment) but positive NPV, so GTI managers may want to explore how sensitive the NPV is to changes in the assumptions. Analysts often begin a sensitivity analysis by developing both pessimistic and optimistic forecasts for each of the model's important assumptions. These forecasts may be based on subjective judgments about the range of possible outcomes or on historical data drawn from the firm's past investments. For example, a firm with historical data available on output prices might set the pessimistic and optimistic forecasts at one standard deviation below and above their expected price.

Table 9.4 shows pessimistic and optimistic forecasts for several of the NPV model's key assumptions. Next to each assumption is the project NPV that results from changing one (and only one) assumption from the base-case scenario. For example, if GTI can sell its product for $225 rather than $200 per unit the first year, the project NPV increases to $960,000. If, however, the selling price is less than expected—say, $175 per unit—then the project NPV declines to −$488,000. A glance at Table 9.4 reveals that small deviations in assumptions about market *share* generate large NPV changes whereas assumptions about market *size* have less impact.

Table 9.4	Sensitivity Analysis of the Gyroscope Skateboard Project (dollar values in thousands except price)			
NPV	**PESSIMISTIC**	**ASSUMPTION**	**OPTIMISTIC**	**NPV**
−$ 558	$8,000	Initial investment	$6,000	$1,030
−$ 343	450,000 units	Market size in year 1	550,000 units	$ 815
−$ 73	2% per year	Growth in market size	8% per year	$ 563
−$1,512	3%	Initial market share	7%	$1,984
−$1,189	0%	Growth in market share	2% per year	$1,661
−$ 488	$175	Initial selling price	$225	$ 960
−$ 54	62% of sales	Variable costs	58% of sales	$ 526
−$ 873	−20% per year	Annual price change	0% per year	$1,612
−$ 115	16%	Discount rate	12%	$ 617

Scenario Analysis and Monte Carlo Simulation

Scenario analysis is a more complex variation on sensitivity analysis. Rather than adjust one assumption up or down, analysts conduct scenario analysis by calculating the project NPV when a whole set of assumptions changes in a particular way. For example, in 2008 many companies wished they had considered a scenario in which simultaneously credit markets freeze up, consumer demand falls, and their stock prices decline by a third. In the GTI example, what if consumer interest in the new skateboard is low, leading to a lower market share and a lower selling price than originally anticipated. If production volume falls short of expectations, cost as a percentage of sales may also be higher than expected.

Developing realistic scenarios requires a great deal of thinking about how an NPV model's assumptions are related to each other. Analysts must ask questions, such as: "If the market doesn't grow as fast as we expect, which other of our assumptions will also probably be wrong?" As with sensitivity analysis, firms often construct a base-case scenario along with more optimistic and pessimistic ones. For instance, consider a worst-case scenario for GTI's new skateboard. Suppose that Murphy's Law kicks in and every pessimistic assumption from Table 9.4 becomes reality. In that case, the project NPV is a disastrous negative $4.9 million. On the other hand, if all the optimistic assumptions turn out to be correct, then the NPV is a positive $11.7 million. Although extreme, these scenarios are still useful in that they illustrate the range of possible NPVs.

There is also an even more sophisticated form of sensitivity analysis. In **Monte Carlo simulation**, analysts specify a range or a distribution of potential outcomes for each of the model's assumptions. For example, a simulation might specify that GTI's skateboard price is a random variable drawn from a normal distribution with a mean of $200 and a standard deviation of $30. Similarly, the analyst could dictate that the skateboard might achieve an initial market share anywhere between 1% and 10%, with each outcome being equally likely (i.e., a uniform distribution). It is even possible to specify the degree of correlation between key variables. The model could be structured in such a way that when the demand for skateboards is unusually high, the likelihood of obtaining a high price increases.

Analysts enter all the assumptions about distributions of possible outcomes into a spreadsheet. Next, a simulation software package takes random "draws" from these distributions, calculating the project's cash flows (and perhaps its NPV) over and over again under different scenarios perhaps thousands of times. After completing these calculations, the software package produces statistical output that includes the distribution of project cash flows (and NPVs) as well as sensitivity figures for each of the model's assumptions.

The use of Monte Carlo simulation has grown dramatically over the past 20 years because of steep declines in the costs of computer power and simulation software.[10] Unfortunately, misuse of simulation analysis has grown as well.

One common mistake is using of the cost of capital to calculate the NPVs from the project cash flows generated in the simulation. The NPVs should be calculated using the risk-free rate to discount cash flows. Why not discount cash flows at the cost of capital? The reason is that discounting at the cost of capital takes into account the risk of the project's expected cash flows; and when a simulation model calculates an NPV, the cash flows represent just one outcome drawn from a large distribution of possible outcomes, not their expected value. Therefore, plotting an entire distribution of NPVs calculated using the cost of capital as the discount rate and then measuring its return and risk by the distribution's mean and variance, respectively, double-counts risk: first in the discount rate and then in the variance of the distribution. A better approach is to calculate NPVs

---

[10]Just a few of the companies that we know have used Monte Carlo simulation include Merck, Intel, Procter & Gamble, General Motors, Pfizer, Owens-Corning, and Cummins Engine.

using the risk-free rate, thereby making the distribution of NPVs free of any prior risk adjustment. As a result, the variance of that distribution more accurately measures the risk of the project.

Interpreting a distribution of NPVs calculated using the risk-free rate has its own problems. For example, analysts who draw inferences about risk by looking at the variance of such a distribution may then fail to consider the opportunities that shareholders have to eliminate some of the risk through diversification.[11] Clearly, the variance of the simulated distribution of one project's NPVs can be reduced by joining it with another project and then rerunning the simulation. If an examination of NPV distributions is part of a firm's project approval process, then employees will soon learn to propose joint projects that have less variability than stand-alone investments.

The bottom line is that Monte Carlo simulation is a powerful, effective tool when used properly. Using simulation to explore the distribution of a project's cash flows—and the major sources of risk driving that distribution—is sensible, but be wary of NPV distributions produced by a simulation program.

Decision Trees

Most important investment decisions are much more complex than simply forecasting cash flows, discounting at the appropriate rate, and investing if the NPV exceeds zero. In the real world, managers face a sequence of future decisions that influence an investment's value. These decisions might include whether to expand or abandon a project, whether to alter a marketing program, when to upgrade manufacturing equipment, and, most important, how to respond to the actions of competitors. A **decision tree** is a visual representation of the choices that managers face over time with regard to a particular investment. Sketching out a decision tree is somewhat like thinking several moves ahead in a game of chess. The value of decision trees is that they force analysts to think through a series of *if–then* statements that describe how they will react as the future unfolds.

Imagine that Trinkle Foods Limited of Canada has invented a new salt substitute, Odessa, that it plans to use in snack foods such as potato chips and crackers. The company is trying to decide whether to spend 5 million Canadian dollars (C$) to test-market in Vancouver, British Columbia, a new line of potato chips flavored with Odessa. Depending on the outcome of that test, Trinkle may spend an additional C$50 million one year later to launch a full line of snack foods across Canada. If consumer acceptance in Vancouver is high, the company predicts that its full product line will generate net cash inflows of C$12 million per year for 10 years.[12] If consumers in Vancouver respond less favorably, Trinkle expects cash inflows from a nationwide launch to be just C$2 million per year for 10 years. Trinkle's cost of capital is 15%.

Figure 9.4 shows the decision tree for this problem. Initially, the firm can choose whether or not to spend the C$5 million on test-marketing. If Trinkle goes ahead with the market test, it estimates the probability of high and low consumer acceptance to be 50%. After the company sees the test results, it will decide whether to invest C$50 million for a major product launch.

The proper way to work through a decision tree is to begin at the end and work backward to the initial decision. Suppose that Trinkle learns one year from now that the

---

[11]Note that calculating a single NPV using the WACC or another appropriate discount rate does not suffer from this problem because the discount rate selected depends on the project's beta, a measure of its systematic risk.

[12]Note that the test begins immediately, the C$50 million investment starts one year later, and the stream of C$12 million annual cash inflows begins one year after that.

FIGURE 9.4

Decision Tree for
Odessa Investment

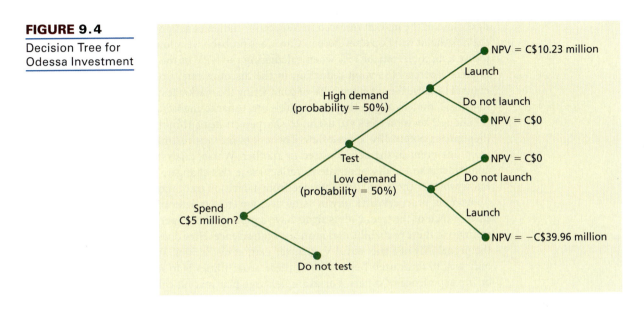

Vancouver market test was successful. At that point, the NPV (in millions of Canadian dollars) of launching the product can be determined as follows:

$$\text{NPV} = -\text{C\$50} + \frac{\text{C\$12}}{(1.15)^1} + \frac{\text{C\$12}}{(1.15)^2} + \frac{\text{C\$12}}{(1.15)^3} + \cdots + \frac{\text{C\$12}}{(1.15)^{10}} = \text{C\$10.23}$$

Clearly, Trinkle will invest if it winds up in this part of the decision tree, but what if initial test results are unfavorable and it still launches the product? In that situation, the NPV is

$$\text{NPV} = -\text{C\$50} + \frac{\text{C\$2}}{(1.15)^1} + \frac{\text{C\$2}}{(1.15)^2} + \frac{\text{C\$2}}{(1.15)^3} + \cdots + \frac{\text{C\$2}}{(1.15)^{10}} = -\text{C\$39.96}$$

Thus, the product should not launch if the test marketing is unfavorable. The best decision to make if the initial test does not go well is to walk away. After the test has been done, its cost is a sunk cost. As of time 1, the NPV of doing nothing is zero.

Now we have a set of simple if–then decision rules that come from the decision tree. If initial test results indicate high consumer acceptance of Odessa, then Trinkle should go ahead with the full product launch to capture a positive NPV of C$10.23 million. But if initial results show that consumers do not like foods flavored with Odessa, Trinkle should not invest the additional C$50 million.

With this information in hand, we now step back and evaluate the project at time 0. We can evaluate today's decision about whether or not to spend the C$5 million on testing. Recall that we calculated the NPVs in terms of year-1 dollars—that is, as of the date of the decision on whether or not to launch the product nationwide. In terms of today's Canadian dollars (millions), the expected NPV of conducting the market test is determined to be

$$\text{NPV} = -\text{C\$5} + 0.5\left(\frac{\text{C\$10.23}}{1.15}\right) + 0.5\left(\frac{\text{C\$0}}{1.15}\right) = -\text{C\$0.55}$$

Spending the money for test-marketing does not appear to be worthwhile. However, there is a subtle flaw in our analysis. Can you spot it? At the present time, when Trinkle must decide whether or not to invest in test-marketing, it does not know what the test results (unavailable for another year) will indicate. So at the end of one year, when the firm chooses whether or not to invest C$50 million for a major product launch, it knows a great deal more. If the market research in Vancouver indicates a high demand for Odessa, then the risk that it will flop elsewhere in Canada is probably very low. If so, does it make sense to use a discount rate of 15% when calculating the NPV of the product launch decision? A mere 1-percentage-point reduction in the discount rate, from 15% to 14%, would be enough to cause the expected NPV of conducting the market test to increase from −C$0.55 to C$0.52, thereby suggesting that Trinkle's test-marketing *would* be worthwhile.

Though decision trees are useful to sharpen strategic thinking, the previous example illustrates a potentially serious flaw. The risk of many investments changes as you move from one point in the decision tree to another. Worse, analysts rarely attempt to make adjustments to the discount rate to reflect these risk changes. This makes it difficult to know whether the final NPV obtained from a decision tree is correct.

Another practical difficulty in using decision trees is determining the probabilities for each branch of the tree. Unless firms have a great deal of experience with similar "bets," estimating these probabilities is more art than science. How does Trinkle Foods know that the probability of a successful Vancouver market test is 50%? Why not 80% or 10%? The only way to form useful estimates of these probabilities is to rely on experience—yours or the experience of others. For example, large pharmaceutical companies have enough experience investing in potential drug compounds to make reasonable estimates of the odds that any particular drug will make it to market.

Concept Review Questions	6. Why might a project that reaches the break-even point in terms of net income be bad for shareholders?
	7. Which variable do you think would be more valuable to examine in a project sensitivity analysis: the growth rate of sales or the allowable depreciation deductions each year? Explain.
	8. You work for an airline that is considering a proposal to offer a new, nonstop flight between Atlanta and Tokyo. Senior management asks a team of analysts to run a Monte Carlo simulation of the project. Your job is to advise the group on what assumptions they should put in the simulation regarding the distribution of the ticket price your airline will be able to charge. How would you go about this task?
	9. Why might the discount rate vary as you move through a decision tree?

9.3 REAL OPTIONS

Why NPV Doesn't Always Give the Right Answer

Only a few decades ago, the net present value method was essentially absent from the world of corporate practice. Today it has become the standard tool for evaluating capital investments, especially in very large firms. Even so, NPV can systematically overstate or understate the value of certain types of investments. These systematic errors occur because the NPV method is essentially static. That is, NPV calculations do not take into account actions by managers to increase the value of an investment once it has been made. When managers can react to changes in the environment in ways that alter an investment's value, we say that the investment has an embedded **real option**. A real option is the right, but not the obligation, to take a future action that changes an investment's value. We will present an in-depth analysis of how option pricing techniques can be used to improve capital budgeting processes in Chapters 18 and 19, so only an overview is presented here. Hopefully, this will be enough to convince you that identifying and valuing—even if only

JOB INTERVIEW QUESTION

Under what conditions might an NPV calculation recommend the wrong investment decision?

conceptually—the real options embedded in most capital investment projects can help managers make better investment decisions.[13]

A simple example shows where NPV can go wrong. Suppose you are bidding on the rights to extract oil from a proven site over the next year. You expect extraction costs to run about $65 per barrel. Say that currently oil sells for $60 per barrel. You know that oil prices fluctuate over time, but you have no unique ability to predict where the price of oil is headed next. So you assume that the price of oil follows a **random walk**, which means prices wander aimlessly—they have no connection to past price changes and no tendency to return to a mean value over time. In this case, your best estimate of the future price of oil is simply today's price. How much would you bid?

An NPV analysis would tell you not to bid at all. If your best forecast of the future price of oil is $60 per barrel, then you cannot make money when extraction costs are $65 per barrel. The expected NPV of this investment is negative no matter how much oil you can pump out of the ground.

A real options approach to the problem yields a different answer. If you own the rights to extract oil, you are not obligated to do so if the price is too low. You reason that you will pump oil only when the market price is high enough to justify incurring the extraction costs. Predicting exactly when the price of oil will be high enough to make pumping profitable is impossible, but historical price fluctuations persuade you that the price of oil will be higher than extraction costs at least some of the time. Therefore, extraction rights at this site are worth more than zero.[14]

The oil extraction problem is analogous to the test-marketing problem in the previous section. In both cases, managers have the option of spending additional resources at a future date. These options add to a project's value in a way that NPV analysis often ignores because of its static approach to decision making. In general, we can say that the value of a project equals the sum of two components, the part captured by NPV and the remaining value of real options:

$$\text{Project value} = \text{NPV} \pm \text{Option value}$$

The NPV may either understate or overstate a project's value, depending on whether the proposed investment creates or destroys future options for the firm. In the oil drilling example, buying extraction rights creates an option—to pump or not to pump oil in the future—and the NPV understates the investment's value. But it is just as easy to imagine projects that eliminate options rather than create them. For instance, by signing a long-term contract to supply a refinery with a certain quantity of crude oil each month, a firm loses its flexibility in the extraction decision.

Types of Real Options

Like Monte Carlo simulation, real options analysis is growing in popularity in many industries. We now turn to a description of common types of real options encountered in capital budgeting decisions: expansion, follow-on investment, abandonment, and flexibility options.

---

[13]Brennan and Schwartz (1985) wrote a pathbreaking paper that demonstrated how option pricing concepts can be used to describe embedded real options. The authors applied option pricing theory to the operation of a mine and described optimal decision rules for when to reopen a closed mine or to shut down a mine that is currently operating. Seventeen years later, Moel and Tufano (2002) showed that managers do indeed seem to make decisions about opening and closing mines in the manner predicted by Brennan and Schwartz.

[14]To determine exactly how much these rights are worth, we must use techniques covered in later chapters. Those chapters also highlight that the inputs used in real options techniques can be difficult to determine in some situations, which helps explain the continued popularity of NPV techniques.

Expansion Options

Expansion Options   What do companies do when one of their investments becomes a huge success? They look for new markets in which to expand that investment. For instance, once Blu-Ray technology gained significant popularity, consumers could rent Blu-Ray DVDs in video stores, grocery stores, and many other places where they were previously unavailable. Likewise for Blu-Ray players: the number of retail outlets selling these players also expanded dramatically.

Naturally, companies invest in expansion only for their most successful investments. As mentioned in the decision-tree problem, the risk of expanding an already successful project is much less than the risk when the project first begins. An NPV calculation misses both of these attributes—the opportunity to expand or not depending on initial success, and the change in risk that occurs when the initial outcome is favorable.

Follow-on Investment Options   A *follow-on* investment option is similar to an expansion option. It entitles a firm to make additional investments should earlier investments prove to be successful. The difference between this and the expansion option is that here the subsequent investments are more complex than a simple expansion of the earlier ones.

Hollywood offers an excellent example of follow-on options. Did you know that the rights to movie sequels are sometimes bought and sold before the original movie is completed? By purchasing the right to produce a sequel, a studio obtains the opportunity to make an additional investment should the first film become a commercial success.

Abandonment Options   Just as firms may invest additional resources to expand projects that enjoy early success, they also may withdraw resources from projects that fail to live up to short-run expectations. In an extreme case, a company may decide to withdraw its entire commitment to a particular project and exercise its *option to abandon*.

In legal systems that provide limited liability to corporations, shareholders have the ultimate abandonment option. A firm may borrow money to finance its operations, but if it cannot generate cash flow sufficient to pay back its debts then management may declare bankruptcy, turn over the company's assets to its lenders, and let the shareholders walk away. Though declaring bankruptcy is not what shareholders hope for when they invest, it protects them against personal liability for a firm's debts. Put another way, investors who buy shares are willing to pay a little more because of the embedded option to abandon (in this case, the *default option*) than they would be willing to pay without that option. We can express this mathematically as follows:

$$\text{Share value} = \text{NPV} + \text{Value of default option}$$

Consider the same situation from the lender's perspective. When lenders commit funds to a corporation, they know that the borrower may default and that the lenders' ability to recover the associated losses does not extend to the shareholders' personal assets. We could even say that an investor who buys a bond from a corporation is simultaneously selling an option to the firm—the option to default. So the price paid by the investor for the bond is effectively net of the proceeds from the option to default. Notice that an option to default is essentially absent in U.S. Treasury securities. Suppose that a Treasury bond and a corporate bond offer the same interest payments to investors. Which one would sell at a higher price?

$$\text{Corporate bond value} = \text{Treasury bond value} - \text{Value of firm's default option}$$

Abandonment options crop up in unexpected places, and it is important for managers to recognize whether a given investment has an attached abandonment option or grants another party the right to abandon. Consider refundable and nonrefundable airline tickets. With a refundable ticket, the traveler has the right to abandon travel plans without incurring a penalty. Such a ticket is more valuable than one that requires a traveler to pay a penalty if plans change.

Flexibility Options   Other options that have recently come to prominence in capital budgeting analyses are collectively known as flexibility options. Three examples illustrate the nature of flexibility options. First, the ability to use multiple production inputs creates option value. An example of such *input flexibility* is a boiler that can switch between oil or gas as a fuel source, enabling managers to switch from one type of fuel to another as prices change. Second, having a flexible production technology capable of producing (and switching between) a variety of outputs using the same basic plant and equipment can be useful. This type of *output/operating flexibility* creates value when output prices are volatile.

Finally, option value can be created by maintaining excess production capacity that can be quickly utilized to meet peak demand. Though costly to purchase and maintain, this *capacity flexibility* can be quite valuable in capital-intensive industries subject to wide swings in demand and long lead times for building new capacity. For example, consider the profit opportunities a multinational company can employ if it has the excess capacity needed to move production around the world in response to movements in the real exchange rate.

The Surprising Link between Risk and Real Option Values

Until now, every valuation problem covered in this text satisfies the following statement: Holding other factors constant, an increase in an asset's risk decreases its price. If two bonds offer the same coupon but investors perceive one to be riskier than the other, then the safer bond will sell at a higher price. If two investment projects have identical cash flows but one is riskier, then analysts will discount the cash flows of the riskier project at a higher rate, resulting in a lower NPV.

A surprising fact is that this relationship does not hold for options. For an explanation, we go back to the oil extraction problem. The current price of oil is $60 per barrel and extraction costs are $65. The expected future price of oil is the same as the current price, so an NPV calculation would say that this investment is worthless.

Consider two different scenarios regarding the future price of oil. In the low-risk scenario, the price of oil in the future will be $64 or $56, with each price equally probable. This means that the expected price of oil is still $60. However, both an NPV and an options analysis would conclude that bidding on the rights to this site is not a good idea because the price of oil will never be above the extraction cost.

Next, think about the high-risk scenario. The price of oil may be $75 or $45 with equal probability, so again we have an expected price of $60. If the price turns out to be $45, extracting the oil clearly does not make sense. But if the price turns out to be $75, extracting oil generates a profit of $10 per barrel. Therefore, a real options analysis would say that bidding for the right to extract the oil is a sensible decision.

Why does more risk lead to higher option values? Observe that in these two scenarios the payoff from extracting oil equals zero whether the price of oil falls to $56 or all the way to $45. At either price, an oil producer would simply decline to incur extraction costs; thus, a huge decrease in the price of oil is no more costly than a small decrease. On the other hand, the payoffs on the upside increase as the price of oil rises. This all means that options are characterized by *asymmetric payoffs*. When the price of oil is extremely volatile, the potential benefits if prices rise are quite large. Yet if oil prices fall precipitously then there is no additional cost relative to a slight decline in prices, since in either case the payoff is zero.

9.4 Strategy and Capital Budgeting

Competition and NPV

Finance textbooks tend to focus on the mechanics of project evaluation: how to calculate an NPV or IRR, how to estimate cash flows, how to select the right discount rate, and so on. This emphasis on technique is not entirely misplaced. Knowing how to apply quantitative discipline to the project selection process is crucial. Nevertheless, experienced managers rarely make major investment decisions based solely on NPV calculations. The best managers have a well-honed intuition that tells them why a particular project would or would not be a good investment. Their business acumen helps them to recognize projects that will create shareholder value, even if the NPV numbers from financial analysts are negative, and to avoid investments that will destroy value, even when the NPV calculations are positive.

No textbook can adequately substitute for the invaluable experience of making many investment decisions over several years and then watching some of them succeed and others fail. However, there are certain common characteristics shared by projects that enhance shareholder value.

Recall some of the most basic lessons from microeconomics about a perfectly competitive market. In such a market, there are many buyers and sellers trading a similar product or service. Because the number of agents is small relative to the whole market, each agent acts as a "price taker." Competition and the lack of entry or exit barriers ensures that the product's market price equals the marginal cost of producing it, and no firm earns pure economic profit.[15] In a market with zero economic profits, the NPV of any investment equals zero: every project earns just enough to recover the cost of capital, no more and no less.

Therefore, if we want to form an intuitive judgment about whether or not an investment proposal should have a positive NPV (before actually calculating it), we must identify ways in which the project deviates from the perfectly competitive ideal. For instance, if the proposal calls for production of a new good, is there something about this good that clearly differentiates it from similar goods already in the market? If the new product is genuinely unique, will the firm producing this good be able to erect some kind of entry barrier that will prevent other firms from producing their own, nearly identical versions of the product, competition that will eventually preclude any pure economic profits?

Competitive advantages of this sort can come in many forms. One firm may have superior engineering or R&D talent that generates a continuous stream of innovative products. Another may excel at low-cost manufacturing processes. Still another may create a sustainable competitive advantage through its unique marketing programs. The main point is that

---

[15]Remember that the notion of "economic profit" is very different from accounting profit. If a firm makes a zero economic profit then it earns just enough to pay competitive prices for the labor and capital that it employs to produce a good or service.

if any project is to have a positive NPV, then advocates of that project should be able to articulate its competitive advantage even before "running the numbers." No matter how positive the project's NPV appears to be on paper, if no one can explain its main competitive advantage in the market then the firm should probably think twice about investing. Similarly, when an investment proposal has a compelling reason for its competitive edge but the NPV numbers come out negative, it may be worth sending the financial analysts back to their desks to take a second look at their assumptions.

We want to emphasize here that, although the numbers are extremely important, they should line up with experienced intuition. When the two are in conflict, managers need to think hard about whether the NPV model is in error or whether the project lacks a true competitive advantage.

Strategic Thinking and Real Options

We conclude this chapter with a return to the topic of real options. The technical aspects of calculating the real option value of a given project can be quite complex. Real options techniques are still relatively new and are used extensively by firms in only a few industries. Though we expect an increasing number of firms to include real options analysis as part of their standard capital budgeting approach, we believe that just thinking about a project from a real options perspective can be valuable even if coming up with a dollar value for a real option proves to be elusive.

Investments generally have option value as long as they are not "all or nothing" bets. Almost all investments fit this description. Managers usually have opportunities subsequent to the initial investment to make decisions that can increase or decrease the value of the investment—decisions that create (or destroy) an investment's option value. To maximize, or at least recognize, an investment's option value, managers should try to describe—before the firm commits to an investment—all the subsequent decisions they will make as events unfold. In other words, managers must articulate their strategy for a given investment. This strategy may consist of a series of statements like these:

- *If sales in the first year exceed our expectations, then we plan to commit another $50 million to ramp up production.*
- *If consumers enjoy sending and receiving files on their cell phones, then we will be prepared to invest additional resources so that our cell phones will be capable of performing other tasks on the Internet.*
- *If our MP3 player cannot hold as many songs as the leading model, then the unit must weigh at least one ounce less than the market leader or we will not commit the resources necessary to manufacture it.*

Such a series of if–then statements is necessary to value a real option, but it also has intangible value in that it forces managers to think through their strategic options before they invest. Identifying a real option is tantamount to identifying future points at which it may be possible for managers to create and sustain competitive advantages.

Concept Review Question	12. Why must manager intuition be part of the investment decision process regardless of a project's NPV (or IRR)? Why is it helpful to think about real options when making an investment decision?

SUMMARY

- All-equity firms can discount their "standard" investment projects at the cost of equity. Managers can estimate the cost of equity using the CAPM.

- The cost of equity is influenced by a firm's operating leverage as well as its financial leverage.

- Firms with both debt and equity in their capital structures can discount their "standard" investments using the company-wide weighted average cost of capital, or WACC.

- The WACC is the company-wide weighted average of the cost of each source of financing used by a firm, where the weights are equal to the proportion of the market value represented by each source of financing.

- A company's WACC and CAPM are connected in that the cost of debt and equity (and any other financing source) are driven by the betas of the firm's debt and equity.

- If a firm wants to make an "unusual" investment—an investment outside its normal line of business—then it should try to estimate the asset beta for the industry by examining pure-play firms.

- To estimate the asset beta for a different industry, an analyst first must unlever the equity beta of any pure-play firm that uses debt. Then she must relever the industry asset beta based on her firm's existing capital structure.

- Several tools exist to assist managers in understanding the sources of uncertainty in a project's cash flows. These tools include break-even analysis, sensitivity analysis, scenario analysis, Monte Carlo simulation, and decision trees.

- The value of many investments includes not just the NPV but also the investment's option value. As a static analytical tool, NPV analysis often misses the value of management's ability to alter an investment in response to environmental changes that may occur after it is made.

- Types of real options include the option to expand, the option to make follow-on investments, the option to abandon, and flexibility options.

- An investment's option value, unlike its NPV, increases as risk increases.

- For an investment to have a positive NPV, it should have a competitive advantage—something that distinguishes it from the economic ideal of perfect competition.

- Valuing an investment's option value requires strategic thinking. Articulating the strategy may be as important as calculating the project's value.

KEY TERMS

asset beta	Monte Carlo simulation	sensitivity analysis
break-even analysis	operating leverage	unlevered equity beta
contribution margin	pure play	weighted average cost of capital
debt beta	random walk	(WACC)
decision tree	real option	
financial leverage	scenario analysis	

QUESTIONS

9-1. When a project's discount rate is based on the firm's beta, why is it important that the project not alter the firm's risk profile?

9-2. Does the tax rate affect a firm's operating leverage?

9-3. Explain when firms should discount projects using the cost of equity. When should they use the WACC instead? When should they use neither?

9-4. If a firm takes actions that increase its operating leverage, we might expect to see an increase in its equity beta. Why?

9-5. Suppose two computer manufacturers produce and sell very similar machines. One company sells its computers through nationwide electronics chain stores, the other sells via its own network of stores. Which of these sales/distribution strategies results in higher operating leverage?

9-6. Why do you think it is important to use the market values of debt and equity, rather than their book values, when calculating a firm's WACC?

9-7. Assuming that there are no corporate income taxes, what is the connection between a firm's WACC and its asset beta?

9-8. What is the relationship between the size of a firm's debt beta and the total amount of debt the firm borrows?

9-9. Suppose that two firms have identical asset betas but very different equity betas. Why might this be so?

9-10. Many high-tech companies use the following compensation strategy to attract key talent: They offer a relatively low base salary (low relative to what employees with a given level of experience and training might earn in another industry) augmented by large incentive-pay packages, including cash bonuses and stock options. Presumably, there is a trade-off at work in the labor market such that high-tech firms could attract the same employees by offering a higher base and lower incentive pay. Which of these two strategies would lead to a higher stock beta, assuming other factors are held constant?

9-11. What is the relationship between the equity risk premium and the aggregate value of the stock market? If the equity risk premium declined suddenly (holding all other factors constant), what would happen to the value of the stock market?

9-12. In what sense could one argue that, if managers make decisions using break-even analysis, then they are not maximizing shareholder wealth? How can break-even analysis be modified to solve this problem?

9-13. Explain the differences between *sensitivity analysis* and *scenario analysis*. Offer an argument for the proposition that scenario analysis offers a more realistic picture of a project's risk than does sensitivity analysis.

9-14. In Chapter 8, we discussed how one might calculate the NPV of earning an MBA. Suppose you are asked to perform a sensitivity analysis on the MBA decision. Which of the following factors do you think would have the greatest impact on the degree's NPV?

   a. The ranking of the school you choose to attend

   b. Your choice of a major

   c. Your GPA

   d. The state of the job market when you graduate

9-15. Suppose that you wanted to model the value of an MBA degree with decision trees. What would such a decision tree look like?

9-16. If you decide to invest in an MBA, what is your follow-on investment option? Your abandonment option?

9-17. Your company is selling the mineral rights to several hundred acres of land it owns that are believed to contain silver deposits. The current price of silver is $5 per ounce but, of course, future prices are uncertain. Would you expect the mineral rights to sell for more or for less if investors believe that silver prices will be more volatile in the future than they have been in the past? Explain.

9-18. Why might an oil company lease land with reserves that will cost $55.00 a barrel to extract when the current price of oil is only $52.50 a barrel? (Assume that the price of oil is fairly volatile.)

PROBLEMS

Choosing the Right Discount Rate

9-1. Puritan Motors has a capital structure consisting almost entirely of equity.

   a. If the beta of Puritan stock equals 1.6, the risk-free rate equals 6%, and the expected return on the market portfolio equals 11%, then what is the cost of equity?

   b. Suppose that a 1% increase in expected inflation causes a 1% increase in the risk-free rate. Holding all other factors constant, what will this do to the firm's cost of equity? Is it reasonable to hold all other factors constant? What other part of the calculation of the cost of equity is likely to change if expected inflation rises?

9-2. Download historical stock price data for the pharmaceutical industry giant, Merck (ticker symbol, MRK). Be sure to check the box indicating that you want monthly data, and use September 1, 1999, as your start date and September 1, 2008, as your end date.

Retrieve data from Yahoo! and download it into an Excel spreadsheet. (The file downloads in "comma delimited" format with a .csv file extension; but once you have the data, save it as an Excel file with the familiar .xls file extension.) Repeat this process using exactly the same settings (e.g., monthly data using the same starting and ending dates) and the ticker symbol SPY, which stands for Standard & Poor's Depository Receipts (SPDRs), commonly called *Spiders*. Returns on SPDRs will closely approximate returns on the S&P 500 index, our proxy for the market portfolio in this problem.

a. Calculate the monthly return on Merck by dividing the adjusted closing price in any particular month by the adjusted closing price the previous month and then subtracting 1. This should yield 108 monthly returns for Merck (you can calculate returns in only 108 of the 109 months, because the previous month's price is needed to calculate the current month's return).

b. Calculate the monthly return on the S&P 500 Index the same way. Paste the returns on the S&P and the returns on Merck into a single spreadsheet (use the "Paste-Special-Values" sequence in Excel).

c. You will run a regression in Excel using the returns on Merck as the dependent (Y) variable and using returns on the S&P 500 as the independent (X) variable. There are two ways to do this. You can use the data analysis function under the Data menu. Click "Data—Data Analysis Regression" to set up the regression. Type in the cell range containing Merck returns for the input Y range; and type in the cell range containing the S&P returns for the input X range.

(The other way to estimate a regression in Excel is to use the "linest" function. We refer the reader to Excel's Help feature for more information on that function.)

The figure to the right of the label "X Variable 1" is the slope of the regression line, and it represents Merck's equity beta. Does it surprise you that Merck's equity beta is less than 1.0? What economic rationale can you give for this finding?

d. Suppose that the risk-free rate is 5% and that the expected return on the market is 10%. What is Merck's cost of equity? Assuming Merck's capital structure is virtually 100% equity, what is its WACC?

e. Now go back and repeat the steps necessary to download monthly data for General Electric (ticker symbol, GE). Calculate monthly returns on GE stock as before, pair them up with monthly returns on the S&P 500 Index, and then use regression analysis to estimate GE's beta. Given that GE is a highly diversified conglomerate, what would you expect GE's beta to be before estimating it? Does your estimate confirm your intuition?

Operating and Financial Leverage

See the problem and solution explained step-by-step at SMARTFinance

9-3. In its 2008 annual report, The Coca-Cola Company reported sales of $31.9 billion for fiscal year 2008 and $28.9 billion for fiscal year 2007. The company also reported operating income (roughly equivalent to EBIT) of $8.4 billion and $7.2 billion in 2008 and 2007, respectively. Meanwhile, arch-rival PepsiCo, Inc. reported sales of $43.2 billion in 2008 and $39.5 billion in 2007. PepsiCo's operating profit was

$6.9 billion in 2008 and $7.2 billion in 2007. Based on these figures, which company had higher operating leverage?

9-4. Suppose a firm's EBIT increases by 12% after sales change from $2.3 million to $2.507 million. What is the firm's operating leverage? If the firm's sales increase to $2.7577 million with EBIT increasing by only 11%, what is the new operating leverage for the firm?

9-5. A firm has no debt and a tax rate of 40%. If the net income changes from $2.5 million to $2.75 million based on a net profit margin of 10% (see Chapter 2), then what is the firm's operating leverage? Suppose the net profit margin goes down to 9% when the net income increases to $2.75 million. What is the new operating leverage?

9-6. A certain firm has fixed costs of $4.5 million with variable costs of $295 per unit. If each unit sells for $450, what is the firm's break-even point? Currently, the firm sells 32,000 units per year, but it believes that 60,000 units per year could be sold if the selling price were lowered to $385 per unit. What is the operating leverage for the firm, and what is its new break-even point?

9-7. ASIC Inc. has assets worth $6.9 million. Two million dollars is financed with debt that costs 10% a year in interest. If ASIC's contribution margin is $175 per unit, then how many units must be sold to cover the interest payments? If ASIC sells 2,500 units this year, how much return on a pre-tax basis (i.e., return based on earnings before taxes) do shareholders receive? How much pre-tax return would they receive if ASIC had no debt?

9-8. Firms A and B have the same asset base of $65 million. Firm A has $20 million of debt that costs 8% annually in interest, and Firm B has $10 million in debt that costs 7% interest annually. Determine the shareholder pre-tax return for both firms based on EBIT values of $0.5 million, $1.0 million, $1.6 million, $3.2 million, and $6.8 million. If Firm C has assets identical to Firms A and B but has no debt, then at what EBIT levels do Firm C's shareholders have an advantage (in terms of pre-tax return) over Firm A's and Firm B's shareholders?

Choosing the Right Cost of Capital

9-9. A firm has an equity multiplier of 2.0 (see Chapter 2). The firm's debt pays 12% interest annually, and common shareholders demand an 18% return. Assuming a 34% tax rate, what is the weighted average cost of capital (WACC) for the firm?

9-10. A firm has a debt-to-equity ratio of 1.0. If we assume that the firm's debt pays 11% interest annually, the equity has a 19% annual return, and the tax rate is 40%, then what is the firm's WACC?

9-11. A firm has an asset base with a market value of $5.3 million. Its debt is worth $2.5 million. If $0.2 million is paid in interest annually and the shareholders expect a 16% annual return, what is the weighted average cost of capital assuming no corporate taxes? What is the WACC if corporate taxes are 45%?

9-12. The risk-free rate equals 5%, and the expected risk premium on the market portfolio equals 6%. A particular company has bonds outstanding that offer investors a yield to maturity of 6.5%. What is the debt beta?

9-13. The risk-free rate equals 5%, and the expected risk premium on the market portfolio equals 6%. A particular company has bonds outstanding that offer investors a yield to maturity of 6.5%. The company also has common stock outstanding (with market value equal to its bonds outstanding) with an expected return of 15%. What is the firm's WACC? What is the beta of the firm's assets? You may assume there are no taxes.

9-14. A firm's assets have a beta of 1.0. Assuming that the debt beta equals 0.0 and that there are no taxes, calculate the firm's equity beta under the following assumptions:
  a. The firm's capital structure is 100% equity.
  b. The capital structure is 20% debt and 80% equity.
  c. The capital structure is 40% debt and 60% equity.
  d. The capital structure is 60% debt and 40% equity.
  e. The capital structure is 80% debt and 20% equity.
  Do you believe that the assumption of a zero debt beta is equally valid for each of these capital structures? Why or why not?

Smart
Solutions
*See the problem and
solution explained step-by-
step at* SMARTFinance

9-15. A diversified firm with investments in many industries is considering investing in the fast-food industry. By looking at data on publicly traded fast-food companies, an analyst discovers the following information for McDonald's Corporation and Wendy's International Inc.
  • The expected return on the market portfolio is 10%.
  • The debt beta for McDonald's and Wendy's is zero.
  • The corporate tax rate is 34%.
  • The equity betas are 0.8 for Wendy's and 1.0 for McDonald's.
  • The debt-to-equity ratio is 0.15 for Wendy's and 0.25 for McDonald's.
  • The risk-free rate is 5%.
  Calculate the asset beta for McDonald's and Wendy's, and illustrate how these could be used to calculate the discount rate for an investment in the fast-food business.

9-16. Belmont Corp. (BNT) has stock that currently sells for $14.17, with a current dividend of $0.65. Assume that BNT's return on equity (ROE) is 12% and that the retention ratio is 75% (see Chapter 4 to determine how this information is used to calculate a growth rate). What is the discount rate implied by this stock price?

9-17. Allied Sales Force (ASF) expects to distribute a dividend of $0.77 (up from $0.70). The current price of ASF stock is $15.40. What is the implied discount rate based on the stock price? Assuming an expected market return of 18% and a risk-free rate of 3%, what is the beta associated with the implied discount rate? Assuming the firm has no debt and a 42% tax rate, what is the firm's equity beta? (Use Equation 9.6.)

9-18. A particular firm has an asset beta of 1.50 with a debt ratio of 60% and a tax rate of 30%. Use Equation 9.6 to answer these questions:
  a. What is the equity beta for this firm?
  b. Based on this equity beta, what is the asset beta for a different firm with a debt ratio of 50% and a tax rate of 40%?

9-19. The asset beta for a particular industry is 0.75. Use Equation 9.6 to estimate the equity betas for the following three firms based on their respective debt ratios and tax rates. Then calculate each firm's cost of equity assuming an expected market premium of 6% and a risk-free rate of 4%.
    Firm A: 75% debt ratio and 35% tax rate
    Firm B: 20% debt ratio and 38% tax rate
    Firm C: 80% debt ratio and 45% tax rate

A Closer Look at Risk

9-20. Alliance Pneumatic Manufacturing, a producer of specialty machine tools, has fixed costs of $200 million per year. Across all the firm's products, the average contribution margin equals $1,200. What is Alliance's break-even point in terms of units sold?

9-21. Refer to the values in Table 9.4. Determine which of the following has the greater impact on the NPV of the gyroscope skateboard project: a 10% increase (over the base case) in the initial selling price or a 10% increase in the year-1 market size.

9-22. T. Nixon Enterprises (TNXN) sells its product for $3.99 per unit. The product costs $1.42 per unit to produce, not including any fixed costs. Assuming fixed costs of $4 million, what is the break-even point? If TNXN projects sales of 1.5 million units at the current price, will TNXN be profitable? TNXN is considering lowering the unit price to $3.49, which would boost projected sales to 2.2 million units. Based on the break-even point, is this a better option?

9-23. E. Craft Industries (ECR) is considering entry into a new market in which it believes it can sell 500,000 units of product. Depending on where ECR chooses to manufacture this product, the fixed costs and the contribution margin will vary. Determine the profitability [i.e., (Units × Contribution margin) − Fixed costs] of each of the following manufacturing facilities.

Facility X: $4.67 contribution margin with fixed costs of $2 million
Facility Y: $3.95 contribution margin with fixed costs of $1.7 million
Facility Z: $2.25 contribution margin with fixed costs of $1.2 million

Which facility should be used for manufacturing the product?

THOMSON ONE | Business School Edition

9-24. Calculate the operating leverage and financial leverage for Mattel Inc. (ticker symbol, MAT) and FedEx Corp. (ticker symbol, FDX) for the last three years. Higher operating leverage and higher financial leverage lead to higher betas. Is this statement consistent with the betas calculated in Problem 6-25?

9-25. Use Equation 9.5 and the equity beta reported on ThomsonONE to calculate the asset beta for International Paper Company (ticker symbol, IP) for the last three years. How has the asset beta changed over this time period?

MINI-CASE: COST OF CAPITAL AND PROJECT RISK

Cascade Water Company (CWC) currently has 30,000,000 shares of common stock outstanding that trade at a price of $42 per share. CWC also has 500,000 bonds outstanding that currently trade at $923.38 each. CWC has no preferred stock outstanding and has an equity beta of 2.639. The risk-free rate is 3.5%, and the market is expected to return 12.52%. The firm's bonds have a 20-year life, a $1,000 par value, a 10% coupon rate and pay interest semi-annually.

CWC is considering adding to its product mix a "healthy" bottled water geared toward children. The initial outlay for the project is expected to be $3,000,000, which will be depreciated using the straight-line method to a zero salvage value, and sales are expected to be 1,250,000 units per year at a price of $1.25 per unit. Variable costs are estimated to be $0.24 per unit, and fixed costs of the project are estimated at $200,000 per year. The project is expected to have a 3-year life and a terminal value (excluding the operating cash flows in year 3) of $500,000. CWC has a 34% marginal tax rate. For the purposes of this project, working capital effects will be ignored. Bottled water targeted at children is expected to have different risk characteristics from the firm's current products. Therefore, CWC has decided to use the "pure play" approach to evaluate this project. After researching the market, CWC managed to find two pure-play firms. The specifics for those two firms are:

Firm	Equity Beta	D/E	Tax Rate
Fruity Water	1.72	0.43	34%
Ladybug Drinks	1.84	0.35	36%

1. Determine the current weighted average cost of capital for CWC.

2. Determine the appropriate discount rate for the healthy bottled water project.

3. Should the firm undertake the healthy bottled water project? As part of your analysis, include a sensitivity analysis for sales price, variable costs, fixed costs, and unit sales at ±10%, 20%, and 30% from the base case. Also perform an analysis of the following two scenarios:

   a. *Best case:* Selling 2,500,000 units at a price of $1.24 each, with variable production costs of $0.22 per unit.

   b. *Worst case:* Selling 950,000 units at a price of $1.32 per unit, with variable production costs of $0.27 per unit.

PART 4

Capital Structure and Payout Policy

The previous chapters provided a framework for deciding how a firm should invest its money. In this part, we examine other related questions: How should managers finance the investments they undertake? Should managers pay for new investments by using cash that the firm generates internally, or should external sources of funds be tapped? Is it better to finance with equity or with debt? If the firm's investments are successful, should the company return capital to shareholders by paying a dividend or should it repurchase shares instead?

Chapter 10 discusses whether financial markets are efficient; that is, do prices in financial markets accurately reflect available information? For many years, there was an almost unanimous view among academics that the answer to this question was yes. However, new evidence has in recent years prompted many scholars and practitioners to rethink their positions on this issue.

Chapter 11 describes the trade-offs firms face when they choose between internal or external financing or between debt and equity. The chapter explains how firms acquire the funds needed to finance investments. The difference between investment needs and internal financing is a firm's financial deficit, and corporations fund this financial deficit in different ways in different countries. American managers rely more on internal funding and external debt, while managers from other countries rely relatively more on loans from banks for their external funding needs.

In Chapters 12, 13, and 14, we explore whether managers can increase the value of a firm by financing its operations with an optimal mix of debt and equity. Chapter 12 presents modern finance's core theoretical model of capital structure and examines how the predictions of that theory match up with practice. We also study how corporate and personal taxation changes the way that capital structure choices affect firm value. Chapter 13 studies the benefits and costs of debt and shows how managers can increase firm value by finding the right balance between these benefits and costs. Chapter 14 ties together capital structure choices and capital budgeting.

Chapter 15 examines the related question of how managers can affect the value of a firm through dividend and share repurchase policies. In Chapter 5 we presented a model that claimed the value of any stock should equal the present value of all dividends the stock will pay through time (or, more broadly, the value of all cash payments made to stockholders). The surprising message of Chapter 15 is that—although payouts are clearly important—payout policy may or may not affect the value of a firm.

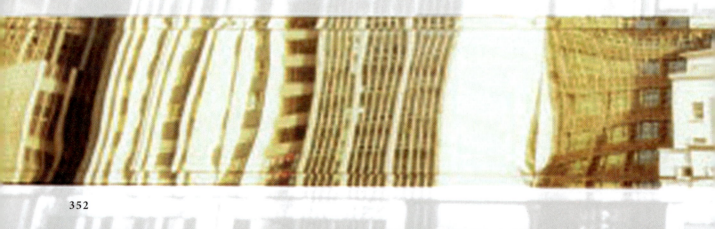

What Companies Do

Massive Short Squeeze Briefly Makes Volkswagen the World's Most Valuable Company

If markets are efficient then stock prices should reflect rational values, but occasionally large misvaluations occur. One dramatic example of misvaluation occurred in late October 2008, when a shortage in tradable shares of Volkswagen AG caused the automaker's stock price to nearly *quintuple* over two trading days—rising from €210 per share on Friday, October 24, to an intraday high of €1,005 on Tuesday, October 28. This briefly gave VW a market capitalization of €296 billion ($383 billion) and made it the world's most valuable company.

This price surge resulted from the Saturday, October 25, announcement by Porsche Automobil Holding SE that it had increased its ownership stake in Volkswagen, which Porsche was in the process of attempting to acquire, from the previously disclosed 35% level to 74.1% by secretly purchasing cash-settled call option contracts (this is legal under German financial regulations). By discreetly purchasing so many option contracts, Porsche had reduced the "free float" of VW to less than 5% of the company's total outstanding shares. This caused panic buying of VW stock by the large number of hedge funds and other investors who had executed "short sales" of VW shares, which they had done by borrowing and then selling the stock in the expectation that the price would fall. When these traders learned of Porsche's actions, they tried to buy VW shares in the open market to cover their borrowings, and this frenzied competition for shares (a "short squeeze," in Wall Street parlance) is what forced VW's stock price to rise so spectacularly.

Sources: Richard Milne, "Porsche Offers to Settle VW Hedging Trades," Financial Times (October 29, 2008); Daniel Schäfer, "Porsche Makes €6.8bn from VW Trades," Financial Times (November 7, 2008).

10

Market Efficiency and Behavioral Finance

In the next few chapters, we ask: "Can financing activities create value for a company in the same way that investment activities can?" Our study of capital budgeting implied that product markets are less than perfectly competitive, and observation of real industries supports this conclusion. Many products are manufactured by relatively few companies, and firms invest in research and development only because they believe that R&D will give them sole access to new investment opportunities. Positive-NPV investment opportunities arise from market imperfections that can protect companies from intense competition.

Do financial markets offer financial managers positive-NPV investment opportunities? We argue in this chapter that they usually do not, for several reasons. First, financial assets are much more similar to each other than are real assets. By comparing the prices of similar financial assets, investors can identify and exploit pricing discrepancies—in the process, changing relative prices in such a way that similar assets offer similar expected returns. Second, the sheer size and transparency of modern financial markets should make them more competitive than markets for goods and services.

An excellent example of the competitiveness of financial markets is the foreign exchange market, which is perhaps the closest thing to a perfectly competitive market in the world today. The trading volume in this market is over $3 trillion *per day*, with literally thousands of traders dealing in the largest currencies. The size, sophistication, and low trading costs of this market ensure that currencies will be perfect substitutes for each other. This means that if traders can exchange 1 U.S. dollar ($) for 2 Swiss francs (SF) or for 100 Japanese yen (¥), then SF1 must be worth ¥50. If any deviation from this pricing relationship occurs, traders will observe and act on the deviation instantly, changing prices so that the pricing discrepancy is quickly eliminated.

A third distinction between financial and real asset markets is that far more analysts study and report on financial assets. Perhaps several hundred business and professional reporters will comment on the technical merits of the products offered by large companies such as IBM, Shell Oil, or Toyota Motors. In contrast, a far greater number, likely thousands, of financial analysts routinely evaluate these companies' debt and equity securities.

In summary, financial markets are larger and more efficient than product markets. Does this imply that there is no gain to be made from creative financing strategies? Not necessarily, but it does imply that there are fewer opportunities to profit from clever financing strategies than from smart capital investment spending and also that the former is generally less profitable. It implies further that existing financial value-creating opportunities occur in financial markets that are less than perfectly competitive or in which there are trading restrictions.

Concept Review Questions	1. Suppose that traders can exchange 1 U.S. dollar ($) for 2 Swiss francs (SF) or for 100 Japanese yen (¥). Explain how competition in financial markets ensures that SF1 will be worth ¥50. Then describe a comparable process for a manufactured product, such as a machine tool. Which process seems more realistic?
	2. Describe how the Internet might push the market for airline tickets closer to the theoretical ideal of perfect competition. How might the Internet have the same impact on the stock market?

10.1 What Is an Efficient Financial Market?

Definitions of Efficiency

Analysts and researchers are very interested in the informational efficiency of financial markets. **Informational efficiency** refers to the tendency for prices in a market to rapidly and fully incorporate new, relevant information. For financial markets, informational efficiency is more important because efficient capital markets incorporate all relevant information into financial asset prices, which in turn helps ensure that promising investments receive funding.

The concept of efficient capital markets is one of the most influential contributions that financial economics has made to modern economic thought. The **efficient markets hypothesis (EMH)**, as formally presented by Eugene Fama in 1970, has revolutionized financial thought, practice, and regulation. The EMH asserts that financial asset prices fully reflect all available information. What do we mean by "all available information"? The answer to this question varies, and we discuss three distinct versions of the efficient markets hypothesis.

The Three Forms of Market Efficiency

The EMH presents three increasingly stringent definitions of efficiency based on the information that market prices reflect: weak-form, semistrong-form, and strong-form efficiency.

Weak-Form Efficiency   In markets characterized by **weak-form efficiency**, asset prices incorporate all information from the historical record—that is, all information about price trends or repeating patterns that occurred in the past. This implies that trading strategies based on analyses of historical pricing trends or relationships cannot consistently yield market-beating returns.

Prices in a weak-form efficient market will be unpredictable and will change only in response to the arrival of new information. In technical terms, this means that prices follow a **random walk**: they wander aimlessly, with no connection to past price changes and no tendency to return to a mean value over time.

Semistrong-Form Efficiency   The second form of market efficiency, **semistrong-form efficiency**, asserts that asset prices incorporate *all publicly available information*. The key point about this form of efficiency is that the prices need only reflect information from *public* sources (e.g., newspapers, press releases, computer databases).

There is both a "stock" and a "flow" aspect to the information processing capabilities of semistrong-form efficient markets: First, the *level* of asset prices should correctly reflect all pertinent historical, current, and predictable future information that investors can obtain from public sources. Second, asset prices should *change* fully and instantaneously in response to relevant new information.

Strong-Form Efficiency   In markets characterized by **strong-form efficiency**, asset prices reflect *all* information, both public and private. This extreme form of market efficiency implies that important company-specific information will be fully incorporated in asset prices with the very first trade after the information is generated.

In strong-form efficient markets, most insider trading would be unprofitable and there would be no benefit to ferreting out information on publicly traded companies. Any data morsel so obtained would already be reflected in stock and bond prices.

Table 10.1 on page 358 describes the three forms of market efficiency and summarizes the key implications of each form.

Does Empirical Evidence Support Market Efficiency?

Ultimately, whether financial markets are efficient is an empirical question. For more than a quarter of a century, the efficient market hypothesis enjoyed overwhelming support among financial economists. However, in recent years a large body of empirical evidence challenging the EMH has caused many former "true believers" to take a fresh look at the efficiency question. It also seems likely that the paralysis and near-collapse of global

Smart
Ideas
Video

Malcolm Baker, Harvard
University

"There is increasing evidence that stock markets aren't perfectly efficient."

See the entire interview at
SMART**Finance**

Table 10.1	Forms of Informational Market Efficiency	
FORM	**DEFINITION**	**EXAMPLE**
Weak form	Financial asset (stock) prices incorporate *all historical price information* into current prices; future stock prices cannot be predicted based on an analysis of past stock prices.	Nothing of value can be gained by analyzing past stock price patterns, since this doesn't help you predict future patterns—renders "technical analysis" useless.
Semistrong form	Stock prices incorporate *all publicly available information* (historical and current); there will not be a delayed response to information disclosures.	The relevant information in an SEC filing will be incorporated into a stock price as soon as the filing is made public.
Strong form	Stock prices incorporate *all information*, private as well as public; prices will react as soon as new information is generated rather than when it is publicly disclosed.	Stock prices will react to a dividend increase as soon as the firm's board of directors votes and before the board announces its decision publicly.

markets in the fall of 2008 has prompted many people to question how efficient modern financial markets truly are.

Adding to this disquiet, there have been several dramatic recent examples of markets surging for an extended period and then collapsing suddenly, the so-called **bubble phenomenon**. Figure 10.1 details one such "boom and bust" cycle, the rise in U.S. technology stock prices from January 1998 to March 2000 and their ruinous decline thereafter. The Nasdaq Composite Index tripled over the 3-year period leading up to March 2000, while the Goldman Sachs Internet Index increased by *600%*. Because there was no comparable rise and fall in "dot.com" company earnings during this period, many have concluded that this (and other) recent market collapses were the result of exploding *price bubbles*. Subscribers to **behavioral finance** argue that bubbles occur when behavioral biases cause investors to bid prices to unsustainable levels. Eventually, the bubble bursts and prices fall dramatically (and often suddenly—consider the housing market during the

FIGURE 10.1

Rational Market Valuation or Price Bubble? Nasdaq and Internet Stock Prices, January 1998 to March 2000

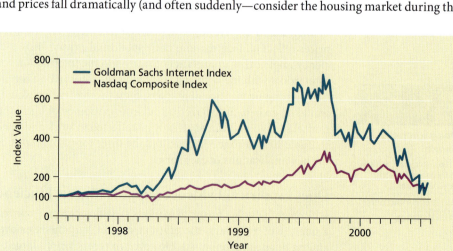

period 2006–2008). To the extent that bubbles do occur, they are interpreted by some as evidence *against* market efficiency.

Not surprisingly, the debate between behaviorists and those who believe strongly in market efficiency has triggered a surge in research. In this chapter, we present a brief synthesis of more than three decades of research on market efficiency.

Concept Review Questions	3. Many people criticize the efficient markets hypothesis as unrealistic but do not then describe what the absence of efficiency would imply. Give a specific example of how a semistrong-form *inefficient* market would react to new information. Does this seem realistic? 4. There is frequently an upward drift in a firm's stock price *prior to* the actual announcement of a takeover bid. What do you think causes this drift, and is it consistent with market efficiency?

10.2 EMPIRICAL EVIDENCE ON MARKET EFFICIENCY

Instead of relying on the three "forms" of market efficiency, Fama (1991) classified empirical tests of market efficiency into three categories: (1) tests for return predictability, (2) event studies (or tests for rapid price adjustment), and (3) tests for private information.

Tests for Return Predictability

Much of the research on market efficiency has examined the validity of the weak-form efficiency prediction that past price changes do not predict future changes or that prices follow a random walk. Research papers studying this aspect of market efficiency are called *tests for return predictability*. We further classify these tests into four categories.

First, *tests of simple trading rules* examine whether an investor can construct a consistently profitable trading strategy based on observed trends in recent stock returns. Second, *tests of the effectiveness of technical analysis* examine whether it is profitable to buy or sell stocks based on historical pricing "patterns" identified by stock analysts. Third, *tests for return predictability* study whether there is an exploitable tendency for stock price changes to continue from one period to the next or to reverse direction each period. And finally, *tests of the performance of newly issued shares* examine whether firms issuing shares to the public underperform stock market indexes over the next several years.

Smart Ideas Video

Laura Starks, University of Texas

"Stock prices of small firms tend to be increasing during the first four days of January, a puzzle called the January effect."

See the entire interview at

SMARTFinance

Tests of Long-Run Returns to Firms Issuing Common Stock As early as 1975, academic researchers began to document the strange result that initial public offerings were, on average, significantly underpriced. For example, an investor who purchased the typical IPO at the offering price and sold the stock at the end of the first day's trading earned an *initial return* that averaged around 15%. Not a bad return for a one-day investment!

Sixteen years later, an equally baffling long-term return anomaly was documented: investors who purchased shares in newly public companies *after* the IPO earned significantly negative abnormal returns over the next several years. In fact, such an investment strategy left investors with 44% less wealth than if they had simply bought the market portfolio. Such a large negative excess return contradicts weak-form efficiency. It raises the question, "Why do investors keep buying shares in IPOs when the average return is so bad?"

Several researchers have cast doubt on the validity and/or interpretation of the findings of negative long-run returns to firms issuing common stock. Brav and Gompers (1997)

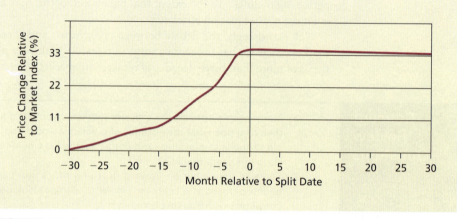

FIGURE 10.2

The First Event Study: Stock Splits

This figure describes the average stock price response to the "event" of a stock split (e.g., when a company distributes two shares to investors for every one share they already own). The stock prices are lined up in "event time," where the month of the stock split is defined as 0. All of the information in the stock split is incorporated into stock prices by the event date and so there is, on average, no tendency for prices to change after the split.

Source: Eugene F. Fama, Lawrence Fisher, Michael C. Jensen, and Richard Roll, "The Adjustment of Stock Prices to New Information," *International Economic Review* 10 (February 1969), pp. 1–21, as presented in Ray Ball, "The Theory of Stock Market Efficiency: Accomplishments and Limitations," *Journal of Applied Corporate Finance* 8 (Spring 1995), pp. 1–21.

find that underperformance is limited to the smallest IPOs that are not backed by venture capital firms. It is unclear whether a separate "new issue" effect exists and whether it would constitute a de facto violation of market efficiency.

Tests for Rapid Price Adjustment

Yet another type of empirical test of market efficiency involves rapid price adjustments. The first **event study** (Fama et al. 1969) examined how stock markets respond to new information releases by analyzing the market's response to stock splits. In a stock split, firms distribute new shares to existing shareholders, which causes a decline in the stock price. For example, in a 2-for-1 split, shareholders receive one new share for every existing share they own, and the stock price drops by roughly 50%. The innovation of this study was to compare the companies in *event time* rather than in calendar time. For each company, the researchers assigned day 0 to the date the stock split was executed, day −1 to the trading day before the split date, day +1 to the trading day immediately following the split, and so on.[1] This allowed for calculation of the average return for each event day simply by summing up all the sample returns from, say, day −1 to day +5 and then dividing by the number of observations.

Figure 10.2 shows that firms that choose to split their stock do so after an extended period in which their stock earns above-market returns. After the split, however, the stock earns returns roughly equal to those of the overall market. This suggests that markets are efficient: investors who buy shares after split announcements do not earn above-market returns.

---

[1]Fama, Fisher, Jensen, and Roll (FFJR) actually used monthly, rather than daily, stock return data because only monthly data were available in the late 1960s. However, because we are discussing FFJR as the paradigm of event studies and because the majority of post-1980 event studies have employed daily data, we will use the term "event day" in our discussion of FFJR's results. Brown and Warner (1985) and MacKinlay (1997) describe and assess event-study methodologies.

EXAMPLE

The employment report released by the U.S. Department of Labor at 8:30 A.M. on the first Friday of every month is perhaps the most intently watched of all economic statistics. A report showing rapid employment growth and declining unemployment often indicates that the Federal Reserve Board will feel pressure to tighten monetary policy and raise interest rates. Conversely, a weak job report typically signals a slowing economy, declining interest rates, and a less restrictive monetary policy. The connection between the employment report and Federal Reserve actions, combined with the influence of interest rates on economic activity and asset prices, means that bond and stock prices often react dramatically to surprises contained in the Labor Department's report.

Imagine the Labor Department's embarrassment when the October 1998 employment report was inadvertently posted on an internal working section of the department's Internet site on Thursday morning, November 5, rather than on Friday, November 6. Almost instantly, a financial analyst at a large brokerage firm noted the statistic, contacted a Labor Department spokesperson for verification, and then revealed the number to the brokerage firm's customers and the business news media. Within minutes of its discovery, the number was broadcast worldwide, and its impact on interest rates and financial asset prices was felt in full. (The report showed a smaller than expected monthly rise in employment.)

During the rest of Thursday, the Labor Department struggled to disclose all the supplementary data that typically accompanies the headline employment numbers. (It also tried to determine how such a breach of security could have occurred.) The lesson for financial markets, however, was clear: Significant information will immediately affect financial markets, even if the information is unexpectedly released at the "wrong" time. The Labor Department also learned its lesson and, as of this writing, no comparable premature information disclosure has occurred since 1998.

Tests for Private Information

Implied in the phrase "tests for private information" is an examination of whether someone, such as a corporate insider or a particularly perceptive mutual fund manager, could earn excess returns by trading on private (nonpublic) information. We categorize these tests into four groups.

Tests of the Profitability of Insider Trading

The most direct test of strong-form market efficiency is whether corporate insiders can earn abnormal profits when they trade in their own firms' securities. As you surely suspect, studies document that insiders *do* earn excess returns on these trades—a finding contrary to strong-form market efficiency.

The studies differ, however, on the critical issue of whether outside investors can earn excess profits by mimicking insider trades after they are publicly disclosed. For example, Jaffe (1974) reports that outsiders can profit by mimicking insiders' trades, a finding that constitutes a rejection of semistrong-form efficiency, whereas Seyhun (1986) argues that investors cannot discover and mimic insider trades as quickly as Jaffe assumes they can.[2]

---

[2]Though it is not a test of market efficiency, the survey of insider trading laws and enforcement around the world provided in Bhattacharya and Daouk (2001) shows that insider trading is a severe problem in almost every market outside the United States and also in a few other advanced industrial countries. In fact, insider trading is so severe in Mexico that Bhattacharya et al. (2000) find that stock prices do not react *at all* to company-specific news announcements. All the information content of the announcement is already embedded in stock prices owing to the previous insider trading.

Tests of Mutual Fund Investment Performance In our experience, students approach the notion of market efficiency with a great deal of skepticism. Surely, they think, smart investors can beat the market if they work hard enough. Research on the performance of professionally managed mutual funds offers perhaps the most compelling evidence that outguessing the market is extremely difficult.

More than 40 years ago, a study reported negative net returns for the majority of mutual fund managers. Net returns in this context equal gross returns minus fund operating costs. The model for assessing mutual fund performance has been used by many subsequent researchers:

$$R_{pt} - R_{ft} = \alpha_p + \beta_{pt}(R_{mt} - R_{ft}) + \mu_p \qquad \textbf{(Eq. 10.1)}$$

Here

$R_{pt} - R_{ft}$ = the excess return (above the risk-free rate R_{ft}) on a managed portfolio;
β_{pt} = the beta of the portfolio during period t;
$R_{mt} - R_{ft}$ = the excess return on the market portfolio during period t;
α_p = the regression alpha or intercept term;
μ_p = an error term

In this framework, the product of a fund's beta and the risk premium on the market, $\beta_{pt}(R_{mt} - R_{ft})$, measures the fund's expected risk premium. Superior investment performance would be returns that reflect more than just compensation for risk. Therefore, testing for superior performance reduces to a test of whether the intercept term, α_p, is significantly greater than zero. To this day, even casual discussions of a mutual fund's performance will often be couched as, "What is the fund's alpha?" The wisdom within the finance profession (at least within academia) was that mutual fund managers, on average, could not beat the stock market on a risk-adjusted basis.[3]

A veritable cottage industry emerged to assess the investment performance of mutual fund managers. Most of these studies separate managerial investment performance into two components: **selectivity** (the ability to pick stocks) and **timing** (the ability to time market turns—getting in before upturns and getting out before crashes). Several important studies claim to document superior mutual fund performance—at least before fund expenses are deducted. Naturally, some mutual fund managers will beat the market over a given period of time even if the average fund manager does not.

An important question for researchers and investors alike is whether the performance of a fund persists over time or whether fund performance, like stock prices, fluctuates randomly. The relative performance of no-load, growth-oriented mutual funds persists in the near term, with the strongest evidence being found for a one-year evaluation horizon. An investor who pursues an investment strategy of buying the funds managed by "hot hands" and avoiding funds managed by "icy hands" (the evil twin of hot hands) can earn risk-adjusted abnormal returns as high as 6% per year. Graham and Harvey (1996) find strong evidence of icy hands among investment newsletters.

It has been shown that individual fund managers who follow a "momentum" strategy do not earn excess returns. Defenders of market efficiency have also attacked studies finding superior (or at least break-even) mutual fund performance. There are two critical biases in most of the tests showing superior performance. The first and most serious is the *survivorship bias*. This involves selecting some period and then comparing the returns

---

[3]We add the modifier "on a risk-adjusted basis" because the higher returns of a fund manager who beats the market simply by investing in risky stocks do not reflect superior stock selection ability on the part of the manager. Instead, the higher return merely compensates investors for the extra risk they take when investing in the fund.

on those mutual funds still in existence at the end of that period to returns of the S&P 500 or some other index. By definition, such a strategy involves examining only *surviving, successful* funds and ignores funds with seemingly equal promise at the beginning of the period that earned subpar returns and were closed down (or merged). Survivorship bias dramatically overstates the returns earned by mutual fund managers. For example, a study by Malkiel (1995) found that nearly 18% of the mutual funds in business in 1982 failed to stay in business until 1992, and the funds that closed earned substantially lower returns than those that survived. The consequence of this is that, if someone were to look back at the historical performance of the mutual funds in existence as of 1992, they would miss the below-average returns of the funds that had gone out of business in prior years, and this bias would cause the average returns of the mutual fund industry to be overstated.

The second bias is the tendency of mutual fund management companies to privately launch a number (say, 10) of "incubator" funds and then, after a few years, to publicly launch those two or three of the funds that have been the most successful. The mutual fund shuts down the seven or eight poorly performing funds, and their returns are not included in the "stellar" fund averages.

Once these two biases are accounted for, mutual funds underperform the S&P 500 even before deducting transaction costs and load fees. Their net return (after fees and expenses) is far worse.

Your first reaction to studies favoring market efficiency may be disbelief. What about Peter Lynch, Warren Buffet, George Soros, or the other investment gurus whose performances have become part of Wall Street lore? Or, for that matter, if mutual fund managers actually subtract value from the portfolios they manage, why have they been so successful over the past decade that today there are over twice as many mutual funds as there are stocks listed on the New York Stock Exchange? Although it is difficult to deny that a few individuals and funds have long-term performance that seems inexplicably high, this is actually what you would expect as a result of the survivorship bias discussed earlier.

To see this, consider the following exercise. At the beginning of a 10-year period (say, the year 2010), survey all 8,000 currently active mutual fund managers and ask each to pick a basket of stocks that he or she expects to outperform the S&P index over the coming year. Market efficiency predicts that, by chance, roughly half of the managers will pick a portfolio that outperforms the S&P in 2010 and half will pick one that underperforms. Those that outperform the index in 2010 are asked to try again in 2011, and so on as long as they continue to beat the market. By the end of the decade, the original 8,000 managers will be whittled down to a mere eight. Put differently, only 0.1% (8/8,000) of managers can be expected to outperform the market 10 years in a row merely by chance, but these eight will be the ones who are lionized as investment gurus.[4]

Tests of Pension Fund and Hedge Fund Investment Performance   Somewhat surprisingly, the investment performance of pension funds (professionally managed funds that invest employee pensions) has attracted far less attention than has the performance of mutual funds, even though pension funds control more assets. Investment policy (the percentage allocation of funds to different asset classes) is far more important than investment strategy in explaining the variation in pension fund returns. Active management yields an average total return that is 1.10% per year *less* than what can be achieved via a passive strategy of

---

[4]Greene and Smart (1999) document this pattern in a *Wall Street Journal* stock-picking contest for which 100 professional investors picked stocks that they expected to beat the market over a 6-month period. After six months, those contestants who beat the market were invited to try again. Market efficiency predicts that 50 analysts would beat the market in the first round, 25 would do so in the second round, and so on. In fact, 53 analysts succeeded in the first round and 27 did in the second round. Hence the pros' success rate is statistically indistinguishable from the outcome predicted by the efficient markets hypothesis.

WHAT COMPANIES DO GLOBALLY

Mutual Fund Fees around the World

In the past quarter-century, a large number of investors have switched from directly purchasing stocks of individual companies to purchasing mutual fund shares instead. These funds offer investors low-cost diversification opportunities and allow savers to allocate fairly small sums across a broad array of asset classes such as growth stocks, international equities, corporate bonds, real estate, and others. The increase in the amount of money invested in mutual funds also suggests that most investors have accepted the idea that it is difficult to "beat the market" by selecting individual stocks and bonds and that they are better served by purchasing shares in professionally managed mutual funds. But just how low-cost are mutual funds, and do costs vary substantially from one national market to the next?

A recently published study documents the fees charged by 46,580 mutual fund classes in 18 countries and empirically examines which factors influence varying cost levels. The study's authors find that mutual fund fees differ substantially across countries, from an asset-weighted average expense ratio for equity funds of 1.05% in Belgium and 1.11% in the United States to 1.92% in Italy and 2.26% in Canada. This is important because the larger the fee, the harder it is for an investor to "keep up with the market." The authors compile three expense ratios for all funds worldwide: (1) the fund's management fee, representing the charges levied by the fund management company; (2) the total expense ratio, which also includes all annual administrative and advisory expenses levied by a fund on its investors; and (3) total shareholder cost (TSC), which also accounts for the "loads" paid by investors to enter and exit a fund. We display the TSC in the following chart.

Results show that fees differ by investment objectives, with larger funds and fund complexes charging lower fees, as do index funds and certain funds selling cross-nationally. Funds selling to institutions and larger accounts have lower fees, whereas funds that are distributed in many countries have higher

(continued)

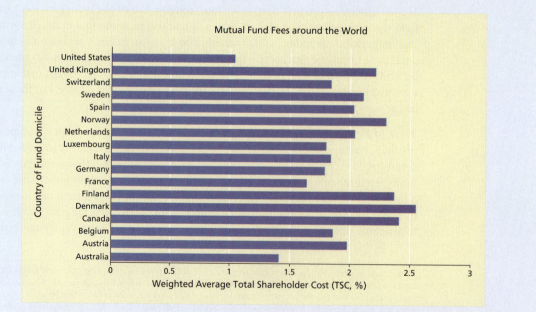

buying the market index. On the other hand, the best pension fund managers produce risk-adjusted excess returns 6% higher than those achieved by fund managers of lesser ability.

One of the most interesting types of professionally managed investment funds to reach prominence in recent years is the **hedge fund**. Hedge funds differ from U.S. mutual funds in their organizational structure (most are partnerships instead of corporations), their generally higher appetites for risk taking, their extensive use of performance-based compensation, and their being largely unregulated. A major empirical study of hedge funds by Ackerman, McEnally, and Ravenscraft (1999) shows that they have consistently outperformed mutual funds but not standard market indexes.

In summary, there is no unambiguous answer to the question of whether professionally managed funds are able to achieve investment returns comparable to that from a naive buy-and-hold investment strategy. Even this lack of conclusive evidence, however, amounts to damning fund managers with faint praise: There is no evidence that they can achieve significantly positive *net* returns (after deducting fees and expenses) for fund shareholders.

Tests of the Stock Picking Abilities of Security Analysts

Do security analysts and investment newsletter writers demonstrate superior stock picking abilities? Many students have heard that the *Value Line Investment Survey* has a reputation for selecting stocks that subsequently outperform the market portfolio, and there is some empirical evidence to support this belief. The question for market efficiency is whether this is a common phenomenon: Can security analysts make recommendations that *consistently* beat the markets?

There is some evidence that they can. For example, brokerage recommendations embody valuable information for which a brokerage firm should be compensated. Additionally, a 2001 study showed that investors who followed the consensus advice of the 4,340 analysts (and 361,620 individual recommendations) in the *Zacks Recommendation Database* from 1985 to 1996 earned excess profits of more than 4% per year. The specific strategy in the study is to buy a stock when analysts move it into a more favorable recommendation category and to short-sell a stock when it moves into a less favorable category. Figure 10.3 shows not only the annual returns on buying and selling stocks that move among the Zacks five recommendation categories but also the average annual return on the market portfolio.

On its face, the study seems to provide striking evidence in favor of security analysts' stock selection ability, which would contradict market efficiency. The catch is that portfolio turnover of up to *400%* per year is required to achieve these returns. Trading costs make this strategy far less profitable. Using a comprehensive and bias-free database covering analysts' recommendations from 1980 to 1996, another study (Metrick 1999) found no significant evidence of stock-picking ability.

On balance, there seems to be little empirical evidence to suggest that the advice offered by security analysts allows investors to consistently beat the market portfolio of stocks. Together with the other empirical evidence surveyed in this section, the EMH appears only somewhat damaged. Before reaching this conclusion, however, we must weigh the evidence marshaled against market efficiency by the followers of behavioral finance.

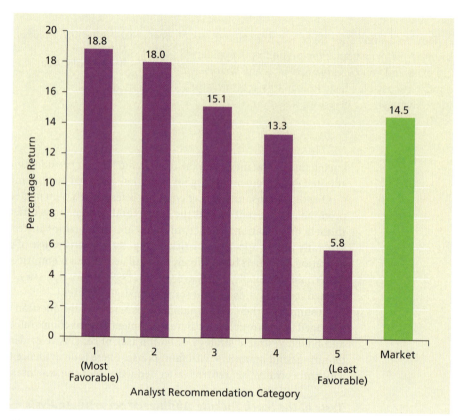

FIGURE 10.3

Can Security Analysts Beat the Market? Returns Earned by Portfolios Formed on the Basis of Consensus Analyst Recommendations, 1986–1996

This figure shows the annualized geometric mean percentage returns that an investor could earn by forming portfolios based on changes in the consensus of analyst recommendations of individual stocks from 1986 to 1996. The consensus forecast is generated using *Zacks Recommendation Database*, which details the recommendations made by analysts at top-tier brokerage firms. The specific trading strategy detailed in the figure involves buying a stock that is moved into a more favorable category and short-selling a stock that is moved into a less favorable category.

Source: Brad Barber, Reuven Lehavy, Maureen McNichols, and Bret Trueman, "Can Investors Profit from the Prophets? Security Analyst Recommendations and Stock Returns," *Journal of Finance* 56 (April 2001), pp. 531–563. Copyright © 2001 Blackwell Publishing. Reproduced with permission of Blackwell Publishing Ltd.

Concept Review Questions

5. What are the strongest pieces of evidence in support of the EMH? Against it?

6. The "Super Bowl Predictor" suggests that the stock market will rise during a year when a former NFL professional football team wins the Super Bowl and that it will fall when a former AFL team wins. This predictor has correctly forecasted the stock market's actual performance roughly 80% of the time since the first Super Bowl in 1967, far better than most human forecasters. What do you think explains this superior predictive performance? Is this predictor consistent with market efficiency?

7. Describe how you would construct an event study that will test the stock market's reaction to CEO resignations and will also examine whether this market reaction is different for voluntary versus involuntary resignations.

8. Several academic researchers have suggested that legalizing insider trading would improve market efficiency by more rapidly incorporating private information into market prices. What do you think would be the costs and benefits of such a legal change?

10.3 THE BEHAVIORAL FINANCE CRITIQUE OF MARKET EFFICIENCY

In recent years, many scholars have advanced an alternative to market efficiency that is known as behavioral finance. This theory asserts that, because traders in financial markets are human beings, they are subject to all the foibles and fads that bedevil human judgment in other spheres of life. Moreover, behaviorists claim that human errors do not simply "cancel out" in markets. Instead, these errors cause prices to deviate far from "fundamental value" in ways that market competition does not eliminate—at least not immediately.

The EMH has long held sway among financial professionals (especially academics) because it provides a logical, internally consistent theoretical model of how markets work and because empirical evidence weighs in its favor. However, the past 20 years have seen the rise of a group of respected economists who reject the EMH as a model of investor behavior and security market performance. Because these economists draw many of their insights from the findings of psychological research, they have become known as *behaviorists*, and their collective research is called *behavioral finance.*

The behavioral finance attack on market efficiency has occurred on several levels. First, behaviorists interpret the empirical evidence surveyed in Section 10.2 very differently than do believers in market efficiency, who for brevity we will refer to as "true believers" throughout this discussion.[5] Behaviorists make a persuasive case that financial markets in general, and stock markets in particular, are simply too volatile for prices to be based on rational valuations. Behaviorists also believe that investors are emotional creatures who process financial information in systematically biased ways. They suggest that human cognitive processes cause investors to overreact to some types of financial information and underreact to others. Additionally, behaviorists point out that the process of arbitrage is both difficult and costly. **Arbitrage** is the process of buying something at a low price in one market and then immediately selling it in another market at a higher price to generate an instant, risk-free profit. Opportunities for such maneuvers supposedly ensure that assets are valued correctly relative to each other.

We now examine the behavioral finance critique of market efficiency in the next three subsections.

Bubbles, Fads, and Cascades: The Empirical Evidence on Behavioral Finance

Few objective observers would disagree with the proposition that financial asset prices tend to be highly volatile. Behaviorists go a step further and claim that financial markets are *irrationally* volatile. As such, they are prone to recurring bubbles, fads, and information cascades. The terms *bubbles* and *fads* are easily understood. An **information cascade** occurs when a piece of "information" rapidly travels through a large group of market participants, influencing trading behavior and being acted on as if it is correct—whether it is or not. All three of these phenomena, if they exist, are inconsistent with long-run market efficiency.

---

[5]To someone trying to objectively weigh the merits of the EMH and behavioral finance, the tendency to interpret the same empirical evidence in fundamentally different ways is disconcerting. The best example of this can be seen by comparing the studies cited in Appendix A of Daniel, Hirshleifer, and Subrahmanyam (1998) with the virtually identical list of papers cited in Table 1 of Fama (1998). Since these are arguably the best academic papers supporting and refuting (respectively) behavioral finance, it is easy to see why a professional consensus has been hard to reach. More recent empirical research supporting behavioral finance includes Hirshleifer and Shumway (2003).

Smart Concepts

See the concept explained step-by-step at

SMARTFinance

FIGURE 10.4

Is This Rational Pricing? Stock Prices versus Earnings and Price/Earnings Ratios for U.S. Stocks, 1871–2000

Upper series, real (inflation-corrected) S&P Composite Stock Price Index (monthly), January 1871 through January 2000; lower series, real S&P Composite earnings, January 1871 through September 1999.

Source: Author calculations using data from S&P Statistical Service; U.S. Bureau of Labor Statistics; Cowles and Associates, *Common Stock Indexes;* George F. Warren and Frank A. Pearson, *Gold and Prices* (New York: Wiley, 1935).

Price/earnings ratio (monthly), January 1881 to January 2000. Numerator, real (inflation-corrected) S&P Composite Stock Price Index; denominator, moving average over preceding 10 years of real S&P Composite earnings. "Peak" years are labeled on the graph.

Source: Robert J. Shiller, *Irrational Exuberance,* p. 6, Fig.1.1 and page 8, Fig.1.2. Copyright © 2005 by Princeton University Press. Reprinted by permission of Princeton University Press.

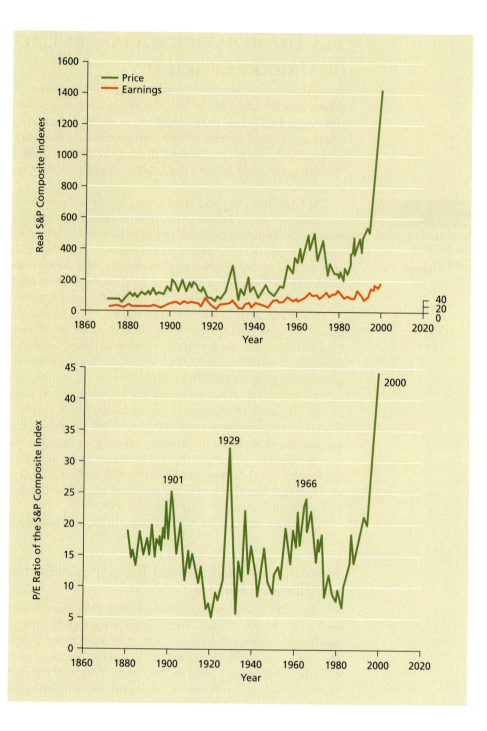

One of the most respected behavioral economists, Robert Shiller, makes the case that stock prices are not determined rationally. Figure 10.4, from Schiller's book, shows the relationship between U.S. stock prices and earnings from 1871 to 2000 as well as the price/earnings ratio of the S&P Composite Index over the same period. Shiller argues that the enormous rise in valuations between 1990 and 2000 was both unprecedented in scale and unexplained by any comparable increase in corporate sales and profits.

Theoretical Underpinnings of Behavioral Finance

It is one thing to marshal empirical evidence against the EMH, as the behaviorists have done, and another thing entirely to develop a full-blown theoretical model to replace the EMH. Although there is not yet a fully iterative model of behavioral finance, behaviorists have explained how markets might be less than fully efficient.

One track of this development of theory has sought to explain how biases in human cognition can cause individual investors to misprice financial assets. The thrust of this research has been to explain investor **overreaction** and **underreaction** to specific information announcements; see Figure 10.5. The second track of theoretical research seeks to explain how these irrational *individual* valuations can affect overall *market* valuations. In other words, even if individual investors make bad valuation decisions, why don't other, more rational investors or arbitrageurs act swiftly to correct any observed mispricing of assets?

Regardless of whether news is positive or negative, **overconfidence** about the precision of information can cause investors to overreact to new information. As the true state of affairs becomes clear over time, investors' beliefs will fall back toward rational valuation,

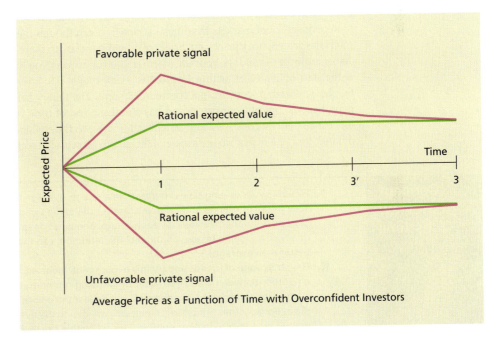

Average Price as a Function of Time with Overconfident Investors

FIGURE 10.5

A Theoretical Explanation of Overreaction and Underreaction

This figure shows how stock prices could overreact to some corporate announcements and underreact to others. When firms announce good news, stock prices should react to the rational expected values shown in the top part of the figure. But because investors are overconfident—in that they believe they have more accurate private information about a firm's real value than they actually do—they drive stock prices above their rational values immediately after receiving the information signal (the good news). Over time, investors realize their mistake, which means that stock prices will drift back to their rational values in later periods. This series of price changes induces overreaction in stock prices with a subsequent reversal as time passes. The bottom part of this figure shows the pattern of price changes that would result from a negative initial price signal.

Source: : Kent Daniel, David Hirshleifer, and Avindhar Subrahmanyam, "Investor Psychology and Under and Overreactions," *Journal of Finance* 53 (December 1998), pp. 1839–1882. Copyright © 1998 Blackwell Publishing. Reproduced with permission of Blackwell Publishing Ltd.

and this causes price changes to reverse over time. For example, a stock price that has fallen in response to negative news will later rise after initially falling below "true value." The opposite will occur for a stock price that has risen above true value.

The **self-attribution bias** has the opposite effect: It can cause investors to underreact to public information signals that contradict their existing beliefs. For example, suppose that an investor who expects a stock to perform poorly receives information contradicting this belief. At first, the investor discounts the value of this information ("I know better than they do"). Over time, as more good news emerges, the investor's opinion gradually changes from negative to positive. If many investors behave this way, stock prices will respond gradually to new information, rising slowly in response to good news and falling slowly after bad news. In other words, the self-attribution bias leads to "continuation" or momentum in stock prices, just the opposite effect of overconfidence.[6]

Assessing Behavioral Finance and Market Efficiency

Behaviorists present persuasive evidence that price bubbles occur for behavioral reasons. The dramatic events of 2008 also support the idea that financial markets suffer occasional bouts of irrationality. On balance, however, we believe that investors and managers are wise to take the efficient markets hypothesis seriously. Even though the evidence challenging the EMH has grown, stock prices and prices of other financial assets are still largely unpredictable. As an example of this, ask yourself whether you (or anyone you have read about) predicted at the start of 2008 that, within 10 months, every major U.S. investment bank would either fail, be acquired, or convert to a commercial bank. The theory behind the efficient markets hypothesis is logically consistent and has stood the test of time very well. Until behavioral finance can offer a consistent and testable alternative to the efficient market model, it will be difficult for the efficient markets view of finance to be replaced by the behavioral view.

Concept Review Questions	**9.** Evaluate your driving skill as better than average, average, or worse than average. Take a poll of friends and relatives, asking the same question. What percentage of people put themselves into each group, and what does this say about the tendency of people to be overconfident? By definition, can the majority of drivers be better than average? **10.** Gather a group of friends and try this experiment. Invite each person to write down a number between 0 and 100 without showing the number to anyone else. You, as the moderator of the experiment, will collect the pieces of paper and calculate the average of these numbers. Next, you will divide the average number by 2. The person who wrote down a number closest to this final value wins a $10 prize. If there is a tie, the proceeds should be equally divided among the winners. If everyone is rational, what number should everyone write down? If some people do not behave rationally (because they do not think carefully enough about the rules of the game), how does that change the strategy of a rational player?

---

[6]See Thaler (2000) for a humorous but informative assessment of how behavioral finance notions are likely to influence economic thought over the next two decades. Among Thaler's predictions: *Homo economicus* will begin losing IQ points (will become less than perfectly informed) and will become a slower learner.

Additionally, Barber and Odean (2002) present striking evidence of overconfidence in their study of online investors. These (mostly young and male) investors generally had been very successful, telephone-based traders prior to going online, but once they began trading over the Internet, their trading increased dramatically and their performance began to trail the overall market by 3% annually. Barber and Odean show that, without regard to whether investors trade online or over the phone, the most active traders earn the lowest net returns. The authors argue that these investors trade too much because they are overconfident in their ability to pick winning stocks.

10.4 WHAT DOES MARKET EFFICIENCY IMPLY FOR CORPORATE FINANCING?

We have surveyed the academic research on market efficiency and concluded that modern financial markets tend to be informationally efficient most of the time. What specifically does this imply for the practice of financial management?

As a manager you might as well assume that you are facing informed, active market participants who will not be fooled by financial gimmicks or "creative accounting." This assumption has specific implications for managerial practices with regard to accounting choices, financing choices, and selection of a corporate strategy for communicating with investors.

How Do Markets Process Accounting and Other Information Releases?

Smart Practices Video

Todd Richter, Managing Director, Bank of America

"I don't necessarily believe that markets are efficient. I believe that markets tend toward efficiency."

See the entire interview at
SMARTFinance

Financial managers tend to devote a great deal of energy and attention to selecting different accounting policies, such as whether to use last-in, first-out (LIFO) or first in, first-out (FIFO) inventory accounting techniques in financial statement reporting. The logic of market efficiency, buttressed by substantial empirical evidence, suggests that this managerial obsession is misplaced for two reasons. First, unless an accounting change affects cash flows, investors will not be concerned with its impact on a company's income statement or balance sheet. Second, if the accounting change merely involves the release, in a new form, of previously disclosed information, then managers can assume that investors will already have processed the new information on their own.

A striking example of the ambiguous role of accounting information involves the disclosure of one of the largest net losses ever reported by a U.S. corporation. In March 2002, AOL Time Warner announced a record loss of $54 billion resulting from a write-off of goodwill. Analysts had known for some time (1) that AOL had grossly overpaid for many of the companies it had acquired and (2) that a large write-off of these excessive acquisition payments was in the works. Thus, the actual stock price response to the announcement of the specific amount was negligible.

This *irrelevance thesis* can be overdone, of course. Financial statements do convey vital information. Also, changes in reporting requirements that affect a firm's cash flows or its ability to borrow can dramatically affect share valuation. In addition, when corporate earnings announcements convey new information about current business conditions and/ or future earnings prospects, the stock price can react strongly.

How Do Markets Respond to Corporate Financing Announcements?

Yet another common but unproductive managerial fixation, according to the EMH, is the attempt by managers to "time" security issues. Several academic studies show that managers on average announce new seasoned equity issues *after* a period in which their firm's stock prices have experienced unusually large increases in value. Another widely noted tendency is an unwillingness to issue new equity at a time when stock prices are believed to be "too low." Both of these behavioral tendencies imply that managers think they know better than the market what the value of their stock "should" be.

Because investors know that managers *may* have superior information about their firm's prospects, there is a clear danger that investors will interpret all managerial actions as being based on inside information, even when managers are not better informed. Investors are not all-knowing, but their interpretations are surprisingly accurate. Studies

WHAT COMPANIES DO

CFO Survey Evidence on Disclosure Habits

Financial regulations mandate that public corporations must disclose a great deal of information about their operations, ownership, and performance. Given these detailed legal requirements, you may be surprised to learn that many corporate managers voluntarily choose to routinely disclose firm-specific information over and above that required by law. In a recently published study, John Graham, Campbell Harvey, and Shiva Rajgopal surveyed 401 executives to learn why they chose to voluntarily disclose financial information about their company, and the key findings are presented in the figure below. The two most important reasons given for voluntary disclosure—cited by over 80% of respondents—were to promote a reputation for transparent/accurate reporting and to reduce the "information risk" that investors assign to their stock.

Responses to the question: Do these statements describe your company's motives for voluntarily communicating financial information?

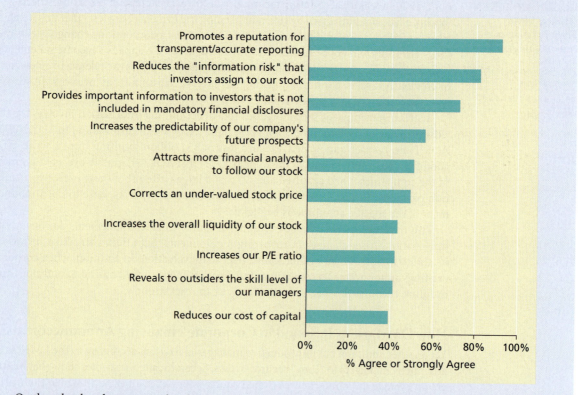

On the other hand, managers also choose not to disclose some types of non-mandated information. The same survey asked managers why they would limit voluntary communication of financial information, and the 401 responses are summarized in the figure at the top of the next page. Executives list the need to "avoid setting a disclosure precedent that may be difficult to continue" as the most important reason for not volunteering information, with the second most important consideration being to "avoid giving away 'company secrets' or otherwise harming our competitive position."

(continued)

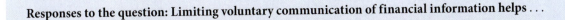

Responses to the question: Limiting voluntary communication of financial information helps . . .

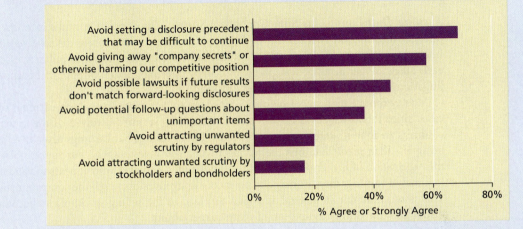

Taken together, these survey responses show that corporate managers carefully consider whether to publicly disclose information not required by law, and will do so if and only if the perceived benefits—such as improving investors' information—exceed the costs of setting up false disclosure hopes and possibly giving away company secrets.

Source: Figures 10 and 11 of John R. Graham, Campbell R. Harvey, and Shiva Rajgopal, "The Economic Implications of Corporate Financial Reporting," *Journal of Accounting and Economics* 40 (2005), pages. 3–73.

have shown that firms raising cash through security issues experience earnings shortfalls in subsequent quarters and that the larger the decline in earnings, the more capital must be raised. Additionally, investors differentiate between the types of announcements of security offers: they usually react negatively to public security offers but react more favorably to privately placed security issues.

How Can Managers Devise a Corporate "Communications" Policy?

Can managers minimize the likelihood that investors will misinterpret their intentions or react to essentially meaningless events? Put differently, how can a manager devise a value-maximizing communication strategy that will credibly (and accurately) convey both positive and negative information to investors and other stakeholders?

We suggest that managers develop a communications strategy with the following four principles in mind: (1) Assume that your words and actions have consequences. (2) Assume that loose lips sink corporate ships. (3) Consider honesty to be the best policy. (4) Listen to your stock price.

Assume That Your Words and Actions Have Consequences As our discussion of financing events makes clear, market participants will react to actions that managers take or to statements they make, so be careful what you do and say. You should try to predict how investors will interpret any particular news announcement and be ready to respond if the actual reaction is other than what you expected.

This is true for both good and bad news. Needlessly withholding good news (i.e., a dividend increase) can lead to the impression that you were sitting on this information until you and other insiders had the opportunity to profit by trading on it. The same is true for bad news. For instance, if you learn that quarterly earnings are less than the market is expecting, your wisest strategy is to disclose this news immediately along with an unbiased assessment of whether you believe the earnings decline is likely to be temporary or permanent.

Assume That Loose Lips Sink Corporate Ships

The opposite mistake is to discuss publicly information that should be kept private, or to prematurely disclose sensitive information. For example, it is often unwise (and sometimes illegal) to publicly discuss early stage merger negotiations, planned security offerings, actual or potential corporate litigation, or personnel issues of almost any kind.[7]

Most corporate managers have also learned not to comment on analysts' earnings forecasts, since this is usually a no-win situation for the executive involved. If the manager confirms an analyst's forecast of unexpectedly high earnings but earnings actually end up being less than predicted, then the manager will anger investors who purchased stock on the expectation of higher profits. On the other hand, a manager who appears to validate a low analyst earnings forecast may end up encouraging investors to sell the company's stock. This is not desirable in general and may also lead to the selling stockholders becoming dismayed if the firm ends up beating analyst expectations.

Consider Honesty to Be the Best Policy

Although this mandate sounds naive, it is actually a core prediction of the efficient markets hypothesis. An investor will rationally form beliefs concerning the trustworthiness of corporate managers based on their observed behavior. Managers who convey good and bad information honestly and promptly and do not try to fool the market with accounting gimmicks or other misleading strategies will be believed, whereas managers with reputations for delaying or overstating will be viewed skeptically.

The same is true regarding a manager's reputation for maximizing shareholder wealth. Investors tend to support managers with a history of acting in the shareholders' best interests and to oppose managers who put their own interests ahead of those of the shareholders.

Listen to Your Stock Price

Most of our discussion thus far has dealt with how managers should convey information to investors. Market efficiency also implies that managers should listen to what the markets *are telling them* in return. Managers should view financial markets as vast information processors that generate unbiased assessments of corporate performance. Markets convey essentially two types of information to managers: (1) reactions to specific corporate announcements; and (2) movements in the firm's stock price relative to the overall market over extended time periods. Both can be informative to the alert manager.

Consider first the stock price reaction to a specific corporate announcement. For example, assume you announce that your firm is planning to acquire another company at a price per share that is 30% higher than the target's closing stock price yesterday. If your firm's stock price rises in response to this announcement, then you should feel reassured that the market believes the takeover is a wise step and that you have negotiated a fair price for the acquisition. If, on the other hand, your firm's stock price falls on the acquisition announcement, then you should realize either that the market believes the acquisition is unwise or that your firm is paying too much, or both. Even though this decline is typically what happens to share prices of the bidding firm, particularly in mergers paid for with stock of the bidding firm, managers often refuse to accept the market's assessment that they are acting unwisely. However, the weight of empirical evidence supports investors more than it does managers.

---

[7]One important exception to this general rule involves the announcement of layoffs. Here, it is almost always best to make *all* the bad news public as soon as legally permissible, for the sake of those who will be asked to leave and those who will be asked to stay.

An equally common conflict between managers and investors occurs when executives articulate a business strategy that seems brilliant to them, yet the firm's stock price languishes. The natural tendency is for managers to bemoan the idiocy of investors. It would often be better for the managers to rethink their strategy's objectives and/or implementation. Unfortunately, examples abound of unwise corporate strategies pursued with heedless passion, though of course the converse is also true. Managers who pursue an unconventional strategy can draw comfort if investors bid up their firm's stock values. In either case, a wise manager should not ignore what the market says about strategic moves.

Concept Review Questions	11. The average stock price response to private security placements is significantly positive, but the average response to almost all public security issues is significantly negative. Why do you think this is? 12. What should a manager do when she firmly believes that a particular corporate strategy is wise, even though the stock market has clearly indicated disapproval of this strategy?

SUMMARY

- In comparison to product markets, financial markets usually are more competitive and efficient because the assets traded tend to be very similar.
- The informational efficiency of financial markets refers to how quickly and fully asset prices incorporate relevant new information.
- In weak-form efficient markets, prices reflect all information available in the record of historical prices. Semistrong-form efficient markets reflect all publicly available information, whether historic or current. In strong-form efficient markets, prices reflect all information—private as well as public.
- The efficient markets hypothesis has been extensively tested, and empirical research has generally found that the major Western stock and bond markets are weak-form efficient and somewhat semistrong-form efficient but not strong-form efficient.
- Most empirical studies find that asset prices respond fully and nearly instantaneously to the release of relevant new information. On the other hand, it is much more difficult to test whether prices are always "accurate" in the sense that they rationally reflect fundamental value at all times.
- Behavioral finance argues that market participants make errors in valuing assets as a result of behavioral biases such as overconfidence and self-attribution. If these cognitive biases are widespread, they can cause prices of financial assets to deviate from fundamental value for long periods of time.
- Research on market efficiency offers several lessons for practicing financial managers. It suggests that managers should not try to "fool" markets by manipulating earnings numbers or through other accounting gimmicks, since investors will usually see through these games.
- Managers should be careful when making public utterances. If a public statement is required, however, it is imperative that managers speak truthfully. Managers also should interpret changes in stock price following release of corporate information as an unbiased market assessment of that information.

KEY TERMS

arbitrage
behavioral finance
bubble phenomenon
efficient markets hypothesis (EMH)
event study
hedge fund

informational efficiency
information cascade
overconfidence
overreaction
random walk
selectivity

self-attribution bias
semistrong-form efficiency
strong-form efficiency
timing
underreaction
weak-form efficiency

QUESTIONS

10-1. How does informational efficiency affect corporate finance and investment decisions? In an efficient market, can a corporate manager enhance shareholder value through changes in financial reporting that have no impact on a company's cash flows?

10-2. List and describe the three forms of informational efficiency.

10-3. What is a random walk, and how does it relate to weak-form efficiency?

10-4. If stock returns follow a random walk with drift, does this mean that investing in stocks is akin to gambling?

10-5. Explain why market efficiency implies that "the stock of an exceptionally well-run company will not necessarily be an exceptionally good investment."

10-6. What types of information are reflected in asset prices under the assumption of semistrong-form efficiency? How is this different from strong-form efficiency?

10-7. Comment on the profitability of trading on inside information in capital markets that are strong-form efficient. What about the profitability of trading on public information?

10-8. Over the long term, stocks of high-tech companies tend to earn higher returns than stocks of public utilities. Does this trend violate market efficiency?

10-9. Distinguish between the types of empirical tests of market efficiency. How does each type actually test market efficiency?

10-10. One investor follows a strategy of buying a stock whenever it hits a 52-week low and holding it for a year before selling it. Another investor follows a strategy of buying a stock whenever it hits a 52-week high and holding it for a year before selling it. Suppose that the first investor's portfolio outperforms the second investor's portfolio over time. Is this inconsistent with efficient markets? Why or why not?

10-11. Give an example of an asset pricing anomaly.

10-12. Explain why the efficient markets hypothesis states that analysts should *not* be able to predict future stock returns based on recurring patterns observed in past stock returns.

10-13. What is an event study designed to test?

10-14. Do empirical studies support or reject the notion that corporate insiders earn abnormal profits on their trades? What about outside investors who mimic their trades? What forms of market efficiency, if any, are supported by these studies?

10-15. In assessing the performance of mutual funds, what does the "alpha" term signify? On average, have actively managed mutual funds historically exhibited positive or negative alphas? What do these results imply about market efficiency?

10-16. What other empirical results have been documented regarding the relationship between active mutual fund performance and market efficiency? What conclusion does Malkiel draw about the performance of actively managed mutual funds?

10-17. Suppose that you are studying the performance of 50 equity mutual funds over the past 10 years. Does the efficient markets hypothesis predict that none of these 50 funds will have a positive alpha? What predictions about alpha does the efficient markets hypothesis offer?

10-18. Have security analysts generally been able to offer valuable stock-picking advice? If they could, why would this pose a challenge to the efficient markets hypothesis?

10-19. What is an asset price bubble? Do you think the rapid rise, and even more rapid subsequent fall, in Nasdaq stock market prices between 1998 and 2000 is evidence of a pricing bubble? Why or why not?

10-20. What is behavioral finance? Describe the two key cognitive biases that investors are prone to, according to behaviorists. How might these biases explain stock market over- and underreaction?

10-21. Describe how Robert Shiller concluded that U.S. capital markets are too volatile to be rational. Do you agree with this assessment? Why or why not?

10-22. What empirical evidence do defenders of market efficiency offer to counter the behavioral finance challenge?

10-23. Briefly describe the four principles of external communications strategy that a corporate manager should consider.

10-24. Why should a corporate manager "listen to the stock price"? If capital markets are efficient and if a company's stock price lags behind those of its peer group, what message should the manager infer?

10-25. A friend insists that he routinely beats the market when picking stocks. Looking in the newspaper, you are able to find that your friend does consistently pick stocks that go up in value slightly, based on closing prices. How might transaction costs affect your friend's performance in the stock market?

10-26. If a stock is incorrectly priced by $0.05 and it costs $0.25 to exploit the opportunity, is the market inefficient?

PROBLEMS

What Is an Efficient Financial Market?

10-1. The stock of Ultrasound Communications Company (UCC) is listed for trading on the NYSE Euronext-Paris stock exchange. For the past several weeks, UCC's stock price has remained around €35 per share. Assume that a competitor, Broadband Telephony Company (BTC), announces that it wishes to acquire UCC in an all-cash tender offer for €60 per share. BTC also announces that it is willing to pay this price for all UCC's shares tendered to it under the offer, and BTC says that UCC's managers support the takeover attempt. If the tender offer is successful, a merger will be effected in three months' time, and UCC will cease to exist as a separate company. Thus, its stock will no longer be listed on the exchange.

    a. What price do you think UCC's stock will sell for immediately after this announcement?

    b. Draw a figure illustrating the likely evolution of UCC's stock price over the next three months.

    c. Suppose that, instead of offering cash, BTC offers to exchange four of its own shares (which recently traded for €15 each) for each outstanding share of UCC. After this announcement, however, BTC shares drop to €12. Answer parts (a) and (b) again under this new scenario.

10-2. You want to measure the cumulative abnormal return (CAR) on a particular stock over a period of time. Assume that the stock has a beta of 1.0, so its expected return equals the market's expected return. Each day, you calculate the return on the stock and subtract the return on the market that day to obtain the daily abnormal return. As time passes, you simply add these daily abnormal returns together to derive the cumulative abnormal return.

    a. Fill in the missing values in the following table.

Day	Stock Return (%)	Market Return (%)	Daily Abnormal Return	CAR
1	2.0	1.8	———	———
2	−0.35	0.1	———	———
3	0.25	−0.15	———	———
4	0.65	0.75	———	———
5	0.53	0.49	———	———

    b. Next, suppose that you gather a sample of stocks that have just reported higher earnings per share figures than anticipated by most analysts. You calculate the CAR for each company over the 30 days preceding the earnings announcement. You continue to follow these firms for the next 30 days, keeping track of the CARs each day. The following three charts plot the average CAR across all stocks in your sample for the 30 days prior to and the 30 days after the earnings announcement. One of these graphs is inconsistent with the notion that markets are efficient. Identify that graph and explain why it violates market efficiency. Also explain why the other two graphs do not necessarily violate market efficiency.

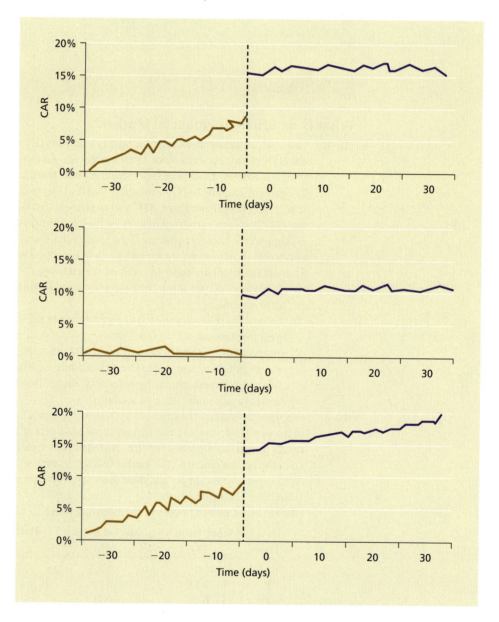

10-3. Stock XYZ has a current price of $70.00 and you own 100 shares. The stock splits 2-for-1 (i.e., 100 shares become 200 shares) and has a closing price the next day of $37.50. Calculate the pre- and post-split value of your stock holdings. Given your findings, and assuming that just after the stock split XYZ also announces that it has been found innocent of any wrongdoing in a multibillion-dollar lawsuit, is the market inefficient?

10-4. A friend has a trading system in which he buys Stock QLM in the morning and then sells the stock in the afternoon of the same day, before the exchange closes. Comparing the opening price and closing price, the evidence over the last five days seems to support your friend's strategy—given that no news about the company has been released over the last five days.

Day	Opening Price	Closing Price
1	$32.00	$32.15
2	32.10	32.15
3	32.15	32.20
4	32.15	32.25
5	32.20	32.25

"Stress test" your friend's trading strategy by buying 100 shares at the opening price and then selling the shares at the closing price. After calculating the profit, convert it to average daily profit and determine if the strategy is still viable after factoring in the trading costs ($10/day). How many shares, on average, would you need to trade each day in order to cover daily overhead of $300 (transaction costs plus the value of your time)?

10-5. A professional trader (trader G) views the price of Stock ABC as either being $25.00 or $45.00 next year with equal probability; trader Q views next year's price to be $25.00 with 60% probability and $45.00 with 40% probability. Determine the expected (mean) future price for both traders (see Chapter 5), and discount the price by 15% to determine the appropriate price for today. At a spot price of $29.50, who will be willing to buy or sell the stock? Assuming that both traders have access to the same public information when determining their price projections, does their trading behavior suggest that the market is inefficient?

10-6. Advisors Inc. will tell 50% of its clients to buy Stock ZZZ and the rest of its clients to short (or sell) Stock ZZZ. Next year, it will do the same with the clients who received the correct advice last year. How many clients must Advisors Inc. start with to receive at least 100 testimonials about the benefit of their advice? (We assume that only investors who receive the correct advice over the 2-year period are willing to give testimonials.) Does Advisors Inc. provide any information beyond what is already publicly available? Does the existence of Advisors Inc. affect the efficiency of the market?

Empirical Evidence on Market Efficiency

10-7. You have been asked to assess the performance, relative to that of the overall stock market, of several mutual fund managers. During the past year, the risk-free interest rate was 3.0% (Rf = 0.03) and the return on the S&P 500 Index was 10% (Rm = 0.10). The following table details each mutual fund's portfolio beta, measured return over the past year, and management fee.

Fund	Portfolio Beta	Return (%)	Management Fee (%)
Aggressive growth	1.60	14.5	1.25
Conservative income	0.90	11.0	0.75
Contrarian	0.40	5.6	1.00

a. Compute the alpha for each fund in two ways: before accounting for the fund manager's fee and on a net basis.

b. Discuss whether each fund manager created value (outperformed the market index) for investors.

10-8. In the 1994 business best-seller entitled Built to Last, James Collins and Jerry Porras described lessons that all corporate managers should learn by studying a set of "Visionary Companies." In the book's first chapter, the authors plotted a graph showing that, over the long term, a $1 investment in a portfolio of visionary firms substantially outperformed a $1 investment in either a portfolio of comparison

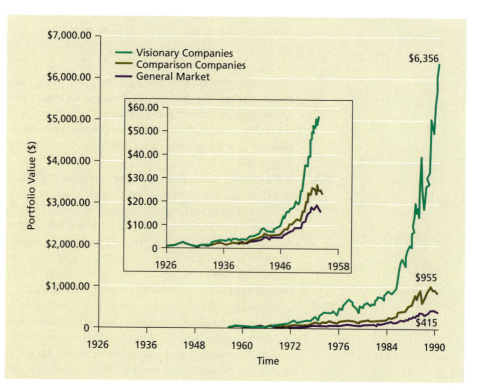

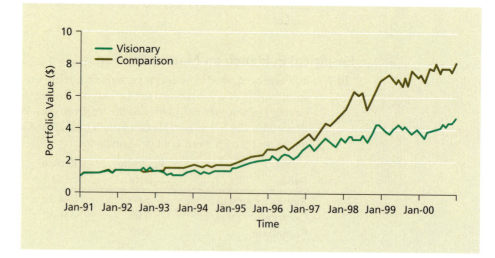

firms from the same industries or the broad market index. We reproduce that graph here in addition to an updated graph that shows the performance of visionary and comparison companies during the 1990s. What lessons about market efficiency can you glean from these diagrams?

10-9. Every day, the Wall Street Journal lists stocks that have reached a 52-week low. A sample of firms appearing on that list on September 4, 2002, appears below. Also shown, for each stock, is the closing price nine trading days later (on September 18).

Firm	9/4/2002	9/18/2002
AAR	$ 6.11	$ 5.05
Albertsons	24.96	25.38
Alcoa	23.14	20.93
American Safety Ins.	8.05	8.05
Ameron International	46.79	47.61
Ashland	27.76	28.62
ATS	1.88	2.05
Boise Cascade	25.85	24.55
Footstar	10.11	10.42
Ford Motor	11.05	10.26
Goodyear	12.87	10.94
Grubb & Ellis	1.30	2.13
Heico	10.09	10.83
Hitachi	51.35	54.13
JLG Industries	8.61	8.71
Longview Fibre	6.15	7.20
Manulife Financial	22.29	21.62
National Semiconductor	15.18	11.93
Oakley	9.70	10.62
Oakwood Homes	1.60	1.70
PCW	1.60	1.44
Sothebys	9.40	7.43
SPS Technologies	27.50	28.03
Stillwater Mining	7.31	6.43
TECO Energy	15.84	15.31
Teradyne	12.19	11.05
Three-Five Systems	5.29	5.20
U.S. Steel	13.13	12.04
ValuCity	1.99	1.90
Vishay Intertechnology	13.37	10.31

a. What fraction of these stocks increased after hitting their 52-week lows, and what fraction continued to decline? Is this consistent with what we would expect if prices follow a random walk?

b. Assuming no dividend payments, calculate the percentage return on each stock from September 4 to September 18. Next, calculate the return on an equally weighted portfolio of these stocks by simply calculating the average return across all firms. Does this return seem consistent with market efficiency? Why or why not?

c. Over the same period, the return on the Nasdaq Composite Index was −1.27%. Does this change your answer to part (b)?

10-10. As a simple test of whether stock prices move randomly, go to Yahoo! (http://www.yahoo.com) and download a few weeks of daily returns for any particular stock. Yahoo! gives you the stock's high, low, and closing prices each day. If stock prices display momentum, then we might expect the closing price to be equal to either the high or the low price for the day. Why? Compare the closing price each day to the day's high price, the day's low price, and the midpoint of the high and low prices. What does this tell you about the tendency of stock prices to move randomly?

10-11. The Super Bowl indicator predicts that the stock market will decline in a year following a Super Bowl victory by a team from the old American Football League (AFL) and that the market will otherwise rise. The following table lists the signal that this indicator gave to investors in each year from 1967 to 2004 as well as the returns on the Dow Jones Industrial Average (DJIA) in the 12 months after each Super Bowl. (There is no prediction for 2003 because the Tampa Bay Buccaneers—an expansion team that had never been part of either the AFL or NFL—won that year.)

Year	Super Bowl Indicator	Subsequent DJIA (%)	Year	Super Bowl Indicator	Subsequent DJIA (%)
2004	Sell	3.1	1985	Buy	33.1
2003	NA	—	1984	Sell	11.2
2002	Sell	−16.8	1983	Buy	3.8
2001	Sell	−3.7	1982	Buy	34.9
2000	Buy	3.6	1981	Sell	−15.4
1999	Sell	8.8	1980	Sell	12.9
1998	Sell	8.9	1979	Sell	6.7
1997	Buy	24.3	1978	Buy	9.0
1996	Buy	25.4	1977	Sell	−20.7
1995	Buy	36.8	1976	Sell	−3.7
1994	Buy	4.7	1975	Sell	38.0
1993	Buy	13.7	1974	Sell	−14.1
1992	Buy	3.2	1973	Sell	−9.9
1991	Buy	13.4	1972	Buy	2.9
1990	Buy	9.7	1971	Sell	5.6
1989	Buy	16.3	1970	Sell	13.0
1988	Buy	9.0	1969	Sell	−14.1
1987	Buy	−6.9	1968	Buy	7.7
1986	Buy	30.1	1967	Buy	0.1

a. Calculate the compound annual percentage return on the DJIA over this period.

b. Suppose that you have followed the Super Bowl indicator every year since 1967. Specifically, when the indicator directed you to buy stocks, you held a portfolio that earned a return comparable to that of the DJIA. In years when the indicator suggested that you should sell stocks, you put your money in Treasury bills earning 4%. (Also assume that you invest in T-bills during 2003, when the indicator does not yield a signal.) Calculate the compound annual rate of return on this strategy.

c. The New England Patriots (a former AFL team) won the Super Bowl in 2005. How did U.S. stocks fare in that year?

d. Is this phenomenon inconsistent with market efficiency? Would you advise investors to follow this indicator going forward?

10-12. Fund TZY has an alpha of 2% when compared to Index ZZZ. The return on Index ZZZ is 12% with an associated beta of 0.8 (the risk-free rate is 2%). A different index, Index XXX, has a return of 14% with an associated beta of 0.9. What is the alpha for Fund TZY using Index XXX? Another index, Index VVV, has a return of 15% with an associated beta of 0.70. What is the alpha for the fund using Index VVV? Which index makes the fund manager look best?

The Behavioral Finance Critique of Market Efficiency

10-13. In September 2001, the month of the terrorist attacks on New York and Washington, D.C., the American Stock Exchange Airline Index declined 47%. However, from the end of September to the end of March the next year, the index rose 55%.

a. How might behavioral finance explain this pattern of returns?

b. From September 30, 2001, through September 19, 2002, the return on the airline index was −44%. Does this seem consistent with your answer to part (a)? From a behavioral point of view, does it appear that investors over- or underreacted to the events of September 11, 2001?

Smart Solutions

See the problem and solution explained step-by-step at **SMARTFinance**

10-14. You have a $30,000 portfolio that consists of equal investments in stocks A, B, and C, each with a current price of $25. After one year, Stock A is worth $40, Stock B is worth $30, and Stock C is worth $12.50. You wish to rebalance your portfolio to equal investments in each stock. How many shares of each stock do you buy and/or sell in order to rebalance the portfolio? A common behavioral hypothesis is that investors sell winners too soon and hold losers too long. Are your rebalancing actions consistent with this hypothesis?

THOMSON ONE | Business School Edition

10-15. Retrieve the daily closing price for Tivo (ticker symbol, TIVO) for the last year and calculate the daily returns. Find the three largest one-day percentage changes in price (either positive or negative). Then search for news released on the day prior to each return. Is the news positive or negative? Does the stock price reaction to the news make sense? Do positive (negative) returns follow positive (negative) news? Are the results consistent with the efficient market hypothesis? In what way are they consistent or not consistent?

10-16. Using the price data from Problem 10-15, can you identify any over- or underreactions related to Tivo stock? Be sure to justify your answer.

MINI-CASE: MARKET EFFICIENCY AND BEHAVIORAL FINANCE

The following table lists the monthly closing net asset value for several mutual funds as well as the monthly risk-free rate and the monthly closing values for the Standard & Poor's Index. Use Equation 10.1 to determine which of the mutual funds, if any, outperformed the market on a risk-adjusted basis.

	Net Asset Value—Close			S&P500	Monthly
Date	ABCAX	DEKVX	JFKZX	Index	Risk-Free Rate (%)
Nov-05	21.80	48.91	16.70	1249.48	0.34
Oct-05	20.85	47.63	15.83	1207.01	0.33
Sep-05	21.00	48.36	16.25	1228.81	0.30
Aug-05	20.40	46.89	16.58	1220.33	0.30
Jul-05	20.27	46.33	17.09	1234.18	0.28
Jun-05	19.67	44.25	16.16	1191.33	0.26
May-05	19.41	43.28	15.85	1191.50	0.25
Apr-05	18.70	41.21	14.92	1156.85	0.25
Mar-05	19.60	41.58	15.45	1180.59	0.25
Feb-05	19.81	42.21	15.78	1203.60	0.23
Jan-05	18.71	41.59	15.62	1181.27	0.21
Dec-04	19.16	44.80	16.35	1211.92	0.20
Nov-04	19.00	42.27	15.76	1173.82	0.19
Oct-04	17.87	39.59	14.97	1130.20	0.17
Sep-04	17.25	39.67	14.31	1114.58	0.15
Aug-04	16.22	38.00	13.54	1104.24	0.14
Jul-04	16.55	36.97	13.74	1101.72	0.14
Jun-04	17.92	39.54	14.92	1140.84	0.13
May-04	17.42	39.42	14.60	1120.68	0.11
Apr-04	16.88	38.11	14.36	1107.30	0.09
Mar-04	17.24	38.16	14.98	1126.21	0.08
Feb-04	16.85	37.96	14.61	1144.94	0.08
Jan-04	16.74	36.98	14.02	1131.13	0.08
Dec-03	16.50	36.16	13.24	1111.92	0.08
Nov-03	15.98	34.08	13.28	1058.20	0.08
Oct-03	15.77	33.88	12.95	1050.71	0.08
Sep-03	8.52	32.79	11.98	995.97	0.08
Aug-03	8.71	33.05	12.25	1008.01	0.09
Jul-03	8.54	32.76	11.65	990.31	0.08
Jun-03	8.36	32.40	10.73	974.50	0.08
May-03	8.30	31.79	10.28	963.59	0.09

What Companies Do
Barclays Bank Passes Up British Government Rescue

An Overview of Long-Term Financing

You know times are strange when a British bank chooses to sell common stock to Middle Eastern sovereign wealth funds rather than accept a capital infusion from the British government. Yet this is precisely what Barclays Bank chose to do, in November 2008, as it was teetering on the brink of insolvency and under government edict to increase its equity capital base. This was after the U.K. Treasury extended a blanket guarantee to all British interbank lending and then purchased £37 billion of stock in Royal Bank of Scotland, Halifax Bank of Scotland (HBOS), and Lloyds TSB.

Rather than accept the government's share purchase offer (and the strings attached to it), Barclays opted for a "private sector" capital raising and sold £7.3 billion worth of ordinary and preferred shares to the Qatar Investment Authority (QIA) and to members of the Abu Dhabi and Qatari royal families. This represented a second "bite of the apple" for QIA, a major Persian Gulf sovereign wealth fund that had participated in Barclays' £4.5 billion capital raising only six months before. Sovereign wealth funds are state-owned funds that invest internationally, and these funds emerged as major investors in Western financial institutions during late 2007 and early 2008—just prior to the collapse of financial stocks in late 2008.

Sources: Jane Croft and Kate Burgess, "Barclays Faces Vote on £7bn Stake Sale," Financial Times (November 23, 2008); Peter Thal Larsen and Kate Burgess, "Barclays Chases £6bn Mideast Cash Boost," Financial Times (October 30, 2008).

11.1 The Basic Instruments of Long-Term Financing

11.2 The Basic Choices in Long-Term Financing

11.3 The Role of Financial Intermediaries in Funding Corporate Investment

11.4 The Expanding Role of Securities Markets in the Global Economy

11.5 Law and Finance: The Importance of Corporate Governance

Long-term financing provides companies with the funds they need to operate and grow. By obtaining financing for the long term, companies establish a financial structure and lock in funding costs. In this chapter we introduce the primary instruments that companies use for long-term financing, and we examine key patterns observed in corporate financial systems. The basic instruments of long-term financing, which are similar worldwide, are common stock, preferred stock, and long-term debt. As the chapter shows, corporations the world over display common tendencies, particularly the near-universal preference to use internally generated cash flow (retained earnings) as the dominant source of new financing.

11.1 THE BASIC INSTRUMENTS OF LONG-TERM FINANCING

Companies have two main sources of corporate long-term financing: equity and debt. **Equity capital** represents an ownership interest, in the form of either common or preferred stock. **Debt capital** is obtained by borrowing via a legally enforceable claim that requires the borrower to make payments that either are fixed or vary according to a predetermined formula. These basic financial instruments exist in most countries, and the rights and responsibilities of the holders of these instruments are very similar worldwide.

Common Stock

Common stock is a general ownership interest in a firm. Holders of common stock have lower priority than a company's debt holders and its preferred stockholders (if any) for claims against the firm's assets. Despite its low priority, common stock is widely held by the public and is a key component of a company's long-term financing.

Table 11.1 details the stockholders' equity accounts of the pharmaceutical company Pfizer, Inc. The table entries provide an excellent overview of the features of common stock. As of December 31, 2008, Pfizer had both common and preferred stock outstanding. Common stock can be sold with or without *par value*. Because many states prohibit firms

Table 11.1 Stockholders' Equity Accounts for Pfizer as of December 31, 2008 and 2007 (millions except preferred stock issued)		
	2008	**2007**
Preferred stock, no par value		
Shares authorized: 27		
Shares issued: (2008, 1,804,000; 2007, 2,302,000)	$ 73	$ 93
Common stock, par value $0.05 per share		
Shares authorized: 12,000		
Shares issued: (2008, 8,863; 2007, 8,850)	443	442
Additional paid-in capital	70,283	69,913
Employee benefits trust	(425)	(550)
Treasury stock, at cost (2008, 2,117; 2007, 2,089)	(57,391)	(56,847)
Retained earnings	49,142	49,660
Accumulated other comprehensive income	(4,569)	2,299
Total shareholders' equity	**$57,556**	**$65,010**

Source: 2008 Pfizer Annual Report (posted at www.pfizer.com).

from selling shares at a market price below par value, there is a clear incentive to set this value low. Pfizer common stock has a low par value, $0.05 per share.[1]

At the end of 2008, Pfizer had 12,000,000,000 common **shares authorized**, meaning that the firm's stockholders have given Pfizer's board of directors the right to sell up to this number of common shares without further stockholder approval. At that time, there were 8,863,000,000 **shares issued** and outstanding (compared with 8,850,000,000 at year-end 2007). The total par value of these shares was $443 million ($0.05/share × 8,863,000,000 shares). Pfizer also listed $70,283 million of **additional paid-in capital**, or capital in excess of par value. This means that the amount the company actually received by selling its shares at market prices over the years added up to $70,726 million ($443 million par value + $70,283 million additional paid-in capital), or an average of $7.98 per share ($70,726 million/8,863 million shares).

Though it does not appear per se in the stockholders' equity section of the balance sheet, a company's **market capitalization** is of great interest to investors. This represents the total value of all shares owned by stockholders and is calculated as market price per share times the number of common shares outstanding. Since Pfizer's stock price was $17.34 per share at the end of December 2008, Pfizer's market capitalization on that date was $153.7 billion ($17.34/share × 8,863 million shares outstanding).

In addition to the shares that were outstanding at the end of 2008, Pfizer has been repurchasing its shares in the open market for years. When it repurchases shares, Pfizer can either retire them or keep them on its balance sheet as **treasury stock**. Treasury stock can be used as payment to employees as part of a compensation package.

Finally, Pfizer's accounts show that the firm had *retained earnings* of $49,142 million at year-end 2008. This represents the cumulative amount of profits that the company has accumulated over the years. Don't be fooled by the balance of this account. Retained earnings do not represent a pool of cash that the firm can use when a need for liquidity arises. Retained earnings simply reflect accumulated profits that were not paid out to shareholders. Some of the retained earnings may be held in the cash account and others may have been used to make capital investments.

Common Stockholders as Residual Claimants

Shareholders of common stock at many companies receive periodic cash distributions in the form of cash dividends. However, firms cannot pay dividends on common stock until they first pay what they owe to creditors and preferred shareholders. Because shareholders hold the right to receive only the cash flow that remains after all other claims against the firm have been satisfied, they are called **residual claimants**. Common stock is risky because it is the junior claim on a firm's assets and cash flows. For this reason, common stockholders generally expect to earn a higher, though more variable, return than do creditors or preferred shareholders.

Stockholder Voting Rights

As residual claimants, stockholders have several rights, the most important of which is the right to vote at any shareholders' meeting.[2] Most U.S. corporations have a single class of common stock outstanding, and every shareholder has the same rights and responsibilities. Most U.S. corporations also have a **majority voting system**, which allows each shareholder to cast one vote per share. It stands to reason that the owners (or owner) of 50.1% of a firm's stock can decide every issue and also elect the people they want to serve on the company's board of directors.

JOB INTERVIEW QUESTION

A firm in financial distress has publicly traded equity and bonds, which are now classified as junk debt. Is the firm's debt or its equity riskier?

---

[1]Outside the United States, par values are often higher because it is common practice for firms in those countries to quote dividend payments and other cash distributions as a percentage of par value.

[2]U.S. public corporations must hold a general shareholders' meeting at least once per year. Additionally, special shareholders' meetings may be held to allow stockholders to vote on especially important questions, such as approving corporate mergers, divestitures, or major asset sales.

A number of states—including California, Illinois, and Michigan—require corporations to use a **cumulative voting system** to elect directors, unless shareholders explicitly vote for a majority system. Other states permit cumulative voting if the corporation's charter allows it. This system gives to each share of common stock a number of votes equal to the total number of directors to be elected. The votes can be given to *any* director(s) whom the stockholder desires. Minority shareholders have a better chance of electing at least some directors under a cumulative voting system because they can concentrate all their votes on just one candidate for the board.

U.S. companies occasionally have two or more outstanding classes of stock, usually with each class having different voting rights. In such cases, corporate insiders generally concentrate their holdings in the superior voting-share class while ordinary investors hold relatively more of the inferior voting-share class. This dual-class capital structure is much more common in other countries than it is in the United States, at least partly because both the New York Stock Exchange and the SEC actively discourage U.S. companies from adopting such a structure.[3]

Proxies and Proxy Contests Shareholders who do not attend the annual meeting may sign a **proxy statement** giving their votes to another party. The firm's incumbent managers generally receive most of the stockholders' proxies, partly because managers can solicit them at company expense. Occasionally, when the firm's stock ownership is widely dispersed, outsiders may attempt to gain control by waging a **proxy fight**. This involves soliciting enough votes to elect a new slate of directors. A study of 97 proxy contests found that firms targeted for the proxy fights generally experienced poor financial performance leading up to the proxy battle. Another study of the effects of 270 proxy contests showed that these clashes usually caused share prices to increase, especially when the targeted firm was ultimately acquired by another company.

A significant fraction of stockholders routinely fail to vote. In some cases, brokers and banks that hold shares in "street name" on behalf of their clients are allowed to vote, and they often side with management. When managers submit a proposal for a shareholder vote that they believe will be closely contested, they can craft the proposal in a way that maximizes the votes cast by brokers and banks. Therefore, managers have a limited ability to manipulate the proxy process to obtain outcomes favorable to their own interests.

Rights to Dividends and Other Distributions A firm's board of directors decides whether or not to pay dividends. Most U.S. corporations that pay dividends pay them quarterly; the common practice in other developed countries is to pay dividends semiannually or annually.

Firms usually pay dividends in cash, but they may also make dividend payments using stock or (on rare occasions) merchandise. Common stockholders have no guarantee that the firm will pay dividends, but shareholders come to expect certain payments based on the company's historical dividend payouts.

Just as shareholders are not guaranteed to receive dividends, they have no assurance they will receive any cash settlement if the firm is liquidated. Yet because of limited liability, shareholders cannot lose more than they invest in the firm. Moreover, there is always upside potential in that a common stockholder can receive substantial returns through dividends and appreciation of the stock price.

---

[3]For most of its modern history, the NYSE automatically delisted any firm that adopted a dual-class capital structure and also refused to list any dual-class company. The exchange was forced to back off this policy in 1986, when General Motors adopted a two-class structure as part of its acquisitions of Hughes and EDS. Two years later, however, the SEC issued a ruling that prohibited publicly traded companies from adopting a dual-class structure, though the ruling did allow firms going public with such a structure to retain it. Google is the most prominent recent example of a U.S. company that went public with a dual-class share structure.

Preferred Stock

Preferred stock investors hold claims that are in most respects senior to those held by common stockholders. The firm promises preferred stockholders a fixed periodic return, stated either as a percentage or as a dollar amount, more or less like interest on debt. In the Pfizer example presented in Table 11.1, the firm had a single class of preferred stock at the end of 2008. Of the 27 million preferred shares authorized, only 1,804,000 shares were outstanding.

The amount of preferred stock issued by U.S. companies had been steadily declining for several decades, until the second half of 2008. In fact, the total value of nonconvertible preferred stock issued publicly by U.S. firms during 2007, $53 billion, represented only 1.4% of the total value of all securities issued. Only 4 of the 30 companies in the Dow Jones Industrial Average index had any preferred stock outstanding at year-end 2007, and even in these cases the preferred stock is a minuscule fraction of the firms' total capital.

Is preferred stock going the way of the VHS video cassette? No. Although it is uncommon for industrial firms, preferred stock is still issued by public utilities, acquiring firms in merger transactions, startups, and companies that wish to attract corporate rather than individual investors. Most dramatically, the total value of preferred stock surged during the last half of 2008 as governments around the world rescued failing banks by directly purchasing preferred stock in huge volumes. The U.S. government bought almost $250 billion worth of newly issued preferred stock in financial institutions during the second half of 2008, including $40 billion each in AIG and Citigroup.

Historically, state agencies have controlled the rates that public utilities in the United States can charge for their services. Some elements of this highly regulated rate-setting process give utilities the incentive to issue a hybrid security like preferred stock. Because it is classified as equity capital, the hybrid increases the firm's credit rating and its debt capacity but does not carry as high a required rate of return as common stock does. Thus many utilities raise capital by issuing preferred stock.

Firms sometimes issue preferred stock in connection with mergers and acquisitions in order to capture certain tax advantages that arise when one company holds another's assets. Because at minimum 70% of the dividends that corporate investors receive are excluded from taxation, corporations rather than individuals own much of the preferred stock issued in the United States.

Like common stockholders, preferred investors hold claims with no fixed maturity date and of a lower priority than debtholders' claims if the firm is liquidated. In most other ways, though, the rights of preferred stockholders resemble those of creditors. For example, preferred shareholders, like lenders, receive contractually specified cash payments that do not vary with the firm's profits. Preferred shareholders also hold a claim that is senior to that of common stockholders, just as lenders do. However, unlike lenders, who can force a firm into bankruptcy if it fails to make scheduled interest and principal payments, preferred stockholders cannot force the firm into bankruptcy if it skips a preferred dividend payment.[4] Finally, because of their preferred status to a claim on company assets, preferred shareholders typically do *not* have the voting rights to which common stockholders are entitled.

Long-Term Debt

Debt is the third of the three instruments used in long-term financing. Because we provide in-depth coverage of long-term debt in Chapter 17, we present only a brief sketch of its key features here, beginning with the various methods of classifying debt.

---

[4]Preferred dividends that are skipped are (in most cases) accumulated and must be paid in full before any common dividends are paid.

Classifying Long-Term Debt   Debt maturity is the simplest method for classifying debt instruments. **Short-term debt** matures in one year or less, and **long-term debt** matures in more than one year.

We can classify long-term debt instruments in terms of various aspects: (1) seniority, (2) security, (3) fixed or floating rate, (4) convertibility/callability, and (5) tradability. In this section we examine all of these debt features.

Seniority   We have stated that debt is always a senior claim to equity, which means that companies must make interest payments before they can pay any dividends. In the event of corporate bankruptcy, all debt claims must be paid in full before anything can be distributed to equity investors. However, there can be differences in seniority status among a firm's debt claims. **Subordinated debt** securities are junior claims to **senior debt**. Holders of subordinated debt are entitled to receive interest or principal payments only if the firm has paid senior debt claims in full. Naturally, subordinated debt offers a higher interest rate than senior debt as compensation for its greater default risk.

Security   Debt can also be classified by whether it is secured or unsecured. Most corporate borrowing from banks and other financial intermediaries is **secured debt**; this means that the loan is backed by assets, called **collateral**, that creditors can seize in the event of default. Loans secured by real property are usually called **mortgages**, and loans extended for the purchase of transportation equipment are often structured as **equipment trust receipts**.

Perhaps surprisingly, most of the publicly traded bonds issued by U.S. corporations are not secured but are backed only by the general faith and credit of the borrowing company. Such bonds are called **debentures**. In many other developed countries, virtually all company borrowing is secured and the corporate bond market is typically quite small.

Fixed or Floating Rate   We also classify debt instruments based on whether they pay fixed-rate or floating-rate interest. Most publicly traded corporate bonds promise **fixed-coupon interest payments**, an unchanging series of (usually semiannual) interest payments over the life of the bond. A corporation that issues a 10-year, 8% coupon rate debenture with a $1,000 principal value promises to make 20 equal semiannual coupon payments of $40 each ($80 per year) for 10 years, at the end of which time the firm will repay the $1,000 principal to the investor.

Although U.S. debentures typically have fixed-coupon interest rates, most bank loans are **floating-rate instruments**. The interest rates charged on these loans periodically change to reflect movements in market interest rates. For example, the interest rates on most large **syndicated bank loans** (loans funded by a large number of commercial banks, called a *syndicate*) increase and decrease with a market interest rate known as **LIBOR**, the London Interbank Offered Rate. The syndicated loan market is the world's largest single corporate financing market, with over $4 trillion in loans arranged during most years. As with all credit markets, the volume of syndicated lending dropped sharply—by almost two-thirds—during 2008.

EXAMPLE

In the midst of extremely tight credit markets, Verizon Wireless announced on December 10, 2008, that it had successfully closed a $17 billion syndicated loan that would allow it to refinance high-cost acquisition debt the company had issued earlier in 2008 to purchase Alltel from two private equity groups. This loan, the largest for a U.S. borrower in 2008, was arranged by a syndicate of Morgan Stanley, Bank of America, and Citigroup and carried an interest rate reported to be 3 percentage points above LIBOR, the base lending rate.

Convertibility/Callability   Corporate bonds are classified by whether they are convertible or callable. Most bonds issued by U.S. corporations are **callable**, meaning that the issuing company has the right to force investors to sell the bonds back to the company at the firm's discretion. This right becomes valuable for corporations when market interest rates decline: it allows the firm to refinance its long-term, fixed-rate borrowing at a lower interest rate.

Obviously, what is good for the issuing corporation is bad for the investor, so callable bonds must offer higher coupon rates than similar noncallable debt. Furthermore, most bonds are protected from being called for several years after they are issued. When the bonds become callable, corporations usually must pay a *call premium* (frequently set at one year's additional interest) to call bonds.

Some corporate bonds grant investors the right to exchange their bonds for shares of stock rather than cash. Called **convertibles**, these bonds offer investors the seniority (relative to equity) and fixed interest rates of a debt instrument and the potential for much higher returns if the underlying stock rises in value. Convertible bonds usually grant investors the right to exchange one bond for a fixed number of common shares. The number of shares per bond is fixed, and the value of the conversion option rises as the price of the underlying stock does. Because the option to convert bonds into shares is valuable, convertible bonds pay lower interest rates than otherwise similar nonconvertible bonds.

Companies can sell convertible bonds that are repaid in shares of another company that the issuing firm happens to own, as the following Example shows.

EXAMPLE

In May 2008, KfW, the German development bank, launched a €3 billion ($4.6 billion) convertible bond that replaced a previous issue floated in 2003. The bonds are convertible into shares of Deutsche Telekom stock, and if fully converted they would represent 4.6% of Deutsche Telekom.

Tradability   Finally, we distinguish those debt instruments that can be traded among investors, called **securities**, from those that are essentially loans offered by financial intermediaries. In our previous discussions, we used the terms "loan," "bond," and "debt instrument" more or less interchangeably. However, the terms and conditions imposed upon a company borrowing from a financial intermediary (in the form of loans or lines of credit) are often quite different from those imposed if the company sold (issued) debt securities as bonds directly to investors.

A bank generally imposes what are called *restrictive covenants*—restrictions placed on a firm by its lenders to keep the firm from defaulting on its obligations. **Loan covenants** are placed on a borrower in an attempt to protect the bank's investment. **Positive covenants** specify what borrowers *must* do, such as provide audited financial statements and maintain minimum debt coverage ratios. **Negative covenants** specify what the borrowing firm *must not* do, such as sell assets without the bank's approval or borrow additional senior debt. Additionally, banks usually monitor a borrower's operating and financial performance over the life of the loan and can intervene when a problem emerges.[5]

---

[5]Public security issues also contain positive and negative covenants, but since there are usually a large number of small investors for any single bond issue, these covenants are difficult to monitor and enforce. Although an agent (trustee) is appointed to represent the investors' interests, less corporate monitoring is generally undertaken with publicly issued debt than with intermediated borrowing.

Borrowing Choices Large corporations have a variety of choices to meet their borrowing needs. As an example, Table 11.2 demonstrates the short- and long-term debt accounts for Pfizer at the end of 2008.

1. The book value of Pfizer's short-term debt of $9,320 million is comparable in amount to its long-term debt of $7,963 million.
2. A large fraction of the short-term borrowing takes the form of **commercial paper**, a short-term instrument sold directly to corporate and individual investors and usually held to maturity. Commercial paper is almost always supported by a standby borrowing arrangement with a commercial bank.[6]

Table 11.2	**Short and Long-Term Debt of Pfizer as of December 31, 2008 and 2007 (millions)**		
		2008	**2007**
Short-term debt[a]			
Commercial paper		$7,800	$4,400
Short-term loans		583	401
Long-term debt: Current maturities		937	1,024
Total		$9,320	$5,825
Long-term debt			
Senior unsecured notes	***Maturities***		
4.55% euro	May 2017	$1,312	$1,291
4.75% euro	December 2014	1,311	1,296
6.60%	December 2028	1,015	764
4.50%	February 2014	836	753
1.21% Japanese yen	February 2011	662	530
1.30% Japanese yen	November 2011	662	—
6.50%	December 2018	624	527
1.85% Japanese yen	February 2016	606	484
4.65%	March 2018	357	300
6.75%	December 2027	309	233
5.63%	April 2009	—	612
3.30%	March 2009	—	297
Other			
Debentures, notes, borrowings, and mortgages		269	227
Total long-term debt		$7,963	$7,314

[a]The weighted-average interest rate for short-term borrowings at December 31, 2008, was 1.9% and was 3.4% as of December 31, 2007.

Source: 2007 Pfizer Annual Report (posted at www.pfizer.com).

[6]According to U.S. Federal Reserve Board statistics, U.S. companies had over $1.43 *trillion* worth of commercial paper outstanding in early December 2008. In order to be exempt from registration as a publicly issued "security," commercial paper must have an original maturity of 270 days or less; most issues have much shorter maturities.

Though investors usually consider commercial paper to be a very safe investment vehicle, during the fall of 2008 the credit crunch became so severe that the commercial paper market nearly dried up, greatly affecting the liquidity management of many well-known firms.

3. The company has numerous publicly traded debentures outstanding with varying maturities, interest rates, and even currencies.
4. The notes to Pfizer's balance sheet (not shown in Table 11.2) indicate that the company has substantial unused borrowing capacity that it could draw on quickly. Pfizer has several different borrowing programs in place that are not being fully tapped, including bank loan arrangements and note-issuance facilities. As one of the world's best known and most respected corporations, Pfizer has access to capital markets around the world.

This section has described the major types of financial instruments that companies use to raise long-term financing. The number of variations on each of these types is truly astonishing. Eighty distinct securities have been introduced in the United States since 1970. Each is designed to fill a specific niche in the market. For example, **catastrophe bonds** distribute interest and principal payments based on whether the issuer, an insurance company, experiences losses of a certain magnitude from a natural disaster, such as a hurricane or an earthquake. Insurance companies sell these bonds in order to redistribute some of the risk of their insurance portfolios.

Concept Review Questions	1. What relationship would you expect between the interest rate offered on a callable bond and the call premium?
	2. Most large Japanese corporations hold their annual shareholders' meeting on the same day and require voting in person. What does this practice say about the importance and clout of individual shareholders in Japanese corporate finance?

11.2 THE BASIC CHOICES IN LONG-TERM FINANCING

Companies the world over face the same basic financing problem: how to fund the projects and activities they need to grow and prosper. This section examines the choices firms face when selecting among financing alternatives, particularly those regarding internal versus external financing.

The Need to Fund a Financial Deficit

Corporations everywhere are often net borrowers, which means they demand more financial capital than they generate internally as retained earnings. Corporations must close this **financial deficit** by borrowing or by issuing new equity securities. Every major company confronts four critical financing decisions on an ongoing basis:

1. How much capital must be raised each year?
2. How much of this must be raised externally rather than through internally generated earnings?
3. How much of the external funding should be raised through borrowing from a bank or another financial intermediary and how much from selling securities directly to investors?
4. What proportion of the external funding should be structured as common stock, preferred stock, or debt?

The answer to the first question depends on the capital budgeting process of a particular firm. A company should ideally raise enough capital to fund all its positive-NPV investment

WHAT COMPANIES DO GLOBALLY

What Do Private Pension Funds and Capital Markets Have in Common?

There is a strong link between the pension system covering most of a nation's citizens and the size of that nation's capital markets. Countries that rely primarily on a privately financed or "funded" pension system tend also to have large capital markets, partly because most of the annual pension fund contributions are invested in the nation's stock and bond markets. The United States, Britain, and Canada had the world's largest private pension funds (measured by total assets) at year-end 2007—totaling $17.077 trillion, $2.002 trillion, and $1.475 trillion, respectively—while Denmark, the Netherlands, and the United States have the largest private pension fund investments expressed as a percentage of GDP (resp. 140.4%, 130.4%, and 123.7%) and as a percentage of overall stock market capitalization (resp. 246.1%, 109.6%, and 85.7%). These five countries also have capital markets that are among the world's largest and most efficient. Most other developed countries, especially the large continental European nations, rely almost exclusively on state-run, "pay as you go" (unfunded) pension systems and have much smaller capital markets. In an unfunded pension system, a younger generation of employed workers supports an older generation of retirees.

These unfunded systems are coming under severe strain, for two reasons. First, declining birth rates in all of these countries are causing the average age of the population to rise rapidly, thus reducing the ratio of employed workers to retirees. Second, most of these countries offer generous payments to pensioners, which can only be supported by equally high taxes on workers. Most countries with pay-as-you-go systems are attempting to switch to a funded system—or at least to increase the role of private financing in pensions—but the following chart makes clear how difficult this transition will be.

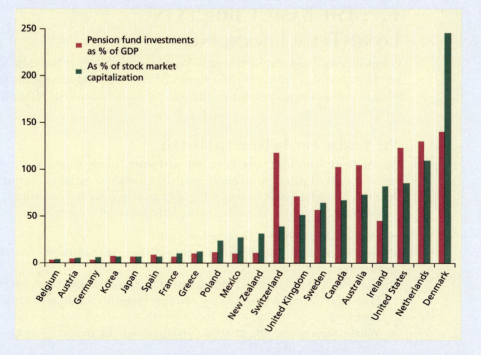

Sources: OECD for all private pension fund assets, 2007 (or most recent); International Monetary Fund for 2007 GDP; World Federation of Exchanges for stock market capitalization and year-end 2007 (or most recent).

projects and cover its working capital needs. The true financing decision begins with question 2, the choice between internal versus external financing.

The Choice between Internal and External Financing

At first glance, the internal/external choice seems to be mechanical. A company's managers might approximate external funding needs by subtracting cash dividend payments from the firm's **cash flow from operations** (net income plus depreciation and other noncash charges). The difference between this internally generated funding and the firm's total financing needs would equal the external financing requirement. The decision is not that simple, however, because management may wish to build up or reduce working capital stocks over time and because dividend payouts are not fixed, though companies prefer not to decrease dividends. Setting this aside, the residual nature of external funding needs implies that they vary considerably from year to year for individual companies. External funding is also highly variable for the U.S. corporate sector as a whole, and the same is true for most other developed economies.

External funding needs tend to peak at the ends of economic expansions and to bottom out during recessions. Intuitively, this makes sense because firms invest little during recessions and much during expansions. Also, internal cash flow is the dominant source of corporate funding in the United States. U.S. businesses regularly finance two-thirds to three-quarters of all their capital spending needs internally.

Over time, other countries are also moving in the same direction. Whereas European corporations relied quite heavily on external funding as recently as the 1970s, the corporate sectors of Western European nations now meet the majority of their total funding needs internally. Japanese corporations still meet up to half of their total financing needs externally, primarily through bank borrowing, but this still implies far lower dependence on external funding than was the case prior to the 1980s.

Once a company determines how much capital it needs to raise externally, it must make the next two additional financing decisions: whether to raise money through financial intermediaries or through the sale of securities, and how to obtain external funding through equity or debt. We discuss the proportions of equity and debt financing in the next two chapters.

Concept Review Questions	3. Why do you think corporations maintain a fixed dividend payout and thus make net external financing the "residual" financial choice, rather than the other way around? In other words, why don't firms make dividends the residual?
	4. Why do you think that corporations around the world rely so heavily on internally generated funds for investment capital? Why do you think firms sometimes simultaneously increase dividends and sell securities?

11.3 THE ROLE OF FINANCIAL INTERMEDIARIES IN FUNDING CORPORATE INVESTMENT

Does it matter whether a company raises capital by dealing with a financial intermediary or by selling securities directly to investors? Shouldn't a bank's money and an investor's money be perfect substitutes? In reality, a corporation's choice between intermediated and security market financing significantly influences its post-financing ownership structure, financial flexibility, and repayment burden. On a broader scale, whether a country emphasizes intermediary or capital market–based financing also influences the key features of its corporate finance system.

What Is a Financial Intermediary, and What Does It Do?

A **financial intermediary (FI)** is an institution, such as a bank, that raises capital by issuing liabilities against itself—for example, in the form of checking accounts or savings accounts. The intermediary pools the capital that's been raised and uses it to make loans to borrowers or, where allowed, to make equity investments in nonfinancial firms. Borrowers repay their loans to the intermediary and have no direct contact with the individual savers who provided funds to the intermediary. In other words, both borrowers and savers deal directly with the intermediary. Because of their role in serving both borrowers and savers, intermediaries specialize in credit analysis and collection. They offer financial products tailored to the particular needs of borrowers and savers.

The most important financial service that banks provide to corporations is **information intermediation**. In financial markets, it is difficult for investors to assess the true creditworthiness of borrowers before lending them money and to monitor how the funds are subsequently used. Faced with such informational and oversight problems, investors would choose either not to lend at all or to do so only at high interest rates. To overcome these problems, a commercial bank can become a **corporate insider**, trusted with confidential information about the borrowing firm's operations and interacting with corporate managers on an ongoing basis. If successful, the bank will be able to first assess and then meet the firm's evolving financial needs.

The Role of Financial Intermediaries in U.S. Corporate Finance

Americans have long distrusted concentrated private economic power, and this has dramatically influenced U.S. financial regulation. Throughout most of the 20th century, policymakers discouraged the growth of large intermediaries (especially commercial banks), in part by imposing on them severe geographical restrictions. Congress passed the **McFadden Act** in 1927 to prohibit interstate banking. The tide began to change when enormous financial institutions formed overseas, making it more difficult for U.S. institutions to compete. After numerous failed attempts to repeal the McFadden Act, in July 2004 Congress finally approved a bill allowing full interstate branch banking. This act prompted an acceleration of the trend toward consolidation in the banking industry. The number of independent U.S. banks declined by more than a third (to 7,540) between October 1992 and December 2005, primarily through mergers.

A second pivotal law affecting the American financial markets was the **Glass–Steagall Act**, which was passed in 1933 in response to perceived banking abuses during the Great Depression. This legislation mandated the separation of investment and commercial banking: it prohibited commercial banks from underwriting corporate security issuances, from providing security brokerage services to their customers, or even from owning voting equity securities on their own account. Banking's corporate financing role was effectively restricted to making commercial loans and providing closely related services, such as leasing. As with the McFadden Act, there were repeated attempts to repeal Glass–Steagall, and these finally succeeded when Congress passed the **Gramm–Leach–Bliley Act** in November 1999.

Nonbank FIs also play important roles in U.S. corporate finance, both as creditors and as equity investors. Insurance companies, for example, provide much of the long-term financing for large real estate development and factory construction. They also directly own roughly 5% of all publicly traded corporate equity. In addition, at least until 2008, specialized finance companies such as General Electric Credit Corporation and General Motors Acceptance Corporation carved out successful niches as secured lenders for major equipment purchases. Finally, public and private pension funds have emerged as by far the single most important class of equity investors in the United States, and these institutions have assumed the role of activist monitors of corporate managers.

The Corporate Finance Role of Non-U.S. Financial Intermediaries

In markets outside the United States, commercial banks typically play much larger roles in corporate finance. In most countries, a handful of very large banks service most large firms, and the size and competence of these banks give them tremendous influence over corporate financial and operating policies. This power is further strengthened by the ability of most non-U.S. banks to underwrite corporate security issues and to make direct equity investments in commercial firms. Whereas the United States, Britain, and a few other nations have promoted the development of a security market–based corporate finance system, most other advanced countries have emphasized intermediated systems.

In many countries, financial intermediaries play extremely important corporate governance roles, distinct from their activities in granting credit and monitoring loan repayment. Commercial banks, in particular, frequently help set client firms' operating and financial policies by serving on corporate boards and monitoring the performance of senior managers. In countries such as Germany, where banks can both directly own large equity stakes and vote the shares they hold in trust for individual customers, financial intermediaries wield tremendous economic power.

In countries with a long tradition of state ownership, where the government owns the enterprise, state-owned banks are usually the chosen vehicle for exercising financial control. For political and historical reasons, however, the United States has chosen to effectively prohibit commercial banks from exercising any significant corporate governance role and has also discouraged other intermediaries (insurance companies, pension funds, mutual funds) from actively monitoring corporate managers.

One of the many ironic outcomes of the extraordinary economic events of 2008 is that the U.S. federal government ended up owning very large (but nonvoting) equity stakes in several of the nation's largest banks. In all likelihood, the government will eventually sell off or redeem these stakes after the financial crisis subsides.

Concept Review Questions	5. What factors might lead to better information intermediation by a financial intermediary as compared to a public financial market? 6. How do you think a bank's incentives change if it is allowed to hold the equity securities of firms in addition to offering them loans? 7. Compare the intermediation services performed by a small community bank and a large corporate pension fund. What do they have in common, and what are their major differences?

11.4 THE EXPANDING ROLE OF SECURITIES MARKETS IN THE GLOBAL ECONOMY

There are significant differences between countries regarding how heavily firms rely on capital markets instead of banks for funding. For example, the corporate financial systems of industrialized countries with legal systems based on English common law—such as Canada, the United States, Britain, and Australia—have large, highly liquid stock and bond markets. Other industrialized countries, particularly those in continental Europe that have legal systems based on German or French civil law, have had much smaller capital markets and rely primarily on commercial banks for corporate financing. Corporate reliance on securities markets rather than commercial banks for external financing has been a transforming trend in today's global economy.

Overview of Securities Issues Worldwide

Table 11.3 presents summary information from the *Investment Dealers' Digest* on primary security issues, both worldwide and for the United States alone, for the years 2005–2008. **Primary issues** are those in which a company makes a first public offering of the security; such issues raise capital for firms. In contrast, in **secondary offerings** investors sell their holdings of already existing securities. Secondary offerings raise no additional capital for the initial issuer.

The total value of primary issues around the world in 2008 was $4.697 trillion, far short of the record $7.511 trillion in 2007. Worldwide security offerings were $1.066 trillion in 1995 and less than $400 billion as recently as 1988. The 19-fold increase in the value of security market financing between 1988 and 2007 was not matched by a remotely comparable increase in world trade, investment, or economic activity. Instead, this increase reflected the trend toward the "securitization" of corporate finance. **Securitization** involves the repackaging of loans and other traditional bank-based credit products into securities that can be sold to public investors. The entries in Table 11.3 show just some of the many securities available.

Unfortunately, this ever-upward climb in the number and value of securities issued around the world was flung sharply into reverse during 2008. Compared to 2007, the total value of securities issued fell 37.5% while the number of issues fell by 39.1% to 13,554. The value of security issuance by U.S. issuers fell even more dramatically, by 42.6% to $2.292 trillion, while the number and value of U.S. initial public offerings fell more sharply still, from 227 IPOs worth $52 billion in 2007 to a mere 29 offerings worth $26 billion in 2008. Worst of all, the U.S. market for mortgage-backed securities (MBS) essentially collapsed, with the value MBS falling 79.7% from $922 billion in 2007 to only $187 billion in 2008.

Security Issues by U.S. Corporations   United States issues have, in most years, been responsible for a relatively steady fraction of worldwide security offerings, ranging from 55% to 75% of the global total. However, the U.S. fraction of global security issuance value fell sharply, to only 48.8%, in 2008.

Looking more closely at the statistics for the United States alone, we can identify several trends that stand out. First, U.S. companies issue far more debt than equity each year. During 2008, U.S. issuers raised $2.060 trillion through debt offerings versus $179 billion of common stock. Debt therefore represented *more than 92%* of the total capital raised by U.S. companies through public security issues in 2008. The common stock issued in 2008 represented less than 8% of the total raised capital. Equity issues have always accounted for a very small share of the total amount of capital raised through public security issues

Table 11.3 Worldwide Securities Issues, 2005–2008

TYPE OF SECURITY ISSUE	2008		2007		2006		2005	
	TOTAL VALUE	NUMBER OF SECURITIES	TOTAL VALUE	NUMBER OF SECURITIES	TOTAL VALUE	NUMBER OF SECURITIES	TOTAL VALUE	NUMBER OF SECURITIES
Worldwide offerings (debt and equity)	$4,697	13,554	$7,511	22,263	$7,290	18,989	$6,259	18,022
Global debt	4,219	11,479	6,634	17,784	6,596	15,587	5,732	14,809
Global equity (excluding U.S.)	478	2,975	689	3,602	426	2,339	315	2,212
U.S. issuers worldwide[a] (debt and equity)	2,292	6,124	3,992	10,662	3,980	9,377	3,555	8,855
All debt[b]	2,060	5,795	3,840	10,005	3,763	8,543	3,373	8,019
Mortgage-backed securities	187	378	922	1,155	1,015	1,362	991	1,353
Convertible debt and preferred stock	59	91	95	173	71	142	41	121
Common stock[c]	179	284	152	657	147	692	141	715
Initial public offerings[c]	26	29	52	227	46	207	39	222

Note: This table details the total value (in billions of U.S. dollars) and number of securities issues worldwide (including the United States) for the period 2005–2008. The data are taken from early January issues of the *Investment Dealers' Digest*.

[a] All figures include Rule 144A offers on U.S. markets.

[b] Includes mortgage-backed securities (MBS), asset-backed securities (ABS), and municipal bonds.

[c] Excludes closed-end funds.

in the United States.[7] If you add in the roughly $1.5 trillion in syndicated bank loans that U.S. companies arrange each year, it becomes clear that firms needing to raise capital externally greatly prefer to issue debt rather than common or preferred stock.

Second, **initial public offerings (IPOs)**, excluding closed-end investment funds, accounted for about 15% ($26 billion of the $179 billion total) of common stock issued by companies in 2008. Initial public offerings involve the first public sale of stock to outside investors. Companies must register IPOs, as well as subsequent **seasoned issues**, with the SEC, and virtually all companies choose to list their stock on one of the organized exchanges so that investors can easily buy or sell the stock. America's IPO market is easily the world's largest and most liquid source of equity capital for small, rapidly growing firms.

The volume of almost every type of security fell sharply during the credit crisis of 2008. Total global bond issuance fell by about 36%, while new issuance of mortgage-backed securities and other structured debt products essentially collapsed. For the first time since 1975, the U.S. initial public offering market suffered three full months without a single IPO being launched.

Smart Ethics Video

Kent Womack, Dartmouth College

"It's very easy for analysts to have conflict of interest problems."

See the entire interview at
SMARTFinance

Security Issues for Non-U.S. Firms

Table 11.3 also reveals a number of patterns in international security issuance. First, international corporate issuers show the same preference that U.S. companies do for issuing debt rather than equity: Debt securities accounted for the vast majority of the capital raised by non-U.S. firms during 2008.

Certain securities, most notably Eurobonds, cannot be offered in the United States but can be sold to international investors. A **Eurobond** issue is a single-currency bond sold in several countries simultaneously. A dollar-denominated bond issued by a U.S. corporation and sold to European investors is an example of a Eurobond. In contrast, a **foreign bond** is an issue that is sold by a nonresident corporation in a single foreign country and is denominated in the host country's currency. A Swiss franc–denominated bond sold in Switzerland by a Japanese corporate issuer is an example of a foreign bond (in this case, a "Heidi" bond). In most years, **Yankee bonds** sold by foreign corporations to U.S. investors are the single largest category of foreign bond issue.

Smart Practices Video

Frank Popoff, Chairman of the Board (retired), Dow Chemical

"A Samurai bond is just an exercise in matching exposure and income."

See the entire interview at
SMARTFinance

A second pattern observable in the international finance data is the rising importance of global equity offerings. **International common stock** issues raised $478 billion in 2008. These are equity issues sold in more than one country by nonresident corporations. This volume has grown steadily over the years and now exceeds that of U.S. domestic equity issuance, though a large fraction of the international total is usually **Yankee common stock** issued by foreign firms in the U.S. market.

The growth in international security issues has kept pace with that in the United States, though it has probably affected non-U.S. economies more because it began from a much smaller base. This is particularly true for the countries of continental Europe. Additionally, the total value of preferred stock issued in 2008 was inflated by the large volumes issued to governments in rescuing failing banks.

Merger and Acquisition Waves

In the last two decades, the value of mergers and acquisitions (M&A) has surged worldwide. Figure 11.1 details the total value of mergers and acquisitions around the world from 1990 to 2008. The global value of M&A hovered around $500 billion from 1990 to 1993. By 1998 it had increased fivefold to $2.5 trillion, and it reached more than $3.4 trillion in 2000 before dropping sharply during 2001–2003. The global value of M&A then rebounded to

---

[7]These are all gross issuance amounts; after accounting for the value of stock removed from public markets through mergers and stock repurchases, net equity issues are often negative.

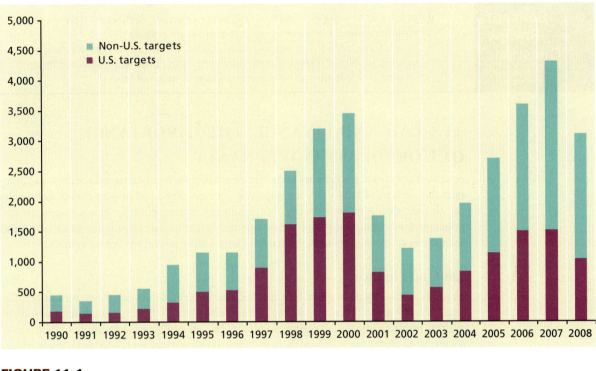

FIGURE 11.1

Global Mergers and Acquisitions, 1990–2008 ($ billion)

a new record of $4.3 trillion in 2007 before dropping to $3.1 trillion in 2008. No comparable period in financial history saw as dramatic an increase in takeover activity as did 2003–2007, and 2007's record volume of $4.3 trillion in announced takeover deals equaled almost 10% of world GDP.

What accounted for this amazing increase in takeover activity in Europe and the United States? Although the root industrial and economic causes of takeover waves are still poorly understood, two things are clear. First, takeover waves tend to occur during periods of rising stock market valuations. As our discussions earlier in this book showed, stock market valuations in Europe and America surged during the 1990s and from 2003 to 2007 before dropping sharply in 2008, and M&A volume generally followed that pattern. As a related phenomenon, merger activity increases when the cost of borrowing is low by historical standards. Second, the increase in mergers and acquisitions activity appears to be tied to the availability of capital that comes with the increasing reliance on capital markets for financing. This is true even though relatively little new common stock is issued each year. As the size and efficiency of public capital markets increase, the demand for firm-specific information disclosure also increases. These factors work to promote the growth of all capital markets, equity as well as debt. As with security issues, the total volume of mergers and acquisitions worldwide fell sharply in 2008, and much of the activity of the second half of the year involved government acquisitions of stock in financial institutions.

In order for a nation's capital markets to grow, however, an effective system of corporate governance must be in place. Academic research clearly documents that effective corporate governance promotes both individual company performance and national economic growth. We conclude this chapter by briefly discussing what this research implies for practicing financial managers.

8. What patterns are observed in U.S. security issues each year? How do these patterns compare to those in international security issues?
9. Why do you think that mergers and acquisitions have grown rapidly during the past two decades? If stock market valuations do not grow as rapidly over the next 10 years, what impact will this have on the total value of M&As?

11.5 LAW AND FINANCE: THE IMPORTANCE OF CORPORATE GOVERNANCE

A nation's **corporate governance** system is the set of laws, regulations, institutions, and practices that determine how a public company will be governed and how control of a company can be contested. A nation's system of corporate governance encompasses both private- and public-sector institutions. Important private-sector institutions include stock exchanges and accounting firms; the public sector provides a nation's legal and regulatory systems.

Law and Finance

Most students are not surprised to learn that a nation's regulatory regime significantly influences the size and efficiency of its capital markets. After all, history influences a citizenry's attitude toward business enterprise, and financial regulations arise naturally in democratic societies to balance the often conflicting rights of corporations and individuals. Most industrial countries have well-established financial regulatory systems, and these are often used as models to set up a regulatory regime in developing and transition countries.

What most students *are* surprised to learn is that the single most important determinant of the size of a country's capital markets is something much more basic than its regulatory framework: the legal tradition on which a nation's commercial code is based. Finance researchers—such as La Porta, Lopez-de-Silanes, Shleifer, and Vishny, among others—have developed what has come to be called the **Law and Finance model** of economic growth. This model states that the most important determinant of capital market development is the degree of legal protection afforded to outside (noncontrolling) investors. This determining factor in turn depends largely on whether a country's legal system is based on English common law or some other legal tradition.

Countries that were once part of the British Commonwealth (e.g., Australia, Canada, India, New Zealand, the United States, and Britain itself) afford great protection to external creditors and minority shareholders, who are thus willing to invest their capital in public companies. Managers may have an incentive to expropriate investors' wealth, but the legal protections offered by *English common law* temper these incentives and give investors legal recourse if they are wronged. Over time, countries with common-law systems have evolved large stock and bond markets. Markets in these countries are characterized by *atomistic* ownership structures—that is, by large numbers of individual investors and low levels of ownership concentration in most public firms. In other words, capital markets have grown large because investors are willing to accept small ownership and creditor positions in public companies.

The other three major Western legal traditions, or families, are *German law, Scandinavian law,* and *French civil law.* The key rules within each legal family pertain to the rights and duties of investors. French civil law offers the weakest legal protections to outside investors; German law and Scandinavian law fall between the civil and common-law systems. Table 11.4 details the impact of a nation's legal traditions on the size of its capital markets, on its economic growth rate, and on the incentive for a citizen to become an entrepreneur (where entrepreneurial incentive is represented by the number

Table 11.4 Law and Finance: An English Common Law System Promotes Capital Market Growth

COUNTRY (1)	EXTERNAL CAP/GDP (2)	DEBT/GDP (3)	GDP GROWTH RATE (%) (4)	DOMESTIC FIRMS/POP (5)	RULE OF LAW (6)	SHAREHOLDER RIGHTS (7)	CREDITOR RIGHTS (8)
Australia	0.49	0.76	3.06	63.55	10.00	4	1
Canada	0.39	0.72	3.36	40.86	10.00	4	1
Israel	0.25	0.66	4.39	127.60	4.82	3	1
United Kingdom	1.00	1.13	2.27	35.68	8.57	4	4
United States	0.58	0.81	2.74	30.11	10.00	5	1
English origin average	**0.60**	**0.68**	**4.30**	**35.45**	**6.46**	**3.39**	**3.11**
Belgium	0.17	0.38	2.46	15.59	10.00	0	2
France	0.23	0.96	2.54	8.05	8.98	2	0
Greece	0.07	0.23	2.46	21.60	6.18	1	1
Italy	0.06	0.55	2.82	3.91	8.33	0	2
Spain	0.17	0.75	3.27	9.71	7.80	2	2
French origin average	**0.21**	**0.45**	**3.18**	**10.00**	**6.05**	**1.76**	**1.58**
Austria	0.06	0.79	2.74	13.87	10.00	2	3
Germany	0.13	1.12	2.60	5.14	9.23	1	3
Japan	0.62	1.22	4.13	17.78	8.98	3	2
Korea	0.44	0.74	9.52	15.88	5.35	2	3
Switzerland	0.62	—	1.18	33.85	10.00	1	1
German origin average	**0.46**	**0.97**	**5.29**	**16.79**	**8.68**	**2.00**	**2.33**
Denmark	0.21	0.34	2.09	50.40	10.00	3	3
Finland	0.25	0.75	2.40	13.00	10.00	2	1
Norway	0.22	0.64	3.43	33.00	10.00	3	2
Sweden	0.51	0.55	1.79	12.66	10.00	2	2
Scandinavian origin average	**0.30**	**0.57**	**2.42**	**27.26**	**10.00**	**2.50**	**2.00**
Sample average (44 countries)	**0.44**	**0.59**	**3.79**	**21.59**	**6.85**	**2.44**	**2.30**

Notes: This table details the relationship between the type of legal system on which a country's commercial code is based and the size of that nation's capital markets for selected countries in 1994. Column 2 shows the ratio of stock market capitalization held by external, minority (noncontrolling) shareholders to GDP, and column 3 provides a similar measure for private-sector debt (bank loans and bonds). Column 4 presents the country's average annual GDP growth rate over 1970–1993, and column 5 is the ratio of the number of domestic firms in a country to its population, in millions. Columns 6–8 present summary measures of the law-and-order traditions in a country (column 6) and of how well its legal code protects the rights of shareholders (column 7) and creditors (column 8). In all three cases, the higher the rating, the better the legal protection accorded investors. Countries with English common law systems, presented first in this table, provide the best legal protections for investors and thus have the largest stock and bond markets. French civil law countries provide the poorest legal protection for outside investors and thus tend to have very small capital markets. German and Scandinavian legal systems fall between these two extremes.

Source: Rafael LaPorta, Florencio Lopez-de-Silanes, Andrei Sheifer and Robert Vishney, "Legal Determinants of External Finance," Journal of Finance 52 (July 1997), pp.1131–1150. Copyright © 1997 Blackwell Publishing. Reproduced with permission of Blackwell Publishing Ltd.

WHAT CFOs DO

CFO Survey Evidence: Factors Affecting Financing Decisions

What are the key factors influencing managers' decisions to raise new capital in the United States, United Kingdom, Germany, Canada, and Japan? This question was recently asked of the chief financial officers of the 300 largest public companies included in the major stock indices of each of these five large OECD countries. Exhibit 1 details the responses received from the 140 CFOs who were asked "to indicate the relative importance of the factors in the exhibit when they are making a financing decision"; Exhibit 2 describes the CFOs' responses to the question, "How frequently does your firm use the following sources of funds to finance a new investment?" The responses were based on a scale of 1 to 5, where 1 = not important and 5 = very important.

Exhibit 1 Relative Importance of Different Factors to Financing Decisions by Country

FACTOR	U.S.	U.K.	GERMANY	CANADA	JAPAN	AVERAGE
Projected cash flow	4.52	4.54	4.57	4.71	4.25	4.52
Financial flexibility	3.65	3.25	3.90	3.76	3.90	3.69
Market value of stock	3.72	3.36	3.28	3.50	3.95	3.56
Corporate tax rate	2.92	3.96	3.45	3.09	3.14	3.31
Transaction costs	3.46	2.87	3.24	3.20	3.25	3.20
Credit rating	2.73	2.83	3.38	2.61	4.24	3.16
Voting control	2.96	2.83	3.12	2.94	3.05	2.98
Bankruptcy costs	1.63	1.83	2.00	1.78	2.57	1.96
Personal taxes	1.44	1.83	2.34	1.48	1.81	1.78

Source: Exhibit 5 in Gil Cohen and Joseph Yagil, "A Multinational Survey of Corporate Financial Policies", Journal of Applied Finance (Summer 2007), pages 57–70. © The Financial Management Association, International, University of South Florida, COBA, 4204 E. Fowler Avenue, Ste. #3331, Tampa, FL 33620-5500 www.fma.org.

Exhibit 2 Frequency of Different Sources of Funds Used to Finance New Investments by Country

SOURCE	U.S.	U.K.	GERMANY	CANADA	JAPAN	AVERAGE
Retained earnings	3.50	3.75	4.00	3.40	4.35	3.80
Long-term debt	3.13	3.19	3.26	3.71	3.57	3.37
Short-term debt	2.79	3.12	2.89	2.73	3.19	2.94
External common equity	3.09	2.50	2.12	3.03	1.90	2.53
Convertibles	1.88	1.58	1.48	1.12	2.10	1.63
Warrants	1.62	1.48	1.12	1.55	1.57	1.47

Source: Exhibit 6 in Gil Cohen and Joseph Yagil, "A Multinational Survey of Corporate Financial Policies", Journal of Applied Finance (Summer 2007), pages 57–70. © The Financial Management Association, International, University of South Florida, COBA, 4204 E. Fowler Avenue, Ste. #3331, Tampa, FL 33620-5500 www.fma.org.

Although numerous differences were observed in the national responses to these two questions, what is striking is just how similar the overall responses were internationally. Executives in every country listed projected cash flow (need for cash) as the most important factor influencing their decision to raise capital, while obtaining/maintaining financial flexibility and concern about the market value of the firm's stock were in most cases the next two most influential factors. Additionally, executives indicated strong reliance on internal financing (retained earnings) relative to external financing sources. CFOs were, in most cases, also more likely to select long- and short-term debt over all other types of external financing (common equity offerings, convertibles, and warrants).

Source: Exhibits 5 and 6 in Gil Cohen and Joseph Yagil, "A Multinational Survey of Corporate Financial Policies," Journal of Applied Finance (Summer 2007), pp. 57–70.

of domestic firms per million inhabitants). The last three columns of Table 11.4 present summary measures of a nation's tradition of law and the effectiveness of its legal system in protecting the rights of outside investors.

The results presented in Table 11.4 are striking: English common-law countries have much larger public equity and debt markets than do countries with other legal systems. Common-law countries also have much more entrepreneurial activity, with an average of 35.45 domestic firms per million citizens versus 27.26 or 16.79 firms per million (respectively) in countries with a tradition of Scandinavian or German law and only 10.00 companies per million in countries with civil law traditions. It is not clear whether entrepreneurs are able to start companies more easily in common-law countries than in others because the laws are more encouraging or because the entrepreneurs are better able to attract external financing, or both. Empirical evidence shows that capital market development and economic growth are indeed positively related.

Applying the Law and Finance Model to Corporate Control
What does the Law and Finance research imply for financial managers in different countries? A lot more than might seem obvious. A key implication of this research is that corporate ownership is likely to be much less concentrated in common-law countries than in other advanced economies, and the evidence supports this prediction. In most continental European countries, a single investor or a single block of shareholders controls either a majority or a large minority of the voting stock in the typical public company. The median voting blocks for the common-law countries Britain and the United States are much smaller.

Who belongs to these voting blocks? Overwhelmingly, they are members of a firm's founding family, and the reason they must retain such concentrated ownership long after the founder's death relates directly to the legal system in place. Founding families in Britain and America tend to divest their concentrated ownership stakes in favor of other investments once the founding generation passes away. In civil-law and German-law countries, families must retain concentrated ownership either to ensure they retain managerial control of the firm or to protect themselves from expropriation by incumbent managers, or both. There is thus a clear cost to continental European families in terms of less-than-optimal wealth diversification. There is also a related loss of economic efficiency in civil-law and German-law countries because the need to preserve concentrated ownership discourages companies from issuing new public securities, particularly stock offerings, which in turn lowers the rate at which companies can grow.

The good news is that ownership structures have become much less concentrated in continental Europe since the mid-1990s, and this is likely to continue apace with capital market growth. However, the practicing financial manager must understand how the corporate governance system of the host nation affects the firm's ability to raise external capital—and on what terms. Multinational firms may consider the legal systems of various countries when deciding where to set up operations or raise capital.

Concept Review Questions	10. What impact do you think a nation's regulatory framework has on its corporate governance system? What does this imply for the newly democratic counties in Central and Eastern Europe?
	11. Why should a nation's legal tradition have such a strong influence on the size of its capital markets? Why do you think the effect is similar for stockholders and bondholders?

SUMMARY

- The three basic instruments of long-term financing in all market economies are common stock, preferred stock, and long-term debt. The way these instruments are used and the degree to which corporations rely on capital markets rather than financial intermediaries for funding differs among countries.

- In almost all market economies, internally generated funds (primarily internally generated earnings) are the dominant source of funding for corporate investment. External financing is used only when needed, and then debt is almost always preferred to equity financing. The difference between a firm's total funding needs and its internally generated cash flow is referred to as its financial deficit.

- Financial intermediaries are institutions that raise funds by selling claims on themselves (often in the form of demand deposits, or checking accounts) and then use those funds to lend to corporate borrowers. Intermediaries thus break, or *intermediate*, the direct link between final savers and borrowers that exists when companies sell securities directly to investors.

- Though financial intermediaries are essential to the smooth running of the U.S. economy, they play a relatively small role proportionately in financing U.S. corporations. This is especially true of large, multinational firms. However, intermediaries are important in the corporate financial systems of most other nations.

- The total volume of security issues has surged 19-fold since 1988, reaching $7.51 trillion worldwide in 2007, and U.S. corporate issuers in recent years accounted for around 50% of the worldwide total. Security issuance plummeted in 2008 as the ongoing credit crisis caused financial markets to freeze up.

- A viable system of corporate governance significantly affects the financial performance of individual companies and entire economies. The legal tradition upon which a country's commercial code is based is especially important; countries with legal systems based on English common law tend to have larger stock and bond markets than do countries with other legal systems.

KEY TERMS

additional paid-in capital	corporate governance	Eurobonds
callable	corporate insider	financial deficit
cash flow from operations	cumulative voting system	financial intermediary (FI)
catastrophe bonds	debentures	fixed-coupon interest payments
collateral	debt capital	floating-rate instruments
commercial paper	equipment trust receipts	foreign bonds
convertibles	equity capital	Glass–Steagall Act

Gramm–Leach–Bliley Act
information intermediation
initial public offerings (IPOs)
international common stock
Law and Finance model
LIBOR
loan covenants
long-term debt
majority voting system
market capitalization
McFadden Act

mortgages
negative covenants
positive covenants
primary issues
proxy fight
proxy statement
residual claimants
seasoned issues
secondary offerings
secured debt
securities

securitization
senior debt
shares authorized
shares issued
short-term debt
subordinated debt
syndicated bank loans
treasury stock
Yankee bonds
Yankee common stock

QUESTIONS

11-1. What role does par value play in the pricing and sale of common stock by the issuing corporation? Why do most firms assign relatively low par values to their shares?

11-2. How can you find the initial proceeds per share received by an issuer of common stock if you know the number of shares issued, the par value per share, and the total additional paid-in capital?

11-3. Assuming you know the number of authorized shares, the number of issued shares, and the amount of treasury stock held by the corporation, how can you find the number of outstanding shares? How does a firm typically end up with treasury stock?

11-4. Why are common stockholders known as *residual* claimants? What does this imply about the risk and required return on common stock relative to other security classes?

11-5. Distinguish between majority and cumulative voting structures. Which is more advantageous to minority shareholders?

11-6. What is a proxy fight? Why does the existing management have an advantage in a proxy fight?

11-7. Why is preferred stock often referred to as a hybrid of common stock and debt? Why would a U.S. corporation rather receive preferred stock dividends than debt interest payments from other corporations as a source of investment income?

11-8. Discuss the basic rights and features of preferred stock. Include in your discussion the topics of seniority of claims relative to other securities, voting rights, callability, and convertibility.

11-9. Why does subordinated debt pay higher interest rates than senior debt? Is most corporate debt from banks and other intermediaries secured or unsecured?

11-10. List and describe the various types of secured debt that constitute corporate borrowing. What mechanisms can be attached to debentures in order to reduce their default risk?

11-11. How are the interest rates typically set on debentures? On loans obtained by both U.S. and non-U.S. corporations? What market rate is typically used to price syndicated bank loans?

11-12. Why are corporate bonds issued by most U.S. companies callable? Does the inclusion of this feature by the corporation have a cost? Is there a cost to the company of issuing convertible rather than straight bonds?

11-13. How are loan covenants used to protect debt holders' investments? Why is the monitoring of these covenants different for intermediated and for public debt?

11-14. What are the key features and costs of commercial paper?

11-15. How should a corporation estimate the amount of financing that must be raised externally during a given year? Once that amount is known, what other decision must be made?

11-16. What is the dominant source of capital funding in the United States? Given this result and the fact that most corporations are net borrowers, what decisions must most managers face in order to address this financial deficit?

11-17. Define the term *financial intermediary*. What role do financial intermediaries play in U.S.

corporate finance? How does this compare to the role of non-U.S. financial intermediaries?

11-18. Discuss the U.S. banking system regulations that have had a major impact on the development of the U.S. financial system. In what ways has the U.S. system been affected (positively and negatively) by these regulations?

11-19. Differentiate between a U.S. commercial bank and the merchant banks found in other developed countries. How have these differences affected the securities markets in the United States versus those in other developed countries?

11-20. What are the general trends regarding public security issuance by U.S. corporations? Specifically, which security type is most often sold to the public? What is the split between initial and seasoned equity offerings?

11-21. Distinguish between a Eurobond, a foreign bond, and a Yankee bond. Which of these three represents the greatest volume of security issuance?

11-22. How does the corporate governance function of financial intermediaries differ between the United States and most other countries?

11-23. How would you describe the recent levels of M&A activity in the United States and elsewhere? What accounts for this change in activity?

11-24. List and briefly discuss the roles played by the key institutions and legal/regulatory systems that make up a nation's system of corporate governance. Apart from legal tradition, which influence do you think is the most important?

11-25. Why does a nation's legal tradition have such a large impact on the size of its capital markets?

Do you think that a nation could change its legal tradition if doing so would promote capital market development?

11-26. How does the concentration of corporate ownership differ between common-law and other countries? Why? What implication do these differences have on the corporate financial manager's ability to raise funds?

11-27. When a firm supplies the capital for a project internally, it is not uncommon to state that the firm is "funding the project from retained earnings." Are retained earnings a true source of funding?

11-28. Firm A is trying to acquire the majority of shares of Firm B. Firm B realizes Firm A's intentions and begins acquiring its own shares on the market as well. To keep the numbers simple, assume that there are 101 shares available and both Firm A and Firm B own 55 shares each. The extra shares have been supplied by investors who are short-selling Firm B's stock. What are the implications for the short-sellers? (*Hint:* Can the short-sellers actually purchase stock to cover their position? Note that short-selling allows an investor to borrow a share of stock and then sell it on the market with the understanding that at some point in the future, the share is to be purchased in the market and returned to the original owner.)

11-29. Despite having net income in excess of the cumulative amount of dividends to be paid, why might a firm still need to borrow money to pay the dividends? (*Hint:* Does net income equate to cash?)

PROBLEMS

The Basic Instruments of Long-Term Financing

11-1. How many shares are needed to elect two directors from a slate of seven if a firm has 10 million shares outstanding and uses cumulative voting in its election?

11-2. Schrell Corporation has 1,700,000 shares of voting common stock outstanding. Recent board actions and their dismal outcomes have raised the ire of many shareholders.

A major group of dissident shareholders that controls 600,000 shares of the common stock wishes to change the composition of the firm's seven-member board to improve the quality of the firm's governance. Management effectively controls the other 1,100,000 shares, many through proxies granted them by shareholders. Management's slate of directors for the upcoming election includes all of the existing directors.

The dissident shareholders want to obtain as much representation as possible in the upcoming election of all seven directors.

    a. If the firm has a *majority voting system*, how many directors can the dissident group of shareholders elect?

    b. If the firm has a *cumulative voting system*, how many directors can the dissident shareholders elect?

    c. If the dissident shareholders decide to wage a *proxy fight* to obtain additional votes, how many additional votes would they need to gain voting control of the board (i.e., control four of seven votes) under majority voting? Under cumulative voting?

11-3. The equity section of the balance sheet for Lopez Digital Entertainment is as follows:

Common stock, $0.50 par	$545,000
Additional paid-in capital	$229,000
Retained earnings	$649,000

    a. How many shares has the company issued?

    b. What is the book value per share?

    c. Suppose that Lopez Digital has made only one offering of common stock. At what price did it sell shares to the market?

11-4. Go to the website for Hewlett-Packard Company (http://www.hp.com), one of the largest marketers of personal computers, printers, and related products and services. Click successively on "HP Corporate," "Investor Relations," and "Annual Reports, Proxy Statements and Forms 10K." Click on the most recent Annual Report and find within it the "Consolidated Balance Sheets." Use the statement to answer the following questions.

    a. How much preferred stock did HP have outstanding at the statement date?

    b. How many shares of common stock was HP authorized to issue? What is its par value?

    c. How many shares of common stock has HP issued? How much did the firm raise from the initial sale of its common stock?

    d. How many shares of common stock did HP hold in its treasury at the statement date?

    e. How many shares of common stock did HP have outstanding at the statement date?

    f. How much retained earnings did HP have at the statement date? By how much did this value change from the previous year? What does this change represent?

Smart Solutions

See the problem and solution explained step-by-step at **SMARTFinance**

11-5. Firm XYZ has 11,500,000 shares outstanding and a current stock price of $42.50. In one week, the firm is expected to split its shares 2-for-1 (i.e., each current share will be worth two new shares). It is not uncommon for market participants to consider a stock split to be a signal of "good news." Consequently, the new shares are anticipated to sell for $22.00 each.

    a. Determine the market capitalization of the firm under its current price.

    b. Determine the market capitalization under the anticipated price after the stock split.

    c. Is there a change in the market capitalization that indicates the market is anticipating "good news" about the company?

11-6. A firm has a stock account of $4,000,000 (at $0.25 par) reported on its balance sheet. Yesterday the firm's stock had a closing price of $22.25. Today, the firm paid a $0.35 dividend and the closing price is $22.00.

    a. Determine the firm's market capitalization at the end of the day yesterday.

b. Determine the firm's market capitalization at the end of the day today.

c. Did the firm's shares lose value or gain value between yesterday and today? Calculate the amount of the loss or gain as part of your answer.

11-7. A firm's preferred stock pays a dividend of $1.40. Assuming there is a 35% personal income tax and a 45% corporate income tax, what is the after-tax value of the preferred dividend to the personal investor and the corporate investor? Reevaluate the corporate investor's after-tax dividend assuming that 90% of the dividend value is exempt from taxes. Given this latter structure, do preferred dividends favor personal or corporate investors? Explain.

11-8. A firm's balance sheet reports $2,000,000 in stock ($1 par) and an account reporting additional paid-in capital of $32,460,000. What is the average price of each share of stock reported in the balance sheet?

The Basic Choices in Long-Term Financing

11-9. Meltzer Electronics estimates that its total financing needs for the coming year will be $34.5 million. The firm's required financing payments on its debt and equity financing during the coming fiscal year will total $12.9 million. The firm's financial manager estimates that operating cash flows for the coming year will total $33.7 million and that the following changes will occur in the accounts noted.

Account	Forecast Change
Gross fixed assets	$8.9 million
Change in current assets	+$2.3 million
Change in accounts payable	+$1.3 million
Change in accrued liabilities	+$0.8 million

a. Use Equation 2.3 and the data provided to estimate Meltzer's free cash flow in the coming year.

b. How much of the free cash flow will the firm have available as a source of new internal financing in the coming year?

c. How much external financing will Meltzer need during the coming year to meet its total forecast financing needs?

11-10. Last year Guaraldi Instruments Inc. conducted an IPO, issuing 2 million common shares with a par value of $0.25 to investors at a price of $15 per share. During its first year of operation, Guaraldi earned net income of $0.07 per share and paid a dividend of $0.005 per share. At the end of the year, the company's stock was selling for $20 per share. Construct the equity account for Guaraldi at the end of its first year in business, and calculate the firm's market capitalization.

THOMSON ONE Business School Edition

11-11. Determine the sources of long-term financing for Google Inc. (ticker symbol, GOOG) and Yahoo! Inc. (ticker symbol, YHOO) for the last three years. What percentage of each firm's permanent financing is long-term debt and what percentage is equity? What are the components of each firm's equity (preferred versus common stock)? What percentage of new equity has been raised internally versus externally for both firms? What are some similarities and differences between the sources of long-term financing for Google and Yahoo!?

Mini-Case: An Overview of Long-Term Financing

KajunKorp currently has 1,500,000 shares of common stock outstanding with a $0.75 par value. The firm issued all 1,500,000 shares via an initial public offering at $11.26 per share. The firm's total common equity balance is $28,649,000 and the firm has no treasury stock. Determine the following balances:

Common stock, $0.75 par: _____
Additional paid-in capital: _____
Retained earnings: _____

Also, KajunKorp estimates that it will need $12,000,000 in additional financing to support new projects in the coming year. The firm's current debt ratio is 30% and it wishes to maintain that percentage. KajunKorp expects to generate EBIT of $6,429,000 and currently has $10,000,000 in outstanding long-term debt with a coupon rate of 7%. Any new debt issued will have the same coupon rate. KajunKorp's tax rate is 35% and the firm currently pays a dividend of $0.10 per share; however, they would like to increase the dividend to $0.11 per share. Determine how much the firm expects to generate in retained earnings during the coming year and how many new shares (if any) of common stock KajunKorp will need to issue at the current stock price of $11.26 in order to finance the equity portion of the additional financing.

12

Capital Structure: Theory and Taxes

What Companies Do
Changing Capital Structures

On May 7, 2008, the pharmaceutical giant, GlaxoSmithKline, announced that it was expanding its planned $6 billion bond offering to $9 billion. Despite signs of a building worldwide financial crisis, Glaxo said its initial bond offering was heavily oversubscribed, so it increased the amount that it planned to borrow by half. The company did not plan to use the proceeds from selling bonds for research and development or an expansion of production capacity. Instead, Glaxo planned to repurchase $9 billion of its outstanding common stock.

Just a week later, GreenFuel Technologies, whose algae farms recycle carbon dioxide to produce biofuels and feed, announced that it had issued equity to a private investor group. Like GlaxoSmithKline, GreenFuel planned to use the proceeds to alter its capital structure, but in this case the company was issuing equity to retire outstanding debt.

These examples illustrate that companies sometimes issue debt or equity, not because they need the money to fund an investment project, but rather because they want to alter their capital structure. This behavior suggests that managers believe that there is an optimal capital structure—in other words, one that maximizes firm value. This chapter and the next explore whether there is such a thing as an optimal capital structure and, if so, what factors determine the optimal mix of debt and equity for a particular firm.

Sources: "Glaxo Bonds Bring Whopping $9 Billion," http://www.fiercepharma.com/story/glaxo-bonds-bring-whopping-9b/2008-05-07 (May 7, 2008); Martin LaMonica, "Algae Maker GreenFuel Technologies Scores Cash and Customer," http://news.cnet.com/8301-11128_3-9944420-54.html (May 14, 2008).

Take a moment to look back at Figure 1.1 on page 7. When CFOs were asked to rank the activities that they managed in terms of their value to the company, capital structure appeared at the top of the list. The term *capital structure* refers to the mix of debt and equity securities that a firm issues to finance its activities. Corporate capital structures vary widely and appear to be linked to particular characteristics of firms and industries. For example, high-tech firms and companies whose primary assets are intangible (e.g., intellectual property) tend to use very little debt. Firms in very stable industries or with large investments in assets with active secondary markets tend to employ much higher debt levels. Table 12.1 lists several prominent U.S. companies and their debt levels in 2009. Note the prevalence of high-tech companies on the list of firms with very little debt. Firms on the high-debt list come from industries such as restaurants, food processing, and consumer products.

Table 12.1 2009 Long-Term Debt-to-Assets Ratios			
LOW-DEBT FIRMS		**HIGH-DEBT FIRMS**	
Accenture	0.01	Colgate-Palmolive	0.36
Apple	0	GlaxoSmithKline	0.39
eBay	0	Kellogg	0.37
Google	0	McDonald's	0.36
Microsoft	0	Target	0.40
Qualcomm	0	DIRECTV Group	0.38
Research in Motion	0.13	Waste Management	0.37
Texas Instruments	0	Yum! Brands	0.55
Yahoo!	0	Caterpillar	0.34

Why do CFOs say that capital structure is so important, and what considerations influence their decisions to raise money via debt or equity? It may surprise you that the most important insights into these questions (important enough to warrant two Nobel Prizes) come from a 50-year-old theory that offers the counterintuitive argument that capital structure decisions are completely irrelevant. Before exploring that theory, we will explore some of the consequences of financing a firm with debt or equity.

12.1 WHAT IS FINANCIAL LEVERAGE AND WHAT ARE ITS EFFECTS?

When firms borrow money, we say that they use **financial leverage**. Similarly, we say that a company with debt on its balance sheet is a *levered firm*, and a company that finances its operations entirely with equity is an *unlevered firm*. In Britain, they refer to debt levering as *gearing*. These terms imply that debt magnifies a firm's financial performance in some way. That effect can be either positive or negative, depending on the returns a firm earns on the money it borrows. A simple example illustrates this principle. Consider the decision facing Susan Smith, chief financial officer of High-Tech Manufacturing Corporation (HTMC), a publicly traded company with no debt and 200,000 outstanding shares of common stock. Analysts expect HTMC to generate a $1,000,000 net cash flow each year for the foreseeable future. Given HTMC's risk, shareholders require a 10% return on their investment. Using the present value formula for a perpetuity, we find the company's value equals

$10,000,000 ($1,000,000 ÷ 0.10). By dividing total firm value by the number of shares outstanding, we see that HTMC's stock price is $50 per share ($10,000,000 ÷ 200,000).

A shareholder suggests to Ms. Smith that, by issuing bonds and retiring some of its outstanding stock, HTMC could increase earnings per share and thereby increase its stock price. To be more specific, the shareholder proposes that HTMC should issue $5,000,000 in long-term debt, at an interest rate of 6%, and use the proceeds to repurchase half the company's common stock (i.e., 100,000 shares). This **recapitalization** would be a dramatic shift in the firm's financing mix. Ignoring for the time being any benefits from financing with debt, HTMC's capital structure would change from 100% equity to 50% debt and 50% equity.[1] In other words, this strategy would convert HTMC's debt-to-equity ratio from 0 to 1.0. Table 12.2 summarizes HTMC's current and proposed capital structures.

Table 12.2 Current and Proposed Capital Structures for High-Tech Manufacturing Corporation

	CURRENT	PROPOSED
Assets	$10,000,000	$10,000,000
Equity	$10,000,000	$ 5,000,000
Debt	$ 0	$ 5,000,000
Debt-to-equity ratio	0	1.0
Shares outstanding	200,000	100,000
Share price	$ 50.00	$ 50.00
Interest rate on debt	—	6.0%

Ms. Smith decides to analyze the proposal to determine whether it results in a higher stock price. She agrees with analysts who expect that HTMC's net cash flow will be $1,000,000 next year, assuming the economy continues to grow at a normal rate. Other outcomes are possible, however. If the economy booms, cash flow will reach $1,500,000. If a recession occurs, cash flow will fall to $500,000. How do shareholders fare under the current and proposed capital structures in each of these scenarios?

First, consider what happens if cash flow equals $1,000,000 as expected. Under the current capital structure, with 200,000 shares and no debt, earnings per share (EPS) equals $5. If HTMC pays out all earnings as a dividend, then shareholders receive $5 on their $50 investment, a 10% return. In other words, an HTMC shareholder who buys a share of stock for $50 earns exactly the required 10% return. But in the case that HTMC issues debt and buys back half its outstanding stock, the firm has 100,000 shares and $5 million in debt. Because the interest rate is 6%, HTMC must pay $300,000 in interest, leaving $700,000 for shareholders. However, with half as many shares outstanding, $700,000 in net cash flow translates into EPS of $7, or a 14% return for shareholders. The first two columns in Table 12.3 summarize these calculations.

So far, the recapitalization plan seems to look rather attractive. But what happens if a boom or a recession occurs? Table 12.3 shows the payoffs to HTMC's investors under those economic scenarios. The middle columns show that if the economy booms and High-Tech's cash flow reaches $1,500,000, shareholders earn more under the new capital structure than the old (EPS of $12 versus $7.50, or a return equal to 24% versus 15%).

---

[1]Later we will see that using debt can reduce taxes because interest is tax-deductible and reducing taxes increases firm value. For simplicity, we ignore that benefit in this example.

Table 12.3 Expected Cash Flows to Stockholders and Bondholders under the Current and Proposed Capital Structures for High-Tech Manufacturing Corporation for Three Equally Likely Outcomes

| CASH FLOW: | NORMAL | | BOOM | | RECESSION | |
| | $1,000,000 | | $1,500,000 | | $500,000 | |
	ALL-EQUITY FINANCING	50% DEBT, 50% EQUITY	ALL-EQUITY FINANCING	50% DEBT, 50% EQUITY	ALL-EQUITY FINANCING	50% DEBT, 50% EQUITY
Less: Interest paid (6.0%)	$ 0	($300,000)	$ 0	($ 300,000)	$ 0	($300,000)
Net income	$1,000,000	$700,000	$1,500,000	$1,200,000	$500,000	$200,000
Shares outstanding	200,000	100,000	200,000	100,000	200,000	100,000
Earnings per share	$ 5.00	$ 7.00	$ 7.50	$ 12.00	$ 2.50	$ 2.00
Return on shares (P_0 = $50/share)	10.0%	14.0%	15.0%	24.00%	5.0%	4.0%

If a recession hits, HTMC shareholders fare worse under the new capital structure than they would have under the old one. In the recession scenario, a 50-50 mix of debt and equity generates EPS of $2 (a return of 4%) whereas with an all-equity capital structure the shareholders receive earnings of $2.50 per share (a return of 5%).

Figure 12.1 illustrates how High-Tech's capital structure affects the relationship between cash flow (before interest) and EPS. In good economic times, the company enjoys higher EPS with the 50-50 capital structure than with the all-equity capital structure. However,

FIGURE 12.1

The Effect of Leverage on the Sensitivity of EPS to Changes in Cash Flow.

For cash flow above $600,000, the levered 50-50 capital structure yields higher earnings per share than does the all-equity capital structure. The reverse is true for cash flow less than $600,000.

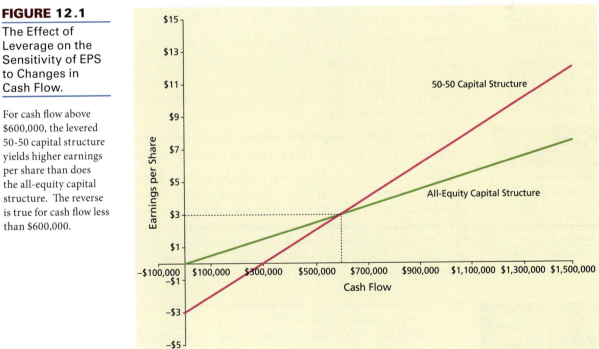

in a recession, HTMC's shareholders earn more under the old all-equity capital structure. Now you see how the terms *leverage* and *gearing* apply to the decision to borrow money: Relative to the all-equity capital structure, borrowing money makes shareholders better off when times are good and the firm's cash flows are high, but shareholders fare worse in bad economic times. Leverage magnifies both the good outcomes and the bad ones.

The lines in Figure 12.1 cross when cash flow equals $600,000. When cash flow exceeds $600,000, HTMC's shareholders earn more with the 50-50 mix than with the current all-equity structure. If cash flow is below $600,000 then the reverse is true: shareholders earn higher EPS with all-equity financing than they would if HTMC were to borrow money.

For the proposed recapitalization, the *break-even level of operating profits*—the level of cash flow yielding the same return on equity (ROE) for both capital structures—occurs when cash flow equals $600,000. It is no accident that $600,000 defines the break-even point here. Notice that if HTMC earns $600,000 on assets of $10 million then its return on assets equals 6%, the same rate that it pays on borrowed funds. If the firm can earn more on its assets than it pays on its debt, then EPS goes up relative to the all-equity case. If cash flow falls short of $600,000 then the firm earns less on its investments than it pays in interest; hence EPS goes down relative to the all-equity case. The slopes of the lines in the figure indicate that debt magnifies the effect on EPS of any change in cash flow. When cash flow changes, EPS changes faster if the firm is levered than if it is unlevered.

What should Ms. Smith do? Suppose she believes that each of the three economic scenarios is equally likely. Based on that view, we can calculate the expected values of HTMC's earnings before interest and taxes, as well as the expected payoffs to shareholders under each capital structure:

$$\text{Expected cash flow} = \left(\tfrac{1}{3}\right)\$1,000,000 + \left(\tfrac{1}{3}\right)\$1,500,000 + \left(\tfrac{1}{3}\right)\$500,000 = \$1,000,000$$

$$\text{Expected EPS (no debt)} = \left(\tfrac{1}{3}\right)\$5.00 + \left(\tfrac{1}{3}\right)\$7.50 + \left(\tfrac{1}{3}\right)\$2.50 = \$5$$

$$\text{Expected EPS (with debt)} = \left(\tfrac{1}{3}\right)\$7.00 + \left(\tfrac{1}{3}\right)\$12.00 + \left(\tfrac{1}{3}\right)\$2.00 = \$7$$

$$\text{Expected ROE (no debt)} = \left(\tfrac{1}{3}\right)10\% + \left(\tfrac{1}{3}\right)15\% + \left(\tfrac{1}{3}\right)5\% = 10\%$$

$$\text{Expected ROE (with debt)} = \left(\tfrac{1}{3}\right)14\% + \left(\tfrac{1}{3}\right)24\% + \left(\tfrac{1}{3}\right)4\% = 14\%$$

JOB INTERVIEW QUESTION

What impact would you expect on a firm's earnings if it raises its debt-to-equity ratio?

Ms. Smith faces a difficult decision. Switching the capital structure from all equity to half equity and half debt raises expected returns to shareholders. But it also makes those returns more variable than in the all-equity case. This example leads us to an important general principle of leverage.

> The **fundamental principle of financial leverage:** *Substituting debt for equity increases expected returns to shareholders but also increases the risk that equity investors bear.*

Because adding debt to the capital structure makes shareholders' claims more risky, they should demand a higher return. Therefore, whether the addition of debt to HTMC's capital structure increases the firm's stock price depends on the relative importance of two offsetting effects: the increase in expected cash flows to shareholders versus the increased discount rate that shareholders will apply to these cash flows. In one special (but important) case, these forces offset each other exactly, which means that changing a firm's capital structure neither raises nor lowers its value.

Smart Practices Video

Mitchell Petersen, Northwestern University

"When firms structure their business, they need to think about trading off operating and financial leverage."

See the entire interview at SMARTFinance

Concept Review Questions

1. What is a recapitalization?
2. What trade-offs do managers face when they consider changing a firm's capital structure?

WHAT COMPANIES DO GLOBALLY

CFO Survey: The Importance of Capital Structure Decisions

Cohen and Yagil surveyed 140 CFOs from the U.S., the U.K., Germany, Canada, and Japan and asked them to rank the importance of investment policy and financing policy to their firms (5 = very important, 1 = not important). The figure below shows the unsurprising result that CFOs view both investment and financing decisions as quite important. Observe, however, that the relative importance of the two decisions varies depending on whether the CFO manages a firm with high leverage or low leverage. In firms that rely more on debt than on equity (i.e., whose debt ratios exceed 50%), CFOs say that managing the firm's capital structure is even more important than how the firm invests its money. Perhaps this reflects the fundamental principle of leverage. The more a firm borrows the more volatile are its earnings, so the importance of paying close attention to capital structure increases.

Source: Gil Cohen and Joseph Yagil, "A Multinational Survey of Corporate Financial Policies," *Journal of Applied Finance* (Spring/Summer 2007), pp. 57–69.

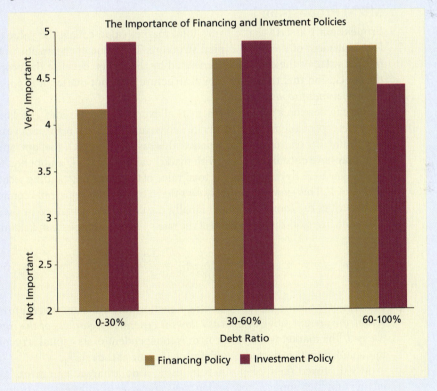

12.2 THE MODIGLIANI & MILLER PROPOSITIONS

In 1958, Franco Modigliani and Merton Miller (hereafter, M&M) published a pathbreaking study that challenged conventional thinking about capital structure.[2] They demonstrated that changes in the mix of debt and equity merely altered the division of a firm's cash flows

---

[2] Franco Modigliani and Merton Miller, "The Cost of Capital, Corporation Finance and the Theory of Investment," *American Economic Review* 48, no. 3 (1958), pp. 261–297.

between its stockholders and bondholders but did not fundamentally affect firm value. This conclusion was predicated on several important assumptions:

1. Capital markets are perfect, meaning that investors and firms face no market frictions such as taxes or transactions costs.
2. Investors can borrow and lend at the same rate that corporations can.
3. There are no information asymmetries.

Although these assumptions clearly do not correspond to conditions in real markets, M&M's conclusions remain significant for two reasons.

First, by understanding why leverage choices have no value impact in perfect markets, managers can see more clearly how market imperfections can lead one capital structure to be preferred over another. Second, the **Modigliani and Miller argument** rests on the principle of *no arbitrage*—a principle that drives many important concepts in finance, from the determination of exchange rates to option pricing. Understanding how this principle applies to the capital structure decision will clarify its use in other areas throughout the book.

M&M Proposition I

Proposition I asserts that a firm's total market value equals the value of its assets and is independent of the firm's capital structure. The value of the assets, in turn, equals the present value of the cash flows generated by the assets. Because the proposition leads to the conclusion that the firm's capital structure does not matter, it is popularly known as the *irrelevance proposition*.

We can develop a simple, mathematical expression of this idea as follows. Assume that investors expect a company to generate a constant cash flow stream each year for the foreseeable future. For convenience, let's denote this cash flow by NOI (net operating income). The firm may have outstanding debt with market value equal to D and/or equity with a market value equal to E. By definition, the total value of the firm's outstanding securities is V, where $V = D + E$. This expression simply says that a firm's value equals the combined value of all the securities the company issues.[3] Finally, the cash flows generated by the firm's assets are risky, and investors discount them at the rate r_A. M&M's Proposition I claims the following:

$$V = (D + E) = \frac{NOI}{r_A} \qquad \text{(Eq. 12.1)}$$

In terms of the firm's capital structure, Equation 12.1 indicates that *the firm's market value equals the present value of the cash flows it generates regardless of the capital structure it chooses.* The market value of any firm is independent of its capital structure and is given by capitalizing its expected net operating income at the rate r_A.

M&M proved their proposition by using a no-arbitrage argument. **Arbitrage** means buying and then immediately selling the same asset at different prices to earn a risk-free profit. In well-functioning markets, arbitrage opportunities arise infrequently and vanish as soon as traders begin to exploit them. The "no-arbitrage principle"—upon which M&M's argument rests—simply states that, in equilibrium, market prices must adjust to a point at which no arbitrage opportunities remain. M&M demonstrate that if a levered firm's value differs from that of an identical unlevered firm, then an arbitrage opportunity exists.

---

[3]We are not speaking of just the value of the firm's equity here. By "value of the firm" we mean the market value of the firm's assets, not just the value of the residual claim that shareholders own.

And arbitrage opportunities can't last very long because traders will quickly exploit them, moving prices and eliminating the opportunity. This means that the values of the levered and unlevered firms must be identical in equilibrium. This result is easiest to show with an example.

Firm Value When Proposition I Holds   Assume that M&M's assumption of a perfect capital market holds, meaning that there are no tax savings or other benefits from issuing debt. Consider two equally risky firms, UnleverCo and LeverCo. Each expects the same operating profit, $100,000 per year in perpetuity. Furthermore, assume that the required return r_A on each firm's assets is 10%, implying a total firm value of $1 million ($100,000 operating profit ÷ 0.10 required return). UnleverCo has no debt outstanding. Instead, it has 20,000 common shares worth $50 each.[4] Note that, because UnleverCo has no debt, the required return on its shares equals the required return on its assets, 10%. We denote the required return on unlevered shares as r_u.

In contrast, LeverCo began life as an all-equity firm but recently issued debt and used the proceeds to retire shares. Assume that it issued $500,000 worth of debt at 6% interest and that it used the debt proceeds to repurchase half of its outstanding equity. This means LeverCo purchased 10,000 shares at $50 each.[5] It therefore has 10,000 shares remaining that should also be worth $50 each, for a total of $500,000.

What return can LeverCo's shareholders expect on their levered shares? Recall that LeverCo will earn $100,000 in operating profits, from which it must pay $30,000 in interest on its debt (0.06 × $500,000). This leaves $70,000 for the firm's 10,000 shareholders, or $7 per share. If LeverCo's shares sell for $50, then investors must expect a 14% return ($7 ÷ $50). We will use r_l to denote the required return on levered equity. Table 12.4 summarizes the two firms' financial characteristics.

Table 12.4   UnleverCo and LeverCo When Proposition I Holds

	UNLEVERCO	LEVERCO
Net operating income (NOI)	$ 100,000	$ 100,000
Less: Interest paid (0.06 × D)	0	30,000
Net income [NOI − (0.06 × D)]	$ 100,000	$ 70,000
Required return on assets (r_A)	0.10	0.10
Total firm value (NOI/r_A)	$1,000,000	$1,000,000
Required return on equity (r_u or r_l)	0.10	0.14
Shares outstanding	20,000	10,000
Market value of equity (E)	$1,000,000	$ 500,000
Interest rate on debt (r_d)	N/A	0.06
Market value of debt (D)	$ 0	$ 500,000

[4] You can derive the $50 stock price in two ways. First, divide total value firm value ($1 million) by the shares outstanding (20,000) to obtain the $50 share price. Second, divide expected operating income ($100,000) by the number of shares to obtain $5 earnings per share; then, because the required return on these shares is 10%, the market price per share must be $50.

[5] To keep this analysis clearly focused on pure capital structure changes, we assume that the firm uses any money raised by issuing debt to retire outstanding equity. This keeps the total value of the firm's assets constant and allows us to examine financial changes in isolation.

Proving Proposition I Using Homemade Leverage Now let's see how an investor could profit if Proposition I does *not* hold and the market value of LeverCo exceeds that of UnleverCo. What happens if investors pay a premium for the shares of levered firms? If the price of LeverCo's shares exceeds $50, then the company's investors must be willing to accept a return below 14%. Let's say that LeverCo's shareholders expect a 12.5% return. This would imply that LeverCo's equity is worth $560,000 ($70,000 net income ÷ 0.125 required return), or $56 per share. Combining the value of LeverCo's debt and equity, we obtain a total firm value equal to $1,060,000. UnleverCo's market value remains $1 million. Table 12.5 summarizes these new conditions.

Table 12.5	Disequilibrium Values for UnleverCo and LeverCo If LeverCo's Required Return Is 12.5%		
		UNLEVERCO	**LEVERCO**
Net operating income (NOI)		$ 100,000	$ 100,000
Less: Interest paid (0.06 × D)		0	30,000
Net income [NOI − (0.06 × D)]		$ 100,000	$ 70,000
Total firm value (NOI/r_A)		$1,000,000	$1,060,000
Required return on equity (r_u or r_l)		0.10	0.125
Shares outstanding		20,000	10,000
Market value of equity (E)		$1,000,000	$ 560,000
Interest rate on debt (r_d)		N/A	0.06
Market value of debt (D)		$ 0	$ 500,000

How can investors profit in this situation? Suppose an investor currently owns 1% of LeverCo's outstanding stock (100 shares worth $5,600) and expects to earn a 12.5% return on that investment, or $700. The investor could earn an arbitrage profit from the following transactions:

Sell 100 LeverCo shares	+$5,600
Borrow $5,000 @ 6%	+$5,000
Purchase 200 UnleverCo shares	−$10,000
Funds remaining	$600

What has our investor accomplished with this series of transactions? Initially, he held 1% of LeverCo's equity. After these transactions are complete, the investor owns 1% of UnleverCo's equity but also has outstanding personal debt of $5,000—an amount that is, not coincidentally, equal to 1% of LeverCo's debt. In other words, the investor uses $5,000 in **homemade leverage** to cover half the cost of buying 1% of UnleverCo's shares.

What return can the investor expect on the new portfolio? Because the expected payoff on each UnleverCo share equals $5, his 200-share portfolio generates $1,000 in cash flow each year. However, he owes $300 in interest on personal borrowings (6% × $5,000), so the net cash flow from the portfolio will be $700 annually. This is exactly the expected annual cash flow from the prior holdings of 100 LeverCo shares. Now we can see that the original portfolio is identical to the new one. *Given that LeverCo finances its operations with 50% equity and 50% debt, holding 1% of LeverCo's stock is equivalent to holding 1% of UnleverCo's stock and financing half of that investment with personal debt.*

In what sense is this an arbitrage opportunity? Recall that after selling LeverCo shares, borrowing money, and buying UnleverCo stock, the investor had $600 in cash left over. That $600 represents his arbitrage profit. The risk and expected return of the new portfolio exactly match the old one, but the new portfolio costs $600 less. Such an arbitrage opportunity will not last very long. As investors sell LeverCo shares so they can buy UnleverCo stock to form the new portfolio, the price of LeverCo shares will fall and that of UnleverCo shares will rise. The share prices will change until the market reaches a new equilibrium in which the total market values of the two firms are identical—just as Proposition I says they should be.

What if the price on LeverCo's shares was originally too *low*? In this case, arbitrage would proceed in the opposite direction. An investor would sell UnleverCo shares and then purchase 1% of *both* the debt and the equity of LeverCo. Purchasing LeverCo's debt and its equity makes the new portfolio just as risky as an investment in UnleverCo shares. After completing this transaction, the investor would have cash remaining because LeverCo's shares are undervalued. However, the purchase of LeverCo shares will push the price up, and in equilibrium the prices of LeverCo and UnleverCo will be equal.

The key point is that, under the assumptions of the M&M model, the profit-maximizing activities of investors will ensure that Proposition I holds. Whether a company uses leverage or not will have no effect on its total market value.

M&M Proposition II and the WACC

Modigliani and Miller established in Proposition I that a firm's market value is not related to its debt-to-equity ratio. In a second proposition, they also dispelled a common misperception about the debt/equity choice. Refer back to the description of UnleverCo in Table 12.4. The table indicates that UnleverCo's shareholders expect a 10% return, but UnleverCo could issue debt at a cost of 6%. Wouldn't it be wise for UnleverCo's managers to raise money from the cheapest source, and isn't that source debt?

M&M's second important insight is that, even though debt is less costly for firms to issue than equity, issuing debt causes the required return on the remaining equity to rise. Based on the core finance principle that investors expect compensation for risk, shareholders of levered firms demand higher returns than do shareholders in all-equity companies. Table 12.4 demonstrates this clearly: even though LeverCo and UnleverCo are essentially identical businesses, LeverCo's shareholders expect a 14% return on their investment—a considerably higher figure than the 10% return required by UnleverCo stockholders. Therefore, when managers are tempted to issue debt because it seems less costly than equity, they do well to remember that adding debt raises the cost of equity (because levered equity is more risky).

We can formalize all of this mathematically as follows. Remember that the required return on the firm's assets is r_A, the interest rate on its debt is r_d, and the market values of its debt and equity are D and E, respectively. M&M's **Proposition II** says that the expected return on a levered firm's equity, r_l, increases with the debt-to-equity ratio:

$$r_l = r_A + (r_A - r_d)\left[\frac{D}{E}\right]$$

(Eq. 12.2)

Observe what Equation 12.2 says about a firm with no debt at all. In that case, the equation implies that the return on equity equals the return on assets, a relationship that we mentioned previously. As debt increases, however, the return on equity rises as well. By replacing equity with debt, a firm does indeed replace a high-cost source of finance with a low-cost one. Yet there is no net benefit from doing so because the increase in the required return on the firm's remaining equity *exactly offsets* the savings from replacing some of the old equity with debt.

JOB INTERVIEW QUESTION

Our firm's cost of equity is 15%, but we can borrow money at 7%. If we need to raise money to fund a new investment, should we borrow money because it's cheaper?

This should not be a surprise; it ties right back to Proposition I. If a firm could lower its total financing costs by substituting debt for equity, then that would increase the firm's value. Proposition I rules this out, so substituting debt for equity (or vice versa) should have no net impact on the firm's financing costs.

With a little rearranging, we can write Equation 12.2 this way:

$$r_A = r_l\left(\frac{E}{D + E}\right) + r_d\left(\frac{D}{D + E}\right)$$

Does this look familiar? It should. It's the expression introduced in Chapter 9 for a firm's weighted average cost of capital (WACC), if we ignore the tax deductibility of interest on debt. Note that the WACC is the discount rate that the firm uses to value its investments in real assets. It is also the return that a firm must earn to satisfy lenders and shareholders. When Proposition II holds, the WACC is independent of capital structure and the term r_A is a constant. But if the WACC is unrelated to leverage then so is the value of the firm, because the WACC is the rate we use to discount the firm's cash flows to obtain its market value. Hence the connection between Propositions I and II.

If you examine Equation 12.2, you may wonder how we can claim that the WACC remains constant even as the debt-to-equity ratio changes. Mathematically, it seems that any adjustment to the terms on the right-hand side of the WACC equation must result in a change on the left-hand side. Thus, changes in capital structure should affect the WACC. But M&M Proposition II implies that *changes in leverage cause an offsetting change in the required return on equity.* That offsetting change would leave the return on assets—the WACC—unchanged. We can see this by calculating the WACC for our two hypothetical firms.

$$WACC_{UnleverCo} = 0.10\left(\frac{\$1,000,000}{\$0 + \$1,000,000}\right) + 0.06\left(\frac{\$0}{\$0 + \$1,000,000}\right) = 0.10$$

$$WACC_{LeverCo} = 0.14\left(\frac{\$500,000}{\$500,000 + \$500,000}\right) + 0.06\left(\frac{\$500,000}{\$500,000 + \$500,000}\right) = 0.10$$

Both firms have a 10% WACC, even though their capital structures vary a great deal. LeverCo finances half its operations with 6% debt. However, because it uses so much debt, LeverCo's shareholders require a 14% return on levered equity, much higher than the 10% return UnleverCo promises its shareholders. *On balance, then, there is no advantage to using all equity or a mix of debt and equity.*

The left-hand graph of Figure 12.2 illustrates M&M's Proposition II: It shows that the rising cost of equity, which accompanies a higher debt ratio, leaves a firm's WACC unchanged. Of course, as a firm borrows more, eventually its creditors may demand a higher return. The right-hand graph of Figure 12.2 illustrates this case. As the debt ratio rises, r_d increases, which causes r_l to increase even faster. Nonetheless, the WACC remains unchanged. In the limiting case when a firm uses 100% debt, r_d equals the WACC. The figure key is as follows:

$$r_A + (r_A - r_d)\frac{D}{E} = r_l = \text{cost of levered equity}$$

$$r_d = \text{cost of debt}$$

$$WACC = r_A = \text{weighted average cost of capital}$$

$$D = \text{market value of debt outstanding}$$

$$E = \text{market value of stock outstanding}$$

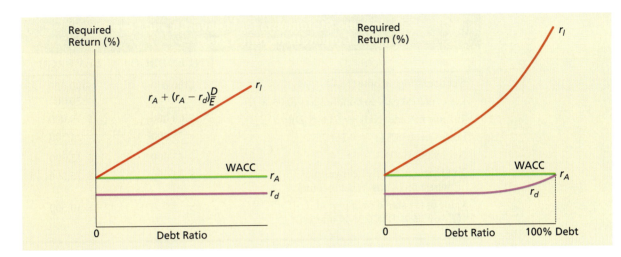

FIGURE 12.2

M&M Proposition II-The Case of Perfect Capital Markets

The required return on equity rises as debt increases, leaving the WACC unchanged. Thus, when capital markets are perfect, WACC = r_A regardless of capital structure.

Concept Review Questions	3. Explain how Propositions I and II are different as well as what they have in common.
	4. What is the difference between levered and unlevered equity? Suppose a shareholder of an unlevered firm, like Intel Corp., wanted the company to include more debt in its capital structure. What action could the investor undertake that would have the same effect as the company borrowing more?
	5. M&M used an analogy of separating whole milk into skim milk and cream to demonstrate the futility—in terms of creating value—of repackaging a firm's cash flows into debt and equity streams. How does this analogy relate to Proposition I? Can separating whole milk into cream and skim components create value? Why or why not?

12.3 M&M AND TAXES

M&M derived their famous propositions by starting with the assumption that firms operate in markets without taxes or transactions costs. In this section, we look at what happens when we introduce corporate income taxes into the M&M framework.

The M&M Model with Corporate Taxes

In the United States and many other countries, firms can deduct interest payments to lenders as a business expense. (Dividends paid to shareholders receive no similar tax advantage.) The interest deduction thus reduces the amount of taxes the firm must pay to the government. Intuitively, this should lead to a tax advantage for debt, meaning that managers can increase firm value by issuing debt.

Table 12.6 illustrates how a 35% corporate income tax rate (T_c) affects firms with and without leverage. Recall that investors expect UnleverCo and LeverCo to generate the same pretax profit of $100,000. After paying $35,000 in corporate income taxes, UnleverCo can distribute $65,000 to its shareholders as a dividend. LeverCo must pay $30,000 in interest to bondholders. As a result, LeverCo's taxable income is just $70,000. It pays $24,500 in taxes and distributes $45,500 to its shareholders.

Table 12.6 Income Statements for UnleverCo and LeverCo with Corporate Income Taxes

	UNLEVERCO	LEVERCO
Net operating income (NOI)	$100,000	$100,000
Less: Interest paid to bondholders (0.06 × D)	0	30,000
Taxable income [NOI − (0.06 × D)]	$100,000	$ 70,000
Less: Tax at 35% (T_c = 0.35)	35,000	24,500
Net income (NI)	$ 65,000	$ 45,500
Total income to private investors (interest on bonds + net income)	$ 65,000	$ 75,500
Value of tax shield each period (T_c × 0.06 × D = 0.35 × interest)	$ 0	$ 10,500

In a sense, a corporate income tax gives the government a claim on a firm's cash flows. Like all other financial claims, the value of the government's claim equals the present value of taxes that the firm pays. Table 12.6 shows that, by using debt, LeverCo reduces its tax bill and thereby reduces the value of the government's claim. By avoiding debt entirely, UnleverCo maximizes its tax bill and the value of the government's stake. This in turn reduces the cash flows available to pay out to investors, ultimately reducing the share price.

We can now compute the value of UnleverCo (V_U) by using the basic M&M valuation formula used before but now modified to discount after-tax net income. Assume that investors still require a 10% return on the firm's assets. Then

$$V_U = \frac{[\text{NOI}(1 - T_c)]}{r} = \frac{\$65,000}{0.10} = \$650,000 \qquad \text{(Eq. 12.3)}$$

In the no-tax world, UnleverCo's market value was $1,000,000. Equation 12.3 shows that the 35% corporate profits tax causes the company's value to drop by $350,000. This represents a wealth transfer from UnleverCo's shareholders to the government.

Equation 12.3 reveals that corporate taxes reduce an unlevered firm's value (compared to its value with no taxes). By issuing debt, a firm can shield some of its cash flows from taxation and hence increase its value. Can we quantify the benefit of this tax shield?

If we assume that the firm always renews its debt when it matures, then the cash flow produced by the interest deduction becomes a perpetuity equal to the tax rate multiplied by the interest paid. To find the perpetuity's present value, we discount the tax shield at r_d, the interest rate on the firm's debt.[6] With these assumptions, we can compute the present value of the interest tax shields as follows:

$$\text{PV(Interest tax shield)} = \frac{T_c \times r_d \times D}{r_d} = T_c \times D = 0.35(\$500,000) \qquad \text{(Eq. 12.4)}$$
$$= \$175,000$$

In other words, the benefit of debt is equal to the tax rate multiplied by the face value of debt outstanding. (Note that Equation 12.4 measures the value of the *benefit* resulting from

[6]We use r_d as the discount rate here because the interest tax shield does not materialize until the firm makes its debt payments, and the debt payments are fixed at an amount D. So the risk of the interest tax deduction is similar to the risk of the firm's debt.

interest tax deductions while ignoring all *costs* associated with using debt.) Hence the value of LeverCo, V_L, equals the value of UnleverCo *plus* the value of the interest tax shields:

$$V_L = V_U + \text{PV(Interest tax shield)} = V_U + T_c D = \$650,000 + \$175,000$$
$$= \$825,000 \qquad \text{(Eq. 12.5)}$$

JOB INTERVIEW QUESTION

If we issue $10 billion in long-term debt and use the proceeds to repurchase shares, what effect (qualitative and quantitative) will this have on our stock price?

What a deal! In essence, the government has given LeverCo's managers a $175,000 subsidy to employ debt financing rather than equity.

It is important to note that shareholders ultimately benefit from the tax benefits of debt financing. Interest deductions reduce the payments owed to the government and increase the cash flows available to shareholders (because shareholders are the residual claimants and receive all cash flows left after all bills and taxes are paid). Therefore, in this example, the $175,000 increase in firm value is reflected in a $175,000 increase in the value of the firm's common stock.

Figure 12.3 illustrates the impact of taxes on firm value. Panel A represents the situation in the original, no-tax case: there, the size of the pie (i.e., the value of the firm) does not depend on how you divide the pie between debt and equity claims. With a corporate income tax, though, a firm's capital structure influences its value: debt determines how much of the pie goes to the government. The more the firm borrows, the smaller is the government's claim and thus the larger are the claims held by private investors. Panel B of Figure 12.3 illustrates this point. At the limit, the government's slice (its tax claim) disappears when the firm finances its operations entirely through debt and pays all its earnings in tax-deductible interest.

EXAMPLE

In 2009, eBay used no debt and its equity had a market value of $13.4 billion. In the absence of debt, this implies that eBay's assets were also worth $13.4 billion. What would happen to the total value of eBay if the firm issued $6.7 billion in long-term debt and used the proceeds to retire half of its equity? According to Equation 12.5, if eBay faces a corporate tax rate of 35% then the recapitalization would create an additional $2.35 billion (0.35 × $6.7 billion) in value for eBay investors!

Smart Concepts

See the concept explained step-by-step at

SMARTFinance

But why should the firm's management stop there? If a 50-50 capital structure increases total firm value by $175,000 (compared to the all-equity case), then the *optimal* leverage ratio for any firm is 100% debt! More than anything else, this implication of M&M's early work created skepticism about their conclusions. How could the theory be correct if it predicted that firms should be so highly levered? Obviously, there must be costs that offset the tax benefit of debt and discourage firms from financing with 100% debt.

The M&M Model with Corporate and Personal Taxes

After M&M published their findings, finance researchers and practitioners faced a quandary. Their best theoretical models said managers either should not worry about the capital structure decision or should borrow as much as possible to minimize taxes. In 1977, Merton Miller offered an explanation for the puzzle. Debt levels had averaged between 30% and 40% of total capital for decades (except during the Depression), in spite of the fact that corporate tax rates had varied from zero to over 50% during the same period. Miller pointed out that legislatures had almost invariably changed corporate and personal tax rates at the same time and in the same direction. Furthermore, in many periods the

FIGURE 12.3

The Impact of Corporate Taxes on Modigliani and Miller Proposition I and Firm Value

Panel A

With no taxes, the size of the pie, or the value of the firm, does not depend on the mix of debt and equity that the firm chooses. Proposition I holds, and capital structure is irrelevant.

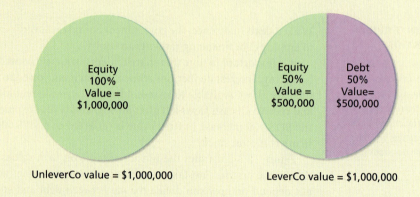

Panel B

With a corporate income tax, a portion of the firm's cash flows goes to the government, diminishing the value of claims held by private investors. The government's slice of the pie shrinks the more debt a firm uses because the government allows deduction for interest payments. A company could shelter nearly all of its cash flows by financing its operations almost entirely with debt. Therefore, capital structure matters because firm value is larger if the firm uses more debt.

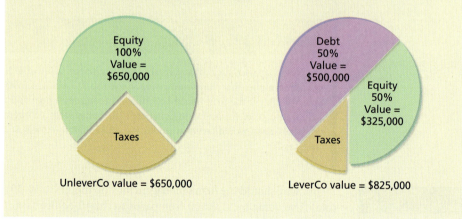

tax rate that investors faced on interest income from corporate bonds exceeded the tax rate they faced on dividends and capital gains from stock. Miller argued that debt's tax *advantage* over equity at the *corporate* level might be partially or fully offset by a tax *disadvantage* at the *individual* level.

Synthesizing differences in corporate income tax rates as well as personal tax rates on interest, dividends, and capital gain, Miller produced the following formula to calculate G_L, the *gains from using leverage*:

$$G_L = \left\{ 1 - \left[\frac{(1 - T_c)(1 - T_{ps})}{1 - T_{pd}} \right] \right\} D \qquad \textbf{(Eq. 12.6)}$$

where

T_c = tax rate on corporate profits (as before)

T_{ps} = personal tax rate on income from stock (dividends and capital gains)

T_{pd} = personal tax rate on income from debt (interest income)

D = market value of a firm's outstanding debt

Equation 12.6 helps resolve the seeming conflict between leverage and taxes. It shows that the capital structure decision can increase, decrease, or have no effect on firm value depending on parameters of the tax code. If, for example, there are no taxes at all ($T_c = T_{ps} = T_{pd} = 0$), then G_L equals zero and the original M&M propositions hold: using debt does not increase firm value. If the government taxes corporations but not individuals ($T_c = 0.35$; $T_{ps} = T_{pd} = 0$), then the gains from leverage, G_L, equal T_cD and an all-debt capital structure emerges as the optimal choice. However, with a high personal tax burden on interest income relative to equity income, the gains from leverage can disappear. Miller (1977) argued that, in the **Miller equilibrium**, the gains to leverage equal zero because personal tax costs exactly offset the gain to interest being tax deductible at the corporate level.

To see how the gains from leverage can even be negative, consider an extreme case with a zero tax rate on income from stocks ($T_{ps} = 0$). This is not as wild as it might sound, since U.S. investors pay taxes on capital gains *only when they are realized*, and taxes on some equity investments can be skipped entirely with careful estate planning. Combine this assumption with a 35% corporate income tax and a 40% personal tax rate on interest income, and debt's tax advantage turns into a disadvantage:

$$G_L = \left\{ 1 - \left[\frac{(1 - 0.35)(1 - 0.0)}{1 - 0.4} \right] \right\} D = (-0.083)D$$

With this set of tax rates, the "gain" from leverage is actually negative! Using debt would actually reduce firm value relative to the case where the firm is financed entirely with equity.

In some cases, the effects of corporate and personal taxes may exactly offset each other. In the example just discussed, if the personal tax on equity income changes from 0% to 7.7%, the gain from leverage is zero and capital structure is again irrelevant.

EXAMPLE

Consider a situation in which the corporate tax rate is 35%, the personal tax rate on interest income is 40%, and the personal tax rate on dividends is 15%. Suppose that a firm finances its operations entirely with equity. In a particular year, this firm earns net operating income of $1 million, or $650,000 after corporate taxes, and it pays out this profit as a dividend. Given the dividend tax rate of 15%, shareholders experience an after-tax gain of $552,500 ($= 0.85 \times \$650,000$).

Now imagine that this firm had financed its operations entirely with debt rather than equity. The entire $1 million operating profit flows to bondholders and escapes corporate taxes entirely. However, bondholders receiving the interest owe $400,000 in personal taxes, netting $600,000 after taxes. Under these conditions, the all-debt capital structure still produces higher returns for investors, but personal taxes on interest lower the debt's tax advantage as compared to the case when governments tax only corporate income.

By changing the corporate and personal tax rates, legislatures change the relative benefits of using debt and equity financing. For instance, lowering the corporate tax rate from 35% to 29% in this Example nullifies the tax advantage of debt.

WHAT COMPANIES DO GLOBALLY

Tax Factors in Emerging Markets

Do tax factors influence capital structure decisions in emerging markets? The answer appears to be a qualified yes. In the first chart below, we plot the ratio of long-term debt as a percentage of total capital (book value) against the corporate tax rate in nine emerging markets as well as in the United States. The upward-sloping line drawn through the data points indicates that there is a tendency for firms facing higher corporate tax rates to rely more heavily on debt, but the R-squared statistic (and visual inspection of the graph) suggests that tax rates do not explain much of the variation in capital structures across countries.

Capital Structures in Emerging Markets
Corporate Tax Rates

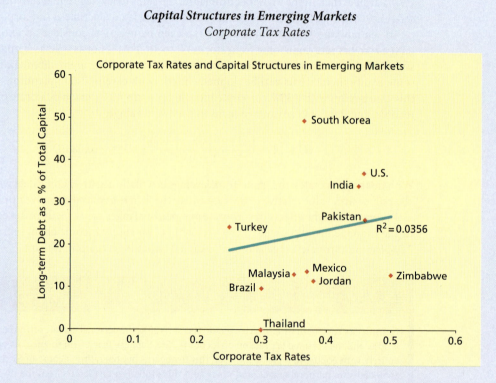

In the second chart, we plot the long-term debt ratio against the net tax advantage of debt as determined by Equation 12.6. First, note that in six countries debt enjoys a net tax advantage but in three countries debt is taxed more heavily than equity once we take personal taxes into account. Second, the correlation between capital structure and taxes is higher here than it was when we considered only corporate taxes (i.e., the R-squared is almost 4 times higher in the second chart). Clearly, however, taxes cannot be the whole story. Firms' capital structure choices vary much more than can be explained by taxes alone.

Source: Laurence Booth, Varouj Aivazian, Asli Demirgüç-Kunt, and Vojislav Maksimovic, "Capital Structures in Developing Countries," *Journal of Finance* 56 (February 2001), pp. 87–130.

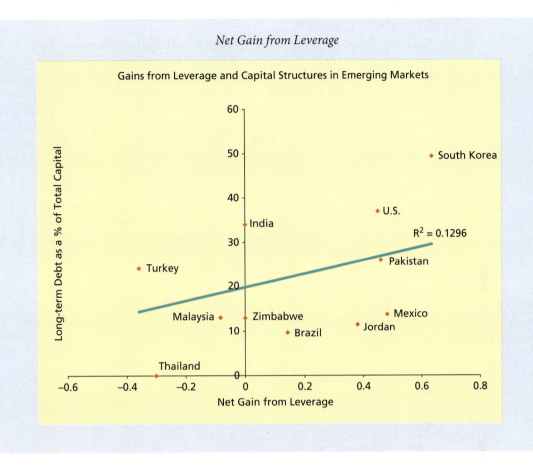

Net Gain from Leverage

Gains from Leverage and Capital Structures in Emerging Markets

When making capital structure decisions, do managers actually consider the personal tax consequences that investors face when receiving interest income? Fewer than 5% of the CFOs responding to the Graham and Harvey (2001) survey said that personal tax factors influenced their thinking about the appropriate amount of debt for their firms. In contrast, roughly 45% said that the level of interest rates was an important consideration in shaping debt policy. At first glance, then, it would seem that personal taxes do not affect firms' capital structures. However, personal taxes may play an indirect but important role in these decisions because the tax treatment of interest income affects the equilibrium interest rate—that is, the rate firms must pay when they borrow (which CFOs cite as being very important).

How does the personal tax treatment of interest affect equilibrium interest rates? Because personal taxes lower investors' after-tax rate of return, they will demand a higher pre-tax return as compensation. This effect is easy to see in the markets. For example, **municipal bonds** issued by state and local governments pay interest that is not taxable at the personal level, and the interest rates on corporate bonds are typically 25%–35% higher than those offered by municipal bonds. In other words, the rate that corporations pay when they borrow is, in equilibrium, higher than it would otherwise be owing to the personal tax treatment of interest, and that in turn influences how much firms borrow. At some point, the interest rate on corporate debt rises enough to compensate investors for their personal tax liabilities. But the higher the rate that companies must pay, the less attractive debt financing becomes (i.e., the tax deduction at the corporate level is offset by higher corporate borrowing rates). When these effects exactly offset, the market is said to be in a Miller equilibrium.

Smart
Ideas
Video

John Graham
Duke University

"Personal taxes push the cost of debt up, and that offsets to some extent the corporate tax advantage of debt."

See the entire interview at
SMARTFinance

Nondebt Tax Shields

Following Miller, several authors developed tax-based extensions of the basic capital structure models. The most important of these, developed by DeAngelo and Masulis (1980), incorporates **nondebt tax shields (NDTS)** as substitutes for debt in corporate financial structures. Their NDTS hypothesis states that each company has an optimal amount of total deductions. Companies that have large deductions from sources other than debt need fewer debt interest deductions to obtain the same amount of total deductions. All else equal, companies with large amounts of depreciation, investment tax credits, R&D expenditures, stock option expenses, and other nondebt tax shields should employ less debt financing than otherwise equivalent companies with fewer such shields.

Figure 12.4 summarizes what we've learned about capital structure so far. The left-hand graph shows the case when markets are perfect and M&M Propositions I and II hold. A firm's capital structure (i.e., its debt-to-assets ratio) can affect neither the value of the firm nor its WACC. The right-hand graph shows the case when the tax code creates an incentive to use more debt. As firms increase debt, firm value rises and the WACC falls. In this situation, the optimal capital structure is 100% debt.

FIGURE 12.4

The Effect of Leverage on Firm Value with and without Taxes

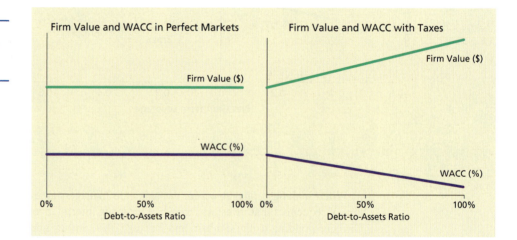

Because firms are not observed financing their operations with 100% debt, we conclude that there must be costs associated with debt that rise as leverage increases. At some point, these costs offset debt's tax advantages, making it optimal for most firms to operate with less than 100% debt. This subject is the focus of Chapter 13.

A Checklist of How Taxes Should Affect Capital Structure

We can summarize four theoretical predictions regarding the impact of taxes on capital structure choices. Other things equal, and assuming that interest is a tax-deductible expense for corporations but that dividend payments are not, the following relationships should hold.

1. *The higher the corporate income tax rate, T_c, the more debt companies will use in equilibrium.* An increase in T_c should cause debt ratios to increase for most firms.
2. *The higher the personal tax rate on equity-related investment income (dividends and capital gains), T_{ps}, the more debt companies will use in equilibrium.* An increase in T_{ps} should cause debt ratios to increase.

3. *The higher the personal tax rate on interest income, T_{pd}, the less debt companies will use in equilibrium.* An increase in T_{pd} should cause debt ratios to fall.
4. *The more nondebt tax shields a company has, the less debt it will use in equilibrium.*

Concept Review Questions	
	6. Holding other factors constant, how do you think corporate capital structures might change if the corporate income tax were abolished?
	7. Over time, institutional investors—especially pension funds, which are effectively untaxed on their investment income—have held an increasing percentage of common stock. What do you think this trend implies for corporate leverage?
	8. In 1964, Britain adopted a corporation taxation system with separate company-level taxation of corporate operating income and personal taxation of distributed profits (dividends). After 1964, debt levels increased in Britain. Offer an explanation of this phenomenon.

SUMMARY

- Financial leverage increases expected earnings per share as well as the volatility of earnings per share.
- Modigliani and Miller (M&M) showed that capital structure is irrelevant in a world of frictionless capital markets. Their Proposition I states that the leverage choice does not affect a firm's value.
- M&M's Proposition II says that, even though the cost of debt is less than the cost of equity, the WACC does not decrease when a firm reduces equity and adds debt to its capital structure. This is because more debt increases the cost of equity, which exactly offsets the advantage of replacing some equity with debt.

- In a world with tax-deductible interest payments and only company-level taxation of operating profits, the optimal corporate strategy is to use the maximum possible leverage. This minimizes the government's claim on profits and maximizes income flowing to private investors.
- When governments impose taxes at both the corporate and personal level, debt's tax advantage usually is lower than when there is a corporate income tax only; in some cases, higher personal taxes on interest income may lead to a net tax disadvantage for debt.

KEY TERMS

arbitrage
financial leverage
fundamental principle of financial
   leverage

homemade leverage
Miller equilibrium
Modigliani & Miller (M&M) argument
municipal bonds

nondebt tax shield (NDTS)
Proposition I
Proposition II
recapitalization

QUESTIONS

12-1. Why is the use of long-term debt financing referred to as using *financial leverage*?

12-2. What is the fundamental principle of financial leverage?

12-3. If a firm borrows money and retires some of its outstanding equity, does the risk of the equity

increase even if the interest rate that the firm is charged on the debt is 0%?

12-4. Examine Table 12.3. What happens if the firm has a 50-50 debt and equity capital structure and the economy goes into a depression, meaning that the firm's cash flows are $0?

12-5. What is the basic conclusion of Modigliani and Miller's Proposition I? What argument do M&M offer as a defense of this conclusion? How is *homemade leverage* used within this argument?

12-6. Following from the conclusion of Proposition I, what is the crux of M&M's Proposition II? What is the natural relationship between the required returns on debt and equity that results from Proposition II?

12-7. In what way did M&M change their conclusion regarding capital structure choice with the additional assumption of corporate taxes? In this context, what explains the difference in value between levered and unlevered firms?

12-8. By introducing personal taxes into the model for capital structure choice, how did Miller alter the previous M&M conclusion that 100% debt is optimal? What happens to the gains from leverage if personal tax rates on interest income are significantly higher than those on stock-related income?

12-9. List and describe the four predictions made by capital structure theory.

PROBLEMS

What Is Financial Leverage and What Are Its Effects?

12-1. As chief financial officer of Magnificent Electronics Corporation (MEC), you are considering a recapitalization plan that would convert MEC from its current all-equity capital structure to one that includes substantial financial leverage. MEC now has 500,000 shares of common stock outstanding, which are selling for $60 each. You expect the firm's annual cash flow, before interest and taxes, to be $2,400,000 for the foreseeable future.

The recapitalization proposal is to issue $15,000,000 worth of long-term debt, at an interest rate of 6.0%, and then to use the proceeds to repurchase 250,000 shares of common stock worth $15,000,000. Assuming there are no market frictions such as corporate or personal income taxes, calculate the expected return on equity for MEC shareholders under the current all-equity capital structure and also under the proposed recapitalization.

12-2. All-Star Production Corporation (APC) is considering a recapitalization plan that would convert APC from its current all-equity capital structure to one that includes some financial leverage. APC now has 10,000,000 shares of common stock outstanding, which are selling for $40 each. You expect the firm's cash flow, before interest and taxes, to be $50,000,000 per year for the foreseeable future.

The recapitalization proposal is to issue $100,000,000 worth of long-term debt, at an interest rate of 6.50%, and then to use the proceeds to repurchase as many shares as possible at a price of $40 per share. Assume there are no market frictions such as corporate or personal income taxes. Calculate the expected return on equity for APC shareholders under the current all-equity capital structure and under the recapitalization plan.

a. Calculate the number of shares outstanding, the per-share price, and the debt-to-equity ratio for APC if it adopts the proposed recapitalization.

b. Calculate the earnings per share (EPS) and the return on equity (ROE) for APC shareholders under the current all-equity capitalization as well as under the proposed mixed (debt and equity) capital structure.

c. Calculate the break-even level of cash flow where earnings per share for APC stockholders are the same under both the current and the proposed capital structures.

d. At what level of cash flow will APC shareholders earn zero EPS under the current and proposed capital structures?

12-3. As chief financial officer of Uptown Service Corporation (USC), you are considering a recapitalization plan that would convert USC from its current all-equity capital structure to one including substantial financial leverage. USC now has 150,000 shares of common stock outstanding, which are selling for $80 each.

The recapitalization proposal is to issue $6,000,000 worth of long-term debt, at an interest rate of 7.0%, and use the proceeds to repurchase 75,000 shares of common stock worth $6,000,000. USC's earnings in the next year will depend on the state of the economy. If there is normal growth, cash flow before interest and taxes will be $1,200,000. Cash flow will be $600,000 if there is a recession, and it will be $1,800,000 if there is an economic boom. You believe that each economic outcome is equally likely. Assume there are no market frictions such as corporate or personal income taxes.

   a. If the proposed recapitalization is adopted, calculate the number of shares outstanding, the per-share price, and the debt-to-equity ratio for USC.

   b. Calculate the EPS and the ROE for USC shareholders, under all three economic outcomes (recession, normal growth, and boom), for both the current all-equity capitalization and the proposed mixed capital structure.

   c. Calculate the break-even level of cash flow where earnings per share for USC stockholders are the same under the current and proposed capital structures.

   d. At what level of cash flow will USC shareholders earn zero EPS under the current and the proposed capital structures?

12-4. Thrifty Pet Insurance (TPI) is an all-equity firm with 500,000 shares outstanding that sell for $40 a share. The firm's current annual cash flow, before interest and taxes, is $5 million; the firm faces a 40% tax rate and has a 40% dividend payout ratio. Calculate TPI's earnings per share and dividend per share (multiply EPS by the dividend payout ratio).

TPI is considering a $10 million debt issue with a coupon rate of 8%. Assuming that the expansion causes a cash flow increase to $8 million, calculate how this debt issue affects the debt-to-equity ratio, the EPS, and the dividend per share. Next, calculate the EPS and dividend per share while assuming that the expansion is instead financed with a stock issue.

12-5. Paulsen Pawn Shops (PPS) has a debt-to-equity ratio of 1.0 and wishes to maintain that ratio even if the firm expands or downsizes. Currently, the stock sells for $25 and there are 300,000 shares outstanding. The existing debt has an annual coupon of $120 per $1,000 bond. Given a current cash flow (before interest and taxes) of $1,650,000 and a tax rate of 40%, what are PPS's earnings per share?

A $5 million expansion of PPS will require a stock and bond issue (assume bonds sell at $1,000 par). How many shares of stock and how many bonds will be required to finance the expansion? What level will the cash flow need to be to maintain PPS's current level of earnings per share?

12-6. A firm's shareholders believe that if its current debt ($2.5 million) were replaced by equity then earnings per share would increase. Assume the debt has a 10% interest rate, the tax rate is 45%, there are 400,000 shares outstanding that sell for $25 a share, and the current EPS is $1.85. Calculate the EPS with no debt. Are the shareholders correct that an all-equity firm would increase the EPS?

12-7. The shareholders of National Brick Yards (NBY) have determined that, if all of its $1 million debt were retired and replaced with stock, then their earnings per share would increase from $0.91 to $0.933. Currently, their EBIT (earnings before interest and taxes) is $4 million, the tax rate is 30%, and the interest on the debt is 10%. The shareholders calculate the current net income to be $2.73 million; distributed over 3 million shares ($10 share price), this amounts to $0.91 per share. The shareholders then calculate the net income to be $2.8 million without the debt; distributed over 3 million shares, this is $0.93. Redo the shareholders' calculations and identify where they are in error. Do the corrected calculations indicate an increase in EPS by eliminating debt?

12-8. A hedge fund manager who owns a large fraction of the common stock of Under Fire Systems (UFS) believes that increasing the company's leverage would improve the return on its stock. The fund manager currently earns a 14% after-tax return on a $5,000,000 investment in UFS stock. If she borrows $2,500,000 at an after-tax rate of 4.5% and invests all of it in UFS stock, what is the debt-to-equity ratio of her investment? What is the manager's after-tax return on the portfolio of debt and UFS stock?

12-9. Richard has $10,000 worth of LAN Inc. stock that earns a pre-tax return of 15%. He also has an outstanding loan of $5,000 on which he pays 8% interest. Richard can deduct the interest he pays for tax purposes, but he must pay taxes at a 40% rate on the return he earns from the stock. What is the net after-tax return on his investment? Suppose he sells $5,000 worth of shares to repay his loan. What is the after-tax return on his new position?

12-10. A firm's EBIT is $2.5 million and it has a 42% tax rate. Calculate how much the government extracts from the firm through taxation if the firm has no debt. If $10 million worth of debt with 10% interest exists, then what is the new amount of taxes paid? How much additional cash can the firm distribute to investors because it has leverage? Calculate this figure as a percentage of the cash flow paid to bondholders.

12-11. Go to Yahoo! and download recent balance sheets for Microsoft (ticker symbol, MSFT), Merck (MRK), Archer Daniels Midland (ADM), and General Mills (GIS). Calculate several debt ratios for each company and comment on the differences that you observe in the use of leverage. What factors do you think account for these differences?

The Modigliani & Miller Propositions

12-12. An unlevered company operates in perfect markets and has net operating income of $250,000. Assume that the required return on assets for firms in this industry is 12.5%. Suppose the firm issues $1 million worth of debt with a required return of 5% and uses the proceeds to repurchase outstanding stock.
  a. What is the market value and required return of this firm's stock before the repurchase transaction?
  b. What is the market value and required return of this firm's remaining stock after the repurchase transaction?

Smart Solutions

See the problem and solution explained step-by-step at **SMARTFinance**

12-13. Assume that capital markets are perfect. A firm finances its operations via $50 million in stock with a required return of 15% and $40 million in bonds with a required return of 9%. Assuming that the firm could issue $10 million in additional bonds at 9% and use the proceeds to retire $10 million worth of equity, what would happen to the firm's WACC? What would happen to the required return on the company's stock?

12-14. A firm operates in perfect capital markets. The required return on its outstanding debt is 6%, the required return on its shares is 14%, and its WACC is 10%. What is the firm's debt-to-equity ratio?

12-15. Assume that two firms, U and L, are identical in all respects except one: Firm U is debt-free, whereas Firm L has a capital structure that is 50% debt and 50% equity by market value. Further suppose that the assumptions of M&M's "irrelevance" Proposition I hold (no taxes or transactions costs, no bankruptcy costs, etc.) and that each firm will have income before interest and taxes of $800,000.

If the required return on assets, r_A, for these firms is 12.5% and if the risk-free debt yields 5%, calculate the following values for both Firm U and Firm L: (1) total firm value, (2) market value of debt and equity, and (3) required return on equity.

Now recompute these values while assuming that the market mistakenly assigns Firm L's equity a required return of 15%, and describe the arbitrage operation that will force Firm L's valuation back into equilibrium.

12-16. Hearthstone Corp. and The Shaky Image Co. are companies that compete in the luxury consumer goods market. The two companies are virtually identical except that Hearthstone is financed entirely with equity and The Shaky Image uses equal amounts of debt and equity. Suppose that each firm has assets with a total market value of $100 million. Hearthstone has 4 million shares of stock outstanding worth $25 each. Shaky has 2 million shares outstanding in addition to a publicly traded debt whose market value is $50 million. Both companies operate in a world with perfect capital markets (no taxes, etc.). The WACC for each firm is 12%, and the cost of debt is 8%.

  a. What is the price of Shaky stock?

  b. What is the cost of equity for Hearthstone? For Shaky?

  c. Suppose that you want to buy 1% of the outstanding Shaky shares, but you do not like the fact that Shaky uses leverage. Assuming that you can borrow and lend at 8%, show how you can trade on your own account to unwind the effects of Shaky's leverage.

  d. Suppose that you want to buy 1% of the outstanding Hearthstone shares, but you wish that the firm's managers were not so conservative in refraining entirely from issuing debt. Demonstrate how you can trade on your own account to create an investment in Hearthstone that is equivalent in terms of risk and return to buying 1% of Shaky's shares.

Smart Solutions

See the problem and solution explained step-by-step at **SMARTFinance**

12-17. An unlevered company operates in perfect markets and has net operating income (EBIT) of $2,000,000. Assume that the required return on assets for firms in this industry is 8%. The firm issues $10 million worth of debt, with a required return of 6.5%, and uses the proceeds to repurchase outstanding stock. There are no corporate or personal taxes.

  a. What is the market value and required return of this firm's stock before the repurchase transaction, according to M&M Proposition I?

  b. What is the market value and required return of this firm's remaining stock after the repurchase transaction, according to M&M Proposition II?

12-18. In the mid-1980s, Michael Milken and his firm, Drexel Burnham Lambert, popularized the term "junk bonds"—bonds with low credit ratings. Many of Drexel's clients issued junk bonds to the public to raise money to conduct a leveraged buyout (LBO) of a target firm. After the LBO, the target firm would have an extremely high debt-to-equity ratio, with only a small portion of equity financing remaining. Many politicians and members of the financial press worried that the increase in junk bonds would bring about an increase in the risk of the U.S. economy because so many large firms had become highly leveraged. Merton Miller disagreed. See if you can follow his argument by assessing whether each of the statements below is true or false.

  a. The junk bonds issued by acquiring firms were riskier than investment-grade bonds.

  b. The remaining equity in highly leveraged firms was more risky than it had been before the LBO.

   c. After an LBO, the target firm's capital structure would consist of very risky junk bonds and very risky equity. Therefore, the risk of the firm would increase after the LBO.

   d. The junk bonds issued to conduct the LBO were less risky than the equity they replaced.

12-19. Currently, a firm has a debt-to-equity ratio of 0.0 and a return on its shares of 15%. Assuming the firm can issue debt at a cost of 10%, determine the ROE at the following debt-to-equity ratios: 0.5, 1.0, and 1.5.

M&M and Taxes

12-20. Herculio Mining has net operating income of $5 million. It has $50 million of debt outstanding with a required rate of return of 6%. The required rate of return on assets in this industry is 12%, and the corporate tax rate is 40%. Assume there are corporate taxes but no personal taxes.

   a. Determine the present value of the interest tax shield of Herculio Mining as well as the total value of the firm.

   b. Determine the gain from leverage if there are personal taxes of 20% on stock income and 30% on debt income.

12-21. An all-equity firm is subject to a 30% tax rate. Its total market value is initially $3,500,000, and there are 175,000 shares outstanding. The firm announces a program to issue $1 million worth of bonds at 10% interest and to use the proceeds to buy back common stock.

   a. What is the value of the tax shield that the firm acquires through the bond issue?

   b. According to M&M, what is the likely increase in market value per share of the firm after the announcement (assuming efficient markets)?

   c. How many shares will the company be able to repurchase?

12-22. Intel Corp. uses almost no debt and had a total market capitalization of about $100 billion in March 2007. Assume that Intel faces a 35% tax rate on corporate earnings. Ignore all elements of the decision except the corporate tax savings.

   a. By how much could Intel managers increase the value of the firm by issuing $50 billion in bonds (which would be rolled over in perpetuity) and simultaneously repurchasing $50 billion in stock? Why do you think that Intel has not taken advantage of this opportunity?

   b. Suppose the personal tax rate on equity income, as faced by Intel shareholders, is 10% and that the personal tax rate on interest income is 40%. Recalculate the gains to Intel from replacing $50 billion of equity with debt.

12-23. SoonerCo has $15 million of common stock outstanding, net operating income of $2.5 million per year, and $15 million of debt outstanding with a required return (interest rate) of 8%. The required rate of return on assets in this industry is 12.5%, and the corporate tax rate is 35%. Within the M&M framework of corporate taxes but no personal taxes, determine the present value of the interest tax shield of SoonerCo as well as the firm's total value. Finally, determine the gain from leverage if there are personal tax rates of 15% on stock income and 25% on debt income.

12-24. The EBIT of Westside Manufacturing is $10 million. The company has $60 million of debt outstanding with a required rate of return of 6.5%. The required rate of return on the industry is 10%, and the corporate tax rate is 30%. Assume there are corporate taxes but no personal taxes.

   a. Determine the present value of the interest tax shield of Westside Manufacturing and also the firm's total value.

   b. Determine the gain from leverage if there are personal taxes of 10% on stock income and 35% on debt income.

THOMSON ONE Business School Edition

12-25. Estimate the gain from leverage for Maxwell Technology (ticker symbol, MXWL) for the last five years. Estimate the tax rate as income taxes paid divided by pre-tax income. Are the changes in the gain from leverage due mainly to changes in the estimated tax rate or to the amount of long-term debt? Repeat the analysis for American Technology Ceramic (ticker symbol, AMK). As a percentage of assets, which firm has the greater gain from leverage? What is driving the difference in the gain from leverage for the two firms?

MINI-CASE: CAPITAL STRUCTURE: THEORY AND TAXES

DataCore Inc. currently has an all-equity capital structure. However, the firm is considering a recapitalization that would structure the firm with 25% debt and 75% equity by issuing an appropriate amount of debt and repurchasing an equal amount of common stock; the debt is expected to have a 5% coupon rate. The firm expects the following scenarios over the next year for EBIT:

Outlook	Probability	EBIT
Good	35%	$800,000
Average	40%	$525,000
Poor	25%	$ 75,000

The firm currently has 200,000 shares of common stock outstanding at $43 per share. The firm is in a 0% tax bracket.

1. Determine the expected earnings before interest and taxes, net income, and earnings per share (a) if the firm maintains its current unlevered capital structure and (b) if it recapitalizes at 25% debt and uses the proceeds to repurchase common stock.

2. Following the assumptions behind M&M's Proposition I, calculate the stockholders' required rate of return of the firm in an unlevered versus a levered state. Calculate the value of the levered firm, separating it into debt and equity components. Also, calculate the weighted average cost of capital (WACC) for the firm in a levered versus an unlevered state.

3. Assuming the firm is in a 35% corporate tax bracket, determine the value of the unlevered firm versus the value of the levered firm.

13

Capital Structure: Balancing the Benefits and Costs of Debt

What Companies Do

Is What's Good for General Motors Good for America?

In his 1953 confirmation hearing as President Eisenhower's Secretary of Defense nominee, former General Motors president, Charles Wilson, was asked whether he could make a decision that was in the best interest of the United States if that decision would have adverse consequences for General Motors. He famously replied that he could not conceive of such a situation, "because for years I thought what was good for the country was good for General Motors, and vice versa."

Congress heard the same refrain 55 years later when CEOs from GM, Ford, and Chrysler appealed for billions in federal assistance to keep the U.S. auto firms from going bankrupt in 2008. Some members of Congress suggested that the auto companies should simply be allowed to go bankrupt, which would allow them to keep operating while restructuring their debts. The auto executives, however, described that option as "pure fantasy," arguing that the costs of going through bankruptcy would be prohibitive because customers would stop buying cars out of fear that warranties would not be honored or replacement parts would be difficult to buy. Rick Wagoner, General Motors' CEO at the time, predicted that, rather than facilitating an efficient reorganization of the company, a bankruptcy filing would lead to GM's liquidation, triggering hundreds of thousands of job losses. Congress ultimately approved up to $25 billion in aid for the industry in 2008, but by early spring 2009 Moody's estimated a 45% chance that Ford, Chrysler, or GM would default on its outstanding debt. Meanwhile, the Big Three were back in Washington seeking more loans from taxpayers. The Obama administration pressured Wagoner to quit and reassured car buyers that the government would stand behind the warranties issued by U.S. auto firms if necessary. Nevertheless, Chrysler filed for bankruptcy protection on April 30, 2009, and GM followed suit on June 1, 2009. Both companies emerged from bankruptcy by mid-summer.

Sources: Lorie Montgomery, "Automakers Press High-Stakes Plea for Aid; Senators Greet CEOs' Request with Skepticism," Washington Post (November 19, 2008), p.A1; Simon Duke, "Moody's Reveals Its Bottom Rung," Daily Mail (London) (March 11, 2009).

13.1 A Conceptual Framework for Trading Off Debt's Benefits and Costs

Does Debt Policy Matter?

In the previous chapter we learned that, in a perfect market, firms' capital structure choices do not matter. That finding stands at odds with what CFOs tell us—namely, that capital structure decisions are extremely important and can have as much influence on the value of a firm as do investment decisions (see, for example, Figure 1.1 on page 7 and Figure 12.2 on page 417). If financial managers believe that capital structure is important, this implies that markets are imperfect in some important way. One of our goals in this chapter is to understand how market imperfections influence capital structure choices, and in turn how those choices affect firm value and the cost of capital.

Is there an optimal capital structure for a particular firm? Figure 13.1 shows that, in the United States, most firms operate with an idea or target capital structure in mind. Of the 392 CFOs surveyed by Graham and Harvey (2001), 44% said that their firm had either a "very strict" or "somewhat tight" capital structure target, and another 37% said that their firms had flexible targets.[1] Fewer than one-fifth of CFOs said that their firm had no target debt ratio or range. In other words, most managers behave as if they believe that some capital structures are better than others, and they try to manage toward a particular target. But what factors determine the optimal capital structure, and how do managers decide what leverage policy will maximize value for their firms?

FIGURE 13.1

Do Firms Have Target Capital Structures?

Source: Graham and Harvey (2001), The theory and practice of corporate finance: evidence from the field, *Journal of Financial Economics*, 60, pp. 187–243, copyright © 2001, with permission from Elsevier.

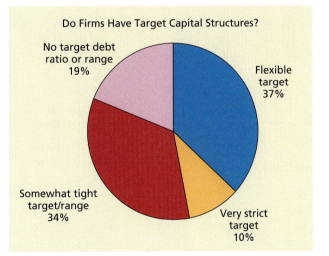

Trading Off Debt's Benefits and Costs

In Chapter 12 we learned that one important market imperfection—taxes—creates an incentive for firms to use debt. When debt interest payments are tax deductible to the corporation but equity payments are not, as has often been the case in the United States and in many other countries, managers often can maximize firm value by using a

---

[1]Graham and Harvey (2001) find that "very strict" or "somewhat tight" capital structure targets are more common among large firms (55%) than small ones (36%) and are also more common among firms with investment-grade credit ratings (64%) than among those with speculative ratings (41%).

FIGURE 13.2

Weighing Debt's
Benefits and Costs
to Find Optimal
Capital Structure

The optimal amount
of debt occurs where
the marginal cost
and marginal benefit
curves intersect. At that
point, total firm value
is at its peak, and the
weighted average cost
of capital (WACC) is at
its minimum.

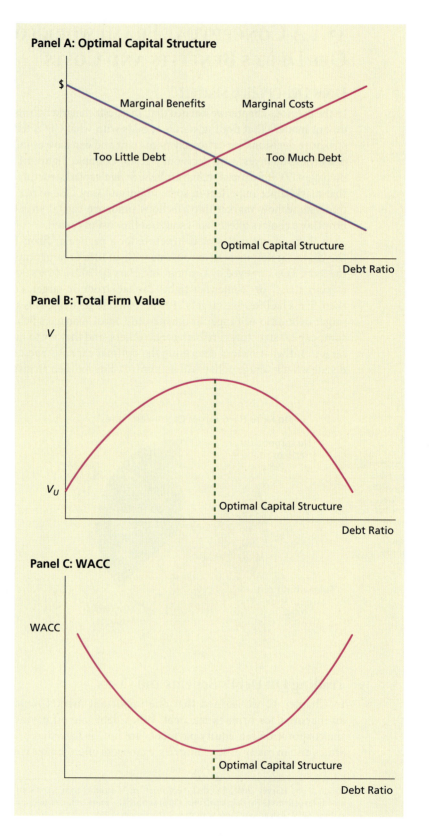

combination of equity and debt, with the debt interest sheltering cash flows from taxes. Even so, most firms do not finance their activities exclusively with debt. This suggests that managers see debt as having costs that at some point offset debt's tax advantages. Based on observing what companies actually do, the optimal capital structure for most firms is apparently one that contains some debt, but not too much.

How do managers trade-off the benefits and costs of debt to establish a target capital structure that maximizes firm value? Figure 13.2 offers a conceptual answer to this question. The blue line in Panel A shows that the marginal benefit of borrowing an additional dollar falls as the firm's overall debt ratio rises. The red line indicates that costs associated with using debt rise as leverage increases. We will explain in the next section why marginal benefits fall and marginal costs rise as debt increases, but for now you can just take the benefits and costs in Figure 13.2 as given. As in any cost–benefit analysis, the optimum occurs when marginal benefits and marginal costs are equal. Therefore, a manager facing these cost and benefit curves would choose a debt level where the two curves intersect. To the left of that point, the firm has too little debt in the sense that marginal benefits exceed marginal costs, so adding more debt would increase firm value. At higher debt levels, debt's marginal costs exceed its benefits, so adding leverage decreases firm value.

Panel B shows the relation between total firm value and leverage. If a firm has no debt, its value equals *Vu*. From that point, if the firm adds debt to its capital structure, its value begins to rise. At some point, firm value reaches a peak, and from that point, adding more debt decreases the value of the firm. The graph shows that, at the same point where the marginal benefit and cost curves in Panel A intersect, firm value reaches its peak. The point at which firm value begins to fall as leverage rises is exactly when debt's marginal costs first exceed its marginal benefits.

At the end of this chapter, we will demonstrate how to find the optimal debt ratio. But how much difference does finding the right capital structure really make in the overall value of the firm? In a recent study, van Binsbergen, Graham, and Yang (2008) estimate that, for the average firm, appropriate debt choices can increase firm value by about 5%. In some companies, like the one described at the beginning of Chapter 14, the increase in value may be 10% or more.

Panel C of Figure 13.2 demonstrates how a firm's weighted-average-cost of capital (WACC) changes as leverage rises. Here, the relation is U-shaped. A firm with no leverage can reduce its WACC by substituting debt for equity, but, eventually, the firm reaches a point where further increases in debt cause the WACC to increase. Naturally, managers want to find the debt ratio that minimizes the cost of capital because doing so maximizes firm value. Therefore, the optimum point in Panel C is the same optimum debt ratio in Panels A and B.

In the next section, we explore in more detail why debt's marginal benefits fall and its marginal costs rise as a firm uses more debt in its capital structure. To begin, we revisit the tax advantage of debt, taking into account some important features of the tax code that we have neglected thus far.

Smart
Ideas
Video

John Graham, Duke University

"Corporate managers trade-off the benefits of debt with the costs of debt."

See the entire interview at
SMARTFinance

| **Concept Review Questions** | 1. How large would the costs of debt have to be in order to justify a firm's decision to operate with 100% equity? |
| | 2. If a firm is operating well below its optimum debt level, then what market forces might prompt it to use more debt? |

13.2 DEBT TAX SHIELDS AND FIRM PROFITABILITY

Panel A of Figure 13.2 asserts that the incremental benefits of additional dollars of debt fall as a firm borrows more. Why is this so? By issuing debt, the firm shields some of its cash flow from corporate taxes because it can deduct interest payments to lenders. If the corporate tax rate is 35% (and if we ignore personal tax issues for the moment), then each dollar that the firm pays in interest reduces its taxable income by a dollar, which reduces its tax bill by $0.35. However, interest deductions only lower taxes to the extent that the firm is profitable.

EXAMPLE

In its fiscal year ending in February 2008, the auto parts retailer Pep Boys—Manny, Moe, & Jack—reported interest expense of $51.2 million. In a profitable year, that amount would have reduced the firm's taxes by $17.9 million ($51.2 × 35%). Unfortunately, like many other firms struggling through the recession, Pep Boys reported a loss in 2008. The U.S. tax code allows a firm that experiences a loss to claim a refund against taxes paid in the prior two years, but only to the extent that the firm earned profits and paid taxes in those two years. Pep Boys lost money in 2007 and 2006, so it could not claim a refund in 2008, and the $51.2 million interest expense that it paid in 2008 didn't reduce its taxes by a penny.

The tax law also allows firms to "carry forward" losses in one year to offset income in up to 20 subsequent years. So if Pep Boys earned a profit in 2009, then the interest it paid in 2008 (as well as in 2009) would eventually reduce its tax bill. But even if the 2009 profit of Pep Boys was large enough to reclaim the $17.9 million tax shield that it missed in 2008, it would not be receiving this tax benefit until a year after it actually paid the interest. If Pep Boys did not return to profitability for several years, it would have to wait even longer to claim the tax break and could lose it entirely. Therefore, the present value (in 2008) of the debt tax shield would be less than $17.9 million.

Smart Ideas Video

Scott Smart, Indiana University

"As firms borrow more, the probability that they will be able to claim the full tax deduction on the incremental interest falls."

See the entire interview at
SMARTFinance

Why does this imply that, as shown in Figure 13.2, the marginal benefit of debt declines as the amount of debt rises? The more debt a firm uses, the higher are the interest expenses that the firm must pay, and therefore the greater the likelihood that the firm will experience losses in at least some years. Figure 13.3 shows that the probability of a loss rises as debt increases. The bigger the loss, the less likely it is that the firm will be able to fully offset the loss against past income, and the longer it may have to wait to fully offset the loss

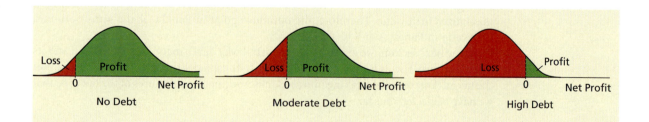

FIGURE 13.3

How Debt Affects the Probability of Profits and Losses

If a firm uses more debt, the probability that it will experience a loss increases and the probability that the firm will enjoy the full tax savings from interest deductions falls. Therefore, as more debt is used, the marginal benefit of using debt falls as shown in the blue line in Figure 13.2.

against future income. Therefore, for each additional dollar of debt used, the probability that the firm will enjoy the full tax benefit for the additional dollar falls, as reflected in the declining benefit curve in Figure 13.2.

Just as the benefits of additional debt fall the more debt a firm uses, the incremental costs of debt rise as leverage increases. In the next two sections, we describe the factors that influence the cost of debt and why these costs rise as firms borrow more.

Concept Review Questions	
	3. Suppose an all-equity firm is sufficiently profitable that the likelihood of it experiencing a loss in the near future is close to zero. For this firm, what does the marginal benefit curve of debt look like?
	4. If the tax law granted firms a tax rebate when they lost money, even when they had not previously earned a profit, then would the marginal benefit curve for debt still decline as debt increased?

13.3 COSTS OF BANKRUPTCY

Direct and Indirect Bankruptcy Costs

A firm is **bankrupt** when it cannot meet its debt obligations, and **bankruptcy** describes the legal process (governed in the United States by federal law) through which creditors' claims are handled. In theory, when a firm fails to pay its debts, creditors can force the firm into bankruptcy and claim its assets. In the U.S., as discussed in Chapter 25, managers often continue to run the firm in bankruptcy, and they may choose to liquidate the firm's assets or to propose a plan to restructure the firm so that it can emerge from bankruptcy as a viable business. If the process of transferring control of a firm's assets from shareholders to creditors were costless, bankruptcy affects the ownership of a firm but not its value, as the following Example illustrates.

EXAMPLE

The resort town of Falling Rivers has granted one-year contracts to two companies—Lo Parking Services and Hi Management—to manage the city's parking lots. The value of these contracts depends on local economic conditions next year. If the economy booms, Falling Rivers will attract many visitors. However, if a recession occurs, then the number of visitors will fall drastically. There is an equal chance (probability $P = 0.5$) that the economy will boom or go into a recession. If a boom occurs, each company will earn a management fee (net of the costs of operating the lots) of $900,000. If a recession occurs, each will net just $200,000.

Each company financed the costs of managing the city's parking lots in part with borrowed money, which must be repaid with interest in one year. At maturity, Lo will owe $106,000 in principal and interest; Hi will owe $270,000. If there is a recession, Hi will be unable to pay its creditors in full and will be bankrupt. In this example, the company's stockholders will lose their investment, and the firm's creditors will receive the $200,000 management fee.

Assume that Hi's stockholders require a return of 11.54% and that its bondholders expect a return of 8%. Both stockholders and bondholders of Lo are willing to accept slightly lower returns because the firm uses leverage more sparingly. Lo's stockholders require an 11% return, and its bondholders require 6%. The following table details the payoffs to security holders of both firms under the additional simplifying assumption that neither firm pays taxes.

	LO PARKING		HI MANAGEMENT	
Item	**Expansion** $(P = 0.5)$	**Recession** $(P = 0.5)$	**Expansion** $(P = 0.5)$	**Recession** $(P = 0.5)$
Cash flow at contract expiration	$900,000	$200,000	$900,000	$200,000
Debt-service payment (interest and principal)	$106,000	$106,000	$270,000	$200,000
Distributions to stockholders	$794,000	$ 94,000	$630,000	$ 0

To value the equity, E, and debt, D, of these two firms, we first compute the expected value of the payoffs to each investor group and then find the present value of the payoffs using the required returns to discount cash flows. The value, V, of the firm is equal to the sum of equity and debt values: $V = E + D$.

$$E_{Lo} = [(0.5 \times \$794,000) + (0.5 \times \$94,000)] \div 1.11$$

$$= \$444,000 \div 1.11 = \$400,000$$

$$D_{Lo} = [(0.5 \times \$106,000) + (0.5 \times \$106,000)] \div 1.06$$

$$= \$106,000 \div 1.06 = \$100,000$$

$$V_{Lo} = \$400,000 + \$100,000 = \$500,000$$

$$E_{Hi} = [(0.5 \times \$630,000) + (0.5 \times \$0)] \div 1.1154$$

$$= \$315,000 \div 1.1154 = \$282,407^2$$

$$D_{Hi} = [(0.5 \times \$270,000) + (0.5 \times \$200,000)] \div 1.08$$

$$= \$235,000 \div 1.08 = \$217,593$$

$$V_{Hi} = \$282,407 + \$217,593 = \$500,000$$

What are the consequences of leverage here? Higher leverage means that Hi's shareholders (and lenders) bear more risk; yet, if the firm goes bankrupt, ownership transfers smoothly (and at no cost) from shareholders to lenders. As a result, both Lo and Hi are worth $500,000, and the fact that one firm borrows more than another is irrelevant when bankruptcy is costless.[3]

In reality, when firms go bankrupt the process of resolving creditors' claims can be very costly and time consuming. Resolving creditor's claims is contentious, and shareholders and managers of a bankrupt firm rarely relinquish control without first trying to renegotiate with creditors. Because the bankruptcy process is costly, investors assess the probability that a firm will go bankrupt as well as the likely costs if bankruptcy occurs, and firm value falls as expected bankruptcy costs rise. Therefore, as a company uses

---

[2]We are actually using a discount rate of 11.541% here. You can double-check that, given the percentages of debt and equity used by each firm and given the required return on each firm's debt and equity, the weighted average cost of capital for managing parking lots is 10%. Given the M&M propositions from Chapter 12, does it surprise you that Hi's WACC is the same as Lo's?

[3]It is worth noting that Hi's bondholders have a *promised* return of more than 24% [($270,000 − $217,593) ÷ $217,593] but an *expected* return of only 8%, so the possibility of default is priced into the bonds today to provide a fair return to bondholders.

more debt, expected bankruptcy costs rise. This means that the marginal cost of using debt increases as more of it is used, as reflected in the red line in Figure 13.2.

Bankruptcy costs fall into two categories. **Direct bankruptcy costs** include fees paid to attorneys, accountants, investment bankers, and other professionals involved in bankruptcy proceedings in addition to other expenses directly tied to bankruptcy filing and administration. Although direct bankruptcy costs can run into the millions of dollars, they are usually small relative to the assets of the firm, especially in high-profile cases involving large, well-known companies. **Indirect bankruptcy costs** are often much greater than the direct costs. Indirect costs include the loss of customers and key suppliers, the time that top managers spend managing the bankruptcy process rather than focusing on their business, the loss of key employees, and missed opportunities to invest in positive-NPV projects.

EXAMPLE

Recall in this chapter's opening vignette that Rick Wagoner, then the CEO of General Motors, argued that it would be disastrous if Congress failed to provide financing for GM and forced the firm to go through bankruptcy, because consumers concerned about warranties would stop buying GM vehicles. That, in turn, would make it impossible for GM to emerge from bankruptcy proceedings as a viable entity. While Wagoner's view may have been overstated, he clearly believed that the indirect costs of bankruptcy were considerably more than the direct costs. The federal government appeared to share that view, because President Obama's administration pledged to stand behind GM vehicle warranties.

If bankruptcy costs reduce a firm's value and if using more debt raises the likelihood that bankruptcy will occur, then bankruptcy costs create a disincentive to use debt. For example, let's return to the Lo Parking and Hi Management Example to see how bankruptcy costs influence the values of those two firms.

EXAMPLE

To illustrate the effects of bankruptcy costs, we use the same assumptions made previously for Lo Parking and Hi Management, with one change: We now assume that if there is a recession and Hi is forced to file for bankruptcy, then the process will be contentious and costly. Instead of receiving the full $200,000 terminal cash flow as in the costless bankruptcy case, the company's creditors will receive only $120,000. In other words, the process of transferring ownership from Hi's stockholders to its creditors is costly and consumes $80,000 of value.

When we recompute the stock and bond values for each firm, it becomes clear that if bankruptcy involves real costs then it reduces the current value of a highly levered firm.

$$E_{Lo} = [(0.5 \times \$794,000) + (0.5 \times \$94,000)] \div 1.11$$

$$= \$444,000 \div 1.11 = \$400,000$$

$$D_{Lo} = [(0.5 \times \$106,000) + (0.5 \times \$106,000)] \div 1.06$$

$$= \$106,000 \div 1.06 = \$100,000$$

$$V_{Lo} = \$400,000 + \$100,000 = \$500,000$$

$$E_{Hi} = [(0.5 \times \$630,000) + (0.5 \times \$0)] \div 1.1154$$

$$= \$315,000 \div 1.1154 = \$282,407$$

$$D_{Hi} = [(0.5 \times \$270,000) + (0.5 \times \$120,000)] \div 1.08$$

$$= \$195,000 \div 1.08 = \$180,556,$$

$$V_{Hi} = \$282,407 + \$180,556 = \$462,963$$

For Hi Management, a costly bankruptcy reduces overall firm value by $37,037.

The Trade-off Model of Capital Structure

How do bankruptcy costs affect firms' decisions about capital structure? If going bankrupt entails costs that reduce firm value, then companies will estimate the expected value of these costs by multiplying the costs if bankruptcy occurs by the probability of going bankrupt. That calculation yields an estimate of "expected bankruptcy costs" which firms will weigh against the tax benefits of debt.[4]

Figure 13.4 illustrates the classic trade-off model of capital structure. The value of an unlevered firm is V_U. Suppose that the corporate tax advantage of debt outweighs any personal tax disadvantage. We know from Chapter 12 that this implies that the optimal capital structure is 100% debt, which the figure illustrates with an upward-sloping blue line. However, from Section 13.1 we know that when a firm encounters losses, some of the value of debt tax shields is lost because the tax benefits are delayed until the firm becomes profitable. This is represented in Figure 13.4 by the difference between the blue line and the solid green curved line. The more debt a firm uses, the more likely it is that the firm will experience a loss and so the present value of lost tax shields rises.

FIGURE 13.4

The Trade-off Model of Capital Structure Incorporating Taxes and Bankruptcy Costs

This model describes the optimal level of debt for a given firm as a trade-off between the tax benefits of corporate borrowing and the increasing bankruptcy costs associated with additional borrowing.

Source: Stewart C. Myers, "The Capital Structure Puzzle," *Journal of Finance* 39 (July 1984), pp. 575–592.

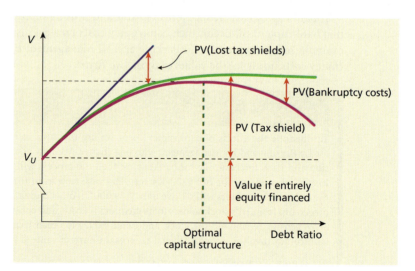

Finally, the gap between the solid green and purple curves in Figure 13.4 shows how expected bankruptcy costs rise with leverage. For a firm with a relatively low debt, the probability of bankruptcy is close to zero; hence the tax advantage of debt dominates and firm value rises with leverage. But as the debt ratio rises, debt's incremental tax benefits become smaller and expected bankruptcy costs increase. Ultimately, the rising bankruptcy costs dominate the tax benefits, and firm value begins to fall as leverage increases. The

---

[4]Because firms with more leverage face a greater probability of going bankrupt (all other things equal), expected bankruptcy costs rise with leverage; this is one reason why the marginal costs of debt rise in Panel A of Figure 13.2.

Smart Ideas Video

Robert Bruner, University of Virginia

"The case of Revco illustrates the principle of too much or too little debt."

See the entire interview at
SMARTFinance

optimal capital structure occurs where the incremental value of additional tax benefits are just offset by the incremental rise in expected bankruptcy costs. It is at this point that firm value reaches a peak. Note that the optimal debt ratio that maximizes firm value is the same optimal debt ratio that occurs where the marginal benefits of debt equal the marginal cost of debt in Figure 13.2.

Equation 13.1 summarizes what we have learned about capital structure and firm value thus far. The value of a levered firm, V_L, equals the value of an unlevered firm plus the present value of debt tax shields minus the present value of expected bankruptcy costs:

$$V_L = V_U + \text{PV(Tax shields)} - \text{PV(Bankruptcy costs)} \qquad \textbf{(Eq. 13.1)}$$

Asset Characteristics and Bankruptcy Costs

Bankruptcy costs, particularly the indirect ones, are likely to be larger for some firms than others. For instance, customers are not likely to abandon a firm in financial distress if the firm's product requires little or no service or if the product typically sells without a warranty. Firms that sell commodities or provide basic services probably face low bankruptcy costs because their customers know that if one firm goes out of business then another, similar firm will be available to provide nearly identical goods and services.

In contrast, firms that produce long-lived, complex products know that if their long-term viability is in question, customers will worry that if the firm goes out of business there will be no one else to provide service or back up the warranty. Because these firms may lose sales if the market perceives bankruptcy risk to be high (i.e., because they face high indirect bankruptcy costs), their optimal capital structure contains more equity and less debt.

If you look back at Table 12.1 on page 413, you can see that firms with complex, long-lived assets typically use very little debt. Google, Qualcomm, and most other high-tech firms borrow very little. In contrast, firms in the high-debt category in Table 12.1 include McDonald's, Target, and Yum! Brands. It seems unlikely that rumors of an impending bankruptcy in the fast-food or retail industries would dissuade consumers from shopping at these firms.

A firm's asset mix also influences its leverage decisions. Companies whose assets are mostly tangible and have well-established secondary markets should be less fearful of financial distress than companies whose assets are mostly intangible. To understand why, consider a firm that is experiencing financial difficulties and wants to sell some of its assets to pay down debt. If its assets are highly specialized or if no secondary market for them exists, then buyers will insist upon fire-sale prices and so the firm will have to liquidate more of its assets to pay a given amount of debt. On the other hand, a firm whose primary assets are tangible goods used in a variety of industries knows that it can sell these assets quickly and without a great loss in value if the need arises. Therefore, trucking companies, airlines, construction firms, pipeline companies, and railroads can all employ relatively more debt than can companies with few, if any, tangible assets. Looking at Table 12.1 again, we see that Accenture, whose assets mostly reside in the intellectual capabilities of its employees and in its brand name, uses far less debt that companies like Waste Management and Caterpillar, whose balance sheets reveal large holdings of tangible assets.

Financial distress can be particularly damaging to firms that produce goods and services that are R&D intensive, for two reasons. First, most of the production expenses are sunk costs, which can be recovered only after a long period of profitable sales. Second, cutting-edge goods require continued spending on research and development in order to ensure market acceptance. A bankrupt firm cannot make such investments. Further, intangible assets such as patents and trademarks are extremely valuable but are unlikely to pass through bankruptcy intact. Apple, Google, and Microsoft are classic examples of companies that invest massive sums in R&D, and Table 12.1 shows that all three firms are essentially debt free!

Smart Ideas Video

Sheridan Titman, University of Texas

"It seems to be the case that the product-market strategies of firms to a large extent dictate how firms are financed."

See the entire interview at
SMARTFinance

Financial distress can also increase production costs for many companies. Suppliers may not extend credit to a company at risk, and the firm may be unable to attract business partners for joint ventures or other risk-sharing projects. Most important of all, a risky firm will have difficulty attracting and retaining talented employees. Firms that depend heavily on the creativity, loyalty, and stability of their workforce are thus highly vulnerable to financial distress and will employ less debt than other firms.

Concept Review Question	5. Revisit the example of the Lo Parking and Hi Management companies on page 442. The required returns on equity and debt are higher for Hi than for Lo. How can the cost of capital for both firms be 10%?

13.4 AGENCY COSTS AND CAPITAL STRUCTURE

Agency Costs of Outside Equity

In 1976, Michael Jensen and William Meckling presented an **agency cost theory of financial structure**. Few papers in the history of finance have had a comparable impact on how we view issues of corporate control, capital structure, or financial contracting. Jensen and Meckling observed that when an entrepreneur owns all of a company's stock, no separation exists between corporate ownership and control. In plain English, this means that the entrepreneur bears all the costs, and reaps all the benefits, of her actions. Once the entrepreneur sells stock to outsiders (so-called outside equity), she bears only a fraction of the cost of any actions she takes that reduce firm value. This gives the entrepreneur a clear incentive to, in Jensen and Meckling's tactful phrasing, "consume perquisites." By selling a stake in her company, the entrepreneur lowers the cost of perquisite ("perk") consumption.

EXAMPLE

The founder of a software company in San Jose, California, must travel to Tokyo to close a sale. The airfare for a first-class seat on Northwest Airlines is $6,500; a seat in coach costs just $700. Assuming there is no additional value to the firm if the entrepreneur buys a first-class ticket, flying in first class lowers the value of the firm by $5,800 ($6,500 − $700).

If the entrepreneur owns all of his firm's shares, then he bears the full cost of this value reduction. On the other hand, if he owns only half the firm's shares and the rest are owned by outside investors, then the cost borne by the entrepreneur is just $2,900. In general, if the entrepreneur sells a fraction α of the firm's shares to outside investors, then he bears just (1 − α) of the cost of any perquisites he consumes. The higher the value of α, the lower a manager's cost of consuming perquisites.

This illustrates a nice deal for the entrepreneur, right? No, not in an efficient market. Informed investors expect the entrepreneur's performance to change after they buy shares, so they are only willing to pay a price that fully reflects the entrepreneur's perk consumption. In other words, shareholders charge the entrepreneur in advance for the perks he will consume after the equity sale. Once again, the entrepreneur bears the full costs of his actions. Society also suffers because these agency costs reduce the market value of corporate assets.

We are therefore at an impasse: selling stock to outside investors creates agency costs that the entrepreneur bears but that also harm society and discourage additional entrepreneurship. On the other hand, selling external equity is vital for entrepreneurs and for society as a whole; doing so allows firms to pursue growth opportunities that would exhaust an entrepreneur's personal wealth. Selling stock also permits entrepreneurs to diversify their portfolios. Given the importance of external equity, a logical next question is: "Is there any way to overcome the agency costs of equity?"

Using Debt to Overcome the Agency Costs of Outside Equity

Jensen and Meckling (1976) point out that using debt helps overcome the *agency costs of outside equity*. It does so in two ways: First, using debt means a firm can sell less external equity and still finance its operations. If agency costs of outside equity rise more than proportionally as α increases, then minimizing outside equity sales will reduce the deadweight agency costs. The second and more important benefit of using debt is that it reduces managerial perquisite consumption. The need to make regular debt-service payments effectively disciplines managers. The cost of excessive perk consumption might well include the entrepreneur losing the company. In Jensen and Meckling's words, external debt serves as a **bonding mechanism**: managers use this debt to convey their good intentions to outside shareholders, who will then pay a higher price for the firm's shares.

JOB INTERVIEW QUESTION

Our firm is thinking of issuing bonds and using the proceeds to buy back shares. What issues should we consider in evaluating this move?

Debt subjects managers to direct monitoring by public capital markets or banks. If lenders doubt management's competence, then they will charge a high interest rate and/or insist on restrictive debt covenants to constrain management's freedom of action. Debt also limits management's ability to destroy value through perquisite consumption or lack of effort. If management fails to operate the firm well enough to cover its debt-service payments, lenders can force the firm into bankruptcy, take control of it, and dismiss the offending managers. By issuing debt, managers risk being replaced, which reduces the agency costs of the manager–stockholder relationship.

Agency Costs of Outside Debt

If debt is such an effective disciplining device, why don't firms use "maximum debt" financing? The answer is that there are also *agency costs of debt*. To see this, remember that bondholders begin taking on an increasing fraction of the firm's business and operating risk as the firm uses more debt. But shareholders and managers still control the firm's investment and operating decisions. This gives managers incentives to transfer wealth from bondholders to themselves and to other shareholders. These incentives can be especially strong when a firm is at risk of going bankrupt.

The Asset Substitution Problem   Financial distress may provide managers with perverse yet rational incentives to play a variety of "games," mostly at bondholders' expense. Two such games—asset substitution and underinvestment—are especially damaging. Both games begin when managers realize the firm will probably not fulfill its obligations to creditors.

Asset substitution consists of promising to invest in a safe asset to obtain a return reflecting low risk but then substituting a riskier asset that offers the possibility of a higher return. To illustrate, let's assume a firm has $10 million in bonds outstanding that mature in 30 days. These bonds were issued years ago when the firm was prospering. The company's operations are currently unprofitable, but its managers believe that the firm can be profitable again once the economy picks up. Despite its problems, the firm still has $8 million in cash on hand that it can invest in one of two projects or simply hold in reserve to partially repay the bonds in 30 days.

The first investment is a low-risk project requiring an $8 million investment that will pay off $8.15 million in 30 days with virtual certainty. This is a monthly return of 1.88%, or an annual return of almost 25%. In other words, it is a positive-NPV project that will increase firm value, but it does not earn a high enough return to fully repay the maturing bonds.

The second investment, given the code name Project Vegas, is basically a gamble. It also requires $8 million, but it offers a 40% chance of a $12 million payoff and a 60% chance of a $4 million payoff. Because its expected value is therefore only $7.2 million, Vegas is a negative-NPV project. The firm's managers would reject it if the firm did not have debt outstanding. However, if Vegas succeeds then its $12 million payoff will allow the company to fully pay off the bonds and pocket a $2 million profit.

Consider the incentives that managers face. Clearly, bondholders would want the managers either to select the low-risk project or to retain the firm's cash in reserve. But this is certainly not in the interests of the firm's shareholders. Because they will lose control of the firm if it cannot fully repay the maturing bonds, shareholders want managers to go ahead with Project Vegas. Thus the shareholders are, in effect, "playing with the bondholders' money." If successful, the project will yield enough for shareholders to pay off the creditors and retain ownership. If Project Vegas is unsuccessful, then the shareholders will default and hand the firm over to bondholders—the same outcome as if the firm had played it safe. Shareholders have everything to gain and nothing to lose from this strategy of substituting a riskier asset for a safer one, and their agent (the manager) controls the firm's investment policy until default actually occurs. As we will see, bondholders can use restrictive covenants that offer some protection against asset substitution, but these only partially solve the problem.

The Underinvestment Problem The second game set up by financial distress is **underinvestment**. Like asset substitution, this game arises when a firm's managers realize that default is likely. Assume that a firm on the verge of declaring bankruptcy gains access to a highly profitable but short-lived investment opportunity. Let's say that a supplier offers to sell its inventory to the company at a dramatically discounted price, provided that the firm pays for the inventory immediately with cash. The inventory will cost $9 million today, but within 30 days the firm can sell that inventory for $19 million, accumulating a net $10 million in cash from the deal. If the firm enters into this transaction then it will earn just enough to pay off its debts, which are due in 30 days. However, suppose the firm has only $8 million in cash on hand today and so shareholders—through stock issuance or dividend reduction—must contribute the additional $1 million needed to purchase the inventory. Accepting this project maximizes overall firm value. Nevertheless, the shareholders rationally forgo the project because they must invest the additional $1 million yet all the benefits accrue to the bondholders.

As you might imagine, experienced lenders know that managers can play games whereby wealth is transferred from bondholders to stockholders, so they take steps to prevent managers from playing these games. Smart investors insist on detailed covenants in bond contracts. These covenants constrain borrowers' actions and limit their ability to expropriate bondholder wealth. Unfortunately, they make bond agreements costly to negotiate and enforce, and they may also prevent managers from making value-increasing investments. For example, if a bond covenant limits a firm's ability to issue additional debt of equal or greater seniority (one of the most common covenants), managers might pass up value-increasing investments if financing attractive projects would require the firm to issue new debt. Other common covenants restrict increases in dividend payments, even for profitable firms.

In any case, the agency costs of debt are real, and they become more important as a firm's leverage ratio increases. Refer back to Figure 13.2 one more time. We have already argued that the marginal costs associated with debt rise as leverage increases as a result of increases in expected bankruptcy costs. The same may be said of agency costs, because managers are most likely to engage in such games as asset substitution when they know that the firm is on the brink of financial disaster. Consequently, when assessing how much debt to use, firms must consider the agency costs of increased debt.

The Trade-off Model Revisited

Jensen and Meckling's (1976) model predicts that, starting from an all-equity position, managers will substitute bonds for stock in order to reduce the agency costs of equity. As this process continues, however, the agency costs of debt begin to rise. The firm's optimal (value-maximizing) capital structure will balance agency costs with the other costs and benefits of debt.

We are now ready to tie together all the threads of the modern "agency cost–tax shield trade-off" capital structure theory. The **trade-off model** expresses a levered firm's value in terms of an unlevered firm's value as adjusted for the present values of tax shields, bankruptcy costs, and the agency costs of debt and equity:

$$V_L = V_U + \text{PV(Tax shields)} - \text{PV(Bankruptcy costs)} - \text{PV(Agency costs)} \qquad \textbf{(Eq. 13.2)}$$

This model provides intuition about how firms establish their optimal capital structures by choosing the debt ratio that maximizes firm value. Figure 13.5 illustrates the model graphically.

FIGURE 13.5

The Trade-off Model of Capital Structure Incorporating Taxes, Bankruptcy Costs, and Agency Costs

The optimal debt ratio maximizes firm value.

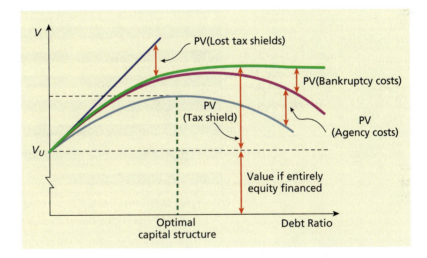

The trade-off model states that a firm's optimal (or target) capital structure depends on a trade-off between the benefits of debt (e.g., tax shields and constraints on managers' perquisite consumption) and the costs of debt (e.g., bankruptcy costs and agency costs). Beyond that intuition, the trade-off model has several quite specific implications.

- *Profitable firms should borrow more than unprofitable firms because they are more likely to benefit from debt tax shields*
- *Firms that own tangible, marketable assets should borrow more than firms whose assets are intangible or highly specialized*
- *Safer firms should borrow more than riskier firms*
- *Companies should have a target capital structure*

Research from the United States and other countries offers substantial support for the prediction that companies should manage toward a target capital structure, as the next What Companies Do Globally feature explains.

Although a great deal of evidence is consistent with the implications of the trade-off model, one glaring inconsistency is that profitable firms tend to borrow less, rather than more as the trade-off model predicts. The next section describes a theory that explains why this might be so.

Smart
Ideas
Video

John Graham,
Duke University

"Is the empirical evidence consistent with the trade-off theory?"

See the entire interview at
SMARTFinance

WHAT COMPANIES DO GLOBALLY

Target Capital Structure

Earlier in the chapter we noted that Graham and Harvey (2001) establish that most U.S. firms—especially large ones—manage toward a target capital structure, which is one of the key implications of the trade-off model. In more recent work with Deutsche Bank, Servaes and Tufano (2006) find that companies around the world followed the same practice. Figure 13.6 shows that a majority of firms in North America, Western Europe, Asia, Oceania, Eastern Europe, the Middle East, and Africa reported that they had a target capital structure.

FIGURE 13.6

Percentage of Firms with a Target Capital Structure, by Region

Source: Servaes and Tufano, The Theory and Practice of Corporate Capital Structure (Deutsche Bank, 2006).

% of Firms with a Target Capital Structure

Concept Review Questions

6. Suppose someone borrows from a bank to buy a new car. A few months later, the borrower realizes that he will have to default on this loan in a few months, after which the bank will repossess the car. What kind of underinvestment problem might occur here?

7. Suppose a commercial bank suffers loan losses so severe that it approaches insolvency. What kinds of asset substitution problems might arise? How might bank regulators act to prevent these problems?

8. Another type of agency problem is overinvestment, in which managers invest in negative-NPV projects to increase the size of the firm (as measured by sales or assets). Explain how debt constrains this behavior.

9. When U.S. auto executives first appeared before Congress in 2008 to request financial assistance, Representative Brad Sherman of California asked: "I'm going to ask the three executives here to raise their hand if they flew commercial." No hands were raised. What fraction of the cost of private aircraft do you think was borne by these CEOs? Is it possible that giving a CEO access to a private jet is a positive-NPV project for a firm?

13.5 THE PECKING-ORDER THEORY

There are two empirical regularities that seem inconsistent with the trade-off model.

1. The most profitable firms in an industry have the lowest debt ratios.
2. Firms issue debt frequently, but equity issues are rare. Announcements of new seasoned equity issues are invariably greeted with a large decline in the firm's stock price, a decline that is often equal to a third or more of the new offering's value.

How can we account for these perplexing facts? One answer was put forward in 1984 by Stewart Myers, who proposed the **pecking-order theory**.

Assumptions Underlying the Pecking-Order Theory

The pecking-order theory is based on four facts that Myers observed about corporate financial behavior. First, dividend policy is "sticky." Managers tend to maintain a stable dividend payment, neither increasing nor decreasing dividends in response to temporary fluctuations in profits.[5] Second, firms prefer internal financing (profits and retained cash) to external financing of any sort, debt or equity. Third, if a firm must obtain external financing, it will issue the safest security first. Finally, as a firm requires more external financing, it will work down the "pecking order" of securities, beginning with safe debt, then progressing through risky debt, convertible securities, preferred stock, and finally common stock as a last resort.

Myers and Nicholas Majluf (1984) provide additional justification for this pecking order that is based on asymmetric information. The authors make two plausible assumptions about managers: (1) a firm's managers know more about the company's current earnings and investment opportunities than do outside investors; and (2) managers act in the interest of *existing* shareholders.

Why are these two assumptions crucial? Assumption (1) about asymmetric information implies that managers who develop or discover a marvelous new positive-NPV investment opportunity cannot convey that information to the market because outside investors don't believe the managers' statements. After all, every management team has an incentive to announce wondrous new projects, and investors cannot immediately verify these claims. Skeptical investors will buy new equity issues only at a large discount from what the stock price would be without informational asymmetries. Corporate managers understand these problems, and in certain cases they will reject positive-NPV investments simply to avoid selling equity to new investors at a discount, which would have the effect of transferring wealth from old to new shareholders.

What a dilemma! Investors cannot fully trust managers, so investors place a low value on common stocks. Managers forgo valuable projects because they cannot credibly convey their private information to existing shareholders. Endemic information problems in financial markets do not have easy solutions.

What, then, must managers do? According to Myers and Majluf, corporations should retain sufficient financial slack or flexibility to fund positive-NPV projects *internally*. **Financial slack** includes a firm's cash and marketable securities holdings in addition to its unused debt capacity. Firms with sufficient financial slack can finesse the information problem because they need never issue equity to finance investment projects. In addition, the optimal investment rule is once again in force, because, by using internal funds, managers

---

[5]See Lintner (1956) and Brav, Graham, Harvey, and Michaely (2005).

can accept positive-NPV projects without harming existing shareholders. This theory also explains why highly profitable firms might retain earnings (Intel is a classic example). Such firms are building both financial slack and financial flexibility.

The pecking-order theory also explains stock market reactions to leverage-increasing and leverage-decreasing events. Firms with valuable investment opportunities find a way to finance their projects internally, or they use the least risky securities possible if financing must be obtained externally. Therefore, only managers who consider the firm's shares to be overvalued will issue equity. Investors understand these incentives and also realize that managers are better informed about a firm's prospects. Hence investors greet the announcement of a new equity issue as bad news: a sign that management considers the firm's shares to be overvalued.[6]

Evidence on the Pecking-Order and Trade-off Theories

**JOB INTERVIEW
QUESTION**

Our firm has identified an investment with a small positive NPV. To fund the investment, we'd have to sell new shares to the public. Should we do it?

The pecking-order theory is consistent with the fact that the vast majority (roughly 90%) of corporate investments in the United States are funded internally through retained earnings. It also explains why profitable firms (which have lots of financial slack) borrow less than unprofitable firms. But the pecking-order theory implies that firms have no target capital structure and that the debt ratios observed in the real world ought to fluctuate randomly. The theory also does not explain the evidence that firms owning more tangible assets typically use more leverage. The What CFOs Do insert on the next page explores these issues further by looking at what factors CFOs say matter most to them when making capital structure decisions.

**Concept
Review
Questions**

10. If you ask senior corporate executives whether their firms' stock prices are overvalued, undervalued, or fairly valued, which do you think would be the most common response? What does this have to do with the pecking-order theory?

11. Do you think that allowing firms to make a rights issue—that is, to sell stock only to their existing shareholders and perhaps at a below-market price—would negate the informational asymmetry problem described by Myers and Majluf?

13.6 SIGNALING AND MARKET-TIMING MODELS

Beginning in the late 1970s, Ross (1977a, 1977b) and others developed a capital structure **signaling model** based on information asymmetries between managers and outside shareholders. These models assume that managers with favorable inside information have an incentive to convey this information to outside investors in order to increase the firm's stock price. Managers cannot simply announce this good news, because shareholders will, quite properly, be skeptical of such statements.

How Signaling with Capital Structure Can Convey Information

One solution to this problem of information asymmetry is for managers of high-value firms (firms with good news to convey) to *signal* this information to investors. They do so by taking some action, or adopting some financial policy, that is prohibitively costly for lower value firms to mimic.

---

[6]This works in reverse, too. The CFO of a Fortune 500 company with billions in cash reserves told us that his company wanted to distribute some of the cash to investors, but management did not want to force investors to pay taxes on high dividend payments and were reluctant to repurchase shares because they thought the firm's stock was overvalued.

WHAT CFOs DO

CFO Survey Evidence

Graham and Harvey (2001) asked U.S. CFOs to rate the importance of several factors in setting capital structures. Figure 13.7 shows their findings. Number one on the list is financial flexibility, which offers some support for the pecking-order theory. However, Graham and Harvey find that the types of firms that value financial flexibility are not necessarily the ones predicted by the pecking-order theory—namely, firms with severe asymmetric information issues. The authors also asked CFOs if they issued equity only when issuing debt was not an option (as the pecking-order theory predicts), but CFOs did not indicate that an inability to issue debt was the reason they issued equity.

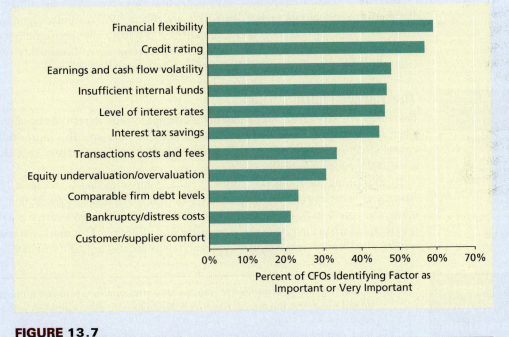

FIGURE 13.7

What Factors Do U.S. Companies Consider When Choosing Debt Policy?

Source: Reprinted from Graham and Harvey, "The theory and practice of corporate finance: Evidence from the field," *Journal of Financial Economics*, Volume 60, Issue 2-3, May/June, pages 187–243, Copyright 2001, with permission from Elsevier.

CFOs said the second most important factor in setting debt policy was their credit rating. Credit ratings reflect the risk of default, so they are closely linked with the probability of bankruptcy. The trade-off model says that expected bankruptcy costs are an important determinant of leverage, so the importance that CFOs place on their credit rating is consistent with that prediction; however, we must note that when asked specifically about bankruptcy costs, CFOs said that they were not particularly important in setting debt policy. The trade-off model also states that safer firms borrow more than risky ones, and third on the list of important items in Figure 13.7 is earnings and cash flow volatility.

For example, suppose that managers have inside information that their firm's investments will generate spectacular cash flows in the future. To credibly convey this good news, the firm's managers can adopt a heavily leveraged capital structure. This commits the firm to paying out large sums to bondholders. Because investors know that only firms with good prospects can afford to take on debt, they recognize a debt issuance as good news and so bid up the firm's shares.

Empirical Evidence on Signaling Models Even though signaling models have intuitive appeal, they enjoy little empirical support. As we have seen, leverage ratios are, if anything, *negatively* related to profitability in almost every industry. Signaling models predict a *positive* relationship.

The signaling model also predicts that, all else equal, companies rich in growth opportunities and other intangible assets should employ more debt than mature firms with mostly tangible assets. Why? Because information asymmetry problems are more severe for growth companies, which thus have a greater need to signal. As we know, asset-rich companies use far more debt than do growth companies.

Even in those research studies that present a best-case scenario for signaling theory, the bottom line is discouraging. Barclay, Smith, and Watts (1995) examine signaling models empirically, finding that they receive support that is statistically significant but economically trivial. "High-quality" firms employ more leverage than "low-quality" ones, after controlling for other factors, but the differences in leverage are minor.

The Market-Timing Model

Baker and Wurgler (2002) argue that firms attempt to time the market by issuing equity when share values are high and issuing debt when they are not. This means that a firm's capital structure simply reflects the cumulative effects of its managers' past attempts to issue equity opportunistically.

By examining the financial histories of U.S. companies that went public after 1972, Baker and Wurgler find that current leverage ratios are related to valuation measures many years previously. This finding suggests that firms with high leverage are those that raised capital when their stock prices were low, and vice versa. This **market-timing model** is intriguing, but it is relatively new and researchers are still testing its predictions.[7]

Concept Review Questions	12. Use a "signaling" argument to explain why students return to school to pursue an MBA and why the market rewards individuals who obtain an MBA with higher salaries.
	13. How might cash dividend payments serve as an effective signal of corporate profitability?

13.7 FINDING THE OPTIMAL CAPITAL STRUCTURE FOR A SPECIFIC COMPANY

Now it's time to pull all of the ideas in this chapter together to show how to find the optimal capital structure for a specific company. Intuitively, we are looking for the crossing point of the marginal benefit and cost curves from Panel A of Figure 13.2 (or, equivalently, the peak in the hump-shaped blue curve in Figure 13.5). The challenge we face is to specify exactly where those curves lie and where they intersect.

---

[7]Leary and Roberts (2007) argue that Baker and Wurgler's evidence is consistent with a dynamic trade-off model.

Let's start with the marginal benefit curve. Most profitable companies in the United States face a marginal federal income tax rate of 35%. If an all-equity firm adds some debt to its capital structure, then each dollar of interest that it pays saves $0.35 in taxes as long as the firm is profitable. We've seen that when a firm incurs losses, the present value of debt tax shields falls, and we know that higher debt levels increase the probability of losses. Therefore, as more debt is added and the probability of losses therefore increases, the marginal benefit of debt curve slopes downward.

Graham (2000) shows how to estimate the present value of tax shields for any firm by running simulations that allow the firm's earnings to fluctuate over time. A marginal benefit function for Alltel, the wireless telecommunications company acquired by Verizon in 2009, appears as the solid line in Figure 13.8. This function is calculated based on Alltel's financial data in 2006 and forward-looking simulations for the next 20 years. The vertical axis shows the tax benefit per dollar of interest expense, and the horizontal axis shows the total interest expense of the company (scaled by book value). Starting on the left, the graph shows that if Alltel had no debt and thus no interest expense, the marginal benefit of adding $1 in interest expense would be $0.35. This simply means that, at low debt levels, Alltel would be sufficiently profitable to take full advantage of the debt tax shield in the same year that it paid interest on the debt. The marginal benefit is flat (at $0.35) up to the point where interest expenses rise to roughly 7% of book value. Beyond that point, the marginal benefit of debt begins to fall because, with more debt, there is an increasing chance that Alltel will experience a loss and fail to capture the full benefit of the tax shield. By the time interest expenses reach approximately 13% of assets, there is almost no tax benefit from debt because the firm is so burdened by debt that it is unlikely ever to earn profit sufficient to benefit from the incremental interest expense tax deductions.

FIGURE 13.8

Marginal Benefit of Debt and Marginal Cost of Debt for Alltel in 2006

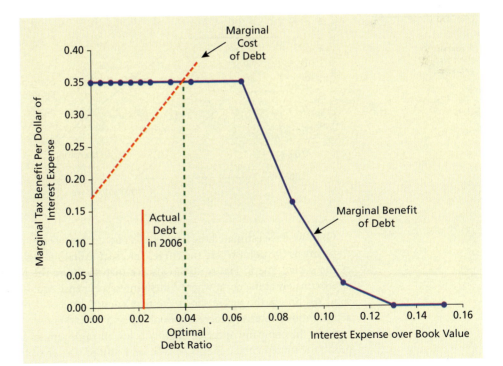

Think about what would happen to the tax-benefit function if Congress passed a law increasing or decreasing the corporate tax rate. At higher tax rates, the deduction for interest expense would shield more income and so the entire function would shift upward.

For example, if the corporate tax rate were 50% then the first dollar of interest paid would reduce taxes by $0.50, rather than the present $0.35. Similarly, if Congress cut tax rates, the curve would shift downward.

With the marginal benefit curve in place, we need a marginal cost curve before we can find the optimal debt ratio. Whereas debt's tax benefits are relatively easy to calculate, the costs of debt are more difficult to measure. To estimate expected bankruptcy costs, one would have to measure the magnitude of these costs when bankruptcy occurs as well as the probability that a firm will experience bankruptcy. Other costs of debt, such as agency costs, are even more difficult to quantify.

Van Binsbergen, Graham, and Yang (2008) develop a clever way to measure the marginal cost curve. They note that changes in the U.S. tax laws over the past several decades have shifted the marginal benefit curve up and down.[8] Assuming that a set of optimizing firms adjust their debt to the optimum level, we can infer where the marginal cost curve lies because it must be located at points that intersect the benefit function. Figure 13.9 illustrates the idea. The figure shows four different marginal benefit functions corresponding to four different tax regimes. The circles on each benefit curve represent the actual debt level chosen by a particular firm at the time that a particular tax scheme was in place. By connecting the dots, we trace out the marginal cost curve.

FIGURE 13.9

Using Variation in Marginal Benefit Curves to Map Out the Marginal Cost of Debt Curve

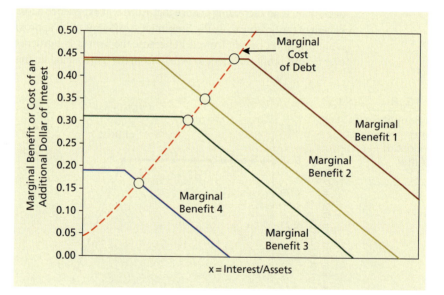

Once we have estimated the benefit and cost curves, we can determine optimal capital structure as the point where the curves intersect. Alltel's marginal cost function appears as the dotted line in Figure 13.8. Observe that it crosses the marginal benefit function approximately at the point where Alltel's interest expense equals 4% of its book value. The solid red line in the figure shows the firm's actual level of debt (to be more precise, the actual ratio of interest expense to book value of assets) chosen by Alltel in 2006. As you can see, the company operated slightly below its optimum leverage at that time. At that point, the incremental benefits of debt were still greater than the costs of debt, so Alltel could presumably have increased firm value by raising debt slightly.

[8] Alternatively, marginal benefit curves can vary across firms in a given year based on firm characteristics. For example, in Figure 13.9, the four marginal benefit curves might represent four different companies in 2006.

Concept Review Questions	14. How would the marginal benefit function for a firm with stable cash flows compare to that for one with volatile cash flows?
	15. How would the marginal cost function for a firm with mostly intangible assets compare to that for one with many tangible assets that could be used as collateral?

Summary

- CFOs claim that capital structure decisions are very important and that their firms manage toward an optimal target debt ratio. Conceptually, the optimal debt ratio occurs where debt's marginal benefits and costs are equal.

- The tax benefits of incremental debt fall as leverage increases because larger interest expense makes it more likely that a firm will lose money, and a firm that loses money must defer realizing the debt tax shield.

- If bankruptcy resulted in a costless transfer of ownership from shareholders to creditors, then bankruptcy would have no important consequence for a firm's capital structure. It is because the bankruptcy process triggers large direct and indirect costs that bankruptcy creates a cost to using debt.

- Creditors know that corporate managers, who operate their firms in the interests of shareholders, have incentives to expropriate creditor wealth by playing certain "games" with the firm's investment policy. Asset substitution is one such game. It involves promising to invest in a safe asset to obtain a return reflecting this risk, but then investing instead in a riskier asset that offers a higher expected return. Creditors protect themselves from these games in several ways, especially by inserting restrictive covenants into loan agreements.

- There are several important agency costs inherent in the relationship between corporate managers and outside investors and creditors. In some cases, using financial leverage can help overcome these agency problems; in others, using leverage worsens the problems. The modern *trade-off* model of corporate leverage predicts that a firm's optimal debt level is set by trading off the tax benefits of increasing leverage against the increasingly severe bankruptcy costs and agency costs of heavy debt usage.

- The *pecking-order* theory predicts that managers will operate their firms in such a way as to minimize the need to secure outside financing—for example, by retaining profits to build up financial slack. These same managers will use the safest source of funding, usually senior debt, when they must secure outside financing. The *signaling* theory predicts that managers will select their firms' leverage levels to signal that the firm is strong enough to employ high debt and still fund its profitable investment opportunities. The *market-timing* model predicts that firms attempt to time the market by issuing equity when share values are high and issuing debt when share prices are low. A firm's capital structure thus reflects only the cumulative effects of its managers' past attempts to issue equity opportunistically.

- By simulating a firm's ability to capture debt tax shields, one can estimate a marginal benefit function for debt. Changes in the tax law shift the benefit function and, in combination with the leverage decisions of actual firms, allow us to infer where the marginal cost function lies. Optimal leverage occurs where marginal benefit and cost functions intersect.

Key Terms

agency cost theory of financial
   structure
asset substitution
bankrupt
bankruptcy

bankruptcy costs
bonding mechanism
direct bankruptcy costs
financial slack
indirect bankruptcy costs

market-timing model
pecking-order theory
signaling model
trade-off model
underinvestment

QUESTIONS

13-1. Empirically, how do bankruptcy costs and agency costs influence capital structure decisions? What are the general relationships between these factors and leverage?

13-2. All else equal, which firm would face higher costs of financial distress: a software development firm or a hotel chain? Why would financial distress costs affect these firms so differently?

13-3. Describe how managers of firms that have debt outstanding and face financial distress might jeopardize the investments of creditors with the "games" of asset substitution and underinvestment.

13-4. Differentiate between direct and indirect costs of bankruptcy. Which of the two is generally more significant?

13-5. What does it mean to use external debt as a "bonding mechanism" for managers? In what way does this mechanism reduce the agency costs of external equity? How can restrictive covenants in bonds be both an agency cost of debt and a way to *prevent* agency costs of debt?

13-6. What are the trade-offs in the agency cost–tax shield trade-off model? How is the firm's optimal capital structure determined under the assumptions of this model? Does empirical evidence support the model?

13-7. What is the main premise underlying the pecking-order theory? What is the "pecking order" of sources of financing? Why is dividend policy so important to this theory? How does the concept of financial slack relate to this theory?

13-8. What type of information is conveyed in a signaling model of capital structure? According to this model, how should leverage affect the market value of firms? Does empirical evidence support the model?

13-9. A CFO says that her firm chooses a capital structure that allows it to maintain a credit rating of AA. She reasons that a credit rating of AAA would be too conservative, but anything less than AA would be too risky. What capital structure model does this firm appear to follow?

PROBLEMS

Costs of Bankruptcy

13-1. Equilibrant Industries is composed entirely of equity and is valued at $1.5 million. Durst Co. has $400,000 worth of debt costing 9% that becomes due next year with interest. Both firms compete in the same market, and next year's expected cash flows for both firms are $300,000 with 50% probability and $3.15 million with 50% probability. What is the expected cash flow of both firms, ignoring taxes and bankruptcy costs? What is the expected equity return for Equilibrant? How much debt is due at the end of the year for Durst? What is the discounted value of Durst's debt? What is the expected return on its equity, assuming that Durst is valued comparably to Equilibrant?

13-2. Raskalnikov Implements Inc. has $700,000 worth of debt due at the end of the year (including interest). The company's expected cash flows (ignoring taxes) for next year are: $1.2 million (30% probability), $2.8 million (50% probability), and $1.8 million (20% probability). Assuming the equity has an expected return of 25% and the firm is valued at $1.772 million, what is the expected return on the firm's debt? Will bankruptcy costs affect the firm's value? What would be the expected return on equity if Raskalnikov had no debt?

13-3. Mellors Management has debt of $1.2 million due at the end of the year (principal and interest). The company's expected cash flows (ignoring taxes) are $1 million with 40% probability and $2 million with 60% probability. Assuming the equity has an expected return of 25% and the firm is valued at $1.4 million, what is the expected return on the firm's debt? How much does the firm's value decrease if bankruptcy costs are $0.5 million? What would be the expected return on equity if Mellors had no debt?

13-4. If firms in a certain industry are expected to have a weighted average cost of capital of 17%, calculate the cost of debt (ignoring taxes) based on the cost of equity provided for the firms below. Assume that each firm is worth $4 million.

Firm A: $2 million of equity with a 24% expected return
Firm B: $2.5 million of equity with a 22% expected return
Firm C: $3 million of equity with a 20% expected return

13-5. If firms in a certain industry are expected to have a weighted average cost of capital of 20%, calculate the cost of equity based on the cost of debt (ignoring taxes) provided for the firms below. Assume that each firm is worth $10 million.

Firm A: $4 million of debt with a 10% expected return
Firm B: $6 million of debt with a 14% expected return
Firm C: $7 million of debt with a 15% expected return

If bankruptcy costs are $1.2 million and if there is only a 10% chance of bankruptcy occurring, then how much value is lost for each firm due to bankruptcy costs?

13-6. You are the manager of a financially distressed corporation with $1.5 million in debt outstanding that will mature in three months. Your firm currently has $1 million cash on hand. Assume that you are offered the opportunity to invest in either of the following two projects.

Project 1: The opportunity to invest $1 million in risk-free Treasury bills with a 4% annual interest rate (a quarterly interest rate of 1% = 4% per year ÷ 4 quarters per year)

Project 2: A high-risk gamble that will pay $1.6 million in two months if it is successful ($P = 0.4$) but will pay only $400,000 if it is unsuccessful ($P = 0.6$).

a. Compute the expected payoff for each project. If you were operating the firm in the shareholders' best interests, which one you would adopt, and why?

b. Which project would you accept if the firm were unlevered? Why?

c. Which project would you accept if the company were organized as a partnership rather than a corporation? Why?

13-7. You are the manager of a financially distressed corporation with $10 million in debt outstanding that will mature in one month. Your firm currently has $7 million cash on hand. Assume that you are offered the opportunity to invest in either of the following two projects.

Project 1: The opportunity to invest $7 million in risk-free Treasury bills with a 4% annual interest rate (or a 0.333% monthly interest rate)

Project 2: A high-risk gamble that will pay $12 million in one month if it is successful ($P = 0.25$) but will pay only $4 million if it is unsuccessful ($P = 0.75$).

a. Compute the expected payoff for each project. Which one would you adopt if you were operating the firm in the shareholders' best interests? Why?

b. Which project would you accept if the firm were unlevered? Why?

c. Which project would you accept if the company were organized as a partnership rather than a corporation? Why?

13-8. A firm has the choice of investing in one of two projects. Both projects last one year. Project 1 requires an investment of $11,000; it yields $11,000 with a probability of 0.5 and $13,000 with a probability of 0.5. Project 2 also requires an investment of $11,000; it yields $5,000 with a probability of 0.5 and $20,000 with a probability of 0.5. The firm is capable of raising $10,000 of the investment required through a bond issue carrying an annual interest rate of 10%.

   a. Assuming the investors are concerned only about expected returns, which project would stockholders prefer? Why?

   b. Which project would bondholders prefer? Why?

13-9. An all-equity firm has 100,000 shares outstanding worth $10 each. The firm is considering a project requiring an investment of $400,000 that has an NPV of $50,000. The company is also considering financing this project with a new issue of equity.

   a. At what price can the firm issue the new shares so that existing shareholders are indifferent to whether or not the firm takes on the project with this equity financing?

   b. At what price would the firm issue the new shares so that existing shareholders capture the full benefit associated with the new project?

13-10. You are the manager of a financially distressed corporation that has $5 million in loans coming due in 30 days. Your firm has $4 million cash on hand. Suppose that a long-time supplier of materials to your firm is planning to exit the business but has offered to sell your company a large supply of material at the bargain price of $4.5 million—but only if payment is made immediately in cash. If you choose not to acquire this material, then the supplier will offer it to a competitor and so your firm will have to acquire the material at market prices totaling $5 million over the next few months.

   a. Assuming that you are operating the firm in the shareholders' best interests, would you accept the project? Why or why not?

   b. Would you accept this project if the firm were unlevered? Why or why not?

   c. Would you accept the project if the company were organized as a partnership? Why or why not?

13-11. Run-and-Hide Detective Company currently has no debt and, for the foreseeable future, expects to earn $5 million in earnings before interest and taxes each year. The required return on assets for detective companies of this type is 10%, and the corporate tax rate is 35%. There are no taxes on dividends or interest at the personal level. Run-and-Hide calculates that there is a 5% chance that the firm will fall into bankruptcy in any given year. If bankruptcy does occur, it will impose direct and indirect costs totaling $8 million. If necessary, use the industry required return for discounting bankruptcy costs.

   a. Compute the present value of bankruptcy costs for Run-and-Hide.

   b. Compute the overall value of the firm.

   c. Recalculate the firm's value under the assumption that firm shareholders face a 15% personal tax rate on equity income.

Agency Costs and Capital Structure

13-12. Magnum Enterprises has net operating income of $5 million. There is $50 million of debt outstanding with a required rate of return of 6%. The required rate of return on the industry is 12%. The corporate tax rate is 40%; there are corporate taxes, but no personal taxes. Compute the value of Magnum assuming that the present value of bankruptcy costs is $10 million.

13-13. Slash and Burn Construction Company currently has no debt and expects to earn $10 million in net operating income each year for the foreseeable future. The required return on assets for construction companies of this type is 12.5%, and the corporate tax rate is 40%. There are no taxes on dividends or interest at the personal level. Slash and Burn calculates that there is a 10% chance the firm will

Smart Solutions

See the problem and solution explained step-by-step at SMARTFinance fall into bankruptcy in any given year and that, if bankruptcy does occur, it will impose direct and indirect costs totaling $12 million. Assume that, in the event of bankruptcy, the firm will reorganize and continue operations indefinitely, with a constant 10% probability of reentering bankruptcy. If necessary, use the industry required return for discounting bankruptcy costs.

   a. Compute the present value of bankruptcy costs for Slash and Burn.

   b. Compute the overall value of the firm.

13-14. Using the data from Problem 13-13, calculate the value of Slash and Burn Construction Company while assuming that the firm's shareholders face a 25% personal tax rate on equity income.

13-15. Assume that the managers of Slash and Burn Construction Company, described in Problem 13-13, are weighing two capital structure alteration proposals, as follows.

Smart Solutions

See the problem and solution explained step-by-step at **SMARTFinance**

Proposal 1: Borrow $20 million at an interest rate of 6% and use the proceeds to repurchase an equal amount of outstanding stock. With this level of debt, the likelihood that Slash and Burn will fall into bankruptcy in any given year increases to 15%, and if bankruptcy occurs then it will impose direct and indirect costs totaling $12 million.

Proposal 2: Borrow $30 million at an interest rate of 8% and use the proceeds to repurchase an equal amount of outstanding stock. With this level of debt, the likelihood of Slash and Burn falling into bankruptcy in any given year rises to 25%, and the associated direct and indirect costs of bankruptcy, should it occur, increase to $20 million.

For each proposal, calculate both the present value of the interest tax shields and the overall value of the firm, assuming there are no personal taxes on debt or equity income.

13-16. Go to the home page for Ford Motor Company (http://www.ford.com) and search for its most recent annual report to shareholders. Within this report, find management's discussion and analysis of financial condition and results of operations. Also find management's discussion about liquidity and capital resources (about halfway through the report). Use that information to answer the following questions.

   a. How large a cash position does Ford hold? How large is this cash position relative to Ford's overall capital structure (also found in the annual report)?

   b. Does Ford's cash position indicate a preference for or against financial slack by Ford's management?

13-17. View the balance sheet information summarized below for Sears Holding Corporation (ticker symbol, SHLD) from January of 2005.

Assets		Liabilities and Equity	
Cash	$3,435	Current liabilities	$2,086
Short-term investments	0	Long-term liabilities	2,096
Other current assets	4,106	Total liabilities	$4,182
Net fixed assets	1,110	Total equity	4,469
Total assets	$8,651	Total liabilities and equity	$8,651

All numbers in millions.

   a. What is Sears's current ratio (see Chapter 2)?

   b. What portion of Sears's liabilities can be paid off immediately with cash?

   c. What is Sears's debt ratio (see Chapter 2)?

   d. Can Sears pay off its long-term debt now? Does this allow Sears financial slack?

13-18. View the balance sheet information summarized below for Gateway Inc. (ticker symbol, GTW) from December of 2004.

Assets		Liabilities and Equity	
Cash	$ 382.972	Current liabilities	$1,122.652
Short-term investments	260.537	Long-term liabilities	404.098
Other current assets	756.108	Total liabilities	$1,526.750
Net fixed assets	372.170	Total equity	245.037
Total assets	$1,771.787	Total liabilities and equity	$1,771.787

All numbers in millions.

a. What is the ratio of Gateway's cash and short-term investments to its long-term liabilities?

b. Considering the ratio from part (a) and Gateway's current ratio (see Chapter 2), does Gateway have significant financial slack?

c. What is Gateway's debt ratio (see Chapter 2)?

13-19. View the information below, which was taken from a recent balance sheet for Microsoft Corporation (ticker symbol, MSFT):

Assets		Liabilities and Equity	
Cash	$ 4,851	Current liabilities	$16,877
Short-term investments	32,900	Long-term liabilities	5,823
Other current assets	10,986	Total liabilities	$22,700
Net fixed assets	22,078	Total equity	48,115
Total assets	$70,815	Total liabilities and equity	$70,815

All numbers in millions.

a. Can Microsoft pay off all of its liabilities with its cash position and short-term investments? Is this an indication of significant financial slack?

b. What is Microsoft's current ratio (see Chapter 2)?

c. Describe the signal that Microsoft may be sending by having debt on its balance sheet.

THOMSON ONE | Business School Edition

13-20. In 2002, United Airlines (ticker symbol, UAUA) filed for bankruptcy. In 2006, United emerged from bankruptcy. What was the change in the book value of equity from before to after the bankruptcy? What was the change in the market value of its equity? What other costs would be relevant when calculating the total cost of United's bankruptcy?

MINI-CASE: CAPITAL STRUCTURE: BALANCING THE BENEFITS AND COSTS OF DEBT

MarCher Industries is considering undertaking a new project with a one-year life. The following table shows each project's expected return under two economic scenarios.

	High-Risk Project	Low-Risk Project
Cash flow (boom)	$1,500,000	$1,000,000
Cash flow (bust)	$ 400,000	$ 500,000

The firm currently has no debt, but it is considering borrowing $870,000 on a short-term basis to help finance its purchase of the project. The firm will owe $900,000, including principal and interest, in one year. There is a 60% chance a boom will occur and only a 40% chance a bust will occur.

1. Calculate the expected value of the high- and low-risk project to MarCher Industries' stockholders if the firm remains unlevered. Which project would the stockholders prefer?

2. Calculate the expected value of the high- and low-risk project to MarCher's stockholders and bondholders, assuming the firm does borrow money to partially finance the purchase of the project. Which project would the bondholders prefer? Which project would the stockholders prefer?

3. Explain why a conflict exists between the bondholders and stockholders.

14

The Link between Capital Structure and Capital Budgeting

What Companies Do

Investors Salivate over Performance Food Group

In January 2008, private equity firm The Blackstone Group announced that it had reached an agreement to acquire Performance Food Group (PFGC) for roughly $1.3 billion. Analysts reported that, at that price, Blackstone valued PFGC at more than 11 times its unlevered cash flow. The stock market responded by boosting PFGC's share price 31% on the news. As part of the deal, PFGC—a supplier for well-known restaurant chains such as T.G.I. Friday's and Outback Steakhouse—would take out a line of credit allowing the firm to borrow up to $1.1 billion, which represented a substantial but presumably temporary increase in the firm's leverage.

How could Blackstone afford to pay a 31% premium, and what role did financial leverage play in this deal? For Blackstone, the PFGC acquisition represented a large capital investment, much like the investments we studied in Chapters 7–9. To determine the value of their investment, Blackstone might have calculated the NPV for investing in PFGC, using the weighted average cost of capital as the discount rate. But because the deal called for rapidly changing capital structure (i.e., a large run-up in debt at the start followed by a reduction as PFGC generated cash flow and paid down the debt), the company's mixture of debt and equity financing was not settled at a particular target level.

In a case like this, where the debt ratio changes each year, applying the weighted average cost of capital can be a bit tedious—but there is a handy valuation method called *adjusted present value* that can be used instead. Adjusted present value separates the investment's value into two components: the value of the investment itself plus the value added by using debt financing. Experts estimated that the financing benefits in this transaction accounted for more than 10% of the total deal value; this in turn means that, in order to justify the 31% premium paid, Blackstone expects to bring about operating changes that would add at least another 20% to the prior value of PFGC.

Sources: van Binsbergen, Graham, and Yang (2008); http://www.bloggingbuyouts .com/2008/01/18/blackstone-pays-1.3-billion-for-performance-food-group/; Melanie Lindner, "Blackstone Scoops Up Performance Food," Forbes.com (January 18, 2008).

14.1 M&M, Capital Budgeting, and the WACC

In this chapter, we pull together many of the ideas from the text's first 13 chapters to address a critical question: How do financing choices affect capital investment decisions? In a world of perfect capital markets, Modigliani and Miller (M&M) proved that a firm's value does not depend on its capital structure. By the same logic, their Proposition I implies that a capital investment project's value will not depend on how the firm finances the project—provided that markets are perfect. But in Chapters 12 and 13 we've seen how financing decisions can affect firm value in light of such market imperfections as taxes. If market imperfections lead to violations of Proposition I (i.e., if firm value does depend on capital structure) then, by extension, the mix of debt and equity that a firm uses to finance an investment project can affect that project's value.

In Chapter 8, we finessed this issue by arguing that analysts should exclude from their capital budgeting spreadsheets any cash flows associated with a project's financing. As an example, we said that if a firm pays for a project's initial outlay by borrowing money, analysts should not deduct interest expenses from the project's cash flows. We argued that by choosing the proper project discount rate, analysts account for financing costs in the denominator of their net present value calculations rather than in the numerator. But what, precisely, does "the proper project discount rate" mean?

Chapter 9 offered one answer to this question by introducing the **weighted average cost of capital (WACC)**. Recall that, in order to calculate the WACC, a firm must determine the after-tax required return on its debt and the required return on its equity. Next, the firm multiplies these rates by the percentage of debt and equity in its capital structure—basing these percentages on market values, not book values. For convenience, we repeat the basic WACC equation here:

$$\text{WACC} = \left(\frac{D}{D+E}\right)(1 - T_c)r_d + \left(\frac{E}{D+E}\right)r_e \qquad \text{(Eq. 14.1)}$$

The WACC method captures the effects of financing choices on a project's value through the discount rate. Because firms can deduct interest payments when they calculate taxable income, the tax code essentially subsidizes the use of corporate debt. The after-tax cost of debt is less than the pre-tax cost as long as the corporate tax rate, T_c, is positive and interest is tax-deductible. In other words, the WACC approach accounts for the tax benefits of interest deductions by reducing the project discount rate for debt-financed investments. This, in turn, increases a project's value because a lower discount rate leads to a higher project value. This line of argument extends to the value of the entire firm. Chapter 12 illustrated how the introduction of corporate taxes caused M&M's Proposition I to break down. With an available tax deduction for interest payments, firms increase their values (or, equivalently, lower their cost of capital) by using more debt.

The WACC accounts for the valuation effects of debt by adjusting the discount rate; therefore, when analysts discount a project's cash flows using the WACC, the cash flows that they discount should ignore financing costs such as interest expense. That is, the cash flows to be discounted should be unlevered cash flows. But there are two other approaches analysts can use to calculate project values when firms use both debt and equity. The first approach, called the **adjusted present value (APV) method**, calculates an investment's value as if it were financed only with equity and then adds the present value of any financing side effects. The second approach, known as the **flow-to-equity (FTE) method**, uses the firm's cost of equity to discount levered project cash flows. Under certain conditions, these methods yield the same estimate of an investment project's value, an estimate that also agrees with that obtained by using the WACC approach. However, each of these approaches has its own advantages and disadvantages, and the valuations that they generate need not be identical in all circumstances.

To see how the WACC, APV, and FTE methods work, let's revisit an earlier example. In Chapter 9 we examined a fast-food company, Lox-in-a-Box Inc., that had a market value of $150 million. Lox-in-a-Box's outstanding equity has a market value of $100 million, so its bonds are worth $50 million. Given the firm's current capital structure (which we will assume is the long-run target capital structure), stockholders require a return of 15% and bondholders a return of 9% on their investment.

Financial managers at Lox-in-a-Box are evaluating an investment opportunity that requires an initial outlay of $60 million. To maintain their target capital structure, the company will finance this investment with $20 million in debt and $40 million in equity.[1] They expect the investment will generate a perpetual pre-tax cash flow stream of $10.8 million per year, starting next year. If the company faces a corporate tax rate of 33% (one-third), then the after-tax annual cash flow, ignoring the interest tax shield, is $7.2 million. To calculate the net present value of this project, discount the unlevered cash flow of $7.2 million using the firm's WACC:

$$\text{WACC} = \left(\frac{\$50}{\$50 + \$100}\right)\left(1 - \frac{1}{3}\right)0.09 + \left(\frac{\$100}{\$50 + \$100}\right)0.15 = 0.12,$$

$$\text{NPV} = -\$60 + \frac{\$7.2}{0.12} = \$0$$

The zero NPV implies that this project offers a minimally acceptable return for Lox-in-a-Box. In the next section we reevaluate this project using the APV method.

Concept Review Questions	1. What information is required to estimate a firm's WACC? How difficult is it to obtain this information? 2. In the Lox-in-a-Box example, does $7.2 million represent the cash flow that goes to stockholders each year? If not, is the stockholders' cash flow higher or lower than $7.2 million?

14.2 The Adjusted Present Value Method

The APV approach begins by calculating the project's unlevered cash flows, just as with the WACC method. However, the adjusted present value method discounts these cash flows using the discount rate that applies if the firm is financed only with equity. In addition, analysts using the APV technique must add (or subtract) the present values of any financing side effects that arise from the firm's use of leverage. The result is the adjusted present value of the investment project:

$$\text{APV} = \text{NPV(Unlevered)} + \text{NPV(Financing effects)} \qquad \textbf{(Eq. 14.2)}$$

---

[1]The company's current debt-to-equity ratio is $50 \div 100 = 0.5$. If the company uses $20 million in debt and $40 million in equity to finance the project, then its debt-to-equity ratio will remain at $0.5(70 \div 140)$.

In Chapters 12 and 13 we learned that debt financing can have many different side effects, which include tax savings due to interest deductions, expected bankruptcy costs, and agency costs. We could also include in this list the fees paid to investment bankers when firms finance projects by issuing new securities as well as special subsidies that may be available, for example, when a government grants below-market loans to companies investing in projects that policy makers want to encourage. In principle, all of these side effects can be accounted for in the NPV(Financing effects) term in Eq. 14.2. Of all these side effects, the easiest to quantify are the tax savings, which also are probably larger than the other side effects (at least for firms with relatively moderate debt levels). For the sake of simplicity, in this chapter we assume—as do most practitioners—that the only material financial side effect that we must measure in an APV analysis is the tax effect.

EXAMPLE

Returning to the Lox-in-a-Box project, we have already determined that the unlevered, after-tax annual cash flow is $7.2 million. The APV method requires that we discount this cash flow at the rate that would apply if Lox-in-a-Box were an all-equity firm. To arrive at this rate, use M&M Proposition II from Chapter 12, making an adjustment for the tax deductibility of interest.

Proposition II expresses the required return on levered equity, r_l, as a function of the required return r_A on the firm's assets, the required return r_d on debt, and the debt-to-equity ratio D/E. Repeating Equation 12.2, we have:

$$r_l = r_A + (r_A - r_d)\frac{D}{E}$$

If the firm employs no debt, then $r_l = r_A$ and we can interpret r_A as the required return on an unlevered firm. Now, to account for the tax effect of corporate interest deductions, we modify this equation as follows:

$$r_l = r_A + (r_A - r_d)\frac{D}{E}(1 - T_c) \qquad \textbf{(Eq. 14.3)}$$

Plugging in known values for Lox-in-a-Box, we have

$$0.15 = r_A + (r_A - 0.09)\,0.5\left(1 - \frac{1}{3}\right)$$

It takes just a little rearranging to determine that the unlevered cost of capital in this equation is $r_A = 13.5\%$. In other words, 13.5% is the equity return that investors would require from Lox-in-a-Box if the firm used no debt. Now use this fact along with the $7.2 million unlevered project cash flow to determine what the NPV of the project would be without debt financing:

$$\text{NPV(Unlevered)} = -\$60 + \frac{\$7.2}{0.135} = -\$6.67$$

This calculation suggests that the project is not worthwhile, but we have not yet taken into account the debt tax shields resulting from the firm financing the project with $20 million in debt. The size of the annual tax shield depends on the tax rate, the cost of debt, and the amount of debt used to finance the project:

$$\text{Annual tax shield} = T_c \times r_d \times D = \frac{1}{3} \times 0.09 \times \$20 = \$0.60$$

(continued)

Lox-in-a-Box will pay lower taxes in perpetuity, by $0.60 million per year, because the debt financing generates $1.8 million in tax deductions ($r_d \times D = 0.09 \times \$20$), and these interest deductions save the firm $0.60 million in taxes each year ($T_c \times \$1.8$ million $= \frac{1}{3} \times \$1.8$ million). Assuming that the interest tax shields are just as risky as the firm's debt, we can calculate the present value of the tax savings by discounting them at 9%:

$$\text{PV(Tax savings)} = \frac{\$0.60}{0.09} = \$6.67$$

Finally, we have everything we need to calculate the project's value using the APV method. The project's APV equals the unlevered NPV ($-\$6.67$ million) plus the present value of tax shields ($6.67 million). In other words, the project APV equals zero. This is the same value that we determined previously with the WACC approach. As before, the APV valuation suggests that the project is barely acceptable.

Given the assumptions made so far, we obtain the same project value whether we follow the WACC or the APV approach. In that case, why do we need two methods? The answer to this question follows shortly, but first we want to examine a third approach for valuing investment projects: the flow-to-equity method.

<table>
<tr><td>**Concept Review Questions**</td><td>3. How is the APV method different from the WACC?
4. Compare the WACC for Lox-in-a-Box to the cost of unlevered equity that we calculated as part of the APV analysis. Why are the two rates different?</td></tr>
</table>

14.3 THE FLOW-TO-EQUITY METHOD

The FTE method differs from the WACC and APV approaches by focusing exclusively on cash flows that flow to shareholders. Whereas the WACC and APV project cash flow calculations ignore interest expense, an FTE analysis deducts interest costs and taxes from project cash flows. We will refer to this type of cash flow calculation as **levered cash flow**. In essence, a flow-to-equity analysis captures the effects of financing in the numerator (i.e., the cash flows) rather than in the denominator. It is important to note that, unlike the WACC method, the FTE discount rate should not be reduced to account for the tax deductibility of interest. Instead, FTE accounts for benefits of interest deductions in the cash flows.

What cash flow does the proposed investment generate for Lox-in-a-Box shareholders? Start with pre-tax cash flow of $10.8 million. Next, deduct annual interest expense, which amounts to $1.8 million ($20 million in debt at 9%). That leaves pre-tax cash flow of $9 million. With a corporate tax rate of 33% (one-third), shareholders are left with $6 million per year in perpetuity.

Because the $6 million annual cash flow we've just calculated flows directly to shareholders, it is appropriate to discount that cash flow at the cost of equity. But take care here: the cost of equity we require to complete the FTE analysis is neither the unlevered cost of equity (13.5%) calculated for the APV analysis nor the Lox-in-a-Box WACC (12%). Instead, we need the rate of return that Lox-in-a-Box shareholders demand, given that the firm maintains a debt-to-equity ratio of 0.5. But that's just the 15% cost of equity we were given at the very beginning (and that can be calculated from actual stock

WHAT COMPANIES DO GLOBALLY

CFO Survey Evidence

How much do companies around the world use APV to value their investment projects? The answer, it turns out, is "not very much." Independent surveys of companies in North America, Europe, and South Africa consistently find that—although firms occasionally use the APV method—few use it as a matter of routine (see Figure 14.1). As you will see later in the chapter, APV is the preferred method when firms do not closely adhere to a target capital structure, such as in leveraged buyout (LBO) situations. Thus, the rather infrequent application of APV may reflect the widespread adoption of target capital structures by firms around the world. Nonetheless, we believe that the APV method is a valuable technique to have in your toolbox and predict that its use will increase as it becomes more widely known.

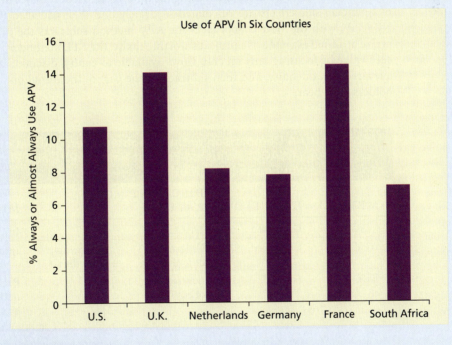

FIGURE 14.1

Use of Adjusted Present Value (APV) in Six Countries

Sources: John R. Graham and Campbell R. Harvey, "The Theory and Practice of Corporate Finance: Evidence from the Field," *Journal of Financial Economics* 60 (2001), pp. 187–243; C. Correia and P. Cramer, "An Analysis of Cost of Capital, Capital Structure, and Capital Budgeting Practices: A Survey of South African Listed Companies," *Meditari Accountancy Research* 16 (2008), pp. 31–52; Dirk Brounen, Abe de Jong, and Kees Koedijk, "Corporate Finance in Europe: Confronting Theory with Practice," *Financial Management* 33 (Winter 2004), pp. 71–101.

market returns). Therefore, the present value of the cash flows that shareholders can claim is $40 million:

$$PV(\text{Cash flows available to equity}) = \frac{\$6}{0.15} = \$40 \text{ million}$$

Does this mean that the project creates $40 million in value for Lox-in-a-Box shareholders? Not quite. Recall that, in order to finance the project, the company planned to use $20 million in debt and $40 million in equity. Therefore, the project's NPV is zero. The value of the project's cash flows available to equity investors exactly matches the initial outlay that stockholders must fund.

Table 14.1 summarizes the three methods. The WACC begins with unlevered project cash flows, discounts them at the WACC, and then subtracts the initial outlay to obtain an NPV. Note that when estimating a project's value using this method, the cash flow calculations essentially assume that the project is financed entirely with equity. The benefit of debt financing comes through in the denominator (discount rate), not the numerator (cash flows). The APV method also starts with unlevered project cash flows, but these cash flows are discounted using the unlevered cost of equity. The present value of financing side effects are calculated separately and then added to the "unlevered NPV." As with the WACC approach, the APV method subtracts the initial outlay to arrive at a final estimate of a project's worth. Finally, the FTE method estimates a project's value by focusing only on cash flows available to equity, discounting those using a levered cost of equity, and then subtracting the part of the initial outlay that equity holders must bear.

Table 14.1	**A Comparison of the Weighted Average Cost of Capital (WACC), Adjusted Present Value (APV), and Flow to Equity (FTE) Methods**			
METHOD	**CASH FLOW**	**DISCOUNT RATE**	**PLUS**	**MINUS**
WACC	Unlevered	WACC		Initial outlay
APV	Unlevered	Unlevered cost of equity	Financing side effects[a]	Initial outlay
FTE	Levered	Levered cost of equity		Part of initial outlay paid for by shareholders

[a] Tax deductions for interest are discounted at the cost of debt to determine financing side effects.

If the three methods lead to the same answers, then why is it necessary to learn all three approaches? As remarked earlier in the text, most firms value investment projects by discounting cash flows at the company's WACC. This is fine as long as two assumptions hold. First, the business risk of the project under consideration should be similar to the business risk of the firm's existing assets. The WACC applies a firm's current costs of debt and equity to arrive at a project discount rate, but those costs reflect the risks of the investments that the firm has already undertaken. Second, the WACC assumes that the investment project does not materially alter the firm's long-run target debt-to-equity ratio. When a company plans to invest in a project with a risk profile that differs markedly from that of its existing assets, or when a new project substantially alters the firm's capital structure, then analysts must make adjustments to the WACC calculations. We illustrated how to do this in Chapter 9.

JOB INTERVIEW QUESTION

How would you value an investment project if you expect the firm to change its target debt-to-equity ratio through time?

As with the WACC, the FTE method assumes that a firm maintains a target debt-to-equity ratio over time. Recall that the FTE calculation discounts a project's levered cash flows using the levered cost of equity. If an investment project causes a firm's leverage to change over time, then the cost of equity will also vary. Much of the research surveyed in Chapters 12 and 13 suggests that managers of most firms tend to act as if they have long-run target debt ratios in mind, even if they "correct" deviations from those targets slowly over time. If this is true, then the WACC and FTE methods are probably appropriate for most capital budgeting decisions.

Finally, the APV approach is the most flexible and can accommodate very different assumptions about the firm's capital structure. Recall that the APV technique calculates the present value of financing side effects as a separate item; therefore, valuing a project under different financing scenarios is easily handled by modifying the NPV(Financing effects) term in Equation 14.2. To calculate the present value of interest tax shields using APV, what analysts need to know is not the mix of debt and equity but rather the amount of debt borrowed to fund the project and the year-by-year debt repayment schedule. Hence APV is the preferred method when analysts expect the firm's debt ratio to vary through time instead of being held constant at a fixed target ratio. Perhaps the most common example of this situation is a leveraged buyout, or LBO. In a leveraged buyout, a group of investors (or a firm) borrows a large sum to acquire an existing business. Initially, the firm may have a capital structure consisting of 90% debt or more. In this situation, there is no expectation that the firm will maintain leverage at such a high level in the long run. Instead, in the early years after the buyout, most of the firm's cash flows go toward paying down the debt. In deciding how much to bid for the target company (and also how much to borrow to pay for the acquisition), LBO investors should use the APV method to capture the time-varying tax benefits of leverage.

In addition to differences between APV and the other two approaches regarding assumptions about the permanence (or lack thereof) of a firm's capital structure, the APV method can account for a broader range of financial side effects. For example, the traditional WACC equation explicitly accounts for only one financial side effect: the tax deductibility of interest. In contrast, we can easily include a wide range of financing side effects in APV calculations, such as the flotation costs of selling debt or equity securities to investors. Therefore, when the side effects of debt are numerous and extend beyond the basic tax advantage discussed here, APV may be the better approach.

Concept Review Questions

5. In a FTE calculation, is the numerator the same as or different from the numerator in a WACC calculation? What about the denominator?
6. What assumption is typically maintained in both WACC and FTE calculations?

14.4 A CHECKLIST FOR THE INTERACTIONS BETWEEN INVESTMENT AND FINANCING DECISIONS

How should practicing financial managers evaluate capital investment decisions, which may range from a small scale (as when replacing old equipment) to a large scale (as when acquiring an entire firm)? We can summarize this chapter's key recommendations for capital investment analysis as follows.

1. Under certain conditions, all three methods (WACC, APV, and FTE) generate estimates of an investment's value that agree. In this case, choose the method that is easiest to apply given the available data.
2. When the firm plans to maintain a constant target debt-to-equity ratio in the long run, use either the WACC or the FTE method.
3. When the firm's debt-to-equity ratio varies over a project's life yet the amount of debt outstanding at any given time is known, the APV method is often easiest to apply.
4. When financing side effects beyond the interest tax shield are an important part of the investment project under consideration, the APV method can often handle these side effects most easily.

SUMMARY

- If the M&M assumption of perfect markets holds, then the basic capital budgeting methods covered in the early chapters of this book work well. In that case, investment and financing decisions are completely separable.
- The most obvious violation of the "perfect markets" assumption is the corporate income tax. The tax deductibility of interest payments tends to increase the value of debt-financed projects relative to those financed entirely with equity.
- The WACC method captures the value of interest tax shields by adjusting the project discount rate downward.
- The APV method estimates a project's value by separating the value of the project itself and the value of financing side effects, such as the interest tax shield. Therefore, the APV accounts for the value of interest tax shields in a separate term, rather than in an after-tax discount rate.

- The FTE approach focuses exclusively on the cash flows available to equity investors. A project's value is the present value of these "levered" cash flows, discounted at a levered cost of equity.
- In most cases, the WACC and FTE methods lead to value-maximizing investment decisions. The APV approach is preferred in certain special cases, such as LBOs.

KEY TERMS

adjusted present value (APV) method
flow-to-equity (FTE) method
levered cash flow

weighted average cost of capital
  (WACC)

QUESTIONS

14-1. Why do violations of the M&M assumption of perfect markets require revisions to our capital budgeting analysis?

14-2. Which valuation method would you use to assess an investment project that involved modernizing a firm's existing plant? The project will not affect the firm's target debt-to-equity ratio.

14-3. If you assume that investment projects are financed entirely with equity, will you tend to overvalue or undervalue these projects?

14-4. List three potential financing side effects for which the APV approach can account.

14-5. Which is higher, the discount rate used in the WACC approach or in the FTE approach?

14-6. In calculating a firm's cost of debt, why is the yield to maturity preferable to the coupon rate on the firm's outstanding bonds?

14-7. Suppose you are calculating the WACC for a firm with outstanding junk bonds. You use the yield to maturity on these bonds as the cost of debt in the WACC formula. Is this correct?

14-8. A foreign government offers your company a below-market interest rate to finance a favored investment in their country. How do you incorporate this factor in your investment analysis?

PROBLEMS

M&M, Capital Budgeting, and the WACC

14-1. A firm has 1,000,000 shares of stock outstanding, and each share is currently worth $20. The stock has a beta of 1.2. The firm also has 10-year bonds outstanding with a par value of $10,000,000, a coupon rate of 6%, and a yield to maturity of 7%. The yield on the bonds is currently 2 percentage points above the risk-free rate and 4 percentage points below the expected return on the overall market. What is the firm's WACC if the corporate tax rate is 35%?

14-2. A project can generate unlevered cash flow of $4 million per year in perpetuity. Suppose the project (and the firm) is financed entirely with equity having a required return of 15%. What is the project's NPV if the initial outlay is $20 million?

14-3. A project can generate unlevered cash flow of $4 million per year in perpetuity. Suppose the firm considering this project finances its operations with an equal mix of debt and equity. The required return on debt is 5%, and the required return on equity is 15%. The marginal corporate tax rate is 30%. What is the project's NPV if the initial outlay is $20 million?

14-4. When calculated using the WACC, Project X has an NPV of $1.3 million. When calculated using the unlevered cost of capital, the NPV becomes −$0.5 million. Based on these two calculations, what is the value of the debt tax shields available within Project X? (*Hint:* Think of how APV is calculated.)

14-5. Torino Corp. is considering a project that will produce annual cash flows of $1.8 million for the next 22 years. The firm has a debt-to-equity ratio of 1.5, where the debt has a yield of 8% and the cost of equity is 18%. Assuming a 38% tax rate, what is the WACC for Torino? Assuming that the project will be funded in the same manner as Torino's existing capital structure, what is the NPV of the project based on a cost of $10 million? How is this NPV affected if the tax rate is reduced to 32%? (*Hint:* Remember to adjust the cash flows and the WACC.)

The Adjusted Present Value Method

14-6. Find a formula for the unlevered cost of equity *r* based on Equation 14.3.

14-7. Smetana's stock currently sells for $13.75 based on a recent dividend of $0.45 and a dividend growth rate of 10% (see Chapter 4). The firm has a debt-to-equity ratio of 50% and a tax rate of 40%. Assuming the debt has a 6% yield, what is the unlevered cost of equity? What is the WACC?

14-8. The NPV of a project based on the cost of equity is −$5.85 million. To complete the APV analysis, the debt shield must be calculated based on a tax rate of 30%.

The firm can issue $10 million of 7% debt over a 20-year period or it can issue $15 million of 6% debt over 15 years (assume that all debt is issued at par). Which debt issue will provide the better APV? Will the project be acceptable?

14-9. A project is expected to produce cash flows of $5 million annually for the next 18 years. The tax rate is currently 35% and the unlevered cost of equity is 16%. The project will cost $22 million, of which $15 million dollars will be raised using 10-year bonds with 8% coupons (sold at par). What is the APV for the project? Suppose the local government provides a tax incentive that lowers the tax rate to 30%. What is the APV now?

14-10. Project Z is expected to produce annual cash flows of $4 million for the next 30 years. Assuming a tax rate of 40% and an unlevered cost of equity of 14%, determine the APV based on a cost of $18 million and no debt financing. Suppose the project can be initiated in a particular locality that features a lower tax rate of 32.5%. What is the APV with this tax incentive included?

14-11. The nation's largest chicken-wing producer, Consolidated Eggleston Inc. (CEI), plans to expand its capacity by building more chicken coops. The expansion project will require an initial outlay of $10 million and will generate an unlevered cash flow of $1 million in perpetuity. CEI uses twice as much equity as debt to finance its operations. Its pre-tax cost of debt is 6%, and its cost of equity is 10%. The marginal corporate tax rate is 30%. Calculate the value of this investment opportunity using the APV method.

14-12. Oogle, a company that designs popular fashions, has $200 million of debt outstanding and $100 million of equity. Investors require a 7% return on Oogle's bonds and 14% on its stock. Oogle's marginal corporate tax rate is 40%. An analyst at the company is using the APV method to value one of Oogle's new investment opportunities. As a first step, the analyst wants to calculate what this opportunity would be worth if it were financed entirely with equity. The analyst reasons that he should use a 14% discount rate at this stage of the analysis. Do you agree? If so, why? If not, what rate would you recommend?

14-13. NanoTubular Inc. is an all-equity firm that makes surfboards from cutting-edge materials. The company has an unlevered cost of equity of 12% and faces a 35% tax rate. NanoTubular is evaluating a proposal to upgrade manufacturing equipment. The table below shows that this investment will require an immediate outlay of $10 million. As part of the financing for this investment, the company plans to borrow $8 million at an interest rate of 8%. Each year the firm will pay interest on the debt and will repay $2 million in principal. The table shows the loan balance and unlevered cash flow for each of the project's 4 years. What is the investment's APV?

Year	Unlevered Cash Flow	Outstanding Debt
0	−$10,000,000	$8,000,000
1	4,000,000	6,000,000
2	3,500,000	4,000,000
3	3,000,000	2,000,000
4	2,000,000	0

The Flow-to-Equity Method

14-14. If an unlevered cash flow is $1.5 million based on a 40% tax rate, what is the levered cash flow if the interest on debt is $1 million annually?

14-15. Suppose that a firm is funded 20% with debt (yield of 9%) and has a 32% tax rate. What is the (levered) cost of equity assuming the unlevered cost of equity is 14%? What is the firm's WACC?

14-16. A firm is funded with 40% debt (9% yield) and has a tax rate of 40%. What is the levered cost of equity if the WACC is 12.06%?

14-17. Quicksand Construction Inc. is examining a potential investment opportunity that will require the company to spend $40 million up front. The company will finance this project with $30 million in equity with a required return of 12% and with $10 million in debt offering a yield of 6%. The project will generate a perpetual cash flow, before interest and taxes, of $2.8 million annually. Assuming a 30% tax rate, value the project using the FTE method.

14-18. An investment project requires an initial outlay of $75 million. A certain firm plans to undertake this investment, financing the up-front cost with $50 million in equity and $25 million in debt. The firm's cost of equity is 16%, and its after-tax cost of debt is 4%. The corporate tax rate is 50%. If the investment generates a perpetual cash flow of $5 million annually after interest and taxes, what is the investment worth according to the FTE method?

14-19. A project under consideration is expected to produce annual cash flows of $6.2 million for the next 30 years. Assuming a tax rate of 40%, $1.4 million in annual interest payments, and a (levered) cost of equity of 17%, determine the net present value using the FTE method based on a cost of $15 million. What does the NPV become if the tax rate falls to 35%?

THOMSON ONE | Business School Edition

14-20. Conduct an Advanced Search using the WtdAvgCostofCapital variable. (*Hint:* Click on Search for Companies and then click the Advanced Search button.) Search for firms that are in the top 10% for the WtdAvgCostofCapital. Select two of these firms. Next, conduct a second search for firms that are in the bottom 10% for theWtdAvgCostofCapital. Select two firms from this group. Comment on why the WtdAvgCostofCapital is so different for the firms in the two different groups. Would these WtdAvgCostofCapital estimates differ if the firms were considering projects that were significantly less risky than the average project for the firm? What adjustments might be made to the WtdAvgCostofCapital estimate to account for this difference in risk?

MINI-CASE: THE LINK BETWEEN CAPITAL STRUCTURE AND CAPITAL BUDGETING

Fiera Corporation is evaluating a new project that costs $45,000. The project will be financed using 40% debt and 60% equity, thus maintaining the firm's current debt-to-equity ratio. The firm's stockholders have a required rate of return of 18.36%, and its bondholders expect a 10.68% rate of return. The project is expected to generate annual cash flows of $13,000 before taxes for the next two decades. Fiera Corporation is in the 36% tax bracket.

1. Determine the firm's weighted average cost of capital (WACC).

2. Calculate the traditional net present value (NPV) of the project using the WACC. Should the project be undertaken?

3. Using Modigliani and Miller's Proposition II, determine the required return on unlevered equity.

4. Use the adjusted present value (APV) method to determine whether or not the project should be undertaken.

5. Use the flow-to-equity (FTE) method to calculate whether or not the project should be undertaken.

What Companies Do
Disappearing Dividends?

Payout Policy

In February 2009, General Electric announced that, for the first time since the Great Depression, it would cut its dividend. The 68% cut from $0.31 to $0.10 per share saved GE $9 billion per year, but it didn't prevent the company from seeing its prized AAA bond rating downgraded just a month later.

GE had plenty of company, as a record number of firms reduced dividends during 2009's first quarter. Standard & Poor's reported that more than 5% of all U.S. public companies cut their dividends that quarter, a 332% increase from the same period in 2008. According to Don Wordell, portfolio manager of the RidgeWorth Mid-Cap Value Fund: "Many companies were paying dividends on unrealistic earnings expectations" that could not be sustained during a recession.

Going against the prevailing wind was software giant Oracle Corp., which reported higher-than-expected first-quarter earnings and announced plans to initiate quarterly dividend payments of $0.05 per share. Oracle CFO Jeff Epstein noted that the company generated $8 billion in free cash flow over the previous year and had more than $11 billion in cash reserves on its balance sheet. At $0.05 per share, Oracle's dividend committed the firm to paying shareholders approximately $1 billion per year, a figure its cash reserves could sustain for several years even if Oracle's ability to generate new cash flow deteriorated.

Sources: Binyamin Appelbaum, "Berkshire, GE Lose Top Credit Rating," Washington Post (March 13, 2009), p. D1; "GE Reduces Dividend for First Time Since 1938," Washington Post (February 28, 2009), p. D2; Stephen Bernard, "S&P: Record Number of Firms Cut Dividends in 1st Quarter," Pittsburgh Post Gazette (April 7, 2009); Stephen Taub, "From the Oracle's Mouth: Its First Div," CFO.com (March 18, 2009).

15.1 PAYOUT POLICY FUNDAMENTALS

Cash Dividend Payment Procedures

A firm's payout *policy* describes the choices its managers make about distributing cash to shareholders. These choices include whether to pay shareholders a regular (recurring) dividend or a one-time "special" dividend, whether to repurchase outstanding shares, and what the size of the cash distribution should be. In the United States, as in most other countries, common shareholders have no legal guarantee that they will receive cash distributions from the firms in which they invest. Instead, a firm's board of directors decides when and how the company will pay dividends or engage in share repurchases. In this chapter, we explore the factors that affect these decisions and how a firm's payout policy affects its value.

Most U.S. firms that pay dividends do so once every quarter. Firms adjust the size of their dividends periodically, but not necessarily every quarter. Figure 15.1 plots the number of dividend changes for 929 public U.S. firms that paid dividends during the 20 quarters from July 2003 to July 2008.[1] Only 81 firms (8.7%) held their dividend constant over this entire period. Clearly the most common practice is to adjust the dividend once per year, with 220 firms (23.7%) implementing exactly five dividend changes in five years and another 245 firms (26.4%) adjusting just slightly more or less often than that. Just 60 (6.4%) of these firms changed their dividend as frequently as twice per year (i.e., 10 or more times), and of these, only eight firms changed their dividend every quarter. Because most companies adjust their dividend infrequently, it appears that firms might "smooth" dividends over time rather than adjusting them up or down each quarter as earnings fluctuate.

FIGURE 15.1

Number of Dividend Changes, July 2003–July 2008

Most firms that pay dividends change the dividend roughly once per year.

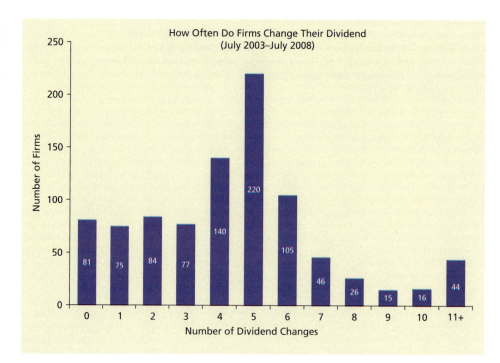

[1]Author calculations using data for public U.S. companies from the Center for Research on Securities Prices (CRSP), excluding closed-end mutual funds, real estate investment trusts (REITs), and other investment companies.

Figure 15.2 provides further evidence on dividend smoothing. The figure plots average earnings and dividends for U.S. nonfinancial firms from 1990 to 2008.[2] Observe that the earnings line dips significantly during the recessions in the early 1990s and in 2001–2002, but in both cases the change in dividends was muted. However, a somewhat sharper reduction in dividends occurred as earnings fell dramatically during the recession that began with the financial crisis in 2007.

FIGURE 15.2

Average Earnings and Dividends for U.S. Nonfinancial Firms

Source: Data provided by Mark Leary.

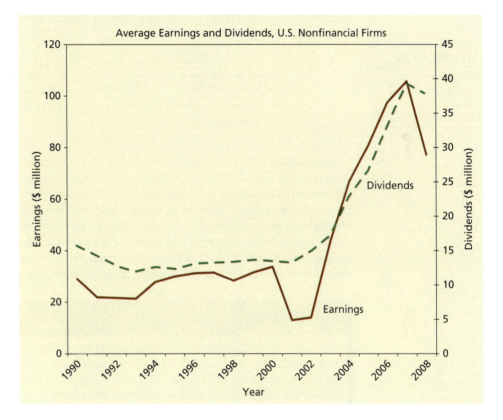

JOB INTERVIEW QUESTION

What happens to a firm's dividend yield as its share price declines?

Investors closely track two ratios related to corporate dividend payments. The first is the **dividend yield**, which equals the annual cash dividend divided by the current stock price. The second ratio related to dividend payments is the **dividend payout ratio**, which equals dividends paid divided by earnings in a given period.

EXAMPLE

On April 14, 2009, Procter & Gamble (PG) announced that it would increase its quarterly dividend payment to $0.44 per share. On the day of that announcement, PG's stock traded for $47.25, so its dividend yield was 3.7% [($0.44 × 4) ÷ $47.25]. The consensus forecast of analysts on PG earnings for the second quarter of 2009 was $0.82 per share, which implies a dividend payout ratio of 54% ($0.44 ÷ $0.82).

[2]The data for 2008 are estimates based on the April 2009 Compustat update. We thank Mark T. Leary of Cornell University for providing data for the figure.

When firms declare dividends, they also establish certain dates that determine which shareholders receive the dividends. *Shareholders of record*, all persons whose names appear as stockholders on the **date of record**, are entitled to the dividend. However, because it takes time to make bookkeeping entries after stocks trade, investors who buy stock on the *record date* will miss the dividend payment. To receive the dividend, an investor must own the stock before the **ex-dividend date**, usually two business days prior to the date of record. Firms distribute dividends on the **payment date**, which usually comes a few weeks after the record date. Figure 15.3 shows a timeline illustrating these events.

FIGURE 15.3

A Timeline Illustrating Important Dates in the Dividend Process

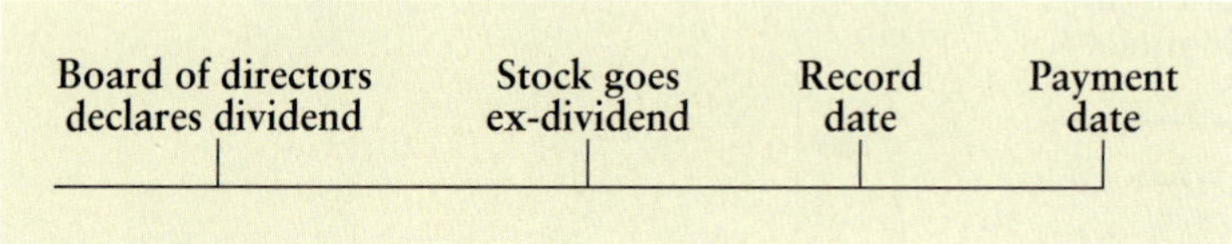

Board of directors declares dividend	Stock goes ex-dividend	Record date	Payment date

In the absence of market imperfections (e.g., taxes and transactions costs) and in the absence of any new information, when a stock "goes ex-dividend" its price should drop by the amount of the dividend. To see why, consider that an investor who buys a stock just prior to the ex-dividend date will receive the dividend a few days later, whereas an investor who buys on the ex-dividend date misses this payment. Therefore, investors who buy on the ex-dividend date will pay less for the stock. For example, suppose a stock that pays a $1 dividend sells for $51 just before going ex-dividend. Once the ex-dividend date passes, the price should drop to $50 (ignoring market imperfections like income taxes).

EXAMPLE

On April 10, 2009, Caterpillar (CAT) announced a $0.42 quarterly dividend to be paid on May 20 to shareholders of record as of Monday, April 20. The ex-dividend date was set two business days prior to the record date, or Thursday, April 16, in this case. Investors who purchased CAT on or before April 15 received the dividend, and those who purchased on April 16 or later missed it. Caterpillar's stock closed at $33.02 on the afternoon of April 15, and it opened the next morning $0.52 lower at $32.50. Thus, the stock price fell after the stock went ex-dividend, with the price decline approximately equaling the amount of the dividend payment.

Research shows that, in the United States and many other countries, the ex-dividend price drop tends to be less than the dividend payment. One explanation for this pattern is related to investor taxes. If a stock priced at $51 falls to $50.30 when the firm pays a $1 dividend, then this may indicate that the investor faces a 30% dividend tax rate and so valued the dividend at only 70 cents in the first place. That is, the $51 represented $50.30 in long-run value plus the after-tax proceeds from the $1 dividend. After the dividend is paid, the $50.30 in remaining long-run value dictates the firm's stock price.

Firms sometimes declare **special dividends** that managers designate as one-time payments resulting from special circumstances (such as an unusually profitable year or a large infusion of cash from an asset sale).

The term *dividend* is sometimes used in settings that are not related to disbursement of cash to shareholders. For example, managers sometimes declare a stock dividend or a stock split. A **stock dividend** is simply a transaction that increases the number of shares that existing stockholders own. For instance, a firm that declares a 20% stock dividend will issue 20 new shares for every 100 shares that an investor owns. However, a 20% stock dividend should not make shareholders 20% wealthier. If a firm pays a 20% stock dividend and nothing else about the firm changes, then the number of outstanding shares increases by 20% and the stock price drops by about 16.7% to 83.3% of its original price (100% ÷ 120% = 83.3%). Thus, the stock dividend neither increases nor decreases the value of investors' shareholdings, i.e., 120% shares × 83.3% price = 100% of original value.

A transaction that is essentially identical to a stock dividend is a stock split. Stock splits, like stock dividends, should have mostly cosmetic effects. When a firm executes a **stock split**, its share price declines because the number of outstanding shares increases. In a 2-for-1 split, the firm doubles the number of shares outstanding but the stock price falls to approximately half its previous level. Managers who implement stock splits generally say they are trying to restore the per-share price of the firm's stock to within a "preferred" trading range that individual investors desire. Such managers believe that they can achieve a higher overall firm value by keeping the stock price low enough to appeal to retail investors.

Intuition suggests that stock splits should not create value for shareholders. After all, if someone gives you two $5 bills in exchange for one $10 bill, you are no better off. A stock split should also have no effect on the firm's capital structure because it changes the number rather than the value of outstanding shares. In spite of this logic, research stretching from Grinblatt, Masulis, and Titman (1984) to Louis and Robinson (2005) documents that stock splits do increase the market value of a firm's equity by about 2.5%. In other words, if a firm whose stock trades for $100 announces a 2-for-1 split, research shows that the stock will fall to roughly $51.25 (so two shares are worth $102.50).

Though most stock splits increase the number of shares outstanding, firms sometimes conduct **reverse stock splits**, replacing a certain number of outstanding shares with just one new share. For example, in a 1-for-2 split, one new share replaces two old shares. A firm whose stock sells at a very low price may initiate a reverse stock split to avoid being delisted owing to the minimum share price requirement of the exchange where the stock trades.

Share Repurchases

Companies can also distribute cash to shareholders by repurchasing some of their outstanding shares. Figure 15.4 demonstrates that share repurchases have grown in importance relative to dividends; in each year from 2005 to 2007, aggregate share repurchases

FIGURE 15.4

Total Share Repurchases Relative to Dividends, 1990–2007

Source: Author calculations from Compustat.

■ Share Repurchases ■ Total Dividends

exceeded aggregate dividends. The repurchase boom began in part because an SEC ruling in 1982 clarified when companies could and could not repurchase their shares without fear of being charged with insider trading or price manipulation.

Companies can use several methods to repurchase shares. In the most common approach, an *open-market share repurchase*, firms buy back their shares in the open market. In a *tender offer*, or *self-tender*, firms offer to buy back a certain number of shares, usually at a premium above the current market price. In a *Dutch auction repurchase*, firms ask investors to submit prices at which they are willing to sell their shares. If the firm wants to buy back 2 million shares, it reviews the offers submitted by shareholders and determines the lowest price at which shareholders will tender 2 million shares. In a Dutch auction, all investors receive the same price when they sell back their shares, even if they expressed a willingness to sell at a lower price in their original offer. When firms announce plans to repurchase shares, their stock prices typically rise, and the positive reaction is much greater for tender offers and Dutch auctions than for open-market share repurchases.

To preview the rest of the chapter, we next present survey evidence about the factors that financial managers say shape their payout decisions. Later in the chapter, we ask whether corporate payout decisions are important. After all, Modigliani and Miller told us that capital structure decisions are not relevant when capital markets are perfect, so why should payout decisions affect firm value? It turns out that, because capital markets are not frictionless, payout decisions are important. Toward the end of the chapter we discuss academic theories that help explain why payout is relevant to firm value.

Factors Affecting Dividend and Share Repurchase Decisions

Brav and colleagues (2005) surveyed 384 CFOs and treasurers and conducted extensive one-on-one interviews with two dozen more to learn how financial executives approach payout policy decisions. Figure 15.5 compares and contrasts executive views on dividends and repurchases. For example, an overwhelming percentage of CFOs agree with the statement that "there are negative consequences to reducing dividends," but fewer than 30% agree with that statement when applied to share repurchases. In other words, CFOs believe that investors view dividends as a commitment made by the firm that must be fulfilled, whereas share repurchases are more discretionary. In that spirit, nearly 80% of CFOs say that they make repurchase decisions *after* investment plans are in place, but

Smart
Ethics
Video

Scott Lee, Texas A&M University

"Generally associated with repurchase announcements is a fairly strong market response."

See the entire interview at
SMARTFinance

Smart
Ethics
Videos

Andy Bryant, Executive Vice President of Finance and Enterprise Systems, Chief Financial Officer, Intel Corp.

"Dividends are probably not the most effective way to return cash to shareholders."

See the entire interview at
SMARTFinance

FIGURE 15.5

CFOs' Views on Dividends and Repurchases

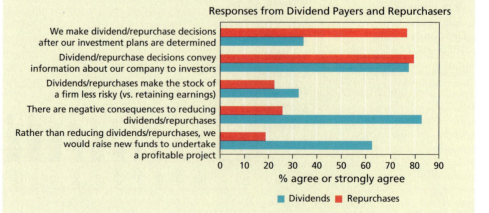

fewer than 35% make the same claim about dividends. Apparently, dividend decisions are as important (or perhaps more important) than at least some investment decisions for these executives. This view is confirmed by the question asking whether CFOs would raise external capital to fund a new investment rather than cutting payout to shareholders. More than 60% of the CFOs say that they would raise external funds rather than cut dividends to finance a profitable new investment, but fewer than 20% say that they would raise capital to avoid cutting repurchases.

As just noted, one key advantage of share repurchases is that they are a flexible form of payout. Managers don't feel that their firm is penalized if repurchases are reduced from one year to the next; they curtail repurchases in order to pursue attractive investments; and they are not generally inclined to raise external funds to maintain repurchase programs. Figure 15.6 reports CFO responses to a set of questions that address separate issues related to corporate share repurchase policy. An overwhelming majority of CFOs (87%) said that they repurchased shares when their stock was a good value (i.e., when the share price was relatively low).[3] Similarly, CFOs said they repurchased shares when buying their own stock was a better investment than other alternatives available to them at the time. But several other factors were important in repurchase decisions, such as offsetting dilution from stock option programs, having excess cash on the balance sheet, and demand by institutional investors that the firm repurchase shares.

FIGURE 15.6

CFOs' Views on Why Firms Repurchase Shares

Source: Reprinted from Brav, Graham, Harvey, Michaely, "Payout Policy in the 21st Century," *Journal of Financial Economics*, volume 77, pg. 483–527, copyright 2005, with permission from Elsevier.

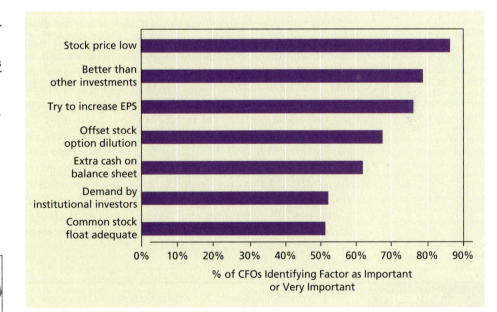

Smart Practices Video

Cynthia Lucchese, Chief Financial Officer, Hillenbrand Industries

"We have to decide how much cash to return as a dividend versus share repurchases."

See the entire interview at **SMARTFinance**

When a firm buys back shares, it reduces the denominator in the earnings per share (EPS) calculation, and more than 75% of the CFOs reported in Figure 15.6 that raising EPS was an important part of their thinking on share repurchases.

Increasing EPS by decreasing shares outstanding sounds like an easy way to create value. After all, won't shareholders place a higher value on a firm's stock if its earnings are higher?

---

[3]In their quarterly CFO survey, Graham and Harvey usually find that CFOs who say their stock is undervalued outnumber by a factor of 10 those who say their stock is overvalued.

The answer is no: as the firm distributes cash to shareholders, not only does the number of outstanding shares fall but also the mix of assets held by the firm changes. For simplicity, assume that a firm owns just two kinds of assets, low-risk cash and high-risk plant and equipment. When the firm distributes some of its cash to investors, its subsequent asset mix is riskier than it was prior to the repurchase, so shareholders will demand a higher rate of return. Moreover, as equity is retired through share repurchases, the company's ratio of debt to equity increases and so financial risk increases as well. The net effect of increasing EPS but also increasing the riskiness and cost of equity is to leave firm value unchanged.[4]

The evidence presented here indicates that dividend decisions are made very conservatively. That is, companies are hesitant to start paying dividends (or to increase the amount of dividends they pay) in part because they know they'll be reluctant to reduce them in the future. In one of the earliest research studies on dividends, Linter (1956) documented several patterns with respect to firms' dividend policies, patterns that are roughly consistent with this conservative view of dividends. In particular:

1. Firms have long-run target dividend payout ratios.
2. Dividend changes follow shifts in long-run, sustainable earnings (not short-run changes in earnings).
3. Managers are reluctant to increase dividends if they might have to be cut later.
4. Managers focus on dividend changes rather than on dividend levels.

Lintner developed a simple empirical model that captured these patterns and estimated firms' target payout ratios as well as the speed with which firms adjusted to those ratios. A slower adjustment speed simply means that firms smooth dividends more as earnings change. You might guess—because firms are placing more importance in recent years on share repurchases and because managers view them as a more flexible tool than dividends for paying cash to shareholders—that firms' target dividend payouts may now be lower (and that adjustments to the target may now occur more slowly) than when Lintner published his findings. Indeed, recent research by Leary and Michaely (2008) finds that, for the period 1950–1983, firms that paid dividends had a target of distributing a little more than one-third of their earnings as dividends; moreover, when their dividend payouts deviated from the desired target, firms made adjustments to close about one-third of that gap each year. But from 1984 to 2002, the target payout ratio appears to have fallen to just 20% of earnings, and likewise the speed of adjustment to that target is much slower. In other words, dividend smoothing increased in recent years.

<table>
<tr><td>**Concept Review Questions**</td><td>

1. What policies and payments constitute a firm's payout policy? Why is determining payout policy more difficult today than in decades past?
2. What do you think the typical stock market reaction is to the announcement that a firm will increase its dividend payment? Why?
3. Well-diversified investors are willing to tolerate great volatility in the prices of stocks they own. Why do you think they might value a constant dividend payment even though the underlying corporate profits on which dividends are ultimately based are highly variable?

</td></tr>
</table>

---

[4]See Oded and Michel (2008) for a complete exposition of this argument.

WHAT CFOs DO

CFO Survey Evidence

Figure 15.7 indicates that firms' priorities with respect to dividends have shifted since Lintner's early research. Brav and colleagues (2005) asked CFOs what specific dividend target (if any) they followed. Nearly 40% said that the level of dividends per share was the key target, rather than the payout ratio (Dividends as a % of earnings), which only 28% identified as their firm's target.

Almost as many CFOs (27%) reported that their target was growth in dividends per share, and a handful of executives said that they managed toward either a target dividend yield or that they had no dividend target at all.

Source: Reprinted from Brav, Graham, Harvey, Michaely, "Payout Policy in the 21st Century," *Journal of Financial Economics*, volume 77, pg. 483–527, copyright 2005, with permission from Elsevier.

FIGURE 15.7

What Dividend Target Do CFOs Aim For?

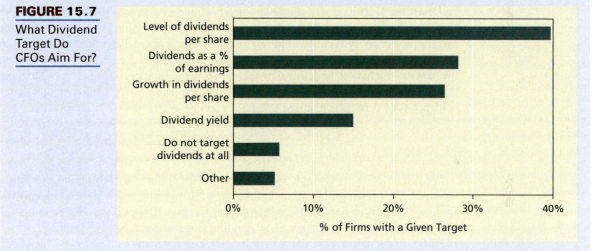

15.2 PAYOUT POLICY IRRELEVANCE IN A WORLD WITH PERFECT CAPITAL MARKETS

Just as they did with capital structure, Miller and Modigliani demonstrated that—in a world of frictionless capital markets—payout policy cannot affect a firm's market value. Value derives solely from the profitability of the firm's assets and the competence of its management team. If payout policy does affect firm value, then it must be because markets are imperfect.

The notion that dividends are irrelevant appears to be a contradiction. After all, we argued in Chapter 4 that a stock's value equals the present value of all its future dividend payments. How, then, do we arrive at a dividend "irrelevance" result? As with capital structure, the answer emerges that a firm's value derives solely from its current and expected future operating profits. As long as the firm accepts all positive-NPV investment projects and has *costless* access to capital markets, it can pay any level of dividends it desires. But if a firm pays out its earnings as a dividend, then it must issue new shares to raise the cash required to finance its ongoing investments. So a company can either retain its profits and finance its investments with internally generated cash flow, or it can pay out its earnings as dividends and raise the cash needed for investment by selling new shares. This dividend irrelevance is best explained with an example.

Consider two firms, Retention and Payout, that are the same size today (January 1, 2010), are in the same industry, and have access to the same investment opportunities. Suppose both companies have assets worth $20 million that will generate a net cash inflow of $2 million by December 31, 2010. Each firm thus earns a 10% return on investment. Furthermore, assume investors require a return, r, of 10% per year and that, at the end of this year, each company will have the opportunity to invest $2 million in a positive-NPV project. Each company currently has 1 million shares outstanding, implying a share price of $20 ($P_{Jan10} = \$20$). Payout's managers want to pay out the firm's earnings as dividends and finance the $2 million investment by issuing new shares. Retention's managers prefer to retain the firm's earnings to fund the $2 million investment program. If each management team pursues its preferred strategy, will the two firms still have identical values next year?

Yes. To see how, we first examine Retention's strategy. Retention's managers finance the $2 million investment project by retaining $2 million in profits. Retention's market value on December 31, 2010, equals the $20 million beginning value, plus the $2 million ($2 per share) in reinvested earnings, plus the investment's net present value. For simplicity, assume that the project's NPV is positive but small enough to be ignored. Retention's year-end 2010 value is $22 million ($20 million + $2 million), or $22 per share ($P_{Dec10} = \$22$), because the firm did not have to issue any new shares in order to finance its investments. Plugging these data into our basic valuation equation from Chapter 4 verifies that Retention's shareholders indeed earn their required 10% return on investment:

$$r = \frac{D_{2010} + P_{Dec10} - P_{Jan10}}{P_{Jan10}} = \frac{\$0 + \$22 - \$20}{\$20} = 10\%$$

We can extend this example indefinitely into the future. In each period, Retention commits to reinvesting all its annual profits (10% return on assets), and shareholders earn an acceptable return because their share values increase 10% each year. Retention never issues new shares, so the number of outstanding shares remains fixed at 1 million.

So far, so good. But what about firm Payout? This company's managers decide to pay a $2 million dividend at the end of the year, so they must raise the $2 million needed for investment by selling new shares. But how many shares must they sell? To answer that, we must deduce what the price of Payout's shares will be on December 31, 2010. After it distributes the dividend, Payout will have assets worth $20 million, exactly what it started with on January 1. With 1 million shares outstanding, the share price will still be $20, so Payout must issue 100,000 new shares to raise the $2 million it needs to undertake its investment project. After the company issues new shares and invests the proceeds, Payout's total market value will equal $22 million ($20 per share × 1.1 million shares outstanding). Payout's market value of $22 million on December 31, 2010, matches Retention's value. We can verify that Payout's original shareholders earn the same 10% return earned by Retention's investors:

$$r = \frac{D_{2010} + P_{Dec10} - P_{Jan10}}{P_{Jan10}} = \frac{\$2 + \$20 - \$20}{\$20} = 10\%$$

Once again, we can repeat this process indefinitely. Each year, Payout distributes all of its net cash flow as a dividend, issuing new shares to finance new investments.

We have shown that the market values of Retention and Payout are equal on December 31, 2010, even though they follow radically different dividend policies. Retention has 1 million shares outstanding worth $22 each, while Payout has 1.1 million shares outstanding worth $20 each. Because both companies have a total value of $22 million, we can say that dividend policy is irrelevant to valuing a firm, at least when markets are frictionless. But what if Retention's investors prefer that the company pay out earnings rather than reinvest them, or if Payout's shareholders prefer that the company reinvest earnings rather than issue new shares? We reinforce dividend policy irrelevance by demonstrating in the following Example that investors can "unwind" firms' dividend policy decisions. In the end, what is true for the firm as a whole is true for each investor: Dividend policy is irrelevant when capital markets are perfect.

EXAMPLE

Consider two investors, Bert and Ernie. On January 1, 2010, Bert owns an 11% stake (110,000 shares) in Retention, whereas Ernie holds an 11% stake (also 110,000 shares) in Payout. By the end of 2010, Bert has received no dividend but he still owns 11% of Retention's outstanding shares, which are now worth $22 each. In contrast, Ernie receives a $220,000 dividend during 2010 but, because Payout issues 100,000 shares to finance its investment opportunity, the shares Ernie owns now represent only a 10% stake in Payout (110,000 ÷ 1,100,000).

If either Bert or Ernie is unhappy with the dividend policy of the firm in which he has invested, he can "unwind" that policy. For example, suppose Bert wishes to receive a dividend. At the end of 2010, Bert can sell 10,000 of his shares for $22 each, generating a cash inflow of $220,000, exactly equal to the dividend that Ernie receives on his investment. In selling some of his shares, Bert creates *homemade dividends*. By the end of the year, Bert owns just 10% of Retention's equity, but that's exactly equal to the ownership stake that Ernie holds in Payout.

Conversely, suppose that Ernie prefers that Payout did not pay dividends. The solution to Ernie's problem is simple. When he receives the $220,000 dividend, he simply reinvests the money by purchasing 11,000 new Payout shares. That would bring his total ownership to 121,000, or 11%, of Payout's shares (121,000 ÷ 1,100,000). In other words, Ernie's position is just like Bert's.

This may seem complex, but the essential points of these examples are simple. If there were no frictions or imperfections in capital markets, then investors would not care whether the firm (1) retains earnings to fund positive-NPV investments or (2) pays dividends and sells new shares to finance investments. In either case, cash flows from the firm's investments—not dividend decisions—determine shareholders' returns.

Concept Review Questions

4. Imagine a firm that has an "intermediate" dividend policy compared to Payout and Retention. This firm pays out half its earnings to shareholders and finances new investment partially through new share issues and partially through retained profits. Describe how dissatisfied shareholders in this firm could "unwind" the dividend policy if they preferred either higher or lower dividends.

5. Managers of slow-growing but profitable firms (e.g., tobacco companies) should pay out these high earnings as dividends. What can they choose to do instead?

6. How do Miller and Modigliani arrive at their conclusion that dividend policy is irrelevant in a world of frictionless capital markets?

7. Utilities worldwide generally have the highest dividend payouts of any industry, yet they also tend to have massive investment programs financed through external funding. How do you reconcile high payouts and large-scale security issuance?

15.3 MILLER AND MODIGLIANI MEET THE (IMPERFECT) REAL WORLD

We just saw that when capital markets are perfect and frictionless, payout decisions do not affect firm value. The core of the idea behind Miller and Modigliani's argument is that operational and investment decisions, not financial policies, are what create value. However, in Figure 15.5 we saw that corporate managers say that maintaining the existing dividend payment ranks *ahead* of investment decisions at many companies. This is the starkest possible rejection of the Miller and Modigliani irrelevance argument because it implies that a financial decision (of maintaining dividends) is more important than the investment decision.[5]

How can this be the case? In the rest of this chapter we discuss several academic theories that explain why payout decisions do matter. Each of these theories describes why a certain market imperfection (taxes, agency costs, etc.) affects payout decisions in general or the choice between dividends and repurchases.

Dividends, Repurchases, and Taxes

Prior to 2003, there was a substantial tax advantage to distributing cash to shareholders via share repurchases rather than dividends. Dividends were taxable as ordinary income when received (at tax rates as high as 40%). In contrast, the only taxpayers who might have an immediate tax liability resulting from a share repurchase were those who sold their shares back to the firm. For these investors, only the difference between the selling price and the original purchase price was taxable, and the applicable tax rate was the relatively low capital gains rate, not the rate on ordinary income. Therefore, the market imperfection of high dividend taxation (relative to share repurchase taxation) encouraged firms to shift payout toward share repurchases.

The Jobs and Growth Tax Relief Reconciliation Act of 2003 reduced the tax advantage for share repurchases by equalizing tax rates on dividends and capital gains at 15%. As a consequence, the friction of dividend taxation decreased, and some firms that had not previously paid dividends began doing so. Figure 15.8 shows the number of new dividend initiations from 2001 to 2006. The reduction in dividend taxation occurred in May 2003, and the figure shows a surge in new dividend payers for several subsequent quarters. Notice, however, that the number of firms initiating dividends fell back toward pre-2003 levels just two years after the tax cuts took effect.

CFO surveys conducted before and after the 2003 tax cuts confirm that tax rates affected the dividend decisions of some firms but certainly not the majority. In February 2003, CFOs of firms that paid dividends and of firms that did not were asked whether impending reductions in the dividend tax rate would cause them to initiate or increase dividend payments. A large majority of both dividend payers and nonpayers said that the tax cut would probably not, or definitely not, prompt them to change their dividend policies. Another survey in June 2003 (one month after the tax cut took effect) produced similar results, with more than 80% of dividend payers and nearly 70% of nonpayers responding that they would not increase or initiate dividends in response to the tax changes. A final survey taken two years later found that a majority of firms still claimed that the dividend tax cut had not influenced their dividend decisions. Only 5%

---

[5]We note that even though the Miller and Modigliani proposition is rejected, it still is a valuable framework within which to think about payout policy. Payout decisions should only matter if there is a relevant market friction. The M&M proposition requires us to establish which market imperfections affect firm value and how they do so.

FIGURE 15.8

Dividend Initiations by U.S. Public Firms, 2001–2006

Dividend initiations increased following the May 2003 dividend tax cut.

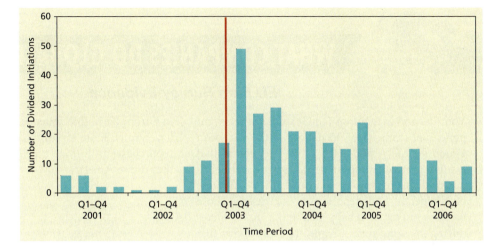

JOB INTERVIEW QUESTION

Would you recommend that our company establish a payout policy by initiating a dividend or by starting a share repurchase program?

of dividend payers and about 20% of nonpayers said that the tax cut had greatly affected their dividend policy.[6]

At the time of this writing it is widely expected that, starting in 2010, dividends will again be taxed at ordinary income levels (which may be as high as 40%) whereas capital gains tax rates will increase less. In such a tax environment, dividends will again be at a material tax disadvantage compared to capital gains, which we expect will contribute to corporations continuing to shift payout away from dividends and toward increased share repurchases.

Agency Cost, Signaling, and Catering Models of Payout

There are several nontax market imperfections that may make corporate payout decisions relevant. This section begins by describing how agency costs (misaligned incentives between managers and stakeholders) can lead to a positive role for payout to play. We concentrate on the **agency cost/contracting model** of dividends (or, more simply, the *agency cost model*).

The agency cost model assumes that firms begin paying dividends in order to overcome the agency problems resulting from a separation of corporate ownership and control. In privately held companies with tight ownership structures, there is little separation between ownership and control. Because agency problems in these firms are minimal, dividends are not that important. Even after a company goes public, it rarely begins paying dividends immediately because ownership remains concentrated for several years after an IPO. Eventually, ownership becomes more widely dispersed as firms raise new equity capital and as the original owners diversify their holdings. With dispersed ownership, few investors have the incentive or the ability to monitor corporate managers, so agency problems can become severe in large, mature firms that generate substantial free cash flow. Managers naturally face temptation to hoard this cash, possibly even spending it on perquisites or negative-NPV projects.[7] Investors understand these temptations and will pay a low price for management-controlled firms that hoard excessive amounts of cash. In contrast, shareholders pay higher prices for companies with more responsive

---

[6]In the year prior to the 2003 tax cut, firms initiating a dividend had been publicly traded for 15.4 years, on average. In the 12 months following the tax cut, the average age of dividend initiators fell to 14 years, rising again over the next 12 months to 16.2 years. All of this evidence suggests that the tax cut prompted firms that would probably have initiated a dividend anyway to do so earlier.

[7]As one financial executive told Brav and colleagues (2005), "extra cash burns a hole in our pocket."

WHAT COMPANIES DO GLOBALLY

EU Firm Survey Evidence

Von Eije and Megginson (2008) studied the payout policies of firms in the 15 nations of the European Union for the period 1989–2006. They found that the fraction of European firms paying dividends declined during this period while the total value of dividends and repurchases increased. Those patterns mirror what happened in the United States during the same period. Figure 15.9 also shows that in Europe (as in the United States) share repurchases have grown more rapidly than dividends, although repurchases in Europe accelerated much later than they did in America.

Source: Henk von Eije and William Megginson, "Dividends and Share Repurchases in the European Union," *Journal of Financial Economics* 89 (2008), pp. 347–374.

FIGURE 15.9

Dividends and Repurchases in the European Union, 1989–2006

As a percentage of total cash payouts to shareholders, share repurchases have been rising relative to dividends in Europe, just as they have in the United States.

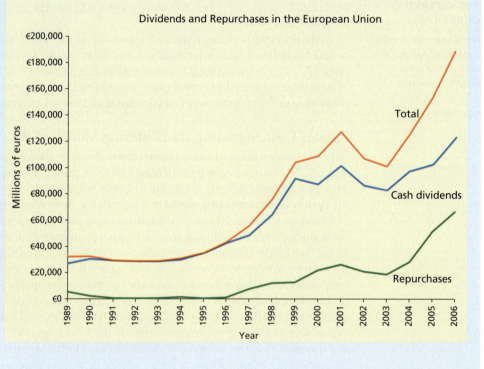

Dividends and Repurchases in the European Union

managers who commit to pay out free cash flow by initiating dividend payments (or aggressively repurchasing shares). This model thus explains why initiating or increasing dividend payments also increases stock prices, at least among firms otherwise subject to agency issues.

The agency cost model predicts that dividend-paying firms are older and larger than nonpaying companies and that they generate more cash as well. It also predicts that dividend payers have fewer growth opportunities. The data for U.S. firms is consistent with these predictions. If we compare U.S. firms that pay dividends with firms that do not, we find that (1) the average market value of dividend payers is much greater than that of nonpayers and (2) payers grow much more slowly. The average age of dividend payers is more than twice the average age of nonpayers.

The **signaling model** of dividends addresses another market imperfection that makes payout policy relevant: asymmetric information. If managers know that their firm is "strong" while investors for some reason do not know this, then managers can pay dividends (or aggressively repurchase shares) in hopes of signaling their firm's quality to the marketplace.[8] For a signal to effectively separate strong firms from weak firms (so that a strong firm can signal its type to the market), it must be costly for a weak firm to mimic the action taken by the strong firm.

According to the signaling models, it is costly for a firm (especially a weak firm) to initiate or increase dividends. For example, a firm that pays out will likely face greater scrutiny from the capital markets if it needs to raise capital in the future, or the firm must expect positive internal cash flow in the near future (as did Oracle in the chapter-opening story); in both of these scenarios, the strong firm has an advantage over the weak firm. An alternative signaling story is based on investors having to pay higher taxes on dividend income, with the weak firm being less able to withstand this cost to their investors. Thus, dividends help investors solve the asymmetric information problem of distinguishing between high-quality and low-quality firms, because high-quality firms are more able to pay dividends. Like the agency cost model, the signaling model predicts that stock prices should rise (resp. fall) in response to dividend increases (resp. cuts). However, the signaling model also predicts that firms with high-growth opportunities will pay higher dividends, contrary to the empirical evidence.

Although there is some evidence supporting the agency and signaling theories, they do not square particularly well with what senior executives *say* about their dividend decisions. Brav and colleagues (2005) explored the agency cost theory by asking CFOs if they paid dividends (in part) to impose discipline on the firm (thereby improving the efficiency of investment decisions) or to attract large investors who would monitor the firm. Recall that the agency cost theory says that dividends solve the agency problems that arise between shareholders and managers due to the separation of ownership and control. Fewer than 15% of the CFOs agreed that these agency-related issues influence dividend policy. Of course, the crux of agency theory is that managers do not always behave in shareholders' best interests, so it may not be surprising that CFOs would not acknowledge the importance of the agency theory in surveys.

Brav and colleagues also inquired about the signaling theory by asking whether firms paid dividends simply to show that they were strong enough to raise external capital or to show that they were strong enough to pass up some profitable investments. Signaling theory asserts that, by imposing costs on themselves that weaker firms cannot afford, high-quality firms signal their true value to investors. However, neither of these motivations received much affirmation from CFOs. Our view is that signaling probably does play a role in explaining some payout decisions (e.g., perhaps Oracle's 2009 dividend initiation) but is less relevant in many cases, so averaged across all firms the survey support for signaling is weak.

The **catering theory** of dividends, proposed by Baker and Wurgler (2004a), predicts that corporate managers cater to investor preferences by paying dividends when investors assign a premium to dividend-paying stocks and by not paying when investors assign a discount to dividend payers. In other words, corporations respond to the whims of

---

[8]The first major dividend signaling paper was by Bhattacharya (1979). Important subsequent signaling models were developed in Miller and Rock (1985), John and Williams (1985), Ambarish, John, and Williams (1987), John and Lang (1991), and Noe and Rebello (1996).

investor preferences regarding whether profits should be distributed as dividends or retained inside the firm. The empirical evidence in Baker and Wurgler (2004b) suggests that the catering theory better explains observed U.S. dividend payments over the period 1963–2000 than do alternative models. Nonetheless, it does not describe why dividends are paid in the first place; nor does it explain what causes investors to change their preferences over time.

Concept Review Question	8. Why are both the signaling and agency theories consistent with the empirical evidence that stock prices fall for firms that cut dividends?

15.4 Payout Policy: Key Lessons

In this chapter we have learned that firms take a conservative approach to paying dividends. The key factor driving dividend payments is the stability of long-run cash flows. Dividends are smoothed and do not vary as much as earnings do from year to year, and once firms start paying dividends they are reluctant to reduce them. Firms that pay dividends tend to be older and larger and produce ample cash flows, and they grow more slowly than firms that do not pay dividends.

Share repurchases, on the other hand, are viewed by managers as being more flexible. Managers say that they are willing to cut back on share repurchases if necessary to finance new investments, whereas managers say that they would raise external capital to fund new investments before cutting dividends.

Not surprisingly, as a percentage of total cash paid to shareholders, repurchases have been gaining ground for many years. In addition to valuing the flexibility of share repurchases, managers appear to engage in repurchases most actively when they perceive their stock to be undervalued.

We also learned that taxes have some influence on dividend decisions, but changes in tax rates do not generally bring about radical and widespread changes in dividend payout. The agency and signaling payout theories help explain payout decisions at some firms, but the empirical evidence so far does not support these theories explaining payout policies for the broad cross-section of companies.

Summary

- Payout decisions are made conservatively. Companies do not initiate or increase dividend payments until they are comfortable that long-run earnings will be stable and reliable. Repurchases may be paid out of stable earnings or when a firm has a temporary increase in cash flows or cash on the balance sheet.
- Public companies regularly pay out some fraction of their profits as dividends, though this fraction has declined over the years. Dividend payments change slowly and do not fluctuate as much as earnings do.
- Share repurchases have grown relative to dividends for several decades. Prior to 2003, share repurchases enjoyed a personal tax advantage relative to dividends. Share repurchase programs are much more flexible than dividend payout commitments.
- Stock splits and stock dividends reduce stock prices. In a 2-for-1 split, for instance, investors receive one new share for every existing share they own, and the stock price falls by roughly half.
- Without market imperfections, dividend policy is irrelevant and does not affect a firm's value.
- Theories related to dividend taxation, agency costs, signaling, and catering offer partial explanations of payout policies.

KEY TERMS

agency cost/contracting model	dividend yield	signaling model
catering theory	ex-dividend date	special dividends
date of record	payment date	stock dividend
dividend payout ratio	reverse stock splits	stock split

QUESTIONS

15-1. What is a firm's dividend yield? How does this compare to that firm's dividend payout ratio?

15-2. What has happened to the total volume of share repurchases announced by U.S. public companies since 1982? Why did that year mark such an important milestone in the history of share repurchase programs in the United States?

15-3. What do *date of record, ex-dividend date*, and *payment date* mean with regard to dividends? Why would you expect the price of a stock to drop by the amount of the dividend on the ex-dividend date? What rationale has been offered for why this does not actually occur?

15-4. What is a *stock dividend*? How does it differ from a *stock split*?

15-5. What factors have contributed to the growth in share repurchase programs by U.S. public companies?

15-6. What does it mean to say that corporate managers "smooth" cash dividend payments? Why do managers do this?

15-7. What is the average stock market reaction to: (a) a dividend initiation; (b) a dividend increase; (c) a dividend termination; and (d) a dividend reduction? Are these reactions logically consistent?

15-8. What are the key assumptions and predictions of the agency cost/contracting model?

15-9. What are the key assumptions and predictions of the signaling model?

15-10. Investor A owns $1,000 worth of stock that does not pay a dividend. Investor B owns $1,000 of an equivalent stock that, after paying a dividend, becomes an investment in stock and cash: $900 in stock and $100 in dividend income. If the tax on capital gains is lower than the tax on dividends, then which investor has the better position: investor A selling 10% of the stock to make an equivalent homemade dividend, or investor B?

PROBLEMS

Payout Policy Fundamentals

15-1. What are alternative ways in which investors can receive a cash return from their investment in the equity of a company? From a tax standpoint, which of these would be preferred, assuming that investors pay a 35% tax rate on dividends and a 15% tax rate on capital gains? What if investors faced the same 15% tax on dividends and capital gains? What are the pros and cons of paying out dividends?

15-2. Delta Corporation earned $2.50 per share during fiscal year 2009 and paid dividends of $1.00 per share. During the fiscal year that just ended on December 31, 2010, Delta earned $3.00 per share, and the firm's managers expect to earn this amount per share during fiscal years 2011 and 2012 as well.

  a. What was Delta's payout ratio for fiscal year 2009?

  b. If Delta's managers wish to hold constant the dividend payout ratio, then what dividend per share will they declare for fiscal year 2011?

15-3. General Manufacturing Company (GMC) follows a policy of paying out 50% of its net income as dividends to its shareholders each year. The company plans to do so again this year, during which GMC earned $100 million in net profits after tax. The company has 40 million shares outstanding.

  a. What is the company's dividend payment per share this year?

  b. Assuming that GMC's stock price is $54 per share immediately before its ex-dividend date, what is the expected price of GMC stock on the ex-dividend date if there are no personal taxes on dividend income received?

15-4. Refer to Problem 15-3, and assume that an investor purchased GMC stock a year ago at $45. The investor, who faces a personal tax rate of 15% on both dividend income and on capital gains, plans to sell the stock soon. Transactions costs are negligible.

  a. Calculate the after-tax return this investor will earn if she sells GMC stock at the current $54 stock price prior to the ex-dividend date.

  b. Calculate the after-tax return the investor will earn if she sells GMC stock on the ex-dividend date, assuming that the stock's price falls by the dividend amount on the ex-dividend date.

15-5. Suppose that GMC pays out 50% of its net income as dividends to its shareholders once each *quarter*. The company plans to do so again this year, during which GMC earned $100 million in net profits after tax. If the company has 40 million shares outstanding, what is the company's dividend payment per share each quarter?

15-6. Global Financial Corporation (GFC) has 10 million shares outstanding, each of which is currently worth $80 per share. The firm's managers are considering a plan to split the company's stock 2-for-1, but they are concerned about the impact this split announcement will have on the firm's stock price.

  a. If GFC's managers announce a 2-for-1 stock split, what exactly will the company do and what will GFC's stock price likely be after the split?

  b. How many total shares of GFC stock will be outstanding after the stock split?

  c. If GFC's managers believe that the "ideal" stock price for the firm's shares is $20 per share, what should they do? How many shares would be outstanding after this action?

  d. Why do you think GFC's managers are considering a stock split?

15-7. Maggie Fiduciary is a shareholder in the Superior Service Company (SSC). The current price of SSC's stock is $33 per share, and there are 1 million shares outstanding. Maggie owns 10,000 shares, or 1% of the stock, which she purchased one year ago for $30 per share. Assume that SSC makes a surprise announcement that it plans to repurchase 100,000 shares of its own stock at a price of $35 per share. In response to this announcement, SSC's stock price increases $1 per share, from $33 to $34, but this price is expected to fall back to $33.50 per share after the repurchase is completed. Assume that Maggie faces marginal personal tax rates of 15% on both dividend income and capital gains.

  a. Calculate Maggie's (realized) after-tax return from her investment in SSC shares, assuming that she chooses to participate in the repurchase program and that all of the shares she tenders are purchased at $35 per share.

  b. How many shares will Maggie be able to sell if all SSC's shareholders tender their shares to the firm as part of this repurchase program and the company purchases shares on a pro rata basis?

  c. If Maggie chooses not to tender her shares, then what fraction of SSC's total common equity will she own after the repurchase program is completed?

15-8. The net income for a firm is currently $1,000,000 and is projected to grow annually for the next four years as follows: $1,200,000, $1,300,000, $1,500,000, and $1,700,000. Assuming the dividend payout ratio is 20% and there are 1,000,000 shares outstanding, what is the current dividend per share? Further assuming that the firm does not change its stated dividend, what is the dividend payout ratio for the next four years? (*Note:* All figures are in thousands.)

15-9. A firm's shares currently sell for $32.48, with 5 million shares outstanding. The firm is considering a 20% stock dividend in which 100 shares become 120 shares. After the stock dividend, at what price will the shareholders' value be unchanged? (*Hint:* Consider shareholder value to be the market capitalization, which equals the number of shares outstanding multiplied by the stock price.) If the stock price became $27.50 after the stock dividend, do the shareholders benefit?

15-10. A firm's shares currently sell for $3.50 with 4 million shares outstanding. The firm plans to reverse split its stock by combining two shares into one share. If the price after this reverse split is $6.52, have shareholders gained or lost value? How much value is gained or lost? (*Hint:* Consider shareholder value to be the market capitalization, which equals the number of shares outstanding multiplied by the stock price.)

15-11. Sunshine Pageants decides that it will use a Dutch auction to repurchase 2 million shares. Investors have submitted the following bids on the price and quantity they are willing to sell shares to the firm:

Price ($)	Shares
24.45	100,000
24.50	200,000
24.60	600,000
24.75	1,100,000
24.95	2,000,000
25.15	2,500,000
25.50	5,000,000

Determine the lowest price at which the firm is able to purchase 2 million shares. (*Note:* If the firm is willing to purchase shares for $25.50, then it must purchase all shares at this price; the goal is to find the lowest price at which the firm can purchase the 2 million shares.) Given the purchase price of the shares, how much extra money do the shareholders receive compared to the schedule of acceptable bids?

15-12. Investor A recognizes $100 in dividend income that is taxed at a rate of 20%. Investor B also wants to recognize the same after-tax revenue as investor A, but investor B owns stock that does not pay dividends. If investor B's stock sells for $12 a share (originally purchased for $7 a share) and if the capital gains tax is 40%, then how many shares must investor B sell?

15-13. A publicly traded firm announces an increase in its dividend, with no other material information accompanying the announcement. What inside information is this announcement likely to convey, and what is the expected effect on the firm's stock price due to the market's assimilation of this information?

15-14. Stately Building Company's shares are selling for $75 each, and its dividend yield is 2.0%. What is the amount of Stately's dividend per share?

15-15. The stock of Up-and-Away Inc. is selling for $80 per share and is currently paying a quarterly dividend of $0.25 per share. What is the dividend yield on Up-and-Away stock?

15-16. Well-Bred Service Company earned $50 million during 2009 and paid $20 million in dividends to the holders of its 40 million shares. If the current market price of Well-Bred's stock is $31.25, calculate the following: (a) the company's dividend payout ratio; (b) the stated dividend per share, assuming Well-Bred pays dividends annually; (c) the stated dividend per share, assuming Well-Bred pays dividends in four equal quarterly payments; and (d) the current dividend yield on Well-Bred stock.

Payout Policy Irrelevance in a World with Perfect Capital Markets

Smart
Solutions
See the problem and solution explained step-by-step at **SMARTFinance**

15-17. It is January 1, 2010, and Boomer Equipment Company (BEC) currently has assets of $250 million and expects to earn a return of 10% during 2010. There are 20 million shares of BEC stock outstanding. The firm has an opportunity to invest in a positive-NPV (minimal) project that will cost $25 million over the course of 2010, and it is trying to determine if it should finance this investment by retaining profits over the course of the year or whether it should pay the profits earned as dividends and issue new shares to finance the investments. Show that the decision is irrelevant in a world of frictionless markets.

15-18. Swelter Manufacturing Company (SMC) currently has assets of $200 million and a required return of 10% on its 10 million shares outstanding. The firm has an opportunity to invest in positive-NPV (minimal) projects that will cost $20 million and is trying to determine if it should withhold this amount from dividends payable to finance the investments or if it should pay out the dividends and issue new shares to finance the investments. Show that the decision is irrelevant in a world of frictionless markets. How is the result affected if a personal income tax of 15% is introduced into the model?

15-19. Assume that it is now January 1, 2010, and you are examining two unlevered firms that operate in the same industry, have identical assets worth $80 million that yield a net profit of 12.5% per year, and have 10 million shares outstanding. Further assume that during 2010 and all subsequent years each firm has the opportunity to invest an amount equal to its net income in (slightly) positive-NPV investment projects. The Beta Company wishes to finance its capital spending through retained earnings. The Gamma Company wishes to pay out 100% of its annual earnings as dividends and to finance its investments with a new share offering each year. There are no taxes or transactions costs to issuing securities.

   a. Calculate the overall and per-share market value of the Beta Company at the end of 2010 and each of the two following years (2011 and 2012). What return on investment will this firm's shareholders earn?

   b. Describe the specific steps that the Gamma Company must take today (1/1/2010) and at the end of each of the next three years (year-end 2010, 2011, and 2012) if it is to pay out all of its net income as dividends and still increase its assets at the same rate as that of the Beta Company.

   c. Calculate the number and per-share price of shares that the Gamma Company must sell today (and at the end of 2010, 2011, and 2012) if it is to pay out all its net income as dividends and still increase its assets at the same rate as that of the Beta Company.

   d. Assuming that you currently own 100,000 shares (1%) of Gamma Company stock, compute the fraction of the company's total outstanding equity that you will own three years from now if you do not participate in any of the share offerings the firm will make during this holding period.

15-20. Investors anticipate that Sweetwater Manufacturing Inc.'s next dividend, due in one year, will be $4 per share. Investors also expect earnings to grow at 5% in perpetuity, and they require a return of 10% on their shares. Use the Gordon growth model (see Equation 4.6 on page 134) to calculate Sweetwater's stock price today.

15-21. Super-Thrift Pharmaceuticals Company traditionally pays an annual dividend equal to 50% of its earnings. Earnings this year are $30 million. The company has 15 million shares outstanding. Investors expect earnings to grow at a 5% annual rate in perpetuity, and they require a return of 12% on their shares.

   a. What is Super-Thrift's current dividend per share? What is it expected to be next year?

   b. Use the Gordon growth model (Equation 4.6 on page 134) to calculate Super-Thrift's stock price today.

15-22. Casual Construction Corporation (CCC) earned $60 million during 2009 and expects to earn $63 million during 2010, in line with the firm's long-term earnings growth rate. There are 20 million CCC shares outstanding, and the firm has a policy of paying out 40% of its earnings as dividends. Investors require a 10% return on CCC shares.

   a. What is CCC's current dividend per share? What is it expected to be next year?

   b. Use the Gordon growth model (Equation 4.6 on page 134) to calculate CCC's stock price today.

15-23. Sam Sharp purchased 100 shares of Electric Lighting Inc. (ELI) one year ago for $60 per share, and he also received dividends of $5 per share since then. Now that ELI's stock price has increased to $64.50, Sam has decided to sell his holdings. What is Sam's gross (pretax) and after-tax return on this investment, assuming that he faces a 15% tax rate on dividends and capital gains?

15-24. Hole Foods Donuts Inc. has generated profits of $2 per share for many years and has consistently paid 100% of those profits to shareholders via a dividend. Investors do not expect Hole Foods Donuts to grow in the future. The company has 200,000 shares of stock outstanding worth $20 per share. Suppose the firm decides to eliminate its dividend and instead use the money to repurchase shares.

   a. Assuming that there are no taxes and that the repurchase announcement conveys no new information to investors about the profitability or risk of Hole Foods Donuts, how do you think the stock price will react to the announcement?

   b. How many shares will Hole Foods Donuts repurchase?

   c. What stock price would you expect for Hole Foods Donuts one and two years after this announcement? What would the stock price have been in the next two years if the company had simply maintained its old dividend policy?

15-25. Jasper Metals Inc. just announced that it will pay its regular quarterly dividend of $3.50 per share.

   a. Does the stock price fall to reflect this payment on the announcement date, the record date, the ex-dividend date, or the payment date?

   b. Assume that there are no market imperfections. By how much will the stock price fall?

   c. Suppose investors must pay a 38% tax on dividends received but pay nothing on capital gains. How would this change your answer to part (b)?

   d. Now suppose that investors must pay 38% in taxes on both dividends and capital gains. In this case, how much would you expect the stock price to fall in response to the dividend?

e. Suppose that, just prior to the dividend announcement, Jasper Metals stock was worth $175 per share. Assume once again that there are no taxes. If you own 50 shares, then what is the value of your investment? How does the dividend payment affect your wealth? If Jasper Metals cancels the dividend and announces that they will repurchase 2% of their outstanding shares, do you care?

THOMSON ONE | Business School Edition

15-26. Using the data found in the Worldscope Income Statement Ratios Report, calculate the dividend payout ratio for the last five years for Ford (ticker symbol, F), General Motors (ticker symbol, GM), DaimlerChrysler (ticker symbol, DCX), Toyota (ticker symbol, TM), and Honda Motor Company Limited (ticker symbol, HMC). How do the payout ratios change over time? How do the dividends per share change over time? Do the payout ratios and dividends per share change in the same direction? How do the earnings per share change over time? Do the dividends per share and earnings per share change in the same direction?

MINI-CASE: PAYOUT POLICY

Yevaud Enterprises has the following historical prices. Each price shown is for the closing day of the month. The prices in the months with splits are the prices after the split has occurred.

Date	Closing Price ($)	Stock Split	Date	Closing Price ($)	Stock Split
Dec-09	79.94	2 for 1	Dec-08	111.63	
Nov-09	124.38		Nov-08	83.75	
Oct-09	100.06		Oct-08	110.88	
Sep-09	125.13		Sep-08	99.75	2 for 1
Aug-09	118.75		Aug-08	88.13	
Jul-09	172.06		Jul-08	91.75	
Jun-09	172.19		Jun-08	85.53	
May-09	128.13		May-08	77.00	
Apr-09	116.94	3 for 1	Apr-08	59.00	
Mar-09	321.25		Mar-08	60.25	
Feb-09	192.00		Feb-08	49.50	
Jan-09	126.44		Jan-08	61.00	

1. If you had purchased the stock for $61 on the last day of January 2008, what rate of return would you have earned had you sold it the last day of December 2009 (after adjusting for the stock splits)?

Yevaud Enterprises has $37 million in assets and expects to generate a return on assets of 12.6%. The stockholders require a 12.6% return on their investment as well. Yevaud can either:

A. invest the entire cash flow generated this year in a new project with a nearly zero yet positive NPV; or

B. pay out the entire amount as dividends and then raise cash for the project by issuing new shares.

The new project will cost $4,662,000 in one year. Yevaud currently has 10,000,000 shares of common stock outstanding.

2. Calculate the value of the firm's stock and the stockholders' rate of return if Yevaud uses alternative A to finance the purchase of the project.

3. How many shares of stock must Yevaud issue in order to finance the new project in one year? Calculate the value of the firm's stock and the stockholders' rate of return if Yevaud uses alternative B to finance the project.

4. Will Yevaud's choice regarding how to raise the money for the project affect the firm's stock price in one year?

5. Assume that you currently own 50,000 shares of stock in Yevaud Enterprises and that Yevaud decided to pursue alternative A. How could you, as a stockholder, generate cash flows equal to those that would have followed from Yevaud's pursuing alternative B? Would this change your percentage ownership of Yevaud's total stock outstanding?

PART 5
Long-Term Financing

In this part of the book we address issues of long-term financing. Chapter 16 describes the investment banking industry and examines how banks assist corporations in the issuance of equity securities directly to investors. We describe the key laws governing public sale of equity securities in the United States, examine the procedures used by firms issuing common and preferred stock, and discuss how the market values of initial public offerings (IPOs) and seasoned equity offerings (SEOs) are determined. Though we focus on U.S. investment banking practices, we discuss international IPO and SEO practices as well. We also cover the wrenching changes investment banking experienced beginning in 2008 and speculate on how these changes will affect security issuance practices in the future.

Chapter 17 examines long-term debt and leasing. Although they may seem disparate, debt and leasing belong together because a lease can be a long-term obligation similar to issued bonds. We describe how bonds are rated with regard to default likelihood and discuss how managers decide whether to refund an outstanding bond issue after market interest rates fall. We also present the special terminology that applies to different types of lease contracts, and we show how managers should decide between borrowing money to buy an asset and financing the asset acquisition with a lease.

What Companies Do

Investment Banks: Crossroads or Crosshairs?

When the British army of Lord Cornwallis surrendered to the upstart Continental army of George Washington at the end of the Battle of Yorktown—effectively ending the American Revolutionary War—the Royal band played the tune "The World Turned Upside Down" to convey their incredulity at the sudden turn of events. In 2008, the American investment banking industry, after two decades of ruling the world of global finance, experienced a series of "The World Turned Upside Down" moments. The top five U.S. investment banks experienced traumatic transitions over the course of the year as the global credit crisis unfolded, their stock prices collapsed, and all of their principal service markets dried up.

By September of 2008, three of the five large investment banks had either filed for bankruptcy (Lehman Brothers) or been acquired under crisis conditions (Bear Stearns by JP Morgan and Merrill Lynch by Bank of America). Two others, Morgan Stanley and Goldman Sachs, finally bowed to the pressure of falling stock prices and evaporating investor confidence in September 2008 when they both filed with the federal government to become commercial banks, subject to the stringent regulatory authority of the U.S. Federal Reserve Board. This change will constrain the operations of Morgan Stanley and Goldman Sachs in many ways, most dramatically by increasing their disclosure requirements and by reducing the amount of leverage they will be allowed to use. In return, the firms will be able to obtain funding by accepting demand deposits from consumers and businesses, and they will gain access to the Federal Reserve's various lending and support programs. Only time will tell whether these changes mark the end of the free-wheeling and highly profitable era of U.S. investment banking.

Sources: Francesco Guerrera, Greg Farrell, and Aline van Duyn, "Morgan Stanley Rallies with Goldman," Financial Times *(October 28, 2008); and Greg Farrell, "Goldman Ponders How to Keep the Legend Intact,"* Financial Times *(December 7, 2008).*

16

Investment Banking and the Public Sale of Equity Securities

Although corporations around the world rely on internal financing for most of their funding, companies also raise large amounts of capital externally each year. This chapter describes how companies obtain equity financing and also shows how investment banks help firms acquire external capital. Chapter 17 examines how firms acquire external debt and lease financing.

Once corporate managers have decided to raise external capital and to raise equity rather than debt, they usually enlist an **investment bank** to help sell the firm's securities. Issuing firm managers can either negotiate privately with individual banks regarding the terms of the equity sale, or they can solicit competitive bids for the business. On behalf of firms, investment banks can then issue shares to a small group of sophisticated investors in a private placement, they can issue new shares to existing shareholders through a rights offering, or they can engage in a much broader public share offering that reaches domestic as well as international investors.

We begin by examining investment banks and the services they offer to corporations. Next, we describe the legal rules governing public security sales in the United States, paying special attention to the disclosure requirements imposed on firms raising equity capital. We then examine equity sales conducted by two types of firms: companies issuing equity for the first time in an initial public offering (IPO) and existing public companies conducting seasoned equity offerings (SEOs). As you might imagine, the dynamics of the process are quite different in IPOs and SEOs. Finally, we conclude the chapter with sections covering private placements and international equity offerings.

16.1 INVESTMENT BANKING

An Overview of the Global Investment Banking Industry

Investment banks (IBs) play an important role in helping firms raise long-term debt and equity financing in the world's capital markets. During the 20-year period before 2008, the global investment banking industry grew dramatically in scale and in the variety of services it provided to corporations. Furthermore, the 1999 passage of the Gramm–Leech–Bliley Act allowed commercial banks to provide investment banking services in the United States (they were formerly excluded from this business by the Glass–Steagall Act of 1933). Table 16.1 presents a **league table**, ranking the world's 15 largest investment banks by the total value of securities underwritten worldwide during 2008.

Several interesting patterns emerge from examining Table 16.1. First, the data reveal just how sharply the volume of worldwide corporate security offerings dropped during 2008: from a record $7.602 trillion during 2007 to $4.697 trillion in 2008, a level not seen since 2002. Second, in sharp contrast to almost all recent years, U.S. investment banks did not dominate the underwriting league table. Instead, European banks occupied five of the top ten slots, including second and fourth. This reflects the turmoil that engulfed American investment banking during 2008, when one of the top five U.S. firms failed (Lehman Brothers), two were acquired (Bear Stearns and Merrill Lynch), and the remaining two converted into regulated commercial banks. European universal banks were also seriously weakened by the credit crisis of 2008 but coped better than their American counterparts. All in all, 2008 marked an abysmal year for security issuance, with the total volume contracting throughout the year before its near total collapse during the fourth quarter.

Bulge bracket firms generally occupy the lead or co-lead manager's position in large new security offerings, meaning that they take primary responsibility for the new offering (even though other banks participate as part of a syndicate) and, as a result, earn higher

Table 16.1   Securities Underwriting League Table for 2008

FIRM RANK 2008 (2007 IN PARENTHESES)	2008 PROCEEDS ($ MILLION)	MARKET SHARE (%)	NUMBER OF ISSUES UNDERWRITTEN	DISCLOSED FEES ($ MILLION)	2007 PROCEEDS ($ MILLION)
1. JP Morgan (1)	455,056	9.7	1,210	1,736	749,887
2. Barclays Capital (2)	401,320	8.5	1,041	1,045	693,314
3. Citi (3)	308,966	6.6	986	1,715	643,867
4. Deutsche Bank (4)	308,588	6.6	807	409	540,099
5. Merrill Lynch (5)	241,203	5.1	852	1,320	459,648
6. Goldman Sachs (8)	229,513	4.9	585	1,122	390,836
7. Morgan Stanley (7)	220,374	4.7	662	773	446,561
8. RBS (6)	213,964	4.6	712	201	452,699
9. Credit Suisse (9)	205,273	4.4	682	594	353,324
10. UBS (10)	204,444	4.4	682	750	332,009
11. Banc of America Securities (11)	203,433	4.3	525	1,004	310,665
12. HSBC Holdings (12)	173,348	3.7	686	220	206,414
13. BNP Paribas (14)	145,409	3.1	446	74	155,453
14. Société Générale (15)	74,130	1.6	146	11	103,563
15. RBC Capital Markets (16)	72,744	1.6	353	277	81,324
Industry Total	**4,697,218**	**100.0**	**13,554**	**13,689**	**7,602,993**

Note: This table presents the global investment banking league table for the year 2008 based on the total value of securities underwritten worldwide. Full credit for each offering is credited to the lead underwriter (book-runner).
Source: Investment Dealers' Digest (January 12, 2009), pg. 31.

fees. You can readily identify the lead investment bank in a security offering by looking at the offering *prospectus*, the legal document that describes the terms of the offering. The lead bank's name appears on the front page, usually in larger, bolder print than the names of other participating banks that are listed below it.

In addition to managing security offerings, investment banks also provide advice for mergers and acquisitions and help syndicate loans. Table 16.2 presents league tables for mergers and acquisitions (M&A) advisory work during 2008 in comparison to 2007. The same set of U.S. and European investment and universal banks dominate M&A advising as dominate securities issuance, but the ordering is somewhat different. American banks still occupy the top ranks of M&A advising, though even here their grip weakened during 2008. Comparing 2008's $2.937 trillion total value of mergers and acquisitions to the vastly larger record $4.169 trillion total value during 2007 also makes clear that the global takeover market declined just as rapidly as did the market for security issuance during 2008. Even more telling, almost half of the value of M&A during the third and fourth quarters of 2008 represented government purchases of newly issued bank stock that were made in an attempt to rescue Western financial systems from collapse.

Table 16.2 Merger and Acquisition (M&A) Advising League Table for 2008

FIRM RANK 2008 (2007 IN PARENTHESES)	2008 VALUE OF TRANSACTIONS ($ MILLION)	NUMBER OF DEALS (ANNOUNCED TARGETS)	2007 VALUE OF TRANSACTIONS ($ MILLION)
1. Goldman Sachs (1)	831,678	344	1,180,725
2. JP Morgan Chase (3)	778,240	382	934,753
3. Citi (4)	705,075	343	874,755
4. UBS (6)	573,985	352	770,945
5. Morgan Stanley (2)	557,992	343	1,142,700
6. Merrill Lynch (5)	515,592	283	807,291
7. Credit Suisse (7)	485,741	328	677,628
8. Deutsche Bank (8)	440,197	283	588,454
9. Barclays Capital (9)	319,890	108	435,991
10. BNP Paribas (17)	268,983	120	150,832
11. Lazard (6)	247,755	210	309,119
12. Rothschild (12)	191,776	289	376,168
13. Centerview Partners (31)	188,074	10	75,791
14. Banc of America Securities (14)	173,634	69	195,053
15. Nomura (10)	138,800	157	399,735
Industry Total	**2,937,345**	**39,654**	**4,169,287**

Note: This table presents the worldwide M&A advising league table for the year 2008, based on the total value of all announced M&A transactions worldwide. Full credit for each offering is credited to the lead underwriter (book-runner).
Source: Investment Dealers' Digest (January 12, 2009), pg. 24.

Smart Practices Video

Todd Richter, Managing Director, Bank of America

"We provide two sets of related services."

See the entire interview at
SMARTFinance

Key Investment Banking Activities

Investment banks provide a broad range of services to corporations. The three principal lines of business are *corporate finance*, *trading*, and *asset management*. Of the three business lines, corporate finance enjoys the highest visibility; it includes security underwriting and M&A advisory work (R. C. Smith, 2001). Corporate finance generally tends to be the most profitable line of business, especially for more prestigious banks, which can charge the highest underwriting and advisory fees. However, corporate finance generates less than one-fourth of a typical IB's revenues even in normal times, and these revenues fell sharply during 2008.

Investment banks earn revenue from trading debt and equity securities in two important ways. First, they act as dealers, facilitating trade between unrelated parties and earning fees in return. Second, they hold inventories of securities and can make or lose money as inventory values fluctuate. Trading revenues usually account for about one-quarter of large banks' revenues; in 2008, however, trading led to enormous losses at most investment banks. Finally, asset management encompasses several different activities, including managing money for individuals with high net worth, operating and advising mutual funds, and managing pension funds. Revenues from asset management exceed those from the other primary investment banking services.

The Investment Banker's Role in Equity Issues

We now turn to the services that investment banks provide to issuing companies, with particular attention to U.S. practices.[1] We focus on common stock offerings, though the procedures for selling bonds and preferred stocks are similar. Investment banks play several different roles throughout the securities offering process, and this section describes the evolution of these roles over the course of an issue. We also describe how issuers compensate IBs for the services they provide.

Although firms can issue stock without the assistance of investment bankers, in practice almost all firms hire IBs to help issue equity. Firms can choose an investment banker in one of two ways. The most common approach is a **negotiated offer**, where the issuing firm negotiates the terms of the offer directly with one investment bank. Alternatively, in a **competitively bid offer**, the firm announces the terms of its intended equity sale and then investment banks bid for the business. Intuition suggests that competitive bidding should be cheaper, but the empirical evidence is mixed. One clear sign that competitive offers are not better and cheaper is that the vast majority of equity sales are negotiated. If the costs of negotiated deals were truly higher, then why would so many firms choose that approach?

Firms issuing securities often hire more than one investment bank. In these cases, one of the banks is usually named the **lead underwriter**, or *book-runner*, while the other leading banks are called **co-managers**. Chen and Ritter (2000) argue that firms often prefer to issue securities with several co-managers because doing so increases the number of stock analysts that will follow the firm after the offering. Firms believe that a larger analyst following leads to greater liquidity and higher stock values. Cliff and Denis (2004) verify the importance of attracting the coverage of top-rated analysts by showing that issuing firms willingly allow their IPO share price to be set low enough to attract excess demand and high trading volume, since this will indirectly compensate the underwriters' star analysts.

Investment bankers sell equity under two types of contracts. In a **best-efforts offering**, the investment bank merely promises to give its best effort to sell the firm's securities at the agreed-upon price but makes no guarantee about the ultimate success of the offering. If there is insufficient demand, the firm withdraws the issue from the market. Best-efforts offerings are most commonly used for small, high-risk companies, and the IB receives a commission based on the number of shares sold.

In contrast, in a **firm-commitment offering** the investment bank agrees to underwrite the issue, meaning that the bank guarantees (**underwrites**) the offering price. The IB actually purchases the shares from the firm and resells them to investors. This arrangement requires the investment bank to bear the risk of inadequate demand for the issuer's shares, but banks mitigate this risk in two ways. First, the lead underwriter forms an **underwriting syndicate** consisting of many investment banks. These banks collectively purchase the firm's shares and market them, thus spreading the risk across the syndicate. Second, underwriters go to great lengths to determine the demand for a new issue before it comes to market, and they generally set the issue's *offer price* and take possession of the securities no more than a day or two before the issue date. These steps help ensure that the investment bank faces only a small risk of being unable to sell the shares that it underwrites.

In firm-commitment offerings, investment banks receive compensation for their services via the **underwriting spread**, the difference between the price at which the banks purchase shares from firms (the **net price**) and the price at which they sell the shares to institutional and individual investors (the **offer price**). In some offerings, underwriters receive additional compensation in the form of warrants that grant the right to buy shares

---

[1]Ljungqvist, Jenkinson, and Wilhelm (2003) and DeGeorge, Derrien, and Womack (2007) document an increasing tendency for security issues around the world to conform to U.S. standards.

of the issuing company at a fixed price. Underwriting fees are substantial, especially for firms issuing equity for the first time. Most U.S. initial public offerings have underwriting spreads of exactly 7% (though lower spreads are common in very large IPOs).[2] For example, if a firm conducting an IPO wants to sell shares worth $100 million, it will receive $93 million, and the underwriter earns the gross spread of $7 million.

EXAMPLE

The underwriting discount for Google's IPO in August 2004 was $2.3839 per share of common stock, deducted from the offering price of $85.00 per share. This gives an underwriting spread of only 2.80%, which is a reflection of both the unusual size of Google's IPO ($2.7 billion) and Google's bargaining power over the underwriters. The spread on Visa's gigantic $19.65 billion IPO in March 2008 was also 2.80%, which was due to the issue's massive size. The Visa offering was the largest in U.S. financial history.

Underwriting spreads vary considerably depending on the type of security being issued. As Table 16.3 indicates, banks charge higher spreads on equity issues than on debt issues. They also charge higher spreads for **unseasoned equity offerings** (i.e., IPOs) than they do for **seasoned equity offerings** (SEOs), which are equity issues by firms that already have common stock outstanding. In general, the riskier the security being offered, the higher the spread charged by the underwriter. Notice that spreads on noninvestment-grade ("high-yield" or "junk") bonds exceed those on investment-grade bonds. Securities that have both debt- and equity-like features, such as convertible bonds and preferred stock, have spreads that are higher than those of ordinary debt but lower than those of common stock.

Table 16.3	Underwriting Spreads for Different Types of Securities		
SECURITY TYPE	AVERAGE FEE (%)	NUMBER OF ISSUES	TOTAL GROSS FEES ($ MILLION)
Debt			
Corporate investment grade debt	0.758	226	504
Long-term corporate high-yield debt	1.377	45	344
Domestic bonds	0.272	4,539	1,372
Agency, sovereign, and supranational	0.100	22	38
Taxable municipal bonds	0.232	161	344
Common stock			
Closed-end funds	5.562	88	1,700
Nonfund initial public offerings (IPOs)	6.739	224	2,843
Seasoned offerings (nonfund/non-IPOs)	4.408	376	2,891
Convertible debt & preferred stock	2.475	69	797
Industry Total	**0.769**	**7,027**	**11,161**

Note: This table presents total underwriting spreads and average underwriting fees charged by U.S. investment banking firms for several different types of security offerings during 2007.
Source: "Underwriting Fees," *Investment Dealers' Digest* (January 21, 2008), pp. 40–41.

[2]Chen and Ritter (2000).

Figure 16.1 shows two additional factors that influence equity underwriting spreads: (1) spreads are higher for smaller, riskier firms compared to larger, less risky firms; and (2) for firms that are similar in terms of risk and size, spreads decline as the offer size increases but only up to a point. It is not surprising that spreads should fall with rising offer size because many underwriting costs—organizing and managing the syndicate, soliciting interest from investors, assuring regulatory compliance—are largely fixed. However, Figure 16.1 shows that, beyond a certain point, increasing the size of an offer does increase the issuing firm's cost.

FIGURE 16.1

Underwriter Spreads for Seasoned Common Stock Offerings

Source: Figure 3 in Oya Altinkilic and Robert S. Hansen, "Are There Economies of Scale in Underwriting Fees? Evidence of rising External Financing costs," *Review of Financial Studies* 13 (Spring 2000), pp. 191–218, by permission of Oxford University Press.

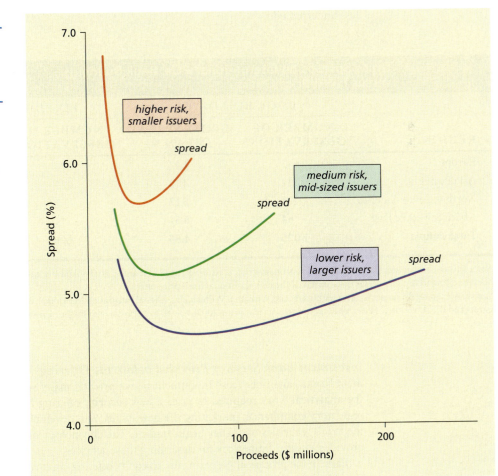

Ljungqvist, Jenkinson, and Wilhelm (2003) show that the spreads on international IPOs are significantly lower than on U.S. initial offers. In part, this reflects differences in underwriting practices across countries. To assess demand for a company's shares and to set the offer price, U.S. underwriters typically use a process, known as **book building**, in which underwriters ask prospective investors to indicate their demand for the offering.[3]

[3]Benveniste and Spindt (1989) explain how investment bankers provide an incentive to reveal investment demand for a firm's shares. When demand for a new issue is particularly strong, investment bankers do not fully adjust the offer price upward to a market-clearing level. This implies that investors who want to buy shares will be rationed, but it also implies that investors who revealed their interest in the stock will be rewarded when trading begins because they will receive shares that immediately increase in value. This information revelation model was tested, with mixed results, in Cornelli and Goldreich (2001, 2003), Aggarwal, Prabhala, and Puri (2002), and Jenkinson and Jones (2004).

Through conversations with investors, the underwriter tries to measure the demand curve for a given issue, and the investment bank sets the offer price after gathering all the information it can from investors. Book building has become increasingly common in international markets, but a method called a **fixed-price offer** also survives. In fixed-price offers, underwriters set the final offer price for a new issue weeks in advance. This imposes more risk on the underwriters, for which they must either charge higher spreads or price the shares far below the expected post-offer price. Table 16.4 lists underwriting spreads on international IPOs. This table shows that underwriters charge significantly *lower* spreads on fixed-price offerings, but the authors find that book-built offerings are less underpriced.

Table 16.4	Gross Spreads on International IPOs: Book Buildings versus Fixed-Price Offers			
	BOOK BUILDINGS		FIXED-PRICE OFFERS	
REGION	NUMBER OF OBSERVATIONS	GROSS SPREAD (MEAN %)	NUMBER OF OBSERVATIONS	GROSS SPREAD (MEAN %)
Europe	645	4.43	370	2.19
Asia Pacific	214	4.10	225	2.21
North & South America	103	5.17	1	5.00
Africa & Middle East	64	6.37	13	2.19
Total sample	**1,026**	**4.55**	**609**	**2.20**

Note: This table examines the difference in gross underwriter spreads for 1,635 non-U.S. initial public stock offerings executed via U.S.-style book-building techniques versus those executed through traditional fixed-price offers.
Source: Alexander P. Ljungqvist, Tim Jenkinson, and William J. Wilhelm, Jr., "Global Integration in Primary Equity Markets: The Role of U.S. Banks and U.S. Investors," *Review of Financial Studies* 16 (Spring 2003), 63–99, by permission of Oxford University Press.

Investment Bank Services Provided before the Offering Precisely how do investment banks earn their fees? Investment banks provide many services, from performing the analytical work required to price a new security offering to assisting the firm with regulatory compliance, marketing the new issues, and developing an orderly market for the firm's securities once they begin trading. The chronology of a typical equity offering provides a useful framework for describing these services.

Early in the process of preparing for an equity offering, an investment bank will help the firm file the necessary regulatory documents, starting with the *registration statement*. This provides detailed information about the securities being offered and the issuing firm. Though document preparation may sound like a trivial undertaking, in fact it is one of the most time-consuming (and expensive) parts of the capital-raising process, especially for IPOs.

While it is preparing the necessary legal documents, the investment bank must also begin estimating the value of the securities the firm intends to sell. This task is much simpler for debt than for equity, and, of course, it is easier to value seasoned equity offerings than to value IPOs. Investment banks use a variety of methods to value IPO shares, including discounted cash flow models and market "comparables." In the latter case, an investment bank compares the firm issuing equity to similar publicly traded firms, often estimating the value of the new stock issue by applying a price-to-earnings or price-to-sales multiple to the issuing firm's current or projected financial results.

One key lesson from the IPO market over the past few years is that pricing new equity issues is not a precise science. Several weeks before the scheduled offering, the firm and its bankers take a whirlwind tour of major U.S. and international cities to assess investor demand for the offering. Affectionately called the **road show**, this process usually lasts one to three weeks and gives managers the opportunity to pitch their business plan to institutional investors. The investment banker's goal in this process is to build a book of orders for shares that is greater (often many times greater) than the amount of stock the firm intends to sell. The expressions of interest by investors during the road show are not legally binding purchase agreements, and the investment bank typically does not commit to an offer price at this point but gives investors a range of prices at which they expect to sell the offer. Given the tentative nature of the demand expressed on the road show, the banker seeks to **oversubscribe** the offering in order to minimize the bank's underwriting risk. Naturally, one way to create excess demand for an offering is to set a low offer price. As we will see, the vast majority of IPOs in the United States and other countries are **underpriced**, meaning that IPO shares typically begin trading at a price higher than the offer price. When firms conduct seasoned equity offerings, they also tend to sell shares at a slight discount to the market price of the outstanding shares, though underpricing is not as severe in SEOs as in IPOs. As the road show progresses, investment bankers adjust the offer price upward, but they almost always leave money on the table—set the offer price below the expected post-issue selling price—in part to reward the investors who reveal their demand for the share issue. Investment banks only partially adjust the offer price upward in response to favorable demand signals from investors.[4]

Investment bankers perform additional services designed to ensure that the firm's securities will be attractive to investors. One such service is "cleaning up the balance sheet," essentially consolidating different classes of stock and other forms of financing that are common in firms issuing equity for the first time. In addition, bankers negotiate **lockup agreements** with the client's managers and directors in which these corporate insiders promise not to sell their personal stock holdings for several months (between 6 and 24 months) after the offering. Bankers require these agreements because insiders typically have private information about the firm's prospects at the time of the equity offering. Insiders have a financial motivation (i.e., higher future prices for their own shares) to communicate positive information to potential investors by retaining shares in the firm after the offering.[5]

Services Provided during and after the Offering
The lead underwriter conducts the stock offering and ensures that participating investors receive their shares, plus a copy of the **final prospectus**, on the offer date. The lead underwriter exercises some discretion over the distribution of shares among syndicate members and the **selling group**, investment banks that assist in selling shares but are not formal members of the syndicate. In oversubscribed offerings, the lead underwriter may exercise a **Green Shoe option** (or **overallotment option**), which is essentially an option to sell up to an additional 15% more shares than originally planned.

Once a firm's securities begin trading, the underwriter may engage in **price stabilization**. This means that, if a new issue begins to falter in the market, the investment bank

---

[4]Hanley (1993).
[5]Several studies examine the importance of IPO lockup agreements. Brav and Gompers (2003) and Aggarwal, Krigman, and Womack (2002) show how managers strategically underprice IPOs in order to maximize personal wealth from selling shares at the lockup expiration. Ofek and Richardson (2003) link the bursting of the Internet bubble to the large number of lockup expirations during the spring and summer of 2000. Finally, Ang and Brau (2003) examine the relationship between insider (i.e., secondary) share sales and lockups and show that insiders accept longer lockup periods in exchange for being allowed to sell more secondary shares in an IPO.

may buy shares on its own account—supporting the market price at or slightly below the offer price. The possibility of having to stabilize market prices gives underwriters an additional incentive to underprice new issues at the outset.

After a share offering is successfully sold, the lead underwriter often serves as the principal **market maker** for trading in the firm's stock. This means the bank will continuously quote bid and ask prices for the new shares, thus "making a market" in the new issue. Corwin, Harris, and Lipson (2004) examine the development of aftermarket liquidity for IPOs and show that trading volumes are typically (and temporarily) very high immediately after the IPO. The lead underwriter also typically assigns one or more research analysts to cover the issuing firm; the research reports these analysts write (which naturally tend to be flattering) help generate additional interest in trading the firm's securities. In fact, some firms choose their investment bankers in large measure based on the reputation of the analyst who will cover the stock once it goes public. Loughran and Ritter (2004) suggest that attracting post-offer research explains why managers are willing to accept significant IPO underpricing. Table 16.5 summarizes the chronology of an investment bank's activities through the IPO process.

Table 16.5   Key Steps in the Initial Public Offering Process

MAJOR STEPS AND MAIN EVENTS	ROLE OF THE UNDERWRITER (U/W)
Initial step	
Select book-running manager and co-manager	Book-running manager's role includes forming the syndicate and being in charge of the entire process.
Letter of intent	Letter specifies gross spread, Green Shoe (overallotment) option, and protects U/W from unexpected expenses. Doesn't guarantee price or number of shares to be issued.
Registration process	
Registration statement and due diligence	After conducting due diligence, U/W files necessary registration statement with SEC.
Red herring	Once the registration statement is filed with the SEC, it is transformed into a preliminary prospectus (red herring).
Marketing	
Distribute prospectus; road show	The red herring is sent to salespeople and institutional investors around the country. Concurrently, company and underwriter conduct a road show and the IB builds a book based on expressed—but not legally binding—demand.
Pricing and allocation	
Pricing; allocation	Once the registration statement has SEC approval, U/W files an acceleration request, asking SEC to accelerate the date the issue becomes effective. Firm and U/W meet the day before the offer to determine price, number of shares, and allocation of shares.
Aftermarket activities	
Stabilization; over-allotment option	Lead U/W supports the stock price by purchasing shares if price declines. Support can only occur at or below the offer price and can continue for only a relatively short period. If stock price goes up, U/W uses overallotment option to cover short position. If price goes down, U/W covers overallotment by buying stock in open market.
Research coverage	Final stage of IPO process begins 25 calendar days after the IPO, when the "quiet period" ends. Only after this can U/W and other syndicate members comment on the value of the firm and provide earnings estimates.

Source: : Katrina Ellis, Roni Michaely and Maureen O'Hara, "When the Underwriter Is the Market Maker: An Examination of Trading in the IPO Aftermarket," *Journal of Finance* 55 (June 2000), pp. 1039–1074.

We conclude this section by highlighting the important conflicts of interest faced by investment bankers. On the one hand, issuing firms want to obtain the highest possible price for their shares, but they also want favorable coverage from their investment banks' analysts. Investors, on the other hand, want to purchase securities at the lowest price possible, but they also value dispassionate, unbiased advice from analysts. Investment bankers must therefore walk a thin line, in terms of both ethics and economics, when attempting to please their constituents. Firms issuing securities are wise to bear this in mind. Investment bankers deal with investors, especially institutional investors, on a repeated basis. They must approach this group each time a new offering comes to the market. In contrast, over the life of a firm, there is just one IPO and perhaps a few SEOs.[6]

Concept Review Questions	1. What are the principal lines of business for top-tier investment banks (IBs)? How do the business strategies of IBs that are affiliated with large commercial banks differ from those of unaffiliated IBs? 2. What are the major sources of revenue for investment banks? 3. What does the term *bulge bracket* mean? What recent regulatory change may create upheaval in the bulge bracket? 4. What services does an investment bank provide before an IPO? After?

16.2 LEGAL RULES GOVERNING PUBLIC SECURITY SALES IN THE UNITED STATES

Security issues in the United States are regulated at both the state and federal levels. The most important federal law governing the sale of new securities is the **Securities Act of 1933** and its amendments. The basis for federal regulation of the sale of securities is the concept of **full disclosure**, which means that issuers must reveal all relevant information concerning the company selling the securities and the securities themselves to potential investors. The other major federal law governing securities issues is the **Securities and Exchange Act of 1934**, which established the U.S. Securities and Exchange Commission (SEC) and laid out specific procedures for the public sale of securities and the governance of public companies.[7]

Given the emphasis that U.S. securities law places on disclosure, it is not surprising that investment banks are required to perform **due diligence** examinations of potential security issuers. This means they must search out and disclose all relevant information about an issuer before selling securities to the public. Investors can sue underwriters if they do not perform adequate due diligence; of course, in such cases the underwriter's reputation suffers as well. The fact that investment banks are willing to underwrite an issue provides valuable **certification** that the issuing company is in fact disclosing all material information.

The principal disclosure document for all public security offerings is the **registration statement**. Firms must file this highly detailed document with the SEC before they can solicit investors. A final revised version must be approved by the commission before an offering can become **effective** and shares can be sold to public investors. There are two

---

[6] A CEO of a company that had recently conducted an IPO told us, "You have two friends in an IPO: your lawyer and your accountant." Notice that the investment banker didn't make the list.

[7] Much of the discussion in this section is based on the legal sections of Ritter (1998) and the updated information from his website (http://bear.cba.ufl.edu/ritter/ipodata.htm). Official information can also be accessed from the SEC's website at http://www.sec.gov.

Smart Ideas Video

Jay Ritter, University of Florida

"The most noteworthy IPO auction was that of Google in 2004."

See the entire interview at
SMARTFinance

basic parts to the registration statement: Part I, the **prospectus**, is distributed to all prospective investors; Part II, **supplemental disclosures**, is filed only with the SEC, although investors can obtain a copy from the commission.[8]

The first, or **preliminary prospectus**, serves as the principal marketing tool during the period from initial filing with the SEC to the time the firm responds to the commission's initial findings. The preliminary prospectus is often called a **red herring**, because it has a standard legal disclaimer printed across its cover in red stating that the securities described therein are not (yet) being offered for sale. An issuing firm may file a half-dozen or more amended prospectuses with the SEC during the registration period preceding an offer.

As the underwriting syndicate responds to SEC feedback, additional prospectuses are printed until the commission allows the offer to proceed to public sale. At that time, a final prospectus is printed that includes the definitive offering price and number of shares being sold. The actual sale of securities cannot occur until each investor receives a final prospectus. Figure 16.2 presents the title page from the final prospectus of Google's IPO in August 2004. Morgan Stanley and Credit Suisse First Boston were the co-lead underwriters for this offering. An additional eight IBs were included in the title page's bulge bracket, including Goldman Sachs, Citigroup, and Lehman Brothers.

None of the key U.S. investment banks involved in Google's IPO still exist in the same form. Lehman Brothers collapsed in September 2008, Merrill Lynch was acquired by Bank of America that same month, Goldman Sachs and Morgan Stanley converted into commercial banks in October 2008, and in January 2009 Citigroup announced its intention to split into two parts.

Material Covered in an Offering Prospectus

The format of the prospectus is highly standardized and informative. The title page presents details about the number of shares being offered and about the underwriting agreement (participants and terms) governing the offering. The next several pages of the prospectus present a thumbnail description of the company and its products, a table detailing the offering and listing how the proceeds will be used, a financial summary of operating results for the past few years, and a simplified balance sheet.

The main part of the prospectus begins with a more detailed portrait of the company as it currently operates and of its recent history; it then proceeds to detail specific "risk factors" that make the offering especially risky. (The risk-factors section of the prospectus can make interesting reading. A prospectus for a chain of funeral homes listed a decline in the U.S. death rate as an important risk factor. A ski resort's prospectus mentioned that "the success or failure of a new business depends greatly on the ability of its management" and "the management has no previous experience in owning and operating a ski resort or any of its amenity services.") The firm must also disclose whether insiders will control a majority of the votes after the offering.

Deeper in the prospectus, investors find more detailed information about the issuer's financial condition, its business strategies, and the experience of its management team. The prospectus also reveals key information about how the firm will be governed after the offer. If the purpose of the offering is to allow an existing shareholder to sell some of her stock, then the issue is a **secondary offering** and raises no capital for the firm. If the shares offered for sale are all newly issued, which increases the number of outstanding shares and raises new capital for the firm, the issue is a **primary offering**. If some of the shares come

---

[8]You can download any prospectus from current and past offerings (going back to the mid-1990s) on the SEC's EDGAR website (http://www.sec.gov/edgar.shtml).

FIGURE 16.2

Title Page from Google's IPO Prospectus.

Reprinted by permission of Google Inc.

Prospectus
August 18, 2004

19,605,052 Shares

Class A Common Stock

Google Inc. is offering 14,142,135 shares of Class A common stock and the selling stockholders are offering 5,462,917 shares of Class A common stock. We will not receive any proceeds from the sale of shares by the selling stockholders. This is our initial public offering and no public market currently exists for our shares. The initial public offering price is $85.00 per share.

Following this offering, we will have two classes of authorized common stock, Class A common stock and Class B common stock. The rights of the holders of Class A common stock and Class B common stock are identical, except with respect to voting and conversion. Each share of Class A common stock is entitled to one vote per share. Each share of Class B common stock is entitled to ten votes per share and is convertible at any time into one share of Class A common stock.

Our Class A common stock will be quoted on The Nasdaq National Market under the symbol "GOOG."

Investing in our Class A common stock involves risks. See "Risk Factors" beginning on page 4.

Price $85.00 A Share

	Price to Public	Underwriting Discounts and Commissions	Proceeds to Google	Proceeds to Selling Stockholders
Per Share	$ 85.00	$ 2.3839	$ 82.6161	$ 82.6161
Total	$1,666,429,420	$46,736,483	$1,168,368,039	$451,324,897

The selling stockholders have granted the underwriters the right to purchase up to an additional 2,940,757 shares to cover over-allotments.

The price to the public and allocation of shares were determined by an auction process. The minimum size for a bid in the auction was five shares of our Class A common stock. The method for submitting bids and a more detailed description of this auction process are included in "Auction Process" beginning on page 34. As part of this auction process, we attempted to assess the market demand for our Class A common stock and to set the size and price to the public of this offering to meet that demand. As a result, buyers should not expect to be able to sell their shares for a profit shortly after our Class A common stock begins trading. We determined the method for allocating shares to bidders who submitted successful bids following the closing of the auction.

The Securities and Exchange Commission and state securities regulators have not approved or disapproved of these securities, or determined if this prospectus is truthful or complete. Any representation to the contrary is a criminal offense.

It is expected that the shares will be delivered to purchasers on or about August 24, 2004.

Morgan Stanley	**Credit Suisse First Boston**
Goldman, Sachs & Co.	**Citigroup**
Lehman Brothers	**Allen & Company LLC**
JPMorgan	**UBS Investment Bank**
WR Hambrecht+Co	**Thomas Weisel Partners LLC**

---

from existing shareholders and some are new, the issue is a **mixed offering**. Google's IPO was a mixed offering.

The final section of an offering prospectus consists of various appendixes. One of the first presents the **cold comfort letter** provided by the firm's auditors that is a simple statement that the company's financial statements were prepared according to generally accepted accounting principles and accurately reflect all relevant information.

Securities can be exempt from registration under certain conditions. Securities with a maturity of less than 270 days are exempt, as are intrastate security offerings and securities issued or guaranteed by a bank.[9] In addition, the sale of unregistered securities is allowed in private placements.

Shelf Registration (Rule 415)

As an alternative to filing a lengthy registration statement and awaiting SEC approval, firms with more than $150 million in outstanding common stock can use a procedure known as **shelf registration** (or **Rule 415**) for the issue. This procedure allows a qualifying company to file a *master registration statement*, a single document summarizing planned financing over a 2-year period. Once the SEC approves the issue, it is placed "on the shelf," and the company can sell the new securities to investors out of inventory (off the shelf) as needed any time during the next 2 years. This has proven to be immensely popular with issuing corporations, which previously had to incur the costs (including costs of delay) of filing separate SEC registrations for each new security issue. In addition to saving time and money, shelf registration allows firms to issue securities in response to changing market conditions.

Shelf registration is especially popular with large firms that frequently need access to the capital markets for funding. Although in principle shelf registration allows companies to reduce their reliance on investment bankers, investment banks continue to be the key link between the firm and capital markets. Shelf registration has been popular with issuers of debt since the program's inception, and recent research shows that U.S. firms have become quite adept at using shelf registration and now issue the majority of seasoned equity under the Rule 415 exemption.[10]

Ongoing Regulatory Requirements for a Publicly Traded Firm

Once a company successfully completes an IPO and lists its shares for trading on an exchange, it becomes subject to all the costs and reporting requirements of a public company. These include cash expenses such as exchange-listing fees and the cost of mailing proxies, annual reports, and other documents to shareholders. Additionally, public companies must hold general shareholders' meetings at least once each year and must obtain shareholder approval for important decisions, such as approving a merger, authorizing additional shares of stock, and approving new stock option plans. By far the most costly regulatory constraints on public companies are the disclosure requirements for the firm, its officers and directors, and its principal shareholders. In essence, the company must report any material change in its operations, ownership, or financing. Once a firm "goes public," life becomes very public indeed.

Concept Review Questions	5. What is the guiding principle behind most of the important U.S. securities legislation? What role does the security registration play in implementing this philosophy?
	6. What is a *red herring*?
	7. What is *shelf registration*? Why do you think this has proven to be so popular with issuing firms?

---

[9]This exemption is why commercial paper (discussed in Chapter 23) invariably has an original maturity of less than 270 days. As it happens, most commercial paper is of much shorter maturity, but the fact that this most important source of short-term financing for top-tier U.S. corporations is specifically designed to be an unregulated financial instrument reveals both the importance of security laws and the lengths to which businesses will go in order to escape such regulation.

[10]Autore, Kumar, and Shome (2008).

16.3 THE U.S. MARKET FOR INITIAL PUBLIC OFFERINGS

Given its role in providing capital market access to entrepreneurial growth companies, the U.S. initial public offering market is widely considered to be a vital economic and financial asset. Indeed, a welcoming IPO market has long been a key building block of America's success in high-technology industries. It is thus not surprising that all the U.S. stock markets compete fiercely for IPO listings. The competition is particularly intense between the two largest, the New York Stock Exchange (NYSE) and the Nasdaq electronic market. Although the number of IPOs (usually a few hundred per year, though a mere 20 during 2008) and the total capital raised ($24 billion to $65 billion) each year between 1995 and 2007 may seem trivial in a $14 trillion economy, IPOs generally represent 30%–40% of all new common equity raised by U.S. corporations each year. In other words, IPOs raise almost half as much external equity capital each year as do established giants such as IBM, Exxon, and General Electric.

Patterns in the U.S. IPO Market

To the uninitiated, a quick survey of the U.S. IPO market reveals some decidedly odd patterns.[11] For example, it is one of the most highly cyclical securities markets. As Table 16.6 makes clear, aggregate IPO volume shows a very distinct pattern of boom and bust. The IPO market boomed throughout most of the 1990s, but it entered truly frothy territory during the "Internet bubble years" of 1999 and 2000. In 1999, for instance, the market saw 457 transactions take place (almost two per business day), and these raised more than $62 billion. The torrid pace continued during the first part of 2000. But when prices of U.S. stocks tumbled, a chill fell over the market. The number of transactions in 2001 was barely one-sixth of 1999's peak, and only about 70 companies attempted to go public during 2002. Though this most recent cycle was among the most dramatic in history, the general pattern was by no means unprecedented, following boom-and-bust cycles from the 1960s, 1970s, and 1980s.

	Table 16.6	Number of Offerings, First-Day Returns, and Gross Proceeds of U.S. Initial Public Offerings, 1975–2008	
YEAR	NUMBER OF OFFERINGS	AVERAGE FIRST-DAY RETURNS (%)	GROSS PROCEEDS ($ MILLION)
1975		−1.5	262
1976	26	1.9	214
1977	15	3.6	127
1978	20	11.2	209
1979	39	8.5	312
1980	78	15.2	962
1981	202	6.4	2,386
1982	83	10.6	1,081

(continued)

---

[11]Loughran and Ritter (2004) summarize pricing and trading patterns for unseasoned issues. Other papers examining overall IPO patterns include Benveniste et al. (2003), Lowry (2003), Bruner, Chaplinsky, and Ramchand (2004), Lowry and Schwert (2004), Henderson, Jegadeesh, and Weisbach (2006), Ivanov and Lewis (2008), and Kim and Weisbach (2008).

Table 16.6 Number of Offerings, First-Day Returns, and Gross Proceeds of U.S. Initial Public Offerings, 1975–2008 *(continued)*

YEAR	NUMBER OF OFFERINGS	AVERAGE FIRST-DAY RETURNS (%)	GROSS PROCEEDS ($ MILLION)
1983	523	8.8	12,047
1984	227	2.6	3,012
1985	215	6.2	5,488
1986	464	6.0	16,195
1987	322	5.5	12,160
1988	121	5.6	4,053
1989	113	7.8	5,212
1990	104	10.8	4,080
1991	273	12.1	12,280
1992	385	10.2	20,970
1993	483	12.8	28,160
1994	387	9.8	16,240
1995	432	21.5	24,460
1996	621	16.7	40,60
1997	432	13.9	28,970
1998	267	22.3	32,200
1999	457	71.7	62,690
2000	385	55.4	65,627
2001	81	13.7	34,368
2002	70	8.6	22,136
2003	68	12.4	10,122
2004	186	12.2	32,380
2005	169	9.8	28,677
2006	164	11.3	30,686
2007	160	13.5	35,197
2008	20	5.3	4,897
1960–69	2,661	21.2	7,988
1970–79	1,537	7.1	6,664
1980–89	2,380	6.8	61,880
1990–99	4,146	21.1	291,531
2000–08	1,303	24.5	264,090
1970–2008	**12,027**	**16.9**	**632,153**

Notes: This table presents summary details about IPOs with an offering price of at least $5 per share sold on U.S stock markets between 1975 and 2008. The table excludes American depositary receipts (ADRs), best-efforts offers, unit offers, Regulation A offerings, real estate investment trusts (REITs), partnerships, and closed-end funds. Average first-day returns are computed as the equally weighted average percentage return from the offering price to the first closing market price.

Source: Jay R. Ritter, "Some Factoids about the 2008 IPO Market," downloaded from his website (http://bear .cba.ufl.edu/ritter/ipodata.htm). Gross proceeds data are from Securities Data Corporation, and exclude over-allotment options but include international tranches, if any.

Another interesting pattern observed in the IPO market is the tendency for firms going public in a certain industry to "cluster" in time. It is common to see bursts of IPO activity in fairly narrow industry sectors, such as energy, biotechnology, communications, and (in the late 1990s) Internet-related companies. Indeed, the last half of the 1990s saw an incredible boom in both the number of Internet companies going public and the valuations assigned to them by the market. Companies such as Netscape, Yahoo!, Amazon.com, and eBay were able to raise hundreds of millions of dollars in equity despite their relatively short operating histories and nonexistent profits. Investors were so eager to purchase shares in these firms that their stock prices often doubled the first day they began trading.

EXAMPLE

The short-term stock price increases for Internet-related IPOs had financial experts scratching their heads in 1999, none more so than the December 9, 1999, debut of VA Linux. The company went public with an offer price of $30 per share; after one trading day, the stock closed at almost $240 per share. For investors who bought shares at the offer price and sold them as soon as possible, the one-day return was an astronomical *700%*. Investors who held on for the long term did not fare as well. After the IPO, the stock closed above $240 only once, and it fell to an intraday low of 54 cents on July 24, 2002. By early January 2009, the company—by then renamed Source Forge, Inc.—saw its stock trading at $1.12 per share.

As recently as the early 1980s, investment banks targeted initial offerings almost exclusively at individual investors, particularly at retail customers of the brokerage firms involved in the underwriting syndicate. Since the mid-1980s, however, institutional investors have grown in importance, and they generally receive half to three-quarters of the shares offered in the typical IPOs and up to 90% or more of the "hot" issues.[12]

A final pattern emerging in the U.S. IPO market is its increasingly international flavor. The largest and most visible of the international IPOs are associated with privatizations of formerly state-owned enterprises. However, both established international companies and non-U.S. entrepreneurial firms are choosing to make initial stock offerings to U.S. investors, either publicly via a straight IPO or to institutional investors through a **Rule 144A offering**. This special type of offer, first approved in April 1990, allows issuing companies to waive some disclosure requirements by selling stock only to sophisticated institutional investors, who may then trade the shares among themselves.

Advantages and Disadvantages of an IPO

The decision to convert from private to public ownership is not an easy one. The benefits of having publicly traded shares are numerous, but so too are the costs. This section describes the costs and benefits of IPOs for U.S. firms. As we discuss more fully in

---

[12]Academic analyses of the strategic share allocation decisions made by investment bankers can be found in Hanley and Wilhelm (1995), Booth and Chua (1996), Aggarwal, Prabhala, and Puri (2002), Ljungqvist and Wilhelm (2002), and Aggarwal (2003). Hanley and Wilhelm, Ljungqvist and Wilhelm, and Aggarwal all find that underwriters typically allocate almost two-thirds of all shares on offer to institutional investors. Ljungqvist and Wilhelm conclude that "discretionary" IPO allocations favoring institutional investors actually work in the best interests of issuing firms. Aggarwal, Prabhala, and Puri document a positive relationship between an IPO's first-day return and the fraction of IPO shares allocated to institutional investors. In other words, institutions receive greater allocations in the "hot" IPOs, those with strong premarket demand.

WHAT COMPANIES DO GLOBALLY

Stock Prices Decline Worldwide during 2008

Investors around the world understand that stock prices can fall as well as rise, so most realize that there will be bad years when virtually all stock markets experience substantial declines. However, nothing in the preceding seven decades could have prepared investors for the carnage to stock portfolios wreaked during 2008, which saw the overall U.S. dollar value of stocks listed on stock exchanges decline by 46.5% from $60.85 trillion on December 31, 2007, to $32.58 trillion on December 31, 2008. Even this measure underestimates the damage that investors outside the United States and Japan experienced after the dollar appreciated during 2008 against all major currencies

except the Japanese yen. This means that local currency losses were even larger than dollar losses for most countries, and the following chart—which details the changes in national stock index values for 50 stock exchanges worldwide—bears this out. Three-fifths (30 of 50) of the national markets experienced declines of more than 46.5%, while only 19 experienced local currency losses smaller than the global dollar average. Iranian investors were the only national group who could view 2008 positively, because the Tehran Stock Exchange was the only national stock market where listed stocks increased in value (by 11%) during 2008.

The *Annus Horribilis*—Stock Price Declines Worldwide during 2008

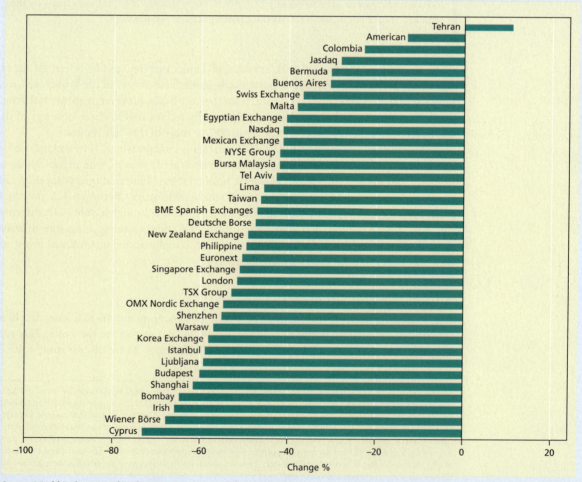

Source: World Federation of Exchanges (www.world-exchanges.org).

Section 16.6, Pagano, Panetta, and Zingales (1998) show that the motivations for going public are significantly different for continental European business owners than for their U.S. counterparts.

Benefits of Going Public   Chapter 2 of the accounting firm KPMG Peat Marwick's publication *Going Public: What the CEO Needs to Know* (1998) suggests the following advantages of an IPO to an entrepreneur.

1. *New capital for the company.* An initial public offering gives the typical private firm access to a larger pool of equity capital than is available from any other source. Whereas venture capitalists can provide perhaps $10 million to $40 million in funding throughout a company's life as a private firm, an IPO allows the company to raise many times that amount in one offering. An infusion of common equity not only permits the firm to pursue profitable investment opportunities, it also improves the firm's overall financial condition and provides additional borrowing capacity. Furthermore, if the firm's stock performs well, the company will be able to raise additional equity capital in the future.

2. *Publicly traded stock for use in acquisitions.* Unless a firm has publicly traded stock, the only way it can acquire another company is to pay in cash. After going public, a firm has the option of exchanging its own stock for that of the target firm. Not only does this minimize cash outflow for the acquiring firm, but such a payment method may be free from capital gains tax for the target firm's owners. This tax benefit may reduce the price that an acquirer must pay for a target company.

3. *Listed stock for use as a compensation vehicle.* Having publicly traded stock allows the company to attract, retain, and provide incentives for talented managers by offering them stock options and other stock-based compensation. Going public also offers liquidity to managers who were awarded options while the firm was private.

4. *Personal wealth and liquidity.* Entrepreneurship almost always violates finance's basic dictum about diversification: real entrepreneurs generally have most of their financial wealth and their human capital tied up in their companies. Going public allows entrepreneurs to reallocate cash from their businesses and to diversify their portfolios. Entrepreneurial families also frequently execute IPOs during times of transition— for example, when the company founder wishes to retire and provide a method of allocating family assets among those heirs who do and do not wish to remain active in the business.

In addition to these benefits, the act of going public generally results in a blaze of media attention, which often helps promote the company's products and services. Being a public company also increases a firm's overall prestige. However, the often massive costs must be weighed against the obvious benefits of an IPO.

Drawbacks of Going Public   KPMG Peat Marwick's going public publication also includes the drawbacks of an IPO for a firm's managers.

1. *The financial costs of an IPO.* Few entrepreneurs are truly prepared for just how costly the process of going public can be in terms of out-of-pocket cash expenses and opportunity costs. Total cash expenses of an IPO, such as printing, accounting, and legal services, frequently approach $1 million, and most of this must be paid even if the offering is postponed or canceled. Additionally, the combined costs associated with the underwriter's fees (usually 7%) and initial underpricing of the firm's stock (roughly 15% on average) represent a large transfer of wealth from current owners to the underwriters and to the new stockholders.[13]

---

[13]The financial costs of an IPO are documented in Ritter (1988) and Lee et al. (1996).

2. *The managerial costs of an IPO.* As costly as an IPO is financially, many entrepreneurs find the unremitting demands made on their time during the IPO process to be even more burdensome. Rarely can CEOs and other top managers delegate these duties, which grow increasingly intense as the offering date approaches. There are also severe restrictions on what an executive can say or do during the immediate pre-offering period, and because the process can take months to complete, the distraction costs of going public are very high. Top executives must also take time to meet with important potential stockholders before completing the IPO and indefinitely thereafter.

3. *Stock price emphasis.* Owners/managers of private companies frequently operate their firms in ways that balance competing personal and financial interests. This includes seeking profits, but it can also include employing family members in high positions as well as other personal benefits. Once a company goes public, however, external pressures build to maximize the firm's stock price; as managerial shareholdings fall, managers become vulnerable to job loss either through takeover or through dismissal by the board of directors.[14]

4. *Life in a fishbowl.* Public shareholders have the right to a great deal of information about a firm's internal affairs, and releasing this information to stockholders also implies releasing it to competitors and potential acquirers as well. Managers must disclose, especially in the IPO prospectus, how and in what markets they intend to compete, information that is obviously valuable to competitors. Additionally, managers who are also significant stockholders are subject to binding disclosure requirements and face serious constraints on their ability to buy or sell company stock.

JOB INTERVIEW QUESTION

What are the pros and cons of doing an IPO?

In spite of these drawbacks, often several hundred management teams each year decide that the benefits of going public outweigh the costs and begin the process of planning for an IPO. In addition to these "standard" IPOs, four "special" types of IPOs warrant attention.

Specialized Initial Public Offerings: ECOs, Spin-offs, Reverse LBOs, and Tracking Stocks

The four special types of IPOs are equity carve-outs (ECOs), spin-offs, reverse LBOs, and tracking stocks. An **equity carve-out (ECO)** occurs when a parent company sells shares of a subsidiary corporation to the public through an initial public offering. The parent company may sell some of the subsidiary shares it already owns, or the subsidiary may issue new shares. In any event, the parent company almost always retains a controlling stake in the newly public company.

A **spin-off** occurs when a public parent company "spins off" a subsidiary to the parent's shareholders by distributing shares on a pro rata basis. Thus, after the spin-off, there will be two public companies rather than one. Conceptually, the stock price of the parent should drop by approximately the amount that the market values the shares of the newly public spin-off, though researchers document significantly positive price reactions for the stock of divesting parent companies at the time of spin-off announcements, perhaps indicating that the market expects the two independent companies

---

[14]Field and Karpoff (2002) show that managers anticipate their exposure to takeover threat. In their sample of more than 1,000 IPOs, at least 53% went public with some form of antitakeover defense in place.

will be managed more effectively than they would have been had they remained together.[15]

EXAMPLE

One of the most puzzling spin-offs ever occurred in March 2000 when 3Com Corp. sold a 5% stake in its subsidiary, Palm Inc., via an equity carve-out. 3Com also announced its intention to spin off the remaining 95% of Palm to existing 3Com shareholders, who would receive 1.5 shares of Palm for each share of 3Com they owned. This gave investors two ways to purchase Palm shares. An investor who wanted to buy 150 Palm shares could buy them directly in the carve-out IPO, or he could purchase 100 shares of 3Com and wait to receive 150 Palm shares after the spin-off. Of course, in the latter strategy the investor would ultimately own 150 shares of Palm and 100 shares of 3Com.

What was puzzling about this spin-off was the behavior of 3Com and Palm shares after the carve-out. Conceptually, the stand-alone value of 3Com shares cannot be negative. Therefore, the price of 3Com shares prior to the spin-off should have been *at least* 1.5 times the price of Palm shares in the carve-out (because anyone who owned 1 share of 3Com would ultimately receive an additional 1.5 shares of Palm). In fact, after a single trading day, Palm shares sold for almost 1.2 times more than 3Com shares were worth! In this case, and in a few other high-tech spin-offs, it seems that only "irrational exuberance" can explain the market's response.[16]

In a **reverse LBO** (or **second IPO**), a formerly public company that has previously gone private through a leveraged buyout goes public again. Reverse LBOs are easier to price than traditional IPOs because information exists about how the market valued the company when it was publicly traded. Muscarella and Vetsuypens (1989) and DeGeorge and Zeckhauser (1993, 1996) study reverse LBOs and find that the LBO partners earn very high returns on these transactions. One reason for this is obvious: only the most successful LBOs can subsequently go public again.

The final type of specialized equity offering, **tracking stocks**, is a recent innovation that may well have already run its course. These are equity claims based on (and designed to mirror, or *track*) the earnings of wholly owned subsidiaries of diversified firms. They are hybrid securities because the tracking stock "firm" is not separated from the parent company in any way, instead remaining integrated with the parent both legally and operationally. In contrast, both carve-outs and spin-offs result in legally separate firms. AT&T conducted the largest common stock offering in U.S. history when it issued $10.6 billion in AT&T Wireless tracking stock in April 2000. As has been true for most other tracking stock offerings, AT&T's stock rose significantly when it announced the Wireless offering. Unfortunately, both parent and tracking stock performed abysmally during the months after the issue, and in July 2001, AT&T Wireless became an independent company; it was acquired by Cingular Wireless in October 2004.

The Investment Performance of Initial Public Offerings

Are IPOs good investments? The answer seems to depend on the investment horizon of the investor and whether or not the investor can purchase IPO shares at the offer price. If an investor can buy shares at the offer price and then **flip** them—sell them on the first

---

[15]Hite and Owers (1983), Miles and Rosenfeld (1983), and Schipper and Smith (1983).
[16]Lamont and Thaler (2002) argue that the inability to short Palm shares allowed this pricing anomaly to persist.

trading day—then the returns on IPOs are substantial.[17] But if the investor buys shares in the secondary market and holds them for the long term, the returns are much less rewarding.

Positive Initial Returns for IPO Investors (Underpricing) Year in and year out, in virtually every country around the world, the very short term returns on IPOs are surprisingly high. In the United States, the share price in the typical IPO closes roughly 15% above the offer price after just one day of trading. Researchers refer to this pattern as **IPO underpricing**, meaning that the offer price in the prospectus is consistently lower than what the market is willing to pay. To capture this **initial return**, an investor must be fortunate enough to receive an allocation of shares from the investment banker and to sell those shares at the first opportunity. Investors who buy IPO shares when open-market trading begins receive much smaller returns, and take on much greater risks, than do investors who participate in the initial offering.

EXAMPLE

On February 19, 2002, shares of Paypal Inc. (ticker symbol, PYPL), the pioneer in Internet payment methods, began trading for the first time. According to the IPO prospectus, Paypal offered its shares for $13.00 to participating investors. At the close of the first day, Paypal shares were worth $18.20, for a one-day return of 40%. However, for investors who could not buy shares from the syndicate and instead bought shares once trading began, the first-day results were not as good. Paypal shares opened the first day of trading at $19.29 before falling 5.7% by the day's end.

The 15% average on one-day IPO returns presents quite a puzzle to financial economists, who in studying these returns have uncovered the following patterns.

1. *Large IPOs tend to be less underpriced than smaller offerings.* The smaller the offering, the more it is underpriced, and best-efforts offers are more underpriced than firm-commitment issues.
2. *Initial returns are higher in "hot-issue markets" than in more normal times.* Anyone wishing to make a case that financial markets are prone to irrational exuberance will quickly seize on initial offerings, for the IPO market does appear especially prone to fads. Partly because of the IPO market's relatively small scale, a small change in investor appetite for new issues can have a profound impact on the reception accorded individual offerings.
3. *The mean initial return is much higher than the median.* Although the "headline" underpricing figures are quite dramatic, only 60%–70% of all IPOs are substantially underpriced, and the median IPO's initial return is roughly half the average value. The

---

[17]Not surprisingly, underwriters tend to discourage flipping because it raises the odds that they will have to help stabilize the price once trading begins. Siconolfi and McGeehan (1998) describe how investment banks try to identify and punish flippers. Krigman, Shaw, and Womack (1999) offer a different assessment of the economic value of flippers. They find that flipping is both a rational response to perceived pricing errors (caused primarily by issuing firms' unwillingness to lower share offering prices in the face of weak demand) and accurately predicts future returns on newly issued shares. Finally, Aggarwal (2003) shows that flippers account for only an average of 19% of immediate post-IPO trading volume (and only 15% of shares offered) and that hot IPOs are flipped more than cold offerings. She also shows that explicit penalty bids are used in only 13% of offerings and are small in size but have an important deterrent effect.

average, in turn, is inflated by a relative handful of extraordinarily popular offerings with initial returns of 50% or more.

4. *The mean return overstates the actual profits earned by most investors.* IPO investors, especially those who are less sophisticated than the institutions that are the investment banks' best clients, face a classic problem of the **winner's curse**. When an IPO is extremely "hot," both sophisticated and unsophisticated investors will demand shares, and the issue will be heavily oversubscribed. In these deals, investors will be rationed—especially "ordinary" investors—receiving only a fraction of the shares they would like. When an IPO is "cold" and the syndicate has difficulty selling the issue to more sophisticated clients, ordinary investors will receive all the shares they request. Because they receive small allocations in hot deals and large allocations in cold deals, unsophisticated players in this market will earn much lower returns than the average one-day return for all IPOs might suggest.

5. *It is unclear whether venture capital backing or the use of a prestigious underwriter increases or decreases IPO underpricing.* Before 1990, venture capital–backed IPOs were less underpriced than other IPO offers, and issues brought to market by more prestigious underwriters yielded lower first-day returns than those handled by lesser-known investment bankers. It is unclear whether this is still true today, but research shows that underwriter prestige and initial return are positively correlated after 1990, though exactly why this has occurred is not understood.[18]

Smart Ethics Video

Jay Ritter, University of Florida

"Every single country in the world has IPOs underpriced on average."

See the entire interview at **SMARTFinance**

The empirical regularities detailed earlier make clear just how expensive going public tends to be for most companies. Significant underpricing means that money is "left on the table" by the owners of a company executing an IPO, since the high initial returns are captured by the original share purchasers rather than by the issuing company. Why IPOs are underpriced is something of a mystery. Presumably, the firms issuing stock would prefer to receive a higher price (with less underpricing) for their shares, and they could choose investment banks with a track record of less underpricing. Competition among investment banks on this dimension might reduce underpricing to an economically insignificant level, on average.

Finance theory offers several possible explanations for the underpricing phenomenon. First, given the problem of the winner's curse, firms may have to underprice shares, on average, to keep relatively unsophisticated players in the market. If the average IPO were not underpriced, then unsophisticated investors would receive large allocations of the IPOs with negative returns and small allocations of those with positive returns, so these investors would eventually drop out of the market. Second, firms could underprice their IPOs in an attempt to achieve higher stock valuations later, when they conduct seasoned offerings. For example, a firm with excellent future prospects might be willing to leave money on the table initially (something a less healthy firm could not afford to do) as a means to convince investors of just how bright its future looks. If investors recognize and respond to this signal of high IPO return, then the long-term value of the firm's shares will be higher and it can recoup the initial underpricing costs in future equity offerings.

Third, a firm might be willing to underprice its shares to generate excess demand for the offering. With excess demand, the firm (or its investment bank) could spread the shares across many different investors, with no single investor holding a large block. A dispersed ownership structure could benefit the firm if it leads to a more liquid market for the shares and hence a lower cost of capital. Managers might selfishly prefer more ownership dispersion because investors who own just a few shares are less likely than those owning large blocks

---

[18]Beatty and Welch (1996).

to threaten managers if the firm's stock performs poorly. In the extreme, managers can create a dual-class equity structure before going public and concentrate their ownership in the share class with greater voting rights (Smart and Zutter 2003). Fourth, firms may underprice to reward investors for revealing information that helps underwriters determine the firm's true market value.

Whatever the case, underpricing is a pervasive phenomenon. However, the long-run performance of IPOs presents a different puzzle.

Smart Ethics Video

Jay Ritter, University of Florida

"By the middle of 2001, 97% of Internet companies were trading below the offer price."

See the entire interview at
SMARTFinance

Long-Term IPO Returns   Early research on the long-run performance of IPOs was not encouraging for investors. It showed that investors who buy IPO shares at the end of the first month of trading and then hold these shares for five years thereafter fare much worse than they would have by purchasing the shares of comparable, size-matched firms.[19] On average, investors' net returns are more than 40% *below* what they would have earned after five years of alternative equity investments.

These findings are controversial because they challenge the notions that investors are rational and financial markets efficient. More recent research casts doubt on this long-run underperformance for IPO shares. Studies conclude that most IPOs do not yield significant long-run underperformance—provided that IPO returns are compared to an appropriate benchmark.[20] In particular, a compelling case is made that much of the observed underperformance can be explained by leverage effects and risk reductions resulting from the IPO itself.[21] Raising new equity capital via an IPO reduces the firm's leverage and its financial risk, so investors will accept a lower required return subsequent to the offering. On balance, we conclude that IPOs tend to earn normal long-term returns.

> **Concept Review Questions**
>
> 8. What patterns have been observed in the types of firms going public in the United States? Why do you think that certain industries become popular with investors at different times?
> 9. What are the principal benefits of going public? What are the key drawbacks?
> 10. Distinguish between an equity carve-out and a spin-off. How might a spin-off create value for shareholders?
> 11. To what does the term *underpricing* refer? If the average IPO is underpriced by about 15%, how might an unsophisticated investor who regularly invests in IPOs earn an average return of less than 15%?
> 12. How does underpricing add to the cost of going public?

16.4 SEASONED EQUITY OFFERINGS IN THE UNITED STATES

Seasoned equity offerings (SEOs) are surprisingly rare for both U.S. and non-U.S. companies. In fact, the typical large U.S. company will not sell new common stock even once per decade, though when an SEO is launched it tends to be much larger than the typical IPO. Seasoned common stock issues must generally follow the same regulatory and underwriting procedures as unseasoned offerings. Seasoned offerings differ from unseasoned ones not just because of the former's large average size but also, and principally,

---

[19]Loughran and Ritter (1995).
[20]See Brav and Gompers (1997), Fama (1998), Brav, Geczy, and Gompers (2000), Eckbo, Masulis, and Norli (2000), Gompers and Lerner (2003), and Eckbo and Norli (2005).
[21]Eckbo, Masulis, and Norli (2000).

because seasoned securities have an observable market value when the offering is priced, which obviously makes pricing much easier. Corwin (2003) finds that, during the 1980s and 1990s, U.S. SEOs were priced at an average of 2.2% below their closing-day market prices, with the discount increasing substantially over time. He also finds that underpricing is greater for larger offers, especially for shares with relatively inelastic demand; this is consistent with the offering exerting temporary downward price pressure on the market.[22] However, ease of pricing does not mean that investors welcome new equity offering announcements, as we now discuss.

Although seasoned equity offerings have traditionally been underwritten and marketed to retail investors in much the same way as IPOs are distributed, a recent study reveals that a dramatic change in SEO marketing has occurred. Today, roughly half of the SEOs marketed in the U.S. and Europe are sold in 48 hours or less in **accelerated underwritings**, which are auctions exclusively targeting investment banks and institutional investors.[23] Figure 16.3 shows how the fraction of global SEOs executed through the three main types of accelerated offers—accelerated book-built offerings (ABOs), bloc trades, and bought deals—grew between 1991 and 2004. As shown, the rapid growth of accelerated underwritings also had a profound competitive effect on traditional nonaccelerated SEO transactions, which are now arranged in a few days rather than weeks, as was the case a decade ago.

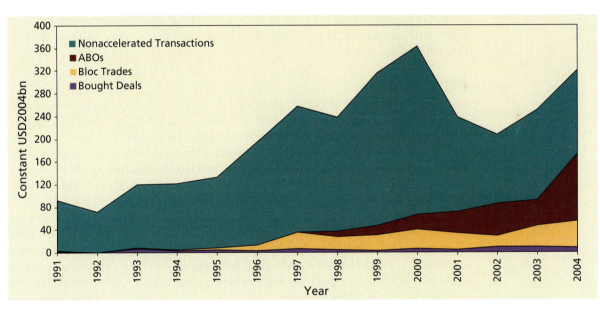

FIGURE 16.3

Global Seasoned Equity Offerings: Total Deal Value by Type, 1991–2004

This chart shows the evolution of global seasoned equity offerings for the 1991–2004 period. The series refer to the total deal value (in billions of constant 2004 U.S. dollars) raised by accelerated book-built offerings (ABOs), bloc trades, bought deals, and all other types of nonaccelerated transactions.

Source: Figure 1 in Bernardo Bortolotti, William Megginson, and Scott Smart, "The Rise of Accelerated Seasoned Equity Underwritings," *Journal of Applied Corporate Finance* 20 (Summer 2008), pp. 35–57.

[22]Altinkiliç and Hansen (2003) and Bortolotti, Megginson, and Smart (2008) document similar levels of SEO underpricing, whereas Loderer, Sheehan, and Kadlec (1991) show that SEOs during the 1970s and 1980s were priced very near their current market price.
[23]See Bortolotti, Megginson, and Smart (2008).

Stock Price Reactions to Seasoned Equity Issue Announcements

One reason corporations issue seasoned equity only rarely is that stock prices usually fall when firms announce plans to conduct SEOs. On average, the price decline is about 3%.[24] In the United States, the average dollar value of this price decline is equal to almost one-third of the dollar value of the issue itself. Clearly, the announcement of seasoned equity issues conveys negative information to investors overall, though precisely what information is transmitted is not always clear. The message may be that management, which is presumably better informed about a company's true prospects than are outside investors, believes the firm's current stock price is too high. Alternatively, the message may be that the firm's earnings will be lower than expected in the future and management is issuing stock to make up for this internal cash flow shortfall.

There is some evidence that SEOs are bad news for shareholders not only at the time they are announced but also over longer holding periods of one to five years. Negative long-run returns following seasoned equity offerings have been documented in Loughran and Ritter (1995), Jegadeesh (2000), and more recent studies. As with long-run IPO returns, however, whether or not long-run returns following SEOs are unusually low depends on the comparison benchmark.

Most equity sales in the United States fall under the category of **general cash offerings**. However, there is a special type of seasoned equity offering that allows the firm's existing owners to buy new shares at a bargain price or to sell that right to other investors. These rights offerings are relatively scarce in the United States but are growing in importance internationally.

Rights Offerings

One of the basic tenets of English common law, and thus of the U.S. commercial laws derived from it, is that shareholders have first claim on anything of value distributed by a corporation. These **preemptive rights** give common stockholders the right to maintain their proportionate ownership in the corporation by purchasing shares whenever the firm sells new equity. **Rights offerings** are stock issues sold exclusively to a firm's existing shareholders. Because this strategy keeps all the gains and losses on share issues "within the family," firms usually price rights offerings well below the current market price in order to ensure that the offering sells out and the firm raises the funds needed. The laws of most American states grant shareholders the preemptive right to participate in new issues unless this right is removed by shareholder consent. However, the vast majority of publicly traded U.S. companies have removed preemptive rights from their corporate charter, so rights offerings by large American companies are quite rare today. Rights offerings are still common in other countries, however.

EXAMPLE

After a decade of extremely rapid growth in capital spending, many telecommunications companies found themselves teetering on the brink of bankruptcy by the summer of 2001. In order to avert financial meltdown, two of the largest European telecoms—British Telecom (BT) and The Netherlands' KPN—took the highly unusual step of launching immense rights

---

[24]Myers and Majluf (1984) provide a theoretical explanation for this negative market response to SEO announcements based on informational asymmetry between managers and investors: investors interpret such announcements as a sign that managers believe the firm's shares are overvalued.

offerings of common stock. BT raised £5.9 billion ($8.5 billion) in June 2001, and KPN issued €5 billion ($4.5 billion) six months later, briefly making these the two largest rights offerings in history. BT sold its shares, which were selling for 435 pence each at the time of the rights issue, for 300 pence each, while KPN priced its new shares at a smaller (but still significant) 4.5% discount to their market price of €5.11 each. In March 2003, France Telecom eclipsed both of these issues with its own €15 billion ($15.8 billion) rights offering. FT shares were sold for €14.50 each, a 28% discount from their market price at the time.

Concept Review Questions	13. What happens to a firm's stock price when the firm announces plans for a seasoned equity offering? What are the long-term returns to investors following an SEO?
	14. Why do you think that rights offerings have largely disappeared in the United States?

16.5 PRIVATE PLACEMENTS IN THE UNITED STATES

As noted earlier, a **private placement** involves the sale of securities in a transaction that is exempt from the registration requirements imposed by federal securities law. A private placement occurs when an investment banker arranges for the direct sale of a new security issue to an individual, several individuals, an institutional investor, or a group of institutions. The investment banker is paid a commission for acting as an intermediary in the transaction. To qualify for a private-placement exemption, the sale of the securities must be restricted to a small group of **accredited investors**, individuals or institutions that meet certain income and wealth requirements. The rationale for the private-placement exemption is that accredited investors are financially sophisticated agents who do not need the protection afforded by the registration process. Typical accredited institutional investors include insurance companies, pension funds, mutual funds, and venture capitalists.

Traditional Private Placements versus Rule 144A Issues

The private-placement exemption is a **transactional exemption**, which means that the securities must be registered before they can be resold or the subsequent sale must also qualify as a private placement. **Rule 144A**, adopted in 1990, provides a private-placement exemption for institutions with assets exceeding $100 million (known as **qualified institutional buyers**) and allows them to freely trade privately placed securities among themselves. The principal reasons for instituting Rule 144A were to increase liquidity and reduce issuing costs in the private-placement market. Another reason was to attract large foreign issuers who were unable or unwilling to conform to U.S. registration requirements for public offerings.

Private placements have several advantages over public offerings. They are less costly in terms of time and money than registering with the SEC, and the issuers do not have to reveal confidential information. Also, because there are typically far fewer investors, the terms of a private placement are easier to renegotiate, if necessary. The disadvantage of private placements is that the securities have no readily available market price, they are less liquid, and there is a smaller group of potential investors than in the public

WHAT CFOs DO

CFO Survey Evidence: Factors that Affect Stock Issuance Decisions

Given the evidence discussed in this chapter that the announcement of new seasoned equity offerings typically causes a firm's stock price to fall sharply, it will likely come as no surprise that corporate managers are reluctant to issue new stock. A recent survey sought to measure what factors managers weighed when making a new stock issuance decision, and the following graph shows the factors that managers feel are the most important to consider when issuing seasoned equity. Almost two-thirds (64%) of respondents expressed concern that a seasoned equity offering will dilute earnings per share, and half of responding managers were concerned about diluting specific large shareholders. Over 60% of respondents voiced concerns regarding the size of a new issue and the likely negative effect that announcement of

such an offering would have on the current price of outstanding shares. Further, about 50% stated they were considering a new stock issue to provide shares for employee stock option programs and to maintain the firm's debt-to-equity ratio near the targeted level. Far smaller fractions of responding managers believed that stock was the least risky source of funds, that recent firm profits would be insufficient to fund company activities, that the firm should issue stock to move toward an industry-standard leverage ratio, or that investors would prefer the company to issue stock rather than bonds.

Source: Reprinted from John R. Graham and Campbell Harvey, "The Theory and Practice of Corporate Finance: Evidence from the Field," *Journal of Financial Economics,* 60, pp. 187–243, copyright © 2001, with permission from Elsevier.

What Factors Do Companies Consider When Issuing Common Stock?

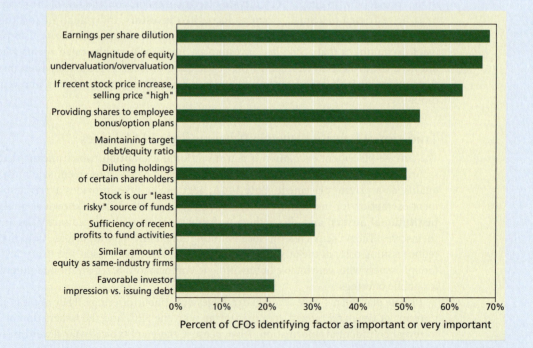

market.[25] There are about 2,500 private placements in the United States most years, and these usually raise $400 to $500 billion in total. Over 90% of these are debt offerings, each with an average value of around $250 million, and Rule 144A issues represent three-fourths of total issues.

<table>
<tr><td>Concept Review Questions</td><td>15. What is a qualified institutional buyer? How does this differ from an accredited investor?

16. What are the relative advantages and disadvantages of private placements compared to those of public offerings of stock and bond issues?</td></tr>
</table>

16.6 INTERNATIONAL COMMON STOCK OFFERINGS

The international market for equity offerings can be broken down into two parts: each nation's market for domestic stock offerings and the international, or cross-border, market for equity offerings. We briefly look at each in turn, beginning with a survey of national markets.

Non-U.S. Initial Public Offerings

Any nation with a well-functioning stock market must have some mechanism for taking private firms public, and the total number of IPOs outside the United States each year usually exceeds the American total by a wide margin. However, until very recently far less money was raised in aggregate by private-sector issuers on non-U.S. markets, because these international IPOs are, on average, very much smaller than those on the Nasdaq or NYSE. This pattern changed dramatically during 2006 and 2007, when large privatization share offerings (to be described shortly) by Russian and Chinese companies pushed London and Shanghai ahead of New York in terms of the highest value of IPOs sold. Yet many of the same investment anomalies documented in the United States are also observed internationally. First, non-U.S. private-sector IPOs also demonstrate significant first-day returns. Figure 16.4 summarizes IPO underpricing studies from 43 different countries; all show significant underpricing, and 24 of these countries have mean initial returns that are greater than the U.S. average.

A second empirical regularity common to both U.S. and international IPOs is that initial international offers also may yield negative long-term returns. However, studies of non-U.S. long-run returns are subject to all the methodological problems bedeviling U.S. studies (and perhaps then some), so it is unclear whether international IPOs truly underperform or not. Third, popular non-U.S. issues also tend to be heavily oversubscribed, and the allocation rules mandated by national law or exchange regulations largely determine which investors capture the IPO initial returns. Fourth, hot-issue markets are as prevalent internationally as in the United States. Finally, taxation issues (particularly capital gains tax rules) significantly affect how issues are priced and/or which investors the offers are targeting.

---

[25]Hertzel, Lemmon, Linck, and Smith (2002) examine private placement (PP) pricing as well as the initial and long-run return to stockholders of companies executing private placements. They find that PPs are sold at an average discount of 16.5% and that news of an impending PP increases the issuer's stock price by 2.4%. Returns become negative over the long term, however, with average three-year abnormal returns between −23.8% and −45.2%, depending on the benchmark used for comparison. Wu (2004) documents that PPs largely fail to improve the performance of issuing firms. She concludes that PPs serve mostly to entrench managers.

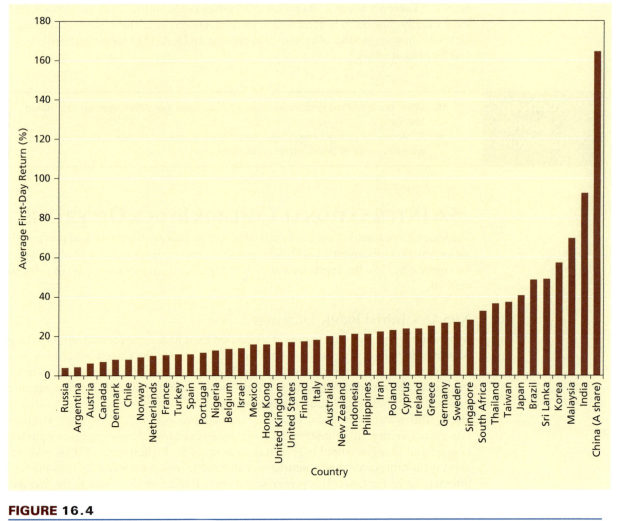

FIGURE 16.4

Average First-Day Returns on IPOs for 38 Countries

Source: Studies cited in Tim Loughran, Jay R. Ritter and Kristian Rydqvist, "Initial Public Offerings: International Insights," *Pacific-Basin Finance Journal* 2 (June 1994), pp. 165–199, updated December 31, 2008, downloaded from Jay Ritter's website (http://bear.cba.ufl.edu/ritter/ipodata.htm), with permission from Elsevier.

International IPO markets do, however, differ in important ways from U.S. markets. For example, many governments impose politically motivated mandates on firms wishing to go public, requiring them to allocate minimum fractions of the issue to their employees or to other targeted groups. Furthermore, the net effect of pricing restrictions in many countries is to ensure that IPOs are severely underpriced; this is especially common in countries where shares must be priced on a par-value basis and/or where minimum dividend payouts are mandated. Some governments (even in advanced economies like Japan's) routinely prohibit firms from making IPOs during periods when market conditions are "unsettled" and/or require explicit permission to be obtained before an IPO can be launched. Many countries require that initial offering prices be set far in advance of the issue, which usually means that offerings that actually proceed tend to be highly underpriced. Finally, non-U.S. entrepreneurs often have different motivations for taking firms public than do owner/managers of U.S. private companies. Whereas many U.S. companies go public in order to acquire the equity capital needed to finance rapid growth, continental European entrepreneurs go public mainly to rebalance their firms' capital structures and to achieve personal liquidity.[26] On a more balanced note, most other countries place fewer restrictions on pre-offer marketing and dissemination of information than do U.S. regulators.

International Common Stock Issues

Although the international market for common stock is not, and probably never will be, as large as the international market for debt securities, cross-border trading and issuance of common stock have increased dramatically since 1990. Much of this increase can be attributed to a growing desire on the part of institutional and individual investors to diversify their investment portfolios internationally. Because foreign stocks currently account for a small fraction of U.S. institutional holdings and of holdings in other developed economies, this total will surely grow in the years ahead.

Besides issuing stock to local investors, corporations have also discovered the benefits of issuing stock outside their home markets. For example, several top U.S. multinational companies have chosen to list their stock in half a dozen or more stock markets. Issuing stock internationally broadens the ownership base and helps a company integrate itself into the local business scene. A local stock listing increases local business press coverage and also serves as effective corporate advertising. Furthermore, having locally traded stock can facilitate corporate acquisitions because shares can then be used as an acceptable method of payment.[27]

American Depositary Receipts and Global Depositary Receipts   Many foreign corporations have discovered the benefits of trading their stock in the United States, though they do so differently than do U.S. companies. The disclosure and reporting requirements mandated by the U.S. Securities and Exchange Commission have historically discouraged all but the largest foreign firms from directly listing their shares on American stock exchanges. For instance, when Daimler-Benz announced in mid-1993 that it would become the first large German company to seek such a listing, the news caused a sensation. Most foreign companies tap the U.S. market through **American Depositary Receipts (ADRs)**. These dollar-denominated claims issued by U.S. banks represent ownership of shares of a foreign company's stock held on deposit by the U.S. bank in the issuing firm's home country.[28]

---

[26]Pagano, Panetta, and Zingales (1998).

[27]It is intriguing that Pagano, Röell, and Zechner (2002) have found that, while many European companies listed abroad (mainly on U.S. exchanges) between 1986 and 1997, the number of U.S. companies cross-listing in Europe declined. Bruner, Chaplinsky, and Ramchand (2004) find that foreign companies going public in the United States experience roughly the same total issuance costs as domestic IPOs. Siegel (2005) studies whether companies from countries with weak corporate governance standards can bond themselves by committing themselves to follow U.S. securities laws when they issue securities on U.S. capital markets; he finds some evidence that such bonding is effective. Doidge, Karolyi, and Stulz (2004) show that foreign companies with shares cross-listed in the United States have significantly higher values than do similar firms that are not cross-listed, which they argue occurs largely because a U.S. listing offers corporate governance benefits.

[28]Jayaraman, Shastri, and Tandon (1993) and Miller (1999) present evidence that listings of ADRs are associated with positive abnormal returns on the underlying shares in their home markets. Muscarella and Vetsuypens (1996) use a sample of "solo splits," or splits of ADR stocks that are not accompanied by splits of the stock in the home-country market, to support a liquidity explanation for cross-listings (i.e., splits lower stock prices and thus increase demand for shares by individual investors). Blass and Yafeh (2001) find that Israeli firms that choose a New York listing over a listing in the home market (Tel Aviv) are younger, more high-tech, and of generally higher quality than their stay-at-home counterparts. Finally, Errunza and Miller (2000) and Lins, Strickland, and Zenner (2005) show that ADRs lower the cost of capital for issuing firms—especially those headquartered in developing countries.

ADRs have proven to be popular with U.S. investors, at least partly because they allow investors to diversify internationally. And because the shares are covered by American securities laws and pay dividends in dollars (dividends on the underlying shares are converted from the local currency into dollars before being paid out), U.S investors are able to diversify at very low cost. Since an ADR can be converted into ownership of the underlying shares, arbitrage ensures rational dollar valuation of this claim against stock denominated in a foreign currency. Figure 16.5 details the rapid growth in market value and trading volume of ADRs on the three major U.S. stock exchanges over the period 1990–2008.

FIGURE 16.5

Trading Volume in Public American Depositary Receipt (ADR) Issues, 1990–2008

Sources: The Bank of New York, "Depositary Receipt Market Review 2004" and "Depositary Receipts (ADRs and GDRs) 2000 Year-End Market Review," both downloaded from the Bank of New York's website (http://adrbny.com).

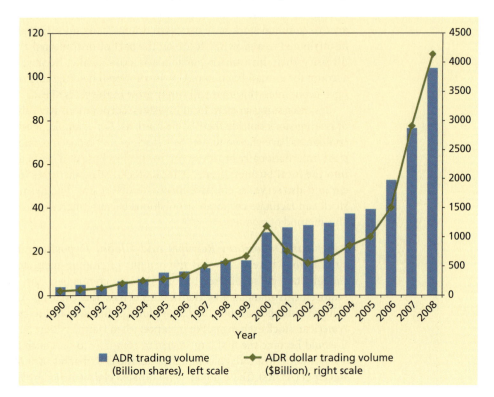

ADRs can be either sponsored or unsponsored. A **sponsored ADR** is one for which the issuing (foreign) company absorbs the legal and financial costs of creating and trading the security. In this case, the company will pay a U.S. depositary bank to create an ADR issue. An **unsponsored ADR** is one in which the issuing firm is not involved with the issue at all and may even oppose it. Historically, unsponsored ADRs resulted from U.S. investor demand for shares of particular foreign companies. Since 1983, however, the SEC has required that all new ADR programs be sponsored, so relatively few unsponsored ADRs still exist.

There are also four different levels of ADR programs, corresponding to different levels of required disclosure and tradability. The least costly—in terms of both required disclosure and out-of-pocket expenses—are Level I and Rule 144A offerings, but the shares offered cannot subsequently be traded on one of the major stock exchanges or Nasdaq.[29] Home-country accounting standards are also allowed for these two types of ADR programs.

---

[29]Karolyi (1998) and Miller (1999).

In contrast, Level II and III programs require the use of GAAP and are significantly costlier to arrange, but these shares can be listed for trading on public markets. As of June 30, 2008, a record 2093 sponsored ADRs from 62 countries were available to U.S. investors; of these, 429 were listed for public trading. China's Baidu.com was by far the most actively traded ADR. Over 805 million Baidu.com ADRs, worth $243.3 billion, traded hands during the first six months of 2008 alone.

Given the success of ADRs, many large international equity issues use this form even for share tranches (portions of the issue) that are destined for sale outside the United States. Large international issues that use ADRs are often called **Global Depositary Receipts (GDRs)** to emphasize their multinational characteristics.

EXAMPLE

To demonstrate how ADRs are created, assume that Bayerische Motoren Werke, the famous German manufacturer of BMW automobiles, wishes to establish an ADR program for its shares on the New York Stock Exchange. In late March 2005, BMW's shares are trading on the Deutsche Börse (formerly the Frankfurt Stock Exchange) at €34.45 per share, and the U.S. dollar/euro exchange rate is $1.3316/€. If BMW wishes to establish an ADR program worth about $100 million, the firm might ask Bank of New York (ticker symbol, BK), one of the two leading ADR issuers, to handle the issue and offer to pay all of BK's issuing and listing expenses—including underwriting fees. Assume further that BK believes the ideal price to trade on the NYSE is about $90 per share. BK would implement this ADR program by taking the following steps.

1. Purchase 2.2 million shares of BMW on the Deutsche Börse at €34.45/share, paying €75.79 million. This represents an investment worth $100,921,964 by Bank of New York (€75,790,000 × $1.3316/€).
2. Create 1.1 million ADRs for listing on the NYSE, with each ADR representing ownership of two BMW shares.
3. Sell the 1.1 million ADRs to American investors at a price of $91.75 per ADR. This is the dollar price implied by BMW's price in euros, the current $/€ exchange rate, and the fact that each ADR is worth two BMW shares (€34.45/share × 2 shares/ADR × $1.3316/€ = $91.75/ADR).

The total proceeds of this offering are $100,921,964, which is exactly equal to the amount BK paid for the shares originally. Holders of these ADRs have a security that is denominated in dollars but that perfectly reflects both BMW's share price in euros and fluctuations in the dollar/euro exchange rate.

To demonstrate how ADRs reflect changes in BMW's stock price, assume that BMW's shares increase by €1.00 per share (to €35.45 each) in early morning trading in Germany. We can compute that the ADRs should rise by $2.66 each (€1.00/share × 2 shares/ADR × $1.3316/€) to $94.41 per share when they begin trading in New York later that day. To demonstrate how ADRs reflect exchange rate movements, assume that BMW's price remains unchanged at €34.45 per share but that the euro appreciates from $1.3316/€ to $1.3509/€ immediately before trading begins in New York. The ADRs should begin trading at $94.41 per share (€34.45/share × 2 shares/ADR × $1.3509/€) when the NYSE opens. In other words, either an increase in BMW's stock price from €34.45 to €35.45 per share (holding exchange rates constant) or an appreciation of the euro from $1.3316/€ to $1.3509/€ (holding BMW's stock price unchanged) can cause the price of each BMW ADR to rise by $2.66, from $91.75 to $94.41.

Share Issue Privatizations

Anyone who examines international share offerings is soon struck by the size and importance of share issue privatizations in non-U.S. stock markets. A government executing a **share issue privatization (SIP)** will sell all or part of its ownership in a state-owned enterprise to private investors via a public share offering. The words *public* and *private* can become confusing in this context; an SIP involves the sale of shares in a state-owned company to *private* investors via a *public* capital market share offering. Since Britain's Thatcher government first popularized privatizations in the early 1980s, there have been almost 950 privatizing share offerings by more than a hundred national governments. These SIPs have raised in excess of 1 trillion.

For our purposes, the most important aspect of privatization programs is the transforming role they have played in developing many national stock markets generally and IPO markets in particular. Share issue privatizations are particularly important for market development because of their size and the way their shares are allocated to potential investors. As Table 16.7 makes clear, SIPs tend to be vastly larger than their private-sector counterparts; in fact, the three largest (and 27 of the 30 largest) public share offerings in world history have all been privatizations. Almost without exception, SIPs have been the largest share offerings in a country's history, and the first several large privatization IPOs generally yield a dramatic increase in the national stock market's trading volume and liquidity. In addition to this difference in size, SIPs also differ from private-sector share issues in being almost exclusively secondary offerings. In other words, the proceeds from SIPs go to the government rather than to the firm being privatized. The sole major exception to this rule to date has occurred in China; almost all Chinese SIPs have been primary offerings.

The importance of SIPs in creating new shareholders derives from the way these issues are generally priced and allocated. Governments almost always set offer prices well below their expected open-market value (they deliberately underprice), thereby ensuring great excess demand for shares in the offering. The issuing governments then allocate shares in a way that ensures maximum political benefit. Invariably, governments favor employees and other small domestic investors (who typically have never purchased common stock before) with relatively large share allocations, whereas domestic institutions and foreign investors are allocated far less than they desire. The net result of this strategy is to guarantee that most of the short-term capital gains of privatization IPOs are captured by the many citizen/investors (who vote) rather than by institutional and foreign investors (who do not). Furthermore, the long-run excess returns to investors who purchase privatizing share issues are significantly positive. All these features help promote popular support for privatization and other economic reform measures the government might wish to enact. In all, privatization share offerings have done as much as any other single factor to promote the development of international stock markets since the mid-1990s.

Concept Review Questions	17. In what ways are non-U.S. (private-sector) initial public offerings similar to U.S. IPOs, and in what ways are they different?
	18. What are American Depositary Receipts and how are they created? Why do you think ADRs have proven so popular with U.S. investors?
	19. In what key ways do share issue privatizations (SIPs) differ from private-sector share offerings? Why do you think governments deliberately underprice SIPs?

Table 16.7 Details of the World's Largest Public Share Offerings

DATE	COMPANY	COUNTRY	AMOUNT ($ MILLION)	TYPE
Nov 87	Nippon Telegraph & Telephone	Japan	40,260	SEO
Oct 88	Nippon Telegraph & Telephone	Japan	22,400	SEO
Oct 06	Industrial & Commcl Bank China	China	21,200	IPO
Mar 08	*Visa*	*United States*	*19,650*	*IPO*
Nov 99	ENEL	Italy	18,900	IPO
Oct 98	NTT DoCoMo	Japan	18,000	IPO
Mar 03	France Telecom[a]	France	15,800	SEO
Oct 97	Telecom Italia	Italy	15,500	SEO
Feb 87	Nippon Telegraph & Telephone	Japan	15,097	IPO
Nov 99	Nippon Telegraph & Telephone	Japan	15,000	SEO
Jun 00	Deutsche Telekom	Germany	14,760	SEO
Nov 96	Deutsche Telekom	Germany	13,300	IPO
Oct 87	British Petroleum	United Kingdom	12,430	SEO
Jul 08	Companhia Vale do Rio Doce	Brazil	12,060	SEO
Nov 00	Nippon Telegraph & Telephone	Japan	11,300	SEO
Jun 06	Bank of China	China	11,190	IPO
Nov 08	*Wells Fargo*	*United States*	*11,000*	*SEO*
Apr 00	*ATT Wireless (tracking stock)*	*United States*	*10,600*	*IPO*
Nov 98	France Telecom	France	10,500	SEO
Nov 97	Telstra	Australia	10,530	IPO
Jul 06	Rosneft (including Yukos)	Russia	10,400	IPO
Nov 04	Telstra	Australia	10,400	SEO
Oct 99	Telstra	Australia	10,400	SEO
Jun 99	Deutsche Telekom	Germany	10,200	SEO
Dec 90	Regional Electricity Companies[b]	United Kingdom	9,995	IPO
Dec 91	British Telecom	United Kingdom	9,927	SEO
Nov 05	China Construction Bank	China	9,200	IPO
Nov 07	Petro China	China	8,900	SEO
Jun 00	Telia	Sweden	8,800	IPO
Feb 07	Sberbank	Russia	8,800	SEO

Notes: This table summarizes the 30 largest public share offerings in history prior to January 2009. Offers are reported in nominal (not inflation-adjusted) amounts and are translated into millions of U.S. dollars using the contemporaneous exchange rate. **Bold italic** type is used to denote private-sector offerings; all other listings are share issue privatizations. Amounts reported for SIP offers are as described in the *Financial Times* at the time of the issue. Private-sector offering amounts are from the *Securities Data Corporation* file or *Financial Times*.

[a]Rights offering in which the French government participated proportionately, so not an SIP in the traditional sense. Though a share offering by a state-owned firm, the share of government ownership did not decline.

[b]Indicates a group offering of multiple companies that trade separately after the IPO.

Source: Table 12 of William L. Megginson and Jeffry M. Netter. 2001. From State to Market: A Survey of Empirical Studies on Privatization, *Journal of Economic Literature* 39, pp. 321–389. Updated by author.

SUMMARY

- Companies wishing to raise capital externally must make a series of decisions, beginning with whether to issue debt or equity and whether to employ an investment bank to assist with the securities sale. This chapter focuses on common stock offerings, but the decisions and issuing procedures are similar for preferred stock and debt securities.

- Investment banks assist companies in selling new securities by underwriting security offerings. Underwriting a security offering involves three tasks: (1) managing the offering, which includes advising the company about the type and amount of securities to sell; (2) underwriting the offering by purchasing the securities from the issuer at a fixed price in order to shift the price risk from the issuer to the investment bank; and (3) selling the securities to investors.

- Firms wishing to raise new common stock equity must decide whether (a) to sell stock to public investors through a general cash offering or (b) to rely on sales to existing stockholders in a rights offering. Rights issues are now fairly rare in the United States, though they remain common in other developed countries.

- Common stock can be sold through private placements to accredited investors, or it can be sold to the public if the securities are registered with the SEC. A company's first public offering of common stock is known as its initial public offering, or IPO. The average IPO in the United States is underpriced by about 15%, and this has held true for several decades. International IPOs are also underpriced. It is unclear whether or not IPOs are poor long-term investments.

- Subsequent offerings of common stock are known as seasoned equity offerings, or SEOs. The announcement of a seasoned equity issue tends to decrease a company's stock price, and there is evidence that firms issuing seasoned equity underperform over the long term.

- The largest share offerings in world history have all been share issue privatizations, or SIPs. Governments have raised over $1 trillion since 1981 through these share offerings, and they have transformed stock market capitalization, trading volume, and the number of citizens owning shares in many countries.

KEY TERMS

accelerated underwritings
accredited investors
American Depositary Receipts
  (ADRs)
best-efforts offering
book building
bulge bracket
certification
cold comfort letter
co-managers
competitively bid offer
due diligence
effective (offering)
equity carve-out (ECO)
final prospectus
firm-commitment offering
fixed-price offer
flip (shares)
full disclosure
general cash offerings

Global Depositary Receipts (GDRs)
Green Shoe option
initial return
investment bank
IPO underpricing
lead underwriter
league table
lockup agreements
market maker
mixed offering
negotiated offer
net price
offer price
overallotment option
oversubscribe
preemptive rights
preliminary prospectus
price stabilization
primary offering
private placement

prospectus
qualified institutional buyers
red herring
registration statement
reverse LBO
rights offerings
road show
Rule 144A
Rule 144A offering
Rule 415
seasoned equity offerings (SEOs)
second IPO
secondary offering
Securities Act of 1933
Securities and Exchange Act of 1934
selling group
share issue privatization (SIP)
shelf registration
spin-off
sponsored ADR

supplemental disclosures	underwrite	unsponsored ADR
tracking stocks	underwriting spread	winner's curse
transactional exemption	underwriting syndicate	
underpriced	unseasoned equity offerings	

Questions

16-1. What preferences do you think common stock shareholders would have regarding a company's source of equity financing?

16-2. Rights offerings are seldom used in the United States to raise equity capital, but they are often used in Europe. How might you explain this fact?

16-3. What do you think are the most important costs and benefits of becoming a publicly traded firm? What questions would you ask before advising whether or not an entrepreneur's firm should go public?

16-4. If you were an investment banker, how would you determine the offering price of an IPO?

16-5. Are the significantly positive short-run and significantly negative long-run returns earned by IPO shareholders compatible with market efficiency? If not, why not?

16-6. Why do investment banks require lockup agreements when they underwrite security offerings? As a potential investor, what would you think if all the shares in an equity offering were being sold by the company's management and none were new shares being sold by the company itself?

16-7. List and describe briefly the key services that investment banks provide to firms before, during, and after a securities offering.

16-8. What are American Depositary Receipts (ADRs), and why have they proven to be so popular with U.S. investors?

16-9. Explain why the underwriting spread on IPOs averages about 7% of the offering price whereas the spread on a seasoned offering of common stock averages less than 5%.

16-10. Discuss the various issues that must be considered in selecting an investment banker for an IPO. Which type of placement is usually preferred by the issuing firm?

16-11. In terms of IPO investing, what does it mean to flip a stock? According to the empirical results regarding short- and long-term returns following equity offerings, is flipping a wise investment strategy?

16-12. What materials are presented in an IPO prospectus? In general, what result is documented regarding sales of shares by insiders and venture capitalists?

16-13. How do you explain the highly politicized nature of share issue privatization (SIP) pricing and share allocation policies? Are governments maximizing offering proceeds, or are they pursuing primarily political and economic objectives?

Problems

Investment Banking

Smart Solutions

See the problem and solution explained step-by-step at **SMARTFinance**

16-1. West Coast Manufacturing Company (WCMC) is executing an initial public offering with the following characteristics. The company will sell 10 million shares at an offer price of $25 per share, the underwriter will charge a 7% underwriting fee, and the shares are expected to sell for $32 per share by the end of the first day's trading. Assume that this IPO is executed as anticipated.

    a. Calculate the initial return earned by investors who are allocated shares in the IPO.

    b. How much will WCMC receive from this offering?

    c. What is the total cost (underwriting fee and underpricing) of this issue to WCMC?

16-2. Continuing from Problem 16-1, assume that you purchase shares in the West Coast Manufacturing Company at the post-offering market price of $32 per share and then hold the shares for one year, after which you sell them for $35 per share. WCMC does not pay dividends, and you are not subject to capital gains taxation. During this year, the return on the overall stock market was 11%. What net return did you earn on your WCMC share investment? Assess this return in light of the overall market return.

16-3. Norman Internet Service Company (NISC) is interested in selling common stock to raise capital for capacity expansion. The firm has consulted First Tulsa Company, a large underwriting firm, which believes that the stock can be sold for $50 per share. The underwriter's investigation found that its administrative costs will be 2.5% of the sale price and its selling costs will be 2.0% of the sale price. If the underwriter requires a profit equal to 1% of the sale price, how much spread (in dollars) is necessary to cover the underwriter's costs and profit?

16-4. LaJolla Securities Inc. specializes in the underwriting of small companies. The terms of a recent offering were as follows:

Number of shares	2 million
Offering price	$25 per share
Net proceeds	$45 million

LaJolla Securities' expenses associated with the offering were $500,000. Determine LaJolla Securities' profit on the offering if the secondary market price of the shares immediately after the offering began were as follows:

a. $23 per share

b. $25 per share

c. $28 per share

The U.S. Market for Initial Public Offerings

16-5. Go to http://www.ipohome.com and find (under "Pricings") information about firms that went public in the first few weeks of 2009. Write down the ticker symbols and offer prices for the firms you select; then go to Yahoo! and download daily price quotes since the IPO date. For each firm, calculate the following:

a. The percentage return measured from the offer price to the closing price the first day

b. The percentage return measured from the opening price to the closing price the first day

16-6. Four companies conducted IPOs last month: Hot.Com, Biotech Pipe Dreams Corp., Sleepy Tyme Inc., and Bricks N Mortar International. All four companies went public at an offer price of $10 per share. The first-day performance of each stock (measured as the percentage difference between the IPO offer price and the first-day closing price) was as follows:

Company	First-Day Return
Hot.Com	45%
Biotech Pipe Dreams	30%
Sleepy Tyme	5%
Bricks N Mortar	0%

a. If you submitted a bid through your broker for 100 shares of each company, if your orders were filled completely, and if you cashed out of each deal after one day, what was your average return on these investments?

b. Next, suppose that your orders were not all filled completely because of excess demand for "hot" IPOs. Specifically, after ordering 100 shares of each company, you were able to buy only 10 shares of Hot.Com, 20 shares of Biotech Pipe Dreams, 50 shares of Sleepy Tyme, and 100 shares of Bricks N Mortar. Recalculate your average return taking into account that your orders were only partially filled.

Seasoned Equity Offerings in the United States

16-7. The Bloomington Company needs to raise $20 million of new equity capital. Its common stock is currently selling for $42 per share. The investment bankers require an underwriting spread of 7% of the offering price, and the company's legal, accounting, and printing expenses associated with the seasoned offering are estimated to be $450,000. How many new shares must the company sell in order to net $20 million?

16-8. GSM Corporation sold 20 million shares of common stock in a seasoned offering. The market price of the company's shares immediately before the offering was $14.75. The shares were offered to the public at $14.50, and the underwriting spread was 4%. The company's expenses associated with the offering were $7.5 million. How much new cash did the company receive?

16-9. After a banner year of rising profits and positive stock returns, the managers of Raptor Pharmaceuticals Corporation (RPC) have decided to launch a seasoned equity offering to raise new equity capital. RPC currently has 10 million shares outstanding, and yesterday's closing market price was $75.00 per RPC share. The company plans to sell 1 million newly issued shares in its seasoned offering. The investment banking firm Robbum and Blindum (R&B) has agreed to underwrite the new stock issue for a 2.5% discount from the offering price, which RPC and R&B have agreed should be $0.75 per share lower than RPC's closing price the day before the offering is sold.

a. What is likely to happen to RPC's stock price when the plan for this seasoned offering is publicly announced?

b. Assuming that RPC's stock price closes at $72.75 per share the day before the seasoned offering is launched, what net proceeds will RPC receive from this offering?

c. Calculate the return earned by RPC's *existing* stockholders on their shares from the time before the seasoned offering was announced until it was actually sold for $72.75 per share.

d. Calculate the total cost of the seasoned equity offering to RPC's existing stockholders as a percentage of the offering proceeds.

International Common Stock Offerings

16-10. Assume that the Rome Electricity Company (REC) wishes to create a sponsored ADR program worth $300 million to trade its shares on the New York Stock Exchange. Also assume that REC is currently selling on the Borsa Italiana (the Italian Stock Exchange, in Milan) for €30 per share and that the current dollar/euro exchange rate is $1.25/€. American Bank and Trust (ABT) is handling the ADR issue for REC and has advised REC that the ideal trading price for utility company shares on the NYSE is about $75 per share (or per ADR).

a. Describe the precise steps that ABT must take in order to create an ADR issue meeting REC's objectives.

b. Assume that REC's stock price rises from €30 to €33 per share. If the exchange rate does not also change, what will happen to REC's ADR price?

c. If the euro appreciates from $1.25/€ to $1.29/€ but the price of REC's shares remains unchanged in euros, what will happen to REC's ADR price?

16-11. Assume that Nippon Computer Manufacturing Company (NCM) wishes to create a sponsored ADR program worth $250 million to trade its shares on Nasdaq. Assume that NCM is currently selling on the Tokyo Stock Exchange for ¥1,550 per share and that the current dollar/yen exchange rate is $0.008089/¥ (or, equivalently, ¥123.62/$). Metropolis Bank and Trust (MBT) is handling the ADR issue for NCM and has advised NCM that the ideal trading price for high-technology shares on the Nasdaq is about $20 per share (or per ADR).

a. Describe the precise steps MBT must take to create an ADR issue that meets NCM's goals.

b. Assume that NCM's stock price rises from ¥1,550 to ¥1,650 per share. If the exchange rate does not also change, what will happen to NCM's ADR price?

c. If the yen depreciates from $0.008089/¥ to $0.008050/¥ but the price of NCM's shares remains unchanged in yen, what will happen to NCM's ADR price?

16-12. Assume that Zurich Semiconductor Company (ZSC) wishes to create a sponsored ADR program worth $75 million to trade its shares on Nasdaq. Assume that ZSC is currently selling on the SWX Swiss Exchange for SF25.00 per share and that the current exchange rate between U.S. dollars and Swiss francs is $0.8264/SF. American Bank and Trust (ABT) is handling the ADR issue for ZSC and has advised the company that the ideal trading price for high-technology shares on the Nasdaq is about $60 per share (or per ADR).

a. Describe the precise steps ABT must take to create an ADR issue meeting ZSC's preferences.

b. Assume that ZSC's stock price declines from SF25.00 to SF22.50 per share. If the exchange rate does not also change, what will happen to ZSC's ADR price?

c. If the Swiss franc depreciates from $0.8264/SF to $0.7850/SF but the price of ZSC's shares remains unchanged in Swiss francs, how will ZSC's ADR price change?

THOMSON ONE | Business School Edition

16-13. Read the prospectus filed on February 15, 2006, by Morgan Hotels Group (ticker symbol, MHGC). (*Hint:* You can access the prospectus under the Filings tab and look for PROSP under Filing Type.) What type of securities did Morgan Hotels offer to the public for sale? What was the total dollar amount of funds raised by Morgan Hotels? If you had purchased this security at its offering price, what would be your total return to date?

16-14. On September 16, 2005, Google, Inc. (ticker symbol, GOOG) filed a prospectus for a seasoned equity offering. Read this prospectus and determine how many shares Google proposed to sell in the secondary offering. What was the proposed secondary offering price relative to the market price of Google at the time of the offering? How much did the secondary offering cost Google in underwriting discounts and commissions?

MINI-CASE: INVESTMENT BANKING AND THE PUBLIC SALE OF EQUITY SECURITIES

PC Unlimited wishes to go public by issuing 20 million shares of common stock at an offer price of $14.63 each. Skrail Underwriters, Inc., will charge a 6.5% underwriting fee.

1. How much will PC Unlimited raise in cash, assuming that all the shares sell?

2. If PC Unlimited wishes to raise $250 million in cash, what proportion of its initial offering must be sold?

3. Assume you purchased shares at the IPO price and then sold them after one year for $36.42 each. What is your after-tax return if you are in the 15% tax bracket for capital gains?

17

What Companies Do

GE Capital Issues AAA-Rated Bonds—at Junk Bond Rates

The default risk of individual corporate bond issues is routinely assessed by bond ratings agencies, which assign a rating that can range from AAA for bonds issued by the most creditworthy corporate borrowers to speculative-grade, C-rated bonds issued by extremely risky companies. Bonds rated BBB and higher are called "investment grade," and bonds with an original issuance rating of BB or lower are referred to as *high-yield bonds* or *junk bonds*. Investment-grade bonds are issued with (and subsequently trade with) lower yield spreads over U.S. Treasury bonds than are junk bonds, and AAA bonds have the lowest yield spreads of all corporate bonds. In early 2007, AAA bonds had an average yield spread of barely 100 basis points (one percentage point) above Treasuries, while junk bond yields hit a record low of less than four percentage points above Treasuries of similar maturity.

This welcoming environment for corporate bond issuers fundamentally changed when the subprime mortgage bond market soured during the summer of 2007, and it became far worse as the global credit crisis deepened throughout 2008. The average yield spread for AAA bonds rose from 204 basis points early in 2008 to a record 523 basis points in December, retreating slightly to 513 basis points in January 2009. Junk bond issuers fared much worse, as yield spreads over Treasuries soared to a record 1,754 basis points (17.54 *percentage points*) in December 2008 before retreating slightly in early 2009.

It was into this unwelcoming market that GE Capital chose to tread in January 2009. The firm decided to issue one of the first bond issues by a financial company borrower since the summer of 2008 that was not explicitly guaranteed by the Federal Deposit Insurance Corporation (FDIC). Despite carrying a AAA credit rating, GE Capital was forced to price its 30-year bond issue at a massive 400-basis-point (four-percentage-point) yield spread over comparable 30-year Treasury bonds. Not only was this yield spread extremely high by historical standards, it was also 100 basis points higher than the price for which existing AAA-rated GE Capital bonds were selling in the secondary market. The lessons from the GE Capital bond offering were clear: Historical pricing norms become far less relevant during a financial crisis, a time during which frightened investors must be offered substantial yield premiums to bear corporate default risk.

Source: Aline van Duyn, "Corporate Bonds Find Hope from New Issues," Financial Times (January 8, 2009). Copyright © 2009 Financial Times Ltd. All right reserved. Reproduced by permission.

Corporations and governments around the world issue long-term debt in order to finance capital investments or to fund current operations. The vast majority of external capital raised by companies each year is debt rather than equity, and most debt is long-term.[1] This chapter examines the key features, costs, advantages, and disadvantages of two sources of capital for business: long-term debt and leasing.

17.1 Characteristics of Long-Term Debt Financing

Long-term debt is the dominant form of long-term, external financing in all developed economies. On the balance sheet, accountants classify debt as long-term if it matures in more than one year. Firms obtain long-term debt by negotiating with a financial institution (or a syndicate consisting of several institutions) for a term loan or by selling bonds.

The Choice between Public and Private Debt Issues

Once a firm's managers decide to employ long-term debt financing, they face a series of practical choices regarding how to structure the debt. The first decision managers make is whether to issue public or private debt. In the United States, public long-term debt offerings involve selling securities (bonds and notes) directly to investors, usually with the help of investment bankers. Firms must register these offerings with the SEC. Most long-term corporate bond offerings take the form of unsecured debentures, and the vast majority of U.S. public debt offerings are **fixed-rate offerings**, meaning they have a coupon rate that remains constant.

Private debt issues usually take one of two forms. **Loans** are private debt agreements arranged between corporate borrowers and financial institutions, especially commercial banks, whereas **private placements** are unregistered security offerings sold directly to *accredited investors*. The best-known and most common form of loan is a *term loan* arranged between a borrower and a single bank. However, much more funding is raised via *syndicated loans* that are arranged for a single borrower but funded by multiple banks. The overwhelming majority of both term loans and syndicated loans extended are **floating-rate issues**, where the loan is priced at a fixed spread above a base interest rate, usually the London Interbank Offered Rate (**LIBOR**) or the U.S. bank **prime lending rate**. The interest rate paid by issuers of floating-rate debt thus moves as the base interest rate changes.

Researchers have analyzed the factors that influence a firm's choice between issuing public or private debt.[2] Relative costs are obviously important, and higher fixed costs for public issues lead to the unsurprising prediction that firms will issue larger offerings publicly and smaller ones privately. However, other factors influence the decision on a public versus private issue, such as the value of ongoing creditor monitoring of the borrower, and whether the borrower has attractive investment opportunities. In general, private borrowing is preferable for firms where growth options represent more of the firm's value than do

---

[1] By definition, governments can issue only debt, because few investors would wish to purchase "government equity" even if such a financial creature existed. Although government debt issuance is an extremely important and interesting topic, we henceforth focus exclusively on corporate debt issuance. Nonetheless, the quantity of sovereign debt that governments around the world are expected to issue during 2009–2010 is enormous. The *Financial Times* predicted in September 2008 that European governments will issue more than $1 trillion in new debt during 2009 and that the U.S. government will issue $2 trillion (Gangahar 2008).

[2] Key early theoretical papers in this literature include those by Diamond (1991) and Rajan (1992). The choice between public and private debt in the United States is examined empirically in Houston and James (1996), Carey (1998), and Krishnaswami, Spindt, and Subramaniam (1999). Anderson and Makhija (1999) perform a similar analysis for Japan.

tangible assets and for companies with nontransparent production processes, because in these firms creditor monitoring helps to ensure that the firm uses funds properly.

Loan Covenants

Long-term debt agreements normally include certain *loan covenants*. These are contractual clauses that place specific operating and financial constraints on the borrower. Debt covenants do not normally place a burden on a financially sound business and typically remain in force for the life of the debt agreement.[3] Covenants allow the lender to monitor and control the borrower's activities to protect itself against the agency problem created by the differing objectives of owners and lenders. Without these provisions, the borrower could take advantage of the lender by investing in riskier projects without compensating lenders with a higher interest rate on their loans.

There are two types of covenants. *Positive covenants* require the borrower to take a specific action, and *negative covenants* prohibit certain actions.

Positive Covenants   Positive covenants specify things that a borrower "must do." Some of the most common positive covenants include the following.

1. The borrower must maintain satisfactory accounting records in accordance with generally accepted accounting principles (GAAP).
2. The borrower must supply audited financial statements.
3. The borrower must pay taxes and other liabilities when due.
4. The borrower must maintain all facilities in good working order.
5. The borrower must maintain a minimum level of *net working capital*. Inadequate liquidity is a common precursor to default.
6. The borrower must maintain life insurance policies on certain "key employees" without whom the firm's future would be in doubt.
7. The borrower is often considered to be in default on all debts if it is in default on any debt to any lender. This is known as a **cross-default covenant**.
8. Occasionally, a covenant specifically requires the borrower to spend the borrowed funds on a proven financial need.

JOB INTERVIEW QUESTION

What are negative covenants and how do they benefit lenders?

Negative Covenants   Negative covenants specify what a borrower "must not do." Common negative covenants include the following.

1. Borrowers may not sell receivables because doing so could cause a long-run cash shortage if the borrower uses the proceeds to meet current obligations.
2. Long-term lenders often impose fixed asset restrictions. These constrain the firm with respect to the liquidation, acquisition, and encumbrance of fixed assets because any of these actions could damage the firm's ability to repay its debt.
3. Many debt agreements prohibit borrowing additional long-term debt or require that additional borrowing be subordinated to the original loan. **Subordination** means that all subsequent or more junior creditors agree to wait until all claims of the senior debt are satisfied in full before having their own claims satisfied.
4. Borrowers are prohibited from entering into certain types of leases in order to limit their additional fixed-payment obligations.

---

[3]Debt covenants have been extensively examined in the finance literature beginning with what remains a classic analysis by Smith and Warner (1979). Subsequent papers include those by El-Gazzar and Pastena (1990), Press and Weintrop (1990), Billett, King, and Mauer (2007), Chava and Roberts (2008), and Roberts and Sufi (2008).

5. Occasionally, the lender prohibits business combinations by requiring the borrower to agree not to consolidate, merge, or combine in any way with another firm because such action could significantly change the borrower's operating and financial risk.
6. To prevent liquidation of assets through large salary payments, the lender may prohibit or limit salary increases for specified employees.
7. A relatively common provision prohibits the firm's annual cash dividend payments from exceeding 50%–70% of its net earnings or a specified dollar amount.

In the process of negotiating the terms of long-term debt, the borrower and lender must agree to an acceptable set of covenants. If the borrower violates a covenant, then the lender may demand immediate repayment, waive the violation and continue the loan, or waive the violation but alter the terms of the original debt agreement.

During the leveraged buyout boom that climaxed in early 2007, many "covenant lite" bonds were issued that contained few, if any, restrictions on borrower activities. As credit markets crumbled in 2008 and 2009, the value of these bonds plummeted owing to the lack of bondholder protections usually offered by covenants. In response, investors demanded that newly issued bonds contain numerous covenants to restrict borrower activities.

Cost of Long-Term Debt

In addition to specifying positive and negative covenants, the long-term debt agreement specifies the interest rate, the timing of interest payments, and the size of principal repayment. The major factors affecting the cost, or interest rate, of long-term debt are loan maturity, loan size, borrower risk, and the basic cost of money.

Loan Maturity   Generally, the yield curve is upward sloping, which implies that long-term loans have higher interest rates than short-term loans. Factors that can cause an upward-sloping yield curve include (1) the general expectation of higher future inflation or interest rates; (2) lender preferences for shorter-term, more liquid loans; and (3) greater demand for long-term rather than short-term loans relative to the supply of such loans. In a practical sense, the longer the term, the greater the default risk associated with the loan; therefore, to compensate for all these factors, the lender typically charges a higher interest rate on long-term loans.[4]

Loan Size   The size of the loan often affects the interest cost of borrowing in an inverse manner because of economies of scale. Loan administration costs per dollar borrowed are likely to decrease with increasing loan size. However, the risk to the lender increases, since larger loans result in less diversification. The size of the loan sought by each borrower must therefore be evaluated to determine the net administrative cost versus risk trade-off.

Borrower Risk   The higher the firm's operating leverage, the greater the volatility of its operating cash flows. Also, the higher the borrower's financial leverage, conveniently reflected in a high financial *debt ratio* or a low *times interest earned ratio*, the greater the volatility of the shareholders' cash flows. The lender's main concern is with the borrower's ability to fully repay the loan as prescribed in the debt agreement. A lender uses an overall assessment of the borrower's operating and financial risk, along with information on past payment patterns, when setting the interest rate on a loan.

---

[4]The debt maturity structure choice for publicly traded U.S. firms is analyzed empirically in Barclay and Smith (1995a, 1995b); Guedes and Opler (1996); Scherr and Hulburt (2001); and Billett, King, and Mauer (2007). International differences in average corporate debt maturity are described and examined empirically in Demirgüç-Kunt and Maksimovic (1999).

Basic Cost of Money   The cost of money is the basis for determining the actual interest rate charged. Generally, the rate on U.S. Treasury securities with equivalent maturities is used as the basic (lowest-risk) cost of money. To determine the actual interest rate to be charged, the lender will add premiums for borrower risk and other factors to this basic cost of money for the given maturity. Alternatively, some lenders determine a prospective borrower's risk class and find the rates charged on loans with similar maturities and terms to firms in the same risk class. Instead of having to determine a risk premium, the lender can use the risk premium prevailing in the marketplace for similar loans.

Concept Review Questions	1. What factors should a manager consider when deciding on the amount and type of long-term debt to be used to finance a business?
	2. What factors should a manager consider when negotiating the loan covenants in a long-term debt agreement?
	3. How can managers estimate their firms' cost of long-term debt prior to meeting with a lender?

17.2 TERM LOANS

A **term loan** is made by a financial institution to a business and has an initial maturity of more than 1 year, generally 5 to 12 years. Term loans are often made to finance permanent working capital needs, to pay for machinery and equipment, or to liquidate other loans.

Term loans are essentially private placements of debt. Firms typically negotiate term loans directly with the lender instead of using an investment banker as an intermediary. An advantage of term loans over publicly traded debt is their flexibility. The securities (bonds or notes) in a public debt issue are usually purchased by many different investors, so it is almost impossible to alter the terms of the borrowing agreement should new business conditions make such changes desirable. With a term loan, the borrower can negotiate with a single lender for modifications to the borrowing agreement.[5]

Companies typically arrange loans with commercial banks as part of a larger, ongoing banking relationship. Large companies often have dozens of these bilateral relationships, but a critical decision for smaller firms is whether to maintain one large banking relationship or several smaller bilateral relationships in order to minimize the risk of not being able to arrange financing during an emergency. The primary benefit of a banking relationship for companies is not lower loan rates so much as the larger amounts that can be borrowed.

The primary lenders making term loans to businesses are commercial banks, insurance companies, pension funds, regional development companies, the U.S. federal government's Small Business Administration, small business investment companies, commercial finance companies, and equipment manufacturers' financing subsidiaries.

Characteristics of Term Loan Agreements

The actual term loan agreement is a formal contract ranging from a few to a few hundred pages. The following items commonly appear in the document: the amount and maturity of the loan, payment dates, interest rate, positive and negative covenants, collateral (if

---

[5]Petersen and Rajan (1994) examine U.S. companies and conclude that fewer, larger relationships are generally preferable to numerous, smaller ones. In contrast, Detragiache, Garella, and Guiso (2000) find that Italian companies must pursue exactly the opposite strategy and maintain multiple bilateral banking relationships in order to ensure funding when needed. Ongena and Smith (2001) show that Norwegian companies frequently terminate their banking relationships as they mature, demonstrating that these firms do not become "locked into" bilateral relationships. On the other hand, Santos and Winton (2008) show that banks do exploit their informational hold over corporate borrowers by increasing loan rates during economic recessions, when firms have fewer external borrowing options.

any), purpose of the loan, action to be taken in the event the agreement is violated, and stock purchase warrants. Of these, payment dates, collateral requirements, and stock purchase warrants require some discussion.

Payment Dates   Term loan agreements usually specify whether the loan payments are made monthly, quarterly, or annually. Generally, these equal payments fully repay the interest and principal over the life of the loan. Occasionally, a term loan agreement will require periodic interest payments over the life of the loan followed by a large lump-sum payment at maturity. This so-called **balloon payment** represents the entire loan principal if the periodic payments represent only interest.

Collateral Requirements   Term lending arrangements may be unsecured or secured. Secured loans have specific assets pledged as **collateral**. The collateral often takes the form of an asset such as machinery and equipment, plant, inventory, pledges of accounts receivable, and pledges of securities. Unsecured loans are obtained without pledging specific assets as collateral. Whether lenders require collateral depends in part on the lender's evaluation of the borrower's financial condition.[6]

Term lending is often referred to as asset-backed lending, though term lenders in reality are primarily cash flow lenders. They hope and expect to be repaid out of cash flow but require collateral both as an alternative source of repayment and as "ransom" to decrease the incentive of borrowing firms to default (because a defaulting borrower would lose the use of valuable corporate assets). Most pledged assets are secured by a **lien**, which is a legal contract specifying under what conditions the lender can take title to the asset if the loan is not repaid and prohibiting the borrowing firm from selling or disposing of the asset without the lender's consent. The liens serve two purposes: they establish clearly the lender's right to seize and liquidate collateral if the borrower defaults; and they serve notice to subsequent lenders of a prior claim on the asset(s).

Not all assets can be readily used as collateral, of course. For an asset to be useful as collateral, it should (1) be nonperishable, (2) be relatively homogeneous in quality, (3) have a high value relative to its bulk, and (4) have a well-established secondary market where seized assets can be turned into cash without a severe price penalty.

Stock Purchase Warrant   The corporate borrower often gives the lender certain financial benefits, usually **stock purchase warrants**, in addition to the payment of interest and repayment of principal. Warrants are instruments that give their holder the right to purchase a certain number of shares of the firm's common stock at a specified price over a certain period. These are designed to entice institutional lenders to make long-term loans, possibly under relatively favorable terms. Warrants are also frequently used as "sweeteners" for corporate bond issues.

Concept Review Questions	4. Suppose that a specialty retail firm takes out a term loan from a bank. Which do you think the bank would prefer to receive as collateral: a claim on the firm's inventory or its receivables? 5. A problem with collateral is that its value is positively correlated with the borrower's ability to repay. Explain.

---

[6]The use of collateral as backing for a loan has been analyzed theoretically by Stulz and Johnson (1985) and Igawa and Kanatas (1990) and has been examined empirically by Booth (1992). This study supports earlier findings that collateral is associated with higher, rather than lower, interest rates (spreads over a base rate) on secured loans. This implies that collateral allows riskier borrowers to receive credit that would not be granted to them through unsecured lending.

17.3 CORPORATE BONDS

A *corporate bond* is a debt instrument indicating that a corporation has borrowed a certain amount of money from institutions or individuals and promises to repay it in the future under clearly defined terms. Firms issue bonds with maturities of 10–30 years (debt securities with an original maturity of 1–10 years are called *notes*) and with a par value (face value) of $1,000.[7] The coupon interest rate on a bond represents the percentage of the bond's par value that the firm will pay to investors each year. In the United States, firms typically pay interest semiannually in two equal coupon payments. Bondholders receive the par value back when the bonds mature.

Popular Types of Bonds

Bonds can be classified in a variety of ways. Here we break them into traditional bonds, the basic types that have been around for years, and new, innovative bonds. Table 17.1 summarizes the traditional types of bonds issued by corporations in terms of their key characteristics and priority of lender's claim in the event of default. Note that the first three types, **debentures**, **subordinated debentures**, and **income bonds**, are unsecured; whereas the last three, **mortgage bonds**, **collateral trust bonds**, and **equipment trust certificates**, are secured.[8]

Over the years, corporations have developed a profusion of new debt instruments designed to attract a unique clientele of bond investors who, it is presumed, would be willing to pay a higher price for a given special feature. A detailed discussion of these new offerings is beyond the scope of an overview chapter, but Table 17.2 surveys the characteristics of a few of them.

Legal Aspects of Corporate Bonds

When they issue bonds, corporations raise hundreds of millions of dollars from many unrelated investors. The dispersion in the investor base creates a need for special legal arrangements to protect lenders.

Bond Indenture A bond **indenture** is a complex and lengthy legal document stating the conditions under which a bond has been issued. It specifies both the rights of the bondholders and the duties of the issuing corporation. In addition to specifying the interest and principal payment dates and containing various positive and negative covenants, the indenture frequently contains *sinking fund requirements* and, if the bond is secured, provisions with respect to a security interest.

Sinking Fund Requirements A positive covenant often included in a bond indenture is a **sinking fund** requirement. Its objective is to provide for the systematic retirement of bonds prior to their maturity.[9] To carry out this requirement, the corporation makes semiannual or annual payments to a trustee who uses the payments to retire bonds by

---

[7]Corporate bonds are occasionally issued that mature in 50 or 100 years.

[8]Although not a direct source of financing for individual corporations, the market for **mortgage-backed securities (MBS)** grew rapidly through mid-2007, at which point it was a $500 billion annual business in the United States alone. MBS offerings are created by pooling large numbers of home mortgage loans and then selling securities backed by these mortgages directly to investors. This market revolutionized home mortgage lending in the United States because it allowed financial institutions to economize on the use of their capital by originating mortgage loans and then selling them to MBS specialists. Unfortunately, the credit crisis that gripped the world during 2008–2009 was triggered by rapidly rising default rates in the U.S. mortgage-backed securities market—especially in the "subprime" segment.

[9]Dunn and Spatt (1984) examine sinking funds theoretically; Dyl and Joehnk (1979), Ho and Singer (1984), Mitchell (1991), Wu (1993), and Jiménez, Salas, and Saurina (2006) examine sinking funds empirically.

Table 17.1 Features of Conventional Bonds

BOND TYPE	CHARACTERISTICS	PRIORITY OF LENDER'S CLAIM
Debentures	Unsecured bonds that only creditworthy firms can issue. Most convertible bonds are debentures.	Seniority is the same as those of any general creditor. May have other unsecured bonds subordinate to them.
Subordinated debentures	Claims are not satisfied until those of the creditors holding certain (senior) debts have been fully satisfied.	Claim is that of a general creditor, but not as high as a senior debt claim.
Income bonds	Payment of interest is required only when earnings are available from which to make such payment. Commonly issued in reorganization of a failed or failing firm.	Seniority is that of a general creditor. Not in default when interest payments are missed, because they are contingent only on earnings being available.
Mortgage bonds	Secured by real estate or buildings. Can be *open-end* (additional bonds issued against collateral), *limited open-end* (a specified amount of additional bonds can be issued against collateral), or *closed-end*; may contain an *after-acquired clause* (property subsequently acquired becomes part of mortgage collateral).	Seniority is on proceeds from sale of mortgaged assets; if not fully satisfied, the lender becomes a general creditor. The *first mortgage* claim must be satisfied before distribution of proceeds to *second mortgage* holders. A number of mortgages can be issued against the same collateral.
Collateral trust bonds	Secured by stock and/or bonds that are owned by the issuer. Collateral value is generally 25%–35% higher than bond value.	Claim is on proceeds from stock and/or bond collateral; if not fully satisfied, the lender becomes a general creditor.
Equipment trust certificates	Used to finance transportation equipment—airplanes, trucks, boats, and railroad cars. A trustee buys such an asset with funds raised through the sale of trust certificates and then leases it to the firm, which, after making the final scheduled lease payment, receives title to the asset. A type of leasing.	Claim is on proceeds from the sale of the asset; if proceeds do not satisfy outstanding debt, trust certificate lenders become general creditors.

purchasing them in the marketplace. This process is simplified by the inclusion of a limited call feature, which permits the issuer to repurchase a fraction of outstanding bonds each year at a "call price." The trustee will exercise this option only when sufficient bonds cannot be purchased in the market place or when the bond's market price exceeds its call price.

The typical life of a U.S. corporate bond is far less than its stated maturity would imply. The reasons for this are the ability of companies to call (and then refinance) bonds and the pervasiveness of mandated sinking funds in long-term U.S. debt security issues. Sinking funds work in such a way that the typical bond issue with, say, $100 million principal amount and a 15-year maturity will probably have only a few million dollars' worth of bonds still outstanding when the last bonds are redeemed 15 years after issuance. Depending on the terms of the sinking fund, the actual average maturity of this issue (the weighted average years outstanding) will probably be less than 10 years, not the 15 years originally stated.

Because sinking funds force corporations to redeem some bonds early, they reduce the risk of default for two reasons. First, sinking funds increase the likelihood that investors will become aware of any financial difficulties encountered by the issuing firm early (when it misses a sinking fund payment) rather than late. This will trigger the demand for effective corrective action, up to and including the removal of the issuing firm's incumbent management team. Second, because at maturity only a fraction of a given bond issue will

Table 17.2   Characteristics of Bonds with Special Features

BOND TYPE	CHARACTERISTICS[a]
Zero (or low) coupon bonds	Issued with no (zero) or a very low coupon (stated interest) rate and sold at a large discount from par. A significant portion (or all) of the investor's return therefore comes from gain in value (i.e., par value minus purchase price) and is paid at maturity. Generally callable at par value. Because the issuer can annually deduct the current year's interest accrual without having to actually pay the interest until the bond matures (or is called), its cash flow each year is increased by the amount of the tax shield provided by the interest deduction. The investor must pay taxes on the implicit interest payments even though no cash inflow is received.
Junk bonds	Debt rated Ba or lower by Moody's or BB or lower by Standard & Poor's. Beginning in the mid-1980s, commonly used by rapidly growing firms to obtain growth capital, most often as a way to finance mergers and takeovers of other firms. High-risk bonds with high yields—typically yielding at least three percentage points more than high-quality corporate debt.
Floating-rate bonds	Stated interest rate is adjusted periodically within stated limits in response to changes in specified money or capital market rates. Popular when future inflation and interest rates are uncertain. Tend to sell at close to par as a result of the automatic adjustment to changing market conditions. Some issues provide for annual redemption at par at the option of the bondholder.
Extendible notes	Debt instruments with short maturities, typically 1–5 years, that can be redeemed or renewed for a similar period at the option of the holders. Similar to a floating-rate bond. An issue might be a series of 3-year renewable notes over a period of 15 years; every 3 years, the notes could be extended for another 3 years at a new rate that is competitive with market interest rates prevailing at the time of renewal.
Putable bonds	Bonds that can be redeemed at par (typically, $1,000) at the option of their holder either at specified dates, such as 3–5 years after the date of issue and every 1 to 5 years thereafter, or when and if the firm takes specified actions such as being acquired, acquiring another company, or issuing a large amount of additional debt. In return for the right to "put the bond" at specified times or actions by the firm, the bond's yield is lower than that of a nonputable bond.

[a]The claims of lenders (i.e., bondholders) against issuers of each of these types of bonds vary, depending on their other features. Each of these bonds can be unsecured or secured.

remain outstanding, the issuing firm's managers will have less incentive to default on the issue or attempt to expropriate bondholder wealth by filing for bankruptcy protection.

Security Interest   Any interest in a property or asset that a lender takes as security or collateral for a loan is called a *security interest*. The bond indenture identifies any collateral pledged against the bond. Usually, the title to the collateral is attached to the indenture, which also describes the collateral's disposition under various circumstances. The protection of bond collateral is crucial to increasing the safety—and thus to enhancing the marketability—of a bond issue.

Trustee   A **trustee** is a third party to a bond indenture and can be an individual, a corporation, or, most often, a commercial bank trust department. The trustee, whose services are paid for by the issuer, acts as a "watchdog" on behalf of the bondholders, making sure that the issuer does not default on its contractual responsibilities. The trustee is empowered to take specified actions on behalf of bondholders if the borrower violates any indenture terms.

Methods of Issuing Corporate Bonds

Public issues of corporate bonds in the United States must be registered with the Securities and Exchange Commission, and large offerings are generally underwritten by an investment banking syndicate. However, there is tremendous variation in actual offering procedures, and this heterogeneity has increased over time as new debt securities have developed. In particular, two financial and regulatory innovations transformed U.S. bond-issuance patterns. First, the introduction of *shelf registration* in the early 1980s allowed corporations to register large blocks of debt securities and then sell them in discrete pieces over the subsequent two years as market conditions warranted. Shelf registration can be used for both debt and equity offerings, but not all companies use this technique for selling stock.[10] In contrast, most companies that can use shelf registration for debt offerings do so.

The second major innovation occurred in 1990, when the SEC created a new private-placement market by implementing *Rule 144A*. This allowed qualified institutional investors (those with assets exceeding $100 million) to trade nonregistered securities among themselves, and corporate issuers soon found that this was a welcoming market for new equity and, especially, debt issues. Because Rule 144A issues offer investors much greater liquidity than do traditional private placements and are less costly than traditional public offerings, U.S. and international corporations sell a total of between $400 billion and $500 billion in securities most years under this rule.

General Characteristics of a Bond Issue

Three characteristics commonly observed in a U.S. bond issue are (1) a call feature, (2) a conversion feature, and (3) stock purchase warrants. Each of these features grants an option, either to the issuer or the investor, that has a significant impact on a bond's value.

Call Feature   The call feature is included in most corporate bond issues and gives the issuer the opportunity to repurchase bonds prior to maturity. The *call price* is the stated price at which bonds may be repurchased. Sometimes the call privilege is exercisable only during a certain period, and usually bonds are not callable in the first few years. Typically, the call price exceeds the par value of a bond by an amount equal to one year's interest. For example, a $1,000 bond with a 10% coupon interest rate would be callable for around $1,100 [$1,000 + (10% × $1,000)]. The amount by which the call price exceeds the bond's par value is commonly referred to as the *call premium*. This premium compensates bondholders for having the bond called away from them and is the cost to the issuer of calling the bonds.

The call feature is generally advantageous to the issuer because it enables the issuer to retire outstanding debt prior to maturity. Thus, when interest rates fall, an issuer can call an outstanding bond and reissue a new bond at a lower interest rate. When interest rates rise, the call privilege will not be exercised, except possibly to meet sinking fund requirements. Of course, to issue a callable bond, the firm must pay a higher interest rate than that on noncallable bonds of equal risk in order to compensate bondholders for the risk of having the bonds called away.

Conversion Feature   The conversion feature of **convertible bonds** allows bondholders to exchange each bond for a stated number of shares of common stock. Bondholders will

JOB INTERVIEW QUESTION

Should a callable bond have a lower or higher yield than a similar noncallable bond? Why would a firm want to issue callable bonds?

---

[10]Autore, Kumar, and Shome (2008).

convert their bonds only when the market price of the stock is greater than the conversion price, hence providing a profit for the bondholder. Because the option to convert into stock is valuable, the interest rate paid on convertible bonds is usually lower than the rate on traditional bonds, all else being equal.

Stock Purchase Warrants Like term loans, bonds occasionally have warrants attached as "sweeteners" to make them more attractive to prospective buyers. As we noted previously, a *stock purchase warrant* gives its holder the right to purchase a certain number of shares of common stock at a specified price over a certain period of time.

High-Yield Bonds

The risk of publicly traded bond issues is assessed by independent agencies such as Moody's and Standard & Poor's (S&P). Both agencies have 10 major *bond ratings* derived by using financial ratio and cash flow analyses. Bonds rated Baa or higher by Moody's (BBB by S&P) are known as **investment-grade bonds**. Bonds rated below investment-grade are known as **high-yield bonds**, **speculative bonds**, or **junk bonds**. As the pejorative name suggests, junk bonds carry a much higher default risk than do investment-grade bonds, but they also offer higher yields. Prior to the late 1970s, such issues were quite rare. Historically, most of these speculative bonds trading in the market were **fallen angels**, bonds that received investment-grade ratings when they were first issued but later fell to junk status.

Junk bond default rates typically peak during recessions. When junk bond default rates rose sharply during the 1990–1991 recession, many commentators wrote off high-yield debt as a viable financing tool. As Figure 17.1 shows, the speculative bond market has prospered since then, at least in terms of the par value of junk bonds outstanding. Default rates rose from 1999 to 2002 and, not surprisingly, rose again during the global recession in 2008.[11] Junk bond investors recognize that they are assuming much of the issuing firm's operating (business) risk when they purchase high-yield debt, but they are willing to do so in return for promised yields that approach the returns earned by stockholders. Of course, a higher *promised* yield may or may not result in a higher *realized* return, because the higher yield reflects a higher likelihood that the borrower will default (in whole or in part) on the bond sometime during its life. In other words, owing to the risk of default and the probability that investors experience losses when default occurs, the expected return on junk bonds is generally well below the promised return (i.e., the yield to maturity).

JOB INTERVIEW QUESTION

Can the yield to maturity on a firm's junk bonds be higher than the expected rate of return on its stock?

After a bond is rated, the rating is not changed unless the likelihood of the company's defaulting on the bond issue changes. It is perhaps surprising that bond issuers themselves pay the ratings companies to issue ratings on newly issued bonds (because bonds are essentially unmarketable without a rating). Additionally, having the issuing firm pay for ratings allows the firm to communicate sensitive information privately to the ratings agency. This information can then be usefully reflected in market data without being disclosed to competitors. Empirical research has shown that bond ratings and, especially, ratings changes convey economically relevant information to investors (Dichev and Piotroski 2001). However, the reputations of all the major ratings agencies were severely damaged during the crisis years of 2008–2009 when many of the bonds—especially mortgage-related securities—that these agencies had rated AAA performed dismally, with some ending up worth a mere 20 cents per dollar of par value.

---

[11]The New York University Salomon Center predicted that 2009 junk bond default rates could reach double digits.

FIGURE 17.1

Par Value Amounts Outstanding and Default Rates for High-Yield Bonds (Junk Bonds), 1971–2008Q3.

Source: Edward I. Altman and Gaurav Bana, "Report on Defaults and Returns on High Yield Bonds: The Year 2002 in Review and Market Outlook." NYU Salomon Center, February 2003, Figure 1.

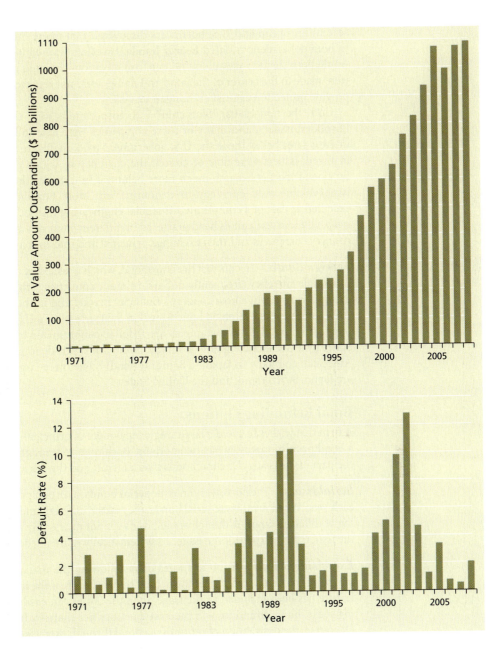

International Corporate Bond Financing

Companies can sell bonds internationally by tapping the *Eurobond* or *foreign bond* markets. Both of these provide established, creditworthy borrowers with the opportunity to obtain large amounts of long-term debt financing quickly and efficiently, in their choice of currency, and with flexible repayment terms.

Eurobonds   A **Eurobond** is issued by an international borrower and sold to investors in countries with currencies other than the currency in which the bond is denominated. A dollar-denominated bond issued by a U.S. corporation and sold to European investors is an example of a Eurobond. The Eurobond market first developed in the early 1960s, when several European and U.S. borrowers discovered that many European investors wanted to hold dollar-denominated **bearer bonds**. Investors wanted bearer bonds because they would both shelter investment income from taxation—because coupon interest payments were made to the bearer of the bond and names were not reported to tax authorities—and provide protection against exchange-rate risk.

Until the mid-1980s, "blue-chip" U.S. corporations were the largest single class of Eurobond issuers, and many of these companies were able to borrow in this market at interest rates below those the U.S. government paid on Treasury bonds.[12] As the market matured, issuers were able to choose the currency in which they borrowed. Later, the Eurobond market became much more balanced in terms of the mix of borrowers, total issue volume, and currency of denomination. Most Eurobond issues, in fact, were executed as part of a complicated financial engineering transaction known as a *currency swap*, wherein companies headquartered in different countries issue bonds in their home-country currencies and then exchange principal and interest payments with each other.

Foreign Bonds   In contrast to a Eurobond, which is issued by an international borrower in a single currency (frequently dollars) in many countries, a **foreign bond** is issued by a foreign borrower in a host country's financial market and in the host country's currency. A Swiss franc–denominated bond issued in Switzerland by a U.S. company is an example of a foreign bond. Other examples are a dollar-denominated bond issued in the United States by a German company (a Yankee bond) and a yen-denominated bond issued by an American company in Japan (a Samurai bond).[13] The three largest foreign bond markets are Japan, Switzerland, and the United States.

Bond Refunding Options

A firm that wishes to avoid a large single repayment of principal in the future or to **refund** a bond prior to maturity has two options. Both require foresight and careful analysis on the part of the issuer. One method is a serial issue, and the other is exercising a call.

Serial Issues   The borrower can issue **serial bonds**, a certain proportion of which mature each year. When firms issue serial bonds, they attach different interest rates to bonds maturing at different times. Although serial bonds cannot necessarily be retired at the option of the issuer, they do permit the issuer to systematically retire the debt.

Exercising a Call   If interest rates drop following the issuance of a bond, the issuer may wish to refund (refinance) the debt with new bonds at the lower interest rate. If a call feature has been included in the issue, then the issuer can easily retire it. In an accounting sense, bond refunding will increase earnings per share by lowering interest expense. Of course, the desirability of refunding a bond through exercise of a call is not necessarily obvious, and assessing its long-term consequences requires the use of present value techniques. This bond refunding decision is another application of the capital budgeting techniques described in Chapters 7 and 8.

Here the firm must find the net present value (NPV) of the bond-refunding cash flows. The initial investment is the incremental after-tax cash outflows associated with calling the old bonds and issuing new bonds, and the annual cash flow savings are the after-tax cash savings that are expected from the reduced debt payments on the new lower-interest bond. These cash flows are the same each year. The resulting cash flow pattern surrounding

---

[12]Kim and Stulz (1988).

[13]Similar issues in Britain would be called Bulldog bonds, and issues in Switzerland and the Netherlands would be referred to as Heidi and Rembrandt bonds, respectively.

WHAT COMPANIES DO GLOBALLY

Islamic Finance: How Do You Sell Bonds When You Cannot Charge Interest?

The past two decades have seen a handful of Muslim countries modify their commercial banking laws to make them consistent with one of the principles of *Syariah* banking: the prohibition on the charging of interest on loans. Several countries have allowed banks to operate under this *Syariah* principle, which is similar to the Catholic church's injunction against usury (charging interest) during the Middle Ages in Europe. Needless to say, bankers have found this restriction on a core source of revenue to be a serious challenge, but many have been able to comply with the religious intent of the laws by structuring loans as investment partnerships—where the bank's return comes in the form of a share of profits—or by structuring loan payments as fees or dividends rather than interest.

While Islamic banking has made few inroads in global markets, it has been relatively successful within the borders of at least some of the countries that have adopted it. But how do you attract international investors to an Islamic bond issue when the *Syariah*-based restriction on payment of interest applies? As it happens, several governments and international development banks have executed successful Islamic finance bond offerings since July 2002. That month, the Malaysian government raised $600 million with the world's first Global Islamic Bond offering targeted primarily at investors in West Asia and the Middle East. The bond issue carried an investment-grade rating, and investors were promised a return (comparable to dividend payments) equal to 0.95 percentage points above LIBOR, funded by rentals from Malaysian government properties.

The second Islamic bond offering was even more intriguing, since the issuer was the government of Iran and this was its first international capital market offering since the fundamentalist regime came to power in 1979. The €500 million issue was assigned a B+ bond rating by Fitch and was priced at 425 basis points over the reference rate for interest-rate swaps of similar risk. Perhaps most surprisingly, the issue was targeted at European investors and sold out very quickly.

The market for Islamic finance expanded rapidly during the five years after 2002, reaching a record issuance total of $30.8 billion worldwide in 2007. By far the largest issuer was the nation of Malaysia, though several other Moslem governments and corporations also issued large *sukuk* bond issues. Despite this promising growth, market analysts bemoaned the fact that no major Persian Gulf national government (especially Saudi Arabia) had chosen to issue Islamic bonds, which would have provided a widely traded benchmark rate against which other *sukuks* could be priced.

The market for Islamic bonds took a dramatic turn for the worse during 2008, with issuance falling 56% to $14.9 billion. Many hopeful issuers, including the governments of Great Britain and Indonesia, were forced to cancel planned offerings, and an executed issue by the Turkish government attracted purchasers for only one-fourth of the bond offering. Two rationales were given to explain the *sukuk* market's contraction during 2008. First, and most obviously, the entire global market for new security issuance contracted sharply that year, though the Islamic bond market contracted by much more. Second, the religious legitimacy of the most important *sukuk* bond market was undermined early in 2008 when a major Islamic scholar in Bahrain ruled that the typical bond structure provided insufficient risk sharing and so the return on the bond was more similar to interest than to the required profit sharing.

Despite these problems, the Islamic finance market seems likely to prosper over the long term. Once issuers adjust bond structures to be fully *Syariah*-compliant and the overall bond issuance market revives, *sukuk* issuance will likely rebound as well.

Sources: John Burton, "Islamic Bond Issues Seen Dropping Further," *Financial Times* (January 22, 2009); Delphine Strauss, "Islamic-Style Turkish Bonds Fail to Appeal," *Financial Times* (January 29, 2009).

this decision is "typical": an outflow followed by a series of inflows. The bond refunding decision can be made using the following three-step procedure.

Step 1. *Find the initial investment* by estimating the incremental after-tax cash out-flow required at time 0 to call the old bond and issue a new bond in its place. Any overlapping interest resulting from the need to pay interest on both the old and new bonds is treated as part of the initial investment.

Step 2. *Find the annual cash flow savings,* which is the difference between the annual after-tax debt payments with the old and new bonds. This cash flow stream will be an annuity, with a life equal to the maturity of the old bond.

Step 3. Use the after-tax cost of the new debt (as the discount rate) to *find the net present value (NPV)* by subtracting the initial investment from the present value of the annual cash flow savings. The annual cash flow savings is a contractually fixed cash flow stream that represents the difference between two contractual debt-service streams, the old bond and the new bond. Therefore, the appropriate discount rate should reflect the risk of the firm's debt (which is tied to these same contractually fixed cash flows). That is, we discount these cash flows at the firm's cost of debt. Moreover, we follow convention and *use the after-tax cost of debt as the discount rate.* If NPV is positive then the proposed refunding is recommended; otherwise, it should be rejected.

Application of this bond refunding decision procedure is illustrated in the Example that follows. First, however, a few tax-related points must be clarified.

Call Premiums The amount by which the call price exceeds the par value of the bond is the **call premium**. It is paid by the issuer to the bondholder to buy back outstanding bonds prior to maturity. The call premium is treated as a tax-deductible expense in the year of the call.

Bond Discounts and Premiums When bonds are sold at a discount or at a premium, the firm is required to amortize (write off) the discount or premium in equal portions over the life of the bond. The amortized discount is treated as a tax-deductible expenditure, whereas the amortized premium is treated as taxable income. If a bond is retired prior to maturity, any unamortized portion of a discount or premium is deducted from or added to pre-tax income at that time.

Flotation or Issuance Costs Any costs incurred in the process of issuing a bond must be amortized over the life of the bond. The annual write-off is therefore a tax-deductible expenditure. If a bond is retired prior to maturity, then any unamortized portion of this cost is deducted from pre-tax income at that time.

EXAMPLE

The Davis Corporation, a manufacturer of industrial piping, is contemplating calling $50 million of 30-year, $1,000 par value bonds (50,000 bonds) issued five years ago with a coupon interest rate of 9%. The bonds have a call price of $1,090 and initially netted proceeds of $48.5 million due to a discount of $30 per bond (50,000 bonds × $970 net per bond). The initial flotation cost was $400,000. The company intends to sell $50 million of 25-year, $1,000 par value bonds with a 7% (coupon) interest rate to raise funds for retiring the old bonds. The flotation costs on the new issue are estimated to be $450,000. The firm is currently in the 30% tax bracket and estimates its after-tax cost of debt to be 4.9% $[0.07 \times (1 - 0.30)]$. Because the new bonds must first be sold and their proceeds then used to retire the old bonds, the firm expects a two-month period of overlapping interest during which interest must be paid on both the old and the new bonds.

Step 1. *Find the initial investment.* Finding the initial investment requires a number of calculations.

a. *Call premium.* The call premium per bond is $90 ($1,090 call price − $1,000 par value). Because the total call premium is deductible in the year of the call, its after-tax cost is calculated as follows:

Before tax ($90 × 50,000 bonds)	$4,500,000
Less: Taxes (0.30 × $4,500,000)	$1,350,000
After-tax cost of call premium	$3,150,000

b. *Flotation cost of new bond.* This cost was given as $450,000.

c. *Overlapping interest.*[14] The after-tax cost of the overlapping interest on the old bond is treated as part of the initial investment and calculated as follows:

Before tax [0.09 × (2 ÷ 12) × $50,000,000]	$750,000
Less: Tax shield (0.30 × $750,000)	$225,000
After-tax cost of overlapping interest	$525,000

d. *Unamortized discount on old bond.* The firm was amortizing the $1,500,000 discount ($50,000,000 par value − $48,500,000 net proceeds from sale) on the old bond over 30 years. Because only 5 of the 30 years' amortization of the discount has been applied, the firm can deduct the remaining 25 years of unamortized discount as a lump sum, thereby reducing taxes by $375,000 [(25 ÷ 30) × $1,500,000 × 0.30].

e. *Unamortized flotation cost of old bond.* The firm was amortizing the $400,000 initial flotation cost on the old bond over 30 years. Because only 5 of the 30 years' amortization of this cost has been applied, the firm can deduct the remaining 25 years of unamortized flotation cost as a lump sum, thereby reducing taxes by $100,000 [(25 ÷ 30) × $400,000 × 0.30].

Summarizing these calculations in Table 17.3, we find the initial investment to be $3,650,000. This means that the Davis Corporation must pay out $3,650,000 now to implement the proposed bond refunding.

Table 17.3   Finding the Initial Investment for the Davis Corporation's Bond Refunding Decision

a. Call premium		
Before tax [($1,090 − $1,000) × 50,000 bonds]	$4,500,000	
Less: Taxes (0.30 × $4,500,000)	(1,350,000)	
After-tax cost of call premium		$3,150,000
b. Flotation cost of new bond		450,000
c. Overlapping interest		
Before tax [0.09 × (2 ÷ 12) × $50,000,000]	$ 750,000	
Less: Taxes (0.30 × $750,000)	(225,000)	
After-tax cost of overlapping interest		525,000
d. Tax savings from unamortized discount on old bond		
[(25 ÷ 30) × ($50,000,000 − $48,500,000) × 0.30]		(375,000)
e. Tax savings from unamortized flotation cost of old bond		
[(25 ÷ 30) × $400,000 × 0.30]		(100,000)
Initial investment		$3,650,000

(continued)

---

[14]Technically, the after-tax amount of overlapping interest could be reduced by the after-tax interest earnings from investment of the average proceeds available from the sale of the new bonds during the interest overlap period. For clarity, any interest earned on the proceeds from sale of the new bonds during the overlap period is ignored.

Step 2. *Find the annual cash flow savings.* Finding the annual cash flow savings requires a number of calculations.

a. *Interest cost of old bond.* The after-tax annual interest of the old bond is calculated as follows:

Before tax (0.09 × $50,000,000)	$4,500,000
Less: Taxes (0.30 × $4,500,000)	$1,350,000
After-tax interest cost	$3,150,000

b. *Amortization of discount on old bond.* The firm was amortizing the $1,500,000 discount ($50,000,000 par value − $48,500,000 net proceeds from sale) on the old bond over 30 years, resulting in an annual write-off of $50,000 ($1,500,000 ÷ 30). Because it is a tax-deductible noncash charge, the amortization of this discount results in an annual tax savings of $15,000 (0.30 × $50,000).

c. *Amortization of flotation cost on old bond.* The firm was amortizing the $400,000 flotation cost on the old bond over 30 years, resulting in an annual write-off of $13,333 ($400,000 ÷ 30). Because it is a tax-deductible noncash charge, the amortization of the flotation cost results in an annual tax savings of $4,000 (0.30 × $13,333).

d. *Interest cost of new bond.* The after-tax annual interest cost of the new bond is calculated as follows:

Before tax (0.07 × $50,000,000)	$3,500,000
Less: Taxes (0.30 × $3,500,000)	$1,050,000
After-tax interest cost	$2,450,000

e. *Amortization of flotation cost on the new bond.* The firm will amortize the $450,000 flotation cost on the new bond over 25 years, resulting in an annual write-off of $18,000 ($450,000 ÷ 25). Because it is a tax-deductible noncash charge, the amortization of the flotation cost results in an annual tax savings of $5,400 (0.30 × $18,000).

Table 17.4 summarizes these calculations. Combining the first three values [(a), (b), and (c)] yields the annual after-tax debt payment for the old bond of $3,131,000. When the values for the new bond [(d) and (e)] are combined, the annual after-tax debt payment for the new bond is $2,444,600.

Subtracting the new bond's annual after-tax debt payment from that of the old bond, we find that implementation of the proposed bond refunding will result in an annual cash flow savings of $686,400 ($3,131,000 − $2,444,600).

Table 17.4 Finding the Annual Cash Flow Savings for the Davis Corporation's Bond Refunding Decision

OLD BOND

a. Interest cost		
Before tax (0.09 × $50,000,000)	$4,500,000	
Less: Taxes (0.30 × $4,500,000)	(1,350,000)	
After-tax interest cost		$3,150,000
b. Tax savings from amortization of discount		
[($1,500,000ᵃ ÷ 30) × 0.30]		(15,000)
c. Tax savings from amortization of flotation cost		
[($400,000 ÷ 30) × 0.30]		(4,000)
(1) Annual after-tax debt payment		$3,131,000

Table 17.4   *(continued)*

NEW BOND

d. Interest cost

Before tax (0.07 × $50,000,000)	$3,500,000
Less: Taxes (0.30 × $3,500,000)	(1,050,000)
After-tax interest cost	$2,450,000

e. Tax savings from amortization of flotation cost

[($450,000 ÷ 25) × 0.30]	(5,400)
(2) Annual after-tax debt payment	$2,444,600
Annual cash flow savings [(1) − (2)]	$ 686,400

[a]$50,000,000 par value − $48,500,000 net proceeds from sale.

Step 3. *Find the net present value (NPV).* Table 17.5 shows the calculations for determining the NPV of the proposed bond refunding. The present value of the annual cash flow savings of $686,400 at the 4.9% after-tax cost of debt over 25 years is computed (using Equation 3.7 on page 80) to be $9,771,792. Subtracting the initial investment of $3,650,000 from the present value of the annual cash flow savings results in a net present value of $6,121,792. Because a positive NPV results, the proposed bond refunding is recommended.

Table 17.5   Finding the Net Present Value of the Davis Corporation's Bond Refunding Decision

Present value of annual cash flow[a]

$$\$686,400 \times \frac{1}{r}\left[1 - \frac{1}{(1+r)^n}\right] = \$686,400 \times \frac{1}{0.049}\left[1 - \frac{1}{(1.049)^{25}}\right]$$

$= \$686,400 \times 14.236 =$	$ 9,771,792
Less: Initial investment (from Table 17.3)	(3,650,000)
Net present value (NPV) of refunding	**$6,121,792**

[a]Annual cash flow savings from Table 17.4 multiplied by a 25-year, 4.9% annuity (Equation 3.7).

Decision: The proposed refunding is recommended because the NPV of refunding of $6,121,792 is greater than $0.

6. What factors should a manager consider when choosing between a term loan and a bond issue for raising long-term debt?
7. What factors might influence the choice between a serial bond issue and an issue with a sinking fund requirement?
8. What factors, other than the current interest rate at which new debt could be sold, should a manager consider when deciding to refund a bond issue?

17.4 SYNDICATED LOANS

A **syndicated loan** is a large-denomination credit arranged by a group (a *syndicate*) of commercial banks for a single borrower. Although syndicated lending has been a fixture of U.S. and international finance since the early 1970s, syndicated loans increased dramatically in size, volume, and importance since the early 1990s. During the 1970s and early 1980s, many syndicated loans were arranged for governments in developing countries. These *petrodollar loans* were funded with the (dollar-denominated) trade surpluses that oil-exporting countries built up following the surge in oil prices in 1974–1975 and 1980–1982. Oil producers deposited their surpluses in global banks, which then "recycled" the funds into petrodollar loans. The "Third World debt crisis" of the early 1980s occurred after developing-country debt loads hit critical levels and the borrowing countries defaulted on some of their interest and principal payments.

The majority of syndicated loans were arranged for Western corporate borrowers even during the 1970s and 1980s, and since that time the market has become overwhelmingly corporate. Almost $5 trillion worth of syndicated loans worldwide were arranged during the record year of 2007, but this total fell by 44% to $2.7 trillion in 2008.[15] The syndicated loan market appeals to borrowers who need to arrange very large loans quickly. Loans for top-tier corporate borrowers are floating-rate credits with very narrow spreads (10–75 basis points) over LIBOR. Typically, lenders structure these loans as lines of credit that borrowers can draw down as needed over four to six years. After that time, the loans generally convert to term credits that firms must repay on a set schedule. One increasingly important use of syndicated lending is to fund debt-financed acquisitions by corporate borrowers, where the ability to borrow large sums quickly and (relatively) discreetly is especially valuable. Table 17.6 provides details of syndicated loans arranged between January 1980 and April 2000, and also of five other loan groupings. *Project finance loans* are limited or non-recourse lending to stand-alone companies, and they are typically arranged to finance large infrastructure projects. *Corporate control loans* are arranged to finance corporate acquisitions or leveraged buyouts, and *general corporate-purpose loans* are raised without a specific fund use being designated. *Capital structure loans* are booked for repayment of maturing lines of credit or for recapitalizations, share repurchases, debtor-in-possession financing, standby commercial paper support, or other unspecified purposes. *Fixed asset–based loans* are intended for mortgage lending or funding purchases of aircraft, property, or shipping.

Specialized Syndicated Lending

Though syndicated loans are used for virtually all types of corporate finance, there are two uses that merit special discussion: Eurocurrency lending and project finance.

Eurocurrency Lending The **Eurocurrency loan market** consists of a large number of international banks that stand ready to make floating-rate, hard-currency loans (typically, U.S. dollar–denominated) to international corporate and government borrowers. For example, a British bank that accepts a dollar-denominated deposit in London is creating a Eurodollar deposit, and by then lending that deposit to another bank or corporate borrower it is making a Eurodollar loan. These loans are often structured as lines of credit on which borrowers can draw. Most large loans (over $500 million) are syndicated, thereby providing a measure of diversification to the lenders.[16] Eurocurrency syndicated

---

[15]Oakley (2008).

[16]Altman and Suggitt (2000) study the default rates in the syndicated loan market, and Megginson, Poulsen, and Sinkey (1995) examine stock market responses to banks' announcements that they are participating in syndicated loans to sovereign or corporate borrowers. Some trends in syndicated lending are described in Jones, Lang, and Nigro (2000), Carey and Nini (2007), and Sufi (2007).

Table 17.6   Characteristics of All Syndicated Loans and Various Loan Categories, January 1980–April 2000

VARIABLE OF INTEREST	ALL SYNDICATED LOANS	PROJECT FINANCE LOANS	CORPORATE CONTROL LOANS	GENERAL CORPORATE-PURPOSE LOANS	CAPITAL STRUCTURE LOANS	FIXED ASSET-BASED LOANS
Number of loans	90,783	4,956	10,795	39,653	25,313	4,680
Total volume (USD million)	$13,298,457	$634,422	$2,292,431	$4,275,803	$5,289,793	$410,175
Loan size (USD million): average	$146	$128	$212	$108	$209	$88
Loan size (USD million): median	$50	$52	$59	$39	$65	$50
Average maturity (years)	4.8 years	8.6 years	5.1 years	4.5 years	3.9 years	8.1 years
Loans with fixed price (%)	5.9%	13.9%	2.7%	4.9%	3.9%	6.2%
Loans priced vs. LIBOR (%)	69.5%	38.8%	84.6%	66.2%	70.8%	72.5%
Loans to U.S. borrowers (%)	55.8%	13.9%	68.8%	50.3%	74.0%	20.4%
Average spread over LIBOR (basis points, bp)	134 bp	130 bp	195 bp	113 bp	135 bp	86 bp
Average number of syndicate banks	10.7	14.5	11.9	9.4	11.5	9.6
Average country risk score	90.0	74.6	95.4	87.3	94.1	82.7

Source: Data are from the CapitalDATA Loanware database, as employed in Stefanie Kleimeier and William L. Megginson, "Are Project Finance Loans Different from Other Syndicated Credits?" *Journal of Applied Corporate Finance* 13 (Spring 2000), pp. 75–87.

WHAT CFOs DO

How to Choose Debt Maturity: CFO Survey Evidence

What factors influence how corporate managers choose the maturity of the bonds that their firms issue? A survey asked 392 chief financial officers this question and examined which theories were best supported by their average responses, which are detailed in the table below. The most popular explanation, expressed by over 63% of respondents, is that managers wish to match the maturity of the debt issued with the useful life of the firm's assets. The second most popular rationale, offered by almost half of respondents, is that managers issue long-term debt in order to minimize the risk of having to refinance debt in "bad times"—periods when long-term rates are relatively high. This reason was especially important to managers of manufacturing and highly levered companies.

The only other factor cited by more than one-quarter of respondents is that managers issue short-term debt while "on hold," waiting for long-term rates to decline. Overall, the responses offer little support for either of the two principal theories of debt maturity choice: (1) that managers issue short-term debt to alleviate the incentive to underinvest in positive-NPV projects; or (2) that managers issue short-term debt to minimize asset substitution problems. Instead, the survey evidence suggests a more pragmatic model of maturity choice: Firms try to match asset and debt maturity and/or to "time" market interest rates. While this pragmatic approach is appealing, it suggests that managers should more broadly consider academic insights related to debt maturity.

What factors affect your firm's choice between short- and long-term debt?

RESPONSES	% IMPORTANT OR VERY IMPORTANT
Matching the maturity of our debt with the life of our assets	63
We issue long-term debt to minimize the risk of having to refinance in "bad times"	49
We issue short-term when short-term interest rates are low compared to long-term rates	36
We issue short-term when we are waiting for long-term rates to decline	29
We borrow short-term so that returns from new projects can be captured more fully by shareholders, rather than committing to pay long-term profits as interest to debtholders	9
We expect our credit rating to improve, so we borrow short-term until it does	9
Borrowing short-term reduces the chance that our firm will want to take on risky projects	4

Source: Table 11 of John R. Graham and Campbell R. Harvey, "The Theory and Practice of Corporate Finance: Evidence from the Field," *Journal of Financial Economics* 60 (2001), pages 187–243, with permission from Elsevier.

loans sometimes exceed $10 billion, and loans of $1 billion or more are quite common. Furthermore, in total size, the Eurocurrency market dwarfs all other international corporate financial markets.

Project Finance   **Project finance (PF) loans** are typically arranged for infrastructure projects—such as toll roads, bridges, power plants, seaports, tunnels, and airports—that require large sums to construct but that, once built, generate significant amounts of free cash flow for many years.[17] Although project finance lending almost always involves the use of syndicated loans, they differ from other types of syndicated credits in two vital ways. First, PF loans are extended to stand-alone companies, sometimes called vehicle companies, created for the sole purpose of constructing and operating a single project. Second, PF loans are almost always limited or nonrecourse credits, backed only by the assets and cash flows of the project, so the sponsors of the project do not guarantee payment of the loan. As described in Kleimeier and Megginson (2000), project finance loans have been employed in many famous recent projects, such as the Eurotunnel under the English Channel, Euro Disneyland in France, the new Athens International Airport, and the Seoul–Pusan High-Speed Rail Project in Korea.

Concept Review Questions	9. What aspect of syndicated lending is most attractive to the lenders?
	10. Why are syndicated loans especially useful for financing takeovers?
	11. How do project finance (PF) loans differ from other types of syndicated loans?

17.5 LEASING

Leasing, like long-term debt, requires a company to make a series of periodic, tax-deductible payments that may be fixed or variable. You can think of a lease as being comparable to secured long-term debt because in both cases there is an underlying asset tied to the firm's financial obligation. The **lessee** uses the underlying asset and makes regular payments to the **lessor**, who retains ownership of the asset. Leasing can take a number of forms. Here we discuss the basic types of leases, lease arrangements, the lease contract, the lease-versus-purchase decision, the effects of leasing on future financing, and the advantages and disadvantages of leasing.

Basic Types of Leases

The two basic types of leases available to a business are *operating leases* and *financial leases*. Accountants also use the term *capital leases* to refer to financial leases.

Operating Leases   An **operating lease** is a contractual arrangement whereby the lessee agrees to make periodic payments to the lessor, often for five years or less, to obtain an asset's services. The lessee receives an option to cancel the lease by paying a cancellation fee. Assets that are leased under operating leases have useful lives that are longer than the lease's term, although (as with most assets) the economic usefulness of the assets declines over time. Computer systems are prime examples of assets whose relative efficiency diminishes with new technological developments. The operating lease is a common arrangement for obtaining such systems as well as for other relatively short-lived assets, such as copiers or automobiles. When an operating lease expires, the lessee returns the asset to the lessor, who may lease it again or sell it. In some instances, the lease contract will give the lessee the option to purchase the asset. In operating leases, the underlying asset usually

---

[17]The early history of PF lending is described in Kensinger and Martin (1988). Brealey, Cooper, and Habib (1996) discuss how PF lending helps mitigate the agency problems that arise between borrower and lender in standard credit relationships; Dailami and Hauswald (2007) describe the contracting terms used in the RasGas Project off the shores of Qatar; Esty (2002) analyzes how PF loans are structured and priced to ensure an adequate return to lenders.

has significant market value when the lease ends, and the lessor's original cost generally exceeds the total value of the initial lessee's payments.

Financial or Capital Leases A **financial** (or **capital**) **lease** is generally for a longer term than an operating lease. Financial leases are noncancelable and therefore obligate the lessee to make payments over a predefined period. Even if the lessee no longer needs the asset, payments must continue until the lease expires. Financial leases are commonly used for leasing land, buildings, and large pieces of equipment. The noncancelable feature of the financial lease makes it quite similar to certain types of long-term debt. As is the case with debt, failure to make the contractual lease payments can result in bankruptcy for the lessee.

Another distinguishing characteristic of the financial lease is that the total payments over the lease period are greater than the lessor's initial cost. In other words, the lessor earns a return by receiving more than the asset's purchase price. Technically, under Financial Accounting Standards Board (FASB) Standard No. 13, "Accounting for Leases," a financial (or capital) lease is defined as having one of the following elements.

1. The lease transfers ownership of the property to the lessee by the end of the lease term.
2. The lease contains an option to purchase the property at a "bargain price." Such an option must be exercisable at a "fair market value" for the lease to be classified as an operating lease.
3. The lease term is equal to 75% or more of the estimated economic life of the property (exceptions exist for property leased toward the end of its usable economic life).
4. At the beginning of the lease, the present value of the lease payments is equal to 90% or more of the fair market value of the leased property.

The emphasis in this chapter is on financial leases because they result in long-term financial commitments by the firm.

Lease Arrangements

Lessors use three primary techniques for obtaining assets for leasing. The method selected depends largely on the desires of the prospective lessee. A **direct lease** results when a lessor acquires the assets that are leased to a given lessee. In other words, the lessee did not previously own the assets that it is leasing. In a **sale–leaseback arrangement**, one firm sells an asset to another for cash and then leases the asset from its new owner. You can see the resemblance of this arrangement to a collateralized loan. In such a loan, the lender gives the firm cash up front in exchange for a stream of future payments. If the borrower defaults on those payments, the lender keeps the collateral. In a sale–leaseback, the firm receives cash immediately (giving up ownership of the asset) and effectively repays this loan by leasing back the underlying asset. Sale–leaseback arrangements are therefore attractive to firms that need cash for operations.

EXAMPLE

Like many firms in the automotive industry, the retail auto parts supplier Pep Boys has experienced steep declines in its business. The firm reported net losses in each year from 2006 to 2009. To deal with its cash flow problems, Pep Boys announced in 2007 that it would engage in a sale–leaseback agreement in which the firm would sell 34 of its stores in exchange for $166.2 million. In return, Pep Boys would agree to lease the properties back from the buyers for 15 years.

Leasing arrangements that include one or more third-party lenders are **leveraged leases**. Unlike in direct and sale–leaseback arrangements, the lessor in a leveraged lease acts as an equity participant, supplying only about 20% of the asset's cost and borrowing the balance of the funds. In recent years, leveraged leases have become especially popular in connection with very expensive assets.[18]

A lease agreement usually specifies whether or not the lessee is responsible for maintenance of the leased assets. Both operating and financial leases generally include **maintenance clauses** specifying who is to maintain the assets and make insurance and tax payments. Under operating leases these costs are typically the lessor's responsibility, whereas under financial leases the lessee is typically responsible for these costs. The lessee often has the option to renew a lease at its expiration. **Renewal options** are especially common in operating leases because their term is generally shorter than the useful life of the leased assets. **Purchase options** allowing the lessee to purchase the leased asset at maturity occur in both operating and financial leases.[19]

The lessor can be one of a number of parties. With operating leases, the lessor is quite likely to be the manufacturer's leasing subsidiary or an independent leasing company. Financial leases are frequently handled by independent leasing companies or by the leasing subsidiaries of large financial institutions, such as commercial banks and life insurance companies. Life insurance companies are especially active in real estate leasing. Pension funds, like commercial banks, have also been increasing their leasing activities.

The Lease Contract

The key items in a lease contract generally include a description of the leased assets, the term or duration of the lease, provisions for its cancellation, lease payment amounts and dates, provisions for maintenance and associated costs, renewal options, purchase options, and other provisions specified in the lease negotiation process. Furthermore, lease contracts spell out the consequences of the violation of any lease provision by either the lessee or the lessor.

The Lease-versus-Purchase Decision

The **lease-versus-purchase** (or **lease-versus-buy**) **decision** commonly confronts firms contemplating the acquisition of new fixed assets. The alternatives available are to (1) lease the assets, (2) borrow funds to purchase the assets, or (3) purchase the assets using available liquid resources. Similar financial analysis applies to alternatives (2) and (3). Even if the firm has the liquid resources with which to purchase the assets, using these resources is viewed as equivalent to borrowing.[20] Therefore, we need to compare only the leasing and purchasing alternatives.

The lease-versus-purchase decision involves application of the capital budgeting methods presented in Chapters 7 and 8. The analysis can be framed in two different ways, but both approaches yield the same answer if done correctly. In one approach, we first list the cash flows associated with the purchase option and the lease option; then we take the differences in cash flows between the two options and calculate the NPV of the incremental

---

[18]For a discussion of why manufacturers may prefer to lease rather than sell their products, see Smith and Wakeman (1985) and Waldman (1997).

[19]For a discussion on determining the appropriate lease rate for a lease that contains various options, see Grenadier (1995).

[20]Consider a company that has $1,000 in the bank earning 8% interest, or $80 per year. If the firm uses this $1,000 to purchase a copier then it will no longer earn the $80 annual interest income. Hence this outcome is equivalent to borrowing $1,000 to buy the copier and paying $80 in interest expense.

cash flow stream using the after-tax cost of debt.[21] The alternative approach is simply to calculate the NPVs of the purchase and lease options separately and then compare them. Note that either method can be used to determine whether the lease option or the purchase option is better, but neither method addresses whether purchasing or leasing is worthwhile in the first place. That is, the analysis merely allows us to make statements about the *relative* merits of buying versus leasing.

EXAMPLE

ClumZee Movers has already conducted a standard NPV analysis and determined that acquiring a new delivery truck would increase firm value. Now, ClumZee needs to decide whether to lease or buy the truck.

The truck costs $25,000 and will reduce operating costs by $4,500 annually over its 5-year life. If ClumZee buys the truck, then it will be depreciated on a straight-line basis, and the truck will have no resale value after five years. Alternatively, the firm can lease the truck for $6,300 per year (with payments at the end of each year). The lease payments are tax-deductible. ClumZee faces a 35% tax rate, and its pre-tax cost of debt is 8%.

Table 17.7 shows the cash flows for both the lease and the purchase option. Under either scenario, the firm realizes $4,500 in savings each year, or $2,925 after taxes [$4,500 × (1 − 35%)]. Under the purchase option, the firm has a large initial cash outflow, but it can also deduct $5,000 per year in depreciation, saving $1,750 in taxes each year ($5,000 × 35%). With the lease option, the firm pays $6,300 per year before taxes, or $4,095 after taxes [$6,300 × (1 − 35%)]. Subtracting the cash flows associated with the purchase option from those tied to the leasing decision and then discounting them at the after-tax cost of debt of 5.2% [8% × (1 − 35%)], we obtain the following incremental NPV of leasing versus buying:

$$\text{NPV} = \$25,000 - \frac{\$5,845}{(1.052)^1} - \frac{\$5,845}{(1.052)^2} - \frac{\$5,845}{(1.052)^3} - \frac{\$5,845}{(1.052)^4} - \frac{\$5,845}{(1.052)^5}$$

$$= -\$166$$

The NPV is negative and so the incremental benefits of purchasing exceed those of leasing. Therefore, ClumZee should buy the truck they need.

Table 17.7   **Lease vs. Purchase Analysis for ClumZee Movers: After-Tax Cash Flows ($)**

| | LEASE OPTION | | | PURCHASE OPTION | | | | LEASE– |
YEAR	COST SAVINGS	LEASE PAYMENT	NET	PURCHASE PRICE	COST SAVINGS	DEPRECIATION TAX SHIELD	NET	PURCHASE OPTION
0	$ 0	$ 0	$ 0	−$25,000	$ 0	$ 0	−$25,000	$25,000
1	$2,925	−$4,095	−$1,170		$2,925	$1,750	$ 4,675	−$ 5,845
2	$2,925	−$4,095	−$1,170		$2,925	$1,750	$ 4,675	−$ 5,845
3	$2,925	−$4,095	−$1,170		$2,925	$1,750	$ 4,675	−$ 5,845
4	$2,925	−$4,095	−$1,170		$2,925	$1,750	$ 4,675	−$ 5,845
5	$2,925	−$4,095	−$1,170		$2,925	$1,750	$ 4,675	−$ 5,845

[21]When analyzing a purchase that is funded by debt, we discount using the *after-tax* cost of debt in order to capture the tax benefit from the interest deduction. Leasing is usually thought of as displacing an equal amount of debt capacity. That is, if we enter a $1,000 lease, this will usually reduce our ability to borrow by $1,000. Because we give up interest tax savings when we give up this debt capacity, the present value of lease payments should be discounted by the *after-tax* cost of debt in order to capture these forgone tax shields. This means that we discount by the after-tax cost of debt when deciding between leasing or buying an asset.

We could reach the same decision by calculating the NPVs of the purchase option and the lease option separately and choosing the one with the higher NPV.

$$NPV(\text{Purchase}) = -25,000 + \frac{\$4,675}{(1.052)^1} + \frac{\$4,675}{(1.052)^2} + \cdots + \frac{\$4,675}{(1.052)^5} = -\$4,871$$

$$NPV(\text{Lease}) = -\frac{\$1,170}{(1.052)^1} - \frac{\$1,170}{(1.052)^2} - \cdots - \frac{\$1,170}{(1.052)^5} = -\$5,037$$

The purchase option is $166 [-\$5,037 - (-\$4,871)]$ less expensive than the lease option. Because the purchase option's NPV is higher, ClumZee should purchase the truck rather than lease it.

It is worth noting that if the lessee and lessor have the same discount rate and same tax rates, then leasing strictly for financial reasons is a zero-sum game. Cash outflows for the lessee represent inflows for the lessor, and vice versa. Only when the two parties have different tax rates or costs of capital can leasing add value purely for financial reasons. Therefore, the lower cost of leasing or buying results from factors such as the differing tax brackets of the lessor and the lessee, different tax treatments for leases versus purchases, and differing risks and borrowing costs for the lessor and the lessee. Moreover, when making a lease-versus-purchase decision, the firm will find that inexpensive borrowing opportunities and high required lessor returns increase the attractiveness of purchasing. Likewise, leasing decisions are affected by many nonfinancial factors such as the risk of obsolescence and the experience and expertise of the lessor in dealing in secondary asset markets.[22] Subjective factors must also be included in the decision-making process. Like most financial decisions, the lease-versus-purchase decision requires a certain degree of judgment and consideration of qualitative factors.

Effects of Leasing on Future Financing

Because leasing is considered a type of debt financing, it affects a firm's future financing ability. Lease payments are shown as a tax-deductible expense on the firm's income statement. Anyone analyzing the income statement would probably recognize that assets are being leased, although the actual details of the amounts and terms of the leases might be unclear. The following sections discuss the lease disclosure requirements established by the Financial Accounting Standards Board (FASB) and the effect of leases on financial ratios.

Lease Disclosure Requirements   Standard No. 13 of the FASB, "Accounting for Leases," requires explicit disclosure of financial (capital) lease obligations on the firm's balance sheet. Such a lease must be shown as a *capitalized lease*, meaning that the present value of all its payments is included as an asset and a corresponding liability on the firm's balance sheet. An operating lease, on the other hand, need not be capitalized, but its basic features must be disclosed in a footnote to the financial statements. Standard No. 13, of course, establishes detailed guidelines to be used in capitalizing leases to reflect them as an asset and corresponding liability on the balance sheet. Subsequent standards have further refined lease capitalization and disclosure procedures, as the following Example shows.

---

[22]Smith and Wakeman (1985), Krishnan and Moyer (1994), Barclay and Smith (1995b), Grenadier (1995, 1996), and Waldman (1997) examine the lease-versus-purchase decision using U.S. data. Lasfer and Levis (1998) perform a similar analysis using British data, and Beattie, Goodacre, and Thomson (2000) examine the choice between operating and financial leases in Britain. To date, no clear-cut patterns are observed, though firm size, tax status, the relative importance of growth options to firm value, and the likelihood of bankruptcy all seem to play a role. As do most subsequent researchers, Schallheim et al. (1987) find that lease rates are significantly higher than otherwise-comparable lending rates, so firms clearly choose leasing for reasons besides lower cost alone.

WHAT COMPANIES DO

Aircraft Leasing Hits Turbulent Skies

Would you lend money to AIG so that the company—whose brush with bankruptcy in Fall 2008 prompted a $100 billion (and counting) federal government bailout—could purchase commercial aircraft to lease to financially troubled airlines? During the spring and summer of 2009, few creditors were willing to fund this transaction, which was extremely bad news for International Lease Finance Corporation (ILFC), AIG's wholly-owned aircraft leasing subsidiary. Whereas ILFC had previously enjoyed very low borrowing costs, it was now paying high interest rates that reflected a large risk premium, if it could obtain financing at all. Coming as it did during a period of extreme stress for the airline industry, this proved too much for AIG, which put ILFC up for sale.

In the 36 years leading up to 2009, ILFC purchased large numbers of aircraft from Boeing and Airbus, plus thousands of jet engines from GE, Rolls Royce, and other manufacturers. ILFC then turned around and immediately leased the planes to airlines that were either unable to finance the aircraft themselves or preferred to specialize in operating rather than owning these complex and expensive pieces of equipment. Since ILFC purchased so many aircraft from both Boeing and Airbus, it was able to buy at a substantial quantity discount—and ILFC passed some of these savings on to airlines in the form of lower lease payments. ILFC supplied planes to the airlines under *operating* leases, meaning that the company did not fully recover the costs of the planes through lease payments, but since it also sold used aircraft, it was able to continuously maintain a very modern fleet of the most popular aircraft. This, plus the vast scale and scope of ILFC's business (the company owned nearly 1,000 operating commercial aircraft in 2009), allowed the company to offer airlines substantial flexibility to rapidly alter their fleet compositions and to change scale in response to expansions or recessions. Since commercial aircraft are among the most fungible of all large capital assets, they traditionally provide excellent collateral, which, in turn, allowed ILFC to access debt markets at very attractive rates.

This virtuous circle of cheap financing promoting low-cost aircraft purchases and subsequent attractive leasing opportunities ended abruptly for ILFC when AIG ceased being a creditworthy borrower. Simultaneously, the world's airlines began losing almost $1 billion per month and, in desperation, slashed their orders for new aircraft, cancelled other orders, and returned aircraft coming off lease back to ILFC and other lessors. In fact, the collapse in demand for new commercial aircraft that occurred in 2008 and 2009 was unprecedented. From combined gross sales for Boeing and Airbus of nearly 3,000 aircraft in 2007 (1,423 for Boeing and 1,458 for Airbus), new orders fell by half in 2008, and then to an annual pace of less than 250 airplanes during 2009. (Net sales were even worse— exactly **one** for Boeing through mid-year and only 11 for Airbus through May 31, 2009!) On top of everything else, in June 2009, Boeing announced yet another delay in delivery of its highly anticipated (but two year past-due) 787 Dreamliner jet, of which ILFC had ordered 74, more than any other customer. In response to Boeing's announcement, Qantas and other carriers cancelled orders for 75 Dreamliners—about 8% of their orders for the new jet—and further delayed the eventual recovery of ILFC and other aircraft lessors.

In was in these trying circumstances that AIG put ILFC up for sale in Spring 2009. Three bidders emerged, and during June 2009, a consortium including the private equity groups Onex and Greenbriar Equity was named the preferred bidder—even though all of the bids reported valued ILFC at less than $5 billion, far below its $7.6 billion book value. While the circumstances facing ILFC were trying, they illustrate that one of the chief benefits of leasing is the sharing of a quantity purchase discount between the lessor and lessee.

Sources: Financial and marketing data from the websites of Boeing (www.boeing.com), Airbus (www.airbus.com/en/), and International Lease Finance Corporation website (www.ilfc.com); news commentary from *Financial Times*, various issues 2007–2009.

EXAMPLE

Altmont Company, a manufacturer of printing equipment, is leasing an asset under a 10-year lease requiring annual beginning-of-year payments of $15,000. The lease can be capitalized merely by calculating the present value of the lease payments over the life of the lease. However, the rate at which the payments should be discounted is difficult to determine.[23] If 10% is used, then the present (or capitalized) value of the lease is found by multiplying the annual lease payment by the expression for a 10-year, 10% annuity due (Equation 3.8 on page 81). This value of $101,385 $\left\{ \$15{,}000 \times \dfrac{1}{0.10} \times \left[1 - \dfrac{1}{(1.10)^{10}} \right] \times (1.10) \right\}$ would be shown as an asset and corresponding liability on the firm's balance sheet, which should result in an accurate reflection of the firm's true financial position.

Leasing and Financial Ratios   Because the consequences of missing a financial lease payment are the same as those of missing an interest or principal payment on debt, a financial analyst must view the lease as a long-term financial commitment of the lessee. With FASB Standard No. 13, the inclusion of each financial (capital) lease as an asset and corresponding liability (i.e., long-term debt) provides for a balance sheet that more accurately reflects the firm's financial status. It thereby permits various types of financial ratio analyses to be performed directly on the statement in a manner that captures all of the firm's fixed obligations and indebtedness.

Advantages and Disadvantages of Leasing

Leasing has a number of commonly cited advantages and disadvantages that should be considered when making a lease-versus-purchase decision. Although not all these advantages and disadvantages hold in every case, several of them may apply in any given situation.

Commonly Cited Advantages

1. Leasing allows the lessee, in effect, to depreciate land, which is prohibited if the land were purchased. Because the lessee who leases land is permitted to deduct the total lease payment as an expense for tax purposes, the effect is the same as if the firm had purchased the land and then depreciated it.
2. The use of sale–leaseback arrangements may permit the firm to increase its liquidity by converting an asset into cash, which can then be used as working capital. A firm short of working capital or in a liquidity bind can sell an owned asset to a lessor and then lease the asset back for a specified number of years.
3. Leasing provides 100% financing. Most loan agreements for the purchase of fixed assets require the borrower to pay a portion of the purchase price as a down payment. Therefore, the borrower is able to borrow (at most) only 90%–95% of the purchase price of the asset.

---

[23]In Standard No. 13, the FASB established certain guidelines for the appropriate discount rate to use when capitalizing leases. Most commonly, the rate used is equal to the rate the lessee would have incurred if funds were borrowed to buy the asset with a secured loan under terms similar to the lease repayment schedule. This simply represents the before-tax cost of a secured loan.

4. When a firm becomes bankrupt or is reorganized, the maximum claim of lessors against the corporation is three years of lease payments—and the lessor, of course, reclaims the asset. The lessor also has higher priority in bankruptcy than do most of the lessee's other creditors, and, therefore, the lessor can charge a little bit less for bankruptcy risk than other creditors would have to charge. If debt is used to purchase an asset, the creditors have a claim that is equal to the total outstanding loan balance.

5. In a lease arrangement, the firm may avoid the cost of obsolescence if the lessor fails to accurately anticipate the obsolescence of assets and sets the lease payment too low. This is especially true in the case of operating leases, which generally have relatively short lives. Of course, the lessee may pay for this expected benefit in the form of a higher lease payment.

6. A lessee avoids many of the negative covenants that are usually included as part of a long-term loan. Requirements with respect to the sale of accounts receivable, subsequent borrowing, business combinations, and so on are not generally found in lease agreements.

7. In the case of low-cost assets that are infrequently acquired, leasing—especially through operating leases—may provide the firm with needed financing flexibility. That is, the firm does not have to arrange other financing for these assets and can obtain them with relative convenience through a lease.

Commonly Cited Disadvantages

1. A lease does not have a stated interest cost. In cases where the return to the lessor is quite high, the firm might be better off borrowing to purchase the asset.

2. At the end of the term of the lease agreement, the lessor realizes the asset's salvage value, if any. If the lessee had purchased the asset, it could have claimed the asset's salvage value. Of course, in a competitive leasing market, if the lessor expects a higher salvage value then the lease payments would be lower.

3. Under a lease, the lessee is generally prohibited from making improvements on the leased property or asset without the lessor's approval. If the property were owned outright, this difficulty would not arise. Of course, lessors generally encourage leasehold improvements that are expected to enhance the asset's salvage value.

4. If a lessee leases an asset that subsequently becomes obsolete, it still must make lease payments over the remaining term of the lease. This is true even if the asset is unusable.

Concept Review Questions	12. Why is it considered important whether a lease is classified as an operating lease or as a financial (or capital) lease?
	13. What factors should be considered when deciding between leasing an asset or borrowing funds to purchase the asset?

SUMMARY

- Long-term debt and leasing are important sources of capital for businesses. Long-term debt can take the form of term loans or bonds. The characteristics of each can be tailored to meet the needs of both the borrower and the lender.

- The conditions of a term loan are specified in the loan agreement. This agreement specifies the rights and responsibilities of both lender and borrower, and the agreement typically lists several positive and negative covenants that the borrower must not violate.

- The conditions of a bond issue are specified in the bond indenture and are enforced by a trustee. These legal agreements are highly detailed and not easily modified, because bonds are held by many individual investors. In contrast, privately placed loan terms can be modified rather easily, because the borrower can negotiate directly with one creditor or a relatively small number of creditors.
- Frequently when interest rates drop, bond issuers make refunding decisions, which involve determining the NPV associated with calling outstanding bonds and issuing new bonds with lower-interest coupons to replace the refunded bonds.
- Syndicated loans are large-denomination credits arranged by a syndicate of commercial banks for a single borrower. These have been increasing in importance in recent years because very large loans can be

arranged quickly and inexpensively and can have flexible borrowing terms.
- Leasing serves as an alternative to borrowing funds to purchase an asset. Operating leases need not be shown on a firm's balance sheet, whereas financial lease obligations must be shown. Firms often make lease-versus-purchase decisions, which involve choosing the alternative with the lower present value of cash outflows.
- Leasing affects a firm's future financing ability. Capital leases must be capitalized and shown as an asset and corresponding liability on the firm's balance sheet, whereas operating leases must only be described in a footnote to the firm's financial statements. Financial analysts view leases as long-term financial commitments. A variety of advantages and disadvantages of leasing are commonly cited.

KEY TERMS

balloon payment	high-yield bonds	prime lending rate
bearer bonds	income bonds	private placements
call premium	indenture	project finance (PF) loans
capital lease	investment-grade bonds	purchase options
collateral	junk bonds	refund
collateral trust bonds	lease-versus-buy decision	renewal options
convertible bonds	lease-versus-purchase decision	sale–leaseback arrangement
cross-default covenant	leasing	serial bonds
debentures	lessee	sinking fund
direct lease	lessor	speculative bonds
equipment trust certificates	leveraged leases	stock purchase warrants
Eurobond	LIBOR	subordinated debentures
Eurocurrency loan market	lien	subordination
fallen angels	loans	syndicated loan
financial lease	maintenance clauses	term loan
fixed-rate offerings	mortgage bonds	trustee
floating-rate issues	mortgage-backed securities (MBS)	
foreign bond	operating lease	

QUESTIONS

17-1. Comment on the following proposition: The use of floating-rate debt eliminates interest rate risk (the risk that interest payment amounts will change in the future) for both the borrower and the lender.

17-2. What purpose do loan covenants serve in a debt agreement? What factors should a manager consider when negotiating covenants?

17-3. What is a debenture? Why do you think that this is the most common form of corporate bond in the United States but is much less commonly used elsewhere?

17-4. How do *sinking funds* reduce default risk?

17-5. What is a trustee? Why do bondholders insist that a trustee be included in all public bond offerings? Why are these less necessary in private debt placements?

17-6. What impact has adoption of Rule 144A had on debt-issuance patterns in the United States?

17-7. Why are most corporate bonds callable? Who benefits from this feature, and what is the cost of adopting a call provision in a public bond issue?

17-8. Why do corporations have their debt rated? Compare the role played by rating agencies and a company's outside auditors.

17-9. What does *investment grade* mean in the context of corporate bond issues? How do these bonds differ from junk bonds, and why have the latter proven so popular with investors?

17-10. What is a Eurobond? Why did these bonds come into existence? Why do Eurobond investors like the fact that these are typically "bearer bonds"? What risk does an investor run from holding bearer bonds rather than registered bonds?

17-11. Explain how uncertainty concerning future interest rates would affect the decision to refund a bond issue.

17-12. What is a syndicated loan? What is a project finance loan? What role does a stand-alone company play in the typical project finance deal?

17-13. What elements must be included in a lease in order for it to be considered a financial (capital) lease?

17-14. How would the availability of floating-rate debt affect the lease-versus-purchase decision?

17-15. For acquiring an asset, what are the key advantages of leasing as compared to borrowing? What are the key disadvantages of leasing?

PROBLEMS

Corporate Bonds

17-1. The initial proceeds per bond, the size of the issue, the initial maturity of the bond, and the years remaining to maturity are shown in the following table for a number of bonds. In each case the bond has a $1,000 par value, and the issuing firm is in the 40% tax bracket.

Bond	Proceeds per Bond ($)	Size of Issue (no. of bonds)	Initial Maturity of Bond (years)	Years Remaining to Maturity
A	985	10,000	20	15
B	1,025	20,000	25	16
C	1,000	22,500	12	9
D	960	5,000	25	15
E	1,035	10,000	30	16

a. Indicate whether each bond was sold at a discount, at a premium, or at its par value.

b. Determine the total discount or premium for each issue.

c. Determine the annual amount of discount or premium amortized for each bond.

d. Calculate the unamortized discount or premium for each bond.

e. Determine the after-tax cash flow associated with the retirement now of each of these bonds, using the values developed in part (d).

17-2. For each of the callable bond issues in the following table, calculate the after-tax cost of calling the issue. Each bond has a $1,000 par value, and the various issue sizes and call prices are shown in the following table. The issuing firm is in the 40% tax bracket.

Bond	Size of Issue	Call Price
A	12,000 bonds	$1,050
B	20,000 bonds	1,030
C	30,000 bonds	1,015
D	50,000 bonds	1,050
E	100,000 bonds	1,045
F	500,000 bonds	1,060

17-3. The flotation cost, the initial maturity, and the number of years remaining to maturity are shown in the following table for a number of bonds. The issuing firm is in the 40% tax bracket.

Bond	Flotation Cost ($)	Initial Maturity of Bond (years)	Years Remaining to Maturity
A	250,000	30	22
B	500,000	15	5
C	125,000	20	10
D	750,000	10	1
E	650,000	15	6

a. Calculate the annual amortization of the flotation cost for each bond.

b. Determine the tax savings, if any, expected to result from the unamortized flotation cost if the bond were called today.

17-4. The initial proceeds per bond, the size of the issue, the initial maturity of the bond, and the years remaining to maturity are shown in the following table for a number of bonds. Each bond has a $1,000 par value, and the issuing firm is in the 35% tax bracket.

Bond	Proceeds per Bond ($)	Size of Issue (no. of bonds)	Initial Maturity of Bond (years)	Years Remaining to Maturity
A	975	50,000 bonds	10	5
B	1,020	25,000 bonds	20	15
C	1,000	100,000 bonds	25	12

a. Indicate whether each bond was sold at a discount, at a premium, or at its par value.

b. Determine the total discount or premium for each issue.

c. Determine the annual amount of discount or premium amortized for each bond.

d. Calculate the unamortized discount or premium for each bond.

e. Determine the after-tax cash flow associated with the retirement now of each of these bonds, using the values developed in part (d).

17-5. The principal, coupon interest rate, and interest overlap period are shown in the following table for several different bonds.

Bond	Principal ($)	Coupon Interest Rate (%)	Interest Overlap Period
A	15,000,000	6.5	2 months
B	20,000,000	7.0	3 months

Bond	Principal ($)	Coupon Interest Rate (%)	Interest Overlap Period
C	15,000,000	6.0	4 months
D	100,000,000	8.0	6 months

a. Calculate the dollar amount of interest that must be paid for each bond during the interest overlap period.

b. Calculate the after-tax cost of overlapping interest for each bond if the firm is in the 40% tax bracket.

17-6. The principal, coupon interest rate, and interest overlap period are shown in the following table for five different bonds.

Bond	Principal ($)	Coupon Interest Rate (%)	Interest Overlap Period
A	5,000,000	8.0	3 months
B	40,000,000	7.0	2 months
C	50,000,000	6.5	3 months
D	100,000,000	9.0	6 months
E	20,000,000	5.5	1 months

a. Calculate the dollar amount of interest that must be paid for each bond during the interest overlap period.

b. Calculate the after-tax cost of overlapping interest for each bond if the firm is in the 40% tax bracket.

17-7. Schooner Company is contemplating offering a new $50 million bond issue to replace an outstanding $50 million bond issue. The firm wishes to take advantage of the decline in interest rates that has occurred since the initial bond issuance. The old and new bonds are described in what follows. The firm is in the 40% tax bracket.

Old bonds. The outstanding bonds have a $1,000 par value and a 9% coupon interest rate. They were issued 5 years ago with a 20-year maturity. They were initially sold for their par value of $1,000, and the firm incurred $350,000 in flotation costs. They are callable at $1,090.

New bonds. The new bonds would have a $1,000 par value, a 7% coupon interest rate, and a 15-year maturity. They could be sold at their par value. The flotation cost of the new bonds would be $500,000. The firm does not expect to have any overlapping interest.

a. Calculate the tax savings that are expected from the unamortized portion or the old bonds' flotation cost.

b. Calculate the annual tax savings from the flotation cost of the new bonds, assuming the 15-year amortization.

c. Calculate the after-tax cost of the call premium that is required to retire the old bonds.

d. Determine the initial investment that is required to call the old bonds and issue the new bonds.

e. Calculate the annual cash flow savings, if any, that are expected from the proposed bond refunding decision.

f. If the firm has a 4.2% after-tax cost of debt, find the net present value of the bond refunding decision. Would you recommend the proposed refunding? Explain your answer.

17-8. High-Gearing Incorporated is considering offering a new $40 million bond issue to replace an outstanding $40 million issue. The firm wishes to thereby take advantage of the decline in interest rates that has occurred since the original issue. The two bond issues are described in what follows. The firm is in the 40% tax bracket.

Old bonds. The outstanding bonds have a $1,000 par value and a 10% coupon interest rate. They were issued 5 years ago with a 25-year maturity. They were initially sold at a $25 per bond discount, and a $200,000 flotation cost was incurred. They are callable at $1,100.

New bonds. The new bonds would have a 20-year maturity, a par value of $1,000, and a 7.5% coupon interest rate. It is expected that these bonds can be sold at par for a flotation cost of $250,000. The firm expects a 3-month period of overlapping interest while it retires the old bonds.

a. Calculate the initial investment that is required to call the old bonds and issue the new bonds.

b. Calculate the annual cash flow savings, if any, expected from the proposed bond refunding decision.

c. If the firm uses its 4.5% after-tax cost of debt to evaluate low-risk decisions, find the NPV of the bond refunding decision. Would you recommend the proposed refunding? Explain your answer.

17-9. Well-Sprung Corporation is considering offering a new $100 million bond issue to replace an outstanding $100 million bond issue. The firm wishes to take advantage of the decline in interest rates that has occurred since the original issue. The two bond issues are described in what follows. The firm is in the 30% tax bracket.

Old bonds. The outstanding bonds have a $1,000 par value and an 8.5% coupon interest rate. They were issued 5 years ago with a 20-year maturity. They were initially sold at a $30 per bond discount, and a $750,000 flotation cost was incurred. They are callable at $1,085.

New bonds. The new bonds would have a 15-year maturity, a par value of $1,000, and a 7% coupon interest rate. It is expected that these bonds can be sold at par for a flotation cost of $600,000. The firm expects a 3-month period of overlapping interest while it retires the old bonds.

a. Calculate the initial investment that is required to call the old bonds and issue the new bonds.

b. Calculate the annual cash flow savings, if any, expected from the proposed bond refunding decision.

c. If the firm uses its 4.9% after-tax cost of debt to evaluate low-risk decisions, find the net present value of the bond refunding decision. Would you recommend the proposed refunding? Explain your answer.

17-10. Web Tools Company is considering using the proceeds from a new $50 million bond issue to call and retire its outstanding $50 million bond issue. The details of both bond issues are outlined in what follows. The firm is in the 40% tax bracket.

Old bonds. The firm's old issue has a coupon interest rate of 10%, was issued 4 years ago, and has a 20-year maturity. The bonds sold at a $10 discount from their $1,000 par value, flotation costs were $420,000, and their call price is $1,100.

New bonds. The new bonds are expected to sell at par ($1,000), have a 16-year maturity, and have flotation costs of $520,000. The firm will have a 2-month period of overlapping interest while it retires the old bonds.

a. What is the initial investment that is required to call the old bonds and issue the new bonds?

b. What are the annual cash flow savings, if any, from the proposed bond refunding decision if the new bonds have an 8% coupon interest rate? If the new bonds have a 9% coupon interest rate?

c. Construct a table showing the NPV of refunding under the two circumstances given in part (b) when (1) the firm's after-tax cost of debt is 4.8% [0.08 × (1 − 0.40)] and (2) this cost is 5.4% [0.09 × (1 − 0.40)].

d. Given the circumstances described in part (c), discuss when refunding would be favorable and when it would not.

e. If the four circumstances summarized in your answer to part (d) were equally probable (each had probability 0.25), would you recommend refunding? Explain your answer.

Leasing

17-11. For each of the loan amounts, interest rates, loan terms, and annual payments shown in the following table, calculate the annual interest paid each year over the term of the loan. Assume that the payments are made at the *end* of each year.

Loan	Amount ($)	Interest Rate (%)	Term (years)	Annual Payment ($)
A	20,000	8.5	4	6,038
B	35,500	7.5	6	7,448
C	152,500	9.5	5	39,207
D	250,000	7.5	10	36,421
E	575,500	6.5	15	59,204

Smart Solutions

See the problem and solution explained step-by-step at **SMARTFinance**

17-12. Shredding Pines Company wishes to purchase an asset that costs $750,000. The full amount needed to finance the asset can be borrowed at 9% interest. The terms of the loan require equal end-of-year payments for the next eight years. Determine the total annual loan payment, and break it into the amount of interest and the amount of principal paid for each year.

17-13. Given the lease payments and terms shown in the following table, determine the yearly after-tax cash outflows for each firm. Assume that lease payments are made at the *beginning* of each year, that the firm is in the 40% tax bracket, and that no purchase option exists.

Firm	Annual Lease Payment ($)	Lease Term (years)
A	250,000	5
B	160,000	12
C	500,000	8
D	1,000,000	20
E	25,000	6

Smart Solutions

See the problem and solution explained step-by-step at **SMARTFinance**

17-14. GMS Corporation is attempting to determine whether to lease or purchase research equipment. The firm is in the 40% tax bracket, and its after-tax cost of debt is currently 6%. The terms of the lease and the purchase are as follows.

Lease. Annual beginning-of-year lease payments of $93,500 are required over the 3-year life of the lease. The lessee will exercise its option to purchase the asset for $25,000, to be paid along with the final lease payment.

Purchase. The $250,000 cost of the research equipment can be financed entirely with a 10% loan (pre-tax). The firm in this case will depreciate the equipment using the straight-line method for three years. The firm plans to keep the equipment and use it beyond its 3-year recovery period.

a. Calculate the after-tax cash outflows associated with each alternative.

b. Calculate the present value of each cash outflow stream using the after-tax cost of debt.

c. Which alternative—lease or purchase—would you recommend? Why?

17-15. Strident Corporation is attempting to determine whether to lease or purchase a new telephone system. The firm is in the 40% tax bracket, and its after-tax cost of debt is currently 4.5%. The terms of the lease and the purchase are as follows.

Lease. Annual beginning-of-year lease payments of $22,000 are required over the 5-year life of the lease. The lessee will exercise its option to purchase the asset for $30,000, to be paid along with the final lease payment.

Purchase. The $100,000 cost of the telephone system can be financed entirely with a 7.5% loan (pre-tax) The firm in this case will depreciate the equipment using the straight-line method for five years. The firm plans to keep the equipment and use it beyond its 5-year recovery period.

a. Calculate the after-tax cash outflows associated with each alternative.

b. Calculate the present value of each cash outflow stream using the after-tax cost of debt.

c. Which alternative—lease or purchase—would you recommend? Why?

17-16. Eastern Trucking Company needs to expand its facilities. In order to do so, the firm must acquire a machine costing $80,000. The machine can be leased or purchased. The firm is in the 40% tax bracket, and its after-tax cost of debt is 5.4%. The terms of the lease and purchase plans are as follows.

Lease. The leasing arrangement requires beginning-of-year payments of $16,900 over five years. The lessee will exercise its option to purchase the asset for $20,000, to be paid along with the final lease payment.

Purchase. If the firm purchases the machine, its cost of $80,000 will be financed with a 5-year, 9% loan (pre-tax). The machine will be depreciated on a straight-line basis for five years. The firm plans to keep the equipment and use it beyond its 5-year recovery period.

a. Determine the after-tax cash outflows of Eastern Trucking under each alternative.

b. Find the present value of the after-tax cash outflows for each alternative using the after-tax cost of debt.

c. Which alternative—lease or purchase—would you recommend? Why?

17-17. Given the lease payments, years remaining until the lease expires, and discount rates shown in the following table, calculate the capitalized value of each lease. Assume that lease payments are made at the beginning of each year.

Lease	Lease Payment ($)	Remaining Term (years)	Discount Rate (%)
A	40,000	12	10
B	120,000	8	12
C	9,000	18	14

Lease	Lease Payment ($)	Remaining Term (years)	Discount Rate (%)
D	16,000	3	9
E	47,000	20	11

THOMSON ONE | Business School Edition

17-18. Read the prospectus filed on December 19, 2008, by Walt Disney Company (ticker symbol, DIS). (*Hint:* You can access the prospectus under the Filings tab and look for PROSP under Filing Type.) What type of debt did Disney offer to the public for sale? What dollar amount of debt did Disney propose to sell? What percentage of the sales price did Disney net (after discounts and commissions)? What did Disney state they would use the funds for? Was the debt secured or unsecured?

MINI-CASES: LONG-TERM DEBT AND LEASING

17A. Nientindoe Corporation (NC) issued $100 million of 7.375% coupon bonds 10 years ago, with a 30-year maturity. Each bond has a par value of $1,000, and they are callable at 104% of par value. Flotation costs were 0.5%, and the bonds were initially sold at par. However, interest rates are currently 6.175% for 20-year bonds, and NC is considering issuing new 20-year bonds and retiring the old bond issue. Because the cash generated by the new bonds would be necessary to pay off the old bonds, there would be a 1.5-month period during which both the old and the new issue would be outstanding. Nientindoe Corporation is in a 35% tax bracket. Flotation costs on the new issue would be 0.25%, and the new bonds would be sold at par.

    1. Determine the initial investment if NC issues new bonds to retire the old bonds. Assume that NC will have to issue enough bonds to cover both the principal and the call premium associated with retiring the old issue.

    2. Determine the annual cash flow savings if NC refunds the old bond issue.

    3. Calculate the net present value of the bond refunding. Should NC refund the old issue?

17B. Barclay Polymers needs to acquire a new extruding machine whose purchase price is $600,000. However, the firm could lease the extruder from Primal Leasing Corporation for a 5-year period and make annual payments of $115,000 at the beginning of the year. If the extruder is leased, then Primal Leasing Corporation would pay all maintenance costs and Barclay would have the opportunity to purchase the asset for $130,000 at the beginning of year 5. If the extruder is purchased by Barclay, then it will be financed with a 5-year loan at an annual rate of 8.75%. Barclay would use the MACRS depreciation method over a 5-year recovery period, would purchase a service contract for $8,000 a year, and would keep the extruder after its recovery period. If the firm pursues the purchase alternative, then it would secure a maintenance contract at an expected cost of $3,000 annually. The firm is in a 35% tax bracket.

1. Calculate the annual after-tax cash outflow for the leasing alternative.

2. Determine the annual interest and principal payments for the purchase alternative.

3. Determine the annual depreciation deduction for the purchase alternative.

4. Calculate the net present value of both the leasing and the purchase alternatives. Which method should Barclay Polymers use to obtain the extruder?

PART 6
Options, Derivatives, and International Financial Management

No area of finance has witnessed more innovation and more explosive growth than the field of derivative securities. Derivatives are financial assets whose values depend on, or derive from, the values of other assets. For example, if your employer grants you the option to buy shares of stock in the company at a fixed price, the value of that option depends on the company's stock price. Derivative securities markets have grown dramatically in the last two decades, in part because these securities help corporations hedge their exposures to different types of risk.

Chapter 18 provides an introduction to options, one of the three main types of derivative instruments. The chapter describes the basic features of put and call options, and it demonstrates how investors can use options and portfolios of options to construct innovative trading strategies. The chapter concludes with a discussion of a method for pricing options called the binomial option pricing model.

Chapter 19 extends the analysis of the previous chapter by exploring many different types of assets that have optionlike characteristics. The chapter begins with an overview of the Nobel Prize–winning Black and Scholes

option pricing model, highlighting the connections between this model and the binomial model from Chapter 18. Next, we show how many different types of securities, such as convertible bonds, have optionlike features, suggesting that knowledge of option pricing techniques is required to value these instruments. The chapter's final section explores how even certain real investment opportunities, such as drilling for oil or expanding a fast-food franchise, can have optionlike traits. For these investments, an option pricing valuation framework may lead to better decisions than the traditional NPV approach.

One of the drivers of explosive growth in derivatives markets is the worldwide expansion of international trade. Chapter 20 focuses on international financial management and addresses the particular challenges faced by multinational corporations. Its emphasis is primarily on the risks that arise when firms do business across national boundaries and in multiple currencies. The chapter begins with a discussion of exchange rates and foreign exchange markets. Then we explore the forces that cause currency values to rise and fall over time and the instruments and strategies that firms can employ to deal with currency-related risk.

584

585

18

What Companies Do

Berkshire Bets on Options

Options Basics

In his March 2008 letter to shareholders, Berkshire Hathaway's chairman, Warren Buffett, disclosed that his company had raised $4.85 billion by selling put options on the Standard and Poor's 500 stock index and several other non-U.S. stock indexes. The announcement surprised many because, just six years earlier, Buffett had famously described options and other exotic financial instruments known as "derivatives" by saying: "In my view, derivatives are financial weapons of mass destruction, carrying dangers that, while now latent, are potentially lethal."

The put options that Buffett sold would require Berkshire to pay out cash if the S&P 500 (and other indexes) in 2019 were below their 2007 levels. Buffett warned shareholders that unrealized gains and losses on these investments could lead to dramatic fluctuations in Berkshire's reported earnings, even though Berkshire could not actually realize losses on these investments for more than a decade.

The warning from the "Sage of Omaha" proved to be prescient. With most stock indexes falling 40% or more in 2008, Berkshire's profits took a beating. By the end of the third quarter, Berkshire reported a liability of $6.72 billion for the put options, or a loss (net of the initial premiums) of $1.87 billion. Publicly, Buffett continued to express confidence that the trades would ultimately be profitable, but investors would have to wait at least until 2019 to see if he was right.

Sources: "Trading Put Options with Buffett," http://seekingalpha.com/article/66749-trading-put-options-with-buffett (March 2, 2008); Alex Crippen, "Berkshire Hathaway Q3 Operating Earnings Fall 19% to $1,335/share," http://www.cnbc.com/id/27596402 (November 7, 2008).

A bit of folk wisdom says, "Always keep your options open." This implies that choices have value and that having the right to do something is better than being required to do it. This chapter shows how to apply that intuition to financial instruments called *options*. In their most basic forms, **options** allow investors to buy or sell an asset at a fixed price during a given period of time. Having the right to buy or sell stock at a fixed price can be valuable—provided the stock price moves in the right direction.

Many commentators see options merely as a form of legalized gambling for the rich. We strongly disagree with that perspective. Options exist because they provide real economic benefits that come in many different forms.

First, as part of the compensation package for managers, options provide incentives for managers to take actions that increase their firms' stock prices, thereby increasing the wealth of shareholders. Abuses may occur when firms award excessive option grants or employees take improper actions in an effort to inflate stock prices and option values. We see these abuses as a corporate governance problem, not a problem with options per se.

Second, a wide variety of options exist that grant holders the right to buy and sell many different types of assets, not just shares of stock in a single company.[1] Sometimes, trading the option is more cost effective than trading the underlying asset. For example, trading a stock index option, which grants the right to buy or sell a portfolio of stocks such as the S&P 500, enables investors to avoid paying all the transactions costs that would result from actually trading 500 individual stocks.

Third, firms use options to reduce their exposure to certain types of risk. Firms regularly buy and sell options to shelter their cash flows from movements in exchange rates, interest rates, and commodity prices. In that function, options resemble insurance much more than they resemble gambling.

Fourth, options facilitate the creation of innovative trading strategies. For instance, suppose that an investor is following a pharmaceutical company that has a genetically engineered cancer drug in clinical trials. The company has invested vast resources in this project, so much so that its future depends entirely on the outcome of these trials. If the tests are successful, the company's stock will skyrocket. If not, the firm may go bankrupt. An investor with choices limited to buying or selling the company's stock must guess whether the clinical trials will succeed or fail. As we will see, an investor who can buy and sell options can construct a trading strategy to profit from a large movement in the firm's stock price regardless of whether that movement is up or down.

One might ask why a chapter on options belongs in a corporate finance textbook. We offer four answers. First, employees of large and small corporations regularly receive options as part of their compensation. It is valuable for both the employees and the employers to understand the value of this component of pay packages. Second, firms often raise capital by issuing securities with embedded options. For example, firms can issue debt that is convertible into shares of common stock at a lower interest rate than ordinary, nonconvertible debt. To evaluate whether the interest savings is worth giving bondholders the opportunity to convert their bonds into shares requires an understanding of option pricing. Third, many capital budgeting projects have optionlike characteristics. As we discussed in Chapters 7–9, a traditional application of the net present value method can generate incorrect accept–reject decisions for projects with downstream options. The best

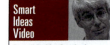

---

[1]Though this chapter focuses primarily on options to buy and sell shares of stock, investors can trade options that grant the right to buy or sell currencies, commodities, fixed-income securities, and many other types of assets at fixed prices.

WHAT COMPANIES DO GLOBALLY

CFO Survey Evidence: Options, Compensation, and Hedging Practices

The role of stock options in executive pay varies widely across countries. The following chart shows that U.S. firms are much more likely to include stock options as a significant portion of the pay package given to senior executives than are firms in other countries. Bryan, Nash, and Patel (2009) investigate differences in executive compensation practices across firms in different countries and find that stock options were more prevalent in countries that had greater institutional protections for shareholder rights and better enforcement of those protections. The study found that characteristics of firms were important, too, with equity-linked compensation such as options playing a bigger role in companies with more growth potential and in larger firms with less free cash flow.

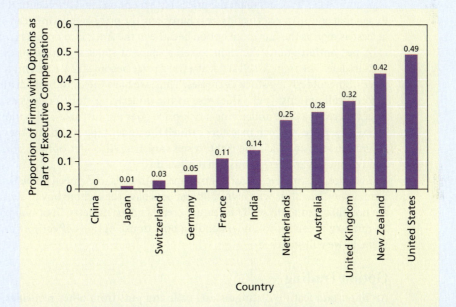

In another study, Cohen and Yagil, in 2007, asked CFOs from the largest 300 companies in the United States, the United Kingdom, Canada, Germany, and Japan how often they used options to hedge financial risks. Executives in Japan reported that they were roughly 50% more likely to use options to hedge risk than their U.S. and Canadian counterparts, whereas German and British CFOs fell in the middle. CFOs from all five countries reported that they were more likely to use forward contracts (discussed in Chapter 20) than options when hedging.

way to develop the ability to recognize which real investment projects have embedded options and which do not is to become an expert on ordinary financial options. Fourth, companies routinely use options to hedge risks they face, such as risk related to movements in currencies or interest rates. Understanding how to hedge risk using options requires fundamental knowledge of how the market prices options.

18.1 Options Vocabulary

An option is one example of a **derivative security**, a security that derives its value from another asset. An option fits this description because its value depends on the price of the underlying stock that the option holder can buy or sell at a fixed price. The asset from which a derivative security obtains its value is called the **underlying asset**. A **call option** grants the right to purchase a share of stock (or some other asset) at a fixed price on or before a certain date. The price at which a call option allows an investor to purchase the underlying share is called the **strike price** or the **exercise price**. Because the option holder can buy the underlying stock at a fixed price, the more the market price of the stock increases, the greater the value of the call option.

Call options grant investors the right to purchase a share for a fairly short time period, usually just a few months.[2] The point at which this right expires is called the option's **expiration date**. An **American call option** gives holders the right to purchase stock at a fixed price on or before its expiration date, whereas a **European call option** grants that right *only* on the expiration date. If we compare the prices of two options that are identical in every respect except that one is American and one is European, the price of the American option should be at least as high as the European option because of the American option's greater flexibility.

A **put option** grants the right to sell a share of stock at a fixed price on or before a certain date. The right to sell stock at a fixed price becomes more and more valuable as the price of the underlying stock decreases. Thus, we have the most basic distinction between put and call options—put values rise as the underlying stock price goes down, and call prices increase as the underlying stock price goes up. Just like call options, puts specify an exercise price at which investors can sell the underlying stock, and they also specify an expiration date at which the right to sell vanishes. Also, put options come in American and European varieties, just as call options do.

The most distinctive feature of options, both calls and puts, can be deduced from the term *option*. Investors who own calls and puts have the right to buy or sell shares, but they are not obligated to do so. This feature creates an asymmetry in option payoffs, and that asymmetry is central to understanding how to use options effectively and how to price them, as we will soon see.

Option Trading

An important feature distinguishing calls and puts from other securities, such as stocks and bonds, is that options are not necessarily issued by firms.[3] Rather, an option is a contract between two parties, neither of whom need have any connection to the company whose stock serves as the underlying asset for the contract. For example, suppose that Tony and Oscar, neither of whom works for General Electric, decide to enter into an options contract. Tony agrees to pay Oscar $3 for the right to purchase one share of General Electric stock for $20 at any time during the next month. As the option buyer, Tony has a **long position** in a call option. He can decide at any point whether he wants to exercise the option or not. If he chooses to **exercise** his option, he will pay Oscar $20, and Oscar will deliver one share of GE stock to Tony. Naturally, Tony will choose to exercise the option only if GE stock is worth more than $20. If GE stock is worth less than $20, Tony will let the option expire unused and will lose his $3 investment.

---

[2]Employee stock options, which typically give workers the right to buy stock at a fixed price for up to 10 years, are an important exception to this rule. Some publicly traded options also have long expiration dates, such as the Long-term Equity AnticiPation Securities (LEAPS) introduced by the American Stock Exchange in 1990.

[3]This is not to say that firms cannot issue options if they want to. Firms do issue options to employees, and they may also sell options as part of their risk management activities.

On the other side of this transaction, Oscar, as the seller of the option, has a **short position** in a call option.[4] If Tony decides to exercise his option, Oscar's *obligation* is to follow through on his promise to deliver one share of GE for $20. If Oscar does not already own a share of GE stock, he can buy one in the market. Why would Oscar agree to this arrangement? Because he receives the **option premium**, the $3 payment Tony made at the beginning of their agreement. If GE's stock rises above $20, Oscar will lose part or all of the option premium because he must sell Tony an asset for less than it is worth. On the other hand, if GE's stock price does not rise above $20, then Tony will not attempt to buy the asset, and Oscar can keep the $3 option premium.

Option trades do not usually occur in face-to-face transactions between two parties. Instead, options trade either on an exchange, such as the Chicago Board Options Exchange (CBOE) in the United States, or in the **over-the-counter market**. Exchanges list options on a limited number of stocks, with a limited set of exercise prices and expiration dates. By limiting the number and variety of listed options, the exchange expects greater liquidity in the options contracts that are available for trading. Furthermore, an options exchange may serve as a guarantor, fulfilling the terms of an options contract if one party defaults. In contrast, over-the-counter (OTC) options come in a seemingly infinite variety. They are less liquid than exchange-traded options, and traders of OTC options face **counterparty risk**—the risk that the counterparty on a specific trade will default on its obligation.

Most investors who trade options never exercise them. An investor who holds an option and wants to convert that holding into cash can do so in several ways. First, one investor can simply sell the option to another investor as long as there is some time remaining before expiration. Second, an investor can receive a **cash settlement** for the option. To understand how cash settlement works, go back to Tony's call option to buy GE stock for $20. Suppose that the price of GE is $30 per share when the option expires. Rather than have Tony pay Oscar $20 in exchange for one share of GE, Oscar might agree to pay Tony $10, the difference between the market price of GE and the option's strike price. Settling in cash eliminates the need for Oscar to buy a share of GE to give to Tony and the need for Tony to sell that share if he wants to convert his profit into cash. Avoiding these unnecessary trades saves transaction costs.

Option Prices

Table 18.1 shows a set of Whirlpool Corp. (ticker symbol, WHR) option price quotations taken from the Chicago Board Options Exchange website on January 23, 2009.[5] The first column indicates that the options being quoted are on Whirlpool common stock. The closing price of Whirlpool on the day that these option prices were obtained was $36.33. The second column illustrates the range of expiration dates available for Whirlpool options. The prices illustrated in the table are for options expiring either in February, March, or June. The third column shows the range of option strike prices available, from $30.00 to $45.00. The fourth and fifth columns give the most recent trading prices for calls and puts.[6] For instance, an investor who wanted to buy a *call* option on Whirlpool stock, with a strike

---

[4]We may also say that Oscar **writes an option** when he sells the option to Tony.

[5]This table shows only a handful of the options contracts available on Whirlpool stock. We have also chosen to exclude from the table the daily trading volume figures that are usually contained in option price quotations.

[6]Two minor institutional details are worth mentioning here. At the CBOE, options expire on the third Saturday of the month. Second, an options contract grants the right to buy or sell 100 shares of the underlying stock, even though the price quotes in the table are on a "per-share" or "per-option" basis. That is, the $4.90 price for a call option expiring in March with a $35.00 strike means that for $490 an investor can purchase the right to buy 100 shares of Whirlpool at $35.00 per share. All the examples in this chapter are constructed as if an investor can trade one option to buy or sell one share. We make that assumption just to keep the numbers simple, but it does not affect any of the main lessons of the chapter.

Table 18.1	Option Prices ($) on Whirlpool Stock				
COMPANY	EXPIRATION	STRIKE	CALL	PUT	
Whirlpool	February	30.00	7.45	1.20	⎫
36.33	March	30.00	8.05	2.05	⎬ Out-of-the-money puts In-the-money calls
36.33	June	30.00	9.65	4.00	
36.33	February	35.00	4.10	2.75	
36.33	March	35.00	4.90	3.90	
36.33	June	35.00	6.85	6.20	⎭
36.33	February	40.00	1.80	5.50	⎫
36.33	March	40.00	2.60	6.70	⎬ In-the-money puts Out-of-the-money calls
36.33	June	40.00	4.65	9.05	
36.33	February	45.00	0.60	9.35	
36.33	March	45.00	1.25	10.35	
36.33	June	45.00	3.10	12.45	⎭

Note: Option quotes retrieved from www.cboe.com on January 23, 2009. Whirlpool's stock price closed at $36.33 that day.

price of $35.00 and an expiration date in March, would pay $4.90. For a March *put* with the same strike price, an investor would pay $3.90.

Options traders say that a call option is **in the money** if the option's strike price is less than the current stock price. For puts, an option is in the money if the strike price exceeds the stock price. Using these definitions, we can say that the call options in the upper six rows of Table 18.1 and the put options in the lower six rows are in the money. Similarly, options traders say that a call option is **out of the money** when the strike price exceeds the current stock price, and puts are out of the money when the strike price falls short of the stock price. Finally, an option is **at the money** when the stock price and the strike price are equal.

Examine the March call option with a strike price of $30.00. If an investor who owned this option exercised it, she could buy Whirlpool stock for $30.00 and resell it at the market price of $36.33, a difference of $6.33. But the current price of this option is $8.05, which is $1.72 more than the value the investor would obtain by exercising it. In this example, $6.33 is the option's **intrinsic value**.[7] You can think of intrinsic value as measuring the profit an investor makes from exercising the option (ignoring transaction costs as well as the option premium). If an option is out of the money, its intrinsic value is zero. The difference between an option's intrinsic value and its market price, $1.72 for the March call, is the option's **time value.** At the expiration date, the time value equals zero.

Suppose that you purchase the March call with a $30 strike price for $8.05. Suppose also that on the option's expiration date, the price of Whirlpool stock has increased from its current level of $36.33 to $40. That's an increase of 10.1%. What would the option be worth at that time? Because the option holder could buy Whirlpool stock for $30 and then immediately resell it for $40, the option should be worth $10. If the option sells for $10, that's an increase of 24.2% from the $8.05 purchase price! Similarly, if Whirlpool's stock price is just $29.99 when the option expires, then the option will be worthless. If you

---

[7]For put options, the intrinsic value equals either $X - S$ or 0, whichever is greater. For example, the intrinsic value of each of the three put options with a strike price of $40.00 is $3.67 ($40.00 − $36.33).

purchased the call for $8.05, your return on that investment would be −100%, even though Whirlpool's stock fell just $6.34, or −17.5%, from the date of your purchase.

JOB INTERVIEW QUESTION

Which is riskier, a share of stock or a call option on that stock?

This example illustrates what may be the most important fact to know about options: *When the price of a stock moves, the dollar change in the stock is generally more than the dollar change in the option price, but the percentage change in the option price is much greater than the percentage change in the stock price.* We have heard students argue that buying a call option is less risky than buying the underlying share because the maximum dollar loss that an investor can experience is much less on the option. That's true only if we compare the $36.33 investment required to buy one share of Whirlpool to the $8.05 required to buy one March Whirlpool call. It is accurate to say that the call investor can lose at most $8.05 while an investor in Whirlpool stock might lose $36.33. But there are two problems with this comparison. First, the likelihood that Whirlpool will go bankrupt and its stock will fall to $0 between January and March is negligible. The likelihood that Whirlpool's stock might dip below $30, resulting in a $0 value for the call option, is much greater. Second, it is better to compare an equal dollar investment in Whirlpool stock and Whirlpool calls rather than compare one stock to one call. An investment of $363.30 would purchase 10 shares of Whirlpool stock, but it would purchase about 45 Whirlpool call options. A portfolio of 45 call options is much riskier than a portfolio containing 10 shares of stock.

Concept Review Questions	1. Explain the difference between the stock price, the exercise price, and the option premium. Which of these are market prices determined by the forces of supply and demand?
	2. Explain the difference between a long position and a short position. With respect to call options, what is the maximum gain and loss possible for an investor who holds the long position? What is the maximum gain and loss for the investor on the short side of the transaction?
	3. Suppose that an investor holds a call option on Nestlé stock. If he decides to exercise the option, what will happen to the total shares of common stock outstanding for Nestlé?
	4. Which of the following would increase the value of a put option: an increase in the stock price, an increase in the strike price, or a lengthening of the expiration period?

18.2 OPTION PAYOFF DIAGRAMS

So far, our discussion of options has been mostly descriptive. Now we turn to the problem of determining an option's market price. Valuing an option is an extraordinarily difficult problem, so difficult in fact that the economists who solved the problem won a Nobel Prize for their efforts. In earlier chapters where we studied the pricing of bonds and stocks, we began by describing their cash flows. We will do the same here, focusing initially on the relatively simple problem of outlining cash flows of options on their expiration dates. Eventually, that will help us understand the intuition behind complex option pricing models.

Call Option Payoffs

We define an option's **payoff** as the price an investor would be willing to pay for the option the instant before it expires.[8] An option's payoff is distinct from its price, or premium, because the payoff refers only to the price of the option at a particular instant in time—the

---

[8]Alternatively, we could define the payoff as the value an investor would receive, ignoring transaction costs, when exercising the option upon its expiration. If the option is out of the money on the expiration date, the payoff is zero.

expiration date. **Payoff diagrams** are graphs that illustrate an option's payoff as a function of the underlying stock price. They are extremely useful tools for understanding how options behave and how they can be combined to form portfolios with fascinating properties.

Suppose an investor purchases a call option with a strike price of $75 and an expiration date three months in the future. To acquire this option, the investor pays a premium of $8. When the option expires, what will it be worth? If the underlying stock price is less than $75 on the expiration date, the option will be worthless. No investor would pay anything for the right to buy this stock for $75 when the investor could easily buy it for less in the market. What if the stock price equals $76 on the expiration date? In that case, owning the right to buy the stock at $75 is worth $1, the difference between the stock's market price and the option's exercise price. Ignoring transaction costs, an investor who owns the option can buy the stock for $75 and immediately sell it in the market for $76, earning a $1 payoff. In general, the payoff on this option will equal the *greater* of (i) $0 if the stock price is less than $75 at expiration and (ii) the difference between the stock price and $75 if the stock price is more than $75 at expiration. The red line in Panel A of Figure 18.1 shows a payoff diagram for the call option buyer, or the long position. This picture, a classic in finance, is known as the **hockey-stick diagram**. It shows that the option will at worst be worth $0 and that at best the option's value is unlimited. The green line in the figure represents the investor's **net payoff**. The net payoff line appears $8 lower than the solid line, reflecting the $8 premium that the investor paid to acquire the option. On a net basis, the holder of the call option makes a profit when the price of the stock exceeds $83.[9]

Panel B of Figure 18.1 shows the payoffs from the seller's perspective, or the short position. Options are a zero-sum game, meaning that profits on the long position always correspond to losses on the short side, and vice versa. The red line illustrates that the seller's payoff equals $0 when the stock price is below $75 and that it decreases as the stock price rises above $75. The incentive for the seller to engage in this transaction is the $8 premium, as illustrated by the green line. If the option expires out of the money then the seller earns an $8 profit. If the option expires in the money then the seller may realize a net profit or a net loss, depending on how high the stock price is at that time. Whereas the buyer of a call option enjoys the potential for unlimited gains, the option seller faces exposure to the risk of unlimited losses. If $8 is sufficient to induce a rational person to sell this option and thereby face the potential of huge losses, then the seller must perceive the probability of a large loss to be relatively low.

Put Option Payoffs

Figure 18.2 shows payoffs for put option buyers (long) and sellers (short), again assuming that the strike price of the option is $75 and the option premium equals $8. For an investor holding a put option, the payoff rises as the stock price falls below the option's strike price. However, unlike a call option, a put option has limited potential gains since the price of a stock cannot fall below zero (because the law provides limited liability for a firm's shareholders). The maximum gain on this particular put equals $75 (or $67 on

---

[9]Observe that, when the stock price is above $75 but below $83, it still makes sense for the investor to exercise the option (or to sell it) because doing so reduces her losses. For example, if the stock price at expiration equals $80 then the option payoff is $5, reducing the net loss to −$3. The careful reader will notice that we seem to be making a major error by comparing the $8 premium paid *up front* to the payoff received *three months later*. At this point, ignoring the time value of money in the graphs is relatively harmless, but rest assured that we will take it into account later when we determine the price of an option.

FIGURE 18.1

Payoff of
a Call Option
at Expiration

In this illustration, the
strike price is $75, and
the option premium
is $8.

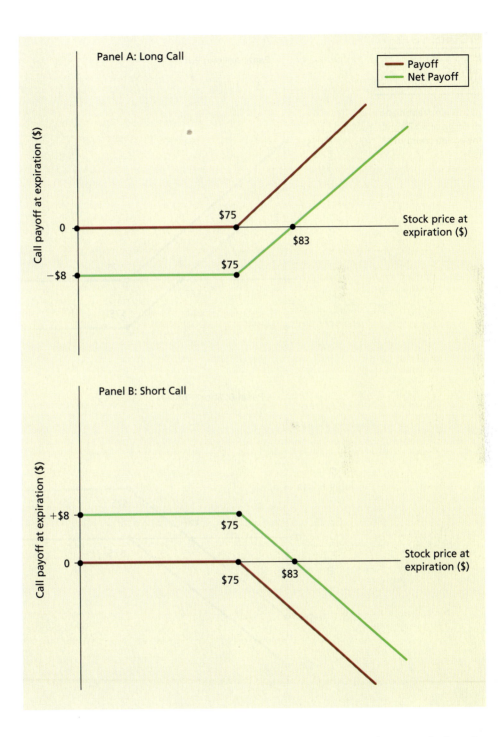

a net basis after subtracting the premium), whereas the maximum loss is, as before, the
$8 option premium.

Again, the seller's perspective is just the opposite of the buyer's. The seller earns a
maximum net gain of $8 if the option expires worthless because the stock price exceeds
$75 on the expiration date, and the seller faces a maximum net loss of $67 if the firm goes
bankrupt and its stock becomes worthless.

FIGURE 18.2

Payoff of
a Put Option
at Expiration

In this illustration, the
strike price is $75, and
the option premium
is $8.

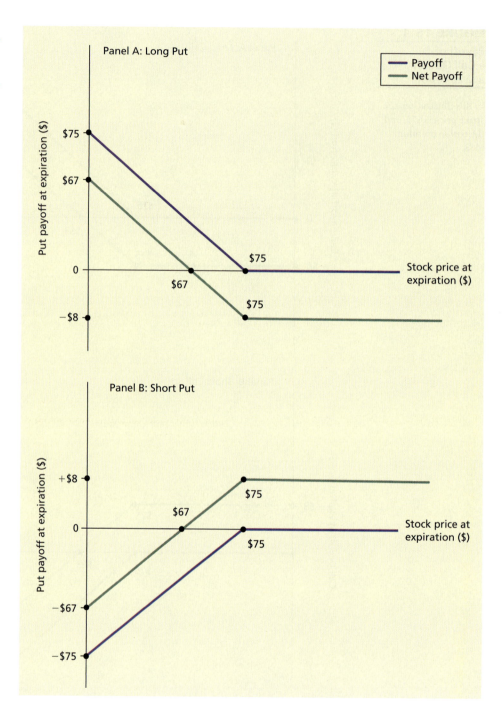

EXAMPLE

Jennifer sells a put option on Electro-Lighting Systems Inc. (ELS) stock to Jason. The option's strike price is $65, and it expires in one month. Jason pays Jennifer a premium of $5 for the option. One month later, ELS stock sells for $45 per share. Jason purchases a share of ELS in the open market for $45 and immediately exercises his option to sell it to Jennifer for $65 (or Jennifer and Jason might agree to settle their contract by having Jennifer pay Jason $20). The payoff on Jason's option is $20, or $15 on a net basis. Jennifer loses $20 on the deal, or just $15 taking into account the $5 premium she received up front.

We must now clarify an important point. Thus far, all our discussions about options payoffs have assumed that each option buyer or seller had what traders refer to as a **naked option position**. A naked call option, for example, occurs when an investor buys or sells an option on a stock without already owning the underlying stock. Similarly, when a trader buys or sells a put option without owning the underlying stock, the trader creates a naked put option. Buying or selling naked options is an act of pure speculation. Investors who buy naked calls believe that the stock price will rise. Investors who sell naked calls believe the opposite. Similarly, buyers of naked puts expect the stock price to fall, and sellers take the opposite view.

But many options trades do not involve this kind of speculation. Investors who own a particular stock may purchase a put option on that stock not because they expect the stock price to decline but rather because they want protection in the event that it does. Executives who own shares of their company's stock may sell call options, even if they think their shares may increase in value, because they are willing to give up potential profits on their shares in exchange for current income. To understand this proposition, we need to examine payoff diagrams for portfolios of options and other securities.

Payoffs for Portfolios of Options and Other Securities

Experienced options traders know that, by combining different types of options, they can construct a wide range of portfolios with unusual payoff structures. Think about what happens if an investor simultaneously buys a call option and a put option on the same underlying stock and with the same exercise price. We have seen before that the call option pays off handsomely if the stock price rises, whereas the put option is most profitable if the stock price falls. By combining both into one portfolio, an investor has a position that can make money whether the stock price rises or falls.

Suppose that Cybil cannot decide whether she expects the stock of Internet Phones Corp. (IPC) to rise or fall from its current value of $30. Cybil decides to purchase a call option and a put option on IPC stock, both having a strike price of $30 and an expiration date of April 20. She pays premiums of $4.50 for the call and $3.50 for the put, for a total cost of $8. Figure 18.3 illustrates Cybil's position. The payoff of her portfolio equals $0 if IPC's stock price is $30 on April 20, and if that occurs then Cybil experiences a net loss of $8. But if the stock price is higher or lower than $30 on April 20, at least one of Cybil's options will be in the money. On a net basis, Cybil makes a profit if IPC stock falls below $22 or rises above $38, but she does not have to take a view on which outcome is more likely.

In this example, Cybil is speculating, but not on the *direction* of IPC stock. Rather, Cybil's gamble is on the *volatility* of IPC shares. If the shares move a great deal, either up or down, she makes a net profit. If the shares have not moved much by April 20, she experiences a net loss. Options traders refer to this type of position as a **long straddle**, a portfolio consisting of long positions in calls and puts on the same stock with the same strike price and expiration

FIGURE 18.3

Payoff of a Long
Straddle

In this illustration,
the strike price is $30,
and the call and put
premiums combined
are $8. By purchasing
a call and a put that
have the same strike
price, an investor can
profit from a significant
change in the underly-
ing stock price in either
direction.

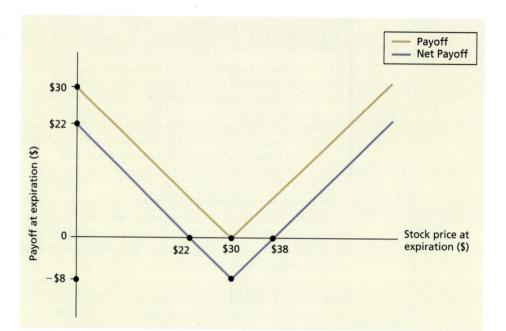

date. Naturally, creating a **short straddle** is possible, too. If Cybil believed that IPC stock would not move far from its current value, then she could simultaneously sell a put and a call option on IPC stock with a strike price of $30. She would receive $8 in option premiums from this trade; if IPC stock were priced at $30 on April 20, then both of the options she sold would expire worthless. On the other hand, if IPC stock moved up or down from $30 then one of the options would be exercised, reducing Cybil's profits from the options sale.

Now let's look at what happens when investors form portfolios by combining options with other securities, such as stocks and bonds. To begin, examine Figure 18.4, which displays payoff diagrams for a long position in common stocks and bonds.[10] A payoff dia-gram shows the total value of a security (in this case, one share of common stock or one bond) on a specific future date on the *y*-axis along with the value of a share of stock on that same date on the *x*-axis. In Figure 18.4, the payoff diagram from holding a share of stock is simply a 45-degree line emanating from the origin because both axes of the graph are plotting the same thing—the value of the stock on a future date.[11]

The payoff diagram for the bond requires a little more explanation. The type of bond we have in mind in this example is very special. It is a risk-free, zero-coupon bond with a face value of $75. The bond matures at precisely the same time as the put and call options expire. The payoff for an investor who purchases this bond is simply $75, no matter what the price of the stock underlying the put and call options turns out to be. Thus, the diagram shows a horizontal line at $75 for the long bond's payoff.[12] Again the payoff from shorting the bond is the opposite of the long-bond payoff diagram.

---

[10]In Figure 18.4 we do not plot the net payoff, which means that the diagram ignores the initial cost of buying stocks or bonds and any revenue obtained from shorting them.

[11]Figure 18.4 also shows the payoff diagram for a short position in stock; as always, it is just the mirror image of the long payoff diagram. When investors *short-sell* a stock, they borrow the share from another investor, promising to return the share at a future date. Short selling therefore creates a liability. The magnitude of that liability is just the price of the stock that the short-seller must return on a future date.

[12]Is it really possible to buy a risk-free bond with a face value of $75? Perhaps not, but an investor could buy 75 Treasury bills, each with a face value of $1,000, resulting in a risk-free bond portfolio with a face value of $75,000. The assumption that investors can buy risk-free bonds with any face value is just a simplification to keep the numbers in our examples manageable.

FIGURE 18.4

Payoff Diagrams for Stocks and Bonds

The bond in this illustration is a risk-free, zero-coupon bond with a $75 face value.

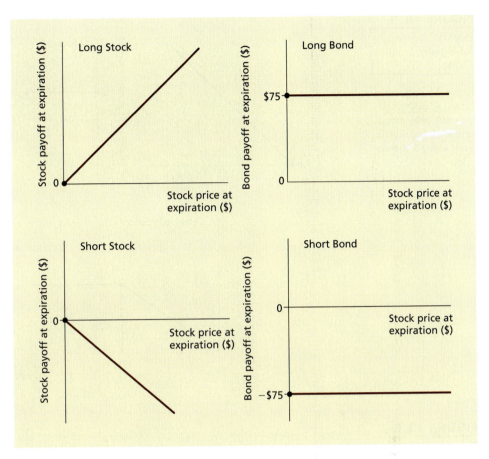

Figure 18.5 illustrates **writing covered calls**, a common trading strategy that mixes stock and call options. In this strategy, an investor who owns a share of stock sells a call option on that stock. By selling the call, the investor receives the option premium immediately. However, the trade-off is that if the stock price rises, the holder of the call option will exercise the right to purchase it at the strike price and so the investor will lose the opportunity to benefit from the stock's appreciation in value. For example, suppose that Michael owns a share of IBM stock. Michael sells a call option on his share to Kathryn for $6. The option has a strike price of $75. As long as the stock price does not rise above $75, Michael will keep the $6 option premium and will retain ownership of his IBM share. If the price rises above $75, however, Kathryn will call the share away from Michael. He will get $75 in cash from Kathryn, but he will not benefit from appreciation beyond that point.

Consider a portfolio consisting of one share of stock and one put option on that share with a strike price of $75. If the stock price equals $75 on the option's expiration date, then the put option will be worthless. Therefore, the portfolio's total value will be $75. Now imagine that the stock price falls to $50. At that point, the put option's payoff is $25, leaving the combined portfolio value at $75. The put option provides a kind of portfolio insurance, for it guarantees that the share of stock can be sold for $75. However, if the stock price rises, the portfolio value will rise right along with it. Though the put option will be worthless, any increase in the stock price above $75 increases the portfolio's value, as shown in Figure 18.6. This strategy is known as a **protective put**.

FIGURE 18.5

Payoff Diagram for Covered Call Strategy

In this illustration, the combined position is the result of holding a long stock and shorting a call with a $75 strike price.

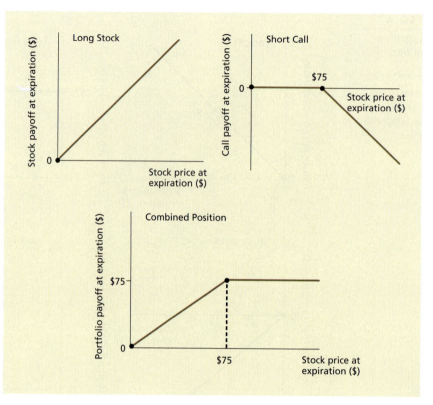

FIGURE 18.6

Payoff of a Put Option and a Share of Stock: A Protective Put

In this illustration, the combined position results from buying a share of stock and a put option with a strike price of $75 on that share.

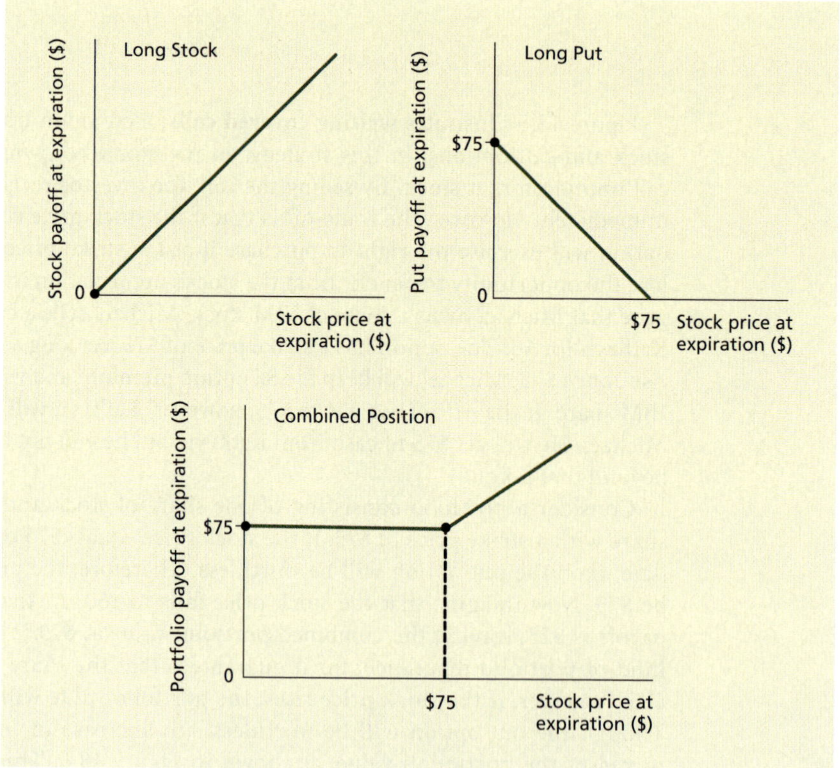

Next, evaluate the payoffs of a portfolio consisting of one risk-free, zero-coupon bond with a face value of $75 and one call option with an exercise price of $75. As Figure 18.7 shows, the bond guarantees that an investor holding this portfolio will have a payoff of at least $75. The payoff can be more if the stock price increases above $75, causing the call value to increase.

FIGURE 18.7

Payoff of a Call Option and a Zero-Coupon Bond

In this illustration, the combined position results from buying a risk-free, zero-coupon bond with a face value of $75 and a call option with a strike price of $75. Notice that the combined position here is identical to that shown in Figure 18.6.

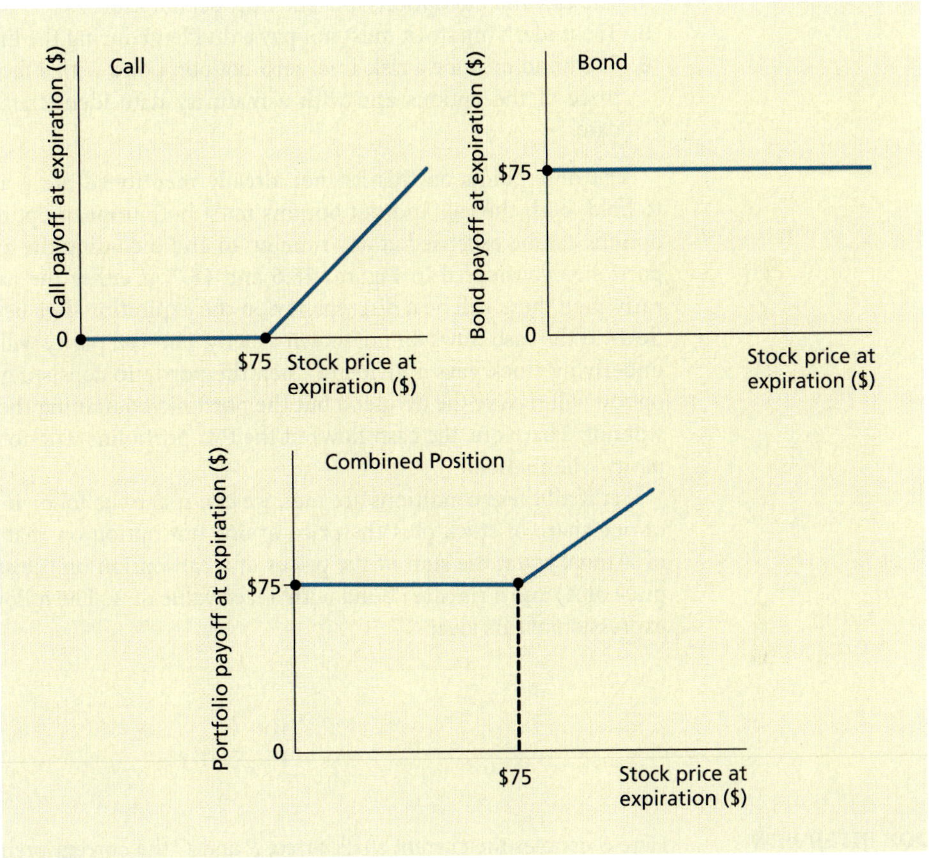

A careful look at Figures 18.6 and 18.7 reveals a surprising fact. The payoffs of the portfolio containing one share of stock and one put option are exactly the same as the payoffs of the portfolio containing one bond and one call option. Both portfolios offer a minimum payoff of $75 and upside potential if the underlying stock price increases. If both of these portfolios offer investors the same cash flows when the options expire, then both portfolios must have the same value today. This link between put and call prices, known as **put–call parity**, is one of the most fundamental results in option-pricing theory. Put–call parity holds only under a rather restrictive set of assumptions, but it nevertheless has many important practical applications.

Put–Call Parity

Using Put–Call Parity to Find Arbitrage Opportunities   Figures 18.6 and 18.7 illustrate that a portfolio of a stock and a put option offers exactly the same future cash flows as a portfolio of a bond and a call option. To be absolutely certain that the cash flows of these portfolios will be identical at the options' expiration date, the following conditions must be met:

1. The call and put options must be on the same underlying stock.
2. The call and put options must have the same exercise price.
3. The call and put options must share the same expiration date.
4. The call and put options must be European options.
5. The underlying stock must not pay a dividend during the life of the options.
6. The bond must be a risk-free, zero-coupon bond with a face value equal to the strike price of the options and with a maturity date identical to the options' expiration date.

The only points on this list not already mentioned are 4 and 5. For put–call parity to hold, both the call and put options must be European options. Recall that American options can be exercised at any time up to and including the expiration date. In the two portfolios considered in Figures 18.6 and 18.7, if either the call or the put is exercised early then there will be a discrepancy on the expiration date between the portfolios' cash flows. If the cash flows do not match exactly, put–call parity will not hold. Similarly, if the underlying stock pays a dividend, then the portfolio consisting of the stock plus the put option will receive the dividend but the portfolio containing the call option and the bond will not. Therefore, the cash flows of the two portfolios will not match exactly, and again parity will not hold.

Yet if all these conditions are met, we can make the following strong claim. The price of one share of stock plus the price of one put option on that stock with a strike price of X must equal the sum of the prices of a call option on the stock (also having a strike price of X) and a risk-free bond with a face value of X. The following is a simple algebraic expression of this idea:

$$
\begin{aligned}
S + P &= B + C \\
&= PV(X) + C
\end{aligned}
$$

(Eq. 18.1)

JOB INTERVIEW QUESTION

How are the prices of puts and calls on the same underlying stock related?

Here S denotes the current stock price, P and C the current premiums on the put and call options (respectively), and B the current price of the risk-free, zero-coupon bond. In the equation's second line we substitute $PV(X)$ for B simply to indicate that, if the bond's face value is $\$X$, then the price of that bond will be the present value of $\$X$ discounted at the risk-free rate.

If you blinked, you may have just missed a significant intellectual leap. Up to now, all our discussions about options have focused on their *payoffs*. Remember, we defined an option's payoff as the price someone would pay for it just before it expired. Determining the market value of an option just before it expires is rather trivial, but in Equation 18.1 we are talking about *option prices at any moment in time*, not just on the expiration date. Because the portfolios on the right- and left-hand sides of Equation 18.1 offer investors identical future cash flows, they must have identical market values on the expiration date, one day before expiration, one week before expiration, and at any other moment in time. One implication of this is that investors who know the market prices of any three of the securities listed in Equation 18.1 can determine what the market price of the fourth security must be to prevent arbitrage opportunities.

EXAMPLE

Mototronics Inc. stock sells for $28 per share. Puts and calls on Mototronics shares are available with a strike price of $30 and an expiration date of one year. The Mototronics call option sells for $6, and the risk-free rate is 5%. What is the appropriate price for the Mototronics put option? Using Equation 18.1, we can derive a price for the put option:

$$S + P = PV(X) + C$$

$$\$28 + P = \frac{\$30}{(1.05)^1} + \$6$$

$$P = \$6.57$$

How can we be sure that $6.57 is the right price for the put option? The reason is that *any other price* would give investors an arbitrage opportunity, a chance to earn unlimited profits without taking any risk. To see how this would work, suppose that the actual market price of the Mototronics put option is $7 rather than $6.57. At that price, the put option is overvalued, so smart investors will sell it. But just selling the put option is not, in itself, arbitrage. Arbitrage means simultaneously buying and selling identical assets at different prices to earn a risk-free profit. Therefore, if the first step in the arbitrage is to sell the put for $7, then traders must also buy an identical asset at a lower price. What kind of asset is identical to a put option? Rearranging the put–call parity equation just a little gives the answer:

$$S + P = PV(X) + C$$

$$P = PV(X) + C - S$$

Put–call parity says that a portfolio containing a share of stock and a put is identical to one containing a bond and a call option. The second equation makes a similar claim. It says that a put option offers cash flows that are identical to those produced by a portfolio containing a bond, a call option, and a short position in the underlying stock.[13] In options lingo, we say that traders can create a **synthetic put option** by purchasing a bond and a call option while simultaneously short-selling the stock.

To exploit the arbitrage opportunity, investors will sell the Mototronics put for $7. Next, to offset the risk of the first trade, arbitrageurs will purchase a bond and a call option and will short-sell the stock. The immediate consequences of these trades are outlined as follows:

Cash Inflows		Cash Outflows	
Sell put	+$7	Buy bond	$\frac{-\$30}{(1.05)^1} = -\$28.57$
Sell stock	+$28	Buy call	−$6

Net cash flow = $7 + $28 − $28.57 − $6 = +$0.43

---

[13]In put–call parity math, a negative sign means "sell" rather than "buy." Therefore, the terms on the right side of the equation, PV(X) + C − S, mean "buy a bond, buy a call, and sell (or sell short) the stock."

FIGURE 18.8

Put–Call Parity Arbitrage

In this illustration, the top diagram shows the payoff from selling a put option. The remaining diagrams illustrate that a portfolio consisting of a long bond, a long call, and a short position in the underlying stock replicates the payoff of a long put position. Thus, if an investor takes all of these positions simultaneously, the payoffs cancel out, and the combined position is risk-free.

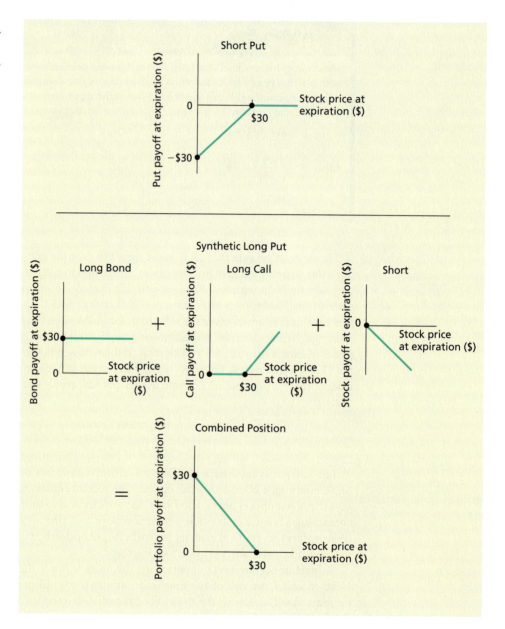

Traders following this strategy pocket $0.43 each time they execute these trades. Notice that $0.43 equals the difference between the put option's theoretically correct price ($6.57) and its actual price ($7). In other words, the arbitrage profits are equal to the pricing discrepancy. What remains to be shown is that the profits from this strategy are truly risk free. Figure 18.8 and Table 18.2 show just that. First look at the figure, whose upper part shows the payoff from taking a short position in the put option. The lower part shows that—by combining a long bond, a long call, and a short stock—an investor creates a portfolio with a payoff identical to a that of a long put option. The short put at the top of the figure and the combined position—the synthetic long put—at the bottom cancel each other out, resulting in a risk-free portfolio.

Table 18.2 Using Arbitrage to Exploit a Mispriced Put

IF MOTOTRONICS STOCK PRICE IS ($)	VALUE OF SYNTHETIC PUT ($)				TOTAL PORTFOLIO VALUE ($)
	VALUE OF (SHORT) ACTUAL PUT IS	VALUE OF LONG BOND IS	VALUE OF LONG CALL IS	VALUE OF SHORT STOCK IS	
10	−20	30	0	−10	−20 + 30 + 0 − 10 = 0
15	−15	30	0	−15	−15 + 30 + 0 − 15 = 0
20	−10	30	0	−20	−10 + 30 + 0 − 20 = 0
25	−5	30	0	−25	−5 + 30 + 0 − 25 = 0
30	0	30	0	−30	0 + 30 + 0 − 30 = 0
35	0	30	5	−35	0 + 30 + 5 − 35 = 0
40	0	30	10	−40	0 + 30 + 10 − 40 = 0

Notes: No matter what value Mototronics stock takes, the value of the actual put that the arbitrageur sold is precisely offset by the value of the synthetic put that the arbitrageur purchased. The arbitrage portfolio consists of short positions in the put option and the stock and of long positions in the bond and the call. The put and call options have an exercise price of $30, and $30 is the bond's face value.

In the first column of Table 18.2 we list a range of prices that Mototronics stock might reach in one year, when these options are expiring. The other columns show the value of the arbitrage transaction at each possible stock price. Take a look at the first row of the table, where we consider what happens if Mototronics stock ends the year at $10. The first trade in the arbitrage strategy was to sell a put option with a $30 exercise price. If Mototronics stock is worth $10, then the investor to whom the put option was sold will exercise it, resulting in a loss to the arbitrageur of $20. The second part of the arbitrage strategy was to buy a risk-free bond with a face value of $30. Clearly, the value of this holding will be $30 in one year. The third part of the trade was to buy a call option with an exercise price of $30. With Mototronics stock at $10, this call will be worthless. The final part of the trade was to short-sell Mototronics stock. At the end of the year, an arbitrageur must return that share to its owner; doing so will cost the trader $10, the current market price of the stock. Adding all this together, we have the following:

Put option	−$20
Bond	+$30
Call option	$ 0
Short stock	−$10
Total value	$ 0

John Eck, President of Broadcast and Network Operations, NBC

"That allowed us to create some doubt around the transaction and allowed us not to have to book the gain up front but to book it as the cash came in."

See the entire interview at
SMARTFinance

In the last column of Table 18.2, we add up the values of these positions and show that—no matter what the year-end price of Mototronics stock turns out to be—the portfolio of securities held by arbitrageurs will be worthless. Holding a portfolio of worthless securities may not seem like much of an investment strategy until you consider that this portfolio generated a net cash inflow up front. Arbitrageurs could engage in this strategy repeatedly, thereby reaping unlimited profits as long as the prices of the securities being traded did not change. Of course, the prices will change, quickly eliminating the arbitrage profit.

5. What would happen if an investor combined the protective put and covered call strategies by simultaneously buying a put option with a strike price of $50 and selling a call option with a strike price of $50? You can assume that the investor already owns the underlying stock.
6. Is selling a call the same as buying a put? Explain why or why not.
7. A major corporation on the verge of going bankrupt is seeking a government bailout. If the company obtains a rescue package from the government, investors expect its stock price to shoot up. If not, the stock price will decline even more than it already has. If investors expect politicians to respond to the firm's request for help in the near future, how will those expectations be reflected in the prices of call and put options on the company's stock?
8. Take another look at the six conditions that must be met for put–call parity to hold. Can you explain why each one of them is necessary?

18.3 QUALITATIVE ANALYSIS OF OPTION PRICING

Factors That Influence Option Values

Before getting into the complex quantitative aspects of pricing options, let's develop some intuition that will help us understand the factors that influence option prices. We begin by taking a closer look at some of the January 23, 2009, price quotations for Whirlpool stock options in Table 18.1. Begin by focusing only on the prices of call and put options that have an exercise price of $45.00. Here are the figures from the table:

Whirlpool	Expiration	Strike	Call	Put
$36.33	February	$45.00	$0.60	$ 9.35
$36.33	March	$45.00	$1.25	$10.35
$36.33	June	$45.00	$3.10	$12.45

You should notice a striking pattern here. The prices of both calls and puts rise the longer the time before expiration. To understand why, think about the call option that expires in February. Currently, this option is out of the money because it grants the right to purchase Whirlpool stock for $45.00, but investors can buy Whirlpool in the open market at $36.33. Buying the February call option requires an investment of just $0.60. The option is inexpensive because there is only a small chance that, in the month remaining before the option expires, Whirlpool's stock price will increase enough to make exercising the option worthwhile. No investor would exercise this option until Whirlpool stock reached at least $45.01, representing an increase of almost 24% from its current price. Investors are not willing to pay more than $0.60 for this option because they doubt that Whirlpool stock will rise that much in one month.

However, the price of the June call option with a strike price of $45.00 is more than five times greater than the price of the February call. The June option expires in about five months, so investors must think that the odds of a 24% increase (or more) in Whirlpool stock over that time period are much higher than the odds of seeing the same move by the third Saturday of February. The same pattern holds for puts. The June put option sells for $3.10 more than the February put option because investors recognize that the chance of a significant drop in Whirlpool stock by February is much lower than the chance of a large decrease over the next five months. We can generalize all this as follows: *Holding other factors constant, call and put option prices increase as the time to expiration increases.*[14]

Next, let's examine the prices of all the Whirlpool calls and puts that expire in March. Here are the figures from Table 18.1:

Whirlpool	Expiration	Strike	Call	Put
$36.33	March	$30.00	$8.05	$2.05
$36.33	March	$35.00	$4.90	$3.90
$36.33	March	$40.00	$2.60	$6.70
$36.33	March	$45.00	$1.25	$10.35

Once again, a clear pattern emerges. The prices of call options fall as the strike price increases, and the prices of put options rise as the strike price increases. This relationship is quite intuitive. A call option grants the right to buy stock at a fixed price. That right is more valuable the cheaper is the price at which the option holder can buy the stock. Conversely, put options grant the right to sell shares at a fixed price. That right is more valuable the higher is the price at which investors can sell. By the same reasoning, call options will rise when the underlying stock price goes up, and puts will rise when the underlying stock price goes down. Summarizing, we can say that *call prices decrease and put prices increase when the difference between the underlying stock price and the exercise price (S − X) decreases.*

Finally, to isolate the most important and most subtle influence on option prices, take a look at one more set of option prices in Table 18.3. The table shows March call and put prices for Whirlpool and Universal Health Services (UHS), a firm that operates hospital and surgical centers. On January 23, 2009, UHS stock traded for $36.10, just $0.23 less than Whirlpool's price. Because the stock prices of these two firms are so similar, we might

Table 18.3	Option Prices ($) for Universal Health Services (UHS) and Whirlpool (WHR)				
COMPANY	**EXPIRATION**	**STRIKE**	**CALL**	**PUT**
UHS	March	30	7.10	0.95
36.10	March	35	3.30	2.45
36.10	March	40	1.30	5.10
36.10	March	45	0.30	9.40
WHR	March	30	8.05	2.05
36.33	March	35	4.90	3.90
36.33	March	40	2.60	6.70
36.33	March	45	1.25	10.35

Note: Option prices retrieved from www.cboe.com on January 23, 2009.

---

[14]There are a few exceptions to this rule. Flip back the calendar to November 2008, and imagine that you own a *European* put option on Circuit City stock. Circuit City's stock trades for pennies a share because the firm has announced that it is going out of business. If the strike price of your put option is $10, then you can make a profit of almost $10 by exercising your option if you can exercise it immediately. But what if the option's expiration date is several months away? The potential for further declines in Circuit City stock, given that it already sells for just a few cents, is negligible, so you would rather exercise your option now and invest the profits in something else. Instead, you must wait to exercise and so lose the time value of money for five months; hence you would pay more for a European option that expires immediately than for one that expires a few months in the future.

expect options written on them to have similar prices, too. In fact, with Whirlpool's price being slightly above the UHS price, we might expect Whirlpool's calls to be a little more valuable (and its puts a little less valuable) than similar puts and calls written on UHS.

Table 18.3 shows that Whirlpool options are quite a bit more valuable than options on UHS, and this holds for both calls and puts. For example, for options with a strike price of $35, the Whirlpool call is worth $1.60 more than the UHS call and the Whirlpool put is worth $1.45 more than the comparable UHS put. With Whirlpool and Universal Health Services stocks trading at nearly identical prices, why are Whirlpool options more valuable?

Figure 18.9 contains a clue to the answer. The graph displays the daily percentage price change in Universal Health Services (red line) and Whirlpool (green line) shares from November 2008 to January 2009 (when we gathered the option prices in the table). A quick glance at the figure shows that Whirlpool stock was generally more volatile than UHS stock over this period. That shouldn't be too surprising because Whirlpool's business, making appliances for the home, is much more sensitive to the business cycle than is the health care business. Looking at Figure 18.9, you can see that the daily changes in Whirlpool shares tended to be sharper than those for UHS stock. For example, Whirlpool's shares moved more than 5% (up or down) on a single day about twice as often as UHS stock did.

FIGURE 18.9

Daily Percentage Stock Price Changes for Universal Health Services (UHS) and Whirlpool (WHR)

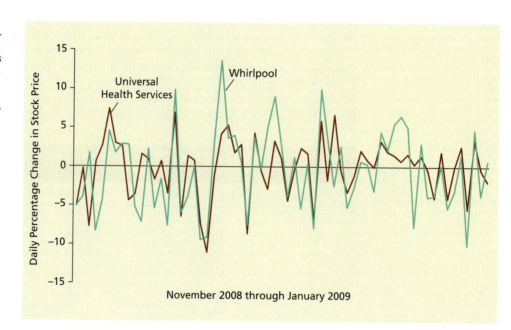

Why should Whirlpool's higher volatility lead to higher call and put option prices? The answer lies in the asymmetry of option payoffs. When a call option expires, its payoff will be zero for a wide range of stock prices. Whether the stock price falls below the option's strike price by $1, $10, or $100, the payoff will still be zero. On the other hand, as the stock price rises above the strike price, the option's payoff increases. A similar relationship holds for puts. The value of a put at expiration will be zero if the stock price is greater than the strike price, and whether the stock price is just above the strike price or far above it does not change the payoff. However, the put option will have a larger payoff the lower the stock price falls, once it falls below the strike price. The bottom line is that *call and put option prices increase as the volatility of the underlying stock increases.*

EXAMPLE

Suppose that you are tracking two stocks, one of which exhibits much more volatility than the other. Call the more volatile stock Extreme Inc. and the less volatile one Steady Corp. At present, shares of both companies sell for about $40. At-the-money call and put options are available on both stocks with an expiration date in three months. Based on the historical volatility of each stock, you estimate a range of prices that you think the shares might attain by the time the options expire. Next to each possible stock price, you write down the option payoff that will occur if the stock actually reaches that price on the expiration date (the strike price is $40 for both options).

The following table gives the numbers:

Stock	Potential Prices	Call Payoff	Put Payoff
Extreme Inc.	$15	$ 0	$25
	25	0	15
	35	0	5
	45	5	0
	55	15	0
	65	25	0
Steady Corp.	30	0	10
	34	0	6
	38	0	2
	42	2	0
	46	6	0
	50	10	0

The payoffs of calls and puts for both companies are zero exactly half the time. But when the payoffs are not zero, they are much larger for Extreme Inc. than they are for Steady Corp. This makes options on Extreme Inc. shares much more valuable than options on Steady Corp. stock.

Summing up, we now know that option prices increase as time to expiration increases and as the volatility of the underlying asset increases. Call option prices decrease the smaller the difference between the stock price and the strike price $(S - X)$, whereas put prices increase as this difference decreases. We are now ready to tie all this together and calculate the market price of calls and puts. We conclude this chapter by studying a simple but powerful tool for valuing options, the binomial option pricing model.

Concept Review Questions

9. Throughout most of this book, we have shown that if an asset's risk increases then its price declines. Why is the opposite true for options?

10. Call options increase in value when stock prices rise, and put options increase in value when stock prices fall. How can the same movement in an underlying variable (e.g., an increase in time before expiration or an increase in volatility) cause both call and put prices to rise at the same time?

18.4 CALCULATING OPTION PRICES

The Binomial Option Pricing Model

Earlier in this chapter, we studied an important relationship linking the prices of puts, calls, shares, and risk-free bonds. Put–call parity establishes a direct link between the prices of these assets, a link that must hold to prevent arbitrage opportunities. A similar logic drives the **binomial option pricing model**. The binomial model recognizes that investors can combine options (either calls or puts) with shares of the underlying asset to construct a portfolio with a risk-free payoff. Any asset with a risk-free payoff is relatively easy to value—just discount its future cash flows at the risk-free rate. But if we can value a portfolio containing options and shares, then we can also calculate the value of the options simply by subtracting the value of the shares from the value of the portfolio.

We will illustrate the binomial model by working through an example that proceeds in three distinct steps. First, we must find a portfolio of stock and options that generates a risk-free payoff in the future. Second, given that the portfolio offers a risk-free cash payment, we can calculate the present value of that portfolio by discounting its cash flow at the risk-free rate. Third, given the portfolio's present value, we can determine how much of the portfolio's value comes from the stock and how much comes from the option. By subtracting the value of the underlying shares from the value of the portfolio, we obtain the option's market price.

Create a Risk-Free Portfolio Assume that the shares of Financial Engineers Ltd. currently sell for $55. We want to determine the price of a call option on Financial Engineers stock with an exercise price of $55 and an expiration date in one year. The risk-free rate is 4%.

The binomial model begins with an assumption about the volatility of the underlying stock. Specifically, the model assumes that by the time the option expires, the stock will have increased or decreased to a particular value. In this problem, we will assume that, one year from now, Financial Engineers' stock price will have risen to $70 or it will have fallen to $40. Figure 18.10 provides a simple diagram of this assumption.[15]

FIGURE 18.10

Binomial Option Pricing

In this illustration, the current stock price is $55, and, in one year, the stock will either rise to $70 or fall to $40. A one-year call option with a strike price of $55 will pay $15 at expiration if the stock price goes up, and it will pay $0 if the stock price goes down.

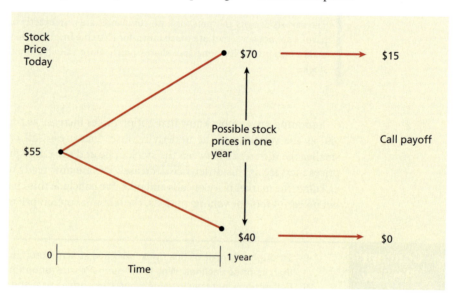

[15]How can we possibly know that the price of Financial Engineers stock will be either $70 or $40? Of course, we cannot know that. Almost any price is possible one year in the future. Very soon we will illustrate that this assumption, which seems completely ridiculous now, isn't really necessary in a more complex version of the binomial model. But let's understand the simple version first.

The call option we want to price has a strike price of $55. Therefore, if the underlying stock reaches $70 in one year, the call option will be worth $15. However, if Financial Engineers stock falls to $40, the call option will be worthless.

Here is the crux of the first step. We want to find some combination of Financial Engineers stock and the call option that yields the same payoff whether the stock goes up or down over the next year. In other words, we want to create a risk-free combination of shares and calls. To begin, suppose we purchase one share of stock and h call options. At the moment, we do not know the value of h, but we can solve for it. Because our portfolio objective is to generate the same cash payment one year from now whether our share of stock rises or falls, we can write down the portfolio's payoffs in each possible scenario and then choose h so that the payoffs are equal:

	Cash Flows One Year from Today	
	If the Stock Price Rises to $70	If the Stock Price Drops to $40
One share of stock is worth	$70	$40
h call options are worth	$15h	$0h
Total portfolio is worth	$70 + $15h	$40 + $0h

A portfolio containing one share of stock and h call options will have the same cash value in one year if we choose the value of h that solves this equation:

$$\$70 + \$15h = \$40 + \$0h$$
$$h = -2$$

The value of h represents the number of call options in our risk-free portfolio. Because h equals -2, to create a risk-free portfolio we must *sell two call options* and combine that position with our single share of stock. Why do we sell options to achieve this objective? Remember that the value of a call option rises as the stock price rises. If we own a share of stock and a call option (or several call options) on that stock, then the assets in our portfolio will be positively correlated, rising and falling at the same time. Recall from Chapter 5 that the only circumstance in which it is possible to combine two risky assets into a risk-free portfolio occurs when the correlation between the two assets is negative (in fact, -1.0). Therefore, if we buy a share, we must also sell call options to create a negative correlation between the assets in our portfolio.

What happens to our portfolio if, in fact, we buy one share of stock and sell two calls? You can see the answer in two ways. First, just plug the value -2 back into the equation we used to solve for h:

$$\$70 + \$15(-2) = \$40 + \$0(-2)$$
$$\$40 = \$40$$

This expression says that the portfolio payoff will be $40 whether the stock price increases or decreases. The other way to see this is to lay out the payoffs of each asset in the portfolio in a table.

	Cash Flows One Year from Today	
	If the Stock Price Rises to $70	If the Stock Price Drops to $40
One share of stock is worth	$70	$40
Two short call options are worth	−$30	$ 0
Total portfolio is worth	$40	$40

The first row of the table is self-explanatory. The second row indicates that if we sell two call options and the stock price equals $70 next year, then we will owe the holder of the calls $15 per option or $30 total. On the other hand, if one year from now the stock price equals $40, the call options we sold will be worthless and we will have no cash outflow. In either case, the total cash inflow from the portfolio will be $40.

Because this portfolio pays $40 in one year no matter what happens, we call it a perfectly hedged portfolio. The value of h is called the **hedge ratio** because it tells us what combination of stocks and calls results in a perfectly hedged position.[16]

Calculating the Present Value of the Portfolio Because the portfolio consisting of one share of stock and two short call options pays $40 for certain next year, we can say that the portfolio is a type of synthetic, risk-free bond. The second step requires us to calculate the present value of the portfolio. Because we already know that the risk-free rate equals 4%, we can determine the present value of the portfolio:

$$PV = \frac{\$40}{1.04} = \$38.46$$

It is crucial at this step to understand the following point. Buying one share of stock and selling two calls yields the same future payoff as buying a risk-free, zero-coupon bond with a face value of $40. Because both of these investments offer $40 at the end of one year with certainty, they should both sell for the same price today. This insight allows us to determine the option's price in the next step.

Determine the Price of the Call Option If a risk-free bond paying $40 in one year costs $38.46 today, then the net cost of buying one share of Financial Engineers stock and selling two call options must also be $38.46. Why? Because both investment strategies are risk-free and offer the same future cash flows, they must both sell for the same price. Therefore, to determine the price of the option, all we need to do is write down an expression for the cost of our hedged portfolio and set that expression equal to $38.46.

From the information given in the problem, purchasing one share of stock costs $55. Partially offsetting this cost will be the revenue from selling two call options. Denoting the price of the call option with the letter C, we can calculate the total cost of the portfolio as follows:

$$\text{Total portfolio cost} = \$55 - 2C = \$38.46$$

Solving for C, we obtain a call value of $8.27.

At this point, it is worth reviewing what we have accomplished. We began with an assumption about the future movements of the underlying stock. Next, given the type of option we want to value and its characteristics, we calculated the payoffs of the option for each of the two possible future stock prices. Given those payoffs, we discovered that, by buying one share and selling two calls, we could generate a certain payoff of $40 in one year. The present value of that payoff is $38.46, so the net cost of buying the share and selling the two calls must also equal $38.46. This implies that we received revenue of $16.54 from selling two calls, or $8.27 each. The following Example repeats the process to value an identical put option on the same underlying stock.

---

[16]The *hedge ratio* can be defined either as the ratio of calls to shares in a perfectly hedged portfolio (the definition we use here) or as the ratio of shares to calls. In this example, the hedge ratio equals either −2:1 (using our definition) or −1:2 (using the alternative definition). Either way, the hedge ratio defines the mix of options and shares that results in a perfectly hedged portfolio.

EXAMPLE

We begin this problem with the same set of assumptions for Financial Engineers given previously. Financial Engineers stock sells for $55 but may increase to $70 or decrease to $40 in one year. The risk-free rate equals 4%. We want to use the binomial model to calculate the value of a 1-year put option with a strike price of $55. We begin by finding the composition of a perfectly hedged portfolio. As before, begin by writing down the payoffs of a portfolio containing one share of stock and h put options:

	Cash Flows One Year from Today	
	If the Stock Price Rises to $70	If the Stock Price Drops to $40
One share of stock is worth	$70	$40
h put options are worth	$0h	$15h
Total portfolio is worth	$70 + $0h	$40 + $15h

Notice that the put option pays $15 when the stock price drops but pays nothing when the stock price rises. Now set the payoffs in each scenario equal to each other and solve for h:

$$\$70 + \$0h = \$40 + \$15h$$
$$h = 2$$

To create a perfectly hedged portfolio, we must buy one share of stock and two put options. Observe that in this problem we are buying options, not selling them. Put values increase when stock values decrease, so it is possible to form a risk-free portfolio containing long positions in both stock and puts because they are negatively correlated. By plugging the value of $h = 2$ back into the equation, we see that an investor who buys one share of stock and two put options essentially creates a synthetic bond with a face value of $70:

$$\$70 + \$0(2) = \$40 + \$15(2)$$
$$\$70 = \$70$$

Given a risk-free rate of 4%, the present value today of $70 is $67.31. It would cost $67.31 to buy a 1-year, risk-free bond paying $70, so it must also cost $67.31 to buy the synthetic version of that bond, consisting of one share stock and two puts. Given that the current share price is $55 and letting P denote the price of the put, we find that the put option is worth $6.16 (rounding to the nearest penny):

$$\text{Cost of 1 share} + 2 \text{ puts} = \$55 + 2P = \$67.31$$
$$\$12.31 = 2P$$
$$\$6.16 = P$$

Take a moment to look over the two examples of pricing options using the binomial approach. Make a list of the data needed to price these options:

1. The current price of the underlying stock
2. The amount of time remaining before the option expires
3. The strike price of the option
4. The risk-free rate
5. The possible values of the underlying stock in the future

JOB INTERVIEW QUESTION

What factors influence the price of an option?

On this list, the only unknown is the fifth item. You can easily find the other four necessary values simply by looking at current market data.

At this point, we pause to ask one of our all-time favorite exam questions. Look back at Figure 18.10. What assumption are we making there about the probabilities of an up and a down move in Financial Engineers stock? Most people see that the figure shows two possible outcomes and guess that the probabilities must be 50-50. This is not true; at no point in our discussion did we make any assumption about the probabilities of up and down movements in the stock. We don't have to know what those probabilities are to value the option, which is convenient because estimating them could be very difficult.

Why are the probabilities of no concern to us? The first answer is that the market already sets the current price of the stock at a level that reflects the odds of future up and down moves. In other words, the probabilities are embedded in the stock price, even though no one can see them directly.

JOB INTERVIEW QUESTION

How does a stock's expected return influence the price of a call option written on the stock?

The second answer is that the binomial model prices an option through the principle of "no arbitrage." Because it is always possible to combine a share of stock with options (either calls or puts) into a risk-free portfolio, the binomial model says that the value of that portfolio must be the same as the value of a risk-free bond—otherwise, an arbitrage opportunity would exist because identical assets would be selling at different prices. Hence, because the portfolio containing stock and options offers a risk-free payoff, the probabilities of up and down moves in the stock price do not enter the calculations. An investor holding the hedged portfolio does not need to worry about movements in the stock because they do not affect the portfolio's payoffs.

Almost all students object to the binomial model's assumption that the price of a stock can take on one of just two values in the future. Fair enough. It is certainly true that the price of Financial Engineers stock one year from today might be $70, $40, or almost any other value. However, it turns out that more complex versions of this binomial model do not require analysts to specify just two final prices for the stock; the model can accommodate a wide range of final prices. To see how this works, consider a slight modification to our original problem.

Rather than presume that Financial Engineers stock will rise or fall by $15 over a year's time, suppose that it may rise or fall by $7.50 every six months. That's still a big assumption. But if we make it, we find that the list of potential prices of Financial Engineers stock one year from today has grown from two values to three. Figure 18.11 proves this claim. After one year, the price of the stock might be $40, $55, or $70. Now let's modify the assumption one more time. Suppose that the price of the stock can move up or down $3.75 every three months. Figure 18.11 shows that, in this case, the number of possible stock prices one year in the future grows to five.

Given a tree with many branches like the bottom one in Figure 18.11, we can solve for the value of a call or put option following the same steps we used to value options with a simple two-step tree. Now imagine a much larger tree, one in which the stock moves up or down every few minutes or even every few seconds. Each change in the stock price is very small, perhaps a penny or two. But as the tree unfolds and time passes, the number of branches rapidly expands, as does the number of possible values of the stock at the option's expiration date. Looking at the tree's terminal nodes, we see that when the option expires in a year, the price of Financial Engineers stock can take any one of hundreds (or even thousands) of different values, so the complaint about the model's artificial assumption of just two possible stock prices no longer applies. Though extremely tedious, solving for the call or put value involves working all the way through the tree and applying the same steps over and over again.

The binomial model is an incredibly powerful and flexible tool that analysts can use to price all sorts of options, from ordinary calls and puts to complex real options embedded

FIGURE 18.11

Multistage Binomial Trees

These trees illustrate that, by allowing the stock price to move at more frequent intervals, but by a smaller amount in each interval, the binomial model can incorporate a wide range of terminal stock prices, not just two.

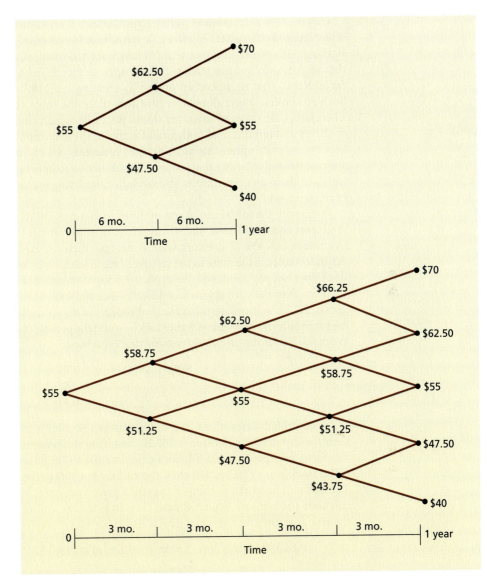

in capital investment projects. The genius of the model is in its recognition of the opportunity to use stock and options to mimic the payoffs of risk-free bonds, the easiest of all securities to price. The binomial model has a close cousin that also makes use of the ability to construct risk-free portfolios using stock and options: the risk-neutral method.

The Risk-Neutral Method

In Chapter 5, we argued that most investors are risk averse and require compensation for risk taking. We briefly mentioned the possibility that an investor might be risk neutral, concerned only about the expected return of an investment and indifferent to its risk. What if all investors are risk neutral? If investors do not worry about risk, then in equilibrium no asset will have to pay a risk premium to survive in the market. The expected return on a share of common stock will be the same as the expected return on a Treasury bill—the risk-free rate.

Clearly, this discussion is purely hypothetical. We live in a world with risk-averse investors, and risky assets do offer risk premiums. However, it is possible to price options starting with the assumption that investors are risk neutral. How can an assumption that we know to be false lead to correct option prices? The answer goes back to arbitrage. Recall that we priced an option by creating a portfolio with a risk-free payoff. Both risk-averse and risk-neutral investors place the same value on a risk-free asset. Therefore, both types of investors would place the same value on the hedged portfolio of shares and options, and both would arrive at the same option price. In other words, because we price options using arbitrage arguments, we can proceed *as if* all investors are risk neutral. Making that assumption allows us to apply the **risk-neutral method**, which leads to an even simpler approach to calculating option prices, as the following example shows.

Begin with the initial conditions outlined in Figure 18.10. The stock price of Financial Engineers equals $55 now, and it may increase to $70 or fall to $40 in a year. The risk-free rate equals 4%. If investors are risk neutral, then the expected return on Financial Engineers stock is the same as the risk-free rate. Therefore, as long as Financial Engineers stock does not pay dividends, the expected price of the stock one year from now must be 4% more than the current price, or $57.20. Once we know that the expected price in one year is $57.20, we can infer what the probabilities of an up and a down move must be. Let the probability of an up move in the stock be p and the probability of a down move be $1 - p$. We can solve for the probabilities using this expression:

$$\$70p + \$40(1 - p) = \$57.20$$
$$p = 0.5733$$
$$1 - p = 0.4267$$

If the probabilities of up and down moves are 57.33% and 42.67% (respectively) then the expected stock price is $57.20, resulting in an expected 1-year return of 4%. Now let's use those probabilities to calculate the value of the call option. As before, if the stock price reaches $70 then the call with a $55 strike price will be worth $15. The call will be worth nothing if the stock price ends up at $40. To value the call, just calculate the option's expected cash flow in one year and then discount that flow at the risk-free rate:

$$\text{Expected cash flow} = \$15p + \$0(1 - p) = \$15(0.5733) + \$0 = \$8.60$$

$$\text{Call value} = \frac{\$8.60}{1.04} = \$8.27$$

Notice that $8.27 is precisely the same call value we obtained using the binomial model, which made no assumption about investors' attitudes toward risk. The binomial model works because it is based on the principle that markets do not allow arbitrage opportunities to exist, at least not for long. Therefore, if a combination of stock and options is risk free, then that combination must sell for the same price as a risk-free bond. If an asset promises a risk-free payoff, then risk-averse and risk-neutral investors will agree on how it should be valued because neither group requires a risk premium on the asset. Thus, if the binomial model works by creating a risk-free portfolio, it does no harm to assume that investors are risk neutral from the start. Whether investors are risk averse or risk neutral, the binomial model's calculations are the same. This opens the door for us to assume that investors are risk neutral, an assumption that gives us a new way to value options.

EXAMPLE

Assuming that investors are risk neutral, let's value the Financial Engineers put option with a strike of $55. If the stock increases to $70, the put is worthless. If the stock falls to $40, the put option pays $15. We already know the probabilities of up and down moves from our risk-neutral valuation of the call option, so we will use those probabilities to calculate the expected cash flow from the put. Once we have the expected cash flow, we can discount it at 4% to obtain the current market price of the put:

$$\text{Expected cash flow} = \$0p + \$15(1 - p) = \$0 + \$15(0.4267) = \$6.40$$

$$\text{Call value} = \frac{\$6.40}{1.04} = \$6.16$$

As expected, the put value obtained from risk-neutral valuation exactly matches the price calculated using the binomial model.

Concept Review Questions	
	11. To value options using the binomial method, is it necessary to know the expected return on the stock? Why or why not?
	12. There is an old saying that nature abhors a vacuum. The financial equivalent is that "markets abhor arbitrage opportunities." Explain the central role this principle plays in the binomial model.
	13. Part of the risk-neutral method involves calculating the probability of an up or a down move in the underlying stock. Do you think these probabilities correspond to real-world probabilities of up and down moves? Explain.

SUMMARY

- The buyer of an option contract has the right (but not the obligation) to buy or sell stock at a fixed price.
- Call options grant the right to purchase shares; put options grant the right to sell shares.
- Options provide a real economic benefit to society and are not simply a form of legalized gambling.
- American options allow investors to exercise their options before the options expire, but European options do not.
- Payoff diagrams show the value of options or portfolios of options on the expiration date. Payoff diagrams are extremely useful in understanding how different options trading strategies work.
- Put–call parity establishes a link between the market prices of calls, puts, shares, and bonds, provided certain conditions hold.

- Put–call parity can be used to calculate the fair value of an option (provided the other prices are known) or to find ways to form synthetic securities.
- Call option prices decrease and put option prices increase as the difference between the underlying stock price and the exercise price decreases.
- Calls and puts both increase in value (usually) when there is more time left before expiration.
- An increase in the volatility of the underlying asset increases the values of calls and puts.
- The binomial option pricing model and the risk-neutral method permit calculation of option prices with a minimal set of assumptions.

KEY TERMS

American call option
at the money
binomial option pricing model
call option
cash settlement
counterparty risk
derivative security
European call option
exercise price
exercise
expiration date
hedge ratio
hockey-stick diagram

in the money
intrinsic value
long position
long straddle
naked option position
net payoff
option premium
options
out of the money
over-the-counter market
payoff
payoff diagram
protective put

put option
put–call parity
risk-neutral method
short position
short straddle
strike price
synthetic put option
time value
underlying asset
writes an option
writing covered calls

QUESTIONS

18-1. Explain why an option is a *derivative* security.

18-2. Is buying an option more or less risky than buying the underlying stock?

18-3. What is the difference between an option's price and its payoff?

18-4. List five factors that influence the prices of calls and puts.

18-5. What are the economic benefits that options provide?

18-6. What is the primary advantage of settling options contracts in cash?

18-7. Suppose you want to invest in a particular company. What are the pros and cons of buying the company's shares as compared to buying their options?

18-8. Suppose that you want to make an investment that will be profitable if a company's stock price falls. Contrast the approach of short-selling the company's stock to that of buying put options on the stock.

18-9. Is buying a call the same as selling a put? Explain why or why not.

18-10. Suppose that you own an American call option on Pfizer stock. Pfizer stock has gone up in value considerably since you bought the option, so your investment has been profitable. There is still one month to go before the option expires, but you decide to go ahead and take your profits in cash. Describe two ways that you could accomplish this goal. Which one is likely to leave you with the higher cash payoff?

18-11. Explain why put–call parity does not hold for American options.

18-12. Look at the Whirlpool call option prices in Table 18.1. For a given expiration date, call prices increase as the strike price decreases. The strike prices decrease in increments of $5. Do the call option prices increase in constant increments? That is, does the call price increase by the same amount as the strike price drops from $35.00 to $30 and so on? Explain.

18-13. Explain the difference between the binomial option pricing model and the risk-neutral method of option pricing.

PROBLEMS

Option Payoff Diagrams

18-1. Draw payoff diagrams for each of the following portfolios (X = strike price).
  a. Buy a call with $X = \$50$, and sell a call with $X = \$60$.
  b. Buy a bond with a face value of $10, short a put with $X = \$60$, and buy a put with $X = \$50$.

c. Buy a share of stock, buy a put option with $X = \$50$, sell a call with $X = \$60$, and short a bond (i.e., borrow) with a face value of $50.

d. What principle do these diagrams illustrate?

18-2. Draw a payoff diagram for the following portfolio (X = strike price): Buy two call options, one with $X = \$20$ and one with $X = \$30$, and sell two call options, both with $X = \$25$.

18-3. Suppose that you buy one Whirlpool call option with $X = \$30$ and one with $X = \$40$. You also sell two Whirlpool calls with $X = \$35$. Using the prices from Table 18.1, determine the net cost of the option portfolio and then draw a new payoff diagram showing the net payoffs at expiration. Over what range of prices would you make money, and over what range would you lose money? What is your maximum possible loss and gain?

18-4. Draw a payoff diagram for each of the following portfolios (X = strike price):

a. Buy a bond with a face value of $80, buy a call with $X = \$80$, and sell a put with $X = \$80$.

b. Buy a share of stock, buy a put with $X = \$80$, and sell a call with $X = \$80$.

c. Buy a share of stock, buy a put with $X = \$80$, and sell a bond with a face value of $80.

18-5. Look at the option prices in Table 18.1. For each row of the table, perform the following calculation: (stock price + put price − call price). According to put–call parity, a portfolio containing a share of stock, a put, and a short call has the same payoff as what security? When you perform this calculation for each row of Table 18.1, do your results seem to indicate that put–call parity holds (at least approximately) or not? Explain. As background information, the annual rate of interest on short-term U.S. Treasury bills was about 0.25% at the time the quotes in the table were obtained from the CBOE website.

18-6. If some of the prices in Table 18.1 fail to satisfy put–call parity, provide an explanation for this apparent violation of the "no arbitrage" principle. Put differently: even if prices in the table do not satisfy parity, is it possible that there is still no arbitrage opportunity to exploit?

18-7. Imagine that a stock sells for $33. A call option with a strike price of $35 and an expiration date in six months sells for $4.50. The annual risk-free rate is 5%. Calculate the price of a put option that expires in six months and has a strike price of $35.

18-8. Suppose that the put option described in Problem 18-7 actually sells for $5. Explain in detail how an arbitrageur could exploit this mispricing to earn a risk-free profit.

18-9. Monitoring option prices in the United Kingdom, you notice that call and put prices on the stock of the British exotic-pet importer Python Inc. seem to be out of alignment. Specifically, the price of Python stock is £55, and the price of 3-month call and put options on Python stock with exercise prices of £60 are £5.75 and £7.25, respectively. The U.K. risk-free rate of interest is 8% (or 2% per three months). How can we exploit this arbitrage opportunity?

18-10. Suppose that an American call option is in the money, so the stock price (S) is greater than the strike price (X). Demonstrate that the market price of this call (C) cannot be less than the difference between the stock price and the exercise price. That is, explain why this must be true: $C > (S − X)$. (*Hint:* Consider what would happen if $C < (S − X)$).

Calculating Option Prices

18-11. A call option expires in three months and has a strike price $X = \$40$. The underlying stock is worth $42 today. In three months, the stock may increase by $7 or decrease by $6. The risk-free rate is 2% per year. Use the binomial option pricing model to value the call option.

Smart
Solutions
*See the problem and
solution explained step-by-
step at* **SMARTFinance**

Smart
Solutions
*See the problem and
solution explained step-by-
step at* **SMARTFinance**

Smart
Solutions
*See the problem and
solution explained step-by-
step at* **SMARTFinance**

18-12. A certain stock sells for $42 today, but in three months it may be worth $49 or $36. Value a 3-month put option with a strike price of $X = \$40$. The risk-free rate is 2% per year.

18-13. Given the call and put prices you calculated in Problems 18-11 and 18-12, check to see if put–call parity holds.

18-14. A put option has a strike price of $90. The underlying stock sells for $88, but in four months it could increase to $95 or decrease to $82. The risk-free rate is 3%, and the put expires in four months. Use the risk-neutral method to value the put.

18-15. A stock sells for $88 now, but in four months its price may rise by $7 or fall by $6. The risk-free rate is 3%. Use the risk-neutral method to calculate the value of a 4-month call with a strike price $X = \$90$. After you have determined the call price, use your answer from Problem 18-14 to check whether put–call parity holds.

18-16. This problem requires you to use the binomial model to price a complex call option with a variable strike price. Suppose that the current price of a particular stock is $80. The stock pays no dividends and has a beta of 1.2. The strike price of a 6-month call option is $78, but the strike price is not fixed. Specifically, the strike price is indexed to the S&P 500, which means that if the S&P 500 changes by x percent then the option's strike price will move in the same direction by x percent. Suppose you believe that the S&P 500 will either rise 20% or fall 10% in the next six months. If the risk-free rate is 4%, what is the value of the call option? (*Hint*: Use the stock's beta to determine the future values of the stock, which will depend on how the S&P 500 behaves.)

18-17. Explain the following paradox. A put option is a highly volatile security. If the underlying stock has a positive beta, then a put option on that stock will have a negative beta and an expected return that is below the risk-free rate. How can an equilibrium exist in which a highly risky security such as a put option offers an expected return below that of a much safer security such as a Treasury bill?

18-18. A stock currently trades for $84. In the next three months it may rise or fall by $5. Similarly, in the subsequent three months the stock price could increase or decrease by $5. Calculate the price of a 6-month put option with a strike price of $87.50, assuming that the risk-free rate of interest is 1% per quarter (roughly 4% per year).

Smart
Solutions

*See the problem and
solution explained step-by-
step at* **SMARTFinance**

18-19. A stock currently trades for $84. In the next three months it may rise or fall by $5. Similarly, in the three months after that the stock price could increase or decrease by $5. Calculate the price of a 6-month call option with a strike price of $87.50, assuming that the risk-free rate of interest is 1% per quarter (roughly 4% per year).

Mini-Case: Options Basics

Suppose Microsoft's common stock is currently (in January) trading for $27.02 per share. The values of several call options, which expire in February and April this year, are as follows:

Symbol	Call Price ($)	Strike Price ($)
February		
MQFBD	7.10	20.00
MSQBX	4.60	22.50
MSQBJ	2.15	25.00
MSQBY	0.40	27.50
MSQBK	0.05	30.00

April

MQFDD	7.20	20.00
MSQDX	4.80	22.50
MSQDJ	2.45	25.00
MSQDY	0.75	27.50
MSQDK	0.15	30.00

1. Which call options are in the money? Which call options are out of the money?

2. Calculate the intrinsic value and time value for each of the call options.

3. Construct a diagram showing the payoff and net payoff for the MSQBJ option from the perspective of a long position and also from that of a short position.

4. Using the concept of put–call parity, determine the price of a put option on Microsoft's stock with a strike price of $27.50 that expires in February. The appropriate risk-free rate of interest is 2.06%. Assume that Microsoft will not pay a dividend and that the options are European options.

5. Assume that in one year Microsoft's stock will have either increased in value to $33 or have fallen to $21.80. Calculate the hedge ratio and the value of a call option with a strike price of $25 and one year to expiration. The appropriate risk-free rate of interest is 2.75%.

6. Assume that one week has passed and Microsoft's stock has risen in value to $28.72. The value of the MSQBJ call option is now $3.80. Calculate the value of a long position in Microsoft's stock versus a long position in the MSQBJ call option, assuming you bought them one week ago and sold them today.

Black and Scholes and Beyond

What Companies Do

Concerns over Taxpayers' TARP Investments Warranted

In response to a growing financial crisis, the U.S. Congress passed the Emergency Economic Stabilization Act on October 3, 2008. The bill created a $700 billion Troubled Assets Relief Program (TARP) that authorized the government to make equity investments in financial institutions. By the end of January 2009, more than 300 financial institutions had participated in the program. Twenty-five of these companies received injections of $1 billion or more from the program, with giants Bank of America, Citigroup, JP Morgan, and Wells Fargo receiving $25 billion each.

In exchange for the infusion of capital, the government received warrants granting it the right to purchase nonvoting common stock in the companies receiving assistance. This meant that if the financial sector recovered, taxpayers might earn a profit on the TARP funds. However, a Congressional Budget Office (CBO) analysis estimated that the value of taxpayers' investments fell 26% during the program's early months. To arrive at this figure, the CBO valued the TARP warrants using a modified version of the Black and Scholes option pricing model, a mathematically sophisticated tool used by option traders since the early 1970s.

Despite its complexity, the Black and Scholes formula is in such widespread use today that there is even a free iPhone app that crunches the numbers automatically.

Sources: U.S. Treasury Department, http://online.wsj.com/public/resources/documents/st_BANKMONEY_20081027.html; Ronald Fink, "Taxpayers Already Down 26% on Their TARP Investments," http://www.financialweek.com/apps/pbcs.dll/article?AID=/20090116/REG/901169973/1028 (February 3, 2009).

In 1973, Myron Scholes and Fisher Black published what might fairly be called a trillion-dollar research paper. Their research produced, for the first time, a formula that traders could use to calculate the value of call options, a pathbreaking discovery that had eluded researchers for decades. Black and Scholes did not have to wait long to see if their formula would have an impact in financial markets. That same year, options began trading in the United States on the newly formed Chicago Board Options Exchange (CBOE). Traders on the floor of the exchange priced options using handheld calculators with the Black and Scholes formula programmed in. From that beginning, trading in options exploded over the next three decades—hence the trillion-dollar moniker given to the original research paper.[1]

This chapter begins with an introduction to the Black and Scholes model. This model has much in common with the binomial model that we studied in the previous chapter, and it is easier to use. Next we discuss how securities issued by corporations often contain embedded options. Understanding the pros and cons of these securities, either from the buyer's or the seller's perspective, requires some facility with option pricing concepts. Finally, we return to the topic of real options to see how analysts use the binomial and Black and Scholes models in a capital budgeting environment.

19.1 THE BLACK AND SCHOLES MODEL

Calculating Black and Scholes Options Values

When you first encounter it, the **Black and Scholes option pricing equation** looks rather intimidating. As a matter of fact, the editor at the journal where Black and Scholes published their prize-winning formula originally rejected their paper because he felt it was too technical. Although the formula uses advanced mathematics, the intuition behind the equation is fairly straightforward. In fact, the logic of the Black and Scholes model mirrors that of the binomial model.

Black and Scholes began by asking a question: If investors can buy and sell stock as well as stock options, does a combination of options and shares exist that provides a risk-free payoff? That should sound familiar, because the binomial model takes the same approach to determine an option's value. However, Black and Scholes's method for valuing options does not mimic the binomial structure exactly.

First, recall from Chapter 18 that the binomial model assumes that, over a given time period, the stock price will move up or down by a known amount. In Figure 18.11 we showed that, by shortening the length of the period during which the stock price moves, we increase the number of different prices that the stock might reach by the option's expiration date. The Black and Scholes model takes this approach to its logical extreme. It presumes that stock prices can move at every instant. If we were to illustrate this assumption by drawing a binomial tree like those in Figure 18.11, the tree would have an infinite number of branches, and on the option's expiration date the stock price could take on almost any value.

Second, Black and Scholes did not assume that they knew precisely what the up and down movements in the stock would be at every instant. They recognized that these movements were essentially random and therefore unpredictable. Instead, they assumed that the volatility, or standard deviation, of a stock's movements was known.

---

[1]Myron Scholes won the Nobel Prize in economics in 1997 for this achievement, an honor he shared with Robert Merton, another researcher who made seminal contributions to options research. Fisher Black undoubtedly would have been a co-recipient of the award, but he died in 1995.

With these assumptions in place, Black and Scholes calculated the *price of a European call option* (on a no-dividend stock) with the following equations:

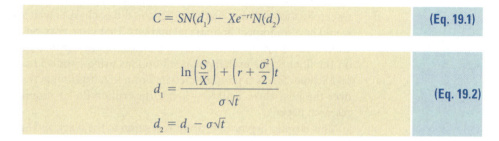

$$C = SN(d_1) - Xe^{-rt}N(d_2) \qquad \text{(Eq. 19.1)}$$

$$d_1 = \frac{\ln\left(\frac{S}{X}\right) + \left(r + \frac{\sigma^2}{2}\right)t}{\sigma\sqrt{t}} \qquad \text{(Eq. 19.2)}$$

$$d_2 = d_1 - \sigma\sqrt{t}$$

Let's dissect this carefully. Most of the terms in the equation we have seen before:

S = current market price of underlying stock
X = strike price of option
t = amount of time (in years) before option expires
r = annual risk-free interest rate
σ = annual standard deviation of underlying stock's returns
e = 2.718 (approximately)
$N(X)$ = probability of drawing, from the **standard normal distribution**, a value that is less than or equal to X

Does this list of variables look familiar? It should, because it is nearly identical to the list of inputs required to use the binomial model. The stock price S, the strike price X, the time t until expiration, and the risk-free rate r are all variables that the binomial model uses to price options. The new item that the Black and Scholes model requires is the standard deviation, σ, of the underlying asset's returns. We illustrate a conventional method for estimating this value in Appendix 19A, but for now assume that you have an estimate of volatility from historical data.

What about the term Xe^{-rt}? Recall from our discussion of continuous compounding in Chapter 3 that the term e^{-rt} reflects the present value of \$1 discounted continuously at r percent for t years. Therefore, Xe^{-rt} simply equals the present value of the option's strike price.[2] With this in mind, look again at Equation 19.1. The first term equals the stock price multiplied by a quantity labeled $N(d_1)$. The second term is the present value of the strike price multiplied by a quantity labeled $N(d_2)$. Therefore, we can say that the call option value equals the "adjusted" stock price minus the present value of the "adjusted" strike price, where $N(d_1)$ and $N(d_2)$ represent adjustment factors. In Chapter 18, we saw that call option values increase as the difference between the stock price and the strike price, $S - X$, increases. The same relationship holds here, although we must now factor in the terms $N(d_1)$ and $N(d_2)$.

In the Black and Scholes equation, d_1 and d_2 are simply numerical values (calculated using Equation 19.2) that depend on the model's inputs: the stock price, the strike price, the interest rate, the time to expiration, and volatility. The expressions $N(d_1)$ and $N(d_2)$

---

[2]Remember, this expression can be written in two ways:

$$Xe^{-rt} = \frac{X}{e^{rt}}$$

If the continuously compounded risk-free rate of interest equals r and the amount of time before expiration equals t, then this is simply the present value of the strike price.

convert the numerical values of d_1 and d_2 into probabilities using the standard normal distribution.[3] Figure 19.1 shows that the value $N(d_1)$ equals the area under the standard normal curve to the left of value d_1. For example, if we calculate the value of d_1 and find that it equals 0, then $N(d_1)$ equals 0.5 because half of the area under the curve falls to the left of zero. The higher the value of d_1, the closer $N(d_1)$ approaches unity (1.0); the lower the value of d_1, the closer $N(d_1)$ approaches zero. The same relationship holds between d_2 and $N(d_2)$. Given a particular value of d, you can find $N(d)$ from a table that shows the cumulative standard normal probabilities, or you can plug d into the Excel function "=normsdist(d)".

FIGURE 19.1

Standard Normal Distribution

The expression $N(d_1)$ equals the probability of drawing a particular (or lower) value, d_1, from the standard normal distribution. In the figure, $N(d_1)$ is represented by the shaded portion under the bell curve. Because the normal distribution is symmetric about the mean, we can write $N(d_1) = 1 - N(-d_1)$.

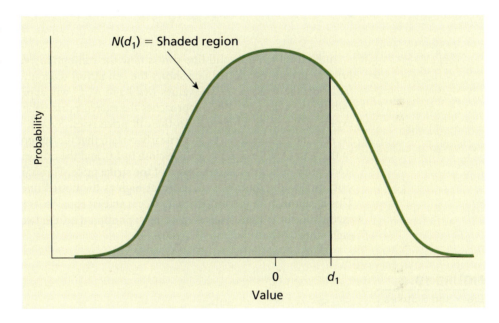

A common intuitive interpretation of $N(d_1)$ and $N(d_2)$ is that they represent the risk-adjusted probabilities that the call will expire in the money. Therefore, Equation 19.1 can be stated verbally as follows: *The call option price equals the stock price minus the present value of the exercise price, adjusted for the probability that the stock price will exceed the strike price when the option expires (i.e., for the probability that the option expires in the money).*

EXAMPLE

The stock of Cloverdale Food Processors currently sells for $40. A European call option on Cloverdale stock has an expiration date six months in the future and a strike price of $38. The estimate of the annual standard deviation of Cloverdale stock is 45%, and the risk-free rate is 6%. What is the call worth? It's worth $6.58, as shown below.

(continued)

---

[3]Recall from statistics that the standard normal distribution has a mean equal to zero and a standard deviation equal to 1.0.

$$d_1 = \frac{\ln\left(\frac{40}{38}\right) + \left(0.06 + \frac{(0.45)^2}{2}\right)\frac{1}{2}}{0.45\sqrt{\frac{1}{2}}} = \frac{0.0513 + 0.0806}{0.3182} = 0.4146$$

$$d_2 = d_1 - \sigma\sqrt{t} = 0.4146 - 0.45\sqrt{\frac{1}{2}} = 0.0964$$

$$N(0.4146) = 0.6608, \qquad N(0.0964) = 0.5384$$

$$C = 40(0.6608) - 38(2.718^{-(0.06)(0.5)})(0.5384) = \$6.58$$

In Figure 19.2, the solid line shows how the call option's value changes as the stock price changes. The dashed line shows the call payoff diagram. When the stock price is far below the strike price, the values $N(d_1)$ and $N(d_2)$ will approach zero and so will the call price. As the stock price approaches the exercise price, the odds that the option will expire in the money increase, so the call price rises. Finally, when the stock price far exceeds the strike price, we can be nearly certain that the option will expire in the money. In that case, $N(d_1)$ and $N(d_2)$ will be close to 1.0, and the call price will (almost) equal the stock price minus the present value of the strike price. Throughout the range of possible stock prices, the solid line is at least as high as the dotted line, and usually it is higher. This means that the option's market price is at least equal to its intrinsic value and usually exceeds intrinsic value. However, at the expiration date, the two lines would lie on top of each other.

FIGURE 19.2

Black and Scholes Call Values for Cloverdale

The figure shows the Black and Scholes call price at different stock prices under the following assumptions:

The call's strike price is $38 ($X = 38$)

The option expires in six months ($t = \frac{1}{2}$)

The risk-free rate is 6% ($r = 0.06$)

The standard deviation of the stock is 45% ($\sigma = 0.45$)

$C = SN(d_1) - Xe^{-rt}N(d_2)$

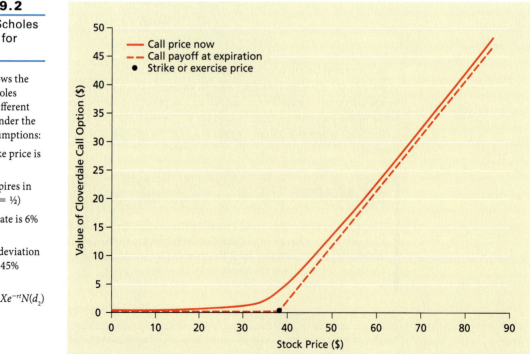

Take another look at Figure 19.2, this time focusing on the slope of the solid line. That slope measures how much the call price changes as the underlying stock price changes. Options traders refer to this as the **option's delta**, and mathematically the delta equals the value $N(d_1)$ from the Black and Scholes equation. When a call option is far out of the money, the solid line in Figure 19.2 is almost flat and the option's delta is close to zero. This means that stock price movements have very little impact on the option's market value, which is not surprising because the odds are high that the option will expire worthless. Conversely, when the option is deep in the money, the slope of the solid line is almost 1.0, and so is the delta. In this case the call's market price moves almost dollar-for-dollar with changes in the stock price. This makes sense, too, because a deep-in-the-money option will almost certainly be exercised. That means the call option holder will almost certainly own the stock eventually, so the option's value should fluctuate in line with the underlying stock.

We can use the concept of an option's delta to make another connection between the Black and Scholes and binomial models. In Chapter 18, we introduced the binomial model's three-step process to value options. The first step was to find a portfolio of stock and options with a risk-free payoff. We denoted the ratio of the number of options to the number of shares in this perfectly hedged portfolio with the symbol h, and we labeled that number the **hedge ratio**. In Black and Scholes's parlance, the ratio $1/N(d_1)$ is equivalent to the hedge ratio from the binomial model. This ratio tells options traders approximately how many options they need to offset the fluctuations of a single common share.

Smart Concepts
See the concept explained step-by-step at
SMARTFinance

EXAMPLE

Let's revisit the Cloverdale call option from the previous Example. Given the parameters in that problem, the market price of the option is $6.58 and the value $N(d_1)$ equals 0.6608. This means that if the price of Cloverdale stock moves by $1 then the price of the call option will move by about $0.66 in the same direction.

Suppose that a mutual fund manager owns 100,000 shares of Cloverdale stock. He plans to sell these shares in a week but is concerned about a potential decline in the value of the shares between now and then. As a hedging strategy, the manager plans to sell Cloverdale call options. He reasons that because call and share prices move in the same direction, he can create a position that is nearly risk-free by purchasing shares and selling calls. But how many Cloverdale calls must he sell?

By taking the reciprocal of $N(d_1)$, the manager discerns that he needs to sell roughly 1.513 calls for each share in his portfolio (or 151,300 total) to construct the hedged position:

$$\frac{1}{N(d_1)} = \frac{1}{0.6608} = 1.513$$

Now suppose that a week passes and Cloverdale's stock price falls from $40 to $38. This means the manager's stock portfolio has declined by $200,000 ($2 per share × 100,000 shares). But what has happened to the value of the options the manager sold? Again we use the Black and Scholes equation to calculate the option's price, but this time with $38 for the stock price and 0.48 years for the time until expiration (one week less than six months). The new call value is $5.20, so the call price dropped $1.38 during the week. Because the fund manager took a short position in call options, the decline in the call price represents a profit of $1.38 per call, or $208,794. That is, the fund manager received $6.58 per call when he sold them and now, a week later, he can buy calls at the lower price to close out his position. Observe that the $208,794 net gain on the option trades approximately offsets the $200,000 decline on the manager's Cloverdale stock. In other words, the manager created a hedged portfolio.

The Black and Scholes model was originally conceived for the purpose of pricing a European call option on an underlying U.S. stock that paid no dividends. Applying the model when the underlying U.S. stock pays dividends requires a small adjustment. Holding all else constant, when a firm pays a dividend its stock price will fall. This effect is largely neutral to shareholders, who experience a decline in their shares but also receive the dividend, but it clearly harms investors holding call options, who are not entitled to receive dividends. If investors expect a firm to pay a dividend during the life of a call, they will pay a lower price for the call than if they did not expect any dividends. A simple way to account for this in Equation 19.1 is to reduce the current stock price (S) by the present value of expected dividend payments. That adjustment makes sense because the current price of the stock overstates, by the amount of the dividend, the value of the underlying claim that option investors have the right to purchase.[4]

With a slight modification to Equation 19.1, we can use the Black and Scholes model to value puts rather than calls. To derive a Black and Scholes equation for a put option, we will use put–call parity. Remember, put–call parity establishes an equilibrium relationship between the price of a call option, C, a put option, P, the underlying stock, S, and a risk-free bond, $PV(X)$. Put–call parity states that

$$S + P = PV(X) + C$$

To put this expression in a form like the Black and Scholes model, replace the term $PV(X)$ with Xe^{-rt}, move the symbol for the stock price to the right-hand side, and replace the symbol for the call price with Equation 19.1. After these steps, we have the following expression:

$$P = Xe^{-rt} + [SN(d_1) - Xe^{-rt}N(d_2)] - S$$

With a little algebraic manipulation, we obtain the *put option formula,*

$$P = Xe^{-rt}[1 - N(d_2)] - S[1 - N(d_1)] \qquad \textbf{(Eq. 19.3)}$$

where d_1 and d_2 have the same definitions as in Equation 19.2. Notice how the terms in this equation have reversed compared to their placement in Equation 19.1. Intuitively, we understand that the terms in the equation switch positions because the circumstances in which a put option is in the money are precisely opposite to those in which a call option is in the money. (A put is in the money when $S < X$, and a call is in the money when $S > X$. In English: a put is in the money when the stock price is below the strike price, and a call is in the money when the stock price exceeds the strike price.) For the same reason, the probabilities $N(d_1)$ and $N(d_2)$ from Equation 19.1 switch in Equation 19.3 to $1 - N(d_1)$ and $1 - N(d_2)$.

Figure 19.3 plots the market value of a Cloverdale put option with characteristics identical to those of the Cloverdale call option illustrated in Figure 19.2. The solid line illustrates how put prices change as the underlying stock price changes, and the dotted line shows the put payoff diagram. The shape of this line is, in many respects, the mirror image of the line in Figure 19.2 for calls. As the stock price falls, the put value increases; as the stock price rises, the put value approaches zero.[5] Unlike a call option, a put option does

---

[4]Option investors have the right to buy a claim on all the firm's future cash flows, except for the dividend that will be paid before the option expires. Fenn and Liang (2001) find a negative correlation between a firm's dividend payout and the quantity of stock options held by the firm's managers. It seems that managers are well aware that paying dividends decreases option values.

[5]As in Figure 19.2, if the stock price is very low then $N(d_1)$ and $N(d_2)$ are close to zero. Consequently, the terms $1 - N(d_1)$ and $1 - N(d_2)$ in the put pricing equation become close to 1.0, so the put value approaches the present value of the strike price minus the stock price. At high stock prices, $N(d_1)$ and $N(d_2)$ approach unity and so $1 - N(d_1)$ and $1 - N(d_2)$ approach zero, as does the put value.

FIGURE 19.3

Black and Scholes
Put Values for
Cloverdale

The figure shows the
Black and Scholes
put price at different
stock prices under the
following assumptions:

The call's strike price is
$38 ($X = 38$)

The option expires in
six months ($t = \frac{1}{2}$)

The risk-free rate is
6% ($r = 0.06$)

The standard deviation
of the stock is 45%
($\sigma = 0.45$)

$$P = Xe^{-rt} \times [1 - N(d_2)] - S(1 - N(d_1))]$$

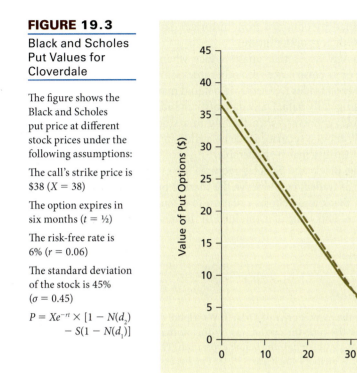

not always sell for more than its intrinsic value. When the stock price is low, the put value
falls below intrinsic value (the dashed line). The interpretation of this phenomenon is as
follows. When the stock price is very low, the option holder is almost certain to exercise
the option, receiving the strike price in cash. However, because this is a European option,
the investor must wait to exercise the option until it expires. The amount by which the
option's price falls below its intrinsic value represents the time value of money the investor
loses by having to wait until expiration to exercise the option.

One of the most interesting aspects of the Black and Scholes equation is what it does not
contain—the expected return on the underlying stock. In other words, it is not necessary
to know what return investors expect on the underlying stock in order to determine an
option's price. This, too, has a parallel in the binomial model. Remember that the binomial
model begins with an assumption about up and down movements in the underlying
stock, but the model makes no assumptions about the probabilities of those movements.
The binomial and Black and Scholes models both depend on the notion that traders can
combine options and shares to create a risk-free portfolio, so the future direction of the
underlying asset does not enter into the pricing mechanics.

Volatility

The Black and Scholes model requires five inputs, four of which can be readily observed
in the market. Only the underlying stock's volatility remains uncertain. For companies
whose stocks have traded in the public markets for a long time, plenty of historical data
exist that analysts can use to estimate volatility, as illustrated in Appendix 19A. Even so,
what is relevant for option pricing is the volatility of the underlying asset over the life of

the option. Estimates of volatility obtained from historical data, even fairly recent data, may or may not be good predictors of the future.

In Chapter 6 we discussed issues that analysts face when using historical data to estimate a stock's variance or its covariance with other stocks, and those same issues apply here. When the stock of interest trades frequently in a liquid market, analysts can gather a reasonably large sample using daily data. Daily data offer the advantage of being the most recent information available. However, when trading in a stock is thin, daily data can generate misleading signals about a security's true volatility; in that case, using weekly or monthly data to estimate volatility may be preferable.

Pricing an option using Black and Scholes requires an estimate of the underlying stock's volatility. However, if traders can observe the market price of an option directly, then they can "invert" the Black and Scholes equation to calculate the volatility implied by the option's market price. The value of σ obtained in this manner is called an option's **implied volatility**.

EXAMPLE

In Chapter 18, we saw that the market price of a March Whirlpool call option with $X = \$35.00$ was $4.90. Suppose that, at the time the option was trading at that price, it had two months (approximately one-sixth of a year) remaining before expiration. The risk-free rate at that time was 0.25% and the price of Whirlpool stock was $36.33. Finally, assume that Whirlpool is not scheduled to make a dividend payment during the life of this option. Given these values, we can use a computer to find the value of σ that would generate a Black and Scholes call value of $4.90. In this case, the implied volatility of the March Whirlpool call is 72.5%. That level of volatility is unusually high for Whirlpool, but remember that the data for this Example were gathered in January 2009 in the midst of the global financial crisis. Stock volatilities were far above normal during this period.

Of course, traders cannot use an option's implied volatility to calculate its price because they must know the price to calculate implied volatility. In other words, traders can use the Black and Scholes equation, along with an estimate of the stock's volatility, to estimate the price of an option; or, if traders know the price of the option, they can use Black and Scholes to find the volatility implied by that price.

Of what practical value is an option's implied volatility if you must first know the option's price in order to calculate it? One application is to use implied volatilities to test the accuracy of the Black and Scholes model. For example, suppose that several call options with different strike prices but the same expiration date trade on the same underlying stock. By observing the market prices of these options, we can determine each option's implied volatility. The Black and Scholes model predicts that the implied volatilities will be identical because all the options share the same underlying asset. If the implied volatilities are not the same but instead reflect a systematic pattern between an option's strike price and its implied volatility, then the Black and Scholes model does not price options correctly at all strike prices.

Early tests of Black and Scholes found that options with the same underlying stock indeed had different implied volatilities, which varied with the exercise price.[6] In particular,

---

[6]See Black (1975), MacBeth and Merville (1979), and Emanuel and MacBeth (1982). Researchers found that plotting implied volatility on the y-axis and the strike price on the x-axis resulted in a slightly U-shaped pattern dubbed the *volatility smile*.

WHAT CFOs DO

CFO Survey Highlights Accounting Application of Black and Scholes

As we learned in Chapter 18, options are an important component of executive pay packages, particularly in the United States. Prior to 2006, U.S. accounting standards did not require companies to treat option-based compensation as an expense like cash salary and bonuses. That all changed with the adoption of Financial Accounting Standards Board Statement 123R, which required firms to place a value on their option grants and to deduct that value as an expense on the income statement. However, FASB did not specify *how* companies should value stock option grants, leaving firms to decide whether they would use Black and Scholes, the binomial model, or some other method.

A 2005 survey of CFOs indicated that about 62% planned to calculate their options expense using Black and Scholes whereas 36% planned to use the binomial approach (see graph below). Since then, however, many companies have switched from the Black and Scholes to the binomial model—in part because the latter can handle factors such as vesting periods, early exercise decisions, and other factors that the Black and Scholes model wasn't designed to consider. Often these factors lead to a lower option value and hence to a lower compensation expense for companies making option grants.

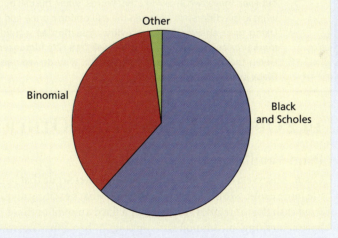

Models Used to Calculate Option-Based Compensation Expense

Smart Practices Video

Myron Scholes, Stanford University, and Chairman of Platinum Grove Asset Management

"Implied volatility is measured by inverting the Black-Scholes model."

See the entire interview at **SMARTFinance**

the implied volatilities of out-of-the-money options seemed much higher than the implied volatilities of at-the-money options. Further tests found that the option prices generated by Black and Scholes were close to actual market prices for at-the-money options but that pricing errors were more substantial for out-of-the-money options.

The existence of a relation between an option's implied volatility and its strike price affects option trading practices in several ways. Some traders adopt speculative strategies, attempting to exploit differences in implied volatility for a single underlying asset. For example, we know that the value of a call option rises with the volatility of the underlying stock. One might therefore argue that, when two options on the same underlying stock have different implied volatilities, the option with high implied volatility is overpriced and/or the option with low implied volatility is underpriced. Traders who hold this belief can take a short position in the first option and a long position in the second to try to profit from any pricing discrepancies. A slightly more sophisticated version of this technique begins with estimating the volatility of an underlying stock by taking a weighted average of the implied volatilities of several options on that stock. The weights might be a function of how close the stock's market price is to the option's strike price, or they might depend on the volume of trading at each strike price. The implied volatilities of some options will naturally be above the weighted average, and others will fall below the average. Traders may take speculative long positions in the options with below-average implied volatilities and short positions in those with above-average implied volatilities.

Why have we invested so much time in valuing ordinary call and put options, given that only a small fraction of business school students become professional options traders? The answer is that options are everywhere, embedded in other corporate securities as well as in capital investment projects. The methods used to price call and put options have much wider applications than it may at first appear.

Concept Review Questions	1. What do the Black and Scholes and binomial models have in common? What are their main differences?
	2. Examine Figure 19.2. When the stock price is very high, the two lines in the figure are virtually parallel. Why?
	3. Look again at Figure 19.2, especially at the portion where the stock price is high. At a given stock price (e.g., $70 in the figure), what is the approximate vertical distance between these two lines? In other words, when the call option is deep in the money, what is the difference between the call option's price and its intrinsic value?
	4. Using your answer to the previous question as a guide, what happens to the market price of a call option if the risk-free rate increases?
	5. Given that options are risky securities, why do we use the risk-free rate in the Black and Scholes equation?

19.2 OPTIONS EMBEDDED IN OTHER SECURITIES

Plain-Vanilla Stocks and Bonds

Casual observers of financial markets sometimes argue that bonds are boring compared to the more exotic world of options. After all, what's exciting about an investment that pays a fixed cash flow at regular intervals for a fixed amount of time? In fact, corporate bonds do have something in common with options. When a firm borrows money, it has the option of defaulting on its loans if cash flow is insufficient to repay the debt. The default option explains why corporate bonds must offer higher yields than government bonds.

Suppose that a company has $250 million in equity financing and $250 million in 3-year, zero-coupon bonds with a current market value of $200 million. The company plans to invest $450 million in cash in an asset of some kind, and it hopes that the asset's future cash flows will be sufficient to offer attractive returns to both stockholders and bondholders. However, both bondholders and stockholders know that if the cash flows are not sufficient even to pay bondholders their $250 million at maturity, then the firm can walk away from its debts and leave bondholders to claim whatever cash they can by selling off the firm's remaining assets.

Figure 19.4 shows that the position occupied by bondholders in this example is identical to that of investors holding a combination of risk-free bonds and a short put option.

FIGURE 19.4

Options Embedded in Ordinary Corporate Bonds

Corporate bond investors hold a position that is equivalent to a portfolio of risk-free debt and a short put option. If the firm's assets are not sufficient to repay its debt at maturity, then the firm puts its assets to the bondholders.

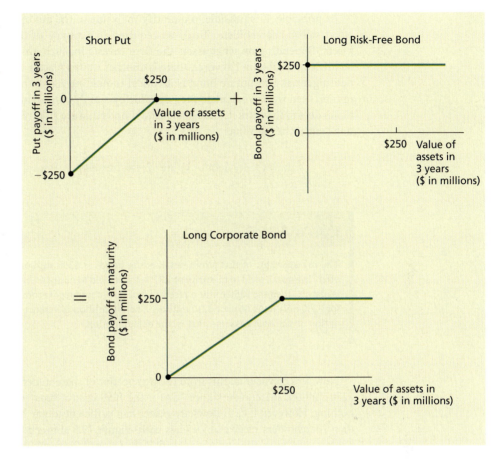

The lower graph in the figure shows a payoff diagram for the firm's bondholders. The underlying asset in this graph is not the value of common stock, such as we have grown used to, but rather the value of the firm's total assets in three years, when the bonds mature. When the value of assets is high, bondholders receive the $250 million they were promised and no more. When the value of assets is low, bondholders receive less than $250 million. How much less depends on the value of the remaining assets.

The upper portion of the figure shows the payoffs from a hypothetical portfolio containing a long position in risk-free government bonds with a face value of $250 million and a short position in put options with a strike price of $250 million. As before, the underlying asset for the put option is not the firm's stock but the firm's assets. The bondholders are, in effect, selling this put option to the firm, so if the firm's assets turn out to be worth less than $250 million then the firm will give the assets to the bondholders for $250 million in cash.[7] The net cash flow to bondholders will equal the $250 million they earn on risk-free bonds, minus any losses they incur on the put option.

---

[7]When firms go bankrupt, bondholders do not usually pay out cash in exchange for the firm's assets. They do something equivalent, however. A bankrupt firm can hand over its assets to lenders, and in exchange the shareholders of the firm can walk away from their debts. In other words, receiving a cash payment of $250 million is equivalent, in economic terms, to having an outstanding debt of $250 million canceled.

In principle, it is possible to quantify the value of the put option that bondholders in effect sell to shareholders. To do so requires an estimate of the volatility of the firm's assets. Depending on what assets the firm invests in, such an estimate may or may not be difficult to obtain. However, there is another way to place a value on the put option. If holding a risky corporate bond is identical to holding a risk-free bond and selling a put option, then we can calculate the put value by simply comparing the market value of the firm's debt to the market value of identical bonds that are risk free. The difference in prices must equal the put value:

$$\text{Value of risky debt} = \text{Value of risk-free debt} - \text{Put value} \qquad \text{(Eq. 19.4)}$$

EXAMPLE

The market value of this firm's outstanding bonds is $200 million, which implies that they offer investors a yield to maturity of 7.72%. If the yield to maturity on 3-year government bonds is just 6%, then the $250 million face value of zero-coupon government bonds would sell today for $250 million/(1.06)³, or $210 million. The $10 million difference equals the value of the put option on the firm's assets—that is, the default option.

Now, let's consider all this from the perspective of shareholders. When the firm borrows $250 million, shareholders know that if the firm cannot repay the loan, they will receive nothing. However, if cash flows are more than sufficient to pay bondholders $250 million, then shareholders receive any excess cash. Figure 19.5 shows a payoff diagram for shareholders. As always, the underlying asset is the value of the firm's assets in three years. Do you recognize this picture? From the shareholders' point of view, they own a claim that is equivalent to a long call option on the underlying assets with a strike price of $250 million.

FIGURE 19.5

Options Embedded in the Stock of a Levered Firm

The shareholders of a levered firm hold a call option. If the firm's assets are worth more than the value of its debts ($250 million in the graph), then shareholders keep the surplus; if not, then shareholders receive nothing when the firm defaults.

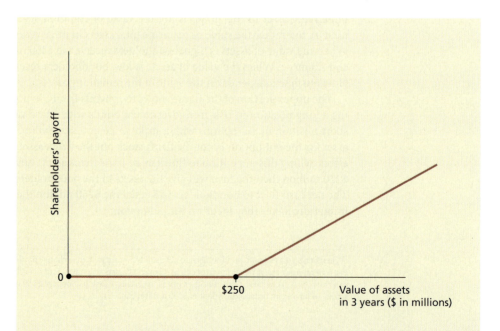

Figure 19.5 contains some unsettling news for bondholders. Suppose that the objective of this firm's management is to maximize the wealth of shareholders. If holding a share of stock in this company is like holding a call option, then maximizing the share price should be analogous to maximizing the value of a call option. What actions might managers take to maximize the call value? We have seen that a critical factor in determining option values is the volatility of the underlying asset. Managers could increase share prices by increasing the volatility of the firm's assets. Once the firm has outstanding debt, its stock behaves like a call option, so *making riskier investments benefits shareholders at the expense of bondholders.*

If it seems far-fetched that managers would intentionally take more risk to increase share values, we offer two pieces of evidence that we hope will persuade you that managers recognize this opportunity. The first piece of evidence is somewhat indirect. When companies enter into loan contracts with banks and other lenders, the companies must often agree to abide by a set of loan covenants designed to protect lenders by, among other things, restricting the uses to which firms can apply borrowed funds. If lenders did not worry that firms might borrow to make risky investments (actually, to make riskier investments than they disclosed when borrowing the money), then there would be no reason for lenders to insist on covenants of this type.

The second piece of evidence is much more direct. In a revealing study, Berger, Ofek, and Yermack (1997) examine the connection between firms' compensation plans and their capital structures. They reason as follows. Suppose a firm chooses to emphasize stock options in the compensation package that it offers to managers. Managers know that the value of these options depends on several factors, one of which is the volatility of the underlying stock. Therefore, managers who receive a great deal of pay in the form of stock options have the incentive to increase not only the price of the stock but also its volatility. One way to increase the volatility of equity is to use more debt in the capital structure. The authors find a positive correlation between the firm's debt-to-assets ratio and the number of stock options held by a firm's CEO. Though a correlation between option compensation and leverage does not prove that managers increase leverage after receiving stock options, it is at least consistent with that hypothesis. In a similar vein, Rajgopal and Shevlin (2002) find that managers of oil and gas firms with employee stock options take greater exploration risks and engage in less hedging than managers without stock options.

Even plain-vanilla investments such as stocks and corporate bonds have optionlike characteristics. Recognizing these characteristics provides unique insights into the forces that influence stock and bond prices as well as into relationships between borrowers and lenders and between managers and shareholders. Now we turn our attention to other types of corporate securities that have more transparent option features.

Warrants

Warrants are securities issued by firms that grant the right to buy shares of stock at a fixed price for a given period of time. Warrants bear a close resemblance to call options, and the same five factors that influence call option values (stock price, risk-free rate, strike price, expiration date, and volatility) will also affect warrant prices. However, there are some important differences between warrants and calls.

1. Warrants are issued by firms, whereas call options are contracts between investors who are not necessarily connected to the firm whose stock serves as the underlying asset.
2. When investors exercise warrants, the number of outstanding shares increases and the issuing firm receives the strike price as a cash inflow. When investors exercise call options, no change in outstanding shares occurs and the firm receives no cash.
3. Warrants are often issued with expiration dates several years in the future, whereas most options expire in just a few months.

4. Although call and put options trade as stand-alone securities, firms frequently attach warrants to public or privately placed bonds, preferred stock, and sometimes even common stock. Warrants that are attached to other securities are called **equity kickers**, implying that they offer additional upside potential on the security to which they are attached. When firms bundle warrants together with other securities, they may or may not grant investors the right to unbundle them and sell the warrants separately.

Even though warrants and options differ in some important respects, the Black and Scholes model can be used to value warrants—provided an adjustment is made to account for the dilution that occurs when firms issue new shares to warrant holders. A simple example will illustrate how to adjust for dilution.

Assume that a small firm has 1,000 shares outstanding worth $10 each. The firm has no debt, so the value of its assets equals the value of its equity: $10,000. Two years ago, when the firm's stock price was just $8, the firm issued 100 shares of common stock to a private investor. Each share had an attached warrant granting a two-year right to purchase one share of stock for $9. The warrants are about to expire, and the investor intends to exercise them.

What would the investor's payoff be if she held ordinary call options (sold to her by another private investor) rather than warrants? Because the price of the stock is $10 and the strike price is $9, the investor would earn a profit of $1 per share, or $100 on the calls. If calls were exercised, then the firm would still have 100 shares outstanding worth $10 each. From the firm's point of view, the call exercise would generate neither a cash inflow nor a cash outflow.

In contrast, if the investor exercises her warrants then two changes take place. First, the firm receives cash equal to the strike price ($9) times the number of warrants exercised (100), or a total inflow of $900. This raises the total value of the firm's assets to $10,900. Simultaneously, the firm's outstanding shares increase from 1,000 to 1,100, so the new price per share can be calculated as follows:

$$\text{New price per share} = \frac{\$10,900}{1,100} = \$9.91$$

JOB INTERVIEW QUESTION

How does the price of a warrant compare to the price of an option with identical characteristics?

The investor's payoff on the warrants is just $0.91, compared to $1.00 on a comparable call option. Fortunately, it's easy to use the Black and Scholes model to value a call option with characteristics similar to those of a warrant and then multiply the call value times an adjustment factor for dilution. If N_1 represents the number of "old shares" outstanding and N_2 represents the number of new shares issued as a result of the warrants being exercised, then the price of the warrants equals the price of an identical call option, $\$C$, multiplied by the dilution factor, $N_1/(N_1 + N_2)$:

$$\text{Warrant value} = \$C\left(\frac{N_1}{N_1 + N_2}\right) \qquad \textbf{(Eq. 19.5)}$$

EXAMPLE

As part of the Troubled Asset Relief Program (TARP), the U.S. government paid Wells Fargo $25 billion in exchange for preferred stock and warrants. The government received 110.3 million warrants, and Wells Fargo had 3,325 million outstanding shares at the time. We will use the Black and Scholes formula and the adjustment factor in Equation 19.5 to value the Wells Fargo warrants. To value the warrants, we must know the price of Wells Fargo stock, the expiration date of the warrants, the strike price, and the risk-free rate. We also need an estimate of Wells

Fargo's volatility. Here are the relevant figures: stock price = \$31.22; strike price = \$34.01; risk-free rate = 2%; expiration = 10 years; standard deviation = 94.7%.[8]

$$d_1 = \frac{\ln\left(\frac{31.22}{34.01}\right) + \left(0.02 + \frac{(0.947)^2}{2}\right)10}{0.947\sqrt{10}} = \frac{(-0.086) + (4.684)}{2.995} = 1.535$$

$$d_2 = d_1 - \sigma\sqrt{t} = 1.535 - 2.995 = -1.459$$

$$N(1.535) = 0.938, \qquad N(-1.459) = 0.072$$

$$C = 31.22(0.938) - 34.01(2.718^{-(.02)(10)})(0.072) = \$27.26$$

$$\text{Warrant} = \frac{3,325}{3,325 + 110.3}(27.26) = \$26.39$$

Convertibles

A convertible bond grants investors the right to receive payment in the shares of an underlying stock rather than in cash. Usually, the stock that investors have the right to "purchase" in exchange for their bonds is the stock of the firm that issued the bonds. In some cases, however, a firm that owns a large amount of common stock in a different firm will use those shares as the underlying asset for a convertible bond issue. In either case, a **convertible bond** is essentially an ordinary corporate bond with an attached call option or warrant.

In February 2007, Xilinx, Inc., announced a sale of 30-year bonds that would generate proceeds for the company of approximately \$0.9 billion. Xilinx's bonds offered investors a coupon rate of 3.125% below the rates on long-term government bonds at the time. How could a technology firm borrow money at a lower rate than the government? Investors were willing to buy Xilinx's bonds despite the low yield because the bonds were convertible into Xilinx common stock. Specifically, each Xilinx bond with a face value of \$1,000 could be converted into 32.076 shares of Xilinx stock.

Convertible bonds offer investors the security of a bond and the upside potential of common stock. If Xilinx's shares increase in value, then the bondholders will redeem their bonds for Xilinx shares rather than cash. To see how far Xilinx's shares would have to rise before bondholders would want to convert, we must divide the value of Xilinx's bonds by the **conversion ratio**, the number of Xilinx shares each bondholder receives upon conversion. The conversion ratio here is 32.0760, so dividing the bond's value by that figure gives us

$$\frac{\$1,000}{32.0760} = \$31.18$$

This represents the **conversion price** of the bonds. In other words, if investors trade a bond worth \$1,000 for 32.076 Xilinx shares, they are effectively paying a price of \$31.18 per share.

---

[8]We estimated the 94.7% figure for standard deviation based on daily data over the 60 trading days prior to the transaction between Wells Fargo and the government. Our calculation probably overstates the value of the warrants because it is not reasonable to expect that the volatility of Wells Fargo stock over the 10-year life of the warrants will remain as high as it was in the months leading up to the TARP bailout. See Appendix 19A for the calculation.

At the time Xilinx issued these bonds, its stock was selling for approximately $25.98 per share. Holding the price of the bond constant, Xilinx's shares would have to rise roughly 20% before bondholders would want to convert their bonds into Xilinx's shares. This 20% figure equals the bond's **conversion premium**. At present, it does not make sense for holders of Xilinx's convertible bonds to trade them for shares of stock. Nevertheless, we can still ask what value bondholders will receive if they do convert. If Xilinx stock sells for $25.98 and if each bond can be exchanged for 32.076 shares, then the conversion value of one bond equals $833.33 (32.076 × $25.98). **Conversion value** is important because it helps define a lower bound on the market value of a convertible bond. For example, suppose that interest rates jump suddenly and the yield on Xilinx's bonds goes from 3.125% to 4.25%. If we forgo the opportunity to convert the bonds, their price would drop to $810.26.[9]

However, the price of Xilinx's bonds cannot dip this low if Xilinx's stock remains at $25.98. If it did drop, then investors could exploit an arbitrage opportunity by purchasing one bond for $810.26 and immediately converting it into 32.076 shares of stock worth $833.33.

In general, we can say that the price of a convertible bond will be, at a minimum, the *higher* of (1) the value of an identical bond without conversion rights or (2) the conversion value. Figure 19.6 demonstrates this pattern for a generic convertible bond with a par value of $1,000 and a conversion ratio of 20. The horizontal line represents the present value of

FIGURE 19.6

The Value of a Convertible Bond

A convertible bond must sell for the greater of its value as a straight bond or its conversion value. If the bond's value is $1,000 and the conversion ratio is 20, then the conversion price equals $50. For each $1 increase in the stock price beyond $50, the bond's conversion value rises by $20.

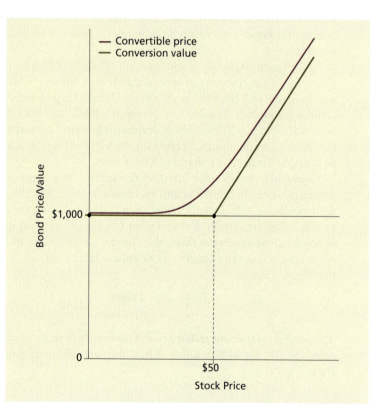

the convertible bond's scheduled interest and principal payments, which for convenience we assume to be $1,000. The upward-sloping line shows the bond's conversion value at different stock prices, and the curve shows the convertible bond's price. When the stock price is very low, the odds that the bonds will ever be worth converting into shares are low, so the convertible bond sells at a price comparable to that of an ordinary bond. As the share price rises, the value of the conversion option increases.

Most convertible bonds have another feature that complicates matters slightly. When firms issue convertibles, they almost always retain the right to call back the bonds. When firms call their outstanding bonds, bondholders can choose (within 30 days of the call) to receive either the call price in cash or a quantity of shares equal to the conversion ratio. Effectively, the call option that firms retain allows them to shorten the conversion option held by bondholders. If a firm calls its bonds, investors will choose cash if the call price exceeds conversion value, and they will choose shares if the opposite is true.

Under what circumstances should a firm call its convertible bonds? If managers are acting in the interests of shareholders, they will never call bonds that are worth less than the call price. Doing so would transfer wealth from shareholders to bondholders. Similarly, if the price of a bond rises above the call price because the underlying stock has increased in value, then firms should call the bonds. If the firm does not call the bonds and the stock price continues to increase, then—when investors ultimately choose to convert their bonds into shares—the firm will be selling stock at a bargain. Again, the result is a transfer of wealth from shareholders to bondholders. Therefore, the optimal policy is to call the bonds when their market value equals the call price.[10]

Convertible securities come in many flavors, and each flavor usually has its own colorful acronym. For example, LYONs (liquid-yield option notes) are zero-coupon bonds, convertible into the shares of the issuing firm, that are both callable by the issuer and putable by the investors. When a bond is putable, investors have the right to force the issuer to redeem their bonds in cash. DECS (debt exchangeable for common shares) are convertibles that automatically convert to shares at a future date. The conversion ratio of DECS can be variable, so bondholders must endure the downside risk of the underlying stock but do not necessarily enjoy all the upside potential. LYONs, DECS, and other exotic convertibles usually offer investors an interest rate that is higher than the dividend yield on the underlying stock. In the late 1990s, several Internet companies issued a new type of convertible bond named *death spiral* convertibles. These convertible bonds promise lenders a fixed dollar amount of shares, which in turn implies a variable conversion ratio. If the underlying share price falls, then the only way to pay lenders a fixed dollar amount of shares is to convert their bonds into more shares. However, as with warrants, convertible bonds create dilution. The name *death spiral* comes from the possibility that, as a firm's share price declines and it issues more shares to convertible bondholders, the subsequent dilution will force share prices even lower.

The lesson from this section is that many types of securities issued by corporations have embedded options, and understanding the characteristics of these options is central

---

[10]Actually, this would be the optimal call policy if firms could force investors to choose cash or shares immediately upon receiving the call. However, because investors have 30 days to decide whether they want cash or shares, the optimal time to call may be when the market value of the bonds exceeds the call price slightly. The reason is that if the firm calls the bonds precisely when the market price hits the call price, the stock price might fall during the 30-day decision period. A decline in the stock price would lower the conversion value, and the firm would be forced to redeem the bonds for cash. Thus, allowing the conversion value of the bonds to rise a little beyond the strike price gives the firm a little "slack" (see Asquith 1995).

WHAT COMPANIES DO GLOBALLY

CFO Survey Evidence

There are several theories that attempt to explain why firms issue convertible bonds. A survey of U.S. CFOs conducted by Graham and Harvey (2001) finds that the most important reason is that firms view convertible bonds as an inexpensive way to issue "delayed" equity. In other words, they expect bondholders to eventually convert to equity, meaning that the company keeps the proceeds from the bond issue rather than having to repay the principal.

More recently, Brounen, de Jong, and Koedjik have surveyed CFOs from several European countries to determine why they issued convertible debt. In addition to the "delayed equity" motivation, the survey asked CFOs whether they issued convertibles because they perceived their stock to be undervalued, because they wanted the ability to call the bonds or force bondholders to convert to equity later, because they wanted to avoid short-term dilution of their existing shareholders, or simply because convertibles can be issued at a lower interest rate than ordinary bonds. As in the United States, European CFOs valued the opportunity to issue delayed equity, but each of the other factors was important to some extent.

From the firm's perspective, other "benefits" of delayed equity include no equity dilution today and no negative market reaction today (as there would be with straight equity issuance).

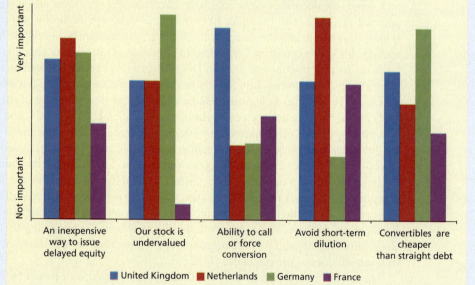

Source: Reprinted from *Journal of Banking and Finance,* 30, "Capital Structure Policies in Europe: Survey Evidence," Dirk Brounen, Abe de Jong, and Kees Koedjik, pp. 1409–1442, copyright 2006, with permission from Elsevier.

to pricing the securities with which they are bundled. But an even broader application of option pricing theory has developed since the mid-1980s, one that is gaining ground in the corporate world: real options. This involves applying the theoretical apparatus developed for financial options to real investment projects with optionlike qualities.

| Concept Review Questions | 6. Using option pricing logic, explain why debt covenants often restrict firms from taking out additional loans without the initial lender's consent. |

Concept Review Questions

6. Using option pricing logic, explain why debt covenants often restrict firms from taking out additional loans without the initial lender's consent.
7. "Firms that wish to save on borrowing costs should always issue convertible bonds, because investors will buy them even though they offer lower yields than ordinary bonds." Comment on this statement.
8. After issuing warrants, what actions might a firm take that would be detrimental to warrant holders?

19.3 OPTIONS EMBEDDED IN CAPITAL INVESTMENTS: REAL OPTIONS

In Chapters 7 and 9, we learned that the NPV rule does not always lead to value-maximizing decisions when firms are considering major investment proposals. The reason is that the NPV approach fails to capture the value of managerial flexibility as the passing of time resolves uncertainty surrounding a particular investment. Managers usually have the option to abandon or to expand an initial investment, and that flexibility often adds to a project's value above and beyond its NPV. Smart managers understand this intuitively; but in recent years tools have emerged that help quantify and refine this intuition.

In this section, we show how to calculate the option value of two capital investment projects. In the first example, which involves oil extraction, we will use the Black and Scholes model to show that oil drilling rights have value even when it is not economic to drill right away. In the second example, we will use the binomial model to quantify the value to McDonald's Corporation of a pilot investment in a new type of storefront, McTreat Spot.

The Option Value of Drilling Rights

Let's return to a problem we studied briefly in Chapter 9. A company has the opportunity to bid for drilling rights for one year on a tract of land. The cost of extracting the oil is $50 per barrel, and the current (and expected future) price of oil is $45 per barrel. Because the cost of drilling exceeds the value of the oil extracted, an NPV calculation shows that the drilling rights have negative value.

Adding a little more structure to this problem, suppose that the annual standard deviation of the price of oil is 30%. Given this volatility, a firm contemplating a bid for the drilling rights can expect that at some point the price of oil may rise to a level that makes drilling profitable. But without knowing when or how high the price of oil may rise, how can the firm quantify the value of the opportunity to drill only when oil prices are sufficiently high?

The right to drill oil is like a call option. By paying the exercise price of $50, the firm has the right to receive one barrel of oil. The option lasts for one year, until drilling rights expire. If we assume that the risk-free rate equals 4%, then this option can be valued using the Black and Scholes model:

$$d_1 = \frac{\ln\left(\frac{45}{50}\right) + \left(0.04 + \frac{(0.30)^2}{2}\right)1}{0.30\sqrt{1}} = -0.0679$$

$$d_2 = d_1 - \sigma\sqrt{t} = -0.3679$$

$$N(-0.0679) = 0.4729, \qquad N(-0.3679) = 0.3565$$

$$C = 45(0.4729) - 50(2.718^{-(0.4)(1)})(0.3565) = \$4.16$$

The value of drilling rights equals $4.16 per barrel, so the firm can determine its bid by multiplying this value by the number of barrels expected in the field. If there are fixed costs of drilling beyond the $50 extraction costs, bidding makes sense only if the total option value exceeds the fixed costs.

Without question, this exercise is an oversimplification of any real-world problem that involves drilling rights. For example, the Black and Scholes calculation assumes that the option exercise occurs on a single date one year in the future. In reality, a firm can decide to pump oil at any time during the year, and it can stop pumping once it has started if the price of oil falls. Modeling this flexibility requires a complex binomial tree, one in which the price of oil moves a little bit each week over the option's life. A complete binomial tree like this will show many different paths that oil prices might take. At each point on each path, the firm must decide whether to begin pumping oil or, if they are already pumping at that point in the tree, whether to stop. Because the binomial valuation approach recognizes that managers have a higher degree of flexibility than contemplated by the Black and Scholes calculation, we expect that a binomial analysis would lead to an option above our current estimate of $4.16 per barrel. Even so, the Black and Scholes model offers a "first cut" at estimating the option value of drilling rights, and it leads the firm to a different conclusion than it would reach from NPV analysis alone.

Mini-Case: Real Options at McDonald's—McTreat Spot[11]

McDonald's Corporation is constantly looking for ways to expand its business by leveraging its various burger-chain strengths (brand management, inventory and cost control, location development, etc.) into new nonburger-store formats. One concept currently under consideration (June 2010) is the McTreat Spot.

The idea behind McTreat Spot is to provide potential customers with convenient places to satisfy their sweet tooth. The current vision of a McTreat Spot is a small kiosk located in high-traffic/high-volume locations like airport concourses and shopping malls, offering ice cream and frozen yogurt products such as sundaes and milkshakes.

There are many uncertainties involved with this new concept. First of all, the company is unsure whether these very small storefronts in high-rent areas can achieve sufficient sales to cover costs and provide a return on capital. Perhaps more important, it is unclear whether customers would like to purchase McDonald's dessert products outside of McDonald's existing stores when faced with specialty-store alternatives (TCBY, Ben & Jerry's, etc.). Finally, as is true in all of McDonald's businesses, there is uncertainty about the overall economy; McDonald's management believes that the McTreat Spot enterprise value will be sensitive to the state of the economy.

Faced with this uncertainty, McDonald's Corporation has decided to test the new store format in selected shopping malls, the Minneapolis Airport, the Circus-Circus Casino in Las Vegas, and even a few Blockbuster Video outlets. Such testing is extraordinarily expensive because each storefront must be uniquely designed and so economies of scale cannot be exploited. In fact, the test stores have negative NPVs on their own (i.e., they use more cash than they generate). But the management at McDonald's knows that they have "strategic" value. The question is this: How much is McDonald's willing

---

[11]We thank Richard Shockley for providing this example. Although this example is based on a real project considered by McDonald's, the numbers are purely hypothetical and are intended only to illustrate how a real options analysis might be applied to the McTreat Spot investment proposal. For an excellent textbook on real options, see Richard L. Shockley, Jr., *An Applied Course in Real Options Valuation* (2007).

to spend in the name of "strategy"? In other words, what is the investment value of the McTreat Spot test stores?

Of course, McDonald's does not disclose detailed financial information on individual projects such as this, but we can construct hypothetical values to illustrate how a financial analyst at McDonald's might approach the problem. First, let's consider what would happen if McDonald's were to launch the new concept without testing. Management feels that the potential market is perhaps 1,000 storefronts, and each would cost $750,000 to outfit and get going. This investment is irreversible; if McDonald's decides to take the big gamble, it would cost $750 million (1,000 × $750,000) up front. Rollout would take two years. At the end of that rollout period, the value of the business would be readily apparent: either it would be a hit, in which case the PV of the free cash flows from operations would be $1.5 billion, or it would be a bust, in which case the PV of the free cash flows from operations would be only $500 million. Management is somewhat sanguine about the project and feels it will be a "hit" with probability 0.40 and a bust with probability 0.60. To an analyst evaluating this problem in June 2010, the problem would look like this:

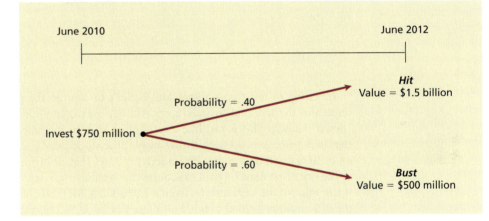

Suppose that McDonald's management assigned a 13% discount rate to this project. At that rate, the NPV of an immediate rollout of McTreat Spot is negative in June 2010:

$$NPV = \frac{0.4(\$1.5 \text{ billion}) + 0.6(\$500 \text{ million})}{(1.13)^2} - \$750 \text{ million}$$

$$= \frac{\$900 \text{ million}}{1.277} - \$750 \text{ million}$$

$$= \$704.8 \text{ million} - \$750 \text{ million} = -\$45.2 \text{ million}$$

In other words, immediate rollout is a value-destroying activity for McDonald's shareholders. The present value of cash inflows from entering this business is only $704.8 million, whereas the cost of entering the business is $750 million.

Even though this hypothetical 2010 NPV of the McTreat Spot concept is negative and the NPV of any test stores would surely be negative, McDonald's management intuitively understands that the test-store program is valuable. The reason is that the test stores generate information in addition to cash flow: by testing for two years, McDonald's can learn the value of a 1,000-store chain *before* investing $750 million. If the test stores indicate that McTreat Spot is a hit, then the firm will spend the capital and take the positive-NPV business. On the other hand, if the test stores indicate that McTreat Spot is a bust, then management will walk away having spent only the cost of the testing program. So the test-store program gives quite a different picture:

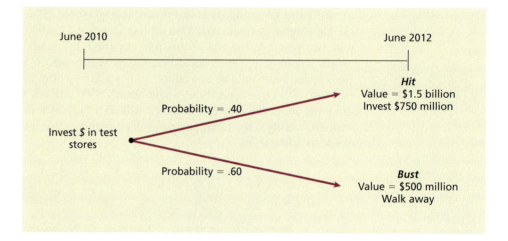

Investing in test stores allows McDonald's to capture the positive NPV in the "up" branch of the tree and to walk away without making an additional investment in the "down" branch. This is just like a call option that an investor can choose to exercise if the stock price goes up or to throw away if the stock price goes down. This option, like an ordinary call option, has an underlying asset that determines its value, and it has a strike price that must be paid to acquire that underlying asset. The underlying asset here is the value of the cash inflows from a 1,000-kiosk McTreat chain, and the strike price is the $750 million needed to build all those kiosks. If McDonald's learns that the value of the business is greater than the $750 million cost, the company will exercise its call option by building 1,000 kiosks at a cost of $750 million. That will allow the firm to take the NPV of $750 million ($1.5 billion minus $750 million) as the payoff in 2012. If McDonald's learns that the value of the business is less than $750 million, then it will let the option die unexercised and the payoff in 2012 will be zero.

Because the test stores create the real option on a 1,000-store chain, we can determine the value of the test-store program itself, which is simply equal to the value of the option it creates plus the NPV of its own cash flows. In other words, we can now answer this difficult question: What is the most McDonald's should spend on the test stores? Recall that, as long as the option value created by the test stores exceeds their cost (their negative NPV), the test stores actually create value for McDonald's shareholders.

McDonald's can value the option created by the test stores using the binomial model. The key issue is to understand the June 2010 value of the underlying asset. The underlying asset is always what you would get if you exercised the option; in this case, exercise of the option results in McDonald's receiving a 1,000-store McTreat Spot chain. The beginning value of the underlying asset is always the value of what you get if you exercise immediately; in this case, it is the June 2010 estimated value of the McTreat Spot chain (which we have determined to be $704.8 million). Our binomial option problem looks like this:

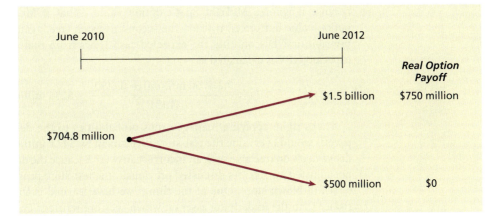

Let's attempt to value this option using the risk-neutral method. Remember, the risk-neutral approach involves choosing the probabilities of the up and down moves in the underlying asset such that the expected return from holding the underlying asset equals the risk-free rate (because that's what risk-neutral investors demand). Suppose that the risk-free rate in this problem is 5%. At this rate, the value of the underlying asset would grow in two years as follows (in millions of dollars):

$$\$704.8(1.05)^2 = \$777$$

Next, let p represent the probability of an up move and $1 - p$ represent the probability of a down move. Setting the expected payoff on the underlying asset equal to the risk-free rate, we determine the following:

$$\$1,500p + \$500(1 - p) = \$777$$
$$1 - p = 0.723$$

Now, use these probabilities to calculate the expected cash flow in 2012 from the call option. The call pays $750 in the up state and pays nothing in the down state, so the expected cash flow is calculated as follows:

$$\text{Expected cash flow from call option} = \$750p + \$0(1 - p)$$
$$= \$750(0.277) = \$207.8$$

Finally, discount this cash flow for two years at 5% to obtain the current price of the call option:

$$\text{Call value today} = \frac{\$207.8}{(1.05)^2} = \$188.4$$

In other words, the most McDonald's should be willing to spend on the test stores (given our assumptions) is $188.4 million. As long as the testing program costs less than this (in capital investment as well as negative free cash flow), then testing creates value for the shareholders.

Consider the errors McDonald's might make if it attempts to value this project using decision trees with management's estimate of the up and down probabilities of 40% and 60%, respectively. In the initial decision tree where we calculated the expected NPV, McDonald's found a negative NPV of −$45.2 million when ignoring the option to walk away if McTreat Spot was not a hit. Focusing on that number alone would be a mistake because it ignores McTreat Spot's option value. What if McDonald's recognized the option value but priced it using the second decision tree, again with the 40% and 60% probabilities? Discounting the expected cash flows from that decision tree at 13%, the expected NPV is calculated as

$$\frac{0.4(\$750 \text{ million}) + 0.6(\$0)}{(1.13)^2} = \$235 \text{ million}$$

That's right: applying management's probabilities to the decision tree of call option payoffs would overvalue the test-store investment by $47.1 million, an error of 25%! Why does a decision tree give such an incorrect answer? Because the decision trees used here are not adjusted for risk. As discussed previously, the test-store program creates a call option on a full-blown store. One of the things we have learned is that call options are much riskier than the underlying asset on which they are written. Therefore, if the underlying asset here, a fully built McTreat Spot chain, has a risk-adjusted required rate of return of 13%, then the required rate of return for the *option* on the McTreat Spot chain must be even higher. How much higher? We cannot know without performing the option valuation. But now that we know the correct option value, we can "infer" the proper discount rate by applying management's probabilities of future outcomes and then solving for the discount rate that provides the option value:

$$\frac{0.4(\$750) + 0.6(0)}{(1 + r)^2} = \$188.4, \quad r = 26.2\%$$

In summary, an expected NPV calculation undervalues the McTreat project because it ignores the project's option value. However, a decision-tree approach to valuing that option using the 40% and 60% probabilities overvalues the option. This is a common pattern. Net present value calculations often understate the value of an investment, but pricing corporate growth options using decision trees leads to overvaluation errors. Analysts must always value real options with the appropriate technology—that is, an option pricing model such as the binomial or the Black and Scholes.

Concept Review Questions	9. In the oil drilling example, how should a firm change its bid if it believes the volatility of oil prices will increase? How would the firm change its bid if it valued the drilling rights using NPV analysis rather than taking an options perspective on the investment?
	10. In the McTreat problem, management believes that the probability of a "hit" is 40%. What effect does this belief have on the option valuation of the investment?

SUMMARY

- Analysts can use the Black and Scholes formula to value a European call on a stock that pays no dividends.
- The Black and Scholes formula requires five inputs: the stock price, the strike price, the risk-free rate, the time to expiration, and the underlying asset's volatility.

- Of the five inputs to the model, only volatility is an unknown that analysts must estimate.
- If analysts can observe the market price of an option, they can use the Black and Scholes equation to solve for the underlying asset's implied volatility.

- When a firm borrows money, both its debt and equity have optionlike characteristics.
- Warrants are similar to call options, though pricing warrants requires an adjustment to the Black and Scholes model to account for dilution.
- Convertible securities combine the characteristics of ordinary bonds with call options.

- Capital investments with optionlike characteristics may be valued using either the binomial or the Black and Scholes model; which valuation approach is appropriate depends on the characteristics of the investment.

KEY TERMS

Black and Scholes option pricing
   equation
conversion premium
conversion price
conversion ratio

conversion value
convertible bond
equity kickers
hedge ratio
implied volatility

option's delta
standard normal distribution
warrants

QUESTIONS

19-1. Project A has a guaranteed payoff of $200 million, which will exactly compensate the debtholders of the firm. Project B has a 50% probability of a $400 million payoff and a 50% probability of a zero payoff. Which project do the debtholders prefer and which project do the shareholders prefer?

19-2. In what sense can the terms $N(d_1)$ and $N(d_2)$ in the Black and Scholes model be interpreted as probabilities that a call option will expire in the money?

19-3. How are the values $N(d_1)$ and $N(-d_1)$ related?

19-4. If all other factors are held constant, what happens to the value of a call option when the risk-free rate increases?

19-5. You observe that the value of a particular put option has increased significantly over the last few days. However, neither the risk-free rate nor the price of the underlying stock has changed. What is the most likely explanation for the change in the put's value?

19-6. In Section 19.2 we learned that buyers of a corporate bond hold an instrument that is equivalent to a risk-free bond and a short put, with the firm's total assets serving as the underlying asset. But the holder of a corporate bond can also be said to hold the following

portfolio: (a) The bondholder owns the assets of the firm (the same way that you might say that the bank owns your car until you have paid it off) and (b) the bondholder sold a call option on the firm's underlying assets. Explain how (a) + (b) is equivalent to a corporate bond.

19-7. In Section 19.2 we also learned that a shareholder of a levered firm essentially owns a call option on the firm's assets. But the shareholder's position can be viewed as the following portfolio: (a) The shareholder owns the firm's assets, (b) the shareholder is short a risk-free bond, and (c) the shareholder owns a put option on the firm's assets with a strike price equal to the risk-free bond's face value. Explain how (a) + (b) + (c) is equivalent to a share of stock in a levered firm.

19-8. In terms of pricing, what are the most important differences between warrants and call options?

19-9. Is the conversion ratio of the Xilinx bonds mentioned in Section 19.2 constant through time? What about the conversion price?

19-10. What elements of the oil drilling problem do not fit the Black and Scholes model very well?

19-11. Why is it inappropriate to use the McTreat project's expected NPV as the basis for a go/no-go decision?

PROBLEMS

The Black and Scholes Model

19-1. Price a 6-month call option with a strike price of $40.00, assuming an annual standard deviation of 30% on returns, a risk-free rate of 5%, and a current stock price of $41.25. Price the associated put using put–call parity. Reprice both options after changing the risk-free rate to 6%.

19-2. Price a 3-month call option with a strike price of $20.00, assuming an annual standard deviation of 20% on returns, a risk-free rate of 5%, and a current stock price of $19.85. Price the associated put using put–call parity. Reprice both options after changing the maturity to one year.

19-3. Suppose a 1-year call option sells for $6.78. The current underlying stock price is $24.02, and the strike price is $25.00. Assuming a risk-free rate of 4%, what is the price of the associated put option?

19-4. Use the Black and Scholes model to value a call option with the following characteristics: the strike price is $55, the underlying stock's price is $65, the risk-free rate is 4%, the time to expiration is six months, and the standard deviation of the underlying asset is 35%. What is the value of $N(d_1)$?

19-5. Recalculate the value of the option in Problem 19-4 assuming that the underlying stock sells for $66. By how much does the call price change? Compare this to the value of $N(d_1)$ in Problem 19-4.

19-6. The following table shows daily closing prices for the common stock of Video Systems and for call options on Video Systems shares during the last week of June. For each pair of consecutive days, calculate the ratio of the dollar change in the price of the option divided by the dollar change in the price of the stock. Next, calculate the ratio of the percentage change in the option price divided by the percentage change in the stock price. What general patterns emerge from these calculations?

Date	Stock	Option
June 28	$17.18	$2.00
June 27	17.08	1.95
June 26	20.07	3.55
June 25	21.17	4.25
June 24	23.08	5.55

19-7. A particular stock sells for $40 and has a standard deviation of 35%. Value a call option on this stock that has three months left before expiration and an exercise price of $55. The risk-free rate is 4%.

19-8. Recalculate the value of the call in Problem 19-7 assuming that the stock price is $41. How much did the call value increase? Compare this to the value of $N(d_1)$ in Problem 19-7.

19-9. Use the Black and Scholes model to value a put option with a strike price of $35 and an expiration date in four months. The underlying stock sells for $40 and has a standard deviation of 55%, and the risk-free rate is 6%.

19-10. Suppose that the current market price of a stock is $63. The standard deviation of the stock's returns is 35% per year, and the risk-free rate is 4%. Calculate the value of a 1-year call option with a strike price of $40. What is the value of $N(d_1)$?

19-11. Recalculate the price of the option in Problem 19-10 using the binomial model under the assumption that in one year's time the stock price will move up or down by one standard deviation, or 35% (up to $85.05 or down to $40.95). What is the value of the hedge ratio, h, in this problem? Draw a connection between this value and the value of $N(d_1)$ in Problem 19-10.

19-12. Repeat the calculations in Problems 19-10 and 19-11 assuming that the call's strike price is $80 rather than $40. Once again, compare the values of $N(d_1)$ and h. Comment on what you find.

19-13. A money manager holds 10,000 shares of stock in a particular company and expects to sell them in one week. She is concerned about the possibility that the stock price might fall before she sells, so she decides to buy 10,000 put options. The current market price of the stock is $70, which is also the strike price of the puts. The standard deviation of the underlying stock is 45%, and the risk-free rate is 3%. The put options expire in four months. One week from today, the manager plans to unwind her position by selling both the shares and the puts at the prevailing market price.

    a. What is the aggregate value of the manager's current holdings in this company's stock?

    b. What will she have to pay for 10,000 puts? After purchasing the puts, what is the total market value of her holdings in both stock and puts?

    c. One week later, when it is time to sell, what will be the market value of her holdings if the stock price has risen to $75? What if the stock price has fallen to $65?

    d. Repeat parts (b) and (c) assuming that the manager bought 20,000 puts rather than 10,000. Comment on how the purchase of twice as many puts affects your answers.

19-14. Using the table below, price 1-year call options using different annual volatilities. The strike price is $30.00, with an underlying spot price of $30.00 and a risk-free rate of 3%.

Volatility	$N(d_1)$	$N(d_2)$	Call Price
20%	0.5987	0.5199	
25%	0.5968	0.4980	
30%	0.5987	0.4801	

19-15. Using the table below, price 1-year put options using different annual volatilities. The strike price is $35.00, with an underlying spot price of $32.50 and a risk-free rate of 3%.

Volatility	$N(d_1)$	$N(d_2)$	Put Price
20%	0.4520	0.3743	
25%	0.4795	0.3815	
30%	0.5012	0.3832	

19-16. A six-month call option with a strike price of $25.00 is selling for $3.50. Assuming the underlying stock price is also $25.00 and the risk-free rate is 6%, what is the implied volatility of the option?

19-17. A three-month put option with a strike price of $25.00 is selling for $4.87. Assuming the underlying spot price is 20.00 and the risk-free rate is 4%, what is the option's implied volatility?

19-18. There are currently 10 million shares outstanding for TKO Inc. Some time ago, TKO issued warrants for 1 million more shares. Assuming call options with the same strike price and expiration date as the warrants are worth $6.98, what are the warrants worth?

19-19. A company with 5,000,000 shares outstanding has issued 1,000,000 warrants that expire in two years and have an exercise price of $50. If the firm's stock price is $55, the standard deviation of the stock is 40%, and the risk-free rate is 3%, what is the market price of one warrant?

Options Embedded in Other Securities

Smart Solutions

See the problem and solution explained step-by-step at **SMARTFinance**

19-20. Company A owns a large block of shares of Company B. Company A issues bonds that at maturity will be converted into shares of Company B (conversion is mandatory). The number of Company B shares that bondholders will receive at maturity is determined by the following schedule:

Price (P) of Company B	Number of Shares Given to Bondholders
$P < 50$	1 share
$50 \leq P \leq 60$	$\dfrac{1}{P}$ shares
$60 < P$	$\dfrac{5}{6}$ shares

Draw a payoff diagram showing the dollar value of what bondholders receive on the *y*-axis and showing the stock price of Company B on the *x*-axis. Then describe how the bonds consist of a portfolio of ordinary bonds and options on Company B's stock.

19-21. Meg and Sons Incorporated has two million shares of common stock outstanding, which sell for $40 per share. The company plans to issue $10 million face value in 5-year notes. Each $1,000 par value bond has 20 attached warrants that grant investors the right to purchase Meg and Sons stock for $55 within five years. If the risk-free rate is 5% and the standard deviation of Meg and Sons shares is 30%, what is the value of the warrants?

19-22. Look again at the Xilinx convertible bonds in Section 19.2.
   a. If the yield to maturity rises to 4.25% immediately after the bonds are issued, what will be the new conversion price?
   b. If the yield does not change but Xilinx stock price rises to $28, what will be the conversion value of the bonds? The conversion premium?

19-23. A company issues 5-year convertible bonds that pay a 6% coupon rate and sell at the par value of $1,000. The conversion ratio of the bonds is 15.
   a. What is the conversion price?
   b. If the current stock price for this company is $60, what is the conversion value of the bonds?
   c. What is the conversion premium?

Options Embedded in Capital Investments: Real Options

19-24. Recalculate the value of drilling rights from Section 19.3 assuming that the standard deviation of the price of oil is 40% rather than 30%. Comment on how your conclusion changes when you value this investment using option pricing logic rather than a net present value approach.

Smart Solutions

See the problem and solution explained step-by-step at **SMARTFinance**

19-25. Value the McTreat Spot option described in Section 19.3 using the binomial method rather than the risk-neutral approach. Verify that either approach results in the same option value.

MINI-CASE: BLACK AND SCHOLES AND BEYOND

A call option on Amazon.com, Inc., is currently trading at $3.20. The option has a strike price of $42.50 while Amazon's stock is trading at $45.22. The annual risk-free rate is 4.50% and the option has 21 days until expiration. You estimate the standard deviation of Amazon's stock to be 42%.

1. Based on the information provided, is the call option correctly valued, overvalued, or undervalued? What is the implied volatility of the call option?

2. If a put option with the same strike price is trading for $1.30, is it currently overvalued, undervalued, or correctly valued?

3. You own 5,000 shares of Amazon.com, Inc.'s common stock, which you plan to sell in two weeks. You are worried the stock will decline over the next two weeks, so you decide to hedge against a decline in the stock price by selling call options on the stock. How many of the call options must you sell to perfectly hedge your stock position?

4. Assume that two weeks have passed and that the value of Amazon's stock has dropped to $43.58. Calculate the value of the call option at this point using the implied volatility calculated previously. Ignoring commissions, calculate the net profit/loss on your overall position in both Amazon's common stock and call options on Amazon's stock.

5. Amazon.com, Inc., recently sold an additional 30 million shares. Before the new issue, the firm had 415 million shares of common stock outstanding. Attached to the new shares were warrants allowing the stockholder the right to purchase one additional share of Amazon.com's stock for $85 for every seven shares of common stock purchased. The warrants expire in two years. Again, Amazon's stock is trading at $45.22 and the annual risk-free rate is 4.5%. Using an estimated standard deviation on Amazon's stock of 35%, determine the value of each warrant.

APPENDIX 19A ESTIMATING VOLATILITY FOR THE BLACK AND SCHOLES MODEL

In this appendix we illustrate how to calculate the standard deviation for a Black and Scholes option valuation. We will use stock price data for Wells Fargo, whose warrants we priced earlier. The first task is to gather historical trading data for Wells Fargo stock. There is no hard-and-fast rule about how much data to gather or about the frequency with which returns should be measured. As is the case with estimating any parameter (such as beta) involving market data, analysts face trade-offs between sample size, data relevance, and the accuracy with which returns can be measured at different frequencies. For instance, if we want our sample to consist of 60 observations then we could choose the last 60 days, weeks, or months. Daily returns probably do a better job of portraying the current state of the company and the market, but daily returns may be subject to measurement problems if the stock does not trade frequently. Weekly or monthly returns solve the measurement problem, but they require us to look so far back to gather 60 observations that some data points may no longer reflect the company's current situation. For example, if a company changed its capital structure significantly in the recent past, then the stock's current volatility could be quite different from the volatility observed just a few months back.

From Yahoo! we downloaded daily closing prices for Wells Fargo stock from August 5, 2009, to the date when the company issued warrants as part of the TARP bailout: October 29, 2009. The closing prices and corresponding dates appear in columns 1 and 2 of Table 19A.1.

Table 19A.1	Calculating the Standard Deviation of Returns for Wells Fargo Stock		
DATE (2008)	**CLOSING PRICE ($)**	**PRICE RELATIVE**	$\ln(P_t/P_{t-1})$
Oct 29	31.22	0.932	−0.070
Oct 28	33.50	1.118	0.111
Oct 27	29.97	0.997	−0.003
Oct 24	30.05	0.987	−0.014
Oct 23	30.46	1.001	0.001
Oct 22	30.43	0.959	−0.042
Oct 21	31.73	1.013	0.013
Oct 20	31.33	1.005	0.005
Oct 17	31.17	0.946	−0.056
Oct 16	32.96	1.017	0.017
Oct 15	32.42	0.995	−0.005
Oct 14	32.59	1.103	0.098
Oct 13	29.55	1.074	0.071
Oct 10	27.52	1.039	0.038
Oct 9	26.49	0.854	−0.158
Oct 8	31.01	1.042	0.041
⋮	⋮	⋮	⋮

Table 19A.1   Calculating the Standard Deviation of Returns for Wells Fargo Stock (continued)

DATE (2008)	CLOSING PRICE ($)	PRICE RELATIVE	$\ln(P_t/P_{t-1})$
Aug 15	28.93	0.986	−0.014
Aug 14	29.33	1.030	0.030
Aug 13	28.47	0.964	−0.037
Aug 12	29.53	0.961	−0.040
Aug 11	30.73	1.048	0.047
Aug 8	29.33	1.040	0.039
Aug 7	28.20	0.957	−0.044
Aug 6	29.47	0.972	−0.029
Aug 5	30.33	NA	NA

0.060 = standard deviation of daily returns (column 4)
0.947 = annualized standard deviation (daily times $\sqrt{250}$)

Next, we calculate the *price relative* on each day, defined as that day's price divided by the price one day earlier:

$$\text{Price relative} = \frac{P_t}{P_{t-1}} = 1 + r_{\text{daily}}$$

Notice that this ratio equals 1 plus the daily return on the stock. To convert this into a continuously compounded return (recall that Black and Scholes assumes continuous compounding), we take the natural logarithm of the price relative. These figures appear in the fourth column of the table. Using this sequence of daily returns, we calculate the standard deviation in the usual way. Finally, to convert our standard deviation from a daily to an annual basis, we multiply it by the square root of the number of trading days (roughly 250) in one year.[12] We thus derive an estimate of annual volatility that can be plugged directly into the Black and Scholes equation.

This method yields a volatility estimate of 94.7% per year, which is an extremely high value. Keep in mind that financial stocks were extremely volatile during the summer and fall of 2008 as the financial crisis deepened. Hence, as a long-run forecast of Wells Fargo volatility, this figure is probably too high—though in the short run it actually underestimated the stock's volatility. By February 2009, the implied volatility on Wells Fargo options was as high as 200%!

---

[12]The reason we convert the standard deviation to an annual basis (via multiplying by the square root of the number of trading days in a year) can be better understood by looking at the conversion for variance. If there are 250 trading days in a year, then the daily variance times 250 equals the annual variance. Take the square root of both sides to obtain the appropriate conversion factor for standard deviation.

20

International Financial Management

What Companies Do

Currency Losses Compound Bad News

In the first quarter of 2009, most U.S. companies reported earnings declines as the global economy slumped. One consequence of the worldwide financial crisis was that many foreign investors sought safety by purchasing U.S. Treasury securities, and that put upward pressure on the value of the dollar. A stronger dollar meant that U.S. products were less attractive to foreign buyers, exacerbating the poor earnings reports in early 2009. For example, Procter & Gamble estimated that the dollar's rise reduced their sales by 5% relative to what they would have achieved with a steady dollar, and Kraft Foods lowered its earnings forecast by $0.16 per share as a result of currency movements.

But a rising dollar was good news for some firms, particularly foreign companies exporting to the United States. Cochlear Limited, the Australian maker of the world's most popular hearing implant, reported that its profits were up 22% owing to appreciation of the U.S. dollar and the euro relative to Australia's currency.

What these cases illustrate is that currency fluctuations can create unexpected gains and losses for companies doing business in many different countries. This chapter explores the factors that cause currency movements as well as the ways that companies can manage those risks.

Sources: Reuters, http://www.reuters.com/article/rbssHealthcareNews/idUSSYU00598620090209 (February 9, 2009); bloomberg.com, http://www.bloomberg.com/apps/news?pid=20601081&sid=afVjBwwjHpOk&refer=australia (February 10, 2009); David Bogoslaw, "Earnings: The Sting of the Strong Dollar," Business Week (February 5, 2009), http://www.businessweek.com/investor/content/feb2009/pi2009024_625664.htm?chan=investing_investing+index+page_top+stories.

Walk down the aisle of a grocery store, visit a shopping mall, go hunting for a new automobile, or check the outstanding balance of your credit card. In each of these activities, chances are that you will be dealing with products and services provided by **multinational corporations (MNCs)**, businesses that operate in many countries around the world. In recent decades, international trade in goods and services has expanded dramatically, and so too have the size and scope of MNCs. Although all the financial principles covered in this text thus far apply to MNCs, companies operating across national borders face additional, unique challenges. Primary among them is coping with exchange rate risk. An **exchange rate** is simply the price of one currency in terms of another, and for almost 40 years the exchange rates of major currencies have fluctuated daily. These movements create uncertainty for firms that earn revenue and pay operating costs in more than one currency. Currency movements also add to the pressures faced by wholly domestic companies that face competition from foreign firms.

This chapter focuses on the problems and opportunities firms face as a result of globalization, with special emphasis on currency-related issues. First, we explain the rudimentary features of currency markets, including how and why currencies trade and the rules governments impose on trading in their currencies. Second, we describe how equilibrium factors that drive currency values—at least for those countries that allow their currency value to float—are constantly responding to market forces. Third, we discuss the special risks faced by MNCs and the strategies they employ to manage those risks. We conclude by illustrating some of the long-term and short-term financial decisions confronting MNCs.

20.1 EXCHANGE-RATE FUNDAMENTALS

We begin our coverage of exchange-rate fundamentals by describing the "rules of the game" as dictated by national governments.

Fixed versus Floating Exchange Rates

Since the mid-1970s, the major currencies of the world have had a floating exchange-rate relationship with respect to the U.S. dollar and to one another. A **floating exchange rate** means that forces of supply and demand continually move currency values up and down. The opposite of a floating exchange rate regime is a fixed exchange-rate system. Under a **fixed exchange rate**, governments fix (or *peg*) their currency's value—usually in terms of another currency, such as the U.S. dollar. Once a government pegs its currency at a particular value, it must stand ready to pursue the economic and financial policies necessary to maintain that fixed value.[1] For example, if demand for the currency increases, the government must stand ready to sell it so that the increase in demand does not cause the currency to appreciate. Conversely, if demand for the currency falls, then the government must be ready to buy its own currency, thereby supporting the exchange rate. In many countries with fixed exchange rates, governments impose restrictions on the free flow of currencies into and out of the country. Even so, maintaining a currency peg can be quite difficult. For example, in response to mounting economic problems, the government of Argentina allowed the peso (which had been linked to the U.S. dollar) to float freely for the first time in a decade on January 11, 2002. Within one day, the peso lost more than 40% of its value relative to the dollar.

---

[1]The fixed exchange-rate system that collapsed in 1973, called the *Bretton Woods system*, was based on the U.S. dollar and had governed international finance since the late 1940s. Under this system, countries established fixed exchange rates (par values) for their currencies versus the dollar, which often did not change for two decades or more.

In addition to using purely fixed and purely floating exchange rate systems, some countries—usually those that are developing—employ several intermediate or hybrid models. A **managed floating-rate system** is a hybrid in which a nation's government loosely "fixes" the value of the national currency in relation to that of another currency but does not expend the effort and resources that would be required to maintain a completely fixed exchange rate. Other countries simply choose to use another nation's currency as their own, and a handful of nations have adopted a *currency board arrangement*. In such an arrangement, the national currency continues to circulate, but every unit of the currency is fully backed by government holdings of another currency—usually the U.S. dollar. In terms of trading volume, the major currencies in international finance today are (in no particular order) the British pound sterling (£), the Swiss franc (SF), the Japanese yen (¥), the Canadian dollar (C$), the U.S. dollar (US$, or simply $), and the **euro** (€). All of these currencies float freely in the market, so the exchange rates between them change constantly.

Exchange Rate Quotes

Figure 20.1 shows exchange rate values quoted in the *Wall Street Journal* on February 10, 2009. Note that the figure states each exchange rate in two ways. The first column reports the exchange rates in terms of the dollar cost of one unit of foreign currency. For example, the exchange rate quote for the Japanese yen indicates than one yen costs .010936 U.S. dollars. When an exchange rate is quoted this way, we will write it as $0.010936/¥. The second column shows the value of each foreign currency relative to one U.S. dollar. Figure 20.1 shows that one U.S. dollar costs 91.44 Japanese yen. In this case, we write the exchange rate as ¥91.44/$. Each of these methods of quoting exchange rates is simply the reciprocal of the other:

$$\frac{\text{Dollars}}{\text{Yen}} = \frac{\frac{1}{\text{Yen}}}{\text{Dollars}} \qquad \$0.010936/¥ = \frac{1}{¥91.44/\$}$$

In expressing "exchange rates," one's location matters. A **direct quotation** is a quote that gives the home currency price of a unit of foreign currency, whereas an **indirect quotation** gives the foreign currency price of one unit of the home currency. Thus, for a trader based in the United States, a direct quotation is $0.010936/¥ and an indirect quotation is ¥91.44/$. A trader based in Japan expresses a direct yen/dollar exchange rate quotation as ¥91.44/$, while $0.010936/¥ is an indirect quotation.

As already noted, most of the world's major currencies float freely in the foreign exchange market, so exchange rates change continuously. The exchange rates in Figure 20.1 were gathered on Monday, February 9, 2009, but on the previous Friday the exchange rate between yen and U.S. dollars was ¥92.01/$. Because one dollar could purchase fewer yen on Monday as compared to Friday (91.44 versus 92.01), we say that the dollar **depreciated** slightly over the weekend. Of course, the opposite is true for the yen. On Friday, February 6, one yen was equivalent to 0.010868 dollars, compared to 0.010936 on February 9, so the yen **appreciated** that weekend. The last column of Figure 20.1 shows how much the U.S. dollar appreciated or depreciated from January 1 to February 9. In the early part of 2009, the dollar appreciated against many currencies including the yen, the euro, and the Swiss franc, but the dollar depreciated relative to the British pound.

We can also distinguish between two types of exchange rates. The exchange rate applying to currency trades that occur immediately is called the **spot exchange rate**. However, in many currencies it is possible to enter a contract today to trade foreign currency at a

FIGURE 20.1

Exchange Rates for Various Currencies versus the U.S. Dollar on February 9, 2009

Source: Wall Street Journal, February 10, 2009, pg. C 12. Reprinted with permission of Wall Street Journal, Copyright © 2009 Dow Jones & Company, Inc. All rights reserved worldwide.

Currencies

February 9, 2009

U.S.-dollar foreign-exchange rates in late New York trading

Country/currency	in US$	— Mon — per US$	US$ vs, YTD chg (%)
Americas			
Argentina peso☆	.2868	3.4868	0.9
Brazil real	.4412	2.2665	-2.1
Canada dollar	.8221	1.2164	unch
1-mos forward	.8220	1.2165	-0.1
3-mos forward	.8219	1.2167	unch
6-mos forward	.8228	1.2154	unch
Chile peso	.001640	609.76	-4.5
Colombia peso	.0004060	2463.05	9.5
Ecuador US dollar	1	1	unch
Mexico peso☆	.0705	14.1904	3.4
Peru new sol	.3112	3.213	2.5
Uruguay peso†	.04420	22.62	-7.2
Venezuela b. fuerte	.465701	2.1473	unch
Asia-Pacific			
Australian dollar	.6803	1.4699	4.6
China yuan	.1462	6.8397	0.2
Hong Kong dollar	.1290	7.7520	unch
India rupee	.02060	48.544	-0.1
Indonesia rupiah	.0000857	11669	7.0
Japan yen	.010936	91.44	0.8
1-mos forward	.010941	91.40	0.8
3-mos forward	.010958	91.26	0.8
6-mos forward	.010985	91.03	0.8
Malaysia ringgit§	.2779	3.5984	4.2
New Zealand dollar	.5408	1.8491	8.4
Pakistan rupee	.01263	79.177	0.1
Philippines peso	.0213	46.926	-1.1
Singapore dollar	.6693	1.4941	4.3
South Korea won	.0007257	1377.98	9.1
Taiwan dollar	.02965	33.727	2.9
Thailand baht	.02856	35.014	0.7
Vietnam dong	.00005724	17469	-0.1

Country/currency	in US$	— Mon — per US$	US$ vs, YTD chg (%)
Europe			
Czech Rep. koruna☆☆	.04697	21.290	10.8
Denmark krone	.1746	5.7274	7.5
Euro area euro	1.3013	.7685	7.3
Hungary forint	.004534	220.56	16.0
Norway krone	.1501	6.6622	-4.2
Poland zloty	.2936	3.4060	14.7
Russia ruble‡	.02790	35.842	17.4
Sweden krona	.1243	8.0451	2.8
Switzerland franc	.8597	1.1632	9.0
1-mos forward	.8602	1.1625	9.0
3-mos forward	.8614	1.1609	8.9
6-mos forward	.8632	1.1585	9.0
Turkey lira☆☆	.6202	1.6124	4.7
UK pound	1.4910	.6707	-2.1
1-mos forward	1.4904	.6710	-2.2
3-mos forward	1.4897	.6713	-2.2
6-mos forward	1.4891	.6715	-2.2
Middle East/Africa			
Bahrain dinar	2.6527	.3770	unch
Egypt pound☆	.1801	5.5525	1.0
Israel shekel	.2478	4.0355	6.8
Jordan dinar	1.4104	.7090	0.1
Kuwait dinar	3.3955	.2945	6.6
Lebanon pound	.0006634	1507.39	unch
Saudi Arabia riyal	.2666	3.7509	-0.1
South Africa rand	.1038	9.6339	2.5
UAE dirham	.2723	3.6724	unch
SDR††	1.4985	.6673	2.8

☆Floating rate †Financial §Government rate ‡Russian Central Bank rate ☆☆Rebased as of Jan 1, 2005
††Special Drawing Rights (SDR); from the International Monetary Fund; based on exchange rates for U.S., British and Japanese currencies.
Note: Based on trading among banks of $1 million and more, as quoted at 4 p.m. ET by Reuters.

fixed price at some future date. The price at which that future trade will take place is called the **forward exchange rate**. For example, a U.S. trader wishing to exchange dollars for British pounds could do so on February 9 at the spot exchange rate of $1.4910/£ (or, equivalently, £0.6707/$). Alternatively, the trader could enter into an agreement to trade dollars for pounds one month later at the **forward rate** of $1.4904/£ (equivalently, £0.6710/$). If the trader chose to transact through a forward contract, no cash would change hands until the date specified by the contract. Though the figure quotes forward contracts only at maturities of one, three, and six months, a much richer set of forward contracts is actually available in the foreign exchange market.

Just as we compared movements in the spot exchange rate from Friday to Monday, we can also examine differences in the spot exchange rate for current transactions and the forward rate for future transactions. For example, look at the rate quotes for Japanese yen. On the spot market, one yen costs $0.010936; however, the exchange rate for trades that will take place 180 days (six months) later is $0.010985/¥. The yen's cost on the forward market is slightly higher than it is on the spot market. Whenever one currency buys more of another on the forward market than it does on the spot market, traders say that the first currency trades at a **forward premium**. The forward premium is usually expressed as a percentage relative to the spot rate, so for the yen we can calculate the 180-day forward premium as follows:

$$\frac{F - S}{S} = \frac{\$0.010985/¥ - \$0.010936/¥}{\$0.010936/¥} = 0.0045 \text{ or } 0.45\%$$

where F denotes the forward rate and S the spot rate, both quoted in terms of $/¥. Recognizing that the yen's 0.45% forward premium refers to a 6-month contract, we could restate the premium in annual terms by doubling the premium, which would yield an annualized forward premium of 0.90%.

If the yen trades at a forward premium relative to the dollar, then the dollar must trade at a **forward discount** relative to the yen, meaning that one dollar buys fewer yen on the forward market than it does on the spot market. Using the same equation, we focus on currency units in terms of ¥/$:

$$\frac{F - S}{S} = \frac{¥91.03/\$ - ¥91.44/\$}{¥91.44/\$} = -0.0045 \text{ or } 0.45\%$$

The dollar trades at a −0.45% forward discount for a 6-month contract (about −0.90% per year). In other words, the forward discount on the dollar is opposite in sign and similar in magnitude to the forward premium on the yen.[2] In general, to calculate the annualized forward premium or discount on a currency based on a forward contract to be executed in N days, use the following equation:

$$\frac{F - S}{S} \times \frac{360}{N} \qquad \textbf{(Eq. 20.1)}$$

EXAMPLE

Using the exchange rate quotes in Figure 20.1, we can calculate the annualized forward discount (or premium) on the Swiss franc (SF) relative to the dollar ($). We will calculate this based on the rate for a 3-month forward contract. The spot rate equals $0.8597/SF, and the 3-month (or 90-day) forward rate equals $0.8602/SF. Notice that the franc buys more dollars on the forward market than it does on the spot market, so it trades at a forward premium. We can determine the annualized premium as follows, given that we are using a 90-day contract:

$$\frac{\$0.8602/SF - \$0.8597/SF}{\$0.8597/SF} \times \frac{360}{90} = 0.0023 \text{ or } 0.23\%$$

The forward discount or premium gives traders information about more than just the price of exchanging currencies at different points in time. The forward premium is tightly linked to differences in interest rates on short-term, low-risk bonds across countries, a relationship that we explore in more depth in the next section.

One last lesson remains to be gleaned from Figure 20.1. In its daily exchange rate table, the *Wall Street Journal* quotes the value of the world's major currencies relative to the U.S. dollar. But what if someone wants to know the exchange rate between British pounds

---

[2]The discount and the premium appear to be identical (in absolute value) here, but you can see that they are different if you carry the calculation out to several decimal places.

and Canadian dollars? In fact, all the information needed to calculate this exchange rate appears in the figure. We simply need to calculate a **cross exchange rate** by dividing the dollar exchange rate for one currency by the dollar exchange rate for the other currency. For example, we can determine the £/C$ exchange rate as follows:

$$\frac{\$1.4910/£}{\$0.8221/C\$} = C\$1.8136/£$$

How can we be sure that one pound buys 1.8136 Canadian dollars simply by taking this ratio? The answer is that if the value of the pound (relative to the Canadian dollar) were different from this number, then currency traders could engage in **triangular arbitrage**, trading currencies simultaneously in different markets to earn a risk-free profit. Because currency markets operate virtually 24 hours per day and because currency trades take place with lightning speed and with very low transaction costs, arbitrage maintains actual currency values in different markets fairly close to this theoretical ideal.

EXAMPLE

Suppose that on February 9, 2009, a trader learns that the exchange rate being offered by a bank in London is C$1.8400/£ rather than C$1.8136/£ as calculated previously. What is the arbitrage opportunity? First, note that the figure C$1.8400/£ is "too high" relative to the theoretically correct rate. This means that in London, one pound costs too much in terms of Canadian dollars; the pound is overvalued, and the Canadian dollar is undervalued. Therefore, a U.S. trader could make a profit by executing the following steps.

1. Convert U.S. dollars to British pounds in New York at the prevailing spot rate. Assume that the trader starts with $1 million, which will be converted to £670,691 ($1,000,000 ÷ 1.4910).
2. Simultaneously, the trader sells £670,691 in London (because pounds are overvalued there) at the exchange rate of C$1.8400/£. The trader will then have C$1,234,071.
3. Convert the Canadian dollars back into U.S. currency in New York. Given the spot rate of $0.8221/C$, the trader will receive $1,014,530 in exchange for C$1,234,071.

After making these trades, each of which can occur in the blink of an eye, the trader winds up $14,530 richer, all without taking any risk. As long as the exchange rates do not change, the trader can continue making profits of this sort.

The preceding Example shows that a trader can repeatedly make a profit if the exchange rates do not change. But exchange rates will change, of course, and they will change in a way that brings the market back into equilibrium. Figure 20.2 illustrates what happens as arbitrage takes place. As traders in New York sell U.S. currency in exchange for pounds, the pound appreciates against the U.S. dollar and so the exchange rate will rise from $1.4910/£ to some new, higher level. Likewise, as traders in London sell pounds in exchange for Canadian dollars, the pound will depreciate against the Canadian currency and the exchange rate will fall below C$1.8400/£. Finally, as traders reap their profits in New York by selling Canadian and buying U.S. currency, the exchange rate between Canadian and U.S. dollars will rise from C$0.8221/$. Though we cannot say exactly how much each of these exchange rates will move, we can say that collectively they will move enough to reach a new equilibrium in which the cross exchange rate in New York and the exchange rate quoted in London are virtually identical.

FIGURE 20.2

Triangular Arbitrage and Foreign Exchange Market Equilibrium

In triangular arbitrage, a trader can earn a risk-free profit by selling a currency where it is overvalued and buying it where it is undervalued. In this case, the British pound is overvalued in London.

Exchange Rates Available in New York	$ per foreign currency
British £	1.4910
Canadian $	0.8221

Exchange Rate Available in London   £1 = C$1.8400

Market Is Not in Equilibrium Because

$$\frac{1.4910}{0.8221} < 1.8400$$

Effects of Arbitragers' Trades

1. Selling US$ and buying £ in New York puts upward pressure on the pound in that market . . . . . . 1.4910 ↑
2. Selling £ and buying C$ in London puts downward pressure on the pound in London . . . . . . 1.8400 ↓
3. Selling C$ and buying US$ in New York puts downward pressure on the C$ in that market . . . . . . 0.8221 ↓
4. The left-hand side of the equation above gets bigger, while the right-hand side gets smaller, until a new equilibrium is reached:

$$\frac{1.4910\uparrow}{0.8221\downarrow} < 1.8400\downarrow \longrightarrow \text{New equilibrium}$$

With this basic understanding of foreign exchange rates in place, let us now turn to some important institutional features of the foreign exchange market.

The Foreign Exchange Market

The **foreign exchange (forex) market** is not a physical exchange but rather an electronic marketplace. In fact, it is the world's largest financial market, with total volume of more than $3 trillion *per day*. The forex market operates continuously during the business week, with trading beginning each business day in Tokyo. As the day evolves, trading moves westward as major dealing centers in Singapore, Bahrain, continental Europe, London, and finally North America (particularly New York and Toronto) come online. Dealers in all these markets quote bid and ask prices for currencies versus the U.S. dollar and, to a limited degree, against other currencies as well. Prices for all the floating currencies are set by global supply and demand. Trading in fixed-rate currencies is more constrained and regulated; it frequently involves a national government (or a state-owned bank) as counterparty on one side of the trade.

The players in the forex market are numerous, as are their motivations for participating. We can break participants in this market into six distinct (but not mutually exclusive) groups: (1) exporters and importers; (2) investors; (3) hedgers; (4) speculators; (5) dealers; and, at times, (6) governments.

Importers and Exporters   Businesses that export goods to or import goods from a foreign country need to enter the foreign exchange market to pay bills denominated in foreign currency or to convert foreign currency revenues back into the domestic currency. Along with all the other players in the market, exporters and importers influence currency values. For instance, if Europeans develop a taste for California wines, then European importers will exchange euros (or perhaps pounds, kroner, francs, etc.) for dollars to purchase wine. Other factors held constant, these trades will tend to put upward pressure on the value of the dollar and downward pressure on European currencies.

Investors   Investors also trade foreign currency when they seek to buy and sell financial assets in foreign countries. In the fall of 2008, the global financial crisis led some investors to seek out the safest possible investments (U.S. Treasury securities). Those who did had to sell their own currency and buy the dollar, putting upward pressure on the dollar relative to other currencies. In general, the pressures exerted on currencies by investors are much larger than those exerted by exporters and importers because investors account for a larger fraction of currency trading volume.

Hedgers and Speculators   Hedgers influence currency values when they take positions that offset the risks of their existing exposures to certain currencies. In contrast, speculators take positions not to reduce risk but to increase it. Speculators sell a currency if they expect it to depreciate and buy if they expect it to appreciate. Some speculators, such as George Soros, have become famous for the enormous profits (or losses) they have earned by taking large positions in certain currencies. When external pressures force a country with a pegged currency to devalue its currency, speculators often take the blame.

Whether or not they deserve blame for causing, accelerating, or exacerbating currency crises, speculators can play a useful economic role by taking the opposite side of a transaction from that of hedgers. Speculators help make the foreign currency market more liquid and more efficient.

Dealers   As in all financial markets, dealers play a crucial role in the foreign exchange business. Most foreign currency trades go through large, international banks in the leading financial centers around the globe: London, New York, Tokyo, and so on. These banks, the dealers, provide a means for buyers and sellers to come together. As their reward they earn a small fee—the bid–ask spread—on each round-trip buy-and-sell transaction that they facilitate.

Governments   Finally, governments intervene in financial markets to put upward or downward pressure on currencies as circumstances dictate. Governments that attempt to maintain a fixed exchange rate with the rest of the world generally must intervene more frequently than those with a floating exchange rate, who intervene only in times of crisis. Currency movements create winners and losers not only across national boundaries but also within a given country. For example, a rise in the value of the U.S. dollar makes U.S. exports more expensive and foreign imports cheaper. Remember, an exchange rate is simply a price: the price of trading one currency for another. Though the financial press dramatizes changes in exchange rates by attaching an adjective such as *strong* or *weak* to a given currency, this practice is rather odd when you recognize that they are just talking about a price. For instance, if the price of apples rises and the price of bananas falls, we do not refer to apples as being strong and bananas as being weak. If the price of apples is high, that is good for apple producers and bad for apple consumers. In the same way, a rise in the value of a particular currency benefits some and harms others. As a result—at least for the major, free-floating currencies—governments are reluctant to intervene because doing so does not unambiguously improve welfare across the board.

Even when governments want to intervene in currency markets, doing so is complicated by the fact that currency values are not set in a vacuum but are linked to other economic variables, such as interest rates and inflation. In the next section, we discuss four parity relationships illustrating the linkages that should hold in equilibrium between exchange rates and other macroeconomic variables.

1. Explain how a rise in the euro might affect a French company exporting wine to the United States. Compare this to the impact on a German firm importing semiconductors from the United States.
2. Holding all other factors constant, how might an increase in British interest rates affect the value of the pound?
3. If someone says, "The exchange rate between dollars and pounds increased today," can you say for sure which currency appreciated and which depreciated? Why or why not?
4. Define spot and forward exchange rates. If a trader expects to buy a foreign currency in one month, can you explain why the trader might prefer to enter into a forward contract today rather than wait a month and transact at the spot rate prevailing then?

20.2 PARITY CONDITIONS OF INTERNATIONAL FINANCE

In this section we discuss the major forces that influence the values of all the world's free-floating currencies. Theory suggests that when markets are in equilibrium, spot and forward exchange rates, interest rates, and inflation rates should be linked across countries. Market imperfections such as trade barriers and transaction costs may prevent these parity conditions from holding precisely at all times, but they are still powerful determinants of exchange-rate values in the long run.

Forward–Spot Parity

If the spot rate governs foreign exchange transactions in the present and the forward rate equals the price of trading currencies at some point in the future, intuition suggests that the forward rate might be useful in predicting how the spot rate will change over time. For example, suppose that a British firm intends to import U.S. wheat for which it must pay $1.80 million in one month. Assume that the pound currently trades at a forward premium and that the prevailing spot and forward exchange rates are as follows:

$$\text{Spot} = \$1.75/\pounds, \quad \text{1-month forward} = \$1.80/\pounds$$

The U.K. firm faces a choice. Either it can lock in the forward rate today, guaranteeing that it will pay £1 million for its wheat ($1.8 million ÷ $1.80/£), or it can wait a month and transact at the spot rate prevailing then. Let us suppose that the U.K. firm in this example is risk neutral. This assumption implies that the firm does not care about exchange-rate risk, and it will decide to enter the forward contract only if it believes that trading at the forward rate will be less expensive than trading at the spot rate in 30 days.

This results in a simple decision rule for the U.K. importer. First, it must form a forecast of what the spot exchange rate will be in one month. Let's call this the *expected* spot rate and denote it by $E(S)$. We can now determine the U.K. firm's decision rule:

1. Enter the forward contract today if $E(S) < \$1.80/\pounds$.
2. Wait and buy dollars at the spot rate if $E(S) > \$1.80/\pounds$.

For example, assume the firm's forecast is that the spot rate will not change from its current level of $1.75/£. Given this forecast, the expected cost of purchasing $1.80 million in 30 days is £1,028,571 ($1.8 million ÷ $1.75/£); given that the firm will need only £1 million if it locks in the forward rate, it makes no sense to wait. Conversely, assume that the U.K. firm believes that the pound will appreciate over the next 30 days to $1.85/£. In that case, the expected cost of paying for the wheat is just £972,973, and the firm should wait. Only if the firm's forecast of the expected spot rate is $1.80/£ (i.e., equal to the current forward rate) will it be indifferent to whether it locks in the forward contract now or waits 30 days to transact at that day's spot rate.

If we look at this problem from the perspective of a U.S. firm that must pay in pounds in 30 days to import some good from the United Kingdom, we derive just the opposite decision rule. For the (risk-neutral) U.S. firm, entering a forward contract to buy pounds makes sense if the expected spot rate in 30 days is greater than the current forward rate [$E(S) > \$1.80/£$]. Clearly, appreciation in the pound increases the cost of importing from Britain; hence, if a U.S. firm expects the pound to appreciate above the current forward rate, then it will lock in a forward contract immediately. On the other hand, if the U.S. firm expects the spot rate to be less than $1.80/£ in 30 days, it will choose to wait rather than lock in at the forward rate.

Now we broaden the example to include all U.S. and U.K. firms who face a future need to buy foreign currency, and we maintain the assumption of risk neutrality. Ideally, U.S. firms who must buy pounds to import British goods could trade with U.K. firms who must buy dollars to import U.S. goods. However, there is a problem because the circumstances under which firms in each country prefer to trade in the spot market (rather than the forward market) are mirror images of each other:

1. If $E(S) > F$, then U.K. firms do not want the forward contract but U.S. firms do.
2. If $E(S) < F$, then U.K. firms want the forward contract but U.S. firms do not.

Equilibrium will occur in this market only when the forecast of the spot rate is equal to the current forward rate. In that case, U.S. and U.K. firms are indifferent to whether they transact in the spot or the forward market. This yields our first parity condition, known as **forward–spot parity**. It says that the forward rate should be an unbiased predictor of where the spot rate is headed. That is, the expected value of the spot rate equals the forward rate:

$$E(S) = F \qquad \text{(Eq. 20.2)}$$

It would certainly be convenient for currency traders if the forward exchange rate provided a reliable forecast of future spot rates. Unfortunately, most studies suggest that this is not the case. Some researchers have found that, on average, the spot rate moves in the opposite direction than that predicted by the forward rate. Other studies find that even though the *direction* of spot rate movements is consistent with that predicted by forward rates, the *magnitudes* are too small. That is, when a currency trades at a forward premium (suggesting it will appreciate on the spot market), the currency does appreciate but not by as much as the forward rate predicted. Finally, virtually all studies of exchange-rate movements find a great deal of "noise," or randomness, in spot-rate movements. Even if spot rates tend to move in the direction predicted by forward rates, they do not do so with a high degree of reliability.

If forward rates do not accurately predict movements in currency values over time, perhaps something else does. Economists have long observed a correlation between currency movements and inflation-rate differentials across countries. Specifically, there is a long-term tendency for the value of a nation's currency to fall if its inflation rate is higher than the inflation rate in other countries. The second parity relationship explains this tendency.

Purchasing Power Parity

One of the simplest ideas in economics is the **law of one price**. This means that, absent any barriers to trade, identical goods trading in different markets should sell at the same price. The law of one price has a natural application in international finance. Suppose that a DVD of a hit movie retails in the United States for $20 and that the identical DVD can be purchased in Tokyo for ¥2,000. Does the law of one price hold? It depends on the exchange rate. If the spot rate of exchange equals ¥100/$ then the answer is yes. A U.S. consumer can spend $20 to purchase the DVD in the United States or can convert $20 to ¥2,000 and purchase the item in Tokyo. We can generalize this example as follows. Suppose the price of an item in domestic currency is P_{dom} and the price of the identical item in foreign currency is P_{for}. If the spot exchange rate quoted in foreign currency per domestic is $S_{for/dom}$, then the law of one price holds if the following is true:

$$\frac{P_{for}}{P_{dom}} = S_{for/dom} \qquad \textbf{(Eq. 20.3)}$$

Naturally, the law of one price extends to any pair of countries, not just the United States and Japan. When Equation 20.3 does not hold, traders may engage in arbitrage to exploit price discrepancies across national boundaries.

EXAMPLE

Suppose that a pair of Maui Jim sunglasses sells for $200 in the United States and for €160 in Italy. Assume that the exchange rate between dollars and euros is €0.85/$. Does the law of one price hold? Apparently not, because the following is true:

$$\frac{160}{200} < 0.85$$

How can arbitrageurs exploit this violation of the law of one price? The displayed inequality reveals that the price of sunglasses in Italy is too low (or, equivalently, that the U.S. price is too high) relative to the current exchange rate. Therefore, suppose that a trader buys sunglasses in Italy for €160 and ships them to the United States. After selling them for $200, the trader can convert back to euros and receive €170 ($200 × €0.85/$). The arbitrage profit is €10. As long as the transaction costs of making these trades are less than €10 and as long as there are no other barriers to trade, then the process will continue until the market reaches equilibrium.

JOB INTERVIEW QUESTION

What happens to the dollar/euro exchange rate if U.S. inflation increases?

Now we will add a new wrinkle to the law of one price. Suppose that prices in different countries satisfy Equation 20.3 not only at one moment in time but *all* the time. We cannot expect this to be the case for every type of good sold in two countries. But if price discrepancies for similar goods become too large, the forces of arbitrage should push them back in line. Of course, the prices of goods and services change every day because of inflation (or deflation), and there is no reason to expect the inflation rate in one country to be the same as in another. If different countries are subject to different inflation pressures, how can the law of one price hold on an ongoing basis? The answer is that the exchange rate adjusts to maintain equilibrium.

EXAMPLE

Suppose that the forces of arbitrage have changed the prices of Maui Jim sunglasses in the United States and in Italy so that the law of one price now holds. Specifically, the U.S. price is $195 and the Italian price is €165.75. If the exchange rate is still €0.85/$, then the law of one price holds because the following equality holds:

$$\frac{€165.75}{\$195} = €0.85/\$$$

Now suppose that the expected rate of inflation in Italy over the next year is 4% but that no inflation is expected in the United States. One year from today, Maui Jim sunglasses will still sell for $195 in the United States, but with 4% inflation the price in Italy will rise to €172.38 (€165.75 × 1.04). If these forecasts are correct, then in a year the exchange rate must rise to €0.8840/$ in order for the law of one price to hold:

$$\frac{€172.38}{\$195} = €0.8840/\$$$

Remember, this exchange rate is expressed in euros per dollar, so an increase from €0.85/$ to €0.8840/$ represents appreciation of the dollar and depreciation of the euro.

JOB INTERVIEW QUESTION

What does the term *purchasing power parity* mean?

Purchasing power parity is an extension of the law of one price. **Purchasing power parity** states that if the law of one price holds at all times, then differences in expected inflation between two countries are associated with expected changes in currency values. Mathematically, we can express this idea as follows:

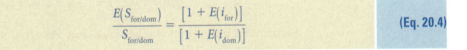

$$\frac{E(S_{for/dom})}{S_{for/dom}} = \frac{\left[1 + E(i_{for})\right]}{\left[1 + E(i_{dom})\right]} \qquad \textbf{(Eq. 20.4)}$$

Here, as before, the expected spot rate is $E(S)$, the current spot rate is S, the expected rate of inflation in the foreign country is $E(i_{for})$, and the expected rate of inflation in the domestic country is $E(i_{dom})$. Observe that the left-hand side of this equation exceeds 1.0 if traders expect the domestic currency to appreciate but is less than 1.0 if traders expect the foreign currency to appreciate. Likewise, the right-hand side of the equation exceeds 1.0 when expected inflation is higher abroad than it is at home, and the ratio falls below 1.0 when the opposite is true. Equation 20.4 thus produces the already familiar prediction that if inflation is higher in one country than another, then the currency of the country with higher inflation will depreciate. The equation also offers the helpful information that traders who want to forecast currency movements should invest resources in forecasting inflation rates.

How accurately does purchasing power parity predict exchange-rate movements? As we have already seen, over the long term there is a strong correlation between currency values and inflation rates. Countries with high inflation see their currencies depreciate over time, whereas the opposite happens for countries with lower inflation. This is no accident. If we did not observe this correlation in the data, then it would be a signal of gross violations of the law of one price and a sign that arbitrage was not working to bring prices back into line.

But purchasing power parity does not fare as well in the short run. Violations of the law of one price do occur frequently, and many studies suggest that they persist from three to four years on average. Once again, arbitrage—or in this case, limits to arbitrage—explain why. When goods' prices in different countries are out of equilibrium, arbitrageurs must trade the goods, moving them across national borders, in order to earn a profit. This process cannot occur without investments in time and money, and for certain goods trade may be impossible because of legal restrictions or physical impediments to transporting goods. Accordingly, there is no reason to expect goods to flow from one market to the other as soon as the law of one price fails to hold. Only if price discrepancies across markets are sufficiently large and persistent will arbitrageurs find it profitable to trade. Hence, purchasing power parity does a good job of explaining long-run movements in currencies but not day-to-day (or even year-to-year) fluctuations.

Interest-Rate Parity

Although it is both time-consuming and expensive to move goods across borders, the same cannot generally be said about purely financial transactions. Large institutional investors can buy and sell currencies rapidly and at low cost, and they can buy and sell financial assets denominated in different currencies just as quickly. **Interest-rate parity** applies the law of one price to financial assets, specifically to risk-free assets denominated in different currencies. Interest-rate parity means that risk-free investments should offer the same return (after converting currencies) everywhere.

To illustrate, assume that a U.S. institution has $10 million that it wants to invest for 180 days in a risk-free government bill. Suppose the current annual interest rate on 180-day U.S. Treasury bills is 4% per year (2% for six months); thus, if the institution chooses this investment, it will have $10.2 million six months later:

$$\$10,000,000\left(1 + \frac{R_{US}}{2}\right) = \$10,200,000$$

Alternatively, the institution might choose to convert its $10 million into another currency and invest abroad. However, even if it invests in a risk-free government bill issued by a foreign government, the institution must enter into a forward contract to convert back into dollars when the investment matures. Otherwise, the return on the foreign investment is not risk-free and will depend on changes in currency values over the next six months.

Suppose for example that the annual interest rate on a 6-month Swiss government bill is 0.55% per year (0.275% for six months). Suppose also that the spot and 6-month forward exchange rates are SF1.3161/$ and SF1.2938/$, respectively. The U.S. institution converts $10 million into SF13,161,000 at the spot rate. It invests the Swiss francs for six months at the Swiss interest rate and enters into a forward contract to convert those francs back into dollars when the Swiss bill matures. At the end of six months, the institution has:[3]

$$\$10,000,000\left(S_{SF/\$}\right)\left(1 + \frac{R_{Swiss}}{2}\right)\left(\frac{1}{F_{SF/\$}}\right) = \$10,200,110$$

Given the prevailing interest rates on short-term, risk-free U.S. and Swiss bonds, and given current spot and forward exchange rates between dollars and Swiss francs, investors are practically indifferent to whether they invest in the United States or Switzerland. In other

---

[3]In this equation we divide by the forward rate to convert Swiss francs back into dollars. Also, the $110 difference between the payoffs on the U.S. and Swiss investment strategies results because we quoted the Swiss interest rate to only two decimals.

words, with respect to short-term, risk-free financial assets, the law of one price holds—and this relationship is called *interest-rate parity*. As usual, we can express interest-rate parity in mathematical terms. Letting R_{for} and R_{dom} denote the respective risk-free rates on foreign and domestic government debt, we obtain the following equation:[4]

$$\frac{F_{for/dom}}{S_{for/dom}} = \frac{(1 + R_{for})}{(1 + R_{dom})}$$

(Eq. 20.5)

What is the intuitive interpretation of this expression? Observe that if the left-hand side of the equation is greater than 1.0 then the domestic currency trades at a forward premium. If domestic investors send money abroad then they will realize an exchange loss (when they convert back to domestic currency) because the foreign currency buys less domestic currency than it did at the spot rate. Domestic investors know this, so they require an incentive in the form of a higher foreign interest rate before they will send money abroad. To maintain equilibrium, the right-hand side must also be greater than 1.0, which means that the foreign interest rate must exceed the domestic rate. The bottom line is that, when a nation's currency trades at a forward premium (discount), risk-free interest rates in that country should be lower (higher) than they are abroad.

As with purchasing power parity, deviations from interest-rate parity create arbitrage opportunities. However, these arbitrage opportunities involve buying and selling financial assets rather than physical commodities. As we know, trade in securities can occur rapidly and much less expensively than trade in goods, so the forces of arbitrage are more powerful in maintaining interest-rate parity than in maintaining the law of one price.

EXAMPLE

Suppose that the 6-month, risk-free rate in the United States is 4% per year (2% for six months) and in Canada is 3.2% per year (1.6% for six months). The spot exchange rate is C\$1.1922/\$, and the 180-day forward rate is C\$1.1862/\$. Interest-rate parity does not hold, as the following equation shows:

$$\frac{C\$1.1862/\$}{C\$1.1922/\$} < \frac{\left(1 + \frac{0.032}{2}\right)}{\left(1 + \frac{0.04}{2}\right)}$$

Because the right-hand side of this equation is "too large" relative to parity, the interest rate in Canada is "too high" or the rate in the United States is "too low." The arbitrage opportunity is as follows: An investor borrows money (say \$1 million) at 4% in the United States, converts the proceeds into Canadian dollars, and then invests them at 3.20%. Six months later, the

---

[4]Be careful to match the term of the forward rate to the term of the interest rate in this expression. For example, if you are comparing interest rates on 180-day government bills, you must use a 180-day forward rate. You can see this by going back to the example of the institution with \$10 million to invest. If you set the expression for the institution's U.S. return equal to that for its Swiss return, then the following equation results:

$$\frac{F_{SF/\$}}{S_{SF/\$}} = \frac{\left(1 + \frac{R_{Swiss}}{2}\right)}{\left(1 + \frac{R_{US}}{2}\right)}$$

investor converts the Canadian dollars back into U.S. currency to repay the loan. Anything left over is pure arbitrage profit.

1. Borrow $1 million in the United States at 4% for six months → must repay $1,020,000;
2. $1 million → converted at spot rate → C$1,192,200;
3. C$1,192,200 invested for six months at 3.20% → (C$1,192,200)(1.016) → C$1,211,275;
4. C$1,211,275 converted to US$ at the forward rate → $1,021,105;
5. $1,020,000 needed to repay U.S. loan → leaves $1,105 arbitrage profit.

The effect of all of these transactions, repeated again and again, is to push exchange rates and interest rates back toward parity. As investors borrow in the United States, the U.S. interest rate will rise from 4% to a higher level. Similarly, as investors purchase Canadian government bonds, the bond prices will rise and the risk-free rate in Canada will fall. When investors sell U.S. dollars to buy Canadian dollars on the spot market, the C$/$ spot rate will fall (the U.S. dollar will depreciate), and just the opposite happens on the forward market as investors sell Canadian dollars to buy U.S. dollars. In terms of the interest-rate parity equation, we can see how these forces drive markets to equilibrium:

$$\text{This ratio is increasing} \leftarrow \frac{\text{C\$1.1862/\$} \uparrow}{\text{C\$1.1922/\$} \downarrow} < \frac{\left(1 + \dfrac{0.032 \downarrow}{2}\right)}{\left(1 + \dfrac{0.04 \uparrow}{2}\right)} \rightarrow \text{This ratio is decreasing}$$

A new equilibrium occurs when the inequality becomes an equality.

The process illustrated in the preceding Example is known as **covered interest arbitrage** because traders attempt to earn arbitrage profits arising from differences in interest rates across countries while "covering" their currency exposures with forward contracts. Implicit in this Example was the assumption that investors could borrow and lend at the risk-free rate in each country. Not all investors can do this, but large, creditworthy institutions can approach this ideal. Moreover, they can execute the trades described in the Example at high speed and at low cost. In the real world, deviations from interest-rate parity are small and transitory.

JOB INTERVIEW QUESTION

If rates on government bonds in Japan are less than rates on U.S. Treasury bonds, is there an arbitrage opportunity?

Real Interest-Rate Parity (the Fisher Effect)

If, after we adjust for currency translation, nominal rates of return on risk-free investments are equalized around the world, then perhaps real rates of return are also equalized. **Real interest-rate parity** means that investors should earn the same real rate of return on risk-free investments no matter the country in which they choose to invest.[5] Recall from Chapter 5 that the real rate of interest is defined as

$$1 + r_{real} = \frac{1 + R}{1 + E(i)}$$

where r_{real} is the real rate of interest, R is the nominal rate, and $E(i)$ is the expected inflation rate. If market forces equalize real rates across national borders, then we can write

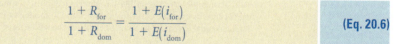

$$\frac{1 + R_{for}}{1 + R_{dom}} = \frac{1 + E(i_{for})}{1 + E(i_{dom})} \qquad \textbf{(Eq. 20.6)}$$

---

[5]Real interest-rate parity is sometimes called the *Fisher effect* after the economist who first recognized the relationship between the inflation rate and nominal and real interest rates.

This equation states that if real rates are the same in the domestic and the foreign country, then the ratio of (1 plus) nominal interest rates in the two countries must equal the ratio of (1 plus) expected inflation rates. If expected inflation is higher in one country than in another, then the country with higher inflation must offer higher interest rates in order to give investors the same real return.

EXAMPLE

Suppose that expected inflation in the United States equals zero and that expected inflation in Italy is 4%. If the 1-year, risk-free rate in the United States is 3%, then what must be the 1-year, risk-free rate in Italy in order to maintain real interest-rate parity?

$R_{\text{Italy}} = 7.12\%$

As with purchasing power parity, real interest-rate parity need not hold at all times: when deviations from parity occur, limits to arbitrage prevent market forces from quickly reaching a new equilibrium. In this case, the limits to arbitrage include the scarcity of risk-free investments that offer fixed real returns (rather than nominal returns). In the United States and a few other countries, governments issue bonds with payouts tied to the inflation rate. These bonds offer investors a way to lock in a fixed real rate. In the long run we expect that real interest-rate parity will hold, at least approximately, but it may not hold in the short run.

We conclude this section with a quick review of the four parity relationships, highlighting how they are linked together. Combining Equations 20.2, 20.4, 20.5, and 20.6 yields the following relationships:[6]

$$\frac{E(S)}{S} = \frac{F}{S} = \frac{1 + R_{\text{for}}}{1 + R_{\text{dom}}} = \frac{1 + E(i_{\text{for}})}{1 + E(i_{\text{dom}})} = \frac{E(S)}{S} \qquad \text{(Eq. 20.7)}$$

The first equality simply restates the forward–spot parity relationship. The second equality is the expression for interest-rate parity, and the third and fourth equalities (respectively) define real interest-rate parity and purchasing power parity. Here we see for the first time that if markets are in equilibrium then spot and forward exchange rates, nominal interest rates, and expected inflation rates are all linked internationally. If we want to understand why currency values change, Equation 20.7 gives us a number of clues. The equation also illustrates how difficult it can be for countries to manage their exchange rates. Attempts to push the exchange rate in a particular direction invariably lead to changes in other macroeconomic variables that policymakers may not desire.[7]

The Asset Market Model of Exchange Rates

The four parity conditions provide important insights into the factors that set relative currency values, but they give an incomplete picture of what will cause exchange rates to

---

[6]Here we have divided both sides of Equation 20.2 by the spot rate. This does no harm to the equality, and it allows us to highlight the connections between forward–spot parity and the other parity relationships.

[7]In October 1997, market pressure was building for a devaluation of the Hong Kong dollar. Hong Kong's currency board reacted by purchasing vast amounts of Hong Kong currency. One consequence of their activity was that overnight interest rates in Hong Kong briefly reached 280%! (See Gerlach 2002 for details.) A year later, a similar spike occurred in Russian interest rates as the government unsuccessfully attempted to support the ruble.

change over time and of how this change will occur. Clearly, all the parity conditions suggest that rising inflation will cause a nation's nominal interest rate to rise and its currency to depreciate. But will this depreciation occur in the spot or the forward market? Will it occur immediately or over time? Moreover, how can we explain the observed tendency of currency traders to react to economic news not covered by the parity conditions—in particular, to news about relative economic growth prospects in two countries?

Before proceeding, we should make a distinction between nominal and real exchange-rate changes. Changes in the *nominal exchange rate* are those that exactly mirror changes in relative inflation rates between two countries, whereas changes in the *real exchange rate* measure changes in the purchasing power of a currency. For example, if inflation is 2% higher in Europe than in the United States, purchasing power parity predicts that the nominal value of the euro (resp. dollar) will fall (resp. rise) by about 2%, leaving the real exchange rate unchanged. If, in fact, the dollar rises by 3% against the euro, then the real value of the dollar has increased.

A model that offers additional insights into the causes of currency movements is the **asset market model of exchange rates**. This model makes a distinction between the demand for a currency as a means of payment (transactions demand) and the demand for currency as a financial asset (a store of value). It predicts that currency values will be set by investors, who demand a currency in order to invest in that country, rather than by traders, who demand a currency in order to pay for exports or imports.

The asset market model is both flexible and powerful, for it can explain the effect that changes in investor expectations can have on relative currency values. For example, assume that investors receive news suggesting that America's economic growth rate over the next several quarters will be higher than expected. In the absence of comparable new information regarding Europe's growth prospects, international investors will increase their demand for dollars on the foreign exchange market either to make direct investments in U.S. businesses or to make portfolio investments in U.S. capital markets. Other things equal, this increased demand for dollars (or, equivalently, the increased supply of euros), in the face of stable demand for euros, will cause the dollar to appreciate and the €/$ exchange rate to rise. Reputation effects also play a role in the asset market model of exchange rates. If a government establishes a reputation for pursuing sound economic policies, that nation's currency will tend to appreciate as investors come to trust the currency as a store of value.

<table>
<tr><td>**Concept Review Questions**</td><td>5. Explain the logic behind each of the four parity relationships.
6. Explain the role of arbitrage in maintaining the parity relationships.
7. In what sense is interest-rate parity an application of the law of one price?
8. An investor who notices that interest rates are much lower in Japan than in the United States borrows in Japan and invests the proceeds in the United States. This is called *uncovered interest arbitrage*, but is it really arbitrage? Why or why not?</td></tr>
</table>

20.3 MANAGING FINANCIAL, ECONOMIC, AND POLITICAL RISK

Any firm that might experience an adverse change in the value of any of its cash flows as a result of exchange-rate movements faces exposure to *exchange-rate risk*. Almost every firm is exposed to exchange-rate risk to some degree, even if it operates strictly in one country and has cash flows in only one currency. Such a firm will face exchange rate risk if (1) it produces a good or service that competes with imports in the home market, or (2) it uses as a production input an imported product or service.

Nonetheless, some types of companies face greater exchange-rate risk than do others. MNCs obviously face this risk in all aspects of their business, but they also have many opportunities to minimize that risk by, for example, moving production facilities to the countries where their products are sold so that costs and revenues can be in the same currency. The greatest exchange-rate exposure occurs when a firm's costs and revenues are largely denominated in different currencies.

As usual, it is easiest to describe the importance of exchange rate risk to an exporter with an example. Assume that the Boeing Co. has just sold an airplane to a Japanese buyer, with the following details. First, Boeing wants to set a price such that it receives $10 million to cover its U.S. dollar costs and generate an acceptable profit. Second, suppose Boeing agrees to receive payment for the aircraft in yen. Third, assume that the current yen/dollar exchange rate is ¥100/$. Therefore, Boeing negotiates a price of ¥1 billion for the airplane, but the company is primarily concerned with the dollars it will collect when payment is made in yen and then converted into dollars on the foreign exchange market.

If Boeing negotiates the terms of this sale at the same time that it receives payment, then it faces no foreign exchange risk. The company will simply exchange ¥1 billion for $10 million on the spot market. In reality, however, Boeing will probably negotiate payment terms months before it actually expects payment from the Japanese customer. This simple fact creates exchange-rate risk, because the exchange rate can move between the dates when Boeing sets the price in yen for the plane and when it receives payment. Because the contract is denominated in yen, Boeing bears this exchange-rate risk. But the risk would not be eliminated by denominating the sales contract in dollars; rather, the risk would simply be shifted to the Japanese buyer.

Suppose that, after Boeing agrees to a price, it must wait six months for payment. In that time, the exchange rate changes to ¥110/$, meaning that the dollar has appreciated and the yen has depreciated. Boeing will still receive the same ¥1 billion but now the amount is worth just $9,090,909. Appreciation in the dollar results in Boeing realizing an *exchange-rate loss* of $909,091. If the yen appreciates—say, to ¥90/$—then Boeing will receive $11,111,111 and will realize an *exchange-rate gain* of $1,111,111.

This exchange rate risk, known as **transactions exposure**, cannot be eliminated, but it can be **hedged** (transferred to a third party) by using financial contracts. Boeing has many hedging options to choose from, including hedging (1) in the forward or futures market, (2) in the currency options market, (3) via swaps, and (4) via money market instruments. Because specific hedging strategies are described in depth in Chapter 27 (one of the web chapters), we will not describe each strategy here. We will demonstrate the use of forward contracts in the discussion that follows after briefly describing other strategies in Table 20.1.

Assume in our example that, instead of remaining unhedged, Boeing books the airplane's sale and immediately afterward asks Citibank to quote a price for yen with delivery to be made in six months. Citibank quotes Boeing a forward price of ¥99/$, which Boeing accepts. Boeing thus *sells yen forward* today, committing itself to deliver ¥1 billion and receive $10,010,101 from Citibank exactly six months from now. Once this forward contract is executed, Boeing is no longer exposed to exchange-rate risk. The risk has not disappeared; it has simply been transferred from Boeing to Citibank. But why would Citibank be willing to assume this risk?

International banks—and, increasingly, other types of financial institutions—are uniquely positioned to bear exchange-rate risk because they can create what amounts to a

WHAT COMPANIES DO GLOBALLY

CFO Survey Evidence

In a survey of CFOs from four European countries, Brounen, de Jong, and Koedijk asked companies whether they had considered issuing debt in a foreign currency and, if so, what factors influenced that decision. A company that earns revenues in a foreign currency can offset some of that risk exposure by generating costs in the same currency, and one way to do that is by borrowing money in the foreign currency.

Apparently, the hedging motivation for issuing foreign debt is important to some firms, especially those in Britain and the United States (the U.S. figures come from Graham and Harvey 2001).

More than 90% of British CFOs and almost as many American CFOs said that "providing a natural hedge" was always or almost always an important factor in their decision to issue debt in a foreign currency. In contrast, CFOs from the Netherlands and Germany put less emphasis on the hedging motive, saying instead that they considered issuing foreign debt because foreign interest rates may be lower than domestic rates.

Source: Reprinted from *Journal of Banking and Finance,* 30, "Capital Structure Policies in Europe: Survey Evidence," Dirk Brounen, Abe de Jong, and Kees Koedijk, pp. 1409–1442, copyright 2006, with permission from Elsevier.

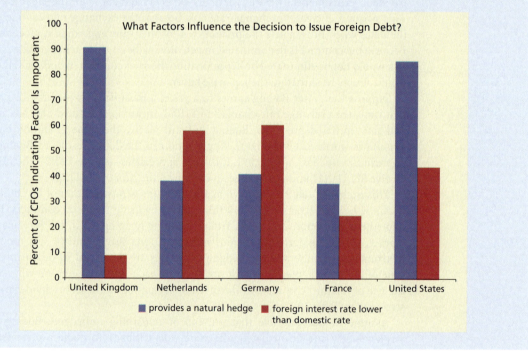

natural hedge, or offsetting risk exposure, as a normal course of their business. This means that they can easily arrange mirror-image positions with other customers. To see this, consider what type of foreign exchange contract a company like Sony might demand from Citibank. The exchange rate risk problem for Sony is the opposite of Boeing's: Sony exports many products from Japan and sells them in the United States. The company receives U.S.

Table 20.1 Exchange-Rate Risk Management and Hedging Tools

TOOL	DESCRIPTION	IMPACT ON RISK EXPOSURE
Borrowing and lending	Borrow money in currency in which payment is to be received and lend in home country's currency. Pay off borrowing when receivable is collected.	Eliminates exchange-rate risk as long as there is no risk of default on the underlying account receivable.
Forward contract	If foreign currency payment is to be received then sell currency forward, locking in a home-country price for foreign currency. If foreign currency payment must be made, buy currency forward.	Forwards eliminate risk but also eliminate opportunity to profit from favorable changes in currency value. No intermediate cash flows, so can be risky unless counterparty is well known.
Futures contract	Used similarly to a forward contract but involves a standardized, exchange-traded financial instrument. Often used for hedging smaller obligations because of their relatively small denominations.	Futures also eliminate both risk and profit opportunity, because futures are an obligation to make or take delivery. Less default risk because exchange traded and "marked to market" each day.
Options contract	Call options are rights (not obligations) to sell a standard amount of currency at a fixed price; puts are rights to sell. If a forward contract payment is to be received, buy a put option to sell forward contract; if payment is to be made, buy a call option.	Options uniquely hedge risk of adverse exchange-rate movements but preserve the potential to profit from favorable exchange-rate movement. Downside: expensive because premium must be paid for both calls and puts whether exercised or not.
Interest-rate swap	Allows the trading of one interest-rate stream (e.g., on a fixed-rate U.S. dollar instrument) for another (e.g., on a floating-rate U.S. dollar instrument).	Permits firms to change the interest-rate structure of their assets/ liabilities and achieves cost savings due to broader market access.
Currency swap	Two parties exchange principal amounts of two different currencies initially; they pay each other's interest payments and then reverse principal amounts (at a preset exchange rate) at maturity. More complex than interest-rate swaps.	All the features of interest-rate swaps, plus it allows firms to change the currency structure of their assets/ liabilities.

dollars as payment, but its costs are in yen and so it would need to *sell dollars forward* (locking in a yen price) in order to cover its costs and make an acceptable profit. Citibank is thus naturally able to buy dollars forward (sell yen) from Sony and simultaneously sell dollars forward (buy yen) to Boeing, thereby netting out the exchange-rate exposure on its own books. This is, of course, a simplified example, because Citibank may not have a perfectly offsetting exposure for Boeing's needs, but in that case it would simply execute its own forward contract with another bank—perhaps with Sony's main bank.

We have discussed how to measure exchange-rate risk as it applies to specific transactions and have briefly discussed one method of dealing with it using a forward market hedge. However, transactions exposure is but one of many types of exchange-rate risk.

Translation and Economic Risk

For MNCs, there are additional complexities involved with operating internationally if they have affiliates or subsidiaries on the ground in a foreign country. One such complication arises when MNCs translate costs and revenues denominated in foreign currencies to report on their financial statements, which naturally are denominated in the home currency. This type of risk is called *translation exposure* or **accounting exposure**. In other words, foreign exchange-rate fluctuations affect individual accounts in the financial statements. A related (and generally more important) risk element is **economic exposure**, which is the overall impact of foreign exchange-rate fluctuations on the firm's value. A firm faces economic exposure when exchange-rate movements affect its cash flows, even those cash flows not specifically tied to transactions in other currencies. For example, a rise in the value of the dollar against the euro makes European wines less expensive to U.S. consumers and also makes U.S. wine more expensive for European consumers. A winery operating in the United States—even one that does not sell directly to foreign customers—may experience a decline in cash flows due to competition from suddenly less expensive European vintners.

What can managers do about these risks? Hedging economic exposure is more difficult than hedging transactions exposure, in part because measuring the exposure is more difficult. For instance, a U.S. winery concerned about the declining prices of foreign wines could engage in currency trades that would result in a profit if the dollar appreciates against the euro. In theory, the profits could offset the decline in earnings that occurs when European wines become less expensive. But exactly how large will these losses be for a given movement in the exchange rate? Increasingly, MNCs manage their economic exposures both by using sophisticated currency derivatives and by matching costs and revenues in a given currency. For instance, a foreign company exporting to Japan might issue yen-denominated bonds, so-called Samurai bonds, to create a yen-based liability that would partially or fully offset the exposure resulting from yen-based receivables. Yet it is important to emphasize that, unless the cash inflows and outflows match exactly, some residual yen exposure will remain.

Political Risk

Smart Practices Video

Herbert Kelleher, Founder, Southwest Airlines

"There is political risk in the United States as well as abroad."

See the entire interview at
SMARTFinance

Another important risk facing MNCs is **political risk**, which refers to actions taken by a government that have a negative impact on the value of foreign companies operating in that country. These negative impacts may include raising taxes on a firm's activities or erecting barriers that prevent a firm from repatriating profits back to the home country. In its most extreme form, political risk can mean confiscation of a corporation's assets by a foreign government.

Political risk has two basic dimensions: *macro* and *micro*. **Macro political risk** means that *all* foreign firms in the country will be subject to political risk because of political change, revolution, or the adoption of new policies by a host government. Thus, no individual country or firm is treated differently. An example of macro political risk occurred when communist regimes came to power in China in 1949 and Cuba in 1959–1960. More recently, the near collapse of Indonesia's currency in late 1997 and early 1998, plus the attendant political and economic turmoil elsewhere in Asia, highlights the real and present danger that macro political risk can pose to MNCs and international investors alike. **Micro political risk**, on the other hand, refers to a foreign government's targeting punitive action against an individual firm, a specific industry, or companies from a particular foreign country. An example is a recent threat by Venezuelan President Hugo Chavez to nationalize industries such as telecommunications and electricity, industries in which U.S. companies such as Verizon have made large investments.

Although political risk can take place in any country—even in the United States—the political instability of many developing countries generally makes the positions of multinational companies most vulnerable in those countries. At the same time, some of the countries in this group have the most promising markets for the goods and services being offered by MNCs. The main question, then, is how to engage in operations and foreign investment in such countries and still avoid (or at least minimize) the potential political risk.

There are both positive and negative approaches that MNCs may be able to adopt for coping with political risk. Negative approaches include taking a trade dispute with a host country to the World Trade Organization or threatening to withhold additional investments from a country unless the MNC's demands are met. Firms may also negotiate agreements with host governments that build in costs the host government must bear if it breaches the terms of the original agreement. Positive approaches for MNCs include working proactively to develop environmental and labor standards in a country and generally attempting to become perceived as a domestic company by the host country's citizenry. In addition, some firms attempt to manage political risks by establishing personal connections with government leaders. Research in this area has generally found that political connections have significant value to shareholders.

Smart Ideas Video

Mara Faccio, Purdue University

"Whether political connections create value depends on how the connections are established."

See the entire interview at **SMARTFinance**

Concept Review Questions	9. Distinguish between transactions exposure, translation exposure, and economic exposure.
	10. Describe how a domestic firm might use a forward contract to hedge its economic exposure. Why does uncertainty about the magnitude of the exposure make this difficult?

20.4 Long-Term Investment Decisions

In Chapters 7 through 9, we emphasized the importance of sound capital budgeting practices for the long-term survival of a corporation. The same lessons covered in those chapters apply to multinational corporations. Whether investing at home or abroad, MNCs should evaluate investments based on their incremental cash flows and should discount those cash flows at a rate that is appropriate given the risk of the investment. However, when a company makes investments denominated in many different currencies, this process becomes a bit more complicated. First, in what currency should the firm express a foreign project's cash flows? Second, how does one calculate the cost of capital for an MNC or for a given project?

Capital Budgeting

Suppose that a U.S. firm is weighing an investment that will generate cash flows in euros. The company's financial analysts have estimated the project's cash flows in euros as follows:

Initial Cost	Year 1	Year 2	Year 3
−€2 million	€900,000	€850,000	€800,000

To calculate the project's net present value, the U.S. firm can take either of two approaches. First, it can discount euro-denominated cash flows using a euro-based cost of capital. Having done this, the firm can then convert the resulting NPV back to dollars at the spot rate. For example, assume that the risk-free rate in Europe is 5% and that the firm estimates the cost of capital (expressed as a euro rate) for this project to be 10% (i.e., there is a 5% risk premium associated with the investment). The NPV, rounded to the nearest thousand euros, equals €122,000:

$$\text{NPV} = -2,000,000 + \frac{900,000}{(1.1)^1} + \frac{850,000}{(1.1)^2} + \frac{800,000}{(1.1)^3} = 122,000$$

Assume that the current spot rate is $1.15/€. Multiplying this by the net present value yields a dollar-based NPV of $140,000 (rounded to the nearest thousand dollars).

In this example, we did not make specific year-by-year forecasts of the future spot rates. Doing so is unnecessary because the firm can choose to hedge its currency exposure through a forward contract. Hedging its currency exposure allows a firm to separate the decision to accept or reject a proposal from specific projections of where the dollar/euro exchange rate might be headed. Of course, the firm may have a view on the exchange-rate question. But even so, it is wise first to consider the merits of the investment on its own. For instance, suppose that this project has a negative NPV but managers believe that the euro will appreciate over the life of the project, increasing its appeal in dollar terms. Given that belief, there is no need for the firm to undertake the project. Instead, it could purchase euros directly, invest them in safe financial assets in Europe, and convert them back to dollars several years later. If the firm wants to speculate on currency movements, it need not invest in physical assets to accomplish that objective.

A second approach for evaluating the investment project is to calculate the NPV in dollar terms, assuming that the firm can hedge the project's cash flows by using forward contracts. To begin this calculation, we must know the risk-free rate in the United States. If that rate is 4% and we recognize that interest-rate parity must hold, then Equation 20.5 can be used to calculate the 1-year forward rate:

$$\frac{F_{\$/€}}{S_{\$/€}} = \frac{1 + R_\$}{1 + R_€}, \qquad \frac{F}{1.15} = \frac{1.04}{1.05}, \qquad F = \$1.1390/€$$

Similarly, we can calculate the 2-year and 3-year forward rates as follows:

$$\frac{F_{\$/€}}{S_{\$/€}} = \frac{(1 + R_\$)^2}{(1 + R_€)^2}, \qquad \frac{F}{1.15} = \frac{(1.04)^2}{(1.05)^2}, \qquad F = \$1.1282/€$$

$$\frac{F_{\$/€}}{S_{\$/€}} = \frac{(1 + R_\$)^3}{(1 + R_€)^3}, \qquad \frac{F}{1.15} = \frac{(1.04)^3}{(1.05)^3}, \qquad F = \$1.1175/€$$

Next, multiply each period's cash flow in euros by the matching spot or forward exchange rate to obtain a sequence of cash flows in dollars (rounded to the nearest thousand dollars):

Currency	Initial Investment	Year 1	Year 2	Year 3
€	2,000,000 × 1.15	900,000 × 1.1390	850,000 × 1.1282	800,000 × 1.1175
$	2,300,000	1,025,000	959,000	894,000

All that remains is to discount this project's cash flows at an appropriate risk-adjusted U.S. interest rate. But how do we determine that rate? Recall that the European discount rate used to calculate the euro-denominated NPV was 10%, or 5% above the European risk-free rate. Intuitively, we might expect the comparable U.S. rate to be 9%, which would represent a 5% risk premium over the current risk-free rate in the United States.

That intuition is roughly correct. To be precise, use the following formula to solve for the project's required return in terms of U.S. dollars:

$$1 + R = (1 + 0.10)\,\frac{1 + 0.04}{1 + 0.05}, \quad R = 8.95\%$$

This equation takes the project's required return in euro terms, 10%, and rescales it to dollar terms by multiplying by the ratio of risk-free interest rates in each country. We can verify that discounting the dollar-denominated cash flows using this rate results in the same NPV (again, rounding to the nearest thousand dollars) that we obtained by discounting the cash flows in euros and converting to dollars at the spot rate:

$$\text{NPV} = \$140{,}000$$

These calculations demonstrate that a company does not have to "take a view" on currency movements when it invests abroad. Whether the company hedges a project's cash flows using forward contracts or whether it calculates a project's NPV in local currency before converting to the home currency at the spot exchange rate, future exchange-rate movements need not cloud the capital budgeting decision.

Cost of Capital

In the preceding example we assumed that the project's cost of capital in Europe was 10%, which translated into a dollar-based discount rate of 8.95%. But where did the 10% come from? We return to the lessons of Chapter 9—namely, that the discount rate should reflect the project's risk. One way to assess that risk is to calculate a beta for the investment. However, calculating the beta for an international project raises some questions for which finance still has no definitive answer.

For example, suppose that shareholders of the U.S. firm investing in Europe hold mostly U.S. stocks in their portfolios. Perhaps the costs of diversifying internationally are prohibitively expensive for many investors. In that case, when a firm diversifies internationally, it creates value for its shareholders. This stands in sharp contrast to when a firm diversifies domestically. Because U.S. investors can easily diversify their own domestic investments, they will not realize any benefit if a firm diversifies on their behalf.

Suppose a firm's shareholders cannot diversify internationally. In that case, when the firm invests abroad, it should calculate a project's beta by measuring the covariance of similar European investments with the U.S. market, not the European market. The reason is that, from the perspective of U.S. investors, the project's systematic risk depends on its covariance with the other assets that U.S. investors already own. A U.S. firm planning to build an electronics manufacturing facility in Germany might compare the returns of existing German electronics firms with returns on a U.S. stock index to estimate a project beta.[8]

In contrast, if the firm's shareholders *do* hold internationally diversified portfolios, then the firm should calculate the project's beta by comparing the covariance of its returns (or returns on similar investments) with returns on a worldwide stock index. This generates the project's "global beta." To estimate the project's required return, the firm should apply the CAPM, multiplying the global market risk premium by the project's beta and then adding the risk-free rate. Because a globally diversified portfolio is less volatile than a portfolio containing only domestic securities, it is likely that the risk premium on the global market will be less than the domestic risk premium.

---

[8]Of course, the U.S. firm would have to worry about the effects of leverage, unlevering the equity betas of German firms with debt on their balance sheets.

EXAMPLE

A Japanese auto manufacturer decides to build a plant to make cars for the North American market. The firm estimates two project betas. The first calculation takes returns on U.S. auto stocks and calculates their betas relative to those on the Nikkei stock index. Based on these calculations, the Japanese firm decides to apply a beta of 1.1 to the investment. The risk-free rate of interest in Japan is 2%, and the market risk premium on the Nikkei index is 8%; hence the project's required return is calculated as follows:

$$R_{project} = 2\% + 1.1(8\%) = 10.8\%$$

The second calculation takes the returns on U.S. auto manufacturers and determines their betas relative to those on a world stock index. It turns out that U.S. auto stocks are more highly correlated with the world market than they are with the Nikkei. Combined with the lower variance of the world market portfolio compared to the variance of the Nikkei, this calculation leads to a higher estimate of the project beta, say 1.3. However, offsetting this effect is that the risk premium on the world market portfolio is just 5%. Therefore, the second estimate of the project's required return is calculated as follows:

$$R_{project} = 2\% + 1.3(5\%) = 8.5\%$$

Concept Review Questions

11. Why does discounting the cash flows of a foreign investment (using the foreign cost of capital) and then converting that into the home currency at the spot rate yield the same NPV as converting the project's cash flows to domestic currency at the forward rate and then discounting them at the domestic cost of capital?
12. What factors determine whether a project's beta will be higher or lower when calculated against a domestic stock index versus a world stock index?
13. Why is it not surprising to find that the risk premium on the world market portfolio is lower than the domestic risk premium?

20.5 SHORT-TERM FINANCIAL DECISIONS

Though the focus in international finance is rightly on long-term investments and economic exposure, managers must also actively measure and manage short-term financial exposures. We have already demonstrated and discussed transactions exposure in the context of exchange-rate risk. We now conclude by looking at several other issues related to short-term financial decision making in an international context.

Cash Management

In its international cash management, a multinational firm can respond to exchange-rate risks by protecting (hedging) its undesirable cash and marketable securities exposures or by making certain adjustments in its operations. Whereas the former approach is more applicable in responding to *accounting* exposure, the latter is better suited for *economic* exposure. Each of these two approaches is examined here.

Hedging Strategies   **Hedging strategies** are techniques used to offset or protect against risk, and they are most applicable to transactions exposure. In international cash management, these strategies include such actions as borrowing or lending in different currencies;

undertaking contracts in the forward, futures, and/or options markets; and swapping assets/liabilities with other parties. We refer the reader to Section 20.3 and Chapter 27 for detailed examples.

Adjustments in Operations   In responding to exchange-rate fluctuations, MNCs can give some protection to international cash flows through appropriate adjustments in assets and liabilities. Two routes are available to a multinational company for responding to economic exposure. The first centers on the operating relationships that a subsidiary of an MNC maintains with *other* firms. Depending on management's expectation of a local currency's position, adjustments in operations would involve the reduction of liabilities (resp., financial assets) if the currency is appreciating (resp., depreciating). For example, if a U.S.-based MNC with a subsidiary in Mexico expects the Mexican currency to *appreciate* in value relative to the U.S. dollar, then local customers' accounts receivable would be *increased* and accounts payable would be reduced. If the Mexican currency were instead expected to *depreciate*, then local customers' accounts receivables would be *reduced* and accounts payables would be increased.

The second route focuses on the operating relationship a subsidiary has with its parent or with other subsidiaries within the same MNC. In dealing with exchange-rate risks, a subsidiary can rely on *intra-MNC accounts*. Specifically, undesirable exchange-rate exposures can be corrected to the extent that the subsidiary can take the following steps:

1. In countries prone to currency appreciation, intra-MNC accounts receivable are collected as soon as possible and payment of intra-MNC accounts payable is delayed as long as possible.
2. In countries prone to currency depreciation, intra-MNC accounts receivable are collected as late as possible and intra-MNC accounts payable are paid as soon as possible.

This technique is known as **leading and lagging**, or simply as "leads and lags." The following Example illustrates its potential effectiveness.

EXAMPLE

Assume that a U.S.-based parent company, American Computer Corporation (ACC), buys parts from and sells parts to its wholly owned Mexican subsidiary, Tijuana Computer Company (TCC). Assume further that ACC has accounts payable of $10 million that it is scheduled to pay TCC in 30 days and also has accounts receivable of (Mexican peso) MP106.5 million due from TCC within 30 days. Because today's exchange rate is MP10.65/$, the accounts receivable are also worth $10 million. Therefore, parent and subsidiary owe each other equal amounts (though in different currencies), and both are payable in 30 days. But because TCC is a wholly owned subsidiary of ACC, the parent has complete discretion over the timing of these payments.

If ACC believes that the Mexican peso will depreciate from MP10.65/US$ to, say, MP12.00/US$ during the next 30 days, then the combined companies can profit by collecting the depreciating-currency (MP) debt immediately but delaying payment of the appreciating-currency (US$) debt for the full 30 days allowed. If parent and subsidiary do this and the peso depreciates as predicted, then the net result is that the MP106.5 million payment from TCC to ACC is made immediately and is safely converted into $10 million at today's exchange rate, whereas the delayed $10 million payment from ACC to TCC will be worth MP120 million (MP12.00/$ × $10,000,000). Thus, the Mexican subsidiary will experience a foreign exchange trading profit of MP13.5 million (MP120,000,000 minus MP106,500,000), whereas the U.S. parent receives the full amount ($10 million) due from TCC and therefore is unharmed. Of course, if the dollar is expected to depreciate against the peso then these steps would be reversed.

This Example demonstrates that the manipulation of an MNC's consolidated intracompany accounts by one subsidiary generally benefits one subsidiary (or the parent) while leaving the other subsidiary (or the parent) unharmed. The exact degree and direction of the actual manipulations, however, may depend on the tax status of each country. Clearly, the MNC would prefer to suffer the exchange-rate losses in whichever country has the higher tax rate. Finally, changes in intra-MNC accounts can also be subject to restrictions and regulations put forward by the respective host countries of the various subsidiaries.

Credit and Inventory Management

Multinational firms based in different countries compete for the same global export markets. Therefore, it is essential that they offer attractive credit terms to potential customers. Increasingly, however, the maturity and saturation of developed markets are forcing MNCs to maintain and increase revenues by exporting and selling a higher percentage of their output to developing countries. Given the risks associated with the latter group of buyers, as partly evidenced by the greater volatility of many developing nations' currencies, the MNC must employ a variety of tools to protect such revenues. In addition to the use of hedging and various asset and liability adjustments (described previously), MNCs should seek the backing of their respective governments in identifying target markets and in extending credit. Multinationals based in a number of Western European nations and those based in Japan currently benefit from extensive involvement of government agencies that provide them with the needed service and financial support suggested here. For U.S.-based MNCs, the international positions of government agencies such as the Export-Import Bank of the United States currently do not provide a comparable level of support.

In terms of inventory management, MNCs must consider a number of factors related to both economics and politics. In the former category, a multinational firm—in addition to maintaining the appropriate level of inventory in various locations around the world—is compelled to deal with exchange-rate fluctuations, tariffs, nontariff barriers, integration schemes such as the EU, and other rules and regulations. Politically, inventories can be subjected to wars, expropriations, blockages, and other forms of government intervention.

Concept Review Questions

14. Assume that a U.S. multinational company has wholly owned subsidiaries in both Britain and Switzerland that trade with each other and the parent regularly. Further assume that the British pound is expected to appreciate versus the dollar and the Swiss franc. How could you profit from this using the technique of "leads and lags"?

15. Assume that your firm has sold a computer to a British company, with delivery and payment (in British pounds) to occur in 30 days. You will receive a fixed payment of £2,000, and the current exchange rate is $1.40/£. What risk do you run by remaining unhedged, and how could you hedge that risk using a forward contract?

SUMMARY

- Large, globally active firms known as multinational corporations (MNCs) dominate international investment and trade today. MNCs tend to be the most dynamic and successful firms in their industry, and most modern international financial and accounting techniques have been designed to meet their special financial needs.

- Exchange-rate movements are linked to differences in inflation rates and interest rates across countries. In general, currency values fall in countries with relatively high inflation.

- Any company that exports a significant amount of goods and services is exposed to exchange-rate risk:

the chance that a change in the home currency's value relative to the currency in the customer's market can impose financial losses on the exporter. Importers can face similar risks, though this is less common because sales are usually denominated in the customer's currency. A variety of hedging techniques have been developed to handle this risk, and the most commonly used is hedging with a forward contract.

- Given the potential danger of loss from exchange-rate fluctuations, MNCs must pay particularly careful attention to their management of cash, accounts receivable, and other short-term assets. However, MNCs can use a variety of techniques not only to survive but actually to profit from these fluctuations.

KEY TERMS

accounting exposure
appreciated
asset market model of exchange rates
covered interest arbitrage
cross exchange rate
depreciated
direct quotation
economic exposure
euro
exchange rate
fixed exchange rate
floating exchange rate

foreign exchange (forex) market
forward discount
forward exchange rate
forward premium
forward rate
forward–spot parity
hedged
hedging strategies
indirect quotation
interest-rate parity
law of one price
leading and lagging

macro political risk
managed floating-rate system
micro political risk
multinational corporations (MNCs)
natural hedge
political risk
purchasing power parity
real interest-rate parity
spot exchange rate
transactions exposure
triangular arbitrage

QUESTIONS

20-1. Define a multinational corporation (MNC). What factors must the manager of an MNC consider that a manager of a purely domestic firm does not face?

20-2. Who are the major players in foreign currency markets, and what are their motivations for trading?

20-3. If an exchange rate is quoted in terms of euros per pound, in what direction would it move if the euro appreciated against the pound?

20-4. Explain how triangular arbitrage ensures that currency values are essentially the same in different markets around the world at any given moment.

20-5. In what sense is it a misnomer to refer to a currency as "weak" or "strong"? Who benefits and who loses if the yen appreciates against the pound?

20-6. What does a spot exchange rate have in common with a forward rate, and how are they different?

20-7. What does it mean to say that a currency trades at a forward premium?

20-8. Explain how the law of one price establishes a relationship between changes in currency values and inflation rates.

20-9. We developed the notion of forward–spot parity by assuming risk-neutral traders. Suppose that managers who make decisions about whether or not to hedge are actually risk averse. How might this alter the logic of forward–spot parity?

20-10. Why does purchasing power parity appear to hold in the long run but not in the short run?

20-11. In terms of risk, is a U.S. investor indifferent about whether to buy a U.S. government bond or a U.K. government bond? Why or why not?

20-12. If the euro trades at a forward premium against the yen, explain why interest rates in Japan must be higher than they are in Europe.

20-13. Suppose that the U.S. Federal Reserve suddenly decides to raise interest rates. Trace out the potential impact that this action might have on (1) interest rates abroad, (2) the spot value of the dollar, and (3) the forward value of the dollar.

20-14. Suppose interest rates on risk-free bonds in the United States are about 4% whereas interest rates on Swiss government bonds are 6%. Can we conclude that investors around the world will flock to buy Swiss bonds? Why or why not?

20-15. A Japanese investor decides to purchase shares in a company that trades on the London Stock Exchange. The investor's plan is to hold the shares for one year and then to sell them at year's end and convert the proceeds into yen. During the year, the pound appreciates against the yen. Does this enhance or diminish the investor's return on the stock?

20-16. Suppose that the dollar trades at a forward discount relative to the yen. A U.S. firm must pay a Japanese supplier ¥10 million in three months. A manager in the U.S. firm reasons that, because the dollar buys fewer yen on the forward market than it does on the spot market, the firm should not enter a forward hedge to eliminate its exchange-rate exposure. Comment on this opinion.

20-17. How is hedging exchange-rate exposure using options different from hedging using forward contracts? What does this suggest about the costs of hedging with options rather than forwards?

20-18. What are some strategies for minimizing the political risk to a firm in a developing country?

PROBLEMS

Exchange-Rate Fundamentals

20-1. A "direct quote" is when an exchange rate is expressed as the cost in domestic currency for one unit of foreign currency. The following quotes are "indirect quotes" (i.e., one unit of domestic currency is valued in terms of the foreign currency):

£2/$
€1.2/$
C$1.25/$

What are the direct quotes corresponding to these indirect quotes?

20-2. Suppose we expect the British pound to appreciate relative to the euro over the next year (i.e., current spot of £0.75/€ and an expected spot of £0.70/€). What is the appreciation rate of the pound and the depreciation rate of the euro?

20-3. If the exchange rates in New York are $1.25/£ and $1.10/€ and if you can exchange euros and pounds in London at the rate €1.20/£, is triangular arbitrage profitable? Illustrate the profit that could be earned by a trader in New York with $1 million.

Smart Solutions

See the problem and solution explained step-by-step at **SMARTFinance**

20-4. On Monday, the exchange rate between the U.S. dollar and the British pound was $1.7423/£ (£0.5740/$). On Tuesday, the exchange rate was $1.7150/£ (£0.5831/$). Which currency appreciated and which depreciated? Calculate both the percentage appreciation of the currency that rose in value and the percentage depreciation of the currency that declined in value.

20-5. Using the data presented in Figure 20.1, calculate the spot exchange rate between Canadian dollars and British pounds (in pounds per dollar).

20-6. Go to http://www.economist.com and then, under the "Markets & Data" section, activate the foreign exchange map. On the menu at the far left, choose the U.S. dollar as the base currency.

  a. Click on the "1-month" selection to show the appreciation or depreciation of the world's currencies relative to the dollar. Does it appear that the dollar is appreciating or depreciating against most of the world's currencies, or is the answer mixed?

b. Next, choose the "1-year" option, and identify (i) two or three countries whose currencies have depreciated the most against the U.S. dollar and (ii) two or three countries whose currencies have appreciated the most. Search the web to find the most recent inflation figures from those countries. What lesson does this illustrate?

20-7. The spot and forward rates for the Japanese yen are:

Spot: $0.008415/¥ (¥118.84/$)
1-month: $0.008446/¥ (¥118.40/$)
3-month: $0.008508/¥ (¥117.54/$)

Supply the forward yen premium or discount (specify which it is) for both the 1-month and 3-month quotes as an annual percentage rate.

20-8. Using the data presented in Figure 20.1, specify whether the U.S. dollar traded at a forward premium or discount relative to the Canadian dollar, the Japanese yen, and the Swiss franc. Use the 3-month forward rates to determine your answer.

20-9. Using the data presented in Figure 20.1, determine the forward premium or discount on the Canadian dollar relative to the British pound, the Japanese yen, and the Swiss franc. Use the 6-month forward rates to determine your answer, which should be expressed as an annual rate.

20-10. Assume that you are quoted the following series of exchange rates for the U.S. dollar ($), the Canadian dollar (C$), and the British pound (£):

$0.6000/C$	C$1.6667/$
$1.2500/£	£0.8000/$
C$2.5000/£	£0.4000/C$

If you have $1 million in cash, how can you take profitable advantage of this series of exchange rates? Show the series of trades that would yield an arbitrage profit, and calculate how much profit you would make.

Parity Conditions of International Finance

20-11. Use the data presented in Figure 20.1 to answer this problem. A particular commodity sells for $5,000 in the United States and ¥600,000 in Japan.
  a. Does the law of one price hold? If not, explain how to profit through arbitrage.
  b. Taking the commodity prices in the United States and Japan as given, at what exchange rate (in terms of yen per dollar) would the law of one price hold?

Smart
Solutions
See the problem and solution explained step-by-step at **SMARTFinance**

20-12. Refer to Problem 20-11. If it costs ¥15,000 to transport the commodity from the United States to Japan, is there still an arbitrage opportunity? At what exchange rate (in yen per dollar) would buying the commodity in the United States and shipping it to sell in Japan become profitable?

20-13. Refer to Problem 20-12. Given shipping costs of ¥15,000, at what exchange rate would it be profitable to buy the commodity in Japan and ship it to the United States to sell? Comment on the general lesson from these last three questions.

20-14. If the expected rate of inflation in the United States is 2%, the 1-year risk-free interest rate is 4%, and the 1-year risk-free rate in Britain is 4.5%, then what is the expected inflation rate in Britain?

20-15. Go to http://www.economist.com and then, under the "Markets & Data" section, find the link for the "Big Mac index." After exploring this part of the site, explain why the Big Mac index might foreshadow changes in exchange rates. What features of the Big Mac would suggest that Big Macs may not satisfy the law of one price?

20-16. Assume that the annual interest rate on a 6-month U.S. Treasury bill is 3%; then use the data presented in Figure 20.1 to answer the following questions.

    a. Calculate the annual interest rate on 6-month bills in Switzerland and Japan.

    b. Suppose that the annual interest rate on a 6-month bill in Japan is 0.5%. Illustrate how to exploit this through covered interest arbitrage.

    c. Suppose that the annual interest rate on a 3-month U.K. government bond is 4%. What then should be the annual interest rate on a 3-month government bond in Switzerland?

    d. Suppose the actual Swiss interest rate is 0.5%. Illustrate how to conduct covered interest arbitrage to exploit this situation.

20-17. Shortly after it was introduced, the euro traded just below parity with the dollar, meaning that one dollar purchased more than one euro. This implies:

    a. that U.S. inflation was lower than European inflation

    b. that U.S. interest rates were lower than European rates

    c. that the law of one price does not hold

    d. none of the above

20-18. Assume the following information is known about the current spot exchange rate between the U.S. dollar and the British pound, inflation rates in Britain and the United States, and the real rate of interest (which is assumed to be the same in both countries):

Current spot rate, $S = \$1.4500/\pounds$ ($\pounds0.6897/\$$)
U.S. inflation rate, $i_{US} = 1.5\%$ per year (0.015)
British inflation rate, $i_{UK} = 2.0\%$ per year (0.020)
Real rate of interest, $R = 2.5\%$ per year (0.025)

Based on these data, use the parity conditions of international finance to compute the following:

    a. Expected spot rate next year

    b. U.S. risk-free rate (on a 1-year bond)

    c. British risk-free rate (on a 1-year bond)

    d. 1-year forward rate

Finally, show how you can make an arbitrage profit if you are offered the chance to sell or buy pounds forward (for delivery one year from now) at the current spot rate of $\$1.4500/\pounds$ ($\pounds0.6897/\$$). Assuming that you can borrow $1 million (or £689,700) at the risk-free interest rate, what would your profit be on this arbitrage transaction?

20-19. The current exchange rate between the United States and Canada is $0.92/C$. A particular item sells for $23.95 in the United States and for C$25.75 in Canada. Shipping costs between the United States and Canada are $300.00 (or C$326.09) per 1,000 units. In which country is the item selling for less money? After accounting for shipping costs, can the price discrepancy be exploited?

20-20. Suppose that the spot exchange rate between the United States and the United Kingdom is $0.89/£ and that the spot rate one year in the future is expected to be $0.90/£. If the expected annual inflation in the United States is 4%, what is the expected annual inflation in the United Kingdom?

20-21. If the expected annual inflation in a foreign country is 7% and the expected annual domestic inflation is 3.2%, then what is the domestic risk-free rate if we assume that the foreign risk-free rate is 12%? If the current exchange rate is 0.75 units of domestic currency per one unit of foreign currency, then what is the expected exchange rate six months in the future and twelve months in the future?

20-22. The U.S. dollar trades at an annual forward premium relative to the euro of 4.3%. If the United States is expected to have −1.0% inflation throughout the year, then what inflation rate can be expected in Europe? If the annual risk-free rate for the United States is 5.4%, what is the annual risk-free rate in Europe?

Managing Financial and Political Risk

Smart Solutions

See the problem and solution explained step-by-step at **SMARTFinance**

20-23. Suppose that the spot exchange rate follows a random walk, which means that the best forecast of the spot rate at some future date is simply its current value. Now suppose that a U.S. firm owes €1 million to a Spanish supplier. If the U.S. firm is risk neutral, describe the circumstances under which the firm will or will not enter into a forward contract to hedge its exposure.

20-24. Classic City Exporters (CCE) recently sold a large shipment of sporting equipment to a Swiss company that intends to sell it in Zurich. The sale, denominated in Swiss francs, was worth SF500,000. Delivery of the sporting goods and payment by the Swiss buyer are due in six months. The current spot exchange rate is $0.7598/SF (SF1.3161/$), and the 6-month forward rate is $0.7729/SF (SF1.2938/$). What risk would CCE run if it remained unhedged, and how could it hedge that risk with a forward contract? Assuming that the actual exchange rate in six months is $0.7000/SF (SF1.4286/$), compute the profit or loss—and state which it is—that CCE would experience if it remains unhedged versus hedging in the forward market.

20-25. A British firm will receive $1 million from a U.S. customer in three months. The firm is considering two strategies to eliminate its foreign exchange exposure. The first strategy is to pledge the $1 million as collateral for a 3-month loan from a U.S. bank at 4% interest. The U.K. firm will then convert the proceeds of the loan to pounds at the spot rate. When the loan is due, the firm will pay the $1 million balance by handing its U.S. receivable over to the bank. This strategy allows the U.K. firm to "monetize" its receivable immediately. The spot exchange rate is 0.6550 pounds per dollar.

The second strategy is to enter a forward contract at an exchange rate of 0.6450 pounds per dollar. This ensures that the U.K. firm will receive £645,000 in three months. If the firm wanted to monetize this payment immediately, it could take out a 3-month loan from a U.K. bank at 8%, pledging the proceeds of the forward contract as collateral. Which of these strategies should the firm follow?

Long-Term Investment Decisions

20-26. The cost of capital in a particular foreign country is 15%. Domestic inflation is expected to be 2.7%, and inflation in the foreign country is expected to be 7%. What is the cost of capital relative to the domestic country? (*Hint:* Look at the relationships established in Equation 20.7.)

20-27. A foreign firm is evaluating a project in the United States by using a cost of capital (based on the U.S. dollar) of 15%. The current exchange rate is $0.85 per unit of foreign currency with a 1-year forward rate of $0.82. What is the domestic cost of capital for the foreign firm? (*Hint:* Look at the relationships established in Equation 20.7.)

20-28. A German company manufactures a specialized piece of equipment and leases it to a U.K. enterprise. The lease calls for five end-of-year payments of £1 million. The German firm spent €3.5 million to produce the equipment, which is expected to have no salvage value after five years. The current spot rate is €1.5/£. The risk-free interest rate is 3% in Germany and is 5% in the United Kingdom. The German firm reasons that the appropriate (German) discount rate for this investment is 7%. Calculate the NPV of this investment in two ways.

a. Convert all cash flows to pounds and then discount at an appropriate (U.K.) cost of capital. Convert the resulting NPV to euros at the spot rate.

b. Calculate forward rates for each year, convert the pound-denominated cash flows into euros using those rates, and then discount the cash flows at the German cost of capital. Verify that the NPV obtained from this approach matches (except perhaps for small rounding errors) that obtained with the first approach as described in part (a).

Short-Term Financial Decisions

20-29. A Canadian firm owes ¥3 million to its Japanese subsidiary. In turn, the subsidiary owes the Canadian firm C$45,000. Both payments are due in 30 days, but managers believe that the yen will appreciate against the Canadian dollar over the next 30 days. Specifically, they expect the spot exchange rate to change from ¥70/C$ to ¥60/C$.

a. If the firm can accelerate one of these payments to the present, which one should it accelerate?

b. What will be the exchange-rate gain from accelerating the payment compared to making the payment in 30 days? (Assume that rates change as expected.)

20-30. A U.S. firm must borrow $1 million to meet operating needs for one year. A U.S. bank offers a 1-year loan at 5% interest. A U.K. bank is willing to lend (in pounds) for one year at 7%, and a Canadian bank offers a loan (denominated in Canadian dollars) at 6%. In all cases, the U.S. firm will repay the loan in a lump sum at the end of the year. If it borrows from a foreign lender, the firm will hedge its currency exposure with a forward contract. The current spot and 1-year forward exchange rates are as follows:

	Foreign Currency per US$	
Country	**Spot**	**1-Year Forward**
Canada	1.1922	1.1802
United Kingdom	0.5760	0.5772

Which loan should the firm accept?

THOMSON ONE | Business School Edition

20-31. Fedex Corporation (ticker symbol, FDX) has been one of the most profitable companies in the world, and McDonald's Corporation (ticker symbol, MCD) is one of the world's largest employers. What geographic regions of the world generate the greatest percentage of revenue for each firm? How would a change in exchange rates impact the reported financial results of these firms? (*Hint:* Under the Financials tab, go to More, then WorldScope, then Geographic Segment.) How are the stock returns for both firms affected by changes in exchange rates? (*Hint:* Under the Prices tab, go to Overviews, then Thomson Market Data, then Stock Performance Overview and click the $ at the top to change the currency used to calculate the returns.) Which of the major currencies yielded the greatest return for each firm over the last five years?

MINI-CASE: INTERNATIONAL FINANCIAL MANAGEMENT

Frog Enterprises recently purchased 50,000 flat-panel monitors from Tokyo Technologies for 2,000 yen each. The invoice, payable in yen, is due in 30 days. The spot rate is 118.15 yen per U.S. dollar, and the 30-day forward rate is 117.757 yen per U.S. dollar.

1. If Frog Enterprises were to buy the yen today, how much would it cost in U.S. dollars?

2. If Frog Enterprises were to engage in a forward contract, how much would it cost in U.S. dollars?

3. Calculate the indirect quote for the spot rate (i.e., how many U.S. dollars will one yen purchase?) and the indirect forward rate.

4. Calculate the annualized forward premium and discount for the yen and the U.S. dollar.

5. Assume that the invoice is due today and that the spot rate for one Canadian dollar is C$1.14/US$. Also, assume the current spot rate is 1CD/107 yen. Does it make sense for Frog Enterprises to buy Canadian dollars and convert them to yen for paying the invoice? Justify your argument numerically.

6. Regarding the previous question, what must be the cross exchange rate (between the Canadian dollar and the yen) in order to make the arbitrage opportunity disappear?

7. Suppose Frog Enterprises could have purchased identical monitors from another company located in England. If the theory of purchasing power parity holds, then how much should each monitor cost in British pounds? (Assume that the spot rate is 0.5634 British pounds per U.S. dollar.)

PART 7

Short-Term Financing Decisions

Financial managers in large corporations spend a significant amount of time dealing with fairly routine short-term financing decisions. One important activity is strategic (long-term) and operational (short-term) financial planning. They work with other managers to convert the firm's goals into a set of financial plans. In addition, the financial manager must oversee the day-to-day management of the firm's current accounts—both assets and liabilities—in order to ensure adequate liquidity. This part of the book includes three chapters that address the financial manager's role in the firm's short-term financing activities.

Chapter 21 describes the financial planning processes. Most firms develop strategic plans that look ahead two to five years or more in addition to detailed operating plans that project inflows and outflows of cash, as well as earnings, over the next year or two. Financial plans help firms identify problems before they arise, and they help managers line up financing before cash shortfalls become critical.

Chapter 22 looks at cash conversion (how cash moves through a firm) and the popular procedures for managing inventory and accounts receivable. How long a firm can delay paying its vendors, how long a firm's goods spend in inventory, and how long the firm must wait before its customers pay for their orders all play critical roles in determining how quickly a firm recovers its cash. When managers determine how much to invest in items such as inventories and receivables, they must consider the costs and benefits of those investments.

Chapter 23 focuses on managing the firm's liquidity. This process is affected by the firm's cash collection procedures and the timing of its cash disbursements, which are affected by the terms under which its suppliers grant credit. In addition, the financial manager must use short-term investing and borrowing in order to maintain the desired cash position (liquidity).

21

What Companies Do
Dell's Challenges and Plans

During 2006, Dell Inc. was still the world's largest PC maker, but in early 2007 Hewlett-Packard bumped it aside, stealing sales and market share with clever advertising and customer-pleasing products. Dell's traditional strengths—a low-cost model of selling computer gear over the Internet, a strong U.S. corporate customer base, and an emphasis on desktop computers—were no longer advantages in a world where laptops dominate and sales growth is strongest in U.S. consumer-oriented stores and in developing nations.

To get Dell back in front, a shake-up occurred in the executive suite on January 31, 2007, and Michael Dell announced his return as CEO. With Dell back in charge, many changes began to take place. In April 2007, Dell unveiled two servers designed to reduce power consumption and improve performance for its corporate customers. In May 2007, the firm announced it would expand in Brazil by building a new plant there and revamping the company's Contact Center and Software Development Centers there. Also unveiled in May were three new consumer systems. Later in 2007, Dell announced plans to sell its PCs through retailers, including 3,000 Wal-Mart stores in the United States and Canada. In addition, it planned to start selling its laptops and desktops at Asian retail chains and stores. To reduce costs, Dell planned to reduce its head count by approximately 10% over the 12 months beginning in June 2007.

In spite of the 2007 shake-up, by the end of 2008, Dell's stock price had fallen 58% since late 2007, versus a 28% slide for Hewlett-Packard, and 54% for Apple. At that time Dell was retrenching ahead of what was likely to be a devastating 2009, as corporate customers were expected to forgo tech upgrades and the margins on "commoditized" PCs were expected to be further squeezed.

In addition to some major personnel changes, Dell was abandoning its regional divisions in favor of four global segments: government, big companies, small companies, and consumers. Although the consumer division introduced flashier, smaller notebooks and gaming machines, it appeared that Dell needed to compete with Apple's iPhone. Some speculated that Dell would deploy its $6 billion in net cash to buy Motorola's handset division, which was expected to soon release a competitive phone using Google's Android platform.

The challenges faced by Dell Inc. illustrate the importance of corporate strategic and financial planning. In its efforts to perpetuate its growth, Dell did not accurately anticipate the strength of competition, the growth of third-world markets, and the general shifts in the tastes and preferences of both consumers and business customers. Though better financial plans might not have prevented the developments Dell faced in 2009, they could have helped Dell develop contingencies that would have allowed the company to more quickly adapt to the changing marketplace and so avoid many of its problems.

Sources: Spencer E. Ante, "The Future of Tech: Dell," Business Week (July 2, 2007), p. 64; "Michael Dell Assumes Duties as Chief Executive Officer of Dell Inc.," Dell Inc. press release, http://www.dell.com/content/topics/global.aspx/corp/pressoffice/en/2007/2007_01_31_rr_0 (January 31, 2007); news summaries from "Dell Inc.: Key Developments" and "Dell Inc.: All Recent News," http://news.moneycentral.msn.com/ticker/sigdev.asp?Symbol=DELL (accessed July 6, 2007); Christopher Helman, "Dell's Re-Reboot," Forbes (February 2, 2009), p. 29.

Strategic and Operational Financial Planning

21.1 Overview of the Planning Process

21.2 Planning for Growth

21.3 Planning and Control

In our experience, almost everyone working in a large corporation encounters two areas of corporate finance on a regular basis. The first is justification of spending plans, or capital budgeting. Chapters 7 through 9 covered the elements of capital budgeting analysis that business professionals in any discipline should know. The second part of corporate finance that touches almost all functional groups in a firm is financial planning. Financial planning encompasses a wide array of activities: setting long-run strategic goals, preparing quarterly and annual budgets, and managing day-to-day fluctuations in cash balances.

In this chapter, we discuss various elements of a firm's financial planning processes. The chapter emphasizes both long-term and short-term financial planning. In Chapters 22 and 23 we consider the operational aspects of short-term financial decisions. The three chapters in Part 7 demonstrate how firms' financial plans must balance the interests and objectives of different business units and functional areas. For example, in setting long-run strategic and financial goals, a firm must prioritize its desires to increase sales and market share; to change or maintain its exposure to financial risk; to achieve production efficiencies; to attract and retain capable employees; and to distribute cash to shareholders. In almost every instance, making incremental progress on one of these objectives means an incremental sacrifice on one or more of the other goals.

Financial planning, particularly long-term planning, is more art than science: the connection between most financial planning models and the objective of maximizing shareholder wealth is tenuous at best.[1] At one level, the advice we would give to a firm constructing a long-term plan is trivial: "Do whatever is necessary to invest in all positive-NPV projects." In practice, a variety of factors make following that advice a major challenge. CFOs usually tell us that they have many more acceptable projects than they can possibly undertake. Limits on capital, production capacity, human resources, and many other inputs make the planning process more complex than simply accepting all projects that look promising. We concede that the theoretical underpinnings of planning models are weak, so in this chapter we focus as much as possible on practice. We describe how firms *actually* build long-term and short-term financial plans rather than argue about how they *should* plan.

21.1 OVERVIEW OF THE PLANNING PROCESS

A long-term financial plan begins with strategy. Typically, the senior management team analyzes the markets in which the firm competes. Managers try to identify ways to protect and increase the firm's competitive advantage in those markets. For example, a firm that competes by achieving the lowest production cost in an industry might seek to determine whether it should make additional investments in manufacturing facilities to achieve even greater production efficiencies. A risk to this strategy is that market demand may turn out to be such that the firm's fixed assets are underutilized. This type of firm, therefore, will try to forecast market demand and develop contingency plans for the possibility that the expected demand does not materialize. If a firm's competitive advantage derives from the value of its brand, it might begin by assessing whether new or expanded marketing programs might increase the value of its brand relative to competitors.

Successful Long-Term Planning

Long-term planning requires more than paying close attention to a firm's existing markets. Even more important is the ability to identify and prioritize *new* market opportunities

---

[1]A number of models—such as economic value added (EVA®) and shareholder value added (SVA)—tie financial decisions and plans to shareholder value. Those widely used models, introduced in Chapter 7, are briefly discussed later in this chapter.

WHAT COMPANIES DO GLOBALLY

How Companies Adjust Financial Plans When a Global Recession Hits

Financial managers always strive to develop clear financial and strategic operating plans, but this activity becomes vital during a recession because a company's very existence may hinge on how effectively it can marshal resources, cut costs, and match output to lower demand. This lesson was brought home to managers in 2008, as the global credit crisis cut demand for goods and services and forced the world's major economies to contract. At the same time, trade credit from suppliers and loans from financial institutions became less available and more costly, so firms with small cash reserves were financially constrained in the sense that they had limited resources to fund current operations and new investments.

A major survey of 1,050 chief financial officers in Europe, Asia, and the United States showed how managers were planning to cope with the deepening recession. The survey found that managers in all countries were planning to cut research and development, marketing, and capital expenditures; to draw down their cash holdings; and to cut dividend payments. These actions are dramatic—for example, recall from Chapter 15 that companies are very reluctant to cut dividends. The survey results, presented in Figure 1, also show that managers in Europe and the United States were planning to reduce personnel but that Asian managers expected to keep employment virtually unchanged. Managers in all three regions were planning to cut marketing expenditures significantly, while managers in Europe and the United States were planning much more drastic cuts in tech spending than were Asian managers. Planned cuts in capital expenditures were less severe in all three regions, ranging from a planned reduction of 2.3% in the United States to 4.1% in Asia. European managers were expecting to draw down their firm's cash holdings much more than were U.S. or Asian managers.

The plans described in Figure 1 were revealing but not especially surprising, since rational managers should cut expenses and conserve cash when demand

(continued)

Figure 1. U.S., European, and Asian Pro Forma Plans for 2009

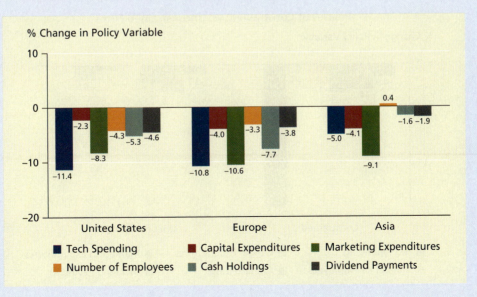

for their output declines. The most striking finding was a dramatic difference in responses planned by financially constrained firms versus unconstrained firms. Responding managers were asked to indicate whether or not their firms were credit constrained, and the results for U.S., European, and Asian managers are summarized (respectively) in Figures 2, 3, and 4. In all three regions, the differential responses

(continued)

Figure 2. Pro Forma 2009 Plans for U.S. Companies

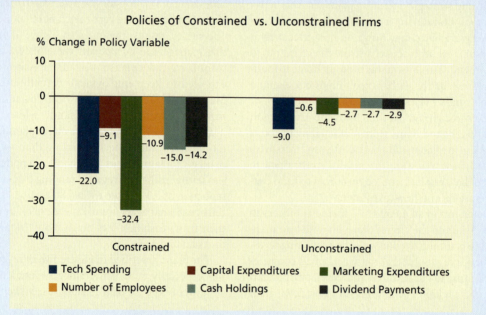

Figure 3. Pro Forma 2009 Plans for European Companies

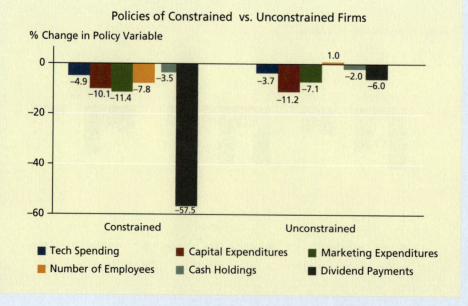

Figure 4. Pro Forma 2009 Plans for Asian Companies

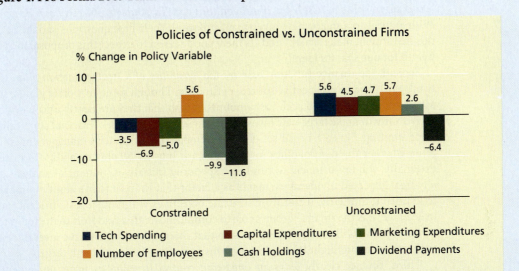

of managers of constrained versus unconstrained companies are dramatic. Managers of financially constrained U.S. companies planned to reduce capital expenditures by 9.1%, staffing by 10.9%, dividend payments by 14.2%, cash holdings by 15.0%, tech spending by 22.0%, and marketing expenditures by almost one-third (32.4%). Managers of unconstrained firms planned dramatically smaller cuts.

Managerial responses for constrained versus unconstrained companies show generally similar—though less dramatic—patterns in Europe as in America, with one major exception. Managers of financially constrained European companies plan to cut dividend payments by a staggering 57.5%, whereas managers of unconstrained firms in Europe plan to reduce cash dividends by only 6.0%. The responses of managers of constrained versus unconstrained firms differ much less dramatically in Asia than in the United States or Europe. However, even managers of constrained Asian firms plan to draw down cash holdings and to cut personnel, tech marketing, and capital expenditures to a greater extent than planned changes in all these variables by managers of unconstrained firms.

Source: Figures 1 and 2 of Murillo Campello, John R. Graham, and Campbell R. Harvey, "The Real Effects of Financial Constraints: Evidence from the Financial Crisis," Duke University working paper (January 2009). Reprinted with permission from the author.

and risks. Successful long-term planning means asking and answering questions such as the following:

1. In what emerging markets might we have a sustainable competitive advantage?
2. How can we leverage our competitive strengths across existing markets in which we currently do not compete?
3. How can we respond to any threats to our current business?
4. In which geographic regions should we produce? Where should we sell?
5. Can we deploy resources more efficiently by exiting certain markets and using those resources elsewhere?

As the firm's senior managers develop answers to these questions, they construct a **strategic plan**. This is a multiyear action plan for the major investments and competitive initiatives that they believe will drive the future success of the enterprise.

The Role of Finance in Long-Term Planning

Finance plays several roles in long-term planning. First, financial managers draw on a broad set of skills to *assess the likelihood that a given strategic objective can be achieved*. With respect to a major new investment proposal, their first questions should be "Does this investment make sense?" and "Is there good reason to expect this proposal to generate wealth for our shareholders?"

Second, the finance function *assesses the feasibility of a strategic action plan*, given a firm's existing and prospective sources of funding. Though some corporate giants, such as Microsoft and Intel, hold such vast amounts of cash that they are nearly unconstrained in their ability to make large new investments, for most companies financial constraints are more limiting. Given a broad set of strategic objectives, financial managers must determine whether the firm's ability to generate cash internally, plus its ability to raise cash externally, will be sufficient to fund new spending initiatives.[2] Financial analysts generally treat expected dividend payments as a factor that limits a firm's ability to make new investments. Similarly, if fulfilling strategic objectives will require a significant increase in leverage, it is the finance group's role to communicate this trade-off to the top management team. We will see in the next section that financial managers have several tools that enable them to highlight the trade-offs firms face when setting growth targets.

Third, finance clearly *plays an important control function as firms implement their strategic plans*. Financial analysts prepare and update cash budgets to make sure that firms do not unknowingly slip into a liquidity crisis. At an even more detailed level, analysts monitor individual items in the cash budget, such as changes in inventories and receivables (our focus in Chapter 22) and changes in payables (our focus in Chapter 23). Here, too, financial managers must evaluate trade-offs.

Fourth, a major contribution of finance to the strategic planning process involves *risk management*. If a firm's strategy calls for making new investments in overseas markets (either producing or selling abroad), then the firm faces a new set of risk exposures. The finance function manages these exposures so that the firm takes those risks that it believes it has a comparative advantage in taking and hedges risks for which it has no advantage. Similarly, more than in any other functional area, the job of finance is to identify problems that could develop in the future if the firm's strategic plans unfold in unexpected ways. Developing "problem scenarios" and options for dealing with them is an important part of finance's risk-management responsibility, which is covered in Chapter 27 (one of the web chapters).

In this chapter, we focus primarily on the second and third roles just described. The next section discusses the financial tools that help managers determine the trade-offs they face when setting future growth objectives.

Concept Review Questions	1. A company decides to compete by making a major investment to modernize its production facilities. Describe two ways in which meeting this objective might force a firm to sacrifice other objectives. 2. Firm A competes in a market in which the demand for its product and its selling price are highly unpredictable. Firm B competes in a market in which these factors are much more stable. Which firm probably creates cash budgets more frequently and monitors them more carefully?

---

[2]Considerations such as these are particularly important when credit market conditions are extremely tight, such as during the credit crisis of 2008 and 2009.

21.2 PLANNING FOR GROWTH

Sustainable Growth

Most firms strive to grow over time, and most firms view rapid growth as preferable to slow growth. Of course, rapid growth does not maximize wealth for all firms at all times, since it's possible for growth to be detrimental to shareholders. Here, though, we put aside the question of whether growth is desirable. Assuming that firms seek growth, they can focus on one or a number of measures of growth.

Popular Measures of Growth Three of the more popular measurements of growth are the accounting return on investment (ROI), economic value added (EVA®), and growth in sales or assets. All of these methods rely on accounting data and are typically measured on an annual basis. We next describe ROI and EVA more fully.

Return on Investment The **accounting return on investment (ROI)** is merely the firm's earnings available for common stockholders divided by its total assets. (In Chapter 2 we referred to this measure by its alternate name, *return on total assets* or ROA.) Return on investment measures the firm's overall effectiveness in using its assets to generate returns to common stockholders.

Firms that use this metric as a measure of growth attempt to maintain ROI above some minimum *hurdle rate* and often raise this standard over time. These firms often set hurdle rates for minimum ROI based on the firm's cost of capital. They assume that if the ROI is greater than the cost of capital (plus perhaps a fudge factor), then shareholder value will be created. The problem with this approach is that it compares the *accounting-based* ROI to an *economic-based* measure of the return demanded by suppliers of capital. Although use of this method has practical appeal, its theoretical roots are shallow at best.

Economic Value Added As noted in Chapter 7, **economic value added (EVA®)** is the difference between net operating profits after taxes (NOPAT) and the cost of funds; when applied correctly, EVA prompts managers to make the same investment decisions that the NPV method directs them to do. The cost of funds is found by multiplying the firm's cost of capital by its investment. Analysts can apply EVA to individual investments or to the entire firm, but its use in financial planning tends to focus on the entire firm or entire divisions.

Firms that employ EVA in the planning process typically build the EVA model into their spreadsheets and evaluate various scenarios by calculating their EVAs. By comparing all positive EVAs, the firm can implement the set of plans with the highest EVA, which should create the most value for shareholders. Although widely examined in the financial literature,[3] EVA's degree of positive correlation with actual share valuations remains unclear. Most agree that the measure is conceptually valid but that it is sometimes difficult to implement because of accrual-based accounting inputs (NOPAT and investment). This disconnect, coupled with its increased computational complexity, tends to result in greater planning focus on growth rates.

Defining Growth Firms frequently set planning goals in terms of *target growth rates*, typically annual growth in sales or assets. For the moment, we set aside the question of whether growth creates or destroys shareholder value. We instead focus on measuring

---

[3]For some critical analyses of EVA, see: Ray D. Dillion and James E. Owers, "EVA® as a Financial Metric: Attributes, Utilization, and Relationship to NPV," *Financial Practice and Education* (Spring/Summer 1997), pp. 32–40; John D. Martin, J. William Petty, and Steven P. Rich, "A Survey of EVA® and Other Residual Income Models of Firm Performance," *Journal of Financial Literature* (Winter 2005), pp. 1–20; and John M. Griffith, "The True Value of EVA®," *Journal of Applied Finance* (Fall/Winter 2004), pp. 25–29.

growth rates in light of their intuitive, computational, and practical appeal. Our goal is to demonstrate a simple model that highlights the trade-offs that firms must weigh when they choose to grow. These trade-offs depend on several factors: how rapidly the firm plans to grow; how profitable its existing business is; how much of its earnings it retains and how much it pays out to shareholders; how efficiently it manages its assets; and how much financial leverage it is willing to bear.

First, let us define what we mean by "growth." A firm's growth can be measured by increases in its market value, its asset base, the number of people it employs, or any number of other metrics. *Our experience suggests that most firms define and measure growth targets in terms of sales*, so we will adopt that convention as well. That is, when we say that a firm plans to grow next year by 10%, we mean that it hopes to achieve a 10% increase in sales.

With sales growth in mind, think about what growth means for a firm in terms of its balance sheet. An increase in sales probably requires additional investments in assets. Certainly, we would anticipate that increased sales volume would require additional investments in current assets, such as inventories and receivables. Over time, increases in sales will also require new investments in fixed assets, such as production capacity and office space. As a shortcut, let us assume that a firm's total asset turnover ratio, the ratio of sales (S) divided by total assets (A), remains constant through time. In other words, any increase in sales will be matched by a comparable percentage increase in assets. Because the balance sheet equation must hold, increases in liabilities and shareholders' equity must equal the increase in assets. So how would we expect increases in liabilities and shareholders' equity come about?

In previous chapters we learned that most companies issue new common shares very infrequently, so we will rule that out as a potential source of new financing. As with inventories and receivables, accounts payable should increase (higher sales volume means higher purchases). We might also expect to see higher accruals and higher short-term liabilities of other types. Similarly, if a firm's business is profitable then its equity account will increase (even if it does not issue any new stock) by the amount of earnings it retains. Figure 21.1 illustrates that the growth in assets must equal growth in these liability and equity accounts over time.

FIGURE 21.1

Sustainable Growth Equality

As a firm grows, it must invest in new assets to support increased sales volume. The investments in new assets must be financed with some combination of increased liabilities and increased equity.

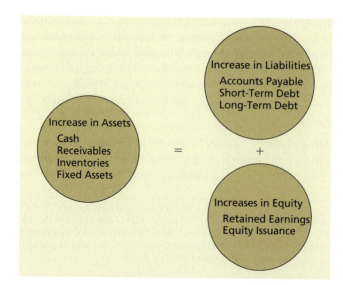

Developing the Sustainable Growth Model   The **sustainable growth model**[4] starts with a balance sheet identity. It then adds a few assumptions and ultimately derives an expression that determines how rapidly a firm can grow while maintaining a balance between its outflows (increases in assets) and inflows (increases in liabilities and equity) of funds. Specifically, the sustainable growth model assumes the following:

1. The firm's only form of equity is common stock (E), and it will not issue new shares of common stock next year.
2. The firm's total asset turnover ratio, S/A, remains constant.
3. The firm pays out a constant fraction, d, of its earnings as dividends.
4. The firm maintains a constant assets-to-equity ratio, A/E.
5. The firm's net profit margin, m, is constant.

   Consider a firm that wants to increase sales next period by g percent. If total assets in the current period equal A and if the asset turnover ratio remains constant, then assets must increase in the next period by gA. This represents a change in the left-hand side of the firm's balance sheet next period—a change that must be balanced by an equal change on the right-hand side.

   Given sales this period of S, a net profit margin (in this case, defined as net income divided by sales) equal to m, and a dividend payout ratio of d, we can determine the firm's retained earnings next period:

$$\text{Retained earnings} = S(m)(1 + g)(1 - d)$$

   The product of S and m yields net profits in the current year. Multiplying this product by $(1 + g)$ results in next year's profits; and multiplying this result by $(1 - d)$ gives next year's retained earnings. This is the amount by which the book equity component of the balance sheet will grow. Next, observe that the ratio of assets to equity (total assets to common stock equity) equals 1 plus the ratio of total liabilities, L, to shareholders' equity:

$$A = E + L;$$

$$\frac{A}{E} = \frac{E + L}{E} = 1 + \frac{L}{E}$$

   Our assuming that the firm maintains a constant assets-to-equity ratio is equivalent to assuming that the ratio of liabilities to equity remains constant. Hence, for each dollar of earnings that the company retains, it can borrow an additional L/E dollars to keep the mix of debt and equity constant. For example, if a firm finances half of its assets with debt and half with equity, then the ratio L/E equals 1.0. If the firm retains \$1 million in earnings in a given year, then it can afford to borrow an additional \$1 million and so maintain the desired mix of debt and equity.

   The increase in liabilities next year simply equals the product of next year's retained earnings and the ratio of liabilities to equity:

$$\text{Increase in liabilities} = S(m)(1 + g)(1 - d)(L/E)$$

   Finally, if the increases in assets must match the increase in the sum of liabilities and equity, then we can write the following equations:

$$\underbrace{gA}_{\text{Assets}} = \underbrace{S(m)(1 + g)(1 - d)}_{\text{Retained earnings}} + \underbrace{S(m)(1 + g)(1 - d)(L/E)}_{\text{Liabilities}}$$

$$= \underbrace{\big[S(m)(1 + g)(1 - d)\big](1 + L/E)}_{\text{Equity + Liabilities}}$$

---

[4]The sustainable growth model was developed by Higgins (1981).

The insight of the sustainable growth model is that there will be some rate of growth, g^*, that keeps the outflows and inflows of funds in balance. This is the *sustainable growth rate*, calculated from the preceding equation and represented as follows:

$$g^* = \frac{m(1-d)\dfrac{A}{E}}{\dfrac{A}{S} - m(1-d)\dfrac{A}{E}}$$

(Eq. 21.1)

Notice how each of the key variables in Equation 21.1 affects the sustainable growth rate:

- *If a firm's profit margin (m) increases then the numerator rises and the denominator falls, so g* increases. Therefore, generating higher profits per dollar of sales provides fuel for a higher growth rate.*
- *Similarly, an increase in the ratio of assets to equity—which can occur only if the firm is willing to accept greater financial leverage—also increases the sustainable growth rate. Firms willing to borrow more can grow more rapidly.*
- *If a firm can increase its total asset turnover ratio (S/A), then the inverse ratio A/S falls and the sustainable growth rate rises. Firms that manage assets more efficiently and generate higher sales volume per dollar of assets can achieve more rapid growth.*
- *Finally, a reduction in dividend payouts (d) also tends to increase g*. When firms retain more earnings, they can finance faster growth.*

EXAMPLE

In 2007, Yahoo! Inc. reported the following financial data:

Sales	$ 6,969.3 million
Net income	$ 660.0 million
Total assets	$12,229.7 million
Total equity	$ 9,532.8 million
Dividends	$0

From these figures, we can determine that Yahoo!'s net profit margin was 9.47%, its assets-to-equity ratio 1.28, its total asset turnover ratio 0.57 (which implies an assets-to-sales ratio of 1.75), and its dividend payout ratio 0.0. Plugging these values into Equation 21.1 yields a sustainable growth rate of a little more than 7.4%. For Yahoo! this meant that the company could increase sales by 7.4% without issuing new shares of common stock and without changing total asset turnover, dividend policy, profit margins, or leverage.

JOB INTERVIEW QUESTION

What are the financial consequences of very rapid growth?

Interpreting the Sustainable Growth Model   It is just as important to understand what the sustainable growth model *does not* say as it is to grasp what it does say. From the previous calculation, should we assume that Yahoo! managers should set as their firm's growth target an increase in sales of 7.4%, equal to the sustainable growth rate? Not at all. Yahoo! managers should decide what rate of growth maximizes shareholder wealth, and then they should use the sustainable growth model as a planning device to help them prepare for the consequences of their growth plans. Suppose that Yahoo! decides it is best for its shareholders if the firm grows at a more rapid rate than 7.4%. In order to do this, Yahoo! must alter one or more of the baseline assumptions of the model. It could seek ways to increase its profit margin, its asset turnover, or its leverage. Yahoo! does not pay dividends, so it cannot use a dividend cut to increase growth.

EXAMPLE

From 2007 to 2008, Yahoo!'s sales actually increased by roughly 3.4%, well less than its 7.4% sustainable growth rate. The sustainable growth model suggests that to finance this relatively slow growth, Yahoo! could experience some combination of lower profit margins, slower asset turnover, and decreased financial leverage. Indeed, by the end of 2008, Yahoo!'s net profit margin decreased by almost 38% (from 9.47% to 5.89%), its total asset turnover decreased by 7% (from 0.57 to 0.53), and its assets-to-equity ratio fell by roughly 5 percentage points (from 1.28 to 1.22).

The sustainable growth model gives managers a shorthand projection that ties together growth objectives and financing needs. It provides hints about the levers that managers must pull in order to achieve growth beyond the sustainable rate. The model also identifies some financial benefits of growing more slowly than the sustainable rate. A firm that expects to grow at a rate less than g^* can plan to reduce leverage or asset turnover, or it can increase dividends. Again, we emphasize that the model does not say anything about how fast the firm *should* grow.

The sustainable growth model also highlights tensions that can develop as firms pursue multiple objectives simultaneously. We have seen that one way to finance faster growth is to increase leverage, so the goals of increasing sales and maintaining the current degree of leverage may be difficult to achieve simultaneously. For the firm to achieve faster sales growth, the marketing group may agree that the firm should offer a wider array of products. Doing so may result in lower inventory turns and reduced total asset turnover. If the firm is unwilling to increase leverage and if expanding the product line means reducing asset turnover, then meeting the sales target will depend on improving profit margins or cutting dividend payout. Compensation issues may further cloud the evaluation of competing objectives: for example, the compensation of the vice president of marketing may be tied to generating additional sales volume, whereas the CFO's compensation may depend on maintaining the firm's credit rating.

The primary advantage of the sustainable growth model is its simple way of linking together various aspects of financial planning. However, the financial planning process generally involves more complex projections. These projections are usually embodied in a set of pro forma income statements and balance sheets that firms use to provide a benchmark against which to judge future performance.

Pro Forma Financial Statements

Periodically, firms produce **pro forma financial statements**, which are forecasts of what they expect their income statement and balance sheet to look like a year or two ahead. Occasionally, firms use these statements to communicate their plans to outside investors (e.g., at the time of an IPO or earnings announcement). Most of the time, however, managers construct pro forma financial statements for purposes of internal planning and control. By making projections of sales volume, profits, fixed asset requirements, working capital needs, and sources of financing, the firm can establish goals to which compensation may be tied. The firm can also predict liquidity requirements with enough lead time to arrange additional financing when needed.

The Sales Forecast   The process of creating pro forma financial statements varies from firm to firm, but there are some common elements. Most pro forma statements begin with a *sales forecast*. The sales forecast may be derived through either a "top-down" or "bottom-up" approach.

Top-down sales forecasts rely heavily on macroeconomic and industry forecasts. Some firms use complex statistical models or subscribe to forecasts produced by econometric modeling firms. In the top-down approach, senior managers establish a firmwide objective for increased sales. Next, individual divisions or business units receive targets that, in aggregate, collectively achieve the firm's overall growth target. Division heads pass down sales targets to product line managers and other smaller-scale units. The sales targets will vary across units within the division, but they must add up to achieve the divisional goal.

Firms that use a **bottom-up sales forecast** begin by assessing demand in the coming year on a customer-by-customer basis. Managers add up these figures across sales territories, product lines, and divisions to arrive at the overall sales forecast for the company. Bottom-up forecasting approaches generally do not rely on mathematical and statistical models.

Not surprisingly, many firms use a blend of these two approaches. For example, a firm may generate a set of assumptions regarding the macroeconomic environment to which all divisions must adhere. It then can generate forecasts from the customer level and aggregate them to an overall forecast for the entire firm that is consistent with the macro assumptions. Some firms produce two sets of forecasts, one that uses a statistical approach and another that relies on customer feedback. Senior managers then compare the two forecasts before setting a final sales objective.

Constructing Pro Forma Statements   Starting with the sales forecast, financial analysts construct pro forma income statements and balance sheets using a mix of facts and assumptions. For example, if a firm's strategic plan calls for major investments in fixed assets, then the analyst will incorporate those projections in the forecast of total fixed asset requirements as well as in the forecast of depreciation expense. In the absence of any specific knowledge of capital spending plans, an analyst may assume that total fixed assets will remain at a fixed percentage relative to sales or total assets; this assumption would, in turn, drive the depreciation line item on the income statement.

Similarly, an analyst can make projections for line items that vary with sales volume. For example, by assuming a constant gross profit margin, the analyst can estimate cost of goods sold directly from the sales forecast. When firms construct pro forma statements by assuming that all items grow in proportion to sales and by extending that percentage to all income statement and balance sheet accounts, they are using the **percentage-of-sales method**. This is a convenient way to construct pro forma statements, and it is usually a good starting point when making financial projections. Such balance sheet items as receivables, inventory, and payables do typically increase with sales, although not always in a linear fashion. For example, a company with $100 billion in sales may not need 100 times as much inventory as a firm with $1 billion in sales.

In constructing pro forma statements, analysts usually leave one line item on the balance sheet as a **plug figure**, which is adjusted after making all other projections. For example, the analyst may make projections for all asset, liability, and equity accounts except for the cash balance; then, when the projections are complete, the analyst simply adjusts the cash account to make the balance sheet balance. Alternatively, the analyst might leave a short-term liability account open to serve as the plug figure. The analyst could, for example, use the line item representing the amount borrowed on a bank line of credit to bring the right-hand and left-hand sides of the balance sheet into equality. If this assumed amount of borrowing on the credit line seems unreasonable, the company may need to recalculate the other assumptions underlying its planning process.

EXAMPLE

Table 21.1 shows the 2010 balance sheet and income statement for Zinsmeister Shoe Corporation. We will use this historical information plus some assumptions to generate pro forma financial statements for 2011. We make the following assumptions:

1. Zinsmeister plans to increase sales by 30% in 2011.
2. The company's gross profit margin will remain at 35%.
3. Operating expenses will equal 10% of sales, as they did in 2010.
4. Zinsmeister pays 10% interest on both its long-term debt and its credit line.
5. Zinsmeister will invest an additional $20 million in fixed assets in 2011, which will increase depreciation expense from $10 million to $15 million in 2011.
6. The company faces a 35% tax rate.
7. The company plans to increase cash holdings by $1 million next year.
8. Accounts receivable equal 8.5% of sales.
9. Inventories equal 10% of sales.
10. Accounts payable equal 12% of cost of goods sold.
11. The company will repay an additional $5 million in long-term debt in 2011.
12. The company will pay out 50% of its net income as a cash dividend.
13. The company plans to use its credit line as the plug figure.

Table 21.1   Financial Statements for 2010 ($ thousand)

ZINSMEISTER SHOE CORPORATION
BALANCE SHEET AS OF DECEMBER 31, 2010

ASSETS		LIABILITIES AND EQUITY	
Cash	$ 10,000	Accounts payable	$ 19,500
Accounts receivable	21,250	Credit line	5,000
Inventory	25,000	Current long-term debt	5,000
Current assets	$ 56,250	Current liabilities	$ 29,500
Gross fixed assets	$ 80,000	Long-term debt	20,000
Less: Accumulated depreciation	20,000	Common stock	20,200
Net fixed assets	$ 60,000	Retained earnings	46,550
Total assets	$116,250	Total liabilities and equity	$116,250

ZINSMEISTER SHOE CORPORATION INCOME
STATEMENT FOR THE YEAR ENDED DECEMBER 31, 2010

Sales	$250,000
Less: Cost of goods sold	162,500
Gross profit	$ 87,500
Less: Operating expenses	25,000
Less: Interest expense	3,000
Less: Depreciation	10,000
Pre-tax income	$ 49,500
Less: Taxes	17,325
Net income	$ 32,175

(continued)

From this set of assumptions and the data in Table 21.1, we can construct the pro forma statements for 2011 shown in Table 21.2. First, Zinsmeister's sales increase to $325 million. Cost of goods sold and operating expenses increase 30% over the prior year (hitting the percentage-of-sales assumptions above). Interest expense is a tricky item. To begin, assume that Zinsmeister will maintain a $5 million balance on its credit line and will retire the current portion of long-term debt. This means that its total outstanding debt during 2011 will be $25 million. At 10%, interest expense should equal $2.5 million. (We shall see that this assumption may change as we continue to build the statements.)

Table 21.2 **Pro Forma Financial Statements for 2011 ($ thousand)**

ZINSMEISTER SHOE CORPORATION
PRO FORMA BALANCE SHEET AS OF DECEMBER 31, 2011

ASSETS		LIABILITIES AND EQUITY	
Cash	$ 11,000	Accounts payable	$ 25,350
Accounts receivable	27,625	Credit line	3,306
Inventory	32,500	Current long-term debt	5,000
Current assets	$ 71,125	Current liabilities	$ 33,656
Gross fixed assets	$100,000	Long-term debt	15,000
Less: Accumulated depreciation	35,000	Common stock	20,200
Net fixed assets	$ 65,000	Retained earnings	67,269
Total assets	$136,125	Total liabilities and equity	$136,125

ZINSMEISTER SHOE CORPORATION PRO FORMA INCOME
STATEMENT FOR THE YEAR ENDED DECEMBER 31, 2011

Sales	$325,000
Less: Cost of goods sold	211,250
Gross profit	$ 113,750
Less: Operating expenses	32,500
Less: Interest expense	2,500
Less: Depreciation	15,000
Pre-tax income	$ 63,750
Less: Taxes	22,312
Net income	$ 41,438
Dividends	$ 20,719

Putting these figures together in the pro forma income statement, we see that Zinsmeister earns a net profit of just over $41 million, half of which it pays out to shareholders.

Next, we build the pro forma balance sheet. Cash is given at $11 million ($10 million in 2010 plus a $1 million increase). Accounts receivable and inventory increase with sales as stated, so current assets increase to $71.125 million. With the additional investment in fixed assets of $20 million (less 2011's depreciation expense), net fixed assets grow to $65 million. Total assets equal $136.125 million.

On the liabilities/equity side, accounts payable increase with sales, the current portion of long-term debt remains at $5 million, total long-term debt declines by $5 million, and common stock does not change. The retained earnings figure for 2011 equals the 2010 figure plus half of 2011's net income. Zinsmeister uses its credit line as the plug figure. That is, given all the assumptions so far, the credit line will decline from $5 million to $3.306 million because otherwise the assets will not balance with the sum of liabilities and equity.

Yet, because the credit line declines, our estimate of interest expense in the income statement is too high. Recall that we predicted interest expense of $2.5 million based on a 10% interest rate on total outstanding debt of $25 million. The pro forma balance sheet now shows long-term and short-term debt of just $23.306 million, so interest expense falls to $2.33 million. A decline in interest expense leads to an increase in profits and retained earnings. Higher retained earnings means that the firm can reduce the line of credit even more, and the cycle repeats. To find the amount of borrowing on the credit line and the corresponding interest expense that reconciles the balance sheet with the income statement, an analyst would need to use an iterative approach, such as Excel's "Solver" function.

The bottom line for Zinsmeister is that its pro forma outlook is quite good. If the company achieves its sales growth target and keeps expenses as well as current asset and current liability accounts in line with historical norms, then it can invest $20 million in new fixed assets while reducing its outstanding interest-bearing debt.

In one sense, this conclusion is hardly surprising. If we take the 2010 data for Zinsmeister and plug it into Equation 21.1, we find that the company's sustainable growth rate is 31.8%. Therefore, the firm's target growth rate of 30% should leave it with some "financial slack." Going through the added steps to build pro forma statements provides the firm with much more information than does the sustainable growth rate alone. With the figures in Tables 21.1 and 21.2 programmed into a spreadsheet, analysts could easily study the effects of changes in any of the assumptions, such as Zinsmeister's ability to pay down debt, or they could identify a need to increase the credit line balance.

A Shorthand Approach for Estimating External Funds Required   We can use the notation defined earlier to present another shorthand approach for estimating the amount of **external funds required (EFR)**—the external financing that a firm will require. Equation 21.2 states that the EFR is a function of three factors. The first term in the equation, $(A/S)\Delta S$, indicates the additional investment in assets required for a firm if it plans to maintain its total asset turnover ratio and increase the dollar volume of sales by ΔS. The second term measures the inflow of funds available to finance this growth. The inflow represented by this second term assumes that the relationship between a firm's sales and its spontaneous liabilities (in this case, accounts payable) remains constant. The third term captures the additional financing inflows that the firm creates internally through retained earnings. Thus, we have

$$EFR = \frac{A}{S}\Delta S - \frac{AP}{S}\Delta S - mS(1+g)(1-d)$$

(Eq. 21.2)

If we apply this shorthand calculation to Zinsmeister, we can determine its external funds required (in thousands of dollars) as

$$EFR = \frac{\$116,250}{\$250,000}(\$75,000) - \frac{\$19,500}{\$250,000}(\$75,000)$$

$$- \left(\frac{\$32,175}{\$250,000}\right)\$250,000(1+0.30)(1-0.50) = \$8,111$$

Under the assumptions of this model, Zinsmeister will require additional external funding of $8.1 million. In the pro forma projections in Table 21.2, Zinsmeister's total external financing actually declines by $6.7 million.[5] Why the discrepancy? Closer examination of the pro forma statements reveals that several of the assumptions in Equation 21.2 do not hold in a more complete analysis. For instance, from 2010 to 2011, Zinsmeister's ratio of assets to sales is not constant, as the equation assumes; instead, the ratio declines from 0.465 to 0.419. Zinsmeister is increasing sales more rapidly than assets, so its funding needs are actually less than Equation 21.2 assumes. When we build projections on an account-by-account basis, the apparent need for external funding predicted by Equation 21.2 turns into a financial surplus, highlighting that Equation 21.2 is just an approximation.

Some Concluding Remarks   This discussion has presented two important points. First, shorthand approaches—such as the sustainable growth model or the equation for determining external funds required—help managers predict whether they should expect a scarcity or a surplus of financial resources, given the firm's growth objectives. Second, firms can construct a more complete picture of their funding requirements by building pro forma income statements and balance sheets. Managers can use any of these models to reduce the risk of experiencing unpleasant financial surprises a year or two ahead.

Besides planning for growth that will occur over a period of years, companies also construct financial plans with shorter time horizons. These plans generally focus on temporary cash surpluses or deficits due to seasonal fluctuations in transactions volume. The next section examines this dimension of financial planning.

Concept Review Questions	3. Describe and evaluate the use of return on investment (ROI) and economic value added (EVA®) as growth targets in financial planning. Why do firms often use annual growth in sales or in assets as a target growth rate? 4. Explain the difference between a firm's *sustainable* growth rate and its *optimal* growth rate. In what circumstances is a firm's optimal growth rate likely to exceed its sustainable growth rate? Under what conditions would you expect the opposite to be true? 5. Current asset accounts, especially cash and inventory, usually increase at a rate that is slightly less than the growth rate in sales. Why? What is the implication of this fact for the sustainable growth model?

21.3 PLANNING AND CONTROL

Short-Term Financing Strategies

In the previous section we observed that most firms establish growth as one of their long-term objectives. It is thus not unusual to observe a distinct upward trend in any company's historical sales volume. However, in a single year many firms experience sharp quarter-to-quarter sales changes due to seasonal factors. Construction-related businesses generate much higher volume in the summer than they do in the winter. In contrast, toy companies experience peak volume in the winter.

---

[5] Table 21.2 includes a $5 million reduction in long-term debt and a $1.7 million reduction in the line of credit. The figures are imprecise because the interest expense and outstanding debt figures in Table 21.2 are not fully reconciled.

Because sales volume tends to fluctuate around a long-term upward trend, we expect to observe the same pattern when we examine a firm's total assets over time. As sales volume grows, so does the firm's need for current and fixed assets. During the year, a firm's investment in current assets will tend to rise and fall with sales. This seasonal pattern creates temporary cash surpluses and deficits that the firm must manage. In the remainder of this section, we use data for Hershey Foods to demonstrate alternative financing strategies.

Hershey Foods' Quarterly Sales and Total Current Assets   Panel A of Figure 21.2 plots quarterly sales figures for Hershey Foods from 1992 through the fourth quarter of 2007. Hershey's fiscal year matches the calendar year, so its quarterly income statements report sales for quarters ending in March, June, September, and December each year. For Hershey, sales usually peak in the third or fourth quarter of each year. Sales troughs

FIGURE 21.2

Quarterly Sales and Total Current Assets for the Hershey Company (1992 through the fourth quarter of 2007)

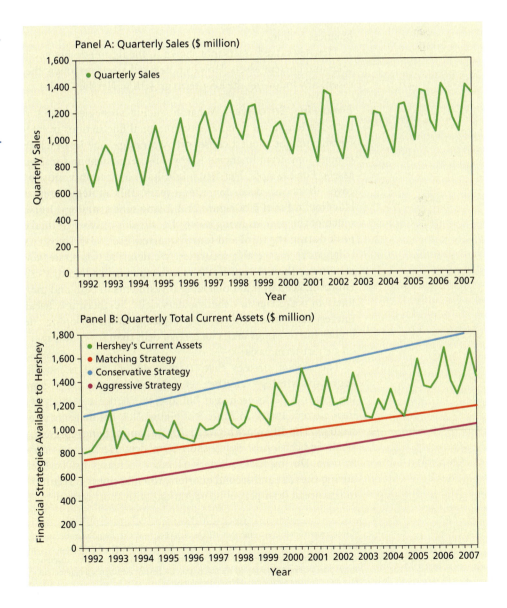

typically occur in the second quarter. Panel A of Figure 21.2 also reveals a gradual upward trend in Hershey sales from 1992 to 1999. That growth trend leveled off from 2000 through 2003 with the U.S. economic recession; it then resumed growth from 2004 through 2006 before leveling off again in 2007.

Panel B of Figure 21.2 plots Hershey's quarterly total current assets over the same period. You can see that the patterns closely match those in Panel A. Hershey's total current assets show the same seasonal pattern (with a lag of one quarter) and the same upward trend of the company's sales. Hershey builds current assets, mostly inventory and receivables, during the third and fourth quarters of each year, and it draws down these items during the first and second quarters.

Because Hershey's total current assets fluctuate around a long-term upward trend, we can think of the company's current assets as containing both a temporary and a permanent component. The temporary component reflects the differences between the seasonal peaks and troughs of Hershey's business. The permanent component represents the sizeable investment in current assets that Hershey maintains even during the quarters when business is slow.

Hershey's fixed assets (not shown in the figure) do not exhibit the seasonal pattern of sales and current assets. However, its fixed assets do follow the long-term upward trend, essentially following the long-term growth in Hershey's sales.

Financing Strategies What financing strategies might Hershey employ to fund both the long-term trend and the seasonal fluctuations in its total current assets? First, Hershey might adopt a **conservative strategy**, one in which the firm makes sure it has enough long-term financing to cover its permanent and seasonal investments in current assets. For example, Hershey might issue long-term bonds to generate enough cash to cover all its cash needs for several years. This strategy is represented graphically by the blue line in Panel B of Figure 21.2. Using such a strategy, Hershey has a cash surplus for much of the year, drawing down that surplus only when total current assets reach their peak during the third and fourth quarters each year. Hershey will invest its excess cash balances in marketable securities. We describe this strategy as conservative because it minimizes the risk that Hershey will experience a liquidity crisis during peak quarters. However, keep in mind that large investments in cash and marketable securities are not likely to make Hershey shareholders rich.[6] Furthermore, because the term structure of interest rates (the _yield curve_) is typically upward sloping, Hershey will generally pay higher interest rates on its long-term debt than it would pay if it were willing to borrow on a short-term basis.

The second strategy that Hershey might adopt is much more aggressive. In this **aggressive strategy**, Hershey relies heavily on short-term borrowing not only to meet the seasonal peaks each year but also to finance a portion of the long-term growth in total current assets. In Panel B of Figure 21.2, the magenta line represents the aggressive strategy. The difference between that line and the one representing Hershey's total current assets indicates how much short-term debt Hershey has outstanding at any moment in time. During peak quarters, Hershey increases its short-term borrowings. But even during the first and second quarters, when business is relatively slow, Hershey continues to finance at least part of its operations with short-term debt. Thus, Hershey uses short-

---

[6]Companies sometimes argue that a large cash reserve is a strategic asset because it enables the firm to make acquisitions quickly as opportunities arise. We agree that, in principle, a cash reserve could have strategic value, but it also enables managers to make value-reducing investments without facing the discipline that comes with raising money in the capital markets. As you will see in Chapter 24, research evidence suggests that managers of acquiring firms generally do not create wealth for their shareholders.

term financing to fund a portion of its long-term, or permanent, growth in total current assets. With this strategy, the company takes advantage of short-term interest rates, which are usually lower than long-term rates. However, if short-term rates rise then Hershey will face increased interest expense. The firm also faces a significant *refinancing risk* in this strategy. That is, if Hershey's financial condition weakens, it may not be able to roll over short-term debt as it had in the past.

A third strategy is the **matching strategy**. Firms that follow the matching strategy finance the permanent component of current assets with long-term financing and finance the temporary or seasonal portion of current assets with short-term debt. The matching strategy is represented by the red solid line in Panel B of Figure 21.2. In the figure, notice that Hershey will increase short-term borrowing during peak periods. It will repay those loans as it reduces its investment in total current assets during slow periods.

The matching strategy is a middle-of-the-road approach. If Hershey finances its short-term assets with short-term debt, then it will have smaller cash surpluses than under the conservative approach but its borrowing costs will be lower, on average. (Because short-term debt is usually lower cost than long-term debt.) Hershey's interest costs will be lower under the matching approach than with the aggressive strategy, but it will face more exposure to refinancing risk and its interest costs will fluctuate more from quarter to quarter.

Regardless of which strategy Hershey decides to pursue, the company will pay careful attention to short-term inflows and outflows of cash. Doing so will allow the company to invest unanticipated cash surpluses and cover unexpected deficits. The primary tool for managing cash flow on a short-term basis is the cash budget.

The Cash Budget

Managers use the tools described in the section on planning for growth (Section 21.2) to make financial projections over horizons of a year or more. However, they also need to monitor the firm's financial performance over shorter horizons. Because it takes cash to operate on a day-to-day basis, firms monitor their cash inflows and outflows very closely, and the primary tool they use for this purpose is the cash budget.

A **cash budget** is a statement of the firm's planned inflows and outflows of cash. Firms use the cash budget to ensure they will have enough cash available to meet short-term financial obligations. Any surplus cash resources can be invested quickly and efficiently. Typically, the cash budget spans a one-year period, with more frequent breakdowns provided as components of the budget. The CFO of Finish Line Inc., a specialty retailer, once described his company to us as a "cash and inventory business." What he meant was that running a successful retail enterprise requires close attention to managing cash flows and inventory. A company like Finish Line needs to know its exact cash position at the end of every business day. For other firms, monitoring cash positions on a weekly or monthly basis may be sufficient. Besides the volume of cash transactions, other factors that determine the frequency with which firms construct cash budgets include the volatility of prices and sales volume and the importance of seasonal fluctuations.

Running out of cash is an ever-present threat at small and medium-size companies. Vulnerable companies include those that are growing rapidly and firms in distress. Even in large corporations, though, astonishing changes in cash reserves can occur over just a few years. For example, in September 2007, General Motors reported cash and marketable security holdings of $30 billion, but over the next six quarters the company's cash reserves fell to $11.6 billion. Although $11.6 billion might seem like plenty of cash, GM reported a net cash outflow of $10.2 billion in just the first quarter of 2009! With the possibility of such dramatic swings in cash holdings, even large firms must monitor their cash positions closely.

As is the case with pro forma financial statements, the key input required to build a cash budget is the firm's sales forecast. On the basis of this forecast, the financial manager estimates the monthly cash inflows from cash sales, receivable collections, and other sources. Naturally, a complete cash budget also contains estimates of cash outflows; some of these vary directly with sales and some do not. Cash outlays include purchases of raw materials, labor and other production expenses, selling expenses, and investments in fixed assets. A cash budget usually presents projected inflows (cash receipts) first. Next come the projected outflows (cash disbursements). Finally, the cash budget shows whether the firm expects a net cash inflow or outflow for the period. Depending on the firm's cash balance at the start of the period, the cash budget will either reveal a need for additional financing or demonstrate that the firm will have surplus cash to invest in short-term marketable securities.

Cash Receipts   **Cash receipts** include all the firm's cash inflows in a given period. The most common components of cash receipts are cash sales, collections of accounts receivable, and other cash receipts. The firm estimates collections of accounts receivable using the past payment patterns of its customers.[7]

EXAMPLE

Consider the cash receipts projections of Farrell Industries, a candy manufacturer, which is developing a cash budget for October, November, and December. Farrell's sales in August and September were $300,000 and $600,000, respectively. The firm forecasts sales of $1,200,000, $900,000, and $600,000 for October, November, and December, respectively. Typically, 10% of Farrell's sales are cash sales and 90% are credit sales; Farrell collects about 60% of each month's sales within the next month but must wait two months to collect the remaining 30% of sales. Bad debts have been negligible. In December, the firm expects to receive a $90,000 dividend from stock it holds in a subsidiary.

Table 21.3 presents the schedule of projected cash receipts. The first row shows total sales in each month. Remember, the figures for October–December are projections. The second row lists cash sales in each month, which (by assumption) equal 10% of total monthly sales. The third and fourth rows report the expected cash inflows from collecting receivables from the previous two months' sales. The next line reports cash receipts not related to sales, and the final line shows total cash receipts each month.

Table 21.3 **Schedule of Projected Cash Receipts for Farrell Industries ($ thousand)**

	AUGUST	SEPTEMBER	OCTOBER	NOVEMBER	DECEMBER
Forecast sales:	300	600	1,200	900	600
Cash sales (10%)	30	60	120	90	60
Collection of accounts receivable					
Previous month (60%)		180	360	720	540
Two months prior (30%)			90	180	360
Other cash receipts					90
Total cash receipts			570	990	1,050

---

[7]We discuss payment patterns more fully in Chapter 22.

For example, consider the month of November. Projected sales are $900,000, which implies that expected cash sales equal $90,000 (0.10 × $900,000). During November, Farrell expects to collect receivables equal to 60% of October's $1,200,000 sales, or $720,000. Farrell also expects to collect the 30% of September $600,000 sales still on the books as receivables, or $180,000. The firm expects no other cash flows in November, so total cash receipts equal $990,000 ($90,000 + $720,000 + $180,000).

Cash Disbursements **Cash disbursements** include all outlays of cash by the firm in the period. The most common cash disbursements are cash purchases, fixed asset outlays, payments of accounts payable, wages, interest payments, taxes, and rent and lease payments. Cash disbursements may also include items such as dividends and share repurchases. It is important to remember that depreciation and other noncash expenses are *not* included in the cash budget. They are not outlays of cash and merely represent a scheduled write-off of an earlier cash outflow. (Depreciation does have a cash outflow effect through its impact on tax payments.)

EXAMPLE

Farrell Industries has gathered the following data needed for the preparation of a cash disbursements schedule for October, November, and December.

> *Purchases:* The firm's purchases average 70% of sales. Of this amount, Farrell pays 20% in cash, 60% in the month following the purchase, and the remaining 20% two months following the purchase. Thus, October purchases are $840,000 (0.70 × $1,200,000). Of that amount, Farrell pays $168,000 (0.20 × $840,000) in cash and then puts $504,000 (0.60 × $840,000) on account to pay in November and $168,000 (0.20 × $840,000) on account to pay in December.
> *Rent payments:* Farrell will pay rent of $20,000 each month.
> *Wages and salaries:* The firm's wages and salaries equal 10% of monthly sales plus $30,000. Thus, October's wages and salaries will be $150,000 [(0.10 × $1,200,000) + $30,000]. The figures for November and December are calculated in the same manner.
> *Tax payments:* Farrell must pay taxes of $75,000 in December.
> *Fixed asset outlays:* The firm will purchase new machinery costing $390,000 and pay for it in November.
> *Interest payments:* An interest payment of $30,000 is due in December.
> *Cash dividend payments:* Farrell will pay cash dividends of $60,000 in October.
> *Principal payments:* A $60,000 principal payment is due in December.

Table 21.4 presents the firm's schedule of projected cash disbursements, based on the preceding data.

Net Cash Flow, Ending Cash, Financing Needs, and Excess Cash We can calculate the firm's net cash flow by subtracting its cash disbursements from its cash receipts for each period. By adding the beginning cash balance to the firm's net cash flow, we determine the ending cash balance for each period.

Table 21.4 Schedule of Projected Cash Disbursements for Farrell Industries ($ thousand)

	AUGUST	SEPTEMBER	OCTOBER	NOVEMBER	DECEMBER
Purchases (70% of sales):	210	420	840	630	420
Cash purchases (20%)	42	84	168	126	84
Payments of accounts payable					
Previous month (60%)		126	252	504	378
Two months prior (20%)			42	84	168
Rent payments			20	20	20
Wages and salaries			150	120	90
Tax payments					75
Fixed asset outlays				390	
Interest payments					30
Cash dividend payments			60		
Principal payments					60
Total cash disbursements			692	1,244	905

Like most companies, Farrell does not want its cash balance to dip below some minimum level at any time. Therefore, by subtracting the desired minimum cash balance from the ending cash balance, we arrive at one of two results: the required total financing or the excess cash balance. If the ending cash balance is less than the desired minimum cash balance, then the firm has a short-term financing need. The firm meets this need with short-term borrowing, typically notes payable. If the ending cash balance exceeds the desired minimum cash balance, then the firm has an excess cash balance that it can invest in short-term marketable securities.

EXAMPLE

Table 21.5 presents the cash budget for Farrell Industries based on the cash receipt and disbursement schedules developed in earlier Examples together with the following additional information: (1) Farrell's cash balance at the end of September is $200,000; (2) notes payable and marketable securities are $0 at the end of September; (3) the desired minimum cash balance is $50,000.

For Farrell to maintain its desired minimum ending cash balance of $50,000, it will have notes payable (short-term borrowing) balances of $226,000 in November and $81,000 in December. In October, the firm will have excess cash of $28,000, which it can invest in marketable securities. The required total financing figures in the cash budget refer to *how much the firm will owe at the end of each month*, but the figures do not represent the monthly change in borrowing. For Farrell, the monthly financial activities are as follows:

October: Farrell invests $28,000 of excess cash.
November: The firm liquidates $28,000 of excess cash and borrows $226,000. Net cash flow of −$254,000 uses all the available cash reserves ($50,000 minimum cash balance from October plus $28,000 excess cash), leaving an ending cash balance of −$176,000. To

Table 21.5   Cash Budget for Farrell Industries ($ thousand)

	OCTOBER	NOVEMBER	DECEMBER
Total cash receipts[a]	570	990	1,050
Less: Total cash disbursements[b]	692	1,244	905
Net cash flow	−122	−254	145
Add: Beginning cash	200	78	−176
Ending cash balance	78	−176	−31
Less: Minimum cash balance	50	50	50
Required total financing (notes payable)[c]		226	81
Excess cash balance (marketable securities)[d]	28		

[a] From Table 21.3.
[b] From Table 21.4.
[c] Values are placed on this line when the ending cash balance is *less than* the desired minimum cash balance. These amounts are typically financed via short-term arrangements and so are represented by notes payable.
[d] Values are placed on this line when the ending cash balance is *greater than* the desired minimum cash balance. These amounts are typically invested in short-term vehicles and so are represented by marketable securities.

cover that negative balance and maintain the desired minimum cash balance, Farrell must borrow $226,000 ($176,000 + $50,000).

December: Net cash flows of $145,000 reduce Farrell's end-of-month borrowing needs to $81,000 (versus November's $226,000). Thus, Farrell repays $145,000 of the amount borrowed.

The cash budget provides the firm with figures indicating whether a cash shortage (financing need) or a cash surplus (short-term investment opportunity) is expected in each of the months covered by the forecast. In our Example, Farrell Industries can expect a cash surplus of $28,000 in October followed by cash shortages of $226,000 in November and $81,000 in December. Each of these values is based on the internal constraint of a minimum cash balance of $50,000.

Because the firm expects to borrow as much as $226,000 during the three-month period, the financial manager should establish a line of credit to ensure the availability of the necessary funds. The maximum amount of borrowing available on the line of credit should actually exceed $226,000 in order to allow for possible forecast errors.

Dealing with Uncertainty in the Cash Budget   Because the cash budget provides only month-end totals, it does not ensure that the firm has sufficient credit to cover intramonth financing needs. For example, what if a firm's disbursements occur before its receipts during a particular month? In that case, its intramonth borrowing needs will exceed the monthly totals shown in its cash budget. To ensure sufficient credit, the firm may forecast its expected receipts and disbursements on a *daily* basis and use these estimates, along with its cash budget, when arranging adequate credit to cover its maximum expected cash deficit.

The monthly cash surpluses and deficits predicted in the budget are affected by virtually all facets of a firm's operations. For example, changes in receivables collection, in payment

JOB INTERVIEW QUESTION

What are the risks of financing a long-term need with a short-term line of credit?

patterns, or in inventory turnover can have a dramatic impact on financing needs. Any action that slows collections from customers or accelerates payments to suppliers will increase monthly financial deficits (or reduce surpluses). In that sense, almost any functional area in the firm can affect, or be affected by, the cash budget.

EXAMPLE

Consider the effect on Farrell Industries of a change in customer payment patterns. In the original Example, Farrell's collection pattern on accounts receivable and its resulting cash position were as follows:

1. 10% cash sales, resulting in a $28,000 cash surplus in October
2. 60% collected one month after sale, resulting in $226,000 total borrowing in November
3. 30% collected two months after sale, resulting in $81,000 total borrowing in December

Now assume that Farrell Industries has a slowdown in its collection pattern, perhaps due to the effects of an economic recession. The new pattern is:

1. 5% cash sales
2. 40% collected one month after sale
3. 50% collected two months after sale
4. 5% uncollectible

This collection pattern changes Farrell's cash receipts to (1) $450,000 in October, (2) $825,000 in November, and (3) $1,080,000 in December. If Farrell's cash disbursements remain unchanged, then the cash budget will show the following:

1. $92,000 total borrowing in October
2. $511,000 total borrowing in November
3. $336,000 total borrowing in December

Comparing these values to the initial collection pattern, it is clear that Farrell's short-term financing requirements have increased.

JOB INTERVIEW QUESTION

What impact would offering customers more generous credit terms have on the cash budget?

The preceding Example demonstrates two important points. First, changes in a firm's collection or payment pattern alter the timing and magnitude of its financing needs. Second, a slowdown (speedup) in collections will increase (reduce) the firm's short-term financing needs. Conversely, with regard to payment patterns, a speedup (slowdown) in payments will likely increase (reduce) the firm's financing needs. The next two chapters focus on the management of current accounts such as inventory, receivables, cash, and payables. By managing these items carefully, firms can increase the profitability of their enterprises and reduce the need for external financing.

In this chapter, we have emphasized the importance of financial planning and have illustrated a few of the most widely used tools of the trade. We end with a word of caution: When firms construct financial plans, they clearly hope to meet the plans' goals. But the value of planning is not just in attaining established goals. Rather, its importance derives from the thinking it forces managers to do—not only about what they expect to occur in the future but also about what they will do if their expectations are not realized.

<table>
<tr>
<td>

Concept Review Questions

</td>
<td>

6. Suppose that a firm follows the *matching* financing strategy. Does this imply that the firm's current assets will equal its current liabilities?
7. Why do firms prepare cash budgets? How do (a) collection patterns and (b) payment patterns affect the cash budget?
8. What can be done to deal with uncertainty in the cash budgeting process? Why might an intramonth view of the firm's cash flows cause a well-prepared cash budget to fail?

</td>
</tr>
</table>

SUMMARY

- Strategic (long-term) financial plans guide firms in preparing operating (short-term) financial plans. For most firms, strategic plans are driven by competitive forces that are not always explicitly financial in nature. However, strategic plans have important financial consequences.

- The finance function partners with other functional units in developing the firm's strategic plan. Once the firm establishes the plan, finance personnel ensure that the plan is feasible given the firm's financial resources. Finance personnel also play a crucial role in monitoring progress and in managing risks associated with financial plans.

- Most firms strive to grow over time. Popular measurements of growth include: (1) achieving accounting return on investment (ROI) in excess of the cost of capital; (2) undertaking only actions that result in positive economic value added (EVA®); and (3) realizing a target growth rate in sales or assets. Target growth rates are widely used because of their intuitive, computational, and practical appeal.

- The sustainable growth model is a tool that is used to determine the feasibility of a target growth rate under certain conditions. When the growth rate that maximizes shareholder value does not match the sustainable rate, the firm must make adjustments to the model's assumptions—such as altering leverage or dividend policy—to achieve the desired growth rate.

- Pro forma financial statements are projected, or forecast, financial statements typically based on historical financial data about the firm. Preparation of these statements begins with a sales forecast that can be developed by using a top-down or a bottom-up approach or a blend of these two approaches. The key inputs to pro forma statements are a mix of facts and assumptions.

- Firms can prepare pro forma financial statements using the percentage-of-sales method, which assumes that all items grow in proportion to sales. Yet certain balance sheet accounts do not typically increase in a linear fashion. As a result, analysts typically use one line item on the balance sheet as a plug figure that can be used to make sure the pro forma balance sheet balances.

- Analysts also can estimate directly the amount of external financing required to fund a firm's anticipated growth by using the equation for external funds required (EFR). This approach, like the preparation of pro forma statements, helps managers determine if they can expect a scarcity or surplus of financial resources, given the firm's growth objectives.

- During the year, a firm's investment in current assets tends to rise and fall with sales. This seasonal pattern creates temporary cash surpluses and deficits that the firm must manage. Three basic financing strategies—conservative, aggressive, and matching—can be used to fund both the long-term trend and seasonal fluctuations in a business. The conservative strategy is the least risky and least profitable, the aggressive strategy is the most risky and most profitable, and the matching strategy falls between the other two in terms of risk and profits.

- A cash budget forecasts the short-term cash inflows and outflows of a firm. For a firm with significant seasonal variations, the financial manager typically prepares the cash budget month by month. This allows the firm to determine peak short-term financing needs and peak short-term investment opportunities, typically over an annual or quarterly period.

- The financial manager must also consider intramonth cash flows to ensure that sufficient credit is available. Changes in collection and payment periods can significantly affect the cash budget's projections.

KEY TERMS

accounting return on investment (ROI)

aggressive strategy

bottom-up sales forecast

cash budget

cash disbursements

cash receipts

conservative strategy

economic value added (EVA®)

external funds required (EFR)

matching strategy

percentage-of-sales method

plug figure

pro forma financial statements

return on investment (ROI)

strategic plan

sustainable growth model

top-down sales forecast

QUESTIONS

21-1. How do you convert return on investment (ROI) into return on equity (ROE)? (*Hint:* See Chapter 2.)

21-2. Is the assets-to-equity ratio equal to the equity multiplier? (*Hint:* See Chapter 2.)

21-3. In what manner does increasing *A* in Equation 21.1 affect the sustainable growth rate? What effect does decreasing *A* have on the sustainable growth rate?

21-4. There is an expression that it is best to operate a business using "other people's money." Given that other people's money is reflected in accounts payable, how do accounts payable affect the external funds required (EFR)? Is the expression correct based on EFR?

21-5. What is the financial planning process? What is a strategic plan? Describe the roles that financial managers play with regard to strategic planning.

21-6. Briefly describe the following popular growth targets: (1) accounting return on investment (ROI), (2) economic value added (EVA®), and (3) target growth rate of sales or assets. Which is most widely used, and why?

21-7. In the sustainable growth model, what does the word "sustainable" mean? In what ways can the sustainable growth model highlight conflicts between a firm's competing objectives?

21-8. With reference to Equation 21.1, explain how each of the variables influences the firm's sustainable growth rate. If high leverage allows a firm to increase its sustainable growth rate, does that mean higher leverage is necessarily good for the firm?

21-9. A firm chooses to grow at a rate above its sustainable rate. What changes might we expect to see on the firm's financial statements in the next year? What changes would result from growing at a rate below the firm's sustainable rate?

21-10. What is the logic of the percentage-of-sales method for calculating pro forma financial statements? On a year-to-year basis, which balance sheet and income statement items do you think will fluctuate most closely with sales, and which items are not likely to vary as directly with sales volume?

21-11. Describe the differences between the *top-down* and the *bottom-up* sales forecast methods. Describe advantages and disadvantages of each. Do you think one approach is likely to be more accurate than the other?

21-12. Why does it make sense to let the firm's cash balance or a short-term liability account serve as the plug figure in pro forma projections? Why not use gross fixed assets as the plug figure?

21-13. Why might pro forma statements and the equation for external funds required yield different projections for a firm's financing needs?

21-14. What is the difference between the conservative strategy, the aggressive strategy, and the matching strategy for funding the long-term trend and seasonal fluctuations in a firm's total current assets? Which strategy is most risky? Which is least profitable?

21-15. How is a cash budget different from a set of pro forma financial statements? Why do you think that firms typically create cash budgets at higher frequencies than they create pro forma financial statements?

21-16. Explain how slower inventory turnovers, slower receivables collections, or faster payments to suppliers would influence the numbers produced by a cash budget.

PROBLEMS

Planning for Growth

21-1. Net operating profit after taxes (NOPAT) is equal to (Revenues − Cost of goods sold − Operating expenses − Depreciation) × (1 − Tax rate) and is a component of economic value added (EVA®), which equals NOPAT less the cost of funds. A project's revenues, operating expenses, cost of goods sold, depreciation, and tax rate are (respectively) $1 million, $150,000, $550,000, $100,000, and 43%. What is the NOPAT for the project? The firm's cost of capital is 16% and the investment for the project is $715,000. What is the EVA for the project for this period? If depreciation can be accelerated to be $150,000, how much will the EVA change? If depreciation remains at $100,000 and operating expenses are reduced to $125,000, how much will the EVA change?

21-2. The firm R.H. Nicholson has a return on equity of 25% based on sales of $6 million, with a $6 million asset base. The company has a debt-to-equity ratio of 1.0 and never pays dividends. What is R.H. Nicholson's sustainable growth rate? The firm is willing to sacrifice some sustainable growth by paying a dividend, but the firm will not allow for a sustainable growth rate below 25%. What is the largest dividend (based on the dividend payout ratio) that the firm can pay? What is the equivalent retention ratio, assuming the dividend is paid?

21-3. Firm PQZ has a net profit margin of 10%, a total asset turnover of 1.5, and an equity multiplier of 1.0 (i.e., there is no debt). Assuming PQZ pays out 35% of its net income as dividends, what is the firm's sustainable growth based on Equation 21.1? Assuming a sales level of $4.4 million (up 10% from the previous year while maintaining the same total asset turnover) and a cost of funds of $375,000, what is the economic value added? Assuming there are no accounts payable because the firm is all equity, what external funds required (EFR) was necessary for the 10% increase in sales?

21-4. Firm QTP currently has sales of $10 million with an asset base of $25 million. QTP has no accounts payable, a net profit margin of 10%, and a dividend payout ratio of 60%. If QTP decides to increase sales by 20%, then what is the effect on external funds required? Assuming that QTP now has accounts payable of $0.5 million, what is the EFR? In addition to having these accounts payable, QTP decides to cut its dividend, making the dividend payout ratio equal to 45%. What then is the associated EFR? Based on the signaling model of dividends (see Chapter 15), should QTP increase or decrease the dividend to indicate its new plan of sales expansion?

21-5. Firm MBK is projecting next year's sales revenue to be $4.424 million (a 12% increase). Current assets, fixed assets, and current liabilities are expected to remain in their current proportions to sales: respectively 20%, 125%, and 16%. The accumulated depreciation is currently $2,037,500 and is expected to be $2.53 million next year. What is MBK's current and expected total asset turnover? What is MBK's current and expected current ratio? Will the future current ratio change if the sales increase by only 10%? (Demonstrate your answer numerically.) Does the change in the total asset turnover ratio violate an assumption within the sustainable growth rate model?

21-6. Eisner Amusement Parks reported the following data in its most recent annual report:

Sales	$42.5 million
Net income	$ 3.8 million
Dividends	$ 1.1 million
Assets	$50.0 million

Eisner is financed 100% with equity. What is the company's sustainable growth rate? Suppose that Eisner issued bonds to the public and used the proceeds to repurchase half of its outstanding shares. This recapitalization would create additional interest expenses of $2 million. Assuming that the company faces a 35% tax rate, what impact would this restructuring have on its sustainable growth rate?

21-7. Use these key financial data from the most recent annual report of Rancho, Inc., to answer the questions that follow.

Sales	$12.7 million
Net income	$ 1.3 million
Total assets	$ 7.6 million
Total equity	$ 5.2 million
Dividends	$ 0.3 million

The firm's CFO wishes to use these data to estimate the firm's sustainable growth rate.

  a. Use the data provided to calculate Rancho's net profit margin, assets-to-equity ratio, total asset turnover ratio, and dividend payout ratio.
  b. Use your findings in part (a) to find Rancho's sustainable growth rate.
  c. Interpret the sustainable growth rate calculated in part (b). Does this rate of growth ensure shareholder wealth maximization? Explain.
  d. If the firm's board feels that shareholders are best served if the firm grows more slowly, then what alterations in each of the baseline assumptions would be necessary to achieve this objective?

21-8. Review the following abbreviated financial statements for the last two years for Norne Energy Corp. All values are expressed in billions of British pounds.

Norne Energy Corp.
Balance Sheet (£ billion)

	2010	2009
Current assets	2.7	2.5
Fixed assets	3.5	3.4
Total assets	6.2	5.9
Current liabilities	1.9	1.8
Long-term debt	2.1	2.2
Shareholders' equity	2.2	1.9
Total liabilities and equity	6.2	5.9

Norne Energy Corp.
Income Sheet (£ billion)

	2010	2009
Sales	7.5	7.1
Net income	0.5	0.4
Dividends	0.2	0.1

  a. What was Norne's sustainable growth rate at the end of 2009?
  b. How rapidly did Norne actually grow in 2010?
  c. What changes in Norne's financial condition from 2009 to 2010 can you trace to the difference between the actual and sustainable growth rates?

21-9. The 2011 sales forecast for Clearwater Development Co. is $150 million. Interest expense will not change in the coming year. Use Clearwater's 2010 income statement, presented below, to answer the questions that follow.

Clearwater Development Co.
Income Statement ($ thousand)

Sales	$125,000
Less: Cost of goods sold	80,000
Gross profit	$ 45,000
Less: Operating expenses	30,000
Less: Interest	10,000
Pre-tax profit	$ 5,000
Less: Taxes (35%)	1,750
Net income	$ 3,250

a. Use the percentage-of-sales method to construct a pro forma income statement for 2011.

b. You learn that 25% of the cost of goods sold and operating expense figures for 2010 are fixed costs that will not change in 2011. Reconstruct the pro forma income statement.

c. Compare and contrast the statement prepared in parts (a) and (b). Which statement will likely provide the better estimate of 2011 income? Explain.

Smart
Solutions

See the problem and solution explained step-by-step at **SMARTFinance**

21-10. Hill Propane Distributors wants to construct a pro forma balance sheet for 2011. Build the statement using the following data and assumptions:

1. Projected sales for 2011 are $35 million.

2. Hill's gross profit margin is 35%.

3. Operating expenses average 10% of sales.

4. Depreciation expense last year was $5 million.

5. Hill faces a tax rate of 35%.

6. Hill distributes 20% of its net income to shareholders as a dividend.

7. Hill wants to maintain a minimum cash balance of $3 million.

8. Accounts receivable equal 8.5% of sales.

9. Inventory averages 10% of the cost of goods sold.

10. Last year's balance sheet lists net fixed assets of $30 million. All of these assets are depreciated on a straight-line basis, and none of them will be fully depreciated for at least three years.

11. Hill plans to invest an additional $1 million in fixed assets that it will depreciate over a 5-year life on a straight-line basis.

12. In 2010, Hill reported common stock and retained earnings of $20 million.

13. Accounts payable average 9% of sales.

Will Hill Propane's cash balance at the end of 2011 exceed its minimum requirement of $3 million?

21-11. Planet Inc. wishes to construct a pro forma income statement and a pro forma balance sheet for the coming year using the following data.

1. Sales are forecast to grow by 5% from $809.5 million last year to $850 million in the coming year.

2. The cost of goods sold is expected to represent 72% of forecast sales.

3. Operating expenses are expected to represent 11% of forecast sales.

4. Depreciation expense on the firm's existing net fixed assets, which currently total $275 million, is expected to remain at $55 million per year for at least four more years.

5. Planet's marginal tax rate is expected to remain at 40%.

6. Planet is expected to continue its policy of paying out 10% of net income as dividends.

7. Planet's net profit margin last year was 5.2%.

8. Planet wishes to maintain a minimum cash balance of $8 million in the coming year.

9. The firm's accounts receivable are expected to equal about 15% of sales.

10. The firm's inventory has historically averaged about 12% of the cost of goods sold.

11. Planet is planning to invest an additional $35 million in fixed assets that will be depreciated on a straight-line basis over a 7-year life.

12. The firm's accounts payable, which totaled $63.5 million at the end of last year, are expected to equal about 11% of cost of goods sold in the coming year.

13. Planet plans to maintain its notes payable of $42 million; this requires annual interest of 5%, which totals $2.1 million.

14. The firm has $80 million of long-term debt that matures as a lump sum, due and payable in full, in five years. Annual interest of $4.8 million must be paid on this debt.

15. Planet has no preferred stock outstanding, and its retained earnings and common stock currently total $250 million.

16. Planet's total assets at the end of last year were $435 million.

a. Use the preceding data to prepare Planet's pro forma income statement for the coming year.

b. Use the data provided and your findings in part (a) to prepare Planet's pro forma balance sheet for the coming year. Use notes payable as the balancing figure and ignore any change in annual interest expense caused by the change in notes payable.

c. Explain the amount of notes payable used as the balancing figure in part (b). Indicate the resulting amount of the plug figure needed to create the balancing figure. Will Planet be able to fund its planned growth internally? Explain.

d. Use Equation 21.2 along with Planet's relevant data to determine its external funds required. Compare this value with the plug figure you found in part (c), and explain in general terms why differences between these two values might result.

21-12. Review the following 2010 balance sheet and income statement for T. F. Baker Cosmetics Inc. The numerical values are in thousands of dollars.

T. F. Baker Cosmetics Inc. Balance Sheet

Cash	$ 5,000	Accounts payable	$10,000
Accounts receivable	12,500	Short-term bank loan	15,000
Inventory	10,000	Long-term debt	10,000
Current assets	$27,500	Common stock	15,000
Gross fixed assets	$65,000	Retained earnings	12,500
Less: Accumulated depreciation	30,000	Total liabilities and equity	$62,500
Net fixed assets	$35,000		
Total assets	$62,500		

T. F. Baker Cosmetics Inc.
Income Statement

Sales	$150,000
Less: Cost of goods sold	120,000
Gross profit	$ 30,000
Less: Operating expenses	15,000
Less: Depreciation	5,000
Less: Interest expense	2,000
Pre-tax profit	$ 8,000
Less: Taxes (35%)	2,800
Net income	$ 5,200

At a recent board meeting, the firm set the following objectives for 2011:

1. The firm would increase liquidity. For competitive reasons, the firm expects accounts receivable and inventory balances to continue their historical relationships with sales and cost of goods sold, respectively, but the board felt that the company should double its cash holdings.

2. The firm would accelerate payments to suppliers. This would have two effects: First, by paying more rapidly, the firm would be able to take advantage of early payment discounts, which would increase its gross margin from 20% to 22%. Second, by paying earlier, the firm's accounts payable balance, which historically averaged about 8.3% of the cost of goods sold, would decline to 4% of the cost of goods sold.

3. The firm would expand its warehouse, which would require an investment in fixed assets of $10 million. This would increase projected depreciation expense from $5 million in 2007 to $7 million in 2011.

4. The firm would issue no new common stock during the year, and it would initiate a dividend. Dividend payments in 2011 would total $1.2 million.

5. Operating expenses would remain at 10% of sales.

6. The firm did not expect to retire any long-term debt, and it was willing to borrow up to the limit of its current bank credit line of $20 million. The interest rate on its outstanding debts would average 8%.

7. The firm set a sales target for 2011 of $200 million.

Develop a set of pro forma financial statements to determine whether or not T. F. Baker Cosmetics can achieve all these goals simultaneously.

Planning and Control

Smart Solutions
See the problem and solution explained step-by-step at SMARTFinance

21-13. A firm has actual sales of $50,000 in January and $70,000 in February. It expects sales of $90,000 in March and $110,000 in both April and May. Assuming that sales are the only source of cash inflow and that 60% of these are for cash and the rest are collected evenly over the following two months, what are the firm's expected cash receipts for March, April, and May?

21-14. Bachrach Fertilizer Corp. had sales of $2 million in March and $2.2 million in April. Expected sales for the next three months are $2.4 million, $2.5 million, and $2.7 million. Bachrach has a cash balance of $200,000 on May 1 and does not want its balance to dip below that level. Prepare a cash budget for May, June, and July given the following information:

1. Of total sales, 30% are for cash, 50% are collected in the month after the sale, and 20% are collected two months after the sale.
2. Bachrach has cash receipts from other sources of $100,000 per month.
3. The firm expects to purchase items for $2 million in each of the next three months. All purchases are paid for in cash.
4. Bachrach has fixed cash expenses of $150,000 per month and variable cash expenses equal to 5% of the previous month's sales.
5. Bachrach will pay a cash dividend of $300,000 in June.
6. The company must make a $250,000 loan payment in June.
7. Bachrach plans to acquire fixed assets worth $500,000 in July.
8. Bachrach must make a tax payment of $225,000 in June.

21-15. Sportif, Inc.'s financial analyst has compiled sales and total cash disbursement estimates for the coming months of January through May. Historically, 60% of sales are for cash with the remaining 40% collected in the following month. The ending cash balance in January is $1,000. The firm's minimum cash balance is $1,000. The analyst plans to use these data to prepare a cash budget for the months of February through May.

Sportif, Inc.

Month	Sales	Total Cash Disbursements
January	$ 5,000	$6,000
February	6,000	8,000
March	10,000	8,000
April	10,000	6,000
May	10,000	5,000

a. Use the data provided to prepare Sportif's cash budget for the four months February through May.
b. How much total financing will Sportif need to meet its financial requirements for the period February through May?
c. If Sportif used the information presented here to prepare a pro forma balance sheet dated the end of May, how much would the firm have in accounts receivable?

21-16. The actual sales and purchases for White Inc. for September and October 2010, along with its forecast sales and purchases for the period November 2010 through April 2011, follow.

Year	Month	Sales	Purchases
2010	September	$310,000	$220,000
2010	October	350,000	250,000
2010	November	270,000	240,000
2010	December	260,000	200,000
2011	January	240,000	180,000
2011	February	280,000	210,000
2011	March	300,000	200,000
2011	April	350,000	190,000

The firm makes 30% of all sales for cash and collects 35% of its sales in each of the two months following the sale. Other cash inflows are expected to be $22,000 in September and April, $25,000 in January and March, and $37,000 in February. The firm pays cash for 20% of its purchases. It pays for 40% of its purchases in the following month and for 40% of its purchases two months later.

Wages and salaries amount to 15% of the preceding month's sales. The firm must pay lease expenses of $30,000 per month. Interest payments of $20,000 are due in January and April. A principal payment of $50,000 is also due in April. The firm expects to pay a cash dividend of $30,000 in January and April. Taxes of $120,000 are due in April. The firm also intends to make a $55,000 cash purchase of fixed assets in December.

a. Assuming that the firm has a cash balance of $42,000 at the beginning of November and that its desired minimum cash balance is $25,000, prepare a cash budget for November through April.

b. If the firm is requesting a line of credit, how large should the line be? Explain your answer.

21-17. Berlin Inc. expects sales of $300,000 during each of the next three months. It will make monthly purchases of $180,000 during this time. Wages and salaries are $30,000 per month plus 5% of monthly sales. The firm expects to make a $60,000 tax payment in the first month and a $45,000 purchase of fixed assets in the second month. It expects to receive $24,000 in cash from the sale of an asset in the third month. All sales and purchases are for cash. Beginning cash and the minimum cash balance equal zero.

a. Construct a cash budget for the next three months.

b. Berlin is unsure of the level of sales, but all other figures are certain. If the most pessimistic sales figure is $240,000 per month and the most optimistic is $360,000 per month, what are the monthly minimum and maximum ending cash balances that the firm can expect for each month?

c. Discuss how the financial manager can use the data in parts (a) and (b).

THOMSON ONE Business School Edition

21-18. Using Equation 21.2, calculate the estimated amount of external funds required for Avon Products (ticker symbol, AVP) for each of the last four years. Do the estimates of the external funds required equal the actual external funds raised by Avon?

21-19. Calculate the sustainable growth rate for Estée Lauder Companies (ticker symbol, EL) for each of the last four years. Compare the sustainable growth rates to the actual growth rates. How and why do they differ?

21-20. Using the percentage of sales method, construct a pro forma balance sheet and income statement for Estée Lauder Companies and Avon Products. Assume that sales will increase by the sustainable growth rate of the previous fiscal year. What plug figure is needed to make the forecasted balance sheet balance?

MINI-CASE: PRO FORMA STATEMENTS AND THE CASH BUDGET

Gobusi Technologies has the following financial statements dated December 31, 2010.

Gobusi Technologies
Balance Sheet as of December 31, 2010

Assets		Liabilities and Equity	
Current assets		Current liabilities	
Cash	$ 50,000	Accounts payable	$ 62,000
Accounts receivable	75,000	Credit line	10,000
Inventory	89,000	Current long-term debt	5,000
Total current assets	$ 214,000	Total current liabilities	$ 77,000
Gross fixed assets	$1,500,000	Long-term debt	185,000
Less: Accumulated depreciation	400,000	Common stock	700,000
Net fixed assets	$1,100,000	Retained earnings	352,000
Total assets	$1,314,000	Total liabilities and equity	$1,314,000

Gobusi Technologies
Income Statement
For the year ending December 31, 2010

Sales	$5,867,000
Less: Cost of goods sold	2,726,000
Gross profit	$3,141,000
Less: Operating expenses	2,617,000
Less: Interest expense	17,575
Less: Depreciation	100,000
Pre-tax income	$ 406,425
Less: Taxes	138,185
Net income[a]	$ 268,240

[a] Gobusi has a dividend payout ratio of 25%.

Gobusi has the following expectations for 2011:

■ *The expected rate of growth in sales is 20%.*
■ *Gobusi expects to lower its cost of goods sold to 42% of sales.*
■ *Operating expenses will remain the same proportion of sales as they were in 2010.*
■ *Gobusi's rate of interest on both short-term and long-term debt is 8%. The firm will retire the current portion of its long-term debt and will keep its credit line at the bank.*
■ *The firm is operating at full capacity with respect to its fixed assets. Therefore, any increase in sales will result in a corresponding increase in fixed assets. Depreciation will be 10% of this increase plus an additional $100,000 depreciation on its existing fixed assets.*
■ *Gobusi is in a 34% tax bracket and expects to maintain its 25% dividend payout ratio.*

■ *The firm expects all other current assets and current liabilities (except the firm's credit line) to remain at 2010 proportions relative to sales. Use the firm's credit line as the plug figure. If there are excess funds, assume that the firm will use them to retire long-term debt.*

1. Determine the firm's sustainable growth rate.
2. Prepare a pro forma balance sheet and income statement for 2011, determine the firm's external financing required, and discuss problems with this method.
3. Prepare a schedule of projected cash receipts, a schedule of projected cash disbursements, and an overall cash budget for the firm for the first quarter of 2011 based upon the following information:

   ■ *The firm's sales during November and December of 2010 were $489,230 and $562,800, respectively. Sales during the first four months of 2011 are expected to be:*

January	*$515,580*
February	*$497,410*
March	*$512,890*
April	*$526,700*

   ■ *Historically, 85% of the firm's sales are on credit, with about 50% of each month's sales collected one month after the sale and the remainder collected two months after the sale.*
   ■ *Inventory purchases are typically 25% of sales and are generally paid 20% with cash; the remainder become accounts payable. Of the accounts payable, 60% are paid one month after the purchase and the rest is paid two months after the purchase. Inventory is typically purchased one month prior to sale.*
   ■ *Rent payments of $120,000 are due each month.*
   ■ *Wages are 10% of sales and are paid in the month incurred, while salaries total $98,000 per month.*
   ■ *Factory overhead is $15,000 a month.*
   ■ *Taxes of $64,000 must be paid in March.*
   ■ *The firm plans a fixed asset expenditure of $300,000 in February.*
   ■ *Interest payments of $8,000 are due in March.*
   ■ *Cash dividend payments of $32,894 are due in March.*
   ■ *As of December 31, 2010, the firm has $50,000 in cash. This is also the firm's target minimum monthly ending cash balance.*

4. Based on the cash budget in question 3, how much short-term financing does Gobusi need during the first quarter of 2011?

22

Cash Conversion, Inventory, and Receivables Management*

What Companies Do

Apple's Superior Cash Conversion Creates Huge Cash Balances

For years Apple has been a leader in cash conversion—a measure of how quickly raw materials can get through the supply chain and be converted into cash. Some refer to this metric as "cash-to-cash" and others call it the "cash conversion cycle." Regardless, shorter cash conversion cycles are preferred because they reflect more efficient cash management.

In its *2008 Supply Chain Top 25*, AMR Research ranked Apple #1, followed by Nokia, Dell, P&G, and IBM. Apple's −62.33-day cash conversion cycle effectively indicates that, through accounts payable, Apple's suppliers provided it with slightly more than two months of financing beyond what was necessary to support its accounts receivable and inventory investments. Of course, minimizing the firm's investment in current assets—particularly accounts receivable and inventory—should allow the firm to free up cash, which can then be deployed to more productive uses. But what if the cash simply accumulates rather than being reinvested or distributed to investors? In Apple's case, the firm's success in preserving cash creates concern among some investors. In early January of 2009, Apple's cash totaled $28.1 billion, among the largest cash hoards in the technology sector.

Many analysts and investors cite CEO Steve Jobs's legendary insecurity over Apple's competitive position as the reason for holding the large cash position. Some believe that Apple should reduce its cash stockpile by issuing a dividend, engaging in a stock buyback, or undertaking significant M&A activity, but most are willing to accept the large cash balance in view of the need to weather the ongoing recession.

Sources: AMR Research, "Supply Chain Top 25: Cash to Cash," http://blogs.amrresearch.com/supplychain/apple (accessed February 11, 2009); Ben Charny, "Investors Look Beyond Apple Disclosure Controversy," Dow Jones Newswires, online.wsj.com/article/BT-CO-20090624-716129.html (posted June 24, 2009; accessed August 13, 2009); Megan Johnston, "Apple's Cash: Its One Sour Cider," Financial Week, http://www.financialweek.com/apps/pbcs.dll/article?AID=/20080225/REG/259088503/1022/opinion (posted February 25, 2008; accessed February 11, 2009).

---

*Professor Dubos J. Masson, CCM, CertCM, of Indiana University, assisted in preparing a large part of this chapter. The authors very much appreciate D.J.'s important contribution.

Smart Practices Video

Vern LoForti, Chief Financial Officer, Overland Storage Inc.

"Working capital management is extremely important because it results in good cash flow."

See the entire interview at **SMARTFinance**

In order to grow and prosper, a firm must manage both its operating assets and its short-term financing. **Operating assets** include cash, marketable securities, accounts receivable, and inventories, all of which the firm needs to support its day-to-day operations. The firm's **short-term financing** consists of accounts payable, commercial paper, and various types of short-term loans used to finance seasonal fluctuations. The firm should efficiently manage and control investments in operating assets because they consume the firm's scarce cash resources. As we saw in Chapter 21, the firm uses short-term financing to fund seasonal fluctuations and to provide adequate liquidity for achieving its growth objectives and meeting its financial obligations. The overall objective is to manage current assets and liabilities as efficiently as possible, minimizing unnecessary operating assets and maximizing the use of inexpensive short-term financing.

What evidence can we cite suggesting that firms spend time and effort trying to economize on their investments in current (operating) assets while taking advantage of relatively inexpensive current liabilities (short-term financing)? Table 22.1 reports the median investment in current assets and current liabilities for a sample of 200 large U.S. companies in existence from 1981 to 2007. In 1981, current assets accounted for 36.6% of total assets for the median firm in this group. By 2007, that figure had dropped to just 26.5%. Over the same period, the importance of current liabilities in financing these firms decreased much less dramatically from 23.1% in 1981 to 22.8% in 2007.

Table 22.1	**Current Assets and Current Liabilities as a Percentage of Total Assets for U.S. Companies, 1981 and 2007**		
YEAR	**CURRENT ASSETS**	**CURRENT LIABILITIES**	**CURRENT RATIO**
For a Sample of 200 Large Firms (median)			
1981	36.6%	23.1%	
2007	26.5%	22.8%	
For the Aggregate Manufacturing Corporate Sector			
1981	32.2%	22.6%	1.42
2007	25.5%	19.7%	1.29

Source: Compustat and authors' calculations.

Smart Practices Video

Jackie Sturm, Director of Finance for Technology and Manufacturing, Intel Corp.

"Inventory loses value every day you hold it."

See the entire interview at **SMARTFinance**

Table 22.1 also shows the aggregate investment in current assets and current liabilities for all U.S. manufacturing firms expressed as a percentage of the aggregate assets of these firms. In 1981, current assets accounted for 32.2% of aggregate corporate assets; current liabilities made up 22.6% of the financing for those assets. By 2007, those figures had changed to 25.5% and 19.7%, respectively. Put another way, the aggregate *current ratio* of U.S. manufacturing firm declined from 1.42 in 1981 to 1.29 in 2007. These figures illustrate both the importance of and the changes in short-term financial management by U.S. firms.

A variety of forces prompted firms in recent decades to find efficiencies in short-term financial management. For example, high inflation in the early 1980s gave a tremendous incentive to reduce investments in non-interest-bearing operating assets. Perhaps even more important were developments in information technology which allowed firms to become much more efficient in managing cash, inventories, and payables, in monitoring receivables, and in establishing short-term loans. With better access to information and

Table 22.2. Operating Cycle and Cash Conversion Cycle for Selected Companies, Fiscal Year 2007

	COMPUTER MANUFACTURERS					OTHER COMPANIES			
	IBM (IBM)	DELL (DELL)[a]	SONY (SNE)	APPLE (AAPL)	HEWLETT-PACKARD (HPQ)	SUPER-VALU (SVU)[b]	POLO RALPH LAUREN (RPL)[c]	GM (GM)	MCDONALD'S (MCD)
Data ($ billion)									
(1) Sales	98.786	61.133	70.513	24.006	104.286	44.048	4.880	181.122	22.786
(2) Cost of sales	57.057	49.462	54.652	15.852	78.598	33.943	2.242	169.001	14.882
(3) Accounts payable	22.273	11.591	18.859	6.230	25.822	3.419	0.652	64.291	1.751
(4) Accounts receivable	30.476	7.693	13.715	4.811	26.191	0.951	0.585	9.659	1.054
(5) Inventory	2.664	1.180	7.997	0.346	8.033	2.776	0.515	20.222	0.125
Time Periods (days)									
(6) Average age of inventory (AAI) $\{(5) \div [(2) \div 365]\}$	17.04	8.71	53.41	7.97	37.30	29.85	83.84	43.67	3.07
(7) Average collection period (ACP) $\{(4) \div [(1) \div 365]\}$	112.60	45.93	41.40	73.15	91.67	7.88	93.76	19.47	16.88
(8) Average payment period (APP) $\{(3) \div [(2) \div 365]\}^d$	142.48	85.53	125.95	143.45	119.91	36.77	106.15	138.85	42.94
Cycles (days)									
(9) Operating cycle (OC) [(6) + (7)]	128.64	54.64	94.81	81.12	128.97	37.73	127.60	63.14	19.95
(10) Cash conversion cycle (CCC) [(9) − (8)]	−12.84	−30.89	−31.14	−62.53	9.06	0.96	21.45	−75.71	−22.99

[a]Fiscal year ending January 2008.
[b]Fiscal year ending February 2008.
[c]Fiscal year ending March 2008.
[d]"Annual purchases" cannot be found in published financial statements and so this value is calculated using "cost of sales" (line 2), which is an approach commonly used by external analysts. Because annual purchases are likely to be smaller than the cost of sales, these APPs may be understated.

the ability to move and dispatch funds electronically, firms today can operate with lower levels of investment in operating assets.[1]

This chapter focuses on the cash conversion cycle and the efficient management of two key operating assets: inventory and accounts receivable. We begin with the cash conversion cycle and the actions that can be taken to manage it. Next, we describe the cost trade-offs in short-term financial management. We then briefly consider the key concerns of the financial manager with regard to inventory before reviewing some popular inventory management techniques. Next we discuss effective accounts receivable management and review two important related concepts, credit standards and credit terms. Finally, we briefly cover some other receivables management activities.

22.1 THE CASH CONVERSION CYCLE

Operating Cycle

A central concept in short-term financial management is the notion of the operating cycle. A firm's **operating cycle (OC)** measures the time that elapses from the firm's receipt of raw materials to its collection of cash from the sale of finished products. As you might expect, operating cycles vary widely by industry. For instance, a bakery—which uses fresh ingredients, keeps finished goods in inventory for only a day or two, and generally sells its products for cash—will have a very short operating cycle. In contrast, semiconductor manufacturers take several months to convert raw materials into finished products, which are sold on credit. The operating cycle for such a firm may extend to six months or longer.

The operating cycle influences a company's need for internal or external financing. In general, the longer a firm's operating cycle, the greater its need for financing. For example, a bakery might pay its suppliers and its employees using the revenues generated each week. The semiconductor manufacturer probably cannot persuade suppliers and employees to wait several months for payment while the firm collects cash from chip sales. Therefore, the semiconductor firm has a greater need for financing day-to-day operations.

The operating cycle encompasses two major short-term asset categories: inventory and accounts receivable. To measure the operating cycle, we use two ratios covered in Chapter 2. First, calculate the *average age of inventory* (AAI) and the *average collection period* (ACP). Next, take the sum of these two items to determine the length of the operating cycle.

Table 22.2 presents the actual operating cycles for some well-known computer manufacturers and a number of other firms. Lines 1 through 5 present data for fiscal-year 2007, and lines 6 through 8 calculate the time periods (in days) for AAI, ACP, and average payment period (APP), respectively. Using the AAI and ACP calculated in lines 6 and 7, line 9 in the table shows the OC for each firm. Note that, among the five computer manufacturers (IBM, Dell, Sony, Apple, and Hewlett-Packard), the make-to-order firm, Dell, has the shortest operating cycle, closely followed by Apple and Sony. IBM's and Hewlett-Packard's respective operating cycles of 130 and 129 days are far longer than the 55- to 95-day range of operating cycles for Dell, Apple, and Sony, which is probably the result of IBM's and HP's more diversified computer businesses. The final four columns show

---

[1]A popular professional certification in the field of treasury and financial management is the Certified Treasury Professional (CTP) credential offered by the Association for Financial Professionals (http://www.afponline.org). More than 15,000 CTPs have passed an exam reflecting the required expertise in the field of treasury and financial management, and they participate in ongoing professional education to maintain the CTP credential.

the operating cycles for four noncomputer firms. Clearly, the operating cycle varies greatly across industries as well as across different types of companies within a given industry.

Cash Conversion Cycle

The elapsed time between the points at which a firm pays for raw materials and at which it receives payment for finished goods is called the **cash conversion cycle (CCC)**. The difference between the operating cycle and the cash conversion cycle indicates the amount of time for which suppliers are willing to extend credit. Most firms obtain a significant amount of their financing through trade credit, as represented by accounts payable. By taking advantage of trade credit, a firm reduces the amount of financing it needs from other sources to make it through the operating cycle.

To calculate the cash conversion cycle, start with the operating cycle and then subtract the average payment period on accounts payable. Here is the formula for the cash conversion cycle:

$$CCC = OC - APP = AAI + ACP - APP \qquad \text{(Eq. 22.1)}$$

JOB INTERVIEW QUESTION

Why do firms attempt to shorten their cash conversion cycles?

As Equation 22.1 shows, the cash conversion cycle has three main components: (1) average age of the inventory, (2) average collection period, and (3) average payment period. It also shows that, by changing any of these time periods, a firm changes the amount of time its resources are tied up in day-to-day operations.

Again referring to Table 22.2, we can see that the cash conversion cycle for each firm is calculated (in line 10) by subtracting the average payment periods in line 8 from the operating cycle calculated in line 9. Reviewing the CCC for the computer manufacturers, we see that IBM, Dell, Sony, and Apple have negative CCCs. This indicates that these firms receive cash inflows ahead of having to make the cash outflows needed to generate those inflows. This desirable state, which is reflected by a negative CCC, is consistent with a "pay up front and we'll manufacture and ship the product to you later" type of business. The other top computer manufacturer, Hewlett-Packard, has a positive but relatively short CCC, which also reflects effective current-account management. It is interesting to note that two of the other firms, GM and McDonald's, also have a negative CCC. Looking at these firms' time periods for AAI, ACP, and APP in lines 6 through 8 (respectively), we can see that their vendors are effectively financing their operations. In other words, the high APPs more than cover the time delays in inventory and accounts receivable. Supervalu and Polo Ralph Lauren have positive CCCs that are due primarily to their relatively lengthy inventory periods. The cash conversion cycles in Table 22.2 demonstrate differences both within and across industries regarding the amount of time for which firms have their money tied up.

EXAMPLE

Reese Industries has annual sales of $5 billion, a cost of goods sold that is 70% of sales, and purchases that are 60% of cost of goods sold. Reese has an AAI of 70 days, an ACP of 45 days, and an APP of 40 days. The 45-day ACP can be broken into 37 days until the customer places the payment in the mail and an additional 8 days before the funds are available to the firm in a spendable form. Thus, Reese's operating cycle is 115 days (70 + 45), and its cash conversion cycle is 75 days (70 + 45 − 40). Figure 22.1 presents Reese's operating and cash conversion cycles on a time line.

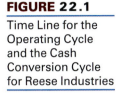

FIGURE 22.1

Time Line for the
Operating Cycle
and the Cash
Conversion Cycle
for Reese Industries

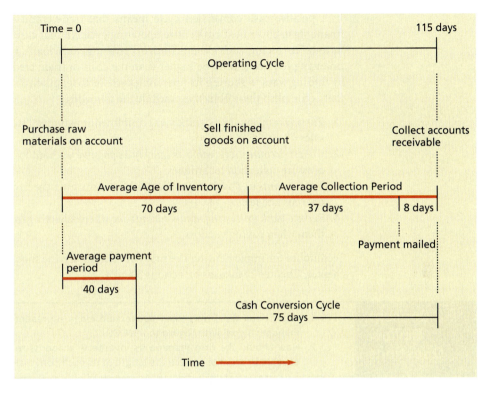

Reese has invested the following resources in its cash conversion cycle, where 0.70 indicates that sales are 70% of cost of goods sold:

Inventory = ($5 billion × 0.70) × (70/365) = $671.2 million

+ Accounts receivable = ($5 billion) × (45/365) = $616.4 million

− Accounts payable = ($5 billion × 0.70 × 0.60) × (40/365)
= $230.1 million

= Resources invested = $1,057 million

If Reese could reduce from 8 days to 3 days the amount of time it takes to receive, process, and collect payments after they are mailed by its customers, then it would reduce its average collection period from 45 days to 40 days (37 + 3). This would shorten the cash conversion time line by 5 days (8 − 3) and thus reduce the amount of resources that Reese has invested in operations. For Reese, a 5-day reduction in the average collection period would reduce the resources invested in the cash conversion cycle by $68.5 million [$5 billion × (5 ÷ 365)].

Shortening the Cash Conversion Cycle

In order *to maximize shareholder value, the financial manager should manage the firm's short-term activities in a way that shortens the cash conversion cycle.* This will enable the firm to operate with minimum cash investment. The firm can find alternative uses for any cash that it is not using to fund the cash conversion cycle—for example, using the cash to pursue more productive long-term investments, using it to pay down expensive long-term financing, or distributing it to the owners as dividends.

A positive cash conversion cycle means that trade credit does not provide enough financing to cover the firm's entire operating cycle. In that case, the firm must seek other forms of financing, such as bank lines of credit and term loans. However, the costs of these financing sources tend to be higher than the costs of trade credit. Thus the firm benefits by finding ways to shorten its operating cycle or to lengthen its payment period. Actions that accomplish these objectives include the following:

1. *Turn over inventory as quickly as possible* while avoiding "stockouts" that result in lost sales.
2. *Collect accounts receivable as quickly as possible* without losing sales because of high-pressure collection techniques.
3. *Pay accounts as slowly as possible* without damaging the firm's credit rating or paying onerous late fees.
4. *Reduce mail, processing, and clearing time* when collecting from customers but *increase* them when paying vendors.

Techniques for implementing the first two actions are the focus of the remainder of this chapter. Chapter 23 focuses on actions 3 and 4.

Concept Review Questions	1. What does the firm's cash conversion cycle represent? Explain the financial manager's goal with regard to the CCC. 2. How should the firm manage its inventory, accounts receivable, and accounts payable in order to reduce the length of its cash conversion cycle?

22.2 COST TRADE-OFFS IN SHORT-TERM FINANCIAL MANAGEMENT

When attempting to manage the firm's short-term accounts so as to minimize cash while adequately funding the firm's operations, the financial manager must focus on competing costs. Decisions with regard to the optimum levels of both operating assets and short-term financing involve cost trade-offs. For convenience, we will view the current-account decision strategies as being revenue neutral and thus will examine their cost trade-offs solely in terms of *minimizing total cost*.

The optimum levels of the key operating assets—cash and marketable securities, accounts receivable, and inventory—involve trade-offs between the cost of holding the operating asset and the cost of maintaining too little of the asset. Figure 22.2 depicts the cost trade-offs and optimum level of a given operating asset. Cost 1 is the holding cost, which increases with larger operating asset account balances. Cost 2 is the cost of holding too little of the operating asset, which decreases with larger operating asset account balances. The *total cost* is the sum of cost 1 and cost 2 associated with a given account balance for the operating asset. As noted, the optimum balance occurs at the point where total cost is minimized.

The table at the bottom of Figure 22.2 provides more detail on the specific costs for each operating asset. For example, consider cash and marketable securities. As the balance of these accounts *increases*, the opportunity costs and tax costs (cost 1) of the funds held in the firm rise. At the same time, the illiquidity and solvency costs (cost 2) fall; the higher the cash and marketable securities balance, the greater the firm's liquidity and the lower its likelihood of becoming insolvent. Hence, the optimum balance of cash and marketable securities is the one that minimizes the total of these two competing costs.

FIGURE 22.2

Trade-off of Short-Term Financial Costs

Smart Concepts

See the concept explained step-by-step at **SMARTFinance**

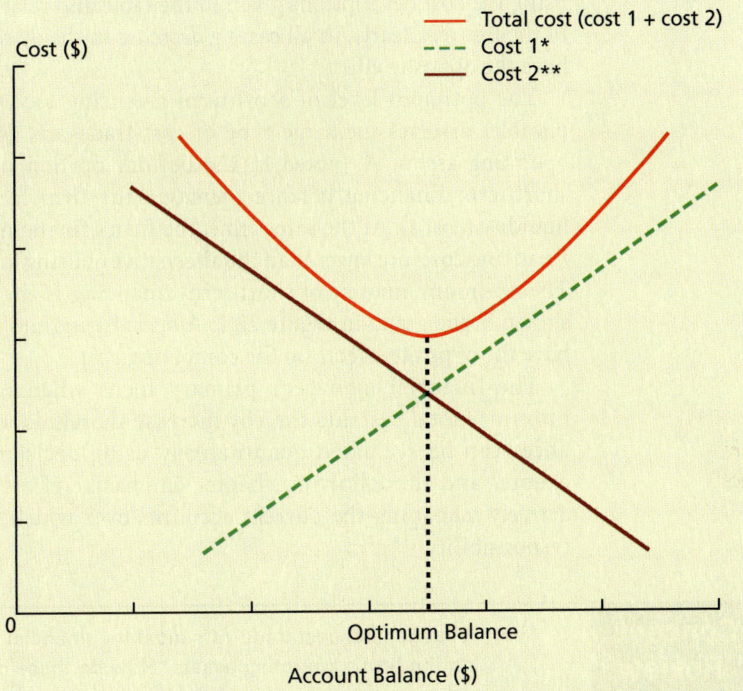

Effect of an Increase in Account Balance

	*Cost 1	**Cost 2
Operating Assets		
Cash and marketable securities	Opportunity cost of funds and tax costs	Illiquidity and solvency costs
Inventory	Carrying cost of inventory, including financing, warehousing, obsolescence costs, etc.	Order and setup costs associated with replenishment and production of finished goods
Accounts receivable	Cost of investment in accounts receivable and bad debts	Opportunity cost of lost sales due to overly restrictive credit policy and/or terms
Short-Term Financing		
Accounts payable, accruals, and notes payable	Cost of reduced liquidity caused by increasing current liabilities	Financing costs resulting from the use of less expensive short-term financing rather than more expensive long-term debt and equity financing

We can evaluate the cost trade-offs for inventory and accounts receivable in similar fashion, using the cost descriptions given in the table and relating them to the two cost functions in the figure. Clearly, in all cases a *decrease* in the operating asset account balance would have the opposite effect.

The optimum level of short-term financing (accounts payable, accruals, and notes payable) involves the same type of cost trade-offs as demonstrated in Figure 22.2 for operating assets. As noted in the bottom portion of the accompanying table, as the short-term financing balance *increases*, the firm faces an increasing cost of reduced liquidity (cost 1). At the same time, the firm's financing costs (cost 2) decline; short-term financing costs are lower than the alternative of using long-term debt and equity financing. The optimum amount of short-term financing is the one that minimizes total cost, as shown in the graph in Figure 22.2. A *decrease* in the short-term financing balance would have the opposite effects on the competing costs.

The financial manager's primary focus when managing current accounts is to minimize total cost and thereby increase shareholder value. Each of these account balances can be evaluated quantitatively using decision models. The remainder of this chapter and the following chapter emphasize effective techniques and strategies for actively managing the current accounts over which the financial manager has direct responsibility.

Concept Review Questions	
	3. What general cost trade-offs must the financial manager consider when managing the firm's operating assets? How do these costs behave as a firm considers reducing its accounts receivable by, say, establishing more restrictive credit terms? How can the firm determine the optimum balance?
	4. What general cost trade-offs are associated with the firm's level of short-term financing? How do these costs behave when a firm substitutes short-term financing for long-term financing? How would you quantitatively model this decision to find the optimal level of short-term financing?

22.3 INVENTORY MANAGEMENT

Inventory is an important current asset. For the typical U.S. manufacturer, inventory represents between 10% and 20% of total assets—a sizable investment. Inventory consists of the firm's stock of raw materials, work in process, and finished goods. Although inventory management is the responsibility of operations managers, it is also a major concern of the financial manager because of the large investments involved.

The firm's goal should be to move inventory quickly in order to minimize its investment. At the same time, it must be careful to maintain adequate inventory to meet demand and to minimize lost sales due to stock outages. The financial manager attempts to maintain optimal inventory levels that reconcile these conflicting objectives. Also, because obsolescence can severely reduce the value of inventories, the firm must carefully control inventory to avoid potential major losses in asset values.

Here we consider the aspects of inventory that concern the financial manager: the amount invested in inventory, and several popular techniques for controlling inventory.[2]

---

[2]For detailed discussions of these and other inventory management techniques, see Thomas E. Vollman, William Lee Berry, David Clay Whybark, and R. Robert Jacobs, *Manufacturing Planning and Control for Supply Chain Management*, 5th Edition (Burr Ridge, IL: McGraw-Hill Irwin, 2005).

Investing in Inventory

A firm must evaluate its inventory investment in terms of associated revenues and costs. Simply stated, additional investment must be justified by additional returns. From a financial point of view, constraining inventory levels improves returns by releasing funds that the firm can use in more profitable investments. In contrast, the production and marketing perspective is that expanding inventories provides for uninterrupted production runs, good product selection, and prompt delivery schedules. The firm needs to balance the conflicting preferences of finance, production, and marketing managers in order to effectively manage inventory.

The financial manager should consider several specific factors when evaluating an inventory system. On the asset side of the balance sheet, inventories represent an important short-term investment. The smaller the level of inventory needed to support the firm's sales, the faster the total asset turnover and the higher the return on total assets (this is consistent with the DuPont system discussed in Chapter 2). More rapid inventory turnover also reduces the potential for obsolescence and resulting price concessions. On the liability side, smaller inventories reduce the firm's short-term financing requirements and thereby lower financing costs and improve profits. The following Example illustrates the key financial trade-off associated with inventory investment.

EXAMPLE

Kerry Manufacturing is contemplating larger production runs to reduce the high setup costs associated with a major product. The firm estimates the total annual savings in setup costs to be $120,000. It currently turns this product's inventory six times a year; with the proposed larger production runs, this turnover should drop to five times a year. If the firm's $30 million cost of goods sold for this product is unaffected by the proposal then, assuming the firm's required return on investments of similar risk is 15%, the analysis would proceed as follows.

Analysis:

Average investment in inventory = cost of goods sold ÷ inventory turnover

Proposed system	= $30.0 million ÷ 5 = $6.0 million
Less: Present system	= $30.0 million ÷ 6 = $5.0 million
Increased inventory investment	$1.0 million
× required return	× 0.15
Annual cost of increased inventory investment	$ 150,000
Less: Annual savings in setup costs	120,000
Net loss from proposed plan	$ 30,000

Decision:

Don't do it; an annual loss of $30,000 would result from the proposed plan.

Techniques for Controlling Inventory

JOB INTERVIEW QUESTION

Why are financial managers in manufacturing firms concerned about inventory?

Although inventory control is an operations/production management task, the financial manager serves as a "watchdog" over this activity. This oversight is important given the firm's typically sizable investment in inventory. Firms commonly use a variety of techniques, discussed below, to control inventory. Although these techniques are typically used by operations and production managers, a good financial manager should understand them.

ABC System A firm using the **ABC system** segregates its inventory into three groups: A, B, and C. The A items are the most costly inventory items, and the B group consists of items accounting for the next largest investment. The C group typically consists of a large number of items accounting for a small dollar investment. Separating its inventory into A, B, and C groups allows the firm to determine the level and types of inventory control procedures needed. Control of the A items should be most intensive because of the high dollar investments involved; the B and C items are subject to correspondingly less sophisticated procedures.

Basic Economic Order Quantity (EOQ) Model A popular tool for determining the optimal order quantity for an inventory item is the **economic order quantity (EOQ) model**. This model could be used to control the firm's big-ticket inventory items such as those included in the A group of an ABC system. The EOQ model considers operating and financial costs and determines the order quantity that minimizes overall inventory costs. The EOQ for a given inventory item is given as

$$EOQ = \sqrt{\frac{2SO}{C}}$$

(Eq. 22.2)

where

S = inventory usage per period (typically one year)
O = order cost per order
C = carrying cost per unit per period

EXAMPLE

Garrison Industries currently uses 16,000 units of an expensive inventory item each year. The firm estimates its order cost to be $500 per order and the carrying cost for this item to be $100 per unit per year. Garrison wishes to estimate the optimal quantity in which to order this item. By substituting $S = 16,000$, $O = \$500$, and $C = \$100$ into Equation 22.2, we calculate the EOQ for this item as

$$EOQ = \sqrt{\frac{2 \times 16,000 \times \$500}{\$100}} = \sqrt{160,000} = 400 \text{ units}$$

By ordering this item in quantities of 400 units, Garrison Industries will minimize its total inventory cost for this item.

Smart Practices Video

Vern LoForti, Chief Financial Officer, Overland Storage Inc.

"You have to have a high level of confidence in those suppliers who are holding that inventory at their warehouse."

See the entire interview at **SMARTFinance**

Reorder Points and Safety Stock The simple EOQ model just presented assumes that inventory is instantaneously replenished precisely at the time the inventory is exhausted. This model implies perfect certainty with regard to the rate of usage and the timing of receipt from suppliers. Assuming a constant rate of usage, a firm can easily estimate a *reorder point* as follows:

Reorder point = Lead time in days × Daily usage

For example, if Garrison Industries uses about 44 units per day (16,000 units per year ÷ 365 days) and if it typically takes the firm four days to place and receive an order, then the firm should place an order when its inventory falls to 176 units (4 days × 44 units).

To allow for faster-than-anticipated rates of usage and/or delayed deliveries, many firms maintain *safety stocks* of inventory. Management determines the size of these stocks by analyzing the probabilities of both increased usage rates and delivery delays. For example, Garrison Industries estimates that a safety stock equal to 2% of its annual usage of the given item will adequately protect against stockouts due to faster-than-anticipated usage and/or order fulfillment delays. Given that estimate, Garrison will maintain a safety stock of 320 units (0.02 × 16,000 units). A variety of more sophisticated models are available for setting both reorder points and safety stocks.

Material Requirements Planning Many manufacturing firms use computerized systems to control the flow of resources, particularly inventory, within the production process. **Material requirements planning (MRP)** is one such system. MRP uses a master schedule to ensure that the materials, labor, and equipment needed for production are at the right places, in the right amounts, and at the right times. The schedule is based on forecasts of the demand for the company's products. The schedule says exactly what will be manufactured during the next few weeks or months and when the work will take place.

Sophisticated computer programs coordinate all the elements of MRP. The computer determines material requirements by comparing production needs to the materials the company already has in inventory. The programs place orders so that items will be on hand when they are needed for production. MRP helps ensure a smooth flow of finished products.

Manufacturing resource planning II (MRPII) expands on MRP. Using a complex computer system, it integrates data from many departments, including finance, marketing, accounting, engineering, and manufacturing. MRPII can generate a production plan for the firm as well as management reports, forecasts, and financial statements. It allows the firm to track and manage key inventory items (typically A items) on a real-time basis. The system also enables managers to assess the impact of production plans on profitability. If one department's plans change, the system transmits the effects of those changes throughout the company.

Just-in-Time System An important and widely adopted inventory management technique, imported from Japan, is the **just-in-time (JIT) system**. JIT is based on the belief that materials should arrive exactly when they are needed for production, rather than being stored on-site. Relying closely on computerized systems such as MRP and MRPII, manufacturers determine what parts will be needed and when before ordering them from suppliers so the parts arrive "just in time."

Under the JIT system, inventory products are "pulled" through the production process in response to customer demand. JIT requires close teamwork among vendors and personnel in purchasing and production; any delay in deliveries of supplies could bring production to a halt. Clearly, unexpected events, such as 9/11, can cause problems for firms using a JIT system. In spite of such risks, a properly employed JIT system can significantly reduce inventory levels and carrying costs, thereby freeing funds for more productive uses.

Concept Review Questions	5. How might the financial manager's view of inventory differ from that of managers in production and marketing? What is the relationship between inventory turnover and inventory investment? Explain.
	6. What is the ABC system? What role does the EOQ model play in controlling inventory?
	7. From the financial manager's perspective, describe the role of reorder points, safety stock, MRP, MRPII, and a just-in-time system in managing a firm's inventory.

22.4 ACCOUNTS RECEIVABLE STANDARDS AND TERMS

Accounts receivable (AR) result from a company selling its products or services on credit and are represented in the cash conversion cycle by the average collection period. This period is the average length of time from a sale on credit until the payment becomes usable funds for the firm. The ACP has two parts. The first, and generally the longer, is the credit period. It is measured as the time from the sale (or customer invoicing) until customers place their payments in the mail. The second is the time from when the customers place payments in the mail to when the firm has spendable funds in its bank account. The first part of the average collection period involves managing the credit available to the firm's customers. The second part involves receiving, processing, and collecting payments. This section discusses customer credit; Chapter 23 discusses receiving, processing, and collecting payments.

As with all current accounts, receivables management requires managers to balance competing interests. On the one hand, managers (generally the cash or treasury managers) prefer to receive cash payments sooner rather than later. That preference leads toward strict credit terms and strict enforcement of those terms. On the other hand, firms can use credit terms as a marketing tool to attract new customers (or to keep current customers from defecting to another firm). This objective argues for easier credit terms and more flexible enforcement.

It is also important to understand that, in many firms, the credit policy is generally not under the control of the financial (cash or treasury) managers but, rather, part of the sales or customer-service functions. For many companies wishing to remain competitive, credit terms are a necessary part of determining the ultimate sale prices for their products and services.

Effective Accounts Receivable Management

Effectively managing the credit and accounts receivable process involves cooperation among sales, customer-service, finance, and accounting staffs. The key areas of concern involve:

1. Setting and communicating the company's general credit and collections policies.
2. Determining who is granted credit and how much credit is extended to each customer.
3. Managing the billing and collection process in a timely and accurate manner.
4. Applying payments and updating the accounts receivable ledger.
5. Monitoring accounts receivable on both an individual and aggregate basis.
6. Following up on overdue accounts and initiating collection procedures, if required.

In the typical company, the credit and accounts receivable departments handle most of these tasks. The cash management or treasury area will usually be responsible for managing the actual receipt of payments. The cash manager usually will also have to collect and organize the remittance data that is sent along with the payments so that the AR department can determine what invoices have been paid. We will cover this *cash application* process in greater detail later in the chapter.

The first decision a company must make is whether it will offer trade credit at all. There are many reasons for offering credit, including increasing sales, meeting terms offered by competitors, attracting new customers, and providing general convenience. In a typical business-to-business environment, a company may have to offer trade credit just to generate sales. This is especially the case for a large company selling to smaller companies, where the smaller company literally needs the credit period in order to sell merchandise so it can pay the supplier. The small company would not usually have access to other types of credit, so if the supplier doesn't offer credit then there is no sale.

As mentioned previously, many companies see trade credit and credit terms as simply an extension of the sales price. They may use credit terms to motivate customers or to compete with other suppliers. In many cases, industry practices dictate whether firms offer credit and under what terms. In today's financial environment, there are also many opportunities for companies to outsource part or all of the credit and accounts receivable process. Some outsourcing alternatives are: use of credit cards, third-party financing, and **factoring**, which involves the outright sale of receivables to a third-party *factor* at a discount.

Once a company has decided to offer trade credit, it must then do the following:

1. Determine its credit standards: Who is offered credit and how much?
2. Set its credit terms: How long do customers have to pay, and are any discounts offered for early payment?
3. Develop its collection policy: How should delinquent accounts be handled?
4. Monitor its accounts receivable on both an individual and aggregate basis: What is the status of each customer and the overall quality of its receivables?

In addition, the firm must have effective cash application procedures in place (these are discussed at the end of Section 22.5).

Credit Standards

The first and most important aspect of accounts receivable management is setting credit standards. This process involves applying techniques for determining which customers should receive credit and how much credit should be granted. Much of the focus is on making sure that a company does not accept substandard customers (i.e., potential defaulters on trade credit). However, a firm must take care not to set the standards so high that potential good customers are rejected. A company's accounts receivable default rates should generally be in line with those of other companies in the same industry if it wants to remain competitive.

Granting Credit to Customers 　In analyzing credit requests and determining the level of credit to be offered, the company can gather information from both internal and external sources. The usual internal sources of credit information are the credit application and agreement and, if available, the company's own records of the applicant's payment history. External sources typically include financial statements, trade references, banks or other creditors, and credit-reporting agencies. Each of these sources involves the internal costs of analyzing the data; some sources, such as credit-reporting agencies, also have explicit external costs (a charge for obtaining the data).

The company must also take into account the variable costs of the products it would be selling on credit. For example, a company selling a product with a low variable cost (e.g., magazine subscriptions) will often grant credit to almost anyone without a credit check. It doesn't have much to lose if payment isn't made, but on the other hand, potential profits are great. Companies selling products with high variable costs (e.g., heavy manufacturing equipment) will typically do extensive credit checks before granting credit and shipping merchandise.

The amount of the credit limit is also an important factor. To reduce some of the costs associated with making credit decisions, a company may routinely grant small levels of credit to new customers and then allow the credit limit to rise as the customer proves to be a good credit risk.[3]

---

[3]The National Association of Credit Managers (NACM; see www.nacm.org) is the primary professional association for credit managers and supports several certification programs.

WHAT COMPANIES DO GLOBALLY

A Working Capital Survey

Each year since 1997, *CFO Magazine* has published a "Working Capital Survey" that ranks 1,000 companies in 35 industries based on two measures of financial efficiency: days (of sales) of working capital and cash conversion efficiency. A recent article by Greg Filbeck, Thomas Krueger, and Dianna Preece assessed (1) whether stock prices of firms that ranked highly in these surveys from 1997 to 2000 rose when the results were disclosed and (2) whether annual stock returns were positively related to these firms' rankings. The authors find that stock prices of highly ranked companies increase significantly on the announcement date. But these returns reverse themselves over subsequent days, and the companies do not significantly outperform matching firms over the year following high-ranked inclusion in the "Working Capital Survey."

Professors Filbeck, Krueger, and Preece also summarize the working capital policies of the companies included in the survey. The following table describes mean, minimum, and maximum values of several financial variables for the 1,094 companies included in the surveys between 1997 and 2000. These companies are quite large on average, with annual sales of $726 million, and their stockholders earn average monthly returns of 0.53%. The companies maintain working capital equal in value to 46.12 days of sales, accounts receivable equal to 43.58 days, inventory equal to 13.53 days, and payables equal to 33.77 days. On the other hand, these average values conceal extremely wide variation in mean levels of the financial values, as shown by high standard deviations of the means and by the extreme minimum and maximum values for each variable.

Financial Data for Firms Included in *CFO Magazine's* "Working Capital Survey," 1997–2000

Variable	Number of Observations	Mean (S.D.)	Minimum	Maximum
Monthly stock return (%)	1,094	0.53% (0.28%)	−12.83%	19.69%
Sales (000)	1,094	$726,746 ($430,108)	$801	$990,701
Days of working capital	1,093	46.12 (42.74)	57.20	872.00
Accounts receivable days sales outstanding	1,092	43.58 (23.36)	0	127.50
Inventory days sales on hand	1,092	13.53 (23.54)	0.60	485.00
Payables days sales outstanding	203	33.77 (21.27)	2.00	182.00

Source: Table 3 of Greg Filbeck, Thomas Krueger, and Dianna Preece, "*CFO Magazine's* "Working Capital Survey": Do Selected Firms Work for Shareholders?" Reprinted with permission from the *Quarterly Journal of Finance and Accounting,* volume 46, no. 2 (Spring 2007), pages 15.

Two popular approaches to the credit-granting process are (1) the five C's of credit and (2) credit scoring.

Five C's of Credit   The **five C's of credit** provide a framework for performing in-depth credit analysis, but they do not provide a specific accept-or-reject decision. This credit-selection method is typically used for high-dollar credit requests. Although applying the five C's does not speed up collection of accounts, it does lower the probability of default. The five C's are defined as follows.

1. *Character* refers to the applicant's record of meeting past obligations. The lender would consider the applicant's payment history as well as any pending or resolved legal judgments against the applicant. The question addressed here is whether the applicant will pay its account, if able, within the specified credit terms.

2. *Capacity* is the applicant's ability to repay the requested credit. The lender typically assesses the applicant's capacity by using financial statement analysis focused on cash flows available to service debt obligations.

3. *Capital* refers to the financial strength of the applicant as reflected by its capital structure. In assessing capital, the lender frequently analyzes the applicant's debt relative to equity and its profitability ratios. The analysis of capital determines whether the applicant has sufficient equity to survive a business downturn.

4. *Collateral* consists of the assets the applicant has available for securing the credit. In general, the more valuable and more marketable the assets are, the more credit lenders will extend. However, trade credit is rarely a secured loan. Therefore, collateral is not the primary consideration in deciding to grant credit. Rather, it strengthens the creditworthiness of a customer who appears to have sufficient cash flows to meet its obligations.

5. *Conditions* refer to current general and industry-specific economic conditions. It also considers any unique conditions surrounding a specific transaction. For example, a firm that has excess inventory of a given item may be willing to accept a lower price or extend more attractive credit terms in order to sell that item.

Credit Scoring   Credit scoring is commonly used with high-volume–low-dollar credit requests. **Credit scoring** applies statistically derived weights for key financial and credit characteristics to predict whether a credit applicant with specific scores for each characteristic will pay the requested credit in a timely fashion.[4] Analysts determine the derived weights using *discriminant analysis*. The specific scores for the applicant are assigned either subjectively by an analyst or by a computer using an expert system. The weighted average score is the sum of the products of the applicant's score and the associated predetermined weight for each characteristic, and the resulting score determines whether to accept or reject the credit applicant. That is, the procedure results in a score that measures the applicant's overall credit strength, and the company uses that score to make the accept-or-reject decision for granting credit. Credit scoring is most commonly used by large credit card operations such as those of banks, oil companies, and department stores.

EXAMPLE

WEG Oil, a major oil company, uses credit scoring to make its consumer credit decisions. Each applicant fills out a credit application. WEG Oil inputs data from the application into an expert system, and a computer generates the applicant's final credit score, creates a letter indicating whether the application was approved, and (if approved) issues the credit card.

Table 22.3 demonstrates the scoring of a consumer credit application, and Table 22.4 describes WEG's predetermined credit standards. Because the applicant in Table 22.3 has a credit score of 83.25, he/she will be extended WEG's standard credit terms (see Table 22.4).

(continued)

---

[4]See Srinivasan, Kim, and Eisenbeis (1987) for a discussion of various analytical methods of credit scoring.

Table 22.3 **Consumer Credit Application Credit Score by WEG Oil**

FINANCIAL AND CREDIT CHARACTERISTICS	SCORE (0 TO 100) (1)	PREDETERMINED WEIGHT (2)	WEIGHTED SCORE [(1) × (2)] (3)
Credit references	80	0.15	12.00
Home ownership	100	0.15	15.00
Income range	75	0.25	18.75
Payment history	80	0.25	20.00
Years at address	90	0.10	9.00
Years on job	85	0.10	8.50
		Total: 1.00	Credit score: 83.25

Notes: In column (1), scores are assigned by an analyst or by a computer based on information supplied on the credit application; scores range from 0 (lowest) to 100 (highest). In column (2), weights are based on the company's analysis of the relative importance of each characteristic in predicting whether or not a customer will pay its account in a timely fashion; the weights must add up to 1.00.

Table 22.4 **WEG Oil's Credit Standards**

CREDIT SCORE	ACTION
Higher than 75	Extend standard credit terms
65 to 75	Extend limited credit; if account is properly maintained, convert to standard credit terms after one year
Lower than 65	Reject application

The purpose of credit scoring is to make a relatively informed credit decision, recognizing that the cost of a single bad scoring decision is small. However, if bad debts from scoring decisions increase, then the company must reevaluate the scoring system. As with the five C's of credit, credit scoring does not speed up the collection of accounts. Instead, scoring allows the firm to quickly and inexpensively identify those customers that are likely to pay their accounts within the stated credit terms. The other advantage to credit scoring is that it is a quantitative approach; it can generally be verified as statistically valid for compliance with fair-credit regulations.

JOB INTERVIEW QUESTION

What financial trade-offs are typically involved when considering a change in credit standards?

Changing Credit Standards The vast majority of sales by U.S. corporations are made on credit. Thus, as a practical matter, it is important to understand how establishing and changing credit standards affect sales, costs, and overall cash flows for a given company. As we discussed earlier, it is essential that firms accurately assess the creditworthiness of individual customers who buy on credit. This does not mean that a firm should extend credit *only* to those customers who are certain to repay their debts. Following such an excessively conservative strategy will cost the company many profitable sales, especially if industry practice is to be more generous in extending credit. Instead, the firm should accept a *degree* of default risk in order to increase sales—but not so much that the additional profit from sales is overwhelmed by additional accounts receivable investment and bad debts. The decision to change credit terms usually rests with the sales or customer-service department. The financial manager is, however, typically responsible for estimating the cash flow and financial impact of a proposed change in credit standards.

Fortunately, measuring the overall financial impact of changes in credit standards is fairly straightforward. Any change will likely yield both benefits and costs; the decision to change standards will depend on whether the benefits exceed the costs. We can describe the general impact of changes in credit standards as follows.

- Relaxing credit standards *will generally yield increased unit sales and additional profits. (The additional profit from relaxed credit standards assumes that each unit is sold at a positive contribution margin. The* **contribution margin** *is a product's price per unit minus variable costs per unit and thus is a direct measure of gross profit per unit sold.) Relaxing credit standards will also yield higher costs from additional investment in accounts receivable and additional bad debt expense.*
- Tightening credit standards *will generally yield reduced investment in accounts receivable and lower bad debt expense at the cost of lower sales and profits.*

It is easiest to demonstrate how to calculate the net effect of changing credit standards by giving an example.

EXAMPLE

Yeoman Manufacturing Company (YMC) produces and sells a CD organizer to music stores nationwide. YMC charges $20/unit and all of its sales are on credit, with customers selected for credit on the basis of a scoring process. With its existing credit standards, YMC expects to sell 120,000 units over the coming year, yielding total sales of $2,400,000 (120,000 units $\times$ $20/unit). Variable costs are $12/unit, and YMC has fixed costs of $240,000 per year.

YMC is contemplating a relaxation of its credit standards and expects the following effects: a 5% increase in sales to 126,000 units; an increase in the average collection period from 30 days (the current level) to 45 days; and an increase in bad debt expense from 1% (the current level) to 2% of sales. YMC plans to keep the product's sale price unchanged at $20/unit, which implies that total sales will increase to $2,520,000 (126,000 units $\times$ $20/unit). If the firm's required return on investments of equal risk is 12%, should YMC relax its credit standards?

To make this decision, YMC's managers must calculate: (1) how much profits will increase from the additional sales that relaxed credit standards are expected to generate; (2) the cost of the marginal investment in accounts receivable; (3) the cost of marginal bad debts; and (4) whether the financial benefits exceed the costs.

1. **Marginal profit contribution from sales.** We are assuming that a 5% increase in sales volume will not cause YMC's fixed costs to increase. Thus, we need to account only for changes in revenues and variable costs. Specifically, we can compute the marginal increase in profits as the increased unit sales volume times the contribution margin per unit sold:

$$\text{Marginal profit from increased sales} = \Delta \text{Sales} \times \text{CM}$$
$$= \Delta \text{Sales} \times (\text{Price} - \text{VC}) \quad \textbf{(Eq. 22.3)}$$

where

Δ Sales = change in unit sales resulting from the change in credit policies
    CM = contribution margin
  Price = price per unit
     VC = variable cost per unit

With the assumptions just detailed for YMC, we can use Equation 22.3 to determine that relaxing credit standards as suggested will yield a marginal profit of $48,000:

$$\text{Marginal profit from increased sales} = 6{,}000 \text{ units} \times (\$20/\text{unit} - \$12/\text{unit})$$
$$= 6{,}000 \text{ units} \times (\$8/\text{unit}) = \$48{,}000$$

2. **Cost of the marginal investment in accounts receivable.** To determine the cost of the marginal investment in accounts receivable, we must calculate the cost of financing the current level of accounts receivable and compare it to the expected cost under the new credit standards. This is more complicated than it sounds. We must first calculate how much YMC currently has invested in accounts receivable based on its current annual sales, variable costs, and accounts receivable turnover. We then repeat this process for the level of sales expected to result from a change in credit standards. Equations 22.4, 22.5, and 22.6 present the steps required. Note that *we use variable costs in calculating investment in accounts receivable because this is the firm's actual cash expense incurred* (and tied up in receivables).

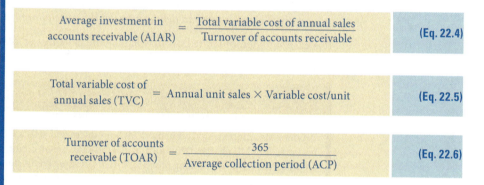

$$\frac{\text{Average investment in}}{\text{accounts receivable (AIAR)}} = \frac{\text{Total variable cost of annual sales}}{\text{Turnover of accounts receivable}} \qquad \textbf{(Eq. 22.4)}$$

$$\frac{\text{Total variable cost of}}{\text{annual sales (TVC)}} = \text{Annual unit sales} \times \text{Variable cost/unit} \qquad \textbf{(Eq. 22.5)}$$

$$\frac{\text{Turnover of accounts}}{\text{receivable (TOAR)}} = \frac{365}{\text{Average collection period (ACP)}} \qquad \textbf{(Eq. 22.6)}$$

We can use these equations to compute the **average investment in accounts receivable (AIAR)** for the current, $\text{AIAR}_{\text{current}}$, and proposed, $\text{AIAR}_{\text{proposed}}$, credit standards. First, we compute the **total variable cost (TVC) of annual sales** under the current credit standards, $\text{TVC}_{\text{current}}$, and the proposed plan, $\text{TVC}_{\text{proposed}}$, using Equation 22.5:

$$\text{TVC}_{\text{current}} = 120{,}000 \text{ units} \times \$12/\text{units} = \$1{,}440{,}000$$

$$\text{TVC}_{\text{proposed}} = 126{,}000 \text{ units} \times \$12/\text{units} = \$1{,}512{,}000$$

Next, we note that the 30-day average collection period under the current plan, $\text{ACP}_{\text{current}}$, is expected to rise to 45 days under the proposed plan, $\text{ACP}_{\text{proposed}}$. This allows us to use Equation 22.6 to compute the **turnover of accounts receivable (TOAR)** under the current, $\text{TOAR}_{\text{current}}$, and proposed, $\text{TOAR}_{\text{proposed}}$, credit terms:

$$\text{TOAR}_{\text{current}} = \frac{365}{\text{ACP}_{\text{current}}} = \frac{365}{30 \text{ days}} = 12.2 \text{ times/year}$$

$$\text{TOAR}_{\text{proposed}} = \frac{365}{\text{ACP}_{\text{proposed}}} = \frac{365}{45 \text{ days}} = 8.1 \text{ times/year}$$

These turnover measures suggest that, if YMC relaxes its credit standards, then the turnover of its accounts receivable will slow down from 12.2 times per year to 8.1 times per year. Clearly, this slowing is attributable to the generally slower paying additional credit customers generated by the relaxed credit standards.

We now have all the inputs required to use Equation 22.4 to compute the $AIAR_{current}$ and $AIAR_{proposed}$:

$$AIAR_{current} = \frac{TVC_{current}}{TOAR_{current}} = \frac{\$1,440,000}{12.2} = \$118,033$$

$$AIAR_{proposed} = \frac{TVC_{proposed}}{TOAR_{proposed}} = \frac{\$1,512,000}{8.1} = \$186,667$$

With these measures, we can now determine the **cost of the marginal investment in accounts receivable**. This amount is the marginal investment in accounts receivable required to support the proposed change in credit policy multiplied by the required return on investment, r:

$$\begin{array}{l}\text{Cost of marginal investment in accounts receivable} = \text{Additional investment} \times \text{Required return}\\[4pt] = (AIAR_{proposed} - AIAR_{current}) \times r\\[4pt] = (\$186,667 - \$118,003) \times 0.12\\[4pt] = \$68,634 \times 0.12 = \$8,236\end{array} \qquad \textbf{(Eq. 22.7)}$$

This value of $8,236 is a cost of adopting the relaxed credit standards; it represents the opportunity cost of investing an additional $68,634 in accounts receivable rather than investing these funds in another earning asset.

3. **Cost of marginal bad debts.** YMC expects that relaxing its credit standards will increase its bad debt expense from 1% to 2% of sales. We can calculate the cost of this by subtracting the current level of bad debt expense from the expected level of bad debt expense under the proposed new credit standards. Equation 22.8 shows the calculations required to determine bad debt expense, and Equation 22.9 shows how to calculate the cost of marginal bad debts if YMC relaxes its credit standards:

$$\begin{array}{l}\text{Bad debt expense (BDE)} = \text{Annual sales (Sales)}\\ \qquad\qquad\qquad\qquad \times \text{Bad debt expense rate (\% BDE),}\\[4pt] BDE_{proposed} = (Sales_{proposed}) \times (\%BDE_{proposed})\\[4pt] \qquad = \$2,520,000 \times 0.02 = \$50,400,\\[4pt] BDE_{current} = (Sales_{current}) \times (\% BDE_{current})\\[4pt] \qquad = \$2,400,000 \times 0.01 = \$24,000;\end{array} \qquad \textbf{(Eq. 22.8)}$$

$$\begin{array}{l}\text{Cost of marginal bad debts} = BDE_{proposed} - BDE_{current}\\[4pt] = \$50,400 - \$24,000 = \$26,400\end{array} \qquad \textbf{(Eq.22.9)}$$

4. **Net profit for the credit decision.** Now that we have calculated the individual financial benefits and costs of changing YMC's credit standards, we can use Equation 22.10 to compute the overall net profit for the credit decision:

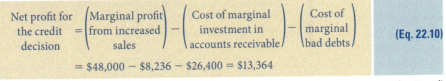

$$\begin{array}{l}\begin{pmatrix}\text{Net profit for}\\ \text{the credit}\\ \text{decision}\end{pmatrix} = \begin{pmatrix}\text{Marginal profit}\\ \text{from increased}\\ \text{sales}\end{pmatrix} - \begin{pmatrix}\text{Cost of marginal}\\ \text{investment in}\\ \text{accounts receivable}\end{pmatrix} - \begin{pmatrix}\text{Cost of}\\ \text{marginal}\\ \text{bad debts}\end{pmatrix}\end{array} \qquad \textbf{(Eq. 22.10)}$$

$$= \$48,000 - \$8,236 - \$26,400 = \$13,364$$

(continued)

Because relaxing YMC's credit standards is expected to yield $13,364 in increased profit, the firm should implement the proposed change. The marginal profit from additional sales will more than offset the total cost of the marginal investment in accounts receivable and marginal bad debts.

Credit Terms

Credit terms are the terms of sale for customers. Terms of *net 30* mean that the customer has 30 days from the beginning of the credit period—typically the end of month (EOM) or date of invoice—to pay the full invoice amount. Some firms offer cash discounts with terms, such as *2/10 net 30*. These terms mean the customer can take a 2% cash discount from the invoice amount if the payment is made within the 10-day *cash discount period*, or the customer can pay the full amount of the invoice within the 30-day *credit period*.

The nature of a firm's business influences its regular credit terms.[5] For example, a firm selling perishable items will have very short credit terms because its items have little long-term collateral value. These firms will typically offer short terms by which the customer has 7–10 days to make payment. A firm in a seasonal business may tailor its terms to fit the industry cycles with terms known as *seasonal dating*. Most managers want their company's regular credit terms to be consistent with its industry's standards. A company will lose business if its terms are more restrictive than those of its competitors; if its terms are less restrictive than those of its competitors, then it will attract customers with poor financial histories that probably are unable to pay under the standard industry terms.

As briefly noted above, a popular method used to lower a firm's investment in accounts receivable is to include a **cash discount** in the credit terms. The cash discount provides a cash incentive for customers to pay sooner. By speeding collections, the discount will decrease the firm's investment in accounts receivable—which is the objective. But the discount will also decrease the per-unit profit because the customer pays less than the full invoice amount. Initiating a cash discount also should reduce bad debts (because customers will pay sooner) and should increase unit sales volume (because customers taking the cash discount pay a lower price for the product). Firms that consider offering a cash discount must perform a cost–benefit analysis to determine if the discount yields sufficient profits.

EXAMPLE

Masson Industries has an average collection period of 45 days: 37 days until the customers place their payments in the mail; and a further 8 days to receive, process, and collect payments. Masson is contemplating a change in its credit terms from *net 30* to *2/10 net 30*. The change is expected to reduce the average collection period to 26 days.

Masson currently sells 1,200 units of its product for $2,500 per unit. Its variable cost per unit is $2,000. It estimates that 70% of its customers will take the 2% discount and that offering the discount will increase sales by 50 units per year but will not alter its bad debt percentage for this product. Masson's opportunity cost of funds invested in accounts receivable is 13.5% per year. Should Masson offer the proposed cash discount? The cost–benefit analysis, presented in Table 22.5, shows that the *net cost* of the cash discount is $2,846. Thus, *Masson should not implement the proposed cash discount.*

---

[5]See Ng, Smith, and Smith (1999) for a discussion of the determinants of credit terms.

Table 22.5 Analysis of Offering a Cash Discount at Masson Industries

Marginal profit from increased sales [50 units × ($2,500 − $2,000)]		$25,000
Current investment in accounts receivable ($2,000[a] × 1,200 units) × (45/365)	$295,890	
New investment in accounts receivable ($2,000[a] × 1,250 units) × (26/365)[b]	178,082	
Reduction in accounts receivable investment	$ 117,808	
Cost savings from reduced investment in accounts receivable (0.135 × $117,808)[c]		15,904
Cost of cash discount (0.02 × $2,500 × 1,250 × 0.70)		43,750
Net profit (cost) from proposed cash discount		$(2,846)

[a]In analyzing the investment in accounts receivable, we use the $2,000 variable cost of the product sold, rather than its $2,500 sales price, because the variable cost represents the firm's actual cash expense incurred and tied up in receivables.
[b]The new investment in accounts receivable is tied up for only 26 days instead of the 45 days under the original terms. The 26 days is calculated as (0.70 × 10 days) + (0.30 × 37 days) + 8 days = 26.1 days, which is rounded to 26 days.
[c]Masson's opportunity cost of funds is 13.5% per year.

Concept Review Questions

8. Why do a firm's regular credit terms typically conform to its industry's standards? On what basis other than credit terms should the firm compete?
9. How are the five C's of credit used to perform in-depth credit analysis? Why is this framework typically used only on high-dollar credit requests?
10. How is credit scoring used in the credit selection process? In what types of situations is it most useful?
11. What are the key variables to consider when evaluating the benefits and costs of changing credit *standards*? How do these variables differ when evaluating the benefits and costs of changing credit *terms*?
12. Why do we include only the variable cost of sales when estimating the average investment in accounts receivable? Why do we apply an opportunity cost to this investment when estimating its cost?
13. What are the key *elements* of a firm's credit terms? What is a key *determinant* of the credit terms offered by a firm?

22.5 COLLECTING, MONITORING, AND APPLYING CASH TO RECEIVABLES

In addition to establishing the firm's accounts receivable standards and terms, the financial manager's responsibilities include collecting and monitoring receivables. The collection and monitoring process is an ongoing activity that is also the responsibility of finance personnel. Here we consider collection policy, credit monitoring, and cash application.

Collection Policy

A company must determine what its **collection policy** will be and how it will implement that policy. As with credit standards and terms, the approach to collections may be a function of the industry and the competitive environment. For many delinquent accounts, a reminder, form letter, telephone call, or personal visit may initiate customer payment. At a minimum, the company should generally suspend further sales to the customer until the delinquent account is brought current.

If these actions fail to generate customer payment, it may be necessary to negotiate with the customer for past-due amounts and report the customer to credit bureaus. It is possible that the company sold the goods with a lien attached, obtained a pledge of collateral against the account, or had other corporate or personal guarantees from the customer. In these cases, the company should utilize these options for obtaining payment. Generally as a last resort, the account can be turned over to a collection agency or referred to an attorney for direct legal action. Obviously, a cost–benefit analysis should be made at each stage to compare the cost of further collection actions against the cost of simply writing off the account as a bad debt.

Credit Monitoring

Credit monitoring involves ongoing review of a firm's accounts receivable to determine if customers are paying according to the stated credit terms. If customers are not paying on time, credit monitoring will alert the firm to the problem. Companies must monitor credit on both an individual and an aggregate basis. Individual monitoring is necessary to determine if each customer is paying in a timely manner and to assess whether a customer is within its credit limits.

Credit monitoring on an aggregate basis indicates the overall quality of the company's accounts receivable. Slow payments are costly to a firm because they increase the average collection period and thereby the firm's investment in accounts receivable. If a company is also using its accounts receivable as collateral for a loan, then the lending institution will generally exclude any past-due accounts from those used as backup for the credit line. Therefore, changes in accounts receivable over time could diminish the company's overall liquidity and increase the need for additional financing. Analysis of accounts receivable payment patterns can also be essential for forecasting future cash receipts in the cash budget.

The three most frequently cited techniques for monitoring the overall quality of accounts receivable are: (1) the average collection period; (2) aging of accounts receivable; and (3) payment-pattern monitoring.

Average Collection Period   The *average collection period* (ACP), also known as *days sales outstanding* (DSO), is the second component of the cash conversion cycle. As noted in Chapter 2, it represents the average number of days that credit sales are outstanding. The average collection period has two components: (1) the time from sale until the customer places the payment in the mail; and (2) the time to receive, process, and collect the payment once it has been mailed by the customer. Equation 22.11 gives the formula for determining the average collection period:

$$\text{Average collection period} = \frac{\text{Accounts receivable}}{\text{Average sales per day}} \qquad \textbf{(Eq. 22.11)}$$

If we assume that the receipt, processing, and collection time is constant, then the average collection period tells the firm how many days (on average) it takes customers to pay their accounts. In applying this formula, analysts must be consistent in their use of the sales period and must adjust for known seasonal fluctuations.

EXAMPLE

P. Scofield Enterprises has an accounts receivable balance of $1.2 million. Sales during the past 90 days were $3.6 million for an average daily sales figure of $40,000. Dividing $1.2 million by $40,000 yields Scofield's average collection period of 30 days.

However, a diligent analyst at Scofield notices that sales have been increasing recently, with average sales over the last 30 days of $45,000 per day. Using this figure in the denominator of Equation 22.11 results in an average collection period of 26.7 days.

The average collection period allows the firm to determine whether there is a general problem with its accounts receivable. However, the ACP can also send misleading signals when daily sales fluctuate. In the preceding Example, suppose that Scofield's credit terms are net 25. Using the most recent month to calculate average daily sales results in an average collection period of 26.7 days, which is right on target given Scofield's credit terms. However, using average daily sales over the past three months yields the longer, 30-day collection period. Therefore, when using this ratio to assess the performance of the collections department, analysts must be aware of the impact of sales fluctuations on their calculations.

If a firm believes that it has a collections problem, a first step in analyzing the problem is to *age the accounts receivable*. By doing so, the firm can determine if the problem exists in its accounts receivable in general or rather is attributable to a few specific accounts or to a given time period.

Aging of Accounts Receivable

The **aging of accounts receivable** requires the firm to break down its accounts receivable into groups based on the time of origin. Aging results in a schedule indicating the portions of the total accounts receivable balance that have been outstanding for specified periods of time. The breakdown is typically made on a month-by-month basis, going back three or four months.

The purpose of aging accounts receivable is to allow the firm to pinpoint problems. For example, if a firm with terms of net 30 has an average collection period (minus receipt, processing, and collection time) of 50 days, then it will want to age its accounts receivable. If the majority of accounts are two months old, then the firm has a general problem and should review its accounts receivable operations. If the aging shows that the firm collects most accounts in about 35 days and that a few accounts are significantly past due, then the firm should analyze and pursue collection of those specific past-due accounts. If the firm has an abnormally high percentage of outstanding accounts initiated in a given month, it may be attributable to a specific event during that time period, such as hiring a new credit manager or selling a substandard product whose quality is being disputed by customer(s) withholding payment.

Table 22.6 provides an example of an *aging schedule*. If the stated credit terms for the company in this example were net 60 days, then the aging schedule would tell us that 80% of the company's receivables are current and 20% are past due.

Payment-Pattern Monitoring

The average collection period and the aging of accounts receivable are excellent monitoring techniques when sales are relatively constant. However, for cyclical or growing firms, both techniques provide potentially misleading results. For example, the average collection period divides the accounts receivable balance by the average daily sales. If the accounts receivable balance is measured during a cyclical firm's high sales period, then the average collection period will be distorted by the cyclical sales peak.

Table 22.6 Sample Aging Schedule for Accounts Receivable

AGE OF ACCOUNTS	ACCOUNTS RECEIVABLE	PERCENTAGE OF ACCOUNTS RECEIVABLE
0–30 days	$1,200,000	50%
31–60 days	720,000	30
61–90 days	336,000	14
91+ days	144,000	6
Total accounts receivable	$2,400,000	100%

Use of the firm's customer payment pattern avoids the problems of cyclical or growing sales when monitoring accounts receivable.

The **payment pattern** is the normal timing in which a firm's customers pay their accounts; it is expressed as the percentage of monthly sales collected in each month following the sale. Every firm has a pattern in which its credit sales are paid. If the payment pattern changes, the firm should review its credit policies.

One approach to determining the payment pattern is to analyze a company's sales and resulting collections on a monthly basis. That is, for each month's sales, the firm computes the amount collected in the month of sale and each of the following months. By tracking these patterns over a period of time, the company can determine the average pattern of its collections using either a spreadsheet or regression analysis. For most companies, these patterns tend to be fairly stable over time—even as sales volumes fluctuate.

EXAMPLE

Consider DJM Manufacturing, which has determined that it collects, on average, 10% of credit sales in the month of sale, 60% in the month following the sale, and the remaining 30% in the second month following the sale. Thus, if sales for the month of January were $200,000, the company would expect to collect $20,000 in January, $120,000 in February, and the remaining $60,000 in March. Table 22.7 shows an example of this approach, which can be extended to develop the cash receipts portion of the cash budget.

Table 22.7 Forecasted Collections for DJM Manufacturing Using Payment-Pattern Monitoring

SALES FORECAST	FORECASTED COLLECTIONS FOR DJM MANUFACTURING				
	JANUARY	FEBRUARY	MARCH	APRIL	MAY
January: $200,000	$20,000	$120,000	$ 60,000		
February: 150,000		15,000	90,000	$ 45,000	
March: 300,000			30,000	180,000	$ 90,000
April: 400,000				40,000	240,000
May: 250,000					25,000
Total projected collections for cash budget:			$180,000	$265,000	$355,000

Notes: This table is created under the assumption that the company collects 10% of each month's sales in the month of sale, 60% in the month following sale, and the remaining 30% in the second month following sale. The first column provides forecasted sales for each month; the remaining columns total up the actual cash flows for each month. In a real-life application, the remaining collections from the prior year's last quarter would be included to complete the projected cash flows in January and February.

Cash Application

Cash application is the process through which a customer's payment is posted to its account and the outstanding invoices are cleared as paid. In most business-to-business environments, the typical application method is known as *open item*. In this approach, the company records each customer invoice in the AR journal and later "matches" received payments to the invoices in order to clear them. This task is complicated by the usual practice of paying multiple invoices with a single check. Ideally, the remittance information accompanying the check should clearly indicate any adjustments, discounts, or allowances taken related to each invoice in that remittance. Unfortunately, the remittance information is sometimes no more than barely legible copies of the invoices with handwritten notes on the adjustments stapled to the check. One of the critical tasks of the accounts receivable department, then, is to figure out what has been paid for so that the outstanding invoices can be closed out.

Some companies are able to use an alternative approach called *balance forward*. In this system, the company applies customer payments to outstanding balances and simply carries forward any unpaid amounts to the next billing period. Examples are utilities and credit card companies, where the only remittance information needed is the customer's account number, the amount of payment, and the date received. These systems generally utilize a scannable remittance document, which allows for automated capture of payment and account information. Automated processing reduces the costs of the cash application process.

Concept Review Questions	14. What is a collection policy? What is the typical sequence of actions taken by a firm when attempting to collect an overdue account?
	15. Why should a firm actively monitor the accounts receivable of its credit customers? Describe how each of the following credit monitoring techniques works: (a) average collection period; (b) aging of accounts receivable; (c) payment-pattern monitoring.

SUMMARY

- The cash conversion cycle has three main components: (1) the average age of inventory (AAI), (2) the average collection period (ACP), and (3) the average payment period (APP). The operating cycle (OC) is the sum of the AAI and ACP. The cash conversion cycle (CCC) is OC minus APP. The length of the cash conversion cycle determines the amount of resources the firm must invest in its operations.

- The financial manager's focus when managing the firm's short-term activities is on shortening the cash conversion cycle. The basic strategies are to turn inventory quickly; collect accounts receivable quickly; pay accounts slowly; and manage mail, processing, and clearing time efficiently.

- When managing the firm's short-term accounts, the financial manager must focus on competing costs.

These cost trade-offs apply to managing cash and marketable securities; accounts receivable; inventory; and accounts payable, accruals, and notes payable. The goal is to balance the cost trade-offs in a way that minimizes the total cost of each of these accounts.

- The large inventory investment made by most firms makes inventory a major concern of the financial manager, who must make sure that the amount of money tied up in inventory—raw materials, work in process, and finished goods—is justified by the returns generated from such investment.

- Operations/production managers use a number of techniques to control inventory. These include the ABC system, the basic economic order quantity (EOQ) model, reorder points and safety stock, material requirements planning, and the just-in-time (JIT) system. Financial managers tend to serve a "watchdog" role over these activities.

- The objective for managing accounts receivable is to balance the competing interests of financial managers, who prefer to receive cash payments sooner, and those of sales personnel, who wish to use liberal credit terms to attract new customers. The key aspects of accounts receivable management include credit standards, credit terms, collection policy, credit monitoring, and cash application.

- When analyzing credit applicants, the firm can gather information from both internal and external sources. Two popular approaches to granting credit to customers are the five C's of credit (for high-volume–low-dollar requests) and credit scoring (for high-volume-low-dollar requests), which is used to make relatively informed credit decisions quickly and inexpensively.

- Companies should perform a cost–benefit analysis of credit standards, credit terms, and other accounts receivable changes to ensure that such policies are profitable. Key variables involved in such an analysis include the marginal profit contribution from sales, the cost of the marginal investment in accounts receivable, and the cost of marginal bad debts.

- The firm's collection policy involves actions aimed at collecting delinquent accounts; these typically include reminders, form letters, telephone calls, or personal visits. If these actions are ineffective, the firm sends negative reports to credit bureaus and may turn over the account to a collection agency or an attorney.

- The three most popular techniques for credit monitoring are the average collection period, aging of accounts receivable, and payment-pattern monitoring. Firms typically make cash application of customer payments using either the open-item method or the balance-forward method.

KEY TERMS

ABC system
aging of accounts receivable
average investment in accounts
   receivable (AIAR)
cash application
cash conversion cycle (CCC)
cash discount
collection policy
contribution margin
cost of marginal investment in
   accounts receivable

credit monitoring
credit scoring
credit terms
economic order quantity (EOQ)
   model
factoring
five C's of credit
just-in-time (JIT) system
manufacturing resource planning II
   (MRPII)

material requirements planning
   (MRP)
operating assets
operating cycle (OC)
payment pattern
short-term financing
total variable cost (TVC) of annual
   sales
turnover of accounts receivable
   (TOAR)

QUESTIONS

22-1. The owner of a hot-dog cart purchases inventory with credit every morning and sells all of the inventory by 2 o'clock in the afternoon. The hot dogs and drinks are sold only for cash. Will the owner have a negative cash conversion cycle?

22-2. How is the cash conversion cycle affected if the operating cycle increases by 10 days and the average payment period also increases by 10 days?

22-3. A firm has the option of writing a check to a supplier (that will take four days to be received and cashed) or using a direct-deposit facility that withdraws the money immediately. Based on the cash conversion cycle, which method of payment should the firm use?

22-4. A furniture store makes an offer that if a purchase over $1,000 is paid in full within 12 months then there is no interest charge (i.e., a 12-month same-as-cash promotion). If the average age of inventory is 60 days and the average collection period is 420 days, how can this financing offer benefit the furniture store?

22-5. If the cash conversion cycle increases (assume the income statement does not change substantially), how does this affect net working capital? (Recall from Chapter 2 that Working capital = Cash + Accounts receivable + Inventory − Accounts payable − Accruals.)

22-6. Describe the impact that aggressive action aimed at minimizing a firm's cash conversion cycle would have on the following financial ratios: inventory turnover, average collection period, and average payment period. What are the key constraints on aggressive pursuit of these strategies with regard to inventory, accounts receivable, and accounts payable?

22-7. What are the principal cost trade-offs that the financial manager must focus on when attempting to manage short-term accounts in a manner that minimizes cash? Prepare a graph describing the general nature of these cost trade-offs and the optimal level of total cost.

22-8. What is the financial manager's primary goal with regard to inventory management? How does this goal compare with the inventory goals of production and marketing?

22-9. What trade-off confronts the financial manager with regard to inventory turnover, inventory cost, and stockouts? In what way is inventory viewed as an investment? Why is it important for the financial manager to understand the inventory control techniques used by operations/production managers?

22-10. What role does the ABC system play in inventory control? What group of inventory items does the EOQ model focus on controlling? Describe the objective and cost trade-offs addressed by the EOQ model.

22-11. Why would a firm extend credit to its customers, given that such an action would lengthen its cash conversion cycle? What key cost trade-offs would be involved in this decision? What typically dictates the actual credit terms the firm extends to its customers?

22-12. Why is using the five C's of credit appropriate for evaluating high-dollar credit requests but not high-volume–low-dollar requests (e.g., department store credit cards)?

22-13. What is credit scoring? In what types of situations is it most useful? If you were developing a credit-scoring model, what factors might be most useful in predicting whether or not a credit customer would pay in a timely manner?

22-14. What are the key variables to consider when evaluating potential changes in a firm's credit standards? Why are only variable costs of sales included when estimating the firm's average investment in accounts receivable?

22-15. If you sell an item costing $16 to a customer for $20 but the customer defaults and does not pay, how much have you actually lost? When quantifying the analysis of potential changes in accounts receivable policy, why are the costs of any bad debts evaluated at the sale price rather than the cost of the sale?

22-16. For a firm contemplating an increase in the cash discount it offers credit customers for early payment, what key variables should be considered when quantitatively analyzing this decision? How do the variables used in this analysis differ from those considered when analyzing a potential change in the firm's credit standards?

22-17. What is credit monitoring? How can each of the following techniques be used to monitor accounts receivable? What are their attributes?
  a. Average collection period
  b. Aging of accounts receivable
  c. Payment-pattern monitoring

PROBLEMS

The Cash Conversion Cycle

22-1. A manager is deciding between two systems to manage the cash conversion cycle (CCC). System A will make the CCC only 60 days, and the cash emerges with a 10% return each rotation through the cycle. System B allows for more customer credit and slows the CCC to 90 days. However, the cash that emerges through each rotation of the cycle has a 13% return. Which system is better? Defend your answer numerically. (*Hint:* Figure out the amount of annual compounding that each system generates.)

22-2. Firm Q currently has sales of $5 million (assume that the cost of goods sold is $4 million, or a 20% gross profit margin) and an inventory turnover of 5.0 (i.e., the firm tends to sell out its inventory five times throughout the year; see Chapter 2). Because of a new promotion, sales are expected to increase by 10% while maintaining the same average inventory. How does this affect the average age of the inventory (AAI), the operating cycle (OC), and the cash conversion cycle? Support your answers with calculations. If the sales promotion offers customers credit (i.e., increases the accounts receivable), how would this affect your previous answer?

22-3. A firm using a LIFO (last in, first out) system for inventory reduces the inventory account, as it is sold, by the amount associated with the cost of the *newest* inventory. A FIFO (first in, first out) system for inventory reduces the inventory account, as it is sold, by the amount associated with the cost of the *oldest* inventory. Suppose there are ten units of inventory. The five oldest units have a book value of $12,000 each, and the five newest units have a book value of $14,000 each. In this period, six units are sold. What is the average age of inventory based on the cost of goods sold for the period, the closing inventory figure, and a 365-day year under a FIFO system and under a LIFO system? Recalculate the AAI under FIFO and LIFO based on an *average inventory* figure, where Average inventory = (Starting inventory + Ending inventory) ÷ 2. How do the conventions of LIFO and FIFO affect the operating cycle? Assuming there are no other changes in the firm's environment, should investors expect a firm's OC to increase after announcing a switch from FIFO to LIFO?

22-4. A firm's average age of inventory is 40 days (assume a 365-day year), and its inventory capacity averages 20,000 units. Assuming it takes 5 days to ship the inventory to the firm when ordered, what is the reorder-point quantity? Is it better to have 5,000-unit capacity trucks (shipping costs of $500 each) deliver the inventory or to have smaller, 2,000-unit capacity trucks (shipping costs of $270) deliver the inventory? If a system can be implemented to speed up the ordering/shipping to 3 days instead of 5 days, would you still use the same truck(s)? Provide numerical support for your decision.

22-5. A firm currently has an average payment period (APP) of 60 days. The average age of inventory is 70 days with an associated cost of goods sold of $340,000. The supplier has offered to decrease the price of the inventory by 5% if the firm pays its bills much earlier. The effect on the APP would be to reduce it to 45 days. How much will the AAI be reduced, and will the change offset the reduction in APP to maintain the firm's cash conversion cycle? If the CCC is reduced by taking the supplier's offer, are there any benefits to the firm in terms of profitability?

22-6. Canadian Products is concerned about managing its operating assets and liabilities efficiently. Inventories have an average age of 110 days, and accounts receivable have an average age of 50 days. Accounts payable are paid approximately 40 days after they arise. The firm has annual sales of $36 million, its cost of goods sold represents 75% of sales, and its purchases represent 70% of the cost of goods sold. Assume a 365-day year.

   a. Calculate the firm's operating cycle.
   b. Calculate the firm's cash conversion cycle.
   c. Calculate the amount of total resources Canadian Products has invested in its CCC.
   d. Discuss how management might be able to reduce the amount of total resources invested in the CCC.

22-7. The cash conversion cycle is an important tool for the financial manager in managing day-to-day operations of the firm. For an investor, knowing how the firm manages its

CCC would provide useful insights about management's effectiveness in managing the firm's resource investment in the CCC. Access Microsoft's annual statement at http://www.microsoft.com, and calculate Microsoft's CCC. Discuss any difficulties you had in obtaining adequately detailed data from Microsoft's website for use in calculating its CCC. Evaluate Microsoft's CCC in light of your calculations.

22-8. A firm is weighing five plans that affect several current accounts. Given the five plans and their probable effects on inventory, receivables, and payables (as shown in the following table), which plan would you favor? Explain.

	Change		
	---	---	---
Plan	**Average Age of Inventory (days)**	**Average Collection Period (days)**	**Average Payment Period (days)**
A	+35	+20	+10
B	+20	−15	+10
C	−10	+5	+0
D	−20	+15	+5
E	+15	−15	+20

22-9. King Manufacturing turns its inventory 9.1 times each year, has an average payment period of 35 days, and has an average collection period of 60 days. The firm's annual sales are $72 million, its cost of goods sold represents 50% of sales, and its purchases represent 80% of the cost of goods sold. Assume a 365-day year.

a. Calculate the firm's operating cycle and cash conversion cycle.

b. Calculate the firm's total resources invested in its CCC.

c. Assuming the firm pays 14% to finance its resource investment in its CCC, how much would it save annually by reducing its CCC by 20 days if this reduction were achieved by shortening the average age of inventory by 10 days, shortening the average collection period by 5 days, and lengthening the average payment period by 5 days?

d. If the 20-day reduction in the firm's CCC could be achieved by a 20-day change in only one of the CCC's three components, which one would you recommend? Explain.

22-10. Bradbury Corporation turns its inventory five times each year, has an average payment period of 25 days, and has an average collection period of 32 days. The firm's annual sales are $3.6 billion, its cost of goods sold represents 80% of sales, and its purchases represent 50% of the cost of goods sold. Assume a 365-day year.

a. Calculate the firm's operating cycle and cash conversion cycle.

b. Calculate the total resources invested in the firm's CCC.

c. Assume that the firm pays 18% to finance its resource investment. By how much could the firm increase its annual profits if (1) it reduced its CCC by 12 days and (2) this reduction were solely the result of extending its average payment period by 12 days?

d. If part (c)'s 12-day reduction in the firm's CCC could alternatively have been achieved by shortening either the average age of inventory or the average collection period by 12 days, would you have recommended one of those actions rather than the 12-day extension of the average payment period specified in part (c)? Which change would you recommend? Explain.

22-11. Aztec Products wishes to evaluate its cash conversion cycle. One of the firm's financial analysts has discovered that, on average, the firm holds items in inventory for 65 days, pays its suppliers 35 days after purchase, and collects its receivables after 55 days. The firm's annual sales (all on credit) are about $2.1 billion, its cost of goods sold represent about 67% of sales, and purchases represent about 40% of the cost of goods sold. Assume a 365-day year.

   a. What are Aztec Products' operating cycle and cash conversion cycle?

   b. How many dollars of resources does Aztec have invested in (1) inventory, (2) accounts receivable, (3) accounts payable, and (4) total CCC?

   c. If Aztec could shorten its cash conversion cycle by reducing its inventory holding period by five days, what effect would that have on the total resource investment found in part (b)?

   d. If Aztec could shorten its CCC by five days, would it be best to reduce the inventory holding period, reduce the receivables collection period, or extend the accounts payable period? Why?

22-12. Go to http://finance.yahoo.com and then input the ticker symbols noted in parentheses following each of the company names listed below. Under the Financials heading in the left-hand column, click on "Income Statement" and then "Balance Sheet" to obtain the most recent income statement and balance sheet for each firm. Use the appropriate financial statement data for each firm to respond to the following instructions and questions.

     Anheuser-Busch Companies, Inc. (BUD)
     Coca-Cola Company (KO)
     Molson Coors Company (TAP)
     PepsiCo, Inc. (PEP)

   a. Use the formulas given in the chapter to calculate the following time periods (in days) for each of the firms:

     (1) Average age of inventory
     (2) Average collection period
     (3) Average payment period

   b. Use the time periods calculated in part (a) to calculate each firm's operating cycle and cash conversion cycle.

   c. Compare the OC and CCC calculated in part (b) for each of the following combinations:

     (1) The two soft-drink companies (KO and PEP)
     (2) The two beer companies (BUD and TAP)

     How would you describe the differences found for each pair of firms?

   d. Compare the OC and CCC for the two soft-drink companies to those of the two beer companies. Explain any differences you observe.

Cost Trade-offs in Short-Term Financial Management

22-13. Geet Industries wants to install a just-in-time (JIT) inventory system in order to significantly reduce its in-process inventories. The annual cost of the system is gauged to be $95,000. The financial manager estimates that, with this system, the firm's average inventory investment will decline by 40% from its current level of $2.05 million. All other costs are expected to be unaffected by this system. The firm can earn 14% per year on investments of similar risk.

   a. What is the annual cost savings expected to result from installation of the proposed JIT system?

   b. Should the firm install the system?

22-14. Sheth & Sons Inc. is considering changing the pay period for its salaried management from every two weeks to monthly. The firm's CFO, Ken Smart, believes that such action will free up cash that can be used elsewhere in the business, which currently faces a cash crunch. In order to avoid a strong negative response from the salaried managers, the firm will simultaneously announce a new health plan that will lower managers' cost contributions without cutting benefits.

Ken's analysis indicates that the salaried managers' bimonthly payroll is $1.8 million and is expected to remain at that level for the foreseeable future. With the biweekly system, there were 2.2 pay periods in a month. Because the managers will be paid monthly, the monthly payroll will be about $4.0 million (2.2 × $1.8 million). The annual cost to the firm of the new health plan will be $180,000. Ken believes that, because managers' salaries accrue at a constant rate over the pay period, the average salaries over the period can be estimated by dividing the total amount by 2. The firm believes that it can earn 15% annually on any funds made available through the accrual of the managers' salaries.

  a. How much additional financing will Sheth & Sons obtain as a result of switching the pay period for managers' salaries from every two weeks to monthly?

  b. Should the firm implement the proposed change in pay periods?

22-15. Firm CFT is trying to determine the optimal amount of a particular inventory item to carry in its warehouse. CFT tends to sell 1,000 units a year, with each unit costing $1,200 and an additional carrying cost of $300. How many units should CFT optimally hold in its inventory? The supplier will ship only 100 units at a given time. Consequently, CFT wants to manage its carrying cost to accommodate this constraint. What carrying cost would make 100 units the optimal quantity? CFT finds that it can only reduce carrying cost to $260. What per-unit cost would make 100 units the optimal amount to hold in inventory? Would it make sense for CFT to negotiate with its supplier for this price?

Inventory Management

22-16. Calculate the average investment in inventory for each of the following situations. Assume a 365-day year.

  a. A firm's annual sales are $18 million, its gross profit margin is 32%, and its average age of inventory is 45 days.

  b. A firm's annual sales are $325 million, its cost of goods sold is 80% of sales, and it turns its inventory 10 times per year.

  c. A firm's annual cost of goods sold totals $120 million, and it turns its inventory about every 70 days.

22-17. GEP Manufacturing is mulling over a plan to rent a proprietary inventory control system at an annual cost of $4.5 million. The firm predicts its sales will remain relatively stable at $585 million and that its gross profit margin will continue to be 28%. GEP expects that, as a result of the new inventory control system, its average age of inventory will drop from its current level of 83 days to about 46 days. The firm's required return on investments of similar risk is 12%. Assume a 365-day year.

  a. Calculate GEP's average inventory investment both (1) currently and (2) assuming it rents the inventory control system.

  b. Use your findings in part (a) to determine the annual savings expected to result from the proposed inventory control system.

  c. Based on your answer to part (b), would you recommend that GEP rent the inventory control system? Explain your recommendation.

22-18. Iverson Industries uses 80,000 units of an "A" item of raw material inventory each year. The firm maintains level production throughout the year, given the steady demand for its finished products. The raw material order cost is $225 per order, and carrying costs are estimated to be $10.50 per unit per year. The firm wishes to maintain a safety stock of 10 days of inventory, and it takes 5 days for the firm to receive an order once it is placed. Assume a 365-day year.

   a. Calculate the economic order quantity (EOQ) for Iverson's raw material.
   b. How large a safety stock (in units) of inventory should the firm maintain?
   c. What is Iverson's reorder point for this item of inventory? (*Hint:* Be sure to include the safety stock.)

22-19. Litespeed Products buys 200,000 motors per year from a supplier that can fulfill orders within two days of receiving them. Litespeed transmits its orders to this supplier electronically, so the lead time to receive orders is two days. Litespeed's order cost is about $295 per order and its carrying cost is about $37 per motor per year. The firm maintains a safety stock of motors equal to six days of usage. Assume a 365-day year.

   a. What is Litespeed's economic order quantity for the motors?
   b. What is its *total cost* at the EOQ?
   c. How large a safety stock (in units) of motors should Litespeed maintain?
   d. What is Litespeed's reorder point for motors? (*Hint:* Be sure to include the safety stock.)
   e. If Litespeed has an opportunity to reduce either its order cost or its carrying cost by 10%, which would result in the lowest total cost at the associated new EOQ?
   f. How much total cost savings will result from the lowest-cost strategy found in part (e) relative to the total cost found in part (b)?

22-20. Vargas Enterprises wishes to determine the economic order quantity for a critical and expensive inventory item that it uses in large amounts at a relatively constant rate throughout the year. The firm uses 450,000 units of the item annually and has order costs of $375 per order; its carrying costs associated with this item are $28 per unit per year. The firm plans to hold safety stock of the item equal to five days of usage, and it estimates that 12 days are needed to receive an order for the item once placed. Assume a 365-day year.

   a. Calculate the firm's EOQ for the item of inventory described in the problem.
   b. What is the firm's total cost based upon the EOQ calculated in part (a)?
   c. How many units of safety stock should Vargas hold?
   d. What is the firm's reorder point for the item of inventory being evaluated?

Accounts Receivable Standards and Terms

22-21. International Oil Company (IOC) uses credit scoring to evaluate gasoline credit card applications. The following table presents the financial and credit characteristics and weights (indicating the relative importance of each characteristic) used in the credit decision. The firm's credit standards are to accept all applicants with credit scores of 80 or higher, to extend limited credit on a probationary basis to applicants with scores higher than 70 and lower than 80, and to reject all applicants with scores at or below 70.

Financial and Credit Characteristics	Predetermined Weight
Credit references	0.25
Education	0.10
Home ownership	0.10
Income range	0.15
Payment history	0.30
Years on job	0.10

The firm needs to process three applications scored recently by one of its credit analysts. The scores for each of the applicants are summarized in the following table.

Financial and Credit Characteristics	Applicants' Scores (0 to 100)		
	X	Y	Z
Credit references	60	90	80
Education	75	80	80
Home ownership	100	90	60
Income range	70	70	80
Payment history	60	85	70
Years on job	50	60	90

   a. Use the data presented to find the credit score for each of the applicants.

   b. Recommend the action that the firm should take for each of the three applicants.

22-22. Barans Company currently has an average collection period of 55 days and annual sales of $1 billion. Assume a 365-day year.

   a. What is the firm's average accounts receivable balance?

   b. If the variable cost of each product is 65% of sales, then what is the average investment in accounts receivable?

   c. If the equal-risk opportunity cost of the investment in accounts receivable is 12%, what is the total annual cost of the resources invested in accounts receivable?

22-23. Melton Electronics currently has an average collection period of 35 days and annual sales of $72 million. Assume a 365-day year.

   a. What is the firm's average accounts receivable balance?

   b. If the variable cost of each product is 70% of sales, what is the firm's average investment in accounts receivable?

   c. If the equal-risk opportunity cost of the investment in accounts receivable is 16%, then what is the total annual cost of the resources invested in accounts receivable?

   d. Suppose that Melton can shorten the average collection period to 30 days by offering a cash discount of 1% for early payment and that 60% of the customers take this discount. Should the firm offer this discount? Assume that its cost of bad debts will rise by $150,000 per year.

22-24. Davis Manufacturing Industries (DMI) produces and sells 20,000 units of a machine tool each year. All sales are on credit, and DMI charges all customers $500 per unit. Variable costs are $350 per unit, and DMI incurs $2 million in fixed costs each year.

     DMI's top managers are evaluating a proposal from the firm's CFO that the firm relax its credit standards to increase its sales and profits. The CFO believes this change will increase unit sales by 4%. Currently, DMI's average collection period is 40 days, but the CFO expects this to increase to 60 days under the new policy. Bad debt expense is also expected to increase from 1% to 2.5% of annual sales. The firm's board of directors has set a required return of 15% on investments with this level of risk. Assume a 365-day year.

   a. What is DMI's contribution margin? By how much will profits from increased sales change if DMI adopts the new credit standards?

   b. Under the current credit standards, what is DMI's average investment in accounts receivable? What would it be under the proposed credit standards? What is the cost of this additional investment?

c. What is DMI's cost of marginal bad debts resulting from the relaxation of its credit standards?

d. What is DMI's net profit (or loss) from adopting the new credit standards? Should DMI relax its credit standards?

22-25. Jeans Manufacturing thinks that it can reduce its high credit costs by tightening its credit standards. However, the firm believes that the planned tightening will result in a drop in annual sales from $38 million to $36 million. On the positive side, the firm expects its average collection period to fall from 58 to 45 days and its bad debts to drop from 2.5% to 1% of sales. The firm's variable cost per unit is 70% of its sale price, and its required return on investment is 15%. Assume a 365-day year. Evaluate the proposed tightening of credit standards, and make a recommendation to the management of Jeans Manufacturing.

22-26. Belton Company is considering relaxing its credit standards to boost its currently sagging sales. The firm expects that its proposed relaxation will increase sales by 20% from the current annual level of $10 million. Managers expect that the firm's average collection period will increase from 35 to 50 days and that bad debts will increase from 2% to 7% of sales if the firm's credit standards are relaxed as proposed. The firm's variable costs equal 60% of sales, and its fixed costs total $2.5 million per year. Belton's opportunity cost is 16%. Assume a 365-day year.

a. What is Belton's contribution margin?

b. Calculate Belton's marginal profit contribution from sales.

c. What is Belton's cost of the marginal investment in accounts receivable?

d. What is Belton's cost of marginal bad debts?

e. Use your findings in parts (b), (c), and (d) to determine the net profit (cost) of Belton's proposed relaxation of credit standards. Should the company relax its credit standards?

22-27. Webb Inc. currently makes all sales on credit and offers no cash discounts. The firm is considering a 2% cash discount for payments within 10 days. The firm's current average collection period is 65 days, sales are 400,000 units, selling price is $50 per unit, and variable cost per unit is $40. The firm expects that the changes in credit terms will result in a sales increase to 410,000 units, that 75% of the purchases will be paid for at the discount, and that the average collection period will fall to 45 days. Bad debts are expected to drop from 1.0% to 0.9% of sales. If Webb's required rate of return on investments of similar risk is 25%, should the firm offer the proposed discount? Assume a 365-day year.

22-28. Microboard, Inc., a major computer chip manufacturer, is contemplating lengthening its credit period from net 30 days to net 50 days. Presently, its average collection period is 40 days; the firm's CFO believes that, with the proposed new credit period, the average collection period will be 65 days. The firm's sales are $900 million, but the CFO believes that the new credit terms will increase sales to $980 million. At the current $900 million sales level, the firm's total variable costs are $630 million. The firm's CFO estimates that, with the proposed new credit terms, bad debt expenses will increase from the current level of 1.5% of sales to 2.0% of sales. The CFO also believes that the increased sales volume and accompanying receivables will require the firm to add more facilities and personnel to its credit and collections department. The annual cost of the expanded credit operations resulting from the proposed new credit period is estimated to be $10 million. The firm's required return on similar-risk investments is 18%. Assuming a 365-day year, evaluate the economics of Microboard's proposed lengthening of the credit period and then make a recommendation to the firm's management.

Collecting, Monitoring, and Applying Cash to Receivables

22-29. United Worldwide's accounts receivable totaled $1.75 million on August 31, 2010. The table below gives a breakdown of these outstanding accounts on the basis of the month of the initial credit sale. The firm extends credit terms of net 30, EOM to its credit customers.

Month of Credit Sale	Accounts Receivable
August 2010	$ 640,000
July 2010	500,000
June 2010	164,000
May 2010	390,000
April 2010 or before	56,000
Total (August 31, 2010)	$1,750,000

a. Prepare an aging schedule for United Worldwide's August 31, 2010, accounts receivable balance.

b. Using your findings in part (a), evaluate the firm's credit and collection activities.

c. What are some probable causes of the situation discussed in part (b)?

22-30. Big Air Board Company, a global manufacturer and distributor of surfboards and snowboards, is in a seasonal business. Although surfboard sales are only mildly seasonal, the snowboard sales are driven by peak demand in the first and fourth calendar quarters of each year. The following table gives the firm's monthly sales for the immediate past quarter (October through December 2010) and its forecast monthly sales for the coming year (calendar year 2011).

Month	Sales ($ million)
Historic	
October 2010	$3.7
November 2010	3.9
December 2010	4.3
Forecast	
January 2011	$3.8
February 2011	2.6
March 2011	2.2
April 2011	1.6
May 2011	1.8
June 2011	1.9
July 2011	2.0
August 2011	2.2
September 2011	2.4
October 2011	4.1
November 2011	4.6
December 2011	5.1

The firm extends credit terms of 2/10 net 30, EOM to all customers. It collects 98% of its receivables and typically writes off the other 2% as bad debts. Big Air Board's historic collection pattern, which is expected to continue through 2011, is 5% collected in the month of the sale, 65% collected in the first month following the sale, and 28% collected in the second month following the sale. Using the data given, calculate the payment pattern of Big Air Board's accounts receivable. Comment on the firm's monthly collections during calendar year 2011.

THOMSON ONE | Business School Edition

22-31. Compute the average age of inventory, average collection period, and average payment period for Cracker Barrel Old Country Store, Inc. (ticker symbol, CBRL), Caterpillar, Inc. (ticker symbol, CAT), Kohl's Corp. (ticker symbol, KSS), and Wal-Mart Stores, Inc. (ticker symbol, WMT) for the last four years. Also calculate the operating cycle and the cash conversion cycle for each of the firms for the same time period. Why are there differences in each of the measures across the different firms? For each firm, comment on how the CCC and each of its components have changed over the last four years. Can you conclude that one firm's cash conversion cycle is "better" simply because it has a lower value?

MINI-CASE: CASH CONVERSION, INVENTORY, AND RECEIVABLES MANAGEMENT

Bracelet Blanks, Inc. (BB) generated $43,803,000 in sales (all on credit) during 2010. The cost of goods sold was 57% of that total. Accounts receivable totaled $3,240,222, inventory totaled $842,020, and accounts payable totaled $1,826,070.

1. Calculate BB's current cash conversion cycle.

2. BB currently uses 3,000 ingots of aluminum each year to manufacture bracelet blanks. The order cost (including shipping) is $5,000 per order, and carrying costs are $75 per unit per year. Determine the economic order quantity, the amount of safety stock, and the reorder point for aluminum ingots assuming there is a 1-week lead time and the firm would like a safety stock of 3%.

3. In an attempt to boost sales, BB is considering relaxing its credit standards by extending more credit to small firms. BB charges $1.50 per unit. Variable costs are $0.5126 per unit and fixed costs are $10,000,000 per year. The relaxation of credit standards is expected to result in a 3.8% increase in sales (the firm has sufficient excess capacity to handle the increase) as well as an increase of three days in the average collection period. They also expect bad debts to rise from the current level of 0% to 0.5% of sales. Assuming that BB requires a 13% return on investments of this type, should the firm relax its credit standards?

4. Additionally, BB currently offers its credit customers terms of net 30. However, it is considering changing the terms to 2/10 net 30 in an attempt to reduce the amount of time it takes to collect its accounts receivable. The firm believes this change alone would decrease the average collection period by five days. BB also expects that 63% of its customers will elect to pay within the discount period and that the increased attractiveness of the terms will increase sales by 1% a year. It is not expected that bad debts will change from the current level of 0% as a result of this change in terms. BB's opportunity cost of funds invested in accounts receivable is 10%. Should the firm offer the cash discount? Evaluate this scenario separately from the one described in question 3.

What Companies Do

The Electronic Payment Revolution?

Liquidity Management*

During the 1960s, a firm was considered efficient if it could process an order in 4 to 7 days, have the product delivered in 14 to 21 days, receive the invoice within a week, and pay within 45 to 60 days. Today a firm is considered "old school" if its customers can't order today, have it shipped to their door tomorrow, get the invoice that same day, and still have 45–60 days to pay!

To address this issue in today's e-everything world, some firms are embracing e-invoicing when making business-to-business transactions. The clunky term for this process is *electronic invoice presentment and payment*, or simply EIPP. The benefits of EIPP include elimination of paper, greatly reduced processing costs, automatic validation of invoice data, and dramatic improvement in on-time payment performance. Enterprise software developers such as PeopleSoft, Oracle, and SAP offer sophisticated packages that tie payments to procurement and make it easier for firms to use EIPP.

It is not surprising that the lack of incentive for firms to speed their payments to vendors has slowed the adoption of EIPP. Clearly, paying faster is contrary to the firm's goal of reducing its resource investment by shortening its cash conversion cycle (CCC). The strategy for increasing the adoption of EIPP being pushed by JP Morgan Xign Corp., a leader in on-demand order-to-pay business software, is for the buyer to agree to pay quickly in exchange for an attractive early-pay discount from the vendor. In addition, by making the transaction and payment electronically, the buyer and seller will reduce their manual labor costs.

Despite the fact that some major companies—such as Dell Inc., Wells Fargo & Co., Office Depot Inc., and Pacific Care Health Systems—have adopted EIPP, so far the acceptance of EIPP has been relatively slow. The problem is that each company that adopts it must convince its customers to sign on. Beth Robertson, a senior research analyst at research and advisory firm Tower Group, suggests that the growth in EIPP will continue to be gradual. She believes that broad technical standards must be established and security issues resolved before there will be widespread adoption of EIPP.

Sources: Julie Sturgeon, "Electronic Payments," CFO (Winter 2003), pp. 52–53; Doug Roberts, "Giving Cash Management a Technology Boost," Financial Executive (December 2003), pp. 62–63; "JP Morgan Chase Closes Acquisition of Xign," Xign Corporation Press Release (May 17, 2007); JP Morgan website, http://www.jpmorgan.com/cm/ContentServer?c=TS_Content&pagename=jpmorgan/ts/TS_Content/General&cid=1159317518404 (accessed February 18, 2009).

*Professor Dubos J. Masson, CCM, CertCM, of Indiana University assisted in preparation of a large part of this chapter. The authors very much appreciate D.J.'s important contribution.

Chapter 22 described the operating and cash conversion cycles and then focused on management of the two key components of the operating cycle: inventory and accounts receivable. Here we shift focus to cash, accounts payable, and liquidity. Clearly, cash is the lifeblood of the firm. Thus it is the primary focus of the financial manager, who must conserve it by gathering cash receipts and making cash disbursements in a cost-effective manner. Additionally, the financial manager conserves cash by using efficient mechanisms for transferring it within and between the firm's operating units. As noted in Chapter 22, short-term financing decisions should result from an analysis of cost trade-offs with the goal of minimizing total cost.

Accounts payable are also an important component of the cash conversion cycle. The firm must manage them in a way that lengthens the payment period while preserving the firm's credit reputation. This strategy will help shorten the cash conversion cycle and reduce the firm's resource requirements. The financial manager also will use other strategies and tools to slow down disbursements.

Of course, all of these cash management strategies are predicated on the firm's ability to maintain adequate liquidity to preserve the firm's solvency. Specifically, the firm must be able to both earn a positive return on idle excess cash balances and obtain low-cost financing for meeting unexpected needs and seasonal cash shortages. This important activity is commonly called **liquidity management**.

Liquidity management plays a role akin to oil lubricating an engine. Without proper liquidity, the economic engine of a corporation will seize up, greatly hampering the ability of the firm to conduct business. This was starkly evident in the period following the credit crisis that began in 2007 and worsened in 2008. For example, GM burned through $6.2 billion in cash in the fourth quarter of 2008 and—although it received $13.4 billion in federal loans between December 31, 2008, and the middle of February 2009—announced in late February 2009 that the bare minimum amount of cash it needed to conduct business was $14 billion. Clearly, the ability to manage cash is crucial to corporate efficiency and even survival.

This chapter emphasizes the key procedures for managing cash, payables, and liquidity. We begin with a discussion of cash management that focuses on *float* in the cash collection and payment system and on the principles of managing the firm's cash position. Next, we consider cash collection, placing emphasis on the types of collection systems, lockbox systems, cash concentration, and various mechanisms for funds transfer. Then we review some key aspects of accounts payable and disbursements: the accounts payable process, cash discounts, disbursement products and methods, and developments in accounts payable and disbursements. Finally, we consider the firm's use of short-term investing and borrowing to maintain adequate liquidity.

23.1 CASH MANAGEMENT

Many companies employ financial specialists known as **cash managers**. One of their primary roles is to manage the cash flow time line related to collection, concentration, and disbursement of the company's funds. The cash manager's job typically starts when a customer (the payer) initiates payment to the company (the payee) in any format (cash, check, or electronic). Because most business-to-business payments are still effected by sending a check in the mail, the collections process usually involves trying to reduce delays in mail, processing, and check collection.

The cash manager is also responsible for assembling or *concentrating* cash from remote collection points into a central account and for initiating payments from the company to its suppliers. The final stage of this process usually involves reconciling the company's various bank accounts and managing all the banking relationships. Any delay in timing on either the collection or disbursement side is generally referred to as *float*.

Float

JOB INTERVIEW QUESTION

What are the cash manager's goals with regard to float when managing a firm's cash receipts and cash disbursements?

Float refers to funds that have been sent by the payer but are not yet usable funds to the payee. Float is important in the cash conversion cycle because its application increases both the firm's average collection period and its average payment period. The primary role of the cash manager on the collections side is to *minimize collection float* wherever possible. On the payments side, trying to *maximize disbursement float* is a common practice that raises an important question: Is it ethical to intentionally pay a supplier after the term within which the firm agreed to pay? This topic will be discussed in greater detail later in the chapter.

We can view float from either the receiving party's (the payee's) perspective or the paying party's (the payer's) perspective. The following list points out that mail float and processing float are generally the same from both perspectives, though the final outcomes are different. The four components of float are defined as follows.

1. **Mail float** is the time delay between when payment is placed in the mail and when payment is received. This float component can range from one day to as many as five days or more, depending on location and other factors.
2. **Processing float** is the time between receipt of the payment and its deposit into the firm's account. In a mail-based system, this involves opening the envelope, separating the check from the remittance advice, preparing the check for deposit, and actually depositing the check at the company's bank. This float component can range from less than one day to three or more days, depending on any processing delays the company may have.
3. **Availability float** is the time between deposit of the check and availability of the funds to the firm. Although this may be related to the actual clearing time of the check, it is ultimately a function of the availability schedule offered by the deposit bank. For most business checks, this ranges from the same day to as many as three business days, depending on where the check is drawn.
4. **Clearing float** is the time between deposit of the check and presentation of the check back to the bank on which it is drawn. This component of float is attributable to the time required for a check to clear the banking system and to have funds debited from the payer's account. In today's clearing system for business checks, availability float and clearing float are generally the same, but there are some exceptions when checks are drawn on banks that are small and/or geographically remote.

In addition to managing the collection, concentration, and disbursement of funds, the cash manager is also responsible for the following duties.

- Financial relationships: *Managing relationships with banks and other providers of cash management services*
- Cash flow forecasting: *Determining future cash flows to predict surpluses or deficits (see Chapter 21)*
- Investing and borrowing: *Managing the investment of short-term surpluses or borrowing for short-term deficits*
- Information management: *Developing and maintaining information systems to gather and analyze cash management data*

Cash management typically resides in the firm's treasury area along with such functions as external financing and risk management. In smaller companies, accounting or clerical staffs may perform the cash management function. The staff's specific cash management tasks related to collection, concentration, and disbursement of funds are described in the following sections.

Cash Position Management

On a daily basis, the primary cash management tasks related to the collection, concentration, and disbursement of funds for the company are generally referred to as **cash position management**. That is, each day the cash manager must determine the amount of funds to be collected, move balances to the appropriate accounts, and fund the projected disbursements. The cash position can be managed with some degree of accuracy many weeks into the future, given proper forecasting of cash flows. Most of the cash management products and services offered by banks and other financial institutions are associated with some part of this process.

At the end of the day, the cash manager must determine (1) whether the company will have a surplus or a deficit of funds in each checking account and (2) how to manage the difference. If the company has a *surplus* of funds, then the money may be placed in some type of short-term investment, such as an interest-bearing account at its bank or a portfolio of marketable securities. However, if the firm has a deficit, then the cash manager must arrange either to transfer funds from investment accounts or to draw on a short-term credit agreement with the firm's bank. The management of these short-term investing and borrowing arrangements is typically the responsibility of the cash manager.

Many companies, especially smaller ones, do not actively engage in cash position management but rather set a **target cash balance** for their checking accounts. The primary approach to determining these target cash balances is based on transactions requirements or a minimum balance set by the bank. The transactions requirement is determined simply by how much cash a firm needs to fund its day-to-day operations. Firms with a high volume of daily inflows and outflows will find that some balances remain in non-interest-bearing checking accounts, regardless of the forecasting ability. Many banks also require a specified minimum balance in customer checking accounts. For smaller companies and banks, this minimum balance is designed to provide adequate compensation to the bank for the services it provides. For larger companies, most banks perform *account analysis*, which compares the value of the balances a firm leaves on deposit to the value of the services it receives from the bank.

A **bank account analysis statement** is a report (usually monthly) provided to a bank's commercial customers that specifies all services provided, including items processed and any charges assessed. It is basically a detailed invoice that lists all checks cleared, account charges, lockbox charges, electronic transactions, and so on. The statement also lists all balances held by the firm at the bank, and includes a computation of the credit earned by the firm on those balances. Under current federal regulations, a bank is not allowed to pay actual interest on corporate checking account balances; however, it can offer an *earnings credit* on these balances that is used to offset service charges. Most companies on account analysis will receive some credit for the transaction balances they leave in the account, and typically the credit will only partially offset the service fees. The balance of fees owed the bank will then be deducted as a service charge for the month in question.

Concept Review Questions	
	1. What is float? What are its four components? What is the difference between availability float and clearing float?
	2. What activities are involved in cash position management? How does the cash manager monitor and take actions with regard to the end-of-day checking account balances?
	3. How do smaller firms that do not engage in cash position management typically set their target cash balance? What is typically detailed in a bank account analysis statement?

23.2 COLLECTIONS

The primary objective of the collections process is to quickly and efficiently collect funds from customers and others. This process includes gathering and disseminating information related to the collections, and in some cases the information may be as important as the money itself. One key requirement is ensuring that the accounts receivable department has the remittance information needed to properly post receipts and update customer files. A secondary requirement is to provide audit trails for the company's internal and external auditors.

As discussed previously, a major delay in the collections process results from *collection float*, which is a function of the mail, processing, and availability floats. The primary goal of collections is to reduce each of these float components as much as possible. Collection float is typically measured in *dollar-days*, or the number of dollars in the collection process multiplied by the number of days of float. For example, $10 million of checks with an average of five days of float would represent $50 million dollar-days of float.

It is important to understand the various payment practices in the U.S. business environment. In the United States, most business-to-business payments are still made via a check in the mail. Many consumer payments are also still made via check, whereas retail establishments must handle cash, debit, and credit cards in addition to checks.

The U.S. business environment is also characterized by a large number of financial institutions: approximately 7,000 commercial banks, 1,200 thrift institutions, and 8,000 credit unions (these figures are based on recent statistics from the FDIC and the NCUA). Historically, the United States has been lacking in true nationwide banking, but bank mergers and expansion of regional branching activities have brought this closer to reality.

Speeding up collections reduces the firm's *average collection period*, which in turn reduces the investment the firm must make in its cash conversion cycle. In our example of the cash conversion cycle in Chapter 22 (Example on page 728), Reese Industries had annual sales of $5 billion and eight days of total collection float (mail, processing, and availability time). If Reese can reduce its collection float time by five days (to three days), it reduces its investment in the cash conversion cycle by $68.5 million [$5 billion $\times$ (5 days $\div$ 365 days)]. A number of popular systems and techniques can be implemented to speed up collections.

The most recent development in the collections area is the implementation of Check 21 legislation (Check Clearing for the 21st Century Act) in 2003/2004. This allows for the creation of digital images of checks that replace the original paper checks. Such images can be cleared much more quickly and efficiently, resulting in significantly reduced clearing times for checks.

Types of Collection Systems

A firm's collection system is primarily determined by the nature of its business. Many high-volume retail establishments, such as fast-food restaurants or convenience stores, receive the bulk of their payments in cash. Other types of retail operations, such as department and variety stores, collect most of their payments by credit card, debit card, or check.

As we have noted, the typical business-to-business payment mechanism is a check mailed in response to an invoice received for products or services. What can complicate the collection process is that one check is often used to pay multiple invoices, and there may be adjustments or partial payments related to those invoices. This makes the information collected by the cash manager of critical importance to the accounts receivable department. Collection systems must take into account the information management requirements related to the payment application process.

WHAT COMPANIES DO GLOBALLY

How Companies Finance Working Capital Needs with Lines of Credit

Financial researchers have developed a clear picture of the working capital practices of U.S. corporations, but far less is known about how companies headquartered in other major countries manage their liquidity needs. A major new survey enriches our understanding of how much cash and marketable securities international companies hold, the purposes for holding these cash balances, and how firms employ lines of credit to finance their operational and precautionary working capital needs. Professors Karl Lins, Henri Servaes, and Peter Tufano surveyed companies in 29 countries, and the results highlight three important points. First, they suggest that international companies pursue liquidity management policies that are generally similar to those followed by U.S. firms. Second, they reveal that corporations everywhere make an important distinction between cash and marketable securities held for operational purposes versus cash and liquid assets held for non-operational and precautionary reasons. And third,

they tell us that lines of credit are vital tools of liquidity management in almost every country.

The following table summarizes managerial responses to two questions about cash holdings and the use of bank lines of credit. Panel A describes the importance of various factors in determining how much "excess cash"—defined as holdings of cash and marketable securities in excess of operating needs—managers choose to hold. For the full sample of companies, total cash holdings amount to 9% of the book value of assets, but cash held for non-operational purposes amount to only 40% of total cash holdings. The most important reason managers give for holding excess cash is to serve as a buffer for possible future cash flow shortfalls, while the need to maintain adequate cash to ensure efficient running of the company is the second most frequently mentioned reason. Managers are also concerned about ensuring the cost and potential availability of funds in case the firm needs to obtain working capital quickly or during an emergency.

(continued)

Survey Responses to Questions about Non-operational Cash and Lines of Credit

Panel A
"In deciding how much excess cash to hold, how important are the following factors?"

Factor	Percentage Responding "Important" or "Very Important"
Cash as a buffer against future cash flow shortfalls	47
Minimal cash ensures efficient running of the company	35
Difference between interest rate on cash and interest rate on debt	35
Time it takes to raise money when funds are needed	31
Level of uncertainty about future investment opportunities	31
Ability to issue debt at a "fair" price when funds are needed	30
Difference between interest rate on cash and cost of capital	26
Size of the undrawn credit facility	23
Transactions costs of raising funds	22

Panel B
"How important are the following factors in deciding on the size of your line of credit?"

Factor	Percentage Responding "Important" or "Very Important"
Credit facility is flexible: Can be drawn and repaid at will	69
Certainty of funding during event risk or acquisition opportunities	60
The fee charged on the credit line	39
The time it takes to raise funds through other means	34
The cost of the credit facility is certain	32
Transaction costs of running funds through other means versus the commitment fee	30

The survey authors also document that lines of credit are the dominant component of corporate liquidity in their global sample of firms, with a median line of credit equal to 15% of book assets. This is very similar to the 16% fraction documented for U.S. firms in other studies. Panel B of the table describes the factors that influence managerial choices about using bank lines of credit around the world. These findings clearly suggest that managers are very concerned about ensuring that credit is available at acceptable cost when needed—especially during periods of financial stress. Finally, the authors conclude that cash and credit lines are used for different purposes, with cash being held principally to meet operational needs and lines of credit serving a precautionary function.

Source: Karl V. Lins, Henri Servaes, and Peter ufano, "What Drives Corporate Liquidity? An International Survey of Cash Holdings and Lines of Credit," Working paper, Harvard University, 2008.

Some types of time-critical transactions, such as real estate closings or high-dollar payments, may be received via wire transfers with same-day value. Other forms of high-volume–low-dollar receipts, especially those of a recurring nature (utility payments, insurance premiums, etc.), may come through the *automated clearinghouse (ACH) system*, which generally offers next-day settlement with fairly low transaction costs. The important thing to understand is that the type of collection system used by a company is usually a function of both the type of business and the customary methods of payment used by that business.

Field Banking System   In a **field banking system**, most collections are made either over the counter (as at a retail store) or at a collection office (often used by utilities). These systems are characterized by many collection points, each of which may have a depository account at a local bank.

The main collection problem in this type of system involves transferring the funds from the local (often small) banks to the main account at the company's primary bank. Many large national retailers find they must maintain hundreds or even thousands of bank relationships as part of their collections system. Typically, the collections in a field banking system are local checks, cash, debit cards, and credit cards. Although debit card and credit card processing is usually highly automated and efficient, checks and cash must be processed and deposited at the local deposit bank. The funds must then be concentrated into the company's main account before the money can be used.

The backbone of this type of system is information management—that is, the company needs to know where the money is before the company can make use of it. Most large retailers utilize *point-of-sale (POS) information systems* that allow them to know on a daily basis how much money has been collected, in what formats (cash, check, debit card, or credit card) it was received, and how much of it was deposited at the local bank. The task of moving this money into a "concentration" account is discussed in the section on cash concentration.

One of the major developments in the area of field banking systems is the increasing use of check-conversion technology. The bulk of field banking check collections are consumer items, which are increasingly being converted into ACH debit transactions, resulting in faster collections at lower costs. Consumer checks can be converted at the point of purchase or later in the processing cycle. Consumer checks that are not converted (or business checks that are not allowed to be converted) can still be imaged (as per Check 21 guidelines) and thus processed more efficiently. Many companies are now using remote deposit capture machines to image checks as early as possible in the collections process.

Mail-Based Collection System   In a **mail-based collection system**, the company typically has one or more collection points that process the incoming mail payments. These processing centers receive the mail payments, open the envelopes, separate the check from the remittance information, prepare the check for deposit, and send the remittance information to the accounts receivable department for application of payment. Companies such as utilities and credit card processors that utilize standardized, scannable remittance information can often process the payments they receive quickly and efficiently using automated equipment. Although many high-volume processors can justify the cost of the equipment needed for automated processing, other companies may find that using a *lockbox* (discussed later) is more cost effective. However, recent developments in payment processing equipment have made automated processing available to smaller companies at a reasonable price.

Electronic Systems   Electronic collection systems, first patented in 2000, continue to develop rapidly as both businesses and consumers better understand their benefits. One of the key developments in this area is **electronic invoice presentment and payment (EIPP)**, introduced in this chapter's opening "What Companies Do" example, in the business-to-business market and **electronic bill presentment and payment (EBPP)** in the business-to-consumer market. In EIPP and EBPP systems, customers are sent electronic bills that they then can pay electronically. Most of these systems are Internet-based and are gradually gaining acceptance in the marketplace. The most successful of the consumer systems offers a consolidator-type service, where customers can go to one site to view and pay all their bills rather than visiting individual billing sites. Electronic payment systems have also gained acceptance in the business-to-business environment.

Some of the primary advantages of using a system such as the EIPP for business-to-business payments are (1) reduced float to the receiving party, (2) lower cost both of receivables processing for the receiver and of payment initiation and reconciliation costs for the payer, and (3) better forecasting for both parties. Though there may be a need to negotiate payment dates and possible discounts for earlier payment, companies that have implemented electronic payments report significant overall savings as a result.

The future for electronic collections systems appears to look good, as more and more companies are implementing some form of electronic invoicing and payment. Many of these systems are implemented by large companies as a means to streamline the billing of their (often smaller) customers and to automate the payment process. Companies that must pay a large number of smaller suppliers are also implementing electronic systems as a means to reduce their overall costs of running accounts payable and disbursement systems.

Lockbox Systems

A **lockbox system** is a popular technique for speeding up collections because it affects three components of float. It works like this: Instead of mailing payments to the company, customers mail payments to a post office box, which is emptied regularly by the firm's bank. The bank processes each payment and deposits the payments into the firm's account. The bank sends (or transmits electronically) deposit slips and enclosures to the firm so the firm can properly credit its customers' accounts.

Lockboxes are typically dispersed geographically to match the locations of the firm's customers. As a result of being near a firm's customers, lockboxes reduce mail time and clearing time. They reduce processing time to nearly zero because the bank deposits payments before the firm processes them. Obviously, a lockbox system reduces collection float, but not without a cost. Therefore, a firm must perform a cost–benefit analysis to determine whether a lockbox system should be implemented. Equation 23.1 presents a simple formula for the cost–benefit analysis of a lockbox system:

$$\text{Net benefit or cost} = (\text{FVR} \times r_a) - \text{LC} \qquad \textbf{(Eq. 23.1)}$$

where

FVR = float value reduction in dollars
r_a = cost of capital
LC = lockbox cost (annual operating cost of the system)

Thus, if the return on the float reduction exceeds the cost of the lockbox system, then the firm should implement the lockbox system.

EXAMPLE

Consider Reese Industries, which has $5 billion in annual sales and eight days of customer collection float in its cash conversion cycle. Reese wants to determine if it should implement a lockbox system that reduces customer collection float to five days. The reduction in float value from decreasing customer float from eight days to five days is $41.1 million [$5 billion × (3 days ÷ 365 days)]. Reese has a cost of capital of 13.5% per year. Thus, the value to Reese of reducing customer float by three days is $5.55 million (0.135 × $41.1 million). If the annual cost of the lockbox system is less than $5.55 million, it would be beneficial to implement the system.

Although large firms whose customers are geographically dispersed commonly use a lockbox system, small firms also may find a lockbox system advantageous. The benefit to small firms often comes primarily from transferring the processing of payments to the bank.

Lockboxes are typically classified as either retail or wholesale. A *retail lockbox* uses standardized, scannable remittance documents in order to highly automate the processing of incoming payments. These types of systems are characterized by high volumes of low-dollar payments, and the key issue is processing the payments at a minimum cost per dollar collected. Given the low-dollar amounts of these payments, availability float is generally not a big issue.

Wholesale lockboxes, on the other hand, primarily process high-dollar payments with nonstandard remittance information. The key issues in this type of system are (1) reducing the availability float related to the large checks and (2) quickly forwarding the remittance information to the accounts receivable (AR) department for application of payment. The current practice for wholesale lockboxes is to make extensive use of imaging technology to quickly and accurately relay copies of the remittance information back to the AR department.

Cash Concentration

In the previous section, lockbox systems were discussed as a means to reduce collection float. With a lockbox system, the firm has deposits in each lockbox bank. **Cash concentration** is the process of bringing the lockbox and other deposits together into one bank, commonly called the *concentration bank*.

Cash concentration has three main advantages. First, it creates a large pool of funds for use in making short-term cash investments. Because there is a fixed-cost component in the transaction cost associated with making marketable security investments, investing a single pool of funds reduces the firm's transaction costs. The larger investment pool also allows the firm to choose from a larger variety of marketable securities. Second, concentrating the firm's cash in one account improves the tracking and internal control of that cash. Third, having one concentration bank allows the firm to implement more effective payment strategies that preserve its invested balances for as long as possible. As bank branch networks continue to expand, more and more companies are choosing banks with large geographic coverage that can simplify concentration by using deposit reconciliation services.

The configuration of a company's cash concentration system is generally a function of the collection system. That is, a company with a *field banking system* will need a way to move money quickly and efficiently from many small deposit banks into its concentration account, whereas a company with several collection centers or lockboxes will typically use wire transfers to quickly move large balances from a limited number of collection points into its concentration account. The type of disbursement system (discussed in a later section) is also an important consideration, because these accounts must be funded either by internal transfer or wire transfer.

Funds Transfer Mechanisms

There are two commonly used mechanisms for transferring cash from the depository banks to the concentration bank: automated clearinghouse debit transfers and wire transfers.

Automated Clearinghouse Debit Transfers The first mechanism is an **automated clearinghouse (ACH) debit transfer**, which is a preauthorized electronic withdrawal from the payer's account and is generally known within the cash management field as an **electronic depository transfer (EDT)**.

The ACH, a computerized clearing facility, makes a paperless transfer of funds between the payer and payee banks. An ACH settles accounts among participating banks; individual accounts are settled by adjustments to the respective bank balances. ACH transfers of this type generally clear in one day.

For cash concentration, an ACH debit is initiated by the concentration bank and sent to each deposit bank, with funds then moving from the deposit bank into the concentration bank. These transfers can be automatically created from deposit information and can then be centrally initiated from the company's headquarters through its concentration bank. A large nationwide retailer can easily concentrate deposits from many small deposit banks into its concentration account by using the daily deposit information gathered from its stores' point-of-sale systems.

Wire Transfers The second funds transfer mechanism is a **wire transfer**. In the United States, the primary wire transfer system, known as *Fedwire*, is run by the Federal Reserve System and is available to all depository institutions. A Fedwire transfer is an electronic communication that removes funds from the payer's bank and deposits the funds in the payee's

Smart Practices Video

Daniel Carter, former Chief Financial Officer of Charlotte Russe

"Each of our stores makes deposits into a local account, which are concentrated back into our corporate account."

See the entire interview at **SMARTFinance**

JOB INTERVIEW QUESTION

What are some of the advantages to a firm of using cash concentration procedures?

bank on a same-day basis via bookkeeping entries in the financial institution's Federal Reserve account. An alternative to Fedwire is the CHIPS system operated by The Clearing House (the New York clearinghouse system). This system transfers over $2 trillion a day between its members, primarily large global banks and financial institutions operating in New York.

Wire transfers can eliminate mail float and clearing float and may provide processing float reductions as well. For cash concentration, the firm moves funds using a wire transfer from each deposit account to its concentration account. Wire transfers are a substitute for ACH debit transfers, but they are generally much more expensive: both the sending and receiving banks charge significant fees for the transaction. Wire transfers are usually used only for high-dollar transfers, where the investment value of the funds outweighs the cost of the transfer.

Selecting the Best Transfer Mechanism The firm must balance the benefits and costs of concentrating cash to determine the type and timing of transfers from its lockbox accounts to its concentration account. The transfer mechanism selected should be the one that is most profitable (i.e., profit per period equals earnings on the increased funds' availability minus the cost of the transfer system). In general practice, most companies use wire transfers for large transfers of funds from lockbox deposits and EDTs for high-volume, low-dollar transfers from small deposit banks.

EXAMPLE

To demonstrate alternative transfer methods, we consider DJM Manufacturing, which needs to transfer $120,000 from its deposit account to its concentration account. It has two choices: an EDT with a total cost of $1, or a wire transfer with a total cost of $15. Because this would be a midweek transfer, the funds would be accelerated by one day using a wire transfer. (*Note:* A Friday transfer would represent three days of funds acceleration.) The firm's opportunity cost for these funds is 7%.

In this Example, the value of moving the funds via wire transfer is the one day of interest that could be earned if the funds arrived in the concentration account today rather than tomorrow. This amount is calculated to be $23.01 (0.07/365 × $120,000). Because the differential cost of wire transfer versus an EDT is $14 ($15 − $1), the company should use a wire in this case because it would result in a net benefit of $9.01 ($23.01 − $14.00).

Given the opportunity cost and transfer fees, we could also determine the minimum amount for which a wire transfer would be beneficial. Take the differential cost of a wire ($14.00) and divide by the daily interest rate (0.07/365); in this case, the minimum transfer amount would be $73,000 [$14.00 ÷ (0.07/365)]. If DJM were transferring funds on a Friday and thus could earn three days of interest, then the minimum transfer amount would be one-third of the standard amount, or $24,333 ($73,000 ÷ 3).

Concept Review Questions	4. What is the firm's objective with regard to collection float? What are the common types of collection systems?
	5. What are the benefits of using a lockbox system? How does it work? How can the firm assess the economics of a lockbox system?
	6. Why do firms employ cash concentration techniques? What are some of the popular transfer mechanisms used by firms to move funds from depository banks to their concentration banks?
	7. How can the cash manager model the benefits and costs of various funds transfer mechanisms to assess their economics? How can this analysis be used to determine the minimum transfer amount?

23.3 ACCOUNTS PAYABLE AND DISBURSEMENTS

Overview of the Accounts Payable Process

The final component of the cash conversion cycle is the *average payment period* (*APP*), which has two parts: (1) the time from the purchase of raw materials until the firm places the payment in the mail, and (2) payment float time (disbursement float). The payment float is the time it takes after the firm places its payment in the mail until the supplier has withdrawn funds from the firm's account. Section 23.1 addressed issues related to payment float time. In this section, we discuss the management of the time that elapses between the purchase of raw materials and mailing the payment to the supplier. This activity is called **accounts payable management**.

Purpose of the Accounts Payable Function   The primary purpose of the accounts payable (AP) function is to examine all incoming invoices and determine the proper amount to be paid. As part of this process, the cash manager matches the invoice to both the purchase order and receiving information to ensure that the goods/services were ordered by an authorized person and that they were actually received. The accounts payable clerk may make adjustments to the invoiced amount for price or quantity differences. Companies usually pay multiple invoices with a single check. A company has the right to make full use of any credit period offered, but intentionally delaying payments or increasing disbursement float is considered to be an unethical cash management practice. Once payment has been authorized (sometimes referred to as "vouchering"), the cash manager is often responsible for the actual payment itself, either managing the preparation and mailing of checks or initiating the electronic transfer of funds.

Types of Payment Systems   The other issue involved with managing disbursements is the choice of a centralized or decentralized payables and payments system. In a *centralized system*, all invoices are sent to a central accounts payable department, where payment is authorized and checks or other forms of payment are initiated. Centralized systems offer many advantages, including easier concentration of funds, improved access to cash position information, better control, and reduced transaction and administrative costs. There are, however, several problems with centralized payables, such as slow payment times (which could damage relationships with vendors or cause missed opportunities for cash discounts) and the need to coordinate between central payables and field offices/managers to resolve any disputes.

Some companies utilize a more *decentralized system* to the payables and disbursements system in which payments are authorized and, in some cases, initiated at the local level. Although this approach generally helps to improve relationships with vendors and enhance local management autonomy, it makes it harder to concentrate funds and obtain daily cash position information, and it increases the chance of unauthorized disbursements.

Cash Discounts

JOB INTERVIEW QUESTION

What is the financial trade-off involved when a firm evaluates whether or not to take an offered cash discount?

When suppliers offer *cash discounts* to encourage customers to pay before the end of the credit period, it may not be in the firm's best financial interest to pay on the last day. Accounts payable with cash discounts have stated credit terms, such as *2/10 net 30*, which means the purchaser can take a *2% discount* from the invoice amount if the payment is made within *10 days* of the beginning of the credit period; otherwise, it must pay the full amount within *30 days* of the beginning of the credit period. The credit period begins at a specific date set by the supplier, typically either the end of the month in which the purchase is made (noted as EOM) or on the date of the invoice. Taking the discount is at the discretion of the purchaser.

When a firm is extended credit terms that include a cash discount, it has two options: (1) pay the full invoice amount at the end of the credit period, or (2) pay the invoice amount less the cash discount at the end of the cash discount period. In either case, the firm purchases the same goods. Thus, the difference between the payment amount without and with the cash discount is, in effect, the interest payment made by the firm to its supplier.

A firm in need of short-term funds must therefore compare the interest rate charged by its supplier to the best rate charged by lenders of short-term financing (typically banks) and then choose the lowest-cost option. This comparison is important because, by taking a cash discount, the firm will shorten its average payment period and thus increase the amount of resources it has invested in operating assets, which will require additional negotiated short-term financing.

To calculate the relevant cost, we assume that the firm will always render payment on the *final day of the specified payment period*—the credit period or cash discount period. Equation 23.2 presents the formula for calculating the interest rate, $r_{discount}$, associated with *not taking the cash discount and paying at the end of the credit period* when cash discount terms are offered:

$$r_{discount} = \frac{d}{1-d} \times \frac{365}{CP - DP} \qquad \text{(Eq. 23.2)}$$

where

d = percent discount (in decimal form)
CP = credit period
DP = (cash) discount period

EXAMPLE

Assume that a supplier to Masson Industries has changed its terms from *net 30* to *2/10 net 30*. Masson has a line of credit with a bank, and the current interest rate on that line of credit is 6.75% per year. Should Masson take the cash discount or continue to use 30 days of credit from its supplier? The interest rate from the supplier is calculated using Equation 23.2:

$$r_{discount} = \frac{0.02}{1-0.02} \times \frac{365}{30-10} = 0.372 = 37.2\% \text{ per year}$$

Thus, the annualized rate charged by the supplier to those customers not taking the cash discount is 37.2%, whereas the bank charges 6.75%. Masson should take the cash discount and obtain any needed short-term financing by drawing on its bank line of credit.

Disbursement Products and Methods

Zero-Balance Accounts   Zero-balance accounts (ZBAs) are disbursement accounts that always have an end-of-day balance of zero. The purpose is to eliminate nonearning cash balances in corporate checking accounts. A ZBA is often used as a disbursement account under a cash concentration system.

A ZBA is designed as follows. Once all of a given day's checks are presented to the firm's ZBA for payment, the bank notifies the firm of the total amount to be drawn, and the firm transfers funds into the account to cover the amount of that day's checks. This leaves an end-of-day balance of $0 (zero dollars). The ZBA allows the firm to keep all operating cash in an interest-earning account, thereby eliminating idle cash balances. Thus, a firm that uses a ZBA in conjunction with a cash concentration system would need two accounts. The firm would concentrate its cash from the lockboxes into an interest-earning account and write checks against its ZBA. The firm would cover the exact dollar amount of checks presented against the ZBA with transfers from the interest-earning account, leaving the end-of-day balance in the ZBA at $0. In many cases, funding of the ZBA is made automatically and involves only an accounting entry on the part of the bank.

A ZBA is a disbursement management tool that allows the firm to *maximize the use of float on each check*. The firm accomplishes this by keeping all of its cash in an interest-earning account instead of leaving nonearning balances in its checking account to cover checks that the firm has written. This allows the firm to maximize earnings on its cash balances by capturing the full float time on each check it writes.

We have discussed only ZBAs in this section. However, banks offer a variety of products. Another common product that achieves the same goal as a ZBA is a *sweep account*, in which the bank "sweeps" account surpluses into the appropriate interest-earning vehicle and liquidates similar vehicles in order to cover account shortages when they occur. Many banks also offer *multitiered ZBAs* that may be used by multidivisional companies or to segregate different types of payments (payrolls, dividends, accounts payable, etc.). This type of account allows the cash manager to better control balances and funding of the master account and associated ZBAs, thus reducing excess balances and transfers.

Controlled Disbursement   **Controlled disbursement** is a bank service that provides early notification of checks that will be presented against a company's account on a given day. For most large cash management banks, the Federal Reserve Bank makes two presentments of checks to be cleared each day. A bank offering controlled disbursement accounts would receive advance electronic notification from the Fed several hours prior to the actual presentment of the items. This allows the bank to let its controlled disbursement customers know as early as possible what will be presented to their accounts. This, in turn, allows customers to determine their cash position and make any necessary investment/borrowing decisions in the morning, before the checks are presented for payment. Controlled disbursement accounts are often set up as ZBAs to allow for automatic funding through a company's concentration account.

Positive Pay   **Positive pay** is a bank service used to combat the most common types of check fraud. Given the availability of inexpensive computers, scanners, and printers, it is not difficult to create excellent copies of corporate checks or to change payees or amounts. The risk to a company issuing checks is that the bank might pay fraudulent items and the fraud would not be revealed until the account is reconciled. When using a positive pay service, the company transmits to the bank a check-issued file, designating the check number and amount of each item to the bank when the checks are issued. The bank matches the presented checks against this file and rejects any items that do not match. It is important to note that several courts have ruled that positive pay is a "commercially reasonable" measure to prevent check fraud. This means that a company that does not use this service when available may find itself liable for fraudulent items accepted by its bank. A recent development in this area is that more companies are using payee/beneficiary verification, or "reverse" positive pay, to make sure that the payee or beneficiary of the check has not been altered. Earlier, more basic positive pay did not include this feature.

Developments in Accounts Payable and Disbursements

Integrated Accounts Payable   **Integrated accounts payable**, also known as *comprehensive accounts payable*, provides a company with outsourcing of its accounts payable or disbursement operations. The outsourcing may be as minor as contracting with a bank to issue checks and perform reconciliations or as major as outsourcing the entire payables function.

One of the most typical approaches to AP outsourcing is to send a bank (or other financial service provider) a data file containing a listing of all payments to be made. The bank will maintain a vendor file for the company and send each vendor payment (in the preferred format) in accordance with the company's remittance advice.

Purchasing/Procurement Cards   Many companies are implementing **purchasing (or procurement) card programs** as a means of reducing the cost of low-dollar indirect purchases. Though companies have been using credit cards for travel and related expenses for many years, they have only recently begun using them to make routine purchases of supplies, equipment, or services. A firm issues purchasing cards to designated employees, but it limits the dollar amounts that may be spent and stipulates which vendors can be used. Companies that have implemented such programs report significant cost savings from streamlining the purchasing process for low-cost items. The other advantage is that the firm can pay the issuer of the purchasing card in a single, large payment that consolidates many small purchases.

Imaging Services   Many disbursement services offered by banks and other vendors incorporate **imaging services** as part of the package. This technology allows both sides of the check, as well as remittance information, to be converted into digital images. The images can then be transmitted via the Internet or easily stored for future reference. Imaging services are especially useful when incorporated with positive-pay services.

Fraud Prevention in Disbursements   In recent years, disbursement fraud—especially related to check payments—has increased significantly. Fraudulent checks can be created with inexpensive scanners, computers, and laser printers. As a result, fraud prevention and control have become even more important in the accounts payable and disbursement functions. Some of the common fraud prevention measures include the following.

- *Written policies and procedures for creating and disbursing checks*
- *Separating check-issuance duties (approval, signing, and reconciliation)*
- *Using safety features on checks (microprinting, watermarks, tamper resistance, etc.)*
- *Setting maximum dollar limits and/or requiring multiple signatures on checks*
- *Using positive-pay services*
- *Increasing the use of electronic payment methods*

Concept Review Questions

8. What is the primary purpose of the accounts payable function? Describe the procedures used to manage accounts payable. What are the key differences between centralized and decentralized payables and payment systems?

9. When is it advantageous for a company to pay early and take an offered cash discount? Under what circumstances would the firm be advised to always take any offered cash discounts?

10. What is the difference between a ZBA and a controlled disbursement account? Are they direct substitutes?

11. What are some of the recent developments in the accounts payable and disbursements area? What role does new technology play in preventing disbursement fraud?

23.4 SHORT-TERM INVESTING AND BORROWING

After determining the company's cash position, the cash manager will generally have either surplus funds to invest or a deficit of funds to replenish via short-term borrowing. Clearly, the goal is to earn relatively safe returns on short-term surpluses and to borrow at reasonable cost to meet short-term deficits. This section reviews some of the key options available to the financial manager for investing short-term surpluses and for borrowing to meet short-term deficits.

Short-Term Investing

Making sure that the company has access to liquid assets when and where they are needed is one of the critical tasks for the cash manager. Although the primary form of liquidity will generally be a company's checking or demand deposit accounts at its banks, these accounts usually do not earn interest and the company should not hold excess balances in them. To earn some type of short-term return, a company will hold some "near-cash" assets in the form of short-term investments, often labeled *marketable securities*. These investments may be either a source of reserve liquidity or a place to maintain temporary surplus funds.[1]

Because such short-term investments are essentially a substitute for cash, *providing liquidity* and *preserving principal* should be the primary concerns. Earning a competitive return is also a consideration; however, care must be taken not to place the underlying principal at risk. Remember that the primary purpose of short-term investments is to maintain a pool of liquid assets as a substitute for cash, not to generate profits for the company. Toward this end, it is important that a company establish policies and guidelines for the management of short-term investments; they should clearly specify the purpose of the investment portfolio and provide recommendations and/or restrictions on acceptable investments and the amount of diversification.

Money Market Mutual Funds   Many large companies will manage their own portfolios of short-term investments, but most companies (especially small ones) use money market mutual funds as an alternative. The **money market mutual funds** are professionally managed portfolios that invest in the same types of short-term instruments in which cash managers invest. They may, in fact, offer even more flexibility and stability than a self-managed fund. Using these types of funds can make sense, especially when the costs of running and managing a short-term portfolio are considered.

In most cases, these funds set their *net asset value* (*NAV*) at a fixed $1 per share in order to preserve the principal value of the fund. As the value of the fund increases, the fund pays investors in additional shares rather than allowing the share price to increase. Commercial money market mutual funds are available from independent companies as well as from most large banks.[2]

Money Market Financial Instruments   Short-term financial instruments are primarily fixed-income securities. They are generally issued in registered form rather than bearer form, yet they are often called "marketable securities." Many of these securities are

---

[1]*Temporary surplus funds* may result from ongoing operations, seasonal performance, sales of large assets, or proceeds from a large securities issue.

[2]It is important to note that money market funds have had some problems. In September of 2008, the Reserve Primary Fund (founded by Bruce Bent, the pioneer of the money market fund concept) was forced to "break the buck" (drop its NAV below $1) as a result of the Lehman Brothers bankruptcy. In late 2008 and early 2009, when T-bill rates effectively dropped to 0%, several large funds prohibited new investment funds as a means to control expenses.

also issued in *discount form*, meaning the investor pays less than face value for the security at the time of purchase and receives the face value at maturity. Table 23.1 lists the more common securities used for money market investments.

Table 23.1 Money Market Financial Instruments		
U.S. TREASURIES	**INTEREST BASIS**	**MATURITY**
Treasury bills (T-bills)	Discount	4, 13, 26, or 52 weeks
Treasury notes (T-notes)	Interest-bearing	2, 5, or 10 years
Treasury bonds (T-bonds)	Interest-bearing	30 years
FEDERAL AGENCY ISSUES	**UNDERLYING ASSETS**	**BACKING**
Government National Mortgage Association (Ginnie Mae)	Home mortgages	Full faith and credit
Department of Veterans Affairs (Vinnie Mac)	VA home loans	Full faith and credit
Federal National Mortgage Association (Fannie Mae)[b]	Home mortgages	GSE[a]—Implied federal backing
Federal Home Loan Mortgage Corporation (Freddie Mac)[b]	Home mortgages	GSE[a]—Implied federal backing
SLM Holding Corporation (Sallie Mae)	Student loans	GSE[a]—Implied federal backing
Federal Farm Credit Banks Funding Corporation	Agricultural loans	GSE[a]—Implied federal backing
Farm Credit System Insurance Corporation	Insurer of Farm Credit Banks	GSE[a]—Implied federal backing
Central Bank for Cooperatives (CoBank)	Loans to agricultural cooperatives	GSE[a]—Implied federal backing
Federal Agricultural Mortgage Corporation (Farmer Mac)	Agricultural loans, rural real estate, and home mortgages	GSE[a]—Implied federal backing
BANK FINANCIAL INSTRUMENTS	**SPECIAL FEATURES**	
Certificates of deposit—CDs (domestic)	Interest-bearing deposits at financial institutions in the U.S.; may be fixed rate or floating rate with maturities from seven days to several years	
Overnight sweep accounts	Interest-bearing accounts used for investing end-of-day surplus funds	
Yankee CDs	Dollar-denominated CDs issued by U.S. branches of foreign banks	
Eurodollar CDs	Dollar-denominated CDs issued by banks outside the U.S.	
Eurodollar time deposits	Nonnegotiable, fixed-rate time deposits issued by banks outside the U.S., with maturities ranging from overnight to several years	
Banker's acceptances	Negotiable short-term instruments used for trade finance	
Bank notes	Unsecured or subordinated debt of the bank (not insured)	
CORPORATE OBLIGATIONS	**SPECIAL FEATURES**	
Commercial paper	Unsecured promissory notes issued by corporations; maturities from 1 to 270 days; usually sold on a discount basis and backed by a credit guarantee from a bank	
Adjustable-rate preferred stock	Tax advantaged for corporate holders because of dividend exclusion rule; dividend rate adjusts to maintain stable pricing	

(continued)

Table 23.1 **Money Market Financial Instruments** *(continued)*

OTHER SHORT-TERM INVESTMENTS	SPECIAL FEATURES
Money market mutual funds	Available directly from funds or through banks
Asset-backed securities	Debt obligations issued by companies that are secured by assets such as receivables, credit card obligations, consumer finance loans, major retailers, and automobile companies
International money market investments	Short-term bills or notes issued by foreign governments, foreign commercial paper, or other types of interest-bearing deposits in foreign currencies
Repurchase agreements (repos)	A collateralized transaction between a securities dealer or bank and an investor; generally backed by Treasuries or agency securities

[a]GSE denotes government-sponsored enterprise.

[b]As of September 2008, Fannie Mae and Freddie Mac were placed under federal government conservatorship (Federal Housing Finance Agency, or FHFA).

U.S. Treasuries   *U.S. Treasury bills* (*T-bills*) are the benchmark of money market financial instruments. The U.S. government issues these short-term securities to finance its activities, and they appeal to a wide range of investors, both domestic and foreign. T-bills are backed by the "full faith and credit" of the U.S. government (making them essentially free of default risk) and have an active secondary market.

T-bills are issued in weekly auctions on a discount basis with maturities of less than one year (usually 4, 13, or 26 weeks). T-bills are available in minimum denominations of $1,000 but are generally traded in round lots of $1 million. Other Treasury instruments such as *Treasury notes* (*T-notes*) and *Treasury bonds* (*T-bonds*) are initially issued as long-term securities, but they may be suitable for a short-term portfolio as they approach maturity.

All treasury securities are registered and issued in *book entry form* (a computer entry at the Federal Reserve Bank rather than a paper certificate) and are exempt from state income taxes.

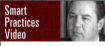

Smart Practices Video

Scott Frame, Federal Reserve Bank of Atlanta

"As subprime mortgages began to fail, the value of securities backed by these mortgages began to plummet."

See the entire interview at

SMARTFinance

Federal Agency Issues   These instruments have some degree of federal government backing and are issued by either federal agencies or private, shareholder-owned companies known as *government-sponsored enterprises* (*GSEs*). Most of the agencies are securitized investments backed by home mortgages, student loans, or agricultural lending. Two of the agencies (Ginnie Mae and Freddie Mac) are backed by the "full faith and credit" of the U.S. government, whereas the rest are backed by the implied intervention of the government in the event of a crisis. Such a crisis actually unfolded in 2008 as U.S. real estate prices plunged, causing a steep decline in the value of mortgage-backed securities. In September of that year, the U.S. government essentially took over Freddie Mac and one of the other large GSEs, the Federal National Mortgage Association (Fannie Mae).

Bank Financial Instruments   U.S. and foreign banks issue short-term *certificates of deposit* (*CDs*) as well as *time deposits* and *banker's acceptances*. Many banks also offer money market mutual funds and sweep accounts in which their customers can invest short-term cash.

Corporate Obligations   The primary corporate obligation in the short-term market is **commercial paper**. Highly-rated corporations typically issue this investment, which is structured as an unsecured promissory note with a maturity of less than 270 days. The short maturity allows for issuance without SEC registration, and commercial paper is usually sold to other corporations rather than the general public. Most issues are also backed by credit guarantees from a financial institution and sold on a discount basis, similar to T-bills. In order to issue commercial paper, a firm must have an investment-grade credit rating, but even then access to this market is sometimes restricted. In the middle of 2007, total commercial paper outstanding in the United States exceeded $2.2 trillion. Early signs of the looming financial crisis appeared that summer, and investors began to have doubts about corporate commercial paper issuers as well as the financial institutions that backed them. Firms found it increasingly difficult to refinance maturing paper, and by June 2009 the market had declined by 45% to just $1.2 trillion outstanding.

The other corporate obligation used for short-term investments is **adjustable-rate preferred stock**. These stocks take advantage of the dividend exclusion (of 70% or more) for stock in one corporation held by another corporation. In order to make this investment suitable for short-term holdings, the dividend rate paid on the stock is adjusted according to some rate index. This will stabilize the price even if interest rates change during the 45-day holding period required to qualify for the dividend exclusion.

Yield Calculations for Discount Instruments (T-Bills or Commercial Paper)[3]

The yield for short-term *discount investments* such as T-bills and commercial paper is typically calculated using algebraic approximations rather than more precise present value methods. In the case of a **discount investment**, the investor pays less than face value at the time of purchase but then receives the investment's face value at its maturity date. There are generally no interim interest or coupon payments during the course of holding such an investment.

Determining the yield of T-bills or commercial paper generally involves a two-step process. In most cases, the rate on the investment is expressed as the discount rate, which is used to compute the "dollar discount" and selling price for the instrument. For example, a 1-year, $100,000 T-bill[4] sold at a 5% discount would sell for $95,000 [$100,000 × (1 − 0.05)]. The investor would pay $95,000 today and receive $100,000 in one year at the maturity date. The yield on this investment would be approximately 5.26% ($5,000/$95,000). Though the calculations for a shorter-term investment are slightly more complicated, they follow the same basic approach. **Money market yield (MMY)** for discount instruments is calculated on a 360-day basis but must be converted to **bond equivalent yield (BEY)** to compare discount instruments to interest-bearing investments, such as bank CDs. Yield calculations are illustrated in the following Example.

---

[3]The calculations demonstrated in this section are the same ones we introduced in our discussion of bond valuation in Section 4.2 of Chapter 4. For convenience as well as custom, we present these formulas a bit differently here.

[4]Although the U.S. government no longer issues T-bills in 1-year maturities, we use a 1-year T-bill here for computational convenience and clarity.

EXAMPLE

We can use two steps to determine the yield on a 91-day, $1 million T-bill that is selling at a discount of 3.75%. Note that the convention in the discount market is to use 360 days when calculating the purchase price and money market yield.

Step 1: *Calculate the dollar discount and purchase price.*

$$\text{Dollar discount} = (\text{Face value} \times \text{Discount rate}) \times (\text{Days to maturity} \div 360)$$
$$= (\$1,000,000 \times 0.0375) \times (91 \div 360) = \$9,479.17$$

$$\text{Purchase price} = \text{Face value} - \text{Dollar discount}$$
$$= (\$1,000,000 - \$9,479.17) = \$990,520.83$$

Step 2: *Calculate MMY and BEY.*

$$\text{Money market yield (MMY)} = (\text{Dollar discount} \div \text{Purchase price})$$
$$\times (360 \div \text{Days to maturity})$$
$$= (\$9,479.17 \div \$990,520.83)$$
$$\times (360 \div 91) = \underline{\underline{3.786\%}}$$

$$\text{Bond equivalent yield (BEY)} = \text{Money market yield} \times (365 \div 360)$$
$$= 3.786\% \times (365 \div 360) = \underline{\underline{3.839\%}}$$

Short-Term Borrowing

Smart
Concepts
See the concept explained step-by-step at
SMART**Finance**

For many companies, a primary source of liquidity is access to short-term lines of credit or commercial paper programs to provide needed funds. This is especially the case for companies in seasonal businesses where large amounts of operating capital may be needed for only a few months of the year. The role of the cash manager in establishing short-term borrowing arrangements is to ensure that the company has credit facilities sufficient to meet short-term cash requirements. Obviously, these arrangements should provide maximum flexibility at a minimum cost. Access to credit can be a major issue for companies in times of financial crisis. Many creditworthy companies had difficulty getting the credit they needed as the financial and credit crises deepened in late 2008 and early 2009. Both bank lending and access to commercial paper markets were severely constrained for most companies.

Most short-term borrowing is done on a variable-rate basis, with rates quoted in terms of a base rate plus a spread. The spread is essentially an adjustment for the relative riskiness and overall creditworthiness of the borrower. The base rate plus the spread are referred to as the **all-in rate**.

Typical base rates include the *prime rate* and *LIBOR (London Interbank Offered Rate)*. The **prime rate** is the rate of interest charged by the largest U.S. banks on short-term loans to the best business borrowers. **LIBOR** is the rate that the most creditworthy international banks that deal in Eurodollars charge on interbank loans.

For bank lines of credit, lending agreements may require *commitment fees* (fees paid for the bank's agreement to make money available) and/or *compensating balance requirements* (minimum deposit balances that must be maintained by the borrower at the

WHAT CFOs DO

CFO Survey Evidence on Bank Lines of Credit

A line of credit is an up-front commitment by a bank to lend to a borrower in the future. For example, a company may arrange to borrow up to $10,000,000 from a bank at any time during the next 30 months. The company must pay a commitment fee to establish this option to borrow, a fee that might cost one-quarter percent (e.g., $25,000 to establish a $10,000,000 credit line). When a firm borrows from the line, it must also pay interest on the amount borrowed, usually a variable interest rate of approximately 100 to 200 basis points (one to two percentage points) above LIBOR, the London Interbank Offered Rate.

Credit lines are designed for temporary borrowing. A company experiencing slow collections one month may draw on the line to pay end-of-month payroll, rather than arrange a new, short-term loan. Or, a seasonal firm may draw on the credit line during its slow quarter, planning to pay back the borrowings plus interest the following quarter. Credit lines are also used as bridge financing for long-term investing. For example, a company may initially fund the purchase of a 10-year asset with a credit line, retiring the line quickly as longer term financing is finalized. More generally, credit lines are a fairly low-cost form

(continued)

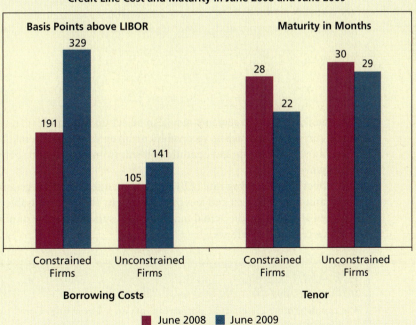

Source: Murillo Campello, Erasmo Giambona, John R. Graham, and Campbell R. Harvey, "Liquidity Management and Corporate Investment during a Financial Crisis," Working paper, Duke University, 2009.

of liquidity insurance, as an alternative to a company needing to accumulate large cash balances. Credit lines usually remain open for two to three years, assuming that the company does not trip a covenant before then.

Companies obtain substantial funding from lines of credit. For example, during the first half of 2009, Campello and co-authors document that borrowing from credit lines represented about one-third of total funds (i.e., the sum of external borrowings and cash flows) used by U.S. companies. The reliance on credit lines varied greatly across firms. More than half of total funding used by unprofitable firms came from lines of credit, compared to only 18% for profitable companies. Alarmingly, in March 2009 unprofitable companies on average had drawn 63% of the maximum available on their credit lines. This extreme borrowing was part of a "run on bank lines of credit" that some researchers argued limited the funds that banks had available to lend through normal channels.

In early 2009 banks responded by raising the cost and reducing the availability of lines to less creditworthy firms. In the graph on the previous page, constrained firms are those for which their CFOs say they are having difficulty borrowing, and unconstrained firms report they are not experiencing difficulty. As shown in the graph, Campello and co-authors document that financially constrained companies saw their interest rates increase in 2009 to 329 basis points above LIBOR, while the interest rate premium for unconstrained companies was only 141 basis points above LIBOR. At the same time, constrained companies saw the tenor (i.e., maturity) of their credit lines shrink from 28 months to only 22 months on average, while the tenor of credit lines for unconstrained companies remained relatively constant at nearly 30 months. This meant that financially constrained firms, the companies that most needed to borrow, would have to renegotiate with their banks or retire their credit lines eight months sooner than their unconstrained counterparts.

Sources: Murillo Campello, Erasmo Giambona, John R. Graham, and Campbell R. Harvey, "Liquidity Management and Corporate Investment during a Financial Crisis," Working paper, Duke University, 2009; M. Campello, J. Graham, and C. Harvey, "The Real Effects of Financial Constraints: Evidence from a Financial Crisis," Working paper, Duke University, 2009; V. Ivashina, and D. Scharfstein, "Bank Lending during the Financial Crisis of 2008," Working paper, Harvard Business School, 2008; and K. Llns, H. Servaes, and P. Tufano, "What Drives Corporate Liquidity? An International Survey of Cash Holdings and Lines of Credit," Working paper, Harvard Business School, 2008.

lending bank). These agreements may also be set up on a multiyear, revolving basis and may use current assets such as receivables or inventory as collateral. In any type of bank lending, most of the terms and conditions result from negotiations between the borrower and the bank.

The **effective borrowing rate (EBR)** on a bank line of credit is generally determined as the total amount of interest and fees paid divided by the average usable loan amount. This rate is then adjusted for the actual number of days the loan is outstanding. A demonstration of this calculation follows.

EXAMPLE

We can determine the effective borrowing rate on a 1-year line of credit with the following characteristics:

CL = credit line, $500,000 total
AL = average loan outstanding, $200,000
CF = commitment fee, 0.35% (35 basis points) on the *unused* portion of the line
 IR = interest rate, 2.5% over LIBOR (assumed to be 5.75%), which equals 8.25%

If we use a 365-day year and assume that no compensating balances are required, then the calculations proceed as follows:

$$EBR = \frac{(IR \times AL) + [CF \times (GL - AL)]}{AL} \times \frac{365}{\text{Days loan is outstanding}}$$

$$= \frac{(0.0825 \times \$200,000) + [0.0035 \times (\$500,000 - \$200,000)]}{\$200,000} \times \frac{365}{365}$$

$$= \frac{\$16,500 + \$1,050}{\$200,000} \times \frac{365}{365} = \frac{\$17,550}{\$200,000} \times 1 = \underline{8.775\%}$$

The effective borrowing rate of 8.775% is about 50 basis points (0.50%) above the 8.25% interest rate as a result of the commitment fee paid on the unused portion of the line.

<table>
<tr>
<td>

Concept Review Questions

</td>
<td>

12. Why are providing liquidity and preserving principal the two primary concerns in choosing short-term investments? What guidelines should be included in a short-term investment policy?

13. What securities are considered to be the benchmark for money market financial instruments, and why? What are some of the popular non–U.S. Treasury money market instruments?

14. What are the key base rates used in variable rate short-term borrowing, and how do they factor into the all-in rate? What other charges might be applicable to short-term borrowing? What effect do they have on the effective borrowing rate (EBR)?

</td>
</tr>
</table>

Summary

- The cash manager's job is to manage the cash flow time line related to collection, concentration, and disbursement of the company's funds. Float can be viewed from the perspective of either the receiving party or the paying party. Mail float and processing float are viewed the same from both perspectives. The third float component is availability float (to the receiving party) and the fourth is clearing float (to the paying party). The receiving party's goal is to minimize collection float, whereas the paying party's goal is to maximize disbursement float.

- Cash managers are also responsible for identifying and quantifying financial relationships, forecasting cash flow, investing and borrowing, and information management. In large firms, they must manage the firm's cash position; in small firms, they set target cash balances based on transactions requirements and minimum balances set by their bank.

- In managing collections, the cash manager attempts to reduce collection float using various collection systems, which include field banking systems, mail-based systems, and electronic systems. Large firms whose customers are geographically dispersed commonly use lockbox systems, although small firms can also benefit from them.

- Firms use cash concentration to bring lockbox and other deposits together into one bank, often a concentration bank. Firms often use automated clearinghouse (ACH) debit transfers (also known as electronic depository transfer, EDT) and wire transfers to transfer funds from the depository bank to the concentration bank.

- The objective of managing the firm's accounts payable is to pay accounts as slowly as possible without damaging the firm's credit rating. If a supplier offers a cash discount, the firm in need of short-term funds must determine the interest rate associated with *not* taking the discount (and paying at the end of the credit period) and then compare this rate with the firm's lowest-cost short-term borrowing alternative. If it can borrow elsewhere at a lower cost, the firm should take the discount and pay early; otherwise, it should not.

- Financial managers use such disbursement products and methods as zero-balance accounts (ZBAs), controlled disbursement, and positive pay. Some of the key developments in accounts payable and disbursements are integrated accounts payable, use of purchasing/procurement cards, imaging services, and a number of measures for preventing fraud.

- The cash manager will hold near-cash assets in the form of short-term investments (often labeled *marketable securities*) to earn a return on temporary excess cash balances. Investment policies and guidelines for management of short-term investments should be established.

- Small companies are likely to invest their short-term surpluses in money market mutual funds. Larger firms will invest in any of a variety of short-term, fixed-income securities; these include U.S. Treasuries, federal agency issues, bank financial instruments, and corporate obligations such as commercial paper and adjustable-rate preferred stock. The yield on discount investments, such as T-bills and commercial paper, is typically approximated by calculating the money market yield (MMY) and converting it into a bond equivalent yield (BEY).

- Short-term borrowing can be obtained through the issuance of commercial paper, primarily by large firms, and through lines of credit. Most short-term borrowing occurs at a base rate—usually, the prime rate or LIBOR—plus a spread reflecting the borrower's relative riskiness. The effective borrowing rate (EBR) can be calculated to capture both the interest costs and other fees associated with a short-term loan.

Key Terms

accounts payable management
adjustable-rate preferred stock
all-in rate
automated clearinghouse (ACH) debit transfer
availability float
bank account analysis statement
bond equivalent yield (BEY)
cash concentration
cash manager
cash position management
clearing float
commercial paper
controlled disbursement

discount investment
effective borrowing rate (EBR)
electronic bill presentment and payment (EBPP)
electronic depository transfer (EDT)
electronic invoice presentment and payment (EIPP)
field banking system
float
imaging services
integrated accounts payable
LIBOR
liquidity management

lockbox system
mail float
mail-based collection system
money market mutual funds
money market yield (MMY)
positive pay
prime rate
processing float
purchasing (or procurement) card programs
target cash balance
wire transfer
zero-balance accounts (ZBAs)

Questions

23-1. What is *float*? What are its four basic components? Which of these components is the same from both a collection and a payment perspective? What is the difference between availability float and clearing float, and from which perspective—collection or payment—is each relevant?

23-2. What is cash-position management? What types of firms set a target cash balance? Why? What is a bank's purpose in requiring the firm to maintain a minimum balance in its checking account? How does this relate to a bank account analysis statement?

23-3. What is the firm's goal with regard to cash collections? Describe each of the following types of collection systems:
  a. Field banking system
  b. Mail-based collection system
  c. Electronic system

23-4. What is a lockbox system? How does it typically work? Briefly describe the economics involved in performing a cost–benefit analysis of such a system.

23-5. Briefly describe the following funds transfer mechanisms:
   a. Automated clearinghouse (ACH) debit transfer
   b. Wire transfer
   Why are wire transfers typically used only for high-dollar transfers?

23-6. What is the goal with regard to managing accounts payable as it relates to the cash conversion cycle? Briefly describe the process involved in managing the accounts payable function.

23-7. How can a firm in need of short-term financing decide whether or not to take a cash discount offered by its supplier? How would this decision change if the firm had no alternative source of short-term financing? How would it change for a firm that needs no additional short-term financing?

23-8. Briefly describe each of the following disbursement products/methods:
   a. Zero-balance accounts (ZBAs)
   b. Controlled disbursement
   c. Positive pay
   How does a ZBA relate to the firm's target cash balance?

23-9. Briefly describe each of the following developments in accounts payable and disbursements:
   a. Integrated accounts payable
   b. Purchasing/procurement cards
   c. Imaging services
   d. Fraud prevention in disbursements

23-10. What is the firm's goal in short-term investing? How does it use money market mutual funds? Describe some of the popular money market financial instruments in each of the following groups:
   a. U.S. Treasuries
   b. Federal agency issues
   c. Bank financial instruments
   d. Corporate obligations

23-11. How is interest paid on a discount investment? What is the money market yield (MMY)? How can the MMY be converted to a bond equivalent yield (BEY)?

23-12. How are the rates on short-term borrowing typically set? What role does the prime rate or LIBOR play in this process? What is the effective borrowing rate (EBR)? How does the EBR differ from the stated all-in rate?

PROBLEMS

Cash Management

Smart Solutions

See the problem and solution explained step-by-step at **SMARTFinance**

23-1. Nickolas Industries has daily cash receipts of $350,000. A recent analysis of the firm's collections indicated that customers' payments are in the mail an average of 2 days. Once received, the payments are processed in 1.5 days. After the payments are deposited, the receipts clear the banking system, on average, in 2.5 days. Assume a 365-day year.
   a. How much collection float (in days) does the firm have?
   b. If the firm's opportunity cost is 11%, would it be economically advisable for the firm to pay an annual fee of $84,000 for a lockbox system that reduces collection float by 2.5 days? Explain why or why not.

23-2. Gale Supply estimates that its customers' payments are in the mail for 3 days and, once received, are processed in 2 days. After the payments are deposited in the firm's bank, the bank makes the funds available to the firm in 2.5 days. The firm estimates its total annual collections from credit customers, received at a constant rate, to be $87 million. Its annual opportunity cost of funds is 9.5%. Assume a 365-day year.

a. How many days of collection float does Gale Supply have?

b. What is the current annual dollar cost of Gale Supply's collection float?

c. If the installation of an electronic invoice presentment and payment (EIPP) system would result in a 4-day reduction in Gale's collection float, how much could the firm earn annually on this float reduction?

d. Based on your findings in part (c), should Gale install the EIPP system if its annual cost is $85,000? Explain your recommendation.

23-3.   NorthAm Trucking is a long-haul trucking company that serves customers all across the continental United States and parts of Canada and Mexico. At present, all billing activities—from preparation to collection—are handled by staff at corporate headquarters in Bloomington, Indiana. Payments are recorded and deposits are made once a day in the firm's bank, Hoosier National. You have been hired to recommend ways to reduce collection float and thereby generate cost savings.

a. Suggest and explain at least three specific ways that NorthAm could reduce its collection float.

b. Assume your preferred recommendation will cut the collection float by four days. NorthAm bills $108 million per year. If collections are evenly distributed throughout a 365-day year and if the firm's cost of short-term financing is 8%, what savings could be achieved by implementing the suggestion?

c. Suppose the annual cost of implementing your recommendation is $100,000. In view of your answer to part (b), should NorthAm implement it?

Collections

23-4.   A particular lockbox system costs $1.25 million annually. Based on a cost of capital of 18%, what is the minimum float value reduction (FVR) that provides a net benefit of zero? What is the FVR if the cost of capital is reduced to 15%? Assuming an FVR of $8.9 million, what cost of capital provides a net benefit of zero?

23-5.   Firm A has annual revenues of $1.6 billion and can reduce its float by four days using a lockbox system. Due to A's significant risk, A has a high cost of capital of 22%. Firm B has annual revenues of $850 million and can reduce its float by three days using a similar lockbox system. Firm B is less risky than Firm A, as evidenced by B's cost of capital of 10%. Assuming the lockbox system costs $2 million, which firm benefits more from using the system? If the two firms merge, making it necessary to have only one lockbox system for the combined firm, then how much is the net benefit of having the lockbox system under this circumstance?

23-6.   Qtime Products believes that using a lockbox system can shorten its accounts receivable collection period by four days. The firm's annual sales, all on credit, are $65 million and are billed on a continuous basis. The firm can earn 9% on its short-term investments. The cost of the lockbox system is $57,500 per year. Assume a 365-day year.

a. What amount of cash will be made available for other uses under the lockbox system?

b. What net benefit (or cost) will the firm receive if it adopts the lockbox system? Should it adopt the proposed lockbox system?

23-7.   Quick Burger Inc., a national chain of hamburger restaurants, has accumulated a $27,000 balance in one of its regional collection accounts. It wishes to make an efficient, cost-effective transfer of $25,000 of this balance to its corporate concentration account, thus leaving a $2,000 minimum balance in the regional collection account. It has the following options:

Option 1: Electronic depository transfer (EDT) at a cost of $2.50 and requiring one day to clear.

Option 2: Wire transfer at a cost of $12 and clearing the same day (zero days to clear).

a. If Quick Burger can earn 6% on its short-term investments, then which of the options would you recommend to minimize the transfer cost? (Assume a 365-day year.)

b. Compare Options 1 and 2, and determine the minimum amount that would have to be transferred in order for the wire transfer (Option 2) to be more cost effective than the EDT (Option 1).

23-8. Firm NBG is trying to determine under what circumstances a wire transfer is beneficial. The cost of a wire transfer is $20. If the transfer speeded up the deposit by three days then, assuming an annual cost of capital of 12.34%, what is the minimum amount that would need to be transferred? If the wire transfer can only speed up deposits by one day, what is the minimum amount that would need to be transferred? NBG's analysis finds that its average daily cash inflows are $38,950 and that the inflows are reasonably steady throughout the week. Should NBG use wire transfers Monday through Thursday when the firm would gain one additional day in deposits? Should NBG use wire transfers on Fridays when the firm would gain three additional days in deposits? How do the answers to the last two questions change during the height of NBG's selling season, when daily average inflow increases to $89,456?

23-9. Firm OPL has average daily cash inflows (Monday through Saturday) of $15,890, $13,267, $20,654, $24,956, $37,923, and $42,516, respectively. A wire transfer deposits money into a concentration account faster by one day if executed Monday through Thursday and by three days if executed Friday. Assuming that the additional cost of a wire transfer is $15.62 and that OPL has a cost of capital of 16% annually, on which days should wire transfers be considered? (*Note:* Saturday inflows should be combined with Monday inflows because banks close too early on Saturday to recognize the cash inflow.)

Accounts Payable and Disbursements

23-10. Assume a 365-day year and that a firm receives the following credit terms from six suppliers.

Supplier	Terms
1	2/10 net 50
2	1/10 net 30
3	2/10 net 150
4	3/10 net 60
5	1/10 net 45
6	1/20 net 80

a. Determine the interest rate associated with not taking the cash discount and instead paying at the end of the credit period for each of the six suppliers' credit terms.

b. In part (a), you calculated the interest rate associated with not taking the discount for each supplier's credit terms. Now you must decide whether or not to take the cash discount by paying within the discount period. To pay early, you will need to borrow from your firm's line of credit at the local bank. The interest rate on the line of credit is the prime rate plus 2.5%. You can get the most recent prime rate from the Federal Reserve at http://www.federalreserve.gov/releases/h15/update. For each supplier's terms, use the current prime rate to determine whether the firm should borrow from the bank or, in effect, borrow from the supplier.

Smart Solutions

See the problem and solution explained step-by-step at **SMARTFinance**

23-11. Access Enterprises is vetting four possible suppliers of an important raw material used in its production process, all offering different credit terms. The products offered by each supplier are virtually identical. The following table shows the credit terms offered by these suppliers. Assume a 365-day year.

Supplier	Terms
A	1/10 net 40
B	2/20 net 90
C	1/20 net 60
D	3/10 net 75

a. Calculate the interest rate associated with not taking the discount from each supplier.

b. If the firm needs short-term funds (which are currently available from its commercial bank at 11%) and if each of the suppliers is viewed *separately*, then which, if any, of the suppliers' cash discounts should the firm *not* take? Explain why.

c. Suppose that the firm could stretch its accounts payable to supplier A (net period only) by 20 days. How would this affect your answer in part (b) concerning this supplier?

23-12. Derson Manufacturing wishes to evaluate the credit terms offered by its four biggest suppliers of raw materials. The prime rate is 7.0%, and Derson can borrow short-term funds at a spread of 2.5% above the prime rate. Assume a 365-day year and that the firm always pays its suppliers on the last day allowed by their stated credit terms. The terms offered by each supplier are as follows:

Supplier	Terms
1	2/10 net 40
2	1/15 net 60
3	3/10 net 70
4	1/10 net 50

a. Calculate the interest rate associated with not taking the discount from each supplier.

b. Assuming the firm needs short-term financing and considering each supplier separately, indicate whether the firm should take the discount from each supplier.

c. If the firm did not need any short-term financing, when should it pay each of the suppliers?

d. If the firm could not obtain a loan from banks and other financial institutions and needed short-term financing, when should it pay each of the suppliers?

e. Suppose that Derson could stretch its accounts payable to Supplier 1 (net period only) to 90 days without damaging its credit rating. What impact, if any, would this have on your recommendation with regard to Supplier 1 in part (b)? Explain your answer.

23-13. Union Company is examining its operating cash management. One of the options the firm is considering is a zero-balance account (ZBA). The firm's bank is offering a ZBA with monthly charges of $1,500, and the bank estimates that the firm can expect to earn 8% on its short-term investments. Determine the minimum average cash balance that would make this ZBA a benefit to the firm. Assume a 365-day year.

Short-Term Investing and Borrowing

23-14. Suppose Treasury bills (face value of $10,000) with maturities of 30 days, 90 days, and 180 days sell at the respective annualized discounts of 4.25%, 4.35%, and 4.92%. What are the respective money market yields for these T-bills? What are their respective bond equivalent yields?

23-15. Suppose that short-term discounts on Treasury bills are "flat" and are set at 3.90% APR for all maturities. Examining 30-day and 180-day T-bills, determine whether the MMYs and BEYs are also "flat."

Smart Solutions

See the problem and solution explained step-by-step at **SMARTFinance**

23-16. Sager Inc. just purchased a 91-day, $1 million T-bill that was selling at a discount of 3.25%.
   a. Calculate the dollar discount and purchase price on this T-bill.
   b. Find the money market yield on this T-bill.
   c. Find the bond equivalent yield on this T-bill.
   d. Rework parts (a), (b), and (c) while assuming the T-bill was selling at a 3.0% discount. What effect does this drop of 25 basis points in the T-bill discount have on its BEY?

23-17. Rosa Inc. has arranged a 1-year, $2 million credit line with its lead bank. The bank set the interest rate at the prime rate plus a spread of 1.50%. The prime rate is expected to remain stable at 5.25% during the coming year. In addition, the bank requires Rosa to pay a 0.50% commitment fee on the average unused portion of the line. Assume a 365-day year.
   a. Calculate the effective borrowing rate on Rosa's line of credit during the coming year assuming the average loan balance outstanding during the year is $1.8 million.
   b. Calculate Rosa's EBR on the line of credit during the coming year assuming the average loan balance outstanding during the year is $0.8 million.
   c. Compare and contrast the effective borrowing rates calculated for Rosa Inc. in parts (a) and (b). Explain the causes of the differences in EBRs.

23-18. Matthews Manufacturing is negotiating a 1-year credit line with its bank, Worldwide Bank. The amount of the credit line is $6.5 million with an interest rate set at 1.5% above the prime rate. A commitment fee of 0.50% (50 basis points) will be charged on the unused portion of the line. No compensating balances are required, and the loan is made on a 365-day basis.
   a. If the prime rate is assumed to be constant at 4.25% during the term of the loan and if Matthews's average loan outstanding during the year is $5.0 million, then calculate the firm's effective borrowing rate.
   b. What effect would an increase in the prime rate to 4.75% for the entire year have on Matthews's EBR calculated in part (a)?
   c. What effect would a decrease in Matthews's average loan outstanding during the year to $4.0 million have on the EBR calculated in part (a)?
   d. Using your findings in parts (a), (b), and (c), discuss the effects on Matthews's effective borrowing rates of interest-rate changes versus changes in the average loan outstanding.

23-19. Firm MGST is reviewing its 1-year line of credit, currently set at 9.15% APR. The credit line is for $1 million, but the firm intends to use only half of it throughout the year. The commitment fee is 42 basis points. Calculate MGST's effective borrowing rate. MGST is considering lowering the credit line to $0.7 million. The commitment fee increases to 55 basis points, but the interest rate lowers to 9.00% APR. Should MGST lower the credit line based on EBR?

23-20. Firm JJBT is considering two plans for a 1-year credit line. Plan A has a fixed rate of 8.25% APR with a commitment fee of 30 basis points. Plan B has a floating rate set 3% above the prime rate (currently 4.75%) with a commitment fee of 45 basis points. JJBT tends to average $450,000 in loans throughout the year but would like a $750,000 line of credit. Calculate the effective borrowing rate for both plans under current conditions. Next, determine the prime rate that sets both plans to the same EBR. Assuming you believe the prime rate will not increase to more than 5.10% over the next year, which credit line would you choose and why? Would your answer change based on a credit line of $500,000 rather than $750,000?

THOMSON ONE | Business School Edition

23-21. Using the Statement of Cash Flows, analyze the short-term borrowing of Dell (ticker symbol, Dell), Wal-Mart (ticker symbol, WMT), Honda (ticker symbol, HMC), and Monster Worldwide (ticker symbol, MWW). Which firms have increased and which have decreased their reliance on short-term borrowing relative to total assets? Can you explain why some of these firms might rely more or less on short-term borrowing relative to assets?

23-22. Using the common-size balance sheets, analyze the cash and short-term investments of Dell, Wal-Mart, Honda, and Monster Worldwide. Which firms have increased and which firms have decreased their cash and short-term investments relative to total assets? Can you explain why some of these firms might need more or less cash relative to assets?

MINI-CASE: LIQUIDITY MANAGEMENT

Foah's Designs sells precious metal jewelry throughout the western half of the United States. It is based in Yakima, Washington, and currently all customers mail their payments to the Yakima office. The average amount of float is 6.5 days. The firm is considering implementing a lockbox system in Los Angeles. Total annual sales that are expected to be routed to the Los Angeles lockbox are $68,000,000, with an average check amount of $1,300. The lockbox system would be administered by California State Bank, which will charge a fee of $0.25 per check and an annual fixed charge of $10,000. Foah's Designs has a cost of capital of 12% per year, and the lockbox is expected to reduce float to 4 days. However, there is some chance that the lockbox will only reduce float to 5 days.

The firm must also decide between using EDT or wire transfers when transferring funds between California State Bank and its local bank, Yakima State Bank. Using the wire transfer method would cost $20 per transfer whereas the EDT method would cost only $1.50 per transfer. However, the wire transfer method would result in the funds arriving at Yakima State Bank one day sooner.

Foah's Designs is also faced with a decision concerning its accounts payable. Foah's purchases its inventory from Jewelry Findings, Inc., on credit. Jewelry Findings' terms of trade are 3/15 net 45, and Foah's Designs normally pays after exactly 45 days. However, it has been considering accessing a line of credit from Yakima State Bank to pay its accounts payable after exactly 15 days instead. The commitment fee on the unused portion of the credit line is 0.3%, and the interest rate on the loan from Yakima State Bank is 8.9%. There are no compensating balance requirements. Assume a 365-day year.

1. Should Foah's Designs implement the lockbox system?

2. Suppose Foah's Designs plans to transfer money on a weekly basis (every Tuesday) from California State Bank to Yakima State Bank. Which transfer method should it use if the interest paid on its funds in Yakima State Bank is 0.5% higher than what they earn from California State Bank?

3. Assuming that Foah's Designs has a $2 million line of credit and that its accounts payable average $1,417,000, determine whether the firm should continuing paying Jewelry Findings, Inc., after 45 days or instead should begin accessing the line of credit from Yakima State Bank.

PART 8

Special Topics

In this section, we take a look at two special topics. Chapter 24 covers one of the most exciting areas of finance—mergers, acquisitions, and corporate governance. Historically, mergers have come in waves, with a huge volume of merger transactions occurring in some years and very few in others. And the same statement can be made looking across countries rather than across time. In most developed economies, mergers and acquisitions are simply part of the economic landscape. Managers know that engaging in a merger is one strategic choice open to them. They also know that, if they do not make choices to increase shareholder wealth, then they themselves may become the target of a takeover attempt. In this chapter, we study some of the motivations for mergers and the tactics that firms use to buy other firms or to defend against unwanted bids.

Chapter 25 explores what happens when a company becomes financially distressed, with particular emphasis on chapter 11 bankruptcy. This chapter is written in the context of the deep recession that lasted from 2007 to 2009 and includes analysis of the Chrysler, GM, LyondellBasell, and Circuit City bankruptcies.

What Companies Do

The Deal That Might Have Been—BHP Billiton's Bid for Rio Tinto Collapses

Had the deal been successfully completed, Australia's BHP Billiton Ltd's $140 billion hostile takeover bid for fellow mining company Rio Tinto plc, launched in November 2007, would have been the third-largest takeover in history. Instead, the bid's failure and withdrawal in January 2009 resulted in the largest failed takeover attempt ever and left the shareholders of both companies feeling bruised. The merger seemed to make sense when launched at the peak of the mining industry's global business cycle. But by 2009 it had fallen victim to plunging share and commodity prices, worldwide economic contraction, opposition from powerful national and business interests intent on scuttling a merger between the world's first- and third-largest mining companies, and the desire of Rio Tinto's management team to remain independent.

When BHP Billiton Ltd approached the board of directors of Britain's Rio Tinto plc on November 7, 2007, with an offer to exchange three BHP shares for each Rio Tinto share, this represented a 14% premium over Rio Tinto's share price the day before. Despite this, Rio Tinto's board immediately rejected the offer as inadequate. Undeterred, BHP followed up with an identical tender offer targeted directly at Rio Tinto's shareholders. It announced that it had lined up a high-powered set of investment and commercial banks to advise BHP on its takeover strategy and to provide financing for a proposed $30 billion buyback of shares in the combined company, to be executed if and when the merger was completed. BHP also described how it would integrate the two companies and predicted that it would be able to generate "synergies"—cost savings, increased sales, and more productive investment spending—of $3.7 billion per year.

Unfortunately for BHP, several large mineral-consuming nations and businesses concluded that the proposed synergies would actually result from price increases for iron ore and other key products, and they challenged the proposed merger on antitrust grounds. These opponents pointed out that a merged BHP–Rio Tinto would control almost 40% of the world's supply of iron ore and would leave just two companies controlling almost 80%. The Chinese state-owned company Chinalco went so far as to pay $14.1 billion in February 2008 to buy Rio Tinto's UK-listed subsidiary to ensure that Chinese interests would be represented in a combined BHP–Rio Tinto. The European Union's Competition Commission also opened a formal investigation of the merger and signaled its plans to oppose the deal in court.

Meanwhile, the market capitalizations of both BHP and Rio Tinto fell by more than a third during 2008 as the global financial crisis pummeled stock prices and slowing growth sharply cut worldwide demand for minerals. In December 2008, BHP was forced to withdraw its offer in order to focus on cutting costs in its own operations. The takeover saga, and the bid's ultimate collapse, left Rio Tinto so badly weakened that the firm was forced to cut its 2009 capital investment spending plans from $9 billion to $4 billion and to search for ways of trimming its $37 billion in debt—which in February 2009 actually exceeded its $36 billion stock market capitalization. The year 2008 saw a record number and value of failed takeover bids, and the BHP–Rio Tinto deal that got away was the largest of them all.

Sources: Lina Saigol, "Investment Banks Seem Too Keen to Join Rio Bandwagon," Financial Times (November 11, 2007); Lina Saigol, "Record Number of Deals Pulled," Financial Times (December 23, 2008); Lex, "Rio Tinto Cuts Capex," Financial Times (January 12, 2009).

24

Mergers, Corporate Control, and Corporate Governance

24.1 Overview of Corporate Control Activities

24.2 Horizontal, Vertical, and Conglomerate Mergers

24.3 Merger and Acquisition Transaction Characteristics

24.4 Rationale and Motives for Mergers and Acquisitions

24.5 History and Regulation of Mergers and Acquisitions

24.6 Corporate Governance

SMARTFinance Use the learning tools at www.cengage.com/finance/smartfinance

797

Corporations have emerged as the modern world's most powerful and productive economic organizations. As corporate power has grown, so has interest in ensuring that these institutions operate in a socially constructive manner that benefits both the firm's owners and society at large. Corporate governance is the term describing the set of laws, practices, and institutions that determine how—and in whose interests—corporations headquartered in a particular country are operated. This chapter will describe corporate governance practices in the United States and in several other important countries. We begin by examining how corporate control is exercised over American corporations.

As its name implies, **corporate control** refers to the monitoring, supervision, and direction of a corporation or other business organization. The most common change in corporate control results from the combination of two or more business entities into a single organization, as happens in a merger or acquisition. A change in corporate control also occurs with the consolidation of voting power within a small group of investors, as found in going-private transactions such as leveraged buyouts (LBOs) and management buyouts (MBOs). Transfer of ownership of a business unit with a divestiture and the creation of a new corporation through a spin-off are other ways to bring about such a change.

The forces effecting changes in corporate control and the resulting impact on the business community present some of the most interesting and hotly contested debates in the field of finance. For example, the corporate control contest for RJR Nabisco captivated corporate America in the fall of 1988, spawned a book and a movie about the takeover, and remains a source of debate for academics and politicians over the social benefit of corporate control activities. We address the causes and consequences of changes in corporate control in this chapter in addition to providing real-world examples of the merger/acquisition process and discussing the technical aspects that a corporate manager must consider before making decisions regarding corporate control changes.

24.1 OVERVIEW OF CORPORATE CONTROL ACTIVITIES

You probably understand what *mergers and acquisitions (M&As)* means in a general sense. However, the common usage of these and other corporate control phrases often has particular connotations. For instance, the popular press often uses the term *takeover* in ways that conjure up images of an unwelcome bidder commandeering control of a corporation through the techniques of high finance. A **takeover**, however, simply refers to any transaction in which the control of one entity is taken over by another. Thus, a friendly merger negotiated between the boards of directors and shareholders of two independent corporations is a takeover, as is a successful entrepreneur selling out her enterprise to a corporation. The terminology of corporate control can be easily misconstrued and must be clearly defined to prevent such ambiguities. In the following discussion, we define many terms and concepts encountered in the corporate control arena.

Corporate Control Transactions

Changes in corporate control occur through several mechanisms, most notably via acquisitions. An **acquisition** is the purchase of additional resources by a business enterprise. These resources may come from the purchase of new assets, the purchase of some of the assets of another company, or the purchase of another whole business entity, which is known as a merger. **Merger** is itself a general term applied to a transaction in which two or more business organizations combine into a single entity. Often, however, the term *merger* is reserved for a transaction in which one corporation takes over another upon the approval of both companies' boards of directors and shareholders after a friendly and mutually agreeable set of terms and conditions and a price are negotiated. There are many different types of mergers, and they (as well as other corporate control activities) can be differentiated according to several criteria. We define mergers by the mode of target integration used by the acquiring firm, by the level of business concentration created by the merger, and by other transaction characteristics for which mergers are commonly known.

There are a number of ways to integrate the assets and resources of an acquired firm into the acquiring company (the acquirer). The following discussion describes the various forms of resource integration that may be used to combine the resources of an acquirer and a target.

Statutory Merger   A **statutory merger** occurs when the acquirer can absorb the target's resources directly, with no remaining trace of the target as a separate entity. Many intrastate bank mergers are of this form.

Subsidiary Merger   Conversely, an acquirer may wish to maintain the identity of the target as either a separate subsidiary or division. A **subsidiary merger** is often the integration vehicle when there is brand value in the name of the target, such as the January 2005 acquisition of Molson by Adolph Coors to form Molson Coors Brewing. Sometimes, separate "tracking" or "target" shares are issued in the subsidiary's name. These shares may be issued as new common shares in exchange for the target's common shares. Alternatively, a new class of preferred stock may be issued by the bidding firm to replace the common shares of the target.

Consolidation   **Consolidation** is another integrative form used to effect a merger of two publicly traded companies. Under consolidation, both the acquirer and target disappear as separate corporations and combine to form an entirely new corporation with new common stock. This form of integration is common in mergers of equals, where the market values of the acquirer and target are similar. Many of these new corporations adopt a name that is a hybrid of the former names, such as the 2001 consolidation of Chevron and Texaco to become ChevronTexaco. (In 2005, the name was changed to Chevron to convey a more unified presence around the world.) But some managers of newly created companies want a "fresh start" with a company name. An example of this occurred in 2000, when the Amsterdam Stock Exchange, the Paris Bourse, and the Brussels Stock Exchange merged to form Euronext.

LBOs, MBOs, and Dual-Class Recapitalizations

Changes in corporate control also occur when voting power becomes concentrated in the hands of one individual or a small group. Going-private transactions are one way to achieve this concentration of control. Just as they sound, **going-private transactions** transform public corporations into private companies through issuance of large amounts of debt used to buy all (or at least a voting majority) of the outstanding shares of the corporation. The acquiring party may be a leveraged-buyout (LBO) firm—such as Kohlberg, Kravis, and Roberts (KKR), which specializes in such deals—the current managers of the corporation (known as a **management buyout**, or **MBO**); or even the employees of the corporation itself through an **employee stock ownership plan (ESOP)**. An LBO that sells shares to the public again in a second initial public offering is known as a **reverse LBO**.

A **dual-class recapitalization** may also concentrate control. Under this form of organizational restructuring, the parties wishing to concentrate control (usually management) buy all the shares of a newly issued Class B stock, which carries "super" voting rights (100 votes per share, for example). Traditional Class A shareholders generally receive some form of compensation, such as higher dividends, for the dilution of their voting power. Dual-class companies are rare in the United States but are common in other countries (see Nenova 2003). The higher stock price typically assigned to the share class with superior voting rights, often called the *voting premium*, has been used as a measure for the private benefits of control in a publicly traded firm.[1]

Tender Offers, Acquisitions, and Proxy Fights

An acquirer can also attain control of a public corporation through a nonnegotiated purchase of the corporation's shares in the open market or by obtaining voting control of other stockholders' shares via proxy. Theoretically, an acquirer can gain control simply through open-market purchases of a target firm's shares, though regulation severely restricts this form of "creeping acquisition" in most developed countries. Generally, an acquirer must explicitly bid for control through a tender offer for shares. A **tender offer** is a structured purchase of the target's shares in which the acquirer announces a public offer to buy a minimum number of shares at a specific price. Interested stockholders may then "tender" their shares at the offer price. If at least the minimum number of shares is tendered, then the acquirer buys those shares at the offer price. The acquirer has the option of buying the shares tendered at the offer price or canceling the offer altogether if the minimum number of shares is not tendered.[2] A two-tiered offer results when the acquirer offers to buy a certain number of shares at one price and then more shares at another price. These offers are especially popular in situations where the acquirer wishes to purchase 100% of the shares outstanding as quickly as possible and offers to buy 51% at a higher price and the remaining 49% at a lower price in an attempt to provide an incentive for shareholders to tender their shares early in order to receive the higher price. A **tender-merger** is a merger that occurs after an acquirer secures enough voting control of the target's shares through a tender offer to effect a merger. Figure 24.1 presents the total number (Panel A) and value (Panel B) of mergers and acquisitions in the United States between January 1962 and December 2008.

Tender offers are often associated with hostile takeovers, but these are the highly publicized minority cases. If mergers are included with tender offers, then the fraction of all acquisitions that are hostile is truly small. Hostile takeovers are rare in countries other than the United States. The world average is 1.01%, with Canada, Italy, Norway, Sweden, the United Kingdom, and the United States having the most.

Here's how tender offers, open market purchases, and proxy fights could be used in combination to launch a "surprise attack" on an unwitting (and often unwilling) target. In the United States, individuals or corporations may own up to 5% of any corporation's stock before they must file a Schedule 13-d form with the Securities and Exchange

---

[1]Dyck and Zingales (2004) define private benefits of control as "the proportion of a firm's value that does not accrue to all shareholders on a per-share basis, but is instead captured by inside shareholders." They find considerable variation in control premiums—higher prices paid for purchases of controlling versus noncontrolling share stakes—among the 39 countries they study. Twelve countries (including the English common law countries of Australia, Britain, Canada, South Africa, and the United States) had control premiums of 2% or less, but 10 had premiums of more than 25%, with Brazil's 65% premium being the highest.

[2]The U.S. tender offer process is regulated by the Williams Act, an amendment to the Securities and Exchange Act. See the discussion of the Williams Act in Section 24.5 for more details on the regulation of tender offers.

FIGURE 24.1

Panel A: Merger and Acquisition Activity in the United States, Number of Deals, 1962–2008

Panel B: Merger and Acquisition Activity in the United States, Total Value of Deals ($ billion), 1968–2008

Source: Mergerstat (downloaded from www.mergerstat.com).

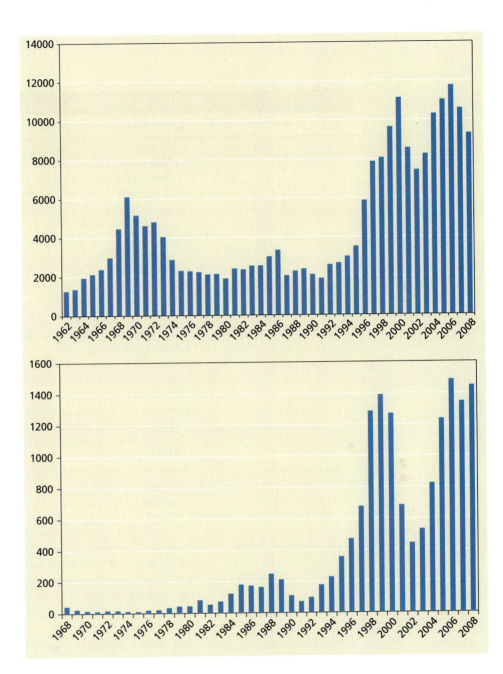

Commission (SEC) identifying themselves as a significant stockholder in the company. Thus, an interested potential acquirer could accumulate a substantial number of shares (known as a *foothold*) without the knowledge of the target's management and then follow several acquisition strategies. To counter such an attack, target firms employ defensive measures, such as **antitakeover amendments** to their corporate charters (also known as **shark repellents**), **poison pills**, the pursuit of **white knights** ("friendly" acquirers who will top the price of an unwelcome bidder), MBOs, stock buybacks, and payment of greenmail (see footnote 4), among other defensive tactics.[3] Table 24.1 describes the most important antitakeover defenses.[4]

Table 24.1	Commonly Used Antitakeover Measures
MEASURE	**ANTITAKEOVER EFFECT**
Fair-price amendments	Corporate charter amendments which mandate that a "fair price," usually defined as the highest price paid to any shareholder, be paid to all of the target firm's shareholders in the event of a takeover
Golden parachutes	Large termination arrangements made for executives that are activated after a takeover
Greenmail	The payment of a premium price for the shares held by a potential hostile acquirer but not paid to all stockholders
Just-say-no defense	Refusal to entertain a takeover offer on the grounds that no consideration offered is sufficient to relinquish control
Pac-Man defense	The initiation of a takeover attempt for the hostile acquirer itself
Poison pills	Dilution of the value of shares acquired by a hostile bidder through the offer of additional shares to all other existing shareholders at a discounted price
Poison puts	Deterrent to hostile takeovers through put options attached to bonds that allow the holders to sell their bonds back to the company at a prespecified price in the event of a takeover
Recapitalization	A change in capital structure designed to make the target less attractive
Staggered director elections	Corporate charter amendments designed to make it more difficult for a hostile acquirer to replace the board of directors with persons sympathetic to a takeover
Standstill agreements	Negotiated contracts that prevent a substantial shareholder from acquiring more shares for a defined period of time
Supermajority approvals	Corporate charter amendments that require the approval of large majorities (67% or 80%) for a takeover to occur
White knight defense	The pursuit of a friendly acquirer to take over the company instead of a hostile acquirer
White squire defense	The sale of a substantial number of shares to an entity that is sympathetic to current management but has no intention of acquiring the firm

---

[3]*Poison pills* are takeover defenses that can be triggered unilaterally by the target firm's board and effectively make a hostile takeover prohibitively expensive to the potential acquirer. These measures are typically adopted *without* shareholder approval.

[4]One notorious practice that was fairly common during the 1980s was for a corporate "raider" to accumulate a large block of shares and then threaten the target with a hostile tender offer and/or proxy fight in order to force the board of directors to repurchase the raider's shares at a premium price. This became known as **greenmail**, which is now outlawed in many states and taxed heavily by the Internal Revenue Service.

Divestitures and Spin-offs

Sometimes, managers prefer to transfer control of certain assets and resources through divestitures, spin-offs, split-offs, equity carve-outs, split-ups, or bust-ups. A **divestiture** occurs when the assets and/or resources of a subsidiary or division are sold to another organization. An example of a divestiture was Guaranty Financial Group, Inc., which (on December 31, 2008) sold its wholly owned subsidiary, Guaranty Insurance Services, Inc., to JLT Insurance Agency Holdings, Inc.

In a **spin-off**, a parent company creates a new company with its own shares by spinning off a division or subsidiary. Existing shareholders receive a pro rata distribution of shares in the new company. For example, on February 11, 2009, the FCC granted approval of the separation of Time Warner Inc. and Time Warner Cable in a spin-off. On February 12, 2009, Time Warner Cable received a favorable IRS ruling and expected the separation process to be completed by the end of the first quarter of 2009. A **split-off** is similar to a spin-off in that a parent company creates a newly independent company from a subsidiary, but ownership of the company is transferred only to certain existing shareholders in exchange for their shares in the parent. *Equity carve-outs* (described more fully in Chapter 16) bring a cash infusion to the parent from the sale of a partial interest in a subsidiary through a public offering to new stockholders. Split-ups and bust-ups are the ultimate transfers of corporate control. As it sounds, the **split-up** of a corporation is the split-up and sale of all its subsidiaries so that it ceases to exist (except possibly as a holding company with no assets). A **bust-up** is the takeover of a company that is subsequently split up.

Concept Review Questions	1. Why are acquired resources integrated into a company in so many different forms? What transaction-specific circumstances might lead to a preference for one integrative form over another?
	2. How does a tender offer differ from a proxy fight? Why might these two corporate control actions be considered different ways to achieve the same objective?

24.2 HORIZONTAL, VERTICAL, AND CONGLOMERATE MERGERS

Mergers may also be classified by the relatedness of the business activities of the merging firms. There are several different classification schemes used for assessing the business relatedness of acquiring and acquired firms, but the most commonly applied scheme is the abbreviated classification offered by the Federal Trade Commission (FTC). In the following paragraphs, we define these FTC classifications as well as others that are used and discuss their importance to our eventual discussion of antitrust laws.

Horizontal Mergers

In a strict sense, the FTC defines a **horizontal merger** as a combination of competitors within the same geographic market; the commission defines a **market extension merger** as a combination of firms that produce the same product in different geographic markets. As interstate commerce and technology have rendered geographic market classification less meaningful over time, the common interpretation of a horizontal merger has loosened to become a merger between companies that produce identical or closely related products in any geographic market. For example, a merger between two electric companies, one in Oregon and the other in Oklahoma, would have once been considered a market extension merger but would now be classified as horizontal.

The classification of mergers is important with regard to the regulatory authority of the FTC and the Department of Justice (DOJ), especially in the case of horizontal mergers. The FTC and DOJ have broad regulatory powers that can be used to prevent any merger that is deemed to be anticompetitive in nature, and the combinations that have the greatest potential to be anticompetitive are horizontal mergers.

EXAMPLE

The failed 1997 merger attempt of Staples and Office Depot illustrates the legal perils facing companies wishing to execute horizontal mergers. Both companies were discount office supply retailers with some overlapping geographic markets and only one major competitor (OfficeMax). FTC and DOJ regulators opposed the merger on the grounds that it would be anticompetitive. Staples and Office Depot countered with an offer to sell all the Office Depot stores sharing the same market as a Staples store and an OfficeMax, making the merger more of a traditional market extension merger than a "strict" horizontal merger. The companies also sought to have their market more broadly defined as general discount retail (such as Target and Wal-Mart) so that the impact of the merger would not appear to be so anticompetitive. The regulators prevailed, however, and the companies had to abandon their proposed merger. Government regulators were less successful in 2004, when they challenged Oracle's proposed acquisition of PeopleSoft in federal court on antitrust grounds. Oracle successfully litigated the case and consummated the PeopleSoft acquisition in early 2005.

Horizontal mergers also have the greatest potential for wealth creation. Firms with similar businesses and assets have the ability to benefit from economies of scale and scope by combining their resources. These mergers also have the greatest *possibility* of realizing cost savings through the reduction or elimination of overlapping resources. **Market power** is another obvious benefit that might arise from a horizontal merger. Increased market power results when competition is too weak (or nonexistent) to prevent the merged company from raising prices in a market at will. Of course, this is exactly the kind of anticompetitiveness that regulators seek to prevent. Yet research by Bittlingmayer and Hazlett (2000), Fee and Thomas (2004), and Shahrur (2005) finds little evidence that horizontal mergers create abusive market power.[5]

Vertical Mergers

A **vertical merger** occurs when companies with current or potential buyer–seller relationships combine to create a more integrated company. These mergers are easiest to think of in terms of steps in the production process. Consider the process of producing and selling finished petroleum products. Petroleum exploration and production is followed by transportation, refining, and end-use sales. If a company in the drilling business acquires a company that refines crude oil, then the driller is moving forward in the production process by purchasing the potential buyer of its crude oil. This type of vertical merger is a **forward integration**. Had a refiner and distributor acquired a driller, then the merger

---

[5]Bittlingmayer and Hazlett present an intriguing analysis of the impact of federal antitrust enforcement actions against Microsoft on the market values of Microsoft's *competitors*. They find these actions reduced competitors' market values by an average of more than $1 billion for each of the 29 events studied between 1991 and 1997. The authors conclude that "financial markets reveal compelling evidence against the joint hypothesis that (a) Microsoft conduct is anticompetitive and (b) antitrust policy enforcement produces net efficiency gains. They also found little evidence that government antitrust enforcement is unambiguously beneficial" (2000, p. 329).

would be a **backward integration**, as exemplified by the 1984 merger between Texaco and Getty Oil. Texaco needed Getty's drilling operations and reserves to complement its own refineries and distribution and marketing outlets in order to be a fully integrated oil company.

There are several obvious potential benefits to vertical integration via merger. One advantage to a vertical merger is that product quality and procurement can be ensured from earlier stages of the production process with backward integration. For instance, a manufacturer of precision surgical devices might wish to ensure the high-quality standards required of an input such as a laser beam by acquiring the company that manufactures the laser beam. Or a manufacturer with great sensitivity to inventory conversion cycles could more efficiently monitor an orderly inventory flow by acquiring a supplier of raw materials. Another advantage to backward integration is the reduction of input prices. The "middleman" and associated price markup are eliminated.

Forward integration may also offer benefits. Whereas backward integration emphasizes inputs, forward integration focuses on output quality and distribution. Providing an outlet for a product is an advantage to forward integration. One reason for Disney's merger with Capital Cities/ABC was to gain access to a television network as an outlet for Disney's television entertainment production.[6] Vertical integration can also be used as a marketing tool. Many retail stores and automobile manufacturers have acquired financing subsidiaries that make it easier for a customer to obtain credit to purchase their products (e.g., HP Financial Services, Investment Arm).

However, there can be disadvantages to vertical mergers. The major disadvantage is the entry into a new line of business. Acquiring managers are likely to have some knowledge of the target firm's business because it is part of the same production process, but similarities do not always imply compatibility. A manager of an automobile manufacturer might find that what works well for manufacturing cars does not work well for renting them (as Chrysler found out with its Thrifty Rent-a-Car unit), even though both businesses revolve around automobiles. Managers might also find that the cost savings from "eliminating the middleman" are not as great as expected. Eliminating the markup might reduce costs for the acquirer, but it also means that the acquired subsidiary is no longer producing profits for the parent company. The acquirer might overlook or underestimate this factor when attempting to value a target. Finally, vertical mergers may also be subject to antitrust regulation, albeit with a smaller probability than occurs with horizontal mergers.

Conglomerate Mergers

The remaining two types of FTC-defined mergers are diversifying in nature. **Product extension mergers**, or *related* diversification mergers, are combinations of companies with similar but not identical lines of business. **Pure conglomerate mergers**, or *unrelated* diversification mergers, occur between companies in completely different lines of business.

Product extension mergers, like market extension mergers, are something of a hybrid classification—in this case, a cross between vertical and purely conglomerate mergers. These mergers are not vertical because they are not between firms in different stages

---

[6]It is interesting that this forward integration strategy proved largely unsuccessful for Disney, as ABC experienced an extended ratings swoon almost immediately after Disney acquired the network. The failure of this strategy was one reason why Disney appeared vulnerable to a hostile takeover attempt launched by Comcast Corporation in early 2004. The takeover attempt eventually fizzled, though Disney was forced to adopt significant changes to its corporate governance rules.

of the production process, but their business operations are still related. The merger between the New York Stock Exchange and Archipelago Holdings, completed in late 2005, is a fascinating example of a product extension merger: the world's largest and most successful stock exchange merged with a much smaller electronic trading company, yet it offered Archipelago shareholders 30% of the combined entity.[7] Managers tend to pursue these types of mergers when searching for a higher-growth business that is not entirely new to them.

Pure conglomerate mergers marry two companies that operate in totally unrelated businesses. Although popular in the 1960s, these mergers have significantly declined in frequency since the 1980s. Andrade, Mitchell, and Stafford (2001) show a steady increase in the fraction of mergers between firms in the same industry, rising from 29.9% during 1970–1973 to 47.8% during 1990–1998. Based on the principles of portfolio diversification, the purpose of conglomerate mergers is to put together two companies that operate in businesses so different that, if some systematic or idiosyncratic event has an adverse effect on one business, then the other business will be minimally (or even positively) affected. Merging the two disparate firms is expected to make earnings and cash flows less volatile. An example of a pure conglomerate merger is Phillips Electronics (maker of TVs and stereos), which acquired their way into the medical devices industry. Phillips stated explicitly that it did so in order to diversify into a growth industry, and it did: they later bought more medical equipment companies. An example of a pure conglomerate run amuck is Ling-Temco-Vought (LTV). Ling had an electrical contracting business, then bought two others, next bought Temco Aircraft, then bought Chance Vought Aerospace, then added the wire and cable company Okonite and bought Wilson, the sports equipment company—which was also involved in meat packing and pharmaceuticals. Ling later spun each of these divisions into separate companies traded on the American Stock Exchange; they soon acquired the trader nicknames "Golfball," "Meatball," and "Goofball," respectively. Ling then added Greatamerica, Post's holding company for Braniff International Airways and National Car Rental, as well as J & L Steel, and it then acquired a series of resorts in Mexico and Colorado. By 1969 LTV had purchased 33 companies, employed 29,000 workers, offered 15,000 separate products and services, and was one of the 40 largest industrial corporations. But after numerous divestitures, what was left of LTV filed for bankruptcy in 2000. The empirical evidence on conglomerate mergers, surveyed in depth in Section 24.4, generally shows that they yield disappointing results.

Other Concentration Classifications

The FTC merger classifications are not always satisfactory for determining the degree of business concentration created by a merger. Compare the following two hypothetical mergers for an illustration of a possible shortcoming of the FTC classification. The first merger pairs two software companies that operate in no other lines of business. The second merger occurs between the companies described in Table 24.2. The acquirer in this merger derives 50% of its revenue from chemicals, 30% from crude oil refining, and 20% from coal mining operations. Chemicals are also the primary line of business for the target at 40% of revenues, followed by 30% from retail drugs and 30% from plastics. In both mergers, the acquirer and target are in the same primary line of business and so the mergers are classified

---

[7]In part, the NYSE pursued this merger as a backdoor way of becoming a publicly traded company, since Archipelago was listed but the NYSE itself was not. Since most of the NYSE's most important competitors are publicly traded, this method of "going public" was very attractive because of its immediacy.

Table 24.2 Level of Business Concentration Resulting from Merger: Example of Various Classifications

LINE OF BUSINESS	ACQUIRER			TARGET			COMBINED		
	REVENUES	%	%²	REVENUES	%	%²	REVENUES	%	%²
Chemicals	$ 500,000,000	50.0	0.2500	$200,000,000	40.0	0.1600	$ 700,000,000	46.7	0.2180
Oil refining	300,000,000	30.0	0.0900	0	0.0	0.0000	300,000,000	20.0	0.0400
Coal mining	200,000,000	20.0	0.0400	0	0.0	0.0000	200,000,000	13.3	0.0178
Retail drugs	0	0.0	0.0000	150,000,000	30.0	0.0900	150,000,000	10.0	0.0100
Plastics	0	0.0	0.0000	150,000,000	30.0	0.0900	150,000,000	10.0	0.0100
Total	$1,000,000,000	100.0	0.3800	$500,000,000	100.0	0.3400	$1,500,000,000	100.0	0.2958

Notes: See Problem 24-13 for an explanation of the "%²" unit.
    Abbreviated FTC classification: horizontal.
    Business overlap classification: medium overlap.
    Change in focus classification: focus-decreasing.

as horizontal mergers under the FTC scheme. But do both mergers have the same level of business concentration? Obviously not—the first merger clearly has more concentration than the second. The need for a finer definition of business concentration in such cases gave rise to the creation of alternative measures, such as degree of overlapping business and change in corporate focus (defined later).

A more finely tuned measure of business concentration revolves around the concept of **corporate focus**. A focused firm concentrates its efforts on its core (primary) business, the opposite end of the spectrum from a diversified firm. A measure known as the **Herfindahl Index (HI)** provides a way quantifying the concept of focus. The HI is computed as the sum of the squared percentages, which in this case is the proportion of revenues derived from each line of business. Thus, the HI exaggerates the difference between focused and diversified firms. A completely focused firm has an HI of 1.00, compared with the diversified acquiring firm in our example, which has an HI of 0.38 ($0.5^2 + 0.3^2 + 0.2^2$). A merger (or divestiture) increases focus if the HI of the merged firm is greater than that of the acquiring firm prior to the merger, preserves focus if the HI does not change, and decreases focus if the HI declines. In our hypothetical mergers, the first merger between the software companies preserves corporate focus whereas the second merger between the diversified companies decreases corporate focus, since the HI declines from 0.380 to 0.296.

Concept Review Questions

3. What is the purpose of classifying mergers by degree of business concentration? Why do you think these classifications have changed over time?
4. Given that conglomerate mergers and corporate diversification have proven to be failures in general, why would any manager pursue these objectives? Can you think of any cases where corporate diversification has worked successfully? What distinguishes these cases from the norm?
5. What is the Herfindahl Index, and what does it measure?

24.3 Merger and Acquisition Transaction Characteristics

Corporate control events can be categorized according to certain defining characteristics of the transactions, including the method of payment used to finance a transaction, the attitude or response of target management to a takeover attempt, and the accounting treatment used when the firms combine.

Method of Payment

Just like any other type of investment, a merger must be financed with capital—including debt, accumulated profits, and newly issued common stock. These components make up the consideration offered in a transaction and sum to the *transaction value*: the dollar value of all forms of payment offered to the target for control of the company. Cash on hand from retained earnings and/or generated from an issue of debt is used in financing a cash-only deal, where the target's shareholders receive only cash for their shares in a public company or the target's owner(s) receives cash for the private enterprise.[8] More rarely, the target receives a new issue of debt in exchange for control in a debt-only transaction.

Bidders almost always offer target firm shareholders a price for their shares that is significantly higher than the target's current market price. The merger premium is the difference between premerger announcement market value and acquisition value. For example, on April 21, 2009, Broadcom announced an unsolicited offer of $9.25 per share for Emulex, a producer of networked storage products for large data centers. Broadcom's offer represented a 40% premium over the market price of Emulex shares one day prior to Broadcom's bid. The bidding firm's stock is the only mode of payment in a stock-swap merger, or **pure stock exchange merger**. The general stock-swap merger involves the issuance of new shares of common stock in exchange for the target's common stock, but payment may come in the form of either preferred stock or subsidiary tracking shares. The number of shares of the surviving firm's common stock that target shareholders receive is determined by the exchange ratio. The surviving firm is either the acquiring firm or the new firm created in a consolidation. For instance, an acquirer with a current stock price of $20 that sets an exchange ratio of 0.75 for a target with a current stock price of $12 and 100 million shares outstanding will issue 75 million new shares in exchange for the target's shares. The transaction value of this merger would be $1.5 billion ($20 × 75 million).[9] An individual who owns 100 shares ($1,200) of the target stock would receive acquirer stock worth $1,500 ($20 × 75 shares), a 25% control premium.

Mergers may also be financed with a combination of cash and securities in transactions known as **mixed offerings**. For example, in January 2005, SBC Communications offered AT&T shareholders a combination of SBC stock worth $18.41 per share plus $1.30/share in cash. Sometimes target shareholders are also offered a choice for the medium of exchange. For example, target shareholders could be offered the choice of either $30 cash

---

[8]Harford (1999) shows that cash-rich acquiring firms make poor bidders. These firms launch more takeover attempts, the attempts are value-destroying in the short term, and the firms underperform other acquirers that also pay with cash. Bank-financed acquisitions are associated with large and significantly positive acquirer announcement returns. Finally, Faccio and Masulis (2005) examine the determinants of the cash versus stock method of payment in European acquisitions of public and private companies during 1997–2000. They find that considerations related to tax, corporate governance and control, and debt financing all play a role in this choice and that the choice will be different in different national markets.

[9]This is under the assumption that the acquirer's stock price remains the same—an optimistic assumption, as we shall see. In most stock-swap mergers, an acceptable range of stock prices and exchange ratios is negotiated from the outset.

or 1.25 shares of the surviving company's shares for each share that they hold. This way, the shareholders can decide whether the exchange ratio is sufficient for them to remain shareholders in the surviving company or whether they should "take the money and run" with the cash offer.

Accounting Treatment

Prior to June 30, 2001, two financial accounting procedures existed for recording a merger in the United States: the pooling-of-interests and purchase methods. However, with implementation of Financial Accounting Standards Board (FASB) Statement 141 and the near-concurrent (December 31, 2001) Statement 142, there is now a single standard method of accounting for mergers. Under this standard, target liabilities remain unchanged, but target assets are "written up" to reflect current market values and also the equity of the target is revised upward to incorporate the purchase price paid. These revised values are then carried over to the surviving firm's financial statements. The intangible asset *good-will* is created if the restated values of the target lead to a situation in which its assets are less than its liabilities and equity. This **goodwill** reflects the premium that an acquiring firm is willing to pay in excess of net asset market value in order to capture synergies from the merger; thus goodwill becomes an intangible asset on the acquiring firm's balance sheet. Going forward, the value of this intangible asset must be evaluated to determine if it has been "impaired" due to a decline in fair value relative to carrying value. If the value of goodwill is impaired, then the amount of the impairment is "written down" from the goodwill account on the balance sheet and charged off against earnings. Otherwise, it remains unchanged on the balance sheet indefinitely. Many large write-downs were taken soon after FASB 142 went into effect at the beginning of 2002. JDS Uniphase, AOL Time Warner, and Nortel Networks all took multibillion-dollar write-downs in 2002 for acquisitions completed in prior years, and the newly renamed MCI Inc. took a $75 billion write-down in early 2004 for acquisitions completed by the company when it was named WorldCom. The following Example details the mathematical treatment of accounting for mergers.

EXAMPLE

Assume that a target firm has 5 million shares outstanding priced at $10 per share. The acquiring firm offers a 20% takeover premium ($12 per share), for a transaction value of equity of $60 million. The acquiring firm wants the R&D capabilities of the target firm and is willing to pay a premium to obtain those capabilities and leverage R&D synergies. The market value of the target's fixed assets is $65 million. Along with the $10 million in current assets, the target has a market value of assets of $75 million. Deducting the $5 million in current liabilities and $25 million in long-term liabilities, the target firm has a net asset value of $45 million. Thus, the acquiring firm is willing to pay $15 million ($60 million less $45 million) for intangible assets that represent the premium paid to acquire the R&D capabilities.

Current assets	$ 10,000,000
Restated fixed assets	65,000,000
Less: Liabilities	30,000,000
Net asset value	$ 45,000,000
Purchase price paid	60,000,000
Less: Net asset value	45,000,000
Goodwill	$15,000,000

(continued)

Further assume that the target firm is treated as a separate reporting subsidiary after the merger. Going forward, the firm must value its intangible assets (goodwill) to determine if the value of $15 million on the balance sheet (shown in the following table) represents a fair value. As long as the firm can demonstrate that the goodwill is fairly valued, then it will remain unaffected on the balance sheet. However, if the value is "impaired" then the value loss must be reported, deducted from the balance sheet, and taken as a write-off against earnings. For example, if two years later the R&D of the subsidiary does not turn out to be as valuable as expected, then the fair market value and net asset value of the subsidiary will be estimated. If the fair market value is estimated at $70 million and the net asset value at $60 million, then the value of goodwill is only $10 million—a $5 million impairment. This $5 million will be deducted from the balance sheet and taken as an intangible asset write-down on the income statement.

	Acquirer ($ million)	Target ($ million)	MERGED ($ MILLION) Subsidiary	MERGED ($ MILLION) Consolidated
Assets				
Current	50	10	10	60
Fixed	350	50	65	415
Goodwill	0	0	15	15
Total assets	400	60	90	490
Liabilities				
Current	50	5	5	55
Long-term	250	25	25	275
Total	300	30	30	330
Owner's equity	100	30	60	160
Total liabilities and equity	400	60	90	490

Shareholder Wealth Effects and Transaction Characteristics

How do the shareholders of companies involved in mergers and acquisitions generally fare? The consensus result obtained in merger studies is that the common stockholders of target firms in successful takeovers experience large and significant wealth gains. Acquirer returns are much smaller and not as generalized, and we discuss the theories offered to explain the cross-sectional differences in acquirers' returns. We also explore the wealth effects of various transaction characteristics.

Returns to Target and Bidding Firm Shareholders

Target Returns   As previously noted, target-firm stockholders almost always experience substantial wealth gains due to the premium offered for giving up control of their company.[10] In an early survey article, Jensen and Ruback (1983) find that, on average, U.S. target-firm common stockholders receive takeover premiums of 29.1% in successful tender offers and 15.9% in successful mergers. More recently, Bhagat and colleagues (2005) find that the average announcement-period abnormal return for target-firm shareholders in 1,018

---

[10]The rare case when a target shareholder receives a negative takeover premium is known as a *takeunder*.

attempted tender offers from 1962 to 2001 is 30.01% when using a 5-day event window and 24.47% when using an event window that begins 90 days before the announcement and ends one day afterward. Andrade, Mitchell, and Stafford (2001) find that the announcement-period abnormal return for target-firm shareholders in 4,256 completed tender offers and mergers during the period 1979–1998 is 16.0% when using a 3-day event window [−1 day, +1 day] and 23.8% when using a window stretching from 20 days before the offer through the merger completion. These authors also show that target returns in all completed M&A deals have remained essentially constant over time, whereas Bhagat and colleagues find that target abnormal returns in tender offers have risen steadily over time. Target returns are also higher when there are multiple bidders and when managerial resistance leads to a higher offer, but takeover premiums are lost when resistance is too great and prevents a takeover.

Acquirer Returns   Results concerning the common stock returns of U.S. acquiring firms are far less conclusive than those for target shareholders, and they are very different depending on whether one examines average percentage returns or overall dollar returns to bidder shareholders. Bhagat and colleagues (2005) find that the average announcement-period abnormal return for the shareholders of firms launching successful tender offers is very close to zero for their entire 1962–2001 study period, with these average returns fluctuating between positive and negative over time. Andrade, Mitchell, and Stafford (2001) document average announcement-period excess returns for successful acquiring-firm shareholders of −0.7% when using a short event window and −3.8% when using an event period that stretches through merger completion.

In Figure 24.2 we present the aggregate dollar returns to acquiring shareholders for acquisitions of U.S. targets announced since 1980. A positive number indicates that acquiring shareholders earned positive returns; a negative number indicates that acquiring shareholders lost value upon announcement of the planned acquisition. The figure shows that acquiring shareholders gained value in acquisitions that were announced during the late 1990s merger boom, perhaps because of the overall euphoria of the stock

FIGURE 24.2

Yearly Aggregate Dollar Return of U.S. Acquiring-Firms' Shareholders, 1980–2007 ($ billion)

Source: Figure 1 in Sara B. Moeller, Frederik P. Schlinemann, and Renee M. Stulz, "Wealth Destruction on a Massive Scale? A Study of Acquiring-Firm Returns in the Recent Merger Wave," *Journal of Finance* 60 (April 2005), pp. 757–782. Updated from 2002–2007 by Graham, Smart, Megginson.

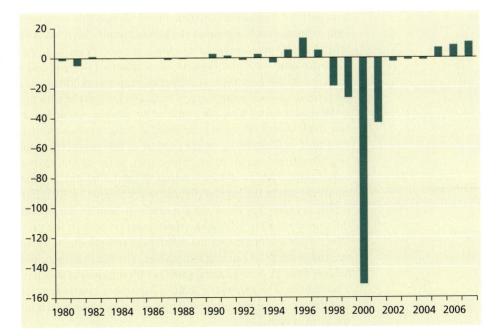

market during that era. However, there was a sharp correction when the Internet bubble burst in 2000, resulting in massive wealth loss for acquiring firms over the period 1999–2004. Moeller, Schlingemann, and Stulz (2005) attribute this wealth loss to 87 "large loss" bidders that each lost at least $1 billion in market value in a single transaction. From 1998 to 2001, acquirers lost $240 billion in total. During this period, the large-loss bidders shed an incredible $397 billion of market value while all other deals increased acquiring-firm wealth by $157 billion in aggregate. These researchers also find evidence of a size effect whereby relatively small bidding firms earn positive returns but larger bidders fare much worse. Over the 2005–2007 period, acquiring shareholders again gained substantial wealth at the time of the merger announcement. Once data become available, it will be interesting to see how acquiring shareholders have fared in 2008 and beyond—after yet another merger wave has crashed.

Combined Returns   An important early study by Bradley, Desai, and Kim (1988; henceforth BDK) computed the capitalization-weighted announcement-period returns to combined bidder and target-firm shareholders and presented these as a measure of the total synergistic gains expected to be realized from the merger. The authors find that the weighted-average return of acquirers and targets consistently ranged between 7% and 8% throughout the period 1962–1984, reflecting a constant anticipated synergistic gain from combining the two firms. But the protective provisions of the 1968 Williams Act seem to have caused a transfer of this consistent gain from acquirer to target-firm shareholders, because acquirer returns were significantly positive prior to the Williams Act and have become slightly negative since. In recent years, several research teams have used the BDK approach to measure total synergistic gains for combined bidder and target-firm shareholders. Andrade, Mitchell, and Stafford (2001) document combined returns of about 2% for merging-firm stockholders when using both short and long event windows; Bhagat and colleagues (2005) find somewhat higher combined returns of around 5% in their sample of tender offers.

Mode of Payment   The mode of payment used to finance an acquisition explains much of the cross-sectional variance in acquirers' returns. Higher returns in cash transactions than in stock transactions observed by both acquirers and targets in tender offers relative to negotiated mergers are attributable to the fact that most tender offers are financed by cash, whereas most negotiated mergers are equity financed. Announcement-period target returns are 13 percentage points greater for cash deals, acquirer returns in cash-financed deals are near zero, and those in stock-financed deals are significantly negative. Long-term results are even more startling: common stockholders in cash tender offers outperform those in stock-swap mergers by 123% through the fifth postacquisition year.

Several theories have been offered to explain the differential returns between cash and stock offers. The most prominent of these revolves around the signaling model first described in Chapter 13. In the context of this model, the mode of payment offered by acquiring firms signals inside information to the capital markets. Managers will finance acquisitions with the cheapest source of capital available. Financing an acquisition with equity signals to the market that managers believe equity is a (relatively) cheap source of capital because they think the acquirer's stock price is overvalued. Receiving this signal, the capital markets will make a downward revision of the value of the acquirer's equity. Other theories concerning the differential returns due to financing method include the tax and preemptive bidding hypotheses. The *tax hypothesis* postulates that target shareholders must be paid a capital gains tax premium in cash offers, which is not required in a stock offer. The *preemptive bidding hypothesis* asserts that acquirers who wish to ward off other potential bidders for a target will offer a substantial initial takeover premium in the form of cash.

Returns to Other Security Holders   Obviously, common stocks are not the only securities affected in corporate control activities. Corporate control events also affect bonds and preferred stocks.[11] A study examining 254 mergers between 1979 and 1997 (with complete data for all the securities of both bidder and target) shows significant wealth changes for bondholders in mergers. There is clear evidence supporting a co-insurance effect in that merging two firms with less than perfectly correlated cash flow streams will benefit the financially riskier firm's bondholders, because the merged cash flows reduce the chance that this firm will default on its debt during a period of operating losses. The bondholders' gain is a wealth transfer from the merging firms' shareholders—especially the financially healthier firm's shareholders—since cash flows that they would have received in the weaker firm's loss period are instead diverted to pay the bondholders' claims. Target bonds that are below investment grade earn significantly positive announcement-period returns, while acquiring-firm bondholders earn negative returns. Corporate managers pursue mergers at least partly to reduce financial risk, benefiting themselves and other fixed claimants (such as bondholders) but harming shareholders.[12]

International Mergers and Acquisitions

During most recent years, roughly two-thirds of the world's mergers and acquisitions involved non-U.S. bidders and targets, and these mergers represented half or more of overall M&A value. In most years, over 85% of all non-U.S. mergers involve European companies, and the European M&A market typically mirrors that of the United States in terms of industries targeted, prices paid (multiples or target firm cash flows offered by the bidder), and frequency of using cash or stock as means of payment. However, Europe's takeover market differs from America's in one important aspect: European bidders are much more likely to resort to hostile bids opposed by target firm managers than are American bidders. This is primarily because poison pills are illegal in Europe, whereas they have been employed by many publicly listed American companies.

It is hard to generalize international mergers and acquisitions. Countries differ with respect to how frequently takeover attempts are launched and also with respect to how often these are friendly versus hostile bids, how often these are cross-border deals (involving a bidder and a target firm in different countries), the average control premium offered, and the likelihood that payment will be made strictly in cash. Table 24.3 presents global average values for these variables—plus national average values for a selected group of 14 countries—derived from a study by Rossi and Volpin (2004) of 45,686 mergers in 49 countries completed between 1990 and 2002. Hostile takeovers rarely occur (except in the United States, Norway, Canada, and Britain), and all-cash bids account for the majority of offers outside of Japan, Canada, and the United States. Over 40% of all M&As are cross-border deals, and this is common everywhere except Japan and the United States. Perhaps surprisingly, the average non-U.S. "takeover" deal involves acquisition of less than one-fourth of the outstanding stock of the target company—although this is sufficient to transfer effective control in many cases.

---

[11]See Wansley, Lane, and Yang (1983), Dennis and McConnell (1986), Lehn and Poulsen (1989), Asquith and Wizman (1990), Macquieira, Megginson, and Nail (1998), and Megginson, Morgan, and Nail (2004). Early empirical research found that some nonconvertible bondholders experienced significant wealth gains but that these gains were driven by the bonds of acquiring firms in nonconglomerate mergers. No financial synergies were realized in conglomerate mergers, and the nonconvertible bondholders in these mergers neither gained nor lost. In general, convertible bond returns were significantly higher than those of nonconvertible bonds. No evidence of significant bondholder wealth losses was systematically observed in LBOs, though specific transactions yielded dramatic bondholder losses. Both convertible and nonconvertible preferred stockholders exhibited significant wealth gains in nonconglomerate mergers.
[12]Billett, King, and Mauer (2004).

Table 24.3 Descriptive Data on International Mergers and Acquisitions, 1990–2002

COUNTRY	VOLUME (%)	HOSTILE TAKEOVER (%)	CROSS-BORDER RATIO (%)	PREMIUM (MEAN)	ALL-CASH BID (%)	NUMBER OF OBSERVATIONS
Australia	34	0.65	27	129.5	60	212
Canada	30	4.60	23	132.9	36	157
France	56	1.68	34	133.4	88	112
Germany	36	0.30	26	116.7	77	13
Hong Kong	34	0.41	39	129.8	93	46
India	2	0.02	56	178.6	67	9
Italy	56	3.04	36	127.7	88	26
Japan	6	0.00	13	99.0	36	73
Norway	61	5.86	37	136.0	76	37
Singapore	34	0.40	31	152.9	85	39
Sweden	62	3.74	35	141.7	71	45
Switzerland	38	1.43	44	111.0	89	9
United Kingdom	54	4.39	23	145.8	64	614
United States	66	6.44	9	144.3	37	2,443
World average	**24**	**1.01**	**43**	**141.6**	**48**	**4,007**

Notes: This table presents descriptive data on international mergers and acquisitions in 49 countries announced between January 1, 1990, and December 31, 1999, and completed by December 31, 2002. Volume is the percentage of the stock of traded companies targeted in a completed deal. Cross-border ratio is the number of cross-border deals as a percentage of all completed deals. Premium is the bid price as a percentage of the closing price of the target four weeks before the announcement. All-cash bid is a dummy variable that equals 1 if the acquisition is paid entirely in cash and 0 otherwise.

Source: Derived from Tables 1 and 2 in Stefano Rossi and Paolo F. Volpin, "Cross-Country Determinants of Mergers and Acquisitions," *Journal of Financial Economics* 74 (November 2004), pp. 277–304. Copyright © 2004, with permission from Elsevier.

Concept Review Questions	6. What are the two most important methods of paying for corporate acquisitions?
	7. What is *goodwill* in the context of merger accounting? What must an acquiring company do if the value of an acquired company is revealed to have declined after a merger?
	8. Who wins and who loses in corporate takeovers? Why do acquiring-firm shareholders generally lose in stock-swap mergers but either benefit or at least break even in acquisitions paid for with cash?

24.4 RATIONALE AND MOTIVES FOR MERGERS AND ACQUISITIONS

The primary objective of any corporation's management team should be the maximization of shareholder wealth. Management should undertake a potential merger or acquisition, like any other investment, as long as its net present value is positive, thereby enhancing shareholder value. However, we know that corporate managers do not always act as proper agents for their shareholders, and agency problems arise when managers engage in behavior that does not maximize value. In this section, we examine both the value-maximizing and non-value-maximizing motives that lead managers to pursue mergers and acquisitions.

Value-Maximizing Motives

Mergers can create value when managers seek to increase operating profit, realize gains from restructuring poorly managed firms, and increase barriers to entry in their industry. These and other value-enhancing objectives can be achieved through mergers and acquisitions that garner access to new geographic markets, increase market power, capitalize on economies of scale, or create value through the sale of underperforming target resources. Mergers can also increase efficiency if they remove inefficient management and transfer control of the firm to more capable managers.[13]

Expansion   Geographic expansion (both domestic and international) may enhance shareholder wealth if the market entered is subject to relatively little competition. Managers considering expansion must first evaluate two mutually exclusive alternatives: internal versus external expansion. Internal expansion into a new market, also known as **greenfield entry**, involves acquiring and organizing all resources required for each stage of the investment. These stages encompass contracting with an engineering firm to build a new plant, hiring new employees to staff the plant, implementing training programs for the new staff, establishing distribution outlets, and so on.

External expansion is the acquisition of a firm with resources already in place. Acquirers pay a control premium to the owners of the acquired firm for relinquishing control, but the payment of this premium ensures that many of the potential problems of greenfield entry are avoided. For instance, external expansion avoids construction delays in the building of a new plant or the inability to adequately staff a new facility. External expansion is often the better option when rapid expansion is desired or when great uncertainty exists about the success of any stage of greenfield entry. International expansion is another good reason to choose external expansion over internal expansion. The business operations, political climate, and social mores differ so greatly between some countries that an acquisition is often the only viable alternative for international expansion.[14] The May 2004 merger between KLM and Air France maintained the separate identities of both airline subsidiaries, at least partly to finesse political sensitivities both in the Netherlands and in France.

Synergy, Market Power, and Strategic Mergers

A **strategic merger** is one that seeks to create a more efficient merged company than the two premerger companies operating independently. This efficiency-enhancing effect is known as **synergy**. Michael Eisner, CEO of Disney at the time, provided the best definition of synergy with his perception of the value created by his company's 1995 merger with Capital Cities/ABC: "1 + 1 = 4." There are three types of merger-related synergies—*operational*, *managerial*, and *financial*. The synergies expected to result from

---

[13]Kini, Kracaw, and Mian (2004) examine the disciplinary role of corporate takeovers using a sample of 279 successful acquisitions of U.S. companies between 1979 and 1998. Their evidence is consistent with the takeover market's serving as a "court of last resort" or as an external source of discipline when internal control mechanisms are weak or ineffective.

[14]Joint ventures and strategic alliances also allow access to foreign markets through existing resources, but these are partnering relationships in which profits must be shared.

WHAT COMPANIES DO GLOBALLY

Survey Evidence: Why Pursue Mergers

What motivates corporate managers to merge with other companies? A study clearly indicates that the most important acquisition motive is to capture potential synergies from combining with another firm. Exhibit 1 reveals that the desire to "take advantage of synergy" is easily the most popular motive for mergers among managers of firms that executed at least one merger during 1990–2001, with 37.3% of respondents listing this as their top-ranked motive. The desire to diversify ranked second, and merging to achieve a specific organizational form through restructuring ranked a distant third choice. No other motive was ranked highly by more than 8% of respondents.

(continued)

Exhibit 1: Motives for Mergers and Acquisitions

This exhibit shows the most important reasons responding firms gave for their mergers and acquisitions during 1990–2001. Respondents could indicate more than one reason, but this exhibit reports only the top-ranked motive.

MOTIVES	n	%
Take advantage of synergy	28	37.3
Diversify	22	29.3
Achieve a specific organizational form as part of an ongoing restructuring program	8	10.7
Acquire a company below its replacement cost	6	8.0
Use excess free cash	4	5.3
Reduce tax on the combined company due to tax losses of the acquired company	2	2.7
Realize gains from breakup value of the acquired firm	0	0.0
Other	5	6.7
Totals	**75**	**100.0**

Exhibit 2: Sources of Synergy

This exhibit presents the source of synergy for those firms directly or indirectly involved in synergy-related mergers. Of the 75 total responses, 69 stated that they were involved in such activities. Although respondents could indicate more than one reason, this exhibit reports only the top-ranked motive for a given respondent.

SOURCE OF SYNERGY	n	%
Operating economies (resulting from greater economies of scale that improve productivity or cut costs	62	89.9
Financial economies (resulting from lower transactions costs and tax gains)	4	5.8
Increased market power (due to reduced competition)	3	4.3
Differential efficiency (due to the acquiring firm's management being more efficient)	0	0.0
Totals	**69**	**100.0**

And what specific synergies are managers looking for in the mergers they implement? As described in Exhibit 2, reduced operating costs resulting from greater economies of scale from combined production are by far the most important synergies that managers hope to capture. Almost 90% of respondents listed this as the top-ranked source of synergy.

Source: Exhibits 2 and 3 of Tarun K. Mukherjee, Halil Kiymaz, and H. Kent Baker, "Merger Motives and Target Valuation: A Survey of Evidence from CFOs," *Journal of Applied Finance* 14 (Fall/Winter 2004), pages 7–24. Copyright © The Financial Management Association, International, University of South Florida, COBA, 4202 E. Fowler Avenue, Ste #3331, Tampa, FL 33620-5500 www.fma.org.

the Disney–Capital Cities/ABC combination proved to be elusive, and this disappointing result is observed in almost half of all mergers.

Synergies   The main sources of **operational synergy** are economies of scale, economies of scope, and resource complementarities. **Economies of scale** result when relative operating costs are reduced because of an increase in size that allows for the reduction or elimination of overlapping resources. A simple example is that Wal-Mart can sell products cheaply because its huge buying power gives it economies of scale: units are cheaper because they buy so many of them. In another example, the cost savings generated from the elimination of overlapping jobs was the reason given for eliminating 7,000 jobs following the 2004 Cingular Wireless acquisition of AT&T Wireless. **Economies of scope** are other value-creating benefits of increased size. The ability of a merged firm to launch a national advertising campaign that would not have been feasible for either of the premerger firms is one such benefit. **Resource complementarities** exist when a firm with a particular operating expertise merges with a firm with another operating strength to create a company that has expertise in multiple areas. A good example of such a complementarity is the planned merger of Pfizer Inc. and Wyeth, announced in January 2009. Benefits of the proposed merger include the combining of Wyeth's drug pipeline with Pfizer's resources, future financial and operating results, diversification, flexibility, and scale. The KLM–Air France merger in 2004 was also driven by a search for resource complementarities—specifically, the desire to combine the two carriers' extensive global route networks to better serve international business customers. Operating synergies are most likely to be achieved in horizontal mergers and least likely to be realized in conglomerate mergers. However, resource complementarities are just as likely to be realized in vertical mergers as in horizontal mergers, because vertical combinations pair companies that specialize in different areas.

Managerial synergies, like operational synergies, cause two firms to have greater value when combined than when they are independent. Managerial synergies, however, result in efficiency gains from the combination of management teams. Similar to resource complementarities, managerial synergies arise when management teams with different strengths are paired. Consider a merger between two retailing firms with differing managerial expertise. The first retailer has a management team that emphasizes revenue growth and excels in recognizing customer trends. The second retailer has a technically oriented management team that excels in cost containment and has perfected inventory control with its superior information systems. A merger between these two firms could have the potential to benefit from managerial synergies with a joint emphasis on and expertise in revenue growth and cost containment, assuming the two management teams can mesh together smoothly.

Financial synergies occur when a merger results in less volatile cash flows, lower default risk, and a lower cost of capital. Because financial synergies are largely the anticipated result of conglomerate mergers, we defer this discussion to the section on the diversification motive for mergers.

Market Power Other, more controversial motives support increasing firm size through mergers and acquisitions. As we have seen, horizontal mergers have the potential to create more efficient companies through size-related operational synergies. Horizontal mergers may also profit from size in another fashion: increased market power. Because horizontal mergers are those that take place between competitors, the number of competitors in an industry will necessarily decline. Presumably, price competition could also decline if the merger creates a dominant firm that has the power to control prices in a market. However, observable gains in pricing power are rare, a fact that is due to intense global competition and governmental regulation.

Consider the Staples–Office Depot merger attempt previously mentioned. The two largest competitors in an industry with only three true competitors attempted to merge. The regulatory authorities denied this merger on the grounds that the merged company would have the power to control prices in the office supplies market, with only one (much smaller) competitor to provide price competition. Regulatory authorities must balance the corporate benefit of increased efficiency against the consumer cost of increased market power when making decisions on allowing a merger to take place—especially a horizontal merger.

Other Strategic Rationales Managers are also motivated to pursue mergers by other strategic reasons. As we mentioned earlier, product quality after a vertical merger can sometimes be more closely monitored. Another strategic motive is defensive consolidation in a mature or declining industry. As consumer demand declines in an industry, competitors may seek each other out for a merger in order to survive the permanent industry downturn. Not only does the merged firm stand to benefit from economies of scale and scope, but it may also benefit from the reduction of competition. Of course, this does introduce the market power issue for regulators. But recent history has seen regulators adopt a more permissive attitude toward defensive consolidation—for example, the consolidation in the U.S. defense industry in the post–Cold War period. It is literally inconceivable that American regulators would have approved the 1997 acquisition by Boeing of McDonnell-Douglas, its sole remaining U.S.-based competitor producing commercial aircraft, during the 1970s or 1980s.

Cash Flow Generation and Financial Mergers

Financial mergers are motivated by the prospect of uncovering hidden value in a target through a major restructuring or the generation of free cash flow from merger-related tax advantages. Many of the highly levered deals of the 1980s were financial mergers aimed at either "busting up" undervalued firms by selling off the assets of the acquired firm for a value greater than the acquisition price or restructuring the acquired firm to increase its corporate focus. A typical financial merger involves a focused acquirer that acquires a diversified firm with some business operations in the acquirer's line of business. The acquirer then sells the noncore businesses and uses the cash flow to pay down the cost of the acquisition.

Tax considerations may also motivate managers to pursue a particular target for a merger. The asymmetrical nature of the U.S. tax code provides an incentive to merge in certain circumstances. Although taxes must always be paid on positive income, negative income (net losses) often leads to tax benefits that are not realized until the firm becomes profitable, and the time value of money erodes the present value of these tax benefits. Merging with a target that has accumulated **tax-loss carryforwards** could shelter taxable income and redistribute that cash flow to other uses. (Tax-loss carryforwards can be charged against future income for up to 20 years.)

The financial merger motive was minimized by a change in the tax code in 1986 that limited the extent to which tax-loss carryforwards could be used after a merger. In general, financial mergers still occur, but their importance in the market for corporate control has declined significantly.

Non-Value-Maximizing Motives

Unfortunately, not all mergers are motivated by the goal of maximizing shareholder wealth. Although the motives of managers may not be intentionally value reducing, some revolve around agency problems between managers and shareholders. We discuss these value-destroying motives next.

Agency Problems   Managers will sometimes intermingle their attempts to derive personal benefits from creating and managing larger corporations with the need to expand through mergers and acquisitions. Academic research confirms the importance of this motive with findings that merger activity is positively related to growth in sales and assets but is not related to increased profits or stock prices. Considering these findings, Mueller (1969) offered the **managerialism theory of mergers**. According to this theory, poorly monitored managers will pursue mergers that maximize their corporation's asset size because managerial compensation is usually based on firm size, regardless of whether or not these mergers create value for stockholders.

Roll (1986) offers a somewhat different rationale with his **hubris hypothesis of corporate takeovers**. Roll contends that some managers overestimate their own managerial capabilities and pursue takeovers in the belief that they can better manage their target than its current management team can. Acquiring managers then overbid for the target and fail to realize the expected postmerger gains, thereby diminishing shareholder wealth. Thus, the intent of the managers is not contrary to the best interests of shareholders (the managers think they will create value), but the result is still value decreasing.

Shleifer and Vishny (2003) present a model of M&A based on stock market misvaluation of the combining firms and of the potential synergies that can be reaped from merging these companies. They assume that investors periodically overvalue some firms, whose managers are then tempted to use their company's stock as currency to acquire other firms that the market has undervalued. In contrast to Roll's hubris hypothesis, Shleifer and Vishny's model assumes that (a) acquiring firm managers are perfectly rational and act in the best interest of their own shareholders, but (b) the stock market is at times (and dramatically) irrational in assigning stock values. Their model explains several empirical patterns, including when stock is likely to be used instead of cash as payment, why takeovers seem to occur in industry waves, and why the short- and long-term return to acquiring firm shareholders is frequently negative.

Another explanation of why bidding-firm managers might pursue value-destroying mergers is Jensen's (2005) model of the **agency cost of overvalued equity**. According to this model, a company's stock becoming significantly overvalued sets in motion a set of organizational forces that inevitably push managers to take actions that destroy part or all of the firm's core value. Once a manager has accepted all positive-NPV investment projects, she will inevitably be enticed to pursue ever larger, negative-NPV projects, such as nonsynergistic mergers. This theory seems to be consistent with the massive losses suffered by acquiring-firm shareholders in the megamergers of the period 1998–2001.[15]

---

[15]Moeller, Schlingemann, and Stulz (2004, 2005).

Diversification As recently as the late 1960s, diversification was actually considered a value-maximizing motive for merger. Over time, however, the capital markets have learned of the failure of corporate diversification strategies, especially those emphasizing unrelated diversification. Given these empirical discoveries, we must now consider that diversification is often a non-value-enhancing motive for merger.

As previously discussed, corporate diversification and conglomerate mergers were an experiment in portfolio theory applied to corporations. The basic premise of corporate diversification is that the combination of two businesses with less than perfectly correlated cash flows will create a merged firm with less volatile cash flows and inherently lower business risk, where bad outcomes in one business can be offset by good outcomes in another business. Diversification supporters contend that these less volatile cash flows make debt service less risky, lowering default risk and the required return on debt. Financial synergy is created by this **co-insurance of debt**, because the debt of each combining firm is now insured with cash flows from two businesses. Other proponents of unrelated diversification cite the existence of internal capital markets as another reason to pursue conglomerate mergers. **Internal capital markets** are created when the high cash flow (*cash cow*) businesses of a conglomerate generate enough cash flow to fund the "rising star" businesses. Since this financing is accomplished internally, underwriting costs are avoided and riskier business ventures can be financed with "cheaper" capital generated from more mature and less risky businesses. Some investment advisors were recommending diversifying mergers in 2008 and 2009 as a means to create an internal capital market for investment, given the limited availability of external funding.

Recent research on corporate diversification highlights the limitations of the diversification motive for merger. Conglomerate mergers are not likely to benefit from any synergies other than financial and so the net effect of conglomerate mergers is zero wealth creation: any wealth gains experienced by bondholders due to financial synergies are merely redistributed from stockholders. Empirical research[16] has generally verified that corporate diversification reduces firm value. The consensus among financial analysts is that corporate diversification does not in and of itself create wealth and that managers should not execute mergers in search of financial synergies. Furthermore, internal capital markets fell into disrepute when it became obvious that managerial control over free cash flow created its own, often severe, agency problems. In particular, capital attained and invested without having to pass a market test is more likely to be used inefficiently. Internal capital markets can also be used to prop up bad divisions rather than fund good ones.

Concept Review Questions	
	9. What characteristics surrounding a merger would lead you to conclude that it is motivated by value-maximizing managers rather than non-value-maximizing managers? What actions could directors or stockholders take to prevent non-value-maximizing mergers?
	10. If you wanted to expand your operations into a foreign country with nebulous laws and an unstable political climate, would you favor internal or external expansion? Why?
	11. What does Jensen's *agency cost of overvalued equity* model predict about the valuation effect of mergers, particularly those paid for with bidding-firm stock? Why do you think that managers might be tempted to pursue size-increasing mergers even when these do not maximize value?

---

[16]See Berger and Ofek (1995), Comment and Jarrell (1995), Lamont and Polk (2002), and Ahn and Denis (2004).

24.5 History and Regulation of Mergers and Acquisitions

Merger activity in the United States has been defined more by waves of concentrated intensity than by continuous activity over time. These waves tend to be positively related to high growth rates in the overall economy and are also related to "industry shocks," or industry-wide events such as deregulation that affect the corporate control activities of whole industries. In this section, we identify the key merger waves in U.S. history and discuss the factors that led to their occurrence as well as the corporate control regulation that has evolved over time.

The History of Merger Waves

The United States has witnessed six major merger waves in its history, most of which have certain similarities. They begin with a robust stock market, and the types of mergers occurring in each wave reflect the current regulatory environment. Activity is generally concentrated in industries undergoing changes (shocks) or facing an altered regulatory environment, and the merger waves tend to end with large declines in the stock market. The following discussion presents an overview of these waves.

The first major merger wave began in 1897 and was largely the result of a growing emphasis on a truly national economy rather than a grouping of regional economies. Merger activity peaked in 1899 in this wave and ended with the stock market crash of 1904. Another merger wave began shortly after World War I, with a zeal for consolidation equal to that of the first wave. Like the first wave, the second wave ended with a stock market decline, the infamous 1929 crash. Conglomerate mergers set the tone for the third merger wave, in the 1960s. Corporations became portfolios of business units; the diversification across different industries was supposed to reduce the risk of the corporation and the volatility of its cash flows in the same manner as portfolio diversification. The push for conglomeration was so great during this wave that approximately 70% of the mergers that took place in the 1960s were either pure conglomerate or product extension mergers. This wave ended with the stock market decline of 1969.

A fascinating and dramatic merger wave occurred in the 1980s. Initiated by the more lax regulatory emphasis of the Reagan administration, the fourth merger wave saw a shift back to corporate specialization and witnessed such occurrences as junk bond financing, hostile takeovers, corporate raiders, greenmail, LBOs, MBOs, and poison pills. Many antitakeover measures were adopted in the 1980s to prevent such hostile takeover attempts. This merger wave differed from previous ones in that it did not end with a major stock market decline; rather, it petered out as the 1980s bull market ended.

Friendly stock-swap mergers became the transaction method of choice in the fifth wave of mergers, which began in 1993 and ended with the sharp drop in takeovers during 2001. Following the trend of corporate specialization from the fourth wave, the vast majority of mergers in this wave occurred between companies in the same industry. Federal regulators remained relatively open to horizontal mergers as merger activity in other countries also led to larger (and supposedly more efficient) foreign competitors. Merger activity in this wave surpassed that in all the others, reaching $3.4 trillion in aggregate transaction value globally in the peak year of 2000. Of this aggregate value, slightly less than $1.8 trillion was generated from deals completed in the United States and about $1.6 trillion from deals outside the United States.

The total value of mergers worldwide fell by more than half between 2000 and 2002, bottoming out at $1.2 trillion worldwide and $439 billion in the U.S. during 2002. The most recent, sixth wave of mergers occurred in 2007–2008. Table 24.4 details the 15 largest corporate mergers of all time.

Table 24.4 Fifteen Largest Corporate Takeovers,[a] Ranked by Transaction Value

ACQUIRER	TARGET	TRANSACTION VALUE ($ BILLION)	YEAR
Vodafone AirTouch PLC (U.K.)	Mannesmann AG (Germany)	202.8	2000
America Online Inc. (U.S.)	Time Warner Inc. (U.S.)	164.7	2001
Royal Bank of Scotland (U.K.)	ABN Amro (Netherlands)	98.0	2007
Pfizer Inc. (U.S.)	Warner-Lambert Co. (U.S.)	89.2	2000
Royal Dutch Petroleum (Netherlands)	Shell Trading and Transport (U.K.)	80.1	2005
Exxon Corp. (U.S.)	Mobil Corp. (U.S.)	78.9	1999
Glaxo Wellcome PLC (U.K.)	SmithKline Beecham (U.K.)	76.0	2000
Travelers Group Inc. (U.S.)	Citicorp (U.S.)	72.6	1998
Sprint (U.S.)	Nextel Communications (U.S.)	71.0	2004
Pfizer (U.S.)	Wyeth (U.S.)	68.0	2009[b]
Sanofi (France)	Aventis (France)	65.7	2004
SBC Communications Inc. (U.S.)	Ameritech Corp. (U.S.)	62.6	1999
NationsBank Corp. (U.S.)	BankAmerica Corp. (U.S.)	61.6	1998
Vodafone Group PLC (U.K.)	AirTouch Communications (U.S.)	60.3	1999
JP Morgan (U.S.)	Bank One (U.S.)	58.8	2004

[a]As of February 18, 2009.
[b]Merger announced in January 2009; not yet completed.

Sources: Mergers & Acquisitions (SDC Publishing), Mergers and Acquisitions Report (Thomson Financial), and *Financial Times* (from www.ft.com).

Regulation of Corporate Control Activities

The legal environment affecting mergers evolved from a state of virtually no regulation during the first merger wave to what is currently a relatively complex nexus of interrelated legal issues, including antitrust enforcement, tender offer regulation, and laws regarding the actions of managers and directors and even actions of state and international regulators. This section addresses these legal issues and their ramifications for the decision to merge.

Antitrust Regulation   Antitrust legislation is intended to prevent an anticompetitive business environment. Obviously, mergers—especially horizontal mergers—often represent the most expedient manner to create corporate giants while simultaneously reducing competition. For this reason, antitrust enforcement seeks to prevent mergers that are deemed to have anticompetitive effects. Antitrust regulation began with the loophole-ridden Sherman Antitrust Act of 1890, was reinforced by the Clayton Act of 1914, and then was further strengthened by the Celler–Kefauver Act of 1950. The level of antitrust enforcement, administered in part by the Department of Justice, tends to be related to the philosophy of the governing executive administration. Following passage of the Celler–Kefauver Act, antitrust laws were relatively strictly enforced until the Reagan administration took office in the 1980s, after which enforcement was and has remained (a few noted cases notwithstanding) more lax.[17] The following sections outline the major aspects of various antitrust

---

[17]Such exceptions include the DOJ's refusal to allow Microsoft and Intuit to merge in 1994 and its continued pursuit of Microsoft for anticompetitive business practices.

laws as well as the guidelines established by regulatory agencies for determining the anti-competitive potential of a merger.

Antitrust Laws   The Sherman Antitrust Act initiated antitrust regulation in 1890 and has been amended and modified many times since. The last major federal antitrust legislation was enacted in 1976, but the interpretation of antitrust laws is a dynamic process in which regulatory agencies maintain an ongoing dialogue on the application of the laws.

Determination of Anticompetitiveness   Much like the business concentration classifications of the Federal Trade Commission, the measures and determinants of anticompetitiveness have evolved over time. The Department of Justice established the first set of merger guidelines for determining anticompetitiveness in 1968 and modified them in 1982, 1984, and 1992. The following guidelines are those currently utilized by the DOJ and FTC.

The 1982 guidelines introduced the use of the Herfindahl–Hirschman Index (HHI), a variant of the Herfindahl Index defined previously, to determine market concentration in the same manner that we used the index to measure business concentration earlier in the chapter. The DOJ determines the anticompetitive effect of a merger by evaluating that merger's impact on the HHI of the industry involved. The HHI is calculated as the sum of the squares of each company's percentage of sales within a market (industry). This HHI is then used to establish a range of concentration levels within a market or industry:

HHI > 1,800	Highly concentrated
HHI = 1,000 − 1,800	Moderately concentrated
HHI < 1,000	Not concentrated

Mergers resulting in an HHI measure in the highly concentrated category are the most likely to be challenged. Consider the example in Table 24.5. The premerger HHI of this industry is 1,450 (moderately concentrated). A merger between Company 7 and

Table 24.5   Determination of Anticompetitiveness: Using the Herfindahl–Hirschman Index (HHI)

	PREMERGER CONCENTRATION			POSTMERGER CONCENTRATION				
FIRM	MARKET SHARE (%)	MARKET SHARE SQUARED	FIRM	MARKET SHARE (%)	MARKET SHARE SQUARED	FIRM	MARKET SHARE (%)	MARKET SHARE SQUARED
1	20	0.0400	1	20	0.0400	1 + 2	35	0.1225
2	15	0.0225	2	15	0.0225	3	15	0.0225
3	15	0.0225	3	15	0.0225	4	15	0.0225
4	15	0.0225	4	15	0.0225	5	15	0.0225
5	15	0.0225	5	15	0.0225	6	10	0.0100
6	10	0.0100	6	10	0.0100	7	5	0.0025
7	5	0.0025	7 + 8	10	0.0100	8	5	0.0025
8	5	0.0025						
Sum		0.1450			0.1500			0.2050
HHI		1,450			1,500			2,050
Concentration		Moderate			Moderate			High

Company 8 would reduce the number of competitors in the industry, but the marginal impact of a merger between the two smallest players in the industry would increase the HHI to only 1,500 and would likely not face a challenge. However, a merger between the two largest firms in the industry would result in an HHI of 2,050—moving this industry from moderately to highly concentrated and likely prompting a challenge by the DOJ or FTC.

Realizing the efficiency-enhancing benefits of economies of scale and scope, which come only from increased size, the regulatory authorities developed an alternative measure to determine the anticompetitiveness of a merger. This alternative, an elasticity measure, offers an advantage over the strict use of the HHI: The elasticity measure does not necessarily deem a merger to be anticompetitive because of fewer competitors in a highly concentrated industry. Instead, an elasticity measure determines if a merged firm will have the market power to control prices in its market. The DOJ uses a "5% rule" to measure elasticity: If a 5% increase in price results in a decline of more than 5% in market demand, then that market is elastic. Elastic markets are less likely to be adversely affected by a merger and also less likely to be strictly governed by the HHI measure.

EXAMPLE

The failed 1997 merger attempt of Staples and Office Depot exemplifies the role of regulatory agencies in preventing what are deemed to be anticompetitive combinations. On September 4, 1996, Staples and Office Depot announced their intent to merge in a $3.4 billion deal. At the time, Office Depot and Staples were the largest and second-largest office supply superstores, respectively. Of the $14.0 billion in sales in this market, Office Depot had a market share of $6.6 billion, followed by Staples with $4.1 billion, and the only other major competitor, OfficeMax, with sales of $3.3 billion.

As permitted under the Hart–Scott–Rodino Act, the Federal Trade Commission (FTC) reviewed the proposed merger for anticompetitive effects and requested more information from the companies at the end of the initial review period. At the end of the second review, the FTC concluded that the proposed merger would have an anticompetitive impact if allowed to be consummated, so it rejected the merger proposal. One of the key points cited by the FTC in its rejection was the market power that the merged firm would be able to wield in those markets where no stores other than Staples or Office Depot existed (the 5% rule). In order to remedy this obstacle, Staples and Office Depot proposed to sell 63 stores to OfficeMax in the geographic market where both Staples and Office Depot were located. The FTC again rejected the merger and threatened to sue the companies in federal court if they attempted to pursue their merger. The FTC further threatened that, even if it could not prevent the merger under the Hart–Scott–Rodino Act through its federal lawsuit, it would continue to pursue the merged firm for antitrust violations.

The managers of both companies continued to fight for their merger, despite the FTC's threats. When presenting their argument to the federal judge assigned to the case, lawyers for the companies presented the companies' willingness to sell off stores in order to satisfy the FTC and enhance competition; they also contended that the FTC had improperly defined their industry when determining the Herfindahl–Hirschman Index. The FTC had limited their industry classification to office supply superstores with three competitors and an HHI of 3,634 (already highly concentrated), which would increase to 6,394 after the merger. Lawyers for the companies, however, stated that the appropriate industry classification should be discount retailers and should include such retailers as Wal-Mart and Kmart in addition to office supply stores. The judge in the case disagreed with the companies' lawyers and sided with the FTC in barring the merger from taking place. The managers of Staples and Office Depot announced their intentions to abandon their merger plans shortly thereafter.

Although merger guidelines have evolved over time and now seem to be less hostile toward horizontal combinations, the DOJ and FTC remain active enforcers of antitrust laws.

Other Antitrust Considerations Managers contemplating a merger now face antitrust scrutiny from sources other than U.S. federal regulators. Globalization and proactive state regulators have created more recent obstacles to merger approval. Individual states have become more active participants in the oversight of anticompetitive business practices since the 1990s. State attorneys general from 14 states joined the antitrust lawsuit first lodged against Microsoft by the Justice Department in 1994. Even after the federal government abandoned its case against Microsoft in 2001 in an effort to settle the case out of court, many of the states refused to abandon their status as plaintiffs against Microsoft.

The Williams Act During the conglomerate merger wave of the 1960s, hostile tender offers became an increasingly frequent and controversial means to facilitate takeovers. The controversy over these tender offers revolved around target shareholders' inability to evaluate the terms of the tender offers in the often short periods of time for which they were open and around the abuses of higher takeover premiums being offered to select shareholders. In response to this controversy, the Williams Act passed in 1967 and was enacted in 1968 as an amendment to the Securities and Exchange Commission Act of 1934. Section 13 of the Williams Act introduced ownership disclosure requirements, and Section 14 created rules for the tender offer process.

Ownership Disclosure Requirements Section 13-d of the Williams Act now requires public disclosure of ownership levels beyond 5%.[18] This section of the act mandates that any individual, group of individuals acting in concert, or firm must file a Schedule 13-d form within 10 days of acquiring a 5% or greater stake in a publicly traded company. This disclosure sends a warning signal to the managers and stockholders of a corporation that a potential acquirer might be lurking about and provides background information on that potential acquirer. Stockholders or managers of the corporation may sue for damages if any material misrepresentation (such as initiating a later takeover attempt when the stated purpose of ownership is for investment purposes) is made on the form.[19]

Tender Offer Regulation Prior to the passage of the Williams Act, tender offers were largely unregulated open calls to the shareholders of public companies to tender (sell) their shares at offered prices. Section 14 changed this free-form nature of the tender offer market to a much more restrictive and structured process. Any party initiating a tender offer must file a Schedule 14-d-1 form (a tender offer statement). Managers of tender offer targets are then required to file a Schedule 14-d-9 form, which contains their recommendation to shareholders on whether to accept, reject, or refrain from supplying an opinion on the offer. Section 14 also provides structural rules and restrictions on the tender offer process. These rules include a minimum tender offer period of 20 days, the right of target share-holders to withdraw shares already tendered at any time during the tender offer period, and the requirement that the acquirer accept all shares tendered and that all tendered shares receive the same price.

Other Legal Issues Concerning Corporate Control Federal securities laws also regulate the actions of managers in corporate control events. The high-profile insider-trading scandals of the 1980s generated a keen interest in these laws, while the 2001 Enron and

---

[18]The threshold was originally 10% but was dropped to 5% in 1970.
[19]It is also illegal to "park" shares, which means engaging another individual to buy shares for you in order to avoid disclosure requirements.

WorldCom scandals prompted Congress to pass the Sarbanes–Oxley Act of 2002. This act primarily targeted accounting practices, but it also mandated significant changes in how (and how much) information must be reported by companies to investors. Individual states have also become more interested in promoting corporate control legislation after witnessing business practices that were perceived as detrimental to the welfare of the electorate. In recent years, many states have developed antitakeover and antitrust laws designed to regulate takeovers of corporations located in their states. We describe the major elements of these other federal and state corporate control laws in the following sections.

Laws Affecting Corporate Insiders A variety of federal securities laws govern the actions of corporate managers and other individuals considered to be corporate insiders during corporate control events. The majority of these laws attempt to prevent informed trading on material nonpublic information (inside information), such as an upcoming takeover attempt known only to the insiders of the acquiring firm. Rule 10-b-5 dictated by the Securities and Exchange Commission outlaws material misrepresentation of information used in the sale or purchase of a security. Trading on inside information about a pending merger is such a material misrepresentation because material information (news of the merger) is being withheld. Also, SEC Rule 14-e-3 specifically forbids trading on inside information in tender offers. The Insider Trading Sanctions Act of 1984 strengthened both SEC rules with triple damage awards. Managers are also restricted from issuing misleading information regarding merger negotiations and may be sued if they deny the existence of merger negotiations that are actually taking place. Finally, Section 16 of the Securities and Exchange Act establishes a monitoring facility for the trading of corporate insiders.

State Laws Individual states have increasingly regulated corporate control activities over the years. Some states have adopted various provisions against takeovers and bust-ups and have formed antitrust agencies that restrict corporate control activities in their states beyond the level of federal regulations.

Antitakeover and anti-bust-up provisions include voting initiatives—such as supermajority voting, which requires that large majorities (usually 67%) approve a takeover—and control share provisions that require the approval of target shareholders before a potential acquirer may even buy a substantial number of shares in the target firm. Fair-price provisions and cash-out statutes are also popular measures that further restrict tender offers. **Fair-price provisions** ensure that all target shareholders receive the same offer price in any tender offers initiated by the same acquirer, limiting the ability of acquirers to buy minority shares cheaply with a two-tiered offer. **Cash-out statutes** are "all-or-none" rules that disallow a partial tender offer/acquisition of a company and the ability to control that company with less than 100% ownership. Business combination rules prevent the bust-up or other major restructuring of a company that is taken over. These provisions are often used in conjunction with each other, and individual state laws must be reviewed when considering a takeover to determine if these provisions are present and, if so, what impact their presence will have on the value of the takeover. The formation of state-level antitrust regulatory boards is an even more recent trend in state corporate control regulation. California has filed antitrust lawsuits and merger injunctions. Other states are following California's lead and have become more active antitrust monitors as well.

International Regulation of Mergers and Acquisitions

International regulatory authorities, especially in Europe, have become a force to be reckoned with for those companies attempting large-scale mergers. The European Commission (EC) first signaled its more stringent antitrust regulatory authority in 1999 when it vetoed the proposed merger of U.S. communications giants WorldCom and Sprint. The EC

WHAT COMPANIES DO GLOBALLY

A Half-Billion Shareholders and Counting

Corporations in most capitalist economies are operated (at least theoretically) in the interest of shareholders, and a firm's stockholders are the ultimate masters of their firms' destinies. But who exactly owns shares in various countries—and how many individual stockholders are there? Traditionally, share ownership has been highly concentrated among the wealthiest citizens in all Western countries, and even more so in developing countries, but the number of individuals owning stock has increased sharply in most countries over the past two decades. There are two reasons for this. First, rising wealth prompted popular demand for stocks as investments, which was met by proliferating mutual fund choices and other consumer-oriented savings vehicles. Second, share issue privatization programs adopted by many governments caused large numbers of citizens to purchase stock for the first time.

A recent academic study by Paul Grout, Bill Megginson, and Ania Zalewska has compiled individual share ownership data for 59 countries—24 developed and 35 emerging countries with stock markets—and a summary of their findings is presented in the following table. Approximately 310 million people own stock directly, meaning that investors hold shares of listed companies directly in their accounts (or in accounts of self-managed pension funds) and/or invest in mutual funds or hedge funds. Perhaps not surprisingly, China and the United States have the largest absolute number of direct shareholders (76.7 million and 62.9 million, respectively), but Canada, Australia, and Japan have the highest percentages of the population owning stock directly (at 37.5%, 35.1%, and 30.8%, respectively). National percentage of "direct" share ownership generally rises with increasing income levels, but the correlation is hardly perfect: over 20% of the population in some middle-income nations such as the Czech Republic own shares directly, while less than 10% of populations of high-income countries—such as Spain and Norway—own stock.

COUNTRY	DIRECT SHARE OWNERSHIP		INDIRECT SHARE OWNERSHIP	
	PERCENT OF POPULATION OWNING SHARES	APPROXIMATE TOTAL NUMBER OF INDIVIDUAL SHAREHOLDERS	PERCENT OF POPULATION CONTRIBUTING TO PENSION FUNDS	NUMBER OF CONTRIBUTORS TO PENSION FUNDS
Argentina	0.52	194,728	28.14	10,816,790
Australia	35.11	7,268,000	—	29,100,000
Brazil	1.62	3,123,425	17.48	5,690,580
Canada	37.52	12,396,020	—	—
Chile	4.24	636,474	48.80	8,043,808
China	5.90	76,700,000	8.92	116,000,000
Czech Republic	29.00	2,963,264	35.30	3,619,428
Estonia	2.60	35,484	38.65	519,726
France	14.70	9,000,000	—	—
Germany	12.50	10,317,000	18.54	15,300,000
Hungary	7.90	2,885,981	39.80	4,015,263

(continued)

COUNTRY	DIRECT SHARE OWNERSHIP		INDIRECT SHARE OWNERSHIP	
	PERCENT OF POPULATION OWNING SHARES	APPROXIMATE TOTAL NUMBER OF INDIVIDUAL SHAREHOLDERS	PERCENT OF POPULATION CONTRIBUTING TO PENSION FUNDS	NUMBER OF CONTRIBUTORS TO PENSION FUNDS
Italy	7.98	4,667,894	3.90	2,279,338
Japan	30.75	39,284,500	8.54	10,870,000
Netherlands	17.05	2,780,889	98.90	16,158,000
Norway	7.30	340,821	5.95	276,303
Poland	2.38	909,000	34.47	13,134,081
Russia	0.14	204,000	4.57	6,503,980
South Africa	2.63	1,275,513	20.71	9,853,055
Spain	5.00	2,152,969	23.29	10,361,201
Sweden	19.70	1,780,530	23.29	10,361,201
Switzerland	20.22	1,508,062	58.47	4,361,740
United Kingdom	15.09	9,060,260	45.50	27,500,000
United States	21.20	62,880,000	20.30	60,160,000
Total		**309,732,545**		**503,268,618**

Additionally, over 503 million people own stock indirectly through pension funds run either by employers or governments. Once more, China and the United States have the largest number of citizens owning stock indirectly, but only 8.9% of China's population is enrolled in pension funds that hold shares. Many low- and middle-income countries have government-run pension plans that cover large fractions of their populations, so indirect stock ownership fractions exceed 25% in several countries, including Argentina, Estonia, Hungary, and Poland.

Impressive though these rising shareholder levels are, it is unclear what their effect has been on corporate governance. In the aggregate, these investors create a political constituency favoring regulation and laws that protect shareholders from corporate misconduct. However, it is extremely difficult for widely dispersed small shareholders to exercise effective control over large corporations, even if the shareholders wish to do so. In addition, the sheer number of people who own stock has increased the worldwide impact of falling stock prices that resulted from the global financial crisis of 2008–2009.

Source: Paul A. Grout, William L. Megginson, and Ania Zalewska, The New Shareholders: Twenty Five Years On," working paper, University of Bath (Bath, England, February 2009). Reproduced with permission from the author.

expressed concerns about the pricing power that the combined firm could have if the second- and third-largest U.S. communications firms (behind industry leader AT&T) merged to become the first- or second-largest communications firm in many European markets. The managers of both WorldCom and Sprint abandoned their effort to merge after the EC's decision. EC competition commissioner Mario Monti created an international stir in 2001 when he denied the petition to merge filed by General Electric and Honeywell, although the merger had already been approved by U.S. antitrust authorities. Monti's stern defense of his position and denial of the petition on appeal sends a clear message that firms with international operations that are considering a merger must take into account antitrust authorities outside the United States, even if the merger is between U.S. firms. Monti caused an even bigger stir when in early 2004 his commission sued Microsoft in an attempt to force the company to uncouple application packages from its operating system (Windows). The commission maintained that this tie gave Microsoft monopoly power. The EC won this court case in 2005, and the top European Union court upheld this ruling in September 2007. Five months later, European regulators imposed a record €899 million ($1.4 billion) fine on Microsoft for failure to comply with demands to end its alleged anti-competitive practices. Adding insult to injury, these regulators opened a new antitrust case against Microsoft in early 2009, seeking to force the company to open up its Explorer Internet software to competing firms.

Concept Review Questions	12. Which industries do you anticipate will experience industry shocks that will spur merger activity in the near future?
	13. How does the dynamic interpretation of antitrust laws affect managers' acquisition strategies? What impact does the involvement of individual states have on the acquisition decision?
	14. Do you believe that increasing global competition will further heighten merger activity?

24.6 CORPORATE GOVERNANCE

Every sovereign nation has a system of corporate governance, though very few countries are content with their system as it currently functions. As noted at the beginning of this chapter, a nation's corporate governance system can be defined as the set of laws, institutions, practices, and regulations that determine how limited liability companies will be run—and in whose interest. This section begins by briefly describing why corporate governance has emerged as the single most important influence on the size and efficiency of a nation's capital markets. We then describe why efficient capital markets are so important: they promote rapid economic growth. Finally, we discuss the role that privatization programs have played in promoting capital markets and corporate governance practices around the world.

Law and Finance: Capital Markets and National Legal Systems

Andrei Shleifer and Robert Vishny can be credited with popularizing interest in corporate governance. The research they initiated, both together and with other colleagues, has examined how a country's legal system—especially whether the system is based on English common law—influences the size, efficiency, and productivity of that nation's capital markets. Using a sample of 49 countries, La Porta, Lopez-de-Silanes, Shleifer, and Vishny (hereafter LLSV) showed in 1997 that countries with poorer investor protection—measured by both the character of legal rules and the quality of law enforcement—have smaller and less liquid capital markets. This is true for both debt and equity markets, suggesting that stock and bond markets are complements rather than supplements and that both require the proper legal infrastructure to reach maturity. LLSV (1997) also show that French civil law countries offer much poorer investor protection than do common-law countries, and in LLSV (1998) the authors describe why this is so. They examine the investor protection characteristics of the world's four basic legal systems (English common law, French civil law, and German and Scandinavian law) and find that the common-law countries offer by far the greatest protection to noncontrolling investors. This study also documents (and provides a rationale for) the fact that ownership concentration is highest in countries offering poor investor protection, which is consistent with the idea that small, diversified shareholders are unlikely to be important in countries that fail to protect outside investors. Because legal systems play such a key explanatory role in explaining cross-country patterns of financial sector development and ownership structures, LLSV's 1998 study and all their subsequent work has been referred to as the *law and finance model* of economic development.

In a specific investigation of the ownership structures of the largest publicly traded companies in the world's developed economies, La Porta, Lopez-de-Silanes, and Shleifer (1999) show that dispersed ownership structures are common only in the United States, Japan, and Britain. Effective family control over even the largest companies, often exercised through pyramidal share ownership structures, is the norm everywhere else. This finding is verified for Western Europe by Faccio and Lang (2002), who analyze the ultimate ownership and control of 5,232 corporations in 13 countries. LLSV (2000) also find that dividend policies in different nations are related to the agency costs of different ownership structures. Empirical studies by LLSV and others support their proposition that a nation's legal system influences the optimal ownership structures of publicly listed companies and that ownership structure "matters." LLSV (1999) find that the size of a nation's government is related to its efficiency, honesty (the legal system again), and the demographic makeup of its citizenry. LLSV (2002) document that countries offering the greatest legal protection for investors also assign the highest valuation to publicly traded shares. The clear implication of this finding is that individual investors are more willing to entrust their savings to capital market investments when they are confident that their wealth will not be expropriated by insiders.

Many other researchers have used the law and finance theoretical framework to explain cross-country differences in financial sector development. Demirgüç-Kunt and Maksimovic (1998) show that in countries whose legal systems score high on an efficiency index, a greater proportion of firms use long-term external financing. Since their measure of efficiency is different from LLSV's, the results are not a direct test of the LLSV hypothesis that common-law countries offer better investor protection than civil-law countries (especially since France receives higher efficiency scores than Britain). Nonetheless, Demirgüç-Kunt and Maksimovic document that an active stock market and large banking sector are associated with externally financed firm growth and that companies in countries with weak financial sectors are unable to fund maximum achievable growth.

Efficient Capital Markets Promote Rapid Economic Growth

There is now little doubt that an efficient financial sector fosters rapid economic development. Rajan and Zingales (1998) provide evidence supporting the positive influence of financial development on economic growth by means of reducing the cost of external financing to firms. They find that financial development is especially important for the process of creating new firms in an economy. Beck, Demirgüç-Kunt, and Maksimovic (2005) show that financial impediments hinder the growth of smaller firms the most. Levine and Zervos (1998) also provide evidence suggesting that banking efficiency is critically important to the development of an economy and that banking services are different from those provided by stock markets. In fact, an entire stream of research has now documented the critical importance of an efficient financial system to sustainable economic growth.[20] The basic themes that emerge from this research are that an efficient financial system is vital and that it is difficult to construct such a system from scratch or in

---

[20]Important recent papers in this literature are Carlin and Mayer (2003), Beck, Demirgüç-Kunt, and Levine (2003), and Claessens and Laeven (2003).

place of existing (typically less effective) systems—because of the determined opposition from entrenched parties.

Rajan and Zingales (2003) describe the amount of national financial development as a function of the degree of interest-group opposition to open markets. Whereas financial development benefits society as a whole, entrenched players such as monopolist producers and owners of financial institutions have strong incentives to stunt development of markets they cannot control. Rajan and Zingales also show that financial development does not increase monotonically over time. In fact, many countries had more developed financial markets in 1913 than they did in 1980. Figure 24.3 presents average values for three measures of financial sector development—bank deposits to GDP, equity issues to gross fixed capital formation, and stock market capitalization to GDP—for 39 mostly Western countries at roughly decade-long intervals from 1913 to 1999. All three measures were higher in 1913 than in 1980, and the 1929 peaks of deposits to GDP and equity issues to gross capital formation had still not been reached again by 1999. Only stock market capitalization relative to GDP is higher today than before the Great Depression.

FIGURE 24.3

The Evolution of Financial Development in 39 Countries over Time, 1913–1999

Source: Table 1 in Raghuram G. Rajan and Luigi Zingales, "The Great Reversals: The Politics of Financial Development in the Twentieth Century," *Journal of Financial Economics* 69 (July 2003), pp. 5–50. Copyright © 2003, with permission from Elsevier.

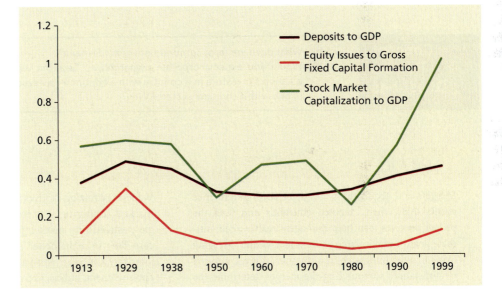

Research findings demonstrating the utility and efficacy of financial markets are important because for many years a debate raged regarding whether a capital market–based system of corporate finance is inherently better or worse than a bank-based system. During the late 1980s and early 1990s, when Japan and Germany appeared to be outperforming major capital market–oriented countries such as Britain and the United States, the academic literature often favored bank-based systems. More recently, however, the weight of opinion has swung strongly in favor of the idea that capital markets have decisive comparative advantages over banks and other financial intermediaries as optimal monitors and financiers of a nation's corporate life. This reassessment has been driven in part by the observation, discussed earlier, that capital markets have been prospering relative to banks for many years now. Additionally, the repetitive nature and massive costs of banking crises in developing and developed countries alike have convinced many observers that banks are inherently fragile institutions whose role in corporate finance should be minimized as much and as quickly as possible.

While experience and observation have driven much of the reassessment of the optimal role of capital markets in corporate finance, academic research has also been important, since it now strongly favors capital markets over banks. The single most important paper in the stream of research documenting that capital markets are essential for good corporate governance is the influential survey article by Levine (1997). Additional papers by Levine and Zervos (1998), Rajan and Zingales (1998), and Demirgüç-Kunt and Maksimovic (1998) all provide direct or indirect support for the optimality of capital markets. Other empirical studies of the impact of financial development on economic growth have documented that the size of the financial system (banks and capital markets) is not as important for growth as is the system's efficiency.

Perhaps surprisingly, the financial turmoil that gripped global financial markets during 2008 and 2009 does not weaken the economic case for large, efficient, and liquid capital markets, even though market valuations and the volumes of securities issuance have fallen dramatically. All corporate financial systems have been badly hurt by the crash, and bank-based systems such as Germany and Japan have declined as much or more than others. Additionally, countries with poorly developed financial markets have suffered the most.

Concept Review Questions	15. What does the term *corporate governance* mean? 16. Would you expect corporate ownership to be more widely dispersed among a nation's investors in a country with a common-law system of corporate law or in one with a civil-law system? Why?

SUMMARY

- Mergers and acquisitions are major corporate finance events that, when executed efficiently and with the proper motives, can help managers realize their ultimate goal of maximizing shareholder wealth. Merging firms may be integrated in a number of ways, and the circumstances surrounding the merger determine the means of integration. Transactions may be hostile or friendly; may be financed by cash, stock, debt, or some combination of the three; and may increase, preserve, or decrease the acquirer's level of business concentration.

- Research on corporate control is bountiful, and major empirical findings include the following. Target shareholders almost always win, but acquirers' returns are mixed. The combined value of merging firms also increases, especially in nonconglomerate combinations. The highest announcement-period returns are found in mergers between well-managed acquirers and poorly managed targets. Long-term performance is highest for focus-increasing deals financed with cash and lowest for diversifying mergers financed with stock.

- Managers have either value-maximizing or non-value-maximizing motives for pursuing mergers.

Value-maximizing motives include expansion into new markets, capturing size economies and other synergies, establishing market power, and generating free cash flow to make better investments. Agency problems result in such non-value-maximizing motives as entrenchment, hubris, and diversification.

- Merger activity occurs in waves spurred by industry-wide events such as deregulation. Domestically, we have witnessed six major merger waves: a turn-of-the-twentieth-century wave of horizontal mergers; a 1920s wave of vertical mergers; the 1960s wave of conglomerate mergers; the 1980s wave that deconstructed many of the 1960s conglomerates; the 1993–2001 wave of deregulation-based mergers and consolidations made in preparation for an increasingly global economy; and the most recent wave in 2007–2008. Antitrust enforcement at the time affects activity in each of these waves.

- Corporate control activities are regulated by federal as well as (increasingly) by state and international authorities. Federal antitrust legislation has been developed over the course of the century, but its enforcement ebbs and flows with the executive administration in office. The Williams Act established disclosure requirements for ownership in public corporations as well as the regulation of tender offers. Federal securities laws also prohibit corporate insiders from trading on the nonpublic information of a pending takeover.

- Corporate governance refers to the set of laws, institutions, practices, and regulations that determine how (and in whose interest) limited liability companies will be run. The law and finance model of economic development asserts that countries with English common-law systems of corporate law will have larger and more efficient capital markets than will countries with civil law commercial codes, because common law offers greater legal protections to individual investors. Ownership of corporate equity will be more widely dispersed in common-law countries for the same reason. Research now conclusively shows that having large, efficient financial markets allows a country to achieve more rapid economic growth.

KEY TERMS

acquisition	going-private transactions	product extension mergers
agency cost of overvalued equity	goodwill	pure conglomerate mergers
antitakeover amendments	greenfield entry	pure stock exchange merger
backward integration	greenmail	resource complementarities
bust-up	Herfindahl Index (HI)	reverse LBO
cash-out statutes	horizontal merger	shark repellents
co-insurance of debt	hubris hypothesis of corporate	spin-off
consolidation	takeovers	split-off
corporate control	internal capital markets	split-up
corporate focus	management buyout (MBO)	statutory merger
divestiture	managerial synergies	strategic merger
dual-class recapitalization	managerialism theory	subsidiary merger
economies of scale	of mergers	synergy
economies of scope	market extension merger	takeover
employee stock ownership plan	market power	tax-loss carryforwards
(ESOP)	merger	tender offer
fair-price provisions	mixed offerings	tender-merger
financial synergies	operational synergy	vertical merger
forward integration	poison pills	white knights

QUESTIONS

24-1. What is meant by a change in corporate control? List and describe the various ways in which a change of corporate control may occur.

24-2. What is a tender offer, and how can it be used as a mechanism to orchestrate a merger?

24-3. Distinguish between the different levels of business concentration created by mergers. Explain how the changing business environment has caused an evolution in the classification of concentration from the original FTC classification to the abbreviated FTC classification and now to the measures of overlap and focus.

24-4. Elaborate on the significance of the mode of payment for the stockholders of the target firm and their continued interest in the surviving firm. Specifically, which form of payment retains the stockholders of the target firm as stockholders in the surviving firm? Which payment form receives preferential tax treatment?

24-5. What is the signaling theory of mergers? What is the relationship between signaling and the mode of payment used in acquisitions? Is there a relationship between the mode of payment used in acquisitions and the level of insider shareholdings of acquiring firms?

24-6. Empirically, what are the wealth effects of corporate control activities? Who wins and who loses in corporate control contests? What explanations or theories are offered for the differences in returns of acquiring firms' common stocks? Why are higher takeover premiums paid in cash transactions than in stock transactions? How do other security holders fare in takeovers?

24-7. Relate the industry shock theory of mergers to the history of merger waves. What were the motivating factors for increased merger activity during each of the six major merger waves?

24-8. Under what conditions would external expansion be preferable to internal expansion? What is the ultimate decision criterion for determining the acceptability of any expansion strategy?

24-9. Delineate the value-maximizing motives for mergers. How are these motives interrelated?

24-10. Define the three types of synergy that may result from mergers. What are the sources of these synergies?

24-11. Explain how agency problems may lead to non-value-maximizing motives for mergers. Discuss the various academic theories offered

as the rationale for motives induced by the agency problem.

24-12. Describe the relationship between conglomerate mergers and portfolio theory. What is the desired result of merging two unrelated businesses? Has the empirical evidence proven corporate diversification to be successful?

24-13. List the federal laws regulating antitrust and anticompetitive mergers. What are the actions governed by each law? How do the regulatory agencies determine anticompetitiveness?

24-14. What is the purpose of the Williams Act? What are the specific provisions of the act?

24-15. What are the restrictions faced by corporate insiders during corporate control events?

24-16. How have individual states become more active monitors of takeover activity?

24-17. What is the law and finance model of economic development, and what are its key predictions? Have these predictions been verified by empirical testis?

24-18. Respond to the following statement: "Countries with large and efficient financial systems will generally achieve higher rates of economic growth than will countries with smaller, inefficient financial sectors."

PROBLEMS

Overview of Corporate Control Activities

24-1. A firm has four divisions—food, cookware, retail, and credit services—that generate revenues of $1.5 million, $3.8 million, $5.7 million, and $3.1 million, respectively. Compute the Herfindahl Index (HI) for the firm. The firm is considering the purchase of a rival retailer, which would increase the retail division's revenues by another $3.2 million. The firm is also considering selling its credit services division. Assuming these two actions occur, what will the HI become? What is the HI if the sale of the credit division does not occur but the rival is acquired?

24-2. HHG Consultants has been asked to analyze Carol & Carroll Co. (C&C), which has one retail division. C&C is concerned that it is not focused on its core mission of sales despite only having one division. Each store is divided into departments: casual clothing (CC), formal clothing (FC), outerwear (OW), shoes (S), and specialty items (SI). C&C's initial impression is that all of the departments contribute equally to sales. However, examination of each department's actual sales reveals that the breakdown is very different: $5.2 billion (CC), $2.7 billion (FC), $3.75 billion (OW), $4.5 billion (S), and $1.7 billion (SI). Compute a Herfindahl Index based on the departments having equal sales and based on the actual sales. Your conclusion concerning the firm's becoming "unfocused" will be based on the actual HI being lower than the equivalent sales HI scenario. What does your analysis find with regard to the focus of C&C's retailing division?

24-3. Firm X has three divisions that generate revenues of $1.3 billion, $2.5 billion, and $5.2 billion. Firm Y is a competitor with three associated divisions that generate $2 billion each. Using a Herfindahl Index to measure focus, determine if both Firm X and Firm Y shareholders would see a merger as an action that would increase or rather decrease focus.

24-4. Shareholders of the firm Up-4-Grabs (U4G) have been offered $36.00 per share in cash for each of their U4G shares currently selling for $29.53. What is the control premium being offered in this cash deal? U4G is also considering a stock-swap offer from another firm, BuyNow Inc. (BYN). BYN will issue one share for every two shares of U4G. At what price will BYN shares be equivalent to the control premium available in the cash offer? When news leaks out about the merger, BYN shares increase to $77.00 and U4G shares increase to $35.24. What control premium does BYN offer now?

24-5. HBABB Corp. has purchased all of the 10 million shares of BOBCO stock for $43.75 a share. BOBCO's net asset value is $350 million. How much goodwill does HBABB need to consider on its balance sheet? Suppose part of the deal requires HBABB to pay $30 million of BOBCO's debt. Refigure the net asset value (i.e., reduce the debt by $30 million) and then recalculate the goodwill. One of your accountants tells you that the net asset value should not be changed and that the $30 million used for BOBCO's debt should be added to the purchase price. Refigure the goodwill calculation and determine if there really is a difference. If there is a difference, which calculation is correct?

24-6. Mega Service Corporation (MSC) is offering to exchange 2.5 shares of its own stock for each share of target firm Norman Corporation stock as consideration for a proposed merger. There are 10 million Norman Corp shares outstanding, and its stock price was $60 before the merger offer. MSC's pre-offer stock price was $30. What is the control premium percentage offered? Now suppose that, when the merger is consummated eight months later, MSC's stock price drops to $25. At that point, what is the control premium percentage and total transaction value?

24-7. Bulldog Industries is offering target Blazerco, as consideration for merger, 1.5 shares of their stock for each share of Blazerco. There are 1 million shares of Blazerco outstanding, and its stock price was $50 before the merger offer. Bulldog's pre-offer stock price was $40. What is the control premium percentage offered? Now suppose that, when the merger is consummated six months later, Bulldog's stock price drops to $30. At that point, what is the control premium percentage and total transaction value?

24-8. You are the director of capital acquisitions for Crimson Software Company. One of the projects you are considering is the acquisition of Geekware, a private software company that produces software for finance professors. Dave Vanzandt, the owner of Geekware, is amenable to the idea of selling his enterprise to Crimson, but he has certain conditions that must be met before selling. The primary condition set forth is a nonnegotiable, all-cash purchase price of $20 million. Your project analysis team estimates that the purchase of Geekware will generate the following marginal cash flow:

Year	Cash Flow
1	$1,000,000
2	3,000,000
3	5,000,000
4	7,500,000
5	7,500,000

Of the $20 million in cash needed for the purchase, $5 million is available from retained earnings with a required return of 12%, and the remaining $15 million will come from a new debt issue yielding 8%. Crimson's tax rate is 40%. Should you recommend acquiring Geekware to your CEO?

24-9. You are the director of capital acquisitions for Morningside Hotel Company. One of the projects you are deliberating is the acquisition of Monroe Hospitality, a company that owns and operates a chain of bed-and-breakfast inns. Susan Sharp, Monroe's owner, is willing to sell her company to Morningside only if she is offered an all-cash purchase price of $5 million. Your project analysis team estimates that the purchase of Monroe Hospitality will generate the following after-tax marginal cash flow:

Year	Cash Flow
1	$1,000,000
2	1,500,000
3	2,000,000
4	2,500,000
5	3,000,000

If you decide to go ahead with this acquisition, it will be funded with Morningside's standard mix of debt and equity at the firm's weighted average (after-tax) cost of capital of 9%. Morningside's tax rate is 30%. Should you recommend acquiring Monroe Hospitality to your CEO?

24-10. Firm A plans to acquire Firm B. The acquisition would result in incremental cash flows for Firm A of $10 million in each of the first five years. Firm A expects to divest Firm B at the end of the fifth year for $100 million. The beta for Firm A is 1.1, which is expected to remain unchanged after the acquisition. The risk-free rate, R_f, is 7%, and the expected market rate of return, R_m, is 15%. Firm A is financed by 80% equity and 20% debt, and this leverage will remain unchanged after the acquisition. Firm A pays interest of 10% on its debt, which will also remain unchanged after the acquisition.

   a. Disregarding taxes, what is the maximum price that Firm A should pay for Firm B?

   b. Firm A has a stock price of $30 per share and 10 million shares outstanding. If Firm B shareholders are to be paid the maximum price determined in part (a) via a new stock issue, then how many new shares will be issued and what will be the postmerger stock price?

24-11. Charger Incorporated and Sparks Electrical Company are competitors in the business of electrical components distribution. Sparks is the smaller firm and has attracted the attention of the management of Charger, for Sparks has taken away market share from the larger firm by increasing its sales force over the past few years. Charger is considering a takeover offer for Sparks and has asked you to serve on the acquisition valuation team that will turn into the due diligence team if an offer is made and accepted. Given the financial information and proposal assumptions that follow, how would you respond to (a) and (b)?

   a. Make your recommendation about whether or not the acquisition should be pursued.

   b. Assume that Sparks has accepted the takeover offer from Charger and that the new subsidiary must now be consolidated within Charger's financial statements. Taking Sparks' most recent balance sheet and a restated market value of assets of $295.6 million, calculate the goodwill that must be booked for this transaction.

**Sparks Electrical Company Condensed
Balance Sheet Previous Year ($ million)**

	2009
Current assets	12.2
Fixed assets	442.5
Total assets	454.7
Current liabilities	10.1
Long-term debt	150.0
Total liabilities	160.1
Shareholders' equity	294.6
Total liabilities and equity	454.7

**Sparks Electrical Company
Condensed Income Statement
Previous Five Years ($ million)**

	2009	2008	2007	2006	2005
Revenues	1,626.5	1,614.1	1,485.2	1,380.5	1,373.4
Less: Cost of goods sold	1,488.1	1,490.9	1,359.5	1,271.4	1,268.0
Gross profit	138.4	123.2	125.7	109.1	105.4
Selling, general, & administrative expenses (SG&A)	41.1	36.8	41.2	35.0	36.1
Noncash expense (depreciation & amortization)	7.3	6.7	7.1	6.6	6.4
Less: Operating expense	48.4	43.5	48.3	41.6	42.5
Operating profit (*EBIT*)	90.0	79.7	77.4	67.5	62.9
Less: Interest expense	11.5	12.0	12.0	12.0	12.0
Earnings before taxes (*EBT*)	78.5	67.7	65.4	55.5	50.9
Less: Taxes paid	24.3	20.8	19.9	16.8	15.3
Net income	54.2	46.9	45.5	38.7	35.6

Assumptions:

- *Sparks would become a wholly owned subsidiary of Charger.*
- *Revenues will continue to grow at 4.3% for the next five years and will level off at 4% thereafter.*
- *The cost of goods sold will represent 95% of revenue going forward.*
- *Sales-force layoffs will reduce SG&A expenses to $22 million next year, with a 2% growth rate going forward.*
- *These layoffs and other restructuring charges are expected to result in expensed restructuring charges of $30 million, $15 million, and $5 million (respectively) over the next three years.*
- *Noncash expenses are expected to remain around $7 million going forward.*
- *Interest expenses are expected to remain around $11.5 million going forward.*
- *A tax rate of 31% is assumed going forward.*
- *Charger's cost of equity is 12%.*
- *Sparks' current market capitalization is $315.7 million.*
- *Charger will offer Sparks a takeover premium of 20% over current market capitalization.*

24-12. Referring to Problem 24-11, assume it is now two years after the acquisition of Sparks and you must perform a "goodwill impairment" test of the subsidiary. Growth expectations have been lowered to 3% going forward. Using the following 5-year projection of cash flows and a 12% cost of equity, estimate the value of the subsidiary beyond year 5, the current value of the subsidiary, the current value of goodwill, and any goodwill impairment. Total assets (excluding intangibles) are now $612.5 million, and total liabilities are $175.0 million.

Cash Flow Projection for Next Five Years ($ million)

	2012	2013	2014	2015	2016
Revenues	1,815.2	1,869.7	1,925.7	1,983.5	2,043.0
Less: Cost of goods sold @ 95% of revenue	1,724.4	1,776.2	1,829.5	1,884.3	1,940.9
Gross profit	90.8	93.5	96.2	99.2	102.1
SG&A expense @ 2% growth rate going forward	23.0	23.5	23.9	24.4	24.9
Noncash expense (depreciation & amortization)	7.0	7.0	7.0	7.0	7.0
Less: Operating expense	30.0	30.5	30.9	31.4	31.9
Operating profit (EBIT)	60.8	63.0	65.3	67.8	70.2
Less: Interest expense	11.5	11.5	11.5	11.5	11.5
Less: Restructuring charges	5.0	0.0	0.0	0.0	0.0
Earnings before taxes (EBT)	44.3	51.5	53.8	56.3	58.7
Less: Taxes paid	13.7	16.0	16.7	17.4	18.2
Net income	30.6	35.5	37.1	38.9	40.5
Free cash flow	54.1	54.0	55.6	57.4	59.0

24-13. Firms AFD, TYU, CHG, and LAN are competitors within an industry. Their respective sales figures are $2.8 billion, $3.9 billion, $4.8 billion, and $2.1 billion. What is the Herfindahl–Hirschman Index (HHI) for the industry? Is the industry considered highly concentrated, moderately concentrated, or not concentrated? Assuming that two more firms—QBC ($3.6 billion in sales) and RTY ($2.7 billion in sales)—are added to the industry figures, does the concentration level of the industry change? (Recompute HHI to determine this.) If the three smallest firms (AFD, LAN, and RTY) merged, would the FTC be concerned? If so, why? (*Note:* The HHI is measured in units of %². For example, 50% × 50% = 2,500%² (or, in decimal form, 0.50 × 0.50 = 0.25). To make the conversion from decimal to percentage form mathematically, multiply the answer by 10,000; using the same example, this yields 0.50 × 0.50 × 10,000 = 2,500.)

24-14. A given market was initially segmented evenly among 20 firms (Phase 1). Five years later, the market was still segmented evenly among competing firms, but there were now only 10 firms (Phase 2). Eventually six firms emerged with equal portions of the market (Phase 3), but a move toward deregulation of the industry has prompted two of the firms to merge. Determine the Herfindahl–Hirschman Index for the three phases. Next, determine whether the merger will cause the industry to be considered "highly concentrated." In a preemptive move (fearing the FTC), the merged firms agree to sell off portions of the market to the other four firms so that the market will be equally divided among all five firms. How does this affect the HHI, and is the merger viable under these circumstances?

THOMSON ONE | Business School Edition

24-15. On November 18, 2005, SBC Communications, Inc., completed its acquisition of AT&T Corporation. The combined company was named AT&T Inc. (ticker symbol, T). Examine the 19-page 8-K report filed on November 18, 2005. How many shares of AT&T Inc. were exchanged for each share of AT&T Corporation? What was the total number of shares issued to the "old" AT&T shareholders? At the time of the merger, what percentage of the "new" AT&T was owned by "old" AT&T shareholders? Did "old" AT&T shareholders receive any additional compensation? Based on the closing stock price on November 17, 2005, what was the estimated value of the merger?

MINI-CASE: MERGERS, CORPORATE CONTROL, AND CORPORATE GOVERNANCE

Jackson Enterprises (JE) is offering a 25% takeover premium to Michael Studios, Inc. (MSI) for the firm's 2 million outstanding shares, which are currently trading for a pre-offer price of $20 per share.

The balance sheet for MSI is:

Assets		Liabilities	
Current	$15,000,000	Current	$ 7,500,000
Fixed	45,000,000	Long-term	25,000,000
Total	$60,000,000	Total	$32,500,000
		Owner's equity	27,500,000
		Total liabilities and equity	$60,000,000

The market value of MSI's fixed assets is $60,000,000.

The sales (in millions) for the industry by company are:

	Sales
ABC	$89
CWC	66
DEF	35
JE	45
KOJ	42
MSI	18
SEE	76

1. Determine the amount Jackson Enterprises is willing to pay in terms of goodwill.

2. If JE's shares are currently trading at $62.43, then how many shares should JE offer for every share of MSI?

3. Assuming that MSI will be treated as a separate reporting subsidiary following the merger, develop the balance sheet for the subsidiary.

4. Calculate the Herfindahl–Hirschman Index for the industry both before and after the proposed merger.

25

Bankruptcy and Financial Distress*

What Companies Do

The Largest Ever Debtor-in-Possession Financing Follows Lyondell's Bankruptcy Filing

In the early months of 2009, there was a surge in the number and value of corporate bankruptcy filings in the United States, as the credit crisis forced many previously struggling companies over the financial cliff into default. One such filing was by Lyondell Chemical, the U.S. subsidiary of the Dutch firm LyondellBasell. Lyondell had $24 billion of debt outstanding and 20,000 employees when it filed for protection from creditors under chapter 11 of the U.S. Bankruptcy Code on January 8, 2009. The company had tried and failed to restructure its debts through private negotiations with its creditors.

Lyondell's single most important concern at the time of its filing was to secure enough *debtor-in-possession* (DIP) financing to be able to execute an orderly bankruptcy process. Without this funding, which gives a new creditor "super-priority" status over existing debts, a bankrupt company would be unable to operate and would likely be forced into a liquidation. Because of its super-priority status, DIP financing has traditionally been fairly easy to arrange. However, market conditions in early 2009 made funding for bankrupt firms extremely hard to obtain. In the end, Lyondell was able to arrange an $8 billion DIP loan, the largest ever, mostly from its existing creditors—but only under extremely onerous terms. Counting fees and interest, the loan's cost approached 20% and set to mature in less than one year later (in December 2009). Perhaps the most controversial aspect of the DIP was its "roll-up" feature, which allowed certain existing creditors to reprioritize their original "pre-bankruptcy" debt in exchange for new cash injections from the DIP loan.

Despite intense opposition from many creditors, Lyondell's proposed DIP loan was approved in U.S. bankruptcy court on February 26, 2009. The judge concluded that this loan offered the best—perhaps the only—hope for Lyondell to avoid liquidation, which experience had shown was likely to yield lower final proceeds for creditors than would a successful reorganization. Lyondell was also given until August 2009 to file a formal reorganization plan, though extensions were possible.

Sources: Nicole Bullock and Anousha Sakoui, "Creditors DIP into Pockets Again to Save Companies," Financial Times (January 29, 2009); Nicole Bullock, "Lyondell Wins Court Approval of Modified Bankruptcy Loan," Financial Times (February 27, 2009).

---

*Joseph A. Guzinski assisted in preparing part of this chapter. The authors very much appreciate Joe's important contribution.

SMARTFinance Use the learning tools at www.cengage.com/finance/smartfinance

A **business failure** is an unfortunate outcome. Although the majority of firms that fail do so within the first few years of life, other firms grow, mature, and fail much later. The failure of a business can be viewed in a number of ways and can result from many different causes. The legal procedure through which troubled firms reorganize or leave the market is **chapter 11** bankruptcy. In what follows, we examine first how and why firms fail. We then look at U.S. bankruptcy law and the ways that a failed business can resolve its difficulties through bankruptcy.

25.1 BANKRUPTCY AND BUSINESS FAILURE

A headline blares that a company has filed for chapter 11 or has "sought the protection of the bankruptcy court." The words themselves signify failure but they do not describe how the firm failed. Is the firm **insolvent** in the sense that its liabilities exceed its assets? Or does the firm have a liquidity problem and is unable to pay its debts? Perhaps the filing is the result of both of these factors, or of other factors entirely.

As a working definition, **financial distress** occurs when a company's cash flows are insufficient to pay its current obligations. Although a firm usually files for bankruptcy because its finances are distressed, the term "bankruptcy" does not really describe a financial condition. Instead, **bankruptcy** refers to a legal process. With certain narrow exceptions,[1] a firm is not required to demonstrate a financial problem in order to file for bankruptcy. All it needs to do is file papers with the court.[2]

Bankruptcy is only one of many avenues a company may employ to address its problems. When a firm experiences financial distress, it may try to solve that problem through changes in operations (e.g., reducing expenditures, selling assets, or even merging with a healthy company) or through financial actions (e.g., raising new capital by selling new securities, exchanging debt securities for equity, reducing payout, or renegotiating with creditors). Filing for bankruptcy is typically a last resort.

Figure 25.1 illustrates the chain of events that may lead to a bankruptcy filing and gives an indication of the percentage of financially distressed firms that follow each of the

FIGURE 25.1

Outcomes of Financial Distress

Source: Karen Wruck, "Financial Distress, Reorganization, and Organizational Efficiency," *Journal of Financial Economics* 27, pp. 419–444 (1990).

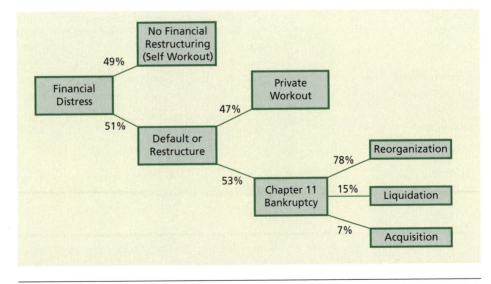

---

[1]The most prominent exception is the "involuntary" case where creditors ask a bankruptcy court to force a company into bankruptcy. In this scenario, the creditors must show that the failed company is "not paying its debts as they come due."
[2]If filing for bankruptcy does not aid any creditors and provides the debtor no relief other than stalling a foreclosure, then the bankruptcy court may rule that it occurred in "bad faith" and thus not recognize the filing.

WHAT COMPANIES DO GLOBALLY

How the United Kingdom, France, Germany, and the United States Handle Corporate Bankruptcy Differently

Despite being very similar in terms of economic development, industrial structure, and financial sophistication, the three largest economies of Western Europe have very different procedures for handling corporate bankruptcies. The following table details the key features of company bankruptcy processes in the United Kingdom, France, and Germany, and also presents corresponding features of U.S. bankruptcy procedures for firms filing under chapter 11 and chapter 7 of the U.S. Bankruptcy Code. Professors Sergei

Davydenko and Julian Franks, who co-authored the study in which this table first appeared, examined how the terms and procedures of bankruptcy in Britain, France, and Germany affect how creditors structure loans to companies in order to best protect their creditor claims in the event borrowers default—and also how these terms and procedures affect the recovery rates creditors achieve when a borrower firm is liquidated.

(continued)

Bankruptcy Procedures in the United Kingdom, France, Germany, and the United States

	UNITED KINGDOM	FRANCE	GERMAN	UNITED STATES	
	ADMINISTRATIVE RECEIVERSHIP	REDRESSEMENT JUDICIAIRE	INSOLVENZORDNUNG (1999 CODE)	CHAPTER 11	CHAPTER 7
Bankruptcy trigger	Default (covenant breach)	Cessation of payments (inability to meet current obligations)	Cessation of payments or over-borrowing	No objective test; solvent firm may enter chapter 11	No objective test
Control rights	Secured creditor	Court-appointed administrator	Creditors under court supervision (secured creditors have more power)	Debtor, creditors collectively; bankruptcy court supervision	Trustee
Automatic stay	None	Unlimited	3 months	Unlimited	None
Super-priority financing	None	Yes	Creditors' approval required	Yes	None
Dilution of secured claims	None	Significant	Limited	Limited	None
Creditor protection score (max = 4)	4	0	3	1	N/A

Notes: Listed are principal bankruptcy procedures in the United Kingdom, France, Germany, and the United States in terms of their main characteristics. The bottom row reports creditor protection scores given by Rafael La Porta, Florencio López-de-Silanes, Andrei Shleifer, and Robert W. Vishny, "Law and Finance," *Journal of Political Economy* 106 (1998), pp. 1113–1150.

Source: Table I of Sergei A. Davydenko and Julian R. Franks, "Do Bankruptcy Codes Matter? A Study of Defaults in France, Germany, and the U.K.," *Journal of Finance* 63 (April 2008), pp. 565–608.

Professors Davydenko and Franks present evidence supporting the widely held notion that Germany and (especially) Britain have creditor-friendly bankruptcy codes that are designed primarily to maximize protection of senior creditor claims. France's bankruptcy code is much more debtor-friendly, designed principally to protect businesses and employees and to allow potentially salvageable companies to reorganize rather than liquidate. Although the authors do not explicitly study U.S. firms, their summary supports the idea that the U.S. code is also quite debtor-friendly and has much the same motivation as the French code.

The differing emphasis on creditor versus debtor rights can be observed by contrasting key features between countries in the table. Control of a debtor firm transfers more or less automatically to secured creditors in the event of borrower default in Britain and Germany, whereas control passes to a court-appointed administrator in France and to a court-appointed **trustee** under U.S. chapter 7. In most cases, debtors retain operating control of defaulting firms that file under chapter 11 in the United States, exerting significant influence on the entire reorganization process. In both France and the United States (chapter 11), companies filing for bankruptcy protection are granted an "automatic stay" of unlimited duration, which prevents creditors from any further enforcement of their claims until a reorganization plan is approved by the court. There is no such automatic stay in the United Kingdom (or under U.S. chapter 7); defaulting German companies are granted a stay of only three months.

Finally, these four countries offer strikingly different protections for secured creditors in terms of whether courts are allowed to dilute their claims during the reorganization process and whether debtors are allowed to arrange "super-priority" financing (new loans with higher priority than existing claims) after filing for bankruptcy. Britain does not allow either super-priority financing or dilution of secured creditor claims (nor does U.S. chapter 7), and German courts are severely constrained in allowing either process. In contrast, super-priority financing is allowed in both France and the United States (chapter 11), and both countries' codes give bankruptcy courts significant discretion to dilute secured creditor claims during reorganization.

various options. For example, of the firms that experience financial distress, 49% manage to resolve the problem without resorting to any kind of financial restructuring. For these firms, operational changes are sufficient to improve the firm's financial condition. Of the 51% of firms that do engage in financial restructuring to deal with financial distress, 47% renegotiate with creditors on their own to resolve the difficulties and 53% file for bankruptcy protection under chapter 11 of the U.S. Bankruptcy Code. Most firms that file for chapter 11 eventually reorganize.

Despite the publicity that the cases receive, business bankruptcies in general and chapter 11 reorganizations in particular do not typically involve many of the larger firms in the economy—although a number of high-profile bankruptcies have occurred in recent years. Table 25.1 lists the all-time largest U.S. bankruptcies.

Table 25.2 shows the number of bankruptcy filings by year and type. Until recently the number of bankruptcy events had been trending downward. Business bankruptcies declined after the mid-1980s, except for an uptick during the 1991 and 1992 recessions. Filings declined further in 2006, following a 2005 change in bankruptcy law that made filing less attractive. In 2007 and 2008 there was an increase in filings that accompanied the severe credit crisis and global recession, and as of this writing the trend is expected to continue in 2009.

Table 25.1 Largest Bankruptcies in U.S. History as of June 6, 2009

COMPANY	DATE OF BANKRUPTCY	DESCRIPTION OF COMPANY	TOTAL PRE-BANKRUPTCY ASSETS ($ MILLION)
Lehman Brothers Holdings Inc.	09/15/08	Investment bank	691,063
Washington Mutual, Inc.	09/26/08	Savings & loan holding company	327,913
WorldCom	07/21/02	Telecommunications	103,914
General Motors	06/01/09	Automobile manufacturing	83,300
Enron Corp.	12/02/01	Energy trading, natural gas	65,503
Conseco	12/18/02	Financial services holding company	61,392
Chrysler LLC	04/30/09	Automobile manufacturing	39,300
Thornburg Mortgage	05/01/09	Real estate investment trust	36,500
Pacific Gas and Electric Co.	04/06/01	Electricity and natural gas	36,152
Texaco, Inc.	04/12/87	Petroleum and petrochemicals	34,940
Financial Corp. of America	09/09/88	Financial services; savings & loans	33,864
Refco Inc.	10/05/05	Brokerage services	33,333
IndyMac Bancorp, Inc.	07/31/08	Bank holding company	32,734
Global Crossing Ltd.	01/28/02	Global telecommunications carrier	30,185
Bank of New England Corp.	01/07/91	Interstate bank holding company	29,773
Lyondell Chemical Company	01/06/09	Global manufacturer of chemicals	27,392
Calpine Corporation	12/20/05	Integrated power company	27,216
New Century Financial Corp.	04/02/07	Real estate investment trust	26,147
UAL Corporation	12/09/02	Passenger airline	25,197
Delta Air Lines, Inc.	09/14/05	Passenger airline	21,801
Adelphia Communications	06/25/02	Telecommunications	21,499
MCorp	03/31/89	Banking and financial services	20,228
Mirant Corporation	07/14/03	Electric services	19,415

Sources: Bankruptcy.com, June 6, 2009 (http://www.bankruptcydata.com) and *Fortune* (for General Motors and Thornburg Mortgage, http://money.cnn.com/galleries/2009/fortune/0905/gallery.largest_bankruptcies.fortune/8.html).

Why do businesses file for bankruptcy? Financial distress does not automatically mean bankruptcy. A firm may try to work out a deal with its creditors by negotiating out of court, rather than filing for bankruptcy.

Bankruptcy, however, gives the debtor firm a major bargaining advantage. Prior to bankruptcy, creditors may threaten litigation or aggressive collection actions. Bankruptcy relieves the debtor of these immediate threats. Without the threat of imminent litigation or collection, the debtor may be in a better position to bargain with its creditors and to restructure its operations.

Thus, while bankruptcy is not a dominant force in the overall economy, it often plays a significant role for firms facing financial failure. An open question is whether bankruptcy reorganizations can be thought of as successful. Answering that question requires an understanding of the basic principles of bankruptcy and how a firm may employ them when it faces failure.

	Table 25.2	Annual Business and Consumer Filings in the United States, 1980–2008		

YEAR	TOTAL FILINGS	BUSINESS FILINGS	CONSUMER FILINGS	CONSUMER FILINGS AS PERCENTAGE OF TOTAL FILINGS
1980	331,264	43,694	287,570	86.81
1981	363,943	48,125	315,818	86.78
1982	380,251	69,300	310,951	81.78
1983	348,880	62,436	286,444	82.10
1984	348,521	64,004	284,517	81.64
1985	412,510	71,277	341,233	82.72
1986	530,438	81,235	449,203	84.69
1987	577,999	82,446	495,553	85.74
1988	613,465	63,853	549,612	89.59
1989	679,461	63,235	616,226	90.69
1990	782,960	64,853	718,107	91.72
1991	943,987	71,549	872,438	92.42
1992	971,517	70,643	900,874	92.73
1993	875,202	62,304	812,898	92.88
1994	832,829	52,374	780,455	93.71
1995	926,601	51,959	874,642	94.39
1996	1,178,555	53,549	1,125,006	95.46
1997	1,404,145	54,027	1,350,118	96.15
1998	1,442,549	44,367	1,398,182	96.92
1999	1,319,465	37,884	1,281,581	97.12
2000	1,253,444	35,472	1,217,972	97.17
2001	1,492,129	40,099	1,452,030	97.31
2002	1,577,651	38,540	1,539,111	97.56
2003	1,660,245	35,037	1,625,208	97.89
2004	1,597,462	34,317	1,563,145	97.85
2005	2,078,415	39,201	2,039,214	98.11
2006	617,660	19,695	597,965	96.81
2007	850,912	28,322	822,590	96.67
2008	1,117,771	43,546	1,074,225	96.10

Source: American Bankruptcy Institute.

Concept Review Questions	1. What is the difference between financial distress and bankruptcy? 2. Does a firm cease to exist when it files for bankruptcy?

WHAT COMPANIES DO

CFO Survey Evidence: Constrained and Unconstrained Firms

Although finance theorists have long drawn a distinction between financially constrained and unconstrained companies—defining the former group as marginally profitable or unprofitable with imperfect access to capital markets—the full practical implications of being financially constrained did not become clear until the severe recession of 2008–2009. A survey conducted in the last quarter of 2008 asked the chief financial officers of several hundred U.S. companies how they changed their firms' plans for 2009 in response to the ongoing financial crisis. Key results of this survey are presented in the following table.

Do Financially Constrained and Unconstrained Firms Adopt Different Policies during a Financial Crisis?

PERCENTAGE CHANGE IN . . .	CONSTRAINED	UNCONSTRAINED	DIFFERENCE[a]
Tech spending	−21.954*** (−5.31)	−8.980*** (−6.13)	−12.974*** (−3.58)
Capital expenditures	−9.062*** (−2.38)	−0.610 (−0.46)	−8.452*** (−2.59)
Marketing expenditures	−32.375*** (−2.49)	−4.520* (−1.78)	−27.855*** (−3.41)
Number of employees	−10.867*** (−5.81)	−2.720*** (−4.81)	−8.148*** (−5.56)
Cash holdings	−14.988*** (−5.85)	−2.740*** (−3.03)	−12.249*** (−5.56)
Dividend payments	−14.176*** (−4.05)	−2.926*** (−3.44)	−11.251*** (−4.63)

Notes: This table displays mean comparison tests of planned percentage changes in various policies of U.S. firms according to whether they are financially constrained or financially unconstrained (*t*-statistics in parentheses).

[a]Difference = Constrained − Unconstrained.

***, **, and * denote (respectively) statistical significance at the 1%, 5%, and 10% (two-tail) test levels.

Source: Table 4 of Murillo Campello, John R. Graham, and Campbell R. Harvey, "The Real Effects of Financial Constraints: Evidence from the Financial Crisis," Working paper, Duke University (May 2009).

As expected, the crisis forced all companies to cut tech spending, capital investment, and marketing programs as well as to reduce employee headcount, draw down cash holdings, and cut dividend payments. However, the survey highlighted that financially constrained firms were forced to make much larger cuts than were healthier, financially unconstrained companies. Unconstrained firms planned to cut marketing and tech spending by relatively modest amounts (by 4.52% and 8.98%, respectively) and to reduce capital investment expenditures by a mere 0.61%. In contrast, constrained companies expected cuts of 32.38%, 21.95%, and 9.06% (respectively) in marketing, tech spending, and capital investment spending. Whereas unconstrained firms only planned to cut staffing by 2.72% and draw down cash holdings by just 2.74%, constrained companies planned to lay off 10.87% of their employees and reduce cash holdings by 14.99%. Finally, unconstrained companies expected to trim dividend payments by 2.93%, whereas constrained firms planned to reduce dividends by 14.18%. As this evidence shows, credit market conditions can alter operating and investment decisions, especially for financially constrained companies.

25.2 THE BANKRUPTCY CODE AND CHAPTER 11

The primary source of bankruptcy law is a statute first enacted by Congress in 1898. Congress completely overhauled bankruptcy law in 1978, and it is this version of the law, with certain amendments, that governs today. It is generally referred to as the **Bankruptcy Code**.

The Bankruptcy Code contains fifteen chapters. Six of these, summarized in Table 25.3, provide the types of relief available in bankruptcy. Although a company may choose to liquidate its assets under **chapter 7**, a firm that wants to survive will seek reorganization under chapter 11.

Table 25.3	Summary of Bankruptcy Code Chapters
CHAPTER	**PROVISIONS**
Chapter 7	This chapter provides for the liquidation of the debtor's assets by a trustee. Available to both individuals and businesses. Over 98% of these cases are filed by individuals.
Chapter 9	A specialized chapter governing bankruptcies of cities and municipalities.
Chapter 11	Provides for reorganization. Though used primarily by firms, it can also be used by individuals. Key aspect: management remains in control.
Chapter 12	A simplified form of restructuring for farmers.
Chapter 13	Permits consumers to repay all or a portion of their debts over time, rather than go through liquidation.
Chapter 15	For multinational situations. Applies to U.S. assets of firms that file primary bankruptcy in another country.

The unique feature of chapter 11 is that management of the firm remains in place as the **debtor-in-possession (DIP)** while the case is pending. This contrasts with chapter 7, where a trustee takes over the debtor's assets with the primary objective of maximizing liquidation value. This feature also distinguishes chapter 11 from insolvency relief in many other industrialized countries, where management is closely supervised or displaced altogether.

The continued role of management in chapter 11 raises the question of whether chapter 11 is a useful tool to address the factors that lead to business failure. The question is often posed: "Is chapter 11 successful?"

"Success" in chapter 11 is a subtle concept. Some of the cases that are filed never propose a reorganization plan and are either dismissed or wind up in chapter 7 liquidation. Even when a firm obtains the approval of its creditors and the court for a plan, the approval itself may not necessarily be an indicator of success. One example: within four months, Goody Family Clothing Inc. went from a celebrated and successful chapter 11 reorganization to filing once again under chapter 11.[3] The pattern is not uncommon.[4] Does a company's failure to meet the terms of its plan of reorganization mean that the chapter 11 procedure was "unsuccessful"?

---

[3]Jamie Mason, "Every Man for Himself," *The Deal*, http://www.thedeal.com/newsweekly/features/every-man-for-himself.php#bottom (March 20, 2009).

[4]Edie Hotchkiss (1995) uses the phrase "chapter 22" to refer to firms that file for chapter 11 a second time. She finds that one-third of the companies in her study restructured again, some outside of court and some within another chapter 11 filing. As examples of "chapter 22" filings, Aloha Air and KB Toys both filed for bankruptcy in 2004 and again in 2008. Levitz Home Furnishings and TWA are examples of "chapter 33" firms (that file for bankruptcy a third time). Edward Altman (2009) attributes these multiple filings to a combination of bad luck (in the sense of an overall slow economy) and of not reducing debt enough when emerging from bankruptcy the first time.

Answering this question requires an understanding of the chapter 11 process and what happens during the beginning, middle, and end of the case. When a company files for chapter 11, an **automatic stay** immediately takes effect. The automatic stay is the protective legal fence that drops around the firm to prevent efforts by creditors to collect on claims.

For a firm on the verge of failing, the immediate relief provided by this automatic stay may help it reorganize successfully. It gives the debtor protection that it did not have prior to commencement of the case. Creditors no longer have the threat of declaring default or pursuing collection actions. The debtor now has some time to evaluate its situation without immediate threat from creditors. In order to take collection action, creditors now have to obtain the permission of the bankruptcy court, and this permission is rarely granted. As a result, a creditor who may have been recalcitrant and unwilling to negotiate with the debtor prior to the bankruptcy filing may now choose to bargain. Furthermore, the case brings all creditors and claims into one forum, perhaps streamlining negotiations.

The automatic stay essentially allows the debtor to consider the financial condition of the entire firm. Outside of bankruptcy, each creditor would be free to pursue its own remedies. Individual creditors could seize individual assets, dismembering the firm and destroying any value it might have as a going concern. The implicit logic behind chapter 11 is the assumption that, over the long term, creditors as a whole will be better off if the entity is allowed to survive, even though individual creditors might not receive as much as they would by pursuing their individual remedies.

The current version of chapter 11 contains many sections that address general reorganizations.[5] The key reorganization tools contained in these sections each address one of three issues that face the failing company: illiquidity, valuation, and management (control).

Illiquidity

In the early stages of a case, a firm filing for chapter 11 frequently faces questions of liquidity. Not only has the firm depleted its cash, but sources of credit have also largely evaporated under such circumstances. Lenders may threaten a declaration of default or covenant violations. As a consequence, the firm faces the loss of revolving lines of credit that it uses to fund daily operations. The lenders may also have liens on cash proceeds from the sale of products produced with their collateral assets.

For an insolvent company, authority to borrow funds may not be enough. So, in order to help the chapter 11 company gain access to loans, the Bankruptcy Code authorizes the company to offer an array of sweeteners to lenders who are willing to lend. With the authority of the bankruptcy court, the chapter 11 firm may offer a *super-priority* to new lenders: the right to be paid ahead of everyone else.[6] If certain conditions are met, a debtor-in-possession lender may be able to leapfrog other secured creditors and receive a lien on all assets of the firm (even those previously pledged to other lenders).[7] This debtor-in-possession financing is often prearranged and kicks in simultaneously with the formal chapter 11 filing.

A company in chapter 11 may also have to deal with suppliers who refuse to extend credit. For example, retailers rely heavily on short-term credit for inventory, and manufacturers use credit to purchase raw materials. If major suppliers become worried about whether they will be paid, they may refuse to ship unless paid in advance—in cash. If the

---

[5]For example, subchapter IV of Title 11 contains 11 sections that deal specifically with railroad reorganizations.
[6]11 U.S.C. § 364(c)(1)–(3).
[7]11 U.S.C. § 364(d).

supplier is owed money by the bankrupt company at the time it files chapter 11, the supplier may demand payment or refuse to ship going forward.

This issue is further complicated by one of the basic principles in bankruptcy: similarly situated creditors should receive the same treatment. Thus, for example, when a company files for chapter 11, the Bankruptcy Code requires that all trade creditors with unpaid accounts at the time of the filing (1) receive the same percentage distribution on their claims and (2) wait until the confirmation of a plan of reorganization sets the terms and timing of their payments. A supplier who knows that its products are essential to the filing company's survival may nevertheless try to use this advantage to secure preferential treatment.

Bankruptcy Courts have devised a rule that allows for certain "critical vendor" payments to be made if the debtor can show that the suppliers in question are integral to the company's survival. If permitted, the debtor may be able to pay key suppliers before other creditors, allowing these suppliers to continue shipping on credit during the chapter 11 process.

Valuation

Valuation is often contentious in bankruptcy. The highest-priority creditors have incentive to argue that the firm's overall value is low, because this implies that their claims constitute a substantial share (perhaps all) of the firm's value. The lower the firm's value, the larger the share that high-priority creditors can argue should be awarded to them. In contrast, low-priority creditors have incentive to argue that the overall firm value is large, because this makes it more likely that some value will be left for them after the higher-priority creditors are paid off. Likewise, management and equity holders usually have incentive to argue that ongoing firm value is high. The Bankruptcy Code provides the debtor with a neutral arbiter—the bankruptcy judge—who ultimately decides which valuation to recognize. It is worth noting that, even though much uncertainty surrounds valuation of a distressed firm, the valuation techniques discussed earlier in this book (discounted cash flow, multiples valuation relative to peer firms, transactions multiples) are still the primary tools of the trade. One reason for this is that valuation experts must often testify in front of the bankruptcy judge, so they tend to rely on traditional, defendable methodologies.

Valuation issues often arise at the earliest stages of a bankruptcy case when the debtor seeks authorization to borrow money. The lender will usually ask for additional collateral, and the question then arises: How much additional collateral is sufficient? At this stage, the debtor's bargaining power is limited—the loan is usually necessary to continue operations. Unsecured creditors, however, may complain out of concern that the new lender has first claim on too much of the debtor's unencumbered assets, thereby leaving less for unsecured creditors in the event the debtor is ultimately liquidated.

The next stage at which valuation becomes an issue is when a secured creditor asks permission of the bankruptcy court to take back its collateral. One of the criteria for relief from the automatic stay is whether the loan balance exceeds the value of the collateral. In this situation, the debtor will seek to demonstrate the highest possible value for the collateral while the secured creditor will do the opposite. Even if the court determines that the collateral's value exceeds the loan balance, it may order the debtor to make periodic payments to offset the projected decline in value that will occur when the collateral is used.

The plan of reorganization is the next stage where the value of the debtor's assets becomes an issue. Under the Bankruptcy Code, the debtor must propose a plan that is in the "best interests of creditors," in other words, a plan that pays more to creditors via chapter 11 restructuring than they would receive in liquidation under chapter 7. At this stage, the debtor may try to minimize the proposed liquidation value of its assets in order to meet this threshold. A reorganization must also be "feasible" in that it is not likely to be followed by liquidation or need of further financial reorganization.

Management

In chapter 11, the debtor's existing management usually remains in place. By law, the filing of the case creates a new entity called the debtor-in-possession. The firm becomes like a trustee—a fiduciary for its creditors. As a practical matter this means that the firm's decisions and actions are subject to review and questioning by the creditor committees and the bankruptcy court, whereas outside of bankruptcy the same decisions would be simply a matter of management discretion. As shown in Figure 25.2, there is a growing number of parties with which management must interact. This time-consuming distraction is a significant cost of financial distress but one that is hard to measure. (As mentioned in Chapter 13, the possibility of experiencing these costs of financial distress if things turn sour are traded off against the benefits of using debt financing when the company chooses its optimal capital structure.)

FIGURE 25.2

The Players in a Corporate Bankruptcy

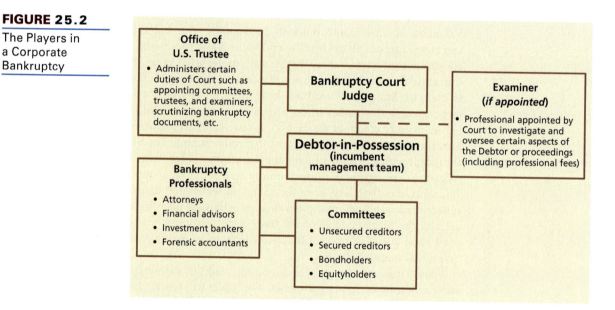

In addition to the court, the firm's management may also have to deal with a committee of creditors. Typically, one committee is appointed to represent the interests of all unsecured creditors, and this committee has the right to participate in the reorganization process. Even though the firm's management initially has an "exclusivity period" of 120 days to propose a restructuring plan within chapter 11, the creditors' committee—as a representative of all unsecured creditors—also has practical negotiating power. The creditors' committee has the power to retain professionals to represent it and to have those professionals paid out of the estate. In some cases, more than one creditor committee may be appointed in order to represent different classes of unsecured debt. In large cases where the firm has a complex capital structure, several committees may be appointed to represent different types of claims. For example, bondholders and suppliers might be represented by different committees.

Unlike creditors, who have well-defined roles under the Bankruptcy Code, the owners of the firm's equity usually struggle to have an effect on the process. This struggle creates a dilemma for management. Under normal circumstances, the owners of the firm—the shareholders or partners—control the firm's management. Management of a firm that has filed for bankruptcy, however, may consider the firm to be insolvent—the firm's liabilities exceed its assets. If the firm is insolvent, the firm's owners are out-of-the-money. Under bankruptcy law, this lack of economic interest leaves the owners of the firm with little ability to influence the outcome of the case. Nonetheless, as mentioned in the next section, shareholders sometimes do receive payments in chapter 11 reorganization.

When ownership and management overlap—as in the case of a company that is closely held—the role of management is more complicated than in a widely held firm. In these situations the question becomes whether management is working to maximize value for creditors or rather to retain ownership of the firm. This issue is further complicated by the Bankruptcy Code's requirement that, absent creditor consent, the owners of the firm receive nothing until everyone else is paid in full. The owners/management may use the protection of the Bankruptcy Code to exact concessions from creditors that will allow the managers to retain their interest.

The rationale behind the Bankruptcy Code's concept of debtor-in-possession is that existing management has experience and knowledge that are crucial to the reorganization's success. This rationale has been subject to much debate. The concern is whether management is working for the creditors or primarily for its own benefit. Moreover, in some cases management is thought to have contributed to the problems that led to distress. Nonetheless, the debtor-in-possession principle, when combined with the Bankruptcy Code's provisions governing lending and valuation, give a failing company the opportunity to stabilize and reorganize.[8]

The Plan of Reorganization

The goal of a chapter 11 case is the filing of a plan of reorganization and its acceptance by creditors and the bankruptcy court. Cases that do not achieve this goal end when the bankrupt firm is acquired or liquidated.

In broad outline, the process of proposing and confirming a plan is straightforward. The debtor files a proposed plan along with a disclosure statement. The disclosure statement is intended to provide background and justification for the plan. The court and creditors have the opportunity to review the disclosure statement. Once the bankruptcy court approves it, the debtor sends the plan and disclosure statement to creditors. The creditors are invited to submit ballots that either accept or reject the plan. The acceptance of a plan by creditors depends on both the number of creditors who vote for it and on the size of their claims. Typically, only creditors that receive something, but not full payment (often, the unsecured creditors), are permitted to vote. Secured creditors have either reached an agreement with the debtor or the plan will pay them in full, according to the terms of their loan. Even if a sufficient number of creditors accept the plan, the debtor must present it to the bankruptcy court for final approval.

The types of reorganization are as varied within chapter 11 as they are outside of it. The plan may change the firm's capital structure by cancelling or diluting old ownership interests and offering unsecured creditors stock or other ownership interests. Terms of loans may be

---

[8]The provisions of chapter 11 allow for two exceptions to the debtor-in-possession concept and the continuation of management control. Creditors may move for the Bankruptcy Court to order the appointment of a chapter 11 trustee if there is evidence of gross mismanagement or wrongdoing. This trustee would have the power to take over operation and management of the firm. The appointment of a chapter 11 trustee is unusual, and in most cases management remains in place. Creditors may also seek the conversion to chapter 7 (discussed later in the text). In chapter 7, a trustee is also appointed but will usually shut down operations and liquidate the company's assets.

changed by reducing principal, reducing interest, and/or granting an **extension** of time for repayment. Unsecured debt is often repaid at a significant discount to face value, though unsecured creditors may also receive an ownership interest in the reorganized firm.

If the firm has not done so during the course of the chapter 11 proceedings, it may propose reducing costs by the sale and closing of facilities or other changes. In addition, the firm may propose a sale as a going concern or a liquidation under the control of existing management.

An important principle of chapter 11 is known as the **absolute priority rule**. Under absolute priority, equity and low-priority creditors can retain no interest in the reorganized company unless all higher-priority creditors are paid in full. As can be seen in Figure 25.3, violations of absolute priority occur, though they have become much less common in recent years.

FIGURE 25.3

Frequency with Which the Absolute Priority Rule Is Violated by United States Bankruptcy Courts in Chapter 11 Reorganizations, 1979–2005

Source: Figure 1 of Sreedhar T. Bharath, Venkatesh Panchapagesan, and Ingrid M. Werner, "The Changing Nature of Chapter 11," Working paper, Ohio State University (October 2007).

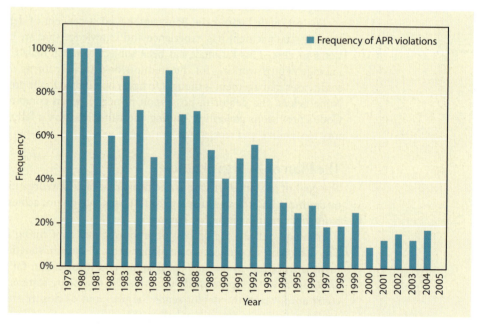

After an initial plan of reorganization is proposed, creditors may reject it. If they do, the debtor then has the option of seeking a **cramdown**, essentially asking the judge to force the creditors to accept the terms of the plan. Unsecured (low-priority) creditors may ultimately accept the cramdown if they perceive the alternative outcome to be that secured creditors will consume all of the proceeds of the plan and unsecured creditors will receive nothing. Depending on the facts in a case, the threat of cramdown is essentially a game of chicken. Will unsecured creditors accept the plan, perhaps even allowing the owners or equity holders to retain an interest, or will they risk letting the secured creditors gobble up whatever value the firm has to offer?

JOB INTERVIEW QUESTION

A distressed company is considering whether to file for chapter 11. What issues must a reorganization plan address with respect to secured creditors? Under what conditions can existing equity holders receive some payment in the plan?

Attractive Features of Chapter 11

For viable firms that are in temporary financial distress, reorganization is viewed as a means of providing breathing space in order to save jobs and avoid disruption to local communities. So that reorganization will be attractive to managers and equity holders,

WHAT COMPANIES DO

Chrysler Crisis

Chrysler entered chapter 11 bankruptcy protection in spring 2009 with liabilities that far exceeded its assets. In fact, its assets were not sufficient to fully repay the face value that was owed to senior creditors (i.e., secured creditors and general unsecured creditors). In most chapter 11 cases, senior creditors are paid in full before lower-priority junior creditors (e.g., employee benefit plans) receive any payment. In the Chrysler case, secured creditors were offered partial payment on their claims (29 cents per dollar of claim) and a lower-priority unsecured claim by the United Auto Workers retiree health-care trust was to receive a $4.5 billion note and a 55% ownership stake in the portion of Chrysler that emerged from bankruptcy. The government's rationale for pressuring secured creditors to accept this deal was an attempt to save tens of thousands of jobs and, in a worst-case scenario, to prevent Chrysler from liquidating.

At the last minute, a small group of Indiana pension plans and consumer advocacy groups filed an appeal with the U.S. Supreme Court. These plaintiffs claimed that the proposed plan was unconstitutional because it put junior creditors' rights ahead of senior creditors': the former received some payment even though the latter had not been paid in full. Ultimately, their appeal was rejected by the Supreme Court, though the Court did not rule on this apparent violation of the absolute priority rule.

These pensions aside, why did the vast majority of secured creditors accept the plan even though they received less than full payment? One reason is that the federal government put senior creditors under severe public pressure to accept the deal. Another reason is that the creditors most likely weighed the odds that if they objected and the initial plan failed, they would receive a smaller payment if Chrysler were to liquidate. In this sense, the senior creditors that accepted the plan blinked in a high-stakes game of chicken.

Congress has provided a number of sources of aid to firms in reorganization. This help comes either from the government or from creditors. They give firms in reorganization advantages relative to firms that continue operating outside of bankruptcy and firms that liquidate. Six major forms of aid are as follows:

1. When reorganizing firms settle liabilities for less than their face value, the amount of debt forgiveness is deducted as a loss by the creditor but is not immediately treated as taxable income to the reorganizing firm. The amount of the debt forgiveness becomes taxable when the reorganized firm becomes profitable by reducing either its tax loss carryforward or its depreciation allowances.

2. Firms reorganizing under chapter 11 have the right to terminate underfunded pension plans, and the U.S. government's Pension Benefit Guaranty Corporation (PBGC) picks up the uncovered pension costs.

3. Firms that reorganize retain most of their accrued tax loss carryforwards, which would be lost if they liquidated. These loss carryforwards shelter the firm from paying taxes on corporate profits for a period in the future if its operations become profitable. They also make reorganized firms attractive merger partners for profitable firms, because if the acquisition is properly structured the profitable firm can use the tax loss carryforwards.

4. A firm's obligation to pay interest to unsecured prebankruptcy creditors ceases when they file for bankruptcy. They do not have to start paying interest again until a reorganization plan is approved, and the unpaid interest does not become a claim against the

firm. This feature clearly gives managers of failing firms an incentive to file for bankruptcy earlier and to delay proposing a reorganization plan.

5. Firms in reorganization can reject contracts that are not substantially completed. Thus, they can rework or reject unprofitable contracts, and the cost of shedding such contracts is small. Although firms are still liable for damages to parties of rejected contracts, such damage claims are unsecured and likely to receive a low payoff rate.

6. Firms in reorganization can reject their collective bargaining labor agreements. Since 1984, however, this step has required the approval of the bankruptcy judge. Nonetheless, this aid has sometimes benefited unionized firms in industries that have a mixture of unionized and nonunionized establishments by enabling them to cut all wages to nonunionized levels. An example is Continental Airlines: after airline deregulation, it filed for bankruptcy in 1983; once reorganized, it was allowed to cut wages by 50% and reduce its workforce by 65%.

EXAMPLE

Although companies are no longer able to unilaterally revoke collective bargaining agreements after they file for bankruptcy protection, the supervising judges allow companies this flexibility frequently enough that the companies are often able to win concessions from their unionized employees by *threatening* to file for bankruptcy. American Airlines used this tactic successfully in April 2003, when it secured $1.8 billion in annual cost savings from its eight principal unions by credibly threatening to file for chapter 11 protection if the wage cuts were not approved.

In fact, three major North American airlines had recently filed for bankruptcy protection in the previous eight months. The second-largest U.S. carrier (UAL Corporation) filed for chapter 11 in December 2002, and the seventh-largest (US Airways) had filed in August—though US Airways emerged from bankruptcy a mere seven months later, only to reenter during 2004. In early April 2003, Air Canada filed for protection from its creditors in the Canadian bankruptcy courts.

This same tactic was used successfully several times during late 2005. Delphi, Delta, and Northwest all pressured their unions to accept dramatic labor cost cuts by threatening to ask the bankruptcy court judge to impose even more drastic cuts unilaterally if the unions balked. Chrysler and General Motors also used this tactic to obtain major concessions from unions (as well as bondholders and auto dealerships) during negotiations in early 2009.

The Success of Chapter 11

A commonly accepted benchmark of success in chapter 11 is a confirmed plan of reorganization. However, another measure of success is whether chapter 11 saved companies that would otherwise have failed. Here, the evidence is not clear. At the very least, chapter 11 can be said to offer a well-defined process that permits creditors and debtors to evaluate the firm's prospects, offer a platform for negotiations where litigation threats are reduced, and perhaps prevent the firm from prematurely forgoing opportunities to survive. A recent study by Kalay, Singhal, and Tashjian (2007) finds that 459 firms filing for chapter 11 between 1991 and 1998 experienced, on average, significant improvements in operating performance after being reorganized, which suggests that the protection afforded by the Bankruptcy Code was valuable for these firms. Figure 25.4 shows their main result: chapter 11 filings are preceded by dramatic reductions in profitability (measured here by the ratio of earnings before interest, taxes, depreciation, and amortization to assets), but after filing the firms' profitability improves noticeably.

WHAT COMPANIES DO

Section 363 Bankruptcy Code Asset Sales

Substantive asset sales often occur under Section 363 of the Bankruptcy Code. Corporate assets sold under Section 363 are "free and clear" of any other interests in the property. The free-and-clear provision allows a debtor to consummate the sale quickly, as competing interests in the property need not be resolved as a condition to the sale. Much like a traditional auction, 363 sale mechanics include an initial bidder (the "stalking horse") who reaches an agreement to purchase assets from the chapter 11 debtor. The buyer and the debtor negotiate an asset purchase agreement, listing the stalking horse as the initial bidder but leaving the transaction open to "higher and better" bids. In principle, most of the assets of a firm can be sold via Section 363. In 2009, General Motors Corp. used Section 363 of the U.S. Bankruptcy Code as a mechanism to separate the healthy parts of the company from its less competitive parts. GM used Section 363 to sell its healthy assets to a new and improved GM, financed by the federal government. This relatively healthy part of GM emerged from chapter 11 in only 40 days. The remaining unhealthy assets were retained in a separate company (Motors Liquidation Co.), with the intent of being gradually auctioned off or liquidated.

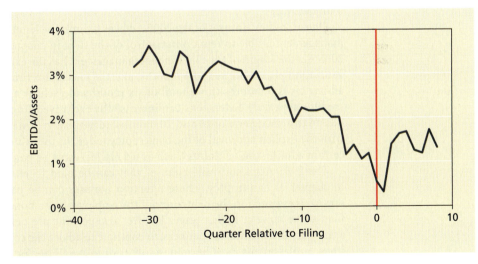

FIGURE 25.4

Firm Profitability before and after Filing for Chapter 11 Bankruptcy

This figure plots the operating income of firms [measured as earnings before interest, taxes, depreciation, and amortization (EBITDA) divided by total assets] that filed for chapter 11 between 1991 and 1998 and successfully reorganized. Quarter 0 is the quarter end before the chapter 11 filing date and quarter 1 is the quarter end after the chapter 11 filing date. After quarter 0, the number of firms for which operating income is calculated declines as firms exit chapter 11. The number of firms falls from 81 firms in quarter 0 to 41 firms by quarter 8.

Source: Avner Kalay, Rajeev Singhal, and Elizabeth Tashjian, "Is Chapter 11 Costly?" *Journal of Financial Economics* 84 (2007), pp. 772–796.

25.3 BANKRUPTCY ACT OF 2005

Relative to the options available to distressed firms in many other countries, the U.S. chapter 11 bankruptcy system has the reputation of being "debtor friendly" in terms of helping companies reorganize and survive. Some argue that the U.S. code is too debtor friendly, allowing too many companies to hide from their creditors by filing for chapter 11 and ultimately destroying firm value. A similar, commonly held sentiment is that U.S. citizens are able to shirk their liabilities and obligations too easily by filing for bankruptcy. Given this sentiment, Congress passed the Bankruptcy Abuse Prevention and Consumer Protection Act of 2005. One early indication that the new Act was viewed as less accommodating by distressed firms was that a number of companies filed for chapter 11 just before the new Act took effect so that they'd be subject to the old law. For example, the auto parts manufacturer Delphi filed under the old law and operated under chapter 11 protection for more than four years.

One of the key features of the 2005 Act was to limit the length of time that incumbent management is able to remain in control of the firm in chapter 11. For example, in the 2005 Act the length of time incumbent management has the exclusive right to file a reorganization plan is limited to 4 months, and the maximum time to obtain consent from all parties is 6 months (for a total of six months of exclusivity to both file and obtain creditor approval). Extensions can increase the exclusive filing and approval time periods up to a maximum of 18 and 20 months, respectively; however, these can occur only with the explicit approval of the bankruptcy judge. In the same vein, under current law certain administrative claims (such as tax claims) must be paid within five years.

The 2005 Act also limits bonuses that can be paid to retain key employees while in chapter 11 bankruptcy. These retention bonuses can be paid only if an employee's service is essential to the debtor and if the employee has a bona fide offer from another firm at the same or higher wage. The Act also permits pre-petition professionals, such as lawyers and investment bankers, to continue to advise the company during chapter 11 (these professionals must be paid in full prior to the filing, for otherwise they'd be considered a creditor, deemed to have a conflict of interest, and thus not able to serve as advisers).

The 2005 Act has led to some dramatic consequences. One feature of the Act was to increase the priority of administrative claims, thereby giving more power to administrative claimants during the bankruptcy process. As described in the following What Companies Do feature, in the case of Circuit City these claimants became part of the creditor committee and ultimately forced Circuit City to liquidate rather than follow the normal chapter 11 process. Though the Circuit City case might be an extreme example, overall the 2005 Act has made chapter 11 less debtor friendly, swinging the pendulum of power away from incumbent management and shareholders and toward creditors.

WHAT COMPANIES DO

Short Circuited

After nearly 60 years in business, the second largest electronics retailer in the United States, Circuit City, filed for bankruptcy on November 10, 2008, just weeks before the traditional holiday selling season. Citing vendor concerns that the company could not continue to pay for its inventory, Circuit City filed under chapter 11 of the Bankruptcy Code and announced that it received $1.1 billion in debtor-in-possession financing to maintain operations as it tried to restructure. CEO James Marcum attempted to reassure customers by stating: "It is important for you to understand that this announcement does not mean that Circuit City is going out of business." Apparently sharing that opinion was Ricardo Salinas Pliego, owner of the Mexican broadcaster, TV Azteca. Just eight days after the bankruptcy filing, Pliego purchased 28% of Circuit City's outstanding equity and was rumored to be willing to purchase a majority stake.

As part of the chapter 11 process, the court appointed a creditors' committee to represent the interests of Circuit City's largest creditors. The list of committee members read like a Who's Who of consumer electronics producers and included names such as Hewlett-Packard, Samsung, LG Electronics, Garmin International, and Toshiba as well as the large mall developer, Simon Property Group. Liquidation specialists offered $900 million for Circuit City's assets and so, in order to keep the firm alive, management had to formulate a reorganization plan to convince creditors that they'd be better off if the firm continued to operate. Ultimately, the creditors decided that they would be better off immediately liquidating the firm, rather than going through a potentially drawn-out chapter 11 reorganization. Therefore, on January 16, 2009, the U.S. Court announced that Circuit City's assets would be liquidated, putting over 34,000 people out of work at a time when U.S. unemployment was climbing toward 10%.

Sources: Andrea Chang, "Picture Gets Fuzzy for Circuit City; The Electronics Chain Files for Chapter 11 amid Growing Doubts about Its Survival," *Los Angeles Times* (November 11, 2008), p. C1; David Ress and Louis Llovio, "The Final Moments of Circuit City," *Richmond Times Dispatch*, http://www.timesdispatch.com/rtd/business/banking/bankruptcies/article/CIRC25_20090124-215712/187917/.

Concept Review Questions	8. What is an automatic stay, and why is it important in chapter 11 proceedings? 9. Did the 2005 Act increase or reduce the power of creditors?

25.4 ALTERNATIVES TO TRADITIONAL CHAPTER 11

Chapter 11 of the U.S. Bankruptcy Code outlines the procedures for reorganizing a failed or failing firm, whether its petition is filed voluntarily or involuntarily. If a workable plan for reorganization cannot be developed, then there are alternatives to a traditional chapter 11. These alternatives include out-of-court workouts, prepackaged bankruptcies, and chapter 7 bankruptcy.

Out-of-Court Workouts

As an alternative to formally filing for bankruptcy, many companies attempt to negotiate a solution with their creditors out of court. In these **workouts**, the debtor company must receive unanimous approval from a given creditor class, rather than the majority or two-thirds of votes required in chapter 11. The advantages of a workout include that they take much less time and hence are less of a distraction for managers, cost less in legal and other fees, and do not cede power to third parties such as a bankruptcy judge. Workout announcements often receive a much more positive capital market reaction than do formal chapter 11 filings, though this may reflect that the "best" of the distressed firms are those most likely to reach a workout agreement with creditors. Many workouts amount to simple renegotiations of credit terms by bankers or other creditors, giving the firm improved terms and/or more time to make payments. In the face of a pending chapter 11 filing, creditors are more likely to agree to workouts if they perceive that more of the firm's value will be preserved by continuing normal operations than under the disruptions associated with a formal chapter 11 filing.

Prepackaged Bankruptcies

Sometimes companies prepare a reorganization plan that is negotiated and voted on by creditors and stockholders before the company actually files for chapter 11 bankruptcy. This process, known as a **prepackaged bankruptcy**, shortens and simplifies the process, saving the company money and frequently generating more for the creditors because there is less spent in legal and related fees, less disruption to the company's business, and less damage to its goodwill (see McConnell, Lease, and Tashjian, 1996).

Regal Cinemas, the largest U.S. movie theater chain, simultaneously filed a voluntary petition for chapter 11 bankruptcy protection and a prepackaged plan of reorganization on October 12, 2001. The reorganization plan gave effective control of the operation of 3,831 movie screens to Denver billionaire Philip Anschutz, who used the theater industry's misfortunes to gain control of two other chains, United Artists and Edwards. The reorganization plan gave Regal's senior debt holders 100% of the reorganized company's stock. As it turned out, Anschutz owned the majority of the senior debt, having bought it for pennies on the dollar from Regal's bankers earlier in the year. Regal Cinemas emerged from bankruptcy in January 2002, an astonishingly short three months after filing!

Chapter 7

Although chapter 11 cases attract the most publicity, most businesses that file bankruptcy choose chapter 7 instead. Chapter 7 is liquidation, and it offers no hope of reorganization. Instead, an officer of the Department of Justice—the United States Trustee—appoints a private party (called a chapter 7 trustee) from a panel of preselected individuals. The chapter 7 trustee takes total control and possession of the firm and all of its assets. Operations are almost always stopped; the management of the firm is no longer in control.

Unless the trustee seeks to recover against former management, management usually has little interest in the chapter 7 process. However, the chapter 7 trustee frequently confronts a challenge from the secured creditors. The secured creditors will ask the Court for "relief from the automatic stay" so that they may resume attempts to take possession and liquidate collateral.

In these situations, one of the chapter 7 trustee's goals is to find some asset that can be liquidated for the benefit of the unsecured creditors. To do this, the trustee may challenge the validity of a secured creditor's lien. If successful, the asset can be liquidated and all of the proceeds used to pay unsecured creditors.

However, the trustee and secured creditors often fight about valuation: whether the asset has any value over and above the lien that encumbers it. The secured creditors will usually contend that it does not and that the bankruptcy estate thus has no interest in the asset. The trustee may contend that the asset has value over and above the lien that encumbers it, arguing that the asset should remain in the estate so that the excess value can be used for distribution to unsecured creditors.

25.5 PRIORITY OF CLAIMS

The chapter 7 trustee has the responsibility of liquidating all the firm's assets and distributing the proceeds to the holders of provable claims. The courts have established certain procedures for determining the provability of claims; these procedures are the *absolute priority* rules mentioned in Section 25.2. The priority of claims, which is specified in chapter 7 of the Bankruptcy Reform Act, must be maintained by the trustee when distributing the funds from liquidation.

In a liquidation, it is important to recognize that if any secured creditors have specific assets pledged as collateral, then they receive the proceeds from the sale of those assets. If these proceeds are inadequate to meet their claim, the secured creditors become unsecured (or general) creditors for the unrecovered amount because specific collateral no longer exists. These and all other unsecured creditors will divide up, on a pro rata basis, any funds remaining after all prior claims have been satisfied. If the proceeds from the sale of secured assets are in excess of the claims against them, the excess funds become available to meet claims of unsecured creditors.

A listing of the priority of claims follows:

1. The expenses of administering the bankruptcy proceedings.
2. Any unpaid interim expenses incurred in the ordinary course of business between filing the bankruptcy petition and the entry of an Order of Relief in an involuntary proceeding. (This step is not applicable in a voluntary bankruptcy.)
3. Wages of not more than $2,000 per worker that have been earned by workers in the 90-day period immediately preceding the commencement of bankruptcy proceedings.
4. Unpaid employee benefit plan contributions that were to be paid in the 180-day period preceding the filing of bankruptcy or the termination of business, whichever occurred first. For any employee, the sum of this claim plus eligible unpaid wages cannot exceed $2,000.
5. Claims of farmers or fishermen in a grain-storage or fish-storage facility, not to exceed $2,000 for each producer.
6. Unsecured customer deposits, not to exceed $900 each, resulting from purchasing or leasing a good or service from the failed firm.
7. Taxes legally due and owed by the bankrupt firm to the federal government, state government, or any other governmental subdivision.
8. Claims of secured creditors, who receive the proceeds from the sale of collateral held regardless of the priorities described earlier. If the proceeds from the liquidation of the collateral are insufficient to satisfy the secured creditors' claims, then the secured creditors become unsecured creditors for the unpaid amount.
9. Claims of unsecured creditors. The claims of unsecured (or "general") creditors and unsatisfied portions of secured creditors' claims are treated equally.
10. Preferred stockholders, who receive an amount up to the par (stated) value of their preferred stock.
11. Common stockholders, who receive any remaining funds, which are distributed on an equal per-share basis. If different classes of common stock are outstanding, priorities may exist.

Despite the priorities listed in items 1 through 7, secured creditors have first claim on proceeds from the sale of their collateral. The claims of unsecured creditors, including the unpaid claims of secured creditors, are satisfied next; finally, the claims of preferred and common stockholders are honored. Also, some unsecured creditors' claims may be subordinated to those of other unsecured creditors. In the event of liquidation, the subordinated creditors do not receive any cash until the claims to which they are subordinated are paid in full. The following Example describes the application of these priorities by the trustee in bankruptcy liquidation proceedings.

EXAMPLE

Table 25.4 presents the balance sheet of Oxford Company, a manufacturer of computer drives. The trustee has liquidated the firm's assets, obtaining the largest amounts possible. The trustee obtained $2.1 million for the firm's current assets and $1.8 million for the firm's fixed assets; thus the total proceeds from the liquidation amounted to $3.9 million. It is clear that the firm is legally insolvent because its liabilities of $5.5 million exceed the $3.9 million asset sale proceeds. The next step is to distribute the proceeds to the various creditors. The only liability that is not shown on the balance sheet is $500,000 in expenses for administering the bankruptcy proceedings and satisfying unpaid bills incurred between the time of filing the bankruptcy petition and the entry of an Order of Relief. Table 25.5 shows the distribution of the $3.9 million among the firm's creditors and illustrates that, once all prior claims on the proceeds to liquidation have been satisfied, the unsecured creditors get the remaining funds. Table 25.6 gives the pro rata distribution of the $1 million among the unsecured creditors. The disposition of funds in the Oxford Company liquidation are shown in Tables 25.5 and 25.6. Because the claims of the unsecured creditors have not been fully satisfied, the preferred and common shareholders receive nothing.

Table 25.4　Balance Sheet for Oxford Company

ASSETS		LIABILITIES AND STOCKHOLDERS' EQUITY	
Cash	$ 100,000	Accounts payable	$ 200,000
Accounts receivable	1,200,000	Notes payable—bank	1,500,000
Inventories	3,150,000	Accrued wages[a]	100,000
Total current assets	$4,450,000	Unpaid employee benefits[b]	110,000
Land	$2,000,000	Unsecured customer deposits[c]	90,000
Net plant	1,500,000	Taxes payable	300,000
Net equipment	1,100,000	Total current liabilities	$2,300,000
Total fixed assets	$4,600,000	First mortgage[d]	$1,400,000
Total	$9,050,000	Second mortgage[d]	800,000
		Subordinated debentures[e]	1,000,000
		Total long-term debt	$3,200,000
		Preferred stock (7,000 shares)	$ 700,000
		Common stock (20,000 shares)	$ 200,000
		Paid-in capital in excess of par	300,000
		Retained earnings	$2,350,000
		Total common stockholders' equity	$2,850,000
		Total	$9,050,000

[a]Represents wages of $2,000 or less per employee earned within 90 days of filing bankruptcy for 150 of the firm's employees.

[b]These unpaid employee benefits were due in the 180-day period preceding the firm's bankruptcy filing, which occurred simultaneously with the termination of its business.

[c]Unsecured customer deposits not exceeding $900 each.

[d]The first and second mortgages are on the firm's total fixed assets.

[e]The debentures are subordinated to the note payable.

Table 25.5	Distribution of the Liquidation Proceeds of Oxford Company	
Proceeds from liquidation		$3,900,000
Expenses of administering bankruptcy and paying bills		$ 500,000
Wages owed workers		100,000
Unpaid employee benefits		110,000
Unsecured customer deposits		90,000
Taxes owed governments		300,000
Funds available for creditors		$2,800,000
First mortgage, paid from $1.8 million proceeds of fixed asset sale		$1,400,000
Second mortgage, partially paid from remaining asset sale proceeds		400,000
Funds available for unsecured creditors		$1,000,000

UNSECURED CREDITORS' CLAIMS	AMOUNT	SETTLEMENT AT 32%[a]	AFTER SUBORDINATION
Unpaid balance on second mortgage	$ 400,000[b]	$ 129,032	$ 129,032
Accounts payable	200,000	64,516	64,516
Notes payable—bank	1,500,000	483,871	806,452
Subordinated debentures	1,000,000	322,581	0
Totals	$3,100,000	$1,000,000	$1,000,000

Table 25.6 Pro Rata Distribution of Funds among the Unsecured Creditors of Oxford Company

[a] The 32% rate is calculated by dividing the $1 million available for the unsecured creditors by the $3.1 million owed the unsecured creditors. Each is entitled to a pro rata share.
[b] This figure represents the difference between the $800,000 second mortgage and the $400,000 payment on the second mortgage from the proceeds from the sale of the collateral remaining after satisfying the first mortgage.

Concept Review Questions

10. How are chapters 7 and 11 in the Bankruptcy Code different?
11. What is the purpose of the absolute priority rule? Why shouldn't the bankruptcy judge be given more discretion?
12. What is the significance of subordinating a claim if a firm is liquidated?
13. Why is payment of the expenses of administering the bankruptcy proceeding given the highest priority?

25.6 PREDICTING BANKRUPTCY

Many analysts attempt to predict the occurrence of bankruptcy using a tool like Altman's **Z score**, named after Professor Edward Altman of New York University. The Z score is the output of a quantitative model that uses a blend of traditional financial ratios and a

**JOB INTERVIEW
QUESTION**

Your firm is considering
lending money to a new
customer. What factors
might you consider in
determining whether to
lend to this customer?

statistical technique known as *multiple discriminant analysis.* In some tests, Z score has been found to be about 90% accurate in forecasting bankruptcy one year in the future and about 80% accurate in forecasting it two years in the future. The model was estimated for manufacturing firms as follows:

$$Z = 1.2(X_1) + 1.4(X_2) + 3.3(X_3) + 0.6(X_4) + 1.0(X_5)$$

where

X_1 = Working capital ÷ Total assets
X_2 = Retained earnings ÷ Total assets
X_3 = Earnings before interest and taxes ÷ Total assets
X_4 = Market value of equity ÷ Book value of total liabilities
X_5 = Sales ÷ Total assets

The guidelines for classifying businesses are: Z score less than or equal to 1.8, high probability of bankruptcy; Z score between 1.81 and 2.99, unsure; and Z score of 3.0 or higher, bankruptcy unlikely.

EXAMPLE

Table 25.7 presents the balance sheet and Table 25.8 depicts the income statement for Poff Industries, a manufacturer of computer power supplies. The company's stock price currently is $3.50 per share.

The company's Z score can be calculated as follows:

$$Z = 1.2(0.052) + 1.4(0.095) + 3.3(0.086) + 0.6(0.418) + 1.0(0.431)$$
$$= 1.157$$

The Z score of 1.157 indicates that the probability that Poff Industries will fail is quite high.

Table 25.7   Balance Sheet for Poff Industries

ASSETS		LIABILITIES AND STOCKHOLDERS' EQUITY	
Cash	$ 100,000	Accounts payable	$ 2,000,000
Accounts receivable	1,000,000	Notes payable—bank	1,500,000
Inventories	3,000,000	Total current liabilities	$ 3,500,000
Total current assets	$ 4,100,000	Mortgage	$ 2,000,000
Land	$ 2,000,000	Debentures	3,000,000
Net plant	2,500,000	Total long-term debt	$ 5,000,000
Net equipment	3,000,000	Preferred stock (100,000 shares)	1,000,000
Total fixed assets	$ 7,500,000	Common stock (1,000,000 shares)	1,000,000
Total	$11,600,000	Paid-in capital in excess of par	1,000,000
		Retained earnings	1,100,000
		Total stockholders' equity	$ 3,100,000
		Total	$11,600,000

Table 25.8 Income Statement for Poff Industries	
Sales	$5,000,000
Less: Cost of goods sold	3,000,000
Less: Selling and administrative expenses	1,000,000
Earnings before interest and taxes	$1,000,000
Less: Interest	500,000
Earnings before taxes	$ 500,000
Less: Taxes (40%)	200,000
Net Income	$ 300,000

Concept Review Questions

14. Why is predicting bankruptcy useful?
15. How are the five factors that determine a Z score related to the financial health of a business?

SUMMARY

- *Financial distress* refers to the condition that a firm's cash flow is insufficient to meet short-term obligations.
- *Bankruptcy* refers to the legal process that firms go through to resolve financial distress.
- Bankruptcy gives the debtor firm (and its management) an opportunity to renegotiate with creditors.
- Chapter 7 of the U.S. Bankruptcy Code governs the process of liquidating distressed firms, whereas

chapter 11 provides a legal process by which distressed firms can attempt to reorganize and emerge from bankruptcy as an ongoing entity.
- Valuation disputes are common in bankruptcy, since each party has incentive for the firm's assets to be valued in a way that is favorable to its own priority status.
- Statistical models have been developed to predict the likelihood that individual firms may go bankrupt.

KEY TERMS

absolute priority rule (APR)
automatic stay
bankruptcy
Bankruptcy Code
business failure
chapter 7

chapter 11
cramdown
debtor-in-possession (DIP)
extension
financial distress
insolvent

prepackaged bankruptcy
trustee
workout
Z score

QUESTIONS

25-1. Discuss why it makes sense to help firms attempt to reorganize rather than liquidate.

25-2. Explain why the option to delay entering bankruptcy has value for corporate managers.

25-3. Why do creditors usually accept a plan for financial rehabilitation rather than demand liquidation of a business?

25-4. "A certain number of bankruptcies are good for the economy." Discuss why you agree or disagree with this statement.

25-5. "A business should always be liquidated when the liquidation value exceeds the business's value as a going concern." Discuss why you agree or disagree with this statement.

25-6. What are the advantages and disadvantages of a voluntary workout to resolve financial distress? What are the advantages and disadvantages of declaring bankruptcy to resolve financial distress?

25-7. A business can be liquidated for $700,000, or it can be reorganized. Reorganization would require an investment of $400,000. If the company is reorganized, earnings are projected to be $150,000 per year, and the company would trade at a price/earnings ratio of 8. Should the company be liquidated or reorganized?

25-8. Explain why the priorities for liquidation are determined as they are. Do you agree with the order?

25-9. Who would use Altman's Z score to predict bankruptcy? Why would the ability to predict bankruptcy be useful to them?

25-10. What is the purpose of a prepackaged bankruptcy? Would a prepackaged bankruptcy be more likely to be used for a liquidation or a reorganization?

25-11. Why would some creditors be willing to subordinate their claims to the claims of other creditors?

PROBLEMS

Bankruptcy Patterns

25-1. Go to http://www.bankruptcydata.com and identify the largest public company bankruptcies during the previous year. Compare the list of the largest bankruptcies in U.S. history presented in Table 25.1 with the current list at http://www.bankruptcydata.com. Have any recent bankruptcies made the list?

Liquidation in Bankruptcy

25-2. A firm has $450,000 in funds to distribute to its unsecured creditors. Three possible sets of unsecured creditor claims are presented. Calculate the settlement, if any, to be received by each creditor in each case shown in the following table.

Unsecured Creditors' Claims	Case I	Case II	Case III
Unpaid balance of second mortgage	$300,000	$200,000	$ 500,000
Accounts payable	200,000	100,000	300,000
Notes payable—bank	300,000	100,000	500,000
Unsecured bonds	100,000	200,000	500,000
Total	$900,000	$600,000	$1,800,000

25-3. A firm has $5 million in funds to distribute to its unsecured creditors. Three possible sets of unsecured creditor claims are presented. Calculate the settlement, if any, to be received by each creditor in each case shown in the following table.

Unsecured Creditors' Claims	Case I	Case II	Case III
Unpaid balance of second mortgage	$1,000,000	$2,000,000	$3,000,000
Accounts payable	2,000,000	1,000,000	3,000,000
Notes payable—bank	3,000,000	2,000,000	1,000,000
Unsecured bonds	1,000,000	3,000,000	2,000,000
Total	$7,000,000	$8,000,000	$9,000,000

Smart Solutions

See the problem and solution explained step-by-step at **SMARTFinance**

25-4. A firm has $8 million in funds to distribute to its unsecured creditors. Three possible sets of unsecured creditor claims are presented. Calculate the settlement, if any, to be received by each creditor in each case shown in the following table.

Unsecured Creditors' Claims	Case I	Case II	Case III
Unpaid balance of second mortgage	$ 2,000,000	$ 2,500,000	$ 5,000,000
Accounts payable	2,500,000	3,000,000	4,000,000
Notes payable—bank	3,500,000	3,500,000	1,500,000
Unsecured bonds	4,000,000	5,000,000	5,500,000
Total	$12,000,000	$14,000,000	$16,000,000

25-5. Keck Business Forms recently failed and will be liquidated by a court-appointed trustee, who will charge $300,000 for her services. The preliquidation balance sheet follows. Assume that the trustee liquidates the assets for $4.8 million, with $2.6 million coming from the sale of current assets and $2.2 million coming from fixed assets. Also assume that the unsecured bonds are subordinate to the notes payable. Prepare a table indicating the amount to be distributed to each claimant. Do the firm's owners receive any funds?

Keck Business Forms Balance Sheet as of December 31, 2010

Assets		Liabilities and Stockholders' Equity	
Cash	$ 100,000	Accounts payable	$1,200,000
Marketable securities	50,000	Notes payable—bank	1,100,000
Accounts receivable	1,100,000	Accrued wages[a]	300,000
Inventories	2,400,000	Unpaid employee benefits[b]	200,000
Prepaid expenses	400,000	Unsecured customer deposits[c]	250,000
Total current assets	$4,050,000	Taxes payable	100,000
		Total current liabilities	$3,150,000
Land	$1,000,000	First mortgage[d]	$1,500,000
Net plant	2,100,000	Second mortgage[d]	1,000,000
Net equipment	2,300,000	Unsecured bonds	2,000,000
Total fixed assets	$5,400,000	Total long-term debt	$4,500,000
Total	$9,450,000	Preferred stock (5,000 shares)	$ 500,000
		Common stock (10,000 shares)	1,000,000
		Retained earnings	300,000
		Total stockholders' equity	$1,800,000
		Total	$9,450,000

[a] Represents wages of $2,000 or less per employee earned within 90 days of filing for bankruptcy for 400 of the firm's employees.

[b] Unpaid employee benefits that were due in the 180-day period preceding the firm's bankruptcy filing, which occurred simultaneously with the termination of its business.

[c] Unsecured customer deposits not exceeding $900 each.

[d] First and second mortgages on the firm's total fixed assets.

25-6. Oxygen Filtration Systems recently failed and will be liquidated by a court-appointed trustee, who will charge $500,000 for his services. The preliquidation balance sheet follows. Assume that the trustee liquidates the assets for $10.2 million, with $5.8 million coming from the sale of current assets and $4.4 million coming from fixed assets. Also assume that the unsecured bonds are subordinate to the notes payable. Prepare a table indicating the amount to be distributed to each claimant. Do the firm's owners receive any funds?

Oxygen Filtration Systems Balance Sheet as of December 31, 2010

Assets		Liabilities and Stockholders' Equity	
Cash	$ 600,000	Accounts payable	$ 2,500,000
Marketable securities	750,000	Notes payable—bank	4,000,000
Accounts receivable	1,750,000	Accrued wages[a]	750,000
Inventories	2,250,000	Unpaid employee benefits[b]	500,000
Prepaid expenses	900,000	Unsecured customer	500,000
Total current assets	$ 6,250,000	deposits[c]	
		Taxes payable	1,000,000
		Total current liabilities	$ 9,250,000
Land	$ 3,000,000	First mortgage[d]	$ 3,000,000
Net plant	5,000,000	Second mortgage[d]	2,000,000
Net equipment	6,250,000	Unsecured bonds	3,500,000
Total fixed assets	$ 14,250,000	Total long-term debt	$ 8,500,000
Total	$20,500,000	Preferred stock (10,000	$ 500,000
		shares)	
		Common stock (20,000	2,000,000
		shares)	
		Retained earnings	250,000
		Total stockholders'	$ 2,750,000
		equity	
		Total	$20,500,000

[a] Represents wages of $2,000 or less per employee earned within 90 days of filing bankruptcy for 400 of the firm's employees.

[b] Unpaid employee benefits that were due in the 180-day period preceding the firm's bankruptcy filing, which occurred simultaneously with the termination of its business.

[c] Unsecured customer deposits not exceeding $900 each.

[d] First and second mortgages on the firm's total fixed assets.

Predicting Bankruptcy

Smart Solutions
See the problem and solution explained step-by-step at **SMARTFinance**

25-7. Sosbee Foods has a Working capital/Total assets ratio of 0.2, a Retained earnings/Total assets ratio of 0.1, an Earnings before interest and taxes/Total assets ratio of 0.25, a Market value of equity/Book value of total liabilities ratio of 0.6, and a Sales/Total assets ratio of 0.8. Calculate and interpret the company's Z score.

25-8. Express Trailers has a Working capital/Total assets ratio of 0.3, a Retained earnings/Total assets ratio of 0.15, an Earnings before interest and taxes/Total assets ratio of 0.20, a Market value of equity/Book value of total liabilities ratio of 0.5, and a Sales/Total assets ratio of 0.75. Calculate and interpret the company's Z score.

25-9. The following balance sheet and income statement are for Weber Industries. The firm's stock currently is priced at $6 per share. Calculate and interpret the company's Z score.

Weber Industries Balance Sheet as of December 31, 2010

Assets		Liabilities and Stockholders' Equity	
Cash	$ 400,000	Accounts payable	$ 5,000,000
Accounts receivable	3,000,000	Notes payable—bank	1,000,000
Inventories	4,000,000	Total current liabilities	$ 6,000,000
Total current assets	$ 7,400,000	Mortgage	$ 4,000,000

Land	$ 1,000,000	Debentures	6,000,000
Net plant	5,000,000	Total long-term debt	$10,000,000
Net equipment	8,000,000	Preferred stock (100,000 shares)	$ 1,000,000
Total fixed assets	$14,000,000	Common stock (500,000 shares)	1,000,000
Total	$21,400,000	Paid-in capital in excess of par	2,000,000
		Retained earnings	1,400,000
		Total stockholders' equity	$ 5,400,000
		Total	$21,400,000

Weber Industries Income Statement
for the Year Ending December 31, 2010

Sales	$6,000,000
Less: Cost of goods sold	3,500,000
Less: Selling and administrative expenses	1,000,000
Earnings before interest and taxes	$1,500,000
Less: Interest	1,100,000
Earnings before taxes	400,000
Less: Taxes (30%)	120,000
Net Income	$ 280,000

25-10. Compute the Z score for General Motors Corporation given the following information for year-end 2004:

GM Financial Information (year-end 2004)

Current assets	$ 55,515,000
Current liabilities	$ 74,892,000
Retained earnings	$ 14,428,000
Total assets	$482,029,000
Total liabilities	$ 451,877,000
Shares outstanding	565,100,304
Share price	$ 29.27
Sales	$ 193,517,000
EBIT	$ 1,192,000

All values in thousands except share price and shares outstanding.

At what share price would GM have a Z score equal to 3.00? How does the future look for GM?

25-11. Compute the Z score for General Motors Corporation given the following information for year-end 2008:

GM Financial Information (year-end 2008)

Current assets	$ 41,224,000
Current liabilities	$ 73,911,000
Retained earnings	−$ 70,610,000
Total assets	$ 91,047,000
Total liabilities	$176,387,000

(continued)

GM Financial Information (year-end 2008)

Shares outstanding	610,500,684
Share price	$ 2.83
Sales	$148,979,000
EBIT	−$ 27,467,000

All values in thousands except share price and shares outstanding.

Based on its Z score, is GM likely to go bankrupt in the near future?

25-12. Compute the Z score for Ford Motor Company given the following information for year-end 2008:

Ford Financial Information (year-end 2008)

Current assets	$ 34,124,000
Current liabilities	$ 49,178,000
Retained earnings	−$ 16,145,000
Total assets	$ 218,328,000
Total liabilities	$ 235,639,000
Shares outstanding	2,412,000,000
Share price	$ 2.29
Sales	$ 146,277,000
EBIT	−$ 13,812,000

All values in thousands except share price and shares outstanding.

What proportion (measured as a percentage) of the Z score is composed of $0.60(X_4)$? Is Ford likely to go bankrupt in the near future?

25-13. Compute the Z score for Wal-Mart given the following information for year-end 2008:

Wal-Mart Financial Information (year-end 2008)

Current assets	$ 48,949,000
Current liabilities	$ 55,390,000
Retained earnings	$ 63,600,000
Total assets	$ 163,429,000
Total liabilities	$ 98,144,000
Shares outstanding	3,925,000,000
Share price	$ 47.12
Sales	$ 405,607,000
EBIT	$ 22,798,000

All values in thousands except share price and shares outstanding.

What proportion (measured as a percentage) of the Z score is composed of $0.60(X_4)$? What proportion (measured as a percentage) of the Z score is composed of $1.00(X_5)$? Is Wal-Mart likely to fail in the near-future?

THOMSON ONE Business School Edition

25-14. In July 2008, IndyMac Bancorp Inc. (ticker symbol, IDMCQ) filed for bankruptcy protection. Calculate Altman's Z score for IndyMac for the years 2004–2007. Was there deterioration in Altman's Z score over this time period? Did Altman's Z score predict IndyMac's bankruptcy? If so, by how many years in advance of the bankruptcy?

25-15. Calculate Altman's Z score for Great Atlantic & Pacific Company (ticker symbol, GAP) for the years 2004–2007. What is the trend in Altman's Z score over this time period? How do the Z scores for Great Atlantic & Pacific compare to IndyMac's?

MINI-CASE: BANKRUPTCY AND FINANCIAL DISTRESS

Flanan Photography Studios, Inc. (FPS) is preparing for a court-ordered bankruptcy and has issued the following preliquidation financial statements.

Flanan Photography Studios, Inc., Balance Sheet as of December 31, 2009

Assets		Liabilities and Stockholders' Equity	
Cash	$ 800,000	Accounts payable	$ 2,600,000
Marketable securities	24,000	Notes payable	2,200,000
Accounts receivable	3,500,000	Accrued wages	700,000
Inventories	4,000,000	Unpaid employee benefits	385,000
Prepaid expenses	1,000,000	Taxes payable	250,000
Total current assets	$ 9,324,000	Total current liabilities	$ 6,135,000
		First mortgage	$ 8,500,000
Land	$10,000,000	Second mortgage	27,000,000
Net plant	28,000,000	Unsecured bonds	28,000,000
Net equipment	32,000,000	Total long-term debt	$63,500,000
Total fixed assets	$70,000,000	Preferred stock (15,000 shares)	$ 1,500,000
Total	$79,324,000	Common stock (1,500,000 shares)	7,500,000
		Retained earnings	689,000
		Total stockholders' equity	$ 9,689,000
		Total	$79,324,000

Flanan Photography Studios, Inc., Income Statement
for the Year Ending December 31, 2009

Sales	$14,420,000
Cost of goods sold	−7,210,000
Selling and administrative expenses	−787,000
Earnings before interest and taxes	$ 6,423,000
Interest expense	−5,715,000
Earnings before taxes	$ 708,000
Taxes (30%)	−283,200
Net income	$ 424,800

TruValue Trustees Services (TTS) has been appointed to oversee the sale and disbursement of funds from the liquidation and will charge $450,000 for the service. TTS can obtain $7,250,000 from the sale of FPS's current assets and $49,850,000 from the sale of fixed assets. Accrued wages represent wages of $2,000 or less per employee, and the wages were earned within 90 days of filing bankruptcy. Unpaid employee benefits represent an amount that was due within the 180-day period preceding the bankruptcy filing. The first and second mortgages are secured by the firm's total fixed assets. The firm's stock is currently trading for $3.25 per share.

1. Calculate the amount to be received by each claimant.

2. Calculate and interpret the firm's Z score.

Key Formulas

Free Cash Flow

A firm's free cash flow (FCF) is derived from operating cash flow (OCF) and changes in asset and liability accounts as:

$$FCF = OCF - \Delta FA - (\Delta CA - \Delta AP - \Delta accruals)$$ (Eq. 2.4)

Present Value of an Ordinary Annuity

The present value of an n-year ordinary annuity of $1 per year is:

$$PV = \frac{PMT}{r} \times \left[1 - \frac{1}{(1+r)^n} \right]$$ (Eq. 3.7)

Present Value of a Perpetuity

The present value of a perpetual stream of $1 annual payments is:

$$PV = PMT \times \frac{1}{r} = \frac{PMT}{r}$$ (Eq. 3.10)

Present Value of a Growing Perpetuity

The present value of a perpetual stream of payments that grows at an annual rate g is:

$$PV = \frac{CF_1}{r - g} \quad (r > g)$$ (Eq. 3.11)

Effective Annual Interest Rate

The effective annual interest rate (EAR) can be derived from the stated rate r (given m compounding periods) as:

$$EAR = \left(1 + \frac{r}{m} \right)^m - 1$$ (Eq. 3.14)

Expected Return on a Portfolio

If the expected returns for individual assets in a portfolio are known, then the expected return of an n-asset portfolio (with individual asset weights w_i) can be found as:

$$E(R_p) = w_1 E(R_1) + w_2 E(R_2) + w_3 E(R_3) + \cdots + w_N E(R_N)$$ (Eq. 5.6)

Measures of Risk

Variance of Returns of a Single Asset

The variance of returns on a single asset i can be derived from a historical return series on N periods as:

$$\text{Variance} = \sigma^2 = \frac{\sum_{t=1}^{N}(R_{it} - \overline{R}_i)^2}{N - 1} \qquad \text{(Eq. 5.4)}$$

Covariance of Returns between Two Assets

The covariance between the returns on two assets, 1 and 2, is calculated using historical return series over N periods as:

$$\text{Cov}(R_1, R_2) = \sigma_{12} = \frac{\left[\sum_{t=1}^{N}(R_{1t} - \overline{R}_1)(R_{2t} - \overline{R}_2)\right]}{N - 1} \qquad \text{(Eq. 5.8)}$$

Correlation Coefficient

The correlation coefficient is a normalized measure of co-movement between two assets, and it is derived from the covariance (σ_{12}) as:

$$\text{Correlation coefficient} = \rho_{12} = \frac{\sigma_{12}}{\sigma_1 \sigma_2} \qquad \text{(Eq. 5.9)}$$

Variance of a Portfolio of Two Stocks

If two stocks are combined into a portfolio then the variance of the portfolio's return, which is usually less than a weighted average of the individual variances, is computed as:

$$\text{Portfolio variance} = \sigma_p^2 = w_1^2\sigma_1^2 + w_2^2\sigma_2^2 + 2w_1 w_2 \rho_{12}\sigma_1\sigma_2 \qquad \text{(Eq. 5.12)}$$

Beta

A stock's beta is a measure of the degree of co-movement between that stock's return and the overall market's return:

$$\beta_i = \frac{\sigma_{im}}{\sigma_m^2} \qquad \text{(Eq. 5.14)}$$

The Capital Market Line

The CML plots the trade-off between an asset or portfolio's risk and return in terms of expected return and standard deviation of return:

$$E(R_p) = R_f + \left[\frac{E(R_m) - R_f}{\sigma_m}\right]\sigma_p \qquad \text{(Eq. 6.1)}$$

The Capital Asset Pricing Model

The CAPM yields a unique expected return for an asset or portfolio as a linear function of that asset's beta (β_i) and the risk-free rate R_f:

$$E(R_i) = R_f + \beta_i \left[E(R_m) - R_f \right] \qquad \text{(Eq. 6.2)}$$

The Fama-French Model

The Fama-French asset pricing model generates expected returns as a function of an asset's sensitivity to a market factor ($R_m - R_f$), a size factor ($R_{small} - R_{big}$), and a book-to-market factor ($R_{high} - R_{low}$):

$$R_i - R_f = \alpha + \beta_{i1}\left(R_m - R_f\right) + \beta_{i2}\left(R_{small} - R_{big}\right) + \beta_{i3}\left(R_{high} - R_{low}\right) \qquad \text{(Eq. 6.3)}$$

Net Present Value

Finance's basic valuation model computes the NPV of a project or an asset, usually by subtracting the sum of a series of discounted cash inflows from a single cash outflow (CF_0):

$$NPV = CF_0 + \frac{CF_1}{(1+r)^1} + \frac{CF_2}{(1+r)^2} + \frac{CF_3}{(1+r)^3} + \cdots + \frac{CF_N}{(1+r)^N} \qquad \text{(Eq. 7.1)}$$

The Weighted Average Cost of Capital [with taxes]

Incorporating corporate taxes allows one to calculate a firm's WACC when it must pay taxes at rate T_c on its income:

$$WACC = \left(\frac{D}{D+E}\right)(1 - T_c)r_D + \left(\frac{E}{D+E}\right)r_E \qquad \text{(Eq. 9.3)}$$

Asset Beta [without taxes]

Asset betas are derived from equity betas as:

$$\beta_A = \left(\frac{D}{D+E}\right)\beta_D + \left(\frac{E}{D+E}\right)\beta_E \qquad \text{(Eq. 9.4)}$$

Equity Beta [with taxes]

When a firm must pay corporate income taxes, the relationship between asset and equity betas (assuming the debt beta is zero) is given by:

$$\beta_E = \beta_A\left[1 + (1 - T_c)\frac{D}{E}\right] \qquad \text{(Eq. 9.6)}$$

M&M Proposition I

Modigliani and Miller's famous Proposition I states that a firm's value (V) is determined by discounting its stream of expected net operating income and is independent of capital structure:

$$V = (E + D) = \frac{NOI}{r_A} \qquad \text{(Eq. 12.1)}$$

M&M Proposition II

Proposition II determines the rate at which the expected return on a levered firm's equity (r_l) must increase as debt is substituted for equity in its capital structure:

$$r_l = r_A + (r_A - r_d)\left(\frac{D}{E}\right) \tag{Eq. 12.2}$$

Value of a Levered Firm [including only corporate taxes]

In the presence of corporate income taxes, the value of a levered firm is equal to the value of an otherwise equivalent unlevered firm plus the value of the interest tax shields on its debt:

$$V_L = V_U + \text{PV(Interest tax shield)} = V_U + T_cD = \$650{,}000 + \$175{,}000$$
$$= \$825{,}000 \tag{Eq. 12.5}$$

Gain from Leverage

In the presence of both corporate and personal taxes, the gain from leverage for a firm is a function of the effective tax rates on corporate profits (T_c), equity income received by investors (T_{ps}), and interest income received by investors (T_{pd}):

$$G_L = \left\{1 - \left[\frac{(1 - T_c)(1 - T_{ps})}{1 - T_{pd}}\right]\right\} D \tag{Eq. 12.6}$$

Put–Call Parity

The put–call parity formula shows the relationship that must hold between the values of the stock price (S), the put (P), the call (C), and the present value of the common exercise price $(\$X)$ of the put and call options in order to prevent arbitrage:

$$S + P = B + C$$
$$= \text{PV}(X) + C \tag{Eq. 18.1}$$

The Black and Scholes Option Pricing Model

The value of a call option, C, is given as:

$$C = SN(d_1) - Xe^{-rt}N(d_2);$$

$$d_1 = \frac{\ln\left(\frac{S}{X}\right) + \left(r + \frac{\sigma^2}{2}\right)t}{\sigma\sqrt{t}} \tag{Eq. 19.1}$$

$$d_2 = d_1 - \sigma\sqrt{t} \tag{Eq. 19.2}$$

where

S = current market price of underlying stock
X = strike price of option
t = amount of time (in years) before option expires
r = annual risk-free interest rate
σ = annual standard deviation of underlying stock's returns
e = 2.718 (approximately)
$N(X)$ = probability of drawing, from the standard normal distribution, a value that is less than or equal to X

The Forward Premium or Discount [exchange rates]

The annualized forward discount or premium of a currency is:

$$\frac{F - S}{S} \times \frac{360}{N}$$

(Eq. 20.1)

The Parity Conditions of International Finance

Forward–Spot Parity

In equilibrium, the forward rate (F) observed for a currency should be equal to the expected future spot exchange rate, $E(S)$, for that currency:

$$E(S) = F$$

(Eq. 20.2)

Purchasing Power Parity

PPP expresses a currency's expected future spot exchange rate [$E(S_{\text{for/dom}})$], relative to today's spot rate ($S_{\text{for/dom}}$), as a function of the relative expected inflation rates in the foreign, $E(i_{\text{for}})$, and domestic, $E(i_{\text{dom}})$, markets:

$$\frac{E(S_{\text{for/dom}})}{S_{\text{for/dom}}} = \frac{\left[1 + E(i_{\text{for}})\right]}{\left[1 + E(i_{\text{dom}})\right]}$$

(Eq. 20.4)

Interest Rate Parity

IRP expresses a currency's forward exchange rate ($F_{\text{for/dom}}$), relative to today's spot rate ($S_{\text{for/dom}}$), as a function of the relative interest rates in the foreign (R_{for}) and domestic (R_{dom}) markets:

$$\frac{F_{\text{for/dom}}}{S_{\text{for/dom}}} = \frac{1 + R_{\text{for}}}{1 + R_{\text{dom}}}$$

(Eq. 20.5)

Real Interest Parity

The real interest parity relationship expresses interest rate parity in real rather than nominal terms:

$$\frac{1 + R_{\text{for}}}{1 + R_{\text{dom}}} = \frac{1 + E(i_{\text{for}})}{1 + E(i_{\text{dom}})}$$

(Eq. 20.6)

Forward Price of an Asset

Given a risk-free rate of interest R_f, the forward price (F) of an asset or commodity to be delivered n periods in the future can be derived from the current spot price (S_0) as:

$$F = S_0(1 + R_f)^n$$

(Eq. 27.1)

Bibliography

Ackermann, Carl, Richard McEnally, and David Ravenscraft. 1999. "The Performance of Hedge Funds: Risk, Return, and Incentives." *Journal of Finance* 54 (June), pp. 833–874.

Aggarwal, Reena. 2003. "Allocation of Initial Public Offerings and Flipping Activity." *Journal of Financial Economics* 68 (April), pp. 111–135.

Aggarwal, Reena, Laurie Krigman, and Kent Womack. 2002. "Strategic IPO Underpricing, Information Momentum, and Lockup Expiration Selling." *Journal of Financial Economics* 66 (October), pp. 105–137.

Aggarwal, Reena, Nagpurnanand R. Prabhala, and Manju Puri. 2002. "Institutional Allocation in Initial Public Offerings: Empirical Evidence." *Journal of Finance* 57 (June), pp. 1421–1442.

Ahn, Seoungpil, and David J. Denis. 2004. "Internal Capital Markets and Investment Policy: Evidence from Corporate Spinoffs." *Journal of Financial Economics* 71 (March), pp. 489–516.

Altınkılıç, Oya, and Robert S. Hansen. 2003. "Another Equity Issue Riddle: Why Is the Bear So Often There?" Working paper, University of Pittsburgh (August).

Altman, Edward. 2009. "Post-Chapter 11 Bankruptcy Performance, Avoiding Chapter 22." Working paper, Stern School of Business, New York University.

Altman, Edward I., and Brenda J. Karlin. 2008. "Defaults and Returns in the High-Yield Bond Market: Third-Quarter 2008 Review." Working paper, Stern School of Business, New York University.

Altman, Edward I., and Heather J. Suggitt. 2000. "Default Rates in the Syndicated Bank Loan Market: A Mortality Analysis." *Journal of Banking and Finance* 24, pp. 229–253.

Ambarish, Ramasastry, Kose John, and Joseph Williams. 1987. "Efficient Signalling with Dividends and Investments." *Journal of Finance* 42 (June), pp. 321–343.

Anderson, Christopher W., and Anil K. Makhija. 1999. "Deregulation, Disintermediation and Agency Costs of Debt: Evidence from Japan." *Journal of Financial Economics* 51 (February), pp. 309–339.

Andrade, Gregor, Mark Mitchell, and Erik Stafford. 2001. "New Evidence and Perspectives on Merger." *Journal of Economic Perspectives* 15 (Spring), pp. 103–120.

Ang, James S., and James C. Brau. 2003. "Concealing and Confounding Adverse Signals: Insider Wealth-Maximizing Behavior in the IPO Process." *Journal of Financial Economics* 67 (January), pp. 149–172.

Asplund, Marcus. 2000. "What Fraction of a Capital Investment Is Sunk Costs?" *Journal of Industrial Economics* 48 (September), pp. 287–304.

Asquith, Paul. 1995. "Convertible Bonds Are Not Called Late." *Journal of Finance* 50 (September), pp. 1275–1289.

Asquith, Paul, and Thierry Wizman. 1990. "Event Risk, Covenants, and Bondholder Returns in Leveraged Buyouts." *Journal of Financial Economics* 27 (September), pp. 195–213.

Autore, Don M., Raman Kumar, and Dilip K. Shome. 2008. "The Revival of Shelf-Registered Corporate Equity Offerings." *Journal of Corporate Finance* 14 (February), pp. 32–50.

Baker, Malcolm, and Jeffrey Wurgler. 2002. "Market Timing and Capital Structure." *Journal of Finance* 57 (February), pp. 1–32.

———. 2004a. "A Catering Theory of Dividends." *Journal of Finance* 59 (June), pp. 1125–1165.

———. 2004b. "Appearing and Disappearing Dividends: The Link to Catering Incentives." *Journal of Financial Economics* 73 (August), pp. 271–288.

Barber, Brad M., and Terrance Odean. 2002. "Online Investors: Do the Slow Die First?" *Review of Financial Studies* 15 (Special), pp. 455–487.

Barclay, Michael J., and Clifford W. Smith, Jr. 1995a. "The Maturity Structure of Corporate Debt." *Journal of Finance* 50 (June), pp. 609–631.

———. 1995b. "The Priority Structure of Corporate Liabilities." *Journal of Finance* 50 (July), pp. 899–917.

Barclay, Michael J., Clifford W. Smith, Jr., and Ross L. Watts. 1995. "The Determinants of Corporate Leverage and Dividend Policies." *Journal of Applied Corporate Finance* 17 (Winter), pp. 4–19.

Beattie, Vivien, Alan Goodacre, and Sarah Thomson. 2000. "Recognition versus Disclosure: An Investigation of the Impact on Equity Risk Using UK Operating Lease Disclosures." *Journal of Business Finance & Accounting* 27 (November/December), pp. 1185–1224.

Beatty, Randolph P., and Ivo Welch. 1996. "Issuer Expenses and Legal Liability in Initial Public Offerings." *Journal of Law and Economics* 39 (December), pp. 545–602.

Beck, Thorsten, Asli Demirgüç-Kunt, and Ross Levine. 2003. "Law, Endowments and Finance." *Journal of Financial Economics* 70 (November), pp. 137–181.

Beck, Thorsten, Asli Demirgüç-Kunt, and Vojislav Maksimovic. 2005. "Financial and Legal Constraints to Growth: Does Firm Size Matter?" *Journal of Finance* 60 (February), pp. 137–177.

Benveniste, Lawrence M., Alexander Ljungqvist, William J. Wilhelm, Jr., and Xiaoyun Yu. 2003. "Evidence of Information Spillovers in the Production of Investment Banking Services." *Journal of Finance* 58 (April), pp. 577–608.

Benveniste, Lawrence M., and Paul A. Spindt. 1989. "How Investment Bankers Determine the Offer Price and Allocation for New Issues." *Journal of Financial Economics* 24 (October), pp. 343–361.

Berger, Philip, and Eli Ofek. 1995. "Diversification's Effect on Firm Value." *Journal of Financial Economics* 37 (January), pp. 39–65.

Berger, Philip G., Eli Ofek, and David L. Yermack. 1997. "Managerial Entrenchment and Capital Structure Decisions." *Journal of Finance* 54 (September), pp. 1411–1438.

Bhagat, Sanjai, Ming Dong, David Hirshleifer, and Robert Noah. 2005. "Do Tender Offers Create Value? New Methods and Evidence." *Journal of Financial Economics* 76 (April), pp. 3–60.

Bhattacharya, Sudipto. 1979. "Imperfect Information, Dividend Policy, and 'The Bird in the Hand' Fallacy." *Bell Journal of Economics* 10 (Spring), pp. 259–270.

Bhattacharya, Utpal, and Hazem Daouk. 2002. "The World Price of Insider Trading." *Journal of Finance* 57, pp. 75–108.

Bhattacharya, Utpal, Hazem Daouk, Brian Jorgenson, and Carl-Heinrich Kehr. 2000. "When Is an Event Not an Event: The Curious Case of an Emerging Market." *Journal of Financial Economics* 55, pp. 69–101.

Billett, Matthew T., Tao-Hsien Dolly King, and David C. Mauer. 2004. "Bondholder Wealth Effects in Mergers and Acquisitions: New Evidence from the 1980s and 1990s." *Journal of Finance* 59 (February), pp. 107–135.

———. 2007. "Growth Opportunities and the Choice of Leverage, Debt Maturity, and Covenants." *Journal of Finance* 62 (April), pp. 697–730.

Bittlingmayer, George, and Thomas W. Hazlett. 2000. "DOS Kapital: Has Antitrust Action against Microsoft Created Value in the Computer Industry?" *Journal of Financial Economics* 55, pp. 329–359.

Black, Fischer. 1975. "Fact and Fantasy in the Use of Options." *Financial Analysts Journal* 31 (July/August), pp. 36–41, 61–72.

Black, Fischer, Michael C. Jensen, and Myron Scholes. 1972. "The Capital Asset Pricing Model: Some Empirical Tests." In *Studies in the Theory of Capital Markets*, edited by Michael C. Jensen (New York: Praeger).

Blass, Asher, and Yishay Yafeh. 2001. "Vagabond Shoes Longing to Stray: Why Foreign Firms List in the United States." *Journal of Banking and Finance* 25 (March), pp. 555–572.

Bonser-Neal, Catherine, and Timothy Morley. 1997. "Does the Yield Spread Predict Real Economic Activity: A Multi-Country Analysis." Federal Reserve Bank of Kansas City *Economic Review* (Third Quarter), pp. 37–53.

Booth, James R. 1992. "Contract Costs, Bank Loans, and the Cross-Monitoring Hypothesis." *Journal of Financial Economics* 31 (February), pp. 25–41.

Booth, James R., and Lena Chua. 1996. "Ownership Dispersion, Costly Information, and IPO Underpricing." *Journal of Financial Economics* 41, pp. 291–310.

Bortolotti, Bernardo, William Megginson, and Scott Smart. 2008. "The Rise of Accelerated Seasoned Equity Underwritings." *Journal of Applied Corporate Finance* 20 (Summer), pp. 35–57.

Bradley, Michael, Anand Desai, and E. Han Kim. 1988. "Synergistic Gains from Corporate Acquisitions and Their Division between the Stockholders of Target and Acquiring Firms." *Journal of Financial Economics* 21 (May), pp. 3–40.

Brav, Alon, Christopher Geczy, and Paul A. Gompers. 2000. "Is the Abnormal Return Following Equity Issuances Anomalous?" *Journal of Financial Economics* 56, pp. 209–249.

Brav, Alon, and Paul A. Gompers. 1997. "Myth or Reality? The Long-Run Underperformance of Initial Public Offerings: Evidence from Venture and Non-Venture Capital–Backed Companies." *Journal of Finance* 52 (December), pp. 1791–1821.

———. 2003. "The Role of Lockups in Initial Public Offerings." *Review of Financial Studies* 16, pp. 1–29.

Brav, Alon, John R. Graham, Campbell R. Harvey, and Roni Michaely. 2005. "Payout Policy in the 21st Century." *Journal of Financial Economics* 77, pp. 483–527.

Brealey, Richard A., Ian A. Cooper, and Michel A. Habib. 1996. "Using Project Finance to Fund Infrastructure Investments." *Journal of Applied Corporate Finance* 9 (Fall), pp. 25–38.

Brennan, Michael J., and Eduardo S. Schwartz. 1985. "Evaluating Natural Resource Investments." *Journal of Business* 58 (April), pp. 135–157.

Brown, Stephen J., and Jerold B. Warner. 1985. "Using Daily Stock Returns in the Case of Event Studies." *Journal of Financial Economics* 14 (March), pp. 205–258.

Bruner, Robert, Susan Chaplinsky, and Latha Ramchand. 2004. "US-Bound IPOs: Issue Costs and Selective Entry." *Financial Management* 33 (Autumn), pp. 39–60.

Bryan, Stephen, Robert Nash, and Ajay Patel. 2009. "Law and Executive Compensation: How the Legal System Affects the Equity Mix in Executive Compensation." *Financial Management* 1 (Winter), pp. 68–94.

Carey, Mark. 1998. "Credit Risk in Private Debt Portfolios." *Journal of Finance* 52 (August), pp. 1363–1387.

Carey, Mark and Greg Nini. 2007. "Is the Corporate Loan Market Globally Integrated? A Pricing Puzzle." *Journal of Finance* 62 (December), pp. 2969–3007.

Carlin, Wendy, and Colin Mayer. 2003. "Finance, Investment, and Growth." *Journal of Financial Economics* 69 (July), pp. 191–226.

Chan, Louis K. D., Jason Karceski, and Josef Lakonishok. 2003. "The Level of Persistence of Growth Rates." *Journal of Finance* 58, pp. 643–684.

Chava, Sudheer, and Michael R. Roberts. 2008. "How Does Financing Impact Investment? The Role of Debt Covenants." *Journal of Finance* 63 (October), pp. 2085–2121.

Chen, Hsuan-Chi, and Jay Ritter. 2000. "The Seven Percent Solution." *Journal of Finance* 55 (June), pp. 1105–1131.

Claessens, Stijn, and Luc Laeven. 2003. "Financial Development, Property Rights, and Growth." *Journal of Finance* 58 (December), pp. 2401–2437.

Cliff, Michel, and David Denis. 2004. "Do Initial Public Offering Firms Purchase Analyst Coverage with Underpricing?" *Journal of Finance* 59 (December), pp. 2871–2901.

Cohen, Gil, and Joseph Yagil. 2007. "A Multinational Survey of Corporate Financial Policies." *Journal of Applied Finance* 17 (Spring/Summer), pp. 57–69.

Comment, Robert, and Gregg Jarrell. 1995. "Corporate Focus and Stock Returns." *Journal of Financial Economics* 37 (January), pp. 67–87.

Cornelli, Francesca, and David Goldreich. 2001. "Bookbuilding and Strategic Allocation." *Journal of Finance* 56 (December), pp. 2337–2370.

———. 2003. "Bookbuilding: How Informative Is the Order Book?" *Journal of Finance* 58 (August), pp. 1415–1443.

Corwin, Shane A. 2003. "The Determinants of Underpricing for Seasoned Equity Offers." *Journal of Finance* 58 (October), pp. 2249–2279.

Corwin, Shane, Jeffrey H. Harris, and Marc L. Lipson. 2004. "The Development of Secondary Market Liquidity for NYSE-Listed IPOs." *Journal of Finance* 58 (October), pp. 2339–2373.

Coval, Joshua D., and Tyler Shumway. 2005. "Do Behavioral Biases Affect Prices?" *Journal of Finance* 60, pp. 1–34.

Dailami, Mansoor, and Robert Hauswald. 2007. "Credit-Spread Determinants and Interlocking Contracts: A Study of the Ras Gas Projects." *Journal of Financial Economics* 86, pp. 248–278.

Daniel, Kent, David Hirshleifer, and Avindhar Subrahmanyam. 1998. "Investor Psychology and Under- and Overreactions." *Journal of Finance* 53 (December), pp. 1839–1882.

DeAngelo, Harry, and Ronald W. Masulis. 1980. "Optimal Capital Structure under Corporate and Personal Taxation." *Journal of Financial Economics* 8 (March), pp. 3–30.

DeGeorge, Francois, François Derrien, and Kent L. Womack. 2007. "Analyst Hype in IPOs: Explaining the Popularity of Bookbuilding." *Review of Financial Studies* 20 (July), pp. 1021–1058.

DeGeorge, Francois, and Richard Zeckhauser. 1993. "The Reverse LBO Decision and Firm Performance." *Journal of Finance* 48 (September), pp. 1323–1348.

———. 1996. "The Financial Performance of Reverse Leveraged Buyouts." *Journal of Financial Economics* 42 (November), pp. 293–332.

Demirgüç-Kunt, Asli, and Vojislav Maksimovic. 1998. "Law, Finance, and Firm Growth." *Journal of Finance* 53 (December), pp. 2107–2139.

———. 1999. "Institutions, Financial Markets, and Firm Debt Maturity." *Journal of Financial Economics* 54 (December), pp. 295–336.

Dennis, Debra, and John McConnell. 1986. "Corporate Mergers and Security Returns." *Journal of Financial Economics* 16 (June), pp. 143–187.

Detragiache, Enrica, Paolo Garella, and Luigi Guiso. 2000. "Multiple versus Single Banking Relationships: Theory and Evidence." *Journal of Finance* 55 (June), pp. 1133–1161.

Diamond, Douglas W. 1991. "Monitoring and Reputation: The Choice between Bank Loans and Directly Placed Debt." *Journal of Political Economy* 99, pp. 689–721.

Dichev, Ilia D., and Joseph D. Piotroski. 2001. "The Long-Run Stock Returns following Bond Ratings Changes." *Journal of Finance* 56 (February), pp. 173–203.

Dimson, Elroy, Paul R. Marsh, and Mike Staunton. 2002. *Triumph of the Optimists: 101 Years of Global Investments* (Princeton, NJ: Princeton University Press).

Doidge, Craig, G. Andrew Karolyi, and René M. Stulz. 2004. "Why Are Foreign Firms Listed in the U.S. Worth More?" *Journal of Financial Economics* 71 (February), pp. 205–238.

Dunn, Kenneth B., and Chester S. Spatt. 1984. "A Strategic Analysis of Sinking Fund Bonds." *Journal of Financial Economics* 13 (September), pp. 399–424.

Dyck, Alexander, and Luigi Zingales. 2004. "Control Premiums and the Effectiveness of Corporate Governance Systems." *Journal of Applied Finance* 16 (Spring/Summer), pp. 51–72.

Dyl, Edward A., and Michael D. Joehnek. 1979. "Sinking Funds and the Cost of Corporate Debt." *Journal of Finance* 34 (September), pp. 887–893.

Eckbo, B. Espen, Ronald W. Masulis, and Øyvind Norli. 2000. "Seasoned Public Offerings: Resolution of the 'New Issues Puzzle.'" *Journal of Financial Economics* 56 (May), pp. 251–291.

Eckbo, B. Espen, and Øyvind Norli. 2005. "Liquidity Risk, Leverage and Long-Run IPO Returns." *Journal of Corporate Finance* 11 (March), pp. 251–291.

El-Gazzar, Samir, and Victor Pastena. 1990. "Negotiated Accounting Rules in Private Financial Contracts." *Journal of Accounting and Economics* 12 (March), pp. 381–396.

Emanuel, David C., and James D. MacBeth. 1982. "Further Results on the Constant Elasticity of Variance Call Option Pricing Model." *Journal of Financial and Quantitative Analysis* 17 (November), pp. 533–554.

Errunza, Vihang R., and Darius P. Miller. 2000. "Market Segmentation and the Cost of Capital in International Equity Markets." *Journal of Financial and Quantitative Analysis* 35 (December), pp. 577–600.

Esty, Benjamin C. 2002. "Returns on Project Financed Investments: Theory and Implications." Teaching note 9-202-102, Harvard Business School (February).

Faccio, Mara, and Larry H. P. Lang. 2002. "The Ultimate Ownership of Western European Corporations." *Journal of Financial Economics* 65 (September), pp. 365–395.

Faccio, Mara, and Ronald W. Masulis. 2005. "The Choice of Payment Method in European Mergers and Acquisitions." *Journal of Finance* 60 (June), pp. 1345–1388.

Fama, Eugene F. 1991. "Efficient Capital Markets: II." *Journal of Finance* 46 (December), pp. 1575–1617.

———. 1998. "Market Efficiency, Long-Term Returns, and Behavioral Finance." *Journal of Financial Economics* 49, pp. 283–306.

Fama, Eugene F., Lawrence Fisher, Michael C. Jensen, and Richard Roll. 1969. "The Adjustment of Stock Prices to New Information." *International Economic Review* 10 (February), pp. 1–21.

Fama, Eugene F., and Kenneth R. French. 1992. "The Cross-Section of Expected Returns." *Journal of Finance* 47 (June), pp. 427–465.

———. 1996. "Multifactor Explanations of Asset Pricing Anomalies." *Journal of Finance* 51 (March), pp. 55–84.

———. 2001. "Disappearing Dividends: Changing Firm Characteristics or Lower Propensity to Pay?" *Journal of Financial Economics* 60 (April), pp. 3–43.

———. 2002. "The Equity Premium." *Journal of Finance* 57 (April), pp. 637–659.

Fama, Eugene F., and James D. MacBeth. 1973. "Risk, Return, and Equilibrium: Empirical Tests." *Journal of Political Economy* 81 (May/June), pp. 607–636.

Fee, C. Edward, and Shawn Thomas. 2004. "Sources of Gains in Horizontal Mergers: Evidence from Customer, Supplier, and Rival Firms." *Journal of Financial Economics* 74 (December), pp. 423–460.

Fenn, George W., and Nellie Liang. 2001. "Corporate Payout Policy and Managerial Stock Incentives." *Journal of Financial Economics* 60 (April), pp. 45–72.

Fernandez, Pablo. 2009. "Market Risk Premium in 2008: A Survey with 2,500 Answers." Working paper, IESE Business School, University of Navarra, Spain.

Field, Laura Casares, and Jonathan Karpoff. 2002. "Takeover Defenses at IPO Firms." *Journal of Finance* 57, pp. 1857–1889.

Gangahar, Anuj. 2008. "Citigroup Rescue Lifts Confidence." *Financial Times* (November 29).

Gerlach, Stefan. 2002. "Hong Kong's Currency Board: Modelling the Discretion on the Strong Side." Working paper, Hong Kong Institute for Monetary Research.

Gompers, Paul A., and Josh Lerner. 2003. "The Really Long-Run Performance of Initial Public Offerings: The Pre-NASDAQ Evidence." *Journal of Finance* 58 (August), pp. 1355–1392.

Graham, John R. 2000. "How Big Are the Tax Benefits of Debt?" *Journal of Finance* 55 (October), pp. 1901–1941.

Graham, John R., and Campbell R. Harvey. 1996. "Market Timing Ability and Volatility Implied in Investment Newsletters' Asset Allocation Recommendations." *Journal of Financial Economics* 42 (November), pp. 397–421.

———. 2001. "The Theory and Practice of Corporate Finance: Evidence from the Field." *Journal of Financial Economics* 60, pp. 187–243.

———. 2002. "Expectations of Equity Risk Premia from a Corporate Finance Perspective." Working paper, Duke University.

Graham, John R., Campbell R. Harvey, and Manju Puri. 2008. "Capital Allocation and Delegation of Decision-Making Authority within Firms." Working paper, Duke University and NBER.

Graham, John R., Campbell R. Harvey, and Shiva Rajgopal. 2005. "The Economic Implications of Corporate Financial Reporting." *Journal of Accounting and Economics* 40, pp. 3–73.

Greene, Jason, and Scott Smart. 1999. "Liquidity Provision and Noise Trading: Evidence from the Investment Dartboard Column." *Journal of Finance* 54 (October), pp. 1885–1899.

Grenadier, Steven R. 1995. "Valuing Lease Contracts: A Real Options Approach." *Journal of Financial Economics* 38 (July), pp. 297–331.

———. 1996. "Leasing and Credit Risk." *Journal of Financial Economics* 42 (November), pp. 333–364.

Grinblatt, Mark S., Ronald W. Masulis, and Sheridan Titman. 1984. "The Valuation of Stock Splits and Stock Dividends." *Journal of Financial Economics* 13 (December), pp. 461–490.

Guedes, Jose, and Tim Opler. 1996. "The Determinants of the Maturity of Corporate Debt Issues." *Journal of Finance* 51 (December), pp. 1809–1833.

Hanley, Kathleen W. 1993. "The Underpricing of Initial Public Offerings and the Partial Adjustment Phenomenon." *Journal of Financial Economics* 34 (October), pp. 231–250.

Hanley, Kathleen W., and William J. Wilhelm, Jr. 1995. "Evidence on the Strategic Allocation of Initial Public Offerings." *Journal of Financial Economics* 37 (February), pp. 239–257.

Harford, Jarrad. 1999. "Corporate Cash Reserves and Acquisitions." *Journal of Finance* 54 (December), pp. 1969–1997.

Harvey, Campbell. 1993. "The Term Structure Forecasts Economic Growth." *Financial Analysts Journal* (May/June), pp. 6–8.

Henderson, Brian J., Narasimhan Jegadeesh, and Michael S. Weisbach. 2006. "World Markets for Raising New Capital." *Journal of Financial Economics* 82 (October), pp. 63–101.

Hertzel, Michael, Michael L. Lemmon, James S. Linck, and Richard L. Smith. 2002. "Long-Run Performance following Private Placements of Equity." *Journal of Finance* 57 (December), pp. 2595–2617.

Higgins, Robert C. 1981. "Sustainable Growth under Inflation." *Financial Management* 10, pp. 36–40.

Hirshleifer, David, and Tyler Shumway. 2003. "Good Day Sunshine: Stock Returns and the Weather." *Journal of Finance* 58, pp. 1009–1032.

Hite, Gailen L., and James E. Owers. 1983. "Security Price Reactions around Corporate Spinoff Announcements." *Journal of Financial Economics* 12, pp. 409–436.

Ho, Thomas, and Donald F. Singer. 1984. "The Value of Corporate Debt with a Sinking Fund Provision." *Journal of Business* 57 (September), pp. 315–336.

Hotchkiss, Edith S. 1995. "Postbankruptcy Performance and Management Turnover." *Journal of Finance* 50 (March), pp. 3–21.

Houston, Joel, and Christopher James. 1996. "Bank Information Monopolies and the Mix of Private and Public Debt Claims." *Journal of Finance* 51 (December), pp. 1863–1889.

Igawa, Kazuhiro, and George Kanatas. 1990. "Asymmetric Information, Collateral, and Moral Hazard." *Journal of Financial and Quantitative Analysis* 25 (December), pp. 469–490.

Ivanov, Vladimir, and Craig M. Lewis. 2008. "The Determinants of Market-Wide Issue Cycles for Initial Public Offerings." *Journal of Corporate Finance* 14 (December), pp. 567–583.

Jaffe, Jeffrey F. 1974. "Special Information and Insider Trading." *Journal of Business* 47, pp. 410–428.

Jayaraman, Narasimhan, Kuldeep Shastri, and Kishore Tandon. 1993. "The Impact of International Cross Listings on Risk and Returns: The Evidence of American Depositary Receipts." *Journal of Banking and Finance* 17, pp. 91–103.

Jegadeesh, Narasimhan. 2000. "Long-Term Performance of Seasoned Equity Offerings: Benchmark Errors and Biases in Expectations." *Financial Management* 29 (Autumn), pp. 5–30.

Jenkinson, Tim, and Howard Jones. 2004. "Bids and Allocations in European IPO Bookbuilding." *Journal of Finance* 59 (October), pp. 2309–2338.

Jensen, Michael C. 2005. "Agency Costs of Over-valued Equity." *Financial Management* 34 (Spring), pp. 5–19.

Jensen, Michael C., and William H. Meckling. 1976. "Theory of the Firm: Managerial Behavior, Agency Costs, and Ownership Structure." *Journal of Financial Economics* 3 (October), pp. 305–360.

Jensen, Michael, and Richard Ruback. 1983. "The Market for Corporate Control: The Scientific Evidence." *Journal of Financial Economics* 11 (April), pp. 5–50.

Jiménez, Gabriel, Vicente Salas, and Jesús Saurina. 2006. "Determinants of Collateral." *Journal of Financial Economics* 81, pp. 255–281.

John, Kose, and Larry H. P. Lang. 1991. "Insider Trading around Dividend Announcements: Theory and Evidence." *Journal of Finance* 40 (September), pp. 1361–1389.

John, Kose, and Joseph Williams. 1985. "Dividends, Dilution and Taxes: A Signalling Equilibrium." *Journal of Finance* 40 (September), pp. 1053–1070.

Jones, Jonathan, William W. Lang, and Peter Nigro. 2000. "Recent Trends in Bank Loan Syndications: Evidence for 1995 to 1999." Working Paper no. 2000-10, Office of the Comptroller of the Currency.

Kalay, Avner, Rajeev Singhal, and Elizabeth Tashjian. 2007. "Is Chapter 11 Costly?" *Journal of Financial Economics* 84, pp. 772–796.

Karolyi, G. Andrew. 1998. "Sourcing Equity Internationally with Depositary Receipt Offerings: Two Exceptions That Prove the Rule." *Journal of Applied Corporate Finance* 10 (Winter), pp. 90–101.

Kensinger, John, and John D. Martin. 1988. "Project Finance: Raising Money the Old-Fashioned Way." *Journal of Applied Corporate Finance* 1 (Spring), pp. 69–81.

Kim, Woojin, and Michael S. Weisbach. 2008. "Motivations for Public Equity Offers: An International Perspective." *Journal of Financial Economics* 87 (February), pp. 281–307.

Kim, Yong Cheol, and René M. Stulz. 1988. "The Eurobond Market and Corporate Financial Policy: A Test of the Clientele Hypothesis." *Journal of Financial Economics* 22, pp. 189–206.

Kini, Omesh, William Kracaw, and Shehzad Mian. 2004. "The Nature of Discipline by Corporate Takeovers." *Journal of Finance* 59 (August), pp. 1511–1552.

Kleimeier, Stefanie, and William L. Megginson. 2000. "Are Project Finance Loans Different from Other Syndicated Credits?" *Journal of Applied Corporate Finance* 12 (Winter), pp. 75–87.

KPMG Peat Marwick. 1998. *Going Public: What the CEO Needs to Know* (KPMG International).

Krigman, Laurie, Wayne H. Shaw, and Kent L. Womack. 1999. "The Persistence of IPO Mispricing and the Predictive Power of Flipping." *Journal of Finance* 54 (June), pp. 1015–1044.

Krishnan, V. Sivarama, and R. Charles Moyer. 1994. "Bankruptcy Costs and the Financial Leasing Decision." *Financial Management* 23 (Summer), pp. 31–42.

Krishnaswami, Sudha, Paul A. Spindt, and Venkat Subramaniam. 1999. "Information Asymmetry, Monitoring, and the Placement Structure of Corporate Debt." *Journal of Financial Economics* 51, pp. 407–434.

Lamont, Owen A., and Christopher Polk. 2002. "Does Diversification Destroy Value? Evidence from the Industry Shocks." *Journal of Financial Economics* 63 (January), pp. 51–77.

Lamont, Owen, and Richard H. Thaler. 2002. "Can the Market Add and Subtract? Mispricing in Tech Stock Carve-Outs." Working paper, University of Chicago.

La Porta, Rafael, Florencio López-de-Silanes, and Andrei Shleifer. 1999. "Corporate Ownership around the World." *Journal of Finance* 54 (April), pp. 471–517.

———. 2000. "Government Ownership of Banks." Working Paper no. 7620, National Bureau of Economic Research, Cambridge, MA.

La Porta, Rafael, Florencio López-de-Silanes, Andrei Shleifer, and Robert W. Vishny. 1997. "Legal Determinants of External Finance." *Journal of Finance* 52 (July), pp. 1131–1150.

———. 1998. "Law and Finance." *Journal of Political Economy* 106, pp. 1113–1150.

———. 1999. "The Quality of Government." *Journal of Law, Economics, and Organization* 15, pp. 222–279.

———. 2000. "Agency Problems and Dividend Policies around the World." *Journal of Finance* 55 (February), pp. 1–33.

———. 2002. "Investor Protection and Corporate Valuation." *Journal of Finance* 57 (June), pp. 1147–1170.

Lasfer, M. Ameziane, and Mario Levis. 1998. "The Determinants of the Leasing Decision of Small and Large Companies." *European Financial Management* (June), pp. 159–184.

Leary, Mark, and Roberts, Michael. 2007. "Do Firms Rebalance their Capital Structures?" *Journal of Finance* 60 (December 2005), pp. 2575–2619.

Leary, Mark, and Roni Michaely. 2008. "Why Firms Smooth Dividends: Empirical Evidence." Working paper, Johnson Graduate School of Management, Cornell University, Ithaca, NY.

Lee, Inmoo, Scott Lochhead, Jay Ritter, and Quanshui Zhao. 1996. "The Costs of Raising Capital." *Journal of Financial Research* 19 (Spring), pp. 59–74.

Lehn, Kenneth, and Annette Poulsen. 1989. "Free Cash Flow and Shareholder Gains in Going Private Transactions." *Journal of Finance* 44 (July), pp. 771–787.

Leuz, Christian, Karl V. Lins, and Francis E. Warnock. Forthcoming. "Do Foreigners Invest Less in Poorly Governed Firms?" *Review of Financial Studies*.

Levine, Ross. 1997. "Financial Development and Economic Growth: Views and Agenda." *Journal of Economic Literature* 35, pp. 688–726.

Levine, Ross, and Sara Zervos. 1998. "Stock Markets, Banks, and Economic Growth." *American Economic Review* 88, pp. 537–558.

Lins, Karl V., Deon Strickland, and Marc Zenner. 2005. "Do Non-U.S. Firms Issue Equity on U.S. Exchanges to Relax Capital Constraints?" *Journal of Financial and Quantitative Analysis* 40, pp. 109–133.

Lintner, John. 1956. "Distribution of Incomes of Corporations among Dividends, Retained Earnings, and Taxes." *American Economic Review* 46 (May), pp. 97–113.

Ljungqvist, Alexander, Tim Jenkinson, and William J. Wilhelm, Jr. 2003. "Global Integration in Primary Equity Markets: The Role of U.S. Banks and U.S. Investors." *Review of Financial Studies* 16 (Spring), pp. 630–699.

Ljungqvist, Alexander P., and William J. Wilhelm, Jr. 2002. "IPO Allocations: Discriminatory or Discretionary?" *Journal of Financial Economics* 65 (August), p. 167.

Loderer, Claudio F., Dennis P. Sheehan, and Gregory B. Kadlec. 1991. "The Pricing of Equity Offerings." *Journal of Financial Economics* 29, pp. 35–57.

Lopez-de-Silanes, F., R. La Porta, A. Shleifer, and R. Vishny. 1998. "Law and Finance." *Journal of Political Economy* 106 (December), pp. 1113–1155.

Loughran, Tim, and Jay R. Ritter. 1995. "The New Issues Puzzle." *Journal of Finance* 50 (March), pp. 23–51.

———. 2004. "Why Has IPO Underpricing Changed over Time?" *Financial Management* 33 (Autumn), pp. 5–37.

Louis, Henock, and Dahlia Robinson. 2005. "Do Managers Credibly Use Accruals to Signal Private Information? Evidence from the Pricing of Discretionary Accruals around Stock Splits." *Journal of Accounting and Economics* 30 (June), pp. 361–380.

Lowry, Michelle. 2003. "Why Does IPO Volume Fluctuate So Much?" *Journal of Financial Economics* 67 (January), pp. 3–40.

Lowry, Michelle, and G. William Schwert. 2004. "Is the IPO Pricing Process Efficient?" *Journal of Financial Economics* 71 (January), pp. 3–26.

MacBeth, James D., and Larry J. Merville. 1979. "An Empirical Examination of the Black-Scholes Call Option Pricing Model." *Journal of Finance* 34 (December), pp. 1173–1186.

MacKinlay, Craig A. 1997. "Event Studies in Economics and Finance." *Journal of Economic Literature* 35, pp. 13–39.

Macquieira, Carlos, William Megginson, and Lance Nail. 1998. "Wealth Creation versus Wealth Redistributions in Pure Stock-for-Stock Mergers." *Journal of Financial Economics* 48 (April), pp. 3–25.

Malkiel, Burton G. 1995. "Returns from Investing in Equity Mutual Funds 1971 to 1991." *Journal of Finance* 50 (June), pp. 549–572.

Maloney, Michael T., and J. Harold Mulherin. 2003. "The Complexity of Price Discovery in an Efficient Market: The Stock Market Reaction to the Challenger Crash." *Journal of Corporate Finance* 9 (September), pp. 453–479.

McConnell, John J., Ronald C. Lease, and Elizabeth Tashjian. 1996. "Prepacks as a Mechanism for Resolving Financial Distress: The Evidence." *Journal of Applied Corporate Finance* 8 (Winter), pp. 99–106.

McConnell, John J., and Chris J. Muscarella. 1985. "Corporate Capital Expenditure Decisions and the Market Value of the Firm." *Journal of Financial Economics* 14 (September), pp. 399–422.

Megginson, William L., Angela Morgan, and Lance Nail. 2004. "The Determinants of Positive Long-Term Performance in Strategic Mergers: Corporate Focus and Cash." *Journal of Banking and Finance* 28 (March), pp. 523–552.

Megginson, William L., Annette B. Poulsen, and Joseph F. Sinkey, Jr. 1995. "Syndicated Loan Announcements and the Market Value of the Banking Firm." *Journal of Money, Credit, and Banking* 27 (May), pp. 457–475.

Meier, Iwan, and Vefa Tehran. 2007. "Corporate Investment Decision Practices and the Hurdle Rate Premium Puzzle." Working paper, http://papers.ssrn.com/sol3/papers.cfm?abstract_id=960161.

Metrick, Andrew. 1999. "Performance Evaluation with Transactions Data: The Stock Selection of Investment Newsletters." *Journal of Finance* 54 (October), pp. 1743–1775.

Miles, James A., and James D. Rosenfeld. 1983. "The Effect of Voluntary Spin-Off Announcements on Shareholder Wealth." *Journal of Finance* (December), pp. 1597–1606.

Miller, Darius P. 1999. "The Market Reaction to International Cross-Listings: Evidence from Depositary Receipts." *Journal of Financial Economics* 51 (January), pp. 103–123.

Miller, Merton H. 1977. "Debt and Taxes." *Journal of Finance* 32 (May), pp. 261–276.

Miller, Merton H., and Kevin Rock. 1985. "Dividend Policy under Asymmetric Information." *Journal of Finance* 40 (September), pp. 1021–1051.

Mitchell, Karlyn. 1991. "The Call, Sinking Fund, and Term to Maturity Features of Corporate Bonds: An Empirical Investigation." *Journal of Financial and Quantitative Analysis* 26 (June), pp. 201–222.

Modigliani, Franco, and Merton Miller. 1958. "The Cost of Capital, Corporation Finance, and the Theory of Investment." *American Economic Review* 48 (June), pp. 261–297.

Moel, Alberto, and Peter Tufano. 2002. "When Are Real Options Exercised? An Empirical Study of Mine Closings." *Review of Financial Studies* 15 (Spring), pp. 35–64.

Moeller, Sara B., Frederik P. Schlingemann, and René M. Stulz. 2004. "Firm Size and the Gains from Acquisitions." *Journal of Financial Economics* 73 (August), pp. 201–228.

———. 2005. "Wealth Destruction on a Massive Scale? A Study of Acquiring-Firm Returns in the Recent Merger Wave." *Journal of Finance* 60 (April), pp. 757–782.

Mossin, Jan. 1966. "Equilibrium in a Capital Asset Market." *Econometrica* 24 (October), pp. 768–783.

Mueller, Dennis. 1969. "A Theory of Conglomerate Mergers." *Quarterly Journal of Economics* 83, pp. 643–659.

Muscarella, Chris J., and Michael R. Vetsuypens. 1989. "The Underpricing of 'Second' Initial Public Offerings." *Journal of Financial Research* (Fall), pp. 183–192.

———. 1996. "Stock Splits: Signaling or Liquidity? The Case of ADR 'Solo-Splits.'" *Journal of Financial Economics* 42 (September), pp. 3–26.

Myers, Stewart C. 1984. "The Capital Structure Puzzle." *Journal of Finance* 39 (July), pp. 575–592.

Myers, Stewart C., and Nicholas S. Majluf. 1984. "Corporate Financing and Investment Decisions When Firms Have Information the Investors Do Not Have." *Journal of Financial Economics* 13, pp. 187–221.

Nenova, Tatiana. 2003. "The Value of Corporate Voting Rights and Control: A Cross-Country Analysis." *Journal of Financial Economics* 68 (June), pp. 325–351.

Ng, Chee K., Janet Kiholm Smith, and Richard L. Smith. 1999. "Evidence on the Determinants of Credit Terms Used in Interfirm Trade." *Journal of Finance* 54 (June), pp. 1109–1129.

Noe, Thomas H., and Michael J. Rebello. 1996. "Asymmetric Information, Managerial Opportunism, Financing, and Payout Policies." *Journal of Finance* 51 (June), pp. 637–660.

Oakley, David. 2008. "Bond and Loan Volumes Slump." *Financial Times* (December 22) (www.ft.com).

Oded, Jacob, and Allen Michel. 2008. "Stock Repurchases and the EPS Enhancement Fallacy." *Financial Analysts Journal* 64, pp. 62–75.

Ofek, Eli, and Matthew Richardson. 2003. "DotCom Mania: The Rise and Fall of Internet Stock Prices." *Journal of Finance* 58 (June), pp. 1113–1138.

Ongena, Steven, and David C. Smith. 2001. "The Duration of Bank Relationships." *Journal of Financial Economics* 21, pp. 449–475.

Pagano, Marco, Fabio Panetta, and Luigi Zingales. 1998. "Why Do Companies Go Public? An Empirical Analysis." *Journal of Finance* 53 (February), pp. 27–64.

Pagano, Marco, Ailsa A. Röell, and Josef Zechner. 2002. "The Geography of Equity Listing: Why Do Companies List Abroad?" *Journal of Finance* 57 (December), pp. 2651–2694.

Petersen, Mitchell A., and Raghuram G. Rajan. 1994. "The Benefits of Lending Relationships: Evidence from Small Business Data." *Journal of Finance* 49 (March), pp. 3–37.

Phoa, Wesley, and Frank Fabozzi. 2002. "Default Curves and the Dynamics of Credit Spreads." In *Professional Perspectives on Fixed Income Portfolio Management*, edited by Frank J. Fabozzi (New York: Wiley).

Press, Eric G., and Joseph B. Weintrop. 1990. "Accounting-Based Constraints in Public and Private Debt Agreements: Their Association with Leverage and Impact on Accounting Choice." *Journal of Accounting and Economics* 12 (January), pp. 65–95.

Rajan, Raghuram G. 1992. "Insiders and Outsiders: The Choice between Informed and Arm's Length Debt." *Journal of Finance* 49, pp. 1367–1400.

Rajan, Raghuram G., and Luigi Zingales. 1998. "Financial Dependence and Growth." *American Economic Review* 88, pp. 559–586.

———. 2003. "The Great Reversals: The Politics of Financial Development in the Twentieth Century." *Journal of Financial Economics* 69 (July), pp. 5–50.

Rajgopal, Shivaram, and Terry J. Shevlin. 2002. "Empirical Evidence on the Relation between Stock Option Compensation and Risk Taking." *Journal of Accounting and Economics* 33 (June), pp. 145–171.

Ritter, Jay R. 1987. "The Costs of Going Public." *Journal of Financial Economics* 19 (December), pp. 269–281.

———. 1998. "Initial Public Offerings." In *Handbook of Modern Finance*, edited by Dennis Logue and James Seward (Boston: Warren Gorham & Lamont).

Roberts, Michael R., and Amir Sufi. 2008. "Renegotiation of Financial Contracts: Evidence from Private Credit Agreements." Working paper, University of Chicago (July).

Roll, Richard. 1986. "The Hubris Hypothesis of Corporate Takeovers." *Journal of Business* 59 (April), pp. 197–217.

Ross, Stephen A.. 1977a. "The Determination of Financial Structure: The Incentive-Signaling Approach." *Bell Journal of Economics* 8 (Spring), pp. 23–40.

———. 1977b. "Risk, Return, and Arbitrage." In *Risk and Return in Finance I*, edited by Irwin Friend and James L. Bicksler (Cambridge, MA: Ballinger), pp. 189–218.

Rossi, Stefano, and Paolo F. Volpin. 2004. "Cross-Country Determinants of Mergers and Acquisitions." *Journal of Financial Economics* 74 (November), pp. 277–304.

Santos, João A., and Andrew Winton. 2008. "Bank Loans, Bonds, and Information Monopolies across the Business Cycle." *Journal of Finance* 63 (June), pp. 1315–1359.

Schallheim, James S., Ramon E. Johnson, Ronald C. Lease, and John J. McConnell. 1987. "The Determinants of Yields on Financial Leasing Contracts." *Journal of Financial Economics* 19, pp. 45–68.

Scherr, Frederick C., and Heather M. Hulburt. 2001. "The Maturity Structure of Small Firms." *Financial Management* 30 (Spring), pp. 85–111.

Schipper, Katherine, and Abbie Smith. 1983. "Effects of Recontracting on Shareholder Wealth: The Case of Voluntary Spin-Offs." *Journal of Financial Economics* 12, pp. 437–468.

Servaes, Henri, and Peter Tufano. 2006. "The Theory and Practice of Corporate Capital Structure." Working paper, Deutsche Bank.

Seyhun, H. Nejat. 1986. "Insiders' Profits, Cost of Trading, and Market Efficiency." *Journal of Financial Economics* 16 (June), pp. 189–212.

Shahrur, Husan. 2005. "Industry Structure and Horizontal Takeovers: Analysis of Wealth Effects on Rivals, Suppliers, and Corporate Customers." *Journal of Financial Economics* 76 (April), pp. 61–98.

Sharpe, William F. 1964. "Capital Asset Prices: A Theory of Market Equilibrium under Conditions of Risk." *Journal of Finance* 19 (September), pp. 425–442.

Shleifer, Andrei, and Robert Vishny. 2003. "Stock Market Driven Acquisitions." *Journal of Financial Economics* 70 (December), pp. 295–311.

Siconolfi, Michael, and Patrick McGeehan. 1998. "Wall Street Boosts Penalty on IPO 'Flips.'" *Wall Street Journal* (July 31), p. C1.

Siegel, Jordan. 2005. "Can Foreign Firms Bond Themselves Effectively by Renting U.S. Securities Laws?" *Journal of Financial Economics* 75 (February), pp. 319–359.

Smart, Scott B., and Chad J. Zutter. 2003. "Control as a Motivation for Underpricing: A Comparison of Dual and Single-Class IPOs." *Journal of Financial Economics* 69, pp. 85–110.

Smith, Clifford W., Jr., and L. McDonald Wakeman. 1985. "Determinants of Corporate Leasing Policy." *Journal of Finance* 40 (July), pp. 895–908.

Smith, Clifford W., Jr., and Jerold B. Warner. 1979. "On Financial Contracting: An Analysis of Bond Covenants." *Journal of Financial Economics* 7 (June), pp. 117–161.

Smith, Roy C. 2001. "Strategic Directions in Investment Banking—A Retrospective Analysis." *Journal of Applied Corporate Finance* 14 (Spring), pp. 111–123.

Srinivasan, Venkat, Yong H. Kim, and R. A. Eisenbeis. 1987. "Credit Granting: A Comparative Analysis of Classification Procedures." *Journal of Finance* 42 (July), pp. 665–681.

Statistical Abstract of the United States. 2002. U.S. Census Bureau, Washington, DC.

Stulz, René M., and Herb Johnson. 1985. "An Analysis of Secured Debt." *Journal of Financial Economics* 14 (December), pp. 501–521.

Sufi, Amir. 2007. "Information Asymmetry and Financing Arrangements: Evidence from Syndicated Loans." *Journal of Finance* 62 (April), pp. 697–730.

Thaler, Richard H. 2000. "From Homo Economicus to Homo Sapiens." *Journal of Economic Perspectives* 14 (Winter), pp. 133–141.

Thompson, Samuel C. 2000. "Demystifying the Use of Beta in Determining the Cost of Capital and an Illustration of Its Use in Lazard's Valuation of Conrail." *Journal of Corporation Law* 25, pp. 241–306.

van Binsbergen, Jules H., John R. Graham, and Jie Yang. 2008. "The Cost of Debt." Working paper, Duke University.

von Eije, Henk, and William Megginson. 2008. "Dividends and Share Repurchases in the European Union." *Journal of Financial Economics* 89, pp. 347–374.

Waldman, Michael. 1997. "Eliminating the Market for Secondhand Goods: An Alternative Explanation for Leasing." *Journal of Law and Economics* 40 (April), pp. 61–92.

Wansley, James, William Lane, and Ho Yang. 1983. "Abnormal Returns to Acquired Firms by Type of Acquisition and Method of Payment." *Financial Management* 12 (Autumn), pp. 16–22.

Warren, Carl S., James M. Reeve, and Jonathan Duchac. 2009. *Corporate Financial Accounting*, 10th ed. (Mason, OH: South-Western Cengage Learning).

Welch, Ivo. 2000. "Views of Financial Economists on the Equity Premium and Other Issues." *Journal of Business* 73 (October), pp. 501–537.

———. 2001. "The Equity Premium Consensus Forecast Revisited." Working paper, Yale University.

Wu, Chunchi. 1993. "Information Asymmetry and the Sinking Fund Provision." *Journal of Financial and Quantitative Analysis* 28 (September), pp. 399–416.

Wu, Yi Lin. 2004. "The Choice of Equity-Selling Mechanisms." *Journal of Financial Economics* 74 (October), pp. 93–119.

Further Reading

Ackert, Lucy F., and Brian F. Smith. 1993. "Stock Price Volatility, Ordinary Dividends, and Cash Flows to Shareholders." *Journal of Finance* 48 (September), pp. 1147–1160.

Adams, Paul D., Steve B. Wyatt, and Yong H. Kim. 1992. "A Contingent Claims Analysis of Trade Credit." *Financial Management* 21, pp. 95–103.

Adler, Michael, and Bernard Dumas. 1983. "International Portfolio Choice and Corporation Finance: A Synthesis." *Journal of Finance* 38 (July), pp. 925–984.

Admati, Anat R., and Paul Pfleiderer. 1994. "Robust Financial Contracting and the Role of Venture Capitalists." *Journal of Finance* 49 (June), pp. 371–402.

Aggarwal, Reena, and Pat Conroy. 2000. "Price Discovery in Initial Public Offerings and the Role of the Lead Underwriter." *Journal of Finance* 55 (December), pp. 2903–2922.

Agrawal, Anup, Jeffrey F. Jaffe, and Gershon N. Mandelker. 1992. "The Post-Merger Performance of Acquiring Firms: A Re-examination of an Anomaly." *Journal of Finance* 47 (September), pp. 1605–1622.

Aharony, Joseph, and Itzhak Swary. 1980. "Quarterly Dividend and Earnings Announcements and Stockholders' Returns: An Empirical Analysis." *Journal of Finance* 35 (March), pp. 1–12.

Akerlof, George. 1970. "The Market for 'Lemons,' Qualitative Uncertainty and the Market Mechanism." *Quarterly Journal of Economics* 84 (August), pp. 488–500.

Alderson, Michael J., and Brian L. Betker. 1995. "Liquidation Costs and Capital Structure." *Journal of Financial Economics* 39 (September), pp. 45–69.

———. 1999. "Assessing Post-Bankruptcy Performance: An Analysis of Reorganized Firms' Cash Flows." *Financial Management* 28 (Summer), pp. 68–82.

Allen, David S., Robert E. Lamy, and G. Rodney Thompson. 1990. "The Shelf Registration of Debt and Self Selection Bias." *Journal of Finance* 45 (March), pp. 275–287.

Altinkiliç, Oya, and Robert S. Hansen. 2000. "Are There Economies of Scale in Underwriting Fees? Evidence of Rising External Financing Costs." *Review of Financial Studies* 13 (Spring), pp. 191–218.

Altman, Edward. 1984. "A Further Empirical Investigation of the Bankruptcy Cost Question." *Journal of Finance* 39 (September), pp. 1067–1089.

———. 2000. "Revisiting the High Yield Market: Mature but Never Dull." *Journal of Applied Corporate Finance* 13 (Spring), pp. 64–74.

Altman, Edward I., and Pablo Arman. 2002. "Default and Returns on High Yield Bonds: Analysis through 2001." *Journal of Applied Finance* 12, pp. 98–112.

Amihud, Yakov, and Baruch Lev. 1981. "Risk Reduction as a Managerial Motive for Conglomerate Mergers." *Bell Journal of Economics* 12 (Autumn), pp. 605–617.

Amihud, Yakov, Baruch Lev, and Nikolaos Travlos. 1990. "Corporate Control and the Choice of Investment Financing: The Case of Corporate Acquisitions." *Journal of Finance* 45 (June), pp. 603–616.

Andrade, Gregor, and Steven N. Kaplan. 1998. "How Costly Is Financial (Not Economic) Distress? Evidence from Highly Leveraged Transactions That Became Distressed." *Journal of Finance* 53 (October), pp. 1443–1493.

Ang, James S. 1993. "On Financial Ethics." *Financial Management* 22 (Autumn), pp. 32–59.

Ang, James S., David W. Blackwell, and William L. Megginson. 1991. "The Effect of Taxes on the Relative Valuation of Dividends and Capital Gains: Evidence from Dual-Class British Investment Trusts." *Journal of Finance* 46 (March), pp. 383–399.

Ang, James S., Rebel A. Cole, and James Wuh Lin. 2000. "Agency Costs and Ownership Structure." *Journal of Finance* 55 (February), pp. 81–106.

Ang, James, and William L. Megginson. 1990. "A Test of the Before-Tax versus After-Tax Equilibrium Models of Corporate Debt." *Research in Finance* 8, pp. 97–118.

Anstaett, Kurt W., Dennis P. McCrary, and Stephen T. Monahan, Jr. 1988. "Practical Debt Policy Considerations for Growth Companies: A Case Study Approach." *Journal of Applied Corporate Finance* 1 (Summer), pp. 71–78.

Arundale, Keith. 2001. "European Private Equity and Venture Capital—Current State of the Market and Prospects for the Industry." Working paper, PricewaterhouseCoopers UK.

Asquith, Paul. 1983. "Merger Bids, Uncertainty and Stockholder Returns." *Journal of Financial Economics* 11 (April), pp. 51–83.

Asquith, Paul, Robert Bruner, and David Mullins. 1983. "The Gains for Bidding Firms from Merger." *Journal of Financial Economics* 11 (April), pp. 121–139.

Asquith, Paul, and David Mullins, Jr. 1983. "The Impact of Initiating Dividend Payments on Shareholders' Wealth." *Journal of Business* 56 (January), pp. 77–96.

———. 1986. "Equity Issues and Stock Price Dilution." *Journal of Financial Economics* 15 (January/February), pp. 61–89.

Aylward, Anthony. 1998. "Trends in Venture Capital Finance in Developing Countries." IFC Discussion Paper no. 36, World Bank, Washington, DC.

Backus, David, Silverio Foresi, Abon Mozumdar, and Liuren Wu. 2001. "Predictable Changes in Yields and Forward Rates." *Journal of Financial Economics* 59 (March), pp. 281–311.

Backus, David K., Silverio Foresi, and Chris I. Telmer. 2001. "Affine Term Structure Models and the Forward Premium Anomaly." *Journal of Finance* 56 (February), pp. 279–304.

Bagwell, Laurie Simon. 1991. "Share Repurchase and Takeover Deterrence." *Rand Journal of Economics* 22, pp. 72–88.

Baker, H. Kent, Gail E. Farrelly, and Richard B. Edelman. 1985. "A Survey of Management Views on Dividend Policy." *Financial Management* 14 (Autumn), pp. 78–84.

Baker, Malcolm, and Paul A. Gompers. 2001. "The Determinants of Board Structure at the Initial Public Offering." Working paper, Harvard Business School.

Baks, Klaas P., Andrew Metrick, and Jessica Wachter. 2001. "Should Investors Avoid All Actively Managed Mutual Funds? A Study in Bayesian Performance Evaluation." *Journal of Finance* 56 (February), pp. 45–85.

Baldwin, Carliss, and Kim B. Clark. 1992. "Capabilities and Capital Investment: New Perspectives on Capital Budgeting." *Journal of Applied Corporate Finance* 15 (Summer), pp. 67–82.

Ball, Ray. 1995. "The Theory of Market Efficiency: Accomplishments and Limitations." *Journal of Applied Corporate Finance* 8 (Spring), pp. 4–17.

Ball, Ray, and Philip Brown. 1968. "An Empirical Investigation of Accounting Income Numbers." *Journal of Accounting Research* 6 (Autumn), pp. 159–178.

Ball, Ray, and S. P. Kothari. 1989. "Nonstationary Expected Returns: Implications for Tests of Market Efficiency and Serial Correlation in Returns." *Journal of Financial Economics* 25 (November), pp. 51–74.

Ball, Ray, S. P. Kothari, and Jay Shanken. 1995. "Problems in Measuring Portfolio Performance: An Application to Contrarian Investment Strategies." *Journal of Financial Economics* 38, pp. 79–107.

Banz, Rolf W. 1981. "The Relationship between Return and Market Value of Common Stocks." *Journal of Financial Economics* 9 (March), pp. 3–18.

Barber, Brad, Reuven Lehavy, Maureen McNichols, and Brett Trueman. 2001. "Can Investors Profit from the Prophets? Security Analyst Recommendations and Stock Returns." *Journal of Finance* 56 (April), pp. 531–563.

———. 2003. "Prophets and Losses: Reassessing the Returns to Analysts' Stock Recommendations." *Financial Analyst Journal* 59 (March/April), pp. 88–96.

Barber, Brad M., and John D. Lyon. 1997. "Detecting Long-Run Abnormal Stock Returns: The Empirical Power and Specification of Test Statistics." *Journal of Financial Economics* 43, pp. 341–372.

Barber, Brad M., and Terrance Odean. 2000. "Trading Is Hazardous to Your Wealth." *Journal of Finance* 55 (April), pp. 773–806.

Barberis, Nicholas. 2000. "Investing for the Long Run When Returns Are Predictable." *Journal of Finance* 55 (February), pp. 225–264.

Barclay, Michael J. 1987. "Dividends, Taxes, and Common Stock Prices before the Income Tax." *Journal of Financial Economics* 19 (September), pp. 31–44.

Barclay, Michael J., and Clifford W. Smith, Jr. 1988. "Corporate Payout Policy: Cash Dividends versus Open Market Repurchases." *Journal of Financial Economics* 22 (October), pp. 61–82.

———. 1999. "The Capital Structure Puzzle: Another Look at the Evidence." *Journal of Applied Corporate Finance* 12 (Spring), pp. 8–20.

Barnish, Keith, Steve Miller, and Michael Rushmore. 1997. "The New Leveraged Loan Syndication Market." *Journal of Applied Corporate Finance* 10 (Spring), pp. 79–88.

Baron, David P. 1982. "A Model of the Demand for Investment Banking Advising and Distributions Services for New Issues." *Journal of Finance* 37 (September), pp. 955–976.

Baron, David P., and Bengt Holmstrom. 1980. "The Investment Banking Contract for New Issues under Asymmetric Information: Delegation and Incentive Problems." *Journal of Finance* 35 (December), pp. 1115–1138.

Barry, Christopher, Chris Muscarella, John Peavy, and Michael Vetsuypens. 1990. "The Role of Venture Capital in the Creation of Public Companies: Evidence from the Going Public Process." *Journal of Financial Economics* 27, pp. 447–471.

Barry, Christopher B., Chris J. Muscarella, and Michael R. Vetsuypens. 1991. "Underwriter Warrants, Underwriter Compensation, and the Costs of Going Public." *Journal of Financial Economics* 29, pp. 113–135.

Bascha, Andreas, and Uwe Walz. 2001. "Convertible Securities and Optimal Exit Decisions in Venture Capital." *Journal of Corporate Finance* 7 (September), pp. 285–306.

Baytas, Ahmet, and Nusret Cakici. 1999. "Do Markets Overreact: International Evidence." *Journal of Banking and Finance* 23, pp. 1121–1144.

Beatty, Anne. 1995. "The Cash Flow and Informational Effects of Employee Stock Ownership Plans." *Journal of Financial Economics* 38 (June), pp. 211–240.

Becker, Kent G., Joseph E. Finnerty, and Joseph Friedman. 1995. "Economic News and Equity Market Linkages between the U.S. and U.K." *Journal of Banking and Finance* 19, pp. 1191–1210.

Bell, Leonie, and Tim Jenkinson. 2002. "New Evidence of the Impact of Dividend Taxation on the Identity of the Marginal Investor." *Journal of Finance* 57 (June), pp. 1321–1346.

Benartzi, Shlomo, Roni Michaely, and Richard Thaler. 1997. "Do Changes in Dividends Signal the Future or the Past?" *Journal of Finance* 52 (July), pp. 1007–1035.

Benoit, Bertrand. 2001. "Neuer Markt Starts to Feel Squeeze." *Financial Times* (July 11), p. 19.

Benveniste, Lawrence M., Walid Y. Busaba, and William J. Wilhelm, Jr. 1996. "Price Stabilization as a Bonding Mechanism in New Equity Issues." *Journal of Financial Economics* 42 (October), pp. 223–255.

Berens, James L., and Charles J. Cuny. 1995. "The Capital Structure Puzzle Revisited." *Review of Financial Studies* 8 (Winter), pp. 1185–1208.

Berger, Allen, and Gregory Udell. 1995. "Relationship Lending and Lines of Credit in Small Firm Finance." *Journal of Business* 68 (July), pp. 351–381.

Berger, Philip, and Eli Ofek. 1996. "Bustup Takeovers of Value-Destroying Diversified Firms." *Journal of Finance* 51 (September), pp. 1175–2000.

Berglöf, Erik. 1994. "A Control Theory of Venture Capital Finance." *Journal of Law, Economics and Organization* 10, pp. 447–471.

Berglöf, Erik, and Enrico Perotti. 1994. "The Governance Structure of the Japanese Keiretsu." *Journal of Financial Economics* 36 (October), pp. 259–284.

Bergstrom, C., and K. Rydqvist. 1990. "The Determinants of Corporate Ownership: An Empirical Study of Swedish Data." *Journal of Banking and Finance* 14, pp. 237–254.

Bernanke, Ben S., and John Y. Campbell. 1988. "Is There a Corporate Debt Crisis?" *Brookings Papers on Economic Activity* 1, pp. 83–125.

Bernard, Victor L., and Jacob K. Thomas. 1990. "Evidence That Stock Prices Do Not Fully Reflect the Implications of Current Earnings for Future Earnings." *Journal of Accounting and Economics* 12 (December), pp. 305–341.

Bernard, Victor, Jacob K. Thomas, and Jeffery S. Abarbanell. 1993. "How Sophisticated Is the Market in Interpreting Earnings News?" *Journal of Applied Corporate Finance* 6 (Summer), pp. 54–63.

Bernardo, Antonio E., and Bhagwan Chowdhry. 2002. "Resources, Real Options, and Corporate Strategy." *Journal of Financial Economics* 63 (February), pp. 211–234.

Bernardo, Antonio E., and Eric L. Talley. 1996. "Investment Policy and Exit-Exchange Offers within Financially Distressed Firms." *Journal of Finance* 51 (July), pp. 871–888.

Bernstein, Peter L. 1999. "Why the Efficient Market Offers Hope to Active Management." *Journal of Applied Corporate Finance* 12 (Summer), pp. 129–136.

Bethel, Jennifer E., and Stuart L. Gillan. 2002. "The Impact of the Institutional and Regulatory Environment on Shareholder Voting." *Financial Management* 31 (Winter), pp. 29–54.

Betker, Brian L. 1995. "Management's Incentives, Equity's Bargaining Power, and Deviations from Absolute Priority in Chapter 11 Bankruptcies." *Journal of Business* 68 (April), pp. 161–183.

Bhagat, Sanjai. 1983. "The Effect of Preemptive Right Amendments on Shareholder Wealth." *Journal of Financial Economics* 12 (November), pp. 289–310.

———. 1986. "The Effect of Management's Choice between Negotiated and Competitive Equity Offerings on Shareholder Wealth." *Journal of Financial and Quantitative Analysis* 21 (June), pp. 181–196.

Bhagat, Sanjai, and Peter Frost. 1986. "Issuing Costs to Existing Shareholders in Competitive and Negotiated Underwritten Public Utility Offerings." *Journal of Financial Economics* 15 (January/February), pp. 223–259.

Bhagat, Sanjai, Andrei Shleifer, and Robert Vishny. 1990. "Hostile Takeovers in the 1980s: The Return to Corporate Specialization." *Brookings Papers on Economic Activity*, pp. 1–72.

Bharadwaj, Anu, and Anil Shivdasani. 2003. "Valuation Effects of Bank Financing in Acquisitions." *Journal of Financial Economics* 67 (January), pp. 113–148.

Bhide, Amar. 1992. "Bootstrap Finance: The Art of Start-Ups." *Harvard Business Review* (November/December), pp. 109–117.

———. 1993. "The Hidden Costs of Stock Market Liquidity." *Journal of Financial Economics* 34 (August), pp. 31–51.

Bianchi, Alessandra. 1992. "Why You Won't Sell Your Business." *Inc.* (August), pp. 58–63.

Bicksler, James, and Andrew H. Chen. 1986. "An Economic Analysis of Interest Rate Swaps." *Journal of Finance* 41 (July), pp. 645–655.

Birnbaum, Jeffrey H. 1999. "Uncle Sam, Venture Capitalist." *Fortune* (May 24), p. 66.

Bjerring, James H., Josef Lakonishok, and Theo Vermaelen. 1983. "Stock Prices and Financial Analysts' Recommendations." *Journal of Finance* 38 (March), pp. 187–204.

Black, Bernard. 1992a. "Agents Watching Agents." *UCLA Law Review* 39, pp. 811–893.

———. 1992b. "Institutional Investors and Corporate Governance: The Case for Institutional Voice." *Journal of Applied Corporate Finance* 5 (Fall), pp. 19–32.

Black, Bernard S., and Ronald J. Gilson. 1998. "Venture Capital and the Structure of Capital Markets: Banks versus Capital Markets." *Journal of Financial Economics* 47 (March), pp. 243–277.

Black, Fischer. 1972. "Capital Market Equilibrium with Restricted Borrowing." *Journal of Business* 64 (July), pp. 444–455.

Black, Fischer, and Myron S. Scholes. 1973. "The Pricing of Options and Corporate Liabilities." *Journal of Political Economy* 81 (May/June), pp. 637–654.

Blackwell, David W., and David S. Kidwell. 1988. "An Investigation of Cost Differences between Public Sales and Private Placements of Debt." *Journal of Financial Economics* 22 (December), pp. 253–278.

Blackwell, David W., M. Wayne Marr, and Michael F. Spivey. 1990. "Shelf Registration and the Reduced Due Diligence Argument: Implications of the Underwriter Certification and the Implicit Insurance Hypothesis." *Journal of Financial and Quantitative Analysis* 25 (June), pp. 245–259.

Blackwell, David, and Drew Winters. 1997. "Banking Relationships and the Effect of Monitoring on Loan Pricing." *Journal of Financial Research* 20 (Summer), pp. 275–289.

Blake, David, and Allan Timmerman. 1998. "Mutual Fund Performance: Evidence from the UK." *European Economic Review* 2, pp. 57–77.

Blouin, Jennifer L., Jana Smith Raedy, and Douglas A. Shackleford. 2004. "Did Dividends Increase Immediately after the 2003 Reduction in Tax Rates?" Working Paper W10301, National Bureau of Economic Research, Cambridge, MA (February).

Bohren, Øyvind, B. Espen Eckbo, and Dag Michalsen. 1997. "Why Underwrite Rights Offerings? Some New Evidence." *Journal of Financial Economics* 46, pp. 223–261.

Bollerslev, Tim. 1986. "Generalized Conditional Autoregressive Heteroscedasticity." *Journal of Econometrics* 31 (April), pp. 307–327.

Booth, James R., and Richard L. Smith, Jr. 1986. "Capital Raising, Underwriting and the Certification Hypothesis." *Journal of Financial Economics* 15 (January/February), pp. 261–281.

Booth, James R., Richard L. Smith, and Richard W. Stolz. 1984. "Use of Interest Rate Futures by Financial Institutions." *Journal of Bank Research* 15, pp. 15–20.

Booth, Laurence, Varouj Aivazian, Asli Demirgüç-Kunt, and Vojislav Maksimovic. 2001. "Capital Structures in Developing Countries." *Journal of Finance* 56 (February), pp. 87–130.

Bortolotti, Bernardo, Frank DeJong, Giovanna Nicodano, and Ibolya Schindele. 2005. "Privatization and Stock Market Liquidity." Working paper, Fondazione Eni Enrico Mattei, Milan (March).

Boubakri, Narjess, and Jean-Claude Cosset. 1998. "The Financial and Operating Performance of Newly Privatized Firms: Evidence from Developing Countries." *Journal of Finance* 53 (June), pp. 1081–1110.

Boutchkova, Maria K., and William L. Megginson. 2000. "Privatization and the Rise of Global Capital Markets." *Financial Management* 29 (Winter), pp. 31–76.

Bower, Nancy L. 1989. "Firm Value and the Choice of Offering Method in Initial Public Offerings." *Journal of Finance* 44 (July), pp. 647–662.

Boyd, John H., and Mark Gertler. 1994. "Are Banks Dead? Or Are the Reports Greatly Exaggerated?" Federal Reserve Bank of Minneapolis *Quarterly Review* (Summer), pp. 2–23.

Bradley, Daniel J., Bradford D. Jordan, Ha-Chin Yi, and Ivan C. Roten. 2001. "Venture Capital and IPO Lockup Expiration: An Empirical Analysis." *Journal of Financial Research* 24 (Winter), pp. 465–492.

Bradley, Michael, Gregg Jarrell, and E. Han Kim. 1984. "On the Existence of an Optimal Capital Structure: Theory and Evidence." *Journal of Finance* 39 (May), pp. 857–878.

Brav, Alon, and J. B. Heaton. 2002. "Competing Theories of Financial Anomalies." *Review of Financial Studies* 15 (Special), pp. 575–606.

Breeden, Douglas T. 1979. "An Intertemporal Asset Pricing Model with Stochastic Consumption and Investment Opportunities." *Journal of Financial Economics* 7, pp. 265–296.

Brennan, Michael J. 1970. "Taxes, Market Valuation and Corporate Financial Policy." *National Tax Journal* 23 (December), pp. 417–427.

Brewer, Elijah, III, and Hesna Genay. 1994. "Small Business Investment Companies: Financial Characteristics and Investments." Working paper, Series no. 94-10, Federal Reserve Bank of Chicago.

Brickley, James A. 1983. "Shareholder Wealth, Information Signalling and the Specially Designated Dividend: An Empirical Study." *Journal of Financial Economics* 12 (August), pp. 187–209.

Brinson, Gary P., L. Randolph Hood, and Gilbert L. Beebower. 1986. "Determinants of Portfolio Performance." *Financial Analysts Journal* 50 (July/August), pp. 39–44.

Bris, Arturo, Alan Schwartz, and Ivo Welch. 2005. "Who Should Pay for Bankruptcy Costs?" *Journal of Legal Studies* 34 (June), pp. 296–341.

Brock, William, Josef Lakonishok, and Blake LeBaron. 1992. "Simple Technical Trading Rules and the Stochastic Properties of Stock Returns." *Journal of Finance* 47 (December), pp. 1731–1764.

Brophy, David J., and Mark W. Guthner. 1988. "Publicly Traded Venture Capital Funds: Implications for Institutional 'Fund of Funds' Investors." *Journal of Business Venturing* 3 (Summer), pp. 187–206.

Brous, Peter A., Vinay Datar, and Omesh Kini. 2001. "Is the Market Optimistic about the Future Earnings of Seasoned Equity Offering Firms?" *Journal of Financial and Quantitative Analysis* 36 (June), pp. 141–168.

Brown, Stephen J., and Jerold B. Warner. 1980. "Measuring Security Price Performance." *Journal of Financial Economics* 8 (September), pp. 205–258.

Bruner, Robert F. 2002. "Does M&A Pay? A Survey of Evidence for the Decision-Maker." *Journal of Applied Finance* 12 (Spring/Summer), pp. 48–68.

Burroughs, Bryan, and John Helyar. 1993. *Barbarians at the Gate: The Fall of RJR Nabisco* (New York: HarperCollins).

Byun, Jinho, and Michael S. Rozeff. 2003. "Long-Run Performance after Stock Splits: 1927 to 1996." *Journal of Finance* 58 (June), pp. 1063–1085.

Calegari, Michael J. 2000. "The Effect of Tax Accounting Rules on Capital Structure and Discretionary Accruals." *Journal of Accounting and Economics* 30 (August), pp. 1–31.

Campbell, John Y., and John Ammer. 1993. "What Moves the Stock and Bond Markets? A Variance Decomposition for Long-Term Asset Returns." *Journal of Finance* 48 (March), pp. 3–37.

Campbell, Katharine. 2001a. "Stock Market Volatility Fails to Put Off Investors." *Financial Times* (June 14), p. 6.

———. 2001b. "Informal Financing Totals $196bn a Year." *Financial Times* (November 15), p. 31.

Cannavan, Damien, Frank Finn, and Stephen Gray. 2004. "The Value of Dividend Imputation Tax Credits in Australia." *Journal of Financial Economics* 73 (July), pp. 167–197.

Carhart, Mark M. 1997. "On Persistence in Mutual Fund Performance." *Journal of Finance* 52 (March), pp. 57–82.

Carpenter, Jennifer N., and Anthony W. Lynch. 1999. "Survivorship Bias and Attrition Effects in Measures of Performance Persistence." *Journal of Financial Economics* 54 (December), pp. 337–374.

Carter, Mary E., and Luann J. Lynch. 2001. "An Examination of Executive Stock Option Repricing." *Journal of Financial Economics* 61 (August), pp. 207–225.

Carter, Richard B., Frederick H. Dark, and Ajai K. Singh. 1998. "Underwriter Reputation, Initial Returns, and the Long-Run Performance of IPO Stocks." *Journal of Finance* 53, pp. 285–311.

Carter, Richard B., and Howard E. Van Auken. 1990. "Personal Equity Investment and Small Business Financial Difficulties." *Entrepreneurship Theory and Practice* (Winter), pp. 51–60.

Chambers, Donald R., and Nelson J. Lacey. 1996. "Corporate Ethics and Shareholder Wealth Maximization." *Financial Practice and Education* 6 (Spring/Summer), pp. 93–96.

Chan, Louis K. C., Narasimhan Jegadeesh, and Josef Lakonishok. 1995. "Evaluating the Performance of Value versus Glamour Stocks: The Impact of Selection Bias." *Journal of Financial Economics* 38 (July), pp. 269–296.

———. 1996. "Momentum Strategies." *Journal of Finance* 51 (December), pp. 1681–1713.

Chang, Eric C., Joseph W. Cheng, and Ajay Khorana. 2000. "An Examination of Herd Behavior in Equity Markets: An International Perspective." *Journal of Banking and Finance* 24, pp. 1651–1679.

Chaplinsky, Susan, and Latha Ramchand. 2000. "The Impact of Global Equity Offerings." *Journal of Finance* 55 (December), pp. 2767–2789.

Chauvin, Keith W., and Catherine Shenoy. 2001. "Stock Price Decreases Prior to Executive Stock Option Grants." *Journal of Corporate Finance: Contracting, Governance, and Organization* 7 (March), pp. 53–76.

Chemmanur, Thomas J., and Paolo Fulghieri. 1994. "Reputation, Renegotiation, and the Choice between Bank Loans and Publicly Traded Debt." *Review of Financial Studies* 7 (Fall), pp. 475–506.

Chen, N., R. Roll, and S. A. Ross. 1986. "Economic Forces and the Stock Market: Testing the APT and Alternative Asset Pricing Theories." *Journal of Business* 59 (July), pp. 383–403.

Chidambaran, N. K., Chitru S. Fernando, and Paul A. Spindt. 2001. "Credit Enhancement through Financial Engineering: Freeport McMoRan's Gold-Denominated Depository Share." *Journal of Financial Economics* 60 (May), pp. 487–528.

Chirinko, Robert S., and Anua R. Singha. 2000. "Testing Static Trade-off against Pecking Order Models of Capital Structure: A Critical Comment." *Journal of Financial Economics* 58, pp. 417–425.

Chowdhry, Bhagwan, and Ann Sherman. 1996. "International Differences in Oversubscription and Underpricing of IPO." *Journal of Corporate Finance* 2, pp. 359–381.

Christie, William G., and Vikram Nanda. 1994. "Free Cash Flow, Shareholder Value, and the Undistributed Profits Tax of 1936 and 1937." *Journal of Finance* 49 (December), pp. 1727–1754.

Christopher, Alistair. 2001. "VC and the Law: Potential Legal Hurdles Involved in Funding the Next Big Thing." *Venture Capital Journal* (February), pp. 43–45.

Cleary, Sean. 1999. "The Relationship between Firm Investment and Financial Status." *Journal of Finance* 54 (April), pp. 673–692.

Coggin, T. Daniel, Frank J. Fabozzi, and Shafiqur Rahman. 1993. "The Investment Performance of U.S. Equity Pension Fund Managers: An Empirical Investigation." *Journal of Finance* 48 (July), pp. 1039–1055.

Cole, Jonathan E., and Albert L. Sokol. 1997. "Structuring Venture Capital Investments." In *Pratt's Guide to Venture Capital Sources*, edited by Stanley E. Pratt (New York: Securities Data Publishing).

Comment, Robert, and William Schwert. 1995. "Poison or Placebo? Evidence on the Deterrence and Wealth Effects of Modern Antitakeover Measures." *Journal of Financial Economics* 39, pp. 3–43.

Conrad, Jennifer, and Gautam Kaul. 1988. "Time Variation in Expected Returns." *Journal of Business* 61 (October), pp. 409–425.

———. 1989. "Mean Reversion in Short-Horizon Expected Returns." *Review of Financial Studies* 2, pp. 225–240.

———. 1993. "Long-Term Market Overreaction or Biases in Computed Returns." *Journal of Finance* 48 (March), pp. 39–64.

Cornell, Bradford, and Alan C. Shapiro. 1987. "Corporate Stakeholders and Corporate Finance." *Financial Management* 16 (Spring), pp. 5–14.

———. 1988. "Financing Corporate Growth." *Journal of Applied Corporate Finance* 1 (Summer), pp. 6–22.

Cornell, Bradford, and Erik R. Sirri. 1992. "The Reaction of Investors and Stock Prices to Insider Trading." *Journal of Finance* 47 (July), pp. 1031–1060.

Corwin, Shane A., and Jeffrey H. Harris. 2001. "The Initial Listing Decisions of Firms That Go Public." *Financial Management* 30 (Spring), pp. 35–55.

Cox, Don R., and David R. Peterson. 1994. "Stock Returns following Large One-Day Declines: Evidence on Short-Term Reversals and Longer-Term Performance." *Journal of Finance* 49 (March), pp. 255–267.

Cox, John C., Jonathon E. Ingersoll, Jr., and Stephen A. Ross. 1981. "The Relation between Forward and Futures Prices." *Journal of Financial Economics* 9 (December), pp. 321–346.

Cox, John C., and Stephen A. Ross. 1976. "The Valuation of Options for Alternative Stochastic Processes." *Journal of Financial Economics* 3 (January/March), pp. 145–166.

Cox, John C., Stephen A. Ross, and Mark Rubinstein. 1979. "Option Pricing: A Simplified Approach." *Journal of Financial Economics* 7 (September), pp. 229–263.

Crabbe, Leland E., and Jean Helwege. 1994. "Alternative Tests of Agency Theories of Callable Corporate Bonds." *Financial Management* 23 (Winter), pp. 3–20.

Crawford, Dean, Diana R. Franz, and Gerald J. Lobo. 2005. "Signaling Managerial Optimism through Stock Dividends and Stock Splits: A Reexamination of the Retained Earnings Hypothesis." *Journal of Financial and Quantitative Analysis* 40, pp. 531–561.

Cumby, Robert E., and David M. Modest. 1987. "Testing for Market Timing Ability: A Framework for Market Forecast Evaluation." *Journal of Financial Economics* 19 (September), pp. 169–189.

Cusatis, Patrick J., James A. Miles, and J. Randall Woolridge. 1993. "Restructuring through Spinoffs: The Stock Market Evidence." *Journal of Financial Economics* 33, pp. 293–311.

Dahiya, Sandeep, Kose John, Manju Puri, and Gabriel Ramirez. 2003. "Debtor-in-Possession Financing and Bankruptcy Resolution: Empirical Evidence." *Journal of Financial Economics* 69 (July), pp. 259–280.

Daniel, Kent, and Sheridan Titman. 1997. "Evidence on the Characteristics of Cross Sectional Variation in Stock Returns." *Journal of Finance* 52 (March), pp. 1–33.

Dann, Larry. 1981. "Common Stock Repurchases: An Analysis of Returns to Bondholders and Stockholders." *Journal of Financial Economics* 9 (June), pp. 113–138.

Dann, Larry, and Wayne Mikkelson. 1984. "Convertible Debt Issuance, Capital Structure Change and Financing Related Information: Some New Evidence." *Journal of Financial Economics* 13 (June), pp. 157–186.

Davidson, Wallace N., III, and Dipa Dutia. 1991. "Debt, Liquidity, and Profitability in Small Firms." *Entrepreneurship Theory and Practice* (Fall), pp. 53–64.

DeAngelo, Harry, and Linda DeAngelo. 1985. "Managerial Ownership of Voting Rights: A Study of Public Corporations with Dual Classes of Common Stock." *Journal of Financial Economics* 14 (March), pp. 33–69.

———. 1990. "Dividend Policy and Financial Distress: An Empirical Investigation of Troubled NYSE Firms." *Journal of Finance* 45 (December), pp. 1415–1431.

DeAngelo, Harry, Linda DeAngelo, and Douglas J. Skinner. 1992. "Dividends and Losses." *Journal of Finance* 47 (December), pp. 1837–1863.

———. 1996. "Reversal of Fortune: Dividend Signaling and the Disappearance of Sustained Earnings Growth." *Journal of Financial Economics* 40 (March), pp. 341–371.

———. 2000. "Special Dividends and Evolution of Dividend Signalling." *Journal of Financial Economics* 57 (September), pp. 309–354.

———. 2004. "Are Dividends Disappearing? Dividend Concentration and the Consolidation of Earnings." *Journal of Financial Economics* 72 (June), pp. 425–456.

DeBondt, Werner, and Richard Thaler. 1985. "Does the Stock Market Overreact?" *Journal of Finance* 40 (July), pp. 793–805.

Dechow, Patricia M., and Richard G. Sloan. 1997. "Returns to Contrarian Investment Strategies: Tests of Naive Expectations Hypotheses." *Journal of Financial Economics* 43 (January), pp. 3–27.

DeLong, Bradford, Andrei Shleifer, Lawrence H. Summers, and Robert J. Waldmann. 1990. "Positive Feedback Investment Strategies and Destabilizing Rational Speculation." *Journal of Finance* 45 (June), pp. 379–395.

———. 1990. "Noise Trader Risk in Financial Markets." *Journal of Political Economy* 98 (August), pp. 703–738.

DeMarzo, Peter M., and Darrell Duffie. 1995. "Corporate Incentives for Hedging and Hedge Accounting." *Review of Financial Studies* 8, pp. 743–771.

Demers, Elizabeth, and Katherina Lewellen. 2003. "The Marketing Role of IPOs: Evidence from Internet Stocks." *Journal of Financial Economics* 68 (June), pp. 413–437.

De Miguel, Alberto, and Julio Pindado. 2001. "Determinants of Capital Structure: New Evidence from Spanish Panel Data." *Journal of Corporate Finance* 7 (March), pp. 77–99.

Denis, David J. 1991. "Shelf Registration and the Market for Seasoned Equity Offerings." *Journal of Business* 64 (April), pp. 189–212.

Denis, David J., Diane K. Denis, and Atulya Sarin. 1997. "Agency Problems, Equity Ownership, and Corporate Diversification." *Journal of Finance* 52 (March), pp. 135–160.

Desai, Hemang, and Prem C. Jain. 1995. "An Analysis of the Recommendations of the 'Superstar' Money Managers at *Barron's* Annual Roundtable." *Journal of Finance* 50 (September), pp. 1257–1273.

———. 1997. "Long-Run Common Stock Returns following Stock Splits and Reverse Splits." *Journal of Business* 70 (July), pp. 409–433.

Dewenter, Kathryn, and Vincent Warther. 1998. "Dividends, Asymmetric Information and Agency Conflicts: Evidence from a Comparison of the Dividend Policies of Japanese and US Firms." *Journal of Finance* 53 (June), pp. 879–904.

Dewing, Arthur Stone. 1953. *The Financial Policy of Corporations* (New York: Ronald Press).

Dharan, Bala G., and David L. Ikenberry. 1995. "The Long-Run Negative Drift of Post-Listing Stock Returns." *Journal of Finance* 50 (December), pp. 1547–1574.

Dhillon, Upinder, and Herb Johnson. 1991. "Changes in the Standard & Poor's List." *Journal of Business* 64 (January), pp. 75–85.

Diamond, Douglas. 1989. "Reputation Acquisition in Debt Markets." *Journal of Political Economy* 97, pp. 828–862.

Dolde, Walter. 1993. "The Trajectory of Corporate Financial Risk Management." *Journal of Applied Corporate Finance* 6 (Fall), pp. 33–41.

Downes, David H., and Robert Heinkel. 1982. "Signaling and the Valuation of Unseasoned New Issues." *Journal of Finance* 37, pp. 1–10.

D'Souza, Julia, and John Jacob. 2000. "Why Firms Issue Targeted Stock." *Journal of Financial Economics* 56 (June), pp. 459–483.

D'Souza, Juliet, and William L. Megginson. 1999. "The Financial and Operating Performance of Newly Privatized Firms in the 1990s." *Journal of Finance* 54 (August), pp. 1397–1438.

Dunbar, Craig G. 2000. "Factors Affecting Investment Bank Initial Public Offering Market Share." *Journal of Financial Economics* 55, pp. 3–41.

Dwyer, Hubert J., and Richard Lynn. 1989. "Small Capitalization Companies: What Does Financial

Analysis Tell Us about Them?" *Financial Review* 24, pp. 397–414.

Dyl, Edward A. 1977. "Another Look at the Evaluation of Investment in Accounts Receivable." *Financial Management* 6 (4), pp. 67–70.

Eades, Kenneth, Patrick Hess, and E. Han Kim. 1984. "On Interpreting Security Returns during the Ex-dividend Day Period." *Journal of Financial Economics* 13 (March), pp. 3–34.

———. 1994. "Time Series Variation in Dividend Pricing." *Journal of Finance* 49 (December), pp. 1617–1638.

Easterbrook, Frank H. 1984. "Two Agency-Cost Explanations of Dividends." *American Economic Review* 74 (September), pp. 650–659.

Easterbrook, Frank H., and Daniel R. Fischel. 1983. "Voting in Corporate Law." *Journal of Law and Economics* 26 (June), pp. 395–427.

Eberhart, Allan, Edward I. Altman, and Reena Aggarwal. 1999. "The Equity Performance of Firms Emerging from Bankruptcy." *Journal of Finance* 54 (October), pp. 1855–1868.

Eberhart, Allan C., William T. Moore, and Rodney L. Roenfeldt. 1990. "Security Pricing and Deviations from the Absolute Priority Rule in Bankruptcy Proceedings." *Journal of Finance* 45 (December), pp. 1457–1469.

Eckbo, B. Espen. 1983. "Horizontal Mergers, Collusion, and Stockholder Wealth." *Journal of Financial Economics* 11 (April), pp. 241–273.

———. 1986. "Valuation Effects of Corporate Debt Offerings." *Journal of Financial Economics* 15 (January/February), pp. 119–151.

Economist, The. 1996. "Remapping South America: A Survey of Mercosur" (October 12).

Edelen, Roger M. 1999. "Investor Flows and the Assessed Performance of Open-End Mutual Funds." *Journal of Financial Economics* 53 (September), pp. 439–466.

Ederington, Louis H., and Jae Ha Lee. 1993. "How Markets Process Information: News Releases and Volatility." *Journal of Finance* 48 (September), pp. 1161–1191.

Ellert, James. 1976. "Mergers, Antitrust Law Enforcement, and Stockholder Returns." *Journal of Finance* 31 (May), pp. 715–732.

Ellis, Katrina, Roni Michaely, and Maureen O'Hara. 2000. "When the Underwriter Is the Market Maker: An Examination of Trading in the IPO Aftermarket." *Journal of Finance* 55 (June), pp. 1039–1074.

Elton, Edwin J., and Martin J. Gruber. 1970. "Marginal Stockholder Tax Rates and the Clientele Effect." *Review of Economics and Statistics* 52 (February), pp. 68–74.

Elton, Edwin J., Martin J. Gruber, Sanjiv Das, and Matthew Hlavka. 1993. "Efficiency with Costly Information: A Reinterpretation of Evidence from Managed Portfolios." *Review of Financial Studies* 6, pp. 1–22.

Engle, Robert F. 1982. "Autoregressive Conditional Heteroscedasticity with Estimates of the Variance of United Kingdom Inflation." *Econometrica* 50 (July), pp. 987–1007.

Esty, Benjamin C. 1999. "Petrozuata: A Case Study of the Effective Use of Project Finance." *Journal of Applied Corporate Finance* 12 (Fall), pp. 26–42.

Fama, Eugene F. 1965. "The Behavior of Stock Market Prices." *Journal of Business* 38 (January), pp. 34–105.

———. 1970. "Efficient Capital Markets: A Review of Theory and Empirical Work." *Journal of Finance* 25 (May), pp. 383–417.

———. 1980. "Agency Problems and the Theory of the Firm." *Journal of Political Economy* 88 (April), pp. 288–307.

———. 1984. "Forward and Spot Exchange Rates." *Journal of Monetary Economics* 14 (November), pp. 319–338.

Fama, Eugene F., and Harvey Babiak. 1968. "Dividend Policy: An Empirical Analysis." *Journal of the American Statistical Association* 63 (December), pp. 1132–1161.

Fama, Eugene F., and Marshall E. Blume. 1966. "Filter Rules and Stock-Market Trading." *Journal of Business* 39 (January), pp. 226–241.

Fama, Eugene F., and Kenneth R. French. 1988. "Permanent and Temporary Components of Stock Prices." *Journal of Political Economy* 96 (April), pp. 246–273.

———. 1989. "Business Conditions and Expected Returns on Stocks and Bonds." *Journal of Financial Economics* 25 (November), pp. 23–49.

———. 1992. "The Cross-Section of Expected Stock Returns." *Journal of Finance* 47 (June), pp. 427–465.

———. 1995. "Size and Book-to-Market Factors in Earnings and Returns." *Journal of Finance* 50 (March), pp. 131–155.

———. 1996. "Multifactor Explanations of Asset Pricing Anomalies." *Journal of Finance* 51 (March), pp. 55–84.

———. 1997. "Industry Costs of Equity." *Journal of Financial Economics* 43 (February), pp. 153–193.

———. 1998. "Taxes, Financing Decisions, and Firm Value." *Journal of Finance* 53 (June), pp. 819–843.

———. 1999. "The Corporate Cost of Capital and the Return on Corporate Investment." *Journal of Finance* 54 (December), pp. 1939–1967.

———. 2002. "Testing Trade-off and Pecking Order Predictions about Dividends and Debt." *Review of Financial Studies* 15 (Spring), pp. 1–33.

Fama, Eugene F., and Michael C. Jensen. 1985. "Organizational Forms and Investment Decisions." *Journal of Financial Economics* 14, pp. 101–118.

Fama, Eugene F., and Merton H. Miller. 1972. *The Theory of Finance* (New York: Holt, Rinehart & Winston).

Fellers, Charles R. 2001a. "Making an Exit: VCs Examine Their Options." *Venture Capital Journal* (May), pp. 40–42.

———. 2001b. "With Companies Faltering, VCs Look at Redemption Exit." *Venture Capital Journal* (June), pp. 34–38.

Fenn, George W. 2000. "Speed of Issuance and the Adequacy of Disclosure in the 144A High-Yield Debt Market." *Journal of Financial Economics* 56 (June), pp. 383–405.

Fernando, Chitru S., Vlaimir A. Gatchev, and Paul A. Spindt. 2005. "Wanna Dance? How Firms and Underwriters Choose Each Other." *Journal of Finance* 60, pp. 2437–2469.

Field, Laura Casares, and Gordon Hanka. 2001. "The Expiration of IPO Share Lock-Ups." *Journal of Finance* 56 (April), pp. 471–500.

Fineberg, Seth. 1997. "Canada's Labor Funds Adapt to Tighter Regs." *Venture Capital Journal* (March), pp. 28–30.

Finnerty, John D., and Douglas R. Emery. 2002. "Corporate Securities Innovation: An Update." *Journal of Applied Finance* 12 (Spring/Summer), pp. 21–47.

Fischer, Edwin O., Robert Heinkel, and Josef Zechner. 1989. "Dynamic Capital Structure Choice: Theory and Tests." *Journal of Finance* 44 (March), pp. 19–40.

Fisher, Irving G. 1965. *The Theory of Interest* (1930; reprint, New York: Augustus M. Kelly).

Foerster, Stephen R., and G. Andrew Karolyi. 2000. "The Long-Run Performance of Global Equity Offerings." *Journal of Financial and Quantitative Analysis* 35 (December), pp. 499–528.

Frankel, Jeffrey A. 1991. "The Japanese Cost of Finance: A Survey." *Financial Management* 20 (Spring), pp. 95–127.

Franks, Julian R., and Walter N. Torous. 1994. "A Comparison of Financial Recontracting in Distressed Exchanges and Chapter 11 Reorganizations." *Journal of Financial Economics* 35 (April), pp. 349–370.

Fraser, Jill Andresky. 1998. "How to Finance Anything." *Inc.* (February), pp. 34–42.

Freear, John. 1994. "The Private Investor Market for Venture Capital." *The Financier* 1 (May), pp. 7–15.

Freear, John, Jeffrey E. Sohl, and William E. Wetzel, Jr. 2000. "The Informal Venture Capital Market: Milestones Passed and the Road Ahead." In *Entrepreneurship 2000*, edited by Donald L. Sexton and Raymond W. Smilor (Chicago: Upstart Publishing).

French, Kenneth R. 1989. "Pricing Financial Futures Contracts: An Introduction." *Journal of Applied Corporate Finance* 1 (Winter), pp. 59–66.

Froot, Kenneth A., David S. Scharfstein, and Jeremy C. Stein. 1993. "Risk Management: Coordinating Corporate Investment and Financing Policies." *Journal of Finance* 48 (December), pp. 1629–1658.

Fung, William K. H., and Michael F. Theobald. 1984. "Dividends and Debt under Alternative Tax Systems." *Journal of Financial and Quantitative Analysis* 19 (March), pp. 59–72.

Galai, Dan, and Ron Masulis. 1976. "The Option Pricing Model and the Risk Factor of Stock." *Journal of Financial Economics* 3 (January), pp. 53–81.

Gande, Amar, Manju Puri, and Anthony Saunders. 1999. "Bank Entry, Competition and the Market for Corporate Securities Underwriting." *Journal of Financial Economics* 54, pp. 165–195.

Garrett, Ian, and Richard Priestley. 2000. "Dividend Behavior and Dividend Signaling." *Journal of Financial and Quantitative Analysis* 35 (June), pp. 173–189.

Garvey, Gerald T., and Gordon Hanka. 1999. "Capital Structure and Corporate Control: The Effect of Antitakeover Statutes on Firm Leverage." *Journal of Finance* 54 (April), pp. 519–546.

Gaughan, Patrick. 1996. *Mergers, Acquisitions, and Corporate Restructurings* (New York: John Wiley & Sons).

Gaver, Jennifer J., and Kenneth M. Gaver. 1993. "Additional Evidence on the Association between the Opportunity Set and Corporate Financing, Dividend, and Compensation Policies." *Journal of Accounting and Economics* 16 (January/April/July), pp. 125–160.

Geczy, Christopher, Bernadette A. Minton, and Catherine Schrand. 1997. "Why Firms Use Currency Derivatives." *Journal of Finance* 52 (September), pp. 1323–1354.

Ghosh, Chimnoy, and J. Randall Woolridge. 1988. "An Analysis of Shareholder Reaction to Dividend Cuts and Omissions." *Journal of Financial Research* 11 (Winter), pp. 281–294.

Gibbons, Michael R., and Patrick Hess. 1981. "Day of the Week Effects and Asset Returns." *Journal of Business* 54 (October), pp. 579–596.

Gibson, Scott, Assem Safieddine, and Ramana Sonti. 2004. "Smart Investments by Smart Money: Evidence from Seasoned Equity Offerings." *Journal of Financial Economics* 72 (June), pp. 581–604.

Gilson, Stuart C. 1989. "Management Turnover and Financial Distress." *Journal of Financial Economics* 25 (December), pp. 241–262.

———. 1997. "Transactions Costs and Capital Structure Choice: Evidence from Financially Distressed Firms." *Journal of Finance* 52 (March), pp. 161–196.

Gilson, Stuart C., Edith S. Hotchkiss, and Richard S. Ruback. 2000. "Valuation of Bankrupt Firms." *Review of Financial Studies* 13 (Spring), pp. 43–74.

Gilson, Stuart C., and Michael R. Vetsuypens. 1993. "CEO Compensation in Financially Distressed Firms: An Empirical Analysis." *Journal of Finance* 48 (June), pp. 425–458.

Gitman, Lawrence J., and John R. Forrester, Jr. 1977. "A Survey of Capital Budgeting Techniques Used by Major U.S. Firms." *Financial Management* 6, pp. 66–71.

Gitman, Lawrence J., and Kanwal S. Sachdeva. 1981. "Accounts Receivable Decisions in a Capital Budgeting Framework." *Financial Management* 10, pp. 45–49.

Goetzmann, William N., and Roger G. Ibbotson. 1994. "Do Winners Repeat?" *Journal of Portfolio Management* 20 (Winter), pp. 9–18.

Goetzmann, William N., Zoran Ivkovic, and K. Geert Rouwenhorst. 2001. "Day Trading International Mutual Funds: Evidence and Policy Solutions." *Journal of Financial and Quantitative Analysis* 36 (September), pp. 287–309.

Golder, Stanley C. 1997. "Structuring the Financing." In *Pratt's Guide to Venture Capital Sources*, edited by Stanley E. Pratt (New York: Securities Data Publishing).

Gompers, Paul A. 1995. "Optimal Investment, Monitoring, and the Staging of Venture Capital." *Journal of Finance* 50 (December), pp. 1461–1489.

———. 1996. "Grandstanding in the Venture Capital Industry." *Journal of Financial Economics* 42 (September), pp. 133–156.

Gompers, Paul, and Josh Lerner. 1996. "The Use of Covenants: An Empirical Analysis of Venture Partnership Agreements." *Journal of Law and Economics* 39 (October), pp. 463–498.

———. 1997. "Ownership and Control in Entrepreneurial Firms: An Examination of Convertible Securities in Venture Capital Investments." Working paper, Harvard Business School.

———. 1998a. "What Drives Venture Capital Fund-raising?" *Brookings Papers on Economic Activity—Microeconomics*, pp. 149–192.

———. 1998b. "Venture Capital Distributions: Short-Run and Long-Run Reactions." *Journal of Finance* 53 (December), pp. 2161–2183.

———. 1999. "An Analysis of Compensation in the U.S. Venture Capital Partnership." *Journal of Financial Economics* 51 (January), pp. 3–44.

———. 2000a. "Money Chasing Deals? The Impact of Fund Inflows on Private Equity Valuations." *Journal of Financial Economics* 55 (February), pp. 281–325.

———. 2000b. "The Really Long-Run Performance of Initial Public Offerings: The Pre-NASDAQ Evidence." Working paper, Harvard Business School (September).

———. 2001. "The Venture Capital Revolution." *Journal of Economic Perspectives* 15 (Spring), pp. 145–168.

Gorman, Michael, and William A. Sahlman. 1989. "What Do Venture Capitalists Do?" *Journal of Business Venturing* 4, pp. 231–248.

Goyal, Vidhan K., Kenneth Lehn, and Stanko Racic. 2002. "Growth Opportunities and Corporate Debt Policy: The Case of the U.S. Defense Industry." *Journal of Financial Economics* 64 (April), pp. 35–59.

Graham, John R. 1996. "Debt and the Marginal Tax Rate." *Journal of Financial Economics* 41 (May), pp. 41–73.

———. 1999. "Herding among Investment Newsletters: Theory and Evidence." *Journal of Finance* 54 (February), pp. 237–268.

———. 2001. "Estimating the Tax Benefits of Debt." *Journal of Applied Corporate Finance* 14 (Spring), pp. 42–54.

Graham, John R., Michael L. Lemmon, and Jack G. Wolf. 2002. "Does Corporate Diversification Destroy Value?" *Journal of Finance* 57 (April), pp. 695–720.

Graham, John R., Roni Michaely, and Michael R. Roberts. 2003. "Do Price Discreteness and Transactions Costs Affect Stock Returns? Comparing Ex-dividend Pricing before and after Decimalization." *Journal of Finance* 58 (December), pp. 2611–2635.

Graham, John R., and Clifford W. Smith, Jr. 1999. "Tax Incentives to Hedge." *Journal of Finance* 54 (December), pp. 2241–2262.

Greene, Jason T., and Charles W. Hodges. 2002. "The Dilution Impact of Daily Fund Flows on Open-End Mutual Funds." *Journal of Financial Economics* 65 (July), pp. 131–158.

Grinblatt, Mark, and Sheridan Titman. 1989. "Mutual Fund Performance: An Analysis of Quarterly Portfolio Holdings." *Journal of Business* 62 (July), pp. 393–416.

Grossman, Sanford J., and Robert J. Shiller. 1981. "The Determinants of the Variability of Stock Market Prices." *American Economic Review* 71 (May), pp. 222–227.

Gruber, Martin J. 1996. "Another Puzzle: The Growth in Actively Managed Mutual Funds." *Journal of Finance* 51 (July), pp. 783–810.

Grullon, Gustavo, and David L. Ikenberry. 2000. "What Do We Know about Stock Repurchases?" *Journal of Applied Corporate Finance* 13 (Spring), pp. 31–49.

Grullon, Gustavo, and Roni Michaely. 2004. "The Information Content of Share Repurchases Programs." *Journal of Finance* 59 (April), pp. 651–680.

Grullon, Gustavo, Roni Michaely, and Bhaskaran Swaminathan. 2002. "Are Dividend Changes a Sign of Firm Maturity?" *Journal of Business* 75 (July), pp. 387–424.

Grundfest, Joseph A. 1990. "Subordination of American Capital." *Journal of Financial Economics* 27 (September), pp. 89–114.

Guay, Wayne, and Jarrad Harford. 2000. "The Cash-Flow Permanence and Information Content of Dividend Increases versus Repurchases." *Journal of Financial Economics* 57 (September), pp. 385–415.

Gul, Ferdinand A. 1999. "Growth Opportunities, Capital Structure and Dividend Policies in Japan." *Journal of Corporate Finance* 5 (June), pp. 141–168.

Gupta, Udayan. 2001. "Truth in Numbers?" *Venture Capital Journal* (May), p. 35.

Habib, Michel A., and Alexander P. Ljungqvist. 2001. "Underpricing and Entrepreneurial Wealth Losses in IPOs: Theory and Evidence." *Review of Financial Studies* 14 (Summer), pp. 433–458.

Hamada, Robert S. 1972. "The Effect of the Firm's Capital Structure on the Systematic Risk of Common Stocks." *Journal of Finance* 27 (May), pp. 435–452.

Hamada, Robert S., and Myron S. Scholes. 1985. "Taxes and Corporate Financial Management." In *Recent Advances in Corporate Finance*, edited by Edward I. Altman and Marti Subrahmanyan (Homewood, IL: Richard D. Irwin).

Hamao, Yasushi, Frank Packer, and Jay Ritter. 2000. "Institutional Affiliation and the Role of Venture Capital: Evidence from Initial Public Offerings in Japan." *Pacific Basin Finance Journal* 8, pp. 529–558.

Hampson, Philip, John Parsons, and Charles Blitzer. 1991. "A Case Study in the Design of an Optimal Sharing Rule for a Petroleum Exploration Venture." *Journal of Financial Economics* 30 (November), pp. 45–67.

Hanley, Kathleen W., A. Arun Kumar, and Paul J. Seguin. 1993. "Price Stabilization in the Market for New Issues." *Journal of Financial Economics* 34 (October), pp. 177–197.

Hansen, Robert S. 1988. "The Demise of the Rights Issue." *Review of Financial Studies* 1, pp. 289–309.

———. 2001. "Do Investment Banks Compete in IPOs? The Advent of the '7% Plus Contract.'" *Journal of Financial Economics* 59 (March), p. 313.

Hansen, Robert S., and Claire Crutchley. 1990. "Corporate Earnings and Financings: An Empirical Analysis." *Journal of Business* 63 (July), pp. 347–371.

Hansen, Robert S., and Naveen Khanna. 1994. "Why Negotiation with a Single Syndicate May Be Preferred to Making Syndicates Compete: The Problem of Trapped Bidders." *Journal of Business* 67 (July), pp. 423–457.

Hansen, Robert S., and John M. Pinkerton. 1982. "Direct Equity Financing: A Resolution of a Paradox." *Journal of Finance* 37 (June), pp. 651–665.

Hardymon, G. Felda, Mark J. DeNino, and Malcolm S. Salter. 1983. "When Corporate Venture Capital Doesn't Work." *Harvard Business Review* (May/June), pp. 114–120.

Harris, Lawrence, and Eitan Gurel. 1984. "Price and Volume Effects Associated with Changes in the S&P 500 List: New Evidence for the Existence of Price Pressures." *Journal of Finance* 41 (September), pp. 815–830.

Harris, Milton, and Artur Raviv. 1991. "The Theory of Capital Structure." *Journal of Finance* 46 (March), pp. 297–355.

Harris, Trevor S., Nahum Melumad, and Toshi Shibano. 1996. "An Argument against Hedging by Matching the Currencies of Costs and Revenues." *Journal of Applied Corporate Finance* 9 (Fall), pp. 90–97.

Hasbrouk, Joel. 1985. "The Characteristics of Takeover Targets." *Journal of Banking and Finance* 9 (September), pp. 351–362.

Haugen, Robert A., and Lemma W. Senbet. 1978. "The Insignificance of Bankruptcy Costs in the Theory of Optimal Capital Structure." *Journal of Finance* 33 (May), pp. 383–393.

Haushalter, G. David. 2000. "Financing Policy, Basis Risk, and Corporate Hedging: Evidence from Oil and Gas Producers." *Journal of Finance* 55 (February), pp. 107–152.

Healy, Paul M., and Krishna Palepu. 1988. "Earnings Information Conveyed by Dividend Initiations and Omissions." *Journal of Financial Economics* 21 (September), pp. 149–175.

Healy, Paul, Krishna Palepu, and Richard Ruback. 1992. "Does Corporate Performance Improve after Mergers?" *Journal of Financial Economics* 31 (April), pp. 135–176.

Heath, David C., and Robert A. Jarrow. 1988. "Ex-dividend Stock Price Behavior and Arbitrage Opportunities." *Journal of Business* 61 (January), pp. 95–108.

Heaton, John, and Robert Korajczyk. 2002. "Introduction to Review of Financial Studies Conference on Market Frictions and Behavioral Finance." *Review of Financial Studies* 15 (Special), pp. 353–361.

Hellmann, Thomas. 1998. "The Allocation of Control Rights in Venture Capital Contracts." *Rand Journal of Economics* (Spring), pp. 57–76.

———. 2002. "A Theory of Strategic Venture Investing." *Journal of Financial Economics* 64 (May), pp. 285–314.

Hellmann, Thomas, and Manju Puri. 2000. "The Interaction between Product Market and Financing Strategy: The Role of Venture Capital." *Review of Financial Studies* 13 (Winter), pp. 959–984.

———. 2002. "Venture Capital and the Professionalization of Start-up Firms: Empirical Evidence." *Journal of Finance* 57 (February), pp. 169–197.

Hendricks, Darryll, Jayendu Patel, and Richard Zeckhauser. 1993. "Hot Hands in Mutual Funds: Short-Run Persistence of Relative Performance, 1974–1988." *Journal of Finance* 48 (March), pp. 93–130.

Hentzler, Herbert A. 1992. "The New Era of Euro-capitalism." *Harvard Business Review* (July/August), pp. 57–68.

Hertzel, Michael, and Richard L. Smith. 1993. "Market Discounts and Shareholder Gains for Placing Equity Privately." *Journal of Finance* 48 (June), pp. 459–485.

Higgins, Robert C. 1977. "How Much Growth Can a Firm Afford?" *Financial Management* 6, pp. 7–16.

Higgins, Robert, and Lawrence Schall. 1975. "Corporate Bankruptcy and Conglomerate Merger." *Journal of Finance* 30 (March), pp. 93–113.

Hillion, Pierre, and Theo Vermaelen. 2002. "Death Spiral Convertibles." Working paper, INSEAD, Fontainebleau, France.

Hines, James R., Jr. 1996. "Dividends and Profits: Some Unsubtle Foreign Influences." *Journal of Finance* 51 (June), pp. 661–689.

Hirschey, Mark, Vernon J. Richardson, and Susan Scholz. 2000. "Stock-Price Effects of Internet Buy-Sell Recommendations: *The Motley Fool* Case." *Financial Review* 35 (May), pp. 147–174.

Hirshleifer, David, Avanidhar Subrahmanyam, and Sheridan Titman. 1994. "Security Analysis and Trading Patterns When Some Investors Receive Information before Others." *Journal of Finance* 49 (December), pp. 1665–1698.

Hirshleifer, Jack. 1958. "On the Theory of Optimal Investment Decision." *Journal of Political Economy* 66 (August), pp. 329–352.

Hoffman, Harold M., and James Blakey. 1987. "You Can Negotiate with Venture Capitalists." *Harvard Business Review* (March/April), pp. 16–24.

Horowitz, Bruce. 2001. "Disney Orders McDonald's Burger Joint for New Park." *USA Today* (January 15).

Hovakimian, Armen, Tim Opler, and Sheridan Titman. 2001. "The Debt-Equity Choice." *Journal of Financial and Quantitative Analysis* 36 (March), pp. 1–24.

Huang, Yen-Sheng, and Ralph Walkling. 1987. "Target Abnormal Returns Associated with Acquisition Announcements: Payment, Acquisition Form, and Managerial Resistance." *Journal of Financial Economics* 19 (December), pp. 329–349.

Huemer, Jason. 1992. "Public Venture Capital: Huge Market Goes Largely Untapped." *Venture Capital Journal* (February), pp. 38–44.

Hughes, Patricia J. 1986. "Signalling by Direct Disclosure under Asymmetric Information." *Journal of Accounting and Economics* 8 (June), pp. 119–142.

Hull, John C., and Alan D. White. 1987. "The Pricing of Options on Assets with Stochastic Volatilities." *Journal of Finance* 42 (June), pp. 281–300.

Ibbotson, Roger G. 1975. "Price Performance of Common Stock New Issues." *Journal of Financial Economics* 2 (September), pp. 235–272.

Ibbotson, Roger G., Jody L. Sindelar, and Jay R. Ritter. 1994. "The Market's Problems with the Pricing of Initial Public Offerings." *Journal of Applied Corporate Finance* 7 (Spring), pp. 66–74.

Ikenberry, David, and Josef Lakonishok. 1993. "Corporate Governance through the Proxy Contest: Evidence and Implications." *Journal of Business* 66 (July), pp. 405–435.

Ikenberry, David, Josef Lakonishok, and Theo Vermaelen. 1995. "Market Underreaction to Open Market Stock Repurchases." *Journal of Financial Economics* 39 (October), pp. 181–208.

Ikenberry, David L., Graeme Rankine, and Earl K. Stice. 1996. "What Do Stock Splits Really Signal?" *Journal of Financial and Quantitative Analysis* 31 (September), pp. 357–375.

Indro, Daniel C., Robert T. Leach, and Wayne Y. Lee. 1999. "Sources of Gains to Shareholders from Bankruptcy Resolution." *Journal of Banking and Finance* 23 (January), pp. 21–47.

Ingersoll, Jonathan E., Jr., and Stephen A. Ross. 1992. "Waiting to Invest: Investment and Uncertainty." *Journal of Business* 65 (March), pp. 1–29.

Ingram, Matt. 2005. "Bankruptcy and Financial Distress: A Literature Review." Working paper, University of Oklahoma (June).

Investment Dealers' Digest. 1997. "Kiss and Tell" (October 27), p. 19.

Ippolito, Richard A. 1989. "Efficiency with Costly Information: A Study of Mutual Fund Performance, 1965–1984." *Quarterly Journal of Economics* 104 (February), pp. 1–23.

Jagannathan, Murali, Clifford P. Stephens, and Michael S. Weisbach. 2000. "Financial Flexibility and the Choice between Dividends and Stock Repurchases." *Journal of Financial Economics* 57 (September), pp. 355–384.

Jain, Bharat A., and Omesh Kini. 1994. "The Post-Issue Operating Performance of IPO Firms." *Journal of Finance* 49 (December), pp. 1699–1726.

Jakob, Keith, and Tongshu Ma. 2004. "Tick Size, NYSE Rule 118, and Ex-dividend Day Stock Price Behavior." *Journal of Financial Economics* 72 (June), pp. 605–625.

James, Christopher. 1987. "Some Evidence on the Uniqueness of Bank Loans." *Journal of Financial Economics* 19 (December), pp. 217–235.

Jarrell, Gregg, James Brickley, and Jeffry Netter. 1988. "The Market for Corporate Control: The Empirical Evidence since 1980." *Journal of Economic Perspectives* 2 (Winter), pp. 49–68.

Jarrell, Gregg A., and Annette Poulsen. 1989a. "Stock Trading before the Announcement of Tender Offers: Insider Trading or Market Anticipation?" *Journal of Law, Economics, and Organization* 5, pp. 225–248.

———. 1989b. "Returns to Acquiring Firms in Tender Offers: Evidence from Three Decades." *Financial Management* 18 (Autumn), pp. 12–19.

Jegadeesh, Narasimhan. 1990. "Evidence of the Predictable Behavior of Security Returns." *Journal of Finance* 45 (July), pp. 881–898.

Jegadeesh, Narasimhan, and Sheridan Titman. 1993. "Returns to Buying Winners and Selling Losers: Implications for Stock Market Efficiency." *Journal of Finance* 48 (March), pp. 65–91.

Jeng, L. A., and P. C. Wells. 2000. "The Determinants of Venture Capital Funding: Evidence across Countries." *Journal of Corporate Finance* 6 (September), pp. 241–289.

Jennings, Robert, and Michael Mazzeo. 1993. "Competing Bids, Target Management Resistance, and the Structure of Takeover Bids." *Review of Financial Studies* 6 (Winter), pp. 883–909.

Jensen, Michael C. 1968. "The Performance of Mutual Funds in the Period 1945–1964." *Journal of Finance* 23 (May), pp. 389–416.

———. 1978. "Some Anomalous Evidence Regarding Market Efficiency." *Journal of Financial Economics* 6 (June/September), pp. 95–101.

———. 1986. "Agency Costs of Free Cash Flow, Corporate Finance and Takeovers." *American Economic Review* 76 (May), pp. 323–329.

———. 1993. "Presidential Address: The Modern Industrial Revolution, Exit, and the Failure of Internal Control Systems." *Journal of Finance* 48 (July), pp. 831–880.

Jensen, Michael C., and George A. Benington. 1970. "Random Walks and Technical Theories: Some Additional Evidence." *Journal of Finance* 25 (May), pp. 156–169.

Jog, Vijay M., and Allan L. Riding. 1986. "Price Effects of Dual-Class Shares." *Financial Analysts Journal* 42 (January/February), pp. 58–67.

John, Kose, and Eli Ofek. 1995. "Asset Sales and Increase in Focus." *Journal of Financial Economics* 37 (January), pp. 105–126.

Johnson, Greg. 2000. "Yankee Bonds and Cross-Border Private Placements: An Update." *Journal of Applied Corporate Finance* 13 (Fall), pp. 80–91.

Jones, Steven L. 1993. "Another Look at Time-Varying Risk and Return in a Long-Horizon Contrarian

Strategy." *Journal of Financial Economics* 33, pp. 119–144.

Jones, Steven L., William L. Megginson, Robert C. Nash, and Jeffry M. Netter. 1999. "Share Issue Privatizations as Financial Means to Political and Economic Ends." *Journal of Financial Economics* 53 (August), pp. 217–253.

Julio, Brandon, and David L. Ikenberry. 2004. "Reappearing Dividends." *Journal of Applied Corporate Finance* 16 (Fall), pp. 89–100.

Kaiser, Kevin M. J. 1996. "European Bankruptcy Laws: Implications for Corporations Facing Financial Distress." *Financial Management* 25 (Autumn), pp. 67–85.

Kalay, Avner. 1982. "Stockholder-Bondholder Conflict and Dividend Constraints." *Journal of Financial Economics* 10 (July), pp. 211–233.

Kalay, Avner, and Marti G. Subrahmanyan. 1984. "The Ex-dividend Day Behavior of Option Prices." *Journal of Business* 57 (January), pp. 113–128.

Kaplan, Steven N., and Bernadette A. Minton. 1994. "Appointments of Outsiders to Japanese Boards: Determinants and Implications for Managers." *Journal of Financial Economics* 36 (October), pp. 225–258.

Kaplan, Steven, and Per Strömberg. 2000. "How Do Venture Capitalists Choose Investments?" Working paper, University of Chicago.

———. 2001a. "Financial Contracting Theory Meets the Real World: An Empirical Analysis of Venture Capital Contracts." Working paper, University of Chicago.

———. 2001b. "Venture Capitalists as Principals: Contracting, Screening, and Monitoring." *American Economic Review* 91 (May), pp. 426–430.

Kaplan, Steven, and Michael Weisbach. 1992. "The Success of Acquisitions: Evidence from Divestitures." *Journal of Finance* 47 (March), pp. 107–138.

Kaplan, Steven N., and Luigi Zingales. 1997. "Do Financing Constraints Explain Why Investment Is Correlated with Cash Flow?" *Quarterly Journal of Economics* 112, pp. 169–215.

Katz, David J. 1990. "Solving the Dilemma of Pricing Secondaries." *Venture Capital Journal* (October), pp. 21–33.

Keim, Donald B. 1983. "Size-Related Anomalies and Stock Return Seasonality: Further Empirical Evidence." *Journal of Financial Economics* 12 (June), pp. 13–32.

Kendall, Maurice G. 1953. "The Analysis of Economic Time Series." *Journal of the Royal Statistical Society*, Series A, 96, pp. 11–25.

Kester, W. Carl. 1992. "Governance, Contracting, and Investment Horizons: A Look at Japan and Germany." *Journal of Applied Corporate Finance* 5 (Summer), pp. 83–98.

Khorana, Ajay. 1996. "Top Management Turnover: An Empirical Investigation of Mutual Fund Managers." *Journal of Financial Economics* 40 (March), pp. 403–427.

Khorana, Ajay, Sunil Wahal, and Marc Zenner. 2002. "Agency Conflicts in Closed-End Funds: The Case of Rights Offerings." *Journal of Financial and Quantitative Analysis* 37 (June), pp. 177–200.

Kinn, Bruce A., and Arnold M. Zaff. 1997. "The Benefits of a Revitalized SBIC Program." In *Pratt's Guide to Venture Capital Sources*, edited by Stanley E. Pratt (New York: Securities Data Publishing), pp. 105–107.

Kleidon, Allan W. 1986. "Variance Bounds Tests and Stock Price Valuation Models." *Journal of Political Economy* 94 (October), pp. 953–1001.

Kliger, Doron, and Oded Sarig. 2000. "The Information Value of Bond Ratings." *Journal of Finance* 55 (December), pp. 2879–2902.

Koch, Adam S., and Amy X. Sun. 2004. "Dividend Changes and the Persistence of Past Earnings Changes." *Journal of Finance* 59 (October), pp. 2093–2116.

Koch, Paul D., and Catherine Shenoy. 1999. "The Information Content of Dividend and Capital Structure Policies." *Financial Management* 28 (Winter), pp. 16–35.

Kogut, Bruce, and Nalin Kulatilaka. 1994. "Operating Flexibility, Global Manufacturing and the Option Value of a Multinational Network." *Management Science* 40 (January), pp. 123–139.

Korajczyk, Robert A., Deborah J. Lucas, and Robert L. McDonald. 1991. "The Effect of Information Releases on the Pricing and Timing of Equity Issues." *Review of Financial Studies* 4, pp. 685–708.

Kothari, S. P., and Jay Shanken. 1992. "Stock Return Variation and Expected Dividends: A Time Series Analysis." *Journal of Financial Economics* 31 (April), pp. 177–210.

———. 1993. "Fundamentals Largely Explain Stock Price Volatility." *Journal of Applied Corporate Finance* 6 (Summer), pp. 81–87.

Kothari, S. P., and Jerold B. Warner. 1997. "Measuring Long-Horizon Security Price Performance." *Journal of Financial Economics* 43, pp. 301–340.

Krigman, Laurie, Wayne H. Shaw, and Kent L. Womack. 2001. "Why Do Firms Switch Underwriters?" *Journal of Financial Economics* 60 (May/June), pp. 245–284.

Kulatilaka, Nalin. 1993. "The Value of Flexibility: The Case of a Dual-Use Industrial Steam Boiler." *Financial Management* 22 (Autumn), pp. 271–280.

Lakonishok, Josef, and Seymour Smidt. 1988. "Are Seasonal Anomalies Real? A Ninety-Year Perspective." *Review of Financial Studies* 1 (Winter), pp. 403–425.

Lakonishok, Josef, and Theo Vermaelen. 1983. "Tax Reform and Ex-dividend Day Behavior." *Journal of Finance* 38 (September), pp. 1157–1175.

———. 1986. "Tax-Induced Trading around Ex-dividend Days." *Journal of Financial Economics* 16 (July), pp. 287–319.

———. 1990. "Anomalous Price Behavior around Repurchase Tender Offers." *Journal of Finance* 45 (June), pp. 455–477.

Lamont, Owen. 1997. "Cash Flow and Investment: Evidence from Internal Capital Markets." *Journal of Finance* (February), pp. 83–109.

Lamont, Owen A., and Christopher Polk. 2001. "The Diversification Discount: Cash Flows versus Returns." *Journal of Finance* 56 (October), pp. 1693–1721.

Lang, Larry, Eli Ofek, and René M. Stulz. 1996. "Leverage, Investment, and Firm Growth." *Journal of Financial Economics* 40 (January), pp. 3–29.

Lang, Larry H. P., and René M. Stulz. 1992. "Contagion and Competitive Intra-industry Effects of Bankruptcy Announcements." *Journal of Financial Economics* 32 (August), pp. 45–60.

———. 1994. "Tobin's q, Corporate Diversification, and Firm Performance." *Journal of Political Economy* 102 (December), pp. 1248–1280.

Lang, Larry, René Stulz, and Ralph Walkling. 1989. "Managerial Performance, Tobin's q and the Gains from Successful Tender Offers." *Journal of Financial Economics* 24 (September), pp. 137–154.

———. 1991. "A Test of the Free Cash Flow Hypothesis: The Case of Bidder Returns." *Journal of Financial Economics* 29 (October), pp. 315–335.

Lasfer, M. Ameziane. 1997. "On the Motivation for Paying Scrip Dividends." *Financial Management* 26 (Spring), pp. 62–80.

Lavelle, Louis. 2001. "Special Report: Executive Pay." *Business Week* (April 16), pp. 75–80.

———. 2002. "Executive Pay: Special Report." *Business Week* (April 15), pp. 80–100.

Lease, Ronald C., John J. McConnell, and Wayne H. Mikkelson. 1983. "The Market Value of Control in Publicly-Traded Corporations." *Journal of Financial Economics* 11 (April), pp. 439–471.

Lee, Bong-Soo. 1995. "The Response of Stock Prices to Permanent and Temporary Shocks to Dividends." *Journal of Financial and Quantitative Analysis* 30 (March), pp. 1–22.

———. 1996. "Time-Series Implications of Aggregate Dividend Behavior." *Review of Financial Studies* 9 (Summer), pp. 589–618.

Lee, Cheng-Few, and Shafiqur Rahman. 1990. "Market Timing, Selectivity, and Mutual Fund Performance: An Empirical Analysis." *Journal of Business* 63 (April), pp. 261–278.

Lee, Chun I., Kimberly C. Gleason, and Ike Mathur. 2000. "Efficiency Tests in the French Derivatives Market." *Journal of Banking and Finance* 24, pp. 787–807.

Lee, Dwight R., and James A. Verbrugge. 1996. "The Efficient Market Thrives on Criticism." *Journal of Applied Corporate Finance* 9 (Spring), pp. 35–40.

Lee, Peggy M., and Sunil Wahal. 2002. "Venture Capital, Certification and IPOs." Working paper, Emory University.

Lee, Susan. 2002. "The Ugly Option." *Wall Street Journal* (April 10).

Lee, Yi-Tsung, Yu-Jane Liu, Richard Roll, and Avanidhar Subrahmanyam. 2004. "Taxes and Dividend Clientele: Evidence from Trading and Ownership Structure." Working paper, University of California at Los Angeles (February).

Leland, Hayne E., and David H. Pyle. 1977. "Informational Asymmetries, Financial Structure, and Financial Intermediation." *Journal of Finance* 32, pp. 371–387.

Lerner, Josh. 1994. "Venture Capitalists and the Decision to Go Public." *Journal of Financial Economics* 35 (June), pp. 293–316.

———. 1994. "The Syndication of Venture Capital Investments." *Financial Management* 23 (Autumn), pp. 16–27.

———. 1995. "Venture Capitalists and the Oversight of Private Firms." *Journal of Finance* 50 (March), pp. 301–318.

———. 1998. "Angel Financing and Public Policy: An Overview." *Journal of Banking and Finance* 22 (August), pp. 773–783.

———. 1999. "The Government as Venture Capitalist: The Long-Run Effects of the SBIR Program." *Journal of Business* 72 (July), pp. 285–318.

———. 2000. *Venture Capital and Private Equity: A Casebook* (New York: John Wiley & Sons).

LeRoy, Christian V., and Stephen F. LeRoy. 1991. "Econometric Aspects of the Variance-Bounds Tests: A Survey." *Review of Financial Studies* 4, pp. 753–791.

Levy, Haim. 1983. "Economic Evaluation of Voting Power of Common Stock." *Journal of Finance* 38 (March), pp. 79–93.

Levy, Haim, and Marshall Sarnat. 1970. "Diversification, Portfolio Analysis, and the Uneasy Case for Conglomerate Mergers." *Journal of Finance* 25 (September), pp. 795–802.

Lewellen, Jonathan. 2002. "Momentum and Autocorrelation in Stock Returns." *Review of Financial Studies* 15 (Special), pp. 533–563.

Lewellen, Wilbur. 1971. "A Pure Financial Rationale for the Conglomerate Merger." *Journal of Finance* 26 (May), pp. 531–537.

Lewellen, Wilbur, Claudio Loderer, and Ahron Rosenfeld. 1985. "Merger Decisions and Executive Stock Ownership in Acquiring Firms." *Journal of Accounting and Economics* 7 (April), pp. 209–231.

Lie, Erik. 2000. "Excess Funds and Agency Problems: An Empirical Study of Incremental Cash Distributions." *Review of Financial Studies* 13 (Spring), pp. 219–248.

Linn, Scott C., and J. Michael Pinegar. 1988. "The Effect of Issuing Preferred Stock on Common and Preferred Stockholder Wealth." *Journal of Financial Economics* 22 (October), pp. 155–184.

Lins, Karl, and Henri Servaes. 1999. "International Evidence on the Value of Corporate Diversification." *Journal of Finance* 54 (December), pp. 2215–2239.

Lipson, Marc L., Carlos P. Macquieira, and William L. Megginson. 1998. "Dividend Initiations and Earnings Surprises." *Financial Management* 27 (Autumn), pp. 36–45.

Livingston, Miles, and Robert E. Miller. 2000. "Investment Banking Reputation and the Underwriting of Nonconvertible Debt." *Financial Management* 29 (Summer), pp. 21–34.

Ljungqvist, Alexander P., and William J. Wilhelm, Jr. 2001. "IPO Pricing in the Dot-Com Bubble: Complacency or Incentives?" Working paper, New York University.

Lo, Andrew W., and A. Craig MacKinlay. 1988. "Stock Market Prices Do Not Follow Random Walks: Evidence from a Simple Specification Test." *Review of Financial Studies* 1 (Spring), pp. 41–66.

———. 1990. "When Are Contrarian Profits Due to Stock Market Overreaction?" *Review of Financial Studies* 3, pp. 175–205.

Lo, Andrew W., Harry Mamaysky, and Jiang Wang. 2000. "Foundations of Technical Analysis: Computational Algorithms, Statistical Inference, and Empirical Implementation." *Journal of Finance* 55 (August), pp. 1705–1765.

Logue, Dennis E., and Seha M. Tiniç. 1999. "Optimal Choice of Contracting Methods: Negotiated versus Competitive Underwriting Revisited." *Journal of Financial Economics* 51 (March), pp. 451–471.

Long, Michael, and Ileen Malitz. 1985. "The Investment-Financing Nexus: Some Empirical Evidence." *Midland Corporate Finance Journal* 3 (Spring), pp. 53–59.

Lorie, James H., and Leonard J. Savage. 1955. "Three Problems in Rationing Capital." *Journal of Business* 28 (October), pp. 229–239.

Loughran, Tim, and Jay R. Ritter. 2000. "Uniformly Least Powerful Tests of Market Efficiency." *Journal of Financial Economics* 55, pp. 361–389.

Loughran, Tim, Jay R. Ritter, and Kristian Rydqvist. 1994. "Initial Public Offerings: International Insights." *Pacific Basin Finance Journal* 2, pp. 165–199.

Loughran, Tim, and Anand Vijh. 1997. "Do Long-Term Shareholders Benefit from Corporate Acquisitions?" *Journal of Finance* 52 (December), pp. 1765–1790.

Lowry, Michelle, and G. William Schwert. 2002. "IPO Market Cycles: Bubbles or Sequential Learning?" *Journal of Finance* 57 (June), pp. 1171–1200.

Lubben, Stephen. 2000. "The Direct Costs of Corporate Reorganization: An Empirical Examination of Professional Fees in Large Chapter 11 Cases." *American Bankruptcy Law Journal* 74 (Fall), pp. 509–552.

Lummer, Scott C., and John J. McConnell. 1989. "Further Evidence on the Bank Lending Process and the Capital Market Responses to Bank Loan Agreements." *Journal of Financial Economics* 25 (November), pp. 99–122.

Lynch, Anthony W., and Richard R. Mendenhall. 1997. "New Evidence on Stock Price Effects Associated with Changes in the S&P 500 Index." *Journal of Business* 70 (July), pp. 351–383.

MacKie-Mason, Jeffrey K. 1990. "Do Taxes Affect Corporate Financing Decisions?" *Journal of Finance* 45 (December), pp. 1471–1493.

Majd, Saman, and Robert S. Pindyck. 1987. "Time to Build, Option Value and Investment Decisions." *Journal of Financial Economics* 18 (March), pp. 7–28.

Maksimovic, Vojislav, and Gordon Phillips. 1998. "Asset Efficiency and Reallocation Decisions of Bankrupt Firms." *Journal of Finance* 53 (October), pp. 1495–1532.

Maksimovic, Vojislav, and Sheridan Titman. 1991. "Financial Policy and Reputation for Product Quality." *Review of Financial Studies* 4, pp. 175–200.

Malkiel, Burton G., and William J. Baumol. 2002. "Stock Options Keep the Economy Afloat." *Wall Street Journal* (April 4), p. A18.

Mandelker, Gershon, and Artur Raviv. 1977. "Investment Banking: An Economic Analysis of Optimal Underwriting Contracts." *Journal of Finance* 32 (June), pp. 683–694.

Manne, H. G. 1965. "Mergers and the Market for Corporate Control." *Journal of Political Economy* 73, pp. 110–120.

Markowitz, Harry. 1952. "Portfolio Selection." *Journal of Finance* 7 (March), pp. 77–91.

Marsh, Paul. 1982. "The Choice between Equity and Debt: An Empirical Study." *Journal of Finance* 37 (March), pp. 121–144.

Martin, John D., and J. William Petty. 1983. "An Analysis of the Performance of Publicly Traded Venture Capital Companies." *Journal of Financial and Quantitative Analysis* 18 (September), pp. 401–410.

Masson, Dubos J., ed. 2001. *Essentials of Cash Management*, 7th ed. (Bethesda, MD: Association for Financial Professionals).

Masulis, Ronald W. 1980. "The Effect of Capital Structure Change on Security Prices: A Study of Exchange Offers." *Journal of Financial Economics* 8 (June), pp. 139–177.

Masulis, Ronald W., and Ashok N. Korwar. 1986. "Seasoned Equity Offerings: An Empirical Investigation." *Journal of Financial Economics* 15 (January/February), pp. 91–118.

Maxwell, William F., and Clifford P. Stephens. 2003. "The Wealth Effects of Repurchases on Bondholders." *Journal of Finance* 58 (April), pp. 895–919.

Mayer, Colin. 1990. "Financial Systems, Corporate Finance, and Economic Development." In *Asymmetric Information, Corporate Finance and Investment*, edited by R. Glenn Hubbard (Chicago: University of Chicago Press).

Mayers, David. 1972. "Non-Marketable Assets and the Determination of Capital Market Equilibrium under Uncertainty." In *Studies in the Theory of Capital Markets*, edited by Michael Jensen (New York: Praeger).

Mayers, David, and Clifford Smith. 1982. "On the Corporate Demand for Insurance." *Journal of Business* 55 (April), pp. 281–296.

McConnell, John J., and Eduardo S. Schwartz. 1992. "The Origins of LYONs: A Case Study in Financial Innovation." *Journal of Applied Corporate Finance* 4 (Winter), pp. 82–89.

McLaughlin, Robyn, and Robert A. Taggart, Jr. 1992. "The Opportunity Cost of Excess Capacity." *Financial Management* 21 (Summer), pp. 12–23.

McQueen, Grant. 1992. "Long-Horizon Mean-Reverting Stock Prices Revisited." *Journal of Financial and Quantitative Analysis* 27 (March), pp. 1–18.

Megginson, William L. 1990. "Restricted Voting Stock, Acquisition Premiums and the Market Value of Corporate Control." *Financial Review* 25 (May), pp. 175–198.

Megginson, William L., Robert C. Nash, Jeffry Netter, and Adam Schwartz. 2000. "The Long-Term Return to Investors in Share Issue Privatizations." *Financial Management* 29 (Spring), pp. 67–77.

Megginson, William L., Robert C. Nash, and Matthias van Randenborgh. 1994. "The Financial and Operating Performance of Newly-Privatized Firms: An International Empirical Analysis." *Journal of Finance* 49 (June), pp. 403–452.

———. 1996. "The Record on Privatization." *Journal of Applied Corporate Finance* 9 (Spring), pp. 403–452.

Megginson, William L., and Jeffry M. Netter. 2001. "From State to Market: A Survey of Empirical Studies on Privatization." *Journal of Economic Literature* 39 (June), pp. 321–389.

Megginson, William L., and Kathleen A. Weiss. 1991. "Venture Capital Certification in Initial Public Offerings." *Journal of Finance* 46 (July), pp. 879–903.

Mello, Antonio S., and John E. Parsons. 1999. "Strategic Hedging." *Journal of Applied Corporate Finance* 12 (Fall), pp. 43–54.

Menyah, Kojo, Krishna Paudyal, and Charles G. Inyangete. 1995. "Subscriber Return, Underpricing, and Long-Term Performance of U.K. Privatization Initial Public Offers." *Journal of Economics and Business* 47, pp. 473–495.

Merton, Robert C. 1973a. "An Intertemporal Capital Asset Pricing Model." *Econometrica* 41 (September), pp. 867–887.

———. 1973b. "Theory of Rational Option Pricing." *Bell Journal of Economics* 4 (Spring), pp. 141–183.

Meulbroek, Lisa K. 1992. "An Empirical Analysis of Illegal Insider Trading." *Journal of Finance* 47 (December), pp. 1661–1699.

Mian, Shehzad. 2001. "On the Choice and Replacement of Chief Financial Officers." *Journal of Financial Economics* 60, pp. 143–175.

Michaely, Roni, and Franklin Allen. 2002. "Payout Policy." In *Handbook of Economics*, edited by George Constantinides et al. (Amsterdam: North-Holland).

Michaely, Roni, and Wayne H. Shaw. 1995. "The Choice of Going Public: Spin-offs and Carve-outs." *Financial Management* 24 (Autumn), pp. 5–21.

Michaely, Roni, Richard H. Thaler, and Kent L. Womack. 1995. "Price Reactions to Dividend Initiations and Omissions: Overreaction or Drift?" *Journal of Finance* 50 (June), pp. 573–608.

Miffre, Joëlle. 2001. "Efficiency in the Pricing of the FTSE 100 Futures Contract." *European Financial Management* 7, pp. 9–22.

Mikkelson, Wayne H., and M. Megan Partch. 1986. "Valuation Effects of Security Offerings and the Issuance Process." *Journal of Financial Economics* 15 (January/February), pp. 31–60.

Mikkelson, Wayne H., M. Megan Partch, and Kshitij Shah. 1997. "Ownership and Operating Performance of Companies That Go Public." *Journal of Financial Economics* 44, pp. 281–307.

Miller, Merton H. 1999. "The History of Finance: An Eyewitness Account." *Journal of Portfolio Management* (Summer), pp. 95–101. [Text of a speech made to the German Finance Association on September 25, 1998.]

Miller, Merton H., and Franco Modigliani. 1961. "Dividend Policy, Growth, and the Valuation of Shares." *Journal of Business* 34 (October), pp. 411–433.

Mitchell, Mark, and Harold Mulherin. 1996. "The Impact of Industry Shocks on Takeover and Restructuring Activity." *Journal of Financial Economics* 41 (June), p. 93.

Mitchell, Mark, and Erik Stafford. 2000. "Managerial Decisions and Long-Term Stock Price Performance." *Journal of Business* 73 (July), pp. 287–320.

Modigliani, Franco, and Merton Miller. 1963. "Corporate Income Taxes and the Cost of Capital." *American Economic Review* 53 (June), pp. 433–443.

Moehrle, Stephen, and Jennifer Reynolds-Moehrle. 2001. "Say Good-Bye to Pooling and Goodwill Amortization." *Journal of Accountancy* 192 (September), pp. 11–20.

Moore, James, Jay Culver, and Bonnie Masterman. 2000. "Risk Management for Middle Market Companies." *Journal of Applied Corporate Finance* 12 (Winter), pp. 112–119.

Morck, Randall, Andrei Shleifer, and Robert Vishny. 1988. "Management Ownership and Market Valuation: An Empirical Analysis." *Journal of Financial Economics* 20 (January), pp. 293–315.

———. 1990. "Do Managerial Objectives Drive Bad Acquisitions?" *Journal of Finance* 45 (March), pp. 31–48.

Morris, Jane Koloski. 1988. "The Pricing of a Venture Capital Investment." In *Pratt's Guide to Venture Capital Sources*, edited by Stanley E. Pratt (New York: Securities Data Publishing), pp. 55–61.

Moskowitz, Tobias J., and Mark Grinblatt. 1999. "Do Industries Explain Momentum?" *Journal of Finance* 54 (August), pp. 1249–1290.

Mukherjee, Tarun K. 1991. "A Survey of Corporate Leasing Analysis." *Financial Management* 20 (Autumn), pp. 96–107.

Mulherin, J. Harold, and Annette Poulsen. 1998. "Proxy Contests and Corporate Change: Implications for Shareholder Wealth." *Journal of Financial Economics* 47 (March), pp. 279–313.

Murphy, Kevin. 1985. "Corporate Performance and Managerial Remuneration: An Empirical Analysis." *Journal of Accounting and Economics* 7 (April), pp. 11–42.

Muscarella, Chris J., and Michael R. Vetsuypens. 1990. "Efficiency and Organizational Structure: A Study of Reverse LBOs." *Journal of Finance* 45 (December), pp. 1389–1413.

Myers, Stewart C. 1977. "The Determinants of Corporate Borrowing." *Journal of Financial Economics* 5 (November), pp. 147–176.

———. 1993. "Still Searching for an Optimal Capital Structure." *Journal of Applied Corporate Finance* 6 (Spring), pp. 4–14.

Nance, Deana R., Clifford W. Smith, Jr., and Charles W. Smithson. 1993. "On the Determinants of Corporate Hedging." *Journal of Finance* 48 (March), pp. 267–284.

Nanda, Vikram. 1991. "On the Good News in Equity Carve-Outs." *Journal of Finance* 46 (December), pp. 1717–1737.

Narayanan, Rajesh P., Kasturi P. Rangan, and Nanda K. Rangan. 2004. "The Role of Syndicate Structure in Bank Underwriting." *Journal of Financial Economics* 72 (June), pp. 555–580.

Nathan, Kevin, and Terrence O'Keefe. 1989. "The Rise in Takeover Premiums: An Exploratory Study." *Journal of Financial Economics* 23 (June), pp. 101–119.

Nichols, N. A. 1994. "Scientific Management at Merck: An Interview with Judy Lewent." *Harvard Business Review* 72 (January/February), p. 91.

Obstfeld, Maurice, and Kenneth Rogoff. 2001. "The Six Major Puzzles in International Macroeconomics: Is There a Common Cause?" In *NBER Macroeconomics Annual 2000*, edited by Ben Bernanke and Kenneth Rogoff (Cambridge, MA: MIT Press), pp. 339–390.

Ojah, Kalu, and David Karemera. 1999. "Random Walks and Market Efficiency Tests of Latin American Emerging Equity Markets: A Revisit." *Financial Review* 34 (May), pp. 57–72.

Opler, Tim C., and Sheridan Titman. 1994. "Financial Distress and Corporate Performance." *Journal of Finance* 49 (July), pp. 1015–1040.

Packer, Frank. 1996. "Venture Capital, Bank Share-holding, and IPO Underpricing in Japan." In *Empirical Issues in Raising Equity Capital*, edited by Mario Levis (Amsterdam: North-Holland), pp. 191–214.

Parrino, Robert, and Michael Weisbach. 1999. "Measuring Investment Distortions Arising from Stockholder-Bondholder Conflicts." *Journal of Financial Economics* 53 (July), pp. 3–42.

Pástor, Lubos, and Robert F. Stambaugh. 2002. "Mutual Fund Performance and Seemingly Unrelated Assets." *Journal of Financial Economics* 63, pp. 315–349.

Petersen, Mitchell A., and Raghuram G. Rajan. 1994. "The Benefits of Lending Relationships: Evidence from Small Business Data." *Journal of Finance* 49 (March), pp. 3–37.

Pettit, Richard, and Ronald Singer. 1985. "Small Business Finance: A Research Agenda." *Financial Management* 14 (Spring), pp. 47–60.

Peyer, Urs, and Anil Shivdasani. 2001. "Leverage and Internal Capital Markets: Evidence from Leveraged Recapitalizations." *Journal of Financial Economics* 59 (March), pp. 477–515.

Phillips, Gordon M. 1995. "Increased Debt and Industry Product Markets: An Empirical Analysis." *Journal of Financial Economics* 37 (February), pp. 189–238.

Poterba, James. 1987. "Tax Policy and Corporate Savings." *Brookings Papers on Economic Activity* 2 (December), pp. 455–515.

Pound, John, and Richard Zeckhauser. 1990. "Clearly Heard on the Street: The Effects of Takeover Rumors on Stock Prices." *Journal of Business* 63 (July), pp. 291–308.

Pratt, Stanley E. 1988. "The Organized Venture Capital Community." In *Pratt's Guide to Venture Capital Sources*, edited by Stanley E. Pratt (New York: Securities Data Publishing), pp. 55–61.

———. 1997. "The Organized Venture Capital Community." In *Pratt's Guide to Venture Capital Sources*, edited by Stanley E. Pratt (New York: Securities Data Publishing), pp. 75–80.

Pringle, John J. 1991. "Managing Foreign Exchange Exposure." *Journal of Applied Corporate Finance* 3 (Winter), pp. 73–82.

Pringle, John J., and Robert A. Connolly. 1993. "The Nature and Causes of Foreign Currency Exposure." *Journal of Applied Corporate Finance* 6 (Fall), pp. 61–72.

Prowse, Michael. 1992. "Is America in Decline?" *Harvard Business Review* (July/August), pp. 34–45.

Prowse, Stephen D. 1990. "Institutional Investment Patterns and Corporate Financial Behavior in the United States and Japan." *Journal of Financial Economics* 27, pp. 43–66.

———. 1996. "Corporate Finance in International Perspective: Legal and Regulatory Influences on Financial System Development." Federal Reserve Bank of Dallas *Economic Review* (Third Quarter), pp. 2–15.

Pulvino, Todd C. 1999. "The Effects of Bankruptcy Court Protection on Asset Sales." *Journal of Financial Economics* 52 (May), pp. 151–186.

Puri, Manju. 1999. "Commercial Banks as Under-writers: Implications for the Going Public Process." *Journal of Financial Economics* 54, pp. 133–163.

Rajan, Raghuram, and Mitchell Petersen. 1997. "Trade Credit: Some Theories and Evidence." *Review of Financial Studies* 10, pp. 661–692.

Rajan, Raghuram, Henri Servaes, and Luigi Zingales. 2000. "The Cost of Diversity: The Diversification Discount and Inefficient Investment." *Journal of Finance* 55 (February), pp. 35–80.

Rajan, Raghuram G., and Luigi Zingales. 1995. "What Do We Know about Capital Structure? Some Evidence from International Data." *Journal of Finance* 50 (December), pp. 1421–1460.

Rau, P. Raghavendra. 2000. "Investment Bank Market Share, Contingent Fee Payments, and the Performance of Acquiring Firms." *Journal of Financial Economics* 56 (May), pp. 293–324.

Ravenscraft, David, and F. M. Scherer. 1987. *Mergers, Sell-Offs, and Economic Efficiency* (Washington, DC: Brookings Institution).

Ravid, S. Abraham, and Stefan Sundgren. 1998. "The Comparative Efficiency of Small-Firm Bankruptcies: A Study of the US and Finnish Bankruptcy Codes." *Financial Management* 27 (Winter), pp. 28–40.

Rawls, S. Waite, III, and Charles W. Smithson. 1989. "The Evolution of Risk Management Products." *Journal of Applied Corporate Finance* 1 (Winter), pp. 18–26.

Reese, William A., Jr. 1998. "Capital Gains Taxation and Stock Market Activity: Evidence from IPOs." *Journal of Finance* 53 (October), pp. 1799–1819.

Richardson, Matthew, and Tom Smith. 1994. "A Unified Approach to Testing for Serial Correlation in Stock Returns." *Journal of Business* 67 (July), pp. 371–399.

Riley, John. 1979. "Informational Equilibrium." *Econometrica* 47 (March), pp. 331–359.

Ritter, Jay R. 1984. "Signaling and the Valuation of Unseasoned New Issues: A Comment." *Journal of Finance* 39, pp. 1231–1237.

———. 1991. "The Long-Run Performance of Initial Public Offerings." *Journal of Finance* 46 (March), pp. 3–27.

———. 1996. "How I Helped Make Fischer Black Wealthier." *Financial Management* 24 (Winter), pp. 104–107.

———. 2001. "The Biggest Mistakes That We Teach." Working paper, University of Florida.

Ritter, Jay, and Navin Chopra. 1989. "Portfolio Rebalancing and the Turn-of-the-Year Effect." *Journal of Finance* 44 (March), pp. 149–166.

Roberts, Harry V. 1959. "Stock Market 'Patterns' and Financial Analysis: Methodological Suggestions." *Journal of Finance* 14 (March), pp. 1–10.

Rock, Kevin. 1986. "Why New Issues Are Underpriced." *Journal of Financial Economics* 15 (January/February), pp. 187–212.

Rodriguez, Ricardo. 1988. "The Wealth Maximization Ordering Quantity: An Extension." *Financial Review* 23 (May), pp. 227–232.

Roe, Mark J. 1990. "Political and Legal Restraints on Ownership and Control of Public Companies." *Journal of Financial Economics* 27 (September), pp. 7–41.

———. 1997. "The Political Roots of American Corporate Finance." *Journal of Applied Corporate Finance* 9 (Winter), pp. 8–22.

Roll, Richard. 1977. "A Critique of the Asset Pricing Theory's Tests, Part I: On Past and Potential Testability of the Theory." *Journal of Financial Economics* 4, pp. 129–176.

———. 1994. "What Every CEO Should Know about Scientific Progress in Economics: What Is Known and What Remains to Be Resolved." *Financial Management* 23 (Summer), pp. 69–75.

Ross, Stephen A. 1976. "The Arbitrage Theory of Capital Asset Pricing." *Journal of Economic Theory* (December), pp. 341–360.

Rubinstein, Mark E. 1973. "A Mean-Variance Synthesis of Corporate Financial Policy." *Journal of Finance* 28 (March), pp. 167–181.

Rutterford, Janette. 1988. "An International Perspective on the Capital Structure Puzzle." In *New Developments in International Finance*, edited by Joel M. Stern and Donald H. Chew, Jr. (New York: Basil Blackwell).

Safieddine, Assem, and Sheridan Titman. 1999. "Leverage and Corporate Performance: Evidence from Unsuccessful Takeovers." *Journal of Finance* 54 (April), pp. 547–580.

Sahlman, William A. 1988. "Aspects of Financial Contracting in Venture Capital." *Journal of Applied Corporate Finance* 1 (Summer), pp. 23–36.

———. 1990. "The Structure and Governance of Venture Capital Organizations." *Journal of Financial Economics* 27 (September), pp. 473–524.

Samant, Ajay. 1996. "An Empirical Study of Interest Rate Swap Usage by Nonfinancial Corporate Business." *Journal of Financial Services Research* 10 (March), pp. 43–57.

Samuelson, Paul A. 1965. "Proof That Properly Anticipated Prices Fluctuate Randomly." *Industrial Management Review* 6 (Spring), pp. 41–49.

Sarkar, Sudipto. 2001. "Probability of Call and Likelihood of the Call Feature in a Corporate Bond." *Journal of Banking and Finance* 25 (March), pp. 505–533.

Schenone, Carola. 2004. "The Effect of Banking Relationships on the Firm's IPO Underpricing." *Journal of Finance* 59 (December), pp. 3–27.

Scherr, Frederick C. 1996. "Optimal Trade Credit Limits." *Financial Management* 25, pp. 71–85.

Schilit, W. Keith, and John T. Willig, eds. 1996a. "The Globalization of Venture Capital." In *Fitzroy Dearborn International Directory of Venture Capital Funds*, 2nd ed. (Chicago: Fitzroy Dearborn), pp. 79–80.

———. 1996b. "Structuring the Venture Capital Deal." In *Fitzroy Dearborn International Directory of Venture Capital Funds*, 2nd ed. (Chicago: Fitzroy Dearborn), pp. 71–77.

Schipper, Katherine, and Abbie Smith. 1986. "A Comparison of Equity Carve-outs and Seasoned Equity Offerings: Share Price Effects and Corporate Restructuring." *Journal of Financial Economics* 15 (January/February), pp. 153–186.

Schoar, Antoinette. 2002. "Effects of Corporate Diversification on Productivity." *Journal of Finance* 57 (December), pp. 2379–2403.

Schultz, Paul. 2003. "Pseudo Market Timing and the Long-Run Underperformance of IPOs." *Journal of Finance* 58 (April), pp. 483–517.

Schultz, Paul H., and Mir A. Zaman. 1994. "Aftermarket Support and the Underpricing of Initial Public Offerings." *Journal of Financial Economics* 35 (April), pp. 199–219.

Schwert, G. William. 1996. "Markup Pricing in Mergers and Acquisitions." *Journal of Financial Economics* 41 (June), pp. 153–192.

Scott, James H., Jr. 1977. "Bankruptcy, Secured Debt, and Optimal Capital Structure." *Journal of Finance* 32 (March), pp. 1–19.

Sekely, William S., and J. Markham Collins. 1988. "Cultural Influences on International Capital Structure." *Journal of International Business Studies* (Spring), pp. 87–100.

Servaes, Henri. 1991. "Tobin's q and the Gains from Takeovers." *Journal of Finance* 46 (March), pp. 409–420.

———. 1996. "The Value of Diversification during the Conglomerate Merger Wave." *Journal of Finance* 51 (September), pp. 1201–1225.

Seyhun, H. Nejat, and Michael Bradley. 1997. "Corporate Bankruptcy and Insider Trading." *Journal of Business* 70 (April), pp. 189–216.

Shah, Kshitij. 1994. "The Nature of Information Conveyed by Pure Capital Structure Changes." *Journal of Financial Economics* 36 (August), pp. 89–126.

Shapiro, Alan C., and Sheridan Titman. 1986. "An Integrated Approach to Corporate Risk Management." In *The Revolution in Corporate Finance*, edited by Joel Stern and Donald Chew (Oxford, U.K.: Basil Blackwell).

Sharpe, William F. 1966. "Mutual Fund Performance." *Journal of Business* 39 (January), pp. 119–138.

Shastri, Kuldeep. 1990. "The Differential Effects of Mergers on Corporate Security Values." *Research in Finance* 8, pp. 179–201.

Shefrin, Hersh. 2002. "Behavioral Corporate Finance." *Journal of Applied Corporate Finance* 14 (Fall), pp. 113–124.

Sherman, Ann Geunther. 1992. "The Pricing of Best Efforts New Issues." *Journal of Finance* 47 (June), pp. 781–790.

Sherman, Ann, and Sheridan Titman. 2003. "Building the IPO Order Book: Underpricing and Participation Limits with Costly Information."

Journal of Financial Economics 65 (July), pp. 3–29.

Shiller, Robert J. 1979. "The Volatility of Long-Term Interest Rates and Expectations Models of the Term Structure." *Journal of Political Economy* 87 (December), pp. 1190–1219.

———. 1981. "Do Stock Prices Move Too Much to Be Justified by Subsequent Changes in Dividends?" *American Economic Review* 71 (June), pp. 421–436.

Shin, Hyun-Han, and Young S. Park. 1999. "Financing Constraints and Internal Capital Markets: Evidence from Korean 'Chaebols.'" *Journal of Corporate Finance* 5 (June), pp. 169–191.

Shleifer, Andrei, and Lawrence Summers. 1988. "Breach of Trust in Hostile Takeovers." In *Corporate Takeovers: Causes and Consequences* (Chicago: University of Chicago Press).

———. 1990. "The Noise Trader Approach to Finance." *Journal of Economic Perspectives* 4 (Spring), pp. 19–33.

Shleifer, Andrei, and Robert Vishny. 1989. "Management Entrenchment." *Journal of Financial Economics* 25 (November), pp. 123–139.

———. 1997a. "The Limits to Arbitrage." *Journal of Finance* 52 (March), pp. 35–55.

———. 1997b. "A Survey of Corporate Governance." *Journal of Finance* 52 (June), pp. 736–783.

Shockley, Richard L., Jr. 2001. "McTreat Spots: Creating Options at McDonald's." Teaching case, Indiana University.

Shyam-Sunder, Lakshmi, and Stewart C. Myers. 1999. "Testing the Static Trade-off against Pecking Order Models of Capital Structure." *Journal of Financial Economics* 51 (February), pp. 219–244.

Sirri, Erik R., and Peter Tufano. 1998. "Costly Search and Mutual Fund Flows." *Journal of Finance* 53 (October), pp. 1589–1622.

Slovin, Myron B., Marie E. Sushka, and Steven R. Ferraro. 1995. "A Comparison of the Information Conveyed by Equity Carve-outs, Spin-offs, and Asset Sell-offs." *Journal of Financial Economics* 37 (January), pp. 89–104.

Slovin, Myron B., Marie E. Sushka, and K. W. L. Lai. 2000. "Alternative Flotation Methods, Adverse Selection, and Ownership Structure: Evidence from Seasoned Equity Issuance in the U.K." *Journal of Financial Economics* 57 (August), pp. 157–190.

Smith, Clifford W., Jr. 1977. "Alternative Methods of Raising Capital: Rights versus Underwritten Offerings." *Journal of Financial Economics* 5 (December), pp. 273–307.

———. 1992. "Economics and Ethics: The Case of Salomon Brothers." *Journal of Applied Corporate Finance* 5 (Summer), pp. 23–28.

Smith, Clifford W., Jr., Charles W. Smithson, and D. Sykes Wilford. 1989. "Managing Financial Risk." *Journal of Applied Corporate Finance* 1 (Winter), pp. 27–48.

Smith, Clifford W., Jr., and René M. Stulz. 1985. "The Determinants of Firms' Hedging Policies." *Journal of Financial and Quantitative Analysis* 20 (December), pp. 391–405.

Smith, Clifford W., Jr., and Ross L. Watts. 1992. "The Investment Opportunity Set and Corporate Financing, Dividend, and Compensation Policies." *Journal of Financial Economics* 32 (December), pp. 263–292.

Smith, Janet Kiholm. 1987. "Trade Credit and Informational Asymmetry." *Journal of Finance* 42 (September), pp. 863–872.

Sneddon, Gregory B., and Jay K. Turner. 1997. "Non-traditional Financing Sources." In *Pratt's Guide to Venture Capital Sources*, edited by Stanley E. Pratt (New York: Venture Economics), pp. 91–96.

Song, Wei-Ling. 2004. "Competition and Coalition among Underwriters: The Decision to Join a Syndicate." *Journal of Finance* 59 (October), pp. 2421–2444.

Sorensen, Eric H., and Thierry F. Bollier. 1994. "Pricing Swap Default Risk." *Financial Analysts Journal* 50, pp. 23–33.

Spence, Michael. 1973. "Job Market Signalling." *Quarterly Journal of Economics* 87 (August), pp. 355–374.

Spiess, D. Katherine, and John Affleck-Graves. 1995. "Underperformance in Long-Run Stock Returns following Seasoned Equity Offerings." *Journal of Financial Economics* 38 (July), pp. 243–267.

Stancill, James McNeill. 1987. "How Much Money Does Your New Venture Need?" *Harvard Business Review* (May/June), pp. 122–139.

Stickel, Scott. 1985. "The Effect of Value Line Investment Survey Rank Changes on Common Stock Prices." *Journal of Financial Economics* 14 (March), pp. 121–143.

Stiglitz, Joseph E. 2002. "Accounting for Options." *Wall Street Journal* (May 3).

Stillman, Robert. 1983. "Examining Antitrust Policy towards Mergers." *Journal of Financial Economics* 11 (April), pp. 225–240.

Strömberg, Per. 2000. "Conflicts of Interest and Market Illiquidity in Bankruptcy Auctions: Theory and Tests." *Journal of Finance* 55 (December), pp. 2641–2692.

Stulz, René M. 1984. "Optimal Hedging Policies." *Journal of Financial and Quantitative Analysis* 19 (June), pp. 127–140.

———. 1988. "Managerial Control of Voting Rights: Financing Policies and the Market for Corporate Control." *Journal of Financial Economics* 20 (January), pp. 25–54.

———. 1990. "Managerial Discretion and Optimal Financing Policies." *Journal of Financial Economics* 26 (July), pp. 1–25.

———. 1996. "Rethinking Risk Management." *Journal of Applied Corporate Finance* 9 (Fall), pp. 8–24.

Subrahmanyam, Avanidhar, and Sheridan Titman. 1999. "The Going-Public Decision and the Development of Financial Markets." *Journal of Finance* 54 (June), pp. 1045–1082.

Sullivan, Ryan, Allan Timmerman, and Halbert White. 1999. "Data-Snooping, Technical Trading Rule Performance, and the Bootstrap." *Journal of Finance* 54 (October), pp. 1647–1691.

Taggart, Robert A., Jr. 1985. "Secular Patterns in the Financing of U.S. Corporations." In *Corporate Capital Structures in the United States*, edited by Benjamin M. Friedman (Chicago: University of Chicago Press).

Targett, Simon. 2001. "Institutional Investment: Should Do More." *Financial Times* (June 14), European Private Equity Survey, p. 5.

Testa, Richard J. 1988. "The Legal Process of Venture Capital Investment." In *Pratt's Guide to Venture Capital Sources*, edited by Stanley E. Pratt (New York: Securities Data Publishing), pp. 66–77.

Thatcher, Janet S. 1985. "The Choice of Call Provisions Terms: Evidence of the Existence of Agency Costs of Debt." *Journal of Finance* 40 (June), pp. 549–561.

Thorburn, Karin S. 2000. "Bankruptcy Auctions: Costs, Debt Recovery and Firm Survival." *Journal of Financial Economics* 58 (December), pp. 337–368.

Titman, Sheridan. 1984. "The Effect of Capital Structure on a Firm's Liquidation Decision." *Journal of Financial Economics* 13 (March), pp. 137–151.

———. 1992. "Interest Rate Swaps and Corporate Financing Choices." *Journal of Finance* 47 (September), pp. 1503–1516.

Titman, Sheridan, and Roberto Wessels. 1988. "The Determinants of Capital Structure Choice." *Journal of Finance* 43 (March), pp. 1–19.

Travlos, Nickolas G. 1987. "Corporate Takeover Bids, Methods of Payment, and Bidding Firms' Stock Returns." *Journal of Finance* 42 (September), pp. 943–963.

Triantis, Alexander J., and James E. Hodder. 1990. "Valuing Flexibility as a Complex Option." *Journal of Finance* 45 (June), pp. 549–565.

Trigeorgis, Lenos, and Scott P. Mason. 1987. "Valuing Managerial Flexibility." *Midland Corporate Finance Journal* 5 (Spring), pp. 14–21.

Tufano, Peter. 1996. "Who Manages Risk? An Empirical Examination of Risk Management Practices in the Gold Mining Industry." *Journal of Finance* 51 (September), pp. 1097–1137.

Tyebjee, Tyzoon T., and Albert V. Bruno. 1984. "A Model of Venture Capitalist Investment Activity." *Management Science* 30 (September), pp. 1051–1066.

Vermaelen, Theo. 1981. "Common Stock Repurchases and Market Signalling." *Journal of Financial Economics* 9 (June), pp. 139–183.

Vijh, Anand M. 1999. "Long-Term Returns from Equity Carve-outs." *Journal of Financial Economics* 51 (February), pp. 273–308.

Villalonga, Belén. 2004. "Diversification Discount or Premium? New Evidence from the Business Information Tracking Series." *Journal of Finance* 59 (April), pp. 479–506.

Vu, Joseph D. 1986. "An Examination of the Corporate Call Behavior of Nonconvertible Bonds." *Journal of Financial Economics* 16 (June), pp. 235–265.

Vuolteenaho, Tuomo. 2002. "What Drives Firm-Level Stock Returns?" *Journal of Finance* 57 (April), pp. 233–264.

Wakita, Shigeru. 2001. "Efficiency of the Dojima Rice Future Market in Tokugawa-Period Japan." *Journal of Banking and Finance* 25 (March), pp. 535–554.

Walker, Ernest W., and J. William Petty II. 1978. "Financial Differences between Large and Small Firms." *Financial Management* 7 (Winter), pp. 61–68.

Warner, Jerold B. 1977. "Bankruptcy Costs: Some Evidence." *Journal of Finance* 32 (May), pp. 337–347.

Warren, Carl S., James M. Reeve, and Philip E. Fess. 2002. *Corporate Financial Accounting*, 7th ed. (Cincinnati, OH: Thomson South-Western).

Wassener, Bettina. 2002. "Tarnished Image in Need of Restoration." *Financial Times* Special Survey of Germany (June 12), p. 2.

Wedig, Gerard J., Mahmud Hassan, and Michael A. Morrisey. 1996. "Tax Exempt Debt and the Capital Structure of Nonprofit Organizations: An Application to Hospitals." *Journal of Finance* 51 (September), pp. 1247–1283.

Wei, Zhang, and Jiang Yanfu. 2002. "The Relationship between Venture Capitalists' Experience and Their Involvement in the VC-Backed Companies." Working paper, Tsinghua University, Beijing.

Weiss, Lawrence A. 1990. "Bankruptcy Resolution: Direct Costs and Violations of Absolute Priority of Claims." *Journal of Financial Economics* 27 (October), pp. 285–314.

Welch, Ivo. 1991. "An Empirical Examination of Models of Contract Choice in Initial Public Offerings." *Journal of Financial and Quantitative Analysis* 26 (December), pp. 497–518.

———. 2000. "Herding among Security Analysts." *Journal of Financial Economics* 58, pp. 369–396.

Wermers, Russ. 2000. "Mutual Fund Performance: An Empirical Decomposition into Stock-Picking Talent, Style, Transactions Costs, and Expenses." *Journal of Finance* 55 (August), pp. 1655–1703.

Weston, Fred J., and Juan A. Siu. 2003. "Changing Motives for Share Repurchases." *Finance* (December 19), Paper 3-03.

Whited, Toni M. 1992. "Debt, Liquidity Constraints and Corporate Investment: Evidence from Panel Data." *Journal of Finance* 47 (September), pp. 1425–1460.

———. 2001. "Is It Inefficient Investment That Causes the Diversification Discount?" *Journal of Finance* 56 (October), pp. 1667–1691.

Williams, Frances. 2001. "Global Foreign Investment Flows 'Set to All by 40%.'" *Financial Times* (September 9), p. 9.

Williams, Joseph. 1988. "Efficient Signalling with Dividends, Investment, and Stock Repurchases." *Journal of Finance* 43 (July), pp. 737–747.

Womack, Kent L. 1996. "Do Brokerage Analysts' Recommendations Have Investment Value?" *Journal of Finance* 51 (March), pp. 137–166.

Wong, Andrew. 2001. "Angel Finance: The Other Venture Capital." Working paper, University of Chicago.

Yeoman, John C. 2001. "The Optimal Spread and Offering Price for Underwritten Securities." *Journal of Financial Economics* 62 (October), pp. 169–198.

Zingales, Luigi. 1994. "The Value of the Voting Right: A Study of the Milan Stock Exchange Experience." *Review of Financial Studies* 7, pp. 125–148.

———. 1998. "Survival of the Fittest or the Fattest? Exit and Financing in the Trucking Industry." *Journal of Finance* 53 (June), pp. 905–938.

Glossary

A

ABC system (Chapter 22)   An inventory control system that segregates inventory into three groups: A, B, and C. The A items require the largest dollar investment and the most intensive control, the B items require the next largest investment and less intensive control, and the C items require the smallest investment and the least intensive control.

absolute priority rules (APRs) (Chapter 25)   Rules contained in chapter 7 of the Bankruptcy Reform Act of 1978 that specify the procedure by which secured creditors are paid first, then unsecured creditors, then preferred shareholders, and finally common stockholders.

accelerated underwritings (Chapter 16)   A seasoned equity offering that takes place in as little as 24–48 hours and is targeted primarily at institutional investors.

accounting exposure (Chapter 20)   Occurs when MNCs translate costs and revenues denominated in foreign currencies to report on their financial statements—which, of course, are denominated in the home currency. This type of risk arises because foreign exchange-rate fluctuations affect individual accounts in the financial statements.

accounting return on investment (ROI) (Chapter 21)   A performance metric calculated by dividing a firm's reported net income by its total assets.

accounts payable management (Chapter 23)   A short-term financing activity that involves managing the time that elapses between the purchase of raw materials and mailing the payment to the supplier.

accredited investors (Chapter 16)   Individuals or institutions that meet certain income and wealth requirements.

accrual-based approach (Chapter 2)   Revenues are recorded at the time of sale and costs when they are incurred, not necessarily when a firm receives or pays out cash.

acquisition (Chapter 24)   The purchase of additional resources by a business enterprise.

activity ratio (Chapter 2)   A measure of the speed with which various accounts are converted into sales or cash.

additional paid-in capital (Chapter 11)   Capital in excess of par value.

adjustable-rate preferred stock (Chapter 23)   A corporate obligation used for short-term investments. These stocks take advantage of the dividend exclusion (of 70% or more) for stock in one corporation held by another corporation. In order to make this investment suitable for short-term holdings, the dividend rate paid on the stock is adjusted according to some rate index. This will stabilize the price, even if interest rates change during the 45-day holding period required to qualify for the dividend exclusion.

adjusted present value (APV) method (Chapter 14)   A method for valuing investment projects or firms that discounts unlevered cash flows at the cost of equity and then adds the present value of any financing side effects, such as the tax shield associated with debt financing.

agency bonds (Chapter 4)   Bonds issued by federal government agencies. Agency bonds are not explicitly backed by the full faith and credit of the U.S. government. Agencies issue bonds to promote the formation of credit in certain sectors of the economy such as real estate, education, and farming.

agency cost/contracting model (Chapter 15)   A theoretical model that explains empirical regularities in dividend payment and share repurchase patterns.

agency cost of overvalued equity (Chapter 24)   Michael Jensen's model of the agency cost of overvalued equity predicts that when a company's stock becomes significantly overvalued, this sets in motion a set of organizational forces that inevitably push managers to take actions that destroy part or all of the firm's core value. A manager's stock is overvalued when she realizes that she cannot, except by pure luck, produce the performance required to justify this stock price.

agency cost theory of financial structure (Chapter 13)   Michael Jensen and William Meckling (1976) observe that if an entrepreneur owns 100% of a company's stock then there is no separation between corporate ownership and control; the entrepreneur bears all the costs, and reaps all the benefits, of his actions.

agency costs (Chapter 1)   The costs that arise because of conflicts of interest between shareholders and managers.

agency problems (Chapter 1)   The conflict between the goals of a firm's owners and managers.

aggressive strategy (Chapter 21)   When a company relies heavily on short-term borrowing, not only to meet the seasonal peaks each year but also to finance a portion of the long-term growth in sales and assets.

aging of accounts receivable (Chapter 22)   A schedule that indicates the portions of the total accounts receivable balance that have been outstanding for specified periods of time.

all-in rate (Chapter 23)   The base rate and the spread.

American call option (Chapter 18)   Gives holders the right to purchase stock at a fixed price on *or before* the expiration date.

American Depositary Receipts (ADRs) (Chapter 16) Dollar-denominated claims, issued by U.S. banks, that represent ownership of shares of a foreign company's stock held on deposit by the U.S. bank in the issuing firm's home country.

angel capitalists (Chapter 26)   Wealthy individuals who make private equity investments on an ad hoc basis.

annual percentage rate (APR) (Chapter 3)   The stated annual rate calculated by multiplying the periodic rate by the number of periods in one year.

annual percentage yield (APY) (Chapter 3)   The annual rate of interest actually earned, reflecting the impact of compounding frequency.

annuity (Chapter 3)   A stream of equal periodic (frequently annual) cash flows over a stated period of time.

annuity due (Chapter 3)   An annuity for which the payments occur at the beginning of each period.

antitakeover amendments (Chapter 24)   Adding defensive measures to corporate charters in order to discourage a hostile takeover.

appreciated (Chapter 20)   The condition of a currency that has increased in value compared to another currency.

arbitrage (Chapters 10, 12, and 27)   The process of buying something in one market at a low price and simultaneously selling it in another market at a higher price to generate an immediate, risk-free profit.

arithmetic average return (Chapter 5)   The average annual return over a period of years.

asset beta (Chapter 9)   A measure of the systematic risk of a real asset based on the covariance of the cash flows

generated by that asset divided by the variance of cash flows from the market portfolio.

asset market model of exchange rates (Chapter 20)   This model makes a distinction between the demand for a currency as a means of payment (transactions demand) and the demand for currency as a financial asset (as a store of value).

asset substitution (Chapter 13)   An investment that will increase firm value but does not earn a return high enough to fully redeem the maturing bonds.

assets-to-equity (A/E) ratio (Chapter 2)   A measurement of the proportion of total assets financed by a firm's equity.

at the money (Chapter 18)   Occurs when an option's strike price equals the price of the underlying stock.

automated clearinghouse (ACH) debit transfer (Chapter 23) A preauthorized electronic withdrawal from the payer's account.

automatic stay (Chapter 25)   Legal protection given to a firm that has filed for bankruptcy; it prevents creditors from taking further action to collect their claims.

availability float (Chapter 23)   The time between deposit of a check and availability of the funds to a firm.

average age of inventory (Chapter 2)   A measure of inventory turnover, calculated by dividing 365 (the number of days in a year) by the turnover figure.

average collection period (Chapter 2)   The average length of time from a sale on credit until the payment becomes usable funds for a firm. Also called the *average age of accounts receivable.*

average investment in accounts receivable (AIAR) (Chapter 22)   An estimate of the actual amount of cash tied up in accounts receivable at any time during the year.

average payment period (Chapter 2)   Calculated by dividing the firm's accounts payable balance by its average daily purchases.

B

backward integration (Chapter 24)   A merger in which the acquired company provides an earlier step in the production process.

balloon payment (Chapter 17)   A term loan agreement that requires periodic interest payments over the life of the loan followed by a large lump-sum payment at maturity.

bank account analysis statement (Chapter 23)   A regular report (usually monthly) provided to a bank's commercial customers that specifies all services provided, including items processed and any charges assessed.

bank discount yield (Chapter 4)   A poor measure of a bond's return that is frequently used by bond traders to communicate with each other about current prices in the market.

bankruptcy (Chapters 13 and 25)   Occurs only when a company enters bankruptcy court and effectively surrenders control of the firm to a bankruptcy judge.

Bankruptcy Code (Chapter 25)   The legal rules governing the process of handling claims against a bankrupt firm.

bankruptcy costs (Chapter 13)   The direct and indirect costs of the bankruptcy process.

basis points (Chapter 4)   Yield spreads on bonds are normally quoted in terms of basis points. One basis point equals one one-hundredth of one percent (i.e., 0.01%). Simply put, 100 basis points = 1.00%.

basis risk (Chapter 27)   The possibility of unanticipated changes in the difference between the futures price and the spot price.

bearer bonds (Chapter 17)   Bonds that both shelter investment income from taxation and provide protection against exchange-rate risk.

behavioral finance (Chapter 10)   Asserts that because traders in financial markets are human beings, they are subject to all the foibles and fads that bedevil human judgment in other spheres of life.

best-efforts offering (Chapter 16)   In a best-efforts offering, the investment bank promises to give its best effort to sell the firm's securities at the agreed-upon price but makes no guarantee about the ultimate success of the offering. If there is insufficient demand, then the firm withdraws the issue from the market. Best-efforts offerings are most commonly used for small, high-risk companies, and the investment bank receives a commission based on the number of shares sold.

beta (Chapter 5)   A standardized measure of the risk of an individual asset that captures only the systematic component of its volatility.

binomial option pricing model (Chapter 18)   This model recognizes that investors can combine options (either calls or puts) with shares of the underlying asset to construct a portfolio with a risk-free payoff.

Black and Scholes option pricing equation (Chapter 19)   A stochastic differential equation relating the time to expiration and the strike price of an option, the current price and the volatility of its underlying stock, and the risk-free interest rate.

board of directors (Chapter 1)   Elected by shareholders to be responsible for hiring and firing managers and setting overall corporate policies.

bond equivalent yield (BEY) (Chapters 4 and 23)   The percentage return on zero-coupon bonds calculated as the difference between the par value and the purchase price.

bond indenture (Chapter 4)   A legal document describing the terms and conditions associated with a particular bond offering.

bond ratings (Chapter 4)   Grades assigned based on degree of risk.

bonding mechanism (Chapter 13)   Shareholders are willing to pay a higher price for a firm's shares, because taking on debt validates a manager's willingness to risk losing control
of her firm if she fails to perform effectively.

bonds (Chapter 1)   Debt with original maturities of more than seven years.

book building (Chapter 16)   A process in which underwriters ask prospective investors to reveal information about their demand for the offering. Through conversations with investors, the underwriter tries to measure the demand curve for a given issue, and the investment bank sets the offer price after gathering all the information it can from investors.

book value (Chapter 4)   The value of a firm's equity as shown on its balance sheet.

bottom-up sales forecast (Chapter 21)   This kind of sales forecast relies on the assessment by sales personnel of demand in the coming year on a customer-by-customer basis.

break-even analysis (Chapter 9)   A calculation that shows conditions under which a project's profits and losses, or cash inflows and outflows, balance out.

bubble phenomenon (Chapter 10)   A rapid rise in the price of an asset or asset class, followed by a steep decline.

bulge bracket (Chapter 16)   Consists of firms that generally occupy the lead or co-lead manager's position in large, new security offerings, meaning that they take primary responsibility for the new offering (even though other banks participate as part of a syndicate), and as a result they earn higher fees.

business failure (Chapter 25)   The circumstance of a firm's inability to stay in business.

bust-up (Chapter 24)   The takeover of a company that is subsequently split up.

C

call option (Chapter 18)   Grants the right to purchase a share of stock (or some other asset) at a fixed price on or before a certain date.

call premium (Chapter 17)   The amount by which the call price exceeds the par value of a bond. Paid by corporations to call bonds after a protection period ends.

callable (Chapter 11)   Bonds that the issuing corporation has the right to force investors to sell back to the firm at the firm's discretion.

cancellation option (Chapter 26)   Option to deny or delay additional funding for a venture fund.

cannibalization (Chapter 8)   Loss of sales of an existing product when a new product is introduced.

capital asset pricing model (CAPM) (Chapter 6)   States that the expected return on a specific asset equals the risk-free rate plus a premium that depends on the asset's beta and the expected risk premium on the market portfolio.

capital budgeting (Chapter 7)   The process of identifying which long-lived investment projects a firm should undertake.

capital budgeting function (Chapter 1)   Selecting the best projects in which to invest the resources of the firm, based on each project's perceived risk and expected return.

capital commitments (Chapter 26)   Commitments that limited partners (investors) make to venture capital and buyout funds. These commitments are then "called" over time, requiring investors to actually pay cash into the fund to allow it to make investments.

capital investment (Chapter 7)   Investments in long-lived assets such as plant, equipment, and advertising.

capital lease (Chapter 17)   A noncancelable contractual arrangement whereby the lessee agrees to make periodic payments to the lessor, typically for more than five years, to obtain an asset's services.

capital market line (CML) (Chapter 6)   Under the assumption of homogeneous expectations, the line connecting the market portfolio to the risk-free rate, which quantifies the relationship between the expected return and standard deviation for portfolios consisting of the risk-free asset and the market portfolio.

capital rationing (Chapter 7)   Choosing a combination of projects that maximizes shareholder wealth, given a set of attractive investment opportunities and subject to the constraint of limited funds.

capital spending (Chapter 7)   Investments in long-lived assets such as plant, equipment, and advertising.

capital structure (Chapter 1)   Distribution of the financial claims on the firm between debt and equity securities; intended to maximize the market value of a firm.

carried interest (Chapter 26)   The performance or incentive fee, expressed as a percentage of the profit earned on the fund's investments that is paid to the general partners managing venture capital and buyout funds. For venture and buyout funds, the carried interest is around 20% of profits.

cash application (Chapter 22)   The process through which a customer's payment is posted to its account and the outstanding invoices are cleared as paid.

cash budget (Chapter 21)   A statement of a firm's planned inflows and outflows of cash.

cash concentration (Chapter 23)   The process of bringing the lockbox and other deposits together into one bank, often called the *concentration bank*.

cash conversion cycle (CCC) (Chapter 22)   The elapsed time between the points at which a firm pays for raw materials and at which it receives payment for finished goods.

cash disbursements (Chapter 21)   These include all outlays of cash by a firm in a given period.

cash discount (Chapter 22)   A method of lowering investment in accounts receivable by rewarding prompt payment.

cash flow approach (Chapter 2)   Used by financial professionals to focus attention on current and prospective inflows and outflows of cash.

cash flow from operations (Chapter 11)   Cash inflows and outflows directly related to the production and sale of a firm's products or services. Calculated as net income plus depreciation and other noncash charges.

cash manager (Chapter 23)   A specialist responsible for managing a firm's cash flow time line related to collection, concentration, and disbursement of the company's funds.

cash position management (Chapter 23) The collection, concentration, and disbursement of funds for the company.

cash receipts (Chapter 21) These include all of a firm's cash inflows in a given period.

cash settlement (Chapter 18) Investor sale of an option for cash eliminates the need for the seller to buy shares to give to the buyer, together with the need for the buyer to sell shares if he wants to convert his profit into cash.

cash-out statutes (Chapter 24) Antitrust "all-or-none" rules that disallow a partial tender offer/acquisition of a company and the ability to control that company with less than 100% ownership.

catastrophe bonds (Chapter 11) Bonds that distribute interest and principal payments that vary according to whether or not the issuer (an insurance company) experiences losses of a certain magnitude from a natural disaster, such as a hurricane or an earthquake. Insurance companies sell these bonds to redistribute some of the risk of their product portfolios. For investors, catastrophe bonds offer unique diversification benefits because the occurrence of natural disasters is not highly correlated with other sources of financial risk (e.g., interest-rate movements, currency movements, business cycles).

catering theory (Chapter 15) Predicts that corporate managers cater to investor preferences by paying dividends when investors assign a premium to dividend-paying stocks and by not paying when investors assign a discount to dividend payers. In other words, corporations respond more or less passively to investor preferences regarding whether profits should be distributed as dividends or retained inside the firm.

certification (Chapter 16) Assurance that the issuing company is in fact disclosing all material information.

chapter 7 (Chapter 25) Section of the Bankruptcy Reform Act of 1978 that details the procedures to be followed when liquidating a failed firm.

chapter 11 (Chapter 25) Section of the Bankruptcy Reform Act of 1978 that details the procedures to be followed when reorganizing a failed or failing firm.

chief executive officer (CEO) (Chapter 1) Hired by the board of directors to be responsible for managing day-to-day operations and carrying out the policies established by the board.

clearing float (Chapter 23) The time between deposit of the check and presentation of the check back to the bank on which it is drawn.

closing futures price (Chapter 27) The price used to settle all contracts at the end of each day's trading.

co-insurance of debt (Chapter 24) The debt of each combining firm in a merger is insured with cash flows from two businesses.

cold comfort letter (Chapter 16) A simple statement that a company's financial statements were prepared according to generally accepted accounting principles and accurately reflect all relevant information.

collateral (Chapters 11 and 17) The specific assets pledged to secure a loan.

collateral trust bonds (Chapter 17) A secured type of bond.

collection policy (Chapter 22) The procedures used by a company to collect overdue or delinquent accounts receivable. The approach used is often a function of the industry and the competitive environment.

co-managers (Chapter 16) Banks other than the lead underwriter when a firm enlists the services of more than one investment bank.

commercial paper (Chapters 1, 11, and 23) The primary corporate obligation in the short-term market. Typically structured as an unsecured promissory note with a maturity of less than 270 days and sold to other corporations and individual investors. Most issues are also backed by credit guarantees from a financial institution, are sold on a discount basis, and are held to maturity.

common stock (Chapter 2) Stockholders' equity.

competitively bid offer (Chapter 16) The less common approach firms can take in choosing an investment banker: the firm announces the terms of its intended equity sale, and investment banks bid for the business.

compound interest (Chapter 3) Interest earned both on the principal amount and on the interest earned in previous periods.

conservative strategy (Chapter 21) When a company makes sure that it has enough long-term financing to cover its permanent investments in fixed and current assets as well as the additional investments in current assets that it makes during the third and fourth quarters each year.

consolidation (Chapter 24)   A merger in which both the acquirer and target disappear as separate corporations, combining to form an entirely new corporation with new common stock.

constant growth model (Chapter 4)   Assumes that dividends will grow at a constant rate forever when calculating the value of a cash flow stream by using the formula for a growing perpetuity.

continuous compounding (Chapter 3)   Interest compounds at literally every moment as time passes.

contribution margin (Chapters 9 and 22)   The sale price per unit minus variable cost per unit.

controlled disbursement (Chapter 23)   A bank service that provides early notification of checks that will be presented against a company's account on a given day.

conversion premium (Chapter 19)   Price to which shares would have to rise before bondholders would want to convert their bonds into shares.

conversion price (Chapter 19)   The market price of a convertible bond divided by its conversion ratio. The conversion price shows the price that a bondholder effectively pays for common stock if the bondholder exercises the conversion option.

conversion ratio (Chapter 19)   Defines how many shares bondholders will receive if they convert.

conversion value (Chapter 19)   The value bondholders receive if they do convert. Conversion value is important because it helps define a lower bound on the market value of a convertible bond.

convertible bonds (Chapters 17 and 19)   The investor is granted the right to receive payment in shares of an underlying stock rather than in cash.

convertibles (Chapter 11)   Corporate bonds that grant an investor the right to exchange the bonds for shares of stock rather than cash.

corporate bonds (Chapter 4)   Bonds with maturities ranging from 1 to 100 years that are issued by corporations.

corporate charter (Chapter 1)   The legal document created at the corporation's inception to govern its operations.

corporate control (Chapter 24)   The monitoring, supervision, and direction of a corporation or other business organization.

corporate finance (Chapter 1)   The science of managing money in a business environment.

corporate focus (Chapter 24)   A focused firm concentrates its efforts on its core (primary) business; the opposite end of the spectrum from a diversified firm.

corporate governance (Chapter 11)   The system that encompasses a nation's body of commercial law, including the institutions, regulations, and practices that influence how—and in whose interest—managers run companies.

corporate governance function (Chapter 1)   Developing an ownership and corporate governance structure for the company, which ensures that the managers act ethically and in the interests of the firm's stakeholders, particularly its stockholders.

corporate venture capital funds (Chapter 26)   Subsidiaries or stand-alone firms established by nonfinancial corporations eager to gain access to emerging technologies by making early-stage investments in high-tech firms.

corporate insider (Chapter 11)   A commercial bank or other financial institution trusted with confidential information concerning a borrowing firm's operations and opportunities.

corporation (Chapter 1)   In U.S. law, a separate legal entity with many of the economic rights and responsibilities enjoyed by individuals.

correlation coefficient (Chapter 5)   A unit-free measure of the co-movement of two assets that standardizes the covariance measure by dividing it by the product of the standard deviations of each asset.

cost of marginal investment in accounts receivable (Chapter 22)   The marginal investment in accounts receivable required to support a proposed change in credit standards multiplied by the required return on investment.

counterparty risk (Chapter 18)   The risk that the counterparty on a specific trade will default on its obligation.

coupon (Chapter 4)   A fixed amount of interest that a bond promises to pay investors.

coupon rate (Chapter 4)   The rate derived by dividing the bond's annual coupon payment by its par value.

coupon yield (Chapter 4)   The amount obtained by dividing the bond's coupon by its current market price (which does not always equal its par value).

covariance (Chapter 5)   A statistical concept that provides a way of measuring the co-movements of two random variables.

coverage ratio (Chapter 2)   A debt ratio that focuses more on income statement measures of a firm's ability to generate sufficient cash flow to make scheduled interest and principal payments.

covered interest arbitrage (Chapter 20)   Occurs when traders attempt to earn arbitrage profits arising from differences in interest rates across countries and so "cover" their currency exposures with forward contracts.

cramdown (Chapter 25)   Used when a reorganization plan fails to meet the standard for approval by all classes, but at least one class of creditors has voted for a reorganization plan; or when the firm is clearly insolvent and the existing equity has no value.

credit monitoring (Chapter 22)   The ongoing review of a firm's accounts receivable to determine if customers are paying according to the stated credit terms.

credit scoring (Chapter 22)   Applies statistically derived weights for key financial and credit characteristics to predict whether or not a credit applicant with specific scores for each characteristic will pay the requested credit in a timely fashion.

credit terms (Chapter 22)   The terms of sale for customers.

cross exchange rate (Chapter 20)   Calculated by dividing the dollar exchange rate for one currency by the dollar exchange rate for another currency.

cross-default covenant (Chapter 17)   In which the borrower is often considered to be in default on all debts if it is in default on any debt.

cross-hedging (Chapter 27)   The underlying securities in a futures contract and the assets being hedged have different characteristics.

cumulative voting system (Chapter 11)   System that gives to each share of common stock a number of votes equal to the total number of directors to be elected.

currency forward contract (Chapter 27)   Exchange of one currency for another at a fixed date in the future.

current ratio (Chapter 2)   A measure of a firm's ability to meet its short-term obligations; defined as current assets divided by current liabilities.

currency swap (Chapter 27)   A swap contract in which two parties exchange payment obligations denominated in different currencies.

D

date of record (Chapter 15)   The date on which the names of all persons who own shares in a company are recorded as stockholders and thus eligible to receive a dividend.

debentures (Chapters 11 and 17)   Unsecured bonds backed only by the general faith and credit of the borrowing company.

debt (Chapter 1)   Borrowed money.

debt beta (Chapter 9)   A measure of the systematic risk of a real debt based on the covariance between return on debt and returns on a diversified portfolio of securities.

debt capital (Chapter 11)   Capital provided by the firm's creditors.

debt ratio (Chapter 2)   A measurement of the proportion of total assets financed by a firm's creditors.

debtor in possession (DIP) (Chapter 25)   The firm filing a reorganization petition.

debt-to-equity ratio (Chapter 2)   A measurement calculated by dividing long-term debt by stockholders' equity.

decision tree (Chapter 9)   A visual representation of the choices that managers face over time with regard to a particular investment.

default risk (Chapter 4)   The risk that the corporation selling a bond may not make all scheduled payments.

deferred taxes (Chapter 2)   Reflect the discrepancy between the taxes that firms actually pay and the tax liabilities they report on their public financial statements.

depreciated (Chapter 20)   The condition of a currency that has decreased in value compared to a different currency.

depreciation (Chapter 8)   A noncash expense that effectively spreads the cost of an asset over several accounting periods.

derivative securities (Chapter 18)   A class of financial instruments that derive their values from other assets.

direct bankruptcy costs (Chapter 13)   Out-of-pocket cash expenses directly related to bankruptcy filing and administration.

direct lease (Chapter 17)   A lessor acquires the assets that are leased to a given lessee.

direct quotation (Chapter 20)   An exchange-rate quote expressed in terms of home currency divided by foreign currency.

discount (Chapter 4)   The difference between a bond's par value and the purchase price when the price is less than par value.

discount investment (Chapter 23)   An investment vehicle for which the investor pays less than face value at the time of purchase and then receives the face value of the investment at its maturity date.

discounted cash flow (DCF) analysis (Chapter 5)   A process of valuing a financial or nonfinancial asset by calculating the asset's cash flows and discounting them at an appropriate rate.

discounted payback (Chapter 7)   The amount of time it takes for a project's discounted cash flows to recover the initial investment.

discounting (Chapter 3)   Describes the process of calculating present values.

divestiture (Chapter 24)   Assets and/or resources of a subsidiary or division are sold to another organization.

dividend payout ratio (Chapters 2 and 15)   The percentage of current earnings available for common stockholders paid out as dividends. Calculated by dividing the firm's cash dividend per share by its earnings per share.

dividend per share (DPS) (Chapter 2)   The portion of the earnings per share paid to stockholders.

dividend yield (Chapter 15)   Computed by dividing a firm's annual dividend per share by its stock price.

double-taxation problem (Chapter 1)   Taxation of corporate income at both the company and the personal levels—the single greatest disadvantage of the corporate form.

dual-class recapitalization (Chapter 24)   Organizational restructuring in which the parties wishing to concentrate control (usually management) buy all the shares of a newly issued Class B stock, which carries "super" voting rights (100 votes per share, for example).

due diligence (Chapter 16)   Examination of potential security issuers in which investment banks are legally required to search out and disclose all relevant information about an issuer before selling securities to the public.

DuPont system (Chapter 2)   An analysis that uses both income and balance sheet information to break the ROA and ROE ratios into component pieces.

E

earnings per share (EPS) (Chapter 2)   Earnings available for common stockholders divided by the number of shares of common stock outstanding.

economic exposure (Chapter 20 and 27)   The overall impact of foreign exchange-rate fluctuations on the

firm's value. Also, the risk that a change in prices will negatively affect the value of all cash flows of a firm.

economic order quantity (EOQ) model (Chapter 22)   A common tool used to estimate the optimal order quantity for big-ticket items of inventory. It considers operating and financial costs and determines the order quantity that minimizes overall inventory costs.

economic profit (Chapter 7)   A measure of profit that incorporates a charge for the capital employed to generate that profit.

economic value added (EVA®) (Chapters 7 and 21)   A copyrighted measure calculated as the difference between a firm's net operating profits after taxes (NOPAT) and its cost of funds. Often used by firms as a growth target.

economies of scale (Chapter 24)   Relative operating costs are reduced for merged companies because of an increase in size that allows for the reduction or elimination of overlapping resources.

economies of scope (Chapter 24)   Value-creating benefits of increased size for merged companies.

effective (Chapter 16)   Status of an offering before any shares can actually be sold to public investors.

effective annual rate (EAR) (Chapter 3)   The annual rate of interest actually paid or earned, reflecting the impact of compounding frequency.

effective borrowing rate (EBR) (Chapter 23)   Generally determined as the total amount of interest and fees paid divided by the average usable loan amount.

efficient frontier (Chapter 6)   Portfolios that maximize expected returns for any given level of volatility.

efficient markets hypothesis (EMH) (Chapter 10)   Asserts that financial asset prices fully reflect all available information (as formally presented by Eugene Fama in 1970).

efficient portfolio (Chapter 6)   A portfolio that offers the highest expected return among the group of portfolios with equal or less volatility.

efficient set (Chapter 6)   A set of portfolios, determined graphically, that offer the highest available expected returns without adding volatility.

electronic bill presentment and payment (EBPP) (Chapter 23)   Customers are sent bills in an electronic format and can then pay them via electronic means.

electronic depository transfer (EDT) (Chapter 23)   The term used in the cash management trade for a preauthorized electronic withdrawal from the payer's account.

electronic invoice presentment and payment (EIPP) (Chapter 23)   A system in business-to-business transactions under which business customers are sent bills in an electronic format and then can pay them via electronic means.

employee stock ownership plan (ESOP) (Chapter 24)   The transformation of a public corporation into a private company by the employees of the corporation itself.

equipment trust certificates (Chapter 17)   A secured type of bond.

equipment trust receipts (Chapter 11)   Loans extended for the purchase of transportation equipment.

equity (Chapter 1)   An ownership interest usually in the form of common or preferred stock.

equity capital (Chapter 11)   Capital provided by the firm's owners. This includes common and preferred stock.

equity carve-out (Chapter 16)   Sometimes known as a partial spinoff, this occurs when a parent company sells a minority (usually 20% or less) stake in a subsidiary for an IPO or rights offering.

equity claimant (Chapter 1)   Owner of a corporation's equity securities.

equity kickers (Chapter 19)   Warrants that are attached to other securities.

equity multiplier (Chapter 2)   A measurement of the proportion of total assets financed by a firm's equity.

equity risk premium (Chapter 5)   The difference (historical or forward looking) between the returns on a portfolio of common stocks and a risk-free asset such as a Treasury bond or bill.

equivalent annual cost (EAC) method (Chapter 8)   Calculates the present value of cash flows for each device over its lifetime.

euro (Chapter 20)   Currency adopted as a continent-wide medium of exchange by 12 of the 15 European Union (EU) nations as a result of the Maastricht Treaty of 1991.

Eurobond (Chapters 11 and 17)   A bond issued by an international borrower and sold to investors in coutries with currencies other than that in which the bond is denominated.

Eurocurrency loan market (Chapter 17)   A large number of international banks that stand ready to make floating-rate, hard-currency loans to international corporate and government borrowers.

European call option (Chapter 18)   Gives holders the right to purchase stock at a fixed price but only on the expiration date.

event study (Chapter 10)   Examination of how stock markets respond to new information releases.

exchange rate (Chapter 20)   The price of one currency in terms of another.

ex-dividend date (Chapter 15)   The date on which the right to receive the dividend associated with a particular stock expires. To capture the dividend paid by a stock, an investor must purchase the stock prior to the ex-dividend date.

executive compensation plans (Chapter 1)   Incentives offered to a manager to encourage her to act in the best interests of the owners.

exercise (Chapter 18)   Purchase of stock in a call option.

exercise price (Chapter 18)   The price at which an option holder can buy or sell a stock on or before the option's expiration date.

expectations theory (Chapter 4)   In equilibrium, investors should expect to earn the same return whether they invest in long-term Treasury bonds or a series of short-term Treasury bonds.

expiration date (Chapter 18)   The date on which the right to purchase an option expires.

extension (Chapter 25)   An arrangement wherein a firm's creditors are promised payment in full, although not immediately.

external funds required (EFR) (Chapter 21)   The expectation of a scarcity or a surplus of financial resources, given the firm's growth objectives.

F

factoring (Chapter 22)   The outright sale of receivables to a third party at a discount.

fair bet (Chapter 5)   A gamble that offers an expected payoff of zero.

fair-price provisions (Chapter 24)   Antitrust rules ensuring that all target shareholders receive the same offer price in any tender offers initiated by the same acquirer, limiting the ability of acquirers to buy minority shares cheaply with a two-tiered offer.

fallen angels (Chapter 17)   Bonds that received investment-grade ratings when first issued but later fell to junk status.

Fama-French (F-F) model (Chapter 6)   A mathematical expression similar to the arbitrage pricing theory.

feasible set (Chapter 6)   A set of points, determined graphically, that represent the expected return and standard deviation for all possible portfolios of two stocks.

field banking system (Chapter 23)   System characterized by many collection points, each of which may have a depository account at a local bank.

final prospectus (Chapter 16)   The part of a firm's security issue registration statement that must be distributed to all prospective investors. The registration statement is the principal disclosure document for all public security offerings. Firms must file this highly detailed document with the SEC before they can solicit investors. A final revised version must be approved by the commission before an offering can become effective—that is, before any shares can actually be sold to public investors.

financial deficit (Chapter 11)   More financial capital for investment and investor payments than is retained in profits by a corporation.

financial distress (Chapter 25)   Occurs when a firm's cash flows are not sufficient to pay its current obligations.

financial engineering (Chapter 27)   The process of using the principles of financial economics to design and price financial instruments.

financial intermediary (Chapters 3 and 11)   An institution that raises capital by issuing liabilities against itself. Also, a commercial bank or other entity that lends to corporations.

financial lease (Chapter 17)   A noncancelable contractual arrangement whereby the lessee agrees to make periodic payments to the lessor, typically for more than five years, to obtain an asset's services.

financial leverage (Chapters 9 and 12)   Using debt to magnify both the risk and expected return on a firm's investments. Also, the result of the presence of debt when firms finance their operations with debt and equity, leading to a higher stock beta.

financial management function (Chapter 1)   Managing the firm's internal cash flows and its mix of debt and equity financing, both to maximize the value of the debt and equity claims on the firm and to ensure that the company can pay off its obligations when they come due.

financial slack (Chapter 13)   Large cash and marketable security holdings or unused debt capacity.

financial synergies (Chapter 24)   A merger results in less volatile cash flows, lower default risk, and a lower cost of capital.

financial venture capital funds (Chapter 26)   Subsidiaries of financial institutions, particularly commercial banks.

financing flows (Chapter 2)   Result from debt and equity financing transactions.

financing function (Chapter 1)   Raising capital to support a company's operations and investment programs.

firm-commitment offering (Chapter 16)   A type of offering in which the investment bankers actually purchase the shares from a firm and resell them to investors.

five C's of credit (Chapter 22)   A framework for performing in-depth credit analysis without providing a specific accept or reject decision.

fixed asset turnover (Chapter 2)   A measurement of the efficiency with which a firm uses its fixed assets, calculated by dividing sales by the number of dollars of fixed asset investment.

fixed exchange rate (Chapter 20)   Occurs when governments fix (or *peg*) their currency's value, usually in terms of another currency such as the U.S. dollar. The opposite of a floating exchange rate.

fixed-coupon interest payments (Chapter 11)   Debt instruments that pay interest at a coupon interest rate that is fixed for the life of the security and does not change when market rates change.

fixed-for-floating currency swap (Chapter 27)   A combination of a currency swap and an interest rate swap.

fixed-for-floating interest-rate swap (Chapter 27) Typically one party will make fixed-rate payments to another party in exchange for floating-rate payments.

fixed-price offer (Chapter 16)   An offer in which the underwriters set the final offer price for a new issue weeks in advance.

fixed-rate offerings (Chapter 17)   Offerings that have a coupon interest rate that remains constant throughout the issue's life.

flip (Chapter 16)   To buy shares at the offer price and sell them on the first trading day.

float (Chapter 23)   Funds that have been sent by the payer but are not yet usable by the payee.

floating exchange rate (Chapter 20)   Occurs when forces of supply and demand continuously move currency values up and down.

floating-rate instruments (Chapter 11)   Loan interest rates that periodically change to reflect changes in market interest rates.

floating-rate issues (Chapter 17)   Debt issues with an interest (coupon) rate that changes periodically.

flow to equity (FTE) method (Chapter 14)   A method for valuing investment projects or companies in which levered cash flows are discounted at the cost of equity.

foreign bond (Chapters 11 and 17)   A bond issued in a host country's financial market, in the host country's currency, by a nonresident corporation.

foreign exchange (forex) market (Chapter 20)   The financial market where investors and other participants trade one currency for another.

forward discount (Chapter 20)   What a currency trades at when it buys less of another currency on the forward market than it does on the spot market.

forward exchange rate (Chapter 20)   The price at which a future foreign currency trade will take place.

forward integration (Chapter 24)   A merger in which the acquired company provides a later step in the production process.

forward interest rate (Chapter 4)   The interest rate expected in a future year. It can be estimated mathematically by evaluating the difference in the returns between similar-risk bonds that differ in maturity by that one future year.

forward premium (Chapter 20)   What a currency trades at when it buys more of another currency on the forward market than it does on the spot market.

forward price (Chapter 27)   In a forward contract, the price agreed upon by two parties today, at which the purchaser will buy a specified amount of an asset from the seller at a fixed date sometime in the future and which has zero net present value.

forward rate (Chapter 20 and 27)   In a currency forward contract, the forward price.

forward rate agreement (FRA) (Chapter 27)   A forward contract in which the underlying asset is not an asset at all but an interest rate.

forward–spot parity (Chapter 20)   Holds that the forward rate should be an unbiased predictor of where the spot rate is headed.

free cash flow (FCF) (Chapters 2 and 4)   The net amount of cash flow remaining after the firm has met all operating needs and paid for investments, both long-term (fixed) and short-term (current). Represents the cash amount that a firm could distribute to investors after meeting all its other obligations.

full disclosure (Chapter 16)   Requires issuers to reveal all relevant information concerning the company selling the securities and the securities themselves to potential investors.

fundamental principle of financial leverage (Chapter 12)   The concept that substituting long-term debt for equity in a firm's capital structure increases both the level of expected returns to shareholders—measured by earnings per share or ROE—and the risk (dispersion) of those expected returns.

fungibility (Chapter 27)   The ability to close out a position by taking an offsetting position.

future value (Chapter 3)   Calculation of what the value of an investment made today will be worth at a specific future date.

futures contract (Chapter 27)   Involves two parties agreeing today on a price at which the purchaser will buy a given amount of a commodity or financial instrument from the seller at a fixed date sometime in the future.

G

general cash offerings (Chapter 16)   Securities that are sold at the market price for cash; most equity sales in the United States fall under this category.

general partners (Chapter 1)   One or more participants in a limited partnership who operate the business and have unlimited personal liability.

geometric average return (Chapter 5)   The compound annual return over a period of years.

Glass–Steagall Act (Chapter 11)   Congressional act of 1933 mandating the separation of investment and commercial banking.

Global Depositary Receipts (GDRs) (Chapter 16)   These are claims issued by international banks representing ownership of shares of a foreign company's stock held on deposit by the bank in the issuing firm's home country. Many large international equity issues use this format for share tranches (portions of the issue) that are destined for sale outside of the issuer's home country and the United States.

going-private transaction (Chapter 24)   The transformation of a public corporation into a private company through issuance of large amounts of debt used to buy all (or at least a voting majority) of the outstanding shares of the corporation.

goodwill (Chapter 24)   An intangible asset created if the restated values of the target in a merger lead to a situation in which its assets are less than its liabilities and equity.

Gordon growth model (Chapters 3 and 4)   The constant growth valuation model named after Myron Gordon, who popularized this formula during the 1960s and 1970s. It views cash flows as an annuity with an infinite life, promising to pay a growing amount at the end of each year.

Gramm–Leach–Bliley Act (Chapter 11)   Congressional act of 1999 that repealed the Glass–Steagall Act.

Green Shoe option (Chapter 16)   An option to sell up to 15% more shares than originally planned. Also called an *overallotment option.*

greenfield entry (Chapter 24)   Internal expansion into a new market.

greenmail (Chapter 24)   Payment made to an acquirer who threatens the target with a hostile tender offer and/or proxy fight in order to gain initial or greater access to the board of directors. Greenmail occurs when the potential acquirer sells his or her shares to the target firm at a premium price that is not offered to other investors.

gross profit margin (Chapter 2)   A measurement of the percentage of each sales dollar remaining after a firm has paid for its goods.

growing perpetuity (Chapter 3)   An annuity with an infinite life, promising to pay a growing amount at the end of each year.

H

hedge (Chapter 1)   An action taken to reduce risk, possibly by transferring that risk to another party via a financial derivative.

hedge fund (Chapters 10 and 26)   A professionally managed investment fund.

hedge ratio (Chapters 18 and 19)   The combination of stocks and options that results in a perfectly hedged portfolio. Also, the ratio of the number of options to the number of shares in a perfectly hedged portfolio.

hedged (Chapter 20)   A hedged position or portfolio is one from which all risk has been removed. Typically, traders create a hedged position by combining assets with returns that are negatively correlated so that their fluctuations offset.

hedging strategies (Chapter 20)   Techniques used to offset or protect against risk.

Herfindahl Index (HI) (Chapter 24)   A measure popularized by Comment and Jarrell (1995) to demonstrate the relationship between corporate focus and shareholder wealth.

high-yield bonds (Chapter 17)   Bonds rated below investment grade (also known as *junk bonds*).

hockey-stick diagram (Chapter 18)   A payoff diagram for the call option buyer showing the long position over a range of stock prices.

homemade leverage (Chapter 12)   Borrowing on personal account.

homogeneous expectations (Chapter 6)   The assumption that all investors have access to the same information and that their estimates of the inputs needed to solve for the optimal portfolio are identical.

horizontal merger (Chapter 24)   A combination of competitors within the same geographic market.

hostile takeover (Chapter 1)   The acquisition of one firm by another through an open-market bid for a majority of the target's shares when the target firm's senior managers do not support (or, more likely, actively resist) the acquisition.

hubris hypothesis of corporate takeovers (Chapter 24)   Richard Roll (1986) contends that some managers overestimate their own managerial capabilities and pursue takeovers with the belief that they can better manage their takeover target than can the target's current management team.

I

imaging services (Chapter 23)   Disbursement services offered by banks and other vendors to allow both sides of the check, as well as remittance information, to be converted into digital images. The images can then be transmitted via the Internet or easily stored for future reference. Imaging services are especially useful when incorporated with positive pay services.

implied volatility (Chapter 19)   The value of σ (sigma) obtained by "inverting" the Black and Scholes equation to calculate the level of volatility implied by the option's market price.

in the money (Chapter 18)   Occurs when a call option's strike price is less than the current stock price.

income bonds (Chapter 17)   An unsecured type of bond.

incremental project (Chapter 7)   A hypothetical project with cash flows equal to the difference in cash flows between large-scale and small-scale investments.

indenture (Chapter 17)   A legal document stating the conditions under which a bond has been issued.

indirect bankruptcy costs (Chapter 13)   Expenses or economic losses that result from bankruptcy but are not cash outflows spent on the process itself.

indirect quotation (Chapter 20)   A way of quoting a currency price that gives the foreign currency price of one unit of the home currency.

inefficient portfolio (Chapter 6)   A portfolio that offers a lower expected return than another portfolio with the same standard deviation.

information cascade (Chapter 10)   Occurs when people observe the actions that others have taken and then pursue the same course of action.

information intermediation (Chapter 11)   Financial service provided to corporations by intermediaries to help assess borrowers and monitor subsequent use of funds borrowed.

informational efficiency (Chapter 10)   The tendency (or lack thereof) for prices in a market to rapidly and fully incorporate new, relevant information.

initial margin (Chapter 27)   The minimum dollar amount required of an investor when taking a position in a futures contract.

initial public offering (IPO) (Chapters 1 and 11)   A corporation offers its shares for sale to the public for the first time; the first public sale of company stock to outside investors.

initial return (Chapter 16)   The gain when an allocation of shares from an investment banker is sold at the first opportunity because the offer price is consistently lower than what the market is willing to bear.

insolvent (Chapter 25)   A firm is *insolvent* when (a) it is not paying its debts as they come due; (b) within the immediately preceding 120 days, a custodian (a third party) was appointed or took possession of the debtor's property; or (c) the fair market value of its assets is less than the stated value of its liabilities.

institutional venture capital funds (Chapter 26)   Formal business entities with full-time professionals dedicated to seeking out and funding promising ventures.

integrated accounts payable (Chapter 23)   Provides a company with outsourcing of its accounts payable or disbursement operations. The outsourcing may be as minor as contracting with a bank to issue checks and perform reconciliations or as major as outsourcing the entire payables function.

interest differential (Chapter 27)   In an interest rate swap, only the differential is exchanged.

interest rate collar (Chapter 27)   A strategy involving the purchase of an interest rate cap and the simultaneous sale of an interest rate floor, using the proceeds from selling the floor to purchase the cap.

interest rate floor (Chapter 27)   A put option on interest rates.

interest-rate cap (Chapter 27)   A call option on interest rates.

interest-rate parity (Chapter 20)   Asserts that risk-free investments should offer the same return (after converting currencies) everywhere.

interest-rate risk (Chapter 4 and 27)   The risk that changes in market interest rates will cause fluctuations in a bond's price. Also, the risk of suffering losses as a result of unanticipated changes in market interest rates.

interest-rate swap (Chapter 27)   A swap contract in which two parties exchange payment obligations involving different interest payment schedules.

internal capital markets (Chapter 24)   Created when the high–cash flow businesses of a conglomerate generate enough cash to fund the riskier business ventures internally.

internal rate of return (IRR) (Chapters 4 and 7)   The compound annual return on a project, given its up-front costs and subsequent cash flows.

international common stock (Chapter 11)   Equity issues sold in more than one country by nonresident corporations.

intrinsic value (Chapter 18)   A measure of the profit an investor makes from exercising an option (ignoring transactions costs as well as the option premium).

inventory turnover (Chapter 2)   A measure of how quickly a firm sells its goods.

investment bank (Chapter 16)   A bank that helps firms acquire external capital.

investment flows (Chapter 2)   Cash flows associated with the purchase or sale of fixed assets and business equity.

investment-grade bonds (Chapter 17)   Bonds rated Baa or higher by Moody's (BBB by S&P).

IPO underpricing (Chapter 16)   Occurs when the offer price in the prospectus is consistently lower than what the market is willing to bear.

J

joint and several liability (Chapter 1)   Each partner is personally liable for all the debts of the partnership.

junk bonds (Chapters 4 and 17)   Bonds rated below investment grade (also known as *high-yield bonds*).

just-in-time (JIT) system (Chapter 22)   An inventory management technique used to make sure that materials arrive exactly when they are needed for production rather than being stored on site. In order to work effectively, it requires close teamwork among vendors and purchasing and production personnel.

L

Law and Finance model (Chapter 11)   This model states that the most important determinant of capital market development is the degree of legal protection afforded to outside (noncontrolling) investors; this, in turn, depends largely on whether a country's legal system is based on English common law or another legal tradition. Countries with English common law commercial codes tend to have larger debt and equity markets than do civil-law countries.

law of one price (Chapter 20)   The idea that identical goods trading in different markets should sell at the same price, absent any barriers to trade.

lead underwriter (Chapter 16)   The investment bank that manages a firm's underwritten security offering and forms an underwriting syndicate consisting of many investment banks. These banks collectively purchase the firm's shares and market them, thus spreading the risk across the syndicate.

leading and lagging (Chapter 20)   Adjustments in the collection and payment of intra-MNC accounts in order to correct for the appreciation and depreciation of currency.

league table (Chapter 16)   A tabular ranking of the world's 15 largest investment banks by the total value of securities underwritten, or for a particular type of debt or equity security.

lease-versus-buy decision   *See* **lease-versus-purchase decision.**

lease-versus-purchase decision (Chapter 17)   The alternatives available are to (1) lease the assets, (2) borrow funds to purchase the assets, or (3) purchase the assets using available liquid resources. Even if the firm has the liquid resources with which to purchase the assets, the use of these funds is viewed as equivalent to borrowing.

leasing (Chapter 17)   Acquiring use of an asset by renting rather than purchasing it.

lending-versus-borrowing problem (Chapter 7)   Choice is offered between cash paid out today in exchange for a larger amount of cash in one year, or cash received today with payback of a larger amount later.

lessee (Chapter 17)   The user of the underlying asset who makes regular payments to the lessor.

lessor (Chapter 17)   The owner of the asset who receives regular payments for its use by the lessee.

leveraged leases (Chapter 17)   The lessor acts as an equity participant, supplying only about 20% of the cost of the asset, and a lender supplies the balance.

levered cash flow (Chapter 14)   Project cash flows calculated by subtracting interest expense and taxes; hence, the cash flows will reflect the effects of debt financing.

LIBOR (Chapters 11, 17, and 23)   The London Interbank Offered Rate.

lien (Chapter 17)   A legal contract that specifies under what conditions a lender can take title to an asset if a loan is not repaid and also prohibits the borrowing firm from selling or disposing of the asset without the lender's consent.

lifetime high prices (Chapter 27)   The highest settlement prices recorded for a contract since its inception.

lifetime low prices (Chapter 27)   The lowest settlement prices recorded for a contract since its inception.

limited liability company (LLC) (Chapter 1)   A form of business organization that combines the tax advantages of a partnership with the limited liability protection of a corporation.

limited partners (Chapter 1)   One or more totally passive participants in a limited partnership who do not take an active role in the operation of the business and who do not face personal liability for the debts of the business.

limited partnership (Chapter 1)   Most of the participants in the partnership (the limited partners) have the limited liability of corporate shareholders, but their share of the profits from the business is taxed as partnership income.

liquidation (Chapter 25)   Winding up a firm's operations, selling off its assets, and distributing the proceeds to creditors.

liquidation value (Chapter 4)   The amount of cash that would be left over if a firm sold all its assets and used the proceeds to pay off all of its liabilities.

liquidity management (Chapter 23)   The process of managing a firm's cash and accounts payable in order to earn a positive return on excess cash balances and obtain low-cost financing for meeting unexpected needs and seasonal cash shortages.

liquidity preference theory (Chapter 4)   States that the slope of the yield curve is influenced not only by expected interest rate changes but also by the liquidity premium that investors require on long-term bonds.

liquidity ratios (Chapter 2)   Measure a firm's ability to satisfy its short-term obligations *as they come due*.

loan amortization (Chapter 3)   A borrower makes equal periodic payments over time to fully repay a loan.

loan amortization schedule (Chapter 3)   Used to determine loan amortization payments and the allocation of each payment to interest and principal.

loan covenants (Chapter 11)   Specifications imposed by a bank on a borrower in an attempt to protect the bank's investment.

loans (Chapter 17)   Private debt agreements arranged between corporate borrowers and financial institutions, especially commercial banks.

lockbox system (Chapter 23)   A technique for speeding up collections that is popular because it affects all three components of float. Instead of mailing payments to the company, customers mail payments to a post office box, which is emptied regularly by the firm's bank.

lockup agreement (Chapter 16)   An agreement that bankers negotiate with a client's managers and directors, stipulating that these corporate insiders will not sell their personal stock holdings immediately after the offering.

long position (Chapter 18 and 27)   Taking a long position in a security is equivalent to buying the security. In a *forward* or *futures contract*, the long position is obligated to pay the forward or futures price of the asset when the contract expires.

long straddle (Chapter 18)   A portfolio consisting of long positions in calls and puts on the same stock with the same strike price and expiration date.

long-term debt (Chapters 2 and 11)   Debt that matures more than one year in the future.

M

macro political risk (Chapter 20)   Risk that applies to *all* foreign firms in a country because of political change, revolution, or the adoption of new policies by the host government.

mail float (Chapter 23)   The time delay between when payment is placed in the mail and when payment is received.

mail-based collection system (Chapter 23)   Processing centers receive the mail payments, open the envelopes, separate the check from the remittance information, prepare the check for deposit, and send the remittance information to the accounts receivable department for application of payment.

maintenance clauses (Chapter 17)   Specifying who is to maintain the assets and make insurance and tax payments.

maintenance margin (Chapter 27)   Margin level required to maintain an open position.

majority voting system (Chapter 11)   System that allows each shareholder to cast one vote per share for each open position on the board of directors.

managed floating-rate system (Chapter 20)   A hybrid system in which a nation's government loosely "fixes" the value of the national currency in relation to that of another currency but does not expend the effort and resources that would be required to maintain a completely fixed exchange rate regime.

management buyout (MBO) (Chapter 24)   The transformation of a public corporation into a private company by the current managers of the corporation.

managerial synergies (Chapter 24)   Efficiency gains from combining the management teams of merged companies.

managerialism theory of mergers (Chapter 24)   Poorly monitored managers will pursue mergers to maximize their corporation's asset size because managerial compensation is usually based on firm size, regardless of whether or not these mergers create value for stockholders.

manufacturing resource planning II (MRPII) (Chapter 22)   Expands on MRP by using a complex computerized system to integrate data from many departments and generate a production plan for the firm along with management reports, forecasts, and financial statements.

margin account (Chapter 27)   The account into which the investor must deposit the initial margin.

market/book (M/B) ratio (Chapter 2)   A measurement that relates the market value of a firm's shares to their book value.

market capitalization (Chapter 11)   The value of the shares of a company's stock that are owned by the stockholders: the total number of shares issued multiplied by the current price per share.

market extension merger (Chapter 24)   A combination of firms that produce the same product in different geographic markets.

market maker (Chapter 16)   A lead underwriter that continuously quotes bid and ask prices for new securities after a share offering is successfully sold.

market portfolio (Chapter 6)   The portfolio that all investors want to hold as required for equilibrium, which in theory consists of every available asset with each asset weighted by its market value relative to the total market value of all assets.

market power (Chapter 24)   A benefit that might arise from a horizontal merger when competition is too weak (or nonexistent) to prevent the merged company from raising prices in a market at will.

market price of risk (Chapter 6)   Maximized by investors as they search for the optimal risky portfolio.

market-timing model (Chapter 13)   Model that predicts that firms attempt to time the market by issuing equity when share values are high and by issuing debt when share prices are low. As a consequence, a firm's capital structure simply reflects the cumulative effects of its managers' past attempts to issue equity opportunistically.

marking-to-market (Chapter 27)   Daily cash settlement of all futures contracts.

material requirements planning (MRP) (Chapter 22)   A computerized system used to control the flow of resources, particularly inventory, within the production–sale process. Uses a master schedule to ensure that the materials, labor, and equipment needed for production are at the right places in the right amounts at the right times.

maturity (Chapter 4)   The limited life of a bond.

McFadden Act (Chapter 11)   Congressional act of 1927 that prohibited interstate banking.

merger (Chapter 24)   A transaction in which two or more business organizations combine into a single entity.

micro political risk (Chapter 20)   Refers to a foreign government's targeting punitive action against an individual firm, a specific industry, or companies from a particular foreign country.

Miller equilibrium (Chapter 12)   An equilibrium in which the corporate tax advantage of debt financing is exactly offset by the personal tax disadvantage of debt.

minimum variance portfolio (MVP) (Chapter 6)   A portfolio of A and B that has less volatility than either A or B.

mixed offering (Chapters 16 and 24)   An offering in which some of the shares come from existing shareholders and some are new. Also, a merger financed with a combination of cash and securities.

mixed stream (Chapter 3)   A series of unequal payments reflecting no particular pattern.

modified accelerated cost recovery system (MACRS) (Chapter 8)   Set forth in the Tax Reform Act of 1986 to define the allowable annual depreciation deductions for various classes of assets.

Modigliani & Miller (M&M) argument (Chapter 12)   The original theoretical model showing that capital structure is irrelevant—it cannot affect overall firm value—in a world with frictionless capital markets and no taxes. M&M assert that the market value of any firm is independent of its capital structure and is given by capitalizing its expected net operating income at a single rate r.

money market (Chapter 1)   The market for debt instruments maturing in one year or less.

money market mutual funds (Chapter 23)   Used by many small companies and some large companies to manage their portfolio.

money market yield (MMY) (Chapter 23)   The yield for short-term discount instruments such as T-bills and commercial paper is typically calculated using algebraic approximations rather than more precise present value methods.

Monte Carlo simulation (Chapter 9)   A sophisticated analysis that provides for calculating the net present value when provided a range or distribution of potential outcomes for each set of assumptions.

mortgage (Chapter 11)   A loan secured by real property.

mortgage-backed securities (MBS) (Chapter 17)   Debt securities that pass through to investors the principal and interest payments that homeowners make on their mortgages.

mortgage bonds (Chapter 17)   A secured type of bond.

multinational corporations (MNCs) (Chapter 20)   Businesses that operate in many countries around the world.

municipal bonds (Chapters 4 and 12)   Issued by U.S. state and local governments. Interest on these bonds is exempt from federal income tax.

mutually exclusive projects (Chapter 7)   When several investments exceed the hurdle rate but only a subset of them can be undertaken at any given time.

N

naked option position (Chapter 18)   Results when an investor buys or sells an option on a stock without already owning the underlying stock.

natural hedge (Chapter 20)   Offsetting risk exposure.

negative covenants (Chapter 11 and 26)   Restrictions a borrower must accept in order to secure a loan.

negotiated offer (Chapter 16)   The most common approach that firms take in choosing an investment banker: the issuing firm negotiates the terms of the offer directly with one investment bank.

net operating profits after taxes (NOPAT) (Chapter 2)   A firm's earnings before interest and after taxes. Mathematically, earnings before interest and taxes (EBIT) $\times$ (1 − tax rate [T]).

net payoff (Chapter 18)   The share price less the amount paid to acquire the call option.

net present value (NPV) (Chapter 7)   The present value of a sequence of cash inflows and outflows. Also, a method for valuing capital investments.

net price (Chapter 16)   The price at which banks purchase shares from firms.

net profit margin (Chapter 2)   A measurement of the percentage of each sales dollar remaining after all costs and expenses (including interest, taxes, and preferred stock dividends) have been deducted.

net working capital (Chapters 2 and 8)   The difference between a firm's current assets and its current liabilities. Often used as a measure of liquidity.

nominal cash flows (Chapter 8)   Amounts that reflect an assumed inflation rate.

nominal return (Chapter 4)   The stated return.

noncash charges (Chapter 2)   Expenses that appear on the income statement but do not involve an actual outlay of cash.

nondebt tax shield (NDTS) (Chapter 12)   Fixed, tax-deductible expenses (such lease payments or depreciation charges) that offer a tax benefit similar to that from debt financing.

normal distribution (Chapter 5)   The probability of investment outcomes forms a roughly bell-shaped curve that is symmetric about its mean, which makes it easy to determine the probabilities of events that fall within certain ranges and allows full description by just two characteristics: the mean and the variance.

notes (Chapter 1)   Longer-term debt instruments with original maturities of less than seven years.

notional principal (Chapter 27)   The hypothetical principal amount.

NPV profile (Chapter 7)   A plot of a project's NPV (on the y axis) against various discount rates (on the x axis). It is used to illustrate the relationship between the NPV and the IRR for the typical project. Also called the *net present value profile*.

O

offer price (Chapter 16)   The price at which banks sell a firm's shares to institutional and individual investors.

opening futures price (Chapter 27)   Price on the first trade of the day.

open interest (Chapter 27)   The number of contracts that are currently outstanding.

operating assets (Chapter 22)   Cash, marketable securities, accounts receivable, and inventories that are necessary for the day-to-day operation of a firm.

operating cycle (OC) (Chapter 22)   Measurement of the time that elapses from the firm's receipt of raw materials for production to its collection of cash from the sale of the finished product.

operating flows (Chapter 2)   Cash inflows and outflows directly related to the production and sale of a firm's products or services.

operating lease (Chapter 17)   A contractual arrangement whereby the lessee agrees to make periodic payments to the lessor, often for five years or less, to obtain an asset's services. The lessee generally receives an option to cancel, and the asset has a useful life longer than the lease.

operating leverage (Chapter 9)   Measures the tendency of the volatility of operating cash flows to increase with fixed operating costs.

operating profit margin (Chapter 2)   A measurement of the percentage of each sales dollar remaining after deducting all costs and expenses other than interest and taxes.

operational synergy (Chapter 24)   Economies of scale, economies of scope, and resource complementarities.

opportunity costs (Chapter 8)   Lost cash flows on an alternative investment that the firm or individual decides not to make.

optimal risky portfolio (Chapter 6)   The portfolio that maximizes the return that investors can expect for a given standard deviation.

option (Chapter 18)   Allows an investor to buy or sell an asset at a fixed price during a given period of time.

option premium (Chapter 18)   The purchase price of the option to buy is kept by the seller if the buyer decides not to make the purchase.

option's delta (Chapter 19)   The slope measures how much the call price changes as the underlying stock price changes.

ordinary annuity (Chapter 3)   An annuity for which the payments occur at the end of each period.

out of the money (Chapter 18)   Occurs when a call option's strike price exceeds the current stock price.

overallotment option (Chapter 16)   In oversubscribed common stock offerings, the lead underwriter may exercise a Green Shoe option (or overallotment option), which is essentially an option to sell up to an additional 15% more shares than originally planned.

overconfidence (Chapter 10)   Investors exhibit this trait when they believe they are better informed about the true state of a company's affairs than is in fact the case.

overreaction (Chapter 10)   The opposite of *underreaction* to corporate news announcements or prior period returns.

oversubscribe (Chapter 16)   When the investment banker builds a book of orders for stock that is greater (often many times greater) than the amount of stock the firm intends to sell. These orders are not legally binding, and typically the offer price is given as a range of prices at which they expect to sell the offer.

over-the-counter market (Chapter 18)   There are a seemingly infinite variety. They are less liquid than exchange-traded options.

ownership rights agreements (Chapter 26)   Specify both the distribution of a firm's ownership and the allocation of board seats and voting rights to the participating venture capitalists investing in that company. Special voting rights often given to VCs include the right to veto major corporate actions and to remove the management team if the firm fails to meet performance goals.

P

paid-in-capital in excess of par (Chapter 2)   The number of shares outstanding times the original selling price of the shares, net of the par value.

participation rights (Chapter 26)   These give venture capitalists the option to participate in any private stock sale the firm's managers arrange for themselves.

par value (Chapters 2 and 4)   The face value of a bond, which the borrower repays at maturity. Also, an arbitrary value assigned to common stock on a firm's balance sheet.

partnership (Chapter 1)   A proprietorship with two or more owners who have joined together their skills and personal wealth.

payback period (Chapter 7)   The amount of time it takes for a given project's cumulative net cash inflows to recoup the initial investment.

payment date (Chapter 15)   The actual date on which a firm mails the dividend payment to the holders of record.

payment pattern (Chapter 22)   The normal timing in which a firm's customers pay their accounts, expressed as the percentage of monthly sales collected in each month following the sale.

payoff (Chapter 18)   The price an investor would be willing to pay for an option the instant before it expires.

payoff diagrams (Chapter 18)   Graphs that illustrate an option's payoff as a function of the underlying stock price.

pecking-order theory (Chapter 13)   A hypothesis, developed by Stewart Myers and colleagues, that assumes managers are better informed about the investment opportunities faced by their firms than are outside investors (asymmetric information) and also assumes managers act in the best interests of existing shareholders.

percentage-of-sales method (Chapter 21)   Constructing pro forma statements by assuming that all items grow in proportion to sales.

perpetuity (Chapter 3)   An annuity with an infinite life, promising to pay the same amount at the end of every year forever.

plug figure (Chapter 21)   A line item left on the balance sheet of a pro forma statement. After all other projections are made, this figure can be adjusted so that the balance sheet balances.

poison pills (Chapter 24)   Defensive measures taken to avoid a hostile takeover.

political risk (Chapter 20)   The actions taken by a government that have a negative impact on the value of foreign companies operating in that country.

positive covenants (Chapter 11 and 26)   Requirements a borrower must meet to secure a loan.

positive pay (Chapter 23)   A bank service used to combat the most common types of check fraud. A company transmits a check-issued file, designating the check number and amount of each item, to the bank when the checks are issued. The bank matches the presented checks against this file and rejects any items that do not match.

preemptive rights (Chapter 16)   These hold that shareholders have first claim on anything of value distributed by a corporation.

preferred habitat theory (Chapter 4)   The effect on the yield curve caused by a desire to invest to match liabilities, despite lower expected returns.

preferred stock (Chapter 2)   Stockholders' equity.

preliminary prospectus (Chapter 16)   The registration statement is the principal disclosure document for all public security offerings. The first part of the registration statement, the prospectus, is distributed to all prospective investors; an issuing firm may file a half dozen or more amended prospectuses with the SEC during the registration period preceding an offer. The first or *preliminary* prospectus serves as the principal marketing tool during the period from initial filing with the SEC to when the firm responds to the commission's initial findings. The preliminary prospectus is often called a "red herring" because there is a standard legal disclaimer (printed in red across the cover) stating that the securities described are not yet being offered for sale. Rather than a single price, the red herring lists a range of prices at which the securities may be offered.

premium (Chapter 4)   The difference between a bond's par value and the purchase price when the price is greater than par value.

prepackaged bankruptcy (Chapter 25)   Companies prepare a reorganization plan that is negotiated and voted on by creditors and stockholders before the company actually files for chapter 11 bankruptcy.

present value (Chapter 3)   Calculation of the value today of a cash flow to be received at a specific date in the future.

president (Chapter 1)   Hired by the board of directors to be responsible for managing day-to-day operations and carrying out the policies established by the board.

price/earnings (P/E) ratio (Chapter 2)   A measurement of a firm's long-term growth prospects by determining the amount investors are willing to pay for each dollar of a firm's earnings.

price stabilization (Chapter 16)   Purchase of shares by an investment bank when a new issue begins to falter in the market, keeping the market price at or slightly above the offer price for an indefinite period.

primary issues (Chapter 11)   Debt and equity security issues that actually raise capital for firms and are thus distinct from secondary offerings, where an investor sells his or her holdings of existing securities.

primary market transaction (Chapter 1)   Sale of securities to investors by a corporation to raise capital for the firm.

primary offering (Chapter 16)   An offering in which the shares offered for sale are newly issued shares, which increases the number of outstanding shares and raises new capital for the firm.

prime (lending) rate (Chapter 17)   The rate of interest charged by the largest U.S. banks on short-term loans to business borrowers with good credit ratings.

principal (Chapter 3)   The amount of money on which interest is paid.

private equity (Chapter 26)   The management of companies acquired through a leveraged buyout by private investment funds using a relatively small amount of equity and a relatively large portion of outside debt might have the potential to rival public corporation. The term commonly applied to buyout funds, though sometimes also broadened to include venture capital funds.

private placements (Chapters 16 and 17)   Unregistered security offerings sold directly to accredited investors.

pro forma financial statement (Chapter 21)   A forecast of what a firm expects its balance sheet and income statement to look like a year or two ahead.

probability distribution (Chapter 5)   A distribution that tells us what investment outcomes are possible and associates a probability with each outcome.

processing float (Chapter 23)   The time that elapses between the receipt of payment by a firm and its deposit into the firm's account.

product extension merger (Chapter 24)   A diversification merger that combines companies with similar but not identical lines of business.

profitability index (PI) (Chapter 7)   A capital budgeting tool defined as the ratio of the present value of a project's cash flows, excluding the initial cash outflow (the initial investment), divided by the initial cash outflow.

project finance (PF) loans (Chapter 17)   Loans usually arranged for infrastructure projects such as toll roads, bridges, and power plants.

Proposition I (Chapter 12)   The "irrelevance proposition," which claims that a firm's value depends only on the cash flows it generates and not on how it is financed.

Proposition II (Chapter 12)   Asserts that the expected return on a levered firm's equity is a linear function of that firm's debt-to-equity ratio.

prospectus (Chapter 16)   The first part of a registration statement; it is distributed to all prospective investors.

protective put (Chapter 18)   By granting the right to sell a share of stock at a fixed price on or before a certain date, a put option provides a kind of portfolio insurance, guaranteeing that the share of stock can be sold for at least that amount.

proxy fight (Chapter 11)   A ploy used by outsiders to attempt to gain control of a firm by soliciting a sufficient number of votes to unseat existing directors.

proxy statement (Chapter 11)   Used by shareholders not attending an annual meeting to give their votes to another party.

public company (Chapter 1)   A corporation whose shares of stock can be freely traded among investors without obtaining the permission of other investors and whose shares are listed for trading in a public security market.

purchase options (Chapter 17)   The lessee may have the option to purchase the leased asset when the lease expires.

purchasing (or procurement) card programs (Chapter 23)   Implemented by companies as a means of reducing the cost of low-dollar indirect purchases.

purchasing power parity (Chapter 20)   An extension of the law of one price. It maintains that if the law of one price holds at all times, then differences in expected inflation between two countries are associated with expected changes in currency values.

pure conglomerate mergers (Chapter 24)   An unrelated diversification merger that occurs between companies in completely different lines of business.

pure play (Chapter 9)   A firm that competes in a single line of business.

pure stock exchange merger (Chapter 24)   A merger in which stock is the only mode of payment.

put option (Chapter 18)   Grants the right to sell a share of stock at a fixed price on or before a certain date.

put–call parity (Chapter 18)   Results when the payoffs of a portfolio containing one share of stock and one put option are exactly the same as the payoffs of a portfolio containing one bond and one call option.

Q

qualified institutional buyers (Chapter 16)   Institutions with assets exceeding $100 million.

quarterly compounding (Chapter 3)   Interest involves four compounding periods within the year and is paid four times a year.

quick (acid-test) ratio (Chapter 2)   Similar to the current ratio except that it excludes inventory, which is usually the least-liquid current asset.

R

random walk (Chapters 9 and 10)   A description of the movement of the price of a financial asset over time. When prices follow a *random walk*, future and past prices are statistically unrelated, and the best forecast of the future price is simply the current price.

ratchet provisions (Chapter 26)   Protect the venture capital group's ownership rights in the event that the firm sells new equity under duress. Generally, these provisions ensure that the venture capital group's share values are adjusted so that entrepreneurs bear the penalty of selling low-priced new stock. For example, if the venture fund purchased shares initially for $1 each and the start-up later sells new stock at $0.50 per share, then a "full ratchet" provision mandates that the venture group receives one new share for each old share, thereby protecting the value of the VC's initial stake (a "partial ratchet" only partially protects the venture group).

ratio analysis (Chapter 2)   Calculating and interpreting financial ratios to assess a firm's performance and status.

rational expectations (Chapter 6)   The assumption that even if investors make mistakes when forming assessments concerning expected returns, their errors are not systematic.

real cash flows (Chapter 8)   Amounts that reflect only current prices and do not incorporate upward adjustments for expected inflation.

real interest-rate parity (Chapter 20)   Asserts that investors should earn the same real rate of return on risk-free investments no matter the country in which they choose to invest.

real option (Chapter 9)   The right, but not the obligation, to take a future action that changes an investment's value.

real return (Chapters 4 and 5)   Approximately, the difference between an investment's stated or nominal return and the inflation rate.

recapitalization (Chapter 12)   Alteration of a company's capital structure to reduce high fixed charges.

redemption option (Chapter 26)   Option for venture capitalists to sell a company back to its entrepreneur or founders.

red herring (Chapter 16)   Nickname often given to the preliminary prospectus because of the standard legal disclaimer (printed across its cover in red) stating that the securities described are not yet being offered for sale.

refund (Chapter 17)   To refinance a debt with new bonds at a lower interest rate.

registration rights (Chapter 26)   The rights of a shareholder of restricted stock to force the company issuing the shares to register with the SEC, which will allow the shareholder to sell shares to outside investors. Without these rights, it would be difficult for restricted shareholders to divest themselves from the company.

registration statement (Chapter 16)   The principal disclosure document for all public security offerings.

reinvestment rate assumption (Chapter 7)   The assumption that intermediate cash flows can be reinvested at a particular rate over the life of an asset or investment project.

renewal options (Chapter 17)   In an operating lease, the lessee often has the option to renew a lease at its expiration.

reorganization (Chapter 25)   The process in bankruptcy designed to allow businesses that are in temporary financial distress but are worth saving to continue operating while the claims of creditors are settled using a collective procedure.

repurchase rights (Chapter 26)   A company's contractual rights to buy from an employee any stock resulting from the exercise of a stock option or other stock grant.

residual claimants (Chapters 1 and 11)   Investors who have the right to receive cash flows only after all other claimants have been satisfied. Common stockholders are typically the residual claimants of corporations.

resource complementarities (Chapter 24)   A firm with a particular operating expertise merges with a firm with another operating strength to create a company that has expertise in multiple areas.

retained earnings (Chapter 2)   The cumulative total of the earnings that a firm has reinvested since its inception.

return (Chapter 5)   The total gain or loss on an investment over a given period of time.

return on common equity (ROE) (Chapter 2)   A measurement that captures the return earned on the common stockholders' (owners') investment in a firm.

return on investment (ROI) (Chapter 21)   A firm's earnings available for common stockholders divided by its total assets. Alternatively called *return on total assets* (*ROA*).

return on total assets (ROA) (Chapter 2) A measurement of the overall effectiveness of management in generating returns to common stockholders with its available assets.

reverse LBO (RLOB) (Chapters 16, 24, and 26) The re-listing, through an initial public offering, of a company that had been purchased by a private equity fund through a leveraged buyout.

reverse stock split (Chapter 15) Occurs when a firm replaces a certain number of outstanding shares with just one new share.

rights offerings (Chapter 16) A special type of seasoned equity offering that allows the firm's existing owners to buy new shares at a bargain price or to sell that right to other investors.

risk management (Chapter 27) The process of identifying firm-specific risk exposures and managing those exposures by means of insurance products. Also includes identifying, measuring, and managing all types of risk exposures.

risk management function (Chapter 1) Managing the firm's exposures to all types of risk, both insurable and uninsurable, in order to maintain the optimum risk–return trade-off and thereby maximize shareholder value.

risk-averse (Chapter 5) A description of the preferences of investors who must be compensated to bear risk or will pay to shed risk.

risk-free bond (Chapter 4) A bond that is certain to make all promised payments on time and in full.

risk-neutral (Chapter 5) Investors who care only about the returns on their investments, totally disregarding risk.

risk-neutral method (Chapter 18) An approach that uses arbitrage arguments to calculate option prices and that assumes investors are risk neutral.

risk-seeking (Chapter 5) Investors who prefer to take risk and hence will be willing to invest in a risky asset even when its expected return falls below that of a safer alternative.

road show (Chapter 16) A tour of major U.S. and international cities taken by a firm and its bankers several weeks before a scheduled offering. The tour's goal is to solicit demand for the offering from investors.

Rule 144A (Chapter 16) Provides a private-placement exemption for qualified institutional buyers and allows them to freely trade privately placed securities among themselves.

Rule 144A offering (Chapter 16) A special type of offer, first approved in April 1990, that allows issuing companies to waive some disclosure requirements by selling stock only to sophisticated institutional investors, who may then trade the shares among themselves.

Rule 415 (Chapter 16) This procedure allows a qualifying company to file a master registration statement, which is a single document summarizing planned financing over a 2-year period. Once the SEC approves the issue, it is placed "on the shelf" and the company can, as needed, sell the new securities to investors out of inventory (off the shelf) any time over the next two years.

S

S corporation (Chapter 1) An ordinary corporation in which the stockholders have elected to allow shareholders to be taxed as partners while still retaining their limited liability status as corporate stockholders.

sale–leaseback arrangement (Chapter 17) One firm sells an asset to another for cash, then leases the asset from its new owner.

Sarbanes–Oxley Act of 2002 (Chapter 1) Legislation passed in the wake of corporate scandals at Enron and other firms that makes sweeping changes affecting the governance and control of public companies.

scenario analysis (Chapter 9) A more complex variation on sensitivity analysis that provides for calculating the net present value when a whole set of assumptions changes in a particular way.

seasoned equity offering (SEO) (Chapter 16) An equity issue by a firm that already has common stock outstanding.

seasoned issues (Chapter 11) Security offerings in which the security for sale already trades in public markets.

second IPO (Chapter 16) In a second IPO (or reverse LBO), a formerly public company that has previously gone private through a leveraged buyout goes public again. Reverse LBOs are easier to price than traditional

IPOs because information exists about how the market valued the company when it was publicly traded.

secondary market transactions (Chapter 1)   Trades between investors that generate no new cash flow for the firm.

secondary offering (Chapters 11 and 16)   An offering whose purpose is to allow an existing shareholder to sell a large block of stock to new investors. This kind of offering raises no new capital for the firm.

secured creditors (Chapter 25)   Creditors who have specific assets pledged as collateral and who receive the proceeds from the sale of those assets.

secured debt (Chapter 11)   A loan backed by collateral.

securities (Chapter 11)   Claims that trade in public markets and entitle investors to some type of claim on a firm's cash flows or assets.

Securities Act of 1933 (Chapter 16)   The most important federal law governing the sale of new securities.

Securities and Exchange Act of 1934 (Chapter 16)   This act, and its amendments, established the U.S. Securities and Exchange Commission (SEC) and laid out specific procedures for both the public sale of securities and the governance of public companies.

Securities and Exchange Commission (SEC) (Chapter 1)   The organization charged with regulating U.S. securities markets.

securitization (Chapter 11)   The repackaging of loans and other traditional bank-based credit products into securities that can be sold to public investors.

security market line (SML) (Chapter 6)   The line plotted for the equilibrium expected returns of all securities.

selectivity (Chapter 10)   Stock-picking ability; one of two components of managerial investment performance.

self-attribution bias (Chapter 10)   Investors with this trait will interpret the arrival of new private information supporting their existing beliefs as important confirmatory evidence, but they will tend to disregard contradictory new evidence as being random noise.

selling group (Chapter 16)   Consists of investment banks that may assist in selling shares but are not formal members of the underwriting syndicate.

semiannual compounding (Chapter 3)   Interest involves two compounding periods within the year and is paid twice a year.

semistrong-form efficiency (Chapter 10)   This version of the EMH asserts that asset prices incorporate all publicly available information.

senior debt (Chapter 11)   Debt that has a higher priority claim than other debts that the firm may have outstanding.

sensitivity analysis (Chapter 9)   A tool that allows exploration of the importance of individual assumptions concerning a project's net present value by determining the impact of changing one variable while holding all others fixed.

serial bonds (Chapter 17)   Bonds of which a certain proportion mature each year.

settlement date (Chapter 27)   The future date on which the buyer pays the seller and the seller delivers the asset to the buyer.

settlement price (Chapter 27)   The closing price of a futures contract at the end of a trading day. This is used to settle all contracts, in a process called "marking to market."

share issue privatization (SIP) (Chapter 16)   A government executing one of these will sell all or part of its ownership in a state-owned enterprise to private investors via a public share offering.

shareholder (Chapter 1)   Owner of common and preferred stock of a corporation.

shares authorized (Chapter 11)   The shares of a company's stock that are authorized by the stockholders to be sold by the board of directors without further stockholder approval.

shares issued (Chapter 11)   The shares of a company's stock that are owned by the stockholders.

shark repellents (Chapter 24)   Antitakeover measures added to corporate charters.

shelf registration (Chapter 16)   A procedure that allows a qualifying company to file a "master registration statement," a single document summarizing planned financing over a 2-year period.

short position (Chapter 18 and 27)   Taking a short position is equivalent to selling the asset. In a forward or futures contract, the short position is obligated to sell the asset to the buyer at the forward or futures price.

short straddle (Chapter 18)   A portfolio consisting of short positions in calls and puts on the same stock with the same strike price and expiration date.

short-term debt (Chapter 11)   Debt that matures in one year or less.

short-term financing (Chapter 22)   Accounts payable, bank loans, commercial paper, international loans, and secured short-term loans that are used by a firm to finance seasonal fluctuations in current asset investments and provide adequate liquidity to achieve its growth objectives and meet its obligations in a timely manner.

signaling model (Chapters 13 and 15)   A capital structure theory that assumes managers know more about a firm's prospects than do investors.

simple interest (Chapter 3)   Interest paid only on the initial principal of an investment, not on the interest that accrues in earlier periods.

single-factor model (Chapter 6)   Just one variable explains differences in returns across securities.

sinking fund (Chapter 17)   A positive covenant, often included in a bond indenture, whose objective is to provide for the systematic retirement of bonds prior to their maturity.

small business investment companies (SBICs) (Chapter 26)   Federally chartered corporations established as a result of the Small Business Administration Act of 1958.

sole proprietorship (Chapter 1)   A business with a single owner.

sovereign wealth funds (Chapter 26)   Government-owned investment funds (not operating companies) that make long-term domestic and international investments in search of commercial returns.

special dividend (Chapter 15)   The additional dividend that a firm pays if earnings are higher than normal in a given period.

speculating (Chapter 27)   Choosing not to hedge a risk exposure, or choosing to overhedge.

speculative bond (Chapter 17)   A bond that carries significant default risk.

spin-off (Chapters 16 and 24)   A parent company creates a new company with its own shares to form a division or subsidiary, and existing shareholders receive a pro rata distribution of shares in the new company.

split-off (Chapter 24)   A parent company creates a new, independent company with its own shares, and ownership of the company is transferred to certain existing shareholders only in exchange for their shares in the parent.

split-up (Chapter 24)   The division and sale of all of a company's subsidiaries, so that it ceases to exist (except possibly as a holding company with no assets).

sponsored ADR (Chapter 16)   An ADR for which the issuing (foreign) company absorbs the legal and financial costs of creating and trading the security.

spot exchange rate (Chapter 20)   The exchange rate applying to currency trades that occur immediately.

spot price (Chapter 27)   A cash market transaction in which the buyer and seller conduct their transaction today.

spot rates (Chapter 27)   Rates that call for immediate delivery.

staged financing (Chapter 26)   Used by venture capitalists to minimize risk exposure.

stakeholders (Chapter 1)   Customers, employees, suppliers, and creditors of a firm.

standard normal distribution (Chapter 19)   A normal distribution with a mean of 0 and a standard deviation of 1.

stated annual rate (Chapter 3)   The contractual annual rate charged by a lender or promised by a borrower.

statutory merger (Chapter 24)   A target integration in which the acquirer can absorb the target's resources directly with no remaining trace of the target as a separate entity.

stock dividend (Chapter 15)   The payment to existing owners of a dividend in the form of stock.

stock option plans (Chapter 26)   Provide incentives for portfolio company managers in virtually all venture capital deals. As part of these plans, the firm sets aside a large pool of stock to compensate current managers for superior performance and to attract talented new managers as the company grows.

stock options (Chapter 1)   Outright grants of stock to top managers or, more commonly, giving them the right to purchase stock at a fixed price.

stock purchase warrants (Chapter 17)   Instruments that give their holder the right to purchase a certain number of shares of a firm's common stock at a specified price over a certain period.

stock split (Chapter 15)   When a firm executes a stock split, its share price declines because the number of outstanding shares increases. For example, in a 2-for-1 split, the firm doubles the number of shares outstanding.

Managers who implement stock splits generally say they are trying to reduce the per-share price of the firm's stock back within a "standard" trading range that individual investors desire.

strategic merger (Chapter 24) Seeks to create a more efficient merged company than the two premerger companies operating independently.

strategic plan (Chapter 21) A multiyear action plan for the major investments and competitive initiatives that a firm's senior managers believe will drive the future success of the enterprise.

strike price (Chapter 18) The price at which a call option allows an investor to purchase the underlying share. Also called the *exercise price.*

strong-form efficiency (Chapter 10) In markets characterized by this kind of efficiency, asset prices reflect all information, public and private.

subordinated debenture (Chapter 17) An unsecured type of bond.

subordinated debt (Chapter 11) Debt claims that are junior to other claims and therefore are entitled to receive interest or principal payments only if the senior debt claims have been paid in full.

subordination (Chapter 17) Agreement by all subsequent or more-junior creditors to wait until all claims of the senior debt are satisfied in full before having their own claims satisfied.

subsidiary merger (Chapter 24) A merger in which the acquirer maintains the identity of the target as a separate subsidiary or division.

sunk costs (Chapter 8) Costs that have already been spent and are not recoverable.

supplemental disclosures (Chapter 16) The second part to a registration statement. It is filed only with the SEC.

sustainable growth model (Chapter 21) Derives an expression that determines how rapidly a firm can grow while maintaining a balance between its sources (increases in assets) and uses (increases in liabilities and equity) of funds.

swap contract (Chapter 27) Agreement between two parties to exchange payment obligations on two underlying financial liabilities that are equal in principal amount but differ in payment patterns.

syndicated (bank) loan (Chapters 11 and 17) A large loan arranged by a group (a *syndicate*) of commercial banks for a single borrower.

synergy (Chapter 24) An efficiency-enhancing effect resulting from a strategic merger.

synthetic put option (Chapter 18) Traders can create this by purchasing a bond and a call option while simultaneously short-selling the stock.

systematic risk (Chapter 5) The proportion of risk that cannot be eliminated through diversification.

T

tailing the hedge (Chapter 27) Purchasing enough futures contracts to hedge risk exposure, but not so many as to cause overhedging.

takeover (Chapter 24) Any transaction in which the control of one entity is taken over by another.

target cash balance (Chapter 23) A cash total is set for checking accounts to avoid engaging active cash position management.

tax-loss carryforwards (Chapter 24) Negative income (net losses) can be used to offset taxes due on future income.

tender offer (Chapter 24) The structured purchase of a target's shares in which the acquirer announces a public offer to buy a minimum number of shares at a specific price.

tender-merger (Chapter 24) A merger that occurs after an acquirer secures enough voting control of the target's shares through a tender offer to effect a merger.

term loan (Chapter 17) A loan, made by a financial institution to a business, with an initial maturity of more than 1 year and generally of 5 to 12 years.

term sheet (Chapter 26) The contract that details all of the economic, control, and ownership terms of an investment proposal that a venture capitalist prepares and presents to the entrepreneur.

term structure of interest rates (Chapter 4) The relationship between yield to maturity and time to maturity.

terminal value (Chapter 8) A number intended to reflect the value of a project at a given future point in time.

time line (Chapter 3) A graphical presentation of values over time.

time value (Chapter 18)   The difference between an option's intrinsic value and its market price.

time value of money (Chapter 3)   The principle of finance that a dollar received today is more valuable than a dollar (euro, pound, franc, or yen) received in the future.

times interest earned ratio (Chapter 2)   Earnings before interest and taxes divided by interest expense; it measures a firm's ability to make contractual interest payments.

timing (Chapter 10)   The ability to time market turns: getting in before upturns and getting out before crashes. One of two components of managerial investment performance.

top-down sales forecast (Chapter 21)   This kind of sales forecast relies heavily on macroeconomic and industry forecasts.

total asset turnover (Chapter 2)   A measurement of the efficiency with which a firm uses all its assets to generate sales; calculated by dividing the dollars of sales a firm generates by the dollars of asset investment.

total variable cost (TVC) of annual sales (Chapter 22)   Calculated by multiplying the annual sales in units by the variable cost per unit; used to estimate the average investment in accounts receivable under a stated policy.

tracking stocks (Chapter 16)   Equity claims based on (and designed to mirror, or *track*) the earnings of wholly owned subsidiaries of diversified firms.

trade-off model (Chapter 13)   A model of capital structure in which managers choose the mix of debt and equity that strikes a balance between the tax advantages of debt and the various costs of using leverage.

trade sale (Chapter 26)   The sale of a portfolio company by a buyout fund to a non-financial or industry buyer.

transactional exemption (Chapter 16)   Requires that securities be registered before they can be resold, or that the subsequent sale must also qualify as a private placement.

transactions exposure (Chapter 20 and 27)   The risk that a change in prices will negatively affect the value of a specific transaction or series of transactions.

Treasury bills (Chapter 4)   Debt instruments issued by the federal government that mature in less than one year.

Treasury bonds (Chapter 4)   Debt instruments issued by the federal government with maturities ranging from 10 to 30 years.

Treasury notes (Chapter 4)   Debt instruments issued by the federal government with maturities ranging from 1 to 10 years.

treasury stock (Chapters 2 and 11)   Common shares that a firm currently holds in reserve.

triangular arbitrage (Chapter 20)   Trading currencies simultaneously in different markets to earn a risk-free profit.

trustee (Chapters 17 and 25)   In bankruptcy, someone appointed by a judge to replace a firm's current management team and to oversee liquidation or reorganization.

turnover of accounts receivable (TOAR) (Chapter 22)   Used to calculate the *average investment in accounts receivable* (AIAR) when evaluating accounts receivable policies; calculated as 365 divided by the *average collection period* (ACP).

two-fund separation principle (Chapter 6)   The principle that says that investors should divide their wealth between two types of investments—a risk-free asset and a portfolio of risky assets.

U

underinvestment (Chapter 13)   A situation of financial distress in which default is likely yet a very profitable but short-lived investment opportunity exists.

underlying asset (Chapter 18)   The asset from which a derivative security obtains its value.

underpriced (Chapter 16)   Refers to the typical situation in which an IPO offering price is lower than its price at the end of the first day's trading.

underreaction (Chapter 10)   When stock prices on average react positively to a dividend initiation, for example, but then an additional positive reaction continues over the next several months.

underwrite (Chapter 16)   The investment banker purchases shares from a firm and then resells them to investors.

underwriting spread (Chapter 16)   The difference between the net price and the offer price.

underwriting syndicate (Chapter 16)   Consists of many investment banks that collectively purchase the firm's shares and market them, thereby spreading the risk exposure across the syndicate.

unlevered equity beta (Chapter 9)   The figure calculated by removing the effects of leverage on an equity beta.

unseasoned equity offering (Chapter 16)   An IPO.

unsecured creditors (Chapter 25)   Creditors who have no specific assets pledged as collateral, or the proceeds from the sale of whose pledged assets are inadequate to cover the debt.

unsponsored ADR (Chapter 16)   An ADR in which the issuing firm is not involved with the issue at all and may even oppose it.

unsystematic risk (Chapter 5)   The proportion of risk that can be eliminated through diversification.

V

variable growth model (Chapter 4)   Assumes that the growth rate dividend will vary during different periods of time when the value of a firm's stock is calculated.

venture capital (Chapter 26)   A professionally managed pool of money raised for the sole purpose of making actively managed direct equity investments in rapidly growing private companies.

venture capitalists (Chapter 1)   Professional investors who specialize in high-risk/high-return investments in rapidly growing entrepreneurial businesses.

venture capital limited partnerships (Chapter 26)   Funds established by professional venture capital firms.

vertical merger (Chapter 24)   Companies with current or potential buyer–seller relationships combine to create a more integrated company.

W

warrants (Chapter 19)   Securities issued by firms that grant the right to buy shares of stock at a fixed price for a given period of time.

weak-form efficiency (Chapter 10)   In markets characterized by this kind of efficiency, asset prices incorporate all information from the historical price record.

weighted average cost of capital (WACC) (Chapters 4, 9, and 14)   The after-tax weighted average required return on all types of securities issued by a firm, where the weights equal the percentage of each type of financing in a firm's overall capital structure.

white knights (Chapter 24)   "Friendly" acquirers who will top the price of an unwelcome bidder to prevent a hostile takeover.

winner's curse (Chapter 16)   Because they receive small allocations in hot deals and large allocations in cold deals, the unsophisticated players in this market will earn much lower returns.

wire transfer (Chapter 23)   The primary U.S. wire transfer system, known as *Fedwire*, is run by the Federal Reserve and is available to all depository institutions.

working capital (Chapter 8)   Refers to what is more correctly known as *net working capital.*

workout (Chapter 25)   A firm that becomes technically insolvent or bankrupt may make an arrangement with its creditors that enables it to bypass formal bankruptcy and many of its attendant costs.

writes an option (Chapter 18)   Sells an option.

writing covered calls (Chapter 18)   A common trading strategy that mixes stock and call options. In this strategy, an investor who owns a share of stock sells a call option on that stock.

Y

Yankee bonds (Chapter 11)   Bonds sold by foreign corporations to U.S. investors.

Yankee common stock (Chapter 11)   Stock issued by foreign firms in the U.S. market.

yield curve (Chapter 4)   A graph that plots the relationship between maturity and yield to maturity for a group of similar bonds.

yield spread (Chapter 4)   The difference in yield to maturity between two bonds or two classes of bonds with similar maturities.

yield to maturity (YTM) (Chapter 4)   The discount rate that equates the present value of the bond's cash flows to its market price.

Z

Z score (Chapter 25)   The product of a quantitative model for forecasting bankruptcy that uses a blend of traditional financial ratios and a statistical technique known as *multiple discriminant analysis.* The Z score has been found to be about 90% accurate in forecasting bankruptcy one year in the future and about 80% accurate in forecasting it two years in the future.

zero growth model (Chapter 4)   The simplest approach to dividend valuation; it assumes a constant dividend stream.

zero-balance accounts (ZBAs) (Chapter 23)   Disbursement accounts that always have an end-of-day balance of zero.

The purpose is to eliminate nonearning cash balances in corporate checking accounts.

zero-coupon bonds (Chapter 4)   Pure discount instruments, such as U.S. Treasury bills, that promise investors a single fixed payment on a specified future date.

Name Index

Company Index

Note: (ex) refers to examples cited in the text; *italicized* page references indicate tables and figures.

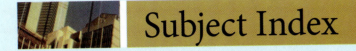

Subject Index

Note: *Italicized* page references indicate tables and figures.